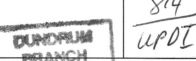
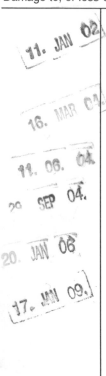

MORE MATTER

POEMS

The Carpentered Hen (1958) · Telephone Poles (1963)
Midpoint (1969) · Tossing and Turning (1977)
Facing Nature (1985) · Collected Poems 1953–1993

NOVELS

The Poorhouse Fair (1959) · Rabbit, Run (1960) · The Centaur (1963)
Of the Farm (1965) · Couples (1968) · Rabbit Redux (1971)
A Month of Sundays (1975) · Marry Me (1976) · The Coup (1978)
Rabbit is Rich (1981) · The Witches of Eastwick (1984)
Roger's Version (1986) · S. (1988) · Rabbit at Rest (1990)
Memories of the Ford Administration (1992) · Brazil (1994)
In the Beauty of the Lilies (1996) · Toward the End of Time (1997)
Bech at Bay (1998)

SHORT STORIES

The Same Door (1959) · Pigeon Feathers (1962)
Olinger Stories (a selection, 1964) · The Music School (1966)
Bech: A Book (1970) · Museums and Women (1972) · Problems (1979)
Too Far to Go (a selection, 1979) · Bech is Back (1982) · Trust Me (1987)
The Afterlife (1994)

ESSAYS AND CRITICISM

Assorted Prose (1965) · Picked-Up Pieces (1975) · Hugging the Shore (1983)
Just Looking (1989) · Odd Jobs (1991) · Golf Dreams: Writings on Golf (1996)

PLAY

Buchanan Dying (1974)

MEMOIRS

Self-Consciousness (1989)

CHILDREN'S BOOKS

The Magic Flute (1962) · The Ring (1964) · A Child's Calendar (1965)
Bottom's Dream (1969) · A Helpful Alphabet of Friendly Objects (1995)

John Updike

MORE MATTER

ESSAYS AND CRITICISM

HAMISH HAMILTON · LONDON

HAMISH HAMILTON LTD
Published by the Penguin Group
Penguin Books Ltd, 27 Wrights Lane, London w8 5tz, England
Penguin Putnam Inc., 375 Hudson Street, New York, New York 10014, USA
Penguin Books Australia Ltd, Ringwood, Victoria, Australia
Penguin Books Canada Ltd, 10 Alcorn Avenue, Toronto, Ontario, Canada m4v 3b2
Penguin Books (NZ) Ltd, Private Bag 102902, NSMC, Auckland, New Zealand

Penguin Books Ltd, Registered Offices: Harmondsworth, Middlesex, England

First published in the United States of America by Alfred A. Knopf, Inc. 1999
Published in Great Britain by Hamish Hamilton Ltd 1999
1 3 5 7 9 10 8 6 4 2

Copyright © John Updike, 1999

The Acknowledgments on pages vii and viii constitute an extension of this copyright page

The moral right of the author has been asserted

Printed in Great Britain by Clays Ltd, St Ives plc

A CIP catalogue record for this book is available from the British Library

ISBN 0-241-14091-9

Acknowledgments

Grateful acknowledgment is made to the following magazines and publishers, who first printed the pieces specified, sometimes under different titles and in slightly different form:

THE NEW YORKER: "The Burglar Alarm" (part I), "The Twelve Terrors of Christmas," "That Syncing Feeling," "Paranoid Packaging," "Hostile Haircuts," "Glad Rags," "Addressing the Scandal Glut," "Car Talk," "Legendary Lana," "Genial, Kinetic Gene Kelly," "Cartoon Magic," "Christmas Cards," "Me and My Books," "A Note on Narayan," "TV in NYC," "Amazon.com," the tributes to William Shawn and Brendan Gill, and sixty-one of the book reviews, including eight published as "Briefly Noted."

THE NEW YORK REVIEW OF BOOKS: "Nadar's Swift Tact," "Big, Bright, and Bendayed," "Verminous Pedestrians and Car-Tormented Streets," "Funny Faces," and the introductions to Edith Wharton's *The Age of Innocence* and Søren Kierkegaard's *The Seducer's Diary*.

THE NEW YORK TIMES BOOK REVIEW: "Lust," "People Fits," "Nightmares and Daymares," "Sirin's Sixty-Five Shimmering Short Stories," and "The Flamingo-Pink Decade."

THE NEW YORK TIMES MAGAZINE: "A Childhood Transgression."

THE NEW YORK TIMES: "The Gentlemen of Summer."

THE LONDON SUNDAY TIMES: "On the Edge of the Post-Human" and "The Short Story and I."

THE NEW REPUBLIC: "Fast Art" and "Cheever on the Rocks."

ART & ANTIQUES: "An Ecstatic State," "The Revealed and the Concealed," "Fun Furniture," and "Acts of Seeing."

ARCHITECTURAL DIGEST: Part II of "The Burglar Alarm" (as "Spat").

MIRABELLA: "The Sistine Chapel Ceiling" and "The Frick."

VOGUE: "Women Dancing" and "Henry Bech Interviews Updike."

ALLURE: "Get Thee Behind Me, Suntan."

PLAYBOY: "M.M. in Brief" and "The Vargas Girl."

MICHIGAN QUARTERLY: "The Disposable Rocket."

FORBES: "The State of the Union, as of March 1992," and "Five Remembered Moments of Reading Bliss."

NEW CHOICES: "Letter to a Baby Boomer."

NEWSWEEK: "The Fifties."

CHICAGO: "Freedom and Equality: Two American Bluebirds," also published as a booklet by the Illinois Humanities Council.

ISLANDS: "The Vineyard Remembered."

USAIR MAGAZINE: "Home in New England" (second part).

HOGAN'S ALLEY: "My Cartooning."

MEDIA EXCHANGE: "Reflections on Radio."

TIME INC.: "Bodies Beautiful."

LIFE: "A Bookish Boy" and "Remembering Pearl Harbor."

CIVILIZATION: "Descent of an Image."

AMERICAN HERITAGE: "Facing Death."

AMERICA: "Accepting the Campion Medal."

WALLACE STEVENS JOURNAL: "Stevens as Dutchman."

THE PARIS REVIEW: "Humor These Days."

LUFTHANSA BORDBUCH: "Print: A Dialogue" and "One Big Bauble."

THE TOKYO-JIN: "On the Edge."

VEJA: "The Sun the Other Way Around."

FOLHA DE S. PAULO: "The Cold."

DER SPIEGEL: "The Old Movie Houses."

FRANKFURTER RUNDSCHAU: "Samson and Delilah and Me."

DIE ZEIT: "A Woman's Burden."

LE NOUVELLE OBSERVATEUR: "Remembering Reading *Don Quixote*."

WORLD ALMANAC: "The Ten Greatest Works of Literature, 1001–2000."

THE IRISH TIMES: "Undelivered Remarks upon Awarding the 1992 GPA Book Award in Dublin."

LONDON OBSERVER: "An Hour of the Day."

ANTAEUS: "Updike and I."

NEW LETTERS: "Remarks on Religion and Contemporary American Literature."

HOUGHTON MIFFLIN: Introduction to *The Best American Short Stories 1984* and notes on "A Sandstone Farmhouse," "Playing with Dynamite," and "My Father on the Verge of Disgrace."

VIKING PENGUIN: Introductions to *Surviving: The Uncollected Writings of Henry Green* and to *Writers at Work: The Paris Review Interviews*, edited by George Plimpton.

RANDOM HOUSE: "V," in *Hockney's Alphabet*, and the introduction to *The Writer's Desk*, by Jill Krementz.

WESTMINSTER JOHN KNOX PRESS: "Religion and Literature," in *The Religion Factor*.

LION PUBLISHING: Introduction to *The Song of Solomon*.

HARPERCOLLINS: "Golf in the Land of the Free," an introduction to *Golf: The Greatest Game*.

PRINCETON UNIVERSITY PRESS: Introduction to *The Seducer's Diary*, by Søren Kierkegaard.

EVERYMAN'S LIBRARY: Introduction to *The Complete Shorter Fiction* of Herman Melville.

FAWCETT BOOKS: Introduction to *The Age of Innocence*, by Edith Wharton.

AURUM PRESS: Introduction to *Writers on Writers*, compiled by Graham Tarrant.

ANDRE DEUTSCH LTD.: Introduction to *Heroes and Anti-Heroes*.

DISNEY CONSUMER PRODUCTS: Introduction to *The Art of Mickey Mouse*, edited by Craig Yoe and Janet Morra-Yoe.

JOHN DANIEL & CO.: Introduction to *My Well-Balanced Life on a Wooden Leg*, by Al Capp.

DELL BOOKS: Introduction to *House of God*, by Samuel Shem.

WHITNEY MUSEUM: Introduction to *The First Picture Book—Everyday Things for Babies*, by Mary Steichen Calderone and Edward Steichen.

ART INSTITUTE OF CHICAGO: "A Case of Monumentality" from *Transforming Vision: Writers on Art*, edited by Edward Hirsch.

SHINCHOSHA INC.: Introduction to my *Self-Selected Stories*.

GALLIMARD: Foreword to the French translation of *Facing Nature*.

EUROGRAPHICA: Foreword to *Love Factories*.

METACOM PRESS: Foreword to *Brother Grasshopper*.

WILLIAM B. EWERT: Foreword to *The Women Who Got Away*.

LORD JOHN PRESS: Introduction to *Concerts at Castle Hill*.

GREENWOOD PUBLISHING GROUP: Foreword to *John Updike: A Bibliography, 1967–1993*, compiled by Jack De Bellis.

EASTON PRESS: Introduction to the four "Rabbit" novels.

THE FRANKLIN LIBRARY: "Special Messages" for Franklin Library Editions of *Memories of the Ford Administration*, *Brazil*, *In the Beauty of the Lilies*, and *Toward the End of Time*.

PROCEEDINGS OF THE AMERICAN ACADEMY OF ARTS AND LETTERS: "Accepting the Howells Medal."

Grateful acknowledgment is made to the following for permission to reprint previously published material:

CITY LIGHTS BOOKS: Excerpt from "The Day Lady Died" by Frank O'Hara, copyright © 1964 by Frank O'Hara. Reprinted by permission of City Lights Books.

CONDÉ NAST PUBLICATIONS: "From the Opinions of a New Yorker" by Robert F. Sisk, copyright © 1925. Originally published in *The New Yorker*, February 21, 1925. Reprinted by permission of Condé Nast Publications.

DOUBLEDAY: Excerpt from *Go Tell It on the Mountain* by James Baldwin, copyright © 1952, 1953 by James Baldwin. Reprinted by permission of Doubleday, a division of Random House, Inc.

FARRAR, STRAUS AND GIROUX, LLC: Excerpt from "Love Lies Sleeping" from

for ROGER ANGELL
and ANN GOLDSTEIN
editors, audiences of one, companions
in the hunt for the elusive *mot juste*
and the fearsome *phrase mauvaise*

Contents

Matter under Review

OTHER CONTINENTS

MEDLEYS

BIOGRAPHIES

THINGS AS THEY ARE

Visible Matter

MOVIES

PHOTOS

ART

Personal Matters

Preface

"MORE MATTER, with less art," Queen Gertrude advises Polonius; she sounds like a modern magazine editor. The appetite in the print trade is presently for real stuff—the dirt, the poop, the nitty-gritty—and not for the obliquities and tenuosities of fiction. A writer is almost never asked to write a story, let alone a poem; instead he or she is invited to pen introductions, reviews, and personal essays, preferably indiscreet. (Pen them, then fax them. Instant modemed communication and rapidly overlapping semes are à la mode.) Human curiosity, the abettor and stimulant of the fiction surge between Robinson Crusoe's adventures and Constance Chatterley's, has become ever more literal-minded and impatient with the proxies of the imagination. Present taste runs to the down-home divulgences of the talk show—psychotherapeutic confession turned into public circus—and to investigative journalism that, like so many heat-seeking missiles, seeks out the intimate truths, the very genitalia, of Presidents and princesses. It is as if, here at the end of a millennium, time is too precious to waste on anything but such central, perennially urgent data. And so it has come to pass that, in the 1990s, as I turned sixty and then reached sixty-two (senior discount at the movies!) and then passed retirement age, instead of devoting myself wholly to the elaboration of a few final theorems and dreams couched in the gauzy genres of make-believe, I have cranked out, in response to many a plausible request, the mass of more or less factual matter, of assorted prose, which Knopf has herewith heroically, indulgently printed and bound, my fifth such collection and—dare we hope?—my last.

In this terminal decade the editor of my favorite magazine, *The New Yorker*, became Tina Brown. It has been my bewildering professional experience to see the editors of that revered journal go from being much older, wiser heads, gray and authoritative, with a shamanistic mystique, to being all—with the friendly exception of Roger Angell—much younger than I, young enough in most cases to be my sons and daughters, with an adult child's willful and mysterious fondness for loud music, late nights, unheard-of celebrities, and electronic innovation. However, Ms. Brown's demeanor toward me, during her tenure, was engagingly benign, and I tried, albeit somewhat arthritically, to dance to her tune—contributing, for instance, to the back-page "Shouts and Murmurs" which she revived from the days of Alexander Woollcott, and answering her call to write about Lana Turner and Gene Kelly, whose videos I was nostalgically happy to view. The magazine's books department passed, through a flurry of interim managers, from the relaxed custody of the late, gravel-voiced Edith Oliver to the more scholastic, tremulously sensitive care of Henry Finder. The kind of books, mostly fiction from Europe and other exotic realms, that I used to be assigned for review yielded to meatier fare, like biographies of such imposing figures as Isaac Newton, Abraham Lincoln, Queen Elizabeth II, and (my last assignment before Ms. Brown's abrupt departure for even greener pastures) Helen Keller. These august subjects subtended areas of knowledge shadowy to me, but the late William Shawn—whose blessed memory has itself recently undergone some biographical elaboration—made it a principle not to assign books to specialists in the field, so I was already habituated, as a reviewer, to being at sea and steering by starlight. Also, on their own intellectual initiative, the new editors composed, in the hope that I might become a Critic at Large, a few bouquets of related titles for me to admire and address; in this volume's section "Medleys," the first two conjunctions were my idea, and the next two theirs. Presciently, they had me tackle the *Titanic* a year before the movie swept all before it. Another ambitious assignment, on Edith Wharton and her cinematic spinoffs, took me uneasily into territory already thoroughly patrolled by Anthony Lane. He and I bumped heads in the dark of a midtown screening room and I beat a quick retreat.

Though *The New Yorker* has always been scrupulously, tirelessly edited, requests to write to a certain specified length and on a certain timely topic much less obtruded upon a writer's consciousness in the days when William Shawn sustained the editorial illusion of a full and ghostly freedom. Reviews were allowed to run until the reviewer felt depleted; now one aims at a shorter length of nine hundred words or a much longer of around three thousand. Snappy or expansive, take your pick. My reviewing habit, hard to break, was to quote extensively; just as the impossibly ideal map would be the same size as the territory mapped, the ideal review would quote the book in its entirety, without comment. In a strange way, the passing of the Cold War has made it harder to frame a literary opinion; the polarities of right versus left and red versus free lent a tension to aesthetic questions miles removed from the Manichaean global struggle. Fiction from the Communist world was inevitably considered from a political angle, but that of Europe and the Americas also crackled with miniature versions of the global clash, the debate, carried on country by country, between Marx and Adam Smith on how one should live. Economic realities, in the form of declining ad revenues, had at last overtaken *The New Yorker*, which for so long seemed exempt from the crasser considerations. Her model for renovation, Tina Brown let it be known, was the magazine edited by Harold Ross—a peppier, saucier, and succincter publication that proclaimed itself not for the old lady from Dubuque. The old lady from Dubuque had become, over the years, one of the faithful subscribers, and then she got doddery. That a doddery contributor like myself might still have a part to play in the redesigned, more sharply angled pages was a comforting thought. I fell in love with the magazine as a child, from what seemed an immense distance. Appearing under the same Rea Irvin–designed title-type and department logos as White and Thurber and Cheever and those magical cartoons was for me a dream come true. It still is.

Let's face it, gentle reader: I set out to be a magazine writer, a wordsmith as the profession was understood in the industrial first half of the century, and I like seeing my name in what they used to call "hard type." The magazine rack at the corner drugstore beguiled me with its tough gloss. The academization and etherealization and latterly the devaluing deconstruction of the writer's trade in the second half of the century have taken me by surprise, though my Harvard education should have prepared me. Journalism has not only its social stimulations but its aesthetic virtues. An invitation into print, from however suspect a source, is an opportunity to make something beautiful, to discover within oneself a treasure that would otherwise have remained buried. When the call comes from beyond one's own language—from a German, French, Brazilian, or Japanese publication—the opportunity is to go back to basics, to write of one's own cultural context more bluntly than would be seemly at home, and to phrase an English that, in regard to the finished product, forms a preliminary stage. My two contributions to the Lufthansa *Bordbuch* (an elegant publication recently trimmed down) appeared in English and German both; otherwise, I explained the cold to Brazilians, my short stories to the Japanese, and my poems to the French with an agreeable sensation of hiding behind a foreign language, as when in my escapades as a cultural ambassador I spoke through a bilingual intermediary. Introducing works by other authors, especially those secure in the lists of immortality, offers the pleasure of another, pedagogic impersonation; the introductions to certain works of Melville, Wharton, and Henry Green gave me the quiet joys of a scholar as he adds his careful modicum to an extensive bibliography. The lecture on New York writing exploited the anthologies of others and marks another occasion when the rustle of mock-professorial robes cosseted my ears. "Religion and Literature" was actually a chapter in a textbook, *The Religion Factor*, published by a Presbyterian press; I took it upon myself, perhaps wickedly, to remind the presumed students of divinity that a once-healthy religion existed outside the Judaeo-Christian belief system and died, as it were, in literature's embrace. The itch to inform is perhaps as pernicious a goad to utterance as the itch to charm.

The invitations to inform or charm that come my way are limited by the meagre number of my areas of supposed expertise. Of golf I have had my say in *Golf Dreams*, though a foreword late to tee off offered itself for inclusion in *More Matter*. Suburban interrelations creep into discussions of dancing, suntanning, and the Fifties. Among living American authors, I take, it may be, an anomalously positive or at least hopeful view of our Republic's progress; hence I am occasionally trusted by the powers that be to expound on matters of state, as the reader can see in the first section. On the strength of my early cartooning ambitions, my single year at an English art school, and my willingness to feel happy in museums, *Art and Antiques*, *The New Republic*, and *The New York Review of Books* have over the years let me write on art and exhibits. One book, *Just Looking*, has already been made of such articles; this present volume holds, in addition to commentary on movies and photographs, those art reviews which did not, it seemed to me, require color illustration, or illustration at all.

As in my other eight-years' gatherings, *Picked-Up Pieces*, *Hugging the Shore*, and *Odd Jobs*, the last section rounds up snippets, some a mere paragraph, pertaining to me and my works. My excuses for this methodical narcissism are that all authorial activity is egoistic anyway and that close students of my work—there are a few—will be interested. In truth, so impenetrably loom the paper mountains of a diligent oeuvre, that interviewers rarely seem aware of my faithful deposits of opinion and autobiography. Again and again I am asked questions already patiently answered in print. Never mind; predator satiation being one of nature's survival techniques, I answer them again, and thus add a bit more superfluous self-description to what we might laughingly call "the record." Some repetition is inevitable, as part of the satiation. The inventory of my rather paltry childhood reading keeps coming round, and I fear the same Henry James quotation is invoked three times; in each case it seemed indispensable, and too choice to paraphrase.

A child begins to play at art in the faith that there is a treasure house where the most accomplished work is stored, to last forever, forever consulted. Intimations of the definitive tinged my creative excitement at its outset, around and under our family dining-room table, with its Tiffany lampshade of many glowing colors. There is a bliss in making sets of things, and in bringing something imperfect closer to perfection—firmly inking in a sketchy drawing, adding a few more verbal enhancements to a final proof. Or, in a review, listing, say, the exotic words in Norman Rush's *Mating* and the savored meals in Ardashir Vakil's *Beach Boy*. The assembly and arrangement of a book like *More Matter* offers such satisfactions—the tactile thrill of the fixed, the interlocking—but any illusion of "permanent form" struggles against the realizations, come upon me late in life, that paper decays, that readership dwindles, that a book is a kind of newspaper, that the most polished composition loses edge to the flow of language and cultural context, that no masterpiece will outlast the human race, that the race is but an incident in the fauna of our planet, that our planet is doomed to die in a hiccup of the sun, that the sun will eventually implode and explode, and that the universe itself is a transitory scribble on the surface, so oddly breached fifteen billion years ago, of nothingness. Wow! *Zap!* Nevertheless, the living must live, a writer must write. Enough said. So bulky a book warrants a brief preface.

J.U.

Large Matters

MATTERS OF STATE

Freedom and Equality: Two American Bluebirds

ON THIS SUNDAY MORNING, all over Chicago, churchgoers are settling to hear a sermon and to sing the praises of the Lord; let us, then, in synchrony sing the praises of freedom and equality, those two bluebirds of hope and aspiration swooping in our American skies. The two concepts nest at the heart of what we like to think makes the United States an exemplary and revolutionary place; yet neither is unambiguous or without its problematical aspects. Equality, I would say, is a practical concept, and freedom a subjective, rather metaphysical one; let us begin closer to the earth, with equality.

"We hold these truths to be self-evident," the Declaration of Independence resoundingly declares in its most famous passage, "that all men are created equal, that they are endowed by their Creator with certain unalienable Rights, that among these are Life, Liberty, and the pursuit of Happiness." And Alexis de Tocqueville's indispensable masterpiece of political analysis, *Democracy in America*, begins, "Among the novel objects that attracted my attention during my stay in the United States, nothing struck me more forcibly than the general equality of condition among the people. I readily discovered the prodigious influence that this primary fact exercises on the whole course of society.... It creates opinion, gives birth to new sentiments, founds novel customs, and modifies whatever it does not produce."

De Tocqueville's visit to the New World consisted of nine months in 1831; when he speaks of equality, it is always against the mental background of the European class system, weakened by revolution and the

Given as the keynote speech of the Chicago Humanities Festival III, "From Freedom to Equality," on November 15, 1992.

rise of capitalism yet by no means extinct, a system that poses the landed aristocracy, with its allies the church and the military, over against the peasantry, with an urban mercantile class uneasily emerging in between. The abolition of such a hierarchical system, rooted in the age of feudalism, produces what to de Tocqueville is a thrilling and menacing absence, a yawning void where reverberations reach into every realm of human activity, even to that of poetry. He tells us, "When . . . the progress of equality had reduced each individual to smaller and better known proportions, the poets, not yet aware of what they could substitute for the great themes which were departing together with the aristocracy, turned their eyes to inanimate Nature. As they lost sight of gods and heroes, they set themselves to describe streams and mountains."

For de Tocqueville, the young United States are a giant social experiment whose results, good and bad, he holds up to his French readership as a guide to their probable future. "In our time," he asserts, "and especially in France, this passion for equality is every day gaining ground in the human heart." Rather surprisingly, to our rhetorical sense of things, he finds the passion for equality more basic and fervent than that for freedom: "The advantages that freedom brings are shown only by the lapse of time, and it is always easy to mistake the cause in which they originate. The advantages of equality are immediate, and they may always be traced from their source. Political liberty bestows exalted pleasures from time to time upon a certain number of citizens. Equality every day confers a number of small enjoyments on every man."

In this day and age we need no reminder that the society of free equals pledged by Jefferson in 1776 and visited by de Tocqueville in 1831 consisted of property-owning white males. The election of government was limited to those who had what was called "a stake in society"; at the least a poll tax was required to vote. The propertyless, and women, and those indigenous Americans called Indians, and African-Americans whether as slaves or freedmen did not enjoy a full stake. De Tocqueville observed the stringent conditions of marriage for women in a society simultaneously puritanical and commercial: "In America," he said, "the independence of woman is irrecoverably lost in the bonds of matrimony. If an unmarried woman is less constrained there than elsewhere, a wife is subjected to stricter obligations." Of the Indians, at a time when remnants of the Cherokee and Choctaw nations still existed in the South, and when the tribes had not yet been harried much beyond the Mississippi, he is chillingly bleak: "It is the misfortune of Indians to be brought into contact with a civilized people, who are also (it must be owned) the most grasping nation on the globe, while they [that is, the Indians] are still semi-barbarian; to find their masters in their instructors, and to receive knowledge and oppression at the same time." The condition of black men and women in 1831 is painted in even grimmer colors. In the North, the rights of freedmen are mostly illusory: "The electoral franchise has been conferred upon the Negroes in almost all the states in which slavery has been abolished, but if they come forward to vote, their lives are in danger. If oppressed, they may bring an action at law, but they will find none but whites among their judges; and although they may legally serve as jurors, prejudice repels them from that office." In the South, de Tocqueville foresees only bloody struggle:

> The Negroes may long remain slaves without complaining; but if they are once raised to the level of freemen, they will soon revolt at being deprived of almost all their civil rights; and as they cannot become the equals of whites, they will speedily show themselves as enemies. . . . When I contemplate the condition of the South, I can discover only two modes of action for the white inhabitants of these States: namely, either to emancipate the Negroes and to intermingle with them, or, remaining isolated from them, to keep them in slavery as long as possible. All intermediate measures seem to me likely to terminate, and that shortly, in the most horrible of civil wars and perhaps in the extirpation of one or the other of the two races.

One's reaction, reading this dire analysis over a century and a half later, is twofold: relief that things are not quite that bad, but sorrow that de Tocqueville's picture still has so much truth in it. In spite of a legal and social revolution which swept the South in the 1950s and '60s, and a nationwide movement toward integration that has given us African-American mayors, judges, generals, sports stars, talk-show hosts, and, the other day, from this state, a United States Senator,* most black babies are born not equal but handicapped in life's contests. They will, generally, leave school earlier, live poorer, go to jail more often, and die sooner than their white counterparts. Nor, as recent events in Los Angeles and Las Vegas show, is race war an impossibility amid the de-facto inequalities of a society still fractured by racial prejudice and the aftermath of black slavery.

Yet, it must be asked, what is meant by being "born equal"? We are born, clearly, unequal, of differing sizes and abilities, in families and communities widely various in their capacities to nurture and encourage, and of two different sexes, sexes of which Nature requires different tasks and to which she has assigned different physiologies and, to some extent, psy-

---

*Carol Moseley-Braun.

chologies. Variety, not equality, is what Nature offers to the naturalist's observation. To insure its continuance, Nature covers a lot of genetic bets; the organisms unequal to the task of survival are eliminated, with their genes, from the vast ongoing struggle.

The U.S. Constitution, in trying to construct a political organism—"a more perfect Union"—that will survive, says surprisingly little about equality; its language is concerned with balancing and dovetailing *un*equal entities—states and the federal authority, the executive, judicial, and legislative branches of government—in creating a structure of power that will be both stable and yet responsive to popular votes. Section 9 of Article I states that "No Title of Nobility shall be granted by the United States," thus eliminating the sanctioned inequality of Old World societies. Article IV, Section 2, asserts that "The Citizens of each State shall be entitled to all Privileges and Immunities of Citizens in the several States," thus assuring, I take it, that no pockets of feudal or totalitarian rule develop in the union of States. In extension of the same principle, we might remind ourselves, the same section asserted that "No Person held to Service or Labour in one State, under the Laws thereof, escaping into another, shall, in Consequence of any Law or Regulation therein, be discharged from such Service or Labour"—a constitutional recognition of the rights of slaveowners, and a basis of the white South's grievances on the long-tormented fugitive-slave issue. Among the amendments, the Fourteenth, passed after the Civil War and Emancipation, extends citizenship to "all persons born or naturalized in the United States" and guarantees that all persons be counted equally in arranging the apportionment of congressional Representatives. The next amendment states that the right of citizens to vote shall not be denied or abridged "on account of race, color, or previous condition of servitude," and the Nineteenth Amendment, ratified in 1920, states that the same right shall not be denied "on account of sex." Thus the right of suffrage was gradually extended beyond the original circle of propertied white men.

Equality is a state of mind. In a poem by Stephanie Brown I find these lines, pertaining to a group of librarians vacationing in Baja:

> It's hard, though, to vacation without hierarchy.
> Someone is the best tennis player, the best storyteller, the best gossip,
>   has the best body, gets along best.

Our equality is a matter of rights, not circumstances. The defense and definition of those rights call into being the prodigious and prodigal number of American lawsuits and lawyers. For rights conflict. My right to peace clashes with my neighbor's right to play his radio at a volume pleasing to him. My right to privacy conflicts with the right of my former girlfriend, a budding novelist, to free speech. My right to hire or rent to whomever I please conflicts with a host of laws forbidding racial, sexist, and ageist discrimination. Affirmative action, in the form of an employment policy or a college admissions policy that attempts to correct a societal imbalance by favoring minorities, produces charges of reverse discrimination. And so on. In a single issue of the *Boston Globe* this fall, we find four California women filing suit against two Las Vegas conventions of Navy aviators where they were sexually harassed; spokespersons for the Philadelphia gay community protesting the closing of adult bookstores in eastern Pennsylvania by the state Attorney General; lesbian activists in Queens protesting a local school board's decision against a new multicultural curriculum; a Massachusetts couple holding a news conference to decry the lack of rights for foster parents; a Boston knickknack store called the Nostalgia Factory asserting its right to offer for sale politically incorrect advertisements, ads from 1890 to 1975 that might today be deemed "sexist, racist, or antianimal rights"; and the Massachusetts Supreme Judicial Court declaring a security emergency to combat "increasingly violent behavior in courthouses and courtrooms." And so the battle of rights goes, a necessary but expensive clamor attendant upon a culture that asserts equality before the law, and therefore hands over to lawyers a proportion of power and treasure unmatched in any other nation. Ours is an invented country, a country of written principles rather than of anciently inherited customs; the courts are the busy, noisy forges wherein our theoretical equality is beaten out, again and again.

The equality that de Tocqueville saw in 1831 as defining the American character was perhaps less theoretical and more organic. The hardship, simplicity, and isolation of the early New England settlements, along with the austere Puritan doctrines, had imposed a levelling. The American wilderness gradually yielded up county after county of small farms, whose proprietors faced much the same challenges and reaped the same harvests. Even in the South, where slavery made large landed estates possible, and the rise of a kind of aristocracy, the laws of inheritance and the eddies of fortune tended to break up extensive properties. "Great landed estates which have once been divided," de Tocqueville observes, "never come together again, for the small proprietor draws from his land a better revenue, in proportion, than the large owner from his." Especially away from the coastal cities, a rough-hewn equality prevailed, and an informality of manner of which de Tocqueville observed, "In democracies manners are never so refined as among aristocratic nations, but on the other hand they are never so coarse. . . . Among a democratic people manners . . . form, as it were, a light and loosely woven veil through which the real feelings and private opinions of each individual are easily discernible. The form and the substance of human actions, therefore, often stand there in closer relation."

This manner of ours, invisible to ourselves, is best noticed by foreign visitors. I recall reading the account of a British tourist who, finding himself standing amid the flat lawns and glaring sidewalks of a suburban development somewhere in Texas, was abruptly addressed by a little boy on a tricycle. "Hi," the little boy said, and the startled Englishman felt that by this one unsolicited syllable of greeting his own Americanization had begun. A French boy visiting my stepson a few years ago came back from a trip to Boston and Cambridge with a curious observation about the variety of clothes the Americans wore on the street: "They dress," he said in his uncertain English, "as if they are not afraid." And it came to me that proper bourgeois dress, like the businessman's gray suit and the smart black dress of a proper Parisienne, does express a certain fear, the fear of being mistaken for someone of an inferior caste, and that the curious global triumph of denim and Levi's is, for the young people from China to Chile who have taken them up, a declaration of freedom, a liberation from caste. Blue jeans and the stencilled T-shirt are what the Mao jacket wanted to be, equality's uniform. Our great national exports, from hamburgers to mass entertainment, project an unprejudiced accessibility; a Coke, Andy Warhol said in one of his profoundly superficial observations, is the same Coke for a rich man as for a poor man. Such a product gives every purchaser what my father used to call "a fair shake"—an expression that has been current since 1825, and derives not from our national propensity to shake hands but from the game of craps. If life is, as the Enlightenment began to perceive, a crapshoot, the most we can ask is a fair shake.

Here are two more minor revelations of the American character. Once, in Kenya, I was in a safari van that broke down. The driver, a black African, and the English passengers in the van sat back waiting in the dusty heat for the notified authorities to send a repairman to us. The Americans in the van, including me, though I know little about engines, insisted on popping the hood and trying to fix the machine themselves. What I remember about the incident is not whether or not we did get the van going but the sick look of horror on the face of the scandalized driver; clearly, we were jeopardizing his position in a chain of command where one did not take unspecified initiatives. He was afraid. He knew what he was, a driver and not a repairman, whereas the Americans were happily willing to go from being docile passengers to dynamic auto mechanics. They felt equal to the task.

On another occasion, in Russia, I was told by a Russian that you could always tell an American by the way he walked down the street. When I asked how, he tried to demonstrate a kind of gunfighter's swagger and said, "Tough guy." Tough guy! Is this where our cherished, hard-won equality has brought us, to toughness as well as to an easy affability and can-do resourcefulness? Looking at the violence of our film entertainments and of our popular music, and at our murder statistics and international image as a bully nation, and at the brutality that rages through our literary classics as well as trash thrillers, we must conclude that toughness is part of the equality package. Class-prone societies create a specialized warrior class to do their enforcing, and a romanticized criminal class; here in our Wild West only the color of the hats distinguishes the lawbreakers from the law enforcers. We are all gunfighters, and not even a Quaker woman, as played by Grace Kelly in the movie *High Noon*, can remain above the fray.

America promises equal opportunity; the opportunity, relatively unhobbled by feudal or socialist restraints, to get ahead. But to get ahead means to leave someone else behind. The ideal is of a level playing field, but in the game there must be winner and losers. Former President Reagan, in a startlingly heartfelt answer to a reporter's question, once said he wanted this always to be a country in which a person can get rich. Not, perhaps, a response that liberals can love, but a vivid and honest egalitarian one, expressing the hope that has brought millions here, and that motivates millions still. Not to serve a king, but to become, in Huey Long's phrase, every man a king. The American conditions of equality and freedom are supposed to liberate the productivity and creativity of each citizen. The incentive is personal gain, usually conceived in material and sensual terms. We are driven, that is, by the inequalities constantly held before us by a celebrity-worshipping, comfort-cherishing culture, by luxury-touting advertisements, by the fanatically engineered expensiveness of American life. Being born equal is a precondition of striving for more; contentment with one's lot is not on the list of American virtues. Ambitiousness is. Greed almost is, or was a decade ago. Equal in our rights, we are free to strive to beat out the other fellow. This is the torque, the twist, the paradox, the stress that makes the explosive democratic engine go.

Freedom is our second bluebird. My early fiction, I notice, was much concerned with its elusive nature. My first novel, *The Poorhouse Fair*, showed the rebellion of the inmates of a charitable institution against their nobly intentioned, even saintly administrator; with an ineffectual hail of rocks, they voted against his benevolent order in favor of the disorder of the previous administrator, a raffish purveyor of blarney called Mendelssohn. Is not such rebellion against a benevolent but confining order a deeply human protest? We have a natural resistance to being told what is good for us. A full third of God's angels rebelled, we read in Milton's *Paradise Lost*, even under Heaven's optimum conditions. We say of people, they need to stretch their wings. With those wings we fly from boredom and stagnation, even at the risk of death. *Live free or die*, New Hampshire's state motto proclaims from a million license plates. We'll take our chances, we say, in this land of the free and home of the brave.

My second novel, *Rabbit, Run*, concerned a young husband who on an impulse runs away from his needy wife and child but runs into, on the other side of the mountain, more entanglements and abridgements of his personal freedom. For there is no absolute freedom, of course. We are not free of our body's needs, of our sexual and emotional compulsions, or of other people from cradle to grave. When one set of interrelations is fled, we blunder into another, and my hero finds, in the end, that freedom is a momentary sensation, a running to nowhere. The contrast, in my first novel, between a cold order and a warm disorder, a soulless welfare state and an entertaining squalor, needed this qualification; our human existence can know no absolute autonomy or social isolation. One man's freedom, as in *Rabbit, Run*, is purchased at the price of other people's suffering, often that of the innocent and helpless, the children among us.

My third novel, *The Centaur*, in deliberate contrast, held up for examination the life of an animal in harness, a plodding half-horse who offers up his life, as many fathers do, so that his child may experience the freedom that safety and shelter afford. Those who consciously settle, in life, for a job and a family role, who accept a limiting and dwindling niche in the social fabric, have located, in acceptance, an inner freedom; they make a virtue of necessity. We are not only free *to* do things but free *from* things. Of the four freedoms that Franklin Roosevelt enumerated, two were active—freedom of speech and of worship—and two were passive: freedom from want and from fear. American society offers less of the last two freedoms than any other major industrial state. In a recent article in the *New York Times Magazine* by Stephen R. Weisman, the word "freedom" comes up in a discussion of the conformity and tight loyalties of Japanese life: "Japanese have a different kind of freedom—a freedom rooted in security, a low crime rate, a sense of belonging that seems to have vanished from many societies." Civilization imposes its discontents for a considerable reward. Camille Paglia, in her thrillingly Nietzschean book *Sexual Personae*, says with characteristic bluntness: "Freedom is the most overrated modern idea, originating in the Romantic rebellion against bourgeois society. But only *in* society can one *be* an individual. Nature is waiting at society's gate to dissolve us in her chthonian bosom." Half animal, half responsible citizen, we each offer up some of our chthonian longings in exchange for freedom from chthonian chaos.

My fourth novel, a country cousin of *The Centaur* called *Of the Farm*, attempted to show an aging mother and an adult son negotiating acceptance of what seems to each the sins of the other. Its epigraph was a lovely quotation from Jean-Paul Sartre:

> Consequently, when, in all honesty, I've recognized that man is a being in whom existence precedes essence, that he is a free being who, in various circumstances, can want only his freedom, I have at the same time recognized that I can want only the freedom of others.

We extend freedom to others in the form of forgiveness, of forbearance. A free society must be a tolerant society. Even the tyrannies of love must be moderated. Every day in this violent nation, as we read in the newspapers, men kill their estranged girlfriends, and estranged husbands kill their former wives and the children of that marriage; there was a recent case of a Cambodian immigrant killing his adult daughter rather than granting her freedom. We are horrified. But is not the other extreme from such murderous possessiveness a cool indifference, a tenuousness in human relationships peculiarly American? There is a sliding-by-ness in American life, an emotional minimalism, that facilitates democratic mobility and permissiveness. "Do what you want" is said often, less often in love than in angry dismissal. To be free, often, is to be alone.

Thus run some of my early reflections on this bottomless matter of freedom, our slippery national shibboleth. "This is a free country," we hear said. "Sweet land of liberty," we sing. Freedom is invoked on all sides of a controversy. James M. McPherson titles his giant history of the Civil War *Battle Cry of Freedom* and begins by pointing out that both sides were fighting, in their minds, for freedom—the South for what Jefferson Davis in 1863 called "the freedom, equality, and State sovereignty which were the heritage purchased by the blood of our revolutionary sires," and the North for what Lincoln, that same year, in the Gettysburg Address, called "a new birth of freedom." In 1861, Lincoln had put the matter more concretely: "We must settle this question now, whether in a free government the minority have the right to break up the government whenever they choose." By the most liberal interpretation, the North was fighting to free the slaves. "As he [Christ] died to make men holy, let us die to make men free," urged "The Battle Hymn of the Republic." In fact there were relatively few abolitionists among the Union soldiers, just as most of the Confederate troops were not slaveowners. Freedom, at any rate, was and is universally cited as the treasure beyond price, worth any ordeal of battle and suffering. Moses Mitchell, a former slave interviewed in the 1930s, when the South was thoroughly segregated and economic conditions for his race were abysmal, nevertheless stated simply, "Here's the idea: freedom is worth it all."

One wonders what percentage of former Soviet citizens now liberated from Communism would agree. Just as de Tocqueville defined equality by its contrast with European aristocracy, for these last forty-five years Americans have been able to define freedom against the example of Communism. "If you don't like it here, go to Russia," protesters were told, and a few—a very few—of them did. The Soviets' gulags and purges and show trials, their absurd censorship and xenophobia, their military invasions of their supposed allies, and finally their stubbornly backward economy all made us feel good about ourselves, and told us what freedom was. It was being not-them, just as equality was having no king and nobility. But now they and their former satellites are reaping the mixed and difficult results of "a free market," whose most visible benefits seem to be near-famine for many and the rapid rise in affluence of former criminals. In his poem "Liberty," Hartley Coleridge asks, "But what is Freedom? Rightly understood, / A universal license to be good." Another Victorian poet, Tennyson, came closer to the dark truth in his quatrain:

> Of old sat Freedom on the heights,
> The thunders breaking at her feet;
> Above her shook the starry lights;
> She heard the torrents meet.

The thunders break and torrents meet under freedom, and many in the former Soviet Union now long for the restrictive good old days of Stalin and Brezhnev.

We are never free from the needs of the body, and hungry and desperate people will usually exchange some of their freedom for food and security. Such an exchange functions as the basis for every society. In the tribal societies that gave rise to the first monarchical civilizations, the exchange left little personal freedom to be enjoyed. What choices, what freedom, did the residents of pharaonic Egypt have, as expressed by the giant suffocation of their pyramids? Yet on the walls of their lesser tombs we see depictions of daily life that imply the same pleasures of gratified appetite and concluded venture, of harvested crop and peaceful mating, that we enjoy. In the Old Testament, and the writings of classic Greece, we find human identity as we understand it, a matter of fateful choice and consequence, but reserved, pretty much, for the kings and chieftains. When the Roman Empire broke up, the mutually protective associations of serf and lord arose, in a landscape of walled towns fed by enfeoffed fields, to form the new social structure. And are not societies still, basically, protective associations? I consider myself, as writers go, a patriotic American and a cheerful taxpayer; but in honesty I pay my taxes not because I understand or endorse the uses the money is put to but for exactly the same reason a Sicilian shopkeeper slips money to the local Mafia—to buy peace, the privilege in his case of not having his windows broken and in my case that of not being sent to jail. Governments are coercive and punitive in the last resort, and American freedom is a relative and not absolute condition. It is not a chemical that can be distilled into pure form; freedom is a coloring, a shimmer, that softens the coercions and hard necessities of being a human creature, a social animal.

Chemically pure water, I once read, is undrinkable. One might say that freedom as Americans have exalted it is so new to the human condition that we have not evolved the biological equipment for it; it frightens us, and afflicts us with agoraphobia and anorexia. Jack Thomas, the biographer of former Boston mayor James Michael Curley, recently advanced the theory "that societies die from intensification of their own first principle, so that Athens dies of an excess of democracy, Sparta dies of an excess of order, and what we're dying of is an excess of liberty." At the outset of the American Revolution, Thomas Paine wrote, "Those who expect to reap the blessings of freedom must, like men, undergo the fatigue of supporting it."

Freedom is choice, and choice is a burden and responsibility, and if an American is free to succeed as few others are, he is also free to fail, to sink, as few outside the impoverished Third World are. Poverty has no sacred status here, as it does in India and some Catholic countries; poverty is a sheer disgrace, and is felt by the poor as such. The genius of our Founding Fathers was to invite Nature's turmoil into the system: to let the torrents of the marketplace shape the economy, and to anoint natural human selfishness—self-interest, the pursuit of happiness—as the system's central energizer. Under recent Presidents selfishness became not merely an energizer but the only idea in the field. The concepts of equality and freedom are bound up together. De Tocqueville thought, citing the equally oppressed citizens of a tyranny, that you can have equality without freedom; but you cannot have, I believe, freedom without equality. Without the sensation of equality, I mean, since absolute equality is impossible and in terms of American dynamics undesirable. But if inequality becomes too great in fact, the sense of any unity will diminish, and I fear that is the present trend.

The gap between the rich and poor is widening, for a great number of reasons, including the Reagan tax cuts. A recent report by the Center on Budget and Policy Priorities declared that during the Eighties those in the richest fifth of our society gained an average income of $7,200, those in the middle fifth gained only $140, and the poorest fifth lost $350. Another recent study, by economists at Harvard and Columbia, studied the richest one percent of Americans throughout our history. At the time of the American Revolution, the country's wealthiest one percent controlled a mere fifteen percent of the nation's wealth; by the time of the Civil War ninety years later, this fraction had doubled, and by 1929 it had climbed to forty-three percent—nearly half of the nation's wealth in the hands of one-hundredth of the population. The Depression, World War II, and post-war boom saw the percentage hold at around thirty percent, and in the 1970s it dropped to a mere eighteen; in the 1980s, under Presidents Reagan and Bush, the percentage doubled, climbing back to thirty-six. The rich got richer.

The loss of equality is felt not in statistics but in our cities, with their Calcutta-like efflorescence of beggary and homelessness, and in the elaborate security systems the affluent erect around themselves. The poor are increasingly visible and the rich ever less so. The cherished small-town America where the front yards had no fences and nobody locked his door because nobody needed to steal is gone, even from Hollywood movies. I grew up in such a town. Not that my family was not aware of local gradations of income and status; we were, painfully. It was the Depression, and we were running scared. Yet we and our neighbors seemed to be all in the same broad boat. As a man who has lived most of his life in small towns I can tell you: If your neighbor is more or less in the same boat you are, it is easy to like him. If he's not, it becomes easier to dislike him, to fear him as a threat.

A sense of equality is necessary to freedom because when a society breaks down into hopelessly unequal blocs the elite in its own defense will seek to contain—that is, to repress—the disaffected. Mostly white police forces already, it seems to many African-Americans and Hispanics, function as an army of occupation and restraint in the big cities. An unequal society is an angry and fearful society, and a fearful society is not a free society. When a man or woman, white or black, is afraid to go into a certain neighborhood, whether it be Bedford-Stuyvesant or South Boston, freedom has been curtailed. Our liberties flourish in an atmosphere of mutual trust, and the legend of equality, blazoned in our documents and coinage, has served to lubricate American motion, and to soothe with hope of betterment the old sore spots of ethnic antagonism. People are naturally optimistic and conservative, and can long defer gratification—the attainment of happiness—if the door to its pursuit is open. But when the door seems locked, when the poor get poorer and the society's assets increasingly accrue to a minority, then we can reconcile ourselves to a world of hostile contending forces, with all the abridgments of liberty that warfare brings with it.

What is the solution? Well, a return to a more progressive income tax would seem a likely beginning, and we have just elected President a man* who promises just that. *The End of Equality*, by Mickey Kaus, proposes that, since the redistribution of income, by such means as welfare, has proved ineffective, an institution from above of compulsory national service, a national health program, and a workfare program to improve public amenities might restore a sense of national community. But I wonder how much can be done from above, from a government already spending well beyond its means.

A sense of contented commonality grows from the private pocketbook upwards. There is a freedom of permission, and a freedom of empowerment. When, say, blacks are permitted to eat at a lunch counter with whites, it is a hollow freedom if they can't afford to pay for the lunch. Nor are women's rights, so-called, very meaningful without women's access to the workplace and the paycheck. It is the freedom of empowerment, the freedom of disposable income, that fleshes out our legal freedoms, and that affects the way a person moves in the world, freely and responsibly. How much empowerment can our planet support? This land of freedom was also a land of plenty, plenty enough to support a great deal of waste and piracy yet still feed mass hopes. This plenty underwrote our confidence, our asserted freedom. We must learn to do, it seems, with less. Certainly we must learn to apportion our national wealth more thoughtfully, with more conscious scruples than laissez-faire economics finds necessary.

The topic of this conference is "From Freedom to Equality." The phrase was meant, no doubt, to conjure up the legal emancipation Abraham Lincoln bestowed upon black Americans and their still-unfulfilled struggle for real equality. I have chosen to meditate on our topics more generally, arriving at the thought that the progression is the reverse: an American degree of personal freedom can flourish only when the economic thrust is not forcing people apart, when men can relax into the assurance that we are all equal in opportunity if not inheritance, before

---

*William Jefferson Clinton.

the law if not at the bank. Such a relaxation is unusual in history and perhaps temporary even on this fortunate continent. Freedom in the American sense may be a luxury to be tasted by a few, in a few remissions of what Hobbes called "the war of every man, against every man." But, I would hope not. Though this century's history abounds in abnegations of freedom and equality, the ideals of the American Declaration of Independence do receive, I think, some new reinforcement from technology; the electronic revolution makes us all a bit harder to bully. As information blankets the globe, tyranny, injustice, and falsehood have become harder to hide. Myself, I am grateful to have been born in the United States in the twentieth century, and devoutly wish that my grandchildren, and their children, will find cause to be grateful in the next century, while our ever-endangered bluebirds continue to sing. Amen.

The State of the Union, as of March 1992

(In Answer to the Question, Proposed by Forbes Magazine, "Why, when Americans have it so good, do we feel so bad?")

THE QUESTION suggests its own answer; because Americans *had* it so good, they feel bad now. Not altogether bad, of course, and not equally bad in all sectors of the society; obviously, there are worse fates on the globe than to be a citizen of the United States. Few residents of our worst ghettos would swap their assets for a one-way ticket back to Africa, Mexico, Eastern Europe, or Vietnam. One would concede that the quality of the life led by the average American, measured in space, leisure, and cost of daily living, compares favorably with that of the average crowded, hard-worked Japanese, and is not markedly inferior to that of the dwellers in such socialized high-tech utopias as Switzerland, Sweden, and the united Germany—all of which, recently, evince their own problems and discontent. Americans still have it good.

But we *should* have it good, with our gorgeous stretch of the planet's real estate and our remarkably enduring and adaptable political institutions. Nature and the Founding Fathers have been kind to us, and World War II was less hard on us than on any other major participant. We emerged from that holocaust with a disproportionate share of the world's wealth and power, and it was inevitable that the proportions be adjusted, as the wounded nations recovered their health and the poorer nations strove to claim their own share of the finite global resources. Nor could

our claim to unsullied international success and virtue be endlessly sustained, as the failed Vietnam intervention and its domestic repercussions
showed us. The post-Vietnam era has read to our generally fortunate
country a number of lessons in reality whose assimilation should make
the United States, in the end, a better—more reasonable, less self-
righteous—global citizen.

I write the above paragraphs, as it happens, on my sixtieth birthday. In
my sixty years of being an American I have seen, through the shifting lens
of my own life, considerable social change. The years began in a small
Pennsylvania town where I was made to feel, threadbare and Depression-
bound though the world around me was, cherished—cherished by a
polity that erected schools for my education, playgrounds for my recreation, libraries for my edification, police stations for my protection. Perhaps my sensation was a trick of egocentric perspective—a child
cannot but feel himself the center of the universe—but certain architectural remains corroborate it. In the nearby city of Reading, the municipal high school was a species of cathedral, looming ornately above its
neighborhood—not merely constructed, but constructed with a flourish
that showed where the society placed its pride. In my little community of
five thousand, the two school buildings were similarly eminent; we
moved through them in steady fashion, after sixth grade graduating from
one to the other, and walking down the main avenue in a new direction.
The importance of our education was a central strand of the town fabric.
The school grounds included a playground and several baseball fields
where one could improvise games under a light canopy of adult supervision. It was a hardscrabble, still rather rural world, but a generous share
of its resources seemed devoted to the young. The school system and its
satellites were the factories, as it were, wherein Americans were made—a
process worth investing in, even in hard times.

Now, we read in the papers and see on the streets, children are the
poorest group of our society—one-fourth live below the poverty line.
Millions live in environments where families are chaotic, the drug dealer
and the pimp the only visible role models, and the police the only agents
of discipline. Public schools, running on tightened budgets, can do little
more than physically restrain the inwash of hopeless, brutalized adolescents. Every major city bears the signs—vandalized playgrounds, dangerous parks, desecrated statues, ubiquitous graffiti—of a common civic
life swamped by the wrathful indifference of young people to whom society offers little but eventual shelter within the world's biggest penal
system. In the middle class, the young, reared on seven daily hours of
television-watching, are simply less educable, as slumping SAT scores

show. Their high schools no longer look like castles but like second-rate airports, low-slung and cut-rate, while the society's riches are reserved, in a curious gerontocratic shift, to the old, with their Social Security, their pensions, their Medicare, and the government entitlements that account for a third of the national budget. A nation where the old are coddled and the young are deprived of both purpose and means is surely one where people are entitled to feel bad.

This has become a nation in which it is increasingly difficult to establish an adult life. For my generation, coming of age in the Fifties, a job, a car, a house, and the appurtenances of family life were not difficult to acquire. A boom was on, but the cost of living was still modestly pitched. When I decided to leave New York (where we were paying $150 a month for a Greenwich Village floor-through) and go live in a New England small town, I figured that by selling six short stories a year I could support a family that had come, by 1960, to include four children. Our first house, not a small one, cost $18,500; our next, a rather grand one, in 1970, what now seems a paltry $80,000. I was fortunate, but not unusual; most of our friends, also in their twenties, owned their houses and had lots of children. These children, coming of age in the Seventies, found housing almost impossibly expensive, and have delayed marriage, by and large, until their thirties. When they marry, both partners work, and even so, they scrape by, with secondhand cars and handed-down furniture.

My generation lived better than its parents, which made us feel good; but we live better than our children, which makes us feel bad. "Diminished expectations" is the name of the new game, domestically as well as internationally. Our present discouragement, which fuels the transient success of such "protest" politicians as Pat Buchanan and Paul Tsongas, is not rooted in statistics but in sensory impressions—the squalor of midtown Manhattan, for instance, where homeless beggars line Fifth Avenue, sidewalks are cluttered with buskers and hustlers and pushcarts, and the Japanese own Rockefeller Center. The triumphant Japanese raid on our domestic automobile market lies at the very heart of our discouragement: our quintessential native industry gutted by an invasion of better-made, lower-priced foreign cars. We sense that the vast Eighties explosion of corporate acquisitions and junk-bond floatings was a storm of meaningless activity that left us without the ability to *make* anything—this having been, as our schoolteachers used to tell us so proudly, citing Henry Ford and the Wright Brothers and Thomas Alva Edison, a nation of makers. The pioneers who perfected the apple-corer have become the flaccid starers at the upstairs Sony. Just the muscle tone of Americans is discouraging to contemplate—either the artificially swollen pecs of exer-

cise freaks or the utterly limp abdominals of junk-food-fed channel
surfers, mainlining electronic visuals. Not many generations ago, this was
a nation of firm-bodied farm folk, and the sheer suety pallor of our
consumerism, of our "service economy," is enough to make us feel bad.

We feel bad about lawyers. We have five percent of the world's population and thirty percent of the world's lawyers, none of them good for anything much but dealing with other lawyers, generating megafees that
cumulatively function like a black hole at the center of the business
world, sucking dollars into it, adding to the cost of every manufactured
item from dental floss to hydraulic presses. We feel bad about bankers. It
turns out they are not colorless, punctilious caretakers of our money but
big spenders, wild and crazy lenders in gold-trimmed cowboy boots, the
wastrels of the Eighties, rolling up billions in bankruptcy without so
much as an "I'm sorry." We feel bad about doctors. The old-fashioned
country GP, with his horse and buggy and little black bag of sugar
pills, has become the white-collar gouger of the urban hospitals, running
thousand-dollar tests on comatose street people and propelling a ruinous
run-up on medical costs the country over. Except for the very rich and
the legally penniless, nobody can afford to get sick in this country. The
well-intentioned Medicaid and Medicare programs have become excuses
for a ruthless rip-off of government tax dollars; breakthroughs in medical technology produce nightmarish prolongations of natural life and a
costly, predatory exploitation of our fear of death.

AIDS adds to the smog of malaise. Our bodily fluids, the lubricant of
intimacy and the nectar of life, have become death potions; the sexual
revolution of the Sixties, however unrealistic its pot-sweetened hedonism, surely didn't deserve this murderous molecular backlash. We are all
potential contaminants of one another; toxicity is thoroughly internalized. We feel bad about pollution—every sort, from HIV to atomic
waste, from the overflowing landfills to the eroding ozone. The human
species, the United States in the forefront, is rapidly using up the world,
while enjoying it less and less. Farms into housing tracts, downtowns into
cardboard shantytowns, small towns into strips of highway junk stores,
urban projects into giant crack houses—the transforming decay spreads,
while the average citizen leads a chicken-coop existence, office cubicle to
sealed car to snug, burglar-proofed quarters where the televised world is
piped in like chlorinated water.

We feel bad because a once-sinewy nation, exultant in the resourcefulness that freedom brings, now seems bloated and zombified, pillaged and
crumbling, all around us. Enough of our original Puritanism remains to
generate self-disgust. Benjamin Franklin's exhortations to thrift haunt us,

in a world that makes debt not merely a necessity but a virtue. On the personal scale, credit-card companies beg us to buy more than we can pay for; on the national scale, professedly conservative, benefits-pinching Presidents yet run up ever more billions in the red, and despite a weak dollar a staggering trade imbalance persists. Americans feel bad, I think, because we have gone from being the globe's chief creditor to being one of the world's biggest debtors, and no amount of soothing statistical analysis from economists can allay our inner conviction that so many negative numbers must add up somewhere, and there must be an eventual reckoning.

Our pessimism dates from the optimism of the Sixties, when John Kennedy told us we would "pay any price, bear any burden, meet any hardship, support any friend" to advance the cause of liberty, and Lyndon Johnson simultaneously launched the War Against Poverty and the war against North Vietnam. Guns and butter, we could afford both—there was nothing America could not do. As recent events show, the Red Menace proved easier to defeat than the internal enemy. There is still a shameful amount of poverty and social derangement in this country, and it is harder than ever to ignore. It takes its revenge in making our cities dangerous and unsightly. Rural poverty can be shut into its countryside, but urban poverty affects the centers of infrastructure and the capitals of wealth and culture. Until the legacy of black slavery is erased, and the myth of white supremacy forgotten, the United States will have a sore spot for politicians to exploit. Strides in race relations have been made in my sixty years, not only on the statute books but in the impalpable realm of popular culture. Black musicians, black comedians, and black athletes are heroes to white as well as black youngsters, an effortless racial mixing takes place at least on television screens, and black men and women can now be seen in business suits all across the country. Nevertheless, the majority of the descendants of the slaves are still sunk at the bottom of the economy, and without a factory job in Detroit or Birmingham to offer them a way up. Large numbers of the white population see blacks as criminals and welfare sponges, and the once solidly Democratic South now delivers solidly for the Republicans, in a vote that must be termed reactionary. And this is another reason for feeling bad. The expanding economy that promised to carry all minorities and immigrants upward with it no longer expands. American openness and generosity, expressed in the unfenced grass of our front yards, now threatens to turn defensive, protectionist, exclusionist, isolationist; the fences are going up, in our minds and on our properties.

The brief euphoria that greeted the effective prosecution of the Gulf

War should be understood, I think, against the background of pessimism. Having been for years bombarded with tales of Pentagon inefficiency and extravagance, we were amazed that the high-priced "smart" weapons actually seemed to work (many didn't, it turns out). Remembering the protests, draft defiance, and miserable combat mire of Vietnam, we were gratified to discover a generation of young men and women who, having signed up basically for a free education in a peacetime military force, were nevertheless willing and able to fight a war. Having associated the military with the disgraced Vietnam policies, we were relieved to see generals we could admire briskly achieving a clearly defined goal against a villainous and boastful opponent. But the aftermath has muddled the victory with stalemate, and the possession of the world's undisputed champion military machine makes Americans, I think, more uncomfortable than not. We are a nation that likes its military glory in spurts, in the service of a crusade, and then set aside; we do not in our hearts aspire to being an international enforcer or a mercenary army for the oil-consuming nations.

What *do* we aspire to? What the Declaration of Independence promises: the pursuit of happiness. The chance to get ahead. Enough space to chase rainbows in. The fact that, compared with the inhabitants of Africa and Russia, we still live well cannot ease the pain of feeling we no longer live *nobly*. American plenty, to taste right, needs a seasoning of idealism; the land's abundance was taken as God's provision for a freer, more equal, less encumbered life than Europe could provide, except to its anointed nobles. Now the land feels encumbered and squeezed and depleted; the ground feels soft and riddled under us; the air is robbed of ozone by the aerosol in the spray cans busy defacing our public monuments with the bloated letters proclaiming gang turf; things don't get better and better every day; and we naturally feel bad.

If I had written these impressions in 1999, there would have been less talk of economic malaise and of Japanese wizardry. I would have felt compelled to mention, however, the President who, though exemplary in many respects, with a continuing high job rating, has shrouded the White House, partly through his own doing, in an atmosphere of scandal and rumor, evasion and counterspin, to the point of national demoralization. Our great Republic deserves better from above, one can't help thinking, than this relentless rain of tawdriness.

Letter to a Baby Boomer

My dear Boomer:

I'm afraid we won't be able to call you "Baby" much longer. Yours is the most famous demographic group in America, and it has been your youthfulness that has characterized you at every stage. In infancy, you popped into being in unprecedented numbers on the great wave of post-war fertility and prosperity between 1946 and 1964. In childhood, you filled the new Levittowns with your tricycles and backyard wading pools, and you imbibed the newly concocted milk and honey of television in such giant draughts that child psychologists feared your brains would be washed away; you were car-pooled everywhere by an army of moms and you hid under your school desks in drills designed to mitigate the effects of atomic war. In your adolescence, you learned to rock-and-roll, and you waitressed on roller skates at the car hop on the edge of town. In your youth, you went to Woodstock, experienced altered states of conscious-ness, protested Vietnam, or fought in it, or both. In your adulthood, you invented Yuppie-ness, health-consciousness, and corporate greed. You thought that, whatever happened, you would never grow old. You went from left-wing revolution under Johnson to right-wing revolution under Reagan without losing your waistlines and fine tanned musculature. Now the first of you are turning fifty, and thenceforth at the rate of one every seven seconds you will be joining the unspeakable pod people, the indis-putably middle-aged, the over-the-hill, the thick-waisted and presbyopic. I write to welcome you, immigrants to life's second half-century, and to offer what guidance I can.

In my own experience, the fiftieth birthday is less traumatic than the thirtieth, which says goodbye to youth, or the sixtieth, which says hello to old age. But my experience is that of another generation, the Silent, or Almost Absent, Generation. We thinly straggled onto the stage during the Depression and World War II—a baby bust. Yet, in our quiet, wary way, we were fortunate, stepping into adulthood as America bestrode the world; our modest expectations were, often, exceeded. Your expectations, nurtured in all those post-war upward trends, were sanguine, but the world began to come apart in 1963, when John Kennedy was shot. Other assassinations and dislocations followed, climaxing in 1968, when your generation, from Chicago to Paris, generously offered to relieve the world's corrupt and doddery leaders of their responsibilities and run things along the utopian lines of love (not war), racial harmony, pot, rock,

Written, in 1996, for *New Choices*, a magazine for the unyoung.

bell-bottoms, LSD, tie-dyed T-shirts, a cozy communal anarchy, and plenty of risk-free sex to go around. While not all points of this ambitious program were instantly adopted, boomer thinking infiltrated the mainstream, and now one of you sits in the White House. The Silent Generation never had a President. Instead, we had Michael Dukakis, Jesse Jackson, and Gary Hart.

Turning fifty for us, perhaps, was no big deal, since we had been born old, or at least born meek. But for you—a rude shock, no doubt. Your first big bite of obsolescence. Your first clear mathematical indication that, unless you haggle and stagger your way to a hundred, the larger part of your life is over. What can I tell you about this territory of the downward slope, of thickening twilight? Well, there is the matter of the winking-out neurons. On your brisk way to perform a minor errand, you forget what the errand was. You stand in the center of the room inwardly waltzing with the ghost of your good intention. About to greet a neighbor at the supermarket, you confidently reach down into a mental pocket that has only a hole in it. Well, let's not forget that forgetfulness is the safeguard of sanity. If we remembered everything all the time, our brains would be clogged and clamorous. The neighbor's name will come to you in the car driving home, and the errand (taking the car to get its inspection sticker, say) will come to you in the middle of the night, when the garage is closed. Neurons die painlessly, and ignorance is bliss. What I didn't realize, until after I turned fifty, was how little information one needs to get by—all those once-memorized baseball stats and stanzas by Henry Wadsworth Longfellow, the sun still comes up without them.

Physical deterioration: you boomers have jogged and bench-pressed and done yoga until you are somatically as gods. Nevertheless, after fifty the air-conditioner gets heavier every year you lift it out of the window. Running up five flights of steps, you will feel on the final landing as if your knees are made of liquid detergent. Sexually (and I know this was important to you), there is a new force of gravity dragging at your angel wings; bed becomes more and more a place to fall asleep in. Indeed, all the old enemies of sleep—a voracious lover, a hilarious party, a fascinating book, a sheer excitement at being alive—slowly lose their puissance, and pale beside the majestic attractions of oblivion. These lessenings are not entirely debits; the remission of romantic fury allows more time for, say, crossword puzzles, and the need to cut a dynamic figure at every weekend party and tennis scramble no longer shoulders aside those household and gardening chores that once appeared so contemptibly marginal. A quaint tidiness creeps over the latter decades, along with a long-dormant interest in the songs of birds and the names of plants. The annual return of barn swallows to our carport, for instance, and their subsequent rearing of three or four swallowettes, have become principal topics of excited conversation between my wife and myself—little natural miracles relieving the level quiet of our days. Over fifty, you shall find, one makes more of less. The muscles of empathy and curiosity strengthen while those of youthful egocentricity weaken. As the old biological missions—mating and begetting, mostly—slacken in urgency, the world itself, in its multifarious and ceaselessly shifting non-human detail, sifts into awareness, imparting an innocent sense of witness like that of childhood.

These surrenders take place inch by inch. A fifty-year-old is still a fierce being—potent, competitive, prone to surges of animal energy. For men and women in the workforce, the decade of the fifties should be a prime time, of vigor fortified by experience, of grave responsibility and maximum salary. But a time tinged, it may be, with an undercurrent of ebbing creativity, as magnetism and savvy pass to a younger generation, who have the new technology in their veins and effortlessly speak the language of the up-and-coming consumer. One is, after fifty, no longer up-and-coming, not even in the sluggish realm of the arts, which allows youthful promise to fortysomething performers who, if athletes, would be already retired. It will be hard for you boomers—for so long the promoters and consumers of the new thing, be it Dylan and the Beatles, miniskirts and safari jackets, PCs and videos—to yield fashion to generations yet younger. Like the flapper generation of the 1920s, you were made much of in your youth, envied and analyzed, deplored and deferred to. But the march of generations did not halt its self-consuming progress for even you, and, though some few of your cadres will ascend in the next decade or two to summits of political and corporate power, most of you have had the bulk of your fun.

Well, but what is fun? It comes in many flavors, and there is, believe it or not, an over-fifty flavor. The majority of your decisions, willy-nilly, for good or bad, are behind you. You have rough-hewn your fates; now self-preservation and a certain sweet, blameless self-solicitude move to the top of the agenda. The quality of life—a side issue in the thick of the battle—becomes a matter of careful consideration and numerous discriminations. Pressing obligations suddenly loom as imaginary. The charms of saying no, of not-doing, for the first time exercise a significant appeal. There are, if you don't panic, terminal satisfactions. Now that your future is no longer infinite, your entire life can be, for the first time, contemplated in its achieved shape, susceptible to a few finishing touches, applied with the fingertips of an artist rather than with a warrior's heavy hand. There is a certain relief in knowing how little remains in your control, how little remains to be proved. In the meantime, that inestimable treasure, that perpetual present in which life is lived, that aware split-second through which all flows, remains in your possession, along with, if you are lucky, health and sanity.

You baby boomers have pushed in a herd down this half-century, cropping the grazing land in each decade. Now you are on your way, collectively, to bankrupt Medicare and the Social Security System. But I address this letter to you in the singular. After fifty, the essential solitude of being a human being can scarcely be hidden; trust me that the chill rather clears the air. Shakespeare's Prospero, upon taking his early retirement, promised, "Every third thought shall be my grave." Which leaves two thoughts, however, to entertain above the ground. You have in your colorful pilgrimage long rehearsed what these thoughts might be: (1) love one another, and (2) seize the day.

The Fifties

THE FIFTIES in my mind's eye are a waxy blue-white, a shining Cold War iceberg drifting by in the wake of the khaki-brown Forties and the grit-gray Thirties. As a child of those two shabby, beleaguered decades, I was happy in the Fifties; I entered them as a penniless high-school senior and left them as a home-owning father of three children and the author of three books, with a fourth, *Rabbit, Run*, submitted to the publisher just as the decade ran out. Many Americans were happy in the Fifties—but not as happy, looking back, as we should have been. The American economy was the world's behemoth. The imbalance of trade was a few billion in our favor, instead of over a hundred billion in annual outflow. Ten dollars bought a four-course meal in Paris, instead of a demitasse and a stale croissant. At home, ten thousand dollars bought a house, and a quarter bought a gallon of gas. You could walk most city streets without a qualm at two in the morning, and as to family values—boy, did we have family values! Divorce rates dropped, along with the age when people got married. Wives churned out new Americans at the highest birth-rate of the century. Night after night, we clustered around the television set watching *Father Knows Best, I Love Lucy, Leave It to Beaver, The Pat Boone Show,* and *The General Electric Theatre*, hosted by an avuncular Ronald Reagan.

In the Fifties, there was the nuclear family, and there were nuclear

---

Written in 1994 as one of six essays describing the six American decades of *Newsweek*'s existence, since February 1933.

weapons, featuring the H-bomb. It took its bow at Eniwetok in 1952 and then, for an encore, at Bikini in 1954. In 1953 the new and rather temporary head of the Soviet Union, Georgi Malenkov, ceremoniously announced, "The Soviet Government deems it necessary to report that the United States has no monopoly in the production of the hydrogen bomb." With H-bombs all around, John Foster Dulles, the Cold Warrior's Cold Warrior, boasted of "massive retaliatory power" and, in 1956, explained brinkmanship: "The ability to get to the verge without getting into war is the necessary art." That same year, Nikita Khrushchev informed a gathering of Western ambassadors at the Kremlin, "History is on our side. We will bury you!," and J. Robert Oppenheimer likened the U.S. and the U.S.S.R. to two scorpions in a bottle. The danger of mutual annihilation was real and dreadful enough, and percolated through every psyche, but by no means dominated life in the decade; the nuclear jitters co-existed with a private optimism and a shy, domestic hedonism. The thought of atomic war, like that of one's own death, was too big to be useful. An editorialist for the French journal *Le Monde* expressed the paradoxical formula: "The balance of terror is more and more the foundation of peace."

Peace it was, with some skirmishes—most painfully, in Korea, a muddy three-year struggle that ended where it began, on the 38th Parallel. It was our first Cold War venture at tactical warfare, and our first fight under the banner of the United Nations. Everything that was awkward and unsatisfactory about the conflict—self-imposed limits, unlovable allies, murky purposes in unfriendly terrain—became unbearably so in Vietnam fifteen years later; in Korea, however, both sides accepted stalemate. MacArthur had wanted to go for an old-fashioned all-out victory, but Truman, confrontational though he was on the home front, always resisted the tempters urging him to set things right in Asia. Two oldish men presided over the Fifties, Truman and Eisenhower, and in retrospect they seem pretty fair Presidents, though the right detested Truman and the left scorned Ike. Sitting on Armageddon, they taught us to live with ambiguity. Eisenhower let the noxious Joe McCarthy slowly self-destruct, and declined to rescue the French in Vietnam. When his turn came in 1959 to "lose" Cuba, as Truman had "lost" China in 1949, he swallowed the pill, and left it to his brash young successor to invade the Bay of Pigs and to test the Vietnamese quagmire.

The Fifties got a bad rap from their successor decade, as conformist, consumeristic, politically apathetic, sexually timid. The decade didn't lack its own internal critics: Sloan Wilson in *The Man in the Gray Flannel Suit*, David Reisman in *The Lonely Crowd*, John Kenneth Galbraith in

The Affluent Society, Allen Ginsberg in *Howl*. My generation, coming into its own, was called Silent, as if, after all the vain and murderous noise of recent history, this was a bad thing.

The Fifties should be understood as, like the Twenties, a post-war decade. The returning veterans had set the tone for the colleges: serious study, leading to the private redoubt of the career, the kids, the collie, and the tract house. As in the Twenties, business interests reasserted control over government. Idealism retreated from the public sector; each man was an island. The general turning-inwards was fruitful for the arts. In painting, the New York School, whether called action painting or abstract expressionism, reversed the artistic current that had always flowed from Europe to these shores, by creating a global—some said an imperial—style. Television, a flickering gray toy at the beginning of the decade, grew to dominate the average family's day and to alter the quality and span of attention. Yet the Fifties adults had grown up in a Gutenbergian universe, and literature was revered as it would not be again. The modernist classics—Eliot and Pound and Joyce and Stevens and Kafka and Proust—loomed as demigods to undergraduates and bohemians. What decade since the Twenties could show a burst of novels as radiant and various as Salinger's *Catcher in the Rye* and McCullers' *Ballad of the Sad Café* (1951), Ellison's *Invisible Man* and O'Connor's *Wise Blood* (1952), Bellow's *Adventures of Augie March* (1953), Nabokov's *Lolita* (1955), Kerouac's *On the Road* and Malamud's *Assistant* (1957), Connell's *Mrs. Bridge* (1958), Roth's *Goodbye, Columbus* and Vonnegut's *Sirens of Titan* (1959), to name but a few? The literary South saw itself in the grip of a renaissance, Jewish-Americans had found their amazing voice, and the phrase "New York intellectual" still meant something.

America's artists and intellectuals, like those of the Twenties, felt mostly a sardonic estrangement from a government that extolled business and mediocrity. "The great problem of America today," Eisenhower said, "is to take that straight road down the middle," and his Secretary of Defense, Charles Wilson, claimed, "What was good for our country was good for General Motors and vice versa." By the middle of the decade, Elvis Presley and Alan Freed's "rock 'n' roll" radio station offered teenagers a musical vehicle for their rebellious instincts, and an outsider style in word and deed was being developed by the "beats." When the generation being piously raised in the nation's Levittowns came to seek a haven from respectability in "sex, drugs, and rock 'n' roll," the site had already been prepared.

The Fifties' condition as a post-war decade helps explain the something prim and Spartan about it. There was a military rigor in its ticky-tacky housing developments and sternly boxy skyscrapers, a kind of platoon discipline in its swiftly assembled families. The nation was still war-hardened. When the nation's young draftees were asked to do battle in Korea, few thought to protest or resist, though few went with enthusiasm. When Senator McCarthy announced that traitorous Communists pervaded the government and that only draconian measures could defeat this inner enemy, many were willing to believe him: blacklists, congressional show trials, and meaningless, redundant loyalty oaths for a time gave patriotism an ugly face. The citizens of the Fifties remembered the Depression and the universal mobilization of the Second World War; they were relatively docile, with more consciousness of duties and less of rights than we have.

How much we have they didn't!—personal computers and home videos, contraceptive pills and AIDS, legalized abortion and pornography, shopping malls and microwave ovens. Most main roads still ran through the center of towns, and in the South segregated schools and Jim Crow laws were still the rule. Black equality was the main domestic issue: Truman desegregated the armed forces in 1950, and Eisenhower reluctantly sent troops to Little Rock to enforce the Supreme Court's 1954 decision outlawing segregated schools, but the national government followed rather than led the way in the civil-rights movement, which took its energy from inspired lonely defiers like Rosa Parks and Martin Luther King. What is hardest to picture about the Fifties is how many less of us there were, a hundred million less: the U.S. census for 1950 counted about 150 million citizens, moving about with no thought of acid rain or cholesterol, in a land where farmland now gone surrounded quiet roadways now jammed. For those who were favored by society, the quality of daily life—in terms of absent dangers and demands, in terms of the purchasing power of a day's wages—was arguably better than that of the faster-paced decades since.

American Chronicle, by Lois and Alan Gordon, fascinatingly lists year by year the expressions that came into use in the Fifties, populating mental spaces until then blank: apartheid, Cinerama, H-bomb, integration, mambo, spaceman, miniaturization, cool jazz, hot rod, panty raid, ponytail, printed circuit, TelePrompTer, drag strip, name-dropper, cookout, countdown, discount house, egghead, girlie magazine, jet stream, split-level, metalinguistics, captive audience, windfall profit, fallout, hard sell, hotline, greaser, hip, togetherness, automated, junk mail, Thorazine, cue card, stoned, blastoff, Third World, fuzz, cop-out, put-on, hero sandwich, headshrinker, meter maid, shook up, funky, beatnik, DNA, lunar probe, news satellite, sex kitten, sick joke, gung ho, joint, chick, and polymorphous perversity.

A decade that had to coin all those terms surely can be forgiven its gauche tail fins and ducktails, its hula hoops and contact-papered Populuxe kitchens. The decade was trying to reinvent pleasure and irony. By the time (1959) a "Nikita doll" could be advertised for sale ("Lifelike figure, in washable-rubberoid, smiles, lolls tongue, says 'Peace' when tilted"), the Cold War iceberg was beginning to melt. In 1959, John Foster Dulles died, along with Billie Holiday and Buddy Holly, and Charles Van Doren and quiz-show producer Dan Enright admitted to having rigged *Twenty-One* and *Tic Tac Dough*, and everyone felt cheated. Also that year, Doris Day, the very symbol of robust Fifties chastity, starred in a sexy feminist film, *Pillow Talk*, with the closet homosexual Rock Hudson, and Marilyn Monroe starred in a transvestite farce, *Some Like It Hot*. Polymorphous perversity had arrived; the hectic Sixties, hot and (in my mind's eye) a psychedelic red, would wreck our Fifties marriages, shatter our faith in the anti-Communist crusade, and leave scarcely a hero standing. What one decade—a bit of a fuddy-duddy, but no fool—had carefully saved, the next recklessly spent. Perhaps the Fifties didn't truly end until November of 1963, when John F. Kennedy was shot, and the demons frozen in the iceberg came out to swarm.

GENDER AND HEALTH

The Disposable Rocket

INHABITING A MALE BODY is like having a bank account; as long as it's healthy, you don't think much about it. Compared with the female body, it is a low-maintenance proposition: a shower now and then, trim the fingernails every ten days, a haircut once a month. Oh yes, shaving— scraping or buzzing away at your face every morning. Byron, in *Don Juan*, thought the repeated nuisance of shaving balanced out the periodic agony, for females, of childbirth. Women are, his lines tell us,

> Condemn'd to child-bed, as men for their sins
> Have shaving too entail'd upon their chins,—
>
> A daily plague, which in the aggregate
> May average on the whole with parturition.

From the standpoint of reproduction, the male body is a delivery system, as the female is a mazy device for retention. Once the delivery is made, men feel a faint but distinct falling-off of interest. Yet against the enduring female heroics of birth and nurture should be set the male's superhuman frenzy to deliver his goods: he vaults walls, skips sleep, risks wallet, health, and his political future all to ram home his seed into the gut of the chosen woman. The sense of the chase lives in him as the key to life. His body is, like a delivery rocket that falls away in space, a disposable means. Men put their bodies at risk to experience the release from gravity.

When my tenancy of a male body was fairly new—of six or so

Written for a special issue of the *Michigan Quarterly Review* (Fall 1993) on this topic, as a companion piece to "The Female Body," incited by the same editors and reprinted in *Odd Jobs*, pp. 70–72.

years' duration—I used to jump and fall just for the joy of it. Falling—backwards, or down the stairs—became a specialty of mine, an attention-getting stunt I was still practicing into my thirties, at suburban parties. Falling is, after all, a kind of flying, though of briefer duration than would be ideal. My impulse to hurl myself from high windows and the edges of cliffs belongs to my body, not my mind, which resists the siren call of the chasm with all its might; the interior struggle knocks the wind from my lungs and tightens my scrotum and gives any trip to Europe, with its Alps, castle parapets, and gargoyled cathedral lookouts, a flavor of night-mare. Falling, strangely, no longer figures in my dreams, as it often did when I was a boy and my subconscious was more honest with me. An air-plane, that necessary evil, turns the earth into a map so quickly the brain becomes aloof and calm; still, I marvel that there is no end of young men willing to become jet pilots.

Any accounting of male-female differences must include the male's superior recklessness, a drive not, I think, toward death, as the darker feminist cosmogonies would have it, but to test the limits, to see what the traffic will bear—a kind of mechanic's curiosity. The number of men who do lasting damage to their young bodies is great; war and car accidents aside, secondary-school sports, with the approval of parents and the encouragement of brutish coaches, take a fearful toll of skulls and knees. We were made for combat, back in the post-simian, East African days, and the bumping, the whacking, the breathlessness, the pain-smothering adrenaline rush form a cumbersome and unfashionable bliss, but bliss nevertheless. Take your body to the edge, and see if it flies.

The male sense of space must differ from that of the female, who has such interesting, active, and significant inner space. The space that inter-ests men is outer. The fly ball high against the sky, the long pass spiralling overhead, the jet fighter like a scarcely visible pinpoint nozzle laying down its vapor trail at forty thousand feet, the gazelle haunch flickering just beyond arrow-reach, the uncountable stars sprinkled on their great black wheel, the horizon, the mountaintop, the quasar—these bring por-tents with them and awaken a sense of relation with the invisible, with the empty. The ideal male body is taut with lines of potential force, a diagram extending outward; the ideal female body curves around cen-ters of repose. Of course, no one is ideal, and the sexes are somewhat androgynous subdivisions of a species: Diana the huntress is a more trendy body-type nowadays than languid, overweight Venus, and poly-morphous Dionysus poses for more underwear ads than Mars. Relatively, though, men's bodies, however elegant, are designed for covering terri-tory, for moving on.

An erection, too, defies gravity, flirts with it precariously. It extends the diagram of outward direction into downright detachability—objective in the case of the sperm, subjective in the case of the testicles and penis. Men's bodies, at this juncture, feel only partly theirs; a demon of sorts has been attached to their lower torsos, whose performance is erratic and whose errands seem, at times, ridiculous. It is like having a (much) smaller brother toward whom you feel both fond and impatient; if he is you, it is you in curiously simplified and innocent form. This sense, of the male body being two of them, is acknowledged in voiced love play and erotic writing, where the penis is playfully given a pet name, an individuation not even the rarest rapture grants a vagina. Here, where maleness gathers to a quintessence of itself, there can be no insincerity, there can be no hiding; for sheer nakedness, there is nothing like a hopeful phallus; its aggressive shape is indivisible from its tender-skinned vulnerability. The act of intercourse, from the point of view of a consenting female, has an element of mothering, of enwrapment, of merciful concealment, even. The male body, for this interval, is tucked out of harm's way.

To inhabit a male body, then, is to feel somewhat detached from it. It is not an enemy, but not entirely a friend. Our being seems to lie not in cells and muscles but in the traces that our thoughts and actions inscribe on the air. The male body skims the surface of those deeps wherein the blood and pain and mysterious cravings of women perpetuate the species. Participating less than the female body in nature's processes, the male body gives the impression—false—of being exempt from time. Its full powers of strength and reach appear in early adolescence, along with acne and sweaty feet, and depart, in imperceptible increments, after thirty or so. It surprises me to discover, when I remove my shoes and socks, the same paper-white, hairless ankles that struck me as pathetic when I observed them on my father. I felt betrayed when, in some tumble of touch football twenty years ago, I heard my tibia snap; and when, between two reading engagements in Cleveland, my appendix tried to burst; and when, the other day, not for the first time, there arose to my nostrils out of my own body the musty attic smell my grandfather's body had.

A man's body does not betray its tenant as rapidly as a woman's. Never as fine and lovely, it has less distance to fall; what rugged beauty it has is wrinkle-proof. It keeps its capability of procreation indecently long. Unless intense athletic demands are made upon it, the thing serves well enough to sixty, which is my age now. From here on, it's chancy. There are no breasts or ovaries to admit cancer to the male body, but the prostate, that awkwardly located little booster to the sperm, shows the strain of sexual function with fits of hysterical cell replication. And all that male-bonding beer and potato chips add up in the coronary arteries. A writer, whose physical equipment can be minimal as long as it gets him to the desk, the lectern, and New York City once in a while, cannot but be grateful to his body, especially to his eyes, those tender and intricate sites where the brain extrudes from the skull, and to his hands, which hold the pen or tap the keyboard. His body has been, not himself exactly, but a close pal, pot-bellied and balding like most of his other pals now. A man and his body are like a boy and the buddy who has a driver's license and the use of his father's car for the evening; you go along, gratefully, for the ride.

Women Dancing

WHAT DO WOMEN WANT? They want, evidently, to dance. Why? Why, in the days of my youth, did girls permit themselves to be seized and clumsily pushed about by sweating, overexcited, embarrassed boys? Not only did they permit it, they dressed themselves in taffeta and tulle and strapless bras to encourage its happening, and wept when it did not.

For tears to be evoked, the importance of dances—school, country-club, Saturday-night, tea, square—as a means of gauging female desirability and mateability must be firmly established in feminine nervous systems. Society, to perpetuate itself in an orderly fashion, needs to arrange controlled outlets for the sexual impulses of the young. In the West, couples dancing became such an outlet, a ritual sublimation. For the male, the opportunity to put at least one of his arms around a female, inhaling her perfume, feeling her body brush against his and her palm moisten in his grip, was its own breathtaking reward.

In *Homage to Blenholt*, by the great Daniel Fuchs, Mendel Munves, a scholarly etymologist, is belatedly taught to dance by the amiable Rita. Taking her into his arms opens him to cosmic speculation:

> Munves pressed her tightly to him and shivered. Ooooh, it felt good. Soft, soft. Women were originally built like a jackknife, like a Westchester roll, and all one short round lump, he was thinking, and when God opened them up straight, the body protruded in round curved masses. He hugged her tighter and tighter, his skinny arm on her shoulders aching.

On the other side of the world, where the Japanese were tentatively imitating this risqué Western custom, the hero of the great Tanizaki's *Naomi* has a harder time of it, at first:

I remember taking Naomi's hand and beginning the one-step, feverish with excitement, but after that, I lost all sense of what was going on. I couldn't hear that music any longer; my steps were chaotic; my eyes were dazed; my heart pounded. It was all so different from dancing to records above Yoshimura's music shop. Once I'd paddled out into this vast sea of people, there was no turning back and no going forward. I didn't know what to do.

Another partner, however, settles him down:

But when I danced with Kirako, I was surprised to find how light she was. Her whole body was soft, like cotton, and her hands were as smooth as new leaves. She quickly got the knack of dancing with me, awkward as I was, and adapted herself to me the way an intelligent horse does to its rider. Lightness carried to this degree is indescribably pleasant.

Though he is supposed to lead, a man dancing is a guest of his female partner, welcomed into her province. Girls take to dancing with a mysterious ease and keenness. Lacking a male partner, they will dance with each other, as we see in that ecstatic painting by George Luks, *The Spielers*, showing two slum girls locked in a musical embrace so energetic that their hair is a blur of brushstrokes. The fondness for conjoined rhythmic motion relates, perhaps, to a gender trait—a female somatic unity, a sense of the entire body as an expressive and erotic means. Men, relatively, are compartmentalized creatures, and in couples dancing the parts—the feet, the tongue, the libido, the diagrammatic brain—go flinging in different directions.

Guide me, master me, the woman's posture says, as she lifts her arms to be danced with. How sweetly forbearing she is, shuffled back and forth in a pathetically stunted version of what Fred Astaire might have sweepingly done with her graceful compliance. Astaire epitomized the romantic hero as dancing man; his reedy voice, his odd face, his slight build, the trifling nature of his screen personae were all small coin within the largesse of his permission, to his female partner, to dance. Even Astaire, paired with a female, became an excuse for her greater suppleness and grace to display itself, to discover itself, in dancing. It is Ginger Rogers' trailing boas and shimmering gowns that stick in the mind as tokens of an indescribable pleasure. We remember her face as coolly averted, not so much from her partner's face as from the naked sensation of dance, an invisible white fire that is engulfing her from below.

The maenads, intoxicated by wine, danced themselves into a murderous frenzy. Eliza Doolittle could have danced all night. Dancing is one of the earliest and most widespread expressions of culture—that is, of human raw material channelled into social form. Stone Age cave paintings show dancing shamans in animal dress. Fertility dances occur from Australia to Alaska. Rain dances reinforce the shaman's danced appeal to the gods. The upper classes of advanced societies tended to leave dancing to the priests and the peasants. "The cultured upper classes of Egypt do not appear to have indulged in any form of social dancing," I read in the *Encyclopaedia Britannica*, and, "Dancing of all kinds was regarded with disfavor by the cultural and intellectual people of Rome." No authorities are cited, but I believe it. The Romans did have war dances, however, in which the priests of Mars danced with weapons, while those of Cybele and Attis gashed themselves with knives and potsherds. The people of the Middle Ages had the dance of death, and the slower-paced *basse danse*. The sixteenth century brought in the galliard, the pavane, the courante, and the volta, whose turns were so violent the lady was sometimes lifted off her feet. The volta was considered impolite until Queen Elizabeth I herself danced it. Dance and indecency go hand in hand. Look at go-go, exotic, and belly dancers. Dancing is both self-exhibition and self-exploration.

Until the twist came along in 1960, it was hard to see your female partner. She was a piece of waved hair, a bare shoulder, a foreshortened upper lip. In the jitterbug, she flew past—and in my high school the boys who could jitterbug were so few the girls jitterbugged with each other. When the twist came along, I was determined not to be left out, and wasn't. Around eleven o'clock on a Saturday night, the Chubby Checker and Fats Domino records were put on the turntable and our suburban dinner parties shucked their small talk and revealed their Dionysian side. The twist was, for women, one of the most ungainly dances ever devised, and yet they did it, as if knowing that in a year or two it would yield to the frug, at which they could show themselves to subtler advantage. In all of the myriad non-contactual dances that have followed rock-and-roll on its proliferating course, the woman becomes alone with her bliss. When happy, little boys jump and start hitting things with sticks; little girls do a dance.

In the West Indies, the black women wrapped their bodies snug around the mambo, its chickenish head-motions and mincing steps, and the steel drums pealed on and on. In New England, in our ethnically mixed little mill town, the young housewives learned the steps to join in at Greek dances, and affected a Melina Mercouri–esque hauteur as they slid along in the braid of moving feet and interlocked hands. In swinging London, in 1969, the dollies in their minis cavorted by the light of a stroboscopic flash, stamping each pose onto the blackness of my retina like a letter of the Egyptian alphabet. In the Shillington (Pennsylvania) Recreation Hall, in 1943 or '4, "Mairsy Doats" and Artie Shaw's slippery "Begin the Beguine" were the records I tried to learn to fox-trot to, not very successfully, though my partner kept murmuring encouragement in my ear. We were eleven, or twelve. My mother, sensing something amiss in my preparations for life, sent me to take dancing lessons in a nearby city, with a plump woman shorter than I though more than twice as old. We strode around her empty studio for an hour each Saturday morning, but it didn't give me twinkling feet.

I have always been excessively afraid of stepping on women's toes. They do get stepped on, but it is not the issue, just as—as Norman Mailer once told me—bloody noses cease to be the issue once you put on gloves and begin to box in earnest. I haven't taken up boxing, and my dancing days are stumbling down to a precious few. This is a sadness to my wife, who took ballet as a tiny girl and loved her Connecticut cotillions. Well, I tell her, life is more than a two-step. But in my heart I fear it is not; we are born (step one) and then we die (step two), and betweentimes the drumbeat of the pulse demands that we act out its rhythm.

In my lovingly preserved images of women dancing they are sweaty and self-forgetful—hopping up and down to, say, the sixth hoarse chorus of Janis Joplin's "Me and Bobby McGee," or being cradled in the dreamy last clarinet run of "Stardust," while the overhead mirror-ball slows. Dancing should be a vacation the body takes from consciousness. I have seen Martha Graham and Margot Fonteyn dance, on the far edge of their long primes, but performance dancing however exquisite has always afflicted me with a slight anxiety—that the shoe will squeak, that the male dancer with his bulging legs and buttocks will drop his quivering burden of ballerina, that some small earthly happenstance will mar the attempted otherworldly perfection. It is the supporting ensemble, in their multiple tutus and undulant anonymity, that override anxiety, and relax the spectacle. Dance should transcend its form. Dance should not be a worry, but worry's cancellation. If women have more worries than men, by compensation they seem to arrive more readily at shedding them.

Once, in Africa, I watched the staging of a so-called native dance. The most conspicuous item of clothing for the females was a set of colorful flat necklaces bounced up and down in picturesque tribal synchrony. Some of the women were young girls, and as I watched I reflected that, this being modern Kenya, they were probably, otherwise dressed, receiving sound neo-colonial educations and preparing for progressive careers in engineering or civil service. One of the girls, one of the bounciest, caught my eye and seemed to read the mind of this elderly *mzungu*; her smile, already broad, broadened further, while her necklaces didn't miss a prehistorical beat. "O body swayed to music, O brightening glance / How can we know the dancer from the dance?" Well, we can't, and that is the beauty of it.

Get Thee Behind Me, Suntan

THE ALLURE OF THE SUN, so irresistible thirty years ago, has come in for nothing but bad press since. Wrinkles, skin cancers, premature epidermal senility—no doubt about the culprit. The young married beauties with whom my then wife and I spent great chunks of summer sunning on a broad beach north of Boston have in the subsequent decades gone from being nut-brown Pocahontases to looking like Sitting Bull, with a melancholy facial fissure for every broken treaty. In one extreme case of sun worship, a devotee who had her husband build her a sunporch over the garage became in her middle years so phototoxic that she now goes outdoors swaddled like a beekeeper. Still, as with the Roaring Twenties, it was a great ride. We all smoked, too, while soaking up the poisonous rays at noon, and drank martinis when the beloved sun sank beneath the yardarm. Feeling glamorous had very little to do with physical conditioning; swatting sand flies was as close as we came to aerobic exercise.

But a tan is, of course, a gesture in the direction of nature, an attempt to be at one with our cosmic roots. Adam and Eve, most memorably portrayed by indoorsy Northern Europeans like Jan van Eyck and Lucas Cranach the Elder, rarely show even the ghost of a tan, but they must in fact have been heavily burnished by that Mesopotamian sun. In race-haunted America, the dark-skinned female offers sexual release—the Polynesian maiden swimming out to welcome the Presbyterian whaler, or the dusky quadroon (her mulatta mother herself born of a master's midnight visit to the slave shack) beckoning from the wrought-iron balcony of a New Orleans bordello. Dorothy Lamour in a sarong, Ava Gardner playing Julie in *Show Boat*. The marginalized tan races were credited with the sexiness that had been discounted by the Protestant ethic. In Hawthorne's refiguration of Puritan psychology, even black hair was suspectly racy, as flaunted by Hester Prynne in *The Scarlet Letter* and Zenobia in *The Blithedale Romance*. Darkness, the subliminal message runs, has something to teach us. Sunbathing in the Sixties was a modestly subversive exploration of the Dionysian potential of American life, which had been underexploited since the Twenties crashed. A woman who would bare herself to the sun, the hovering implication was, might bare herself to you.

A tan in a man is a less provocative affair. The notion, indeed, of a man with time to spend in the vain exercise of lying in the sun is somewhat repellent, except perhaps in Florida, California, and the Hamptons, where a tan registers as conspicuous consumption: solar leisure demonstrates monied clout. In my own odd case, sunning was the only known remedy for a skin condition, psoriasis, and the sensations of flattening out on the warm sand or the backyard blanket, of closing my eyes under a crimson fury of protons, and even of sunburn welling up on my nose and collar bones became associated in my warped mind with healing, with normality. As early as chilly April, I would resort to the back dunes of the great beach that, it is not too much to say, had brought me to live in this particular New England town. With a winter boost from the Caribbean, the sun cure more or less worked, enough for me to participate without undue embarrassment in the pleasures of the scantily clad bourgeoisie, during those years of assassination and sit-in, of Asian intervention and student protest, of riot and rally and rock-and-roll. The bikini had achieved acceptance among young matrons, and there was a stately frieze effect as they paraded back and forth in front of the horizon with their cherubic sprats and toddlers.

Frying our children was not the least of our sins in that heedless time. But, let it be said in mitigation, suntan lotion was applied (mostly the fashionable, ochre-tinted, sunscreen-free Bain de Soleil) to our offspring's tender hides, and the sociable, spectacular effects of beachgoing must have had some positive influence on their developing minds. It was a carnival under the dome of heaven, every fair day. Sand and sea are superb babysitters. Even for ten-year-olds, an hour or two of quiet amusement can be managed, if friends are near. We camped in family groups, amid the alien hordes of teenagers with Frisbees and retirees in aluminum chairs. I, one of the few young husbands present, tried to blend in innocuously, as if I were an honorary female, going topless.

Established on our blankets, with plastic cooler and plastic toys in place, we then received and paid visits, sharing lotion and gossip and the pervasive, radiant sense of well-being. Sunlight drenched us in its deceptive goodness. Salt sparkled on our skin. Drying hair took on a mussed, wild-woman look that was very attractive. I, as my psoriasis spots wilted beneath the hammering of ultraviolet rays, suppressed shouts of sheer happiness at being so naked in this American space, at feeling so free. Perception fragmented into bright shards. History, personal and global, became mere background noise.

Tagging along in my wife's social orbit, I was exposed to one after another sunbathing housewife, lazing in her little pool of beach paraphernalia. There were baked shoulders, freckled clavicles, creamy midriffs, sand-encrusted rumps and thighs. Bare feet, over a summer, take on a two-tone look, the insteps and toes tanning but the tougher sides, heels, and soles resisting the sun's delicate dye. Tanned toes! And the little blush of pink that appears on the thin skin beneath the eyes when the two noontide hours have been absorbed and it is time to pack up the cooler, sand pails, towels, and kids and return to the suburban realities of the broiling car, the shady yard, the kitchen full of expectant appliances, the living room with its rustling drawn shades, and the upstairs bathrooms where the beach sand reluctantly eddies down the drains.

We lived, in tune with the Zeitgeist, without many frills. Rather than wear sandals, we hotfooted it across the parking lot, complaining every time. The same frazzled towel served several. A French au pair who shared one summer with us had to be weaned from her expectation of changing rooms and seaside amenities. No, Albertine, we just get in the station wagon in our bathing suits and come back wet and sandy and cranky. This is America. We waited three hundred years to take off our clothes. In apology to the red Indians, we are going to acquire their color. Black is beautiful, and if not black, brown, and if not brown, bistre, and if bistre cannot be mustered, we will make do with pink enough to show that it hurts. Albertine, as I remember, was blonde and six feet tall, and had skin the white of Sèvres china, and moved in high-heel clogs with a gently awkward distaste across the rocky parking lot, the crooked old boardwalk, the burning loose sand and then the flat wet sand. She was, seen now through the shimmer of more than thirty bygone summers, a sweet good sport, come here among the redmen to taste steamed clams and corn and to improve her already charming English.

So, what did it mean, all that sun-soaked *temps perdu*? What remains, save the continuous crop of keratoses patiently harvested by the dermatologist with his bottle of liquid nitrogen and the plastic surgeon with his cunning knife? The memory of a sensation of cosmic rapport remains. The sense, as one stretched out on the bare sand (its reflective qualities increased the exposure), of being encased in a giant jewel, a universe of atomic activity. One with the sun. Along with many of my generation, I had moved from a pinched and affrighted childhood to a post-war ease, when the middle class suddenly had the time and means to sample hedonism. The backyard pool, the side-yard barbecue, the second car, the sec-

ond home on the shore or in the mountains all were signs of Fifties affluence, as innocent as Barbie dolls and pastel refrigerators at first. But by
the Sixties, consumerism had shifted inwards, to a hunger for luxuriant
feelings as well as objects and an impatience with conventional limits to
self-fulfillment. Sunbathing would seem a harmless self-indulgence, but
it was symptomatic: those American women lying with closed eyes and
browning legs were hatching something. They joked that, with a grain
of sand inside them, they could be making pearls. Many of them did
have, by the early Sixties, the Pill inside them, and seeds of discontent.
The sexual revolution created by women—men allegedly have always
been sexual anarchists—was on the way, and, in its wake, its sobering
hangover of feminism.

Italian Renaissance frescoes show Adam as distinctly darker, a reflection of the sex-role division that plants men in the outdoors, laboring or hunting or fighting, and women inside the house, tending the
hearth and the family. When women took to acquiring tans, the relatively
androgynous hard-body look was born, replacing the milky, zaftig Marilyn Monroe body type. *I am tough*, those female tans murmured to whoever would listen. *I can do without shelter.* The barefoot, make-up–less
sunbathers scorned their mothers' perms and pampered, housebound
look. It may not be too much to say that, in offering their bodies to the
sun, these Sixties matrons were already proving unfaithful to the gods
of domesticity, including their husbands. The flight from the spotless
kitchen had begun. If the first acts of rebellion took the form of adultery, with the relatively conservative yen to be married to a (slightly) different man, the dreams of the sunbathers could and did evolve beyond
heterosexual attachment entirely, toward an Amazonian paradise of self-
sufficient women. Perhaps that society already existed on the beach, and
I, a puppyish wrong-sex tagalong, did not realize what I was witnessing.
Out of suburbia, matriarchy. These women were donning bronze armor.

Deliberate exposure to the sun's rays is, as far as I know, a purely
twentieth-century phenomenon. Pirates and yeomen of old suffered
the burning glare stoically. Hats had broad brims; our ancestors, their
daguerreotypes reveal, kept at least their foreheads pale. The world's
beaches rimmed the continents with wasteland, except where the thrifty
Scots perpetrated in the dunes a game called golf. It would make sense, as
the century closes, if sunbathing were consigned to the follies of the past,
along with therapeutic bleeding and trial by ordeal. But I see on the
streets, metropolitan and rural, evidence that young women and men are
still willing to trade their epidermal futures for a passing ruddy glow.

Tanning parlors have replaced the old-fashioned sunlamp as an artificial aid; the sun-kissed look is still negotiable on the bourse of human appeal, for the primitive reason that health is attractive and its absence not.

Now that old age has removed my stock from the trading lists, it would be churlish to regret those hours spent mindlessly cooking myself into self-esteem. The chips—the bits of DNA driven crazy by an excess of ultraviolet—are called in gradually. Skin cancers appear at exposed places one never thought of at the time—the nostril wings, and the tops of the ears, and the knees and elbows. The edges of the lips and eyebrows seem to have been especially vulnerable. The lower half of my nose was burned so severely that it lost all its melanin and now exists in a permanent pink state, constantly peeling in little dry flakes I pick at as compulsively as I used to puff cigarettes. Fresh warts and old scars mingle in the mottled wreck of the backs of my hands. My first keratosis appeared in the center of the back of my right hand (the one never covered by a golf glove) when I was in my thirties, and I didn't know what it was, this tiny tower of dry white cells, and imagined when it fell off one day, outside of Seward's Store on Martha's Vineyard, that I would see it no more. It returned, and its scar of removal is still rough to the touch.

But, hey, bodies are to use, right? The sun won't be there forever—the heavens are full of its exploding and collapsed brothers—and in making contact with it, while it was still golden and lusty, along the tingling length of our whole prone or supine selves, we seized the day, we used what was there. We worshipped and arose transformed, if only minutely, in our topmost layer, and temporarily, doomed as we all are to fade.

V

V FOR VENEREAL, of course, and for victory. These days it is the venereal diseases which are achieving victory: a few decades after penicillin banished syphilis and gonorrhea to the backwash of pathology, AIDS and herpes—both with palliations but without cure—have reattached a high price tag to sex. The existence of venereal disease at all argues against Providence and in behalf of a demonic Nature, which hormonally incites

---

Written for *Hockney's Alphabet*, a compilation edited by Stephen Spender, illustrated by David Hockney, and published in this country by Random House (1991) in association with the American Friends of AIDS Crisis Trust. The letters were assigned. Julian Barnes got U. Susan Sontag had W.

us to mate and then invents a spirochete, a gonococcus, and a viral group that thrive at the thrilled point of contact. "Love has pitched his mansion in," Yeats wrote, "the place of excrement." The place, certainly, of humid and susceptible membranes. As the *Encyclopaedia Britannica* puts it in its usual level-headed fashion, it all seems natural and mild enough: the microörganism behind gonorrhea simply has "a predilection for the type of mucous membranes found in the genito-urinary tract and adjacent area"; the "delicate" syphilis microbe, like all of us, is saddled with "a requirement of moisture for life and transmission." HIV, in its burglarious transactions with the human immune system, just can't help itself, and is doing, in rhythm with its macrocosmic carriers, what comes naturally. In the meantime, our venery, as blessed by Freud, feels inextricably bound up with our vitality and even our virtue, as well as our vanity and, in love's cause, occasional villainy. It does seem hard that, having so recently absorbed Freud's blessing, we should now have to flinch from Nature's curse.

Lust

THE WORD originally meant pleasure and then was modulated to signify desire and, specifically, sexual desire. How can sexual desire be a sin? Did not God instruct Adam and Eve to be fruitful, and to multiply? Did He not say, having created woman from Adam's rib, that "therefore shall a man leave his father and his mother, and shall cleave unto his wife, and they shall be one flesh"? The oneness of flesh is itself a vivid metaphor for copulation. The organic world is soaked in sex; Lucretius, in his epic *On the Nature of Things*, begins by saluting Venus: "Yea, through seas and mountains and tearing rivers and the leafy haunts of birds and verdant plains thou dost strike fond love into the hearts of all, and makest them in hot desire to renew the stock of their races, each after his own kind."

Venus alone, in the rousing translation of Cyril Bailey, is "pilot to the nature of things"—without her aid nothing "comes forth into the bright coasts of light, nor waxes glad nor lovely." Two millennia after Lucretius and his fellow Latin celebrants of all-powerful love, Freud and his followers have reconfirmed the helplessly sexual nature of humankind, and have announced the harmfulness, not to say the futility, of sexual repression. How strangely on modern ears falls the notion that lust—sexual desire that wells up in us as involuntarily as saliva—in itself is wicked!

One-eighth of a series of sins for the *New York Times Book Review*.

With what nervous hilarity did we greet Jimmy Carter's famous confession: "I've looked on a lot of women with lust. I've committed adultery in my heart many times." Carter was running for President at the time; his opponent, the incumbent Gerald Ford, was a more typical post-Freudian man; asked how often he made love, he healthily responded, "Every chance I get." Impotence, frigidity, unattractiveness—these are the sins of which we are truly ashamed.

But to the early Christian moralists, of whom Sts. Paul and Augustine are the greatest, the body was a beast to be tamed, not a master to be served. In that decadent, brutal first-century Roman world, sex possibly did not seem to Paul a very big deal; the world was about to be dissolved in the Second Coming of Christ, and procreation, of such concern to the Old Testament God, was practically irrelevant. The seventh chapter of Paul's first letter to the Corinthians considers briskly the topic the Corinthians had proposed: "It is good for a man not to touch a woman." Paul concurs, with a famous qualification: "I say therefore to the unmarried and widows, It is good for them if they abide even as I. But if they cannot contain, let them marry: for it is better to marry than to burn." Augustine had had more experience of burning than Paul: in Carthage's "cauldron of dissolute loves," his *Confessions* tell us, he fell "in love with loving." Some chapters after he sketches his youthful life and his concubine, he confides to God, "I had prayed to you for chastity and said 'Give me chastity and continence, but not yet.' For I was afraid that you would answer my prayer at once and cure me too soon of the disease of lust, which I wanted satisfied, not quelled."

His youth passed, and the worst of the burning, and he evolved, as an African bishop beset by Donatists and Pelagians, a pessimistic theology that virtually identified human sexuality with original sin. Though Augustine's fiercer insistences (upon infant damnation and predestination, say) reminded other Christians of the Manichaeanism to which he had been a convert for a time, his theology became one of the foundations upon which the church instituted a thousand-year war against the flesh—for saints, mortification, and for the laity, regulation.

It tests the patience of a Protestant to peruse the *Catholic Encyclopedia*'s article on "Lust," with its fussy, imperturbable bureaucratic obstinacy and orderliness. An alleged order, described as natural and rational, is repeatedly invoked:

> A lustful action is a disordered use or pursuit of sex pleasure not only because it defeats the biological, social, or moral purpose of sex activity, but also because in doing this it subjects the spiritual in man to values of the grossly material order, acting as a disintegrating force in the human personality.

Lust leads to "blindness of mind, rashness, thoughtlessness, inconstancy, self-love, and excessive attachment to the material world." The pitfall of venereal sin resides in "merely sensible" pleasures such as "delight in the touch of a soft object," let alone a human kiss: "The Church has condemned a proposition that states that a kiss indulged for the sake of carnal pleasure and that does not involve danger of further consent is only venially sinful." That is, a kiss is *mortally* sinful. Sexual activity has but two legitimate ends, "the procreation of children and the promotion of the mutual love of spouses in marriage." Narrow and pedantic is the way: we are invited to consider two sinners against the sexual order, "a prostitute who plies her trade for monetary gain without any physical enjoyment, and . . . a married man enjoying normal conjugal intimacy but with no motive except that of physical pleasure." The first sins "against the sex order without a sin of lust," the second commits "a sin of lust without a sin against the sexual order." With pleasure, without pleasure—the whole scene seems damned. What right-thinking man or woman would not quickly abandon so treacherous a minefield for the monastery and the nunnery?

But of course the gospel of Freud has triumphed; the nunneries are drying up, and priests are being hauled into court for their numerous offenses against chastity. Sex is a great disorderer of society—the old ascetics were not wrong about that. The embarrassingly detailed religious prohibitions which strike the modern liberal as outrageous and ridiculous—against masturbation, contraception, homosexuality, and so-called sodomy—were patchwork attempts to wall in the polymorphous-perverse torrents which, in our time, have conspicuously undermined those confining but as yet unreplaced institutions, marriage and the male-headed family. Pornography and its slightly more demure cousin, advertising, present an ideal world, and the claims of the ideal strain and stress imperfect reality. Citizens' private sexual expectations do spill over into society, producing divorce, out-of-wedlock pregnancies, and a rise in literally mortal venereal disease. The conscientious medieval lovers who in the throes of the sex act had to consider whether their concupiscent sensations (*concupiscentia*) were remaining in line with "right reason" (*rectam rationem*) are matched by the modern lovers who must keep asking themselves which bodily fluids might infect what susceptible membranes with HIV. The old nay-sayers were right in pointing out that sex has consequences; it is not a holiday from reality.

The sin of lust was defined by St. Thomas as a misalignment in regard to God's procreative purposes; another serene systemizer, Spinoza, wrote in his *Ethics*, "Avarice, ambition, lust, etc., are nothing but species of madness." Madness, presumably, is to be avoided, as a deviation from an Aristotelian norm of sane moderation. Of the seven deadly sins, gluttony and sloth are sins of excess, of quantity rather than quality, since the human animal must both eat and rest. It must lust, also, one might say, or else sublimate.

Is lust not, as Freud and Augustine darkly agree, central to our Promethean human nature? Lust, which begins in a glance of the eye, is a searching, and its consummation, step by step, a knowing. Not only does the sexual appetite join us to "the beasts of the field" and our chthonian mother—"the Mother of All Living," wrote Robert Graves, "the ancient power of fright and lust"—but it calls into activity our most elegant faculties, of self-display, social intercourse, and idealization. We are attracted not merely to the bodies of others but to their psyches, the shimmering non-material identities that used to be called souls. Romantic love, which Denis de Rougement convincingly described as a pernicious heresy, rarefies lust into an angelic standoff, a fruitless longing without which our energizing, ubiquitous dreamland of song, film, and fiction would be bereft of its main topic. This endless celebration of love and its frustrations amounts to a popular religion, giving dignity and significance to the vagaries of lust.

Love is supposedly eternal, whereas lust is a physical process that has an end. It rhymes with "dust," a number of poets have noticed. Andrew Marvell begs his "Coy Mistress" to succumb ere "your quaint honour turn to dust; / And into ashes all my lust." But Shakespeare wrote the definitive treatise, in his Sonnet 129, beginning, "Th' expense of spirit in a waste of shame / Is lust in action." Lust is, he goes on, "a swallow'd bait" and "A bliss in proof, and proved, a very woe; / Before, a joy proposed; behind, a dream." Yet none, he concludes, "knows well / To shun the heaven that leads men to this hell."

The Bible, actually, is rather soft on lust. Jesus's plea for the adulterous woman and His fondness for female company, high and low, give a genial tinge to His ministry.* The Old Testament contains erotic poetry and a number of erotic episodes; King David's lusting after Bathsheba, spied at

---

*A reader of the *New York Times Book Review* wrote to point out that Jesus also said, in the Sermon on the Mount as recorded by Matthew, "Whosoever looketh on a woman to lust after her hath committed adultery with her already in his heart. And if thy right eye offend thee, pluck it out, and cast it from thee: for it is profitable for thee that one of thy members should perish, and not that thy whole body should be cast into hell." As elsewhere in Matthew, Jesus presents an uncharacteristically fierce face. In the Hemingway story "God Rest You Merry, Gentlemen," a sixteen-year-old boy, tormented by "that awful lust," takes Christ's words to heart and cuts off his penis.

her bath from a rooftop, led to adultery and the murder of her husband, Uriah the Hittite, but not to any permanent loss of David's status as God's favorite. "The thing that David had done displeased the Lord," and the Lord killed the illicit couple's firstborn child, but then Bathsheba gave birth to Solomon. Out of lust, wisdom. If God created the world, He created sex, and one way to construe our inexhaustible sexual interest is as praise of Creation. Says the Song of Solomon: "The joints of thy thighs are like jewels, the work of the hands of a cunning workman."

In admiring another, and in yearning to make our flesh one with the other's, we are stepping out of our skins into a kind of selflessness and into a sense of beauty. Without lust on the planet, what would wax glad and lovely? Liberal truisms on the joy—nay, the downright virtuousness—of sexual activity are very easy to write in this day and age. What we may lose in this ease is a sense of the majestic power that Augustine and others felt—the power of lust to bind souls to this transient, treacherous world and to drive men and women to extremes of obsession. Sex loses something when we deny its tragic underside. T. S. Eliot wrote of Baudelaire, "He was at least able to understand that the sexual act as evil is more dignified, less boring, than as the natural, 'life-giving', cheery automatism of the modern world. For Baudelaire, sexual operation is at least something not analogous to Kruschen Salts." Humanly enough, some sense of the forbidden—of what Freud spoke of as an "obstacle . . . necessary to swell the tide of libido to its height"— gives lust its savor, its keenness. Such is the confusion of this fallen world, where sins lie intermixed with the seeds of being.

The Song of Solomon

OF ALL THE BIBLE'S CHAPTERS, none is more surprising and pagan than the Song of Solomon—in Hebrew, "Shir Hashrim," which the Vulgate translated as "Canticum Canticorum" and some English versions as the "Song of Songs." Its dating is difficult. After the Babylonian Exile of the sixth century B.C., Hebrew was slowly replaced by Aramaic as the language of Palestine; to judge by the proportion of Aramaicized expressions, the Song of Solomon comes fairly late in the process, around the third century B.C. Its references to Solomon, who reigned in the tenth century B.C., partake of the fabulous and folkloric. His wedding is not elsewhere mentioned in the Bible; the lovers use his golden reign as one of the idyllic settings in which their love is exalted. Yet ancient elements exist in the text. Tirzah, evoked along with Jerusalem, had not been the capital of Israel since the century after Solomon. Certain formulae ("His left hand should be under my head, and his right hand should embrace me") and the emphasis on the spring season and the dialogue form all suggest a derivation from Mesopotamian fertility rites, celebrating a marriage between the king and a goddess, that date back to the third millennium B.C. A modern Arabic term, *wasf*, denotes ritual exchanges of songs praising the beloved's beauty, songs that persist at Middle Eastern betrothal ceremonies, like Western toasts.

The Song, which never once mentions God, was included in the Bible most probably because, like Proverbs and Ecclesiastes and Job, it was a treasure of Hebrew literature. No other love poem from this literature survives. Its attribution to Solomon gave it the protection of a revered historical name. An early commentator, Rabbi Akiva (d. 135 A.D.), claimed that "the whole world is not worth the day on which the Song of Songs was given to Israel; for all the writings are holy, but the Song of Songs is the holiest of the holy." Nevertheless, he read it allegorically, as really about the love between God and Israel. Christian commentators, with more of an anti-sexual bias than the Hebrew scribes, for two millennia sought to explain away the Song's carnal content; the beloved's two breasts became Moses and Aaron in one interpretation, and the Old and New Testaments in another. A Bible I bought in England in 1955 blandly heads the verses, at the top of the page, "The church's love of Christ" and "Christ's love of the church."

Now, one would hope, Christians can read the Song as a hymn to human love, including a virtual worship of the body of the other. Three voices speak: a young female, called the Shulamite; her lover, from whom she is intermittently separated; and a chorus. The chorus, one theory runs, consists of the women in Solomon's harem, wherein the sun-blackened Shulamite has been enlisted though she longs for her shepherd lover; she searches the city for him and is captured by watchmen who beat her and take away her veil. But it is impossible to make such a cogent dramatic situation fit every verse; the lovers' voices change tense and context in a manner that seems—not inappropriately—delirious. The Song of Solomon has traditionally been printed without differentiating the speakers, compounding a confusion that no translation can totally eliminate. The original Hebrew is, according to the introduction by Ariel and Chana Bloch to their 1995 translation, exceptionally compressed, elliptical, and rich in rare words and *hapax legomena*—words that occur nowhere else and whose meaning must be conjectured. It is also the most vernacular Hebrew in the Bible, and contains a number of words of Per-

sian and Greek origin, as well as similarities with the pastoral idylls of
Theocritus, a Greek poet who wrote in Alexandria in the first half of the
third century B.C.

Though the Blochs, among others, have provided modern translations,
the Song in most minds remains cast in the King James Version. Phrases
of its ringing archaic English still permeate the language: "I am black, but
comely"; "Stay me with flagons, comfort me with apples"; "The voice of
the turtle is heard in our land"; "Take us the foxes, the little foxes, that
spoil the vines: for our vines have tender grapes." The Song's erotic magnificence crests in well-known verses near the end:

> Thy navel is like a round goblet,
> which wanteth not liquor:
> thy belly is like an heap of wheat
> set about with lilies.
> Thy two breasts are like two young roes
> that are twins.

In the next verses, however, the Jacobean rendition of Hebraic concreteness strikes the contemporary ear as absurd:

> Thy neck is as a tower of ivory;
> thine eyes like the fishpools in Heshbon,
> by the gate of Bath-rabbim:
> thy nose is as the tower of Lebanon
> which looketh toward Damascus.

In another verse, a shift in the language has betrayed the poetry: "My
beloved put in his hand by the hole of the door, and my bowels were
moved for him." But love includes earthiness as well as exaltation, and its
spiritual fever embraces the extravagant and does not shun the grotesque.

"I have eaten my honeycomb with my honey," the lover avows. He
exclaims, "How beautiful are thy feet with shoes," and likens the joints of
her thighs to jewels. He finds the beloved as "fair as the moon, clear as
the sun, and terrible as an army with banners." And she, even more rapturous, wants him to lie all night between her breasts. Her hands upon the
handle of the lock she opens to him are wet with myrrh. She conceives
him in terms of hard, towering substances: "His legs are as pillars of marble, set upon sockets of fine gold," and his countenance "is as . . . excellent as the cedars" of Lebanon. And she to him is "a garden inclosed . . . a
spring shut up, a fountain sealed." The ecstasy of reciprocated desire
need not wait for Freudian interpretation; these voices are dizzily
drenched in perfumes, fruits, spices—all of the nature around them

brings metaphors to the feast of their senses. The speed of their heart-beats lives in the rapidity of their crowding similes; the mutual outpour-ing ends with the Shulamite's cry

> Make haste, my beloved,
> and be thou like to a roe or to a young hart
> upon the mountains of spices.

This anticipates the last utterance of the New Testament, in Revelation: "Surely I come quickly. Amen. Even so, come, Lord Jesus." The yearning for love fills the cosmos.

The Bible would be the poorer if it lacked the Song of Solomon. Such a burst of sensual rapture and erotic passion helps ground Biblical humanism on the human creature that exists, under the great frowning imperatives of Creation. Carnal passion has its natural place in the annals of Israel; Judaism recognized that the body is the person, a recognition extended in the strenuous Christian doctrine of the bodily resurrection. A world-picture must include everything that is the case, and the love frenzy of the young—the Shulamite is so young she is accused of having no breasts—completes, along with the cynicism of Ecclesiastes, the despair of Lamentations, the problematics of Job, and the plagues and war-fury of Numbers, the picture. We might even say that, in this era of irrepressible sexual awareness, we trust the Bible a bit more because it contains, in all its shameless, helpless force, the Song of Solomon.

LITERATURE

Religion and Literature

By "RELIGION" I mean humankind's transactions with what it believes to be the supernatural. The relation between religion and literature is ancient and far from incidental. Accountants invented writing, to keep track of goods shipped and received, but priests soon took it in hand. The earliest written language, Sumerian, appears around 3100 B.C., in the form of business and administrative texts and school exercises; lists of gods and kings, however, occur early. Sumerian texts from the second millennium before Christ include the range of religious literature to be found also in the Jewish Old Testament—creation myths, epics about early kings, lamentations, hymns, and proverbs.

The best-known Sumerian epic, and the world's most ancient work of enduring literature, is the story of Gilgamesh. Gilgamesh was, in Sumerian tradition, an early ruler of the city-state of Uruk, the builder of the city's mighty walls. To not only the Sumerians but to the Assyrians and Babylonians, who absorbed the language and civilization of Sumer, Gilgamesh was both a hero-king and a god, worshipped as a deity of the underworld. Figurines in his image are found in the tombs of the Sumerian dead. His story existed in a number of versions; although some fragments go back to the late third millennium B.C., the epic has descended to posterity primarily in the form of twelve broken tablets in the Akkadian language of Babylonia, from the seventh century B.C.

The story, in its emphasis on male love and the fear of death, seems surprisingly modern and secular. It deals with, in order: the taming of a wild man, Enkidu, by a temple prostitute, Shamhat; the intense love that

---

A chapter from *The Religion Factor: An Introduction to How Religion Matters*, edited by William Scott Green and Jacob Neusner (Westminster John Knox Press, 1996).

springs up between Enkidu and King Gilgamesh after a combat between the two, which Gilgamesh wins; their journey together to slay a forest monster, Huwawa; Gilgamesh's rejection of an offer of marriage from Ishtar, the goddess of love; Enkidu's death; Gilgamesh's inconsolable mourning and his journey to visit Utnapishtim, the sole survivor of the Babylonian flood, who tells Gilgamesh how to avoid death with a magic plant, which a serpent steals from him. The Babylonian tablets end with a grim report from Enkidu on conditions in the underworld.

The tale is unclear at many points and certainly disjointed. What we may observe about it, as typical of early literature, is (1) the inclusion of fabulous elements from a credulous cosmology that populated the world with spirits and divine emissaries; (2) the ambiguous nature of the hero, whose elevation to the status of king falls well short of the tranquil well-being of the deathless gods; (3) the metaphysical nature of the hero's quest, as he explores a hostile, inhuman, and confusing world. His is the poignance of being "two-thirds a god, one-third a man, the king."* A hero, it could be generalized, is a mortal on the way to becoming a god; outside the bounds of the story, in Sumerian religion, Gilgamesh has become a god, but within the story he suffers doubt, fear, and loss. He seeks an answer to the appalling mystery of personal death. His anguish and vulnerability arouse empathy in us still, but to the teller's audience and to the scribes who committed the tale to writing, his significance derived from his legendary kingship, his divine antecedents (his father was a mortal but his mother was the goddess Ninsun), and his larger-than-human status.

The fortunes of royalty primarily concern the bard, for, by a basic term of the archaic social contract, the king's well-being determines that of the tribe or state. The monarch's health includes our own. In a number of societies studied by anthropology, the king must die, as the year dies, so that the world can be renewed; a sickly king is put to death, rather than be allowed to drag his kingdom down into unhealth with him. A trace of such magical thinking remains in the morbid fascination the British public expresses toward its royalty, especially the morally suspect Prince Charles, and in the relatively recent withholding, from the American public, of the extent of President Roosevelt's and President Kennedy's physical infirmities. The tales of kings, even their mere names in a chronological list, deliver vital information to the present moment. Literature, in its first, oral forms, acquaints the listeners with their collective case history.

---

*Translation by David Ferry, *The Epic of Gilgamesh* (Farrar, Straus and Giroux, 1982).

What, we might wonder, about Gilgamesh made him the most popular of his culture's heroes? The surviving literature holds no more than clues. He built the protective walls of Uruk and attempted to solve the problem of death; though he failed to retain the magic herb of immortality, this attempt was also, construably, for the general benefit. Like the suffering King of the Jews centuries later, he met death on mankind's behalf. More murkily, in the fragments that remain, the hero on several occasions spurned seduction by the feminine principle, manifested by Ishtar and Siduri: he held fast to the ideal of masculine comradeship and patriarchal purity against, it may be, representatives of an older matriarchal order. He enacted the warrior's necessary desertion of the nurturing mother to join the father's martial world. Gilgamesh is seen, in our glimpse of him, as a rebel against nature, a seeker after the supernatural.

As civilizations arose on the planet, they generated writings of pervasively religious character. The Egyptian *Book of the Dead*, the collective name given to a fund of charms, spells, and formulas to be used by the deceased in their passage to the afterworld, contains items as old as the earliest anecdotes of Gilgamesh. Although—as visitors to the Nile know—images and inscriptions devoted to the deities are omnipresent on the walls of temples, tombs, and funerary stelae, few complete mythic narratives emerge from the Egyptian ritual texts and devotional poems; the Greek historian Plutarch is the source of the famous legend of Isis and Osiris. In India, Sanskrit literature begins, in about 1500 B.C., with the Vedas—hymns to the gods of the invading Aryan peoples, employed in the liturgy of these invaders' religious ceremonies. As Sanskrit over the next millennium became a purely literary language, employed by an educated elite, two immense national epics were spawned, the *Mahabharata* and the *Ramayana*. These sprawling accounts of dynastic struggles abound in fantastic and religious elements; the fraternal heroes of the *Ramayana* collectively compose the seventh avatar of the Hindu god Vishnu, and the *Mahabharata* contains one of the world's great religious texts, known as the *Bhagavad-Gita* (*Song of God*), preached on the eve of battle by Vishnu's divine incarnation, Lord Krishna. In China, the *I Ching* dates from the twelfth century before Christ, and the published sayings of Lao-tzu and the *Analects* of Confucius from the sixth.

The point needs no belaboring: creation myths, hymns to divinity, liturgical formulas, spells, charms, and essays in theosophic wisdom compose much of each culture's early literature. What can easily be overlooked or minimized, however, is the supernatural ingredient in the two Homeric epics, the *Iliad* and the *Odyssey*, which form the fountainhead of Western humanism. The events around which accumulated the legends of the Trojan War occurred in approximately 1200 B.C.; the Homeric telling of them was written down four to five centuries later. Homer—to give the authors of the epics a single name—was dealing with a world that was, to him, archaic. His treatment of the gods is sometimes light-hearted, and he was chastised by Renaissance critics as, compared with the Roman Virgil, irreverent.

Yet we are not allowed to forget that the Trojan War was an event determined in the sky. Eris, the goddess of discord, was excluded from the nuptials of King Peleus and the sea-nymph Thetis and takes her revenge by throwing into the festivities a golden apple inscribed, "For the fairest." Hera, Aphrodite, and Athena each claim the prize, and ask Zeus to adjudicate. He passes the buck to a mortal, Paris, son of Priam, King of Troy, who awards the prize to Aphrodite on her promise of giving him for wife the fairest woman of earth. This is Helen, the wife of King Menelaus of Sparta; Paris, as a guest in Menelaus's palace, persuades Helen to elope with him. Menelaus and his brother Agamemnon, King of Mycenae, organize a Greek invasion fleet to reclaim Helen, and the Trojan War has begun. The launch of the fleet is delayed by another affront to a female divinity: Agamemnon has slain a stag sacred to Artemis, and she denies a favoring wind and inflicts pestilence on the lingering troops until Agamemnon sacrifices to her his daughter Iphigenia. The subsequent fortunes of war are repeatedly influenced by the sympathies of the gods: Poseidon, the god of the sea, and the slighted goddesses Hera and Athena favor the Greeks; Aphrodite and her lover Ares, the god of war, favor the Trojans; Zeus and Apollo are uneasily neutral.

Homer assumes his audience to be acquainted with this theological context. The *Iliad* opens by relating how Agamemnon, in taking as a spoil of war the daughter of Chryses, the priest of Apollo, has offended this god. Yielding up his fair captive, Agamemnon replaces her with another, Briseis, who had belonged to Achilles. Achilles, furious, withdraws from the war and remains in his tents. Achilles's anger and his final triumphant reënlistment in the Greek cause, which brings about the death of Hector, the son of King Priam and the leader of the Trojan forces, form the basic curve of action—occupying a mere forty days—of this saga of Bronze Age war. The *Iliad* ends when the semi-divine Achilles (the son of Peleus and Thetis), in bowing to Priam's plea that he give decent burial to Hector's corpse, restores himself to the sacralized order of noble civility. As if to a kind of father, Achilles tells the aged Priam:

> I myself am minded
> to give Hector back to you. A messenger came to me from Zeus,
> my mother, she who bore me, the daughter of the sea's ancient.

> I know you, Priam, in my heart, and it does not escape me
> that some god led you to the running ships of the Achaians.*

The *Odyssey* more marvellously makes us feel the enveloping religious pressures. Odysseus wanders through a Mediterranean populated by gods and the offspring of gods: Scylla, Charybdis, Aeolus, Polyphemus, Calypso, and Circe all have their divine pedigrees and prerogatives. Aeolus controls the winds, and Circe is a sorceress who turns men into swine and directs Odysseus to Hades, the underworld, where he interviews a host of spectres, including his own mother and a number of his companions-at-arms at the siege of Troy, now among the dead. The animosity of the sea god, Poseidon, repeatedly delays Odysseus's return home, which is achieved only with the help of his patroness, the goddess Athena. When he at last arrives in Ithaca after his ten years of tortuous travel, she greets him in the disguise of a young shepherd. After hearing him recite a string of lies about how he came to these shores, she laughs in affectionate delight and, revealing herself in the form of a tall and radiant woman, caresses him and fondly exclaims, "What a wonderful liar you are, indeed!"† She goes on:

> "Any man, or even any God, who would keep pace with your all-round craftiness must needs be a canny dealer and sharp-practised. O plausible, various, cozening wretch, can you not even in your native place let be these crooked and shifty words which so delight the recesses of your mind? Enough of such speaking in character between us two past-masters of these tricks of trade—you, the cunningest mortal to wheedle or blandish, and me, famed above other Gods for knavish wiles. And yet you failed to recognize in me the daughter of Zeus, Pallas Athena, your stand-by and protection throughout your toils!"‡

Such tender teasing and gleeful collusion approach love between a goddess and her pet mortal. Swathing him in mist, coaching his wife, Penelope, and darting here and there in disguise, Athena engineers the hero's slaughter of his wife's suitors and his final return to the connubial bed. For all the fearful carnage that accompanies his return and the loss of all his shipmates on the way, the *Odyssey* is, in its happy outcome, a comedy, demonstrating how a man's native wits and courage, reinforced by a supernatural guardian who is like a shadow-self, can win out against all peril. Civil and domestic order are restored.

---

*Translation by Richmond Lattimore, *The Iliad* (University of Chicago Press, 1951).

†Translation by Robert Graves, *The Greek Myths* (Penguin Books, 1955), vol. 2, chap. 171.

‡Prose translation by T. E. Lawrence, *The Odyssey* (Galaxy, 1956).

The *Odyssey's* mingled world of gods and men is a benign vision wherein nature's harsh imperatives and men's fragile aspirations achieve a pact; the gods personify and humanize the natural forces amid which we are otherwise helpless and negligible. Nature is a live field of latent supernature. The *Odyssey's* hero, placed in this ambiguous field, achieves not merely the transient triumphs of a Gilgamesh but a basis for personal happiness.

The three great tragic dramatists of Athens in the fifth century B.C.—Aeschylus, Sophocles, and Euripides—together trace a decline in the reality of the gods. Greek drama began as ritual devoted to a latecomer among the gods, Dionysus, god of fertility and wine. A god of the poor, he consoled them with violent and ecstatic rites. As part of the god's festivals, dithyrambic—irregular and rapturous—hymns were sung by a chorus, with improvisations by a leader from the chorus.

Aeschylus is credited by Aristotle with adding a second actor and thereby inventing drama. His dramas remain simple in structure, with the chorus still prominent and the action close to theological debate. *Prometheus Bound,* for instance, portrays the stationary sufferings of the Titan who, amid Zeus's successful overthrow of the Titans, gave mankind fire; for his punishment he is nailed and shackled to a rock in the Caucasus Mountains, where eagles tear at his liver. This punitive Zeus is not the beneficent, if lecherous and distractable, god of Homer but a cruel tyrant—"the mind of Zeus is hard to soften with prayer, and every ruler is harsh whose rule is new," Prometheus is told, and "only Zeus is free."* Yet Zeus is himself subject to the rulings of the Fates, and Prometheus foresees his own eventual release.

The question of justice, in a universe ruled by a pantheon seemingly arbitrary and ruthless in its dispensations, bears upon such legendary situations as that of the family of Agamemnon, who was murdered on his return from Troy by his wife, Clytemnestra, and her lover, Aegisthus. Plays on the topic were composed by both Sophocles and Euripides, and by Aeschylus in the trilogy called the *Oresteia.* As the trilogy proceeds, Orestes, Agamemnon's son, returns from the safety of exile and, with his sister Electra's connivance and encouragement, kills his mother and her lover in revenge for his father's murder. But matricide is a heinous crime, and a sequence of wrongs reaching into the past makes simple moral judgments impossible. Clytemnestra argues in her own defense that

---

*Translation by David Grene, *Prometheus Bound,* by Aeschylus, in *Complete Greek Tragedies* (University of Chicago Press, 1959), vol. 1.

Agamemnon sacrificed their daughter Iphigenia to further the invasion of Troy, and then he brought a concubine, Priam's daughter Cassandra, home with him. Aegisthus for justification can look back to the unspeakable crime committed against his father, Thyestes, by Thyestes' brother Atreus, who, in the guise of hospitality, fed him his own slaughtered children. Agamemnon and Menelaus are the sons of Atreus, whose royal house is rightfully cursed: "A house that God hates," Cassandra says, "guilty within of kindred blood shed."*

Aeschylus's chorus, contemplating this tangle of atrocity and suffering, offers the consolation that "Zeus . . . has laid it down that wisdom comes along through suffering. . . . From the gods who sit in grandeur grace comes somehow violent." The trilogy as a whole concludes the matter within the framework of belief, as Athena persuades the Furies to give up their pursuit of the guilt-haunted Orestes and to accept, in return, shrines and worship within Athens. Thus the darkest and most nebulous of the gods are brought within a religious system; Athena assures the Furies, "No household shall be prosperous without your will."† The bloody workings of taboo and revenge morality achieve a precarious truce with civic light and reason.

Sophocles, perhaps thirty years younger than Aeschylus, introduced a third actor into drama and diminished choral expostulation to make room for more interplay among characters. In recasting the myths of the heroic age, he retained the supernatural framework with an appearance of conviction. His *Antigone* concludes, "There is no happiness where there is no wisdom; No wisdom but in submission to the gods."‡ Indeed, of the three great Attic playwrights he provides the most vivid sense of workaday Greek religion—its dank and gloomy oracular caves, its decaying rustic shrines, its bloody sacrifices and desperate auguries, its ghosts and prophetic dreams, its sense of purity and abhorrence of pollution, its ritualized libations and lavations, its localized sacred spaces rimmed with uncertainty and terror.

The gods in Sophocles, however, come in for some severe indictments. The hero of *Philoctetes* asks, "How can I praise, when praising Heaven I find the Gods are bad?"** *The Women of Trachis* ends,

---

*Translation by Richmond Lattimore, *Agamemnon*, by Aeschylus, in ibid.

†Translation by Richard Lattimore, *The Eumenides*, by Aeschylus, in ibid.

‡Translation by Dudley Fitts and Robert Fitzgerald, *Antigone*, by Sophocles, in ibid., vol. 2.

**Translation by David Grene, *Philocletes*, by Sophocles, in ibid.

> You see how little compassion the Gods
> have shown in all that's happened; they
> who are called our fathers, who begot us,
> can look upon such suffering. . . .
> You have seen a terrible death
> and agonies, many and strange, and there is
> nothing here which is not Zeus.*

Yet Sophocles does not condemn the divine dispensations. Two of his last plays, *Oedipus at Colonus* and *Philoctetes*, show the redemption of cursed social outcasts and imply a benign providence. His version of the Orestes story, *Electra*—even though a character in it perceives that "there are times when even justice brings harm with it"†—proceeds inexorably to its merciless denouement. Neither Electra nor Orestes has any second thoughts or reservations; they force Aegisthus to look upon the face of his slain mistress, and Orestes marches him off, vowing,

> I must take care that death
> is bitter for you. Justice shall be taken
> directly on all who act above the law—
> justice by killing. So we would have less villains.

The chorus appears to agree, proclaiming that the house of Atreus has come at last "to freedom, perfected by this day's deed."

If Sophocles accepts the creaking divine framework as the necessary adjunct to human heroism, Euripides, a mere ten years younger, rebels and presents religion as a nightmare. In his nineteen surviving plays, a roiling mass of barbaric violence borrowed from the old legends is intensified and warped by human psychology, portrayed with an insight and depth that remain strikingly modern. Two of his best plays, *Hippolytus* and *The Bacchae*, show gods—Aphrodite, Dionysus—ruthlessly destroying mortals—Hippolytus, Pentheus—who fail to honor them. "O, if only men might be a curse of Gods!"‡ the dying Hippolytus exclaims. The chorus bewails the loss of faith bred by "the inflexible hearts of the Gods":

> The care of God for us is a great thing,
> if a man believe it at heart:
> it plucks the burden of sorrow from him.
> So I have a secret hope
> of someone, a God, who is wise and plans;

---

*Translation by Michael Jameson, *The Women of Trachis*, by Sophocles, in ibid.
†Translation by David Grene, *Electra*, by Sophocles, in ibid.
‡Translation by David Grene, *Hippolytus*, by Euripides, in ibid., vol. 3.

> but my hopes grow dim when I see
> the deeds of men and their destinies.

The religious impulse is poignantly analyzed:

> The life of man entire is misery:
> he finds no resting place, no haven from calamity.
> But something other dearer still than life
> the darkness hides and mist encompasses;
> we are proved luckless lovers of this thing
> that glitters in the underworld.

Or, as the love-crazed Queen Phaedra observes, "I think that our lives are worse than the mind's quality would warrant." In the drama of Euripides, internal demons have replaced deified Furies.

Insofar as the gods of Greek religion personify natural forces, they cannot be exonerated from these forces' cruelty. The tender collusion between Odysseus and Athena is not, as it were, a repeatable experiment. As often as not, the gods destroy us. Euripides' retelling of the Orestes story in the two plays *Orestes* and *Electra* feverishly ripples and ramps through the permutations of a vengeful matricide demanded by Apollo and furiously urged by a sexually deprived princess kept in rags by a wicked stepfather. "I accuse Apollo. The god is the guilty one,"* Orestes cries in the wake of his murder of his mother. In a wryer mood, when Menelaus asks why Apollo has not helped him in his misery, Orestes blasphemously jests, "Oh, he will. In his own good time, of course. Gods are slow by nature." The whole stately "matter of Troy" comes close to parody in its enactment by earthbound neurotics; Menelaus and Helen are serenely selfish and diffident in the wake of the vast slaughter on their behalf. The majestically fraught tower of revenge murders, descending to tormented Orestes from Atreus and even Atreus's grandfather Tantalus, loses its barbaric seriousness with the anachronistic announcement that judicial courts exist: "Legal action, not murder. That was the course to take."

Relieved of reverence, the author achieves all sorts of startling and lurid turns. For the first time in the evolution of Greek drama, we become aware of the playwright as a personality—devastating in his insights, careless in his construction, rather cynically sensational in his effects. While he has no use for the gods as moral guides, Euripides has much theatrical use for them; the device of the *deus ex machina*, wherein a god is lowered by machinery to terminate an otherwise unresolvable plot,

---

*Translation by William Arrowsmith, *Orestes*, by Euripides, in ibid., vol. 4.

is frequently and shamelessly exploited. In two plays, *Helen* and *Iphigenia in Tauris*, heroines of the Trojan tragedy are implausibly rescued from their old roles to star in a newly invented genre, romantic comedy. In winning through to the purely human, with the old religious figurations shrunk to private devils, Euripides enters into the problematical freedom of modern authorship.

For, without the gods, what significance, what direction, do human adventures have? The cowering, wavering, haunted, brutal, frantically scheming Orestes of Euripides is no hero in the old sense, no king on his way to becoming a god. There is no longer an upward arrow in human affairs, only the lateral arrows between lovers and haters, mates and rivals, hunters and the hunted. Orestes displays a vivid variety of characteristics but not the god-sent grandeur of an ancestor, a prototype. In *Electra*, he states the muddled case:

> Alas,
> we look for good on earth and cannot recognize it
> when met, since all our human heritage runs mongrel. . . .
> How then can man distinguish man, what test can he use?*

Religion created Greek literature and died within its embrace. In the Mediterranean regions, now Christian and Islamic, where Zeus/Jupiter and his fellow-gods were for two thousand years the objects of joyful celebration and fervent prayer, the temples are empty ruins, their incomparable beauty testifying to an idealism paradoxically sponsored by an erratic, immoral, dimly conceptualized pantheon. The gods and heroes live only in literature, where they continue to inspire retellings of their stories as various as Eugene O'Neill's *Mourning Becomes Electra*, James Joyce's *Ulysses*, and the recent synoptic *Marriage of Cadmus and Harmony*, by the Italian Roberto Calasso. They haunt us in paintings and children's books, in manufacturers' trademarks and Freudian terminology.

The literature of the Judaeo-Christian religion still speaks for itself, although intimate familiarity with the Bible diminishes from generation to generation. In my childhood home, which was of average Protestant piety, Biblical characters were as familiar, and as frequently mentioned, as relatives on a distant farm. Elijah's chariot of fire and Joseph's coat of many colors brightened our stock of mental imagery; adjurations such as Christ's parable of the talents and Paul's advice on the position of women stimulated our thoughts and familial conversation, in a household that included my maternal grandparents.

---

*Translation by Emily Townsend Vermeule, *Electra*, by Euripides, in ibid.

The Biblical hero is typically a stalwart of faith: Abraham, Moses, Daniel, David, Job, Jesus Christ, Peter, and Paul keep faith with God, even when He glowers. At the heart of the Judaic and Christian religions respectively, Abraham's willingness to sacrifice his son Isaac at God's behest and God's willingness to let His son, Jesus, be crucified echo the sinister familial murders of Greek legend—but, in both cases, with a redemptive intercession from above. In the thousand years between the Emperor Constantine's public conversion and Dante's composition of *The Divine Comedy*, the Christian faith ruled the mind of Europe, and the hero of faith took forms as various as El Cid and St. Francis.

When there appeared a hero whose faith was perceived as excessive and misplaced, however lovably and entertainingly so, a new era, if not an absolutely post-Christian era, began. Such a hero was the protagonist of Miguel de Cervantes's *Don Quixote*, published in two parts in 1605 and 1615 and commonly considered the first modern novel. As the deluded don acts out the visions of knightly romances, his faith wins only a series of beatings, though it also enables him, one could say, to sustain the beatings buoyantly.

A contemporary of Cervantes, William Shakespeare, born a generation later but arrived at greatness somewhat earlier than the Spanish author, is a playwright who reminds us of Euripides in his wealth of invention and psychological insight, and in the sense he gives of a near-chaotic, feverish overflow, and in his apparent skeptical removal from the religious creed of his time. God is invoked, ghosts appear, and curses are laid, but the events in Shakespeare seem purely human, in all the contradictory richness of which human nature is capable—a torrential spillage of self-importance beneath an enigmatic heaven. At times, as with Euripides, Shakespeare seems overwhelmed by disgust at the human spectacle, so the drama becomes ineffective: for example, *Timon of Athens*, *Troilus and Cressida*, and the immense *King Lear* display an almost unbearable piling-on of calamities. The first two have Greek milieux, and the third contains the Euripidean lines

> As flies to wanton boys, are we to the gods;
> They kill us for their sport.

Not that skepticism and pessimism are Shakespeare's only notes, or that he necessarily expressed them in his personal life. In an age when atheism was punishable by death, he was probably conventionally obser-vant,* just as he was, from the little we know about him, a property-

---

*As an Anglican, presumably—though G. K. Chesterton expressed the fond belief that Shakespeare was a Roman Catholic, and some few scholars argue likewise.

acquiring bourgeois and a good team member of the Globe theatrical company. A writer's professed religious convictions do not necessarily control the religious content of his writing. Jonathan Swift's being an Anglican priest did not mute the savage indignation of his satire, nor did Alexander Pope's being a Roman Catholic stop him from being, in his poetry, the proponent of a bloodless and melioristic Deism. Milton's announced determination, in *Paradise Lost*, "to assert eternal Providence, and justify the ways of God to Men," did not prevent him from glorifying God's enemy Lucifer, this religious epic's most vivid and eloquent character.

The twentieth-century reader will find little orthodox comfort in the fiction of such professedly Christian novelists as Graham Greene, Muriel Spark, Evelyn Waugh, Flannery O'Connor, François Mauriac, and Georges Bernanos. It is a bleak world they display, often comic in its desolation and inconsequence—not the world of arrived faith and its consolations but a fallen world whose emptiness, perhaps, has led these authors to make the leap of faith. Given the limits of hagiography and the ineffability of God, isn't that all a novelist can be expected to deliver—*this* world, in its pain and mangled glory?

Graham Greene, writing as a critic, detected a divide between this century and the preceding:

> After the death of Henry James a disaster overtook the English novel. . . . For with the death of James the religious sense was lost to the English novel, and with the religious sense went the sense of the importance of the human act. . . . Even in one of the most materialist of our great novelists— in Trollope—we are aware of another world against which the actions of the characters are thrown into relief.*

James was not himself a believer, but he retained an instinctive religiosity that gave his society novels the weight and interest of moral drama. The English Victorians, speaking broadly, wrote out of a consensual Christian sensibility that supports not only Charles Dickens's extremes of good and evil characters and his sentimentally providential endings but George Eliot's more agnostic investigations of human motive and fulfillment.

The modernists, confronted with the rubble left when Darwin, Marx, Freud, and the higher criticism† shook Victorian Christianity to its foundations, proposed to make a religion of art itself. The Jesuit-trained

---

*"François Mauriac," in *Collected Essays* (Viking, 1983).

†As opposed to the lower criticism, which sought to establish merely correct Biblical texts through comparison of manuscripts, the higher criticism investigated the Bible with the same methods used on secular texts, seeking to establish authenticity, time of

James Joyce created, on the outline of the *Odyssey*, a giant novel of quotidian Dublin in 1904 as packed with arcane references and rigorous schematics as any ancient book of spells. Marcel Proust, isolated and enfeebled, poured his life into a verbal cathedral of remembrance. The excesses and sufferings of Proust and Franz Kafka and Arthur Rimbaud resembled the self-mortifications of saints. The idea of the writer as priest—performer of marvels and supplier of values—went back to Flaubert and perhaps, in essence, to Wordsworth, who presented his religious perceptions in a secular vocabulary of personal sensation. The American poet Wallace Stevens expressed it bluntly: "In an age of disbelief, or, what is the same thing, in a time that is largely humanistic, in one sense or another, it is for the poet to supply the satisfactions of belief, in his measure and in his style."*

The satisfactions of belief, however, stem from assertions about the nature of reality rather than qualities of measure and style. "To see the gods dispelled in mid-air and dissolve like clouds is one of the great human experiences," Stevens goes on to say, and, with passionate subtlety, "It is important to believe that the visible is the equivalent of the invisible."† It is important, but difficult. Such an equivalence suggests the Hindu *yuganaddha*—"a state of unity obtained by perceiving the identity of the phenomenal world and the absolute."‡ This is low-energy metaphysics, cold fusion.

Yet it remains curiously true that the literary artist, to achieve full effectiveness, must assume a religious state of mind—a state that looks beyond worldly standards of success and failure. A mood of exaltation should possess the language, a vatic tension and rapture. Even a grimly tragic view, like that of *King Lear*, Samuel Beckett, Céline, and Herman Melville, must be expounded with a certain rapt celebrative air. The work of literary art springs from the world and adheres to it but is distinctly different in substance. We enter it, as readers, expecting an intensity and shapeliness absent in our lives. A realm above nature is posed—a supernatural, in short. Aesthetic pleasure, like religious ecstasy, is a matter of inwardness, elevation, and escape.

---

authorship, chronology, and sources, using relevant data from linguistics and archaeology. The scholars, French and German, scandalized many Christians by taking such a scientific approach to writings long thought to have been literally dictated by God.

*"Two or Three Ideas," in *Opus Posthumous* (Knopf, 1969).

†Ibid.

‡Mircea Eliade, *A History of Religious Ideas*, vol. 2, translated by Willard R. Trask (University of Chicago Press, 1982).

Fiction: A Dialogue

SCENE: *An antiseptic think tank in the California desert. The curving white walls, marked off in rectangles by barely discernible rows of rivet heads, support some computer terminals with their cables and attachments; framed prints of works by Klee, Mondrian, and Escher; and sparkling bouquets of fresh-picked, minuscule desert flowers, held in gilded wall vases mounted on brackets. The participants in the dialogue, which has been arranged by a special branch of NASA devoted to the explanation of American civilization to alien life forms, are Farquhar, an obscure belle-lettrist originally from Indiana, and Chokchöq, an emissary from Mars. Chokchöq is russet in color, metallic in sheen, and antlike in form, only with many more legs. The neural circuitry developed over aeons to coördinate this wealth of legs (each of which has a number of swivelling knees) and the three prehensile antennae that spring from the alien creature's head account for, evolutionists speculate, its phenomenal brainpower; in* Homo sapiens *the parallel development is traced to the opposable thumb, bioptic vision, and the upright stance.*

Farquhar is seated in a Naugahyde balloon chair; Chokchöq remains low to the floor except during especially animated discourse. Both participants are miked, and wear headphones relaying simultaneous translation. Since the Martian has no ears, his headphones are plugged into a four-prong electrical receptacle drilled into his skull, which has no nerves.

CHOKCHÖQ: Explain to me again, O obliging Earthling, about fiction. It consists of stories concerning persons that never existed yet that often bear strong resemblances to persons the author has memorably known?

FARQUHAR: Not exactly, my extraterrestrial friend. Put it this way: Fictional persons are objectifications of actual impressions of life received by the author. Because they are not actual, the author is free to invade their privacy and confide to us their thoughts and sensations, however evanescent and trivial. Thus he—or she, for the females of our species excel at producing fiction—provides the reader with an image of life more close-textured and vivid than any reality-bound genre, such as history, sociology, and even autobiography, can provide. Fiction is realer than real, one could say.

CHOKCHÖQ: One could, if one accepts quantification of the unquantifiable.

FARQUHAR: Sorry, we're a bit at the mercy of the translators here. Let's have a few examples. (*Think-tank technicians in gray jumpsuits shift cables and offload into Chokchöq's neural circuitry the digitized texts of* Ulysses, *by James Joyce, and* War and Peace, *by Count Leo Tolstoy. The transmission, marked by a faint ticking, takes seventeen seconds. Chokchöq's eyelids, which operate sideways, blink twice.)*

CHOKCHÖQ: This Napoleon, he was an actual person? This Dublin was an actual city?

FARQUHAR: Yes, well, but they've been *re-created*; the information isn't the point. Fiction is directed at neurons more complicated than the fact-collecting ones. Fiction aims to give the illusion of *experience*, so we know what it's like to be *alive*.

CHOKCHÖQ: How curious. On Mars, we know we are alive as soon as the nurses, while we are still in the larval stage, feed us pap that has been chewed by the queen.

FARQUHAR: Exactly. Fiction is experience that has been chewed by somebody else. Here, try these on for size. (Middlemarch *and* Madame Bovary *are offloaded. Twelve seconds of feathery ticking.)*

CHOKCHÖQ: I see. Fiction is about the difficulties of being female. On Mars, only our queens are allowed egos. We have found that more than one queen for every million workers and nurses distresses the social equilibrium.

FARQUHAR: Hold on, old boy—fiction can be about men, too. To wit— (Robinson Crusoe, Remembrance of Things Past, *and* The Trial *course through the Martian's input receptacle. Forty full seconds of ticking pass, during which his blinking becomes rapid and his many-elbowed antennae reach out to pluck a bunch of desert flowers from the wall.)*

CHOKCHÖQ: I see. Much anxiousness. Male unease in the universe is the topic.

FARQUHAR: I hate to be seeming quarrelsome, you know, but there isn't really *one* topic of fiction—it's about everything and almost nothing at the same time. It's an appeal to the whole soul. It's existential, it's onto-logical, it's accidental, it's sublime. It's as broad as life, as high and as deep, as shallow and bittersweet and murky, even. It's a mirror out for a walk, if you can picture that. Here, have a little change of pace. The French call these *nouvelles. (The complete short stories of Anton Chekhov, Katherine Mansfield, Guy de Maupassant, Machado de Assis, and Ernest Hemingway are downloaded in twenty-one seconds. With a startlingly unstoppable gesture, Chokchöq stuffs the bouquet of desert flowers into his face and chews. His jaws, like his eyelids, work sideways. His nose is hard and plow-shaped, from digging underground cities.)*

CHOKCHÖQ: Much humanness. Humanity appears to be a cosmic breed which never wearies of looking into the mirror. A rather *soft* mirror, in the case of fiction. It shows little of the digestive process, the laws of physics, and the productive labor of the proletariat, and gives inordinate attention to the erotic and the conversational. *(His antennae are locating another flower-bunch on the circular white wall.)*

FARQUHAR: Now, wait a minute there, chum. What's wrong with love and talk, heh? Make the world go round, don't they? The thing about fiction you're not getting is, it's *delicious.*

CHOKCHÖQ: *(having finished the second bunch; flecks of pink and blue plant tissue adhere to the metallic sheen of his mandibles):* More delicious, perhaps, for the writer than the reader. I am given to understand that for every reader on this planet there are three would-be writers.

FARQUHAR: Got you there, my ultralunar Ferdinand. Our latest critical theories demonstrate that the distinction between writers and readers is entirely illusory. The writer is a reader, reading what he writes as he goes along, watching the text create itself, and the reader as he reads creates the story in terms of scenery he can imagine, faces he can see— it's the story of his life! There's nothing like it, fiction, for immaterial interpenetration; it expands the sympathies and gives us more lives to lead than our own. It's life under the microscope, slice by slice, but also it's life in the empyrean, among the stars! Hey! *(getting carried away)*— if you guys had had some fiction on Mars you would have come out of your crummy, overregulated tunnels ages ago, where we could have seen you, and you wouldn't have blown up that Magellan probe the other year. You wouldn't be so cruel, xenophobic, and paranoid, frankly.

CHOKCHÖQ: *(clasping Farquhar's head with two of his prehensile tentacles and opening his russet jaws to an alarming width):* You insult our Martian way of life! *(The watchful technicians shoot megabolts of electricity, six seconds' worth, through the computer cable and stun the space alien. As he sinks onto his back, appendages feebly waving, Chokchöq emits faint rasping sounds which the translator renders as:)* Wow! That fiction packs a wallop! Still, I'm not sure you Earthlings will have much luck exporting it.

Print: A Dialogue

SCENE: *The spirits of Johannes Gutenberg and Bill Gates hang above the Frankfurt Book Fair. Both are the size of barrage balloons, silvery and lightly tethered. Such morphing is no problem for the magical software of Mr. Gates, but the great enlargement poses a problem for Herr Gutenberg, since so little is known about him, and that mostly from lawsuits. The shadowy details make enormous dark patches in his inflated image. Vagueness in, vagueness out, as the saying goes.*

Beneath these two hovering spirits there sprawls the Fair, a bustling market of the publishing industry—books, stalls, posters, salesmen, even authors, quaint doomed creatures carefully shepherded about, by vivacious publicity facilitators wearing miniskirts and spike heels, from one ill-attended press conference to another. There is a constant hubbub, as on a sinking ship's deck, of people keeping one another's courage up.

GUTENBERG *(marvelling):* What a circus! This commodity must be as precious as gold!

GATES: Cheap as dirt, actually. And on the way out. It's called print. You invented it, or so history claims, *faute de mieux.*

GUTENBERG: Printing was one of my sidelines—I was a goldsmith, by trade. Such fine work I used to do! After the intricacies of a signet ring or a necklace clasp, the technology of movable type seemed a game. One engraved the punches of hardened steel—this was an old process—and then punched the copper matrices, and then poured the type, of lead strengthened with tin and zinc; the hard part, the stroke of genius, was the adjustable mold, of two L-shaped pieces. Letters, you see, are not all of the same width, but it was important that the pieces of type be the same height and the same *depth*—else the inked impression would be hopelessly uneven.

GATES *(impatient with all this obsolete technology):* Yeah, yeah. I remember a similar problem arose when I was mapping the first version of Microsoft Basic—

GUTENBERG *(who is slightly deaf, from all those years of gold-hammering):* The thing about those first books, we wanted them to be *beautiful,* just like the finest manuscripts. The Bible and the Psalter had to have ornamental initials, in two sections, each linked separately and reassembled for each impression—it was tedious, but we thought if the books reflected God's glory less fully than the manuscripts the monks turned out nobody would take them seriously. This idea of mass production, of many different books, of new books all the time, it came later, after Fust foreclosed and took everything from me, and Peter Schoeffer, that traitor, went over to him, with all that I had taught him.

GATES: Lawsuits, don't mention them. Microsoft must have sixty going at any one time. These information revolutions, they don't come friction-free.

GUTENBERG: What is this Microsoft? The title of a romance? The angels tell me that, once people lost interest in religion, they began to read fables called romances, and all sorts of Godless mischief ensued, for which my invention was to blame.

GATES: Microsoft is bigger than a book, by a factor of billions. It makes programs, which are ways to make a book, among other things. A program is the software, and the hardware are those little boxes you see down there, with the shining faces.

GUTENBERG: Ah, I thought perhaps those were a new species of human being—heads without bodies. I see they are often consulted, like sages, and the alphabets attached to them are often caressed.

GATES: They're better than heads, actually. The circuits are more logical than a brain's circuits—no sex, no religion, no funky old anger and fear. No ego. Pure computing and memory. And communication— wow, do they communicate! And we're just at the beginning! If this were the print revolution, we're not even at the year 1500. The presses haven't begun to roll, man!

GUTENBERG *(peering down politely):* And what are they communicating?

GATES *(momentarily at a loss):* Why, you know—*stuff.* Information. Anything you communicate any other way, but faster. Bank statements. Airline reservations. Love letters, if you're into that, and the significant other is also on the Internet. Pornography, for that matter—virtual sex and violence, in a year or two, they say. *Data.* See that woman, there? She's pulling up the latest sales figures from New York, though it's still three in the morning there. That guy in the booth next to her? He's filing a press release that in four seconds will be printed out in Singapore!

GUTENBERG *(grasping at the familiar concept):* Printed, ah. And on what sort of press? Our press, before that rascal Fust took everything, had been an old wine press.

GATES: No more presses, Mr. G. Just the touch of light. No more lead molds and messy old ink balls leaking lampblack and linseed oil. It's all bytes and pixels and lasers now—no human muscle needed.

GUTENBERG *(squinting down):* And yet these glowing faces—what do you call them?—

GATES: Computer screens.

GUTENBERG: And yet these screens contain what seem to be letters, though very unbeautifully formed. Crude and hateful to the eyes though they are, a monk in his scriptorium could make sense of them, and set to copying them. How have letters survived your electric revolution?

GATES: Merely as a human convenience. The computers don't use them, they talk to themselves and to each other in *bits,* the smallest possible unit of information. A bit is the presence or absence of a pulse of electricity in an instant of time, or else the presence or absence of a charge of static electricity in a memory device. Doesn't sound like much, but they add up to quite a web of input and output as they move around through systems of built-in switches called, funnily enough, *gates*. It's hard to explain to a late-medieval mind, and you can't see a thing without a microscope, but, believe me, it works. When these machines do math, it's not at all like you and me doing math: they run a sort of guess through a series of loops enough times until they close in on the answer. They work on a hexadecimal base of sixteen instead of ten, which goes back, primitively enough, to our fingers and toes. Fingers and toes! Before the computers flash the answer, they translate it back into ten base, for our convenience. Letters are like numbers—they're an *interface*. That's another concept for you, interface. It's like, say, oh, the Church in your day was an interface between men and God. Or the printed page became an interface between one man's brain and another's voice. The alphabet was an interface between spoken language and the human eye. Already, there are computers that can take in and put out spoken language. Already, a generation or two has come along that can't be bothered to read; it absorbs all of its information from television and musical tapes. When you think about it, the printed page was an awful lot of *work*, and not a healthy use of your body, sitting and staring like that. Face it, friend, even at the height of the print era, only a tiny fraction of mankind read, and most did it for business purposes. It strained the eyes, overexcited the brain, and was anti-social. Do you follow me?

GUTENBERG: But . . . those people staring at their luminous screens, are they not reading? What does the material that holds the letters matter, whether it be stone, papyrus, vellum, rag paper, paper made of wood pulp, or raw light? These words made of electric impulses, do they not need a source of electricity nearby and, as you say, a computer to render them visible? Though I see a number of computers small enough to be portable—

GATES: Laptops, we call them.

GUTENBERG: —I see none as small and light as a modern book, which requires no electricity, and which can be entered—

GATES: Accessed.

GUTENBERG: —by simply opening its bound, sequentially numbered pages. How could information, or intellectual adventure in its many sorts, be more handily and—since one does not need to be a goldsmith to desire traces of eternal harmony in the objects of everyday human use—pleasingly packaged?

GATES *(holding up a small, exquisite, iridescent disk, a CD-ROM):* In my hand, Johannes, I hold thousands of pages, reduced to magnetized digits. Already, the sales of paper encyclopedias, in their many ponderous volumes, are withering beneath the appeal of these shimmering disks, which, in the flicker of a few computer keys, will yield not only the desired information but illustrative pictures in sixty-four-color display, diagrams that can be explored like three-dimension models, and specimens of music, played aloud! Access and amplitude—these are the virtues of digitized information. The card catalogues of entire libraries—the bulging, groaning repositories of the fading, crumbling fruit of your revolution—have been reduced to computer memory, exhaustively searched in a twinkling! No more fumbling at dog-eared pages! You had your day, old fellow—your five centuries, I should say—and now we must pack up your clumsy, dust-collecting, forest-wasting printed matter. This Fair beneath us is in truth a wake, just as, in the words of your great German philosopher Nietzsche, churches are but the tombs and sepulchres of God.

GUTENBERG *(hesitantly):* Perhaps the book, like God, is an idea some men will cling to. The revolution of print pursued a natural course. Like a river, print flowed to its readers, and the cheapness of the means permitted it, where the channel was narrow, to trickle. This electronic flood you describe has no banks; it massively delivers, but what, to whom? There is something intrinsically small about its content, compared with the genius of its workings. And—if I may point out a technical problem—its product never achieves autonomy from its means of delivery. A book can lie unread for a century, and all it needs to come to life is to be scanned by a literate brain. This CD-ROM of yours—what machine will be able to read it a hundred years from now? The very speed and momentum of your revolution erode its contact with the earth. You speak of this global Internet as if it transcended human brains; but man is still the measure of all things.

GATES *(collapsing with a hiss):* Oh? Who sayssss?

A Different Ending

Scene: The tomb of the Capulets, Juliet lies as if dead upon her bier. Romeo, bereft, is about to take poison.

ROMEO: Eyes, look your last;
   Arms, take your last embrace; and lips, O you
   The doors of breath, seal with a righteous kiss
   A dateless bargain to engrossing death!
   Though desperate pilot, now at once run on
   The dashing rocks thy seasick weary bark.
   Here's to my love! *(Lifts phial to drink.)*

   Enter Friar Laurence, catches his arm.

FRIAR: Pray, stay thy sad intent!
   Thank Heav'n I come, i' th' nick o' time. How oft
   Tonight have my old feet stumbled at graves.
   Attend me now. A letter sent to Mantua,
   In care of Friar John, an incident of plague
   Sealed fast at its source, never to arrive.
   Had you received this missive so ill-fortuned,
   You would have found spelled plain therein a plot
   Of benefice to thee and to thy love,
   Who lies here only seeming lost to death.
   The faithful child, she took, at my instruction,
   A potion mixed of cunning banes and phlegms
   And essences to hold her deep entranc'd,
   Beyond the tremble of a pulse, for two
   And forty hours, at the end of which
   Appointed spell, having eluded by
   The poignant hazard of this medicinal ruse
   That scheduled wedding with the noble Paris
   Which she detested and her family urged,
   She will, were the potion exact, awake,
   To be thence spirited away by you
   To Mantua and happy life thereafter.

A "one-minute" play done for the benefit of the American Repertory Theatre in Cambridge, Massachusetts.

Look, e'en now, her eyes like candles flicker,
And dawning blood ousts night's pall from her cheek!
ROMEO *(amazed as she stirs):*
Her body gives this tangled tale its proof.
JULIET *(sitting up):*
Good friar. And Romeo, as guaranteed.

The lovers embrace.

FRIAR*:* Come, Romeo, to Mantua escape,
And there possess your bride by night and day
And grow habituate, as sea to moon,
Revolving on the constant miracle
Of Juliet's bright face, until old age
Shall bend to earth a uniòn so rich
In seasons reaped and little Montagues!
JULIET*:* As heirs shoot forth, our elders, now so wroth,
Shall fondly vie in lavishing forgiveness.
ROMEO *(looking around uneasily):*
Indeed, this monkish plot has saved the day.
And yet, it doesn't leave much of a play.

Curtain.

THE BURGLAR ALARM

I.

A CREW OF YOUNG MEN came one day and threaded wire through hith-erto unviolated plaster and wood, "snaking" it from floor to floor, from basement to attic, with much grunting and shouted consultation; then they placed high in certain strategic corners of our rooms tidy vanilla-colored boxes, little rectangular eyes that glow red when we, in moving about, cross their electric vision. A panel at the front door, and another on the second-floor stair landing, winks one of its vertical row of small green lights when, in an unseen room, a body moves. It arouses guilt, this spying apparatus, this Geiger counter detecting bodily activity, and also provokes pleasure, as does anything that puts us in a fresh relation with the familiar. Standing in the front hall, we picture the boy of the house slouching from his desk to his stereo, perhaps scratching his armpit or picking his nose: the blinks do not take a photograph, they just register the fact that the house is shared—haunted, in a sense. A curtain blowing, or a picture falling from a nail, would also trigger the system, which, as long it is not activated, signals no alarm, merely mutely comments, blink-ing green.

When, with a numerical code only we know (hush! keep it secret! don't tell even the cleaning lady!), the alarm is activated, the light at the top of the row glows red. Then, we are safe. The rooms and doors are watched. An owl fluttering into the attic or a groundhog burrowing into the cellar would be detected, as would a burglar or rapist furtively prying open the window of the mudroom off the kitchen, or a Nazi arrogantly kicking in the front door. Behind this door, in the entrance hall, the panel beeps—a high-pitched, batlike whine—for a number of seconds, so that those who live here, who have a right to come through the front door, can dart to the panel of numbers and punch in the code and thus reassure the system that there is no burglar, no owl, no Nazi; that we are its friends, privy to its secret. We are benign bodies. Our motion must be allowed. We belong here. The system bestows distinct status upon us, in the manner of a headwaiter who lifts the velvet rope and quickly ushers a chattering, insouciant party to a prime table. The system resembles a set of antibodies, but also a team of obsequious doormen.

At night, having raided the refrigerator and cruised through the piano room one last time, we (we! you and I, you in your pale-blue robe and fluffy bunny slippers or else your feet bare and your pink toes unaware, like solemn babies, of how adorable they are) punch the alarm on, at the upstairs panel, and retreat to the bedroom as to a castle tower guarded by ruddy-cheeked pikemen and a deep moat, or, better, by a tenuous unsleeping dragon, its thin nerves of wire coiled about our warm oblivion, threaded through the studs and sills, its tiny red eyes alert throughout the night—the tall hour of midnight, the wee morning hours, the gray-blanched approach of dawn that gradually, filteringly picks out more and more details of our so-well-protected bedroom. The first one of us to stir deactivates the alarm, else he or she, heading thoughtlessly toward the kitchen, trips an invisible thread and suddenly is surrounded by an enormous voice, a remorseless frightened honking designed to terrify the interloper.

For the dragon has a voice; his voice is the most of him. "Huge" is the adjective that comes first to mind to describe this overwhelming noise; "anxious" is the next; "tireless" is the third; and then the mind shuts down, and the impulse, seizing homeowner as well as interloper, is to flee, to get out the door and into the woods, away from the noise. The crew that installed the alarm ran tests. The young man at the head of the crew, when the voice came on, became so panicked that he couldn't remember the code, the number we had agreed on. (*He* knows it, come to think of it—our secret number. Suppose burglar-alarm installers become burglars? Crime will be unstoppable! Suppose police turn dishonest, and servants ungrateful? Chaos will return!) Finally, he recalled the number we had chosen, or we shouted it to him—shouted through the thick of the terrible noise—and blessed silence returned. Blessed, because silence was now the reverse, the weird-looking negative image, of this huge outcry that would be henceforth, from this day forward, protecting us.

We were advised to run tests, now and then, to make sure that our protection is not imaginary. We are shy about it; it feels like a game. We call the police; we warn them we will be testing. You (you in your tasteful Saturday at-home outfit, the softened pre-shrunk blue jeans, the pre-dirtied white tennis sneakers, the combs that pin your abundant glossy hair into a workwomanlike bun, the sweatshirt decaled with an image of Minnie Mouse and, on the back, a feminist slogan) stand at the front-door panel while I, imitating a burglar, an invader in a black ski mask, stealthily enter the basement, or jimmy open the mudroom door, or slither into the attic window. In every case, the vigilant vanilla box sees me and the enormous voice comes on—honking, heaving, wailing, ululating. The noise takes possession of the house: it flattens the furniture against the wainscoting, bleaches the carpets, alchemizes the family silver into tin, turns the television set, the stereo, the VCR, the IBM PC, the microwave oven into two-dimensional junk. No fencible treasure is worth the price of this terrible noise, this protest that rings out all over the neighborhood and sets obscure signals blinking in the distant, bored police station. The tests at last over, we meet in the front hall. Your hair was somehow come undone and looks straggly. Dazed, I wonder how Minnie Mouse ever managed to walk in those ridiculously loose high-heeled shoes.

Our neighbors' burglar alarm keeps testing itself. When it comes on, there is an abrupt power drain that causes our microwave to skip a beat and our personal computer to lose everything in its short-term memory. Since their house is empty, the alarm bleats on and on, until the bored police at last arrive and shut it off. When they do, it feels like a dog being shot: a dog that has been hit by a car and is yowling in anguish until the policemen arrive and put it out of its misery. Perhaps our neighbors' house is truly being ransacked, every time. We have never asked. The neighborhood is an unfriendly one—houses scattered through the woods. In the summer we cannot see one other, in the winter we avert our eyes; each house would like to imagine it is the only one in the area. Perhaps our neighbors' alarm goes off now and then out of sheer loneliness. Perhaps our own will start to answer it some night, when we are snug and oblivious in our beds, yanking us from sleep with the suddenness that causes heart attacks.

But our dragon has been on good behavior so far. We sleep serene in its coils. Once, you (you with your mind still fuzzily full of *Masterpiece Theatre*, its ideal English villages, its exquisitely cast and scarcely intelligible character actors) forgot to punch the extra digits that take our bedroom out of the system, so that then, coming to bed—innocently, dreamily—you triggered that astonishing voice in all its monotonous merciless protest. It took some seconds for our brains, flattened by noise as they were, like ferns fossilized within a great weight of shale, to realize what had happened, to rush to the panels and deactivate, to rush to the telephone and head off the waves of policemen that would theoretically come crashing in upon us. In such a call, one must speak a code number, which if varied by a single digit carries some distinctly other meaning, such as "I am being held hostage and everything I say should be ignored. Come anyway. Be careful. They are armed."

I have the impulse, often, to turn the alarm on and walk about casually, to tease the thing, to test if it is still there. How do we know, as the silent weeks and months go by, if it has not died or lost interest? The lights on the panels still glow and blink, but that may be deceptive. I asked the young man who headed the installation team how one replaced the little lights when they wore out, and he looked me over—my gray hair, the wattles at my throat—and repressed a smirk. "They burn out in about forty years," he told me. As far as I was concerned, they were immortal. Like the rocks outside, like the clouds overhead, the burglar alarm is realer, longer lasting, than you and I. At night when we come in late, the boy of the house asleep or away (I in my tuxedo and you in your great-grandmother's matched pearls, your wide-shouldered spangly party dress with the low-slung belt, and your delectable silver sandals), the little red light staringly greets us, and the panel makes its warning whine, and then all the green lights in the row happily blink when we punch the deactivating code and prove ourselves once again worthy, "in," of select status, O.K. people, among the very few—at night, my dear, I am trying to say, when we enter, it seems clear that the burglar alarm, ever vigilant, so lean and ready and possessive, and the plump round furnace, churning out motherly heat in the basement, are the true couple of the house. We are guests, homeless ghosts that come and go. We have been robbed.

II.

THE BURGLAR ALARM and the furnace keep fighting. Early in the morning, when with a snort and rumble the furnace comes on and heat begins to pour in palpable sheets from the radiators, the alarm feels suddenly imposed upon, and lets out its enormous, heart-stopping wail. The sound seizes us in our bed and lifts us up, aglow with surging adrenaline, into the dawn darkness, our dazed brains flooded by images of rapine, theft, air raid, disaster. There must be, at the other end of the house, or at the bottom of the stairs, or transfixed at the basement door, a sneaker-clad cat burglar or, worse, a political terrorist in a ski mask or, worst, a homicidal maniac with a chain saw or meat cleaver, his jibbering face hideously squeezed into one thigh of some pantyhose.

The dawn peace of the house, oddly, co-exists with the noise of the alarm, like one layer of a sandwich under another, or cool water under hot. We blunder into the dusky, howling hall and in a tangle of trembling fingers punch on the control panel the numbers that cause the alarm, with a sharp little terminal whine, to cease. The tiny green lights on the panel bob off and on rapidly in a code we cannot read.

We listen. Our hearts are thumping audibly, and the furnace is muttering to itself, scraping at its throat like an old smoker, tapping like an idiot mechanic at something in the pipes. The system is old but the boiler is new: that must be the problem. The new boiler is putting out so much steam the pipes are overstimulated and the radiators are gushing clouds of heat that the alarm's infrared eyes misread as warm bodies. But this is just theory; the fact may be that another presence elsewhere in the house is tiptoeing toward us, sliding toward us sideways, drawn pistol glinting. Something creaks. Another thing rustles. In the east, dawn besmirches the sky like an industrial disaster. Our teeth feel the need to be brushed. The children who used to live in the house are gone—gone to Arizona, to Brooklyn, to Ulan Bator. If they were here, we would not feel like such children ourselves: scared, stunned, scuzzy-mouthed. Innocent, and yet not. If we were truly innocent, why would the alarm and the furnace be fighting this way? For they must be fighting about *us*.

The telephone rings. Somewhere far away, in a sealed-off, bombproof room, our burglar alarm has a connection. A woman is under orders to dial our number. She says, "Yes?" She sounds weary and wary. We assure her we are all right, we are fine; but she doesn't believe us until we go downstairs and fumblingly find a little card and read off some numbers to her. Then she hangs up, without wishing us well. These numbers make us, to her, real people, just as the burglar alarm, by our theory, thinks people are clouds of heat from the radiator.

We are too stirred up to go back to bed. I tiptoe down into the basement, to check on the furnace, lest it feel neglected—lest it feel we are catering to the burglar alarm behind its back. A dark and jealous god, it is snuffling to itself; it snorts, sighs, and then sings a curious high note, as high as its deep voice will allow, while its one eye, a small round window, flickeringly blazes. The furnace is making heat and sending it through the walls. When the burglar alarm was installed, perhaps one of its wires became involved with a thermostat wire, creating what electronics engineers call a "spike." This is another theory of ours.

The repairmen come, dressed like lawyers, in three-piece suits. Naturally, each wants to make the best possible case for his client. The furnace has been checked out repeatedly. The ferocious knocking merely means the water is trapped somewhere in the system, possibly where a valve is stuck, or where the house's settling over the years has reversed the pitch of a stretch of pipe. Unless we want to go to the considerable additional expense of installing a condensate overflow tank and ripping out some walls, we and the burglar alarm will just have to live with a little knocking, a little vibration. Vibration, after all, means vitality. "If the furnace is dead," the plumber tells us, "you won't get the vibration, but you won't get any heat, either." We glance toward the burglar alarm, hoping it overheard, hoping it will start to make allowances.

The alarm repairman, warming to his client's case, preaches that to get a little, you have to give a little. "We can shut down the zones that seem to be tripping, but then you're cutting down on your protection. The interloper can waltz right in through these zones into your bedroom." We huddle closer together, frightened by the "the," the definiteness of the article, which makes the hypothetical interloper real. The alarm system's advocate is sceptical of our radiator-heat-gusts/ghosts theory of activation; he crouches in front of a radiator and the red eye of the sensor on the front hall wall fails to blink. We turn up the thermostat and the radiator fails to produce. The repairman, in his tailored chalkstripes, turns on us a suspicious eye, only slightly red. His question need not be stated: can all this quarrel, this nocturnal tripping and wailing, have been our dreaming imaginations? He makes a handsome concession to our anxieties; he puts a bit of tape over one facet of the sensor's polyfaceted eye, like partial blinders on a horse, and leaves, counselling mutual tolerance, in a wide world of give and take.

We pray that our sanguine counsellors are right. The two systems must learn to live together; between them they warm us and protect us from harm. They must think of us and our welfare, and be calm. Their worst fights, evidently, take place when we are out of the house. Then, in those three or four hours while we are soaking our fatigued spirits in the soy sauce of a Chinese meal and the effluvium of Martin Scorsese's latest travail, the furnace and the burglar alarm really go at it—alarm after alarm, while the neighbors gather about the wailing, empty, darkened house in horror and indignation and the police cars come and go in a futile parade of spinning blue lights. It is like a fire without the fire. From her far-off bunker the weary, wary woman calls our number and gets no answer; so she telephones the neighbors, the local police, the Coast Guard, and in final desperation the 800 number for American Express.

From afar, we hear the howling. Stopping on our way back from the Chinese meal and American movie to buy our breakfast granola at the local 7-Eleven, we faintly hear from the parking lot the insistent cry that, as a mother knows her baby's wail in the tumult of a nursery, we know to be our own house. Home, home we speed—you crouched forward toward the dashboard in your low-key evening-out outfit, the hound's-tooth checks of your boxy wool jacket shaping my admiration as a waffle iron shapes running batter, your two severe bracelets, one to a wrist, clamped in place like impeccable manacles. Pulling up with a screech of brakes, we distribute laughing reassurances to the mob of neighbors milling in the blue lights. We enter the yelling hall, punch the code, tell the weary woman our numbers, grovel before the police and the neighbors, and take public vows that it will never happen again. This is humiliating, my darling. Other people's furnaces and burglar alarms get along, or at least suffer each other in stoic uncomplaint. Why must ours be this way? *"Why?"* you ask aloud, when we are alone at last. *"Do* something!"

"What the hell can *I* do?" I ask. "I'm no electronics engineer. All I do is pay the bills. Bills and bills. The alarm wasn't my idea in the first place. All it does is make everybody think we have something worth stealing."

"It was supposed to make me feel more se*cure*, all those nights you work in town late—what are you *doing* in there, anyway? You come home smelling like a distillery, that silly smile on your face—"

"Any smile on my face looks silly to you."

"Well you should have *seen* yourself with that cop, doing that disgusting 'ah shucks' routine you have, he was *not* amused."

"Yeah, well, I don't think your la-di-da Lady of the Manor manner went over that hot, either, and the neighbors, they all get up at five-thirty and were no doubt dead asleep—"

"Then *fix* it, *fix* it, get it *fixed*, you idiot! It was *your* idea to get the new boiler, the old one was *fine*, just a little dirty, you're just such a *sucker* with these plumbers, they talk you into any crazy thing and you just stand around blushing, saying, 'Oh, well.' Other people, other men—"

"Other men, other men, if they're so great why didn't you marry one? Do me a favor, could you? Just shut up. Shut up and let's go to bed."

"I *won't* shut up, I *won't* go to bed. How can I sleep? It might do it again! It's *hor*rible, it's *ter*rifying—"

"Oh, boo hoo." Steam is coming from my ears. And you, quite wonderfully, have slipped off your Ferragamos and begun to wail. The telephone rings. It is the weary woman, far away. She says the system is still reporting trouble.

THE GLITTERING CITY

New York Reflected in American Writing after 1920

THE PREVIOUS LECTURER, Louis Auchincloss, has talked to you about Edith Wharton; I hope it will not unforgivably trespass upon his territory if I begin by reminding you that a pivotal scene toward the end of Wharton's *The Age of Innocence* takes place in this very institution, which she describes as being, in the 1870s, **the queer wilderness of cast-iron and encaustic tiles known as the Metropolitan Museum.** The star-crossed lovers, Ellen Olenska and Newland Archer, for privacy retreat to the room where, and I quote, **the 'Cesnola antiquities' mouldered in unvisited loneliness.**

They had this melancholy retreat to themselves, and seated on the divan enclosing the central steam-radiator, they were staring silently at the glass cabinets mounted in ebonized wood which contained the recovered fragments of Ilium.

"It's odd," Madame Olenska said, "I never came here before."

"Ah, well—. Some day, I suppose, it will be a great Museum."

"Yes," she assented absently.

And then the novel takes a great leap, thirty years forward in time, and Newland Archer, we read, **had just got back from a big official reception for the inauguration of the new galleries at the Metropolitan Museum, and the spectacle of those great spaces crowded with the spoils of the ages, where the throng of fashion circulated through a series of scientifically catalogued treasures, had suddenly pressed on a rusted spring of memory.**

"Why, this used to be one of the old Cesnola rooms," he heard

Given on December 5, 1995, as one of a series of talks titled overall "Art Creates a City," at the Metropolitan Museum of Art in New York City.

someone say; and instantly everything about him vanished, and he was sitting alone on a hard leather divan against a radiator, while a slight figure in a long sealskin cloak moved away down the meagrely-fitted vistas of the old Museum.

The Age of Innocence was published in 1920; that same year a first novel called *This Side of Paradise*, by F. Scott Fitzgerald, was making a sensation, as were, in New York City, young Fitzgerald and his bride, Zelda. A Midwesterner and a Southerner, they suddenly became, in this first year of Prohibition, symbols of the new generation, and they obliged gossip columnists with a series of inebriated pranks: in André Le Vot's biography we read: **Zelda dived fully dressed into the Pulitzer fountain, naked into the one on Union Square, and danced on a carbaret table; Scott blanked out on a drunken brawl and came to the next morning to see a headline reporting that "Fitzgerald Knocks Officer This Side of Paradise."**

For Wharton, a native New Yorker, the city was a place of inexorable change, little of it for the better; for Fitzgerald, it was a site of giddy enchantment and romance, potential and fulfilled. Remembering his year of urban conquest a dozen years later, in a wryly modulated essay called "My Lost City," Fitzgerald wrote, **From the confusion of the year 1920 I remember riding on top of a taxi-cab along deserted Fifth Avenue on a hot Sunday night, and a luncheon in the cool Japanese gardens at the Ritz with the wistful Kay Laurel and George Jean Nathan, and writing all night again and again, and paying too much for minute apartments . . . The first speakeasies had arrived, the toddle was** *passé*, **the Montmartre was the smart place to dance and Lillian Tashman's fair hair weaved around the floor among the enliquored college boys. . . . When bored we took our city with a Huysmans-like perversity. An afternoon alone in our "apartment" eating olive sandwiches and drinking a quart of Bushmill's whiskey presented by Zoë Atkins, then out into the freshly bewitched city, through strange doors into strange apartments with intermittent swings along in taxis through the soft nights. At last we were one with New York, pulling it after us through every portal. . . . And lastly from that period I remember riding in a taxi one afternoon between very tall buildings under a mauve and rosy sky; I began to bawl because I had everything I wanted and knew I would never be so happy again.**

New York, then, makes you cry even when it fulfills your dreams.*

---

*This sentence in its cadence reminds me of another, by Jennifer Egan, in her short story "Emerald City" from the collection of the same name (1996): "And it struck him that

Speaking with less romantic egoism through his character Nick Carro-
way, Fitzgerald in *The Great Gatsby* gives a more subdued and penetrating impression of New York's charms for the stranger: **I began to like
New York, Nick writes, the racy, adventurous feel of it at night, and
the satisfaction that the constant flicker of men and women and
machines gives to the restless eye. I liked to walk up Fifth Avenue
and pick out romantic women from the crowd and imagine that in a
few minutes I was going to enter into their lives, and no one would
ever know or disapprove. Sometimes, in my mind, I followed them
to their apartments on the corners of hidden streets, and they
turned and smiled back at me before they faded through a door into
warm darkness. . . . Again at eight o'clock, when the dark lanes of the
Forties were five deep with throbbing taxicabs, bound for the the-
ater district, I felt a sinking in my heart. Forms leaned together in
the taxis as they waited, and voices sang, and there was laughter
from unheard jokes, and lighted cigarettes outlined unintelligible
gestures inside. Imagining that I, too, was hurrying toward gayety
and sharing their intimate excitement, I wished them well.**

Thus are expressed the two contradictory sensations of living in this
ultimate American metropolis: the excitement and pleasure induced by so
many active, proximate presences, and the concomitant sense of exclusion from almost all of the activity, breeding the inevitable suspicion that
other people are having the fun, with their gaiety and unheard jokes. In
"My Lost City" Fitzgerald remembers fondly a sense of inclusion in the
apartment of his Princeton friend Edmund Wilson: **But that night, in
Bunny's apartment, life was mellow and safe, a finer distillation of all
that I had come to love at Princeton. The gentle playing of an oboe
mingled with city noises from the street outside, which penetrated
into the room with difficulty through great barricades of books.** This
cozy apartment, this domestic beachhead in New York, reappears in Wilson's youthful novel *I Thought of Daisy*, but as an embarrassment because
it is not bohemian enough. Our hero has brought back to it Rita
Cavanagh, the fictional embodiment of Wilson's real-life love object
Edna St. Vincent Millay: **I was ashamed of the prospect disclosed,** he
tells the reader. **There were a large and comfortable couch, sets of
books in glass-doored bookcases, Whistler's "Battersea Bridge," and
a drawing by Leonardo, which I had brought up with me from college, a small mahogany desk, a green carpet and a French clock.**

---

this was New York: a place that glittered from a distance even when you reached it."
Fitzgerald's essay ends, "Come back, come back, O glittering and white!"

Besides, the maid had been there that morning and everything was swept and neat. I was afraid that she would see at once—if she had not already guessed—that I was really not one of them, that I had never paid their price. The Greenwich Village of this novel, published in 1929 but with a gestation period the whole decade long, is a kind of club, cozy and exhilarating; the narrator finds, he says, hope and excitement amid the variety and gayety of the Village, so densely intermingling, so vivaciously chattering about me: the Italian and Russian painters; the intelligent amateur actors; the mad baroness who kept a restaurant; the radical journalists and agitators, who, despite the homely forthright style of their writings, not infrequently turned out, when one met them, to be engagingly shy, and sometimes to possess personal charm to a degree almost cloying; the pretty Jewesses with thick red lips and glossy black bobbed hair; the austere and handsome women managers of theatres and magazines, with their dignity of Mother Superiors; and the megalomaniac lunatics whom it was the thing rather to like.

There is an epic tint to the Village's polymorphous babble of free spirits; the narrator describes how, among those tangled irregular streets to the west of Washington Square, I caught occasionally, from the taxi, a glimpse, almost eighteenth century, of a lampless, black-windowed street-end where the street urchins, shrieking in the silence, were stacking up bonfires in the snow—those lost corners of the old provincial city, where the traffic of the upper metropolis no longer gnashed iron teeth, no longer oppressed the pavements with its grindings and its groans—where those soft moans and hoots of the shipping washed the island from the western shore. There they had come, those heroes of my youth, the artists and the prophets of the Village, from the American factories and farms, from the farthest towns and prairies—there they had found it possible to leave behind them the constraints and self-consciousness of their homes, the shame of not making money—there they had lived with their own imaginations and followed their own thought. Alas, even this haven of heroic philosophers is not safe from money: I did not know that I was soon to see the whole quarter fall a victim to the landlords and the real estate speculators, who would raise the rents and wreck the old houses—till the sooty peeling fronts of the south side of Washington Square, to whose mysterious studios, when I had first come to live in the Village, I had so much longed some day to be admitted, should be replaced by fresh arty pinks—till the very guardian façades of the north side should be gutted of their ancient

grandeurs and crammed tight with economized cells . . . till finally
the beauty of the Square, the pattern of the park and the arch, the
proportions of everything, should be spoiled by the first peaks of a
mountain range of modern apartment houses . . . dominating and
crushing the Village. Neither Wilson nor Fitzgerald stayed in New
York: by 1921 Fitzgerald and Zelda had taken their captivating *folie à
deux* to Paris, and when returned from Paris they rented a grand house
outside of Wilmington; Wilson, originally a refugee from Red Bank,
New Jersey, drifted north, to Cape Cod and his ancestral home in Talcottville, in upstate New York.

One who did stay was Wilson's friend Dawn Powell, a refugee from
central Ohio. She was twenty when she arrived, in 1918. Her recently
published journals spell out the battering that life in New York gave
her—the drinking, the romantic fever, the high cost of living, the
enmeshed bitchiness of the envy-ridden literary scene. Nevertheless, her
youthful gratitude for her New York liberation endured. In 1931 she
wrote a cousin still in Ohio, **New York City** [is] **the only place where
people with nothing behind them but their wits can be and do everything. . . . The very *best* people think to be able to do as you damn
please, not caring what anyone thinks, is the mark of aristocracy.** A
Powell novel of Ohio like *Dance Night* is claustrophobic and sombre, yet
weighted with the tender authority of the well-known; a novel of New
York like *Turn, Magic Wheel* is giddy, hectic, with all its sadness and silli-
ness excused by the latent mysteries of the magnificent metropolitan setting. Glittering little poems to the city decorate the narrative: **New York
twinkled far off into Van Cortlandt Park, spangled skyscrapers piled
up softly against the darkness, tinseled parks were neatly boxed and
ribboned with gold like Christmas presents waiting to be opened.
Sounds of traffic dissolved in distance, all clangor sifted through
space into a whispering silence, it held a secret.** The sense of whispering secrecy comforts Powell, and one might speculate that men, more
confident of being able to be genuine, to do as they damn please, anywhere in the American breadth, are less loyal to New York's concentration of mysteries and clangor than are women. In *Turn, Magic Wheel*
Dawn Powell has her hero awake and feel **sorry for the country with its
poor morning sky bereft of clangor blended into its blue. . . .** Scar-
**latti, a laundress in the basement yard singing over her clothes-
hanging, the swish of a broom on stone and hydrant splashing over
cement court, the endless flow of trucks and streetcars and fire
engine all translated into a steady throb in the walls of his fourth-
floor room, a perpetual dynamo that operated the life of Manhattan.**

Perhaps people from Ohio were especially prone to an impression of New York as a dynamo, as a sublime concentration of energy. The poet Hart Crane, from Garrettsville and then Cleveland, spent only a few years in New York City, in the mid-Twenties, first as an advertising copywriter and then as a pure poet, dedicating himself to a large multiple-faceted poem, *The Bridge*, which would take the Brooklyn Bridge as its central subject and symbol and extend the rhapsodic note of Walt Whitman's "Crossing Brooklyn Ferry" into the twentieth century. The opening apostrophe "To Brooklyn Bridge" begins:

> How many dawns, chill from his rippling rest
> The seagull's wings shall dip and pivot him,
> Shedding white rings of tumult, building high
> Over the chained bay waters Liberty—
>
> Then, with involate curve, forsake our eyes
> As apparitional as sails that cross
> Some page of figures to be filed away;
> —Till elevators drop us from our day . . .
>
> I think of cinemas, panoramic sleights
> With multitudes bent toward some flashing scene
> Never disclosed, but hastened to again,
> Foretold to other eyes on the same screen;
>
> And Thee, across the harbor, silver-paced
> As though the sun took step of thee, yet left
> Some motion ever unspent in thy stride,—
> Implicitly thy freedom staying thee!

And so on. The pitch of eloquence is so high, and the verbal compression so great, that the exact meaning of many lines eludes at least this reader; nevertheless, the feeling remains that Crane more than any other twentieth-century poet caught the overpowering essence of New York, the fractured magnificence of it, the grandeur of its engineering, its sheer multitudinousness:

> Performances, assortments, résumés—
> Up Times Square to Columbus Circle lights
> Channel the congresses, nightly sessions,
> Refractions of the thousand theatres, faces . . .

And yet New York exhausted this fervent devotee—in 1923, his first year there, he is writing his mother, **The plain fact was, and still is—that New York takes such a lot from you that you have to save all you can**

of yourself or you simply give out. A month later, he is writing another correspondent, **Most of my friends are worn out with the struggle here in New York. If you make enough to live decently on, you have no time left for your real work,—and otherwise you are constantly liable to starve. New York offers nothing to anyone but a circle of friendly and understanding brothers,—beyond that it is one of the most stupid places in the world to live in.** By the end of 1925, Crane had left the city, and in April of 1932, having been living in Mexico, he apparently dove to his death in the Caribbean from the deck of the ship that was bringing him back to New York.

The disadvantages of life in this city have remained fairly constant in the last seventy-five years. In early 1925, the first issue of a new magazine called *The New Yorker* included in its slender sheaf of facetious pages this squib, entitled "From the Opinions of a New Yorker":

> **New York is noisy.**
> **New York is overcrowded.**
> **New York is ugly.**
> **New York is unhealthy.**
> **New York is outrageously expensive.**
> **New York is bitterly cold in winter.**
> **New York is steaming hot in summer.**
> **I wouldn't live outside New York for anything in the world.**

The New Yorker, as it slowly gained prestige and circulation under the editorship of the Colorado-born Harold Ross, did add, I think it not too much to say, a sliver of additional panache to the city's cultural self-consciousness. In its elegant covers, its *au courant* cartoons, its "Talk of the Town" chatter, and its frequently local stories both fictional and non-fictional, this magazine nominally devoted to New York's prototypi-cal citizen—figured forth as a Knickerbocker dandy—reinforced the notion, put forth resoundingly by Walt Whitman and sustained in the fiction of O. Henry and Horatio Alger, that to live in New York was a special adventure, for the habitués to relish and the outlanders to envy. Over the decades, but especially in its earlier decades, *New Yorker* fiction communicated a situational excitement, a sense that life in New York, though far from painless, was life in a state of electric arrival, arrival at a center where wistful feelings of relativity and irrelevance, so prevalent in such disgruntled provincial fiction as Sherwood Anderson's and Sinclair Lewis's, were left behind. The New York setting needed no justification and little preamble. It celebrated itself in voices as various as Leonard Q. Ross's stories about the night-school education of the redoubtable

Hyman Kaplan, John McNulty's page-long tales told by amiable barflies, and J. D. Salinger's exhaustive explorations of his ultra-urban Glass family. Irwin Shaw's celebrated story of 1939, "The Girls in Their Summer Dresses," brought home from Europe the sparkling Hemingway bleakness: **Fifth Avenue was shining in the sun when they left the Brevoort,** it begins. **The sun was warm, even though it was February, and everything looked like Sunday morning—the buses and the well-dressed people walking slowly in couples and the quiet buildings with the windows closed.** As our central couple, Michael and Frances Loomis, seek ways to fill the appetizing immensity of a New York Sunday, they reveal, as inexorably as a Hemingway couple in a Paris hotel or on a Swiss railway platform, a nagging irritant between them— Mr. Loomis's propensity for girl-watching, which he describes in terms that amount to a series of optimistic advertisements for the charms of New York: **I love to walk along Fifth Avenue at three o'clock on the east side on the streets between Fiftieth and Fifty-seventh Streets,** he confesses to his wife. **They're all out then, shopping, in their furs and crazy hats, everything all concentrated from all over the world into seven blocks—the best furs, the best clothes, the handsomest women, out to spend money and feeling good about it.** In another celebrated story, "Children Are Bored on Sunday," of 1948—a story which takes place entirely within the glowingly detailed interior of this museum—Jean Stafford's heroine wanders from one artwork to another, longing for a man and a drink and worried that she is insufficiently sophisticated for her metropolitan setting: she reflects back to a cocktail party where **that modern apartment, wherever it had been, while the cunning guests, on their guard and highly civilized, learnedly disputed on aesthetic and political subjects, the feeling of spring had boldly invaded, adding its nameless, sentimental sensations to all the others of the buffeted heart.** The heart, and the seasons, are not quite excluded from this marvellous, rectilinear milieu. John O'Hara's "Memo to a Kind Stranger" begins, with a cozy generalizing sweep reminiscent of O. Henry, **It is a strange thing, although it probably is just as well for everybody, that in New York City alone there are millions of people walking the streets who are in love, but not a single one of those millions ever gives much thought to the fact of having this one thing in common with so many others.** O'Hara had come to New York in 1928 and quickly learned the ropes, as he indirectly tells us in this inventory from the 1935 novel *Butterfield 8*: **She**—his heroine, Gloria Wandrous—**became one of the world's heaviest drinkers between 1927 and 1930, when the world saw some pretty heavy drinking.**

The Dizzy Club, the Hotsy-Totsy, Tommy Guinan's Chez Florence, the Type & Print Club, the Basque's, Michel's, Tony's East Forty-third Street, Tony's West Forty-ninth Street, Forty-two West Forty-nine, the Aquarium, Mario's, the Clamhouse, the Bandbox, the West Forty-fourth Street Club, McDermott's, the Sligo Slasher's, the News-writers', Billy Duffy's, Jack Delaney's, Sam Schwartz's, the Richmond, Frank & Jack's, Frankie & Johnny's, Felix's, Louis', Phyllis's, Twenty-one West Fifty-third, Marlborough House—these were places where she was known by name and sight. To a remarkable extent O'Hara's imagination remained loyal, through his long exile, to the Pottsville, Pennsylvania, of his youth; in his copious output there is relatively little New York, but, a strange mix of crudeness and hypersensitivity, he was equipped as few are to pick up on the vibrations from its many social strata. There is nothing but its title, "By Way of Yonkers," to identify this vignette of 1937 as specifically New York, but the description brings a whole stratum of the population excitingly with it: **The door was opened and a girl came in. She had on a black cloth coat, gunmetal stockings, black patent-leather pumps, and a Cossack hat. She had a neat, short nose with jigsaw nostrils and her eyes were bright and black and probably the long eyelashes were basically her own. She was a little taller than short, and in a few years she would be fat.** In the single arresting image "jigsaw nostrils" we feel not only her still fitly formed youth and beauty but an implication of mass manufacture—a race of good-looking, bright-eyed girls spread through the city's huge, furtively erotic picture puzzle. She seems to be a hooker, and her boyfriend a down-on-his-luck former bootlegger; but their exchange is tender nevertheless, and ends in tears.

If John O'Hara was the quintessential *New Yorker* short-story writer of the Thirties and Forties, John Cheever was that of the Fifties. Cheever wrote about the city first as a resident, come to New York in his early twenties in the early Thirties, and then, after his move to Scarborough in 1951, from a commuter's perspective. In his lyrical work a wonderful primal glitter is increasingly subject to a dark and desperate tarnish. "The Bus to St. James's" begins with the city in its morning innocence: **The bus to St. James—a Protestant Episcopal school for boys and girls—started its round at eight o'clock in the morning, from a corner of Park Avenue in the Sixties. The earliness of the hour meant that some of the parents who took their children there were sleepy and still without coffee, but with a clear sky the light struck the city at an extreme angle, the air was fresh, and it was an exceptionally cheerful time of day. It was the hour when cooks and doormen walk dogs, and** when porters scrub the lobby floor mats with soap and water. Traces of the night—the parents and children once watched a man whose tuxedo was covered with sawdust wander home—were scarce. In "The Five-Forty-Eight," written a bit earlier in the mid-Fifties, it is evening, and raining, and our hero, Blake, a commuter, is being pursued by an unbalanced young woman, his former secretary, whom he has slept with and then fired. **He listened for a minute—foolishly—as he walked, as if he could distinguish her footsteps from the worlds of sound in the city at the end of a rainy day. Then he noticed, ahead of him on the other side of the street, a break in the wall of buildings. Something had been torn down; something was being put up, but the steep structure had only just risen above the sidewalk fence and daylight poured through a gap. Blake stopped opposite here and looked into a store window. It was a decorator's or an auctioneer's. The window was arranged like a room in which people live and entertain their friends. There were cups on the coffee table, magazines to read, and flowers in the vases, but the flowers were dead and the cups were empty and the guests had not come. In the plate glass, Blake saw a clear reflection of himself and the crowds that were passing, like shadows, at his back. Then he saw her image—so close that it shocked him. She was standing only a foot or two behind him.** Scott Fitzgerald's awareness of other lives closely passing in anonymous provocation, **the constant flicker of men and women and machines,** has become in Cheever more sinister; the sense of a soaring New York is now a monotonous, meaningless something being torn down and something else being put up; the flowers in the shop window are dead, the teacups are empty, and the imitation of a home environment is horribly false. The chance romantic encounter sung by Fitzgerald has become in his disciple Cheever a shocking shadowy closeness to a woman with vengeance in her heart.

Unease, in fact, was always part of *The New Yorker*'s version of urbanity, present in Thurber's sharply captioned, woozily drawn cartoons and E. B. White's gently skeptical "Notes and Comment." White wrote the affectionate book-length tribute titled *Here Is New York*, saying of the city that **It is to the nation what the white church spire is to the village— the visible symbol of aspiration and faith, the white plume saying the way is up**, but he also spoke for metropolitan bemusement and anxiety. In his short story "The Door" White imagines himself as a rat systematically frustrated and bewildered by scientific experiments in conditioned reflexes: **Everything (he kept saying) is something it isn't. And everybody is always somewhere else. Maybe it was the city, being in the city, that**

made him feel how queer everything was and that it was something else. A little poem by the novelist Ben Ray Redman appeared in the magazine in 1955, titled "Portrait of a Friend" and ending with the lines

> Rhode Island creased
> His temple in the west,
> Cannes hid between two chins,
> And, for his sins,
> Manhattan lay
> Heavy across his chest.

And now what of those who did not voluntarily arrive from Ohio or Minneapolis or, like White, Mt. Vernon, and who could not retreat to farms in Maine or, like Cheever, to an old farmhouse in Ossining? They numbered and number in the millions, these to whom the city, in its unfashionable neighborhoods and boroughs, looms as a doom, an ineluctable fate. In his 1930 novel *Jews Without Money*, Mike Gold, who had been born on the Lower East Side as Irwin Granich, wrote: **New York is a devil's dream, the most urbanized city in the world. It is all geometry angles and stone. It is mythical, a city buried by a volcano. No grass is found in this petrified city, no big living trees, no flowers, no bird but the drab little lecherous sparrow, no soil, loam, earth; fresh earth to smell, earth to walk on, to roll on, and love like a woman. Just stone. It is the ruins of Pompeii, except that seven million animals full of earth-love must dwell in the dead lava streets.** Gold had become a Communist at the age of nineteen, was made editor of the *New Masses* in 1928, and urged "proletarian realism" upon others, a realism yearning for a revolutionary Messiah: **You will destroy the East Side when you come, and build there a garden for the human spirit.** Henry Roth's *Call It Sleep* of 1934 also concerns the poor of the Lower East Side, but is a more modernist, subjective work, Joyceanly full of dialogue and dialect and compressed, epiphanic word-pictures. To the novel's boy hero, David Schearl, rats are not a metaphor but a frightening presence in a cellar where, pursued by a policeman, he takes shelter: **He dipped his foot into night, feeling for the stair, found it, pulled the door shut behind him. Another step. He clung to the wall. A third. The unseen strands of a spider's web yielded against his lip. He recoiled in loathing, spat out the withered taste. No further. No! No further. He was trembling so, he could barely stand. Another step and he would fall. Weakly, he sat down.**

Darkness all about him now, entire and fathomless night. No single ray threaded it, no flake of light drifted through. From the

impenetrable depths below, the dull marshy stench of surreptitious decay uncurled against his nostrils. There was no silence here, but if he dared to listen, he could hear tappings and creakings, patterings and whispers, all furtive, all malign. It was horrible, the dark. The rats lived there, the hordes of nightmare, the wobbly faces, the crawling and misshapen things.

Call It Sleep does not strive for a political overview but gives us, in an often overwrought prose, the very taste and sound and sensations of growing up in the devil's city of lava. Across the East River, in the Williamsburg section of Brooklyn, Daniel Fuchs grew to young manhood. In the mid-Thirties he published three novels remarkable for their easy, luminous style and Olympian good humor. In the first and most ambitious of them, *Summer in Williamsburg*, the novel's autobiographical central observer, Philip Hayman, puzzling over the suicide of a neighbor, tells himself, **If you would really discover the reason, you must pick Williamsburg to pieces until you have them all spread out on your table before you, a dictionary of Williamsburg. And then select. Pick and discard.** Such a Joycean aesthetic detachment, much cooler than Roth's fury of rendition, takes Williamsburg, with its brutal gangsters and strangled amours, as a massive datum distilled into word-pictures of a strange tranquillity: **On Sunday, the sun floats down tranquilly to cover with its glaring brightness the pavements and the buildings. The streets are deserted, their inhabitants jamming the subways for Coney Island or else seeking the dark coolness of moving picture houses. Williamsburg becomes for the day like a bright painting in its motionlessness, and somehow this creates an atmosphere in which you may like to bathe sleepily.** Fuchs eventually turned, as if with a shrug, from novel-writing; he made money betting on horses and selling short stories to magazines, including *The New Yorker*, and wound up in Hollywood, where one of his scripts won an Academy Award. His Williamsburg tenement-dwellers are always escaping to the movie houses, and their amusements are haunted by awareness of the glamorous life an island away: Philip, sitting in a girlfriend's apartment watching a party, thinks, **Parties on July nights and sweat. Dim lights and a red board floor losing its wax in a crazy design from dancers' heels . . . As the girls danced Philip would see where the stockings stopped. He looked for the little soft roll of flesh above the rubber garters.** But across these sweaty amusements falls a vision: **At a Park Avenue penthouse the lovely gentlemen glide over the carpets with their hands nonchalantly in their pockets while their heads stick out above high wing collars like chrysanthemums. Fascinating** women in liquid gowns flow and ebb as they move from group to group of men.

The New York rich may forget the poor, but the poor cannot forget the rich. In James Baldwin's novel of 1953, *Go Tell It on the Mountain*, his hero, John, the son of a Harlem preacher, likes to venture south into Central Park, and stand upon a knoll from which he can see the skyline: **Then he, John, felt like a tyrant who might crumble this city with his anger; he felt like a tyrant who might crush the city beneath his heel . . . He remembered the people he had seen in that city, whose eyes held no love for him. And he thought of their feet so swift and brutal, and the dark gray clothes they wore, and how when they passed they did not see him, or, if they saw him, they smirked. . . . And certainly perdition sucked at the feet of the people who walked there; and cried in the lights, in the gigantic towers; the marks of Satan could be found in the faces of the people who waited at the doors of movie houses; his words were printed on the great movie posters that invited people to sin. It was the roar of the damned that filled Broadway . . . *Broadway:* the way that led to death *was* broad, and many could be found thereon; but narrow was the way that led to life eternal, and few there were who found it. But he did not long for the narrow way, where all his people walked; where the houses did not rise, piercing, as it seemed, the unchanging clouds, but huddled, flat, ignoble, close to the filthy ground, where the streets and the hallways and the rooms were dark, and where the unconquerable odor was of dust, and sweat, and urine, and homemade gin. In the narrow way, the way of the cross, there awaited him only humiliation forever . . . but here, where the buildings contested God's power and where the men and women did not fear God, here he might eat and drink to his heart's content and clothe his body with wondrous fabrics, rich to the eye and pleasing to the touch.** To this son of Harlem, midtown New York is a temptation to rage and to sin, a glittering torment beseeching him, in his words, **To hurl away, for a moment of ease, the glories of eternity!**

And now I can hear you thinking, *This lecturer has just about used up his allotted time, and hasn't gotten us past the 1950s. He hasn't shown us a single slide, and hasn't even mentioned my favorite New York novel, which is Tom Wolfe's* The Bonfire of the Vanities.

Have no fear; the end approaches. Art holds the mirror up to nature, and recent mirrors are so broken or cloudy that New York seems scarcely reflected. In Saul Bellow's 1969 novel, *Mr. Sammler's Planet*, James Baldwin's sense of New York as drastically divided and unholy returns from the other side; Artur Sammler, a scholarly, elderly, Anglicized Polish Jew, traverses a New York in which he helplessly watches a **powerful Negro in a camel's-hair coat, dressed with extraordinary elegance**, pick pockets on the Riverside bus, deliberately, brazenly, **with the effrontery of a big animal.** Sammler intends to report this criminal activity to the police, and goes to a phone booth on Riverside Drive. But: **Of course the phone was smashed. Most outdoor telephones were smashed, crippled. They were urinals, also. New York was getting worse than Naples or Salonika. It was like an Asian, an African town, from this standpoint. The opulent sections of the city were not immune. You opened a jeweled door into degradation, from hypercivilized Byzantine luxury straight into the state of nature, the barbarous world of color erupting from beneath.** Bellow, who wove some lovely images of New York into *Herzog*, and in *Seize the Day* fashioned a moving elegy for upper Broadway, finds little good to say for New York City as of 1969; the menacing Negro is finally brought down, but in a sickeningly barbarous fashion, bludgeoned unconscious by a sack of sharp-edged abstract sculptures wielded by an athletic, merciless Israeli. Bellow's word "Byzantine" is suggestive: the New York of the Twenties and Thirties, at least the Greenwich Village, offered the stimulation and openness of a Greek city-state; the bastion metropolis of the Forties and Fifties had a serious Roman grandeur, an imperial air of global mission; and now we have the Byzantine decades of the Peppermint Lounge and Plato's Retreat, of multiplying bathhouses and spreading AIDS, of junk bonds and jailed millionaires, of ubiquitous beggary and homelessness, of luxury and squalor separated by a thin jewelled door. Well, New York has never been a *nice* town. In his recent novel *The Waterworks*, E. L. Doctorow describes the city of 1871 as **everyone securing his needs in a state of cheerful degeneracy.** Boston and Philadelphia had their religious, utopian pretensions, but Edith Wharton boasted of **New York, where people seem from the outset to have been more interested in making money and acquiring property than in Predestination and witch-hunting.** John Adams, visiting in 1774, said, **There is very little good breeding to be found . . . At their entertainments there is no conversation that is agreeable; there is no modesty, no attention to one another. Their talk is very loud, very fast, and altogether.** Of the hundreds of local voices that have sought print in the Byzantine luxury and squalor, let me mention and briefly cite three postmoderns: Frank O'Hara, Donald Barthelme, and Paul Auster.

O'Hara, like many another sensitive gay man from the provinces, found happiness in New York. His passions for music, for art, for words, and for companionship were sated here; New York was for him what it had been for Walt Whitman: **City of orgies, walks and joys.** He was an art critic and a curator at the Museum of Modern Art during the heroic days of Abstract Expressionism, when New York supplanted Paris as the world's art capital. He wrote poems at odd moments, often misplacing them soon after the process; lunch hour was a favorite time, and a favorite topic. A poem like the well-known "The Day Lady Died" has the texture of a diary:

> It is 12:20 in New York a Friday
> three days after Bastille day, yes
> it is 1959 and I go get a shoeshine
> because I will get off the 4:19 in Easthampton
> at 7:15 and then go straight to dinner
> and I don't know the people who will feed me

The happenstance facticity of city life patters above an underlying bliss, culminating in the moment when

> Everything
> suddenly honks: it is 12:40 of
> a Thursday.
> Neon in daylight
> is a great pleasure.

The Whitmanesque rapture lives again in him; "Rhapsody" asks:

> 515 Madison Avenue
> door to heaven? portal
> stopped realities and eternal licentiousness
> or at least the jungle of impossible eagerness

and concludes:

> I have always wanted to be near it
> though the day is long (and I don't mean Madison Avenue)
> lying in a hammock on St. Mark's Place sorting my poems
> in the rancid nourishment of this mountainous island

The banality and frivolous muchness of New York life are benign in O'Hara, as they are in the poems of his friend John Ashbery—an element in which the individual ego transparently swims, taking rancid nourishment.

The short stories of Donald Barthelme recast these qualities in satire, with an undercurrent of despair. A Texan, Barthelme was one of the most loyal literary immigrants since Dawn Powell. Like O'Hara, he was an aficionado of the art world; collage, surreal juxtapositions, and a deadpan Pop Art comedy characterize his work. He was an expert parodist, taking off on older modes of written narrative from fairy tales to nineteenth-century novels; the underlying message is, *We are at the end of narrative*, and his own disjointed tales are told in a curt tone bordering on impatience. *Let's cut the guff*, his style says. In "The Glass Mountain," a story consisting of a hundred numbered sentences, a glass mountain is posited at the corner of Thirteenth Street and Eighth Avenue. As the hero climbs it with climbing irons and two plumber's friends, his human friends hoot from the base and the mountain, a patent symbol of Manhattan ambition, reveals a certain beauty to its climber: **Touching the side of the mountain, one feels coolness. Peering into the mountain, one sees sparkling blue-white depths.** But what he finds at the top is, quote, **only a beautiful princess,** and he throws her headfirst to his vicious acquaintances at the mountain's base. City life, as experienced with a number of interchangeable princesses, has a final unanswerable flatness. From "The Indian Uprising": **I spoke to Sylvia. "Do you think this is a good life?" The table held apples, books, long-playing records. She looked up. "No."** In the story titled "City Life," **Elsa and Ramona entered the complicated city. They found an apartment without much trouble, several rooms on Porter Street. Curtains were hung. Bright paper things from a Japanese store were placed here and there.** By the story's end, Ramona is an unmarried mother and gives herself to civic introspection: **Ramona thought about the city. —I have to admit we are locked in the most exquisite mysterious muck. This muck heaves and palpitates. It is multidirectional and has a mayor. To describe it takes many hundreds of thousands of words. Our muck is only a part of a much greater muck—the nation-state—which is itself the creation of that muck of mucks, human consciousness.**

The Barthelme stories cited all come from the late 1960s; to the mid-Eighties belongs Paul Auster's *New York Trilogy*—three novels, his first three, now bound as one. They are exquisitely bleak literary games written under the influence of the *nouveau roman* and the genre of detective fiction. Mysteries are not solved, however, but allowed to dangle and multiply, as symbols of the existential mysteries. New York—where Auster took up residence after four years in France—is an ideally vacuous arena for self-referential behavior and reflection. **New York,** we read in the first novel, *City of Glass,* **was an inexhaustible space, a labyrinth** of endless steps, and no matter how far he walked, no matter how well he came to know its neighborhoods and streets, it always left him with the feeling of being lost. Lost, not only in the city, but within himself as well. The characters, some of whom are called Paul Auster, give the impression of being, with their stark, forgettable names, refractions of a single solipsistic character. One of them, Stillman, tells another, Quinn, I have come to New York because it is the most forlorn of places, the most abject. The brokenness is everywhere, the disarray is universal. You have only to open your eyes to see it. The broken people, the broken things, the broken thoughts. Of a hotel lobby it is said, The place seemed blank, a hell of stale thoughts. Though the novels hold much precise topography and street layout, from Harlem to City Hall, the details are ghostly, bloodless, maps without sensations; one character, it develops, has been spelling out, with his daily walks, letter forms on the map of the Upper West Side. The streets feel eerily empty, like those in Richard Estes' meticulous photorealist cityscapes, or those in Kurt Vonnegut's 1976 novel *Slapstick*, which presents a post-plague Manhattan called the Island of Death, or Skyscraper National Park.

So the brimming city where one used to come to find oneself is now a monstrous blank in which to lose oneself; the nation's intellectual capital has become a hell of stale thoughts. A vision like Auster's may lie, of course, in the beholder, but there is no doubt, I think, that in the seventy-five years since 1920 the city's bounty and glory are more enigmatically phrased than they were, say, for Edmund Wilson, who came here to exercise his brain, or for Scott Fitzgerald, who came to parade his bride and cash in his dreams. Rather than end this skimming survey on a down note, let me proclaim that the city survives its reflections—it is still here, around us, the buildings, the population, the golden lit windows, the ginkgo trees, an infinite conflux of phenomena whose constant stir is not unhopeful or uninspiring. Each day the streets awaken to freshness, as in these beautiful stanzas by Elizabeth Bishop:

> Earliest morning, switching all the tracks
> that cross the sky from cinder star to star,
>   coupling the ends of streets
>   to trains of light,
>
> now draw us into daylight in our beds;
> and clear away what presses on the brain:
>   put out the neon shapes
>   that float and swell and glare

down the gray avenue between the eyes
in pinks and yellows, letters and twitching signs.
　　Hang-over moons, wane, wane!
　　From the window I see

an immense city, carefully revealed,
made delicate by over-workmanship,
　　detail upon detail,
　　cornice upon façade,

reaching so languidly up into
a weak white sky, it seems to waver there.

*Two books provided invaluable help in assembling the materials of this talk,
or reading:* Remarkable, Unspeakable New York: A Literary History, *by
Shaun O'Connell (Beacon Press, 1995), and* New York: Poems, *edited by
Howard Moss (Avon, 1980).*

GEOGRAPHICAL, CALENDRICAL, TOPICAL

On the Edge

THOSE OF US who live outside New York and visit it only from time to time approach the city limits with a number of anxieties. In my father's day it was the fear of being cheated and swindled by a "city sharper," a resident of the city more quick-witted and less scrupulous than a simple, moral country person. Now it is fear of being mugged and assaulted by an "inner-city" resident socially and economically disadvantaged to the point of violent behavior. In my father's day the fear was of being dazzled by the city's bright lights; now we fear being caught in the darkness of a power outage or, worse yet, a riotous collapse of the city's tenuous, precariously maintained order. The traffic jams, the burst water mains, the failed electric cables, the dust of construction and deconstruction, the thousand daily crimes and quarrels all seem prophetic of a total disaster drawing near, when the city's ethnic tensions and overburdened social structures explode into total rage and anarchy.

New York, we say, with comic understatement, is a tough town. The toughness can be seen on the faces not only of its homeless beggars and its jaded policemen but on those of its aristocrats and beauties. Nobody can be trusted; nothing is sure. A cornice from a crumbling skyscraper can fall on your head; a demented beggar can lurch at your wallet; a knife can flash out of a crowd waiting for the traffic light to change. A few years ago, a beautiful model had her face slashed by men hired by her disgruntled West Side landlord. The crime horrified a public inured to most crimes; it struck at the heart of New York's image of itself as the place where Americans with brains or beauty can come and sell their wares. It is a city of winners as well as of losers, where the Dutch, the

---

Written for a special New York issue of *The Tokyo-jin*, a Japanese magazine.

English, the Irish, the blacks, and the Jews came to better their lives, and where now Haitians, Senegalese, Koreans, Eastern Europeans, Middle Easterners, and Central Americans still pour in, in a seemingly endless circus of hope and hustling, of dangerous and laborious freedom.

An outsider's feeling of New York as a kind of Hell is so instinctive that he is perpetually surprised, in his visits, by the renewed discovery that the city holds many cozy places and gentle people; that the flavor of New York, in fact, is fundamentally innocent, in the way that the first attempts at civilization—Ur, Harappa—must have seemed innocent, there on the edge the desert. The social contract is constantly being tested, as a new invention. To be in New York is to be on the edge—the edge of safety, and the edge of other worlds.

The American Academy of Arts and Letters, for instance, sits in a neighborhood—once-fashionable West 155th Street—where Spanish is heard on the street more than English, and the crack trade thrives. Nevertheless, learned meetings and celebrations go on. Most of the Academicians, old and frail as we tend to be, are brought in from the rest of Manhattan by limousine, and limousined safely back. However, one afternoon, anxious to go to the airport and get home to Boston, I ventured out of the building onto upper Broadway, hoping to hail a taxi. Sometimes, returning from a fare in the Bronx, taxis can be seen, though in nothing like the teeming, heedless numbers of midtown Manhattan. Today, however, there were none, and a fellow-Academician, becoming worried about me, offered me a ride to New Rochelle, one of New York's suburbs, and then back south to the airport. This would have been a long way around. Above all, the Academician sternly warned me, don't get lured into one of the unlicensed, unmarked gipsy cabs that might stop for me.

No sooner said, than a dented old car pulled up, one of the bloated boatlike Detroit models built before the Arab oil boycott and the influx of Japanese automobiles changed the spacious American way of thinking about private motorized vehicles. These gas-guzzling relics of our old optimism, becoming antiques, have fallen to the poor. The driver was a young black. Very young, quite black. He rolled down the window enough for me to ask him how much he would charge to take me to La Guardia Airport. He thought a while, as if the idea of going to the airport was new to him, and said, "Seventeen dollars." This was surprisingly cheap—no more than most cab rides would have cost—so I opened the door and hopped in, happy.

Yet my heart was beating, for wasn't I slightly off the beaten track, a white-haired, white-skinned gent of sixty in the depths of an illegal cab?

The driver took me along a winding series of streets in Harlem. Suppose he decided to drive me into an empty lot or cul-de-sac, and demand money? Who would come to my rescue? Out of the windows, I saw only black people—black men standing around on street corners talking and waiting for something to happen, black women shopping and pushing black babies in strollers. A world I had no part in, yet one full of life; even the shop signs, in bold reds and yellows, had a vibrant demotic energy, a black accent. Signs of violence were everywhere—shuttered-up shop windows, garish graffiti, burned-out tenement buildings, glittering fragments of shattered glass on the pavement. Society had shown these people little consideration; why would they show me any?

I studied the back of my driver's head. He had shaved his skull. His ears were exquisite—little baroque flowers of beige flesh, the tips in close to the hairless skull—and his hands on the steering wheel, equally so. Emboldened by his physical delicacy, I cleared my throat and asked him, as we passed an especially thick assembly of people, gathered on the sidewalk in what seemed a party mood, what those people were doing there. In this world I was as much a tourist as a visiting Japanese. He looked over at the festive crowd, loosely arranged in a line, and told me, "Welfare."

"At six-thirty at night?" I asked.

He nodded wordlessly. He was concentrating, I realized, on how to get me to the airport. The smooth oval of his skull was entirely devoted to the practical objective. He was young, it came to me, younger than my own sons, and possibly less at home in English and in New York than I had assumed. Not all blacks, after all, came to our shores on seventeenth-century slave ships; they still come, voluntarily now, from the beautiful and profitless quarters of the tropical world. He was good at steering us through Harlem, but once on the major roads to the airport he seemed nervous. My advice became welcome. We worked at the problem together—he cleverly ignored the one bad turn I suggested—and arrived at the Delta Shuttle terminal, which is not easy to find. When I gave him a twenty-dollar bill and with a little wave indicated he should keep the change, he smiled for the first time. It was a sweet, hopeful, vulnerable smile, with enviably healthy mauve gums.

He had been afraid of me—afraid at least that I would not give him, after our terse bargain on upper Broadway, a tip—much as I, at first, had been afraid of him. Our fears had been baseless. For every dire thing that happens in New York, a hundred—a thousand—successful small transactions like this take place. The city remains a great learning experience, a center of education in how to be an American. Americans like me, who live far from its vitality and menace, its glamour and squalor, owe it to ourselves to visit it from time to time. We visit it at our physical peril, but stay away at our spiritual peril.

People Wrapped to Go

AN OUT-OF-TOWN FRIEND writes:

I don't get to New York as often as would be good for me, and when I'm there I don't always take the subway, but lately I've had several rides, and was struck by a new, to me, feature of their interiors: little bundles, wrapped up in plastic and vinyl, that upon closer inspection turn out to be sleeping people. Homeless people, presumably, making a home where they can, in a corner of a moving subway car, and sleeping, like swans with their heads neatly tucked under their wings, in a swaddling darkness created by the carefully meditated arrangement of a nylon parka or a green garbage bag. The first such bundle I encountered was so small, so headlessly huddled and tidily wrapped, that only when I noticed the legs sticking out below did its nature—its contents—dawn on me. This was a human being. I started back, in revulsion, as if a chair, say, had begun to breathe and dance, and then took my cue from the impassive, accustomed, in-town faces of my fellow-passengers. They were used to this, it was part of the texture of their daily lives. They ignored it, and I tried to. Yet, I have noticed, these bundles get room—people don't sit down next to them if they have a choice, and except at the rush hours a surrounding emptiness pads the peculiar and pathetic shelter that these wanderers have carved for themselves from the hurtling mass of metropolitan transit.

A nearly empty car heading up toward Columbia and beyond held two such artifacts the other day: a remarkably dainty entity, neatly folded and as snugly opaque as a Christmas package, at one end, extruding two legs one of which wore a jogging sneaker and the other merely a fuzzy athletic sock, and a large black man in the center of the car, slumped asleep on the slick orange bench seat, tilting and righting himself at every stop and start of the train, yet keeping his eyes squeezed shut. It must have been a truly miserable doze, yet he never made the sensible adjustment of moving his body to an end seat, where he could have braced himself on one side. Perhaps in his dreams he thought the train was more crowded than

An unpublished "Notes and Comment" submitted to *The New Yorker* in April 1991.

it was. His chin dug into his chest, his head jerked and flopped with the changing momentum of the train, and his hands, one in a thick brown glove and the other in a glove the lobster red of a barbecue mitt, lay defenseless beside his thighs, along with a boyish leather cap with earflaps. He had property: a besmirched duffle bag rode between his tired shoes. At the end of the car, the feet of the other homeless bundle changed position, the foot with the sock resting on the running shoe for a moment, as if in sudden inspiration, like the gesture of a person about to venture a bright remark at a cocktail party. The black man with mismatching gloves looked as if he could be or had been strong, and he took up a lot of psychological space in the train. We scattered other passengers—black and white, Hispanic and Asian—looked at him with dull and wary eyes, and looked away. Nobody knew what to do about him, any more than the United Nations knows what to do about the Kurds.

Suddenly it seems the world is full of countries that just don't work. Iraq is a murderous mess, with tens of thousands of homeless families looking to the conquering UN armies for the only food and protection in sight, and the one secure citizen is the one mostly responsible for it all, Saddam Hussein. But not just Iraq. Albanians fleeing their country overwhelm Italian ports, Eastern Europeans in general are trying to jump ship. The U.S.S.R., our former fellow-superpower, is in some kind of meltdown. There used to be friendly countries and countries we didn't like, but all appeared to have a system that made the use of a collective noun feasible: "they," "we." Now many of the contracts that held people within boundaries, and defined their routes to the human necessities, seem to be dissolving, and it isn't so much a question of good and evil or wise and unwise but of order and chaos, with chaos gaining. Basic services are not being maintained. This country startled itself and the world with how well it could still manage a war. But the concrete in our bridges keeps crumbling, and our subways carry back and forth to nowhere figures out of Samuel Beckett, reduced to a minimum that mocks our pretensions to civilization and brotherhood.

One Big Bauble

CHRISTMAS IN NEW YORK CITY is a brave and somewhat bizarre affair. Like almost everything in America but the landscape and the Native Americans, the holiday was imported. The New England Puritans and the Dutch settlers of New Amsterdam had little use for it, as a pagan and then papist intrusion in the Christian calendar. But in 1823 Clement Clark Moore, a New York clergyman and professor at the Episcopal General Theological Seminary, published a poem, "A Visit from St. Nicholas," which created the American Christmas. Known to every schoolchild, the poem begins with the famous couplet,

> 'Twas the night before Christmas, when all through the house
> Not a creature was stirring, not even a mouse;

and goes on to evoke a St. Nicholas totally removed from the austerities of medieval sainthood—

> He had a broad face and a little round belly
> That shook, when he laughed, like a bowl full of jelly.
> He was chubby and plump, a right jolly old elf,
> And I laughed when I saw him, in spite of myself . . .

This fat, laughable Santa Claus is the patron saint of the Christmas spree which merchants and even grave-faced economists encourage—a frenzy of buying meant to reach its highest pitch in Manhattan, the nation's grandest *souk*. The Knickerbocker New York of Clement Moore's time, amiably confused with the snow-bedecked London of Dickens' *Christmas Carol*, is a religiously neutral evoker of the season's magic; the inspector of Christmas windows will find many a top hat and hoop skirt bedecking mannequins whose faces are alight, beneath a tall haloed gas lamp, with the joys of carolling or of being drawn through Central Park in a one-horse sleigh.

But contemporary New York is raucously multi-ethnic and post-Christian, a site for the worship of Mammon and Dionysus rather than of the baby Jesus. Specifically Christian notes, in fact, are rare in the city's seasonal decorations. Long gone are the days when the Jewish owners of emporiums like Bloomingdale's and Stern's made crèches, with tenderly smitten shepherds and resplendent, gift-bearing magi, the centerpiece of their display windows. The windows of Bergdorf Goodman in 1995, for instance, contained enigmatic scenes of set tables and similar posh decor,

---

Written for Lufthansa Airline's *Bordbuch*, with photographs by Frieder Blickle.

all coated with an artificial frost whose sparkle and whiteness presumably signified Christmas in the current minimalist code. Those of Saks were devoted to "The Little Snowman of Rockefeller Center," with a series of windows occupied by nodding reindeer and slowly twirling snowmen. Symbolized by Santa Claus, evergreens, angels, and baubles, Christmas belongs to everyone. In his novel *Operation Shylock* Philip Roth salutes Irving Berlin for having secularized the two major Christian holidays with a pair of popular songs, "White Christmas" and "Easter Parade," that leave Christ quite out of it. Christmas in New York offers foreign tourists an excellent study in the accommodations of the American melting pot.

One out of four New Yorkers is Jewish; Jewish energy and intelligence and warmth set the city's tone, or, rather, have conformed to and strengthened a tone that was always there, a tone of mercantile brashness that was haughtily noted by Bostonians and Philadelphians while the colonies were still ruled by a king across the ocean. The eight days of Hanukkah have been blended with Christmas into the "holiday season," and the Hanukkah menorah and the Nordic pine tree have merged with the camels carrying the magi across the Sinai Peninsula and Tiny Tim and Rudolph the Red-Nosed Reindeer—a welter of acceptable Christmas imagery available to window-dressers as elements of the message intended to excite holiday spending.

New York is also home to one of the world's greatest concentrations of people of sub-Saharan African blood, and black-faced Santa Clauses, in white beards and mustaches, can be seen on many a street corner. How many of these are, behind their beards, Black Muslims does not bear looking into. In an age of weakening Christian orthodoxy, the vigorous dogmas of political correctness and ethnic diversity are enforced everywhere. Of two ten-foot wooden soldiers standing guard on the south side of Rockefeller Center in 1995, one was female and one was black. Snowmen, once a common symbol of the season, have become, in their ineluctable whiteness, something of an embarrassment. Deep in the maze of tunnels beneath Times Square, a trio of black men in Santa Claus outfits were playing Christmas carols, in jubilant Caribbean rhythms, on steel drums.

The center of New York's Christmas observance bears, on maps, the rather recessive name of Sunken Plaza. It is a rectangular area in front of the RCA Building in Rockefeller Center, where ice skaters go round and round beneath the great golden figure of a horizontally floating Prometheus. At Prometheus's back, above his elegantly marcelled Art Deco head, there is erected each year the gigantic Christmas tree whose lighting, in early December, marks the beginning of the holidays in the metropolis. This year the tree, a seventy-five-foot Norway spruce, came from the grounds of a nunnery in New Jersey, the Sisters of Christian Unity, many of whom attended the ceremony, along with the mayor and thousands of citizens and tourists seeking to be infected by the Christmas spirit. The nuns referred to their departed tree in the feminine gender, as when one nun said, "I haven't seen her since she was cut."

You approach the skating rink by walking down the Promenade, a sloping pedestrian way decorated with angels fashioned of white wicker. A security guard, with his own beatific smile, stood ready to defend the angels from any who might think them worth stealing. A half-block to the west, in the Radio City Music Hall, the Rockettes danced in their famous line of high-kicking bare legs, in a heavily patronized Christmas show also featuring animals, both real and simulated. A half-block to the east, across Fifth Avenue, St. Patrick's Cathedral, one of the few city churches that still manage to hold their own with the surrounding architecture, opened its bronze portals to those seeking a more intimate, specifically religious "take" on the season. A few blocks up the Avenue, the city had hung a giant three-dimensional snowflake at the intersection of 57th and Fifth. Directly behind the cathedral, on Madison Avenue, the New York Palace—a Helmsley hotel occupying the block-long brownstone edifice once shared by Random House and the Catholic Diocese of New York—rose to the occasion by outlining itself in ribbons of tiny white lights, like an enormous Christmas package; this theme, of the building as self-wrapped package, was also presented, along Fifth Avenue, by the jeweller Cartier.

Small white "champagne" lights are ubiquitous, like clouds of gnats in a damp pine woods in the heat of summer. The little streaks and splashes of them, and the plastic evergreens that ornament the window of many a haberdashery and boutique, seem, under the towering stone mass of midtown, a bit perfunctory. This year, one store along the Promenade, BREE, displayed an arrangement of crossed sticks and an entwining, sinuous wreath curiously suggesting both a dollar sign and a crucifixion. Along Rockefeller Plaza, the little half-street that connects 48th and 51st Streets to the west of Fifth Avenue, a racy shop called Sylvie Bluelips resorted, for the seasonal supernatural note, to mannequins of a comic extraterrestriality: one had an eyeball for a belly-button and wore great triangular earrings spelling the word SEXY. HAVE A SEXY XMAS is not quite yet an official greeting.

This central territory of Christmas is also heavy media country: the Associated Press and Time Warner have their fortresses in the shadow of the RCA Building, and at its base tourists cluster to gaze and grimace into the windows at the *Today Show*, the NBC network's gifts to break-fasting America. Christmas, in a world ever more shaped by the images that television beams forth, seems a giant commercial, thrust upon us helpless viewers as inflexibly, as mercilessly, as all those other commercials that deaden the mind of a hucksterized society.

It is in the little byways of Manhattan that a certain poignance and intimacy still attach to the holiday. The wreath in the steamy restaurant window, the luxuriously bearded Santa cut-outs softening the grim lines of a police station, the cold and lonely treks of the tree-deliverer and the nativity players—these are among the images our photographer has captured in the less well-lit streets away from Rockefeller Center. In the hearts of the city's millions, Christmas struggles to keep a personal meaning. In the great Main Post Office on Eighth Avenue, adults take time to peruse and answer sheafs of letters written to Santa Claus by New York children; where they once used to ask for toys, they now ask Santa simply for clothes. A grim world of deprivation lives lurks beneath the glitzy surface of Christmas in New York; and the contrast is not exactly concealed, in this city of street people housed on the sidewalks in cardboard boxes and plastic garbage bags. The tireless, inescapable begging ("Change, spare change?" comes the muttered litany) is seasonally reinforced by the monotonous ringing of the Salvation Army volunteers. These institutional beggars, incidentally, once as common a Christmas sight as red suits and false beards, have been banned from many of the country's shopping malls, as unsightly intrusions on the malls' private property. New York is one of the few cities left where the downtown still functions as a shopping center. In midtown Manhattan, beggars, police, shoppers, tourists, and jostling teenagers from Harlem and the boroughs mingle in an open-air carnival shot through with the smell of chestnuts heating over charcoal grills and the sound of carols leaking from swinging doors.

As a child I more than once travelled, with a family member, to see Christmas in New York, where the displays of the department stores lifted into a realm of more exalted enchantment the nodding dolls and the circling electric trains of the store windows in my home city in Pennsylvania. I still try to visit New York in December, and to admire once more the baroque opulence of the huge artificial Christmas tree erected in the Metropolitan Museum of Art, with its magnificent carved crèche and firmament of angels, from eighteenth-century Naples. The month is generally a raw time of year in Manhattan, as the calendar's shortest days press on the brave display of consumerism. The tinsel shivers in the wind off the rivers that surround this narrow, rocky island. In a city so fathomlessly layered, Christmas does not penetrate very conspicuously into the subways, or transfigure the tall, granite-faced buildings much above the ground floor. Yet I have never been disappointed in my visits; something of Christmas unobtainable elsewhere exists here. The holiday hustle suits a hustling town; it raises the ante and ups the tempo. The fantastically abundant lights of the island become Christmas illuminations—Manhattan a single glittering bauble, a brave extravagance.

The Twelve Terrors of Christmas

1. Santa: the Man. Loose-fitting nylon beard, fake optical twinkle, cheap red suit, funny rummy smell when you sit on his lap. If he's such a big shot, why is he drawing unemployment for eleven months of the year? Something scary and off-key about him, like one of those Stephen King clowns.

2. Santa: the Concept. Why would anybody halfway normal want to live at the North Pole on a bunch of shifting ice floes? Or stay up all night flying around the sky distributing presents to children of doubtful deservingness? There is a point where altruism becomes sick. Or else a sinister cover-up for an international scam. A man of no plausible address, with no apparent source for his considerable wealth, comes down the chimney after midnight while decent law-abiding citizens are snug in their beds—is this not, at the least, cause for alarm?

3. Santa's Helpers. Again, what is *really* going on? Why do these purported elves submit to sweatshop conditions in what must be one of the gloomiest climates in the world, unless they are getting something out of it at our expense? Underclass masochism one day, bloody rebellion the next. The rat-a-tat-tat of tiny hammers may be just the beginning.

4. O Tannenbaum. Suppose it topples over under its weight of bomb-shaped ornaments? Suppose it harbors wood-borers which will migrate to the furniture? There is something ghastly about a tree—its look of many-limbed paralysis, its shaggy and conscienceless aplomb—encountered in the open, let alone in the living room. At night, you can hear it rustling and slurping water out of the bucket.

5. Tiny Reindeer. Hooves that cut through roof shingles like linoleum knives. Unstable flight patterns suggesting to at least one observer "dry leaves that before the wild hurricane fly." Fur possibly laden with disease-bearing ticks.

6. Electrocution. It's not just the frayed strings of lights any more, or the corroded transformer of the plucky little Lionel. It's all those battery packs, those electronic games, those built-in dictionaries, those robots a-sizzle with artificial intelligence. Even the tinsel tingles this year. And isn't it somehow terrible, the way shed tinsel shivers in the gloomy ice-clogged gutters?

7. The Carols. They boom and chime from the vaulted ceilings of supermarkets and discount malls—and yet the spirits keep sinking. Have our hearts grown so terribly heavy, since childhood? What has happened to us? Why don't they ever play our favorites? What *were* our favorites? Tum-de-tum-tum, angels on high, something something, sky.

8. The Specials. Was Charlie Brown's voice always so plaintive and grating? Did Bing Crosby always have that little pot belly, and walk with his toes out? Wasn't that Danny Kaye/Fred Astaire/Jimmy Stewart/ Grinch a card? Is Vera-Ellen still alive? Isn't there something else on, like wrestling or *Easter Parade*?

9. Fear of Not Giving Enough. Leads to dizziness in shopping malls, foot fractures on speeded-up escalators, thumb and wrist sprain in the course of package manipulation, eye and facial injuries in carton-crowded buses, and fluttering sensations of disorientation and imminent impoverishment.

10. Fear of Not Receiving Enough. Leads to anxious scanning of UPS deliveries and to identity crisis on Christmas morning, as the piles of rumpled wrapping paper and emptied boxes mount higher around every chair but your own. Three dull neckties and a pair of flannel-lined work gloves—is this really how they see you?

11. Fear of Returns. The embarrassments, the unseemly haggling. The lost receipts. The allegations of damaged goods. The humiliating descent into mercantilism's boiler room.

12. The Dark. Oh, how early it comes now! How creepy and green in the gills everybody looks, scrabbling along in drab winter wraps by the phosphorous light of department-store windows full of Styrofoam snow, mock-ups of a factitious 1890, and beige mannequins posed with a false jauntiness in plaid bathrobes. Is this Hell, or just an upturn in consumer confidence?

That Syncing Feeling

WHAT'S ALL THIS lip-syncing? The nation's most adored TV show rarely purveys an episode without Bill or Phylicia or the kids mouthing air, rolling their eyes, and demonstrating labial stops while some pop classic from the bulging vaults unfurls on the sound track. Filmgoers still humming over Jessica Lange's spirited mime of the entire Patsy Cline discology in *Sweet Dreams* can now dig Dean Stockwell's eerily sensitive mock-rendition of "In Dreams" in *Blue Velvet*. From lurid go-go caves to sun-splashed kindergartens, lip-syncing seems to be the Eighties mode of self-expression, just as the oil glut is the Eighties economic fact, and the trash glut the overriding civic problem. When you think about it, there exists both a glut of post–Beach Boys pop classics and a contemporary oversupply of selves needing expression, and lip-syncing must be Nature's way of mopping up both in one beautiful act of recycling. Lip-syncing wastes no wax and does not ask that society shoulder the housing costs of any new creativity. The other arts, also bedevilled by overpopulation and excess backlog, would do well to find equivalents of the lip-sync solution. How about:

Brush-sync. Acquire a large reproduction of an already accredited painting and without dipping your brushes in paint trace every stroke, right on the poster or giant Polaroid print. Where the brushstrokes are loaded, think gumbo. Pro*ject* gumbo. Where the texture thins, dip the dry brush frequently into a cup or dish devoid of turps. In the case of action painting, dribble-sync from the appropriate aerial distance, with facial expressions copied from sardonic photojournalism essays in Fifties issues of *Life*. For the ultimate artistic adventure, sneak into a museum late at night and *brush-sync directly on actual masterpieces.*

Type-sync. Go through the motions of typing, or else firmly type on a keyboard welded solid, while periodically extracting photocopied pages of an admired manuscript from the platen. Lean energetically into erasures and manual insertions. Great piano-sync passages from old films such as *Tonight We Love*, starring Cornel Wilde, may offer attitudinal guidance and indicate attainable levels of simulated emotion. A number of celebrated modern manuscripts are available in published form. That of *The Waste Land* offers an opportunity to sync not only Eliot tapping and scratching at the various stanzas but then to sync Pound making marginal comments and pencilling his brilliant, slashing deletions. The *Ulysses* manuscript is bulkier and more expensive, and tracing page after page of Joyce's Jesuit-schooled handwriting may grow tedious; but there are some fun bits with colored crayon in the "Ithaca" episode.

Think-sync. Sit prolongedly. At moments abruptly leap up and pace the room, stare out a window, chew a pencil eraser, furrow the brow. Take deep, brain-oxygenating breaths; wince when a chain of hypothetical thought is broken by an imagined interruption. Do not shy from extending for days and even weeks this exercise in participatory appreciation and vicarious achievement. At the end, feign scribbling on a piece of paper, or silently mouth with a contorted expression of triumph, *"Cogito, ergo sum"* or *"*$E = mc^2$*"* or "Absolute power corrupts absolutely" or *"Le silence éternel de ces espaces infinis m'effraie."*

Syncing feels so good. Why be yourself, with that same old boring Social Security number, when you can sync your way out? History has had its fun; art is tired of trying not to repeat itself. The eternal return is cosmic-sync, and Nietzsche or a simulacrum may be next week's guest on the *Cosby Show* mouthing air in time with "Also Sprach Zarathustra."

Paranoid Packaging

MAYBE THE MADNESS began with strapping tape. Its invention seemed to excite people, so that packages arrived more and more impenetrably wrapped, in layer upon layer of the tough, string-reinforced stuff. Where tearing fingers used to do the job, an X-Acto knife and a surgical precision had to be mustered. Domestic injuries mounted, but the tape kept coming, along with flesh-colored plastic tape that wouldn't tear—just stretched, like tortured flesh—no matter how hard you pulled.

Then, one day, in the long twilight of the Reagan Presidency, the cereal and sugar boxes that had always said PRESS HERE ceased to yield, when pressed, the little pouring holes we remembered from childhood. Rather, our thumbnails broke, and turned purple overnight. Padded book envelopes, which used to open with an easy tug on the stapled turned-over flap, were now taped *over* the staples. The taping was tenacious, multi-layered. Postal regulations, some said: too many clerks were calling in sick from cutaneous contact with half-bent staple ends. At some juncture under Bush, with everybody distracted by bulletins from the Gulf War, the self-sealing book envelope was promulgated. Now there was no hope of a tidy opening and a thrifty reuse; nothing less than a hatchet or a machete would free the contents, in a cloud of fast-spreading gray fluff.

All this time, child-proof pill bottles had been imperceptibly toughening and complicating, to the point where only children had the patience and eyesight to open them. Though the two arrows were lined up under a magnifying glass and superhuman manual force was exerted, the top still declined to pop off. Similarly, the screw-tops on the can of creosote and the bottle of Liquid-Plumbr refused to slip into the grooves that in theory would lift them up—up and free. Instead, they rotated aimlessly no matter how much downward and sideways, or semi-circular, pressure was applied. Occasionally an isolated householder did enjoy a moment of success with these recalcitrant containers; manufacturers, swiftly striking back, printed the instructions in even smaller type or, less readably yet, in raised plastic letters. The corporations, it seemed, did not want their products released into use—any upsurge in demand might interfere with their profit-enhancing downsizing programs.

The little bags of peanuts with which the downsizing airlines had replaced in-flight meals became, as the Clinton administration warily settled into the seats of power, impossible to open. The minuscule notch lettered TEAR HERE was a ruse; in truth, the plastic-backed tinfoil, or tinfoil-backed plastic, had been reinforced in that very place. Mounting frustration, intensified by the claustrophobia, cramping, and fright normal to air travel, produced dozens of cases of apoplexy and literally thousands of convulsively spilled peanuts. Even the little transparent sacs of plastic cutlery for airplane meals (when these were actually served) proved seamlessly resistant, and yielded up their treasure only when pierced from within by a painstakingly manipulated fork.

Such consumer-resistant packaging devices were all as bows and arrows before the invention of gunpowder, however, once the maker of Vanish, a brand of mystery-crystals alleged to clean toilet bowls, came up with a red child-resistant cap, shaped like a barred O, a three-dimensional Θ, whose accompanying, arc-shaped directions commanded TO OPEN: SQUEEZE CENTER WHILE PULLING UP. Well, good luck, Mr. and Mrs. America: squeeze until your face turns red, white, and blue. No amount of aerobic finger exercise will ever instill the squeeze-power needed to release those crystals into that murky toilet bowl.

Either as a nation we have grown feeble, or the policy of containment, once preached as the only safe tactic for dealing with the Communist menace, has now refocussed upon the output of capitalism, in all its sparkling, poisonous, hazardous variety. The corporate powers that control our lives have apparently decided, in regard to one product after another, to make it, advertise it, ship it, *but not to let us into it*. Be it aspirin, creosote, salted peanuts, or Vanish, it is too wonderful for us—too potent, too fine. We rub the lamp, but no genie is released. We live surrounded by magic caskets that keep their tangy goodness sealed forever in.

This little "Shouts & Murmurs" for The New Yorker *attracted more mail than any magazine piece I have ever published. Kindred complaints poured in—against rupture-proof bubble wrapping, heat-sealed plastic magazine wrappers, red cellophane pull-strips with unfindable ends, chain-stitched pet-food sacks without directional indications, little tinfoil seals on the spouts of orange-juice cartons that adhere as if soldered. Many of the correspondents were elderly and arthritic. Alicia Dillon, of Pascagoula, Mississippi, reported jumping in frustration upon a pill bottle that, even so, remained impregnable. Dolores Webster, of Reno, Nevada, had been battling for six months with a container of Lysol that continued to defy her best efforts: "I tried and tried. I live alone so had to do it myself—it's still in the bathroom, unopened." John F. Grimm, of West Bethesda, Maryland, had a legal proposal: "It has long been my contention that every CEO of every company that produces products for public consumption should, by law, be compelled annually to open one sample of every product produced by his organization. He should have to do this without assistance, without wearing glasses or contacts, and in a location where spillage will produce uncomfortable results."*

Hostile Haircuts

Now that I am sixty, I see why the idea of elder wisdom has passed from currency. My thoughts have become not only fewer and smaller but more spiteful and timorous. The impression has been growing upon me that I am surrounded by hostile haircuts. When African-American males first began to cut their hair in skullcapping muffins sharply differentiated from shaven sides sometimes ornamented with X's and other brandlike symbols, I assumed that, within a long history of experimentation that ranged from conking to the Afro, an intraracial code was being playfully augmented, with no special message for me. When young white men, however, took up the same style, menace began to emanate as surely as from a crowd of Marine crew-cuts or FBI-style tight trims. Prior to 1960, now that I think upon it, all men's haircuts expressed a slight hostility, a simmer of close-clipped individual militance whose subtext was "Don't mess with [muss] me." On the distaff side, those lacquered hairdos from Forties Hollywood were as virginity-defensive as iron chastity belts; the height of untouchability was reached with the beehive, which abruptly collapsed into the limp ironed hair of the counterculture, signalling a state of stoned acquiescence.

Honestly, I don't recall feeling especially threatened by Sixties long hair, at least not after my sons, still cherubically freckle-faced, adopted it. True, some male faces, wearing a scruffy tangle down to their shoulders,

with a beard thrown in for good measure, appeared the opposite of paci-
fied. Wasn't facial hair, the evolutionists argued, a trait worth preserving
because men could scare each other with it in battle? My main sensation,
however, of the long-hair era was the disconcerting sexual confusion,
with its revelation of latent adrogyny within myself, of being unable to
gender-identify an attractive figure from the back, as it sashayed along
with locks flowing down to its slender, swaying hips. Now, seeing a young
male whose ostentatiously full-bodied locks have been cropped on the
sides in what I think of as normal fashion but have been encouraged
to flourish in the middle to form a Samsonesque mane, complete with
extended nape curls, I have no trouble recognizing hostility. This haircut
wants me to drop dead.

When the sweet-mannered bespectacled young woman at the local
library shaved off all her head of hair but a tuft she dyed cerise, I rather
desperately tried to believe she was not out to get me. She continued to
twinkle behind her glasses, and to stamp the due date. The Seventies
Mohawk, after all, had been somewhat defused by splashes of color, its
fierce statement removed to a theatrical realm of outrageous costume. In
the movie *The Last of the Mohicans*, I am assured by a with-it critic, Daniel
Day-Lewis sports a "really terrific head of hair . . . rock-star hair . . .
greasy enough to shine with rebel integrity, yet not so disgusting that we
start wondering what Hawkeye smells like." Native American haircuts
(hostile to white invaders and swindlers) are a grease-layer's thickness
removed from rocker haircuts (hostile to family values, bourgeois repression, and regular hours). English punk haircuts (hostile to the upper class
and fans of foreign soccer teams) are to be distinguished from American
punk haircuts (hostile to Mom, Dad, and high-school dress codes). One
day, the young woman wore a bandana over her cerise topknot, meaning
either that the head librarian had spoken sternly to her, or that she was
experimenting with degrees of hostility, as Venetian blinds experiment
with degrees of sunlight.

Not all haircuts are hostile in the same way. Sinead O'Connor's is
screamingly, overtly hostile, for instance, whereas Ross Perot may even
think his is friendly. Ted Koppel's swooping bang is slyly but purposefully
hostile—a shield of hair interjected to protect his frontal lobes from
insidious waves of interviewee blather. Bill Clinton's hair, closely mod-
elled on the opossum fur of his beloved Arkansas, manages to say yes and
no to hostility at once, appearing both cuddly and spiky and in any case
composed of an unidentifiable salt-and-pepper substance, like spill-proof
carpeting. On *Wall Street Week*, Louis Rukeyser's lopsided smile is hostile, but his haircut is defensive, and begs for our mercy; in response, we

feel hostile toward *it*—its simpering, whitening, overlook-me comb-over. It's a hairily cruel world. Snip or be snipped. We're all butting for psychological space, and leading with our warheads.

Glad Rags

To THOSE OF US who were alive and sartorially active at the time, it was saddening to read in *Vanity Fair* recently the allegation, by "New York socialite" Susan Rosenstiel, that in 1958 J. Edgar Hoover was parading around in a Plaza Hotel suite wearing women's clothes: "He was wearing a fluffy black dress, very fluffy, with flounces, and lace stockings and high heels, and a black curly wig." I was saddened to think that future generations, trying to grasp the peculiar splendor and excitement of high-echelon cross-dressing during Eisenhower's second term, will imagine that dowdy bit of black fluff, with its fussy flounces and matching wig, to have been *très à la mode*, when the truth is we all considered J. Edgar something of a frump.

Ike, for instance, dear Ike with his infallible instincts, would never have let himself be caught in lace stockings, even though he did have the legs for them. I remember, within a month of Saint-Laurent's 1958 collection for Dior, Ike coming out in a stunning cobalt-blue wool trapeze, with white open-backed heels and a false chignon. That very day, if memory serves, he had sent five thousand Marines to Lebanon, and not a hair was out of place. It was with this outfit—or was it a belted A-line from the previous year?—that he sported a flowered silk neck-cloth, when scarves were still thought to be strictly for babushkas. He was very conservative as to hemlines, however; when Saint-Laurent lifted skirts to the knee in 1959, the President waited three months for Congress to decide the issue and then, losing all patience, switched to Balenciaga with a stroke of his pen. Thenceforth, to the very end of his administration, he stuck with long-waisted day dresses in neutral duns and beiges.

John Foster Dulles, on the other hand, favored a slinky-pajama look, and pastel pants suits with a touch of glimmer in the fabric. Oodles of bangles, upswept blond wigs, and pompommed mules. For all his staunch anti-Communism, he was oddly partial to red, though I believe on good authority that Sherman Adams at least once took Foster aside and made the point that bright colors did not become a big-boned frame. Sherman, though he was undone by vicuña, lingers in my mind's eye as a creature of whimsical ostrich-feather boas and enchantments in lightly starched lemon voile. Neil McElroy, the Secretary of Defense, vied with Senator Dirksen for the title of Most Quietly Elegant; at a time when bell-shaped skirts and full-sleeved blouses were controlling the silhouette, McElroy denounced Pentagon cost run-ups in a shimmering jade-green sheath, side-slit to the thigh and topped by a cloth-buttoned brocade linen bodice with shoelace shoulder straps. Foster Dulles's brother Allen also preferred the slim look—tailored suits of pencil-striped wool, the jackets sharply cinched at the waist, with wide lapels piquantly emphasizing the bosom of a padded corselette.

That terrible weekend after Sputnik, to rally our spirits Ike commandeered a ballroom at the Mayflower and sent down the directive: *Glad rags only.* My God, what floods of organdie and tulle, ruffles and ruchings and appliquéd beadwork! Present-day Washington, with its dreary cutbacks, has no concept of our kind of style. Of course, the U.S. had half the world's refrigerators then, and the national debt was peanuts. I went up to Allen, who in the spirit of the occasion had forsaken his pinstripes for a so-called "corolla" gown by Capucci of dusty-rose taffeta, with a real rose stuck in his silver-dusted wig, and asked him, "For Heaven's sake, Allen, what *ever* are we going to do about the Soviets and this terrible Cold War?"

Eavesdropping as he always was, J. Edgar came up to us in some perfectly inappropriate, pathetic little frock of cocoa crêpe gathered in front to a ribbon bowknot. That winsome bulldog-puppy face of his was crowned by a grotesque paste tiara, and the spike heels of his patent-leather pumps kept sticking in the parquet floor.

Allen suavely elbowed him aside and spoke *sotto voce* to me. "Mr. Under-Secretary"—I was always being Under-Secretary of something or other in those giddy years—"not to worry, though the Commies have the rocket power for now. Our top-secret reconnaissance flights, I can inform you, have come back with photographs of Khrushchev in an evening dress of gold-threaded silk chiffon and of Mikoyan in a two-piece, low-backed outfit of velvet and shirred georgette. If this is the game they want to play, we'll outspend the bastards right into the ground!"

Addressing the Scandal Glut

AT THE DECEMBER 1993 MEETING of the OCSD (Organization of Celebrity Sleaze Distributors), the chairman was in an understandable dudgeon. "Too much, too much," he moaned, adding for the benefit of the Francophone members of the global organization, *"Embarras de richesses.* This Clinton thing on top of this Jackson thing—all the news programs are complaining they have no slot left for the sports and the weather, let alone the stock report and Somalia. Surveys show that nearly a third of the sleaze consumers are under the impression that Cliff Jackson, the Arkansan former Clinton friend and fellow Oxford student now allegedly devoting his life to embarrassing the President, is one of the former Jackson Five and close kin to the world's twelfth-highest-paid entertainer and most famous sexual cipher."

An average consumer extraordinaire, known to the organization under the acronym ACE, volunteered into his table mike, "I do find that lately I have some trouble distinguishing Larry Patterson, one of the state troopers who claim to have arranged liaisons and scooped dog turds for the then Governor, from Larry Feldman, the attorney for the unnamed father, a Beverly Hills dentist, of the pop singer's thirteen-year-old accuser. After I read, in *Vain Affairs,* all thirty-two and a half columns of Maureen Worth's masterpiece of investigative journalism 'Nightmare in Neverland,' my capacity to take in alleged facts from Arkansas was definitely impaired. And when I realize that I might soon have to scan the two million words of Senator Packwood's diary, my heart, frankly, quails. Maybe it was following all the twists and turns of the Burt Reynolds–Loni Anderson split-up last summer that weakened my concentration. Some days," his testimony sadly concluded, "everybody seems to be called Pam and Vic and to be laughing into a flash-bulb."

"It's the Hollywood divorces," eagerly interjected a prominent industry spokesperson. "They're overproducing tawdry revelations by a factor of two to three. Couldn't a quota be imposed, just till the national reserves are somewhat depleted?"

"Why should Hollywood be the one to shut down?" indignantly queried an esteemed West Coast monger. "We've been *there* for you distributors when the rest of the planet was drying up. Let the New York gossip mills go to a four-day week. After all, this glut began with Mia and Woody, on top of that Amy Fisher thing."

The delegates from the Big Apple were characteristically quick to respond. "It ain't us," they chorused, "it's da foreign imports. Put the restrictions on London—widdout those royals and Mick Jagger, light sweet crude goes back up to twenty bucks a barrel. If that don't do it, slap tariffs on Monaco. It's like their attitude is 'What's a bodyguard for if not to make a princess pregnant?' "

"Too many wildcatters," a Midwestern representative opined. "Virginia fertility doc uses own sperm, impregnates hundreds," he recited, sarcastically. "Once-mousy Florida housewife receives breast implants, beds hundreds while sheriff's-deputy husband takes graphic notes in closet and lawyer's son videotapes trysts in Dad's office."

"Things have gotten so bad," blurted ACE, rendered bold by his proximity to the great and near-great, "that some days I can no longer tell Carla Bruni from Marla Heasley."

"One is a leggy Italian model who has denied having an affair with Mick Jagger, who is presently reconciled with his wife, the former model Jerry Hall," impatiently advised a *National Quagmire* higher-up, "and the other is Wayne Newton's ex-fiancée, who claims to have been kept a 'prisoner of love' on his Las Vegas ranch by the insanely jealous yet compulsively unfaithful bankrupt millionaire entertainer."

"Gushers, gushers, everywhere!" wailed the chairman. "And to think I once thought that, with Ted and Julia and now Donald safely married, there might be a shortage! Why can't celebrities just *behave*, at least till we get a handle on this supply-and-demand thing?"

"Whaddeya think they are, inhuman?" snarled a highly placed staffer for the weekly *Peephole*. "Listen, here's an idea. If we can't cut production, what about—"

The chairman adroitly completed his thought for him: "Upping consumption! Yes! Redesign the consumer for improved insatiability! Wider bodies, twin carburetors, more ponderous cams, more sludge in the engine! We'll start with this one." Assisted by his minions, he pounced on ACE. "Have you ever heard," he murmured into the goggle-eyed little fellow's helpless ear, "of guzzling?"

Manifesto

I'VE NEVER BEEN SOFT ON FOREIGNERS, but this here arrest of Mr. Hugh Grant for trying to make a friend in Los Angeles has got me so darn mad I've gone and joined the local militia. Armed Citizens of Cranberry Corners doesn't have much of a ring, some say, but we like the acronym ACCC. Sounds like an Uzi automatic mowing down a bunch of pests from the Vice Squad, doesn't it?

I mean, is a man's brand-new white BMW his castle, or not? So, the windows were getting steamed? It's not as if he was parking at a bus stop or next to a fire hydrant. It was 1:30 a.m., on Hawthorne Avenue. "Engaging in a lewd act"? Come on, Officers Terry Bennyworth and Ernest Caldera, of the understandably notorious LAPD. How you think you got here, to the surface of the planet Earth? A lewd act, every one of us.

That is, excepting for these test-tube or intra-vitro babies that are in the papers all the time, and don't you think the government won't be poking its nose and its microscopic tweezers in there, splicing a tax-compliance gene into the poor tiny helpless thing's DNA?

You could have knocked me over with a feather when Dan Rather, or maybe Diane Sawyer, explained that there was a crime called soliciting for sex. And another called sexual harassment. Where was I when the government passed these outrageously unconstitutional laws, product of a clear conspiracy to bring heterosexuality into disgrace and create a secret oligarchy of Ivy League eunuchs? Out in the cranberry bogs, that's where I was, tending to business in my hip-waders, floating the harvest to shore.

We've been such patsies, up to now. We've been so damn *good*. The wetlands bleeding-hearts and their Department of Interior musclemen always after us about breaking up the nests of the fan-tailed egrets. Then the clean-water freaks in their armored helicopters crabbing about our gelatinous insecticides drifting out to sea and smothering the mackerel. Yeah, yeah, we said. We'll comply. We'll toe the line. God forbid a single fan-tailed egret or ugly spiny-finned mackerel should make a little sacrifice so millions and millions of loyal Americans can celebrate Thanksgiving properly, with the traditional fare.

They make you feel a*shamed*, of doing a day's honest work and trying to bring something positive, something edible, into people's lives. Be a teenage mother on welfare or a former draft-dodger, they fall all over you, they build ramps all over the post office for you, they even elect you President. But go out there under the broiling sun, armed with just a wooden cranberry rake, and do daily battle with the fruit-eating water mites, they treat you like a criminal. Regulation this, regulation that, and seven layers of taxation besides.

Now it's like there were two *me*s—the old oppressed me, the patsy me, a guy about two feet tall and shrinking, and then the post-LA (lewd act) me, with the fog lifted from my brain and my head seven feet off the ground. This afternoon, on our secret parade ground, we have bazooka practice and then dressage, in case underhanded government tactics bring back the cavalry.

I feel strong. I feel clean. If I ever feel a twinge of trepidation, like during one of our free-form mine-planting sessions, all I have to do to get my blood boiling again is to think of that poor young Englishman being booked, staring out at the camera hollow-eyed from being up past his bedtime and rudely pulled out of what he thought was his own BMW by officers of the law Bennyworth and Caldera and still trying to digest the sushi and saki he consumed a few hours before at the trendy Matsuhisa restaurant with his *Nine Months* director Chris Columbus.

Chris Columbus! What an irony!! If this is what freedom means, the real Chris Columbus could have stayed in Genoa. I've got Hugh Grant's mug shot tattooed on my right forearm, where I can see it. On the other forearm, Divine Marie Brown, looking bored. She knows the drill, we know the drill, but poor Mr. Grant? He thought he was visiting a free country, where soliciting for sex was a normal human act.

They do anything to put a crimp into that pretty boy's sheepish grin, we'll be ready. Cranberry Corners as you've known it will cease to exist.

Car Talk

A HUMAN BEING has vocal cords, a tongue, teeth, and, for expressive reinforcement, eyes and hands; a car has nothing but its horn and lights. Yet cars do talk; they can say "Howdy!" (a brief, deft toot) and "I hate you!" (a firmer, sustained blast) and "Do it!" (a flicker of the headlights). As their drivers are sealed ever more inaccessibly into a casing of audio-tapes, cell phones, and deafening air-conditioning, automobiles for the sake of their own survival are evolving increasingly complex speech patterns. There is a distinct difference, to the attuned ear, between the highly respectful honk used in a service station during an annual car inspection in response to the command "Sound your horn" and the just perceptibly more urgent, less deferential beep that announces to the inhabitants of a domicile that a summoned taxi or car-pool van somewhat impatiently awaits.

Meaning is often, as with other languages, a matter of context. The polite, minimal sounding of the horn—the automotive equivalent of a throat-clearing—that declares simple presence ("Howdy!") in non-threatening circumstances, becomes, while one is passing on a four-lane highway an automobile that has an aura of wanting to change lanes with an abrupt swerve, more admonitory—something like "Watch it, buddy! You've got two tons of moving metal right here in your blind spot!"

If no response is indicated, the same utterance, more insistently intoned, takes on a suggestion of rebuke and heightened anxiety: "Hey, you're riding me into the median strip!" And if the swerve does take place, within inches of one's front fender, a strengthened intonation moderates the meaning to, roughly, "You crazy blind idiot, go back to driving school!" Then, if no penitent reverse-swerve communicates regret, the next level of volume declares, "You bastard—you cut me off! Drivers like you should be in jail, and I'd ram you right in your saucy little vanity plate if I didn't hate fussing with the insurance agent and weren't already late for the dentist!"

As with birdsong and insect stridulation, impressive amounts of information are packed into virtually indistinguishable sounds. In city traffic, one moderate toot, not quite deferential, informs the car ahead at an intersection that the light has changed from red to green. "Let's go, day-dreamer!" might be a translation. The same toot, amplified by a few decibels, points out to a truck being slowly unloaded that double parking is illegal and obstructive, or to a taxi that passengers should not be dumped in the middle of Fifth Avenue. Another few decibels suggest to an errant pedestrian, "I'd be within my rights to run you over," or to a messenger on a bicycle, "Having thin wheels, Lycra shorts, and a Walkman on your head doesn't make you immune to the laws of physics. Someday you're going to get squashed, and don't look for me among the mourners!"

The highest, most prolonged volume of the horn transcends communication. It expresses—at, say, the mouth of the Lincoln Tunnel—frustration to the point of insanity. The noise can be read as existential protest, a frantic desire on the part of automobiles to opt out of their very condition of car-ness, as cattle at the chute of the slaughterhouse bellow to be released from their condition of steer-ness.

Car lights, too, say more than they used to. Having the controls on a stalk behind the steering wheel has considerably enhanced their eloquence. Flashed lights, for instance, once only hinted that a police car was lurking around the corner, but now, flicked demurely, say "Do it" and "Thank you," much as the Italian word *prego* says both "Here you are" and "You're welcome."

Headlights lit in broad daylight used to mean, "We're all in a funeral procession. Don't muscle in." But now such headlights, enlarging in the rearview mirror, cry out, "Here I come, hell for leather, and possibly crazed on drugs! Get out of my way!" Red tail-lights, braked into luminescence, can mean not only "I'm braking" but "Stop tailgating, I do beg you!" The latter can be reacted to before it is consciously understood. As in other highly evolved languages, signifiers can signify opposites: at night, high-beam lights in your eyes either mean that the offending driver has forgotten to switch to the low beam or he is telling you that *you* have. Even turned-off lights can say something: in a locked car parked in your favorite curbside spot near home, their message reads, "Tough luck, kid. I got here first."

Thus a situational and gestural linguistics of considerable complexity has grown up in a mere hundred years of automobile traffic. In the next century, we may expect vocabulary to increase and grammar to ramify to the point that human drivers can spare themselves the vocal outbursts and exchanges which occasionally still mar the subtle conversational pattern of the streets.

The Gentlemen of Summer

BASEBALL is in the doghouse, this summer of 1995, and golf basks in the limelight, at least for this weekend of the U.S. Open at Shinnecock Hills. Golf is so popular, we read, that on Long Island, west of the privileged and precious old Shinnecock links, men arise at three in the morning to get in line for a round at one of the Bethpage State Park public courses, while at the same once-ungodly hour other addicts are finishing up a round at the new, well-patronized *illuminated* nine-hole, seventeen-acre layout, in Deer Park, called Heartland Golf Park. An issues-minded alert *New York Times* editor asks me, Is golf stealing our national heart away from gritty, greed-sullied baseball?

On network television, with the LPGA and the Seniors getting tube time along with the regular tour pros, golf is hard to escape on a weekend. Viewers, players, equipment sales, advertising revenue—the numbers are all up. In baseball, though some franchises are still whistling a brave tune, the main ascending curves trace fan indifference and the time it takes to play a game. All those changes of pitcher and fussy squints in for the catcher's sign—the whole game seems so narcissistic, so obsessive-compulsive. I confess that I, in my New England fastness, have not once, this strike-delayed season, sat down to watch nine innings, even though the Boston Red Sox are, to universal amaze, leading their division. Televised golf, however, each weekend, exerts upon me a magnetic pull, especially as Sunday shadows lengthen and the leaders, between commercials for Maxfli and Calloway, are lining up their $40,000 putts.

Who would have thought, back in the black-and-white days, that tournament golf would televise so well? Golf is certainly the worst spectator sport in the world; you are never in the right spot, and if you are you can't see over the intervening heads. But television vaults over the crowds and puts us in the right spot again and again, with a flickering sequence of drives and irons and putts that form a single field of action—a kind of Shakespearean weave of scenes as opposed to baseball's (or soccer's or football's) fixed proscenium stage. The inaction problem, so conspicuous in baseball telecasts, is solved by flicking, in the control booth, to another group, another green.

And golf is so pretty, with its sculpted scenery and non-violent, non-uniformed participants swinging and tapping along their spectator-lined paths, to the drawled music of commentary in Southern or British voices. And the PGA players are such gentlemen, so assiduous in their courtesies to each other's putting lines, so gracious in defeat and modest in victory, shaking their opponents' hands in one motion and in the next sweeping their wives and children into their arms while the camera's eye fights back a tear. Tired of sex, violence, and the savage media assault on family values? Watch televised golf for glimpses of Republican heaven.

Still, bulldozers, don't turn that baseball stadium into another pitch-and-putt course quite yet. There's room for both these grassy sports in our national heart. And in our national terrain, there's more room for baseball than for golf. For every child with easy access to a golf course, there must be a hundred who can join a baseball game on some imperfect diamond or other. Both sports hark back to an older, more bucolic America; but baseball was the workingman's off-hours idyll, and golf the domain of the well-off and their caddies. There are evidently enough well-off Americans on Long Island to make public golf a nightmare of crowding and sleeplessness, while the sixty-eight private clubs are as full-up as rush-hour buses.

Golf is locked into certain financial and topographical limits; to many among its growing television audience, it must be a purely electronic game, and its players apparitions of sheer celebrity, conjured from bytes and algorithms. Those polite young pros in pastel slacks are out of this world, in a shaved green corporate-sponsored Oz. Baseball, with its team interdependence and intimidation factor and latent violence, its razzing and chatter and slides in the dirt, still presents a pattern of the life most of us live.

Bodies Beautiful

EVER SINCE THE REVIVAL of the modern Olympic Games in 1948, the Cold War has framed and accented their competition. The easy domination of the United States, the only major nation to emerge strong and well-fed from the Second World War, gradually yielded to increasingly

Written for the official souvenir program of the 1992 Olympic Games.

impressive showings from the Soviet Union—first in women's and winter events and then in almost all events, gaining even two victories in the Americans' own sport of basketball—and remarkable performances from some of the Communist countries of Eastern Europe, especially the German Democratic Republic. When last heard from, in 1988, East Germany, a country of not seventeen million, out-medalled the United States in gold, silver, and bronze. Every four years, it would be muttered throughout the free world that the catch-as-catch-can methods of free-enterprise athletic training could not compete with the professionalized rigor with which the fanatic robots of Communism sifted and hardened the athletic talent of their countries. On the other side, it could be muttered that were it not for its African-American track stars the United States might as well stay home—which it did do, for political reasons, in 1980.

There was nothing robotic, in truth, about the way Katerina Witt of East Germany flirted and flowed her way to two gold medals in figure skating, or the way Sergei Bubka came out of the Ukraine to carry pole vaulting—an American gold-medal monopoly from 1896 to 1968—to new heights, or the way the U.S. hockey team of 1980 upset the heavily favored Russians, or the way Greg Louganis has turned men's diving, these last two Olympics, into his personal showcase. Individual performance under pressure is still the name of the game, or Games; there must be and always will be opportunity for the brilliant performer from the so-called Third World—the Brazilian triple-jumper, the Ethiopian marathoner, the hundred-meter butterfly specialist from Suriname. The democracy of the Games served the world well during the four decades of East-West tension—it provided, when few other venues existed, a place where men and women from both sides could meet, take each other's measure, speak a universal language of motion and speed, and even photogenically embrace in the exhausted aftermath.

But now the Cold War is over. East Germany no longer exists, and, incredibly, not the Soviet Union either. All the lands long frozen behind the Iron Curtain are in varying states of thaw and disarray, and the United States, with its own hangover from the post-war decades of militancy and opulent military expenditure, is a shadow of its former self—Europe's bedraggled Western annex, or from another angle the northernmost Latin American nation. With the old Communist-capitalist dualism no longer present to lend drama, what use will the world have for the Olympic Games? They will serve, I suggest, as a quadrennial source for televised images of humanity at its most physically exalted.

What the mind and spirit retain of the past recent Olympics are the superhuman feats of legerity—the hummingbird flickerings of the astonishingly supple girl gymnasts, the suspensefully prolonged downward glide of the ski jumper as he daringly leans parallel to his floating skis, the taut mid-air tumbling of the platform diver, the twinned swoops and entwined twirls of the pairs skaters. These demonstrations of the magic that sufficiently fearless and well-conditioned human beings can perform constitute a revelation, of the sort that circuses and theatres provided in the past.

Historically, the Games were founded, in the Greece of the seventh century before Christ, as exercises fundamentally religious, set off by vows, ceremonies, sacred truces between warring sovereignties, and the pious exclusion of women not only as competitors but as spectators, except for the priestesses of Demeter. So it is not surprising that television, that glittering mesmerizer of the global village, has recovered, in its visual packaging of the Games, the ancient sense of the body sublime. The best moments of action—captured, rerun, slowed to a dreamlike pace—rival in graphic brilliance those montages of high-energy images characteristic of the commercials with which, in the consumeristic countries, broadcasts of the Games are heavily interlarded. Running, the sport at the historic heart of the competitions, televises indifferently; racing of all sorts, whether in water or on skis, offers to our eyes a repetition of strenuous gestures, while the camera prefers the isolated arabesque, the elaborate lone motion.

Thanks to the electronic handmaiden who carries them to us, the Games ever more closely approach the condition of the Dionysian dance—an abstract rapture of our physical species, in its plurality of color and sex, as it angelically defies gravity. Political allegiance falls away; the ideal human form remains, vital and precise, at the center of this age-old celebration.

Golf in the Land of the Free

GOLF is a game of space and America is a spacious land—even more so one hundred years ago, when the USGA was founded. Not for the U.S., once the pawky old game took root here, the thrifty Scots use of waste linksland by the sandy shore. Forests and farms went under to the shovelling crews and horse teams and then the bulldozer and the front loader to

An introduction to *Golf: The Greatest Game* (HarperCollins, 1994), marking the hundredth anniversary of the USGA.

make space for the booming drive, the elevated tee, the glimmering water hazard, the cunning dogleg. This largeness of scale—the epic earthworks that carve a winding green firmament beneath the firmament of cloudy blue—is one of the game's powerful charms. The tennis court is a cage by comparison, and the football field a mirthless gridiron. Only base-ball also consecrates a meadow to play, and not one so wide and various, besprinkled with flowers, studded with trees, haunted by wildlife—a giant humming odorous piece of nature. The same course, played ninety times a summer, is never the same; the wind, the wetness of the soil, the thickness and tint of the foliage all affect the flight of the ball and the condition of the lie. Playing golf, we breathe natural amplitude.

The tools of the game answer to this amplitude—the little hard ball, engagingly dimpled all over, and the hawk-faced clubs, with their woolly hoods. When else does a person move an object so far and high with mere musculature, marvellously leveraged by the mechanics of the swing? What a beautiful thing a swing is, what a bottomless source of instruction and chastisement! The average golfer, if I am a fair specimen, is hooked when he hits his first good shot; the ball climbs into the air all of its own, it seems—a soaring speck conjured from the effortless airiness of an accidentally correct hit. And then he or she, that average golfer, spends endless frustrating afternoons, whole decades of them, trying to recover and tame the delicate wildness of that first sweet swing. Was ever any sporting motion so fraught with difficulty and mystery? The golf swing is like a suitcase into which we are trying to pack one too many items—if we remember to keep our heads still, we forget to shift our weight; if we remember to shift our weights, we lift our heads, or stiffen the left knee, or uncock the wrists too soon. A playing partner of mine has had good fortune with the four-part formula "Low, slow, inside out, and finish high." But this is one too many thoughts for me, to hold in the perilous two seconds or so between the stately takeaway and the majestic follow-through. The swing thought that worked so well last Wednesday flies out of my head on Sunday. "Arms like ropes," "soft from the top," "turn your back," "hit with your feet," "throw your hands at the hole," "keep the right elbow close to the body," "touch first the left shoulder with your chin and then the right," "think oily"—all have worked for me, if only for a spell. The excitement of hitting the ball and seeing where it will go is too much for me. Of all sports, golf least favors an excitable dis-position. You don't have to look as sleepy as Fuzzy Zoeller, or be as expressionless as Davis Love III, but it takes more than a dash of phlegm to apply one's talents steadily over the length of eighteen holes.

This, too, this drawling quality of good golf, seems well suited to our national character. Laconic, cool, easy in the saddle, eyes dryly squinting at the distant horizon—these attributes belong equally to the cowboy and the good golfer. Who is more American, Gary Cooper or Sam Snead? Our champions, from Frances Ouimet to Ben Hogan on up to Fred Couples, tend to be terse types who let the clubs do the talking. Once American golfers, basking in the electronic sunshine that Arnold Palmer turned on, became personable on television and productive of gracious on-the-spot interviews, the underexposed Europeans began to win our championships.

Among the benisons golf bestows upon its devotees is a relative hush. One says "good putt" or "too bad" or "two up and three to go" and there is no obligation to say much more; a worshipful silence attends the long walks between shots, the ignominious searching of the rough, the squatting appraisal of a treacherous, critical putt. Golf is a constant struggle with one's self, productive of a few grunts and expletives but no extended discourse; it is a mode of meditation, a communion with the laws of aerodynamics, a Puritan exercise in inward exhortation and outward stoicism. Since its rules can be infracted in the privacy of a sand bunker or a sumac grove, it tests the conscience. And it is the only professional game that, under the stress of ever bigger bucks and crowds, hasn't lost its manners.

How much poorer my sense of my native land would be if I had not, at the age of twenty-five, fallen in love with golf! Many landscapes have been engraved in my memory by the pressures of this or that golf shot. The magnificent view, for instance, from the fourth tee of the Cape Ann public course in Essex, Massachusetts—of salt marshes interwoven with arms of steel-blue tidal inlet, cottage-laden peninsulas, and strips of glowing white beach—takes fire in my mind's eye from the exaltation of a well-struck drive drawing into the leftward curve of the fairway, taking a big bound off the slope there, and winding up in fine position to set up a birdie on this scenic patsy of a par-five. In Florida, where can one draw close to the original landscape, so thoroughly paved-over and air-conditioned, but on a golf course, as one strives to retrieve the ball from the edge of a mangrove swamp, or hit it cleanly out of a nest of dried-up palm fronds? The secrets of a locale declare themselves in the interstices of a golf game: the sun-baked spiciness of Caribbean underbrush, the resiny scent and slippery lie beneath a stand of Vermont pines, the numerous anthills of Pennsylvania, like so many cones of spilled coffee grounds. And I am not a golf tourist—the same course day after day holds adventure enough for me, and strangeness enough, and inexhaustible matter for thought. Until I played golf, for instance, I scarcely knew what grass was—its varying lengths, breadths, resiliencies, and degrees of resistance, gloss, uprightness, and just plain friendliness, as it sits your ball up or snuggles it down, and as it returns your stare as you trudge the length of the long fifteenth fairway to the pot bunker where your errant three-wood has found, in an ocean of grass, a single lonely island of depressed, depressing sand.

People, too, yield up their nuances to golf. As it happened, several of my early, formative playing partners were women: my first wife's aunt, who put a club into my hand and gave me my first tips (hit the ball with the back of your left hand, she said, and take the putter back as many inches as the putt is feet long); a Japanese widow, somewhat my senior, who told me, after an adequate but unsweet shot, "Not you. Not fly like bird"; an Englishwoman, as smart and spiky as her kiltied shoes, who kept the ball stolidly in the center of the fairway and beat me hollow on her green and soggy layout in suburban London. It was a lesson in feminism to pace the course with these determined females. In the seaside Massachusetts town where I spent my prime, my faithful partners were a local druggist, a pediatrician, and the Baha'i owner of an automatic car-wash. Reduced each Wednesday to the same innocence and ineptitude, we loved one another, it seems not too much to say; at least we loved the world we shared for those four hours, a common ground outside of whose boundaries we had little to communicate. A priest without his collar, a movie star without his agent, and a Martha's Vineyard hippie without his shoes have been some of my other playing companions, all enjoyable, as the differences between us were quickly subdued to the shared glories and frustrations of the sport of golf.

No other game, to my knowledge, provides so ready and effective a method of handicapping, which can produce a genuine match between gross unequals. On the ski slopes, the daughter quickly outspeeds the father; at the backgammon table, the mother consistently outsmarts the son; but on the golf course, we play our parents and our children with unfeigned competitive excitement, once the handicap strokes are in place on the card. Golf is a great social bridge, and a great tunnel into the essences of others, for people are naked when they swing—their patience or impatience, their optimism or pessimism, their grace or awkwardness, their life's motifs are all bared. Like children trying to walk and bear cubs trying to climb a tree, they are lovable in their imperfection and then all the more lovable in their occasional triumphs of muscle and will. The putt that wobbles in, the chip that skids up close, the iron that climbs like a rocket and sinks like a plumb line—we cheer such momentary feats as if they were our own. Golf is a competitive experience, yes, but also an aesthetic one—a mutual appreciation that burns away the grit of selfish aggression or sublimates it into a hovering *bonhomie*.

On a golf course, I feel free—free of my customary worries, left back at the clubhouse and the parking lot, and free even of the physical limits placed on my body, as I try to imagine this or that soaring, unerring shot. In Michael Murphy's mystical yet practical *Golf in the Kingdom*, the acolyte-narrator relates of his critical midnight lesson with the guru Shivas Irons, "As I fell into the focus Shivas wanted, my body widened until it embraced the ball all the way to the target. He had said that the club and the ball are one. 'Aye ane fiedle afore ye e'er swung [all one field before you ever swung],' . . . and sure enough I became that field." The spirit of golf is transcendental and free. Americans are not the only people to treasure freedom—all people treasure it, even when they dare not name it—but here above all is freedom proclaimed as a national ideal. After the game's slow American start a century ago (our first golf course, St. Andrew's in Yonkers, was founded in 1888, fifteen years after Canadians formed the Montreal Golf Club), the United States took to golf with such a vengeance that, from the Age of Jones up through the Age of Nicklaus, it seemed we had invented it. A curious number of that long era's stars (Byron Nelson, Ben Hogan, Jimmy Demeret, Lee Trevino, Ben Crenshaw) came from Texas, the American superstate, with the widest-open spaces and a superabundance of those hot days which bring out golf's subtlest juices. Now the Europeans are in the game, and not just our old cronies the English and the Scots; Germany has produced a superstar and Spain several. In golf as in every other international activity the United States must prove itself anew, and this is a good thing. On the first tee, all men, and all nationalities, are equal, and after the eighteenth green, there is no arguing with the scorecard.

Complexity and simplicity: in the tension between them lies the beauty of the real. Golf, which generates more books, more incidental rules, more niceties of instruction, and more innovations in equipment than any other game, yet has a scoring system of divine simplicity: as all souls are equal before their Maker, a two-inch putt counts the same as a 250-yard drive. There is a comedy in this, and a certain unfairness even, which make golf an apt mirror of reality. But its reflection is a kindly one, with some funhouse warps and waves in the glass; it is life without the weight. Or so it has seemed to me, on many a dewy morning and many a long-shadowed afternoon spent in those bonny pieces of America set aside for this grand and gracious form of play.

The Vineyard Remembered

As soon as the ferryboat from Woods Hole socketed itself in the creaking, groaning slip at Vineyard Haven, summer had begun—super-summer, the Martha's Vineyard distillation of that widespread American season. Once, in my exuberance at coming onto the island, with my four children shrieking in the back seat, I pushed the down button on the automatic convertible top; in retracting, it struck a ceiling in the hold and I spent the next month trying to get it fixed. The canvas top was like a bat wing with a broken bone, limp and creepy. Still, we had fun that month—the very air on Martha's Vineyard was fun. It tugged us in our rented Sailfish across Chilmark Pond or Tisbury Great Pond to South Beach and, on a different tack, back; it made the wild roses bob in the hollows back from the dunes. In this salt air, cedar shingles somehow weathered an even silver, instead of the blotchy brown you saw on the mainland. On the mainland, dreadful things happened—traffic jams and Red Sox games and muggings and droughts—but on the Vineyard the worst eventuality was a sunburned nose or a footful of splinters from turning cartwheels on a sun-bleached porch.

We used to rent a house "up-island," in the Sixties and early Seventies, when some of the old left-wing libertarians like Max Eastman and Roger Baldwin were still around, presiding over the remnants of a vacation society that favored nude sea-bathing, beach clambakes, and long cocktail hours. The counterculture had arrived on the Vineyard in the Thirties; a venerable ritual was "getting clayed" in the oozy pit at the base of the cliff at Windy Gates. There was no law against wearing a bathing suit as you coated yourself in the primal muck, but it was frowned upon. It was astonishing, how thoroughly the clay came off, even out of your hair, in the pounding, aerated surf. I saw enough naked bodies, those summer months on the Vineyard, to populate the walls of a Hindu temple. It was back to basics, up-island; Vineyard Haven and Edgartown were nice places to visit, to buy Solarcaine or see a movie, but one wouldn't want to live there. Too citified. They had sidewalks, and some stores liked you to wear shoes.

Martha's Vineyard includes a hundred square miles in its roughly triangular shape (actually, it looks on the map like an open-mouthed dwarf doing the split, with Gay Head as one thick shoe and Chappaquiddick Island the other); it is the largest island off the East Coast except for

---

Written for *Islands* magazine, 1996.

Long Island, which is welded fast at one end to the New York megalopolis. The free-floating Vineyard is large enough to have distinct regions, yet so small that within a month a vacationing family manages to visit most of them: staid, pretty Edgartown, the poshest town; Gay Head, with its polychrome clay cliffs and dusky Wampanoag Indians; Menemsha, a little sunset-facing port and the mercantile center of Chilmark; West Tisbury, a village in the island's central flatlands, hosting a general store and, every August, the Dukes County Agricultural Fair; Vineyard Haven, a dry town where the tourists from Woods Hole disembark into a bustle of rentable bikes and motor scooters; Oak Bluffs, a cheerfully wet alternative disembarkation point whose populace includes a Portuguese enclave, the surviving Methodists of a gingerbread-cottage encampment, the descendants of Baptist missionaries to the Indians, and a vacationing elite of African Americans that goes back to the Depression. Oak Bluffs, with its Methodist tabernacle, seaside bandstand, and antique but still-functioning indoor carrousel, is a nineteenth-century resort preserved under several coats of twentieth-century tackiness; the veneers burn away during Illumination Night, a traditional summer celebration when the cottagers hang out on their little porches an enchanting galaxy of paper lanterns.

Such quaint spectacles, an unstrident ethnic diversity, and scenery from Winslow Homer's America—all this was well worth a pricey rental and the luxury tax of "island prices." It was good for the children, their mother and I thought, to see the world in such friendly miniature. Hitchhiking was considered safe, and fishing off Menemsha Dock was free. For me, there was a collegial aspect, since many of the New York vacationers worked in the publishing and literary trades. Carly Simon, the island's most celebrated troubadour, was a daughter of the co-founder of Simon and Schuster; her fellow-troubadour and onetime husband, James Taylor, was associated with the other summer strain, the Boston and Cambridge professoriat. Hollywood aristocracy was represented by Katharine Hepburn and James Cagney, tucked out of sight on the Island's north shore; the arrival of John Belushi and Jacqueline Kennedy postdated my heyday as a summer visitor, but there was no end of authors—William Styron, John Hersey, Art Buchwald, Lillian Hellman, Philip Rahv, Bernard Malamud, Philip Roth, Robert Crichton—and we could not always avoid one another. Nor, in truth, did we wish to. But the Vineyard's bottom line was not celebrity but geography; it was a real place, of cemeteries and farms, cliffs and coves, stone walls and shingled shacks, wherein everyone felt younger and dressed in cut-offs and sandals.

I write about it, I notice, with an uneasy mix of the past and present tense. In the last twenty years, I am told, there have been more building, more tourist buses, more beach pollution, more pressure from the teeming mainland. The ultra-rich come and create walled enclaves and more severely patrolled private beaches. In my last summers, such pockets of Edenic innocence as the nude section of Lucy Vincent Beach—bequeathed to the island as a beach for Vineyarders—were invaded by sightseers in shoes and socks and nothing else. There is talk of the Wampanoags' opening gambling casinos, the way Native Americans do these days. There are development projects, and organized furors of resistance. President Clinton has vacationed there twice; he and his family might not upset the local ecology, but what about his entourage and all those Secret Service men?

It is a familiar story, the country over: the rustic island, far from a paradise for its working inhabitants (winters on the Vineyard are famously dreary), becomes cherished, then fashionable, and finally spoiled. On to the next. But we are running out of islands. Martha's Vineyard floats in my memory as a state of happiness, an escape into a cleaner, rarer air, with a bouquet of mist, hay, salt, skin, and fermented grapes.

The Sun the Other Way Around

IN THE BEGINNING, for me, Brazil was cinema: Carmen Miranda hissing and chattering like a steam radiator about to explode beneath her towering hat of fruit in *The Gang's All Here* (1943); José Carioca darting about with his parrot break and jaunty cane, flicking cigar ash all over the splashy cartoon scenery, in Disney's animated *Saludos Amigos* (1943); Hope and Crosby and Lamour taking their gags and songs south in *Road to Rio* (1947); the stunning and sombre fable of *Black Orpheus* (1959). I saw this last film after college, and long after Franklin Roosevelt's Good Neighbor Policy had ceased to stimulate Hollywood to the outpouring of maraca bands, conga lines, and Latin lovers that bewitched my gullible adolescence with visions of the livelier, hotter, more undressed, more carefree existence led "down South American way," as a popular song put it.

Mexico, of course, was our immediate neighbor south of the border, but its images were tinged with a certain harsh melancholy, a tragic

---

Written for the twenty-fifth anniversary publication of the journal *Veja: Reflexoẽs para o futuro.*

undertone blended of ancient Aztec savagery and our own military skirmishes in that death-obsessed land. The United States knew Mexico too
well to romanticize it thoroughly. Central America—those unhappy little "banana republics" in whose muddled affairs our Marines and unofficial filibusters so often felt obliged to intervene—was also a touch too
real, too involved with our material practicalities, to serve as a never-
never-land, although a catchy song of the 1940s did proclaim, pre-
Sandinistas, "Managua, Nicaragua, what a wonderful town!"

But Brazil—ah, Brazil! Just the name was honey on the tongue, fizz in
the brain. We had never made war on Brazil, or on Portugal for that matter. The old Spanish-English struggle for empire didn't apply; at a splendid geographical and historical remove Brazil floated like a smiling twin
nation in its tropical hemisphere. It was another big country, fat with
minerals and forest, a "melting pot" and land of opportunity. It had the
same endlessness of territory where innocent Indians could be imperi-
ously brushed aside, the same ebullient population of former slaves, the
same glitter of coastal metropolises. But with a charming difference—a
United States without Puritanism, without heating bills, and without
a superpower's stern global responsibilities. A vast indolent fecundity, a
perpetual samba, a promiscuous and color-blind Carnaval, a constant
music in which African rhythms lull rather than excite, insinuate rather
than assault—this is our image of Brazil. We picture pastel ruffles and
bright fruit, brown flesh beautiful in rags, the green Amazon and white
beach sands.

The image persists: just a few days ago, in the *Boston Globe*, we New
Englanders could read how the cinema actress Amy Irving, divorced by
the Hollywood magnate Steven Spielberg, found happiness and release
from inhibition in the land of her new spouse, the Brazilian director
Bruno Barreto. "Brazilian culture has changed me," the actress is quoted
as saying. "It's changed the temperature of my blood; it's changed my
own attitude toward sexuality. Sex over there is so natural, while this
country is so sexually repressed that you cannot even know how sexually
repressed you are until you get out." Brazil to her has been a rebirth: "In
my previous incarnation I was a 'princess' who was married to the Prince
of Hollywood, and there were certain standards I had to live up to. . . .
It was almost like being a politician's wife. Now I'm ready to show that
I'm actually much more a free spirit than people think." And was not
the same true, on a higher cultural plane, of another North American
princess, the poet Elizabeth Bishop, who in Brazil shed her New
England, Nova Scotian self and dared taste, as if for the first time, the
pleasure of life? In "Questions of Travel" she brightly asked:

What childishness is it that while there's a breath of life
in our bodies, we are determined to rush
to see the sun the other way around?
The tiniest green hummingbird in the world?

In Edith Wharton's last novel, *The Buccaneers*, which concerns the marital adventures of five American girls, one of them is part Brazilian, and is seen by another as "enveloped in a sort of warm haze unlike the cool dry light in which Nan's sister and the Elmsworths moved."

A "warm haze"—Brazil remains, for me, one of the few places on earth where facts have not ousted possibilities, where there is still room for the imagination. At least, I felt free to locate a novel there, after no more than a week's visit last year. No doubt I was presumptuous. It must gall thoughtful, earnest Brazilians to see their nation's real functioning swaddled in amiable myth, concealed by the masks and costumes of Carnaval. We read, in the North American newspapers, not only of Amy Irving's sexual arousal in Brazil but of corruption in the highest places, of rampant crime and inflation, of the assassination of homeless children—many indications, in short, of an economy in continual crisis and a society failing to fulfill the promise of its rich land and its rich-natured people.

Nevertheless, from a balcony in Rio, I saw the white crescent of swarming beaches, and the green-topped breadloaf mountains—the postcards are true, these things exist. Carnaval exists: though I had arrived too late for it, the television in my hotel room played for hours—in the middle of the night!—reruns of sweating samba dancers under their loads of feathers and fake pearls, grinning, gyrating, saucily straddling the camera lens. I was struck, as I watched, by what hard work it must be to samba all night long. The dancers' grins wore the glaze of exhaustion. All around me, people seemed to be working hard, distracted by an excess of tasks, struggling to keep up. This was an unanticipated impression. In Ouro Prêto, before dawn, people set up an entire market on the square outside my window, while I slept, and in the evening dismantled it all again. In São Paulo, gray buildings to the horizon spoke of a world of urban struggle and grim endeavor. The people I met—journalists, editors, photographers—were all hustling, hurrying, their feet a blur on an invisible treadmill. One woman exclaimed to me, "We work so *hard*, and it's not *fun*!" Even the middle-aged joggers on the beach, and younger counterparts playing volley ball with their feet, seemed to be in thrall to a strenuous routine. The cinema of Brazil, from within, moved faster than I had expected, less tropically. I had the impression of people running ever faster just to stay in place, and in this, too, Brazil mirrors my own country; global competition has upped the pace and lowered the rewards. We are all racing against the exhaustion of the planet by our voracious, increasingly desperate species. Had I stayed two weeks instead of one, I might have become too discouraged, too saturated by reality, to write my flight of fancy called *Brazil*.

The Cold

A BRAZILIAN once told me, before I was setting out to visit his fabulous country, "Americans don't understand inflation, and Brazilians don't understand the cold." Now, I hear, there is no more inflation in Brazil; but there is still plenty of cold in North America. Recent temperatures in New England have been around zero Fahrenheit; in parts of the Midwest they have been thirty and forty degrees below zero; and even in Florida, where perpetual summer is supposed to reign, temperatures have gone below freezing, to the peril of oranges, strawberries, and alligators.

Cold is an absence, an absence of heat, and yet it feels like a presence— a vigorous, hostilely active presence in the air that presses upon your naked face and that makes your fingers and toes ache within their mittens and boots. Cold is always *working*, it seems—busy freezing water in the ponds and rivers, knitting intricate six-sided snowflakes by the billions, finding cracks around the walls and windows of your house, forcing furnaces in the cellar to roar away. Cold fights you—it doesn't want your automobile engine to ignite in the morning, and once your car is on the highway it clogs its path with snow and slush. A whole secondary world of dirt, of sand and salt, is called into being by the cold, and an expensive and troublesome array of wearing apparel—mufflers, earmuffs, wool-lined boots and gloves, parkas, leggings, long underwear, and knitted face-masks. If for some of these items words do not exist in Brazilian Portuguese, be grateful.

These thick and clumsy items of winter wear complicate every social gathering with their extra bulk. Because of them a special room in restaurants and theatres and schools exists, a room called, though almost no one wears cloaks any more, the cloakroom. When I was a schoolchild, the cloakroom was a narrow and exciting transitional chamber where the concept of undressing stirred a certain rowdiness; there was a powerful semi-sexual smell to the cloakroom, of wet wool and snow-chilled

---

Written for the Brazilian newspaper Folha de S. Paulo.

rubber, that I have never forgotten. For adults, the tip to the cloakroom attendant adds one more expense to an already expensive evening on the town. I once was in Russia in late November, and pitied the little grand-motherly women who tottered back and forth under the heaps of heavy coats entrusted to their care by opera-goers.

In Brazil, the skin is beneath the clothes, and, often, not very far beneath—the naked self and the dressed self do not pose a drama-tic dichotomy. In a winter climate, there is a multiplicity of wraps—a padded, furry armor is peeled away, indoors, to reveal a butterfly clad in less ponderous clothes, somewhat as the well-to-do women of Arabia and Iran gaily strip off, in the homes of their friends, the drab garbs of purdah to reveal flashing Paris fashions. Thus, duplicity is created. The cold, in seeking to freeze the body, makes one, puritanically, seethingly aware of it, as each limb and body part struggles to keep warm in its dark place of concealment.

The cold generates a whole code of shelter and warmth: the fireplace hearth was, before central heating, the center of the house, the place where all the family members gathered. The burning, crackling log fire still signals hospitality and festivity, and ancient ceremonies of alcohol and caffeine consumption revolve about the notion of "warming up." A sense of oneself as a brave and resourceful survivor attends the dweller in a cold climate. With the camaraderie of soldiers on dangerous missions, muffled strangers greet each other on the snowbound, windswept street. Cold challenges the blood; it sets the cheeks to tingling and the brain to percolating. By making the indoors cozy, it encourages intellectual activity. On the map of Europe, the statistics for readership go down as the latitude becomes southerly; a warm climate invites citizens outdoors, to the sidewalk café, the promenade, the brain-lulling beach. I like winter because it locks me indoors with my books, my word processor, and my clear and brittle thoughts.

There is a visual poetry that goes with the cold. Ferns and stars of frost mysteriously appear on the windows and take their place in a child's mythology, along with icicles, snowmen, snowballs, and Santa Claus in his gliding sleigh. Snowsuits, which were dark wool outfits in my own childhood, have become, in the age of Dacron and Gore-Tex, wonder-fully bright and gaudy, so that children clustered at a bus stop on a cold morning look like a pack of little circus clowns. (Adolescents—girls as well as boys—display their bravado in dressing as skimpily as possible, in sneakers and cotton T-shirts, and in my college days at Harvard it was a mark of shame to venture forth on even the coldest day wearing any coat heavier than a sports jacket, with shirt, tie, and khaki pants.) A wealth of special sports equipment—sleds, ice skates, skis, snowboards—emerges to harvest fun from the cold. The drama of snowplows, working all night to heave up great white mounds along the roadways, adds to the excitement, and television weathermen, pompously padding their predictions with all manner of computer graphics, work up an almost hysterical excitement as another winter storm approaches. The sight of the world made new and fantastic by a sparkling fresh snowfall repays many days of numbing discomfort. And nature, even when locked most deeply in the cold's embrace, gives off signs of persistent activity—chirping birds, swelling buds, the tracks of fox and deer.

The cold has the philosophical value of reminding men that the universe does not love us. Cold as absolute as the black tomb rules space; sunshine is a local condition, and the moon hangs in the sky to illustrate that matter is usually inanimate. Most of the body's caloric intake is consumed in its effort to maintain body temperature. The cold is our ancient companion; prehistoric men developed their art and technology on the edge of ice-age glaciers. To return back indoors after exposure to the bitter, inimical, implacable cold is to experience gratitude for the shelters of civilization, for the islands of warmth that life creates.

Matter under Review

INTRODUCTIONS

To *"The Seducer's Diary," a chapter of* Either/Or

SØREN KIERKEGAARD'S METHOD, dictated by his volatile and provocative temperament, resembles that of a fiction writer: he engages in multiple impersonations, assuming various poses and voices with an impartial vivacity. The method is, in one of his favorite words, *maieutic*—from the Greek term for midwifery—like that of his beloved model Socrates, who in his questioning style sought to elicit his auditors' ideas rather than impose his own. *Either/Or*, Kierkegaard's first major work, was a bulky, two-volume collection of papers ostensibly found by the editor, "Victor Eremita" ("Victor Hermit"), in the secret compartment of a writing desk to which he had been mysteriously attracted in the shop of a secondhand dealer. Some time after its acquisition, he tells us, he took a hatchet to a stuck drawer and discovered a trove of papers, evidently composed by two distinct authors. As arranged and published by Victor Eremita, the first volume consists of aphorisms, reflections, and essays by "A," a nameless young man who styles himself an aesthete, and the second volume of two long letters to this first writer, with some final words, composed by an older man, "B," who is named William and has been a judge. The last item in the first volume is a narrative, "The Seducer's Diary," which "A," deploying the same mock-scholarly documentary specifics as Victor Eremita offers in regard to the whole, claims to have discovered and to be merely editing. The overall editor ironically complains that this complicates his own position, "since one author becomes enclosed within the other like the boxes in a Chinese puzzle."

Either/Or's intricate, arch, and prolix medley, published in Copenhagen in February of 1843, made a significant stir and eventually required a second edition, to which Kierkegaard considered (but decided against) appending this postscript:

> I hereby retract this book. It was a necessary deception in order, if possi-
> ble, to deceive men into the religious, which has continually been my task
> all along. Maieutically it certainly has had its influence. Yet I do not need to
> retract it, for I have never claimed to be its author.

In dealing with an author so deceptive, so manifoldly removed in name
from his own words, we need to insist that there were events of a sore
personal nature behind so prodigiously luxuriant a smokescreen. In brief,
Kierkegaard had, just before the surge of literary activity bound into
Either/Or, broken off a year's engagement with a woman, Regine Olsen,
ten years younger than himself. Externally, their engagement appeared a
happy one, uniting two youngest children of prosperous Copenhagen
households. Michael Pederson Kierkegaard was a retired merchant, and
Terkild Olsen a state councillor—an *Etatsraad*—and a high official in
the Ministry of Finance. Young Kierkegaard, then a university student,
first saw Regine when she was fourteen, in May of 1837, at a party of
schoolgirls in the home of the widowed mother of another girl, Bolette
Rørdam, whom Kierkegaard was pursuing. According to the lightly fictionalized account in the "Quidam's Diary" section of *Stages on Life's Way*
(1845), Kierkegaard began to spy on the girl, frequenting a pastry shop
along the route whereby Regine went to her music lessons:

> I never dared sit by the window, but when I took a table in the middle of the
> room my eye commanded the street and the opposite sidewalk where she
> went, yet the passersby could not see me. Oh, beautiful time; Oh, lovely
> recollection; Oh, sweet disquietude; Oh, happy vision, when I dressed up
> my hidden existence with the enchantment of love!

Yet she is not mentioned in his journal until nearly two years after the
first meeting: "Sovereign of my heart, 'Regina,' kept safe and secret in the
deepest corner of my breast." In the summer of 1840, now twenty-seven,
Kierkegaard passed his theological examination and made a pilgrimage to
West Jutland, the desolate birthplace of his father, who had died in 1838.
Soon after returning, on September 8, he went to the Olsens' house,
found Regine alone, and proposed with such abrupt passion that she said
nothing and showed him the door. Two days later, however, with her
father's consent, she accepted. Writing an account in his journal nine
years later, Kierkegaard confessed, "But inwardly—The next day I saw I
had made a blunder. As penitent as I was, my *vita ante acta*, my melancholy: that was enough. I suffered indescribably in that period." For a
year, the formal attachment held: fond letters went back and forth; calls
upon their extensive families were made; the couple strolled together up
Bredgade or on the Esplanade; and Kierkegaard, preparing himself for a

respectable post in the church or university, gave his first sermon and wrote his philosophical dissertation, *On The Concept of Irony, with Continual Reference to Socrates.*

Regine, though, observed how her fiancé "suffered frightfully from his melancholy," and her friends sensed "something sad hanging in the air." On August 11, 1841, he sent her back her ring, with a note that said, "Forget him who writes this, forgive a man who, though he may be capable of something, is not capable of making a girl happy." Regine resisted rejection, taking the bold step of calling upon him in his rooms; he was out. For two months the engagement dragged on, while he defended and published his thesis; then, in October, in response to a plea from her father, he met her for an exchange that he later reported as follows:

> I went and talked her round. She asked me, Will you never marry? I replied, Well, in about ten years, when I have sown my wild oats, I must have a pretty young miss to rejuvenate me. She said, Forgive me for what I have done to you. I replied, It is rather I that should pray for your forgiveness. She said, Kiss me. That I did, but without passion. Merciful God!
>
> To get out of the situation as a scoundrel, a scoundrel of the first water if possible, was the only thing there was to be done in order to work her loose and get her under way for a marriage.

Two weeks later, Kierkegaard left Copenhagen for Berlin and began, with *Either/Or,* the flood of volumes in which he pondered and dramatized such matters as marriage, the ethical versus the aesthetic, dread, and, increasingly, the severities of Christianity. In his mind Regine was the muse and object of much of his production, and it shocked him when, two years after their break, she accepted an earlier suitor, Johan Frederik Schlegel, and they became betrothed, marrying in 1847. To the end of his life Kierkegaard wrote of Regine in his journals; four weeks before his death in early November 1855 he put it succinctly: "I had my thorn in the flesh, and therefore did not marry."

Was this "thorn in the flesh" the religious melancholia he had inherited from his father, or was it somehow physical? The child of elderly parents, he was frail and slight, with an erratic gait and a bent carriage noted by acquaintants and caricaturists, but he possessed no apparent deformity that would explain his self-description as "in almost every way denied the physical qualities required to make me a whole human being." His sexual experience may have been confined to a single drunken encounter with a prostitute in November of 1836.* Though he extolled

---

*See *Søren Kierkegaard,* by Peter Rohde, translated from the Danish by Alan Moray Williams (London: George Allen & Unwin Ltd., 1963), pp. 42–43. Rohde bases his

marriage for many pages, there is little trace, in his surviving love letters or reminiscences, of carnal warmth. His later theology endorses celibacy and declares a frank hostility to the sexual instinct. "Woman," he wrote in 1854, "is egoism personified. . . . The whole story of man and woman is an immense and subtly constructed intrigue, or it is a trick calculated to destroy man as spirit." He once complained of Regine that she "lacked a disposition to religion." His hero, Socrates, had been married to a legendary shrew, Xanthippe, and European philosophy was ever after dominated by bachelors, one of whom, Kant, succinctly defined marriage as "the union of two persons of different sexes for the purpose of lifelong mutual possession of their sexual organs." Kierkegaard's breaking the engagement perhaps needs less explaining than the conventional impulse that led him into it.

His attempt to set right, in writing, the botch of his relation with Regine taught him, he wrote, the secret of "indirect communication." As he came to frame the matter, "The Seducer's Diary" was part of his campaign to portray himself as a scoundrel and thus make their break easier for her. His journal of 1849 claims that he wrote it "for her sake, to clarify her out of the relationship." In 1853 he notes that it was written "to repel" her and quotes his *Fear and Trembling*: "When the baby is to be weaned, the mother blackens her breast."

"The Seducer's Diary," then, is a work with a devious purpose and an uneasy conscience. A number of details connect the real Regine with the fictional Cordelia Wahl. When the Seducer writes, "Poor Edward! It is a shame that he is not called Fritz," the allusion is not only to a comedy by Scribe but to Regine's other suitor, Schlegel, who was called Fritz. The hero's long and loving stalking of a girl too young to approach provides, in fiction as in the reality, a peak of erotic excitement. The little party of girls that occasioned Kierkegaard's first glimpse of Regine is evoked with a piquant vividness but placed much later in the affair, as its cold-hearted dissolution nears. No doubt a number of particulars spoke only to Regine.

And yet a cool shimmer of falsity plays over the finespun fabric. The Seducer's desire seems curiously abstract. Contemporary readers, especially younger readers, may be put off by his tone of sexist condescension; under the name of a seduction he conducts a perverse sort of educational

---

supposition upon a journal entry of November 10, 1836, reading "My God, my God . . ." and "That bestial giggling . . ." As an episode in SK's rowdy, hard-drinking student life at the time, it seems not unlikely, though several Kierkegaardians took indignant issue with the allegation. In any case, SK was no seducer in the usual sense.

experiment. Seeking to "teach her to be victorious as she pursues me," he retreats before her, so that she will know "all the powers of erotic love, its turbulent thoughts, its passion, what longing is, and hope." In an artful teasing that is close to torture, he labors at "cheating her of the essentially erotic" and thus bringing her to a new power and certain freedom, "a higher sphere." He mentions Pygmalion, but he reminds us more of heartless Dr. Frankenstein, in one of Romanticism's first masterpieces. The nineteenth century was Romantic from beginning to end; the eighteenth century's man of reason yielded as a cultural ideal to the man or woman of sensibility, of feeling. As the old supernatural structures faded, sensation and emotion took on value in themselves; the Seducer exults in the turbulence of his awakening love. "How beautiful it is to be in love; how interesting it is to know that one is in love." He likens himself to a bird building its nest on "the turbulent sea" of his agitated mind and proclaims, "How enjoyable to ripple along on moving water this way—how enjoyable to be in motion within oneself."

Inner turbulence is a piece of nature's magnificent turbulence, and the female an emissary of this same worshipped nature: "Woman is substance, man is reflection. . . . In a certain sense man is more than woman, in another sense infinitely much less." Women were both the objects of romantic desire and, in their susceptibility to love, Romanticism's foremost practitioners. Female psychology became an object of fascination to seducers and their chroniclers. Nineteenth-century novelists from Jane Austen to Henry James embraced as a patently major theme the sentimental education of their heroines; the outcome could be comic and triumphant, as for Austen's Emma Woodhouse and George Eliot's Dorothea Brooke, or tragic, as for Emma Bovary and Anna Karenina. Kierkegaard would not have been aware of these novels, but Mozart's opera *Don Giovanni* was much on his mind, and he breathed the same dandyish intellectual atmosphere that produced Byron's *Don Juan* and Stendhal's superb study of erotic psychology, *On Love*. Even the classic texts supplied touchstones and handbooks: "The Seducer's Diary" cites both Ovid and Apuleius's *Amor and Psyche*.

In the vast literature of love, "The Seducer's Diary" is a curiosity—a feverishly intellectual attempt to reconstruct an erotic failure as a pedagogic success, a wound masked as a boast, a breast blackened to aid a weaning. It sketches a campaign of hallucinatory cleverness: "If I just keep on retreating before her superior force, it would be very possible that the erotic in her would become too dissolute and lax for the deeper womanliness to be able to hypostatize itself." Yet a real enough Copenhagen, with its tidy society and sudden sea views, peeps through, and a real love is memorialized, albeit with a wearying degree of rationalization not unlike the tortuous *Winkelzüge* with which Kafka, Kierkegaard's spiritual heir, was to fend off Felice and Milena in his letters to them. Kierkegaard did succeed, in "The Seducer's Diary" and his other apologetic versions of the engagement, in immortalizing Regine. "I shall take her with me into history," he told his journal. She outlived him, and then her husband, and was remembered by the Danish critic Edvard Brandes, who saw her in her middle age, as "radiantly beautiful—with clear, roguish eyes and a svelte figure." She lived into the next century, until 1904, and as a white-haired celebrity gave gracious and modest interviews, recalling those dim events of over sixty years before, when she was but eighteen. Her fame was a vestige of her old suitor's convoluted gallantry. If our impression is that she behaved with the greater dignity, consistency, and human warmth in the affair, it was Kierkegaard who created the impression.

To The Complete Shorter Fiction *of Herman Melville*

1. Melville's Situation 1853–56

HERMAN MELVILLE turned to writing fiction for magazines in some desperation, and it is surprising, given his preference for big, willful novels, that he was so good at it. No anthology of classic American short stories can do without a Melville entry, usually "Bartleby, the Scrivener," and it is a rare collection of novellas that ignores "Benito Cereno." A scion of distinguished gentry on both his father's and mother's side, and married to a daughter of the wealthy Chief Justice of Massachusetts, Melville rather disdained the commercial aspect of his profession. In 1849 he wrote his father-in-law, concerning *Redburn* and *White-Jacket*, two books rapidly turned out in the wake of the disastrously overambitious *Mardi*:

> They are two jobs, which I have done for money—being forced to it, as other men are to sawing wood . . . Being books, then, written in this way, my only desire for their "success" (as it is called) springs from my pocket, & not from my heart. So far as I am individually concerned, & independent of my pocket, it is my earnest desire to write those sorts of books which are said to "fail"—Pardon this egotism.

In the late spring of 1851, while his work on *Moby-Dick* was competing with the demands of his 160-acre farm, Arrowhead, in the hills of western

Massachusetts, and of a household that included his wife, his mother, two or three unmarried sisters, an infant son, and various servants, he wrote to his fellow-author Nathaniel Hawthorne, the man above all others to whom he opened his heart:

> Dollars damn me; and the malicious Devil [a pun on "printer's devil," the boy who took copy from the author to the printer] is forever grinning in upon me, holding the door ajar. My dear Sir, a presentiment is on me,—I shall at last be worn out and perish, like an old nutmeg-grater, grated to pieces by the constant attrition of the wood, that is, the nutmeg. What I feel most moved to write, that is banned,—it will not pay. Yet, altogether, write the *other* way I cannot. So the product is a final hash, and all my books are botches.

Melville was not yet thirty-two when he described his presentiment, and it did not come true immediately. His struggle to support himself and his family with his pen continued for some more years. His last novel, *The Confidence-Man*, was published in 1857. Before its publication, he travelled, at his father-in-law's expense, to Glasgow and Liverpool, and then the Holy Land, Greece, and Italy. Upon returning, he limped through three seasons on the lecture circuit, and in 1860 travelled to San Francisco on the clipper ship captained by his brother Thomas. In 1863 he exchanged Arrowhead for his brother Allan's house at 104 East 26th Street in New York, where he lived until his death. In 1866, his last commercially published volume, the poems *Battle-Pieces*, appeared, to slighting notices, and he accepted an appointment as a district inspector in the United States Customs Service in New York City. His heroic attempt to be an American writer was over, though he composed poetry to the end of his life, privately publishing three more volumes. His lifetime earnings from all his books have been estimated as about $5,900 from the United States and $4,500 from Great Britain.

And yet his first two books, *Typee* and *Omoo*, which described his adventures as a sailor footloose in the Pacific, made his debut sensational. He developed fast; in the same confessional outpouring to Hawthorne of May 1851, he wrote:

> I am like one of those seeds taken out of the Egyptian Pyramids, which, after being three thousand years a seed and nothing but a seed, being planted in English soil, it developed itself, grew to greenness, and then fell to mould. So I. Until I was twenty-five, I had no development at all. From my twenty-fifth year I date my life. Three weeks have scarcely passed, at any time between then and now, that I have not unfolded within myself. But I feel that I am now come to the inmost leaf of the bulb, and that shortly the flower must fall to the mould.

If the reception of *Moby-Dick*, published in the fall of 1851, had been much less enthusiastic than he had hoped or than this masterpiece deserved, the fate of *Pierre* the following year had been devastating. Eight months after its release, Harper's, its publisher, reported sales of 283 copies, out of an edition of 2,310; Melville's lifetime royalties on the book amounted to $157. The negative reviews did not stop at calling the book "intolerably unhealthy" *(Graham's)* and "repulsive, unnatural, and indecent" *(American Whig Review)*; they impugned Melville's sanity. The *Boston Post* called *Pierre* "the craziest fiction extant. . . . It might be supposed to emanate from a lunatic hospital rather than from the quiet retreats of Berkshire." *The Southern Quarterly Review* reported: "That Herman Melville has gone 'clean daft,' is very much to be feared; certainly he has given us a very mad book, my masters. . . . The sooner this author is put in ward the better." HERMAN MELVILLE CRAZY, ran a headline in the *New York Day Book* of September 1852, above a paragraph claiming that he "was really supposed to be deranged, and that his friends were taking measures to place him under treatment." Such allegations could not have but wounded one who at the age of twelve had seen his father die in a raving delirium and whose own nervous state was a topic of concern and gossip throughout his extended family. Melville's father, Allan Melvill (sic), pressed by his debts and business reverses, strained his health and in January of 1832, in Albany, progressed from feverishness and sleeplessness into an "excitement," according to his brother-in-law Peter Gansevoort, that became "an alienation of mind." The "deranged man" was visited by his brother Thomas, who found him "at times fierce, even *maniacal*" and who refused to hope for his recovery because "in all human probability—he would live, a *Maniac*!" His widow, Maria, wrote in the family Bible that "my dear Allan by reason of severe suffering was depriv'd of his Intellect. God moves in a misterious way."

His son Herman's mental health was keenly watched. A Berkshire neighbor, Sarah Morewood, in 1851 wrote a friend, apropos of Melville's writing binges, that he did not "leave his room till quite dark in the evening—when he for the first time during the whole day partakes of solid food—he must therefore write under a state of morbid excitement which must injure his health." At her Christmas party, when she remarked to him that his reclusive life led friends to think he was insane, he replied that he had long ago come to the same opinion. *Pierre* contains a nightmarish description of a writer scribbling himself into near madness. Many who knew Melville remarked upon his mood swings, from depression to a manic ebullience; these swings can be felt in the gusty outpourings of his prose. Laurie Robertson-Lorant in her biography claims, "In our day he would almost certainly be diagnosed as manic-depressive and put on medication." His wife, Elizabeth, noted in her brief biography of her husband, "We all felt anxious about the strain on his health in the spring of 1853." That same year, his mother, urging her brother Peter to procure her son a foreign consulship, wrote, "This constant working of the brain, & excitement of the imagination, is wearing Herman out." Overuse rendered his eyes "as tender as sparrows," and in the mid-1850s he developed disabling rheumatism and sciatica.

The Melville men were fragile. Herman's older brother, Gansevoort, had died at the age of thirty, in London, after a decline as precipitous as their father's; before dying, he had written Herman how he felt he was "breaking up." The hovering threat of disintegration did not leave Melville in later life, when employment and bequests eased his circumstances. The long poem *Clarel*, published in 1876 at his uncle Peter Gansevoort's expense, took a toll. Elizabeth, who was ever solicitous of her delicate, moody husband, wrote to Kate Gansevoort in 1877 that the "poor fellow he has had so much mental suffering to undergo (and oh how *all* necessary) I am rejoiced when anything comes into his life to give him even a moment's relief." In the same year, Melville ended a letter to one of *Clarel*'s few sympathetic readers, John Hoadley, "N.B. *I aint crazy.*" In Book Three of that poem, the Wandering Jew proclaims,

> Go mad I cannot: I maintain
> The perilous outpost of the sane.

From the surviving evidence, Melville took *Pierre*'s emphatic, even scandalous, failure sanely. He had written of his hero, who is similarly threatened by hereditary insanity and whose labors and conflicts so closely parallel his own,

> In that lonely little closet of his, Pierre foretasted all that this world hath either of praise or dispraise; and thus foretasting both goblets, anticipatingly hurled them both in its teeth. All panegyric, all denunciation, all criticism of any sort, would come too late for Pierre.

Elizabeth, years later, reported that her husband had thought the reception of Pierre "a joke": although "it might have affected his literary reputation, it concerned him personally very little."

After completing *Pierre* in the spring of 1852, he gave himself, for the first time since 1849, a vacation from writing; but he was on the lookout for new ideas. During a summer of bucolic activity and family excursions, he travelled with his father-in-law to Nantucket, where he heard the story of one Agatha Hatch Robertson, the daughter of a lighthouse-keeper who had saved a sailor, married him, became pregnant by him, and waited seventeen years for his return, only to discover that he had married a second time. Touched by the tale enough to solicit a transcript, Melville offered it, with detailed suggestions on its rendition as fiction, to Hawthorne, who in 1851 had left the Berkshires for eastern Massachusetts. "This thing lies very much in a vein," Melville wrote, "with which you are peculiarly familiar . . . Besides the thing seems naturally to gravitate to you." He followed this overture with a personal visit, that fall, to Hawthorne, now back in Concord, where he had bought the Alcotts' spacious house, Hillside. The relation, though still amiable, had cooled, to judge from Melville's rather formal summation: "I greatly enjoyed my visit to you, and hope that you reaped some corresponding pleasure." Hawthorne had returned the materials and urged Melville to write the story of Agatha himself. This he proceeded to do, in the winter of 1853, under the title "The Isle of the Cross." Presumably this is the "new work, now nearly ready for the press," of which his mother wrote in April of 1853, and to which Melville alludes in a November letter to Harper and Brothers as "the work which I took to New York last Spring, but which I was prevented from printing at that time." The nature of the prevention is unspecified, and any manuscript has vanished. Nor did he deliver on his proposal, in the same November letter, for a "book—300 pages, say—partly of nautical adventure, and partly—or, rather, chiefly, of Tortoise Hunting Adventure"; he claimed it to be "now in hand, and pretty well towards completion [and] ready for press some time in the coming January."

Amid these aborted projects, however, a number of more modest works did begin to appear in print, though anonymously. Anonymity, or a pseudonym, was customary for magazine contributors, and possibly not displeasing to Melville; he had suggested to his British publisher that *Pierre* be brought out as "By a Vermonter" or "by Guy Winthrop." In early October of 1852, he had received a circular letter inviting authors to contribute to a new magazine, *Putnam's Monthly Magazine*, edited by George Palmer Putnam, a cousin of Allan Melvill's wife, Sophia. A letter by Hope Savage Shaw, Elizabeth Shaw Melville's stepmother, reveals that by the early summer of 1853 Herman had been "persuaded" by "the Harpers" to write for their magazine. He was not a total stranger to journal publication. At the age of nineteen he had published two "Fragments from a Writing Desk" in the May 4 and May 18, 1839, issues of the *Democratic Press, and Lansingburgh Advertiser*—at that point his hometown paper. To *Yankee Doodle*, which was edited by an acquaintance, Cornelius Mathews, Melville in 1847 contributed the successive installments of "Authentic Anecdotes of 'Old Zack' " (issues of July 24, July 31, August 7, August 14, August 21, August 28, and September 11). For

Evert Duyckinck's weekly *Literary World* he wrote five anonymous reviews, chief among them "Hawthorne and His Mosses," so expansive that it was run in two issues, those of August 17 and August 24, 1850. *Harper's New Monthly Magazine* for October 1851 carried a chapter from *Moby-Dick*, "The Town-Ho's Story," which was also printed in the *Baltimore Evening Sun* of November 8. Between 1853 and 1856 the following fourteen stories were published as specified:

"Bartleby, the Scrivener: A Story of Wall Street," *Putnam's*, November and December 1853.

"Cock-A-Doodle-Doo! or the Crowing of the Noble Cock Benevantano," *Harper's*, December 1853.

"The Encantadas or Enchanted Isles," *Putnam's*, March, April, and May 1854.

"Poor Man's Pudding and Rich Man's Crumbs," *Harper's*, June 1854.

"The Happy Failure: A Story of the River Hudson," *Harper's*, July 1854.

"The Lightning-Rod Man," *Putnam's*, August 1854.

"The Fiddler," *Harper's*, September 1854.

"The Paradise of Bachelors and the Tartarus of Maids," *Harper's*, April 1855.

"The Bell-Tower," *Putnam's*, August 1855.

"Benito Cereno," *Putnam's*, October, November, and December 1855.

"Jimmy Rose," *Harper's*, November 1855.

"I and My Chimney," *Putnam's*, March 1856.

"The 'Gees," *Harper's*, March 1856.

"The Apple-Tree Table or, Original Spiritual Manifestations," *Harper's*, May 1856.

In addition, the novel *Israel Potter: His Fifty Years of Exile* was serialized in nine numbers of *Putnam's*, from July 1854 to March 1855.

The order of publication was not necessarily the order of writing. Merton M. Sealts, Jr., in his "The Chronology of Melville's Short Fiction, 1853–1856," argues that "Bartleby," though the first to be published, was probably written, in the summer of 1853, after three shorter, less accomplished essays at short fiction—"The Happy Failure," "The Fiddler," and "Cock-A-Doodle-Doo!" These, he believes, are the "three articles which perhaps may be found suitable to your Magazine" that Melville submitted to *Harper's* with a letter dated August 13 and which Sealts persuasively ascribes to the year 1853. The eleven-month delay between submission and publication was not unusual for *Harper's*; "The 'Gees," according to Sealts, was likely submitted in September of 1854 and held for fourteen months.

The only known editorial rejection suffered by Melville in this period was of "The Two Temples." The *Putnam's* editor, Charles F. Briggs, wrote the author in May of 1854, "I am very loth [sic] to reject the Two Temples as the article contains some exquisitely fine description, and some pungent satire, but my editorial experience compels me to be very cautious in offending the religious sensibilities of the public, and the moral of the Two Temples would array against us the whole power of the pulpit, to say nothing of Brown, and the congregation of Grace Church." Putnam himself asked his cousin-in-law to revise the story and resubmit it, but Melville did not.

In the dollars of the day, he was paid well—$5 a page from *Putnam's* and as much as $100 from *Harper's* for a group of stories. For *Israel Potter* he received $421.50. His total earnings for these years of piecework have been calculated as $750; this does not include the $300 advance given him by Harper and Brothers for the "Tortoise Hunting Adventure," a project whose lineaments we may recognize, much shrunken, in "The Encantadas." (For financial comparison, consider that he was paid, in his modest post as customs inspector, $4 a day or $1,200 a year; that an apple cost a penny and a book ordinarily a dollar; that his 160-acre farm was assessed at $4,000 in 1863; and that his brother-in-law, Lemuel Shaw, Jr., left an estate of over $300,000.)

Magazines were on the rise—"the most saleable of all books nowadays," Melville admitted to his British publisher. *Harper's*, with a circulation of a hundred thousand, was criticized for extensively serializing such English authors as Dickens and Thackeray; *Putnam's* was founded as a magazine specifically devoted to the work of American writers. It published the longest and most ambitious of Melville's short pieces, in addition to works by Thoreau, Cooper, Longfellow, Lowell, Charles A. Dana, and Horace Greeley. Aimed at an educated, politically liberal (that is, anti-slavery) readership that never exceeded twenty thousand, it was sold by George Putnam in 1855 and went into receivership in 1857. When it was revived in 1868, its prospectus asked, "And where . . . is Herman Melville? Has that copious and imaginative author . . . let fall his pen just where its use might have been so remunerative to himself, and so satisfactory to the public?" Melville wrote the editors, "You may include me in the list of possible contributors," but he never did contribute.

In putting together a book of his short pieces, he chose only those that had appeared in *Putnam's*. His original title was *Benito Cereno & Other Sketches*; the selection was, in this order, "Benito Cereno," "Bartleby," "The Bell-Tower," "The Encantadas," and "The Lightning-Rod Man." Sealts believes that, if *Putnam's* had published "I and My Chimney" before the end of 1855, it would have been included. The book's publisher was Dix and Edwards—the purchaser, as it happened, of *Putnam's*. In discussions, Melville—to quote a letter of his—"volunteered something about supplying some sort of prefatory matter, with a new title of the Collection," then decided that "both steps are not only unnecessary, but might prove unsuitable," and reversed himself again, providing "The Piazza" as an introductory essay/story/sketch/article and as the occasion of the new title. The date of composition can be assumed to lie between January 19, 1856, when the elaboration seemed unsuitable, and February 16, when it was submitted. *The Piazza Tales* appeared in May of 1856. Melville was already immersed in the composition of his last novel, *The Confidence-Man*, which Dix and Edwards were also to publish, after declining to give him a requested advance for it. Joshua Dix's partner George William Curtis, a popular writer who acted as an adviser to *Putnam's*, told Dix to "decline any novel from Melville that is not extremely good," but wrote of the proposed short-story collection, "I don't think Melville's book will sell a great deal, but he is a good name upon your list. He has lost his prestige,—& I don't believe the Putnam stories will bring it up. But I suppose you can't lose by it. *I* like the Encantadas, and Bartleby, very much." In the event, *The Piazza Tales* sold a disappointing 1,047 copies, only three-fifths of the number needed to break even. Within a year, the firm, and along with it *Putnam's Monthly Magazine*, fell to the Panic of 1857. The bankrupt company offered Melville the opportunity to buy the plates of both his books, but he responded: "Sell them without remorse. To pot with them, & melt them down." His career as a professional tale-teller was over.

2. The Piazza Tales *and Other Tales*

The Piazza Tales was not reprinted until 1922, when, as part of the great Melville revival, the British firm of Constable brought his complete works back into print. In the seventy-five years since, a full weight of twentieth-century scholarship and commentary has fallen upon these and Melville's other short pieces; scarcely a story lacks its scholarly champions and its denigrators, and the interpretations called forth by their puzzles are legion. Many students first come to Melville through the stories. Like his four novels of the 1850s, they manifest a densely figured prose, a penchant for pedantry and ambiguity, a saturnine humorousness, and an undertow of nihilism; but in briefer doses these traits menace the young reader more mildly. *The Piazza Tales* form an entertainingly mixed bag: in order, (1) a man adds a piazza to his country farmhouse and then walks up a mountain toward a distantly gleaming cottage that he imagines as a fairyland, (2) a good-natured, elderly lawyer hires, and then somehow cannot fire, a pale scrivener who declines to perform any tasks beyond strict scrivening, (3) an American sea-captain, moored off a desolate Chilean island, boards an eerily depopulated and deteriorated Spanish merchant-ship whose cargo includes black slaves, (4) a householder not unlike the piazza-builder testily repels a lightning-rod salesman who shows up in a thunderstorm, (5) a cluster of cindery islands in the Pacific plays host to great tortoises, many sea-birds, pirates, occasional adventurers and madmen, and a lonely half-breed widow called Hunilla, (6) a Renaissance "mechanician" named Bannadonna rears a great bell-tower whose bells are to be rung by an intricate robotic mechanism.

It is not for an introducer to disclose the outcomes of these suspenseful situations, or to pose critical judgments that might cramp the reader's enjoyment. *The Piazza Tales*, and Melville's other stories, still elude settled verdicts and excite a vital variety of reactions. Even the least of them, "The 'Gees," has been variously seen as a piece of racism, as an attack on nineteenth-century racist ethnology, as "a metaphor for the majority of the human race," as a parable of capitalist exploitation, and as "an example of how Melville can be read as a master of satire." One might generalize, however, to the effect that as a group these magazine pieces of the mid-Fifties are brownish and sombre in color, etched rather than painted. Compared with the exhilarating prose of *Typee*, *Omoo*, and *Moby-Dick*, their language feels chastened, at times stiff and halting. The stories testify to both a creeping exhaustion and a stubborn, innate vigor. The writer of *Moby-Dick* was exalted by Shakespearean possibilities that had opened up to him; the short-story writer—post-*Pierre*, deserted by Hawthorne, and the object of pitying scheming within his own family—sees failure everywhere.

"So my poem is damned, and immortal fame is not for me! I am nobody forever and ever. Intolerable fate!" Thus begins "The Fiddler," one of the first of his ventures into the sketch length; another of the early group, "The Happy Failure," ends, "But it's all over now. Boy, I'm glad I've failed. I say, boy, failure has made a good old man of me. It was horrible at first, but I'm glad I failed. Praise be to God for the failure!" So speaks the hero, the narrator's elderly uncle, who has just torn apart his world-saving invention, a mechanical swamp-drainer, and who owes some traits to the obsessed Ahab and some to Herman's bankrupt uncle Thomas. Do we believe him? Or is his claim of wisdom through failure a crowing as inutile and finally grating as that of the noble cock Benevantano in "Cock-A-Doodle-Doo!"? Surrounded by a culture of optimism, of which Emerson sounded the purest note, Melville found himself obliged to doubt: "I was not wholly at rest concerning the soundness of Merrymusk's views of things, though full of admiration for him."

His autobiographical persona, in such fictionalized reports from Arrowhead as "I and My Chimney," "The Apple-Tree Table," and "The Piazza," is disconcertingly elderly, considering that Melville was then in his mid-thirties, with a wife who was bearing him a new child every two years. Sons, in any condition of male activity, are absent from these sketches, and daughters, where they appear, are already grown. "I and My Chimney," composed during his period of severe sciatica, limns such an interfering and inimical wife that Elizabeth felt obliged to defend herself with a marginal note on the printed copy preserved in a binder: "All this about his wife, applied to his mother—who was very vigorous and ener-getic about the farm, etc. The proposed removal of the chimney is purely mythical." Wife, mother, and sisters are merged into one big, threatening woman. Dr. Oliver Wendell Holmes treated Melville in June of 1855 and for his trouble got lampooned as the architect Scribe, enlisted in the female conspiracy to do away with a warming, homely chimney that, if not an outright phallic symbol, represents, with its irregularities and "secret recesses," his masculine privacy. Curtis—apparently blind to the story's darker side, including a pun on "ash-hole"—wrote to Dix calling it "a capital, genial, humorous sketch by Melville, thoroughly magazin-ish." In its conclusion, the hero, rather than leave his chimney unde-fended, stays at home for seven years. Like Bartleby, he will not be moved from the seat of his identity, however uncomfortable it is. The titular heroes of "Bartleby" and "Benito Cereno" assume a defensive catatonia that strains credibility and the reader's patience.

Warner Berthoff, introducing the *Great Short Works of Herman Melville*, says of the stories:

> One after another presents an action of withdrawal, resignation, defeat; of stoic endurance and passive suffering; of isolated and constricted spirits living on, though sometimes with a strange cheerfulness, after wrenching disasters; of measures taken—usually too eccentric to be generally service-able—against hardly avoidable catastrophe.

Newton Arvin, whose short biography of 1950 remains one of the most acute and vivid, had little use for the tales:

> During the two or three years that follow [*Pierre*], Melville has the air of consciously sparing himself; sparing himself by attempting only short and unexacting flights or by leaning heavily on some bookish source . . . Few of

the tales themselves are anything but thin, pale, insubstantial, and fatally easy to forget. . . . It is Melville whipping himself on, without a moment's support from his deeper nature, to be a disposable and pliant writer for *Harper's* and *Putnam's*, to furnish the magazines with the literary staples they will pay for . . . He has an unhappy air, all the while, of supposing that there is a formula for doing this if he can only lay his hand on it; that there is a tone of genteel informality, of essayistic levity, out of Lamb or Leigh Hunt, that will buoy up almost any matter on its smooth surface.

Edwin Haviland Miller, in his rather relentlessly psychological biography of 1975, sees the stories as studies in regression:

Despite the comic surfaces of many of these short stories, perhaps intended as a sop for the magazine audience, Melville depicts with almost frightening consistency a wasteland in which nothing grows and no one matures. The characters—or caricatures of humanity—are frozen, despite their chronological ages, in infantile responses or flee from life.

Annihilation, becoming "nobody," is, in Miller's reading, these characters' ultimate goal.

We are, perhaps, after a century of literary wastelands, able to read not only a personal predicament but a general truth in Melville's blasted islands, bedevilled slave ships, misshapen houses, falling towers, ticking tables, ghastly factories, sickly cottages, and blank brick city walls. The appetite for truth is what gives Melville's narratives their persistent interest and, even under the spell of discouragement, their untoward verbal energy. The form and style of truth deeply concerned him. "Truth uncompromisingly told will always have its ragged edges," he wrote in *Billy Budd*. "Truth is ever incoherent," he wrote to Hawthorne in November of 1851, responding with feverish gratitude to the older writer's favorable letter (now lost) concerning *Moby-Dick*. Melville's letter of response is amazing in its unembarrassed ardor, which becomes religious ecstasy:

Whence came you, Hawthorne? By what right do you drink from my flagon of life? And when I put it to my lips—lo, they are yours and not mine. I feel that the Godhead is broken up like the bread at the Supper, and that we are the pieces. Hence this infinite fraternity of feeling.

In the next paragraph, he catches himself:

My dear Hawthorne, the atmospheric skepticisms steal into me now, and make me doubtful of my sanity in writing you thus. But, believe me, I am not mad, most noble Festus! But truth is ever incoherent, and when the big hearts strike together, the concussion is a little stunning. Farewell. Don't write a word about the book. That would be robbing me of my miserly delight. I am heartily sorry I ever wrote anything about you—it was paltry. Lord, when shall we be done growing?

While the extent of Melville's homosexuality will be ever uncertain, this is a love letter, no doubt—so passionate a one that the "farewell" is spoken, perhaps, in self-protection. He saw Hawthorne as a fellow "big heart," a partner in the whale-hunt for truth. "For unless you own the whale," he writes in *Moby-Dick*, "you are but a provincial and sentimentalist in Truth. But clear Truth is a thing for salamander giants only to encounter; how small the chances for the provincials then?"

Melville's grand-spirited truthfulness makes him fruitful and frustrating to his legion of interpreters. The paired sketches, "The Paradise of Bachelors" and "The Tartarus of Maids," have prompted a good deal of overinterpretation. Together, they form the most ambitious of three double sketches composed in the fall and winter of 1853–54. All three draw, in one of their halves, from a journal Melville kept during a visit to London from October 1849 to January of 1850; all are about, one way or another, poverty and riches. The point of "Poor Man's Pudding and Rich Man's Crumbs" seems clear enough. The complacent meliorism of the poet Blandmour, whose orotund praise of "Poor Man's Pudding"—a savorless concoction of rice, milk, and salt—is debunked by the narrator's experience of eating some in a poor woodcutter's household; and the narrator's experience in "Rich Man's Crumbs" debunks the complacent satisfaction which his suavely uniformed guide takes in the charity thrown to London's poor—scraps of a magnificent royal banquet the night before. The misery of the poor is held up for our pity and indignation in both panels of the transatlantic diptych, and the moral is professed as "if ever a Rich Man speaks prosperously to me of a Poor Man, I shall set it down as— I won't mention the word."

"The Two Temples," denied publication for its satire on Broadway's Grace Church, contrasts the narrator's rude exclusion from the ecclesiastical temple and his warm reception, though he finds himself penniless, in a London theatre. The target must be the Pharisaism of upper-class American Christianity, contrasted with English warmth and guilt-free spontaneity. A refined British hedonism is foremost in "The Paradise of Bachelors," a wholly admiring and grateful remembrance of a boozy, loquacious bachelor's dinner staged in London, on December 21, at the Erechtheum Club, which Melville altered in the telling to a chamber of the Temple; the literary men of the actual party have been changed to lawyers and erudite gentlemen hobbyists. Melville's love of food, drink, and male companionship are nowhere more lavishly displayed. "We were a band of brothers," he says, brothers who, in a long evening of steady oral indulgence, evinced "nothing unmannerly, nothing turbulent." They do not even sneeze when taking snuff from a great silver horn decorated with goats' heads. Removed from "the thing called pain, the bugbear styled trouble," the men talk and tipsily watch the decanters gallop around the table until, at midnight, the grateful guest, in "a burst of admiring candor," pronounces the Temple "the very Paradise of Bachelors!" Yet Robertson-Lorant, in her biography, says flatly, "Melville portrays these privileged 'bachelors' as morally stunted, selfish parasites." They may be that in her view, or any progressive modern view, but little in the celebrative, rather fawning Melville text bears out such a condemnation.

"The Tartarus of Maids," describing a frigid January visit to a paper mill staffed by pale young women, does invite, with such place-names as the Devil's Dungeon, Black Notch, and Blood River, an allegorical interpretation. Even so, Edwin Miller's Freudian equivalences ("The mills produce paper in nine minutes with apparatus that resembles the sexual reproductive organs. The tale is a grotesque mockery of the birth and sexual process") slight Melville's main thrust, which is to provoke pity for the miserably paid maiden wage-slaves, along with a shuddering awe at the powerful, inexorable machines. "Machinery—that vaunted slave of humanity—here stood menially served by human beings." The prominent humanitarian and Marxist dimension of the sketch is ignored in the search for Freudian puns; in Robertson-Lorant's reading, a piston inevitably becomes "phallic," the rags torn and pulped to make paper become the "rags women used to stanch the flow of menstrual blood," and the narrator, a "seedman" who, in need of envelopes for his product, descends through Dark Notch into a "Devil's Dungeon," becomes a spermatozoon on legs. Yet the frozen, blood-drained tint of the whole, wherein the maidens have become as pale and blank as the paper they make and the ice around them, does not reinforce such eroticization. Here are two worlds, Melville's juxtaposition implies, both—bachelor bliss, maiden misery—real. His closing sentences restore the visitor to "inscrutable nature"; with non-committal dichotomy he exclaims, "Oh! Paradise of Bachelors! and oh! Tartarus of Maids!"

Melville, overall, says neither yea nor nay. In 1851, when he was at the peak of his powers, Sophia Hawthorne wrote her sister that "he is a boy in opinion—having settled nothing as yet." Melville broke into capital letters when he came to the conclusion of his poem of 1860–61, "The Conflict of Convictions":

YEA AND NAY—
EACH HATH HIS SAY;
BUT GOD HE KEEPS THE MIDDLE WAY.
NONE WAS BY
WHEN HE SPREAD THE SKY;
WISDOM IS VAIN, AND PROPHESY.

On the great issue of the time, black slavery, he issues no comforting wisdom or prophecy. Having served on whalers with racially mixed crews, and famously dwelled among brown-skinned cannibals, he championed Polynesians against missionary incursions and drew heroic portraits of the heathen harpooners in *Moby-Dick*. But his attitude toward the bristling facts of race in the New World remained dramatic rather than didactic.

"Benito Cereno" is both a visit to the heart of darkness and a call for black power. The narrator, Captain Delano, expresses a benign white racism: "In fact, like most men of a good, blithe heart, Captain Delano took to negroes, not philanthropically, but genially, just as other men to Newfoundland dogs." As Delano wanders the ship, he observes a "slumbering negress . . . lying, with youthful limbs carelessly disposed, under the lee of the bulwarks, like a doe in the shade of a woodland rock." The passage goes on:

> Sprawling at her lapped breasts was her wide-awake fawn, stark naked, its black little body half lifted from the deck, crosswise with its dam's; its hands, like two paws, clambering upon her; its mouth and nose ineffectually rooting to get at the mark; and meantime giving a vexatious half-grunt, blending with the composed snore of the negress. . . . There's naked nature, now; pure tenderness and love, thought Captain Delano, well pleased.

Watching the faithful Babo shave Captain Cereno, Delano meditates with satisfaction upon the "something in the negro which, in a peculiar way, fits him for avocations about one's person . . . taking to the comb and brush congenially as to the castinets, and flourishing them apparently with almost equal satisfaction." Beyond this there is "a certain easy cheerfulness . . . as though God had set the whole negro to some pleasant tune" and "the docility arising from the unaspiring contentment of a limited mind, and that susceptibility of blind attachment sometimes inhering in indisputable inferiors." Such impressions have led to the consoling American myth of black-white friendship, the white hand being the one generously extended; the action of "Benito Cereno" dispels such impressions in declaring the simple, though often obscured and (to whites) shocking truth that the enslaved do not love their enslavers.

Melville, "a boy in opinion," is among the least prejudiced and pater-nalistic of authors; he rarely seems—compared with, say, Dickens and Hardy—to be trying to sell us something. An exception, possibly, is the Hunilla episode of "The Encantadas," "Sketch Eighth: Norfolk Isle and the Chola Widow," where all the pent-up affect of the aborted Agatha story attempts to force itself on the inarticulate heroine. But, if instances of Melville's verbal magic are wanted, this episode provides one in the lit-tle oval picture of her life's disaster that Hunilla creates for herself when, to watch her husband and brother head out to sea in their crudely fash-ioned catamaran, she in her seaside thicket pushes back some branches:

> They formed an oval frame, through which the bluely boundless sea rolled like a painted one. And there, the invisible painter painted to her view the wave-tossed and disjointed raft, its once level logs slantingly unheaved, as raking masts, and the four struggling arms undistinguishable among them; and then all subsided into smooth-flowing creamy waters, slowly drifting the splintered wreck; while first and last, no sound of any sort was heard. Death in a silent picture; a dream of the eye; such vanishing shapes as the mirage shows.
>
> So instant was the scene, so trance-like its mild pictorial effect, so distant from her blasted bower and her common sense of things, that Hunilla gazed and gazed, nor raised a finger or a wail.

The unreality of a dreadful event is portrayed with a visual and psycho-logical accuracy that glistens. This glisten, which momentarily suspends the reader's mind in its fine surprise, touches also the little bug who, in Melville's retelling of a well-known New England legend, crawls at last out of "the apple-tree table":

> There, half in and half out of its crack, there wriggled the bug, flashing in the room's general dimness, like a fiery opal.
>
> Had this bug had a tiny sword by its side—a Damascus sword—and a tiny necklace round its neck—a diamond necklace—and a tiny gun in its claw—a brass gun—and a tiny manuscript in its mouth—a Chaldee manuscript—Julia and Anna could not have stood more charmed.

It is sad, for the reader as well as for the narrator and his daughters, that this "seraphical bug" "did not long enjoy its radiant life; it expired the next day." We are put in mind of Melville's own marvellous unfolding, which he likened to that of a seed taken from a pyramid and which, he prophesied to Hawthorne, would too soon come to its inmost leaf.

3. Other Short Works

His literary ambitions were not born solely of the sea. The heading "Fragments from a Writing Desk" would have allowed frequent contributions to the *Democratic Press, and Lansingburgh Advertiser.* Only two, however, appeared, on May 4 and May 18, 1839, the month before Melville shipped out on his first ocean voyage, to Liverpool and back on the trading vessel *St. Lawrence.* The first "fragment" shows the nineteen-year-old essayist to be healthily interested in local girls and to have a dandyish prose style, heightened by self-parody. His insecurities masked by a persona, he boasts of his physical beauty and of his mind—"Why, sir, I have discovered it to be endowed with the most rare and extraordinary powers, stored with universal knowledge, and embellished with every polite accomplishment." Melville's formal education had been sharply truncated by the family's financial misfortunes, but the houses of his youth had been well stocked with books, and he garnishes his wordy flights with quotations from Thomas Campbell, Shakespeare, Lord Byron, Sir Walter Scott, Milton, and Coleridge. Granted that those teenagers of the era who were literate at all were capable of considerable flourishes, a paragraph like his fourth, which is all one sentence, shows a precocious virtuosity.

The second "fragment" tells a tale that holds our interest to its anti-climactic end; like the last story Melville wrote, "The Piazza," it follows a romantic interest to its ultimate disillusion. A voice is what his vision of feminine perfection lacks, and a voice is what Melville above all had. She bends upon him "Andalusian eyes," which are unexpected even though Washington Irving had made Spain fashionable. Ten years later, when Melville had entered upon fame with *Typee* and *Omoo*, a New York journalist wrote of "Herman Melville, with his cigar and Spanish eyes." Melville was the dark-eyed son of blue-eyed races. The opulent apartment he imagined in Lansingburgh—"its atmosphere was redolent of the most delicious perfumes. The walls were hung round with the most elegant draperies, waving in graceful folds, on which were delineated scenes of Arcadian beauty. . . . Chandeliers of the most fanciful description, suspended from the lofty ceilings by rods of silver, shed over this voluptuous scene a soft and tempered light"—anticipates that described, with a more sinister tint, in the forty-sixth chapter of *Redburn: His First Voyage.* Wellingborough Redburn could have stepped right out of these upstate daydreams, though he seems younger than nineteen.

Literary success brought Melville literary friends. Evert Duyckinck, the urbane, Episcopalian, sociable editor (with his brother George) of

The Literary World, introduced Melville, on his Manhattan visits, into the circle of Duyckinck's Saturday-night suppers, called the Tetractys Club, or "Knights of the Round Table." A member of the circle, Cornelius Mathews, edited *Yankee Doodle*, a humorous weekly billed as "the American *Punch*," and he invited Melville to contribute some satirical pieces on Zachary Taylor, the hero of the day for his victories in the Mexican-American War. At seven installments and nine "anecdotes," the series runs on too long, losing the modest verve with which it began. Like many Northern liberals, Melville saw the war as an imperialist aggression fostered by a pro-Southern national government to expand the potential territory for slavery. Taylor was himself a slaveholder and had spent most of his military career waging war against Indians; neither Melville nor anyone else could foresee that, when placed in office, in 1850, as the twelfth President of the United States, the crusty old soldier would show the pro-slavery interests a resistant mettle that, had he not died within a few months of his inauguration, might have altered the course of events leading up to the Civil War. Melville's satire in any case makes no use of political argument; what comes through, besides an aristocratic disdain of the popular "Old Rough and Ready," is a protest against the Barnumization of American culture. P. T. Barnum had opened his American Museum in New York City in 1841; Melville pictures him, four times, seeking to obtain Old Zack's relics (his pants, his tobacco box) for display and "the satisfaction of the curious." American celebrity-worship here provokes an early lampoon, complete with advertising's typographical fireworks. In parodying the diction of a physiognomist, Melville attains a certain Melvillian grandeur:

> His eye is Websternian, though grey. The left organ somewhat affects the dexter side of the socket, while examined by a powerful telescope several minute specks are observable in the pupil of the sinister orbit. But this detracts not from the majesty of its expression: the sun even has its spots.

While a comic sense presides over the grandest of Melville's fictions ("There are certain queer times and occasions in this strange mixed affair we call life," he says in *Moby-Dick*, "when a man takes this whole universe for a vast practical joke, though the wit thereof he but dimly discerns"), topical jesting is not his forte. Taken neat, his humor has a bitter taste; we are in the bleak territory, rife with fustian and fraudulence, of *The Confidence-Man*. Nevertheless, these "Authentic Anecdotes of 'Old Zack' " are recognizably by Melville (they show his characteristic interest in costume, for example) and constitute his only significant magazine appearance in the 1840s.

"Hawthorne and His Mosses," published in the summer of 1850, belongs among his uncollected sketches because of its imaginative fever and fictional frame, being ostensibly written by "a Virginian spending July in Vermont," who has had Hawthorne's *Mosses from an Old Manse* urged upon him by "a mountain girl, a cousin of mine." His written response describes the encounter of two sensibilities, or, rather, the ravishment of one by the other; it is among the most personal, as well as the most exalted, of literary appreciations. A number of its sentences are inscribed in the commonplace-book of the American sublime:

> The world is as young today, as when it was created; and this Vermont morning dew is as wet to my feet, as Eden's dew to Adam's.

> Believe me, my friends, that Shakespeares are this day being born on the banks of the Ohio.

> But it is better to fail in originality, than to succeed in imitation.

> For genius, all over the world, stands hand in hand, and one shock of recognition runs the whole circle round.

A prey exists in the empyrean of art, and its name is Truth: "For in this world of lies, Truth is forced to fly like a scared white doe in the woodlands; and only by cunning glimpses will she reveal herself, as in Shakespeare and other masters of the great Art of Telling the Truth,—even though it be covertly, and by snatches."

The playful tone of some other of the few book reviews Melville had done for the *Literary World* reveal the tepidity of the respect he bore such American predecessors as Fenimore Cooper and Francis Parkman. In Hawthorne's short stories he descried a brain and heart Shakespearean in penetration, in honest darkness, in shining truth. The discovery leads to patriotic exhortation: "The truth is, that in our point of view, this matter of a national literature has come to such a pass with us, that in some sense we must turn bullies, else the day is lost." The exhortation, penned on the point of noon of the century's day, Melville above all addressed to himself; the inspiration of Hawthorne's example fed directly into *Moby-Dick*, another sea-tale in progress, which became more metaphorical, metaphysical, and "wicked" thanks to Hawthorne's perceived virtues, foremost his "great power of blackness." Like an ongoing tale, the essay acquires a second wind—the Virginian confesses that, in his haste to praise, he had not read all the *Mosses*, and finds fresh reason, twenty-four hours later, for "love and admiration" in what he has now read.

> But already I feel that this Hawthorne has dropped germinous seeds into my soul. He expands and deepens down, the more I contemplate him; and further, and further, shoots his strong New-England roots into the hot soil of my Southern soul.

This famous, even notorious declaration tells the nub of the story. The story's sequels—the masterpiece created, scorned, and, for seventy years, neglected; the intense friendship kindled and then cooled—ask a different telling. In the meantime, to be "admired by every one who is capable of admiration," Melville's effusion marks a dramatic moment, of one genius hailing another, in a setting no longer provincial.

After the failure of *The Confidence-Man*, Melville turned exclusively to poetry. But toward the end of his life, and especially after his retirement from the customs service in 1885, prose crept back, in the unlikely form of long headnotes to his poems. Among his papers, but not published until the Constable edition of his works, were a number of sketches, or "characters," attached to poems, all more or less work in progress; five of them, titled "The Marquis de Grandvin," "Daniel Orme," and three concerning "Jack Gentian," can be found in Berthoff's collection. The only such extended sketch, however, that Melville printed in his lifetime is "John Marr," which, with its poem, introduced *John Marr and Other Sailors, with Some Sea Pieces*, privately published in 1888 in an edition of twenty-five. Marr, described in a lecturer's present tense, is imagined to have retired to the Midwestern prairie fifty years earlier, in 1838. Isolated with his rich sea-memories among people whose unwillingness to listen "seemed of a piece with the apathy of Nature herself," Marr, like Melville in the heart of New York City, finds a "shadowy fellowship" in old shipmates:

> Ye float around me, form and feature:—
> Tattooings, ear-rings, love-locks curled;
> Barbarians of man's simpler nature,
> Unworldly servers of the world.
> Yea, present all, and dear to me,
> Though shades, or scouring China's sea.

Melville died, in bed, in 1891. Elizabeth Shaw outlived him by fifteen years and—in no wise resembling the destructive termagant wife of "I and My Chimney"—carefully, lovingly tended his literary estate, overseeing the new editions of four novels (*Typee, Omoo, White-Jacket, Moby-Dick*) in 1892, and preserving and arranging his unpublished papers. Prominent among the latter were the many leaves of *Billy Budd*, a headnote which had reached novella length before Melville wrote "End of Book, April 1891." The text was first published in an edition by Melville's first biographer, Raymond Weaver, in 1924, and revised by him in 1928. The manuscript was donated by Mrs. Eleanor Melville Metcalf, Melville's granddaughter, to Harvard, and is kept in Houghton Library;

from it a "literal text," including all of Melville's not always harmonizable markings, was prepared by F. Barron Freeman, in 1948, and another version, in 1962, by Harrison Hayford and Merton Sealts. The manuscript shows that Melville did not number his divisions but separated them with a figurative device; certain paragraphs have no clear location; and in the absence of a fair copy a definitive version is impossible.

Billy Budd has excited the most admiration and commentary of any work by Melville except *Moby-Dick*. It has the translucence and the loose weave of last works—of Shakespeare's *Tempest* and Tolstoy's "Hadji Murad," of Henry Green's *Doting* and Hemingway's *A Moveable Feast*. A lifetime sifts into it. Whenever Melville ventures onto shipboard, the reader feels the deck beneath his feet. The nautical setting of the H.M.S. *Bellipotent*, with its wartime society of sailors, is closely allied to that of the American frigate *Neversink* in *White-Jacket*: both ships have villainous masters-at-arms; *Billy Budd* is dedicated to the most admired figure in *White-Jacket*, Jack Chase; and it was while serving upon the *Neversink*'s original, the *United States*, that Melville learned, in 1844, of his cousin Lieutenant Guert Gansevoort's involvement in a drumhead verdict aboard the *Somers*. But *White-Jacket* was written, in a rush of memory and opinion, by a confident young writer coming into his highest powers, whereas the author of *Billy Budd* is feeling his way back into fiction after the long hiatus of a failed literary career.

The manuscript shows much revision, during which the story wandered far from the poem that it was designed to elucidate. The Billy of the poem, with his rhythmic slang and his fond memory of Bristol Molly, is an earthy brother of the tale's angelic, not to say Christly, foretopman. A less stylized story might have less readily absorbed the overt Biblical allusions which link Billy with both unfallen Adam and the crucified Christ. Melville proceeds a bit arthritically, in a prose that puts us in mind now and then of Henry James's studied gropings, to present, as in his other headnotes, his "characters." There are three: Billy the Handsome Sailor, limned with an unprecedented homoerotic relish; John Claggart, the master-of-arms, a man of estimable appearance yet with a pallid complexion that, though "not exactly displeasing, nevertheless seemed to hint of something defective or abnormal in the constitution and blood"; and the captain, Edward Fairfax Vere, once dubbed "Starry" by a kinsman in recognition of his stellar qualities, an "exceptional character" almost imperceptibly marred—in parallel with Billy's occasional stutter and Claggart's clammy complexion and protuberant chin—by what an unnamed sailor calls "a queer streak of the pedantic running through him . . . like the King's yarn in a coil of navy rope."

These three delicately flawed characters are struck one against the other in an action of operatic starkness. Indeed, an opera has been made of the story, by Benjamin Britten. A perfect captain, perhaps, could have averted tragedy, or at least put it off—as those around him suggest he should—to an admiral's hearing. But Vere's "streak of the pedantic" forces, in the context of 1797, the year of the Great Mutiny, an absolute resolution. Before seeing his will enacted, however, he attempts reconciliation with the innocent culprit in a scene Melville preferred not to write, as if fearing to commit sacrilege. Vere "may," he tells us,

> have caught Billy to his heart, even as Abraham may have caught young Isaac on the brink of resolutely offering him up in obedience to the exacting behest. But there is no telling the sacrament, seldom if in any case revealed to the gadding world, wherever under circumstances at all akin to those here attempted to be set forth two of great Nature's nobler order embrace. There is privacy at the time, inviolable to the survivor; and holy oblivion, the sequel to each diviner magnanimity, providentially covers all at last.

The tortuous grammar of this splendidly equivocating passage contains the poignant torque of an ideal father-son relationship's being posed by a man whose own father died raving when he, the son, was twelve, and whose two sons died, one a suicide and one an invalid vagabond, within their father's lifetime. The analogy of Abraham and Isaac and the language of sacrament suggest a yet greater reconciliation: between the life-long seeker and God, in spite of cruelties witnessed on one side and an implacable starry silence maintained on the other. "God bless Captain Vere!"—Captain Truth. For Melville, the captain of a ship, being in absolute command as God presumably is of the universe, poses questions in essence theological. Nor does the circumambient horizon of the sea— "the intense concentration of self in the middle of such a heartless immensity," as Ishmael puts it in *Moby-Dick*—but encourage speculations of a perilous profundity. Like Billy Budd, Melville when a sailor on a man-of-war was a top-man, at home on the highest yards, enjoying the widest view. "There you stand," says Ishmael, "a hundred feet above the silent decks, striding along the deep, as if the masts were gigantic stilts, while beneath you and between your legs, as it were, swim the hugest monsters of the sea, even as ships once sailed between the boots of the famous Colossus at old Rhodes." Ishmael admits that he was sometimes an indifferent lookout, distracted as he was by "the problem of the universe revolving in me." Melville instinctively aspired to the grandest scale, and even in his shorter works offers vast inklings and the resonance of cosmic concerns.

To The Age of Innocence, *by Edith Wharton*

THE AGE OF INNOCENCE, considered by many to be Edith Wharton's best novel, was begun when the author was fifty-seven and published, in October of 1920, when she was fifty-eight. She had come to the writing vocation tardily, after an upbringing in New York society and after some years of an increasingly unhappy marriage to a Bostonian, Edward Wharton. She was twenty-nine when her first short story was published, and six more years passed before her first book, a non-fiction collaboration called *The Decoration of Houses*, appeared. Yet, as the new century settled in, she, despite the many distractions of an active social life and travel schedule, and bouts of ill health on both her and her husband's part, had settled into a daily routine of morning writing and a steady, even copious, production of fiction. *The House of Mirth* in 1905 was her first masterpiece; *Ethan Frome* (1911) and *The Custom of the Country* (1913) followed, among many other well-received, if less well-remembered, titles. Against the grain of her social class, she had become a thoroughly professional, widely read, critically esteemed writer. Still, the brilliance and fullness of *The Age of Innocence*, coming so relatively late in her career, suggest a special renewal.

For a novelist, the halls of memory and imagination are adjacent spaces. An exemplary work of fiction is generally the fruit of a new grasp the author has taken of the riches within. Toward the end of the war, in Paris, Wharton had remarked to Bernard Berenson, *"Je me cherche, et je ne me retrouve pas."* Her search for herself had been a process of many steps, beginning with her ardent exploration of her father's library in the Jones house on West 23rd Street. Edith Jones's marriage to the amiable but somewhat feckless and, in the end, mentally unstable Teddy Wharton had been another step, which had left her deeply informed on a favorite theme, the unsatisfactoriness of marriage, especially a socially presentable marriage of mismatched spirits. Teddy Wharton might have been an admirable husband for a less intellectually ambitious and formidably achieving woman than his wife; as it was, they tried each other sorely. Their sex life (for which Edith's prim and imperious mother had prepared her by telling her to look at Greek statues and exclaiming, "You can't be as stupid as you pretend") went from poor to nonexistent. Edith executed another step in her self-education by taking a lover, Morton Fullerton, in 1909. Her ties to Teddy, who on his side had turned to adultery and embezzlement from his wife's assets, weakened along with her ties to the United States; in 1911 she sold the Mount, a splendid house she had built in Lenox, Massachusetts, not ten years before, and became a Parisian. Her divorce followed two years later. World War I possessed her, as it did her adopted country; manifesting a prodigious organizational prowess, she founded and ran hostels for refugees, workshops for women unemployed because of the war, hospitals for tubercular patients, and a rescue committee for a thousand children of Flanders. Except for some battlefield journalism, later collected in *Fighting France*, her own work languished, and not just for reasons of time and energy. "These four years," she wrote in 1918, "have so much changed the whole aspect of life that it is not easy to say now what one's literary tendencies will be when the war is over." Weary of Paris, she bought a small estate twelve miles to the north, named Pavillon Colombe after the two soiled doves, Venetian actresses and courtesans, whose lovers had installed them there in the eighteenth century. In that same year of 1919, she found and leased a suitable winter home—a ruined convent on a hilltop in Hyères, on the Riviera, which an American architect promised to render habitable. "I am thrilled to the spine," Wharton wrote to a friend. "I feel as if I were going to get married—to the right man at last!"

In these new and congenial settings, then, amid the flurry of creativity with which she tackled fresh challenges of interior decoration and gardening, the writer set herself to fulfill a contract with the American magazine *Pictorial Review*, which offered the great sum of $18,000 for the serialization of a novel. Wharton always had several novels cooking at once, but she and the editors settled on a new idea. As R. W. B. Lewis explains in his biography of Wharton,

> It bore the working title "Old New York" and the scene was laid in 1875. The two main characters, Langdon Archer and Clementine Olenska, are both unhappily married. Falling in love, they "go off secretly," Edith explained, "and meet in Florida where they spend a few mad weeks" before Langdon returns to his pretty, conventional wife in New York, and Clementine to an existence, separated from her brutish husband, in Paris.

As the reader will see, the eventual *Age of Innocence* departed from this scenario in a number of particulars, including the chief characters' first names and the situation for which Florida is a background. Dividing her year amid four places of residence, including her last, extended stay in her apartment on the rue de Varenne, Wharton pushed the novel forward and delivered it on schedule, in April of 1920; Rutger Jewett, her editor at Appleton and Company, wrote her, "Do you marvel that I bow low before such energy?"

New York society had been her milieu and of course had figured in her fiction before; *The House of Mirth* and *The Custom of the Country* both dramatize the charms and cruelties of the Manhattan upper crust. But she had never before approached the topic so deliberately, with the wisdom of her (like her hero's) "readings in anthropology" and the personal sense of history which the world war had inflicted upon her. According to Berenson, she told him that "before the war you could write fiction without indicating the period, the present being assumed. The war has put an end to that for a long time. . . . In other words, the historical novel with all its vices will be the only possible form for fiction." The 1870s had been the decade of Edith Jones's growing from the age of eight to that of seventeen; in *The Age of Innocence* she reached back across the ocean toward an era long dead, as seen by a self long outgrown. Not that she had ever broken completely with her past; as Louis Auchincloss points out in his *Edith Wharton: A Woman in Her Time*, her fund-raising for her war charities had enlisted the rich old families, so that her list of directors "reads like a blue book of New York society." Distressed by much of the contemporary world, she found the nineteenth century, she wrote a friend, "a blessed refuge from the turmoil and mediocrity of today—like taking sanctuary in a mighty temple."

She set her agent and former sister-in-law, Minnie Jones, to researching the dates and details of opera performances, balls, assemblies. Her own memories fleshed out a precisely etched reconstruction of brownstone New York, of Newport before the great cottages, of Florida in a primitive, idyllic stage of development. The author's voice more than once reminds us that this is a past time, when the telephone is just a gadget and the horse-and-carriage the only conveyance. Yet the insistent historical details, including characteristically Whartonian particulars of décor and costume, do not distance or muffle the passions and intimate presence of the three principal characters: Ellen Olenska, Newland Archer, and his wife, May. Rather, the historical distance unclutters the carefully lit stage: these New Yorkers stroll up and down Fifth Avenue as if it were a village street, and are always encountering each other, in a world scarcely larger or less economically populated than the Starkfield of *Ethan Frome*. The décor is lush, but the plot is simple and its action mostly in the realm of the emotions. Though the poor and unfortunate figured in Wharton's awareness, and movingly appear in *The House of Mirth* and several short stories, the train holding Newland and May on their honeymoon trip to Rhinebeck is described as simply "shaking off the endless wooden suburbs"; no "social question" is allowed to arise and let the reader doubt the importance of how this man and his two women, amid their material comforts, dispose of their romantic needs. Wharton's wartime reading had gone back to basics—the older German literature, the Old Norse sagas, the New Testament—and the directness of myth entered her new novel.

The Age of Innocence has classic lines, and reminds us of other classics. Like *Anna Karenina*, it pulses with the sexuality of its polite, thoroughly clad protagonists, and with the awesome sacrilege of Victorian adultery. Like *The Princess of Clèves*, it embodies the romantic paradox expressed by its heroine: "I can't love you unless I give you up." Like *The Scarlet Letter*, it shows a Europeanized woman, married to a sinister older man, beckoning to a son of a Puritan society with the allurements of a richer life "over there." Like much of Henry James, and especially *The Ambassadors*, it deals with the effect of European corruption upon the purer American soul and with the terror of a man, like James's Strether, confronting the fact that he has missed "the flower of life" and is "a man to whom nothing was ever to happen." Surely James was much on Wharton's mind, as he was often a guest in her home and a passenger in her automobile, and the intense—but rarely mannered and never unclear— stylistic refinement of *The Age of Innocence* is some kind of riposte, across the English Channel, to his ghost. And, like *A Farewell to Arms*, by a third American in love with Europe, her novel ends with a man walking back to the hotel alone.

But the new sharpness and the strange poetic *steepness* revealed by the crystalline perspective of this novel owe much, I felt upon a recent rereading, to Proust. Proust and Wharton, though they lived but blocks apart and had a number of friends (including André Gide and Walter Berry) in common, never met; she was, however, among the early enthusiasts for *Swann's Way*, which came out in 1913. She and Berry had been enthralled by the book, to the point of making the names of the aristocratic Guermantes part of their vocabulary; she sent a copy to Henry James, who was slow to warm but eventually pronounced it "a new vision" by "a new master." She herself wrote, after Proust's death in 1922, that "his endowment as a novelist . . . has probably never been surpassed." By the time she was working on *The Age of Innocence*, only the second volume of Proust's immense work (*Within a Budding Grove*, in 1918) had followed the publication of *Swann's Way*, but, though the sprawling social commentary of *The Guermantes Way* was still to come, Wharton had read enough to learn his lesson of social analysis, with his flashes of comedy and presiding philosophical temper. Proust's simultaneously telescopic and microscopic view; his recognition that grandeur and absurdity co-exist; his sense of society's apparent rigidity and actual fragility—these inform Wharton's enchanted caricature of her own tribe, brought to life in her delicately farcical elaboration of Mrs. Manson Mingott's absurd girth and mansion surreally located among "the quarries, the one-story saloons, the wooden greenhouses in ragged gardens, and the rocks from which goats surveyed the scene." The van der Luydens' mummified sacerdotal status, and Lawrence Lefferts' hardworking hypocrisy, and Mr. Welland's tyrannical hypochondria, and Mrs. Lemuel Struthers' inexorable rise all have the serio-comic savor of Proustian data. Of course, the material was Edith Wharton's already, but Proust's example gave her a new angle on it, a slant both more impudent and lofty than hers hitherto; her earlier treatments of society are relatively caustic and fearful, still full of girlhood resentments. At a time in her creative life when she needed fresh direction, she learned from Proust the dignity of nostalgia and the value of each character as a specimen, an index to the species and to broad laws of behavior. She learned from him, one might say, how to leap: the impending marriage she describes, of the daughter of the kept woman Fanny Ring and the son of the old-breed Archers, spans worlds, as did Proust's marriage (still in manuscript) of Gilberte Swann, the daughter of a Jew and a courtesan, to the Marquis de Saint-Loup.

The romantic heart of *The Age of Innocence*, however, beats with an ardor that Proust might endlessly anatomize but could not persuasively re-create. Edith Wharton might be brusque and aloof in person—with a mouth, an unkind observer said, "shaped like a savings box"—but she was a writer of unstinting empathy. Her portrait here of a man in love, with his unconscious slippage, his changeable internal weathers, his resolves and irresolution and unquellable obsession, though it lacks any specifics of male lust, is extraordinary, and beautifully modulated toward its highest pitch. What could more forcefully express the mystery of erotic bewitchment than Archer's way of forgetting what Ellen looks like, and his telling her, in italics, *"Each time you happen to me all over again"*? Ellen Olenska is one of the splendid women of American fiction—alluring, conflicted, vulnerable, blithely and touchingly truthful—and we see her entirely through his eyes, in a few hurried encounters; she speaks but a sibylline modicum of words in the course of the novel. May Archer, the third principal, barely escapes the author's impulse to make her a simpleton exclusively composed of upper-class prejudices; but in a few critical scenes she is allowed to move beyond her limitations into a more generous and intuitive femininity. She is seen as a glorious young archer, literally, and, unlike Archer, she hits her targets; she *acts*. The excited and not unsympathetic warmth that exists between women—in this case, cousins—competing for the same man is conveyed, but always in indirect testimony; our masculine narrator hears of, but never overhears, May and Ellen talking. On the other hand, Wharton confidently gives us a number of stag conversations, over brandy and cigars.

The novel glitters with epigrammatic moments, sequins of comedy— "Mrs. Lovell Mingott had the high color and glassy stare induced in ladies of her age and habit by the effort of getting into a new dress"—and jewels of hard wisdom: "A woman's standard of truthfulness was tacitly held to be lower: she was the subject creature, and versed in the arts of the enslaved." The novel treasures and polishes its incidents, as Archer's mind returns to his few, infatuated glimpses of Ellen, shaping them into fetishes and precious symbols. No scene is more poignant, more memorably loaded with widening significances, than the lonely lovers' meeting in the old Metropolitan Museum, "a queer wilderness of cast-iron and encaustic tiles"; the two seek seclusion in a deserted room containing the "Cesnola antiquities," fragments of vanished Ilium. Ellen, in the awkwardness of this chaste assignation, wanders over to a case:

> "It seems cruel," she said, "that after a while nothing matters . . . any more than these little things, that used to be necessary and important to forgotten people, and now have to be guessed at under a magnifying glass and labeled: 'Use unknown.' "
> "Yes; but meanwhile—"
> "Ah, meanwhile—"

The historical perspective Wharton achieved—the passions of the past, imprisoned in the conventions of the past—widens here into an archaeological vista wherein our poor dry fragments will be someday labelled "Use unknown." Our lives, so full of feeling and yearning and egotism, and of the beauty and magnetism with which Nature equips us to accomplish her ends, are but a magnificent "meanwhile," whose most glowing possibilities must often be sealed with a renunciation. *The Age of Innocence*, beneath its fine surface, holds an abyss—the abyss of time, and the tragedy of human transience.

To Surviving: The Uncollected Writings of Henry Green

HENRY GREEN was a novelist of such rarity, such marvellous originality, intuition, sensuality, and finish, that every fragment of his work is precious, as casting a reflected light upon his achievement, the nine novels and the memoir that he published in his lifetime. There is not much uncollected Green, really; he was not a worker on Grub Street, piling up copy every week. Through the Thirties he was a man fully engaged in his business at the London office of H. Pontifex & Sons, able to produce only one novel, *Party Going*, in the decade. The Forties saw him become an auxiliary fireman in the blitz and its aftermath, with one day in three devoted to his business—in spite of all, his most productive period. In the Fifties, growing famous, he ventured out into the world of journals and the BBC, and even managed a few such extracurricular chores as a translation from the French, a paean to Venice, and a friendly note for an exhibition of Matthew Smith. But, though these peripheral compositions are interesting, and in some cases revelatory, his art and his claim to fame are all but entirely concentrated in his novels. We read these previously uncollected pieces, lovingly marshalled by his grandson, for an answer to the question the editor Edward Garnett posed to the twenty-year-old Henry Yorke after reading his first novel, *Blindness*: "How did you ever come to write any thing so good?"

In England the literary vocation is usually the prerogative of the middle class, even when, like Evelyn Waugh, the successful writer puts on upper-class airs. The Yorkes not only enjoyed a venerable aristocratic background but owned a Birmingham factory. By Green's own account, in *Pack My Bag* and the autobiographical tidbits he released in later life, he was an unprepossessing, overweight, rather sad and solitary youngster, fond of fishing and reading. At Eton, he did not do as well as his two older brothers, Philip and Gerald, and his beginning a novel while there was, according to his schoolmate Anthony Powell, "an undertaking not regarded over seriously by relations and friends." At Oxford, he was on the billiards team, drank and went to the movies a great deal, and eventually failed to graduate, allegedly because he could not learn Anglo-Saxon and "for the rest discovered that literature is not a subject to write essays about." But he did manage, while still at Oxford, to complete his novel, to show it to Edward Garnett, and to get it published by Dent in 1926. He was then twenty-one. We search his juvenile writings for clues as to his possession so young of a defined and venturesome style and an imagination that, in *Blindness*, ranges impressively beyond the mind of his schoolboy hero into the thoughts and feelings of a middle-aged woman, a defrocked and decrepit clergyman, and a young girl wasting away in unnatural isolation.

The oldest piece here, "The Type,"* which begins in the form of a play and lapses into the voice of fiction, was unearthed five years after its

---

*Omitted, finally, from *Surviving*.

composition and sent by Green to his first mentor, the young Oxford don Nevill Coghill, with a note saying, "It must be about the first thing I ever wrote and on finding it this evening it made me laugh so much I had to send it on. Really it isn't bad you know for sixteen years." In *Pack My Bag* Green remarks, "Any account of adolescence is necessarily a study of the fatuous," and yet one is struck, in this sketch of schoolboy cruelty and snobbery, by a lack of egotistic center; though Brown might be guessed to be closest to the writer, he merges with a pack of boys evoked disinterestedly, and the drama ends in the mind of the schoolmaster, Brown dismissed.

A tendency toward authorial invisibility and a universal empathy thus were early manifested; Green's juvenile effort is to create, as he when mature would consummately do in *Living, Loving*, and *Concluding*, a field of characters, mingled with their environment like small creatures coming and going in a meadow. In "Bees," the earliest published piece here, from an Eton magazine when the author was seventeen, a sunk clergyman—kin perhaps to the miserably eccentric Parson Entwistle of *Blindness*—retreats from the world of men into that of bees, a vision of adult despair carried out naïvely but with a brave completeness, right to the final ironical amorous twist, which the school authorities deleted. The adult writer's voice, in its compression and obliquity, can be already heard in an admirably pawky sentence like "He detected an insult in the butcher boy's whistling as he delivered the meat." And in the next piece chronologically, "Arcady" from 1925, the style is full at work, its cunningly limp convolutions searching for a simultaneous precision of emotion and sensation: "The air inside drooped with folded wings at the shut windows & the scent she used, sweeping through the streets that swirled in eddies of changing light, talking nervously she & I of what was coming." It is an exercise, directed to Coghill, and leaves a rather mannered and priggish impression, yet in its deflationary account of the deadness of a date of which both parties had unreal expectations—a barren night at the theatre ("Hysterical laughter when the curtain came down to cover the emptiness that was left . . . Then a scene with a bed upon the stage with the tumult of my fears storming within me")—there is, remarkable in a nineteen-year-old, that terrible tender honesty with which Green was ever to gaze at human romance. "Adventure in a Room" contains the embryo of *Blindness*; one would love to know what incident gave Green, a painterly writer of great visual acuity, his fantasy of blindness, and what frustration "exasperated" him, an advantaged youth of seemingly callow character, "into a desperate striving after the beautiful."

The two stories about giants are quaint surprises, childish and familial; yet they lead us to reflect that part of Green's unique effect, as we read his fiction, is the largeness that his diction gives his characters, a statuesque magnification achieved by the studied piling-on of some words and the withholding of others. For the first time, in "Monsta Monstrous," we see the withholding of articles, with incantatory, epic effect:

> Mountains are in Wales but he strode over these and often knocked over the tops of them, till he came where they fell before plains and sat down on the last mountain and let his feet rest in the plain, resting the toes in a river to cool them (and they were hot with knocking) and sat there looking at the smallness before him. Toes made floods immediately.

"Saturday" extends articlelessness into the sensations of a young working-class woman and the territory of his great second novel, *Living*:

> No blind was over window. Sun came by it. And she turned head over from sun toward them sleeping and did not see them. She smiled. Head on bolster was in sunshine.
> Life was in her belly. Life beat there.

The growing writer's next venture is again into the mind of a young woman, one of his own age and class, and it failed to become a novel. He discussed *Mood*, with liberal quotation, thirty years later, in the essay "An Unfinished Novel." He tells us that he was in love with the model for Constance Ightham, his heroine, and the images with which he furnishes her stream of consciousness have a variety and an assurance lacking in the almost comically primitive giant's world of Maggie Cripps, who was transformed into Lily Gates in *Living*. He may have loved Constance but didn't admire her, as he admired the rougher-hewn Maggie, and perhaps admiration for a character is more sustaining than love. At any rate, *Mood* was abandoned and *Living* became his second novel, though eventually and with visible artistic difficulty Green did incorporate in his third novel, *Party Going*, his own social set, which included (his son's memoir tells us) Aly Khan. "Excursion," with its railroad terminal and crowd confusion, seems a dry run at *Party Going*, on the plebeian level; without any of the gaudy color and giddy comedy of the upper-class interactions within the terminal hotel, the panorama stays inertly, wanly gray, though Green by this time (1932) has his style and sympathies in place.

These early pieces show, in sum, a self-effacing, broadly empathetic author assembling a style that with a seemingly casual sensitivity can register a wide range of visual, vocal, and emotional nuances. Green is unusual, for his class and nation, in his strong democratic tastes—for football and pub talk, and those experiences of factory and firefighting that broke down class barriers—and his avant-garde propensities. He was sent to France in 1923, before going to Oxford at the age of eighteen,

and along with the language he imbibed there, it seems, a certain continental approach to art: Proust and Céline were high among his artistic
heroes, and his novels never give the impression of being merely social
news. A certain abstract shimmer, a veil as it were of transcendent
intention, adds lustre to all his pictures, and piquancy to his prose. Each
paragraph has something of a poem's interest and strangeness.

The uncollected pieces of the Forties show him functioning at full tilt,
bringing to the inferno of blitzed London a descriptive power of almost
lurid virtuosity. Fire meets an ice of visual exactitude:

> Already it would have been possible to read in the reddish light spread by a
> tall building sixty yards away, the top floors of which, with abandon, in reck-
> lessness, with fierce acceptance had exchanged their rectangles for tiger-
> striped hoops, great wind-blown orange pennants, huge yellow cobra
> tongues of flame. . . . There must have been a gas main alight beneath the
> debris for whitish yellow flames were coming out, as I could now see five
> yards away round a great corner, in darker blue, of sculptured coping stone,
> curved in an arc up which this yard-high maple leaf of flame came flaring,
> veined in violet, then died, then flared again.

The prose is not easy; it must be read and read again, until the picture
comes clear. From this decade comes also Green's most considered and
passionate piece of criticism, his "Apologia" for the idiosyncratic prose of
C. M. Doughty's *Arabia Deserta*. Green exalts qualities we would not
ordinarily think of him as aspiring to: monumentality, purity, magnificence. Doughty's prose represents "the magnificent in written English";
Doughty is "harsh, simple to the point of majesty, and not clear, that
is his sentences meander." Green considers the point that the rhythms
of this prose derive from Arabic and says that others who also knew the
language—T. E. Lawrence, Gertrude Bell, Wilfrid Blunt—have "an elegance that is too easy." Doughty is not easy: "When he passes on a tale,
he treats it as a man will granite that he has to fashion." "He is often
obscure. He is always magnificent." As if to cinch this professed admiration for a meandering, majestic, difficult prose, Green ends his essay with
one of the most defiantly tangled and impenetrable sentences ever committed by a careful writer to print.*

---

*"Then, if they do learn to write in the idiom of the time, as Doughty without doubt
wrote in the idiom of the real Arabia, and not of Araby, can we at last have the silence of
those Sunday reviewers to whom, of his generation, we can almost certainly lay the charge
that he was not reprinted for thirty years, and for whom, in our own generation, we resent
the patronage they extend to us in phrases which, like those sung from the minaret on the
last page of the *Seven Pillars of Wisdom*, have, from constant repetition, only a limited
meaning even to those so deaf as to be able to hear, and none at all to those who, on read-

This yearning for the majestic surprises us but explains an enduring-ness, a resistant hardness, a something graven that distinguishes Green's prose from the lucid, efficient, common-reader prose of many of his con-temporaries; one such, Anthony Powell, recalled of his old friend Yorke that "he had a passion for Carlyle (an author tolerable to myself only in small doses), and (a taste I have never acquired) Doughty's *Arabia Deserta*; both indicated a congenial leaning towards obscure diction." This leaning would seem to be at the opposite pole from Green's marked fondness for demotic speech; but colloquial diction too, as we can see in an orgy of it like "The Lull," can be obscure, and needs to be reread for the meaning to soak in. Green might be writing of himself when he says of Doughty that in a miraculous way he "puts words together which, entering by our ears if they are read out loud, or slipping by our eyes if they are scanned in print, express their meaning in our bones." In his striving for a prose that, coming at us at an unexpected slant, penetrates to bone-deep meaning, Green was in the company of, among others, Ronald Firbank, Rose Macaulay, and Virginia Woolf. But it is Henry James he cites on "the effort really to see and really to represent, [which] is no idle business in face of the constant force that makes for muddle-ment." Though he elsewhere deplores the late James style, it seems truer of James and himself than of Doughty that "his style is mannered but he is too great a man to be hidden beneath it."

As Green was precocious so was his decline into silence premature. His last novel, the impeccable but attenuated *Doting*, was published in 1952, when he was only forty-seven. It is difficult, given the oblique invitation of its title, not to take "The Great I Eye" as autobiographical, and to con-sider its profoundly hungover hero as a pilgrim on the path of Green's own decline. The muddle of Jim's spotty memories of last night's flirta-tions, nudity, and drunkenness doesn't quite become a story; the prose loops out to include what seem stray images:

> When drunk the trouble one caused spread ripples, several dry walnuts thrown at the time into a water tank hung with green ferns; & where the ripples met, leering faces of his green friends mirrored in the base over and over again in the repeated olympic bracelets; linked arms for false amity, a symbol of old games.

Old games, perhaps, are wearing the player down, "one's body that did not forgive. Always the same. The feeling it couldn't go on like it; misery, anxiety, death death death." A casual despair flecks Green's multiplying personal statements during the Fifties: he told the *New York Herald*

---

ing the words, sigh recognition of the old trick it was on the part of Lawrence to close his book in that fashion, remembering how there is not one such in all Arabia Deserta?"

Tribune in 1950, "I write at night and at weekends. I relax with drink and conversation. In the war I was a P.F.C. fireman in London, the relaxation in fire stations was more drink and conversation. And so I hope to go on till I die, rather sooner than later. There is no more to say." *Rather sooner than later!* John Pomfret, the hero of *Nothing*, published in 1950, ends the novel by wanting "Nothing . . . nothing."

Yet Green's descriptions of the processes and strategies of writing for *The Listener* show a loving pride in his craft, and the handful of book reviews he consented to do reveal a love of the written word that was broad and voracious; he boasted of reading a novel a day. He undertook literary chores, offering *Vogue* some pages of thrillingly purple prose on Venice, and sharing with *Esquire* some alarmingly tough male thoughts on love. Having come increasingly to believe that dialogue was the best way to carry a story, he was attracted to playwriting. After *Doting*, he spent a great deal of time and energy on a political farce, *All on His Own-some*, which though it passed through several drafts was never produced; nor has it been included in this collection. Based upon the not unfamiliar conceit of one potent man left in a world of women, it seems at once hectic and static. Even Green's dialogue, without the embedding descriptions of scenes and poses, refuses to kindle into mental pictures and psychological resonance. The two unpublished short stories "The Jealous Man" and "Impenetrability" have a new, slack tone; the teller, so delicately and elusively felt a presence in his best fiction, moves to the foreground. The first story feels like a fable spun in an Oriental bazaar, and the second like a BBC chat. The BBC, which broadcast a number of talks by Green, might have done even more; surely the play *Journey Out of Spain*, with a little trimming, could have been broadcast on radio. It is a play of voices purely, with no need of scenery, and charmingly renders one of those near-disastrous yet in the end harmless and even rejuvenating scrapes that foreign travel involves. The device of the monologues is excellent, and the unexpected emergence of the Fixer into the limelight shows a touch of Green's impish social reach: "English people are O.K. but they cannot understand. Maybe they do not wish."

Green's own emergence as a *Paris Review* interview subject deserves its place here among the works of invention. His droll turn as a deaf codger is carried off with an explosive precision like that of highly honed farce:

> After fifty, one ceases to digest; as someone once said: "I just ferment my food now." Most of us walk crabwise to meals and everything else. The oblique approach in middle-age is the safest thing. The unusual at this period is to get anywhere at all—God damn!

The interviewer, Terry Southern, seems more deeply deaf than the subject; nevertheless, Green manages to enunciate a number of interesting confidences, from why he preferred to keep his writing side hidden from business associates to the way he carried in his head the *"proportions"* of a novel in progress and reworked the first twenty pages "because in my idea you have to get everything into them." His proclamation of the purpose of art is almost hierophantic: "to produce something alive, in my case, in print, but with a separate, and of course one hopes, with an everlasting life on its own." This credo returns, later in the discussion, with some specific articles of faith: if the book has a life of its own, "the author must keep completely out of the picture" ("I hate the portraits of donors in medieval triptychs") and there will be discrepancies, for "life, after all, is one discrepancy after another." Though Green gave some later interviews in which he appeared depressed and dazed, he was in good form during that session with Southern, and stated with a beautiful crispness why fiction, in its forms, must keep moving on:

> I think Joyce and Kafka have said the last word on each of the two forms they developed. There's no one to follow them. They're like cats which have licked the plate clean. You've got to dream up another dish if you're to be a writer. . . . It isn't that everything has been done in fiction—truly nothing has been done as yet, save Fielding, and he only started it all.

The interview ends with mention of a book under way, a factual account of the blitz to be called *London and Fire, 1940.* The first section of that uncompleted work, with an opening sentence very like the one Green confided to the interviewer, is this collection's last substantial item, and restores us to the flourishing Greenian universe, with its ingenuously compacted sentences—"That innocent child could never have even guessed how much of a child one fireman he saw before him was swishing past"—and its glowing full palette:

> . . . we saw a parrot coloured group of rich women and one or two men with rods and wader. The little river dark red with peat tumbled through an emerald field to the slate dark sea ribboned with white capped waves as far as a breakout in dark clouds, edged with sulphur yellow, turned a streak of waste waters below to brightest aluminium.

At its highest pitch Green's writing brings the rectangle of printed page alive like little else in English fiction of this century—a superbly rendered surface above a trembling depth, alive not only with the reflections of reality but with the consolations of art. He thought about art with a French, or modernist, concentration, and in the final pages here comes up with an un-Aristotelian statement of art's therapeutic powers: "Living one's own life can be a great muddle, but the great writers do not make it plain, they palliate, and put the whole in a sort of proportion. Which helps; and on the whole, year after year, help is what one needs." Help is what art gives us, with its "sort of proportion," and what Green gave, and gives, in those ten volumes to which this now adds a glinting, uneven, but in part priceless eleventh.

To The Best American Short Stories 1984

GIRDING MY LOINS for this editorial task, I read the collection of fifty years ago, *The Best Short Stories 1934*. It came out when I was two, and its contents were written in my infancy and perhaps conceived before I was. It contained thirty stories, selected single-handedly by Edward J. O'Brien, who also managed, from his address on Banbury Road in Oxford, to edit an annual British counterpart as well. Some of the authors whose works he reprinted in 1934 are still well remembered—William Faulkner most emphatically so. Indeed, against the general impression that Faulkner was an unappreciated author until his last years may be set the fact that throughout the Thirties and Forties, an annual *Best* without a Faulkner story in it was more the exception than the rule. Also represented in 1934 were Erskine Caldwell, Morley Callaghan, Langston Hughes, and Allen Tate (with an odd sad tale as stilted as his poetry). Some others of the honored names ring fainter bells—Manuel Komroff; Marquis Childs; Vincent Sheean; William March, author of *The Bad Seed*; Alvah C. Bessie, of the blacklisted "Hollywood Ten"; and both Whit Burnett and Martha Foley, who together edited *Story* magazine and who are one of two married couples present in the collection, since Tate's wife, Caroline Gordon, also has a short story among the thirty. A good third of the writers in that year's *Best* were quite unknown to me, though they had produced some of the collection's gems—for example, Eugene Joffe's "Siege of Love" and Alexander Godin's "My Dead Brother Comes to America." Perusal of the volume's index of "Distinctive Short Stories in American Magazines" reveals that O'Brien could have reprinted, but chose not to, "The Red Pony," by John Steinbeck, and "A Clean, Well-Lighted Place," by Ernest Hemingway, along with works by Sherwood Anderson, Gertrude Stein, Conrad Aiken, and Thomas Wolfe.

A number of the stories he did select struck this belated reader as, really, atrociously written, in a hard-breathing, toss-it-all-in style of portentous flashbacks and parenthetical urgencies more fashionable then (see Faulkner and Wolfe) than now. Zestful formal experimentation co-existed in 1934 with tame, Tarkingtonish stories of domestic misadventure. One entry (Louis Mamet's "The Pension," reprinted from *The Anvil*) was virtually a play, a little piece of agitprop set in a heartless factory of murderously defective machines. But vernacular monologue, with its dramatic ironies and oral humor, was a popular form, and rural scenes predominate, redolent of a raw poverty more shocking, perhaps, now than then. "Bad time now in America," a bankrupt immigrant tells an out-of-work stranger on a park bench. Bums and bumming were commonplace in 1934; a policeman kicks a body in Lincoln Square, and to his chagrin discovers it to be a dead body, a starved man wearing religious medals, a Roman Catholic like himself ("The Sacred Thing," by Paul Ryan). Two of the stories (Alvah Bessie's "No Final Word" and Alan Marshall's "Death and Transfiguration") harrowingly portray birth-labor under primitive conditions; in one, the mother dies, and in the other, the infant.

The Best Short Stories 1934 reflects a harsh world, but not a hopeless or narrow one. No doubt thanks in part to O'Brien's selecting hand, there is a vigorous ethnic and geographical variety: two of the stories have black heroines, another (*not* by Saroyan) concerns an Armenian community in California. The sandy coast of Florida, waiting for its boom, and the clammy marshes and decayed villages of new Hampshire's meagre coast are evoked with a specificity that puts us squarely there. Western desert rats and Southern gentry, New York jazz musicians and strong silent women of the prairie are conjured up, and there is no interchangeability of milieu or persona. Less homogenous than today's America, that of 1934 feels more consciously democratic, in the range of types and accents that authors felt empowered to bring to life. Hollywood movies of the time, of course, also embody this hopeful richness of types, each distinct to the point of caricature and functioning within the bounds of an assigned social "place," yet all nevertheless embraced by the egalitarian myth, all available to one another's admiration and imagination. In a nation still composed of more or less closed and insular regions, classes, and immigrant groups, a writer arising anywhere had something to deliver—a report to the nation at large as to conditions in Asheville, or upper Michigan, or Mississippi, or Harlem, or Fresno.

Yet it must be admitted that many of *The Best Short Stories 1934* could appear in this present selection with scarcely a jarring note and that a surprising number of this year's stories are rural or small-town in locale. Surprising, that is, because many more Americans live in cities or their suburbs than elsewhere, and the most influential short-story writers of the last decades—J. D. Salinger in the Fifties, Donald Barthelme in the Sixties, Ann Beattie in the Seventies—were all urban sensibilities. Yet urbanity, and the exhilarations of big-city life, seemed in notable recession in the short fiction of 1983, and the charms of Southern aunts and country-flavored reminiscence in notable resurgence. Perhaps Americans no longer trust and adore their cities; or perhaps most writers now live on campuses, where bucolic appearances are artificially preserved. Or the short story could be a basically conservative form. A Thirties painting or a Thirties automobile looks more dated than a Thirties story. Like women's skirts, short prose fiction can only go up and down so much, and this season we are somewhere between the racy Donald Barthelme mini and the wide-swinging Harold Brodkey maxi with its heavy folds and multiple pleats.

All of nine of *The Best Short Stories 1934* came from *Story* magazine, now long defunct. Two more came from *The American Mercury*, one from *Scribner's Magazine*, and two from *Vanity Fair*, which has recently been rendered, for a time at least, de-defunct. Some of the magazines represented—*Harper's, The Atlantic Monthly, Prairie Schooner, The Yale Review, Commonweal*—are still with us, in revised formats. Conspicuously absent from O'Brien's sources is *The New Yorker*, though the magazine was nine years old in 1934 and had turned the corner into solvency and fashionability. Arthur Kober and John O'Hara have a few *New Yorker* contributions listed in the index of also-rans, marked mostly with one star (the minimum in O'Brien's rather fussy rating system), and that's about it for the publication that has come to dominate the short-fiction market and (with the exception of John Gardner's volume) recent *Best* collections. In 1948—the inverse of our year and the one, of course, in which Orwell wrote *1984*—*The New Yorker*, with three stories to still-functioning *Story*'s two, does not loom overwhelmingly; but two of the three are classics that lent their titles to memorable books: "The Enormous Radio," by John Cheever, and "The Second Tree from the Corner," by E. B. White. Since 1980 the guest editors of this series have picked nearly half of their *Best* from *The New Yorker*. With some determination I have held my own quota to five, or one-quarter.

Fifty years have seen the number of general magazines that publish fiction greatly shrink, and the field of weekly national magazines that print fiction shrink to one. I wonder, could any young writer now support himself or herself and a family, as I did in my twenties, by selling six or so short stories a year? The magazines that pay significant (four-figure) amounts for short fiction cannot presently be more than a dozen, and of those perhaps four (*The New Yorker, The Atlantic Monthly, Esquire*, and *Playboy*) are open to what we might call artistic adventure. For Faulkner, short stories were bread and butter; for Scott Fitzgerald, in the palmy days of George Lorimer's *Post*, they were an avenue to glamorous excess. Now, for the bright young graduates that pour out of the Iowa Writers' Workshop and its sister institutions, publishing short stories is a kind of accreditation, a certificate of worthiness to teach the so-called art of fiction. The popular market for fiction has shrivelled while the academic importance of "creative writing" has swelled; academic quarterlies, operating under one form of subsidy or another, absorb some of the excess. Short fiction, like poetry since Kipling and Bridges, has gone from being a popular to a fine art, an art preserved in a kind of floating museum made up of many little magazines. The populist flavor of *Best Short Stories 1934*—the sense of a pluralistic people trying to explain themselves to themselves—is not likely to be tasted by a reader of *Best American Short Stories 1984* in the year 2034.

Enough of the past and the future. The present facts are these: Shannon Ravenel sifted out of 1,428 eligible stories published in 539 issues of 141 different periodicals a mere 120, which she forwarded to me and which I then sifted, shuffled, and squeezed to make these twenty. Nineteen, actually: I have added on my own Mavis Gallant's "Lena," because in the course of my year's casual reading I had especially liked it and because I thought a volume describing itself as "Selected from U.S. and Canadian Magazines" should contain at least one story by a Canadian. Who better to welcome from the north than the annually amazing Ms. Gallant, whose talent, exercised for many years in Parisian exile, is as versatile and witty as it is somber and empathetic?

Ms. Ravenel's batch contained two stories by me and one by my mother, Linda Grace Hoyer; I instantly disqualified myself as an interested party and set all three aside. Of what remained, I had hoped that perhaps half could be dismissed at a skimming glance; but in fact almost every one of the stories compelled a reading through to the end. I made three piles—largest to smallest, "No," "Maybe," and "Yes." I leaned away from candidates that seemed to be fragments of novels or parts of a greater whole, and also from stories that seemed to be thinly disguised memoirs, even when they were as elegant and illuminating as those by Jamaica Kincaid and Andrea Lee. I asked that something feel invented, that there be something freestanding and, if seemingly remembered, yet willfully distorted about the stories considered, whether written in the first or the third person. Even so, so many of the stories I ended up choosing were composed in the first person that I considered deviating from the traditional alphabetical-by-author order in order to distribute them, lest one many-headed ego seem to be chanting this book. But in the end the alphabetical order seemed as good as any, and to have the advantage of being patently arbitrary. Even the anthologist's lowly art must have that sacred pinch of the accidental, of the *given*. Had I arranged these myself, for instance, I might have put side by side Ms. Gallant's "Lena" and Norman Rush's "Bruns"—both character portraits in exotic settings—to point up, a bit pedantically, the sex-reversal of author and narrator in each. In an age when an unbridgeable chasm and a permanent state of war are often said to loom between the sexes, it is gratifying to observe how easily Ms. Gallant, here and elsewhere, assumes the dry, wry, faintly harried voice of a woman-baffled male, and to observe how Mr. Rush's anthropologist, curiously, *because* she speaks in such a relaxed, brusque, unsentimental, "mannish" manner, is somehow all the more persuasively female and fit to wear the large breasts she casually admits to.

Making a selection like this turns out to be a kind of Rorschach test, pulling our secret proclivities from us. I was drawn to stories about funerals and passed over a number about baseball. I would rather read about sleazy people than genteel ones. My tolerance for, in print, violence and nature description is rather high. I like those relatively rare stories that are about people at work, such as the dentist (in "Morrison's Reaction") or the young woman who, in Mary Morris's "Copies" (admired but not chosen for inclusion here), winds up happily pinned between one of her boyfriends and the flashing, throbbing, pulsing body of a color Xerox Model 2200. In a way, I want—perhaps we all want—facts, words I can picture. I want stories to startle and engage me within the first few sentences, and in their middle to widen or deepen or sharpen my knowledge of human activity, and to end by giving me a sensation of completed statement. The ending is where the reader discovers whether he has been reading the same story the writer thought he was writing. Two chains of impression have been running in rough parallel; the ending—"the soft shock at the bottom of the story, the gasp of the dimly unfolding wings of finished symmetry" (to quote another story just barely excluded from this collection, "The Dealer's Yard," by Sharon Sheehe Stark)—confirms or dissolves the imagined partnership. The ending of James Salter's "Foreign Shores," for instance, returns us not to poor passive Truus, our ostensible heroine, but to Gloria, and we realize that the story has been about her, her failures of the heart, all along. And the ending of Jeanne Schinto's "Caddies' Day," which ends this book, lifts a grubby and inconsequential-seeming scene from the underworld of childhood into timeless significance: the caddies' casual brutality and the little heroine's stubborn adherence to the menacing shack (a stickiness like that of the ants and bottles so insistently mentioned) add up to a celebration of—we venture to guess—our prepubescent pest's eventual sexuality. To explain, as I have just done, one's sensation of rightness slightly spoils it; the *echt* ending is finer than analysis. It is an inner release, as Aristotle said, of tensions aroused. A narrative is like a room on whose walls a number of false doors have been painted; while within the narrative, we have many apparent choices of exit, but when the author leads us to one particular door, we know it is the right one *because it opens*. Wright Morris's splendid "Glimpse into Another Country" shows a set of rather confusing events amiably experienced by an elderly man whose actions are themselves confused, yet at the end, when another addled person affords him recognition and lifts her hand to wave, the gesture is identified and welcomed as "assurance," and we remember that at the outset he had headed to New York for "something in the way of assurance"; we realize, furthermore, that a great deal of what might appear to be our random, inefficient, and extravagant human activity is in fact a quest for reassurance. "You're okay, right, girlie? Right?" the heroine of "Caddies" is complimented, having stoically endured her little trial. And the family of protagonists in Susan Minot's "Thorofare," having bravely executed, in seven individual styles, their bizarre ritual of disposal, feel "something lofty" in their departing procession. The good ending dismisses us with a touch of ceremony, and throws a backward light of significance over the story just read. It *makes* it, as they say, or unmakes it—a weak beginning is forgettable, but the end of a story bulks in the reader's mind like the giant foot in a foreshortened photograph.

The ending of Lee K. Abbott's "The Final Proof of Fate and Circumstance" troubled me, as having somehow too many words, and the particular disconcerting word *fellow* arriving out of the blue; but I decided that this is Mr. Abbott's blue, and that this attempt at rendering in words a father-son rapport wraps up well enough so delicate and grappling a reformulation of heroic stoicism and comradely love, in a Southern atmosphere where grown men refer to their father as "my daddy." Sexual love and its distress of the social order is a common theme of novels; the more elusive matter of comradeship, within a family or social circle, is relatively low-octane but it can comfortably propel the compact form of the short story. Mr. Abbott deals with a son's love for his father; Andre Dubus's "A Father's Story" tells of a father's for his daughter. Ms. Minot shows a family assembled to scatter a mother's ashes; Mary Ward Brown's "The Cure" assembles three daughters at a mother's deathbed. Jonathan Penner's "Things to Be Thrown Away" reveals itself, in the end, to be about the helpless love of brother for brother. Paul Bowles's "In the Red

Room" presents, at a level of understatement almost beneath thermal detection, that original hotspot, the Oedipal triangle, and Donald Justice's "The Artificial Moonlight" almost as coolly sketches that tenuous but tenacious erotic web, the group of young adult friends. In this case the friends' total history becomes a demonstration of the stunning work of time, as, like wind erosion, it slowly carves lives into unforeseeable shapes.

Time, that immense invisible in our midst, is part of the substance of narrative, as it is of music; from the standpoint of our subjectivity, death is time's ultimate fruit, and perhaps I need not be embarrassed or surprised that so many of these stories deal with death—deaths in the family, more or less close, and deaths as experienced or longed for by the subjects of Dianne Benedict's "Unknown Feathers" and Mary Hood's "Inexorable Progress." Also there were Molly Giles's "Rough Translations," whose heroine, Ramona, tries in vain to plan a good-taste funeral for herself, and Amy Hempel's "In the Cemetery Where Al Jolson Is Buried," wherein one young woman confronts another, just as young, dying in the hospital. In our heavily paved and sanitized world, death is an astounding visitor, a piece of nature that will not quite go away. Paradoxically, the merciful machinery of modern science does everything to prolong and give financial importance to dying. Several of the *Best* stories of fifty years ago dramatized how difficult it was to come into the world; a more contemporary theme seems to be how difficult it is to leave it. The heroines of "The Cure" and "Inexorable Progress" and Cynthia Ozick's "Rosa" are all burdened with life; euthanasia and gerontology figure in the Eighties short story as distinctively as live-in lovers, Little League, shopping malls, television, and rickety extended families of stepparents and stepsiblings.

Equable distribution of theme, milieu, or authors by sex or degree of fame was not one of my conscious concerns; I tried to enter each microcosm as it rotated into view and to single out those that somehow, in addition to beginning energetically and ending intelligibly, gave me a sense of deep entry, of entry into life somewhat below the surface of dialogue and description; this nebulous sense of deep entry corresponds to the sensation we get in looking at some representational paintings that render not merely the colors and contours but the heft and internal cohesion of actual objects, which therefore exist on the canvas not as tinted flat shapes but as palpables posed in atmosphere. Skill alone cannot produce this extra fidelity to the real; it needs passion. Nor is it a matter of literal realism; Kafka has it more abundantly than Zola. In this collection, "Unknown Feathers" takes us into the center of a real dying, though it is hard to know how many of the events—the wife chopping the bed legs, the nun climbing the tree—are hallucinations. Joyce Carol Oates quickly and forcefully introduces the reader into the nervous systems of her heroines but does not always bother to tie up loose ends in the "real" world that frames their tensions; in "Nairobi" we do not know exactly what Ginny has been doing with her life up to now or why Oliver needs to have a presentable companion at his meeting. We do know, however, that we are experiencing an act of prostitution, performed with the not-quite-invulnerable inner distancing whereby the prostitute preserves her dignity. The atmosphere, as in Robbe-Grillet's mechanical renderings of circumstance, is fear; the tentative "puckish kiss" at the end is pathetic. The reassurance delivered in this instance—"You were lovely up there"—is in its dimissive past tense a cold far cry from "You're okay, right, girlie?"

The inner spaces that a good short story lets us enter are the old apartments of religion. People in fiction are not only, as E. M. Forster pointed out in his *Aspects of the Novel*, more sensitive than people one meets; they are more religious. Religion and fiction both aver, with Kierkegaard, that "subjectivity is truth"; each claims importance for the ephemeral sensations of consciousness that material science must regard as accidents, as epiphenomena. Fictional technique and the craft of suspense are affected: without a transcendental ethics, of what significance are our decisions? It pleased me to hear, in "A Father's Story," the grave, responsible voice of a convinced Roman Catholic, quite free of the impishness and hysteria that so often attend this faith's manifestations in twentieth-century fiction. With no unnatural stretching, a supernatural dialogue emerges from a tawdry dilemma, an automotive mishap and its cover-up. Lena, in Mavis Gallant's more satiric world, is also a faithful Catholic, but entirely, one feels, to suit her earthly purposes and vanity. "Inexorable Progress" begins in church, and "Bruns" ends with an act of sacrifice, a saintly feat ghastly and even sadly comic in its modern context. Not just Christianity haunts these imagined spaces: Paul Bowles describes, with an eerie indirection and softness of tone, a blood-soaked private shrine; Susan Minot, a rite of water and bone and air; and Cynthia Ozick, a private religion involving rapturous and lengthy communication with one of the dead. And surely there is something numinous about the serpent ("This old snake just comes and goes when the spirit moves him") that makes itself at home in the untidy hovel of Madison Smartt Bell's "The Naked Lady."

Bell's story is the strangest in this selection, but I liked it the instant I read it, for its delicate misspellings and cheerful voice—a descendant of those vernacular voices that used to tell so many stories in this country, from Mark Twain to Ring Lardner, from John O'Hara to Eudora Welty. Bell's two heroes are no more sociologically placeable than a pair of

Beckett clowns; but their fire in the cave of being seems securely lit, and we rejoice to see their slow upward progress, like that of our remote ancestors. Ozick's "Rosa" is at the opposite pole—an exercise in several high styles, loosely translated from the Polish and the Yiddish, as well as a very funny rendering of a star-crossed courtship among feisty oldsters. It should be read, ideally, as a sequel to her much bleaker and shorter story "The Shawl," which appeared in *The Best American Short Stories 1981*. In a few minimal pages, "The Shawl" told of the infant Magda's death by electrocution on a concentration-camp fence, of the shawl that the then-fourteen-year-old Stella stole and with which Rosa, rather than be shot for screaming, stifled herself. In these hellish circumstances Rosa voted for life, and she votes again for life here, in the gaudier hell of a broiling Florida populated by lascivious homosexuals, potential muggers, and garrulous retirees from the garment industry.

> In the street a neon dusk was already blinking. Gritty mixture of heat and toiling dust. Cars shot by like large bees. It was too early for headlights: in the lower sky two strange competing lamps—a scarlet sun, round and brilliant as a blooded egg yolk; a silk-white moon, gray-veined with mountain ranges. These hung simultaneously at either end of the long road. The whole day's burning struck upward like a moving weight from the sidewalk. Rosa's nostrils and lungs were cautious: burning molasses air.

Such gorgeous prose, abrupt in rhythm and replete with metaphor, has already been had from Bellow and Malamud, Fuchs and Elkin; in a woman's hands it becomes even more highly colored, more outrageously figured. So much clotted brilliance is thinned enough to flow by injected dialogue of laconic veracity:

> "I got my own troubles," Rosa said.
> "Unload on me."

One has to love Ms. Ozick for daring a bravura style in an age when many short-story writers are as tight-lipped as cardplayers on a losing streak— in faithful reflection, no doubt, of the *Weltgeist*, the post-Vietnam cool, cautious and anti-inflationary. Experience itself, in an age when so much is reported and exposed, has been cheapened. In the stories of, say, Bobbie Ann Mason and Frederick Barthelme, the people seem to be glancing away from television at the events of their own lives with the same barely amused, channel-changing diffidence. So one is grateful to Lee K. Abbott for his own bravura style and his willingness to stand up for filial love, and to Lowry Pei, whose "The Cold Room" melts into an old-fashioned love story—guy meets girl, guy dumps other girl, guy maybe gets right girl. One sits up when Stephen Kirk, showing an alarming intimacy with dental procedures, in "Morrison's Reaction," turns a three-hour appointment into a battle as strenuous and gruesome as Beowulf's long tug on Grendel's arm. One smiles, if wistfully, when, in Rick DeMarinis's "Gent," a twelve-year-old boy comes to see that his own mother is trouble—what they used to call a hot number. This story, incidentally, was one of many told from the standpoint of children (often with baroque titles such as "The Man Who Gave Brother Double Pneumonia" and "Frankenstein Meets the Ant People") but one of the few that seemed to me to catch childhood without hyperbole or condescension and to indicate with precision the links of dependence and imperception that connect it to the adult world. Our information about each other remains, in the midst of a sophistication glut, wonderfully faulty, and for this reason we read short stories. Each is a glimpse into another country: an occasion for surprise, an excuse for wisdom, and an argument for charity.

To Writers at Work: The Paris Review Interviews, *edited by George Plimpton*

THE PARIS REVIEW interviews, of which this is the seventh hefty collection, offer the writer some special temptations: as much tape, time, and space as he or she wants to fill; interviewers more knowledgeable and pointedly interested than your usual harassed professional journalist; and the opportunity to peruse and edit the transcript, to eliminate babble and indiscretion and to hone finer the elicited aperçus. This editorial process has evolved to the point that in this volume we are told how Philip Larkin conducted his interview entirely by mail, John Barth made his shorter every time it was returned to him to make it longer, and Milan Kundera concocted his, in the interviewer's somehow enabling presence, with "typewriter, scissors and glue." Even among those writers submissive to the old-fashioned question-and-answer procedure, signs of resistance were noted. John Ashbery gave his interviewer an "impression of distraction, as though he wasn't quite sure just what was going on or what his role in the proceedings might be." Arthur Koestler complained of a cold, moaned when the tape recorder was set up, refused to be photographed, and came fully alive only when he suddenly emitted "a very peculiar noise, a wailing falsetto half-yodel" that beckoned his wife to bring more malt whiskey to lubricate his ordeal. Kundera, we are told, "hates to talk about himself," and some such disclaimer figures in almost every one of these thirteen encounters. And yet, in the thirty years since the *Paris Review* began to offer its temptations, few writers of distinction have finally resisted, and this "Writers at Work" series now forms an unparalleled roll-call of the century's literary lights. Malcolm Cowley, who heads up, by right of seniority, this present volume, in 1957 introduced the first, whose senior interviewee was E. M. Forster, whose baby was Françoise Sagan, and whose middle-aged voices included those of William Faulkner, Thornton Wilder, James Thurber, Alberto Moravia, Georges Simenon, and Nelson Algren.

As Alfred Kazin pointed out in introducing the third volume of this series, wise men such as Socrates and Buddha were interrogated in antiquity, and Boswell interviewed Johnson and Eckermann Goethe. But until the twentieth century it was generally assumed that a writer had said what he had to say in his works. Among the causes of the uneasiness so drolly noticeable in these writer-interviewer tussles is the fear, far from unjustified, that the writer's words as distractedly dictated, under random verbal prodding from a stranger, into a tape recorder will be taken as a worthy substitute for the words he has with such labor and love and hope of imperishability written down and ushered into print. Writers take words seriously—perhaps the last professional class that does—and they struggle to steer their own through the crosswinds of meddling editors and careless typesetters and obtuse and malevolent reviewers into the lap of the ideal reader. So to clutter the written record with an interview seems something of a desecration, or at the least a misuse, of language, and spendthrift besides. Also, one of the satisfactions of fiction or drama or poetry from the perpetrator's point of view is the selective order it imposes upon the confusion of a lived life: out of the daily welter of sensation and impression these few verbal artifacts, these narratives or poems, are salvaged and carefully presented. The creative writer uses his life as well as being its victim; he can control, in his work, the self-presentation that in real life is at the mercy of a thousand accidents. Philip Larkin's poetry, for instance, does not stammer, and Raymond Carver's tirelessly polished stories ("It's something I love to do," he says, "putting words in and taking words out") have nothing of the messiness of the experiences they describe. Also again: an interview, in our age of fast cultural food and the thirty-second sell, may give its consumer a sensation of duty done by that particular author. Kundera and Philip Roth, in the following pages, are especially zealous in directing attention away from themselves to their written work, and in acting as their own best critics. But any interview, however stringently controlled, and however many months go by in its adjustment and elaboration (months and months, in Roth's case), remains intrinsically informal if not chaotic and perforce grapples with the questions someone else asks rather than (as in the practice of art) the groping, truly interesting questions that one asks oneself.

Art of many sorts stems from a pose, from an unlifelike convention that releases inhibition and permits an absentee, as it were, enactment of human truths suppressed in normal social workings. Posing as Venus or Eve or Euphrosyne, a young woman in the most muffled of Victorian times could display her naked body to the artist and thence to his audience of gallery-goers. Music and the dance put on parade ecstasies otherwise confined to the intimacy of the bedroom or the prayer stall. The writer, even the lyric poet, in picking up his pen and posing at his desk, puts on a disguise that frees him to speak. Our appetite for interviews such as these thirteen derives in part from the hope that the disguise will slip, the constructed authorial persona will be poked away, and the "real" person behind the words will be as ignominiously revealed as a shapeless snail without its shapely shell. Roth (whose defense of the free-world writer against the charge of triviality is worth the price of this book in itself) takes the opportunity to explain how manipulated, how invented, how aesthetically determined are the autobiographical-seeming first-person novels that have made his fame. "What may be taken by the innocent for naked autobiography is, as I've been suggesting, more than likely mock-autobiography or hypothetical autobiography or autobiography grandiosely enlarged." The writer is an impersonator, he insists, and cites many examples, most fondly the personally generous Jack Benny's radio impersonation of a miser called Jack Benny. "It excited his comic imagination to do this," and as a writer you need to "torture and subvert" your own biography to give it "that dimension that will excite your verbal life." Edna O'Brien, when faced with the blunt question "Is the novel autobiographical?," usefully distinguishes between emotions, which the author must have experienced, and incidents, which are often fabricated—"But any book that is any good must be, to some extent, autobiographical, because one cannot and should not fabricate emotions." John Ashbery, asked if there is a close connection between life and poetry, makes a distinction along a somewhat different plane: "In my case I would say there is a very close but oblique connection. . . . I don't want to bore people with experiences of mine that are simply versions of what everybody goes through. For me, poetry starts after that point. I write with experiences in mind, but I don't write about them, I write out of them. I know that I have exactly the opposite reputation, that I am totally self-involved, but that's not the way I see it." May Sarton excitingly confides that "I'm only able to write poetry, for the most part, when I have a Muse, a woman who focuses the world for me," but quickly Platonizes the revelation: "She may be a lover, may not. In one case it was a person I saw only once, at lunch in a room with a lot of other people, and I wrote a whole book of poems." Importuned by the autobiographical question, William Maxwell calmly answers, "I don't feel that my stories, though they may appear to be autobiographical, represent an intention to hand over the whole of my life. They are fragments in which I am a character along with the others. They're written from a considerable distance. I never feel exposed by them in any way." Writers, who have developed ways of profitably using their lives and what of their world their lives permit them to see, have perhaps less than the normal need to boast and to boost the ego; the package has already been delivered. "I have always been averse to talking about myself," Ashbery simply states.

Along with our reprehensible interest in the "real" people behind the impersonations goes a curiosity about their working "secrets," the magic that has enabled them to be writers while the bulk of humanity, each soul laden with its story to tell, is denied access to print. There can be few surprises in this line: manuscript accumulates pretty much by way of the same patient labor as other products. It *is* surprising that Ashbery composes his poems right on the typewriter, and that Raymond Carver for years was so pressed for space and peace that he would write sitting in his car, and that Eugene Ionesco dictates like a pasha of industry: "I sit comfortably in an armchair, opposite my secretary. Luckily, although she's intelligent, she knows nothing about literature and can't judge whether what I write is good or worthless. I speak slowly, as I'm talking to you, and she takes it down." Unsuspected depths of the writing travail are revealed by Carver's "twenty or thirty drafts of a story" and "forty or fifty drafts" of a poem, and by Roth's six months of eight-hour days that produce at the end one page ("Usually it doesn't come to more than one page") of sufficiently lively sentences, and by Larkin's optimum average of three poems per year, and by his last fallow decade—truly his last, for Larkin, like Koestler, has died since being interviewed. With eerie prescience he serenely estimated, while still in his early sixties, "It's unlikely I shall write any more poems."

Beyond the trivial mechanics of tools and schedule, the engines of creation are difficult to inspect; Kundera's concern with musical counterpoint, John Barth's early baptism in "the ocean of rivers of stories," Roth's search for "the liveliness," Ionesco's faith in dreams as "reality at its most profound"—these fascinating sidelights do not illuminate the fierce practicality of composition, the translation of one's own interests, by way of a superior structural sense and a certain detached selflessness, into language interesting to others. The theories and enthusiasms behind significant art are available as well to intelligent artistic dullards. Ashbery, the most diffident and fatalistic of those who here discuss the artistic process from the inside, quotes Kenneth Koch: "It's rather hard to be a good artist and also be able to explain intelligently what your art is about. In fact, the worse your art is, the easier it is to talk about."

What can be talked about, with no fear of compromising one's own privacy or the private throes of imagination, is the past; these interviews seem most relaxed and valuable in their living glimpses of figures now legendary. Who now, besides Malcolm Cowley, is left to describe how "You forgave Hart [Crane] a great deal because he was so kind and helpful. But then he'd get drunk and start throwing furniture out of the window. Or he'd stagger around the house with a lighted kerosene lamp"? In a few offhand words Cowley brings Hemingway, Faulkner, Pound, Fitzgerald, and Ford Madox Ford back to human scale, wheezing after girls, telling stories in the backwoods manner, sneaking alcohol in the kitchen, filling a room with their enthusiasms. Few of us can look forward to being a "national scholarly resource" on Cowley's scale, but we all become living archives, witnesses to what can be no longer witnessed. Koestler, asked if his friend George Orwell was a happy man, testifies with startling force: "That was the last thing he was." Maxwell remembers the old *New Yorker* art meetings, when Harold Ross would "lean forward and peer at the drawing with his lower lip sticking out." May Sarton saw Virginia Woolf enter a party in London: "She came into the room like a dazzled deer and walked right across—this was a beautiful house in Regent's Park—to the long windows and stood there looking out. My memory is that she was not even introduced at that point, that she just walked across, very shyly, and stood there looking absolutely beautiful." Tristan Tzara is a name that, for Americans at least, has all but melted into cultural history; but Ionesco movingly recalls: "I met Tzara at the very end of his life. He, who had refused to speak Romanian all his life, suddenly started talking to me in that language, reminiscing about his childhood, his youth, and his loves." Even the close-mouthed Larkin loosens up when he remembers the youthful Kingsley Amis and his funny faces, "his Edith Sitwell face, and so on." A whole lost world of New York poets comes back in Ashbery's recalling:

Actually the one poet I really wanted to know when I was young was Auden. I met him briefly twice after he gave readings at Harvard, and later on in New York saw a bit of him through Chester Kallman who was a great friend of Jimmy Schuyler's but it was very hard to talk to him since he already knew everything. I once said to Kenneth Koch, "What are you supposed to say to Auden?" And he said that about the only thing there was to say was "I'm glad you're alive."

And out of her conjugal acquaintance with Robert Lowell, Elizabeth Hardwick distills a revealing sexual insight: "He liked women writers and I don't think he ever had a true interest in a woman who wasn't a writer— an odd turn-on indeed and one I've noticed not greatly shared."

It is the female interviewees in these pages who, perhaps not surprisingly, most warmly extol literature in general. Hardwick testifies: "As I have grown older I see myself as fortunate in many ways. It is fortunate to have had all my life this passion for studying and enjoying literature and for trying to add a bit to it as interestingly as I can. This passion has given me much joy, it has given me friends who care for the same things, it has given me employment, escape from boredom, everything. The great gift is the passion for reading. It is cheap, it consoles, it distracts, it excites, it gives you knowledge of the world and experience of a wide kind. It is a moral illumination." Edna O'Brien remembers with rapture her first encounters with the writing of Hemingway, Joyce, and Woolf; she regrets that "literature is no longer sacred" and ends by asserting that it is (at the least) "the next best thing to God." May Sarton also speaks of her poetry in religious terms: "In the inspired poem something is given," and each new surge of her poetry requires a Muse whereby "the deepest source is reached." The men are more guarded (and none is quite as willingly shrewd and amusing as Miss Hardwick in discussing the writings of others, the "literary scene"), but each of them at some point lets slip a pledge of allegiance, a confession of pleasure and pride that circumstances have enlisted him in this vocation:

COWLEY: Writing becomes its own reward. What do you need from others—except a little money—if you have satisfied the stern critic in yourself?

KOESTLER (*Stands and walks to bookcase*): Whenever I get depressed, which I often do, I come over here and look at this. My comforter. If ever I wonder what on earth it was all for, here is the evidence. The thirty books I've written plus all the translations.

MAXWELL: If you get it all down there's a serenity that is marvelous. I don't mean just getting the facts down, but the degree of imagination you bring to it. . . . Writing fiction was, and still is, pure pleasure.

LARKIN: I can't understand these chaps who go round American universities explaining how they write poems: it's like going round explaining how you sleep with your wife.

IONESCO: People who don't read are brutes.

ASHBERY: Of course, my reason tells me that my poems are not dictated, that I am not a voyant. I suppose they come from a part of me that I am not in touch with very much except when I am actually writing. The rest of the time I guess I want to give this other person a rest, so that he won't get tired and stop.

KUNDERA: A novel is a meditation on existence, seen through imaginary characters. The form is unlimited freedom. Throughout its history, the novel has never known how to take advantage of its endless possibilities.

BARTH: Nearly every writer I know was going to be something else, and then found himself writing by a kind of *passionate default.* . . . After I had written about a novel's worth of bad pages, I understood that while I was not doing it well, *that* was the thing I was going to do.

ROTH: What I want is to possess my readers while they are reading my book—if I can, to possess them in ways that other writers don't. Then let them return, just as they are, to a world where everybody else is working to change, persuade, tempt, and control them. The best readers come to fiction to be free of all that noise, to have set loose in them the consciousness that's otherwise conditioned and hemmed in by all that *isn't* fiction.

CARVER: Good fiction is partly a bringing of the news from one world to another. That end is good in and of itself, I think. . . . It just has to be there for the fierce pleasure we take in doing it, and the different kind of pleasure that's taken in reading something that's durable and made to last, as well as beautiful in and of itself.

Such testimonials to the intrinsic worth and beauty of their activity are worth eliciting, in an age when so many men and women resent their work and regard it ironically. An artist of any sort, in our society and most others, is a privileged person, allowed to stand apart from some of the daily grind and supposed to be closer to the gods, the divine sources of tribal well-being. Once upon a time everyone participated in the dance, and submitted to the signifying tattoo. As the gods recede, the distances between the artist and the other tribal members grow greater, and to lessen the distance, perhaps, interviews like these are sought and, however uneasily, granted.

To Writers on Writers, *compiled by Graham Tarrant*

WRITERS, those self-consuming solitaries, are fascinated by other writers. They know how curious and, in the sought-for fusion of word and thing, arduous the trick of their trade is, and yet how commonly available the tools are—a little learning, a little imagination. They eye each other with a vigorous jealousy and suspicion. They are swift to condemn and dismiss, as a means of keeping the field from getting too crowded. To Rebecca West, Evelyn Waugh was "a disgusting common little man." Thomas Carlyle confided to his diary of Charles Lamb, "A more pitiful, rickety, gasping, staggering, stammering tomfool I do not know." According to Lord Byron, Robert Southey was "a dirty, lying rascal," and according to Robert Southey, Percy Bysshe Shelley was "a liar and a cheat" who "paid no regard to truth, nor to any kind of moral obligation."

All these condemnations are skimmed from the first pages of Graham Tarrant's piquant and savory anthology. Such keen appraisals are based, one gathers, not just on perusal of a rival's works but on personal acquaintance, and in this respect the English writers have an advantage over their American counterparts, who inhabit a larger and less clubbable country. True, for a few years in the middle of the last century the social circles of Hawthorne, Melville, and Emerson intersected; but of the three only Melville hungered for the rub of genius on genius. Hawthorne was a natural recluse and Emerson's relations with even his disciple Thoreau were a bit wary and lofty. Melville felt it a flaw in Emerson that he emanated "the insinuation that had he lived in those days when the world was made, he might have offered some valuable suggestions." The remark is coolly catty; cattiness in general eludes the heavy-pawed Americans. Emerson thumped Swinburne as "a perfect leper and a mere sodomite," Pound likened Chesterton to "a vile scum on a pond," and Dorothy Parker put away Somerset Maugham with "That old lady is a crashing bore." Henry James came closer to the right drawled note in his description of Carlyle as "the same old sausage, fizzing and sputtering in his own grease." James Russell Lowell's verdict on Pope, "careless thinking carefully versified," is a handsome put-down, though it doesn't make us laugh with its justice, as does Cyril Connolly's saying of George Orwell, "He would not blow his nose without moralising on the state of the handkerchief industry."

A writer, it could be, takes less comfort in being praised (the reviewer was fooled or lazy, possibly) than in a colleague's being panned. I enjoyed this assemblage of choice quotations an indecent amount, considering that nine-tenths of them are uncomplimentary or adverse. Familiars of the mysteries of the literary trade are inhibited by no mystique or timid reverence for other adepts; it takes one to know one, as the saying goes. How beautifully *seen*, for example, is V. S. Pritchett's evocation of William Butler Yeats descending the stairs with his "short, pale and prescient nose" and a birdlike air "suggesting one of the milder swans of Coole and an exalted sort of blindness." Just above it on the page we have Edith Sitwell's very vivifying vision of D. H. Lawrence as "a plaster gnome on a stone toadstool in some suburban garden" and "a bad self-portrait by Van Gogh," with "a rather matted, dank appearance . . . as if he had just returned from spending an uncomfortable night in a very dark cave." Sitwell in turn was seen through Dylan Thomas's Blakeian eyes as "a poisonous thing of a woman, lying, concealing, flipping, plagiarising, misquoting, and being as clever a crooked publicist as ever." Her latest book is to him her "latest piece of virgin dung." To Samuel Johnson, Rousseau was simply "a very bad man."

From the admission that a good writer might be a scoundrel it is but a short step to the speculation that a writer is *necessarily* something of a scoundrel. A raffish and bitter scent clings to the inky profession. Seeing truly and giving the human news frankly are both discourtesies, at least to those in the immediate vicinity. The writer's value to mankind irresistibly manifests itself at some remove of space and, often, time. In the meantime, his or her contemporaries are apt to see in him or her a bore, a charlatan, a sneak, an idler, a snob, a drunk. It is not just social friction or personal envy that gives the sharp edge to so many of the following appraisals; writers, with their own inside experience of poetry and fiction, are especially quick to sniff out the personality behind the writings of another. Noël Coward detected in John Osborne "a conceited, calculating young man blowing a little trumpet." Osborne, having viewed two of Shaw's greatest plays, pronounced him "the most fraudulent, inept writer of Victorian melodramas ever to gull a timid critic or fool a dull public." Neither pronouncement is fair, but, then, fairness becomes a secondary issue on any battlefield.

Writing is life and death to writers. An intense competition rages for the pale limelight of literary publicity and for the never-large and presently dwindling body of serious readers. To be sure, there are some generous words in this array: Jack London expresses his surprising debt to Kipling, Valéry his startlingly high opinion of Poe, Tolstoy his tender feelings toward Chekhov, Raymond Chandler his respect for Somerset Maugham. But the section "Praise Be!" is a brief bland course almost lost in the midst of a peppery feast, affording the reader a chance to refresh his palate for the next wave of stinging delicacies. Not even Virgil, Dante,

Shakespeare, and Goethe are spared the hot sauce. A greater number of acute comments on literary matters and persons will scarcely be found in six dozen tomes of studious criticism, and Mr. Tarrant is to be complimented upon his locating in the vast gravel-beds of word-minded words so many gems.

To Heroes and Anti-Heroes, *a collection of photographs by members of the Magnum Photo-Journalists' Coöperative*

THE POST-WAR ERA, with its intricate avoidance of global holocaust and its many shades of political gray, has not conduced to the creation of heroes and anti-heroes. Che Guevara, for instance, would seem to have been a hero to the photographer, Elliott Erwitt, who caught his youthful and lightly bearded face bathed in the unabashed radiance of Hollywood publicity stills, but to others he was, as he seems in the image by René Burri, a tousled-haired kid mischievously playing at soldier while brandishing a cigar in imitation of his big brother. Mao Zedong projected a heroic image, all right, which we can see here in its Long March guise and in its head-of-state maturity, in proximity to a still-youthful Deng Xiaoping. But, since the great Chairman's demise, revulsion has been expressed within China as well as without at some of his revolutionary measures, and the moment when Mao was an idol to university students from Berkeley to Burma seems forever by. We are attracted, rather, as "truer to life," to the unposed profile captured by New China Pictures, in which the Chairman seems curiously soft and semi-formed, chinless and doll-like. A still-living political figure frequently caught in Magnum's focus is the irrepressibly pop-eyed and chronically unshaven Yassir Arafat, with a heap of striped cloth spilling from his head; it is hard to picture any turn in world events which will make him appear, visually, heroic.

Faces tell us less about good and evil than we imagine. Much of our response to an image of a personality is preconditioned. Without knowing anything of these men's history, we might pick Klaus Barbie as the most distinguished and benign physiognomy in this array, and we would certainly be touched by the tender images of Stalin carrying his young daughter Svetlana and of Hitler reaching out to the little girl who has apparently just given him a bouquet. There are not many evil-looking men here, and most of them are American Presidents—Nixon as a black-hatted gangster, Johnson and Humphrey posed behind the podium in a sly clench of dissimulation, Herbert Hoover exuding white-tie arrogance as millions stand in breadlines. The handsomest men, to my eye, are not the movie stars but the industrialist Gianni Agnelli, South Africa's Minister of Foreign Affairs R. Pik Botha, and the pro-Nazi magnate Alfred Krupp, with his industrious minions and Mephisthophelean glower. The ugliest, most grotesquely creased and reptilian visage herein belongs to the book's one saint, Mother Teresa. Some of the hero/villain oppositions posed by this book's make-up are studies in ambiguity. Allende and Pinochet wear a kindred grimness. Saddam Hussein and Bush both look starry-eyed and less than real. And Winnie Mandela—does she look like a heroine, anti-heroine, or both?

If our era has trouble generating heroes and anti-heroes, the camera is one of the reasons—along with television and the endlessly prying free press, it brings us too close to our living leaders and artistic stars, shows us their moles, their dewlaps, their foolish flashbulbed on-camera grins, and their shifty eyes and full mouths in moments of violated privacy. We see they are not icons. In the olden days of monarchies, royal images circulated only as profiles on coins, and nothing was minted that would overhumanize the subject. When I was in college, T. S. Eliot was represented in anthologies almost invariably by the same expressionless profile; my colleague Philip Roth repeats one stern photograph on jacket after jacket with a kindred sacralizing effect. Throughout the Soviet Empire, in its pre-Gorbachev stability, the image of Lenin was distributed very widely but with a distinct narrowness of expression and pointed sameness of salient attributes—the jaunty goatee, the bald dome, the steely gaze with its bead on the coming workers' paradise. It is an image all edges, with which to slice up the future.

Some of these Magnum images, often those we have seen reproduced before, do present an iconic force, a realer-than-real crystallization that stamps itself on our memory. Camus, Faulkner, and Matisse by Cartier-Bresson, Mishima by Elliott Erwitt, Jomo Kenyatta by Ian Berry, Billy Graham by Arnold, Sartre and Simone de Beauvoir by Barbey, a wonderfully puzzled-looking Einstein by Ernst Haas, an at-attention Ike by Wayne Miller, and a wailing Joplin by Elliot Landy. Cornell Capa caught a doubly iconic image of President John Kennedy and, in foreboding foreground profile, his successor, Lyndon Johnson, with the Presidential seal in central focus. Our knowledge of the abrupt assassination that will in an instant transfer the power of the seal from one man to the other enters into the photograph, and becomes part of its aesthetic force. Would Gilles Peress's dramatically shadowed portrait of Salman Rushdie strike us quite so strongly without our knowledge of the engulfing shadows that have subsequently hidden this author from sight? A few very photogenic men, like Rushdie, Churchill, and the Ayatollah Khomeini, are consistently iconic in the image they project. In the photograph by Abbas, the Ayatollah looms above the dowdy other Iranians in the photo with a higher order of vividness—so much so that we check his edges to make sure he is not a cardboard cutout, a mounted poster.

We live in an age of images, of signs. Castro's beard and cigar seen from below, Khrushchev's bald head seen from behind, de Gaulle's *képi* seen from above are enough to identify them. Charlie Mingus and Pablo Casals are subsumed by the photographer in the stringed instruments they mastered. The reality and the image become interchangeable: Anwar Sadat is hidden by microphones but his iconic self stands forth above his head; Jesse Jackson's exuberant arms-up gesture occurs simultaneously with its broadcast version on television. Photographs of images of Tito, Reagan, and Gandhi serve, in this book, for photographs of the men themselves. Guy Le Querrec very wittily captures the business of image-making in operation, as he shows Mitterrand reading the newspaper while the sculptor extracts his head from the cerebral activity and from the tangled heroics on the tapestry behind him. In a number of portraits a peculiar poignance is generated by the juxtaposition of a living person with a visual artifact—Borges and a blind-looking bust, Spiro Agnew and a less beamish Abraham Lincoln, Picasso appearing angry and stunted next to a slave by Michelangelo, Berenson looking beatific over the hip of a reposing Venus.

Though the camera can catch indelible images, its basic procedures work against heroism. It has a democratic and inclusive eye; it is no respecter of celebrities. Again and again, studying these pictures of the famous, our eyes go to the side, to the faces caught by accident in the frame. Nasser and Castro, at the height of their pride as Third World gadflies and glamour-boys, walk down a street in New York, and it is the deadpan policemen guarding them, and the sullen anonymous faces pressed into the telephoto shot with them, that pique our curiosity. Elsewhere, Sadat and Arafat sit upon a stage; are those watchful men behind them the bodyguards who will so dismally fail to protect Sadat not long hereafter? President Nkrumah of Ghana shakes hands with an African chief, but our eye goes to the anxious young face between them, with his tilted pillbox hat and embroidered caftan and elegant eye-whites. Khrushchev, ruler of world Communism, comes to Hollywood, and it is the perky actress, a girlish Shirley MacLaine, daring to pat his bald forehead, whom the camera "loves," as they say—she, and the amiably bored Louis Jourdan gazing off the photograph's edge. Who is that man stepping out so smartly behind Adolf Hitler? Who are those chunky giggling women flanking Yuri Gagarin? Who, for that matter, is the young dog stretching itself behind William Faulkner's back, and that kitten on Albert Schweitzer's wrist? Our eye, like a kitten, is drawn toward the liveliest spot on a photograph, the spot in motion, and that is often not the subject's face. The portrait painter of old directed our attention along the proper flow-lines, and combed superfluous energy out of the canvas. As on a theatrical stage, everything in the painting was a prop, with its assured use.

But a photograph can't help taking in the surroundings, the setting, and these trappings can frame the hero in absurdity. The Pope dwarfed by his limousine, the Shah by his throne and robes, Hirohito by the stadium in which he is emerging like a mole in a morning coat—the comedy of grand eminence makes us irreverent. Eichmann and his empty chair, like a terrible contaminant surrounded by curtains, arouses another emotion, a Beckettian dread, an inkling of deadly emptiness. James Dean asleep before a floodlit mansion out of cinematic dreamland, Nelson Rockefeller good-naturedly coping with the garbagy indignation of some constituents—these images also have a surreal aptness. Politicians usually work in a crowd, and musicians too; there is a natural pictographic drama that, for Herbert von Karajan and Mick Jagger, comes with the job. And it seems effortlessly fitting, too, to capture Walt Disney in Disneyland, Dr. Spock with a child, Churchill on a landing craft, and Maurice Chevalier near the Arc de Triomphe. Landscape, oddly, figures in rather few of these images; the great and famous function mostly in cities. Pasternak sulking at Peredelkino and the Nixons throwing bizarre shadows among the pyramids do set off Nature to some effect, engendering a visual subtext concerning space and freedom: Nixon and Pasternak, in their different ways, are not free. In one of the few photographs here where color really adds something, a violet Himalayan mountainscape in the background mystically sets off the figure of the Dalai Lama.

The concept of heroism belongs to a world of black-and-white, a world that ebbed after 1945. Once color became the rule for Hollywood motion pictures, they ceased to throw off stars with the lambent crispness and marmoreal beauty of Gable, Cooper, Crawford, Garbo, and those dozens of other divinities etched on the skyey screen in platinum and carbon. And once peace, however uneasy, descended upon the globe, heroes and anti-heroes became harder to find. To anyone with a memory of World War II, heroism and wickedness—good and evil embodied—are live categories. Heroes abounded, from the RAF pilots of the Battle of Britain to the Marines and infantrymen who fell to Axis bullets at Guadalcanal and Stalingrad. The leaders of that epic conflict were heroic—Churchill and Roosevelt both ringingly eloquent, unflinchingly self-confident, lordly in their righteousness as they opposed the diabolical and implacable Hitler, whose black deeds outraced even the calumnies of war propaganda; for the slaughterhouse thoroughness of his Final Solution, and his final frenzied disregard of the German people he had led into ruin, were not fully revealed until the war ended. Around Hitler a rabble of lesser devils teemed, as colorful as comic-book villains—fat vain Goering, tiny shrill Goebbels, pale wispy Himmler, drooling anti-Semites like Streicher, crazy men like Hess, and merciless monocled Prussian generals, not to mention that ridiculous bully Mussolini and the subhuman Japanese automatons led by Tojo.

Even at the hottest passages of the Cold War—Greece, Korea, the Berlin Blockade, the Cuban Missile Crisis, the various spy trials and exposés, Vietnam, Afghanistan—devil-theories did not dominate diplomatic relations or, I believe, the popular mentality. Perhaps Americans had too recently, in the war against Hitler, seen the Russians as fellow-heroes to cast them as anti-heroes. And there was something disarming, on both sides, about the geographical amplitude both the superpowers enjoyed, with so much of the world, except at the Bering Strait, between them. And of course the fact of atomic weapons was a great inhibitor. For whatever combination of reasons, real enmity—the sanctioned hatred and black-and-white stylization that the war spirit needs—did not exist between the Russians and Americans. They had seen too many of our movies, perhaps, and we had read too many of their novels. Stalin, for all the rumored and real atrocities he inflicted upon the Soviet people, was a somewhat ambiguous figure, with a twinkle in his eye and a curve to his mustache. The anonymous 1923 photograph of the newly elected General Secretary captures a curious delicacy, an abstracted distance. The odor of idealistic intentions never quite left him. Khrushchev, even while he was banging his shoe and threatening to bury us, was lovable, really, and Brezhnev seemed a good old boy, a crafty power broker with whom Nixon felt more camaraderie than with most of his fellow-Americans. Nixon has recently become the hero of an opera, and his kind of heroism—a knot of inner conflicts, tensions, and contradictions enlarged upon the worldwide publicity screen—is what the post-war years can offer. Gorbachev could be cast as such a hero, but not Reagan.

As the Cold War melts, consider a personage like General Wojciech Jaruzelski, photographed at stiff attention by Bruno Barbey. Hero? Not to us, or to most Poles. Anti-hero, then? Well, it could be said that he took the steps necessary to save Poland from losing what independence she had at the time, and without which there would be no transition to the better, freer Poland that exists. His face is a prim and rather blank face, a bit like Eichmann's, a bit like Jean Genet's. Its moral shade is as in-between as the tint of his sunglasses. The faces of political leaders almost never look evil, because all leaders think they are doing the right thing. A private individual, raised with the Ten Commandments and a bourgeois superego, may experience guilt over some actions, and even the steady self-dislike that warps a visage; an artist might be painfully conscious of plagiarism and selling out, and grow a visible cloud on his expression. But national leaders, immersed in contending pressures, daily faced with choices all of which have a "down side" adversely affecting thousands if not millions, can commit mistakes but not, in the realm of their decision-making, sins. Even Hitler's plunges into genocide figured in his mind as measures beneficial to his chosen constituency, the German "Aryan" people. We have no photograph here of Pol Pot, but if there were one, his face would no doubt be serene, numbed by the chloroform of sincere doctrine and settled policy. The most murderous leader in this volume, Hitler and Stalin and Mao excepted, must be Idi Amin, and it is true that, as photographed by Abbas, he does look menacing, and his uniform megalomaniacal. Yet his predecessor and successor, Dr. Milton Obote, wears a menace of his own, and in fact both men permitted and urged horrors in the miserable history of warfare among the tribes of Uganda.

History, as we now conceive it, is anti-heroic—a matter, for historians of the annalist school, of the little anonymous lives, of market records and statistics, of life-styles and technology. The study of "great men" savors now of the barbaric, the credulous, the regressive. No more Napoleons, no more Davids to paint them on horseback. Instead, grindingly dull memoirs as an eventual fruit of office, and in the meantime a mob of paparazzi popping away during scheduled photo opportunities.

It may be better so. Heroes and anti-heroes are created by our need for them; this need arises in times of emergency, despair, and martial rallying. If we, and the cameras in the skillful hands of Magnum's world-roving photographers, see relatively few heroes around, the shortage should not be too loudly mourned. The times that breed heroes are trying times for the unheroic multitudes. A reluctance to confer the adoration that makes heroes, and to feel a blind hatred for opponents and rivals, augurs a growth of judiciousness and empathy within the run of mankind, and an advance for the civil co-existence that we all, on this shrinking planet, must try to encourage.

To The Art of Mickey Mouse,
edited by Craig Yoe and Janet Morra-Yoe

IT'S ALL IN THE EARS. When Mickey Mouse was born, in 1927, the world of early cartoon animation was filled with two-legged zoömorphic humanoids, whose strange half-black faces were distinguished one from another chiefly by the ears; Felix the Cat had pointed triangular ears and Oswald the Rabbit—Walt Disney's first successful cartoon creation, which he abandoned when his New York distributor, Charles Mintz, attempted to swindle him—had long floppy ears, with a few notches in the end to suggest fur. Disney's Oswald films, and the Alice animations that preceded them, had mice in them, with linear limbs, wiry tails, and ears that are oblong, not yet round. On the way back from New York in the train, having left Oswald enmeshed for good in the machinations of Mr. Mintz, Walt and his wife, Lillian, invented another character, based—the genesis legend claims—on the tame field mice that used to wander into Disney's old studio in Kansas City. His first thought was to call the mouse Mortimer; Lillian proposed instead the less pretentious name Mickey. Somewhere between Chicago and Los Angeles, the young couple concocted the plot of Mickey's first cartoon short, *Plane Crazy*, co-starring Minnie and capitalizing on 1927's Lindbergh craze. The next short produced by Disney's fledgling studio—which included, besides himself and Lillian, his brother, Roy, and his old Kansas City associate, Ub Iwerks—was *Gallopin' Gaucho*, and introduced a fat and wicked cat who did not yet wear the prosthesis that would give him his name of "Pegleg Pete." The third short, *Steamboat Willie*, incorporated that brand-new novelty, a sound track, and was released first, in 1928. Mickey Mouse entered history, as the most persistent and pervasive figment of American popular culture in this century.

His ears are two solid black circles, no matter the angle at which he holds his head. Three-dimensional images of Mickey Mouse—toy dolls, or the papier-mâché heads the grotesque Disneyland Mickeys wear—make us uneasy, since the ears inevitably exist edgewise as well as frontally. These ears properly belong not to three-dimensional space but to an ideal realm of notation, of symbolization, of cartoon resilience and indestructibility. In drawings, when Mickey is in profile, one ear is at the back of his head like a spherical ponytail, or like a secondary bubble in a computer-generated Mandelbrot set. We accept it, as we accepted Li'l Abner's hair always being parted on the side facing the viewer. A surreal optical consistency is part of the cartoon world, halfway between our world and that of pure signs, of alphabets and trademarks.

In the sixty-five years since Mickey Mouse's image was promulgated, the ears, though a bit more organically irregular and flexible than the classic 1930s appendages, have not been essentially modified. Many other modifications have, however, overtaken that first crude cartoon, born of an era of starker stylizations. White gloves, like the gloves worn in minstrel shows, appeared after those initial Twenties movies, to cover the black hands. The infantile bare chest and shorts with two buttons were phased out in the Forties. The eyes have undergone a number of changes, most drastically in the late Thirties, when, as some historians mistakenly put it, they acquired pupils. Not so: the old eyes, the black oblongs with a nick of reflection in the sides, *were* the pupils; the eye-whites filled the entire space beneath Mickey's cap of black, its widow's peak marking the division between these enormous, all-but-merged oculi. This can be seen clearly in the face of the classic Minnie: when she bats her eyelids, their lashed shades lower over the full width of what might be thought to be her brow. But all the old animated animals were built this way, from Felix the Cat on; Felix had lower lids, and the Mickey of *Plane Crazy* also, ringing in the enormous eyeballs that rest upon the animal snout. So it was an evolutionary misstep that—beginning in a 1938 ornamentation, by Ward Kimball, on the program for a company field day—replaced the shiny black pupils with entire oval eyes, containing pupils of their own. No such mutation has overtaken Pluto, Goofy, or Donald Duck. The change brought Mickey closer to us humans, but also took away something of his vitality, his alertness, his bug-eyed cartoon readiness for adventure. It made him less abstract, less iconic, more merely cute and dwarfish. The original Mickey, as he scuttles and bounces through those early animated shorts, was angular and wiry, with much of the impudence and desperation of a true rodent. He was gradually rounded to the proportions of a child, a regression sealed by his Fifties manifestation as the genius of the children's television show *The Mickey Mouse Club*, with its live Mouseketeers. But most of the artists in this album of recent takes on the image, though too young to have grown up, as I did, with the old form of Mickey, have instinctively reverted to it; it is the bare-chested primal Mickey, with his yellow shoes and oval buttons on his red shorts, who is the icon, beside whom the later Disney version is a mere mousy trousered pipsqueak.

Minnie Mouse, with eyes at half-mast

A. Mickey as he appeared in Plane Crazy *(1928) with goggle eyes.* **B.** *Mickey in animated cartoons of the early Thirties, with solid oblong pupils.* **C.** *Mickey with eye rims and nicked pupils, in graphic art of the early Thirties.* **D.** *Without eye rims, in a comic strip of 1934, drawn by Floyd Gottfredson.* **E.** *Mickey with oblong humanoid eyes, as invented by Ward Kimball, on a studio outing invitation in 1938.* **F.** *Mickey in a comic strip of the Seventies, with eyes devolving toward earlier shape.*

His first manifestion had something of Chaplin to it: he was the little guy, just over the border of the respectable. His circular ears, like two minimal cents, bespeak the smallest economic unit, the overlookable democratic man. His name has passed in the language as a byword for the small, the weak—"a Mickey Mouse operation" means an undercapitalized company or a minor surgery. Children of my generation—wearing our Mickey Mouse watches, playing with our Mickey Mouse dolls, following his running combat with Pegleg Pete in the daily funnies, going to the local movie-house movies every Saturday afternoon and cheering when his smiling visage burst onto the screen to introduce a cartoon— felt Mickey was one of us, a bridge to the adult world of which Donald Duck was, for all of his childish sailor suit, an irascible, tyrannical member. Mickey didn't seek trouble, and he didn't complain; he rolled with the punches, and surprised himself as much as us when, as in *The Little Tailor*, he showed a warrior resourcefulness and won, once again, a blushing kiss from dear, virtually identical Minnie. His modest, decent nature meant that, as Disney's mythopoeic Golden Age yielded to its slicker Silver, Mickey would yield the starring role to combative, sputtering Donald Duck and to Goofy, with his gawshes and gawkiness. Save for an occasional comeback like the Sorcerer's Apprentice episode of *Fantasia*, and 1990's rather souped-up semi-short *The Prince and the Pauper*, Mickey was through as a star by 1940. But, as with Marilyn Monroe when her career was over, his life as an icon gathered strength. The America that is not symbolized by that imperial Yankee Uncle Sam is symbolized by Mickey Mouse. He is America as it feels to itself—plucky, put-upon, inventive, resilient, good-natured, game.

Like America, Mickey has a lot of black blood. This fact was revealed to me in conversation by Saul Steinberg, who, in attempting to depict the racially mixed reality of New York streets for the super-sensitive and race-blind *New Yorker* of the 1960s and '70s, hit upon scribbling numerous Mickeys as a way of representing what was jauntily and scruffily and unignorably there. From just the way Mickey swings along in his classic, trademark pose, one three-fingered gloved hand held on high,

Mickey in his jiving mood, strutting onstage

he is jiving. Along with round black ears and yellow shoes, Mickey has soul. Looking back to such early animations as the Looney Toons' Bosko and Honey series (1930–36) and the Arab figures in Disney's own *Mickey*

Mickey in full turban in Mickey in Arabia, *1932*

in Arabia of 1932, we see that blacks were drawn much like cartoon animals, with round button noses and great white eyes creating the double arch of the curious widow's-peaked brows. Cartoon characters' rubberiness, their jazziness, their cheerful buoyance and idleness all chimed with popular images of African Americans, already embodied in minstrel shows and in Joel Chandler Harris's tales of Uncle Remus, which Disney was to make into an animated feature, *Song of the South*, in 1946. Up to 1950, animated cartoons, like films in general, contained caricatures of blacks that would be unacceptable now. In fact, *Song of the South* raised objections from the NAACP when it was released. In recent reissues of *Fantasia*, two Nubian centaurettes and a pickaninny centaurette who shines the others' hooves have been edited out. Even the superb crows section of *Dumbo* makes us uneasy. But there is a sense in which all animated cartoon characters are more or less black. Steven Spielberg's hectic tribute to animation, *Who Framed Roger Rabbit?*, has them all, from the singing trees of Silly Symphonies to Daffy Duck and Woody Woodpecker, living in a Los Angeles ghetto, Toonville. As blacks were second-class citizens with entertaining qualities, so the animated shorts were second-class movies, with unreal actors, who mocked and illuminated from underneath the real world, the cinema of live actors.

Of course, even in a ghetto there are class distinctions. Porky Pig and Bugs Bunny have homes that they tend and defend, whereas Mickey started out, like those other raffish stick figures and dancing blots from the Twenties, as a free spirit, a wanderer. Richard Schickel has pointed out, "The locales of his adventures throughout the 1930s ranged from the South Seas to the Alps to the deserts of Africa. He was, at various times, a gaucho, teamster, explorer, swimmer, cowboy, fireman, convict, pioneer, taxi driver, castaway, fisherman, cyclist, Arab, football player, inventor, jockey, storekeeper, camper, sailor, Gulliver, boxer," and so on. He was, in short, a rootless vaudevillian who would play any part that the bosses at Disney Studios assigned him. And though the comic strip, which still persists, has fitted him with all of a white man's household comforts and headaches, it is as an unencumbered drifter whistling along on the road of hard knocks, ready for whatever opportunity waits at the next turning, that he lives in our minds.

Cartoon characters have soul as Carl Jung defined it in his "Archetypes of the Collective Unconscious": "Soul is a life-giving demon who plays his elfin game above and below human existence." Without the "leaping and twinkling of the soul," Jung says, "man would rot away in his greatest passion, idleness." The Mickey Mouse of the Thirties shorts was a whirlwind of activity, with a host of unsuspected skills and a reluctant heroism that rose to every occasion. Like Chaplin and Douglas Fairbanks and Fred Astaire, he acted out our fantasies of endless nimbleness, of perfect legerity. Yet, withal, there was nothing aggressive or self-promoting about him, as there was about, say, Popeye or Woody Woodpecker. Disney, interviewed in the Thirties, said, "Sometimes I've tried to figure out why Mickey appealed to the whole world. Everybody's tried to figure it out. So far as I know, nobody has. He's a pretty nice fellow who never does anybody any harm, who gets into scrapes through no fault of his own, but always manages to come up grinning." This was perhaps Disney's image of himself; for twenty years he did Mickey's voice in the films, and would often say, "There's a lot of the Mouse in me." Walt's humble Missouri beginnings harked back to mice, whom the Nazis, maligning the Mickey-inspired Allied legions (the Allied code word on D-Day was "Mickey Mouse"), assailed as "the most miserable ideal ever revealed. . . . Mice are dirty."

But was Disney, like Mickey, just "a pretty nice fellow"? He was until crossed in his driving perfectionism, his Napoleonic capacity to marshal men and take risks in the service of an artistic and entrepreneurial vision. He was one of those great Americans, like Edison and Henry Ford, who invented themselves in terms of a new technology. The technology—in Disney's case, film animation—would have been there anyway, but only a few driven men seized the full possibilities. In the dozen years between *Steamboat Willie* and *Fantasia*, the Disney Studios took the art of animation to heights of ambition and accomplishment it would never have reached otherwise, and Disney's personal zeal was the animating force. He created an empire of the mind, and its emperor was Mickey Mouse.

The Thirties were Mickey's conquering decade. His image circled the globe. In Africa, tribesmen painfully had tiny mosaic Mickey Mouses inset into their front teeth, and a South African tribe refused to buy soap unless the cakes were embossed with Mickey's image, and a revolt of some native bearers was quelled when the safari masters projected some Mickey Mouse cartoons for them.* Nor were the high and mighty immune to Mickey's elemental appeal—King George V asked that all the film showings he attended include a dose of Mickey Mouse, and Franklin Roosevelt was similarly partial. But other popular phantoms, like Felix the Cat, have faded, whereas Mickey has settled into the

---

*For these and other facts I am indebted to *Mickey Mouse: Fifty Happy Years*, introduced by David Bain and edited by Bain and Bruce Harris (Harmony Books, 1977). Another valuable source was *Enchanted Drawings: The History of Animation*, by Charles Solomon (Alfred A. Knopf, 1989).

national collective consciousness. The television program revived him for my children's generation, and the theme parks make him live for my grandchildren's. Yet survival cannot be imposed through weight of publicity; Mickey's persistence springs from something unhyped, something timeless in the image that has allowed it to pass in status from a fad to an icon.

To take a bite out of our imagination, an icon must be simple. The ears, the wiggly tail, the red shorts give us a Mickey. Other cartoon characters are inextricably bound up with the draughtsmanship of the artists who make them move and squawk, but Mickey has floated free, and become a Claes Oldenburg sculpture. It was Oldenburg's work that first alerted me to the fact that Mickey Mouse had passed out of the realm of commercially generated image into that of universal artifact. The basic configuration, like that of hamburgers and pay telephones, could be used as an immediately graspable referent in a piece of art. The young Andy Warhol committed Dick Tracy, Nancy, Batman, and Popeye to canvas, but not, until 1981, Mickey; perhaps Pop Art could most resonantly recycle comic strips with a romantic appeal to adolescents. Mickey's appeal is pre-romantic, a matter of latency's relatively schematic manipulations. Hajime Sorayama's sculpturelike piece of airbrush art and Gary Baseman's scribbled scraps [both in *The Art of Mickey Mouse*] capture textures of the developmental stage at which Mickey's image penetrates. Sorayama, by adding a few features not present in the cartoon image— supplying knobs to the elbows and knees and some anatomy to the ears— subtly carries forward Disney creativity without violating it. Baseman's reference to Mouseketeer ears is important; their invention further abstractified Mickey and turned him into a kind of power we could put on while remaining, facially, ourselves. The ancient notion of a transforming hat—crowns, dunce caps, "thinking caps," football helmets, spaceman gear—acquired new potency in the age of the television set, which sported its own "ears," gathering magic from the air. As John Berg's painting shows, ears are everywhere. To recognize Mickey, as Heinz Edelmann's drawing demonstrates, we need very little. Round ears will do it. A new Disney gadget, advertised on television, is a cameralike box that spouts bubbles when a key is turned; the key consists of three circles, two mounted on a larger one, and the image is unmistakably Mickey. Like yin and yang, like the Christian cross and the Islamic crescent, Mickey can be seen everywhere—a sign, a rune, a hieroglyphic trace of a secret power, a current we want to plug into.

Milton Glaser's charming reprise of Mickey wearing glasses, though still engaged in his jivey stride, lightly touches on the question of iconic mortality. Usually, cartoon figures do not age, and yet their audience does age, as generation succeeds generation, so that a weight of allusion and sentimental reference increases. To the movie audiences of the early Thirties, Mickey Mouse was a piping-voiced live wire, the latest thing in entertainment; by the time of *Fantasia* he was already a sentimental figure, welcomed back. *The Mickey Mouse Show*, with its faintly melancholy pack-leader Jimmie Dodd, created a Mickey more removed and marginal than in his first incarnation. The generation that watched it grew up into the rebels of the Sixties, to whom Mickey became camp, a symbol of U.S. cultural fast food, with a touch of the old rodent raffishness. Politically, Walt, stung by the studio strike of 1940, moved to the right, but Mickey remains one of the Thirties proletariat, not uncomfortable in the cartoon-rickety, cheerfully verminous crash-pads of the counterculture. At the Florida and California theme parks, Mickey manifests himself as a short real person wearing an awkward giant head, costumed as a ringmaster; he is in danger, in these Nineties, of seeming not merely venerable kitsch but part of the great trash problem, one more piece of visual litter being moved back and forth by the bulldozers of consumerism.

But never fear, his basic goodness will shine through. Beyond recall, perhaps, is the simple love felt by us of the generation that grew up with him. He was five years my senior, but felt like a playmate. I remember crying when the local newspaper, cutting down its comic pages to help us win World War II, eliminated the Mickey Mouse strip. I was old enough, nine or ten, to write an angry letter to the editor. In fact, the strips had been eliminated by the votes of a readership poll, and my indignation and sorrow stemmed from my incredulous realization that not everybody loved Mickey Mouse as deeply as I did. In an account of my boyhood written over thirty years ago, "The Dogwood Tree," I find these sentences concerning another boy, a rival:

> When we both collected Big Little Books, he outbid me for my supreme find (in the attic of a third boy), the first Mickey Mouse. I can still see that book, I wanted it so badly, its paper tan with age and its drawings done in Disney's primitive style, when Mickey's black chest is naked like a child's and his eyes are two nicked oblongs. Losing it was perhaps a lucky blow; it helped wean me away from hope of ever having possessions.

And I once tried to write a short story called "A Sensation of Mickey Mouse," trying to superimpose on adult experience, as a shiver-inducing revenant, that indescribable childhood sensation—a rubbery smell, a licorice taste, a feeling of supernatural clarity and close-in excitation— that Mickey Mouse gave me, and gives me, somewhat dulled by the years, still. He is a "genius" in the primary dictionary sense of "an attendant spirit." His vulnerable brave bare black chest, his touchingly big yellow shoes, the mysterious seamless fly at the back of his shorts where his tail came out, and the little cleft cushion of a tongue, red as a valentine and glossy as candy, always peeping through the catenary curves of his undiscourageable smile. Not to mention his ears.

To My Well-Balanced Life on a Wooden Leg, *by Al Capp*

FAME IS PERISHABLE; the populace, that insatiable herd, moves on to fresh fodder, leaving the cropped field to cultural historians. Yesterday's baseball player, however, still has his statistics, and last decade's movie star can see her girlish films on late-night television (or rent them down at the video store); but what does even the greatest comic-strip artist have? His old strips, which can be bound into books, as Al Capp's were and will be again; but it's a dry sort of immortality. Part of the power and charm of the newspaper comic strip is that it be constantly renewing itself before our eyes— that it arrive with our coffee and cereal, and be relished in less than a minute and not seen again for twenty-four hours, when its little adventure moves forward another notch, like a big cogwheel that the full diurnal sweep of our ticking lives has barely budged. *Li'l Abner*—as I recall from the days, beginning when I could read, when I never missed a strip— always ended its episodes in the middle of the week, and began another the next day, so as not to have readers wander away during the weekend.

How masterfully, in the reckless variety and headlong outrageousness of his invention, did Capp play upon his millions of readers! One had to have heard Caruso sing and one had to take in *Li'l Abner* with the daily news to appreciate the order of achievement. In its heyday of the Thirties, Forties, and Fifties, no other strip so knowingly teased its vast American audience; no other cartoonist threw out such a wealth of winks and mugging over the heads of his guileless characters. Harold Gray's *Little Orphan Annie* and Chester Gould's *Dick Tracy* were by comparison utterly two-dimensional, single-minded and humorless even in their grotesquerie; once you had encountered Capp's parody *Fearless Fosdick*, you could never again read *Dick Tracy* with a straight face. The note of parody, and of self-parody, was latent in Dogpatch's mise-en-scène—this rangy sweet-natured simpleton with his tiny parents and pet pig in their rickety shack, this pure-minded virgin with her voluptuous barefoot body all but popping from its tattered shorts and polka-dot blouse. The anatomical juiciness of Daisy Mae and flea-ridden Moonbeam McSwine, drawn with such loving brio, was itself a bold and unusual joke, in the chaste ranks of the "funnies." When Capp's hillbilly Candide encountered delegates from the wicked outer world, or found within Dogpatch representatives of national trends, the richness of social and philosophical commentary approached the Voltairean.

Between the demise of *Krazy Kat* and the onset of *Pogo*, what comic strip other than *Li'l Abner* could be said to contain irony or to provide intellectual pleasure? The adventure-comic strips of the period generally presented a wooden superman—Mandrake the Magician, the Phantom, Smilin' Jack, Joe Palooka—left over from a simpler time, an era of stark myths and inflexible draughtsmanship. Capp, with his rollicking abundance of fanciful grotesques and topical allusions, broke this mold, and until near the end, when the strip did seem to careen listlessly out of control, he dizzyingly worked on the edge of what was possible in a lowbrow art form.

His penetration of the mass market was not based on a single smart idea. Sadie Hawkins Day escaped Dogpatch to become a woman-empowering rite at colleges and country clubs. Marryin' Sam became a pervasive phrase. Kickapoo Joy Juice was another. Shmoo dolls appeared in every dime store to question, with their bulbous bottoms and worried eyes, our human ability to live in a utopia. The parody *Fearless Fosdick* took on the vitality of an independent saga as its unflinching hero, living on breadcrusts and as full of holes as a slice of Swiss cheese, carried police duty to the gory extremes of Counter-Reformation sainthood. The real perils of the Depression and World War II found eerie equivalents in Teetering Rock, in the rain cloud that went everywhere with Joe Bfstplk, in the knotty, dwarfed, Gandhi-like body of wisdom that emerged from the cave of Ole Man Mose. Dogpatch, so tiny and innocent in conception, grew endlessly, sprouting ever-new enclaves and freaks of nature as Capp's gift for burlesque metaphor ramified and flourished. *Li'l Abner* was a comic strip with fire in its belly, and a brain in its head.

It is not surprising that Al Capp wrote; his strip, for all its bravura drawing, brimmed with literary wit. He wrote the book for a musical comedy based on *Li'l Abner*, and for eight years supplied the story line for *Abbie an' Slats*. At various points he was a columnist for the Daily News Syndicate and a regular syndicated radio commentator. The pieces in this book, subtitled as "memoirs," were selected from a larger batch left behind at his death in 1979. A few appeared in magazines, as stated in the table of contents; most went unpublished, though all here are shaped as stories, with more than mere memoiristic intent. "Van Schuyler's Greatest Romance" verges on the fictional, and feels imaginary in some details: the opportune death of the Polish lady and the timely separation of the wooden leg seem events from a comic strip, and there is an O. Henryish symmetry in the coming-together of the two would-be Normies. Yet the heart of the story, the pain of the non-normal and the specific pain of

Capp's own amputated leg—"I really don't think it's a joke. It's quite an inconvenience"—is searingly real. The loss of his left leg at the age of nine was the central fact of Al Capp's story as he saw it, and as he tells it in these engaging, basically cheerful autobiographical essays.

An artificial leg is completely covered by long trousers, so it was very easy, meeting Capp at a party and falling captive to his unassuming manner and talkative charm, to forget that he was in any way handicapped. But he didn't forget it and, as the remarkable childhood essay that begins this collection shows, he experienced his crippling accident—a moment's slip off of an ice wagon into the path of a trolley car—as a permanent banishment from the paradise of the normal. "There came a great noise—a great cry—a crash—and darkness. And the gate of the garden closed." That his physical impairment intensified his artistic creativity is easy to say. In the remarkable comic strip that he drew for the benefit and comfort of World War II amputees, Capp shows his father saying it* with an expression of smugness we are not meant, I think, to forgive. In this autobiographical strip, he draws himself as looking almost exactly like Li'l Abner.

He gave himself, as Li'l Abner, a pair of fine long legs that could outrun Daisy Mae's every Sadie Hawkins Day. The ebullient, at times raunchy exaggeration of bodies that is one of Dogpatch's striking features related, surely, to the intensified somatic awareness induced by Capp's missing limb and its painful, awkward substitute. "Short Skirts" is ostensibly about sex but it is virtually about legs. In a surreal sentence, two young women walk toward the twelve-year-old narrator: "Their dresses were of a light color, and ended quite a bit above the knee, and then the legs came down, and down, and down." As one of his own legs did not. The seductive Ula on her porch has "long, long, long legs"; she signals to the now thirteen-year-old onlooker by gesturing with them. Too good to be true, she is a nurse and instantly guesses and discounts his own artificial leg, and for practical reasons which she enunciates is willing to make love with the virgin boy. He flees, though his adolescence as elsewhere described was extensively preoccupied with the longing for girls and with stratagems for concealing his amputated leg from them. By bringing his fantasies into the realm of practicable reality, Ula strips him of a certain developed power, his armor of pretense and artifice. Art is a stratagem, a fabricated reality wherein the artist comes to feel most at home. It was

---

*A panel depicts Capp's middle-aged parents, seated in easy chairs, discussing their maturing son. The mother says, in comic-strip caps, "There's been a great **change** in Al since his accident—he's **really buckled down** to studying art." Replies the father, with a cigar tilted in his smile, "It's **Nature's law of compensation**. The loss of **some** of his physical activity has resulted in increasing his **mental activity!! It never fails!!**"

perhaps inevitable that Capp met his wife in an art school, where she already inhabited, in a sense, the developing comic strip of his life. Catherine Wingate Cameron Capp became the first assistant to work on *Li'l Abner*; she did backgrounds and lettering and named Daisy Mae and Pansy Yokum.

We learn a fair amount about Al Capp in these memoirs. His father was an ineffective schemer, who should have been a cartoonist, and his maternal grandfather was a grand rabbi. The sketch of the marrying-off of Aunt Mildred reveals a family pride (and a happy escape from it) that qualifies his portrait of himself as a Bridgeport, Connecticut, ragamuffin. We learn, from the comic-strip autobiography, that he did once travel in the South before inventing Dogpatch. He scarcely needed to; the early Thirties didn't lack for hillbilly music or literary reports from the Southern backwoods like Erskine Caldwell's *Tobacco Road* (1932) and William Faulkner's *Sanctuary* (1931). Capp first drew hillbilly characters when working as art assistant to Hamilton Fisher, creator of *Joe Palooka*; while Fisher was on vacation in late 1933 Capp inserted some mountain folk in the other man's strip. Shortly thereafter he invented *Li'l Abner* and sold it to United Features Syndicate. As the strip succeeded, Fisher felt that the characters were rightfully his, adding fuel to a feud reflected in this collection's "I Remember Monster."

"My Life as an Immortal Myth," the latest as well as the longest piece here, uneasily parades Al Capp's international celebrity and hints at some of the discontents that clouded his last years. "To have my daily square full of cartoons discussed in the *Art Review*, as reverently as Rothko's empty squares!" The world of the Sixties and Seventies out-zanied Dogpatch, and Capp found himself, in ultra-liberal Cambridge, sounding like a conservative. Begun in the Depression, his comic strip ended in depression. Many strips outlive their creators, perpetrated by ghostly other hands, and some die with them, but Capp himself laid *Li'l Abner* to rest, after forty-three wide-eyed years, in which the ageless, prelapsarian hero not only married but became a father. The slow ticking of daily installments had moved Li'l Abner toward mortality. It was sad to see him vanish from the funnies, where Mandrake and the Phantom still soldier on. But his make-believe life had been intimately bound up with his creator's, and fostered a mutual exchange of energy. Curiously, Capp here and there writes " 'em," and, in one place, "li'l," as if these Yokumisms had become his standard English. Dogpatch was not only his creation but his language, his mask, his prosthesis, his compensation, his magic garden.

AMERICAN PAST MASTERS

Reworking Wharton

THE BUCCANEERS, by Edith Wharton, completed by Marion Mainwaring. 407 pp. Viking, 1993.

More than fifty years after her death, Edith Wharton is having a lively time of it. A dozen of her novels and short-story collections sell briskly in paperback. Even if she had never written a word of fiction, she would be remembered as a shaper of American taste, with such enduring texts as *Italian Villas and Their Gardens* and (with Ogden Codman, Jr.) *The Decoration of Houses*. The Mount, the mansion that she built to put her theories on architecture, décor, and landscaping to the test, is being restored to an approximation of its elegant condition during her inhabitancy (1902–11) and ornaments the Berkshires as a tourist attraction and the home of a Shakespeare company. With the years, the weaker of Wharton's imaginative works have sunk deeper into the shadows and the stronger have climbed to a refulgent height. R. W. B. Lewis, in his very fine 1975 biography of Wharton, described the uncertainty of "enlightened critical opinion" as to "whether *The House of Mirth* could be adjudged a masterpiece or whether it fell just short of that final accolade"; introducing the Signet paperback version in 1984, he was pleased to announce that, "in some inexplicable way, *The House of Mirth* has become a masterpiece." Concerning *Ethan Frome* and *The Age of Innocence*, there has never been much doubt; their perfection and power shone forth immediately. The latter won the Pulitzer Prize, and the former has become compulsory reading for American schoolchildren. If there is a more highly regarded female American author of the twentieth century, her name doesn't come readily to mind.

Nurtured and matured in a social milieu almost uniformly unsympathetic to the notion of a literary vocation, and wherein a proper woman's full and adequate duties consisted of homemaking and an incessant socializing, Wharton took up writing rather late and distractedly. After the age of forty, however, she applied herself to the craft with an almost vengeful energy and consistency of purpose, aristocratically holding herself to the exacting standards of what she called "that dispassionate and ironic critic who dwells within the breast." Enthralled by books and storytelling since childhood, and a cheerful and conscientious student to the few literary tutors that chance threw her way, she became a thorough professional—perhaps too professional, in her last decades. Feminists can rejoice in her female martyrs and feckless males, but readers of any gender must admire "her fearless way of looking life in the eyes"—to use her own words about the French novelist Hortense Allart. The plight of women is her dominant topic, but she portrays the war within womanhood quite unsentimentally. Her moral poise and cosmic pessimism did not permit her to blame any one sex for life's tragic side. Her own female trials—undereducation (save in "modern languages and good manners," her memoir *A Backward Glance* allows), stifling and unfulfilling marriage, neurasthenic illness and breakdown—came early, and were followed by a long, gathering triumph of best-selling fame and expatriate pomp. Her vigorous example is eminently useful, and many are the uses to which her work has been lately put. In the last year, two movies based upon her books have been released—*Ethan Frome* and *The Age of Innocence*—and films of *The Custom of the Country* and *The Buccaneers* are in the works. *The Buccaneers*, her last, unfinished novel, which was first published in 1938, the year after her death, has just been reissued in a version "completed" by Marion Mainwaring.

The scrupulous "Note" supplied to the 1938 original edition of *The Buccaneers* by Wharton's long-time friend Gaillard Lapsley, resonates with the decorums of a less meretricious era of publishing:

> The remarkable novel here submitted to the public is neither complete nor finished in all its parts. There are some parts so characteristically achieved that I am confident Mrs. Wharton would never have retouched them. Others again are evidently either provisional or at most just blocked in; and this is as you would expect, for the novel had been growing in her mind for a number of years before she ever wrote a word of it.

The decision to publish at all, Lapsley goes on to say, was taken only after he and "three of her friends, to whom she had also been in the habit of showing her work while it was in progress," had unanimously agreed.

> It was not only that the incomplete text contained some work too good to be kept back, so good indeed that she would herself probably have been satisfied with it, but because the unfinished passages have their interest and

value too. Indeed the very disparity of the several parts of the text affords an insight into the way in which she worked.

And for ten pages more he discusses, with a fastidious critical dispassion, the virtues and faults of *The Buccaneers* as he sees them. In contrast, Ms. Mainwaring's afterword is less than 150 words long; it acknowledges, besides a few additions to Lapsley's emendations and some unspecified political corrections "when [Wharton] referred to race in terms offensive to modern readers," only that "the passages I have interpolated in the original text serve to reconcile discrepancies in the narrative or prepare for later developments." Any caring reader would have welcomed a franker, fuller discussion from Ms. Mainwaring of the difficulties she faced, and the rationale of her solutions. Instead, we have a text that in no typographical way discriminates between her words and Wharton's, and that asks us to accept this bastardization as a single smooth reading unit, wrapped in a jacket by John Singer Sargent and a puff by Leon Edel. In truth, the last quarter of the novel is Ms. Mainwaring's, based upon a synopsis that Wharton had drawn up early in its composition, and which the honest 1938 edition appends to the last of the author's own written words.

The Buccaneers as it was left is a pretty mess—an ambitious canvas spottily covered with pastel sketches. It wasn't just the infirmities of age that prevented Edith Wharton from completing it but its own internal contradictions and proliferating loose ends. A novel should grow its complications from a stout central stem, and the stem here was manifold from the start. Wharton's synopsis states:

> This novel deals with the adventures of three American families with beautiful daughters who attempt the London social adventure in the 'seventies—the first time the social invasion had ever been tried in England on such a scale.
>
> The three mothers—Mrs. St. George, Mrs. Elmsworth, and Mrs. Closson—have all made an attempt to launch their daughters in New York, where their husbands are in business, but have no social standing (the families, all of very ordinary origin, being from the south-west, or from the northern part of the state of New York). . . . So, though admired at Saratoga, Long Branch and the White Sulphur Springs, they fail at Newport and in New York, and the young men flirt with them but do not offer marriage.

Shades of Consuelo Vanderbilt, who married the Duke of Marlborough; of Consuelo Yznaga, who became the Duchess of Manchester; and of Jennie and Leonie Jerome, who married Lord Randolph Churchill and the Irish baronet Sir John Leslie, respectively, when Wharton was a girl. The world of New York society, which had been Wharton's element and of which she had first written scornfully, in the *The House of Mirth* (1905) and *The Custom of the Country* (1913), and then ruefully, in *The Age of Innocence* (1920) and *The Mother's Recompense* (1925), is here, following upon *A Backward Glance* (1934), approached nostalgically, in a flurry of period detail and a misty mood of forgiveness. The horrors of the upper-class marriage mart, so mordantly portrayed in her earlier novels, are played for gentle comedy. We open in Saratoga, at the height of the racing season:

> Mrs. St. George . . . sat on the wide hotel verandah, a jug of iced lemonade at her elbow and a palmetto fan in one small hand, and looked out between the immensely tall white columns of the portico, which so often reminded cultured travellers of the Parthenon at Athens (Greece). On Sunday afternoons this verandah was crowded with gentlemen in tall hats and frock-coats, enjoying cool drinks and Havana cigars, and surveying the long country street planted with spindling elms; but today the gentlemen were racing, and the rows of chairs were occupied by ladies and young girls listlessly waiting their return, in a drowsy atmosphere of swayed fans and iced refreshments.

Mrs. St. George reflects, with a Whartonian precision as to fashion and décor, fondly back to the days when crinolines were still worn, "Newport had not yet eclipsed all rival watering-places," and dresses were not outrageously low-cut in the newest Parisian style: "What, for instance, could be prettier, or more suitable for a lady, than a black alpaca skirt looped up like a window-drapery above a scarlet serge underskirt, the whole surmounted by a wide-sleeved black poplin jacket with ruffled muslin undersleeves, and a flat 'pork-pie' hat like the one the Empress Eugénie was represented as wearing on the beach at Biarritz?" But an entire novel cannot spend itself on a verandah in preoccupation with such momentous questions; Mrs. St. George, while "her thoughts moved during the endless sweltering afternoon hours, like torpid fish turning about between the weary walls of a too-small aquarium," is also running mental inventories of the charms and marital prospects of her two daughters, eighteen-year-old Virginia and sixteen-year-old Annabel, or Nan, compared with those of the two Elmsworth girls, Elizabeth and Mabel (Lizzy and Mab), and the lone Closson daughter, Conchita.

These five marriageable girls present a problem to the author, too: how to make them easily distinguishable to the reader, and how to trace memorably their fivefold fortunes. Had Wharton lived and found strength to bring *The Buccaneers* to a consummate fullness and finish, she might have demonstrated how, though at the length of a Victorian three-decker. As it is, Mab drops almost entirely out of sight, Lizzy is only very fitfully vivid, and Nan's gradual emergence as the heroine turns her lovely older sister into a brittle blond stick. In solving the initial problem of draughtsmanship, Wharton drew upon the "dusky" tinge introduced into the Closson ménage by Mrs. Closson, a remarried Brazilian widow—or, the vicious rumor is, divorcée—whose two children, Teddy and Conchita, "bear a queer exotic name like Santos-Dios." As if a touch of the Brazilian brush weren't distinguishing enough, Wharton gives olive-skinned Conchita tallness and red hair. Virginia, "pure and luminous as an apple blossom," is a blonde, so that leaves brunetteness to the third young lady who is freshly "out," Lizzy. The two junior girls, not quite nubile, are relatively dim, though Mab is assigned a certain boniness and a laugh that "showed too many teeth" and Nan a volatile, inquisitive intensity that suggests a budding author. One feels that Wharton has exhausted her first inspiration when she triumphantly rallies her five creations for this group display in the Saratoga dining-room, on an evening when two young men—a rare and precious commodity, usually vended in Newport—have arrived to gladden their prospects:

> Ah, but there they were, the girls! . . . The fancy had taken them to come in late, and to arrive all together, and now, arm in arm, a blushing bevy, they swayed across the threshold of the dining-room like a branch hung with blossoms, drawing the dull middle-aged eyes of the other guests from lobster salad and fried chicken. . . . Seeing them through the eyes of the new young men, Mrs. St. George felt their collective grace with a vividness almost exempt from envy. To her, as to those two foreigners, they embodied "the American girl," the world's highest achievement; and she was as ready to enjoy Lizzy Elmsworth's brilliant darkness, and that dry sparkle of Mab's, as much as her own Virginia's roses and Nan's alternating frowns and dimples. She was even able to recognize that the Closson girl's incongruous hair gilded the whole group like a sunburst.

This vision forms the novel's bright heart: "the American girl," beloved of Howells and James, the chimerical creation of the new continent, looming at the threshold of the American century with her captivating innocence and perilous freedom. Here she is bathed in a glowing backward glance from the gritty decade of the Depression, cast by an elderly Parisienne who herself was once an American girl. But a vision does not a novel make, and as Wharton executes her intended plot a continued multiplication of elements diffuses the action to the consistency of froth.

Laura Testvalley, Nan's monitory but winning governess, whose descriptive adjectives "small" and "brown" suggest a direct descendancy from Jane Eyre, and whose odd name the author—she tells us in *A Backward Glance*—found herself helpless to change, arrives in Saratoga, and in next to no time, it seems, Conchita is married to Lord Richard Marable, a younger son of the Marquess of Brightlingsea. Soon the other girls are in England to try their luck at landing noble husbands. The expedition is comically successful. Like bluefish when they are running, the lords scarcely need bait to take the hook: Lord Seadown, Lord Richard's more staid older brother, snaps up Virginia St. George, after nibbling at Lizzy Elmsworth, and Nan, small fry though she is, attracts the appetites of both Guy Thwarte, son of the baronet Sir Helmsley Thwarte and heir to the lovely old manor called Honourslove, and of the Duke of Tintagel, who is so enchanted to find "a girl who doesn't know what a duke is" that he and Nan marry before she realizes she doesn't know what a duchess is, either. It turns out that she doesn't like being one. Her plight echoes that of Undine Spragg as the Marquise de Chelles, captive for ten months of the year in the boring damp galleries of the Château de St. Desert, but the echo is a weak one, since Wharton knew the French better than she did the English, and limned their brand of past-obsessed stuffiness with a more amusing vividness; also, the heroine of *The Custom of the Country*, unlike wan Nan, is a seasoned battler whose predicaments are never merely pathetic. The plotter of *The Buccaneers*, wearying at last of matchmaking (the Elmsworth girls have had to settle for non-titled rich men: dark-browed Lizzy for a rising Conservative MP, Hector Robinson, and many-toothed Mab, back in America, for a widower from Magnesia, Illinois, named Caleb Whittaker), turns to freeing Nan from an unhappy marriage to a duke so she can enter a happy one with a future baronet. At this point Edith Wharton's failing hand dropped the pen, and Marion Mainwaring, half a century later, has rushed to the rescue.

And who is Ms. Mainwaring? A native of Wollaston, Massachusetts, she has lived much of her life in London and Paris, and her short and eclectic list of previous publications includes translations of Turgenev and a 1954 murder mystery, *Murder in Pastiche*, composed in the styles of nine famous mystery-writers and, according to the *New York Times* reviewer, "a brilliantly achieved tour de force." Before considering her job of completion, we should admit that the original author was not finding the going easy. Sensing that her saga lacked something, she kept adding on. The guardian figure of Miss Testvalley is doubled, in London, by the advisory spinster Jacky March, an American once jilted by the empty-headed Marquess of Brightlingsea; in a tiny Mayfair house expressive of her diminished expectations, she ekes out her life in the margins of fashionable London and acts as "the oracle of transatlantic pilgrims in quest of a social opening." Wharton, having constructed and furnished, with her incomparable flair for interior decoration, a number of grand English homes (Honourslove, the Cotswold seat of the Thwartes; Longlands, the ducal country residence; Folyat House, the duke's London abode), late in her working of *The Buccaneers* set up yet another, Champions, "the Glenloe place in Gloucestershire," where Nan, as a refugee duchess, takes shelter with the hearty, peripatetic Lady Glenloe and her two daughters, Corisande and Kitty. These two young ladies bring the nubility problem around once more; Sir Helmsley intends his darkly handsome son, back from three years creating a family fortune in Brazil (that country again!), to marry one of them, he doesn't care which.

Redundancy abounds, generating rafts of throwaway characters. The three American fathers, left in their native dust by the emergence of a number of more colorful, titled English fathers, have nothing to do but silently supply money to feed their daughters' romantic buccaneering. Although Wharton took care to establish all three men as shady operators, inscrutably riding the roller coaster of Wall Street manipulation, she forgot to have any of them go bankrupt, and thus denied the reader a classic Whartonian moment, when the untrustworthiness of men stands naked in the marketplace. What a splendid scene it is, in *The House of Mirth*, when Lily Bart's careworn father, having laughed at his daughter's reasonable wish to sweeten the luncheon table with twelve dollars' worth of lilies-of-the-valley each day, is asked by his free-spending wife if he is ill.

> "Ill?—No, I'm ruined," he said.
> Lily made a frightened sound, and Mrs. Bart rose to her feet.
> "Ruined—?" she cried; but controlling herself instantly, she turned a calm face to Lily.
> "Shut the pantry door," she said.
> Lily obeyed, and when she turned back into the room her father was sitting with both elbows on the table, the plate of salmon between them, and his head bowed on his hands.
> Mrs. Bart stood over him with a white face which made her hair unnaturally yellow.

Indeed, the disgraced Mr. Bart does shortly die, and his wife follows not long after. The lack of a mother, and the social guidance and protection a mother provides, becomes Lily's tragic flaw, whereas the presence of mothers, in *The Buccaneers*, is a nuisance—the Americans are ineffectual society sloths and the British are aristocratic harridans.

Comedy is, perhaps, a natural mode for aged authors. The momentousness of being alive—the majestic awfulness—is felt most keenly by the young, and human existence comes to seem, as death nears and perspective lengthens, gossamer-light, "such stuff / As dreams are made on." *The Buccaneers* can hardly keep a straight face as it pushes its dolls back and forth in the elaborate patterns of attraction and courtship. The characterizations* we tend to remember are the comic ones: the poor young Duke of Tintagel, with his timid scruples, his "naturally inexpressive face," and his wistful penchant for winding clocks; the dashing old wastrel and artist manqué Sir Helmsley Thwarte, with his baroque and catty epistolary style; and Colonel St. George, whose obtuse pride it is to cleave to his house on Madison Avenue (once owned by a member of the Tweed ring) even after his wife has discovered "that no one lived in Madison Avenue, that the front hall should have been painted Pompeian red with a stencilled frieze, and not with naked Cupids and humming-birds on a sky-blue ground, and that basement dining-rooms were unknown to the fashionable."

By way of completing the mare's nest that Wharton left behind, Ms. Mainwaring inserted a short chapter, numbered IX, that attempts to soften with some transitional information the jolt when Wharton abruptly transposed the action, in Chapter VIII, to England. In Chapters XXVI, XXVII, XXVIII, and XXIX, while the plot thickens, or fails to thicken, around Annabel, the waif Duchess of Tintagel, Mainwaring adds a paragraph or two, including, as her confidence as a pseudo-Wharton grows, some airy dialogue. From Chapter XXX on, everything, except for four pages in Chapter XXXII, is Mainwaring's. It was her principal task to flesh out the latter part of Wharton's synopsis:

> Sir Helmsley Thwarte, the widowed father of Guy, a clever, broken-down and bitter old worldling, is captivated by Miss Testvalley, and wants to

---

*Wharton shows, throughout, little of her ability to snap a character down on the page with a startling sharpness; e.g., from *The House of Mirth*: "Mrs. Peniston was a small plump woman, with a colourless skin lined with trivial wrinkles. Her gray hair was arranged with precision, and her clothes looked excessively new and yet slightly old-fashioned. They were always black and tightly fitting, with an expensive glitter: she was the kind of woman who wore jet at breakfast. Lily had never seen her when she was not cuirassed in shining black, with small tight boots, and an air of being packed and ready to start; yet she never started."

marry her; but meanwhile the young Duchess of Tintagel has suddenly decided to leave her husband and go off with Guy, and it turns out that Laura Testvalley, moved by the youth and passion of the lovers, and disgusted by the mediocre Duke of Tintagel, has secretly lent a hand in the planning of the elopement, the scandal of which is to ring through England for years.

Sir Helmsley Thwarte discovers what is going on, and is so furious at his only son's being involved in such an adventure that, suspecting Miss Testvalley's complicity, he breaks with her, and the great old adventuress, seeing love, deep and abiding love, triumph for the first time in her career, helps Nan to join her lover, who has been ordered to South Africa, and then goes back alone to old age and poverty.

There is a suggestion here of Prospero burying her conjuror's wand; for the first time in her own career, the author had determined to let love triumph, and then, through a proud alter ego, retire. But the text she produced had already somewhat compromised her synopsis. Sir Helmsley as we know him is scarcely "broken-down and bitter," nor is Miss Testvalley ever really established as a "great old adventuress," though some passages are devoted to detailing her antecedents as the granddaughter of the Italian revolutionary Gennaro Testavaglia, and to the thankless work that an exile's poverty has thrust upon her—being a governess in a succession of stately homes. Miss Testvalley's failure to fill in the outlines of Wharton's conception of her is one of the deficiencies that set the novel to drifting. Our attention rarely rests on Miss Testvalley; it goes by default to Nan and her rather fantastic plight as girl proprietress of the ducal domains. But Nan has not been adequately groomed to receive the mantle of heroine, in the line of such statuesque protagonists as Jane Austen's Emma Woodhouse and George Eliot's Dorothea Brooke, whose moral educations attain an epic import.

Ms. Mainwaring brings what she can to the plot's gaps. She has a fonder eye for English scenery than Wharton, and supplies a number of scenic vignettes:

> A string of barges glided by, outstripped by a rowing-boat. . . . The unresting, changeable river had frolicked past the bungalow at Runnymede some miles ago. Around the next bend, it would surge grandly, mightily, past the Houses of Parliament.

> Guy, on horseback, and Sir Helmsley (whose injury rendered the saddle impossible) in a light and narrow cabriolet, could make the journey from Honourslove cross-country along lanes that tunnelled through overarching hedges, and wide smooth grassy rides, and stubbly old rights-of-way through fields, in half the time it took carriages and wagons obliged to follow the roundabout road that linked a dozen villages.

Having thoroughly traversed the original text, Mainwaring tidily picks up a number of the *objets* that Wharton tossed into her scenes, as if to make them yield a vitality the thin characterizations withhold:

> The stuffed birds rescued from the fire in the old Champions shared the new glossy-oak library with trophies of post-conflagration Glenloe travels. On the book-shelves, Voyages and Explorations jostled witch-masks, scrimshaw-work, and *guislas*, and a corner of the Feraghan rug was occupied by an enormous and handsome globe of the world which, unlike its counterpart at Allfriars, had lost some of its varnish as the result of much fingering by intending travellers with itineraries to plot.

The new broom sweeps differently. Guy's dead Brazilian wife, the most minimal of figments, is deftly animated as "Paquita: six weeks out of a convent when they married; poignantly sweet, innocent, and incurious." The Elmsworth sisters, unconscionably neglected by Wharton, are called back by Mainwaring; Lizzy becomes quite a dizzy schemer, in a plot suddenly bristling with spiky little developments. A montage of rapid scenes races to wrap up the scattered implications of Wharton's studied tableaux; the original stately *andante* quickens to Mainwaring's sprightly *allegro*, and a moony, post-Freudian light begins to illuminate the characters' psyches. We gain sudden access to Nan's dreams, in one of which she is Proserpine, lowering herself into a black hole, "carefully gathering in the folds of her simple Grecian chiton, to return to the Duke." Wide awake, she throws herself on her bed and moans, "I am in love. I never knew. . . . And what am I to do . . . ? I didn't know. . . ." Our hero, too, is now awash in a "turmoil of emotions": "Guy felt as if he were wallowing in the trough of the waves: not the mild ripples of the moonlit Thames, but the mountainous breakers of an ocean sea." Grammar itself dissolves, under a rain of ellipses: "They would have been under the same roof. . . . Probably better that he hadn't gone . . . he might not have kept to his resolution. . . . Was she still there?—He couldn't very well go now, himself. . . . Besides, he didn't want to see her for the last time in a crush. . . ." The physiognomies of our protagonists reflect the romantic sea-change. Guy sadly observes "the violet smudges beneath the great dark eyes" with which Nan stares at him "with a white intensity"; away from such lurid glimpses, he cannot stop picturing "her face, dimpling or wet with tears, a rainbow face." His very voice disintegrates: with his goal of cohabitation in sight, Guy, under his new management, produces an unsuave stutter: "I d-do. . . . But I will never c-c-consort, never have any but the unavoidable business contacts, with anyone, anywhere, where Annabel isn't honored."

We smile at this hasty obeisance to the social pressures and forms so gravely felt in Wharton and Henry James. The antipodean South Africa that Wharton envisioned, in a serenely colonial era, as a refuge for her unmarried lovers is deftly transposed to less racially awkward climes by Guy's avowal to Miss Testvalley: "If Annabel were to be unhappy, or I to be unhappy *for* her, we wouldn't stay! We'd go to Canada, or Australia— New Zealand—where life is different. I'm a working man. A civil engineer. I care no more than Annabel does about society." Edith Wharton never pretended not to care. In *The Age of Innocence*, when Newland Archer promises to take his illicit love, Ellen Olenska, to a place "where we shall be simply two human beings who love each other, who are the whole of life to each other; and nothing else on earth will matter," she answers, "Oh, my dear—where is that country? Have you ever been there?"

The Mainwaring completion, conscientious though it is, partakes of the blithe social anarchy of Iris Murdoch's world, where dreams and amorous fits are free to seek their fulfillment in a comfortably bohemian monied class. The female heart, in Wharton's world sternly restrained by the whalebone of Victorian morality, is uncorseted and free in Mainwaring's late-twentieth-century garb. The sacred unmentionable in Wharton and James, the fact of sexual congress, is given a vulgar, matter-of-fact voicing: "Lizzy politicly treated the question as a simple request for information. 'Nan is certainly in love with Guy Thwarte, but I don't think there's anything "going on." ' " Mainwaring places our focus on Annabel's love match—Guy sees girl, Guy gets girl—whereas Wharton evidently intended to focus on Miss Testvalley's renunciation of marriage to Sir Helmsley: "The great old adventuress . . . goes back alone to old age and poverty." Renunciation was Edith Wharton's métier; her readers, more sentimental than she, complained of her refusal to provide her heroines with happy endings. As Marion Mainwaring has it, Miss Testvalley's loss is a mere footnote to Nan's gain, a shadow swallowed in the sunset glow as the young couple heads toward the colonies and sexual happiness forever after. The holiday, the Shakespearean comedy of mating, which Wharton proposed for herself toward the end of her life has been invaded by the general moral holiday of the last decades. A project that verged on the trivial has been completed into thorough triviality.

Our estranging distance from the austere ideological frame in which Wharton's moral dramas occur could be gauged, too, in the worthy motion picture of *Ethan Frome* released earlier this year. The makers of this respectful, visually beautiful adaptation, unable to believe that Ethan and Mattie would attempt joint suicide without even a single evening in the sack together, provided one, by golden candlelight, with whimpering and open-mouthed kisses; thus they unwittingly gave to Wharton's comfortless ending the jolly aspect of a man's successfully establishing himself at home with both his wife and his mistress. Of course, it might be argued that on the sexual scale of 1911, when the novel appeared, let alone that of the 1880s, when its catastrophe is supposed to have occurred, the few embraces and kisses that Ethan and Mattie do share in Wharton's lean text constitute the equivalent of contemporary copulation, as breathily demonstrated on the screen. A delicacy of indication possible on the printed page, in the tiny theatre of the easy chair, becomes untrustworthy in the massy cineplex. Ethan's lameness, a souvenir of the fateful night of failed suicide, is tersely, suggestively described by Wharton's narrator as "checking each step like the jerk of a chain," but in the film, the actor Liam Neeson, under John Madden's direction, performs a twisted gyration with each step that rivets the viewer's mind to orthopedic considerations. Even the film's color, though subdued, provides a warmth and a New Englandy charm that soften Wharton's harsh vision. This wintry tale is a steel etching on a stark white ground (the town, like some stopover in *The Pilgrim's Progress*, is called Starkfield) whose bleakness is beyond the 1990s' ken. We are invited into the final stage of Puritanism, which renounces God Himself. A living hell: that is how Mrs. Hale, speaking for the residents of Starkfield, complacently sums up Ethan Frome's household. "The way they are now, I don't see's there's much difference between the Fromes up at the farm and the Fromes down in the graveyard; 'cept that down there they're all quiet, and the women have got to hold their tongues."

The modern film-makers have introduced a specifically Christian note into this grim Aeschylean tale. In place of Wharton's vaguely industrial narrator/observer, whose slow discovery of the Frome scandal is the novel's structural masterstroke, there now is the young Reverend Mr. Smith, a bumbling innocent fresh from works of mercy in the Boston slums. When last seen in the film, Zenobia Frome is placing a marked Bible in the docile hands of the paralyzed Mattie Silver. Yet Christianity is strikingly absent from the major works of Edith Wharton; her characters, though conventionally churchgoing, never think of turning to God in their moments of crisis. She, like many of the late Victorians and Edwardians, harbored an atheism more determined than ours, because it was more consciously and deliberately acquired, in a milieu more insistently Christian.

Edith Wharton, née Jones, had been given a usual upper-class Episcopal upbringing, which in her adolescence her inquisitive mind tried to explore with wide reading of sermons and other religious literature. The doctrine of the Atonement troubled her, in its bloody illogic, and God, according to Lewis's biography, appeared to be "simply one of the 'dark fatalities' with which mortal existence was burdened." Her best friend in girlhood was Emelyn Washburn, the daughter of the rector of Calvary Church, in Gramercy Park. Egerton Winthrop, one of the few intellectual companions of her young womanhood, introduced her to Darwinism and "the naturalist theory of the implacable power of the environment." She retained a lifelong interest in science; her tastes in art, architecture, and landscape favored the rationalist eighteenth century. Her favorite novelist was Stendhal, author of the epigram, "The one thing that excuses God is that he does not exist." In 1902, at the age of forty, she was reading Schopenhauer and remarking in a letter, "How strange it is to rummage in all that old metaphysical lumber." By 1908, as she hesitated above and then plunged into the delicious abyss of her adulterous affair with Morton Fullerton, it was Nietzsche who comforted and strengthened her, in his contempt for Christian morality and his pagan mysticism. The journal she kept during this period of sexual rebirth—birth, one could say, since her marriage with Wharton had been virtually sexless— remarks that it was "salutary now and then to be made to realise 'Die Umwerthung aller Werthe' [the reëvaluation of all values] and really get back to a wholesome basis of naked instinct." In another entry, she mused, "How strange to feel one's self all at once 'Jenseits von Gut und Böse' [Beyond Good and Evil]." Succumbing to the adept roué Fullerton (a minister's son, as it happened) "would hurt no one—and it would give me my first last draught of life."

It was in the wake of her Nietzsche-flavored defiance of her marriage vows, and during a period of increasingly erratic behavior by her husband, that she composed the icy backwoods triangle of *Ethan Frome*. Of the exalting raptures with Fullerton that her journal and poems record there is little trace except a faint echo between the names Morton and Mattie, and the rosy vividness with which Mattie Silver's physical being is made alluring in Ethan's eyes. (It is droll to conceive, as Lewis's biography does, of the amiable, aging *bon vivant* Teddy Wharton as the original of pinch-mean, hypochondriacal Zeena Frome, who has the novel's best lines, and in the film receives the best performance, by Joan Allen.) "I have drunk of the wine of life at last," Wharton wrote in her journal, at the age of forty-six. "I have known the thing best worth knowing, I have been warmed through and through, never to grow quite cold again until the end." But no mere discovery of hot-blooded love among her own possibilities deflected the author from the relentless design of *Ethan Frome*, its illustration of the crushing confinement that nature and society impose upon the individual life. This is naturalism as it came to the late nineteenth century; for all the horrors that the twentieth century has witnessed, such starkness now seems naïve. The materialist premises of science have grown somehow airy, so that physicists speak of finding "the God particle," and the electronic texture of popular culture unweights misery, spliced as it is among the television commercials. The inexorable financial logic of Frome's captivity, spelled out by Wharton with the care of an accountant, melts away in this day of credit cards and billion-dollar budget shortfalls. The denouement of frozen fates, in the novel so devastating, so majestic in its pain, in the movie becomes merely puzzling; Liam Neeson's broad face in the final close-up looks nothing but puzzled, perhaps by the mysteries of the New England accent that kept eluding his Irish tongue. The movie seems a kind of willful child obstinately clutching its unhappy ending when a happy one lies just around the corner, or just to one side of the big elm at the bottom of the sledding hill. And Wharton did cling to her unhappy endings; she refused to let the sad conclusion of *The House of Mirth* be changed for the play version, though it meant, she wrote in *A Backward Glance*, that the play would fail: "In spite of Fay Davis's exquisite representation of Lily Bart I knew that (owing to my refusal to let the heroine survive) it was foredoomed to failure." Emerging from the theatre with her after the Broadway opening, William Dean Howells told her, "Yes—what the American public always wants is a tragedy with a happy ending."

It takes a robust organism to entertain the tragic view. In her memoir Wharton claimed, "I am born happy every morning." She was especially happy during the composition of *Ethan Frome*: it was "the book to the making of which I brought the greatest joy and fullest ease." There was much for the artist in her to enjoy. Her imagination, removed from the arch conversation of polite society, carved wonderfully laconic and suggestive country dialogue. As in the happiest narratives, incidents are effortlessly efficient: Zeena's trip to the doctor in Bettsbridge serves to give Mattie and Ethan their opportunity and then to motivate Mattie's banishment. The red glass pickle-dish from Philadelphia, a wedding present to the Fromes, adorns the mock–marital table of Ethan and Mattie, and then shatters to seal their parting. Wharton moves with assurance among the homely country details of housekeeping and hardscrabble farming. The humiliating pains and exiguous emphases of poverty— Zeena mourns more over the shards of her pickle dish than over any human ruin—were mysteriously accessible to this rich woman, transferred from some enduringly felt deprivation amid her life of outward comforts. It remains difficult to account for the depth of Wharton's pessimism and her capacity to terrify. I read her three most highly considered novels—*The House of Mirth, Ethan Frome, The Age of Innocence*—at widely separated ages, yet experienced in each a sickening, stunning drop into the void. Lily Bart's muddled arrival at the purity of death and Ethan Frome's dogged shouldering of a love-crazed moment's wreckage are matched in *The Age of Innocence* by the way an entire world vanishes between the penultimate chapter and the last; the young lovers we have been suffering with day by day suddenly have their lives behind them, wasted and lost, as far as our sentimental valuation goes.

The present motion picture of *The Age of Innocence*, directed and partly written by Martin Scorsese, does not yet establish Wharton as the chief lode, now that E. M. Forster has been all but mined out, for the *Masterpiece Theatre* school of polite costume drama. There is a playfulness in Forster, a flickering lightness, which feeds the camera as Wharton's polished relentlessness does not. Scorsese, known for his shock effects, begins with thunderous music and gargantuan unfolding roses, as if to overwhelm the audience into admitting that these stiff, pokey, thoroughly clothed New Yorkers of the 1870s contain volcanic passions. Violent camera effects—a stage curtain descending in sharp downward perspective, helicopterish aerial views of Gilded Age banquet spreads—keep jolting this tale, Wharton's most efficient and exquisitely balanced, of covert social maneuver. The movie is flamboyantly sumptuous, where Wharton's repeated point, in her fiction and autobiography both, about the society in which she was raised was how relatively restrained and even Spartan it was—the prudent, conformist descendants of Dutch and English merchants entertaining each other at quiet dinners. It was not until the advent, in the 1880s, of big money from the West, "soon to be followed by the lords of Pittsburgh," that Manhattan got vulgar. From the opulent, giddy look of Scorsese's panning shots, we might be at one of Caligula's orgies.

As with the film of *Ethan Frome*, there are problems of accent and deportment. Of the three principals, only Daniel Day-Lewis, flattening his British accent and pinning down his Mohican good looks with a thin white bow tie, seems, in the role of Newland Archer, to belong to the last century. Michelle Pfeiffer and Winona Ryder, though both are described in the press handout as ardent Wharton readers, radiate twentieth-century vibes and seem lovely but miscast. Pfeiffer—who admirably carried off the exotic rôles of Madame de Tourvel in *Dangerous Liaisons* and a Soviet damsel in distress in *The Russia House*—makes no attempt at the "trailing slightly foreign accent" Wharton ascribes to Ellen Olenska; instead, she does a kind of Grace Kelly imitation and in moments of urgent expression falls into the laid-back cadences of her native California. And Ryder, with her shiny eyes and elfin protruding ears, seems far from the "frank forehead" and "Diana-like aloofness" of the impervious May Welland. Perhaps styles of women as well as of women's clothes change; both actresses seem to be suppressing their natural twitches and the nervous, ironic sensitivity they have evolved under modern conditions, wherein the rules must be improvised rather than assimilated. But then who since Bette Davis and Olivia de Havilland *has* looked at home in hoop skirts, or a "skirt looped up like a window drapery"?

Nevertheless, the film gathers strength as it goes along—strength taken directly from Wharton. Startlingly at first, a voice reads passages of her prose to us—a voice oddly close to that of Archer's obtuse mother, but presumably that of the omniscient author. Such blunt interpolation seems clumsy, but then we relax into it, as if a cinematic adaptation could be simply a reading-aloud of the condensed text, lavishly illustrated by gorgeous faces, scenery, and period interiors—a super–slide show. There are some mishaps: Wharton, trying to understand the blind force of utter conventionality, wrote words about May that, when broadcast from the screen, sound like a sneer, and provoked an uncomfortable laugh from the audience. But at the climax of the plot—the hero's near-simultaneous realizations that all his social circle has been conspiring to break up a liaison he has not yet achieved, and that his wife has scared off Ellen with a premature claim of pregnancy—the audience was still. May's white bony face as she innocently, unchallengeably confesses her triumph becomes a monstrous luminous hammer pounding Archer into his fate.* The terse dialogue is almost exactly Wharton's; after two hours of visually powerful false flourishes, authentic power arrives from the heart of the novel— from the heart, ultimately, of the little girl to whom her father seemed lonely and unfulfilled and her mother cool and implacably conventional. Lewis in his biography writes,

> The relationship between George Frederic [Jones] and Lucretia [née Rhinelander], in their daughter's version of it, provided Edith Wharton with the first and compelling instance of what would become one of her central themes: the larger spirit subdued and defeated by the smaller one.

In reworking Wharton, how tied should the workers be to the cruel overseer within her who denied her characters happiness, after bringing

---

*In coining this image, I must have been influenced by Wharton's own language in describing the moment: "And then, as he was silent, she went on, in tones so clear and evenly-pitched that each separate syllable tapped like a little hammer on his brain. . . ."

them tantalizingly close to it? There was, for me, a momentary ambiguity at the end of Scorsese's film: it appeared unclear which building, on the Paris set, Newland's son entered to visit the now quite middle-aged Ellen Olenska, who has befriended the girl who will be his bride. When his father, having asked him to go on alone but saying that he might follow, rose from his bench and took a few stooped steps, it seemed possible that Hollywood might exercise its prerogative and give us "a tragedy with a happy ending"—have Archer do what any red-blooded widower would do, that is, take the *ascenseur*, give his hostess a hug, and spend the rest of his life with Michelle Pfeiffer. He is only fifty-seven, as he reminds himself. His timidity seems merely perverse, even in the text, which offers a few hurried reasons—a wish to keep Ellen as she was thirty years ago, a fear that the sparkling milieu of Paris formed a "rich atmosphere that he already felt to be too dense and yet too stimulating for his lungs." They are not persuasive, at least to the reader for whom Newland Archer, a few pages back, has come alive in his infatuation, his glimpse of other possibilities than respectability's confinement.

It is rather as if Edith Wharton, a thorough expatriate by 1920, were closing the shutters on a ghostly representative of the New York of her girlhood. It is too cruel, too imperious; perhaps it is realism, or at least naturalism. But abnegations that seem fitting in Starkfield feel willful in the monied circles of New York and Paris. She denies her characters the liberation that she herself found. Although during her lifetime and after she suffered much invidious comparison with Henry James, she was, it might be asserted, the more normal human being, with more real social and sexual knowledge; she can conjure out of her own nature people too full-blooded to be subjected to Jamesian torments of design. They rebel, or invite us to urge them to rebel, there in their two-dimensional prisons of print. Lily Bart, unlike Milly Theale, could rise up and live a life, if the author would permit it. There was an iron vein in Wharton that her adaptors will have to work with, or work around. Marion Mainwaring has given the semi-tragedy of Laura Testvalley a happy ending belonging to a subsidiary plot; Scorsese, the film finally makes clear, has piously followed the author's intention, a renunciation in the classic French style of Madame de La Fayette's *Princesse de Clèves*. It could have gone, our illusion is, the other way. Contradictory possibilities are a sign of life, and Wharton's work abounds with them.

The Key-People

MAIN STREET & BABBITT, by Sinclair Lewis. 898 pp. The Library of America, 1992.

Sinclair Lewis is at last fading from the bookshops. About ten of his twenty-three titles are still in print, but I recently found not even a paper-back *Babbitt* on store racks where works by Jack London, Edith Wharton, Theodore Dreiser, and Scott Fitzgerald were being plenteously offered to *fin-de-siècle* buyers. Have his novels gone the way of Booth Tarkington's and Zona Gale's—souvenirs of a Midwestern America whose power to charm or to oppress has faded into cultural history? Even the Library of America's shiny new edition of *Main Street* (1920) and *Babbitt* (1922)— the two novels that contributed bywords to the English language—has something half-hearted about it, something thin. In a format that has permitted editions of over fifteen hundred pages, and that cheerfully accommodates four novels at a time, Lewis's texts, along with copious notes by the book's editor, the late John Hersey, occupy fewer than nine hundred pages. Why not a third novel—say, *Arrowsmith* (1925), which followed *Babbitt* on the Lewis production line and won him his warmest contemporary praise and a (refused) Pulitzer Prize, or *Elmer Gantry* (1927), which in lively fashion told the considerable amount that Lewis knew about American religion, or *Dodsworth* (1929), the last novel of Lewis's great decade and considered by many critics his best written and most deeply felt, as it takes one of his crass Midwesterners into foreign settings and a Jamesian mood of quiet defeat? The Library of America's policy of carrying no introductions to its selected classics prevents us from sharing the editorial rationale behind this relatively parsimonious volume; we are left to conclude that Lewis is a dwarf classic. Melville, by contrast, for all the hurry and derangement of some of his prose, gets a complete, three-volume treatment, including the virtually unreadable *Mardi* and the quaint oddity *Israel Potter*. Edith Wharton and Willa Cather, contemporaries and admirers of Lewis's, have been awarded sev-eral plump volumes each, as have Jack London and Richard Wright. The Library of America, one imagines, is getting near the bottom of its barrel of crème de la crème, and offers with the wry shrug of a depleted mer-chant these two literary products in which an awkward, homely, hyperac-tive, crudely ambitious scribbler from small-town Minnesota managed to strike a national nerve and in the bargain delivered most of what life had taught him.

For this reader, both novels were slow going. The conflicts in neither lend themselves to sweeping dramatization—to illustration, rather, so that what we get are level stretches of minor incidents. It is not just *Main Street*'s heroine, Carol Kennicott, who longs to get out of Gopher Prairie, with its dreary buildings and hard winters and impassioned petty gossip and self-righteous Republican selfishness; it is the reader as well. And yet this novel, with all its vacillations and ambiguities of artistic purpose, has a reach of greatness to it, a sense of human softness and helpless witness, which the brisker, more polished satire and sentimentality of *Babbitt* lack. Its well-known story is simple: Carol Milford, a young woman of good looks, good family, and directionless idealism, leaves her job as a St. Paul librarian to marry Dr. Will Kennicott, a "thick tall man of thirty-six or -seven," who practices in Gopher Prairie, a Minnesota town of some three thousand surrounded by lakes and wheat farms. Anticipating her impressions of the town's isolation and provinciality, Kennicott, a loyal native, urges, "Come on. Come to Gopher Prairie. Show us. Make the town—well—make it artistic. . . . Make us change!" She tries, but her feeble attempts, such as throwing a relatively jazzy party, organizing a dramatic group, and sitting on the town library committee, fall short and flat, and eventually she leaves, to live with her small son in Washington, D.C., as a clerk in the Bureau of War Risk Insurance. Although she forms friendships in the capital and comes to feel "that she was no longer one-half of a marriage but the whole of a human being," when Dr. Kennicott, after a year, comes re-wooing with uncharacteristic cunning and tact, she returns to Gopher Prairie and bears him a daughter.

The publishing firm of Alfred Harcourt expected that the novel might sell twenty thousand copies; in a little over six months it had sold 180,000. It was, according to Mark Schorer's biography of Lewis, "the most sensational event in twentieth-century American publishing history." Its popular success was matched by its praise from literary lights. The young F. Scott Fitzgerald wrote Lewis:

> I want to tell you that *Main Street* has displaced *Theron Ware* in my favor as the best American novel. The amount of sheer data in it is amazing! As a writer and a Minnesotan let me swell the chorus—after a third reading.

H. L. Mencken, at the peak of his power and prestige, had met Lewis at least once, at a party where, according to the exaggeration-prone George Jean Nathan, "a tall, skinny, paprika-headed stranger" put a stranglehold on both men and announced that he was the best writer in the country and had just written "the gottdamn best book of its kind that this here gottdamn country has had and don't you guys forget it!" Three days later, Mencken wrote Nathan:

> Grab hold of the bar-rail, steady yourself, and prepare yourself for a terrible shock! I've just read the advance sheets of the book of that *Lump* we met at Schmidt's and, by God, he has done the job! It's a genuinely excellent piece of work. Get it as soon as you can and take a look. I begin to believe that perhaps there isn't a God after all.

The popular success of the book derived, my suspicion is, not from Mencken's approbation or the novel's revelation of small-town narrowness (such American exposés, after all, go back to Hawthorne, who wrote a short story called "Main Street") but from the identification of many female readers with the heroine. Their lives, like hers, were stuck in domestic routines and puritanical, provincial, mercantile, male-dominated societies, and all their rebellious impulses came, like Carol's, to little more than a few unsuitable friendships, a flirtation or two, vaguely good works, and poetic daydreaming.

I remember my mother's copy of *Main Street*, as it sat on the shelves of our little family library, in the dusty company of Fitzgerald's *This Side of Paradise*, H. G. Wells's *Tono-Bungay*, and W. H. Hudson's *Green Mansions*. We did not own many books, and they consisted mostly of my mother's college texts and subsequent purchases. The bold spine, blue with an orange mock-label—a distinctive format that Harcourt gave all of Lewis's books—had an aggressive air, and I more than once in boyhood pulled it out and read the opening pages, in which Main Street is ironically evoked as "the climax of civilization" and the college-age Carol is described standing in relief on a hill "where Chippewas camped two generations ago," her taffeta skirt bellied by a prairie breeze "in line so graceful, so full of animation and moving beauty, that the heart of a chance watcher on the lower road tightened to wistfulness over her quality of suspended freedom. . . . A girl on a hilltop: credulous, plastic, young." My mother's maiden name was carefully inscribed inside. She had not been among the first waves of purchasers; her edition, which has now descended to me, was from the thirteenth printing, in January 1921. She was seventeen then; probably she bought the book a few years later, secondhand. Its spine is rubbed and worn as if by several readings. I felt there was something frightening about the book, and something intimately related to her. Not that she ever pressed *Main Street* upon me; her repeated recommendation, when I got to be a teenager, was *Madame Bovary*. I avoided reading both volumes. I did not want to know about my mother's unhappiness; I wanted her to be happy, and to stand still, and to let me grow up in a calm and child-centered atmosphere. When, after her death, her *Main Street* came into my hands, I looked through it for a marginal note in her writing, even some underlining, that would bear out my intuitive, dread-filled sense of her closeness to Carol Kennicott with her "quality of suspended freedom," her mood of longing and discontent. I found nothing, not a mark, not even a "How true!" or a "Yes" or an asterisk next to Carol's eloquent feminist plaint to Guy Pollock in Chapter XVI:

> "I think I want you to help me find out what has made the darkness of the women. Gray darkness and shadowy trees. We're all in it, ten million women, young married women with good prosperous husbands, and business women in linen collars, and grandmothers that gad out to teas, and wives of underpaid miners, and farmwives who really like to make butter and go to church. What is it we want—and need? . . . I think perhaps we want a more conscious life. We're tired of drudging and sleeping and dying. We're tired of seeing just a few people able to be individualists."

It is commonly said that Carol Kennicott is based on Lewis's first wife, born Grace Livingstone Hegger—a smart New Yorker who was working at *Vogue* when he courted her. In her copy he inscribed, "To Gracie, who is all the good part of Carol." The novel originally had a male central character, the languidly disaffected lawyer Guy Pollock, who was apparently based upon a brief acquaintance Lewis made in his home town of Sauk Centre in 1905, an eccentric young attorney called Charles T. Dorion. When Lewis and his bride visited Sauk Centre in 1916, the shift to a female protagonist began. Schorer conjectures, "It was as if, in 1916, seeing his wife and his father and his brother Claude, together, he had asked himself, 'Suppose Grace had married a man like Claude or my father instead of me, and suppose they . . . stayed here?' "

Grace in fact didn't have to cope long with life in Sauk Centre, but another woman Lewis knew well and loved did: his stepmother, Isabel Warner Lewis, whom the novelist later described as "more mother than step-mother" and "psychically my own mother." (His own mother, whom he strikingly resembled, had died when he was six.) Just as the fictional Dr. Kennicott took Carol away from St. Paul, Dr. Edwin Lewis brought Isabel from Chicago, where she had been the daughter of the house in which he roomed as a medical student. Carol's busy but unsatisfying club life echoes Isabel Lewis's vigorous involvements in the Musical Club, the Congregational Church, the Order of the Eastern Star, the local library, the Embroidery Club, and a self-improvement group called the Gradatim Club. "Pleasantly ambitious" was how Lewis described his stepmother, and her town involvements seem to have been triumphant. But perhaps there was an underside of painful adjustment as the Chicago girl came to Sauk Centre, which her youngest and most observant stepson helplessly witnessed. The communal institutions of Gopher Prairie—its churches, lodges, and betterment campaigns—form a comically small theatre for Carol Kennicott's portentous social agonies; to a local boy, however, and to the earnest settlers of the vast prairie, such organizations undoubtedly loomed in a sizable scale. Carol's curiously hectic and variable adventures in attaching herself to the small-town fabric gain dignity and peril if they are felt not as a city wife's visit to the boondocks but as a maternal figure's efforts to make a place for herself in an alien environment.

Imagining *Main Street* as a small boy's point of view helps account for Will Kennicott's oscillations, in the style of a father, between being a boor and being a hero, and for Carol's virtual sexlessness. Mary Austin, a contemporary writer and friend of Lewis's, early remarked, "One wonders if he was fully aware of how much of Carol Kennicott's failure to find herself in Gopher Prairie was owing to the lack of sex potency, a lack which he records without relating it to any other of her insufficiencies." Her frigidity drives her husband into the arms of the plump, "messy-minded" Maud Dyer; Maud is inferior in almost every regard except that, he admits to himself, "she's got more life to her than Carol has." To Carol he cries, "I don't expect you to be passionate—not any more I don't," and insists, "No matter even if you are cold, I like you better than anybody in the world." She is a Madame Bovary without lovers. The author heads her toward a succession of possible flames—Guy Pollock, Miles Bjornstam, Erik Valborg—but nothing kindles; the defiant, yea-saying, ruinous affair that the reader awaits never develops. Even a year on the loose among handsomely uniformed men in Washington generates no romance for Carol. Not only Maud Dyer but Bea Bjornstam and, at another level of intelligence and social status, Vida Sherwin Wutherspoon seem to be set forth as contrasts: all these women find their life's meaning in their relations with a man, while Lewis's feminism disdains any such resolution of his heroine's discontent. Yet he no more knows what to do with her than she knows what to do with herself. Unable to conceive of any better fate for her, the author brings her back, her burden of motherhood doubled, to Gopher Prairie, to the common-sense, pragmatic, conservative American practicality that was, after all his forays into satire, socialism, and building Pre-Raphaelite castles in air, what Lewis knew best and trusted most. Having mentally entertained his heroine's restless unhappiness, he safely ends by remarrying her to Dad.

* * *

Main Street is subtitled *The Story of Carol Kennicott*, but insofar as it portrays purposeful action it is the story of Will Kennicott; he wins and transplants Carol, ministers to the realities around them, and makes money out of the prairie. After she rebels, he knows when to indulge her and when to reconquer her. Similarly, *Babbitt* might be called the story of Myra Babbitt, the eponymous George F.'s almost invisible wife. It is she who is the effective agent of the surrounding society. It was she, we are told, who initiated the engagement, against Babbitt's better judgment; it was she, as the daughter of the hard-nosed real-estate man Henry Thompson, who determined Babbitt's professional career; it is she who contains his middle-aged rebellion by ignoring it and then, with a divinely inspired attack of appendicitis, brings him back into the warm fold of Babbittry. Her first appearance in the novel excites one of its most memorable sentences: "She was a good woman, a kind woman, a diligent woman, but no one, save perhaps Tinka her ten-year-old, was at all interested in her or entirely aware that she was alive." Toward the end, precariously ill and about to be taken to the hospital, she offers to die, in the novel's most moving, nakedly emotional scene:

> He was on his knees by the bed. While she feebly ruffled his hair, he sobbed, he kissed the lawn of her sleeve, and swore, "Old honey, I love you more than anything in the world! I've kind of been worried by business and everything, but that's all over now, and I'm back again."
>
> "Are you really? George, I was thinking, lying here, maybe it would be a good thing if I just *went*. I was wondering if anybody really needed me. Or wanted me. I was wondering what was the use of my living. I've been getting so stupid and ugly—"
>
> "Why, you old humbug! Fishing for compliments when I ought to be packing your bag! Me, sure, I'm young and handsome and a regular village cut-up and—" He could not go on. He sobbed again; and in muttered incoherencies they found each other.

The reader, against all the doctrinal trends of this most celebrated satire of middle-American values, finds himself rejoicing that Babbitt will be after all allowed into the right-wing Good Citizens' League and will resume his daily rounds of professional chicanery and family-bound routine. *Babbitt*, though it was published less than two years after *Main Street*, was written by a different man—one much better positioned to extol the joys of conformity and humble drudgery. The phenomenal success, both popular and critical, of *Main Street* had lifted Lewis up from the limbo of struggling free-lancers into a dizzying limelight, and launched him on the life of rootless travel and reckless living whose details are summed up in the harrowingly crowded thirty-six-page bio-graphical chronology that Hersey provided for the Library of America. *Babbitt* was composed in Cornwall, Kent, Paris, Rome, London, and For-est Hills, while Lewis's marriage to Grace was showing stress and his drinking was becoming, occasionally, a problem.

In the wake of *Main Street* he had gone on a lecture tour of the Mid-west, taking notes on the middle-sized cities—"not NY or Chi but the cities of 200,000 to 500,000," he explained in a letter to Mencken—that were to be the scene of his next novel, whose central figure was to be "a Solid Citizen, one George F. Babbitt." Lewis continues, "The book is not altogether satire. I've tried like hell to keep the boob Babbitt from being merely burlesque—hard tho that is at times, when he gets to orating before the Boosters' Club lunches. I've tried to make him human and individual, not a type." The novel never declares exactly where its city of Zenith is—much farther east than Gopher Prairie, certainly, and east of Chicago—but Cincinnati seems to have been especially fruitful for his researches. From there he wrote Alfred Harcourt in 1921, "Bully time, met lots of people, really getting the feeling of life here. Fine for *Babbitt*." When the book was further along, he wrote a friend that "it was very use-ful for me to go to Cincinnatti [sic]—it gave me a renewed sense of the exact flavor of a large American city of today." Between Sauk Centre High School and Yale, Lewis had spent six months at the academy of Oberlin College, and later credited that interim as giving him "a notion of the Eastern Middlewest, in which is situate Zenith."

But Ohio is never named; Zenith belongs to a state of the American mind. It materializes on the novel's first page as a vision of towers, "sturdy as cliffs and delicate as silver rods," and of limousine-laden high-ways, "a city built—it seemed—for giants." George F. Babbitt, however, is discovered asleep on his sleeping porch, his face "babyish in slumber, despite his wrinkles and the red spectacle-dents on the slopes of his nose." For the next seven chapters and ninety pages, the author follows Babbitt through his rounds, returning him to the sleeping porch and enclosing his unconscious form within another omniscient overview of the city. The mock-epic note and the absurdist diurnal inventory are so strikingly reminiscent of another novel published in 1922, Joyce's *Ulysses*, that one wonders if Lewis, in his wide reading, had encountered any of the *Little Review* excerpts. He was not above borrowing tricks from the avant-garde; some surprising stream-of-consciousness passages appear in *Main Street*.

Babbitt's specimen day concluded, Lewis embarks upon a series of set-pieces, asking us alternately, and even simultaneously, to laugh at Bab-bitt's crass speechifying and opinionating and to sympathize with his longing for something beyond all this. He recurrently dreams of "the fairy child, a dream more romantic than scarlet pagodas by a silver sea . . . She was so slim, so white, so eager! She cried that he was gay and valiant, that she would wait for him, that they would sail—" Closer to earth and to Zenith, he cherishes a sentimental friendship with the introverted, Guy Pollock–like Paul Riesling: "He was an older brother to Paul Riesling, swift to defend him, admiring him with a proud and credulous love passing the love of women." If Mark Schorer's exhaustive yet tart biography has a dominant point about Sinclair Lewis, it is his loneliness, his inability to make and keep friends. *Babbitt*'s attempt to show an intense male friendship comes through with a poignant unreality surpassing that of the fairy child. Paul has his own discontents—"I ought to have been a fiddler, and I'm a pedler of tar-roofing"—and a wife, Zilla, who is more troublesome, expensive, and nagging than Myra Babbitt. Babbitt's slide out of Babbittry is accelerated by his dismay when Paul shoots Zilla (nonfatally) and is sentenced to three years in jail. Into Paul's place as a tempter to apostasy briefly steps an old college classmate, Seneca Doane, a former corporation lawyer who "had turned crank, had headed farmer-labor tickets and fraternized with admitted socialists." A certain furtive respect for Doane, plus a new daring that allows Babbitt to acquire a mistress, Tanis Judique, and to party night after night with her bohemian set, leads him to resist when Vergil Gunch, a staunchly pro-business coal dealer, presses him to join the right-wing Good Citizens' League. This resistance is about to cost the Babbitt-Thompson Realty Company some profitable shady dealing with the Street Traction Company when Myra's appendix opportunely restores the social order.

A happy ending of sorts ensues. Ted Babbitt, George's son, elopes with the girl next door, Eunice Littlefield, whom the senior Babbitt has always seen in a glimmering light: "Eunice was a midge in the sun. . . . The agreeable child dismayed him. Her thin and charming face was sharpened by bobbed hair; her skirts were short, her stockings were rolled, and, as she flew after Ted, above the caressing silk were glimpses of soft knees which made Babbitt uneasy, and wretched that she should consider him old. Sometimes, in the veiled life of his dreams, when the fairy child came running to him she took on the semblance of Eunice Littlefield." So the son wins the fairy girl. Bravely, stoutly, Babbitt gives his blessing and releases the boy, whose only aptitude is mechanical, from the paternal imperative to fulfill Babbitt's own frustrated hope of becoming a lawyer: "Take your factory job, if you want to. Don't be scared of the family. No, nor all of Zenith. Nor of yourself, the way I've been. Go ahead, old man! The world is yours!" Thus raggedly does the heritage of dreams descend through the generations.

My father as well as my mother figured in my ominous early sense of Sinclair Lewis's world. A schoolteacher and deacon, my father didn't make it into the Babbitt circles of our little town—he was never invited, for instance, to join a fraternal lodge—but he hovered on their edge, both admiring and skeptical. The jargon of boosterism, of getting ahead, was much in his mind, as a code he could not quite crack. (Curiously, an Updike plays a peripheral part in *Babbitt*—Horace Updike, "Zenith's professional bachelor," a suave, slender man Babbitt's exact age of forty-six—and two of Lewis's few close friends in young manhood were named Upson and Updegraff.) One of my first thoughts about fiction, arrived at in the near-perfect literary vacuum of my early adolescence, was that it was wrong, morally and aesthetically, to write of common American life as Lewis did, satirically. Life was life, I figured, intricate and problematical everywhere. I must have had my family's complicated socio-economic struggles in mind; it was as if Lewis were peering in our windows and sneering. When at last I came to read *Babbitt*, it was because its central character's name rhymed with that of a fictional character of my own. The parallels astonished me—the bondage to one's father-in-law's business, the baffled love for one's son, the dips into low life, and the scared skid home.

When, in 1930, Lewis became the first American to win the Nobel Prize, Sherwood Anderson found the result "depressing," writing to a friend, "Dreiser has had real tenderness in him. Lewis never. It seems to me that Lewis must have got it out of European dislike of America rather than liking." Yet, at least in *Main Street* and *Babbitt*, lack of overt tenderness is not the fault. Not only are the two central malcontent dreamers given the author's sympathy but their entire constricting milieu is finally endorsed as being without a practical alternative, and the milieu's enforcers are perceived as basically decent folk. Babbitt's lunch-table companions at the Zenith Athletic Club, as rowdy a crowd of capitalist small fry as one could wish, with Vergil Gunch at their head, are lovably silent in regard to Babbitt's grief over Paul Riesling, and win him back to the Good Citizens' fold as tactfully as Will Kennicott woos back Carol. Accused of hating Main Street and its inhabitants, Lewis insisted on his "love of Main Street, from a belief in Main Street's inherent power." To a correspondent who said he would rather live in Gopher Prairie than New York, Lewis mildly suggested that he try it for three years, adding, "Mind you, I *like* G.P., all the G.P.'s; I couldn't write about them so ardently if I didn't." To be sure, his idealism had turned from a youthful immersion in Christianity, which lasted into his second year at Yale, to socialism, and he has telling points to make about Main Street's mercantile exploitation of the farmers, its ferocious resistance to any farmers' coöperative that would diminish its middleman's role, the savage war upon striking workers that galvanizes Zenith's nicer sort, and the conspiratorial venality of the real-estate game. Yet none of these points, however clearly made on his map of society, sink into the fabric of his characters' lives and determine their dooms. Where Dreiser is much his superior is in making the weight of society palpable, as it crushes those who stray from their niche, like Hurstwood in *Sister Carrie*, or who aspire too high, like Clyde Griffiths in *An American Tragedy*. Our depths of wanting and the world's depths of denial were impressed upon Dreiser with a force that the more intellectually nimble Lewis felt mainly in his head. A doctor's son (John O'Hara was another) gains a precocious sense of a community's sufferings, but at a slightly clinical and superior remove. A Yale education— and Lewis had a genuinely scholarly side—added to the remove; he became an anthropologist among his own people.

Lewis's star rose in the very year, 1920, when William Dean Howells died. Though the younger writer was to speak dismissively of Howells in his Nobel Prize acceptance speech, the two Midwestern bards of middle-class America had much in common, besides diligence, socialist leanings, and popular success. Their instinct was to write comedies; their sense of American life was of a dull but smiling surface over which blame and woe were so evenly distributed as almost to evaporate. Where Lewis has potential villains, like Gunch in *Babbitt* or Will Kennicott's odiously interfering Uncle Whittier and Aunt Bessie in *Main Street*, the plot tames them and moves on to portray other conflicts and crises, which, in turn, as crises do in real life, blow over. Life, usually, goes on. Neither Howells nor Lewis believes in catastrophes as typical; their realism is a network of ripples in a shallow pond. Excused from disaster (except to minor characters such as Fern Mullins and Bea Bjornstam in *Main Street*), the reader moves through a world lifelike in its brilliant parts yet in sum lacking life's total resonance, and faintly tepid and inconsequential therefore.

For all the abrasive pronouncements that attended his well-lubricated peregrinations as a world-class author, Lewis was not a political radical, even to the extent that Shaw and Mencken were. Carol's distaste for Gopher Prairie is almost entirely aesthetic: the buildings are plain and ugly, the movies at the downtown theatre are idiotic, the dramatic arts are in sorry shape, and there is not a single cathedral or great museum in sight. It is Henry James's catalogue of not-theres (in his book on Hawthorne) all over again, with little consideration of what America *was* offering its eager immigrants in those pre–World War I years, and how that freedom and opportunity were being warped by capitalist exploitation. Nor does much seem wrong with Zenith that an honest traction company and a Dante Society wouldn't fix. According to Vergil Gunch, "I suppose Dante showed a lot of speed for an old-timer—not that I've actually read him, of course—but to come right down to hard facts, he wouldn't stand one-two-three if he had to buckle down to practical litera-ture and turn out a poem for the newspaper-syndicate every day, like Chum [T. Cholmondeley Frink, the local poetaster] does!"

The names! The slang! One wonders if Hemingway had Lewis in mind when he advised his sister in a letter, "All slang goes sour in a short time." (In a letter to Maxwell Perkins he said, of Lewis, "If I wrote as sloppily and shitily [sic] as that freckled prick I could write five thousand words a day year in and year out.") In Mark Twain and Ring Lardner, the slang and idiom have the charming music of an exotic tongue preserved by transcription; Lewis uses slang from above, as a protest on behalf of the King's English. Did men ever greet each other as noisily as Babbitt and Paul Riesling do?

> "How's the old horse-thief?"
> "All right, I guess. How're you, you poor shrimp?"
> "I'm first-rate, you second-hand hunk o' cheese."

Even a character we are meant to respect, like Will Kennicott, talks to himself in cornpone accents:

> "By golly, she's taking an awful big chance, though. You'd expect her to learn by and by that I won't be a parlor lizard. . . . Be switched if sometimes I don't feel tempted to shine up to some girl that has sense enough to take life as it is; some frau that doesn't want to talk Longfellow all the time, but just hold my hand and say, 'You look all in, honey. Take it easy, and don't try to talk.' "

The awkward jocosity of American ice-breaking—"You can call me Sam—anyway, I'm going to call you Carrie, seein' 's you've been and gone and married this poor fish of a bum medic that we keep round here"—looks blatant in print. Queneau-like phonetic spellings give a surreal look to American pronunciation: "Jever realize that?," "Have smore chicken," "frinstance," "Speaknubout prices," "But zize [as I was] saying." The bright motley of such diction keeps us from taking these characters quite seriously, and makes us wonder if Lewis, American though he was, took them seriously enough.

Perhaps his long stays and ultimate death in Europe enacted a deeper escapism. It is surprising to read, in Hersey's sketch and Schorer's biogra-phy, how much of Lewis's mature energy went into plays—not just writ-ing them, but acting in them, sometimes opposite the fairy-child ingenue of his early dotage, Marcella Powers. He was a tireless and eventually tiresome mimic. Drunk or sober, he tended to perform—to clown and to monologue—when a little calm interaction was called for. The beginnings of his narrative art lay in his family's barn, where he would play alone for hours with, as he confided to his journal at the age of seventeen, "the old 'key-people,' i.e., keys which I used as semi-dolls, or, better, as puppets in many a play hour. They lived, died a number of times, fought battles, had houses ect. ect. [sic]." This memory of solitary boyish make-believe, while Sauk Centre bustled about its business and the prairie stretched to the horizon, seems as sad as Sinclair Lewis usually looks in his photographs. A connection might be made between the little metal key-people and the plethora of characters who, no two notched quite alike, clatter through his novels. From *Babbitt* on, his technique was to assemble pages of thumbnail portraits, expert testimony, detailed plans of fictional houses and locales—"Sheer data!"—before he began to write, not trusting to his powers of improvisation, or to an invisible and silent mulling. In artistic procedures so methodical, the method tends to take over; his characters do sometimes seem animated notes, with their best bits left back in the notebooks. Seventy years after their composition and sensational success, his two masterpieces have a tinny, unintegrated feeling. There was dreaming on the one hand, and the world on the other; the dreamers had his sympathies, but the world had the facts. The facts remained somewhat repellent.

Laughter from the Yokels

THE IMPOSSIBLE H. L. MENCKEN: *A Selection of His Best Newspaper Stories*, edited by Marion Elizabeth Rodgers. 707 pp. Doubleday, 1991.

The generations for whom H. L. Mencken was an exhilarating cultural presence have passed, or are reluctantly passing, on; Mencken's prose has passed into the care of scholars who were born after the Sage of Baltimore ceased to write, in 1948. Indeed, Marion Elizabeth Rodgers, the editor of *Mencken and Sara: A Life in Letters* (1988) and now of *The Impossible H. L. Mencken*, looks from her jacket photograph to have been born after Mencken died, in 1956. She has done a thorough and affectionate job of sifting through approximately three thousand of his newspaper articles, and choosing, arranging, and introducing 174—nearly seven hundred big pages' worth—as they appeared, from 1908 to 1948, in the *Baltimore Evening Sun*, the *Baltimore Sun*, the *Chicago Sunday Tribune*, the *New York Evening Mail*, and the *New York American*. A number of Mencken's editorial columns were later published, with revisions, in *The Smart Set* and *The American Mercury*, of which he was an editor, and then collected in one of his six volumes of *Prejudices*, but many of his news reports, dispatched from political-party conventions, the Scopes trial in Tennessee, a Pan American Conference held in Havana in 1928, and such datelines as London and Jerusalem, have never been reprinted. At least two-thirds of this volume's contents, Ms. Rodgers estimates, "have not been seen since their first appearance in the newspapers where they were praised or damned over sixty years ago."

There is more here to praise than to damn. A few typos and opaque sentences mar the editor's—and her typists'— accomplishment of translating "old newsprint which looks like so many fleas on a page" into book type. The title comes on too strong, and implies a presumably slimmer companion volume entitled *The Possible H. L. Mencken*. Ms. Rodgers's introduction and headnotes admirably explain the historical context of Mencken's reportage and, in some instances, act as a helpful corrective to his not infrequently violent and myopic opinionizing; Gore Vidal, however, has contributed a superfluous foreword that strives to match Mencken sneer for sneer. "For several decades," Mr. Vidal lets us know, "I have been trying to convince Europeans that Americans are not innately stupid but merely ignorant and that with a proper education system, et cetera. But the more one reads Mencken, the more one eyes suspiciously the knuckles of his countrymen, looking to see calloses [sic] from too constant a contact with the greensward." Prohibition, the foreword assures us, "made the United States the world's joke-nation, a title still unceded," while God is put in His place as "the Big Fella in the Sky." Not all sneers are of equal value. Mencken's sneers convince us that he has concrete, if squintingly perceived, objects in view; Mr. Vidal's seem in contrast quite abstract, rooted in nothing less airy than a belief that sneering becomes him. His foreword serves, perhaps involuntarily, to illustrate the perils of Menckenism pursued in a void, without Mencken's old newsman's interest in the nitty-gritty of American life.

To the reader of the 1990s, indurated by the shocks and swoops of the New Journalism as electrifyingly practiced by Norman Mailer, Tom Wolfe, and their lessers, much of Mencken's journalism may seem rather low on voltage. Writing tidily to his daily quota of two to three thousand words, he hymns the ways of cooking Chesapeake crab, and lists 252 "bald-headed geniuses." Behind his cigar smoke and swirling rhetoric, Mencken was something of an affable pedant. Ms. Rodgers's introduction tells us that in 1896, at the age of sixteen, "he graduated from the Baltimore Polytechnic with the highest marks ever achieved by any pupil in the history of the school." Pre-eminent academic prowess is rather rarely given to the scatterbrained souls who take up the practice of literature; another example that comes to my mind is D. H. Lawrence, who at the age of nineteen placed among the top dozen in the all-England King's Scholarship examination. Both prize scholars became roarers, shamelessly reckless in their assertions because, it may be, they knew that they were smarter than everyone else, including professors. Has any writer ever insisted more than Mencken upon other people's stupidity? "Stoneheads," "jackasses and morons," "ignoramuses," "numbskull," "ox," "pestiferous idiot"—these are epithets lifted from adjacent essays on two new-fangled insults to Mencken's intelligence, the telephone and the radio. In the next essay, movies are dismissed as "fodder for half-wits." He concedes (in 1929—as if Chaplin and Eisenstein and Carl Dreyer did not already exist) that someday "someone with an authentic movie mind will make a cheap and simple picture that will arrest the notice of the civilized minority." When that happens, "the movies will split into two halves. . . . There will be huge, banal, idiotic movies for the mob . . . and there will be movies made by artists, and for people who can read and write."

The split between the civilized minority and the barbaric remainder became, during the Scopes trial of 1925, an abyss over which Mencken gazed with horror at the specimens of *Homo neanderthalensis* who had "fought every new truth ever heard of, and . . . killed every truth-seeker who got into their hands." The "great masses of men," he decides, are "immortal vermin," who, "even in this inspired republic, are precisely where the mob was at the dawn of history. They are ignorant, they are dishonest, they are cowardly, they are ignoble." As he warms to his topic, the vermin shrink to microörganisms virtually begging for the mercy of extermination:

> The popularity of Fundamentalism among the inferior orders of men is explicable. . . . The cosmogonies that educated men toy with are all inordinately complex. To comprehend their veriest outlines requires an immense stock of knowledge, and a habit of thought. It would be as vain to try to teach to peasants or to the city proletariat as it would be to try to teach them to streptococci.

"What all this amounts to," he goes on, "is that the human race is divided into two sharply differentiated and mutually antagonistic classes, almost two genera—a small minority that plays with ideas and is capable of taking them in, and a vast majority that finds them painful, and is thus arrayed against them. . . . The intellectual heritage of the race belongs to the minority, and to the minority only." How can we tell one genus from another? Luckily, a ready test exists: Beethoven. "Of the 110,000,000 so-called human beings who now live in the United States, flogged and crazed by Coolidge, Rotary, the Ku Klux and the newspapers, it is proba-ble that at least 108,000,000 have never heard of him at all. . . . The fact saves good Ludwig's bacon. His music survives because it lies outside the plane of the popular apprehension, like the colors beyond violet or the concept of honor."

Mencken's persuasion that everything human he disliked arose from the downright stupidity of most other people considerably limited his insight into the forces operating in a democracy. He makes no attempt to understand the rationale of Fundamentalism—that is, the perception (hidden from many liberal clergymen) that to admit that the Bible is inac-curate in a single detail is to negate it as a divine handiwork and thus to imperil the only local intellectual structure that lends individual lives sig-nificance and comfort. Mencken describes a meeting of Tennessee Holy Rollers, grippingly, as an orgy of "poor half wits"; for him, witnessing it—first from afar in the woods, and then up close, the reporter calmly smoking a five-cent cigar—was "like peeping through a knothole at the writhings of a people in pain." That Mencken, with the aid of Beethoven and a stein of beer, was able to keep smiling in a universe bereft of God didn't really make him a more complex organism than those still in the grip of Christianity's rococo doctrines. He too readily assumed simplicity for any mechanism not his own. In discussing the "American language," he avers that "philologists spend a lot of time studying the dialects of the Eskimo, the Hausa and the Navajo, not one of which has even a refined grammar." Is this true, or is it truer that many small and dying languages in fact possess a grammar more inflected than that of widely spoken, well-worn tongues like English and Mandarin Chinese? Certainly there is a grammar, an elaborated and complicating one, in popular culture to which Mencken was, in the case of jazz, deaf and, in that of the cinema, blind.

Though ostensibly a specialist in the follies of the booboisie, he often misread popular tides; he predicted that Hoover would lose in 1928 and—initially—that he would win in 1932. He never understood Roo-sevelt's strength; he never cared to contemplate the economic despera-tion, in a nation whose workforce was one-fourth unemployed, that Roosevelt was addressing. He scorned "the New Deal schemes to uplift the downtrodden and bring in Utopia at home." He voted for Landon and Willkie, and thought that they both lost because they weren't right-wing enough: "It is impossible to beat a demagogue by swallowing four fifths of his buncombe, and then trying to alarm the boobs over the little that is left." Mencken implied that Hoover lost in 1932 not because of the Depression but because of Prohibition:

> They [the electorate] don't much care what he has to say about the budget, or the gold standard, or farm relief, or any other such tiresome matter, but they remember with relentless tenacity how shabbily he tried to fool them on prohibition. That is the one question that really interests them. It is the only honest issue in the campaign.

"Prohibition" is the longest entry in the compilation's index; Mencken alludes to it in almost every column. It was for him, and the generation he influenced, a sore point and a touchstone, a supreme instance of government gone awry, a triumph of Baptist buffoons over the rights of amiable hedonists: "Whatever lies above the level of their [the *Homo nean-derthalensis* specimens'] comprehension is of the devil. A glass of wine delights civilized men; they themselves, drinking it, would get drunk. *Ergo*, wine must be prohibited. The hypothesis of evolution is credited by all men of education; they themselves can't understand it. *Ergo*, its teaching must be put down." In his fierce dispatches from the Scopes trial, the parallel infringement of liberty is drummed home:

> I sincerely hope that the nobility and gentry of the lowlands will not make the colossal mistake of viewing this trial of Scopes as a trivial farce. . . . Deeper down there are the beginnings of a struggle that may go on to melo-drama of the first caliber, and when the curtain falls at least all the laughter may be coming from the yokels. You probably laughed at the prohibition-ists, say, back in 1914. Well, don't make the same error twice.

Not that, in the era that saw the rise of fascism and Stalinism, such alarums were uncalled-for; what is curious in Mencken is his adamant lack of sympathy with Roosevelt's successful attempt to hold the American nation together, or with any politician's attempt to achieve practical ends. He himself disavowed any "lust to improve the world." He explained in 1925 that he described the Fundamentalists, "dwelling luxuriously upon their astounding imbecilities, their pathetic exploitation by mountebanks," out of no wish to change matters. "Such spectacles do not make me indignant; they simply interest me immensely, as a pathologist, say, is interested by a beautiful gastric ulcer." Democracy seemed to him an incurable disease; he defined it, in a report from the 1920 Republican convention, as "the domination of unreflective and timorous men, moved in vast herds by mob emotions." Twenty years later, reporting from the Democratic convention, he reflected how, since the days of Jackson, "judicious men . . . warned that giving the vote to incompetent, despairing and envious people would breed demagogues to rouse and rally them, and that the whole democratic process would thus be converted into organized pillage and rapine. It has come to pass under Roosevelt, and no one seems to be able to fetch up a plausible remedy."

Many Presidents and seekers of the Presidential office are caricatured in these screeds, with hilarious gusto and with an unrestrained candor that would burn a hole in the editorial page of most contemporary newspapers. Some of Mencken's flights—his examination of Warren Harding's language, termed "Gamalielese" ("It reminds me of a string of wet sponges; it reminds me of tattered washing on the line; it reminds me of stale bean-soup, of college yells, of dogs barking idiotically through endless nights. It is so bad that a sort of grandeur creeps into it"), and his rapturous obituary of William Jennings Bryan—are anthology pieces, monuments of American satire. But his obituary of Calvin Coolidge strikes, amid its humor, a rueful note of self-confrontation. Our stolid, laconic thirtieth Chief Executive had been amply limned by Mencken before; in 1924 he called him "the vacuum in the White House," in 1931 he wrote that the former President had all the character of "a cast-iron dog on a lawn." However, when Coolidge unexpectedly died—having seemed to be "precisely the sort of man who would live to a vast and preposterous age, gradually mummifying in a sort of autogenous vacuum"— Mencken mainly recalled the man's luckiness, and marvelled at the ease with which Coolidge had slipped up the political ladder into the highest office: "No man ever came to market with less seductive goods, and no man ever got a better price for what he had to offer." The journalist inevitably notes Silent Cal's failure to tackle any of the nation's problems during his tenure, and his notorious ability to sleep long hours: "Wrapped in a magnificent silence, his feet upon his desk, he drowsed away the lazy days." But Mencken then asks himself if this narcoleptic inactivity was altogether bad, and concludes not: "The worst fodder for a President is not poppy and mandragora, but strychnine and adrenaline. We suffer most when the White House bursts with ideas." In retrospect the country will remember of Coolidge "only the grateful fact that he let it alone. . . . If the day ever comes when Jefferson's warnings are heeded at last, and we reduce government to its simplest terms, it may very well happen that Cal's bones . . . will come to be revered as those of a man who really did the nation some service." Mencken, with some abashment, confronts in Coolidge his ideal President—the one who does nothing.

This fitted Mencken's anarchic credo, put forth in 1924: "I believe that all government is evil, and that trying to improve it is largely a waste of time." In the spirit if not the exact language of the *Berkeley Barb* four decades later, when Vietnam and pot had produced the greatest invitation to scofflawry since Prohibition, he scorns the *"Polizei"* and praises criminals: "Try to imagine a race so broken to the yoke that it no longer produced highwaymen! God help the United States if it ever comes to that." A column on the Constitution ringingly begins, "All government, in its essence, is organized exploitation, and in virtually all of its existing forms it is the implacable enemy of every industrious and well-disposed man." Public servants are comically corrupt peddlers of buncombe: "The one aim of all such persons is to butter their own parsnips. They have no concept of the public good that can be differentiated from their concept of their own good." Such an insight can be effortlessly extended abroad: "Politics in Latin America, as in the United States, is idealistic only in words. Fundamentally, it is simply a struggle for jobs, with the hindmost left to the Devil." Perceptions so clear-eyed leave little scope for indignation, which is bred of disillusion, and in fact Mencken, except where his own existence was molested by prohibitions on liquor or reading matter, did not wax indignant. He waxed poetic.

Ms. Rodgers in her introduction quotes Mencken as claiming, "I am at my best in articles written in heat and printed at once." The urgencies of newspaper work curbed his natural verbosity and pedantry, while giving his robust and combustible mind display space. The pending deadline licensed his disinclination for intricate second thoughts, and the hasty compression of mental effort produced many marvellous verbal flowers. It is one thing to accuse public leaders of buncombe; it is another, and finer, to call their receptive followers "buncombophagi." The stale metaphor "counting noses" for the voting process takes on bizarre vitality as Mencken lets himself run with it: "The [Scopes] case will be decided by counting noses—and for every nose in these hills that has ever thrust itself into any book save the Bible there are a hundred adorned with the brass ring of Bryan." His rolling periods, studded with German words and revivals from obsolescence like "aurochs" (the extinct European bison, used loosely to mean "ox" or "average American"), were inimitable, except by S. J. Perelman, who took them to their logical conclusion of a laugh in every sentence. There are plenty of laughs here. Deploring the English diet in general, Mencken found good words for English mutton, and decided that it is "the product of English grass— unquestionably the best grass on this piebald ball. Ah, that the English nobility and gentry could dine as well as their sheep!" Of Truman's cam-

paign in 1948 he wrote, "If there had been any formidable body of cannibals in the country he would have promised to provide them with free
missionaries fattened at the taxpayers' expense." No journalist practicing
today can hit quite so orotund and jocular a note, not because none are as
clever as Mencken but because none can, in this age of airplanes and
round-the-clock CNN, luxuriate in his peculiar distance from the shared
national life.

"I believe my chances in Germany would have been at least as good as
they have been in America, and maybe a great deal better. I was born here
and so were my father and mother, and I have spent all of my 62 years
here, but I still find it impossible to fit myself into the accepted patterns
of American life and thought. After all these years, I remain a foreigner."
Mencken confided this to his diary not in the gemütlich days of the
Weimar Republic but in the ninth year of Hitler's dictatorship, with the
United States launched on a mighty war to relieve the world of the patterns of German thought as they had developed. It was not his German
ancestry that held him aloof; Dreiser was of more recent immigrant
blood than he, and identified wholly with American striving. It was something, possibly, about Baltimore. "The city into which I was born in 1880
had a reputation all over for what the English, in their real-estate advertising, are fond of calling the amenities," begins the fourth chapter of his
autobiographical *Happy Days*. For twenty-four years, he boasts in *The
Impossible H. L. Mencken*, in the column "On Living in Baltimore," he
kept an office in Manhattan, yet continued to commute the "four long
hours" to his native city, where he lived in one house for forty years. Even
now, does not this cozy semi-major city exercise a powerful gravitational
force? Does not the work of its two leading literary residents, Anne Tyler
and John Barth, exhibit a kindred sense of happy insulation, of brimming
sufficiency in an exemplary province? When Mencken writes about Baltimore virtues, it is of the horsecars and old stables and the "unutterably
charming" neighborhoods; when he writes of New York, it is as a tourist,
marvelling at the luxury hotels and the well-stocked shops, the ceaseless
construction and the traffic jams. "Baltimore is agreeable to me. . . . New
York irritates me." In his stubborn conservatism and jubilant loathing of
people different from himself, he was—dare we say it?—a yokel.

Stevens as Dutchman

WHAT COULD BE MORE SLAVISHLY STEVENSESQUE than these stanzas of "Cloud Shadows," a poem I wrote at the age of twenty-one?

> That white coconut, the sun,
>   is hidden by his blue leaves,
> piratical great galleons.
>
> Our sky their spanking sea,
>   they thrust us to an ocean floor,
> withal with certain courtesy.

Stevens was fascinating to me because I came from a suburb of Reading, Pennsylvania, and discovered about halfway through my adolescence that a great modern poet had been born and raised in the heart of the city, on North Fifth Street. His brother, Judge Stevens, still sat on the Berks County bench, and the head librarian at the Reading Public Library, Miss Ruth, remembered him fondly as her handsome high-school classmate. She thought it a pity, she spontaneously confessed, that he had married Elsie—Elsie Moll, a beautiful local girl of lesser caste and lesser largeness of mind.

But I had to go to Harvard to read his work—in Edwin Honig's seminar on modern poetry, which I took my senior year. My paper on Stevens got a C+, though I had put myself heartily into it, reading all of *Harmonium* and the Faber and Faber *Selected Poems*. Honig said I tried to cover too much. Better from narrow to broad than from broad to narrow, was the life-lesson this comedian as the letter C taught me.

I loved the high color in Stevens, the rollicking vocabulary, the bearish delicacy, the tirelessness of the onrolling blank verse, and the rare glimpses of Berks County terrain—

> From a Schuylkill in mid-earth there came emerging
> Flotillas, willed and wanted, bearing in them
> Shadows of friends, of those he knew. . . .

and

> One of the limits of reality
> Presents itself in Oley when the hay,
> Baked through long days, is piled in mows.

Written for a special issue of *The Wallace Stevens Journal.*

If Stevens could climb up from this pedestrian, workaday land of farmers, factory workers, and square-headed Pennsylvania Dutchmen into the bluest heights of modernist aestheticism, then the path was trod, and could be followed. A distinctly "Dutch" earthiness, I seemed to perceive, lay at the root of Stevens's fanciful sublimations, and a certain familiar stubbornness and industriousness at the heart of his productivity, which grew as he aged. Reading, a city of factories and railroad yards set squarely among exiguous but tidy and decorated and solid brick row houses, a city built between the gritty Schuylkill and the looming profile of Mt. Penn (surprisingly ornamented by a twelve-story pagoda), had bred not merely a poet but a superpoet, whose sense of mental adventure was present in the grandiloquent drift and the exuberantly mixed vocabulary of lines like

> Nota: his soil is man's intelligence.
> That's better. That's worth crossing seas to find.
> Crispin in one laconic phrase laid bare
> His cloudy drift and planned a colony.
> Exit the mental moonlight, exit lex,
> Rex and principium, exit the whole
> Shebang. Exeunt omnes. Here was prose
> More exquisite than any tumbling verse:
> A still new continent in which to dwell.

I was still provincial and unlettered enough to treasure his lusher verse, above all "Sunday Morning," which bids farewell to faith with a Lutheran gravity and ends with images that might have come right from the hilly fertile landscape of home:

> Deer walk upon our mountains, and the quail
> Whistle about us their spontaneous cries;
> Sweet berries ripen in the wilderness;
> And, in the isolation of the sky,
> At evening, casual flocks of pigeons make
> Ambiguous undulations as they sink,
> Downward to darkness, on extended wings.

My youthful sense, in connection with Stevens, of personal discovery and delight has been somewhat stolen from me by his great academic popularity in these recent decades. He has eclipsed in favor, I believe, almost all of the other stars of Honig's curriculum—Cummings, William Carlos Williams, Moore, Frost, even Eliot. His later, less lush poems, lit by mental moonlight and thought to be rather dry and circular in the Fifties, have been hoisted into great esteem by such connoisseurs of the American sublime as Harold Bloom. But I, perhaps, am still too Dutch to believe in the relentless essentialism of such efforts as "Notes toward a Supreme Fiction," wherein we are told:

> How clean the sun when seen in its idea,
> Washed in the remotest cleanliness of a heaven
> That has expelled us and our images . . .

Enough such lines put me in mind of Peter Davison's epigram on Stevens: "He mouthed and chewed ceaselessly upon the real, without, it seems, often tasting it."

And yet, even such a cursory inspection of his work as this brief tribute has prompted reminds me of how his poems are always a step ahead of the reader, always bearing from an oblique angle upon a momentous central matter, always demanding direct quotation and rendering paraphrase apologetic. His handsome *Collected Poems*, opened anywhere, opens onto greatness—onto an Epicureanism of the noblest sort, a stoic love of a dissolving world, a continuous concern with the highest use that poetry can be put to, a persistent reconstruction of reality through the workings of language and the mind, a delicious and elevating labor that puts the thought of death to sleep.

Wilson as Cape Codder

The Forties, by Edmund Wilson, edited by Leon Edel. 369 pp. Farrar, Straus and Giroux, 1983.

This, the third volume in the posthumous, decade-by-decade publication of Wilson's diaries and notebooks, shows the great critic, after the hectic Twenties and sombre Thirties, settling down. In this decade, he reached fifty; published a best-seller, *Memoirs of Hecate County*; met and married his fourth and final wife, Elena Mumm Wilson; fathered his third child, Helen Miranda; acquired the house in Wellfleet, Massachusetts, that he was to call home to the end of his life; and found employment with *The New Yorker*. Many of the pages of his Forties journals, indeed, are working notes for articles (on post-war Europe, on the Zuni Indians) which appeared in that magazine. Other pages concern an ambitious and intricate novel, *The Story of the Three Wishes*, that he never wrote, or register the "death, illness, and decay of old friends," or contain shapely paragraphs upon the weather and wildlife of his beloved Cape Cod. He closely observes the sex life of horseshoe crabs, and does not entirely neglect to describe his own. It is a pleasure for readers who have followed this restless and sometimes gloomy intellect thus far through the journals he maintained to see him at last happily married and situated, geographically and professionally, where he can exercise in relative freedom and comfort his phenomenal curiosity and powers of judgment. The book, like its predecessors, is attractively produced in the compact Wilsonian format, and admirably edited, with just the right amount of helpful elucidation, by Professor Edel.

The Critic in Winter

THE SIXTIES: *The Last Journal, 1960–1972*, by Edmund Wilson, edited with an introduction by Lewis M. Dabney. 968 pp. Farrar, Straus and Giroux, 1993.

The last installment of Edmund Wilson's journals is, at over nine hundred pages, the bulkiest of the lot; the lot comprises seven chunky volumes, if one adds *A Prelude* and *Upstate*, which Wilson himself annotated and expanded, to the five chronological volumes, beginning with *The Twenties*, that were posthumously published. Leon Edel, who edited the journals of the previous four decades, has yielded the editorship to Lewis M. Dabney; Mr. Dabney, the editor of *The Portable Edmund Wilson*, has topped up this terminal tome with two appendices, more than thirty pages of biographical sketches of persons mentioned by Wilson, a foreword, an excellent introduction, and a fuller and jollier set of chapter heads than Mr. Edel ever saw fit to provide. The journal entries extend into the Seventies, up to those of June 11, 1972, the day before Wilson died, at the age of seventy-seven. Dying and decay are the overall theme. The first notation reads:

> Jan 1, 1960. At my age, I find that I alternate between spells of fatigue and indifference when I am almost ready to give up the struggle, and spells of expanding ambition, when I feel that I can do more than ever before.

This poem to his wife, Elena, appears on the final page:

> Is that a bird or a leaf?
> Good grief!
> My eyes are old and dim,
> And I am getting deaf, my dear,
> Your words are no more clear
> And I can hardly swim.
> I find this rather grim.

As the reader plows, or swims, through these rather grim pages, he is sustained by the transparent, always refreshing element of Wilson's lucid mental outlook. The journals are not quite literature, yet they have an unpreening frankness and an energetic curiosity that stimulates our appetite for literature. We feel readier for reading after traversing these journals, and for reading as well the scribbled texts of society and nature. Wilson was a journalist first and last, and he takes notes on the New Yorkers and Cape Codders around him as eagerly and amusedly as he observes the Hungarians and Israelis he visits on assignment. His isolated upbringing in Red Bank, New Jersey, as an only child with a deaf mother and a disturbed father, left him a grateful, exuberant diner at life's feast. At his home in Wellfleet, on Cape Cod, he writes, "Our life is so quiet and monotonous that a visit like that of the Pipeses seems to me wildly exciting and probably puts a strain on my nerves. I invariably drink too much." In Naples, Florida, appalled by the arid social landscape, he observes, "Peculiar footlessness of ideas that pass through my head here—importance of being somewhere where people are doing something. Otherwise, just nature, nothing." His trips to New York City, even when his frail health scarcely permitted him to stay awake at dinner parties, were frenzies of social engagement and renewed acquaintance. As if seeking out the company of his family's ghosts, he insisted on spending much of each summer at his family's old house in Talcottville, in upper New York State, though his wife refused to accompany him for more than two weeks in August. Here, in this depressed region populated by juvenile delinquents and members of the John Birch Society, among aging old friends and acquaintances enlisted as chauffeurs (Wilson never learned to drive), he still saw some action. The juvenile delinquents noisily drag-raced past his house, and at one juncture he found three of them "drinking beer and drunk" on his front porch. He confronted them impressively:

> I appeared to them with the old gun that the Civil War collector in Boonville had offered to buy as a relic, and they immediately took to their heels. After that, when they gathered I bawled them out, and finally got rid of them.

On another local front, he managed, though riddled with somatic complaints that would shortly kill him, to work up an attraction for his young dentist's wife, and to persuade him to allow him considerable liberties. At the age of seventy-five he reënacts, with a free spirit from the late Sixties, his conquests of the Roaring Twenties:

We finished three bottles of Moselle, a pint of Johnnie Walker (partly by me after she left), and by her the beginning of a bottle of gin. I told her that she would have been quite at home in the twenties.

She—discreetly called "Z" in this passage but elsewhere identified as Anne Miller—gave him lessons in open-mouthed kissing; they earnestly discussed the purpose of pubic hair, and, while she sat "almost completely" undressed and "cross-legged" on his bed, he "stroked her brown body delightfully." Having described the heartening episode with Wilsonian thoroughness, he lets drop into the journal a *cri de coeur*: "—wonderful to feel a wet, gluey, reeking cunt."

Sex, so long his heavy preoccupation, receives a mixed blessing in farewell:

> The last lusts gutter out.
> A force that keeps driving, nagging one that one has no memory of creating oneself.
> That all this fuss should be made about getting one's penis into a woman—filling people with rapture and despair and stimulating them to all kinds of heroisms and excesses.
> Yet homosexuals don't seem to have flowered and borne fruit, don't seem to have fully matured: Auden with his appetite for Tolkien.

Each of the handsome uniform volumes in which Farrar Straus Giroux has brought out the journals bears a contemporary photograph of Wilson: even back when he had a hairline, his face was marked by a high, luminous brow and a bulldog expression. The force of his character, as much as his erudition and taste, enabled him to dominate American criticism. In this journal he remarks of a professorial friend that he has "no large imaginative grasp or intellectual penetration." Wilson's masculine will toward penetration drives him to seek the live psychological presence behind the text. His judgments have the decisiveness, and sometimes the peremptory impatience, of a self-assured gentleman. He was unintimidatable; he would tackle any topic or language. There were intellectual stratagems and niceties that simply never occurred to him—he owed no literary friend a friendly lie, there was no text to which he owed automatic deference. Turning in his old age to the most exalted classics, he finds both Goethe and Tolstoy wanting. Making his way in German through the second part of *Faust*, he writes that Goethe "often irritates and bores" him: "He seems to have no sense of form whatever—simply strings endless incidents and creatures together. . . . Really he has all the characteristics of Germans—egoism, blind self-assertion, pomposity, lack of consideration for others." His resolutely ad-hominem approach rings almost deafeningly in this day of gingerly deconstruction. Against Tolstoy's late works he brings the startlingly basic charge of implausibility: in 1961 he notes of "The Death of Ivan Ilyich," "I do not care for this story as much as many people do: I don't believe that a man like Ivan Ilyich could ever look back on his life and find it so empty and futile; I don't believe that Tolstoy, in the period when he was writing his great novels, would have ever invented such a character." Seven years later, he returns to the charge: "I don't believe in these late stories of Tolstoy's, always intended to prove something and incompletely invented. . . . It begins, perhaps, in *Anna Karenina*. Would she really have thrown herself under that train? I have never quite believed it."

Authors in their style and behavior exasperate him but also give him comradely comfort. He reads Macaulay in the dead of night and finds "quite fortifying" the dying historian's rounding-out his narrative "with the same high morality and thoroughness" as throughout. On the night of his seventy-fourth birthday, depressed by "not being able to make love, not being able to swim or take much exercise and now, with my lower teeth gone, not being able to eat anything but the softest food," Wilson wakes after bad dreams "feeling horrible." The medicine is at hand: "But [I] read Macaulay and somewhat regained my equanimity and my inspiration to live." Balzac, though Wilson laments his "preposterous" improbabilities and oppressive "murkiness and squalor," becomes the critic's faithful companion, novel after novel, like a raffish buddy indulged for his irrepressible vitality by a superior, more serious friend. "Happily sunk in Balzac again" is one of the last journal entries.

Wilson's final twelve years were productive. In 1960, he was publishing *Apologies to the Iroquois* and fending off prosecution for tax delinquency, an embarrassment that was to flavor his pessimistic introduction to *Patriotic Gore* and inspire his book-length diatribe *The Cold War and the Income Tax*. As the decade wore on, he pursued his interest in the Dead Sea Scrolls, in Hungary and its language, in Canada and its literature, in the history of upper New York State. Books and articles were generated from all these interests; his travels in Europe in 1963 and 1964 fattened a reissue of *Europe Without Baedeker*; his Jerusalem visit of 1967 figured in an amplified reissue of "The Dead Sea Scrolls." A collection of three plays—one old, two new—was brought out; his youthful novel *I Thought of Daisy* was reprinted with the even more youthful story "Galahad." To raise money for his tax troubles, he sold his papers to Yale; perhaps this valedictory move stimulated his delving into his journals to produce *A Prelude* and *Upstate*. *Upstate* became a modest best-seller. Two more collections—*A Window on Russia* and *The Devils and Canon*

Barham—followed, the latter after his death. Wilson was, in short, the model of an elderly, honored author industriously tidying up his desk. Yet his journals record a fearful struggle with physical deterioration—fitful impotence, virtual toothlessness, gout, heart attacks—and a dark apathy in regard to his life and to life itself.

His intimations of "the relative feebleness and futility of human lives" form a bass undertone to his scurry of socializing, drinking, award-receiving, reading, and writing:

> When you realize that it won't be so long before you fade out of life, the activities of so short-lived human beings begin to seem rather futile and the beings themselves flimsy. Does it really matter that much? And all that energy and worry expended on merely getting themselves reproduced!

> The subjects we study with such care seem of transitory unreal interest. . . . Is it worth it to impose the order—bound to be superficial and specious—of literature and scientific theory on the mess of our human exploits?

> . . . *the flimsiness of human life*. Surrounded by the void of the universe, we agitate ourselves, one sometimes feels, to very dubious purpose. Our little lives soon go out, and is it really at all surprising that in order to fulfill our immediate desires, we should put out other lives, send them off into the void? Eventually, we shall go blank—what difference does it make if they do?

> A feeling, the older I get—which I never expected to have—that earthly matters are hardly worth the effort . . . Soon I'll be fading out of it, why bother to read books, meet people, travel to foreign countries?

He had not expected to have such a feeling, this man of insatiable curiosity and appetite, and keeps returning to it in his journals, as if the sensation of indifference and removal is in its way precious; it is as close as Wilson comes to mysticism—St. John of the Cross's "dark night of the soul," Buddhism's Nirvana and non-attachment, the *"lauter Nichts"* ("pure Nothing") that summed up God for Meister Eckhardt. Wilson, the descendant of Presbyterian divines, has worked through to the opinion of Ecclesiastes: "I have seen all the works that are done under the sun; and, behold, all *is* vanity and vexation of spirit."

Six months to the day before he died, he inscribed this journal entry:

> *December 12, 1971, Wellfleet*. When I look back, I feel quite definitely divided from my earlier self, who cared about things in a way I no longer do. All that comedy and conflict of human activity—one gets to feel cut off from all that. One cannot even imagine any more the time when one had

once participated. One ought perhaps to have died before reaching this point, when one still had the illusion of participating. All that energy expanded [sic] to peter out! One looks down on an empty arena. What were we all doing there?—running about, jostling and shouting, exchanging vital gossip—involved in great world wars now as trivial and futile as we used to think the Balkan wars were.

His dismissal of the two world wars, like his famous description, in the introduction to *Patriotic Gore*, of any war as no more moral than a battle between two voracious sea slugs, transfers to the relativities of real politics the Swiftian scorn he had come to feel for mankind: "Reading the newspapers, and even the world's literature, I find that I more and more feel a boredom with and scorn for the human race." But acedia breeds inactivity, and activity was Wilson's nature. Reading those same newspapers, he discovered a surprising exemplar:

> *The knowledge that death is not far away*, that I shall soon disappear like a puff of smoke, has the effect of making earthly affairs seem unimportant and human beings more and more ignoble. It is harder to take human life seriously, including one's own passions and achievements and efforts. In my tendency toward this state of mind, I have found Pope John fortifying. When over 80 and knowing he is doomed [by cancer], he gives all the energy left him to his council which will modernize the Church.

Not that Wilson in his decline went soft on religion. Though his work on the Dead Sea Scrolls brought him into friendly contact with intelligent Jesuits, he stopped reading a book by Father Martin D'Arcy with the remark "I can't enter into the point of view of someone who talks about this love between God and the human race." He sat Wilfrid Sheed down at a party and complained "that I couldn't even understand the idea about Christ: sent down by the Father to suffer and redeem the human race. If you believe this, you will be forgiven. What sense does this make?" He commented on the moon landing, "Heaven and God are not up there," and marvelled that "we have not yet completely sloughed off the absurdities of those old theologies . . . that have been hanging around our lives for thousands of years." A Wilson to whom human religiosity would have seemed less bizarre might have been, in some respects, a more sensitive critic, and one who would not so often have resorted to a tone of incredulous arraignment in his appraisals; but a brisk and dauntless rationalism was his religion—his version of Presbyterian rectitude—and it is hard to imagine him otherwise. In what he called "the dark defile of age," he stoically paid the price of an illusionless depression, relieved by generous helpings of alcohol. When a Boston hospital offered him a pacemaker to regularize the beat of his failing heart, he refused it as another useless illusion, confiding to his journal, "I don't want electrodes attached to my heart, and I suspect that this is simply the latest medical fad."

The events of the tumultuous Sixties but lightly dented his carapace and tended to confirm his impression "that all the horrors of a hateful, convulsive and chaotic civilization are closing in on you from every side." He took a visit to the Kennedys' White House rather sourly in stride. He was anti-Vietnam, within a larger opposition to the whole Cold War and the taxes that financed it. In the "sunlit hell" of Naples, Florida, he observed that "our enthusiam for McGovern was coldly received" by one of the rich retirees of their acquaintance. He felt claustrophobic in this retirement paradise: "The people here are almost incredible, and yet they represent the American Dream. I said that it was like living in prison." The liberating social revolutions of his last decade no more engaged him than the new writing of the period—though he took a keen fancy to the comedy team of Nichols and May, especially to Elaine May, and kept going to the movies. He went alone to *Campus Confidential* ("frankly pornographic to a degree that I didn't know was possible for a publicly shown film") and in his last month gave two popular movies the briefest possible review: "Two movies: *Godfather* and *French Connection*, bang bang." In 1961 he wrote:

> I find that I am a man of the twenties. I still expect something exciting: drinks, animated conversation, gaiety: an uninhibited exchange of ideas. Scott Fitzgerald's idea that somewhere things were "glimmering."

Yet Wilson's creative art—foremost, his two books of fiction, *I Thought of Daisy* and *Memoirs of Hecate County*—does not glimmer; it glowers. Shadows of the macabre, of dissolute behavior and mental breakdown are what one remembers. His imagination was saturnine, and the resonance—the *gravitas*, as they say now—of his criticism derives in part from a tug from below the lucid expository surface. As the shadows close around him in these journals, Wilson seems, with his Balzac, his martinis, and his night thoughts, grouchily at home.

An Ohio Runaway

DAWN POWELL AT HER BEST, edited by Tim Page. 452 pp. Steerforth Press, 1994.

The reputation of Dawn Powell may be doomed to a perpetual state of revival. She is too good a fiction writer—too deft, funny, knowing, compassionate, and poetic—to be altogether forgotten, yet is not, in a sense, emblematic enough to be one of the permanent exhibits in the zoo of academically imposed American novelists. Hemingway, Faulkner, and Fitzgerald are the great flashing beasts of her era, with Sinclair Lewis and John Steinbeck lumbering unignorably beside; even Erskine Caldwell, Nathanael West, and Thornton Wilder have signature themes and tics to vivify them in a survey course. Dawn Powell might have found space in the anthologies had she been, like Katherine Anne Porter, Dorothy Parker, and Mary McCarthy, at her best in the short story. Though she did write short stories, including seven that appeared in *The New Yorker* between 1933 and 1940, even the best feel sketchy; she needed the big canvas of the novel, with its room for multiple viewpoints and a lofty perspective, to express her sense of the world.

Born in Ohio in 1897, Powell belongs, in her own, lighter vein, with Theodore Dreiser and Willa Cather and those other Midwestern writers who felt something epic in the national shift from rural to urban, from provincial sequestration to metropolitan liberation. Her mother died when she was six, and her father was a travelling salesman; she and her two sisters were lodged with a variety of "very prim strict relatives," as she put it. Several times, Dawn ran away. "The best time to run away is September," she once wrote, and "There's something about farm life that gives you the strength to run anywhere in the world." When Dawn Powell was young, there was only one non-provincial place in America to run to: New York City. She came to New York in 1918, after graduating from Lake Erie College in Painesville, Ohio, a few months before the Armistice. She was only twenty, and never ceased to be a patriotic New Yorker. In 1931 she wrote her favorite cousin, Jack F. Sherman: "New York City [is] the only place where people with nothing behind them but their wits can be and do everything . . . What I mean, friend, is that you can be yourself here and it's the only place where being genuine will absolutely get you anywhere you want."

These hearty avowals are quoted by Tim Page in his introduction to *Dawn Powell at Her Best*, which he has edited and Steerforth Press, of

South Royalton, Vermont, has attractively published. Although five of Powell's novels have been reissued in paperback since 1989, this is the first reissue in hardcover. The volume holds two novels, *Dance Night* and *Turn, Magic Wheel*, eight short stories, and a brief but pithy autobiographical essay, "What Are You Doing in My Dreams?" Both novels come endorsed by their author: in 1957 Powell told the *New York Herald Tribune* that of her works *Dance Night* was her favorite; elsewhere she described *Turn, Magic Wheel* as "very likely my best, simplest, most original book." Between them, they cover her two literary terrains, Ohio and Manhattan. *Dance Night* (1930) is one of six novels that take place in Ohio, and—not counting her very first novel, *Whither*, published in 1925—*Turn, Magic Wheel* (1936) is the first of a spirited sequence set in New York City, most often among the bohemians of Greenwich Village. The author changes personality depending on her locale; *Dance Night* partakes of Sherwood Anderson's wistful mood of small-town disquiet and projects the blurred largeness and helpless emotional force of childhood impressions, whereas *Turn, Magic Wheel* has the giddiness and acidity of Evelyn Waugh and Aldous Huxley in such smart, edgy romps as *Vile Bodies* and *Antic Hay*—send-ups of modern sophistication from a modern, sophisticated standpoint. As Edmund Wilson pointed out in his own attempt, in 1962, to revive Powell's fading reputation, "She is closer to this high social comedy than to any accepted brand of American humor." By this time, Powell, whose last novel was published the same year, could be likened as well to Muriel Spark and Anthony (no relation) Powell. Her novels feel English in their matter-of-fact expertness, their quickness to set a large cast of characters in motion, their disinclination to moralize, and their subordination of psychological and natural detail to a colorful social weave. Human nature is nature enough; no portentous bears or marlins or whales need apply to Dawn Powell's casting office.

Mr. Page, whose introduction is a model of measured homage by a recent convert to the Powell cult, betrays his youth when he asserts that *Dance Night* is "a dingy portrait of a tiny boomtown in the last years of the 1920s." The fictional community of Lamptown has as one of its few social centers an openly functioning saloon; therefore, the time of action predates Prohibition, which took effect early in 1920. Since the First World War is never mentioned, and never shadows the thoughts of the young male characters, the time can be pushed back further; one may reasonably suppose Lamptown to derive from impressions of life in Shelby, Ohio—home of the Shelby Electric Company, manufacturer of some of the first incandescent lightbulbs—that Dawn received between

1910, when her maternal aunt, Orpha May Steinbrueck, took her in after she ran away from her father and stepmother, and 1914, when she went off to college. Shelby, in the northern middle of the state, was not only a factory town but a busy transfer point for the New York Central, Baltimore & Ohio, and Pennsylvania railroads. Mrs. Steinbrueck lived directly opposite the railroad junction. The constant switching and rumbling of trains lends Lamptown the romance of distant places and brings to a number of its female citizens specific romances with the itinerant, rakish trainmen.

Lamptown has an excess of factory girls. "Nine hundred girls, all young and lively there at the Works with no men's factory around to give them beaux": so says Mrs. Pepper, a travelling corset purveyor. Young Nettie Farrell complains, "Every time a new man comes to town it's like dividing a mouse up for a hundred cats." The mob of unmated females fills Lampton's air with yearning and provides the patronage for the novel's central institutions, the Bon Ton Hat Shop, where Nettie works as assistant to the proprietress, Elsinore Abbott, and the Thursday-night dances at the Casino, which are managed by the travelling dance instructor Harry Fischer. The Casino Dance Hall is situated above Bauer's Chop House; it faces the Bon Ton and Bill Delaney's Saloon and Billiard Parlor to form the novel's conveniently compact stage of action. Morry Abbott, the son of Elsinore and her husband, Charles, a travelling candy salesman, finds comfort talking to a new arrival in town, Jen St. Clair, a fourteen-year-old foundling-home girl adopted by Bill Delaney and his termagant of an ancient mother. A cat's cradle of frustrated desire is woven among the doorways and stairways of this tiny downtown: Jen loves Morry; Morry is seduced by Nettie and by Grace Terris, the "easy" waitress at Bauer's Chop House, but neither seduction takes; both Mrs. Pepper and Mrs. Abbott are in love with the dashing dancing master, Fischer; Jen is taken up by the town's one-man wealthy class, young and feckless Hunt Russell, who has inherited the lamp works; Morry falls in love with Jen's beautiful blonde young sister, Lil, when she is at last released from the orphanage.

But Morry, a broad-shouldered seventeen-year-old who lies in bed reading Jules Verne while his mother and Nettie run the shop downstairs, is less convincing as a lover than as a love object; female desire — a mighty topic, though Victorian prudery found it as awkward as does feminist purism now — is Dawn Powell's theme, in all its varieties of risk and pain. Even old Mrs. Delaney, in her sharp-tongued effort to discourage Morry's lackadaisical attentions to Jen, crackles with the force of it: "Old ideas and wild blood in her and outside of that I trust no young girl.

They're all alike, crazy to get into trouble, always stuck on the boys."
The factory girls, we are told, "write their addresses on the crates that are
shipped out from the factory and they get answers back sometimes from
all over the world. That little Tucker girl they say went all the way to
Australia to marry a man she'd never seen." Nettie, in a remarkable scene
of desperate sexual predation, defies not only propriety but Morry's
seething dislike of her:

> He would like to have taken her by the neck and shook her like a dog would
> shake a hen, but all he could do was to sink his teeth into her round shoul-
> der and bite as hard as he could. Nettie stopped kicking him and began to
> whimper childishly. . . . "Now do be quiet about it," Nettie whispered warn-
> ingly, and didn't even bother to put up her hands in protest when he started
> tearing her blouse again.

Charles Abbott's paranoid, sadistically expressed suspicions that his wife
is unfaithful are not wide of the mark; when he is disposed of, in a wonderfully downplayed moment of violence, Elsinore and her rival for
Harry Fischer's affections, Mrs. Pepper, become hefty, sisterly cruisers
on the dry-goods circuit, on the lookout for "Fine-looking Men" in hotel
lobbies and parlor cars. The sexual imperative outlasts and outshines
motherhood: Elsinore reflects of Morry that "even as a baby he'd been a
stranger—oh yes, part of her in some curious way that made his presence
always welcome, but nonetheless he was a stranger. She wondered if
other mothers were perpetually astonished at their maternity and secretly
a little skeptical of the miracle." And Morry comes to see that his
mother's is "the face of a stranger" and to realize that "there was no place
for him in his mother's life, that there never had been, and he'd flush with
shame to remember his fierce tenderness for his mother as a frantic lover
might blush who realizes in cool retrospect that the beloved was always
indifferent to him."

No human affections survive Dawn Powell's rueful, sympathetic analysis: in this she suggests Proust. Morry is awakened from his infatuation
with Jen's younger sister, Lil, by the perception that "romance was
between a man and love, not between a man and woman"; Jen sees that
"always she would be left because people didn't care for you the way you
cared for them." Childhood itself is a "dreadful cage": "Nothing in life
was possible unless you were old and rich, until then you were only small
and futile before your tormentors." It's a hard world, Lamptown, and
from an inventory of its frustrations and disillusions one could hardly
imagine why Dawn Powell is considered a comic novelist. But such an
inventory leaves out her animated grasp of mundane details, from the

tricks of the millinery trade to the sweaty dazzle of a small-town dance hall, and the driving vitality of her characters' rapt, wily, self-serving talk. Here is the sluttish waitress Grace, dreaming up a future for herself and her asset of "personality":

> "I'm going away, too, believe me. And not to work in any Lamptown dump, either, I'm going to Detroit to work in a big cafeteria. Say, there's a town. A fella was in here the other day, a big bicycle salesman, and he says there's nothing Chicago has got that Detroit hasn't got. He says they got money to burn up there, fellas crazy for a girl with a little life in her, believe me, I'm not sticking in this dump after what this fella told me. He said why a girl with my personality wouldn't have to take nothin' from nobody up there in Detroit, why he says, Gracie, I've seen girls with only half your personality driving their own automobiles in Detroit and you take this Belle Isle, there's nothin' like it this side of New York City, he was sayin'."

Had Henry Green's *Living* been published earlier than 1929, and achieved wider circulation, one might propose an influence. Not only does Powell have Green's lovely ear for talk, and his eye for our essential egoism, but some of her sentences, like his, overflow punctuation, so brimful are they of the moment:

> Her nose quite red Nettie whirled into the back room and for several minutes Elsinore and Mrs. Pepper heard her banging drawers shut and whistling shrilly to indicate how well under control was her temper.

Such poetic hurry is rarer in *Turn, Magic Wheel*, as is our feeling that the author is lost within the richness of her bleak material. Dawn Powell here has donned her New York self, and shows a practiced hand. Perhaps too practiced—there is a slight forcing and a touch of condescension in such a bright vignette as this:

> Lüchow's was filled with a lodge banquet and in every room middle-aged men grimly wore paper hats and clinked glasses with their big wives. The orchestra played polychrome waltzes and a fat man was stirred to get up and holding his stomach in, danced marvelously with a thin toothy girl who arched her scanty behind the way her crowd at Montclair always did.

Dance night is every night now, and the magic wheel of love turns as fast as a pinwheel. In the bigger Manhattan environment, Powell's characters seem somewhat smaller and their predicaments more capriciously self-induced. Yet an earnest examination of the literary vocation is afoot, as well as a satire on mid-Thirties literary life, and amid the swiftly rung changes of a booze-lubricated love farce are excoriating scenes, shocking in their nakedness, of the desperation to which love reduces women. Like *Dance Night*, the novel pivots upon a male protagonist—not adolescent, sluggish Morry Abbott, with his furtive bookishness and vague architectural aspirations, but a red-haired, mentally hyperactive, young, short, and faintly dandified ("a rather nonchalantly Prince of Wales way of wearing his clothes") novelist, Dennis Orphen. The name invites us to consider Orphen (who will return in later novels) something of an alter ego, since Powell thought of herself as an orphan, and the aunt who came closest to being a mother was named Orpha. Orphen's present problem is that he has for the last three years attached himself to Effie Callingham, the former wife of the Hemingway-calibre writer Andrew Callingham, and has betrayed their friendship by writing a novel closely based upon her. According to Edmund Wilson, the à-clef problem is one that Powell avoided; he "almost never found [her] exploiting a personality . . . whom he was able to recognize." But what writer does not recognize Orphen's sensations when real life rises up and incredulously confronts its image in art?

> When he came into the apartment he found Effie already there, the book in her hands, and Dennis had his first swift realization of what the words must mean to her. Why, he thought, meeting her stricken eyes, this was not merely writing. This was a living woman he was putting on the market, the living Effie. He felt guilty and angry.

Confrontation of another sort occurs when Effie takes him to the home of her rich friends the Glaenzers, which he has previously rendered in print out of his imagination and her confidences; the fit is so exact that he has "a nauseating sense of entering the looking glass, of dreaming true." Orphen is relieved to see that one niche contains not the "terra-cotta madonna" he had described in his novel but "a large hideous Chinese vase filled with gloomy lilies."

Such Nabokovian games with reality and mimicry are nice, and Powell's satirical creation of the publisher MacTweed and his minions matches Waugh's heartless partnership of Old Rampole and Mr. Benfleet in *Vile Bodies*. Mr. MacTweed is described as "lifting his horrendous piratical gray eyebrows by specially developed muscles at the top of his skull—certainly no ordinary temporal muscles could undertake such a mighty task very frequently." His minions are all "tallish young men with sleek mouse-colored hair, large mouths filled with strong big white teeth good for gnawing bark or raw coconuts but doubtless taxed chiefly by moules or at the most squab, nearsighted pleasant eyes under unrimmed glasses that might be bifocal . . . and agreeable deep voices left over from old Glee Clubs." The barbs directed at then-fashionable proletarian fiction, the caricatures of the parties and puffery that accompany a book's publication, the comic ubiquity in Manhattan of literary ambitions, the delirious inflation of the mythical, Europe-dwelling Callingham—all these japes are cheerfully executed by a writer who shunned publicity and never enjoyed high sales, but they have taken on, as satire does, a dated, somewhat petty air.

It is as a celebration of love's monstrous spell that *Turn, Magic Wheel* is still fresh and astounds, moves, and enlightens us. Marian, a younger woman who stole Callingham from Effie fifteen years before, returns to New York, fatally ill with cancer, and Effie becomes her only comforter. Marian, in dying, operatically echoes Effie's own infatuation with a love object who, we do not need his eventual arrival on the scene to realize, is the epitome of obtuse and cruel male self-centeredness. And Effie at last realizes it too, even as she shares with her dying rival childhood photos of Callingham, and they dote together over "the funny little face of him!" and his appearance at five, in a Fauntleroy outfit:

> A smile, tender and wishful, played about Marian's fine bluish lips, it sang through her eyes and the hands so lovingly lingering over these mementoes, a little lullaby of a smile, an emanation from the small scraps themselves, for it fluttered across Effie's lips also, delicate, fleeting, an odd little ghost of lost happiness.

The several scenes in the hospital, as the two women draw close in their shunned love, display a harrowing extreme of poignance and gallant folly. Effie wins free of her erotic shackles, but Marian rapturously dies in them as Callingham at last manages to visit her: "When he saw her lying there he had slipped suddenly to the floor, buried his face on the pillow beside her and so she had died." And the reader's own romantic disposition, even after this travesty, finds satisfaction in the happy amorous ending that the author bestows upon Dennis Orphen. Effie is described in Mr. Page's introduction as Dennis's mistress, but we never see them make love; the red-haired author's lovemaking is all with wanton, gorgeous, silly, married Corinne, who—in another confrontation of truth with incredulous reality—blurts out her adulterous passion to her husband and is not believed. "Poor Honeybaby," he says. "For a few minutes there the poor kid went clean out of her mind."

There is no suggestion, in this charade of amorous delusions, that Dawn Powell would have had it any other way. She continued her own marriage, to Joseph Gousha (with whom she shared the care and expense of their handicapped son), while carrying on an extended open liaison with Coburn "Coby" Gilman. Bohemian freedoms were part of New York's enchantment, an enchantment of which she remains a principal singer. The city is more than its geography and buildings; it is the secret eroticism that a place so purely human concentrates, like a perfume pressed from a thousand flowers. The galvanic sexual currents of *Turn, Magic Wheel* spin off from the metropolis's pooled energies. The life-force that in the Lamptowns of the world must struggle against prudery and poverty and class stratification and the onus of being too fully known is strengthened by an impersonal metropolis that reflects back a chosen self:

> Effie got up and looked out the window into the gathering night, twin churches in twin duncecaps of illuminated spires across the street, a skyscraper emptied of workers now threaded with a single row of hall lights, and far-off flaming red sky over Broadway. Outside blurred suddenly into a shadowy reflection of herself in the windowpane, herself with churches, skyscraper, and red sky spreading over the ghostly outline of her head.

Give us your lonely, your misunderstood, your sexually malcontent, your stubborn provincial dreamers: responding to this siren call, Dawn Powell stayed loyal to New York with an ardor beside which that of celebrants like Scott Fitzgerald and E. B. White appears fickle. Such loyalty was in effect a loyalty to the human roil, which she saw with an unhappy child's skepticism and macabre intimations. In the oneiric memoir that ends this anthology, she writes of how, when she thought she was back in Ohio, her "heart began thumping with a kind of terror, the terror of discovering you're human which is worse than any fear of the supernatural."

Powell's heroines, like Jen and Effie, arouse sympathy but do not inspire emulation; her lesser female characters tend to be needy, rapacious, and deluded, and are portrayed with a raking frankness that if from a male author might rouse the charge of misogyny. Her empathy with male impatience and resentment in regard to the fair sex is alarmingly thorough. Not that her men, as they boast and blunder their way through these novels and short stories like "Audition" and "Every Day Is Ladies' Day," are saints; they are so feckless as to make one puzzle over her predilection for male viewpoints. Pervasively sharp-eyed, Powell does not shape her plots to any clear moral; she once said, "My characters are not slaves to an author's propaganda. I give them their heads. They furnish their own nooses." The image reveals a hangman's vision, belied by the far-from-disheartening bustle of her books. If not pleased by life, she was amused by it. The terror of discovering she was human found mitigation in the very place where humanity was densest.

Happiness, How Sad

THE COMPLETE FICTION OF W. M. SPACKMAN, edited with an afterword by
Steven Moore. 634 pp. Dalkey Archive Press, 1997.

William Mode Spackman was born in Coatesville, Pennsylvania, in
1905 and died in 1990, in Princeton, New Jersey. Having grown up in
Wilmington, Delaware, and attended Princeton as an undergraduate and
graduate student, he became a bard of the posher precincts of the Middle
Atlantic region, to which his travels and arcadian imagination annexed
various handsome regions of France and Italy. He is among the most
transatlantic of American writers; at the same time he remained proudly
conscious of his roots in the Quaker aristocracy of the Main Line.
Graduating from Princeton with honors in French and Italian literatures
in 1927, he won a Rhodes Scholarship, and for three years studied Greek
philosophy and ancient Greek and Roman history at Balliol College,
Oxford. Quotations from Greek and Latin and phrases of French and
Italian are liberally sprinkled throughout his fiction. Before his last year
at Oxford, Spackman married an Episcopal bishop's daughter, Mary Ann
Matthews, whose first American ancestor had been one of Cromwell's
lieutenants. In this same year of 1929 he lost a great deal of money in the
stock-market crash; his parents, in Steven Moore's words, "owned a large
hardware store with a substantial steel operation."

Spackman, it would seem, was in his blueblood fashion a victim of the
Depression. His mature fiction offers a series of blithely monied, cavalierly attractive (and single) heroes whom one might conjecture to be
Spackman unbound—a shining collegian never chastened by reality. He
returned from England to teach classics at New York University for a
year and to get a master's degree at Princeton; then, Moore tells us, "he
spent the rest of the Thirties working as a copy-writer and account
executive for various public relations agencies in New York City." Not a
bad life, while millions were going hungry, but for a gourmet sensibility
like his surely distasteful. In a blunt afterword to his first novel, *Heyday*
(1953), he describes its subject as "the young American upper class in that
era of its disaster, the 1930s." He goes on to characterize the class of 1927
as "perhaps the last generation brought up in those traditions of moral
competence and severe pride in the individual which progressive education and the welfare state have nearly stamped out by now forever." Yet,
aside from the hero of his last novel, who claims amid his pastoral pursuits to be a political journalist (of a witheringly caustic bent), his pro-

tagonists' moral competence and severe pride are almost entirely eclipsed by their sizable capacity for self-indulgence, notably in the areas of sex, food, and fancy property. As a writer Spackman sought what Henry James, in *The Golden Bowl*, termed "the convenience of a society so placed that it had only its own sensibility to consider."

World War II—to continue with the somewhat scanty facts—found Spackman in the Rockies, where he had gone for his wife's health. He did service as director of the Office of Public Information at the University of Colorado in Boulder, and toward the war's end studied Russian at the Navy Language School there. In 1945 the university hired him as an assistant professor of classics, a post he resigned the year that *Heyday*—written during a sabbatical leave in France—was published, to mixed reviews and with some editorial censorship of the English edition. He wished to dedicate himself to writing and was dissatisfied with the way in which literature was taught, a dissatisfaction he expressed in his next commercially published book, a collection of essays titled *On the Decay of Humanism*, brought out by the Rutgers University Press in 1967. There was, the same year, a privately printed book of poems. Though Moore doesn't say so, there must have been an amount of that Quaker hardware money left, for Spackman spent many months of the post-war decades living abroad, and in his spare time he "designed and built two Queen Anne houses for himself and his family, even the rough carpentry and panelling, and later remodeled a modern-style house as well as a large seaside villa in France."

The talent deflected by the Depression ran afoul, eventually, of the 1970s' feminist movement. Spackman finished the novel *An Armful of Warm Girl* in 1955 and saw it rejected over the years by fifteen publishers. When he submitted the book to Knopf in the early Seventies, he was told, according to Moore, "that the advent of the feminist movement made his novel unpublishable at that time." But in 1977 the editors of *Canto*, a new literary magazine, ran *An Armful of Warm Girl* as the entire contents of their second issue, and Gordon Lish, an *Esquire* editor, urged the book again on Knopf, which brought out the *Canto* text in the spring of 1978, when its author was seventy-three. In the next eight years Knopf published three more short novels—*A Presence with Secrets* (1980), *A Difference of Design* (1983), and *A Little Decorum, for Once* (1985). A fifth, *As I Sauntered Out, One Midcentury Morning*, was in the editorial works when death overtook Spackman, who was a notable example of geriatric blooming or of neglected genius, depending on how you look at it.

His American companions in the Dalkey Archive editions include Djuna Barnes, William Gass, Gilbert Sorrentino, and Gertrude Stein.

Two foreigners he would be especially happy to greet in the lifeboat of paperback survival are Aldous Huxley, whom he imitated as an under-graduate in a scandalous contribution to the *Nassau Lit*, and Raymond Queneau, a French soulmate who with similar bonhomie and impudence skated along the edge where language becomes life. In the pages of encomiums that Dalkey Archive has assembled, Spackman is likened to Nabokov, Fitzgerald, Anita Loos, Cole Porter, Henry James, Laurence Sterne, Henry Green, and Ronald Firbank. Carolyn See, reviewing *A Little Decorum, for Once* in the *Los Angeles Times*, provided *la phrase juste*: "a literary stylist of dizzying refinement."

Dizziness, prolonged, becomes acute discomfort, and plowing through these six short novels tests a reader's mettle. Better, of course, if they had been scattered over Spackman's lifetime and that of his potential audi-ence. Each is rich in wit and implication and verbal nuance, and the effect is of a banquet of desserts, the chocolate mousse sinking down indistin-guishably into the crème caramel. One begins to weary of reaching for the French or Italian dictionary to make sense of some dialogue; one begins to shudder at the approach of another fey verbal grapple, with the female prettily babbling and the man yielding up either inarticulate grunts or else bullying lectures on the charms and high humanist value of copulation and sexual duplicity. Spackman can be simultaneously pre-cious and sententious, a combination to turn the best-disposed reader sullen. A sense of professorial activity creeps into the blithest of plots: the author lifts his head from the lectern to thrust his epigrams suddenly at us; he snipes at his perceived rival on the faculty, T. S. Eliot, in almost every novel; and his favorite kind of affair is one between a worldly-wise man and a girl young enough to be his tutorial pupil.

Heyday, his first novel, is presented in the Dalkey omnibus with revi-sions that Spackman made well after its not very successful publication; in a number of spots, bracketed ellipses indicate additions he intended to make but never did. The characters are of an age, recent graduates of Princeton or an equivalent female institution, and are struggling to make do in New York in the Depression, "which by 1931 was deepening and spreading about us like an arctic twilight everywhere." The young men, a decade younger than the generation Fitzgerald had romanticized, find that "everything the College had polished us to attain—the easy good manners, the charm, the intelligence, the stations in life hereditary to the ruling caste whose blossoming generation we had been told we were—all this vanished . . . our training and competence nothing, our prerogatives nothing, our intelligence with nothing to be applied to." Nevertheless, they seem to find plenty to drink, Prohibition or not, and carry on flirtations and seductions in such cushy venues as nightclubs and weekend houses. The dialogue is sometimes about revolution but usually about who will sleep with and/or marry whom. Moore in his afterword admires how Spackman differentiates among the speaking styles of his principal heroines—"Kitty's offbeat emphases, Stephanie's lan-guor-ous drawls, Jill's childlike prattle"—but the book's two heroes, the cousins Mike and Webb Fletcher, are so similar that the novel remains a clumsy muddle, as Mike's story is smotheringly enclosed by Webb's first-person narrative. Mike meets Kitty Locke in the first sentence and marries her in the last paragraph. The happy ending arrives with muted trumpets: "Is there a law against at least going through the motions? and who's to say the motions are not the thing itself?" There are fine images and vivid moonlit moments, but the prose is not infrequently strained by its epoch-spanning ambitions. Mike asks himself,

> What is this alien and night-enshrouded era in which I find myself? What am I doing here? Or here? Along what echoing avenues, past what weed-grown and deserted lots, what empty corners, have I made my unaccompanied way?

As critics in 1953 pointed out, this Ivy League smart set was a fragile vehicle in which to capture the leaden weight of the Depression.

Something happened to Spackman between writing this novel and composing the next, *An Armful of Warm Girl*, and I can only think that the something was a transformative encounter with Henry Green. Green is favorably cited in Spackman's criticism more than any other English-language author; an eloquent put-down of Henry James states:

> To understand how far in professional discipline James fell short, one need only contrast his output with that of a really disciplined writer, Henry Green's . . . Green is of course more gifted than James. But the point is how he has disciplined and worked at his gifts: the pauses between novels are not pauses but an intense and endless examination of his art, so that every novel has been something wholly and astonishingly new.

Green—like Spackman, of the "ruling caste"—had a capacity for love of the lesser castes that Spackman evinced only in his fondness for quoting black jazz lyrics. The English writer commands a breadth and variety not found in the American, whose oeuvre holds no working-class *Living*, no middle-class *Back* or *Caught*, no upstairs-downstairs *Loving*. With defensive self-awareness Spackman explained, in the opening chapter of *On the Decay of Humanism*, that "writers work each within the home domain of his disposition, with its private topography and vistas and its selected fauna." The fauna in Spackman's terrain are affluent men and women doing courtship dances, captured with a Greenian precision of fluttering utterance and insistent sensual detail. No more sweating to be a Darwinian Fitzgerald or a patrician Steinbeck: everything is to be oblique, indolent, Watteau-esque. In Green's subtly mandarin style—derived from the Continental avant-garde and Charles M. Doughty's curious adaptation of Arabic cadences into English—Spackman found a way to flow, picking up every vagary and hesitation of the human voice and bending syntax to imbue descriptive prose with the feathery breath of speech. Many earnest readers are relatively blind to Green's charm, but to some few workers in the literary field his fiction comes as an eye-opener. No American writer was more thoroughly captivated than Spackman.

The hero of *An Armful of Warm Girl*, Nicholas Romney, is a gruff Philadelphia private banker in his fifties, whose wife, once "a delicious Main Line deb," abruptly announces she wants a divorce. We keep expecting her to make an appearance in the novel, or their divorce proceedings to meet a significant snag, but the joke is on us; they figure as no more than "a manuscript-size communication from his wife's lawyers which he merely bundled off to his own (who were the same men anyhow)." Romney has swiftly departed Chester County for New York City, where he happens to own a charming, charmingly furnished eighteenth-century house on Barrow Street, and settles into bachelorhood, pursuing a lady of his own generation while being pursued by an actress friend, Morgan, of his daughter, Melissa. His bank seems to run itself while he is thus reëntered in the lists of Cupid, though his vanished estate stimulates a pang and a burst of Greenian eloquence as he drives away:

> In his meadows, in the flash and dazzle of the morning, his fat black cattle grazed through the jingleweed, his white guineas ran huddling. In his parks of oak and hickory the woods' high crowns discharged their splintered emeralds of light, the dogwoods shook out in flower, pink or cream, their weightless sprays. In his grove his great-grandfather's beeches, nave on nave, shone in their argent elegance, his glossy peacocks straggled, his grandfather's marble folly reared its Palladian ruins, studded with busts of ottocento celebrities, now seriously begrimed. In his box maze glittered the fantailed Cytherean tumbling of his doves.
>
> And all this, by one pretty woman's perversity, now done with, unreal; as lost to him as if by disseizin; plundered; *gone!*

The Cytherean doves are almost signature Green; but the word "disseizin" is Spackman swank, along with "gerent," "ullaged," "merchets," "tallage," "scavo," "oestrous," "frusts," "appas," and "co-parceners"—all from this novel alone. (Spackman perpetrated, in a critical piece, one of the funniest footnotes ever, noting of a writer who used the word "visionary," that "instead of 'visionary' a birthright speaker would use the natural and colloquial 'autanagnoristic.'")

Spaced through the novel are four dialogues between Melissa and a teasingly unnamed former roommate that take Green's idiom of natural indirection to a dreamlike extreme. They are brushing their washed hair outdoors, by a sundial, in a Sapphic idyll like that of the two housemaids dancing in Green's *Loving*.

> "*Not* dry?"
> "Here?"
> "Where?"
> "Here!"
> Melissa crooned, "Where, *here?*" approaching to touch deftly the cascading gold.
> "And all in under."
> "Well, no, not."
> "Oh Lissa *hell*!"
> "*Still* wants brushed," pronounced her guest in their private bogus Pennsylvania Dutch.
> "Because husbands, what a creature they are," the hostess chafed, brushing in mad anguish once more. "Because I mean everybody always calls everybody else irresponsible when who knows what it is, responsibility I mean, well goodness!"
> "Mmm."
> "So unfair!"
> "Oh darling men," Melissa sang, "darling, darling men," turning in idle dance about the dial, sleek arms tenderly flailing.*

Sexual mischief, amid much talk of "responsibility," is being woven. The keynote of the novel, as with Green's last, is doting. Women's voices wind and babble luxuriously; one emerges from the telephone in a "charming little diamond of a cry . . . that happy voice, that cascade of light and jewelled syllables." The source of the voice, Mrs. Barclay, figures in Romney's mind as "the lovely untrustworthy thing," "the charming thing," and "you heavenly thing"—all within a few pages. One of the younger enchantresses exclaims to another, "I mean what else is there but love one ever really thinks of!" In this novel, little else. Laden though it is with

---

*Apropos of dialogue—the novel and one passage of *Heyday* employ a device common on the stage and in the movies but rare in fiction: one side of a telephone conversation is given, with the other represented by ellipses. It is tantalizingly hard to make sense of, even by Spackman's sly standards, and he did not use the device in later novels.

amusing passages and exquisite images, *An Armful of Warm Girl* feels in the end faintly brittle in its glitter, a bit programmatic in its celebration of Eros. The Greenian mannerisms, transplanted to America, turn a touch florid and cloying:

> So they gazed at each other through a haze of angels. She murmured, "Must go, caro," in virgin revery, "darling literally fly," not stirring.

The inverted, blurred syntax can seem obstructive and unearned— concocted, as it were, under an insufficient pressure of local reality.

Realer and graver is Spackman's next novel, *A Presence with Secrets*, which Moore considers the author's best, if less entertaining than *An Armful of Warm Girl*. That novel's Nicholas Romney bears the last name of an English portrait-painter, and at one point reflects upon his "lifetime's delight in the mere look, the mere tournure, of women, in the posed and lovely portraits they always somehow made him half-think they were."*

The hero of *A Presence with Secrets*, Hugh Tatnall, is a painter in fact, world-famous, a thirty-seven-year-old Princetonian who lives abroad and whose serial seductions are prettily fused with the parade of a portraitist's sitters. The opening of the novel finds him in Florence and in bed with his most recent conquest, the young Rosemary Decazalet, who has fallen into his arms under the stimulus of a political riot which is surging through the city. Rosemary is under the care of Tatnall's present mistress, Alexandra Fonteviot, a married Anglo-Irishwoman who with her husband rents half of the apartment Hugh has inherited from his roguish rich uncle. (The Continental uncle figures in Spackman's imagination as powerfully as the eastern-Pennsylvania grand seigneur.) Alexandra has vanished in the riot, and Hugh, as he lies there with the sleeping Rosemary, is supposed to be helping her husband find her. He dozes a little, rekindles the coal fire, looks out the window at the dark, suddenly sinister city, reflects upon his year-old affair with Alexandra, furtively tries to contact the frantic husband, and returns to bed, wondering what Rosemary will say when she wakes up. These thirty-five pages are the summit of Spackman's art; he described them in an interview as "starting out stylistically as if I were doing a pastiche of Henry Green." The rosiness of the seducee's name and of the restless firelight pay an open debt to the last page of Green's *Back*. Here, Hugh tends to the fire:

---

*And, again: " 'Not from Wiltshire, that Romney,' this Romney said, but I mean to say he picked some damn' delicious women to sit to him. As every brush-stroke makes plain he knew, too!"

On whose incandescent hummocks of ember he took his time shaking from the scuttle dribblings of fresh coal. Culm, it appeared: soft dusts kindled instantly, showering sparks, then soon the whole hearth glowed again, strewing its roses deep into the room's vaults of shadow, so that when he turned round at last and found great innocent eyes dolefully upon him, those crimsons fluttering in her cheek anyone would have taken for hopeless blushing, so deep among the bed's canopies of night had the hearth distributed its insubstantial emblems.

The room's hyperreal atmospherics congeal around a central concern of Spackman's—the mystery of the other, the strangeness that survives the sexual encounter and is even intensified by it. The coal fire, the old Florentine bed, the city outside, the fate of Alexandra, and the sleeping girl are all ominous latencies, explosive in their potential but silent, close to us, one with Hugh's breathing lungs and churning brain, so that the mystery of his own aliveness is strongly conveyed. He too in his body is a presence with secrets.

The novel thereafter drops all its characters but Tatnall, who seems a different person as he becomes a cool killer in an episode of Breton kidnapping, and then the object of a Quaker funeral, where an old friend (as in *Heyday*, one Princeton alumnus narratively enclosing a scarcely distinguishable other) named Simon Shipley takes advantage of the occasion to seduce one of Hugh's former mistresses. Spackman confessed to the interviewer how he had "cobbled a novel together" of three disparate novella ideas, casting his painter in all three. The second and third panels of the resulting triptych have their qualities, but nothing like the charged resonance of the first. Rosemary in her sleep outweighs most Spackman heroines awake.

The sexual seethe in his novels, though central, is rather cramped and abstract: his treatment lacks the spaciousness bestowed in the novels of Iris Murdoch, where love makes its way through generously individuated personalities, and also lacks the slurping, comically physical concreteness found in the memoiristic wet dreams of Henry Miller or Casanova. Spackman's women are oddly unparticularized, conjured mostly by epithets like "angel arm" and "lovely apparition." One is described as "such a lovely decorative piece to take around the night spots." The menus of the meals with which men court them are more detailed than their faces, pieces of perfection with nary a tic or a mole. Spackman, perhaps, was enough of a philosopher to be less interested in individual women than in the Platonic idea behind all of them, or the hermeneutical problem they pose to men whose brains are numbed by lust. "Why, then, you're a terrible damn' sex, aren't you?" gruff Nicholas Romney genially exclaims, and is told by Mrs. Barclay that she "wished he had somehow learned to distinguish between a woman and an entree." More and more, in the later novels, as the contemporary din of feminist anger leaked through to the septuagenarian novelist, the "woman question" is raised, like a boxer's fending arm:

> "Patronize" implied a value-judgment he never made. Simply he felt women should be thought of as ballerinas; they then responded with every grace. What more they were, *than* that, one discovered as they decided one deserved.

> The immemorial trope was, all a woman existed for was to fall in love, and the shocking thing was so many still believed it.

> Had I for instance so much as thought about Carla's side of it? Even generally: what *was* it, to be a woman, apart from being the woman a woman is in your arms?

Uneasy now with the implications of sexual marauding, Spackman was tempted to forget that the function of fiction is not to render verdicts or effect social justice but to give evidence, and the truthful impressions of a male chauvinist better serve both noble ends than a squirmy political correctness.

Spackman came late to publication, and tried to rise to it with a proportion of backlogged manuscript to fresh inspiration that must be guessed at. His three later books, probably composed in his old age, all begin on a higher note than they sustain. *A Difference of Design*, his personal retelling of James's *The Ambassadors*, a book he found irritating enough to write at length about ("The Jamesian-male shilly-shally of Strether is excessive, and the endless bleating of Bilham is really not to be borne at all. . . . There is not enough physical presence bestowed on Mme. de Vionnet to suggest that she had ever been in anybody's bedroom"), is hilarious and lovely in its opening invasion of the mind of the Comtesse de Borde-Cessac, his flighty equivalent of Mme. de Vionnet. The idea of Strether (here named Sather) being sexually irresistible is already droll, before the Comtesse mulls it over in her vaporing style:

> He was a man like any other. Tall élancé easy urbane. For an American, not un-elegant. Comme un autre. Disabused-looking. A little I thought wary-looking too? A *little* greying. Really I felt nothing much about him one way or the other. And now in five minutes am I so uneasy, I said to myself, shocked, that I can't think what I could merely turn round again and say to him?

I felt I was—I could not understand *how* I felt.

It was as if he—It was as if that terribly self-assured gaze had somehow—But was I some helpless savage, tranced by the spinning of a sorcerer's wheel?

—I felt as if suddenly my neck and my shoulders lay naked. I was appalled.

He could reach out I said to myself and touch me and I could do nothing *nothing*.

But as the rich jest of a Jamesian novel where sex is more than a distant rumor wears thin, the romantic action by itself attenuates. The parody ceases to be much of one, and we realize how relentlessly the characters in Spackman, just as in James, keep discussing and savoring their rather stagnant situations.

A Little Decorum, for Once has the sprightly idea of a hero and old rake who is a well-known author. We find Scrope Townshend in the immediate wake of a heart attack (Spackman had one in 1975, when he was seventy), giving his daughter Sibylla palpitations by reaching out by telephone, even from the depths of intensive care, to his women. As in *An Armful of Warm Girl*, there are two—a young devotee and an old flame, in this case a Danish sociologist who studies Scrope on weekends and a magazine editor who eventually accompanies him to France. But the novel's erotic interest lies less with Scrope than with a ménage à quatre brewing between Sibylla and her husband, Alec Urquhart, and her friend Amy Hallam and Amy's live-in lover, Charles Ebury, who are poets and writers and professors intellectually in bed with each other already; there is also some sweaty intercourse between Amy's younger sister Amanda and "a gangling boy named Richard Scrope Townshend III," Scrope's grandson. More than the earlier novels, this one declares the sexual happiness of having multiple lovers. Scrope quotes Ovid: "Binas habeatis amicas, said Ovid—have two loves, and you're a slave to neither." Adultery, therefore, becomes a marital aid: "With two loves you grow *tired* of neither, and, as things go between men and women, you therefore stay married. And the social structure preserves its stable decencies." The reconciliation of social decorum with instinctive human promiscuity was a problem that preoccupied Spackman, generating more than a little sophistry. Charles reinforces Scrope, saying of adultery, "It was a branch of civilized deportment you had to *acquire* the traditions of, being unfaithful wasn't just something you did by light of nature, as between consenting illiterates, you had to read up on it." And if you read the Marquis de Sade, you learn that two might not be nearly enough: the id craves bodies and bodies, in all their apertures. Though the literary jabs and self-caricature of Spackman's mirror-lined novel tend to fall aslant or flat, the author seems smugly at peace with himself.

Yet sombre countercurrents break through his genteelly orgiastic idyll. "Yes. Well. Happiness, how sad," says one of Hugh Tatnall's old mistresses in offhand eulogy, and in describing student-faculty relations Charles Ebury says or thinks (Spackman is so casual with his quotation marks it is not always easy to tell), "For what sad fumbling!" Death haunts the fringes of Scrope's flings, and Spackman's last novel, *As I Sauntered Out, One Midcentury Morning*, was left in ragged and unpublished shape by his own death. His last is the least mannered of the six, and begins with a clarion recollection by the narrator, Johnnie Coates, of his adolescent affair with a neighbor, an Italian older woman, Carla Montaperti, during a summer spent at the Cap Nègre home of his uncle, who is also named, in one of Spackman's doublings, John Coates. Carla is an exemplary Spackman heroine, all sexual readiness under a silken robe of Continental decorum. When her eighteen-year-old admirer finally breaks through to the waiting paradise, she tells him:

> "Ahi, the time I have had wiz you! So slow, so innocent?—when there I was for you? And what was I there for you *for*, timido mio!" Had I put my little Americans to the trouble I'd put her to? Or were the little stupids helpless themselves! Had they taught me nothing at all? Madonna, che nazione d'incapaci!

Johnnie's subsequent life of Princeton bonvivacity, Pennsylvania squirearchy, substantial inheritance, and marriage seems tame after this authoritative adulteress; like Newland Archer in Edith Wharton's *The Age of Innocence*, Coates passes up a chance, in middle life, to see her again, though the reader longs for it.

Two short stories, neither very satisfactory, round out *The Complete Fiction of W. M. Spackman*. His favorite if not exclusive theme of pre- and post-coital discourse needed some space in which to display its shimmering colors, though even at their short length his novels risk monotony. The focus is brilliantly sharp but narrow. The men are all well-heeled *beaux hommes* with a surprising stock of classical quotations; the uniformly adorable women almost all wax exclamatory in French and Italian. Spackman took as models, besides Green, venerables such as Ovid, Congreve, Racine, and French examples of what he termed "the novel of dissected motivations that is one of our glories, from *La Princesse de Clèves*, *Manon Lescaut*, and *Les Liaisons Dangereuses*, to Stendhal and Proust." His spiritual home was the Enlightenment, where libertinism thrived within neoclassic décors. In this way, perhaps, he was loyal to the eighteenth-century Quakers from whom he inherited aristocratic wealth, a distrust of Puritanism, and the vision or memory of a sensible benignity by whose cool light hedonism could appear crisp and even prim.

Cheever on the Rocks

THE JOURNALS OF JOHN CHEEVER, edited by Robert Gottlieb. 399 pp. Knopf, 1991.

Published as a big and glossy book, these journals make a rather different impression from that of the excerpts published in three two-part batches in *The New Yorker* over the last sixteen months. In the magazine's pages they seemed a gesture partly sentimental that reminded its faithful readers of how luminously and jauntily Cheever's fiction had filled those same columns in bygone decades. The journals were a resurrection of sorts, and for all their fragmentariness and disconcerting emotional nakedness they shone with an ardor, an easy largeness, a swift precision that no living contributor to the magazine could quite muster. No sullen minimalism or intellectual coquetry here. "How the man could write!" said we to ourselves, as the discrete paragraphs, chosen by unexplained editorial fiat, jogged from a marvellously evoked landscape to an enigmatic marital spat to a Saturday-night suburban debauch to a Cheeveresque Sunday morning:

> To church: the second Sunday in Lent. From the bank president's wife behind me drifted the smell of camphor from her furs, and the stales of her breath, as she sang, "Glory be to the Father, and to the Son, and to the Holy Ghost." . . . The rector has a plain mind. If it has any charms, they are the charms of plainness. Through inheritance and cultivation he has reached an impermeable homeliness. His mind and his face are one. He spoke of the impressive historical documentation of Christ's birth, miracles, and death. The church is meant to evoke rural England. The summoning bells, the late-winter sunlight, the lancet windows, the hand-cut stone. But these are fragments of a real past. World without end, I murmur, shutting my eyes. Amen. But I seem to stand outside the realm of God's mercy.

The Cheever prose was back, and thrilling; and thrilling, too, was the scandalous frankness of his revelations, confided in many disconsolate moods to his journal, of severe marital discontent, drastic alcoholism, and repressed homosexuality. In a book of nearly four hundred pages, however, the disjointedness, presented in such bulk and without a single clarifying note, begins to frazzle the brain, and the circularity of Cheever's emotions to depress the spirit. Disjointedness is to be expected in a magazine, and conclusiveness is not to be expected in *The New Yorker*, but between hard covers, as the hours go by, we begin to ask where we are and where we are going.

An editorial decision has been made to present the cream of the journals—one-twentieth of their bulk, we are told in an afterword by the editor, Robert Gottlieb—as an extended prose poem, as unannotated emanations from deep within the quiet desperation of a modern American male. Perhaps this was the only editorial decision that could have been made, given the determination to expose the journals at all, less than ten years after Cheever's death. Many living are mentioned, often indecorously, and must be protected. The dates and locales of these notations, even if knowable, would not add much, though it *is* confusing to have our hero suddenly in Russia or Iowa or Boston with no explanation of how he got there. Lovers come and go so mysteriously in these notations we are not always certain of even their sex. Is the "M." of page 86, dining with Cheever at the Century Club in 1957, the same "M." as on page 346, sharing with Cheever "a motel room of unusual squalor" in 1978? Certain books and stories can be glimpsed as they go by, in the process of creation, but literary matters are among the least of Cheever's problems, as the journals have it. We are at sea, amid waves of alcohol, gloom, domestic tension, and radiance from the natural world.

A journal, even when cut to five percent of its bulk, reflects real time, where we can experience how sluggishly our human adventure unravels and how unprone people are to change. In a novel, Cheever's alcoholism would have been introduced, dramatized in a scene or two, and brought to a crisis in which either it or he would have been vanquished. In these journals, the decades of heavy drinking, of hangovers and self-rebukes and increasingly ominous physical and mental symptoms, just drag on. His life is measured out in belts, or "scoops." On a page from 1968, he describes his preparations for an amorous tryst: "Two scoops for the train, a scoop at the Biltmore, a scoop upstairs, one down—five as well as a bottle of wine with lunch and brandy afterward. We rip off our clothes and spend three or four lovely hours together, moving from the sofa to the floor and back to the sofa again. I don't throw a proper hump, which disconcerts no one"—or would have surprised, he might have added, no medical expert. It was a wonder he could ambulate, let alone copulate. On the next page, he makes a stab at bringing his drinking and his writing into meaningful relation:

I must convince myself that writing is not, for a man of my disposition, a self-destructive vocation. I hope and think it is not, but I am not genuinely sure. It has given me money and renown, but I suspect that it may have something to do with my drinking habits. The excitement of alcohol and the excitement of fantasy are very similar.

In this same year, he rereads two old journals, and comments, "High spirits and weather reports recede into the background, and what emerges are two astonishing contests, one with alcohol and one with my wife. With alcohol, I record my failures, but the number of mornings (over the last ten years) when I've sneaked drinks in the pantry is appalling." Any connection between his besottedness and his wife's physical and emotional rejections is dimly descried: "Mary is depressed, although my addiction to gin may have something to do with her low spirits." At one moment, "Mary talks as if she had a cold, and when I ask if she has she says she's breathing through her mouth because I smell so horrible." He goes on, rather primly, "I seem to suffer from that degree of sensibility that crushes a man's sense of humor." Again and again in these lachrymose journals, he is innocently wounded:

> In the afternoon mail there is a letter saying that two pieces have been bought. I am jubilant, but when I speak the good tidings to Mary she asks, oh, so thinly, "I don't suppose they bothered to enclose any checks?" I think this is piss, plain piss, and I shout, "What in hell do you expect? In three weeks I make five thousand, revise a novel, and do the housework, the cooking, and the gardening, and when it all turns out successfully you say, 'I don't supposed they bothered to include any checks.' " Her voice is more in the treble then ever when she says, "I never seem able to say the right thing, do I?"

Granted, Mary Cheever, with a fine mind of her own and a formidable father, may not have been easy to impress, but what she had to cope with in the post-cocktail hour seems safely out of the diarist's line of vision. "She hates me much of the time, but naturally I can't understand why anyone should hate me." Her adverse moods baffle him: "I don't understand these sea changes, although I have been studying them for twenty-five years." His contest with alcohol similarly remains a standoff. In 1959 he observes, "Year after year I read in here that I am drinking too much, and there can be no doubt of the fact that this is progressive. I waste more days. I suffer deeper pangs of guilt. I wake up at three in the morning with the feelings of a temperance worker." In 1971, still drinking, he notes, "The situation is, among other things, repetitious."

Nor does he find much change in his work. As early as 1952 he writes,

"As a part of moving I have had to go through some old manuscripts and I have been disheartened to see that my style, fifteen years ago, was competent and clear and that the improvements on it are superficial. I fail to see any signs of maturity, of increased penetration; I fail to see any deepening of my grasp. I was always in love. I was always happy to scythe a field and swim in a cold lake and put on clean clothes." Nearly twenty years later, with some marvellous fiction to his credit, he tells his journal, "I've never much liked my work." He thought enough of an adverse remark of his daughter's to record it: "During dinner, Susie says, 'You have two strings to play. One is the history of the family, the other is your childlike sense of wonder. Both of them are broken.' We quarrel. She cries. I feel sick."

In 1970, after the disappointing reception of the rather punchy *Bullet Park*, an entry begins with the unforgettable cry "Whatever happened to Johnny Cheever? Did he leave his typewriter out in the rain?" His perversely contented stuckness, as he rotates in a mire of drink and marital distress, varied by rather forced spurts of child-cherishing and nature-worship but gradually deepening into phobia, artistic impasse, and vicious behavior, should be overwhelming, and it does tax our patience. But in fact even at his lowest ebb Cheever can write like an angel and startle us with offhand flashes of unblinkered acumen. And there is, beneath the apparently futile churning of these jottings to himself, a story, which we know not from any editorial guidance in reading the journal excerpts but from the biographies by Susan Cheever and Scott Donaldson and his letters as edited by his son Ben.

Cheever did, in the spring of 1975, stop drinking. The novel he then wrote, *Falconer*, and the handsome volume of *Collected Stories* that he allowed Robert Gottlieb to assemble and publish won him the greatest financial and critical success of his life. At the same time, he came out of the closet, and the (mostly) suppressed homosexual urges so darkly alluded to in the earlier journals blossomed into lewd romps, mostly with "M.," recorded as frankly and joyfully as a psychotherapist could wish: "When we met here, not long ago, we sped into the nearest bedroom, unbuckled each other's trousers, groped for our cocks in each other's underwear, and drank each other's spit. I came twice, once down his throat, and I think this is the best orgasm I have had in a year." For those of us who faithfully followed Cheever's fiction, an oblique announcement of this breakthrough appeared in a short story, "The Leaves, the Lion-Fish, and the Bear," published in the November 1974 *Esquire* but never collected in hardcover. Its string of feebly connected episodes included the adventure of two married men, Larry Estabrook and Roland Stark, who are caught overnight in a motel near Denver by a snowstorm; they drink, get down to their underwear, do away with the underwear, make love, and feel great about it next morning. The writer strives mightily to bring gay sex within the bounds of his accustomed moral universe:

> The ungainliness of two grown, drunken, naked men in one another's arms was manifest, but Estabrook felt that he looked onto some revelation of how lonely and unnatural man is and how bitter, deep, and well concealed in his disappointments.
>
> Estabrook knew he had done that which he should not have done, but he felt no remorse—felt instead a kind of joy seeing this much of himself and another. . . . When he returned home at the end of the week, his wife looked as lovely as ever—lovelier—and lovely were the landscapes he beheld.

On the long-stormy marital front, a relative peace set in: the alcoholic cure entailed his return to his house in Ossining, where Mary ministered to Cheever as the infirmities of old age descended upon his hard-used body and where she resigned herself not only to awareness of her husband's bisexuality but to the frequent attendance of his chief homosexual lover, the loyal "M."—identified as Max Zimmer in Scott Donaldson's biography. Cheever died at home, surrounded by his family, a few weeks after having been "brought to climax" in his bathroom by this lover, while carpenters were building a studio for Mary:

> Desperately ill as he was, Cheever got out of bed and into the bathroom, where, protected from the possible view of the carpenters, he was brought to climax. "Adiós," John said when Max left. "Adiós."

This sunset saga, in which selfishness and selflessness, pathos and pride inscrutably mingle, exists in the journals, as edited, in only the vaguest way. The break with drink, which involved an impulsive flight from his teaching post, at Boston University—an escape he could not afterwards remember—is signalled by the abrupt entry, "On Valium for two days running, and I do feel very peculiar, but it's better, God knows, than sauce." The entry before that on the page, presumably composed as Cheever was hitting bottom, is yet one of the most evocative and complex, with its backward and forward motions:

> And I think of L. in the morning, the lovely unfreshness of her skin. It was the light scent of a young woman who has made love and slept through one more night of her life . . . but in our nearness I am keenly aware of the totality of our alienation. I really know nothing about her. We have told each other the stories of our lives—meals, summer vacations, lovers, trips, clothing, and yet if she stood at a crossroads I would have no idea of the way she would take. It is in loving her that I feel mostly our strangeness.

After he sobers up, a certain acerbity appears in his prose: "Reading Henry Adams on the Civil War. I find him distastefully enigmatic. I find him highly unsympathetic, in spite of the fact that we breathed the same air." He takes the train up the Hudson to Saratoga and Yaddo, nostalgically thinks back to how he used to sneak into the toilet with his flask, and says, "Alcohol at least gave me the illusion of being grounded." The alcohol, the suppressed homosexuality, the unharmonious wife perhaps made up the "knot" in himself, "some hardshell and insoluble element" that has "functioned creatively, has made of my life a web of creative tensions."

A true artist, he feared more than the ruin of his life the loss of his creativity. And, for whatever reason, the best and indispensable John Cheever was written when all his conflicts were unresolved, in those parched morning hours stolen from the day's inebriation and the night's fretful longings. His last superb stories were "The Ocean" and "The Swimmer" from the early Sixties; his best novel was the first, *The Wapshot Chronicle* of 1957. *Falconer*, although a brave leap into themes hitherto sublimated—chemical addiction, homosexual love, fratricide, captivity—fails to lift its burden of *bizarrerie*; I myself prefer to it his last, slim fable, *Oh What a Paradise It Seems*, and I was struck, reading these journals, by how deeply Cheever, like his elderly hero in that tale, Lemuel Sears, cherished ice-skating. Ice-skating was his exercise, his Wordsworthian hike, his rendezvous with sky and water, his connection with elemental purity and the awesome depths above and below, while he clicked and glided along, in smooth quick strokes (I imagine) like those of his prose. Saul Bellow is the contemporary writer he mentions most often, with affection ("He is my brother") and admiration: "Read Saul. The wonderfully controlled chop of his sentences. I read him lightly, because I don't want to get his cadence mixed up with mine." As soon confuse traffic noise with a babbling brook; Cheever's sentences dash and purl with a headlong opalescence:

> Snow lies under the apple trees. We picked very few of the apples, enough for jelly, and now the remaining fruit, withered and golden, lies on the white snow. It seems to be what I expected to see, what I had hoped for, what I remembered. Sanding the driveway with my son, I see, from the top of the hill, the color of the sky and what a paradise it seems to be this morning—the sky sapphire, a show of clouds, the sense of the world in these, its shortest days, as cornered.

His metaphors spring startlingly from a settled, instinctive reading of natural signals. Of a face: "A broad, Irish face, florid with drink. The large teeth, colored unevenly like maize. Long, dark lashes, and what must have been fine blue eyes, all their persuasiveness lost in rheum." Of a room: "His office is furnished with those modest antiques you find in small hotels. His desk, or some part of it, may have come into the world as a spinet." A sky: "It is one of those days when the massiveness of the clouds, travelling in what appears to be a northerly direction, gives one the feeling of a military evacuation, a hastening, a change in campaign maneuvers." A night: "The cold air makes the dog seem to bark into a barrel. Bright stars, house lights, rubbish fires."

One wishes to quote on and on, erecting a glowing verbal shield against the dismaying personal revelations of these journals. Rarely has a gifted writer's life seemed sadder. His loneliness is irreducible, and lifelong:

> And walking back from the river I remember the galling loneliness of my adolescence, from which I do not seem to have completely escaped. It is the sense of the voyeur, the lonely, lonely boy with no role in life but to peer in at the lighted windows of other people's contentment and vitality. It seems comical—farcical—that, having been treated so generously, I should be stuck with this image of a kid in the rain walking along the road shoulders of East Milton.

He was a New Englander, and kept a Puritan ruthlessness toward himself. His journals, though used partly as workbooks for his fiction, and partly as therapy ("Rows and misunderstandings, and I put them down with the hope of clearing my head"), primarily record his spiritual transactions with that God whose Episcopalian manifestation, though faithfully visited on Sunday mornings, remained discreetly hidden behind the minister's manner and the bank president's wife's camphorous furs. The God of Cheever was a jealous God, manifest in frequently used words like "obscene" and "unspeakable crime" and the "venereal dusk" that enwraps one of the writer's last fictional alter egos, the old poet Asa Bascomb in "The World of Apples." Though of a religious disposition, Cheever had no theology in which to frame and shelter his frailty; he had only inflamed, otherworldly sensations of debasement and exaltation. Perry Miller, in his anthology *The American Puritans*, tells us, "Almost every Puritan kept a diary, not so much because he was infatuated with himself but because he needed a strict account of God's dealings with him. . . . If he himself could not get the benefit of the final reckoning, then his children could."

One hopes that Cheever's three children have indeed benefitted; like Noah's, they have gazed upon their father naked. Ben, the older son— who has already edited, with helpful explanatory notes, a book of his father's letters—in a brief and engagingly honest introduction to the *Journals* describes how, while alive, Cheever offered him a volume of the journals to read.

> I told him I liked it.
> He said he thought that the journals could not be published until after his death.
> I agreed.
> Then he said that their publication might be difficult for the rest of the family.
> I said that I thought that we could take it.

Though Ben expresses surprise at how little he appears in the journals, he and his younger brother figure benignly, as innocents who distract Cheever from his dreadful *cafard*. Their older sibling, Susan, appears with a touch of menace, and their mother takes a brutal drubbing, as a romanticized love object who fails to fill her husband's bottomless needs: "Mary says that my presence is repressive; she cannot express herself, she cannot speak the truth. I ask her what it is that she wants to say and she says, 'Nothing,' but what appears in some back recess of my mind is the fear that she will accuse me of being queer. . . . I feel that she does not love me, that she does not even imagine a time when she might." Ben's introduction compliments her on her courage in letting these *Journals* be published; some might construe it as a long-suffering wife's revenge.

To speak personally, this old acquaintance and keen admirer of Cheever's had to battle, while reading these *Journals*, with the impulse to close his eyes. They tell me more about Cheever's lusts and failures and self-humiliations and crushing sense of shame and despond than I can easily reconcile with my memories of the sprightly, debonair, gracious man, often seen arm in arm with his pretty, witty wife. His confessions posthumously administer a Christian lesson in the deep gulf between outward appearance and inward condition; they present, with an almost unbearable fullness, a post-Adamic man, an unreconciled bundle of cravings and complaints, whose consolations—the glory of the sky, the company of his young sons—have the ring of hollow cheer in the vastness of his dissatisfaction. Comparatively, the journals of Kierkegaard and Emerson are complacent and academic. And Cheever's journals make much of his fiction seem timid, arch, and falsely buoyant. (Not that the journals don't hold fiction; as Cheever's letters showed, he was an inveterate embroiderer, who would not only bend but break the truth to round out a story.) Alfred Kazin shrewdly wrote (in *Bright Book of Life*), "My deepest feeling about Cheever is that his marvelous brightness is an effort to cheer himself up." In the light of the journals, we can be grateful for the effort. Passages here, in their unstructured emotion, reach higher and certainly descend lower than anything in the fiction, but it is the repute of his fiction which will determine if, some time in the next century, a scholarly edition of the complete journals, as has been done for Hawthorne's notebooks, will seem warranted. It would be nice to have names and locations filled in, and a soothing undercurrent of footnotes. A leavening of duller, more dutiful daily entries might relieve the superheated, rather hellish impression this selection makes. For now, we have a literary event, a spectacular splash of bile and melancholy, of clean style and magical impressionability.

Sirin's Sixty-Five Shimmering Short Stories

THE STORIES OF VLADIMIR NABOKOV, translated from the Russian (where not composed in English or French) by Dmitri Nabokov in collaboration with the author. 659 pp. Knopf, 1995.

Return trips to Paradise are risky. The prose of Vladimir Nabokov did loom as a paradise for me when I began to read, in *The New Yorker* over forty years ago, the reminiscences that became chapters of *Speak, Memory* (1951), and the short stories about the touching Russian-émigré professor Timofey Pnin, eventually collected in the quasi-novel *Pnin* (1957). What startling beauty of phrase, twists of thought, depths of sorrow, and bursts of wit! This was a rainbow prose that made most others look flat and gray. *Lolita* sensationally followed in 1958, and I settled into an enraptured readership as, capitalizing upon this breakthrough into best-sellerdom, the exquisite but industrious author mingled new productions in his adopted English with lovingly supervised translations from his large oeuvre in his native Russian. The publication now, eighteen years after Nabokov's death, of his collected stories, under the editorship of his son and favorite translator, Dmitri Nabokov, offers a threat as well as a treat: a threat, that is, to dull and dampen a faithful reader's old ardor with a ponderous assembly of short fiction already relished in the four handy collections, of thirteen items each, which the senior Nabokov had issued while alive.

And, in truth, *The Stories of Vladimir Nabokov* is not an easy read—hard to hold, and rather dense and rich for systematic, consecutive perusal. For those who stay with it, though, the volume recapitulates a brave career. Dmitri, faithful to his father's numerical superstitions, has found an additional, uncollected thirteen stories, bringing the total to sixty-five. Of these, only nine were written in English; one was written in French, in Paris, while the Nabokovs were in transit to America, and the rest in Russian, between 1920 and 1940, within the diaspora that had besprinkled Europe with refugees from the Communist revolution.

Berlin, with over a hundred thousand émigrés, was the capital of this floating world, and here Nabokov lived from 1923 to 1937. The stories written in this period mostly deal, then, with a remembered, enchanted Russia or an observed population of expatriates, heavy on forlorn eccentrics whose behavior partakes of the provisional nature of their citizenship. Aleksey Lvovich Luzhin (a family name Nabokov would use again) is, in "A Matter of Chance," a waiter on a German train who takes cocaine and for five years has been out of touch with his beloved wife; Captain Ivanov, in "Razor," has found employment as a barber, and into his shop one day strays his Soviet torturer; Lavrentiy Ivanovich Krushevnitsyn, in "Lik," wanders France as an actor playing a Russian in a French play, and aptly represents the typical exile, going through the motions on the rickety stage of a borrowed country. There is something charming in the way that Nabokov, an aristocratic scion and autocratic artist, so sympathetically, even gaily, lent his imagination to the boarding-house milieu of impecunious exile. His stories appeared in such émigré dailies as *Rul'*, in Berlin, and *Poslednie Novosti*, in Paris, for compensation that but modestly augmented his earnings as a tutor and tennis coach.

Yet, surprisingly, happiness is a recurrent theme. The very oldest tale here, "The Wood-Sprite," recalls "happiness, the echoing, endless, irreplaceable happiness." In "A Matter of Chance," an aged princess knows "that happy things can only be spoken of in a happy way, without grieving because they have vanished." The narrator of "Beneficence" becomes aware of "the world's tenderness"—"the world does not represent struggle at all . . . but shimmering bliss, beneficent trepidation, a gift bestowed on us and unappreciated." The hero of "Details of a Sunset" muses, "Oh, how happy I am, how everything around celebrates my happiness," and that of "The Thunderstorm" falls asleep "exhausted by the happiness of my day." All this from a writer who had recently lost his homeland, his fortune, and his father, shot on a Berlin stage when Vladimir was twenty-two. Yet the blissful undercurrent continues to run strong in the later fiction: the narrator of "Ultima Thule," a fragment of the last novel Nabokov attempted in Russian, relates that "in moments of happiness, of rapture, when my soul is laid bare, I suddenly feel that there is no extinction beyond the grave."

A strictly non-sectarian fascination with a possible afterlife, and with the precise anatomy of the moment when life becomes death, figures in a novella like "The Eye" and infuses with a queasy transcendence such creations in English as *Pale Fire* and *Ada*. Nabokov was a kind of late Wordsworthian Romantic, ascribing a metaphysical meaning to the bliss that reality inspired in him. Not so much reality, perhaps, as its conscious apprehension: he was a poet of consciousness, of, as he put it in "A Busy Man," "the burden and pressure of human consciousness, that ominous and ludicrous luxury." The mind in its shimmering workings provided his topic and permeated his narrative manner. His stories bubble with asides on their own progress or unravelling. "The Reunion" holds a superb description of the mental process of recalling a forgotten word. "Parting with consciousness," he tells us in "Mademoiselle O," was "unspeakably repulsive to me."

His youthful passions for lepidopterology, chess, and poetry fused to form a prose of unique intensity and trickiness. The visual pursuit of butterflies, in the field and under the examining light, trained his eyes to a supernatural acuity. Eyes in these short stories are themselves observed microscopically. The heroine of "Sounds" (his first fully achieved story, from 1923) is told, "Your eyes were limpid, as if a pellicle of silken paper had fluttered off them—the kind that sheathes illustrations in precious books." In "Wingstroke," another lady's eyes "sparkled as if they were dusted with frost," and a male angel's are "elongated, myopic-looking . . . pale-green like predawn air." In "Revenge," we find "wonderful eyes indeed, with pupils like glossy inkdrops on dove-gray satin." And so on, up to the English-language "Vane Sisters," of whom Cynthia has "wide-spaced eyes very much like her sister's, of a frank, frightened blue with dark points in a radial arrangement." In "Recruiting," we learn that self-portraits are difficult "because of a certain tension that always remains in the expression of the eyes." This tension in Nabokov's case generated an unfailing cascade of bejewelled details, expressed with a language inventively straining at the limits of the expressible.* Sensory minutiae— bicycle tracks in the sandy path of a manorial estate, reflections in a Berlin puddle—encode the mingled miracles of being and perception.

---

*And straining, needless to say, the resources of the translator, even when that happens to be a bilingual father-son team. Without knowing Russian, one can only guess at the strenuous felicities arrived at; at some points, however, something a little beyond the edge of English is produced. What is meant, in "The Admiralty Spire," by a barber's "taking aim with his comb and flipping my hair over with a linotype swing"? Can the verb "pimp" be transitive, as in (from "A Slice of Life") "she and she alone pimped them together"? Do we get the picture intended, in "Mademoiselle O," with "Eyed shadows move on the garden paths"? Just asking.

His love of chess and his invention of chess problems encouraged a taste for "combinational" complexity that can be mechanical and cumbersome. In this book, "Ultima Thule" and "Solus Rex," pieces of an abandoned novel rather than stories in any case, felt like symbolizations of grief and lost kingdoms too remote from their autobiographical referents. When Nabokov too successfully suppressed the personal note, his deceptive designs could seem merely cruel. Of Ivanov, a weak-hearted tutor in "Perfection," we are told that "His thought fluttered and walked up and down the glass pane which for as long as he lived would prevent him from having direct contact with the world." That glass pane sometimes masks with its reflective brightness the display case holding Nabokov's human specimens. Yet he can be movingly empathetic and direct, as in "An Affair of Honor" and "A Slice of Life," so limpidly free of combinational tricks as to feel Chekhovian. No one can paint a better word-picture. Here is his old dog Box, tossed into a reminiscence:

> His grizzled muzzle, with the wart at the puckered corner of the mouth, is tucked into the curve of his hock, and from time to time a deep sigh distends his ribs. He is so old and his sleep is so thickly padded with dreams (about chewable slippers and a few last smells) that he does not stir when faint bells jingle outside.

When he began to write stories in English, Nabokov sacrificed nothing of verbal ingenuity, but addressed his American audience in distinctly émigré accents—his floating world, swallowed in Hitler's Europe, had to be explained. "The Assistant Producer" and "A Forgotten Poet" have the voice, like his little book on Gogol, of an essay, with an impudent, madcap accent. "The Vane Sisters," with its purely American characters, is too spookily clever for words, but "Scenes from the Life of a Double Monster" and "Lance" show that, had he chosen, he could have tweaked and deepened the shorter form as impressively as he did the novel in his amazing imported English.* "Sirin," his Russian pen-name, means "bird of paradise"; it was Nabokov's preening gift to stir paradisiacal intimations wherever he alighted.

---

*The editor, by the way, though scrupulous in reproducing his father's bibliographical notes, omits one elucidative feature of *Nabokov's Dozen* (in paperback, *Spring in Fialta*), wherein each story is followed by the date and place of writing, enabling us to trace the writer's American progress from Boston, where he wrote "The Assistant Producer" in 1943, to Ithaca, New York, where he wrote "Lance," the last of his published short stories, in 1952.

NORTH AMERICAN CONTEMPORARIES

Recruiting Raw Nerves

OPERATION SHYLOCK: *A Confession*, by Philip Roth. 399 pp. Simon and Schuster, 1993.

Some readers may feel there has been too much Philip Roth in the writer's recent books—*The Facts*, subtitled *A Novelist's Autobiography*, with an eight-thousand-word afterword by the novelist's recurrent character Nathan Zuckerman (1988); *Deception*, a breezy love story, with wide margins, involving an American novelist called Philip living in London and conversing with a number of women in gusts of pure dialogue (1990); and *Patrimony: A True Story*, the gritty, moving account of Roth's father's slow death from a brain tumor and of his own coincidental open-heart surgery (1991). Such readers should be warned: there are *two* Philip Roths in his new novel, *Operation Shylock: A Confession*. The first one, an aging author minding his own business in New York and Connecticut, hears from friends in Israel that another Philip Roth has been in the news and is delivering a lecture in Jerusalem's King David Hotel on the topic "Diasporism: The Only Solution to the Jewish Problem." After a sleepless night, Philip the First (let's call him) telephones the hotel and, upon inquiring if this is Philip Roth, is told, "It is, and who is this, please?"

The question is a profound one, and the concept of the double, in this novel, is never again as electrically spooky as in the long-distance phone call that is apparently answered by the caller. Later, in Jerusalem, Philip I meets Phillip II, and finds the resemblance only approximate:

> I saw before me a face that I would not very likely have taken for my own had I found it looking back at me that morning from the mirror. . . . It was actually a conventionally better-looking face, a little less mismade than my

own, with a more strongly defined chin and not so large a nose, one that, also, didn't flatten Jewishly like mine at the tip. It occurred to me that he looked like the after to my before in the plastic surgeon's advertisement.

We seem to have, at first blush, the figure of a nicer brother, like handsome, earnest Henry Zuckerman in *The Counterlife* (1987). At least since *Portnoy's Complaint* (1969), Roth's refractory central persona has been haunted by a moral shadow, the decent, civic-minded, asexual non-writer who is innocent of blame—blame from used and abandoned shiksas, and blame, in the exhaustively investigated case of Nathan Zuckerman, from outraged Jewish critics of the author's allegedly anti-Semitic fictions. But Philip II, "the Hollywood version of my face so nebbishly pleading with me to try to calm down," is no mere shadow. The closer Philip I looks, the more exact the resemblance becomes, down to the "nub of tiny threadlets where the middle button had come off his jacket—I noticed because for some time now I'd been exhibiting a similar nub of threadlets where the middle button had yet again vanished from *my* jacket." The perfection of the duplication infuriates the original, whose charge of personality appropriation meets a wall of fawning verbosity. When Philip I demands, "Who are *you* and what are *you*? Answer me!," the answer comes back, "Your greatest admirer." Philip II supplies a cascade of grievances on the author's behalf ("*Portnoy's Complaint*, not even nominated for a National Book Award!") and of fluent babble about Jung's mystical theory of "synchronicity" and his own theory of Diasporism, which would solve the dangerous problem of Israel by returning its million European Jews to Europe. In addition, he bursts into tears, twice, and reveals, without tears, that he (Philip II) is terminally ill with cancer.

If the repercussions and complications of this self-on-self grapple don't absolutely defy summary, they certainly don't invite it. The book is a species of international thriller: Philip I witnesses some of the trial of the alleged concentration-camp demon John Demjanjuk, ponders the purported diary of the Jewish martyr Leon Klinghoffer, and winds up, against his better judgment, performing as a spy in Athens and elsewhere for the Israeli intelligence service, the Mossad. *Operation Shylock* is, too, something of a medical thriller, and exhibits Roth's knowing way with pathology, no less masterly than Thomas Mann's. Philip I is slowly recovering from paralyzing mental distress induced by his taking Halcion in the aftermath of a botched knee operation, and the novel's Gentile femme fatale is a Chicago nurse called Jinx Possesski, whose descriptions of hospital life are authoritatively harrowing. Philip II, the lover who has saved her from the anti-Semitism contracted after her prolonged exposure to Jewish doctors, wears a penile implant to compensate for the ill

effects of cancer therapy, and the novel's father figure, a Mossad eminence bearing the genial name Louis B. Smilesburger, gets about on
forearm crutches, has "that alarming boiled look of someone suffering
from a skin disease," and shows a bald head "minutely furrowed and
grooved like the shell of a hard-boiled egg whose dome has been fractured lightly by the back of a spoon." Roth's habitual polarities goy/Jew
and hedonism/altruism have been augmented by sick/well and disinte-
gration/integration. Jinx is trumpeted as "a voluptuously healthy-looking
creature . . . somebody who was *well*."

The novel is also a psychological thriller, centered on Philip I's frenzied and not unparanoid responses to the excessive stimuli of a few days
in Israel—responses which are to be construed, we are told at the end, as
steps in his recovery from the Halcion overdose and its sensations of disintegration. This particular infirmity, Roth-readers will recall, figured
in the last paragraph of *The Facts*, when Nathan Zuckerman assures the
author, "I am distressed to hear that in the spring of 1987 what was to
have been minor surgery turned into a prolonged physical ordeal that led
to a depression that carried you to the edge of emotional and mental dissolution." Roth's oeuvre presents an ever more intricately ramifying and
transparent pseudo-autobiography: the first-person voice goes back to
Goodbye, Columbus (1959), the layered self-referentiality to *My Life as a
Man* (1974), the serialized formalization of an alter ego to *The Ghost
Writer* (1980). He should be commended for facing the fact that a fiction
writer's life is his basic instrument of perception—that only the imagery
we have personally gathered and unconsciously internalized possesses the
color, warmth, intimate contour, and weight of authenticity the discrimi-
nating fiction-reader demands. Rousseau's *Confessions* opened the door to
the nineteenth-century novel, and Proust's autobiographical *Remembrance of Things Past* could be said to have closed it. In the post-Proust,
postmodern, post-objective world of American fiction, Roth stands out as
a working theorist of fictional reality; beginning as a marvellously precocious and accomplished realist, he has tested the limits of realism: he has
feverishly paced its boundaries and played games with its presumptions.
The act of writing has become his fiction's central dramatic action. In this
novel, which purports to be a confession, Philip II is a study in ongoing
character creation; when he entertainingly and circumstantially describes
his seamy career as a private detective in Chicago, his auditor, Philip I,
feels doubts that echo the reader's own:

> I thought, He's got it all down pat from TV. If only I'd watched more
> "L.A. Law" and read less Dostoyevsky I'd know what's going on here, I'd
> know in two minutes what show it is exactly. Maybe motifs from fifteen

shows, with a dozen detective movies thrown in . . . Maybe it was the in-flight movie on El Al.

However, taking the trouble to invent a profession and to crib details from other, often equally fictional sources does, by drawing on the edges of the writer's imagination, make possible a wider personal truth—a dreamier level, as it were, of confession. Philip II, implausible and rad-dled as he is, is more of a character than Philip I, who seems, it must be allowed, slightly stiff. Like a Hemingway hero, Philip I has his dignity to protect, a certain virtue to uphold. Perhaps his neck is stiff from the effort of not letting his head be turned by all the compliments directed at him in the course of *Operation Shylock*. Along with his doppelgänger's slavish flattery, he hears himself described by an old Palestinian friend, George Zaid, as a model non-Israeli Jew: "A Jew who has never been afraid to speak out about Jews. An independent Jew and he has suffered for it too." Zaid and Philip I were fellow graduate students at the Univer-sity of Chicago in the Fifties, and Zaid, now a professor in Israel, teaches *Portnoy's Complaint* to his students "to convince them that there are Jews in the world who are not in any way like these Jews we have here." The alluring Jinx Possesski reads Philip I's palm and, after assuring him that, according to his creases, his "sexual appetite is quite pure," tells him, "if I were reading the hands of a stranger and didn't know who you were, I would say it's sort of the hand of a . . . of a great leader." Clinchingly, Smilesburger, who by his final appearance has metamorphosed into the embodiment of enduring Jewish manhood ("The this-worldliness. The truthfulness. The intelligence. The malice. The comedy. The endurance. The acting. The injury. The impairment"), compliments Philip I on his spying assignment and his writing both: "First through our work together and then through your books, I have come to have considerable respect for you. . . . You are a fine man. . . ."

It's a stretch to wrap your mind around this paragon, whereas grotesque, sketchy Philip II has problems we can grasp: he is dying of cancer, he has been cursed with the name and appearance of a celebrity without being one, he must resort to a phallic prosthesis to satisfy his sexy girlfriend, he is enough tormented by the condition of post-Holocaustal Jewry to have developed some crackpot schemes to remedy it. Through the plot's tangle and the steam of righteous indignation emitted by Philip I, this figment attracts our wonder and pity; his last days, and his incredi-ble little afterlife as a dead sexual partner, commemorated in a letter from the faithful Jinx, stick in our minds, as images of the human condition quite apart from being a writer. "I AM THE YOU THAT IS NOT

WORDS," Philip II tells Philip I, in capitals. For a writer, to be without words is to be without defenses, without immortality. Philip II is not the nice side of Philip I but his sick side, his mortal side, given phantasmal reality through the projective magic of fiction.

This magic is amply displayed in *Operation Shylock*, which, under the mysterious intensity of its inspiration, is as scrupulously written as it is elaborately developed. The passages introducing the characters, especially the female characters, are brilliantly, lushly evocative. Here is Jinx:

> Her whitish blond hair was worn casually pinned in a tousled bun at the back of her head, and she had a wide mouth, the warm interior of which she showed you, like a happy, panting dog, even when she wasn't speaking, as though she were taking your words in through her mouth, as though another's words were not received by the brain but processed—once past the small, even, splendidly white teeth and the pink, perfect gums—by the whole, radiant, happy-go-lucky thing.

George Zaid's wife, Anna, appears thus in their cavelike village home:

> Anna was a tiny, almost weightless woman whose anatomy's whole purpose seemed to be to furnish the housing for her astonishing eyes . . . intense and globular, eyes to see with in the dark, set like a lemur's in a triangular face not very much larger than a man's fist, and then there was the tent of the sweater enshrouding the anorexic rest of her and, peeping out at the bottom, two feet in baby's running shoes.

Yet, once they have been so vividly introduced, the characters turn out to be talking heads, faces attached to tirades. The novel is an orgy of argumentation; Roth, like Bernard Shaw, is as happy to shape an aria around a perverse or frivolous argument as around a heartfelt one. "That lubricious sensation that is fluency" seizes even our sensible Philip I as, too often mistaken for Philip II, he fervently expounds his double's theory of Diasporism, "calling for the de-Israelization of the Jews, on and on once again, obeying an intoxicating urge." One of the book's few taciturn characters, a Mossad strong-arm man, complains to him, "You speak too much. You speak speak speak." Though both Philips do much waxing wroth over a range of issues, the de-Israelization of the Jews—the claim that the embattled and therefore combative state of Israel has poisoned the Jewishness of the Diaspora—forms the dominant topic, argued from a pro-Jewish standpoint by Philip II and from a pro-Palestinian standpoint by George Zaid:

> "What *happens* when American Jews discover that they have been duped, that they have constructed an allegiance to Israel on the basis of irrational

guilt, of vengeful fantasies, above all, *above all*, based on the most naive delusions about the moral identity of this state? *Because this state has no moral identity.* It has *forfeited* its moral identity, if ever it had any to begin with. By relentlessly institutionalizing the Holocaust it has even forfeited its claim to the Holocaust! The state of Israel has drawn the last of its moral credit out of the bank of the dead six million—this is what they have done by breaking the hands of Arab children on the orders of their illustrious minister of defense."

Though such views are put in the mouths of fictional characters, Roth's Jewish critics will not excuse him from their vigorous expression. "Name a raw nerve and you recruit it," Smilesburger tells Philip I after he has read this book. The ominous case of Salman Rushdie flickers into the author's mind: "Will the Mossad put a contract out on me the way the Ayatollah did with Rushdie?" If there were a Jewish Ayatollah, he might have issued his fatwa long ago, in the wake of those youthful short stories about goldbricking Jewish soldiers, bullying rabbis, Short Hills nouveaux riches, and little Jewish boys who can't understand why, if God could make the world in six days, He couldn't also impregnate a virgin.

Relentlessly honest, Roth recruits raw nerves, perhaps, because they make the fiercest soldiers in the battle of truth. Moral ambiguity, Semitic subdivision, has always been his chosen briar patch. His searching-out of Jewishness is of a piece with the searching-out of himself that has consumed so many pages and so many pleading, mocking, mocked alter egos. This, his most extended consideration of Jewishness, takes as its reference points not God's covenant with Abraham or the epic of Moses but affectionate memories of the Diaspora Jews of his boyhood's Newark. The myths of personal history have replaced those of a people's history. The only significant Old Testament reference is to Jacob's night-long wrestle with an unknown presence, which pairs nicely as an epigraph with Kierkegaard's assertion, "The whole content of my being shrieks in contradiction against itself." Jacob's struggle with *another*, which gave Israel its name as "he who wrestles with God," has become, in echo of Christian self-abnegation, the self's struggle with itself.

Never impressionistic in his style, Roth began with sensory facts, arranged and presented in a prose not quite colloquial, but simple and clear. From *Goodbye, Columbus*:

> I watched her move off. Her hands suddenly appeared behind her. She caught the bottom of her [bathing] suit between thumb and index finger and flicked what flesh had been showing back where it belonged. My blood jumped.
>
> That night, before dinner, I called her.

Under the stress of the intricate questions his later fiction poses, his sentences stretch, and turn a bit stentorian: "However heroic the cause had seemed to Michael amid the patriotic graffiti decorating his bedroom walls in suburban Newton, he felt now as only an adolescent son can toward what he sees as an obstacle to his self-realization raised by an obtuse father mandating an outmoded way of life." A diagrammatic grayness creeps in as the complications thicken: "And what was *I* thinking? I was thinking, What are they thinking? I was thinking about Moishe Pipik and what *he* was thinking. . . . This is what I was thinking when I was not thinking the opposite and everything else." Not that Roth has quite forgotten the tricks of sensory actualization. Philip I sleeps with the delectable Jinx, and tells us nothing about the experience until, in the next chapter, while riding in a taxi, he remembers "that wordless vocal obbligato with which she'd flung herself upon the floodtide of her pleasure, the streaming throaty rising and falling, at once husky and murmurous, somewhere between the trilling of a tree toad and the purring of a cat." Later still, the experience washes back upon him less pleasantly: "I smelled her asleep in my trousers—she was that heavy, clinging, muttony stench and she was also that pleasingly unpleasing brackishness on the middle fingers of the hand that picked up the receiver of the ringing phone." But such sensory reconstructions are rarer, and get rarer as the story goes on.

Somewhere after Philip I sleeps with Jinx, the novel stops pretending to coherence and becomes a dumping-ground, it seems, for everything in Roth's copious file on Jewishness: a slangy American anti-Semitic monologue recorded by Philip II as a "workout tape" for his Anti-Semites Anonymous program, the touchingly bland and banal journal of Leon Klinghoffer (fictional), searing testimony in the Demjanjuk trial (actual), and pages of uninterrupted discourse on the saintly nineteenth-century rabbi Chofetz Chaim and his desire that Jews abstain from *loshon hora*—evil speech—especially against other Jews. Perhaps the novel, whose events are centered on a few days in January of 1988, was too long in the working, and accumulated an awkward number of subsidiary inspirations. The headlines that haunt it—Demjanjuk, Klinghoffer, and the case of Jonathan Pollard, the U.S. Navy officer who spied for Israel—also date it, as everything on the far side of the end of the Cold War is, for the time being, dated.

Operation Shylock, though it is as hot and strenuous as *Deception* was cool and diffident, shares with the previous novel an album quality, a sense of assembled monologues and interviews. Roth has taken to entrusting his message to the eloquence of his characters rather than the movement of the plot. Plot be damned, he as good as says. Pausing midway to take stock on behalf of Philip I, he writes, "The story so far is frivolously plotted, overplotted, for his taste altogether too freakishly plotted, with outlandish events so wildly careening around every corner that there is nowhere for intelligence to establish a foothold and develop a perspective."

Well, a theorist might argue, life isn't packaged in plots any more. And why shouldn't a novel be a series of interviews, in this interview-mad age? Jinx Possesski's pilgrimage from working-class Catholic to fourteen-year-old hippie to born-again Protestant to anti-Semitic nurse to atheist consort of an anti-Zionist Jewish prophet is livelier than most tales you will read in *People* or hear on *Donahue*. But Roth, in his furious inventiveness and his passion for permutation, has become an exhausting author to be with. His characters seem to be on speed, up at all hours and talking until their mouths bleed. There are too many of them; they keep dropping out of sight, and when they reappear they don't talk the same. The plot is full of holes, and Roth, who becomes increasingly difficult to distinguish from Philip I, leaves out, for fully discussed security reasons, the crucial chapter in which he goes to Athens and spies for Israel and demonstrates, despite vicious rumors to the contrary, that he is a "loyal Jew" full of "Jewish patriotism."

This hard-pressed reviewer was reminded not only of Shaw but of *Hamlet*, which also has too many characters, numerous long speeches, and a vacillating, maddening hero who in the end shows the right stuff. Writing of *Hamlet*, T. S. Eliot coined, or gave fresh circulation to, the phrase "objective correlative," saying, "The supposed identity of Hamlet with his author is genuine to this point: that Hamlet's bafflement at the absence of objective equivalent to his feelings is a prolongation of the bafflement of his creator in the face of his artistic problem." Again, "In the character Hamlet is the buffoonery of an emotion which can find no outlet in action; in the dramatist it is the buffoonery of an emotion which he cannot express in art." All of Roth's work, and the history of mutual exacerbation between his work and his Jewish audience, lies behind the pained buffoonery of *Operation Shylock*. His narrowing, magnifying fascination with himself has penetrated to a quantum level of indeterminacy, where "what Jung calls 'the uncontrollability of real things' " takes over. The authorial ego's imaginative "self-subverting," which in the Zuckerman sequence conjured up counterlives of compelling solidity, in *Operation Shylock* slices things diaphanously thin. Still, this Dostoevskian phantasmagoria is an impressive reassertion of artistic energy, and a brave expansion of Roth's "densely overstocked little store of concerns" into the global marketplace. It should be read by anyone who cares about (1)

Israel and its repercussions, (2) the development of the postmodern, deconstruction-minded novel, (3) Philip Roth.

Doctorpoe

THE WATERWORKS, by E. L. Doctorow. 255 pp. Random House, 1994.

This artful Gothic entertainment draws upon Doctorow's fascination with historical New York and his strong sense of social malaise — of dark forces conspiring behind the scenes. The tale takes place in 1871 and is told by a man whose only given name is McIlvaine and whose occupation of newspaper editor is belied by a windy, philosophical style and a romantic predilection for the three dots of ellipsis. One of the paper's free-lance contributors, Martin Pemberton, claims to have spotted his dead father, a crusty robber baron, riding with some other dazed-looking old men in a municipal omnibus up Broadway; while pursuing the mystery, young Pemberton disappears. The winding trail, cunningly spun out with flashbacks and foreshadowings, leads eventually to a diabolically clever (wouldn't you know!) scientist called Sartorius, who is undertaking advanced experiments in human biology upon waifs and millionaires, within aeries hidden in an East Side orphanage and the Croton waterworks. Everything turns, drips, and pours in this humid narrative, which is most interesting in its casually worn period detail and least persuasive in Doctorow's effort to inflate Boss Tweed and his villainous metropolis into cosmic symbols of "this other disordered existence . . . that our ministers warn us against . . . that our dreams perceive" (ellipses his).

Excellent Humbug

HENRY AND CLARA, by Thomas Mallon. 358 pp. Ticknor & Fields, 1994.

Historical fiction doesn't dominate the best-seller list the way it used to, but its appeal to high-minded novelists seems stronger than ever. Of this season's best-sellers, the two most distinguished novels, Caleb Carr's *The Alienist* and E. L. Doctorow's *The Waterworks*, are both located in nineteenth-century New York City; artful, thoroughly modern Bobbie Ann Mason and Annie Dillard have in recent years produced novels that take place before the authors were born. Perhaps, much as the postmodern architect has all the evolved forms of the previous ages to play with, the present-day writer feels free to treat the past as a toy store, amply stocked with incidents, settings, and characters. There is a danger. Near the beginning of this century, in 1901, Henry James with eloquence and fervor set forth to Sarah Orne Jewett, whose historical novel *The Tory Lover* had just been published, the reasons why her attempt was ill-advised:

> The "historic" novel is . . . condemned even in cases of labour as delicate as yours, to a fatal *cheapness*, for the simple reason that the difficulty of the job is inordinate . . . You may multiply the little facts that can be got from pictures and documents, relics and prints as much as you like—*the* real thing is almost impossible to do and in its essence the whole effect is as nought: I mean the invention, the representation of the old CONSCIOUSNESS, the soul, the sense, the horizon, the vision of individuals in whose minds half the things that make ours, that make the modern world were non-existent. You have to *think* with your modern apparatus a man, a woman—or rather fifty—whose own thinking was intensely otherwise conditioned, you have to simplify back by an amazing *tour de force*—and even then it's all humbug.

Nevertheless, contemporary authors keep trying, and one reason may be that what James so fondly called "the palpable present-*intimate* that throbs responsive" no longer throbs responsive for fiction writers. Twentieth-century experience, now that Joyce has captured its suffocating clutter and the *nouveaux romanciers* and the American minimalists have exposed its desolating inconsequence, repels the imagination that would take human experience as a significant subject; it is in the past, and especially the relatively handy nineteenth-century past, that the sensation of importance can be regained, along with derring-do, beginnings and endings, romantic passion, and costumes dyed in supernatural colors.

Thomas Mallon, in his third novel, *Henry and Clara*, has done an amazing, somewhat sinister thing. He has found, tucked into the crevices of the glaringly lit assassination of Abraham Lincoln, two close witnesses and eventual victims of the event, and has enlarged them into movingly tragic figures. Present in the State Box at Ford's Theatre with President and Mrs. Lincoln on the night of April 14, 1865, were Major Henry Rathbone and Clara Harris, who had been invited when the announced attendance of General and Mrs. Grant fell through. The substitute couple can be found in full accounts of the fatal night. Carl Sandburg in his three-volume biography of Lincoln gives the facts:

In the carriage into which the President and his wife stepped was a betrothed couple. Henry Reed Rathbone, assigned by Stanton to accompany the President, had brought along his fiancée, Miss Clara Harris. For them the future was bright this evening. He was twenty-eight years old, of a well-to-do clan of Rathbones at Albany, New York, a major of volunteers since November of '62, a trusted War Office attaché. His sweetheart was the daughter of Judge Ira Harris of Albany, since 1861 United States Senator from New York.

Gore Vidal in his novel *Lincoln* mentions "the daughter of Senator Harris of New York and her fiancé, Major Rathbone, the best company that Hay could find at such short notice." After Booth entered the box and fired a bullet into the back of Lincoln's skull, he grappled with Major Rathbone, slashing him with a knife, on his way to the edge of the box and his famous, leg-breaking leap onto the stage. Rathbone survived his wound, and he and Miss Harris passed out of history's glare and back into obscurity.

But Mr. Mallon, a former Vassar professor who is now the literary editor of *Gentleman's Quarterly*, has pursued them into the shadows and uncovered, or invented, a compelling, vibrantly Victorian story. Henry and Clara were not an ordinary betrothed couple: they had been raised in the same household since Henry was eleven and Clara thirteen, when the widower Ira Harris married Pauline Rathbone, the widow of a former mayor of Albany. Their respective spouses had died within a few weeks of one another, and the wedding took place three years later. From such facts of record, and the chronology of births and deaths among the Rathbones and Harrises, and Henry Rathbone's military record, and a splendid general saturation in the social and political history of the period from 1845 to 1883, Mr. Mallon has constructed a poignantly accursed romance, discouraged by both parents and then blighted by Henry and Clara's inadvertent presence at the great President's martyrdom. The dust jacket displays an old lithograph that shows them there, in the flag-festooned box—uniformed Henry gesticulating, bonneted Clara clutching her breast, Mary Lincoln baring her plump shoulders, the bearded President tilting back his head and weakly lifting one hand as the bullet enters, and a scowling John Wilkes Booth thrusting out the smoking gun. They are all the same size, these five who loom to posterity in such different proportions, and among the charms of this ingenious, deeply felt novel is the democratic restoration of the historically invisible couple to full human size and complexity.

Their affair, like their century, is rooted in Romanticism. Clara, a lovely dark-haired sister to Jane Eyre and Emma Bovary, is shown early on as fascinated by her impulsive young stepbrother's volatile and Byronesque moods; when they at last consummate their mutual attraction, she reaches up for him and recalls moments from her girlhood, "summer nights . . . when there would be a storm, and she would put her arms out the window and try to coax the lightning down." He is lightning to her, and, if the author never succeeds in making Henry, with his surliness and scornfulness and fixation on his flashy mother, attractive to the reader, he does convincingly convey Clara's enthrallment, which carries her through considerable delay and family resistance to their engagement and, after the war, marriage.

Perhaps one should have attempted a historical novel of one's own to appreciate the skill with which Mr. Mallon navigates the lengthy stretches of time in which these real events take place—Clara is ten when she first appears in the novel and thirty-one when she marries—and distills suspense and a sense of development from the excessively large population that annals of the past provide. American politics is especially troublesome for the historical novelist because elections keep changing the cast of characters; Presidents from Millard Fillmore to Chester Arthur serve as background figures to Henry and Clara's love and marriage, most of them twitched into life with a knowing touch or two. Lincoln, the most important of them—Clara is taken up as a pet of the Lincoln household—seems underanimated, as if the grandest character in American history had to be subdued lest he run away with the story. There is a nice mezzotint evenness, a steel-engraving stiltedness, to the overall picture. The period details are generously supplied, but they rarely, even in the thick of the heavily documented Civil War, detract from the central erotic and psychological drama of the loving couple. Of a sickly Rathbone cousin we are told, "Hot brandy and sweat walks had done no good": how much study of outmoded therapies went into that lightly tossed-in "sweat walks"? As the newlyweds embark on their long-deferred honeymoon in 1867, Clara's sisters chatter:

> [Lina says] "I love to think of what she'll be wearing once she and Henry get to London. They say that bodices have dropped to the point where the women there are hardly wearing anything at all above the waist. Do you think Clara is too old to be décolletée?" Louise, fingering the paper rose at her neck, said she didn't know, and Lina, undiscouraged, asked, "Did you hear that Tom Thumb has managed to raise a mustache?"

It is not surprising that Mr. Mallon has all his paper roses and period trivia in place; he has demonstrated, in his sweeping survey of diaries, *A*

Book of One's Own (1984), and his discursive study of plagiarism, *Stolen Words* (1989), and, indeed, in his second novel, *Aurora 7* (1991), a formidable pedantry. Stylistically, he is, like Nicholson Baker if not with the same antic effect, a precisionist, one who—in *Aurora 7* especially— hones a multitude of details to a gleaming, smoothly oiled fit. Parties among the ante-bellum Albany well-to-do, the feverish society of wartime Washington, the sights and sounds and conveyances of the well-trafficked Grand Tours in the Gilded Age, the resources of pre-Freudian psychiatry—we feel confident that he has them right enough, however precariously assembled of multiplied "little facts . . . pictures and documents, relics and prints" or, as an author's note acknowledges, "contemporary newspaper accounts; military records; pension files; census reports; alumni reports; State Department documents in the National Archives."

All this dry academic drudging enabled Mr. Mallon to come up with something missing from his previous two novels, which, for all their wit and compass, were rather bloodless. Not this one. A keystone of his researches must have been the single surviving letter from the historical Clara Harris, which is preserved in the New-York Historical Society. Dated April 25, 1865, it is figuratively soaked in blood:

> Henry has been suffering a great deal with his arm, but it is now doing very well,—the knife went from the elbow nearly to the shoulder, inside,— cutting an artery, nerves & veins. He bled so profusely as to make him very weak. My whole clothing as I sat in the box was saturated literally with blood, & my hands & face—You may imagine what a scene.

At the novel's stunningly rendered, foreshadowed but unforeseeable climax, she again feels blood on her face. Like characters in a Greek tragedy, Henry and Clara have blood as their element. Henry assures her, after he deflowers her, "that the blood was nothing to worry about"; at war, a dying young soldier attracts Henry's gaze, red blood bubbling from the wound in his chest "like a strange flower from a latitude we have never seen"; when Henry himself is wounded, amid the slaughter in the crater at Petersburg, "his wound . . . bled amazingly little, the mud having acted as a natural poultice." Even the couple's amorous passion, as it is remembered by Clara after marriage and the night at Ford's Theatre have quelled it, is a kind of fury, a savage tussle—"the shouts and scratchings, the games and sometimes terrible language." Yet this violence was their happiness: "She was sure these things were 'abnormal,' had always been sure of that, but they had always been normal to her and Henry, and that was the only standard she had held them against, all through the days when they banished the world and made her—made the two of them together—happy."

Such a vision of happiness, and such an imaginative reconstruction of a relationship intimately marked by murder and incest—incest, self-love turned heterosexual, was the Romantics' ultimate daydream—tap a bloody darkness which Mr. Mallon has previously sublimated into comic inklings of doom. Artie Dunne, the graduate-student hero of his first novel, *Arts and Sciences* (1988), is tormented by destructive impulses and "sweaty frights" while he pursues his meek course as an upwardly mobile Irish-American grind; Gregory Noonan, the eleven-year-old hero of *Aurora* 7, is empathetically caught up in the near-disaster of Scott Carpenter's 1962 space mission and mirrors it with an impulsive, rather mystical flight of his own. Artie Dunne suffers from the "renewed conviction that something awful was going to happen to him." In *Aurora* 7 a character closely resembling Mary McCarthy (who gave Mr. Mallon's first novel a friendly boost) thinks, "Something terrible must be about to happen." As *Aurora* 7 airily weaves back and forth between past and future and catches dozens of characters in its shimmering web, the something terrible becomes the God of the Bible and of the Roman Catholic catechism, as He arbitrarily kills and saves human lives, and lurks at the limits of astronomy with His inscrutable act of Creation. In *Arts and Sciences*, the something terrible circles around an indecision, on the part of the incredibly wimpy protagonist (his weight is given as one hundred ten pounds, eleven ounces), between homosexuality and heterosexuality, not to mention that between belief and unbelief and between careerism and idealism.

How much more substantial and gripping it is to have, in *Henry and Clara*, these winsome autobiographical traces dismissed and the something terrible reified as a definite, infamous historical event, whose anticipation and retrospective illumination keep us turning the pages with a pounding pulse—for there is "a secret" (in Mr. Mallon's brilliant phrasing) "sewn into the violence of that night." The voluminous muffling and verbose affective indirection of Victorian life take the place of the Irish-American Puritanism, with its secrets and suppressions and unconscionable impulses, that Mr. Mallon elsewhere evokes. His successful creation of a female point of view, including a stubborn attraction to male ferocity, anchors and channels his fondness for centrifugal, layered, intellectually circumscribed plots. The book is still a little quote-heavy; we didn't need, at the very end, *two* citations from Byron, epitaphizing characters who have been made amply vivid by their full-blooded actions.

For all his aptitude, Mr. Mallon has been slow to sidle up to fiction;

there has been a curious retardation to his career. *Arts and Sciences*, set in 1973–74 and transparently based on impressions gathered at that time, when the author was a first-year graduate student at Harvard, was not published until 1988, so late it had to bear the apologetic subtitle *A Seventies Seduction*. Three years later, *Aurora 7* told of a boy the author's age in the year 1962. By continuing this pastward trend into his own prehistory—by daring "to simplify back by an amazing *tour de force*"— Mr. Mallon has found forms expressive of his modern disquiet and given his furtive, ominous themes grandeur. He has shown himself to be, at the age of forty-three, one of the most interesting American novelists at work. Sometimes the long way round is the only way home.

The Good Book as Cookbook

MILLROY THE MAGICIAN, by Paul Theroux. 432 pp. Random House, 1994.

Paul Theroux's new novel reverses the black mood of his last one, *Chicago Loop*, with a brilliant display of imagistic legerdemain and Biblical cuisine; *Millroy the Magician* is the story of a strikingly bald, luxuriously mustached modern Jesus, told by a skinny little Lolita from Cape Cod, who sucks her thumb even though she is fourteen going on fifteen. Jilly Farina is her name, and she catches the eye—the eyes, which change color like the lights in a discothèque—of Millroy the Magician at the Barnstable County Fair. Her father, Dada, was supposed to take her, but she finds him lying "black-out drunk" in his trailer, so she goes alone, and by that night is living in Millroy's Airstream instead of keeping unhappy company with her abusive and dismal grandmother, Gaga. Jilly's subsequent adventures with Millroy have the polychrome brightness of an Anne Tyler novel, pursued with an ambitious metaphysical agenda and at rather excessive length. The novel is literally and strenuously wonderful, a showcase of Theroux's limber powers of vision and imagination. Millroy's magic pops out at the reader from the first pages:

> I had seen him once with Dada and not forgotten. He had invited a small girl from the audience and turned her into a glass of milk and drank her. . . . Using a pair of tongs, he fed himself fiery sponges and chomped on them, then made a torch and chewed on those flames. Smoke and fire flew out of his mouth and seemed to singe his mustache. . . . I could see that these were real flames he was eating, and I was near enough to feel the heat.

Eating is what Millroy is all about; he tells Jilly, "I want to eat you," and magically transports her from a wicker basket onstage into his trailer, in whose darkness, that first night, she feels "swallowed up by this stranger, Millroy."

It takes great tact on the writer's part, and considerable suspension of disbelief on the reader's, to repress the pedophiliac unsavoriness of this abduction. Nabokov's *Lolita* put its unsavoriness up front, costumed in Humbert Humbert's rollicking confessional prose and mitigated by the flaws in his captive nymphet's innocence. Theroux, a more schematic writer, keeps insisting on Jilly's utter innocence, to that point where she often seems to be truly, as she says, "a blank":

> "I'm nothing," I had said.
> He had not denied it, which made me feel awful.
> "I'm a blank."
> "Yes." And gave me his thankful face again. "I wouldn't have you any other way."

Night after night, for a year and a half, we are meant to believe, the two share close quarters with no more intimacy than the magician's sudden outbursts of conversation and the outcries of his occasional nightmares. He invades Jilly's body in the form of the food he feeds her, and the sexual metaphor becomes obscene only late in the book, when he tries to force a "finger" of melon into her mouth, and she resists, so that "the fruit squashed like poor weak flesh as he probed with it. I resisted, and then I licked it a little."

Millroy, who confesses, "I was once so fat I was imprisoned in the darkness of my body," has evolved a health diet on the basis of the Bible, which he and Theroux have ransacked for a stunning number of alimentary texts. Ezekiel 4:9 offers a bread recipe: "Take thou also unto thee wheat, and barley, and beans, and lentils, and millet, and fitches, and put them in one vessel, and make thee bread thereof." "Comfort me with apples" (Song of Solomon 2:5), properly interpreted, urges the consumption of apricots. Leviticus 7:23 enjoins, "Eat no manner of fat" and, three verses farther on, "Ye shall eat no manner of blood"—so much for deep-frying and steak tartare. The eleventh chapter of Leviticus, with its well-known list of dietary abominations, constitutes, according to Millroy, "an environmentalist's charter, and it's also a sort of antishopping list." A vegetarian who declines to eat anything with a face or a mother, Millroy is still "looking for guidance" on the many passages in Numbers devoted to the preparation of roast lamb, and translates the meat that Jesus consumes in Luke 11:37 as a mistranslation of a general term for "food."

Nuts, grains, fruits, and fish with scales, he preaches, are Bible-approved fare. Numbers 11:5 remembers "the fish, which we did eat in Egypt freely; the cucumbers, and the melons, and the leeks, and the onions, and the garlic." Isaiah likens the daughter of Zion to "a lodge in a garden of cucumbers" (1:8) and ordains, "For butter and honey shall every one eat" (7:22). Moses promised a land of milk and honey, and Jesus after His resurrection dines upon broiled fish and honeycomb. On fairly attenuated Biblical precedent, Millroy recommends eating flower bulbs ("Consider the lilies of the field—consider that they have edible rootstocks") and flowers—"marigolds, calendulas, borage, sunflowers, chive blossoms." He interprets Mark 1:6, wherein John the Baptist "did eat locusts and wild honey," to mean that he ate the seedpods of the honey locust, that is, carob, and ventures that "Manna was probably a lichen, one of the several lecanoras." Not even the condiments go unsacralized: Jesus mentioned the spice cumin, and Numbers specifies "bitter herbs." To drive home the spiritual importance of regular elimination, Millroy regularly cites Isaiah 16:11: "My bowels shall sound like a harp."

Disguising Jilly as a boy called Alex or Sandy or Rusty, Millroy leaves Cape Cod and joins a Boston children's television show, which he soon dominates with his supernatural cookery. Fired for harping too much on bowels, he refashions a restaurant near Park Square into the Day One Diner, serving such salubrious and venerable items as "Jacob Pottage, Ezekiel Bread, Daniel Lentils, Nahum's Fig Bars, Bethel Barley Cakes."* Then he goes back to television as an evangelist, lauding his Biblical diet in an increasingly successful Sunday-morning program. He enlists a number of children—some from the old television show, some from the city streets—whom he calls the Day One Sons and Daughters, and with their help founds restaurants in cities throughout the nation. He becomes a celebrity, hounded by admirers, enemies, and the press, to whom his constant companion Jilly, still skinny and neuter enough to pass for a boy, becomes a matter of intense curiosity. The Sons and Daughters resent her, and the Day One movement runs into the same pattern of public persecution and internal treachery that brought an end to Christ's earthly ministry.

The "Day One" section is much the longest of the book—too long, at more than two hundred pages. We read so often about the diner's menu

---

*Not altogether without precedent: Post Toasties were originally labelled "Elijah's Manna," and Dr. John Harvey Kellogg had powerful evangelical and reformist tendencies, implemented at his Battle Creek Sanitarium and merrily portrayed in T. Coraghessan Boyle's novel *The Road to Wellville*.

of "melons, honey, Ezekiel bread, almonds, pistachios, figs, apricots, barley porridge, grapes and . . . mashed seed pods" that we begin to hunger
for a Big Mac. Developments unfold with a treacly slowness, as the
author seeks to extract suspense from a situation too fanciful to bear
much examination. A pre-publication puff from V. S. Naipaul calls *Millroy the Magician* "one of the more bewitching of Mr. Theroux's many
inventions," and the word "invention" catches out a chronic weakness, a
sense we have of Theroux's novels as contraptions, as cleverly elaborated
ideas rather than transmuted experiences. *My Secret History*, a beautiful
and rueful *Bildungsroman*, did *not* feel like this; *Picture Palace* and *Chicago
Loop*, say, did. *The Mosquito Coast*, concerning a Yankee inventor who
builds a giant ice-making machine in the jungles of Honduras, shares
with *Millroy* an adolescent narrator; a wonder-working, non-stop-talking
protagonist, full of complaints about modern America; and a sad underlying theme of atrocious parenting. In its apocalyptic, Grand Guignol ending, Allie Fox, the inventor, turns into a talking head, a broken doll, as if
we have been watching a marionette show.

The Day One movement is a contraption that Theroux fiddles with
too long. Energetically he demonstrates his mastery of Biblical cuisine
and of daytime television programming and of the speech patterns of
urban black youth while his bald Romeo and immature Juliet (at fourteen, Jilly/Alex is about Juliet's age) languish in a kind of bemused torpidity; she keeps feeling blank and Millroy keeps spouting magic and
recipes. He is interesting less as himself than as a latter-day Christ. The
rise and fall of the Day One movement is an ingenious, impudent, and
not necessarily irreverent recasting of the New Testament, and in this
form reflects considerable heat.

The parallels are legion. We see Millroy turning water into wine and
back again in the tent at the Barnstable County Fair. He performs the
miracle of the loaves and fishes several times during the novel. The Sons
and Daughters are the disciples, called from the ghetto to be fishers of
men. The thronging opportunists with their plans to expand and com-
mercialize the Day One message are the money changers in the temple;
at one point, Millroy permits himself to lay angry hands upon a promoter,
a man named Veazie. Jilly tells us, "After his anger drained away—it took
almost until nighttime—Millroy seemed smaller but more complicated,
and none of us knew what to say." Theroux's parodic account emphasizes
those moments in the Gospels when Christ's uncertainties and fears can
be glimpsed. Millroy has nightmares about a giant crab eating him, and
Jilly in the dark hears him cry out "Don't, please"—a version of Jesus's
plaintive "Let this cup pass from me." Awake, he confesses to her, "I have

moments of doubt," and she observes, "His face was rumpled with shadow and his whole head had creases so deep I almost did not recognize him." The curious driftingness of Christ's ministry—the way that miracles were pulled from him reluctantly, from a preoccupied passivity— is enlarged and clarified in the mirroring tale of Millroy, whose name holds an echo of a millenary "king" and of a millstone's dreadful weight. Jesus said, "Touch me not"; Millroy gets "rattled when people touch him, especially women." He extols Christ's frequent "look-no-hands" magic, done purely with words. (Millroy's real ambition, we are surprisingly informed late in the novel, was to be a writer.) Performing magic drains him physically. "Miracles and magic are the last resort," he says. "I only do it when I'm desperate." Jilly in her implausible innocence is some kind of safeguard against the underlying desperation of being an itinerant miracle-worker. The Last Supper surreally becomes a shared meal in the Airstream trailer as it rocks and lurches amid Boston traffic; Millroy tears off one of his fingers and slices it into neat little disks, saying, "This is not meat. It is Millroy." His crucifixion takes the form of his being handcuffed to his car's steering wheel, with his ankles manacled too, by a Vermont policeman. But, as you might expect, Millroy escapes.

Toward the end of this elaborately constructed "Day One" section, which is liveliest in its allegory, Jilly flees back to Cape Cod, and regains there a spark of mundane reality, in revisiting her girlhood's impoverished loneliness:

> I pedaled past the old grassy airport to Gaga's. Nothing had changed since my last visit. . . . The house looked weatherbeaten and silent, the roof slightly crushed and sloping, the window shades pulled down, the tall orangy daylilies and some deep blue pansies at the corner of the porch brightening it, and clusters of heavy, mumbling bees clinging to the pink blossoms of the hollyhocks and making the stalks sway.

Such touches of landscape revive the long-dormant innermost story of *Millroy the Magician*, the sentimental life of its two strangely matched main characters. When the pair abruptly flies from Massachusetts to Hawaii, Theroux, the best-travelled of contemporary novelists, conjures up this new place with the vividness of discovery, in Jilly's Huck Finn–like voice:

> It rained most nights, and in the daytime the road and the foliage steamed in the sunlight. Dolphins plopped and played in the sea below our front porch. We heard them gasp and take sucking breaths, we saw them toss themselves in the air. Our palm trees rattled, their lower fronds thumping like brooms against our walls, and sometimes a big splintery brown

frond dropped onto the tin roof. The cockroaches flew with a papery flutter, and the cane spiders scuttled with no sound at all. Heavy mangoes dropped to the damp earth like a punch in the stomach.

"Magic is the power to see," Millroy says, and Jilly sees with the ominous ambivalence of her new mood: "In the distance where the water met the sky, a shadow surfaced from the ocean and sealed the horizon in a streak of darkness, the first stain of night." She has turned fifteen, and Millroy is putting a heavier erotic pressure on her. He says "I love you"; his hand on her is cold and clawlike; his superhuman feats frighten and repel her. A complicated interchange of vulnerabilities and powers takes place in this magic landscape of the U.S.'s farthest reach. If the "Day One" section was too long, this last, "The Big Island," is too short, attempting to do too much, especially on its very last page, which leaps great gulfs and concludes on a note I took to suggest the parting cry of Revelation: "Even so, come, Lord Jesus." Hawaii means more to Theroux, our impression is, than he has given himself space to tell us.

Nevertheless, a tenderness exists in this novel, and a jubilation, not hitherto conspicuous among this earnest and prolific author's qualities. His fiction has tended to cast a chill. There is a fastidiousness in Theroux that, when expressed in the factual accounts of his travels, from *The Great Railway Bazaar* to *The Happy Isles of Oceania*, has exposed him to charges of snobbery and scornfulness. Happily, this scornfulness—or sharp honest eye for grotesquerie and shabbiness—emanates in *Millroy the Magician* from a visionary protagonist who cannot be blamed for seeing almost all Americans as diseased and misshapen, poisoned as they are by cigarettes, meat, and chemicalized food. Toxins, toxins, are what Millroy perceives on all sides, with their sad effects: "Hersh worries me most. That face. Lungs full of toxins. I'd love to hook him up and monitor his emissions, just to show him the printout. Hickle's body's too big for his suit; it's as though he's been sealed into it. You know his feet are swollen." Like Jesus strolling among the sinners, Millroy walks the restaurant districts of nocturnal Boston and peers into the windows of the "pizza joints, burger places, ice-cream parlors, and fancier restaurants—French bistros, Chinese, Indian, Thai, sushi bars, Cajun cafés and Italian delicatessens," marvelling at the junk people put into their mouths, "fascinated by dabs of mustard in the corners of a mouth, or mayonnaise on lips, gravy on a chin; and a splat of ketchup on a forehead . . . people sucking on big swollen cups of Coke." These lost souls have "Fat Voices, Smoker's Face, Sitter's Hips, water retention, porky necks, belly sacks, swags and bags." Parker, the murderous, creepy hero of *Chicago Loop*, was a food purist, too, revolted by the American cuisine, but he crossed over into the mire and was devoured; in contrast, Millroy and his effervescent jeremiads afford the author a conduit for satire, a zestfully distasteful panorama of a burgerized America full of self-created gargoyles, dough-balls, and dyspeptics. Long a globe-trotter and dweller in England, Theroux has come back to America. There is nothing in the book funnier or more surprising than Millroy's outburst of indignation when he is invited to expand his operations overseas:

"I have seen overseas. Overseas is small and dirty. . . . Overseas people eat bad food, gorge themselves on fat and die young. Overseas people squat in hideous cold toilets or in the elements and hurry their bowels, their eyes popping. Overseas kitchens are black with soot. Overseas people hardly wash. They have flat feet, corrupt breath, rotten flesh, no muscle tonus. . . . I have seen their narrow streets and chipped sinks. I will never go overseas again. I will never have to. Overseas is overpriced, overwhelming, over there. It is riddled with opportunistic germs. Overseas is a health risk. I have been there for you. God has placed his hand upon America. This is the Promised Land."

He is not being, we gather from the fervor, entirely ironic.

Him and Who?

U & I: *A True Story*, by Nicholson Baker. 179 pp. Random House, 1991.

Mr. Baker extends the delightful mini-realism of his two short novels *The Mezzanine* and *Room Temperature* into this book-length essay, a close and self-pitiless examination of his relationship with a mental figment derived from a fractional perusal and a few personal glimpses of the author John Updike. The younger writer looks to "Updike" less to learn how to write than to learn how to be a writer; he focusses therefore on the behavioral aspects of his topic's oeuvre—dedications, prize-acceptance speeches, prefaces to special editions of his novels, even the phrases on copyright pages. Before composing this peculiar *hommage*, Mr. Baker resolved not to consult the works of its titular co-hero, and his memory, bracketed addenda reveal, usually tricked him. He marvels, for instance, at Updike's creative use of the word "pool" to signify the head of a dandelion, when the word really employed was the unremarkable "poll," as in "poll tax" and "to pollard." Mr. Baker's own vocabulary glit-ters on the verge of fireworks: he can be "as *tarabiscoté* as George Saints-bury or Henry James" while he goes about "impanating"—placing in bread—"doings in linear sentences." His scrupulous wrestle with the impalpable can be quite comic, but his basic point is serious: out of the books of others we sift a book of our own, wherein we read the lessons we want to hear.

Mayhem at the Hospital

WE EXPECT THE WORLD of doctors. Out of our own need, we revere them; we imagine that their training and expertise and saintly dedication have purged them of all the uncertainty, trepidation, and disgust that we would feel in their position, seeing what they see and being asked to cure it. Blood and vomit and pus do not revolt them; senility and dementia have no terrors; it does not alarm them to plunge into the slippery tangle of the interior organs, or to handle the infected and the contagious. For them, the flesh and its diseases have been abstracted, rendered coolly diagrammatic and quickly subject to infallible diagnosis and effective treatment. *The House of God* is a book to relieve you of these illusions; it does for medical training what *Catch-22* did for the military life—displays it as farce, a melee of blunderers laboring to murky purpose under corrupt and platitudinous superiors. In a sense *The House of God* is more outrageous than *Catch-22*, since the military has long attracted (indeed, has forcibly drafted) detractors and satirists whereas medical practitioners as represented in fiction are generally benign, often heroic, and at worst of drolly dubious efficacy, like the enthusiastic magus, Hofrat Behrens, of Thomas Mann's *The Magic Mountain*.

Not that the young interns and residents and nurses conjured up by Samuel Shem are not sympathetic; they all bring to the grisly funhouse of hospital care a residue of their initial dedication, and the most cynical of them, the Fat Man, is the most effective and expert. Our hero, Roy Bausch, is possessed of a buoyant innocence and a persistent—for all the running hypochondria of his hectic confessional narrative—health. Three windows look out of the claustral hospital onto the sunlit lost landscape of happiness: sex, boyhood nostalgia, and basketball. The sex is most conspicuous, and in the orgies with Angel and Molly acquires an epic size and pornographic ideality. A glimpse of Molly's underpants becomes, in one of the book's many impetuous parlays of imagery, a sail bulging with the breath of life:

An introduction to the 1995 edition, marking a million copies sold, of *The House of God*, by Samuel Shem, M.D.

SAMUEL SHEM   :   313

... in the instant between the sit down, there's a flash of the fantasy triangle, the French panty bulging out over the downy *mons* like a spinnaker before the soft blond and hairy trade winds. Even though, medically, I knew all about these organs, and had my hands in diseased ones all the time, still, knowing, I wanted it and since it was imagined and healthy and young and fresh and blond and downy soft and pungent, I wanted it all the more.

In the prevailingly morbid milieu spurts of lust arrive from a world as remote as the world of Bausch's father's letters, with their serenely illogical conjunctions. Sexual activity between female nurses and male doctors figures here as mutual relief, as a refuge for both classes of caregiver from the circumambient illness and death, from everything distasteful and pathetic and futile and repulsive about the flesh. It is the co-ed version of the groggy camaraderie of the novice interns: "We were sharing something big and murderous and grand."

The heroic note, not struck as often or blatantly as the note of mockery, is nevertheless sounded, and is perhaps as valuable to the thousands of interns who have put themselves to school with the pedagogic elements of Shem's distinctly didactic novel: the thirteen laws laid down by the Fat Man; the doctrines of gomer* immortality and curative minimalism; the hospital politics of TURFING and BUFFING and WALLS and SIEVES; the psychoanalysis of unsound doctors like Jo and Potts; the barrage of medical incidents that amounts to a pageant of dos and don'ts. It would be a rare case, I imagine, that a medical intern would encounter and not find foreshadowed somewhere in this *Gray's Anatomy* of dire possibilities.

Useful even to its mostly straight-faced glossary, *The House of God* yet glows with the celebratory essence of a real novel, defined by Henry James as "an impression of life." Sentences leap out with a supercharged vitality, as first-novelist Shem grabs the wheel of that old hot-rod, the English language:

> The jackhammers of the Wing of Zock had been wiggling my ossicles for twelve hours.

> From the ruffled front unbuttoned down past her clavicular notch showing her cleavage, to her full tightly held breasts, from the red of her nail polish and lipstick to the blue of her lids and the black of her lashes and even to the twinkly gold of the little cross from her Catholic nursing school, she was a rainbow in a waterfall.

---

*A far-gone, usually elderly patient, from the acronym GOMER: Get Out of My Emergency.

We felt sad that someone our age who'd been playing ball with his six-year-old son on one of the super twilights of summer was now a vegetable with a head full of blood, about to have his skull cracked by the surgeons.

We have here thirty-year-old Roy Bausch's belated *Bildungsroman*, the tale of his venture into the valley of death and the truth of the flesh, ending with his safe return to his eminently sane and sanely sensual Berry. Richard Nixon—the most fascinating of twentieth-century Presidents, at least to fiction writers—and the mounting Watergate scandal form the historical background of the novel, pinning it to 1973–74. *The House of God* could probably not be written now, at least so unabashedly; its lavish use of freewheeling, multi-ethnic caricature would be inhibited by the current terms "racist," "sexist," and "ageist." Its Seventies sex is not "safe"; AIDS does not figure among the plethora of vividly described diseases; and a whole array of organ transplants has come along to enrich the surgeon's armory. Yet the book's concerns are more timely than ever, as the American health-care system approaches crisis condition—ever more overused, overworked, expensive, and beset by bad publicity, as grotesqueries of mismanagement and fatal mistreatment outdo fiction in the daily newspapers. As it enters its second million of paperback sales, *The House of God* continues to afford medical students the shock of recognition, and to offer them comfort and amusement in the midst of their Hippocratic travails.

Tummy Trouble in Tinseltown

I'M LOSING YOU, by Bruce Wagner. 319 pp. Villard, 1996.

Bruce Wagner knows his Hollywood, and writes like a wizard. His new novel is an inconclusive tangle, but, then, so is life. Like *Force Majeure*, its predecessor of five years ago, *I'm Losing You* deals with the Los Angeles of aspiring losers and contemptible winners, two populations about equally whacked-out by drugs, disease, and advanced personal dysfunction. Wagner is a screenwriter *(White Dwarf, Nightmare on Elm Street 3: The Dream Warriors*, and *Scenes from the Class Struggle in Beverly Hills)* and the author of the television series *Wild Palms*; he thinks in twenty-five-thousand word bursts and believes in many-levelled plot interweave. The episodes of *Force Majeure* were unified by the central, winsome persona of Bud Wiggins, an L.A.-reared, thirtysomething scriptwriter, a postmodern heir of Scott Fitzgerald's downtrodden scribbler Pat Hobby. *I'm Losing You* has no such continuous hero, just a force-field of explosively dissatisfied wannabes and has-beens who appear and disappear like percolating bubbles on a polluted stream.

These people are not well. The novel begins with a seventy-year-old divorcée, Serena Ribkin, lying "bedridden in her frazzled palace with a bad case of colon cancer," and ends with Perry Needham Howe, a fortyish producer of a successful television cops-and-robbers show called *Streets*, who is enjoying a remission from stage-four adenocarcinoma and contemplating the strange fate of his nine-year-old son Montgomery: Montgomery, as he was dying, seven years ago, of a "medulloblastoma the size of Children's Hospital," became a savant, keeping perfect time in his head. Another child is born blind; a third is murdered. In the cast of dozens, tied together by glutinous strands of kinship, fornication, and chance encounter, other grim fates include nervous breakdown, suicide, heart attack, syphilis, AIDS, being bitten by one's AIDS-ridden sister, and a disastrously infected root-canal job:

> Bacteria got in the blood, attacking a congenitally weakened valve in her heart. It festered there before unleashing a shower of emboli to effervesce the brainstem, blocking supply of blood to the pons—the area commanding movement. When the tide rolled out, death of tissue left her marooned—"locked-in," went the jargon—a Big Star cognitively undamaged, sensoria intact, dungeoned in a useless body, a catheterized sandcastle princess on a wide dead sea.

This immobilized Big Star is called Oberon Mall. The characters tend to have coined-sounding, Pynchonesque names: Zev Turtletaub, the powerful and sadistic producer; Taj Wiedlin, his abused assistant; Troy Capra, the porn director; Kiv Giraux (once Kim Girard), his sweet and hopeful and pregnant star; Stocker Vidra, the celebrated lesbian novelist; Ursula Sedgwick, a homeless mother; Chet Stoddard, a former talk-show host; Gina Tolk, a kleptomaniacal masseuse; Moe Trusskopf, a personal manager; Leslie Trott, "fag dermatologist and celebrity adept"; Calliope Krohn-Markowitz, psychotherapist to the mighty. The Ribkins—the dying Serena; her slimy son, Donny, an agent; and her former husband, Bernie, a producer "once semi-famous for a series of zombie films made in the early seventies" and now "desperate to re-enter the Business"—echo, in a harsher key, the nuclear Wiggins configuration in *Force Majeure*.

The plots enacted by this colorful mob are not so many: bodies fall apart, relationships go bad, and almost everybody has a script or a movie idea that he or she cannot quite sell. The presence, in the Hollywood community, of global fame and fortunes measured in the hundreds of millions depresses the vast majority who have neither. The masses mill about in the gloom beneath the stars, a few of whom—Holly Hunter, Jodie Foster, Richard Dreyfuss—put a gingerly footstep into the novel's tawdry action; a very stern and extensive disclaimer warns us away from supposing that these "incidental appearances" have anything to do with "the actual conduct of real-life persons." Wagner's verbal animation rarely flags in his grisly tour of broken dreams and metastatizing cancers, but this reader found himself counting the pages left to go in a wasteland so unrelievedly cratered. No character holds center stage for long, and relatively few engage our sympathies. Two old movie hands, Bernie Ribkin and Severin Welch, inspire affection via the tenacity with which they cling to their devious hopes in a recycled Hollywood where they haven't a clue. Welch, a onetime gag writer for Bob Hope, is seventy-six and has been waiting for fifteen years to hear back from Paramount on an adaptation of Gogol's *Dead Souls* he once submitted; in his cluelessness he has taken to taping and transcribing the broken, staticky cellular-phone conversations he picks up on his Radio Shack scanner, "scaling heights of cellular Babel." Gina Tolk, as well as filching material posses-sions, appropriates people's energies during her massages, gathering souls into her web with a hilarious, avid poetry: she rubs Donny Ribkin after his mother has died, and feels "the residue of her on him like blue smokey tentacles." Nevertheless, she confides to her journal, "I like his energy; it's orange in hue and looks like kelp—or sleepy eels—floating on the surface of a pinkish coral reef." She is one of the few to whom the sludgy Hollywood scene, its "apocryphal opulence and squalor," is not barren, but teeming.

Wagner is another triumphant gleaner. His prose, out from under the constraints of script manufacture, writhes and coruscates. His revelry in brand names and film trivia extends to the verge of the present, with allu-sions to this year's smash movie *Mission: Impossible* and ditto novel *Primary Colors*. He loads his sentences to the point of the surreal:

> They were lunching at the Barney Greengrass aerie, on the terrace that overlooked the windswept postcard of Beverly Hills—one of those crisp, automatic days that trigger nostalgic dominoes of déjà vu.

Severin Welch's Beachwood Canyon home is a "low-tech shagscape"; Bernie Ribkin's fat lover, Edie, becomes the homely Eastern city of his childhood:

> It was strange, but something about her, something chalky and carnal, took him back to those whitewashed yards of Baltimore. His cousin's faces floated up as he rode the pale, doughy, mole-flecked country of her flesh,

smelled the cooking of ancient neighborhoods in her hair, saw dreary store-fronts in the bone beneath her breast.

The dominant metaphor for life in Hollywood is bodily refuse. In a book wherein the religious systems are more sci-fi than orthodox, a page is devoted to the Torah's fine discriminations concerning the uncleanness of menstruation. Corpses, human ("The rabbis called the human corpse 'the father of fathers of impurity' ") and animal, descriptively recur. Stocker Vidra sends her former lover, Katherine Grosseck, a doctor's bag containing her (Stocker's) excrement. Ass-kissing, rimming, and buggery are acts and figures of speech in the rings of this foul-mouthed hell. "Let us negotiate the amount of *genie shit* you will suck through your pretty little mouth to get there," Zev tells Taj. Vomiting, too, is an expressive act, performable at will; perhaps this is a somewhat special feature of Wagner's universe. Anyone who can write of "the star-speckled vomitus of the Big Bang" sees a lot in emesis. Zev, having tied Taj blindfolded in a bathtub, "gilded him with throw-up. The producer regurgitated a warm rhythmical hail of egesta." The entirety of *I'm Losing You* is an out-pouring of material indigestibly rich, presented in somewhat scattered fashion.

Soap and Death in America

GAIN, by Richard Powers. 353 pp. Farrar, Straus and Giroux, 1998.

Our so-called age of information has bred an impulse to stuff a novel so full of data that it can hardly waddle. Joyce, Pynchon, and Gaddis have their youngish American heirs in William T. Vollmann, David Foster Wallace, and—at a higher level of refinement—Richard Powers. Powers, a polymath whose previous novel, *Galatea 2.2*, brilliantly and, what's more, movingly imagined a computer, called Helen, whose artificial intelligence expanded into the realm of soul, will, and personality, has in *Gain* taken as his protagonist an American corporation named Clare.

The founder, the English merchant Jephthah Clare, comes to these shores in 1802, fleeing financial embarrassment in one of his own packet traders; he and his wife and three children make the journey on a cargo of Wedgwood china, which he sells upon arrival in Boston to set himself up as a trader. An inventive risk-taker, a devotee of the long and hazardous haul, he prospers until, in 1828, the Tariff of Abominations slashes trade. Only a certain English item, Pech's Soap, can be profitably imported, and

the profit soon dissolves in "the flood of imitations." Rescue arrives in
the form of a taciturn, recently widowered Irish candlemaker, Robert
Emmet Ennis, whose superior product is noticed by Resolve Clare, one
of Jephthah's three sons; Ennis converts his fatty skills to those of a
soapmaker. The Clare sons—hard-headed Samuel, pious Resolve, and
botany-minded Benjamin—become "J. Clare's Sons . . . Manufacturer &
Wholesaler of All Imaginable Soaps and Candles / Unguent to Cleanse
the Multitudes / Light to Lighten Them." Soap—its chemistry, its
distribution, its packaging, its advertising, its growingly far-flung offshoots—becomes the stuff of our saga, generation after generation,
boom after crash, triumph after crisis, Manifest Destiny after Civil War,
innovation after innovation, detergents after soapflakes.

The details of doing business are generally left out of novels, even
those involving businessmen—though Howells made a stab at it in
The Rise of Silas Lapham—and Powers does a truly illuminating job of
describing how a Boston soap manufacturer exploits and endures the
twists of our struggling democracy's economy to become a multinational
chemical giant. The homeliness of the basic product and the slenderness
of the advantage whereby one product wins out over another (e.g., Benjamin brings back from the Antarctic Wilkes Expedition a tropical plant,
Utilis clarea, whose scent becomes the crucial ingredient of Clare's Native
Balm, a soap, stamped with a Indian brave's head, of allegedly vast emol-
lient and curative properties) contrast with the increasing scope and complexity of financial operation. Powers scatters epigrammatic business tips
through his pages of exposition:

> Progress demanded the destruction of much that had once been considered
> wealth. . . . The waters had constantly to leave behind the landscape they
> drained. . . . So, too, any forward-looking enterprise had to be ready to cast
> off what had once been its mainstay.
>
> The real purpose of business . . . lay not in getting but in spending.
>
> As always, a firm's worth lay in how many outstanding loans it could
> generate.
>
> Money was the salt of human activity, its refrigeration. It retarded the
> spoilage of your day's efforts. . . . The history of humanity was the history of
> higher and higher orders of convertibility.

But is all this instruction, this entertaining illustration of basic principles,
fiction enough? What does the effort of inventing Clare do that could
not be done by a shrewd and animated history of a real corporation
like—all mentioned in the text—Procter & Gamble, Lever Brothers,
Squibb, or Colgate?

Soap is only half of *Gain*; the other half concerns Laura Rowen Bodey, the forty-two-year-old mother of a daughter, Ellen, and a son, Tim. She also has an ex-husband, Don, a married lover, Ken, and a job at a realty firm, New Millennium. She lives in Lacewood, a prosperous Illinois city (pop. 92,400) one hundred fifty miles south of Chicago, which for more than a century has been home to Clare's national headquarters. We meet Laura as she attends the funeral of her daughter's best friend, who mysteriously wasted away at the age of twelve. Before long, Laura herself is told that she has cancer. Lacewood seems to be a cancer-prone town. Near Clare headquarters is a landscaped pond that somehow never freezes. Clare has branched out from soap into all sorts of chemical marvels—detergents, fertilizers, pesticides. Uh-oh.

The progress of Laura's illness, detailed with the same avid factuality as the chemistry of soap, is on collision course with the progress of Clare International; the two histories are set forth in alternating brief chapters interspersed with telling scraps of advertising and promotional matter clipped from the two centuries since 1802. Oddly, the collision—a lawsuit—when it comes, after three hundred pages of meticulous data distribution, is muffled to the point of a non-event. Laura looks around her house and finds Clare products everywhere:

> Who told them to make all these things? But she knows the answer to that one. . . . Wasn't she born wanting what they were born wanting to give her? Every thought, every pleasure, freed up by these little simplicities, the most obvious of them already worlds beyond her competence.

Laura and the author seem inclined to the view that life, and not Clare, is the villain. "No punishment bigger than living," she thinks toward the end. Her resignation from life is less moving than that of Helen the computer, whom we saw labor to acquire consciousness, connection by connection. We like Laura, but her world feels a bit out of the box, furnished with standard sitcom fixtures. Her relationship with her growing daughter interests her, and the reader, most; Don's stubborn loyalty irritates her, and Ken is hardly even a cipher. Powers's characters have love lives rather incidentally; the breath of carnal passion barely fogs the cool daily details his Lacewood residents live through. Laura's descent, like Clare's rise, is sheer process—a study in chemistry. This intricately, intelligently, and accurately constructed fictional mechanism yet lacks the spark that would make it go on its own. The author, off above the clouds with his omniscience, is unignorably present in every high-tech touch, every shift of narrative gears, every typographical oddity. The rapid fluctuation between Laura's medical weepie and the saga of American industry, with jazzy commercial breaks in between, makes it hard to get close to any character. We never quite dwell among these people; we just collect a few pages of evidence and hurry on. The prose seems not so much written as administered, in short, doselike paragraphs and compressed sentences with an occasional tang of the precious:

Its appeal cut across social strata, from Astor to ash tender.

Lather now lent luster to the name Clare.

Not that Powers's achievement, in describing the rise of the corporations that pollute every corner of our world with souped-up molecules and mind-numbing slogans, isn't formidable: formidable is just what it is. Sensuous and involving it is not. When, in the tale of Laura's valiant attempt to maintain her motherhood and self-respect amid the horrors of chemotherapy, humanity makes itself felt, the overview quickly reduces it to negligible size.

Awriiiighhhhhhhht!

A MAN IN FULL, by Tom Wolfe. 742 pp. Farrar, Straus and Giroux, 1998.

Tom Wolfe's novel is, like its hero, Charlie Croker, burly. The book weighs in as a 742-page bruiser whose jacket vaunts the author's name in letters so big that the "o" in "Tom" is cut out and the eye of the semi-glossy portrait of Croker on the cover stares through. A book to muscle aside all the others on the "New Releases" table. A book that defies you not to buy it. Croker, a sixty-year-old former Georgia Tech football star become a millionaire Atlanta real-estate developer and owner of a twenty-nine-thousand-acre plantation maintained for shooting quail in, excites Wolfe's excitable prose to raptures of anatomical specification: "He flexed and fanned out the biggest muscles of his back, the latissimi dorsi, in a Charlie Croker version of a peacock or a turkey preening . . . his massive neck, his broad shoulders, his prodigious forearms; but above all he was proud of his back. . . . 'I got a back like a Jersey bull!' "

This is a muscular novel; a present-day Georgia Tech football star, Fareek "the Cannon" Fanon, "wore a black polo shirt . . . wide open at the throat, revealing the long, thick pair of muscles that came down the sides of his neck and inserted at the clavicle." Fanon's coach, Buck McNutter, is no beanpole either: "His neck, which seemed a foot wide, rose up out of a yellow polo shirt and a blue blazer as if it were unit-welded to his trapezius muscles and his shoulders." And, on the other side of the continent, in the working-class California town of Pittsburg, thirty miles east of Oakland, an idealistic but ill-starred young man named Conrad Hensley has developed a formidable upper body from toting eighty-pound blocks of frozen food in a warehouse of Croker Global Foods:

> He liked the way the T-shirt stretched across his chest and his shoulders, which were highly defined . . . He pulled the T-shirt out of his pants and slid it up over his ribs so as to bare his midsection, and he tensed his abdominal muscles until they popped out like a six-pack. He was . . . *cut, ripped,* as the bodybuilders liked to put it, from wrestling with all those tons of frozen product at Croker Global . . . Then he lifted his forearms and hands and made two fists . . . His forearms were positively gorged with muscle.*

All these bodies—not to mention those of the young women, "perfect boys with breasts," with their "loamy loins" and "cloven hindquarters" and thighs that "tapered down to where they inserted into the knees"— illustrate the sociological fact that America in the 1990s is mad about conditioning, and give a certain pumped-up sheen to the teeming cast of characters. Another *fin-de-siècle* fact seems to be the persistence of rap music, and Wolfe, never a quiet writer, gets more poetry and thematic harmony out of flat, hostile, usually obscene rap lyrics than I would have thought possible. The book contains a vision of hell, which is the Santa Rita Rehabilitation Center, a converted array of old army barracks out- side of Oakland; each night after lights are out, the jail's rapmaster launches verses into the air, which stinks of caged and sleepless men. A relatively tame sample is:

> Yo, sugar!—think 'at's a ruby
> You got stuck inside yo' crack?
> The fuck, yo' booty turned to gold
> While you was lyin' on your back?

More than twenty-five years ago, Wolfe chastised his contemporaries with ignoring most of the American reality, the brawling socio-economic and power-crazed vastness of it, concerning themselves instead with triv- ial introspective exercises. *A Man in Full* is a brave and energetic attempt to practice what he preached. He gives us Atlanta as an image of a mixed- blood nation, where black and white and Asian uneasily, busily co-exist. Wolfe's portraits of Americans with African ancestry range from the dap- per, pale-brown, Stravinsky-loving lawyer Roger White II, called since

---

*The inscrutably distributed ellipses are all part of Wolfe's prose.

college Roger Too White, to the brutal, almost unintelligible inmates of the Santa Rita jail. Wolfe's renditions of black talk encompass the confident rhythms of a slick clergyman, the irony-layered banter of two ambitious college-educated "brothers," the elaborate deference of an anachronistic Uncle Tom, the sullen non-compliance of a ghetto-bred "homey", and teasing talk among young women (" 'It's know-it time, girlfriend' "). Anthologies in African-American literature are not apt to enshrine passages from this jumpy comedy by a white native of Richmond who wears a white planter's suit; nevertheless, in a strange but honorable way Wolfe has attempted a Great Black Novel. Knowing, of course, his own temerity, he has worked hard on the novel's black sections, making them morally elaborate as well as intensely observant. There is no mooning about slavery or jazz; instead, a crisply animated survey of the current situation takes in a crack house, a big-city mayor's office, a black athlete's truculent triumph, an inferno of incarcerated young black men. The most sympathetic and nervously responsive character in the book is Roger Too White, who manages in the end to unbutton his prim shell and reclaim solidarity with his people. A sentimental pilgrimage, some might say, that comes round to white America's favorite Negro, Booker T. Washington: " 'I see that Booker T. was right all along,' said Roger." But the book cannot be denied its admirable determination to see, with however blue an eye, the United States whole, as a nation whose black thirteen percent interacts with the rest, economically, culturally, and personally.

Plot. There is a great deal of it, spreading like kudzu, sending eager tendrils everywhere. Charlie Croker, that Georgia cracker turned plutocrat, has overreached, building Croker Concourse, including a forty-story skyscraper, outside Atlanta, and is badly bankrupt, while maintaining his baronial life-style in the face of ever fiercer attempts on the part of PlannersBanc, his principal creditor, to reclaim their squandered hundreds of millions. Fareek Fanon, that new, African-American installment of football muscle, is alleged to have raped the eighteen-year-old daughter of another Atlanta baron, Inman Armholster. Coach Buck McNutter wants Fareek on his team, and Wesley Dobbs Jordan, Atlanta's black mayor, doesn't want race riots; nor does the white business establishment. Meanwhile, for reasons that take five hundred pages to dawn, we are made privy to the drab life of Conrad Hensley, who after being laid off by Croker Global Foods winds up in jail, where his only comfort is a volume of Epictetus and other Stoics. He becomes a devotee of Zeus, and, sure enough, Zeus one critical night ordains an earthquake that . . . but leave Wolfe's tale its baroque turns. He concocts a good, if sometimes laborious read, which becomes perfunctory and implausible only toward the end. The laboriousness derives, in part, from the worked-up quality of many scenes, masterpieces of creative journalism but a little thick for sustaining suspense and characters we can care about. The preeningly expert architectural details, the avid sartorial specifics, the infallibly lively decors in all their dubious taste, the price tag attached to everything worn or inhabited, the painstakingly spelled-out accents, the explosive onomatopoetics—"*Brannnnng! Brannnnng! Brannnnng!*" "*Woooo-eeeeeee! Hegh-heggghhhhhh,*" "Ahhhhhhhhhhh ahhhhhhhhhhhh ahhhhhhhhhhh," "Su-perflyyyyyyyyyyyyyyyyy!," "*eye eye eye eye eye eye eye eye,*" "*Scrack scrack scrack scraccckkk scracccck,*" "*glug glug glug glugluglug,*" "Awriiiighhhhhhhht!"—all remind the reader of the vigilant, mischievous, but rather disapproving presence of the writer, for whom America comes down to noise, trash, and vanity.

There is relatively little of Wolfe's celebrated Toryism, though he does put in the mouth of a fictional (I assume) director of Atlanta's High Museum a hilarious stretch of Foucault-speak, and he does suggest that hippies make poor parents. The novel, which is prefaced by two pages of breathless thanks to all those who guided and supported the author through his perilous tour of "the telling details of contemporary American life," proceeds by set pieces: a plantation quail hunt, the majestic and elaborate operation of bringing a stud stallion into contact with a mare in the plantation's brick breeding barn, the gabbly social ritual of a museum benefit, the grisly workout of a "shithead" (a loan defaulter) in a bank's conference room, an exercise class as painfully experienced by a fifty-three-year-old cast-off wife, a fashionable restaurant, a rattlesnake capture—we are surrounded by a modern equivalent of the Cyclorama, "an immense circular mural, a full 360 degrees, illustrating the Battle of Atlanta during the Civil War." For good measure, Wolfe "does" greater Oakland to a T, and when the hero of a subplot, the scheming loan officer Raymond Peepgass, briefly travels to the Bahamas, Wolfe does Nassau. So much local information, so many well-lit settings, so much *news* do not quite knit into a novel powered by the human spirit as it gropes and struggles for focus. Wolfe has perhaps too many opinions for a novelist; his characters have a hard time breaking out of the illustrative mold in which they are cast. The physically perfect, periwinkle-eyed Serena Croker, our hero's twenty-eight-year-old second wife, hovers at his side so blankly that one expects from her at last some revelatory motion, of betrayal or rescue; but she turns out to be a mere gold-digger, as labelled, who disappears when the gold does.

Still, Wolfe loves, or wants to love, Charlie Croker. I must confess that every time I have tried to read *Bonfire of the Vanities*, the blatancy of its icy-hearted satire repelled me. *A Man in Full* is warmed by the Southern setting. Wolfe remains Southerner enough to respect the old macho notion of Southern manhood—narrow, maybe, bigoted and brutal, but also gallant and life-loving—and traces its collapse here with a certain regret, even as he piles tribulations upon Charlie Croker's balding, bull-necked head. Yet Wolfe has become Northerner enough to make us feel that Charlie is a specimen under glass; his non-U pronunciations are steadfastly spelled out—"sump'm" for "something," "far fat" for "fire fight"—in a way that a Faulkner character would be spared. For Faulkner, Southern life was life; for Wolfe, it is a provincial curiosity, though one he cherishes. The lush landscape moves him to nature lyricism; the suburban luxury of Atlanta's Buckhead neighborhood sets off idyllic catalogues of sunsplashed antiques and shrubs. He is, disarmingly, dazzled, and something of this dazzlement rub off. Eleven years in the making, and encumbered with too many subplots, *A Man in Full* touches us with its grand ambition: a talented, inventive, philosophical-minded journalist, coming into old age, has gone for broke in this populous cyclorama of an Atlanta still at war. For a time, I wondered why, doing so much justice to sex ("God's cosmic joke") and greed, Wolfe had left religion out of the human equation. But the novel turns out to be *all* about religion, culminating in renunciation and non-attachment; the world in its baubles has been conjured up only to be dismissed with a wave of a dandy's hand. In a post-Christian world, Wolfe offers us, at considerable explanatory length, the nobility of Stoicism.

This is high-minded, but *A Man in Full* still amounts to entertainment, not literature, even literature in a modest aspirant form. Like a movie desperate to recoup its bankers' investment, the novel tries too hard to please us. Wolfe's exclamatory interjections ("Packs! Dens! Utterly primitive animal turfs!" "Brute sexual energy! A herd of young male animals!" "More thrashing! Looser teeth! Blood! Bone fragments!") are like surges of background music, telling us what to feel, not trusting us to react without supervision. "Literature's a sort of dessert," a minor character, an old professor, tells the pilgrim Conrad. We want dessert to be choice. Wolfe shares a name with another profuse, all-including Southern writer who failed to be exquisite. Such failure would not seem to be major, but in the long run it is. Henry James, composing in 1900 a preface for his youthful novel *Roderick Hudson* a quarter century after he wrote it, recalled intricate difficulties and spelled out modernism's demanding criterion for the new century:

> The greater complexity, the superior truth, was all more or less present to me; only the question was, too dreadfully, how make it present to the

reader? How boil down so many facts in the alembic, so that the distilled result, the produced appearance, should have intensity, lucidity, brevity, beauty, all the merits required for my effect? . . . It is only by doing such things that art becomes exquisite, and it is only by positively becoming exquisite that it keeps clear of becoming vulgar, repudiates the coarse industries that masquerade in its name.

Stones into Bread

THE GOSPEL ACCORDING TO THE SON, by Norman Mailer. 243 pp. Random House, 1997.

The Bible is like a once-fearsome lion that, now toothless and declawed, can be petted and teased. The allegedly sacred text has become a toy for scholars and poets; on my shelves alone sit, among volumes recently received, versified, closer-to-the-Hebraic versions of Genesis and Exodus (by Everett Fox) and the Song of Solomon (by Ariel and Chana Bloch). Seven years ago David Rosenberg—in his own words— "restored and translated a lost version of the Hebrew Bible" called *The Book of J*, which he and Harold Bloom hypothesize was composed by a woman.* In *The Lost Book of Paradise* (1993) he gives us an even more hypothetical reconstruction, whose original—of which traces allegedly exist in the Song of Solomon—is lost or else "placed under a taboo of forgetfulness." It begins with Adam saying, in the centered lines so popular since the advent of the computer:

If I spoke to her in breaths
lips inspire lips
to press
to drink there
as all words swallowed like seeds
by the earth
to rest there, pregnant
for the namer
as I for you, each naming
like your kiss, a pressing claim
to memory . . .

---

*For a thoughtful and thorough dismissal of *The Book of J*, see Chana Bloch's "Shakespeare's Sister" in *The Iowa Review* (Fall 1991).

Well, maybe so, though the sensibility behind this Ur-text seems twentieth-century valentine. Elsewhere, to appease modern gender-sensitivity, "inclusive-language" versions of the Bible are promulgated, with God turned into a He-She. Even in contemporary Christian church services, the masculine pronouns of the resolutely patriarchal Bible are freely neutered: "worthy of all men to be received" in Timothy 1:15 commonly drops the "men," and "If any man sin" in 1 John 2:1 becomes "if any one sin." Unchained by Luther from the lectern and from Latin, the Good Book is open to tweakings by modern novelists from Kazantzakis to Lagerkvist. Just last year, Walter Wangerin, Jr., published the 850-page retelling, *The Book of God: The Bible as a Novel*. The novelist Reynolds Price has put himself to school with the Gospels' *koiné* Greek, and essayed new renditions in *A Palpable God* (1978) and *Three Gospels* (1996). In the latter volume he translated Mark and John entire and provided a third entity, an "Apocryphal Gospel," a synthetic invention of his own. And now Norman Mailer has produced a life of Jesus conceived as an autobiography.

One of Mailer's irrepressible strengths has been his ability to become interested, and then quickly expert, in almost anything. Ancient Egyptians, the CIA, Lee Harvey Oswald, Pablo Picasso, astronauts, prize-fighters, sex, politics—all have stimulated his organs of verbalization. Still, a retelling of the Gospels from Jesus's point of view may find even Mailer's nimblest admirers off balance. He came to it, he told an interviewer for the Random House magazine, *At Random*, by way of his present wife, who was reared as a Free Will Baptist in Arkansas. On visits to her native small town, he would accompany his father-in-law to an adult Bible class, where, as a Jew, he was regarded as a rarity and "approached with the most curious kind of respect": he was invited to shed light on New Testament passages puzzling to these hard-shell Christians. Reading the Gospels for himself, he found them in part remarkable but, "Where you don't have a wonderful sentence, what you get is some pretty dull prose and a contradictory, almost hopeless way of telling the story. So I thought this account, this wonderful narrative, ought to be properly told." Who better to do it—to repair the botch perpetrated by the literary committees of early Christians—than Norman Mailer? He said to himself, "If I can write about Isis and Osiris and Ra, then certainly the New Testament is not going to be that difficult to do."

And he wasn't half wrong. His gospel is written in a direct, rather relaxed English that yet has an eerie, neo-Biblical dignity. Some of the sentences may be a bit too simple ("We were eating with much joy"; "He left the porch. He was weeping. He wept") and some not simple enough

("Tears stood forth in my eyes like sentinels on guard") but the tone as a whole is quietly penetrating. Where the serene ghostly voice of Jesus is coming from is perhaps a question better left alone, but Mailer tackles it at the outset: after complaining of the exaggerations and inaccuracies in the Gospel accounts, "written many years after I was gone," Jesus tells the reader, "So I will give my own account. For those who would ask how my words have come to this page, I would tell them to look upon it as a small miracle." Jesus is setting the record straight, although he* is hopeful rather than certain that he can do it: "I would hope to remain closer to the truth" than Mark, Matthew, Luke, and John, who were all "seeking to enlarge their fold," some appealing to Gentiles, some to Jews.

Mailer's synoptic gospel runs to 242 well-leaded pages, which is not much shorter than the four canonical Gospels altogether in such modern translations as those by E. V. Rieu and Richmond Lattimore. It is almost five times longer than the "Apocryphal Gospel" by Price, and makes a stronger impression; Price took a glancing, minimalist approach, interposing into the traditional narrative a few poetic details—a post-Resurrection appearance to Judas, a post–Last Supper dance, some Freudian touches in the forty days in the wilderness. A number of Price's extra flourishes were added from the apocryphal, non-canonical Gospels ascribed to Thomas and James. Mailer is surprisingly submissive to the canonical material; his additions and emphases derive not from esoteric texts but from a personal fictive reshaping.

His Jesus is very much a carpenter, whose fourteen years of apprenticeship to Joseph are lovingly described; his effort "to find communion with the wood" informs his ministry metaphorically and extends to his being offended, in his last hours, by the crude carpentry of the cross, "nailed together with slovenly blows of the hammer." He and his family are Essenes—the white-clad, strictly observant Jewish sect usually congregated in groups of celibate men. The celibacy does not prevent Joseph from fathering four brothers of Jesus, but it does settle the issue much vexed by modern explorers of the Savior's life: the extent of his sexual activity. This Jesus has some "lustful thoughts" in the night, but God reinforces his chastity by pointing out the faith-weakening effects upon Solomon of his seven hundred wives and three hundred concubines. The Devil in the wilderness accuses God the Father of being secretly in love with Jezebel, and Jesus's later encounter with Mary Magdalene is given a heated treatment. While a virtual anthology of Biblical erotica tumbles through his head, Jesus manages to keep the harlot in proportion: "By

---

*Uncapitalized, as in Mailer and the King James version of the New Testament.

half she was gentle, and that half belonged to God." Rather daringly, Mailer combines in one discourse Jesus's two best-known, widely disparate pronouncements on lust: the tolerant admonition, in John, that "he that is without sin among you, let him first cast a stone" at a woman taken in adultery, and his harsh pronouncement, in Matthew (inspiring many a self-castration), that "it is profitable for thee that one of thy members should perish, and not that thy whole body should be cast into hell." The lustful can find forgiveness or damnation in the Gospels, depending on where they look; either the Gospel writers were of differing minds, or Jesus himself was, humanly enough.

Mailer's macho sense of *virtus*, of virtue as a kind of physical fluid, works well with the many incidents of Jesus's healing. In the *At Random* interview Mailer speaks of himself as being, in his celebrity, "half a man and half something else"; this sense of one man inside another becomes affecting as Jesus, still doubtful of his powers and his mission, haltingly lets God's power flow through him. Some miracles are rationalized: that of the loaves and the fishes is explained as the breaking of the available bread and dried fish into "exceedingly small" pieces. Jesus's first miracle, turning the water into wine at the wedding in Cana, is oddly reconstructed; whereas in the Bible his mother urges him to perform it, receiving the rebuke "Woman, what have I to do with thee? mine hour is not yet come," in Mailer he doesn't tell her anything but silently transforms the barrels of water by eating a single red grape with "much contemplation of the Spirit who resided within." The miracle-worker's strength repeatedly ebbs to lethargy as he copes with the world's endless supply of suffering. The acts of healing are strenuous, and by no means assured of success; accosted in Jerusalem by a man blind from birth, Jesus is almost comically dismayed:

> When I looked at the eyes of this blind man, however, I saw nothing with which to begin, not even a sightless eye on either side of his nose. There were nothing but two hollows beneath his brow. "I believe," I said to my Father. "Now help my unbelief."

With the application of some spittle and clay, he succeeds; but the Pharisees disbelieve, and beat the former blind man when he insists on the miracle's reality. The forces of destruction are gathering; a sense of peril, of miracles shakily performed and a mission dimly perceived, has been woven into Mailer's gospel from the start. The birth of Jesus occasions the slaughter of the innocents and leaves Jesus haunted by the feeling that his true kinship is with "these children and the life they never had." Mailer's first-person voice only fitfully convinces us that we are occupying Jesus's psychological center. To do more would have indeed been a miracle. Any attempt to extend the portrait of the central personality in the overlapping third-person accounts of the New Testament must solve the conundrum of Jesus's consciousness: was he an omniscient God or a fallible human being groping toward a martyr's death? Totally omniscient, he would have been engaged in a passionless charade; yet, without some foreknowledge and cosmic intention, he scarcely deserves worship. The early church entertained a wide variety of views—the Docetists maintained that his body had been an apparition; the Adoptionists claimed that he was a mere mortal adopted as the Son of God at his baptism or, even, after his resurrection. The Western, Roman branch of Christianity has favored the human side, Eastern Orthodoxy the more remote, iconic Christ Pantocrator. A settled though explosively inclusive formula was reached in 451, at the Council of Chalcedon, with the phrasing "perfect in deity and perfect in humanity . . . in two natures, without being mixed, transmuted, divided or separated." Four centuries earlier, Paul, as translated in the New Revised Standard Version, beautifully crystallized the mystery in Philippians: "Christ Jesus . . . though he was in the form of God, did not regard equality with God as something to be exploited, but emptied himself, taking the form of a slave, being born in human likeness." Without such an emptying, the suffering would not be real, nor the Christian answer to the theological problem of suffering— that God descended to suffer with us—persuasive.

It is laid upon each Christian worshipper to exalt a man who confessed to fatigue, who gave way to moods, who on occasion wept, who impulsively withered a fig tree, who founded his church on a pun, who waved away centuries of Judaic observance, who consorted with publicans and tax collectors and women of dubious reputation, who kept asking his disciples who they thought he was, who begged God to relieve him of his coming ordeal, and who on the cross asked God why He had forsaken him. This God, the human being fatally afflicted with a supernatural mission, does walk through this gospel composed by a skeptical, unconverted Jew, whose mother (he told *At Random*) as a girl in New Jersey endured the cat-call of "Christ-killer" from her Irish Catholic schoolmates; she could never understand how her son could have so many Irish friends.

The level amiability of *The Gospel According to the Son* is its marvel and perhaps its weakness. Mailer has written an account that, I believe, his Baptist father-in-law can read without discomfort. This is not one of those lives of Jesus (for example, A. N. Wilson's) that pause to scoff and debate probabilities. The major miracles, including that of the Resurrection, are rolled into the tale; Mailer, whose fiction more than once evokes mystical effluvia, makes himself at home with the Biblical devils, and assigns the Devil himself an extended speaking part. Theologically, Mailer opts for Manichaeanism: his Jesus says, in summary, "God and Mammon still grapple for the hearts of all men and all women. As yet, since the contest remains so equal, neither the Lord nor Satan can triumph." Manichaeanism is, of course, an age-old heresy, weakening God to make sense of the world's mixed and woeful condition. Of more individual provenance is Mailer's equation of Satan and Mammon. No deity, "mammon" is simply the Aramaic word for "riches."

Mailer makes Judas a Sixties radical—a rich kid who has become a militant socialist. "I hate the rich," he tells Jesus. "They poison all of us. They are vain, undeserving, and wasteful of the hopes of those who are beneath them. They spend their lives lying to the lowly." Judas becomes a disciple not because he believes the Master's promises of salvation but because these promises will give the poor courage. Mailer has a narrow basis for this in John 12:3–5. When Jesus accepts the extravagant favor of the anointment with spikenard (his feet in John, his head in Mark and Matthew), it is specifically Judas who protests that the precious perfume should have been sold and the proceeds given to the poor. In the gospel according to Mailer, after Jesus accepts the luxurious touch with the observation that the poor are with you always, Judas departs and prepares to betray his Master. The moral crux—one's obligations to the less fortunate versus the value of ceremony and an instinctive, joyous selfishness— is exposed by the modern gospeller but then pragmatically fudged. "Many roads lead to the Lord," he writes, and, "The truth need last no longer than a shaft of lightning in order to be the mightiest truth of all."

The original Gospels evince a flinty terseness, a refusal, or inability, to provide the close focus and cinematic highlighting that the modern mind expects. In Mark, the moment of crucifixion comes in an introductory clause to a gambling match that nameless Roman soldiers are holding over the confiscated clothes: "And when they had crucified him, they parted his garments, casting lots upon them, what every man should take." In comparison, medieval and modern depictions seem melodramatic. The crucifixion is cheapened, I think, by Mailer's added specifics. The pain appears in Technicolor: "Within my skull, light glared at me until I knew the colors of the rainbow; my soul was luminous with pain." In addition to the seven traditional utterances from the cross, we have this wheedling dialogue, amid metaphorical lava and lightning:

> I cried out to my Father, "Will You allow not one miracle at this hour?" When my Father replied, it was like a voice from the whirlwind. He

said in my ear, and He was louder than my pain: "Would you annul My judgment?"

I said: "Not while breath is in me."

But my torment remained. Agony was written on the sky. And pain came down to me like lightning. Pain surged up to me like lava. I prayed again to my Father: "One miracle," I asked.

Easy enough it is, for a critic, and lazy, to cling to the sacrosanct King James Version and to snub a fresh and in its way fervent rendition of a Biblical narrative. But Mailer, serious as he is, and provocative as some of his shadings are, does not give us what, say, the English writer Jim Crace gives us in his 1997 novel *Quarantine*. There, Jesus's forty days in the wilderness—an ordeal placed, in the three older Gospels, between his baptism and the start of his ministry—are dramatized with an archaeological command of the texture of life in Herod's Palestine and with a troubling heterodoxy. Jesus is reconceived as "Gally," a "boy" besotted with prayer and visions whose program of total deprivation kills him in thirty days; a sextet of other characters—four religious pilgrims, a stranded merchant, and his wife—radically transform the terms of the traditional account, including the person of Satan. Such an assaultive retelling, far from smoothing the rough spots in the Gospel account, raises new ones. Crace is a writer of hallucinatory skill and considerable cruelty. The beatings and thievery of the ancient world, its intimate murderous commerce with animals, and its bestial treatment of women are not stinted, nor the compromised quality of religious experience, nor the deadly beauty of desert mountains. In one temptation, according to Matthew and Luke, Satan asks Jesus to turn stones into bread; Jesus refuses, and Crace, too, leaves the stones the dignity of their stoniness.

Barney Looks Back

BARNEY'S VERSION, by Mordecai Richler. 355 pp. Knopf, 1997.

Now that novelists, like everyone else, live longer, we can expect more geriatric novels. Hitherto, the elderly have received relatively short shrift in the dispensations of fiction; your typical romantic heroine is in her twenties, and a viable hero may be as old as forty, though even his few gray hairs make us—as they would with the hero of a pornographic film—a bit uneasy. Novels are about mating, and the elderly need not apply. But apply they will, henceforth, in all the vigor that modern medicine allows, bursting with regrets and anecdotes and the wisdom of the long view, while pressing upon us videos of old pornographic films in which they once starred. By the demographics of it, the middle of our century now comes in for intense retrospective attention; of Philip Roth's last two novels, for instance, *Sabbath's Theatre* revives with a passionate fullness a boy's impressions of World War II and Thirties swing, and *American Pastoral* extends the effort of resurrection to virtually the entire industrial Newark of the aging narrator's youth. Don DeLillo, a mere sixty-one, is too young to be geriatric, but he begins the massive unearthing of *Underworld* with a fifty-page reconstruction of a baseball game played at the ardently remembered Polo Grounds on October 3, 1951. The Fifties, indeed, are getting more literary respect this time around than when they were occurring.

Barney Panofsky, the vociferous, reprehensible, beguiling narrator of *Barney's Version*, takes as the point of departure for his belated memoirs the Paris of the early Fifties, where he and a number of other young Canadians and Americans were making their first grabs at art and fame. More than four decades later, a companion of the time and a fellow-Montrealer of Barney's, the esteemed but contemptible novelist Terry McIver, is publishing his memoirs, and its inaccuracies have goaded Barney to set down, in arresting fits and starts, "the true story of my wasted life." Wasted? In fact, Barney has made a fortune as the founder and head of Totally Unnecessary Productions, which produces commercials and serial schlock for television. Twenty-two in 1950, he is three years older than Richler—a kind of scapegrace elder brother. A loyal acquaintance of Barney's, Irv Nussbaum, sums him up as "one of your real wild Jews. A *bonditt*. A *mazik*. A devil."

Richler has always been what the Psalmist calls "a ready writer," but much of his writing has been done for films, and the rest lies for most Americans over the horizon that coincides with the Canadian border. For those who, like me, have some catching up to do, *Barney's Version* is a propitious place to begin—a rollicking novel laden with rue, a self-portrait of a creative personality who never found a creative outlet that he could respect, a paean to the pleasures and perils of drink, a celebration of ice hockey and tap-dancing, a lament for a multicultural Montreal now torn and depressed by Québécois separatism, a broad window into the bustle of Canadian Jewry, an intermittent disquisition on authorship, an extended meditation on the relations between the sexes, and even a murder mystery, with an uproarious solution. Bernard "Boogie" Moscovitch was the most promising of the many aspiring literary lights in Barney's mid-century Paris, one to whom Barney, aspiring only to artistic company, attached himself with an loyalty unshaken by Boogie's addiction to drugs, drink, mean put-downs, and publisher's advances never delivered upon. Even Boogie's sleeping with Barney's second wife, in a Laurentian lakeside cottage, sours but does not squelch their comradely drinking bout afterwards. Boogie goes into the lake to clear his head, and disappears; Barney is charged with his murder and, though not convicted, is believed by many to be guilty. What happened to Boogie? This is the novel's underlying riddle, and might have served as its title. Well, what happened to Boogie you wouldn't believe.

The book is more cunningly plotted than its dishevelled surface (with numerous memory lapses and factual errors corrected in footnotes by Barney's meticulous older son) leads the reader to expect. All that matters in Barney's life eventually comes around for a reckoning. He divides his tale into three sections named after his three wives. The first, a faux-Wasp waif called Clara, he marries in Paris and soon leaves, driven away by her mad mixture of frigidity with him and promiscuity with others. Despairing of his return, she commits suicide, and eventually she enjoys a Plath-like posthumous glory on the strength of sketches and poems that no one took seriously at the time.

The Second Mrs. Panovsky, never otherwise named, is met and wed back in Montreal, in 1958, and this misbegotten marriage, wounded by Barney's falling in love with someone else at their wedding, generates the densest comedy and pathos of the novel. The Second Mrs. is a Jewish-Canadian princess from central casting, with self-important arriviste parents and a propensity to sustained prattle—she has a mind like a shopping list. Not since the late Stanley Elkin and the early Philip Roth have I seen a writer take such uninhibited delight in caricaturing Jewish types, from ghetto Yiddish-speaker to superproper pseudo-Gentile, with all shapes of excessive energy in between. The Second Mrs. Panofsky is a gabby bore, yet Barney allows that she, like his old friend Hymie Mintzbaum, "possessed that quality I most admire in other people—an appetite for life." Cruelly neglected and spurned by her husband from the start, she is not without her touching utterances: "Barney, I want you to give us a chance. I want you to tell me what I could do to make you happy." To which he replies, like many another emotionally absent husband, "ImhappyImhappy."

Barney's third marriage, the longest, to Miriam, the vision of grace whom he sighted at his second wedding, is yet the briefest and dimmest in the novel. Happiness, except in Tolstoy, doesn't bear much describing. What entertains and affects us in *Barney's Version* is the headlong, spendthrift passage of a life, redeemed from oblivion in the unbridled telling. The edge of the grave makes a lively point of vantage.

People Fits

SELECTED STORIES, by Alice Munro. 545 pp. Knopf, 1996.

The Canadian Alice Munro has managed to earn a sizable literary reputation on the strength of her short stories. This is not an easy feat; Raymond Carver was the last American to do it, and Donald Barthelme before him, with Eudora Welty and Flannery O'Connor and Katherine Anne Porter making their names when short fiction was still a prime component of the popular culture. Munro's stories, which began to appear in *The New Yorker* about twenty years ago, were from the start characterized by ambition: a well-meditated complexity and multiplicity of plot, an intense clarity of phrase and image, an exceptional psychological searchingness and honesty. There was a grittiness to Munro, and a bold reach. We learn of one of her not-quite-interchangeable heroines: "Gloria once took a creative-writing course, and what the instructor told her was: Too many things. Too many things going on at the same time; also too many people." Another relates, of her housewifery, "In my own house, I seemed to be often looking for a place to hide—sometimes from the children but more often from the jobs to be done and the phone ringing and the sociability of the neighborhood. I wanted to hide so that I could get busy at my real work, which was a sort of wooing of distant parts of myself."

Such a wooing took, in Munro's early stories, a reminiscing, autobiographical approach. Through the shuffle of fictional variations a recognizable heroine emerges. She is born to a hardscrabble rural life in the country around Lake Huron. One or the other of her parents dies young; but there is an animated family background of aunts and uncles and ancestors. Bright, she attends college and marries a man of superior social status; she and her husband move to British Columbia, usually Vancouver, and have children. But something about him—snobbishness, brittleness—is deeply unsatisfactory; they quarrel a lot, and eventually she takes a lover, usually an earthy workingman-type,* and the marriage

---

*"For Bea there was nothing like this—nothing like watching a man work at some hard job, when he is forgetful of you and works well, in a way that is tidy and rhythmical, nothing like it to heat the blood" ("Vandals"). And the heroine of "Miles City, Montana" remembers, of rescuing turkeys in a flood: "The job was difficult and absurd and very uncomfortable. We were laughing. I was happy to be working with my father. I felt close to all hard, repetitive, appalling work, in which the body is finally worn out, the mind sunk (though sometimes the spirit can stay marvellously light), and I was homesick in advance

is wrecked. Our now husbandless heroine has affairs and pursues a life of bohemian independence, whether she is identified as a television actress ("Simon's Luck"), a bookstore owner ("Differently"), or an editor ("Dulse"). We like her, of course, as she moves gimlet-eyed and rabbit-eared through a world of romantic possibilities, marital fury, poignant offspring (daughters, as a rule), and unignorable signs of aging. She is neither virtuous nor a victim; what she is is vital. North of the United States' noisy moralizing and fondness for crusades, things in Canada are what they are, from "the hard-hearted energy of sex" to the Nature that "never deceives us; it is always we who deceive ourselves."

With loving clarity Munro shows how the realities of the world come and enfold a young girl. In the first story in this collection, "Walker Brothers Cowboy," the girl accompanies her father, a travelling salesman, on a swing that ends at the house of an old female acquaintance, Nora. Full of pent-up sexual energy, Nora seizes the girl as a dancing partner, "laughing and moving with great buoyancy, wrapping me in her strange gaiety, her smell of whisky, cologne, and sweat." But the married sales-man abashedly declines to dance with Nora, and as they drive away the girl feels her "father's life flowing back from our car in the last of the afternoon, darkening and turning strange . . . into something you will never know, with all kinds of weathers, and distances you cannot imag-ine." The heavy strangeness of adult life takes the form, in "The Ottawa Valley," of ancestral turf, the recitation of melancholy old poetry, and the mother's refusal to promise that she will recover from Parkinson's dis-ease. In "Royal Beatings," the daughter, growing in wiles and ways, par-ticipates with her father and stepmother in an invigorating rite of teasing and physical punishment, tears and making up: afterwards, "they will be embarrassed, but rather less than you might expect considering how they have behaved. They will feel a queer lassitude, a convalescent indolence, not far off satisfaction." And in the unusually forthright Christmas tale "The Turkey Season," the girl, now fourteen, learns how to gut turkeys ("It was deathly cold in there, in the turkey's dark insides") and glimpses the possibility of a homosexual romance between her boss and a thuggish new employee.

The "wooing of distant parts" of herself has led Munro, in her later stories, into reconstruction of the world of her ancestors. These stories, in their freedom of range, their intricately arranged surprises, and their historical imagination, are like few others. One must go back to Tolstoy's

---

for this life and this place. . . . This raw life angered [my husband]. My attachment to it angered him. I thought that I shouldn't have married him."

"Hadji Murad" and Chekhov's "In the Ravine" for comparable largeness; of contemporary story-writers, only the Mark Helprin of *A Dove from the East* comes to mind. Customary domestic realism, in its frequent vein of personal witness, sets a high standard of authenticity; we ask of short fiction less that it transport us than that it ring true. Munro triumphantly dares herself to transport the reader to a muddy, unruly Ontario town of the 1870s ("Meneseteung"), as experienced through the sensibility of the town's one poetess; to a factory town of the World War I years and afterwards ("Carried Away"); to the raw "bush" of the Ontario frontier in the 1850s ("A Wilderness Station"); and to the isolated, mountainous Albania of the 1920s ("The Albanian Virgin"). The Albanian part of this last story is thrilling in its transmuted anthropology, but the heroine's arrival at a well-lit Canadian bookstore very like the one in "Differently" seems relatively lame. Bringing the historically remote into relation with the present and adjusting her themes of sexual magnetism and mishap to settings of repressed, pre-Freudian mores are problems that Munro solves not always without visible effort. "Carried Away," presenting the sexual history of a small-town librarian, ends in hallucination and a perhaps unnecessarily surreal collage of moments. The most effective, for me, of these reconstructions is "A Wilderness Station," with its evocation, in brilliantly mimicked letters, of the brutality, stoicism, and chaos of the time when God-fearing men and women were improvising their way into the New World wilderness, and then with its swooping updating by way of a Stanley Steamer excursion of 1907, recollected in 1959. The Steamer is a magic carpet: "It did not make a beastly loud noise coughing and clanking like other cars but rolled along silently more or less like a ship with high sails over the lake waters and it did not foul the air but left behind a plume of steam."

Munro's sense of the imperious vagaries of the sex drive leads her to violences of subject as well as of technique. Two of these stories ("Carried Away," "Fits") have gruesome decapitations in them, and in another ("Vandals") a vicious spate of vandalism is visited upon the house of a new widow by a girl she trusted. In "Labor Day Dinner," violent death suddenly looms, at the end of a holiday trip by a typically complicated, crosscurrent-prone family, in the form of a narrowly missed crossroads collision: "The big car flashes before them, a huge, dark flash, without lights, seemingly without sound. It comes out of the dark corn and fills the air right in front of them the way a big flat fish will glide into view suddenly in an aquarium tank." The adults in the front seat are so stunned that the child in the back asks them, upon arrival, "Are you guys dead? Aren't we home?"

Good questions. Being alive and home is not a clear-cut condition. The moral of "Fits," in which a number of adults behave in unaccountable ways, is that "People can take a fit like the earth takes a fit." Munro's later stories probe the tectonics of human earthquakes. "White Dump" reveals dense and groaning layers of sensibility: a little five-seater airplane flight is for one character a birthday celebration, for another a terrifying premonition of her dying, and for a third the commencement of an affair that makes her feel "rescued, lifted, beheld, and safe." Not that love is any panacea in Munro's yearning world; in one of the sternest of her many stern asides, she has a character reflect that "love is not kind or honest and does not contribute to happiness in any reliable way." Her view of our human struggle for happiness—often a mere flight from *un*happiness—partakes of the austere Presbyterianism of Ontario's Scots settlers. She quotes the preacher Thomas Boston: "The world is a wilderness, in which we may indeed get our station changed, but the move will be out of one wilderness station unto another." As well as a spirited, acutely perceptive tale-teller, Munro is an implacable destiny-spinner, whose authorial voice breaks into her fiction like that of a God who can no longer bear to keep quiet.

OVERSEAS

Mandarins

WATERMARK, by Joseph Brodsky. 104 pp. Farrar, Straus and Giroux, 1992.

THAT MIGHTY SCULPTOR, TIME, by Marguerite Yourcenar, translated from the French by Walter Kaiser. 211 pp. Farrar, Straus and Giroux, 1992.

The notion of a few exquisitely informed, aristocratically self-pleasing mandarins presiding above literary culture savors of *fin-de-siècle* decadence—the end of the *last* century, when Henry James and Oscar Wilde and Walter Pater projected from on high a lavender aura which became the ultraviolet modernism of Pound and Eliot, Rilke and Valéry. These men issued bulletins from beyond—beyond academic conventions, beyond commercial hopes, beyond the general earthbound sensibility. Since the deaths of Jorge Luis Borges and Vladimir Nabokov, few such remain. Yet here and there in the contemporary flood of books occasional volumes appear for no reason save to offer us the highest kind of satisfaction written communication can give. With no rousing tale to tell or sweeping thesis to illustrate and prove, they seek out those readers who, in Annie Dillard's phrase, "like, or require, what books alone have." Our pleasure resides in the writer's rare sensibility and curious fund of information; we are flattered to be in his or her company.

When, in 1987, Joseph Brodsky received the Nobel Prize, the Swedish Academy cited his work's "great breadth, in time and in space." His poems and prose essays—collected in *Less Than One* (1986)—both suggest a wish to range widely, to range *free*, over a globe that until 1972, when he was expelled from the Soviet Union, had to be mostly imagined. Since then, he has done his share of roaming—in England, Istanbul, Mexico, and many of the United States. Though he is the present Poet Laureate of this country, Brodsky still seems somewhat to hover (unlike, say, Auden snug on St. Mark's Place), as if wary of getting his feet stuck fast to any point of the map. Every winter, we learn in his book-length essay *Watermark*, he spends his Christmas vacation in Venice, the least rooted city in the world, floating as it does on water. "It's only proper," he tells us, "for the likes of me to regard America as a kind of Purgatorio." Purgatory, we know, is a better place to be than a certain other, but it's basically a way-station; Brodsky's winter trips to Venice are "forays into [his] version of Paradise."

As the punning title warns us, the essay is in part a meditation upon water, as it takes the protean forms of oceans, canals, ripples, reflections, fog, and tears.

> I always thought that if the Spirit of God moved upon the face of the water, the water was bound to reflect it. Hence my sentiment for water, for its folds, wrinkles, and ripples, and—as I am a Northerner—for its grayness. I simply think that water is the image of time, and every New Year's Eve, in somewhat pagan fashion, I try to find myself near water, preferably near a sea or an ocean, to watch the emergence of a new helping, a new cupful of time from it.

In the musical fashion of a poem, the water theme recurs, so insistently that even the "fluently flapping" hands of Venetians giving directions remind the writer of fish. The theme mounts to a rather compressed and schematic coda: "Water equals time and provides beauty with its double. Part water, we serve beauty in the same fashion. By rubbing water, this city improves time's looks, beautifies the future. That's what the role of this city in the universe is. Because the city is static while we are moving. The tear is proof of that. Because we go and beauty stays." That Venice itself is perishable and fragile is factually noted, but all the poignance attaches to our own flow deathwards, while the beauty of these lacy, aqueously mirrored façades remains.

Brodsky has written *Watermark* in his adopted English, which is adequate to all but the most artful word-carving, the working of an image to the utmost. It is just this kind of carving, however, that interests him. For example:

> Assuming that beauty is the distribution of light in the fashion most congenial to one's retina, a tear is an acknowledgement of the retina's, as well as the tear's, failure to retain beauty. On the whole, love comes with the speed of light; separation, with that of sound. It is the deterioration of the greater speed to the lesser that moistens one's eye.

It is not always easy to follow the ornate curves of his thought. Of Pasiphaë, who mated with a bull, we read, "And perhaps she yielded to those dark urges and did it with the bull precisely to prove that nature neglects the majority principle, since the bull's horns suggest the moon." Of Ezra Pound we are told, "I also liked his 'make it new' dictum—liked it, that is, until I grasped that the true reason for making it new was that 'it' was fairly old; that we were, after all, in a body shop." A body shop? Some of his idioms seem trans-idiomatic ("My Italian, wildly oscillating around its firm zero, also remained a deterrent") and more than a bit British ("Lobbing spanners into each other's machinery is something democracy is awfully good at"). Written English is a relatively informal language, but it does observe some decorums; we are shocked to be suddenly told, of the husband of a coveted Venetian woman, that he was "a scumbag of an architect." A ready irritability lurks beneath the elaborately polished sentences: in tourist season, "the shorts-clad herds, especially those neighing in German, also get on my nerves," and, on the next page, the reader is jarred by the aggressive cleverness of "Bipeds go ape about shopping and dressing up in Venice." Brodsky is not conspicuously grateful for the hospitality he receives, whether from the scumbag architect or from Ezra Pound's mistress, Olga Rudge, and he leans a little out of his way to register distaste for homosexuals, whether they are the "gay English charges" of his New York editor or, in Venice, "a bunch of giggling, agile, homosexual youths inevitable these days whenever something mildly spectacular takes place." Just a passing glance at modern art taps deep reserves of pent-up indignation:

> If this place is reality (or, as some claim, the past), then the future with all its aliases is excluded from it. At best, it amounts to the present. And perhaps nothing proves this better than modern art, whose poverty alone makes it prophetic, and a poor man always speaks for the present. Perhaps the sole function of collections like Peggy Guggenheim's and the similar accretions of this century's stuff habitually mounted here is to show what a cheap, self-assertive, ungenerous, one-dimensional lot we have become, to instill humility in us.

The poet's frequent note of strangulated eloquence eases into clarity when he tells personal anecdotes. His evocation of touring an antique, privately owned palazzo is delightfully surreal: "It was a long succession of empty rooms. . . . I had the sense of walking not so much in standard perspective as in a horizontal spiral where the laws of optics were suspended. Each room meant your further disappearance, the next degree of your nonexistence." Concerning the cold of the Venetian winter, he is so heartfelt as to be funny:

Only alcohol can absorb the polar lightning shooting through your body as you set your foot on the marble floor, slippers or no slippers, shoes or no shoes. . . . Everything emanates cold, the walls especially. Windows you don't mind because you know what to expect from them. In fact, they only pass the cold through, whereas walls store it.

His Italian bedmate and he draw lots to decide "who would have to sleep by the wall," and when she loses she wins a loving portrait: "She would bundle up for the night—pink woolen jersey, scarf, stockings, long socks—and, having counted *uno, due, tre!* jump into the bed as though it were a dark river." He goes on to relate that the thermal miseries of that winter affected his chest, which had suffered cardiac surgery, and his obliging inamorata put him on the train to Paris, and he "lived to tell the story, and the story itself to repeat." Miserable as the city had made him, he longed to return. His intellectual and aesthetic fervor for Venice is intense enough to defy death, and there is a mandarin heroism to that. We read *Watermark* enraptured by its gallant attempt to distill a precious meaning from life's experience—to make a spot on a globe a peephole into universal circumstance, and to fashion of one's personal chronic tourism a crystal whose facets reflect an entire life, with exile and ill health glinting at the edges of planes whose direct glare is sheer beauty.

The mandarin tone came naturally to the late Marguerite Yourcenar, a Belgian-born writer doomed to be forever known as the first woman elected to the Académie Française—an honor she had not courted but, in fact, sought to avoid. She also belonged to the Académie's American equivalent, the (as it was then called) National Institute of Arts and Letters; she was a naturalized American citizen, who had resided here since 1940, and since 1950 on Mount Desert Island, in Maine, with her companion and translator, Grace Frick. Her independent remoteness kept her aloof from literary fashion in both French and English, though one novel, *Memoirs of Hadrian*, achieved best-sellerdom in the early Fifties. Aloofness was her métier; it was said of her that she employed the formal *vous* even when addressing her dog. A learned student of not only the classic world but the religions and cultures of India and Japan, she formed a philosophical overview compounded of Stoicism, Oriental mysticism, and remnants of her Catholic upbringing. This height of vantage lends her fiction a certain monologic, epigrammatic coolness but gives an engaging variety and openness to her posthumous collection of essays, *That Mighty Sculptor, Time*. Walter Kaiser, in an afterword that suavely matches her own elegant, marmoreal tone, assures us that, "although the publisher has chosen to defer its appearance until now," his translation was completed before the author's death and was carried forward with her customary collaboration. "To discuss the dilemmas of translation with Marguerite Yourcenar," Mr. Kaiser fondly tells us, "was to be shown unnoticed subtleties in both languages; to wander off with her into the worlds of Greece and Rome, India and Spain, Japan and the Low Countries, medieval England and Renaissance Italy, all of which are encompassed in these essays, was to receive an incomparable education."

As that sentence indicates, her topics are miscellaneous. The earliest essay, a tribute to an obscure writer and cherished friend, Jeanne de Vietinghoff, dates from 1929; the most recent, a few pages on the Day of the Dead, which is observed in America as Halloween, was composed in 1982. All the essays, even the briefest, have the virtues of dignified diction and careful thought; many have the considerable charm of a hard-won historical sense worn lightly, with a quickening of fine discriminations into lively images. In writing of a Renaissance translation, by Florent Chrestien, of an obscure Greek didactic poet, or poets, known as Oppian, Yourcenar says:

> Every translator who is more than a mere laborer transposes, even without meaning to: for the noble Greek hexameters, like beautiful stallions with flowing manes, Florent Chrestien substitutes his alexandrines with their rather panting rhythm, racing one after the other, yoked together by rhyme, like hounds let loose two by two in the grass.

Warmed by these animal similes, she goes on to animate the zoological innocence that had descended upon Europe after the days of the Roman Empire and its circuses of exotic fauna: "Florent has a thousand years of uninterrupted medieval hunting behind him—that world, at once enticing and forbidding, of the haunted forest of werewolves and fairy hinds. . . . He had never seen the great wild beasts of Africa and Asia which were so familiar to the contemporaries of Oppian; at most he might have looked at the scrawny, caged lions in the moats of the Louvre. Thus, he cannot avoid giving to those creatures, which for him were half fabulous, the fantastic splendor of a coat of arms or a bestiary."

The passage holds two of her stately passions: a sympathy for animals and a pleasure in history's glacial movement, with its cumulative shifts of sensibility. Where other historical novelists seek the trappings of antiquity, she was after, in a realm beyond "melodrama or pastiche," the mental state, the voice. In her conversations with Matthieu Galey, collected as *With Open Eyes* (1984), she speaks of revising her book about Hadrian a number of times, until she had his voice, "the melody of his being." Her ear was tuned to nuances within the remote classical world: "People in

Rome made fun of young Hadrian for speaking with what they identified as a 'Spanish' accent. . . . If you compare him with Augustus or Julius Caesar, the difference is striking. They don't resemble him at all, these two clever Italians." In an essay titled "Tone and Language in the Historical Novel," she remarks how few sources, prior to the nineteenth century, record "*conversation* in all its spontaneity, its disjointed logic, its complex byways, its lacunae, and its unarticulated implications without passing through tragic or comic stylization or lyric outburst." The search for "tonal authenticity" led her to "sub-literary documents . . . which haven't undergone the filtering or rearranging literature entails"; by way of illustration she includes some reports, by an informer and a scribe, of the fragmentary, agonized, obscene utterances of the philosopher Fra Tommaso Campanella as he was being interrogated and tortured in Naples, in 1600.

This same textual immediacy, where the muffled past allows itself to be overheard, she finds in the Venerable Bede's famous account of a seventh-century Saxon debate over conversion to Christianity, and in Albrecht Dürer's account, in his journal, of a dream he had in June of 1525. She attempts to fabricate the immediacy of voice in a series of monologues by Michelangelo and some models he used in painting the Sistine Chapel, and in a retelling of the Easter story's high points as if "we found them in Dostoevsky or Tolstoy." Phenomena remote in time and space—the sexuality that pervades Hindu epics and temple reliefs; the samurai ethic that yields to the attractions of defeat and suicide—become, through Yourcenar's sensitive survey, internal sensations, so that we feel, in the Indian instance, "the pulsation of a joy which courses through plant, animal, god, and man." This repeated movement of her discourse, from the historically remote to the palpably intimate, is the inverse of a tendency in Brodsky, who amid a throng of closely observed particulars seems, in prickly fashion, to shy from human contact, preferring the geometric, ricocheting acquisitions of the eye, which Venice above all places lavishes upon him.

One takes away from Marguerite Yourcenar's elevated essays an incongruous coziness—a glisten of fur, a feeling of live pelts drawing closer. The passion she allows herself most often is an indignation at man's cruelty to animals. In the idyll of Krishna among the milkmaids, the presence of cows signifies that "divine ecstasy and human happiness cannot do without the calm contentment of the humble creatures who are exploited by man and who share with him in the adventure of living." When asked to contribute to a collection entitled *Angry Women*, she directs her anger against fur-laden fashion models:

These young people, whom any eye endowed with double vision sees dripping with blood, wear the spoils of creatures who once breathed, ate, slept,
sought partners for their amorous sport, loved their young, sometimes so
much as to get themselves killed in order to protect them, and died, as Vil-
lon would have said, "to pain"—that is, in pain, as we all shall; but these
creatures died a death savagely inflicted by us.

She deplores the slaughterhouses that do their bloody business out of
sight: "We do not see those creatures contorted with pain; we do not hear
their bellows, which even the most ardent lover of steak would find intolerable." She argues that "there would be fewer martyred children if there
were fewer tortured animals, fewer sealed trains carrying the victims of
whatever dictatorship to their deaths if we had not become accustomed
to cattle cars in which animals die without food or water en route to
the slaughterhouse, fewer human game felled with guns if the taste for
and habit of killing were not the prerogative of hunters." Man's much-
deplored cruelty to man is rarely related to his cruelty to other species;
Yourcenar makes a connection which, once made, seems obvious. That a
sense of history detached and broad enough to include our speechless
cohorts in vitality can devolve into a righteous anger so simple, so close
to a child's first moral perceptions, shows how refreshing mandarinism
still can be.

Proust Died for You

How Proust Can Change Your Life, by Alain de Botton. 202 pp. Pantheon,
1997.

Alain de Botton is described on the dust jacket of *How Proust Can
Change Your Life* as living in London and Washington, but his name and
passion for codification savor strongly of the Gallic. His curious, humorous, didactic, and dazzling book bears the subtitle *Not a Novel*; it contains, however, more human interest and play of fancy than most fiction.
Its discourse, broken into such instructive chapters as "How to Love Life
Today," "How to Suffer Successfully," and "How to Open Your Eyes,"
elucidates the lessons of a very long novel, *Remembrance of Things Past*,
by Marcel Proust. De Botton has plainly spent much time within that
great work and, further, has made himself privy to many minutiae concerning Proust himself. We learn, for instance, that Proust's Paris tele-

phone number was 29205; that he often tipped not fifteen or twenty percent but 200 percent of a restaurant bill; that his skin was so sensitive he couldn't use soap but would wash with "finely woven, moistened towels, then pat himself dry with fresh linen (an average wash requires twenty towels, which Proust specifies must be taken to the only laundry that uses the right non-irritant powder, the blanchisserie Lavigne, which also does Jean Cocteau's laundry)"; that he was so attached to his mother that, well past the age of thirty, he gave her detailed reports on his sleep, his "peeing," and his bowel movements; that he was always cold and often kept his fur coat on during dinner parties. We also learn a fair amount about Proust's relatives: his father, Dr. Adrien Proust, wrote thirty-four books of his own, including some well-known manuals on hygiene and physical fitness; Marcel's younger brother, Dr. Robert Proust, the author of *The Surgery of the Female Genitalia*, was so celebrated for his prostatectomies that in the trade they were called "proustatectomies," and he was so hardy that he survived being run over by a five-ton coal wagon.

Such details are not idly marshalled. After depicting Marcel's grotesquely extreme sensitivity, de Botton makes the point that "feeling things (which usually means feeling them *painfully*) is at some level linked to the acquisition of knowledge." Proust puts it: "Happiness is good for the body, but it is grief which develops the strengths of the mind." The painter Elstir, in the novel, formulates the principle thus: "We cannot be taught wisdom, we have to discover it for ourselves by a journey which no one can undertake for us, an effort which no one can spare us." De Botton examines five Proustian characters who suffer *un*successfully, concocting false solutions to their discomforts which in fact prolong them. The chapters "How to Be a Good Friend" and "How to Put Books Down" show from passages in Proust's novel and life how a realistic, even cynical estimate of the value of friendship can fitly support extravagant efforts of cordiality and flattery (his friends coined "the verb *to proustify* to express a slightly too conscious attitude of geniality, together with what would vulgarly have been called affectations, interminable and delicious"), and how the most passionate devotion to an author, such as Proust paid to John Ruskin, properly stops short of idolatry, as when Proust concluded that Ruskin was frequently "silly, maniacal, constraining, false, and ridiculous." De Botton writes as one narrowly saved from idolatry; he wryly describes a pilgrimage made to the drab village of Illiers, now called on road signs "Illiers-Combray" in tribute to Proust's enchanted fictional village. Madeleine sales are brisk there, and the house of Proust's Tante Amiot ("Tante Léonie" in the novel) re-creates "in its full aesthetic horror the feel of a tastelessly furnished, provincial bourgeois nineteenth-century home." The "solitary, curiously oily-looking madeleine" on display reveals itself, upon scrupulous inspection, to be plastic.

De Botton, who is of Swiss birth, writes in English but with French wit and dispassion. His second book, *The Romantic Movement*, was a novel analyzing in terms of self-help the amorous delusions illustrated by a London affair. His penchant for aphoristic laws of human behavior understandably draws him to Proust, since such laws are Proust's own goal. This son and brother of doctors wrote a novel full of closely diagnostic observations, a novel which presents overall, in its demonstration of involuntary memory and its recovery of the past, a cure for the universal malady, time. The reader emerges from the last pages of the last volume, *Time Regained*, with a sensation of having triumphantly undergone therapy. Composed as an act of personal salvation by a desperately frail and neurasthenic man, the work embodies his cure—the discovery of his message as a writer. De Botton vividly sketches his hero's sad condition prior to this discovery. Proust's own appraisal of himself at the age of thirty ran, "Without pleasures, objectives, activities or ambitions, with the life ahead of me finished and with an awareness of the grief I cause my parents, I have little happiness." Kafka and Joyce, those other epic comedians of modernism, each at least had a circle of friends and critics who recognized their genius; whereas even those closest to Proust saw him as a hopeless snob and dilettante, and were taken unawares by the beauty, sweep, and satiric force of his masterpiece. De Botton, in emphasizing, with his amusing but straight-faced pedagogical foppishness, Proust's healing, advisory aspects, does us the service of rereading him on our behalf, providing of that vast sacred lake a sweet and lucid distillation.

Camus Made New

THE STRANGER, by Albert Camus, translated from the French by Matthew Ward. 123 pp. Knopf, 1988.

This new translation of Camus's short classic supersedes that of Stuart Gilbert, which was released in 1946. Gilbert was an Englishman, and he rendered the narrative voice of Meursault, the novel's somewhat Hemingwayesque hero, in an almost chatty prose containing plenty of commas, periphrasis, and expressions like "chap" and "old boy." Mr. Ward is a young American who, in the words of his introduction, has "attempted to venture further into the letter of Camus's novel." Where Gilbert ended the first section with "And each successive shot was another loud, fateful rap on the door of my undoing," Mr. Ward has it, "And it was like knocking four quick times on the door of unhappiness." Where the older translation ends with "howls of execration," the newer has "cries of hate." The effect of the closer, simpler rendering is to make Meursault seem even stranger—more alien and diffident—than the explanatory confider of the British version. Meursault becomes not so much an exponent of illusionless hedonism as a psychological study who is brought, through a gratuitous, sun-dazzled act and its merciless social consequences, to a rapport with his dead mother and a recognition of his fraternity with "the gentle indifference of the world"—a softening internalization of Gilbert's grander phrase "the benign indifference of the universe."

Omniumgatherum

COMPLETE COLLECTED ESSAYS, by V. S. Pritchett. 1319 pp. Random House, 1991.

Eight earlier collections—two hundred three essays—in one giant volume of over thirteen hundred pages, without a word of preface. Pritchett's great critical gift, exercised through much of this century, is at bottom dramatic: an ability to see authors as actors, performing on a bright, populated stage. The stage is given great breadth and depth by the critic's reading, a reading comprehensive not only in the literature of the British Isles but in that of France, Russia, and the Iberian Peninsula. European history to him is one long, lively anecdote, and books are a set of excuses for warm and worldly gossip. His style, perfected in the narrow spaces in which British critics are required to deliver judgment, giddily skips into the lyric: "Fun in English literature is as regular as muffins; the honest bell rings in the sad fog of the London Sunday and we stir ingenuously between one indigestion and the next, in our drowsy chairs." The erudite, manic adventurer Richard Burton "is an almost pestiferous pursuer of whatever can be turned into a footnote." In Hardy, "we are always struck by the largeness of the panorama and by the narrowness of Hardy's single, crooked, well-trodden path across it." Leaving the obvious unstated, the essays can seem cryptic and teasingly compressed. The quirky, witty tone suddenly yields declarations of a confidently generalizing human wisdom: "Remove the vices of a novelist and his virtues vanish too"; Ouida "is not the first novelist to have delusions of grandeur . . . for when one is dealing in fantasy, it is not unnatural to help oneself." It was a happy circumstance of a dire time that the shortages of wartime England included a shortage of new books and that Pritchett was therefore obliged to reread for review the classic productions of Fielding and Swift, Richardson and Scott. Certain writers, such as Smollett and Ouida and Thomas Hood, may have received from him the last intelligent consideration they will ever get. Few of the significant imaginers of the last several centuries go unmentioned here; the index to this huge volume gives us access to an encyclopedic wealth of shrewd appraisals and vivid reconstructions, wherein Sir Victor's love of literature and love of life are indistinguishable.

Man Is an Island

NOT ENTITLED: *A Memoir*, by Frank Kermode. 263 pp. Farrar, Straus and Giroux, 1995.

Frank Kermode's memoir, *Not Entitled*, is an oddly beautiful, or beautifully odd, book—a witty and rueful exercise in self-deprecation, with only the most indirect hints that this abject confessor to failure and dereliction is an esteemed critic and venerated professor. Far from being untitled, he has been knighted for his services to English literature. A thoughtful student of the Bible and seventeenth-century poetry, an unintimidated intimate of modern French critical analysis, he is the least stodgy of thorough scholars and the fairest-minded, levellest-headed of book reviewers. Yet it is as an inadequate son, faulty pupil, indifferent Navy man, bad interviewee, and dupe of more worldly others that he principally figures in his own accounts. He speaks of his "inveterate conviction that I was far from being a good teacher," and charges himself with *jemenfoutisme*, which my French dictionary defines as "casualness, utter indifference." Perhaps, taking the word as *je-m'en-foutisme*, we could call it "don't-give-a-fuckism."

Kermode's life, as he here construes it, came in three parts: his birth, childhood, and youth in Douglas, the snug metropolis of the Isle of Man, an anomalous bit of ancient Scandinavia floating in the Irish Sea; his years of wartime service in the British Navy, under a series of mad or corrupt captains; and his subsequent literary and pedagogic careers, which he characterizes in terms of a quietly frantic wandering from post to post and of two well-publicized resignations—one from the CIA-sponsored magazine *Encounter* in 1967, and the other from the King Edward VII Professorship of English Literature at Cambridge in 1982. Both these terminated involvements illustrate personal traits he describes as a "reluctance to disregard the wrong road" and a "habit of deference that has been a curse largely because the only way to break it seems to be by intemperate action." His sheepishly brilliant career was achieved amid recurrent sensations of alienation and a tropism toward the outsider position that must go back to the Isle of Man.

"To be Manx was to be, in an admittedly not deeply wounding way, exiled from the life and language of the English," Kermode writes. The Manx language was dying by the time when, in 1919, the author was born, though it persisted in phrases and songs. His parents, lower-class if class distinctions need be applied among the twenty thousand insular souls of Douglas, are portrayed tenderly, fellow-prisoners of the something ominously unsatisfactory, if not "deeply wounding," about their son's childhood:

> Part of the difficulty these kind people experienced in rearing me was that I was generally unable, with my best efforts, to do things that other children seemed to manage without much thought, certainly without the terror that immobilised me at the prospect of failing in tasks where success was the norm, such as tying shoelaces.

The comedy of this sentence does not erase its sadness; the child, at the center of considerable parental expectations, was "fat, plain, short-sighted, clumsy, idle, dirty," and, as he moved through school as the perennial youngest in his classes, bullied. A negotiable scholastic aptitude was slow to bloom, hampered by bad eyes and a paralyzing general misery, but had blossomed by his mid-teens. In 1937 he won a scholarship to the University of Liverpool, on condition of his becoming a schoolteacher—possibly, as his mother fondly hoped, on the Isle of Man. Kermode had more venturesome ambitions, but perhaps it took the great dislocations of the coming war to thoroughly un-Man him. The chapter on his provincial growing-up, flavored by the exotic peculiarities of the island (also discussed in his essays "The Faces of Man" and "The Men from Man," included in his collection *The Uses of Error*), has the weight of the often pondered, with no false tinge of the idyllic or, on the other hand, of the plaintive. The child was not too blind or self-absorbed to notice, for example, how his father, "still the curly-headed athlete, sat for hours spitting blood into a bowl from his suddenly sunken mouth . . . his youth deserting him early." Our trials of emergence take place while our still-young parents are embarking upon the trials of decline.

The vast annals of World War II cannot hold many warrior reminiscences more weirdly detached from the grand aims than Kermode's. Part of the absurdist impression, no doubt, stems from his own modesty and fondness for minimization. He spent more than five years on ships any one of which could have been sunk. In considering his academic career, he does speak with a bit of edge of those non-veterans, "ordinary members of the Life Club," who have "no idea of what it feels like to confront people ruthlessly dedicated to the idea of ripping you apart or drowning you." He saw relatively little battle, and dwells upon the maniacal, besotted career Navy men under whom he served on various futile-sounding missions. But at sea near Gibraltar he watched a Catalina piloted by Canadians successfully court destruction by steering into friendly guns, and a boatload of Allied sailors board a burning merchant ship which thereupon exploded. "It may be interesting to note," he writes, "that none of the people who died in this little action need have done so." He felt, in North Africa, no connection with the campaigns in progress (against the Afrika Korps) or about to be launched (the invasion of Sicily): "To all concern with such matters I was immune, but in spite of many superficial distractions I knew myself to be radically unhappy, having no horizon of unhappiness that I could ever hope to cross." He discovered then in himself a capacity for dissoluteness, "a sort of unconsidering recklessness, of pleasure in self-destructiveness." Assignments in the United States and Australia brought some relief, whose pleasurable details are, with an excess of post-war discretion, suppressed: "I omit details of the happiness of Portland. . . . Of the pleasures of [Sydney] I shall not write here, but they were not negligible." He was among the armed multitudes in the Pacific spared the invasion of Japan by the dropping of the atomic bombs ("The general opinion was that it saved our lives, and we were unethically pleased about this"). The Navy left him, in 1946, with dim professional prospects, an addiction to bridge, a healthy appetite for liquor, and a literary vocation whose chief fruit was the winning of a *New Statesman* competition for the translation of a Ronsard sonnet.

In the lively sketches of academic and literary personalities and predicaments that follow, it is possible to detect the boy from Man, where England was called simply "away" or "across." His libel-proof but vehement account of his theoretically exalted professorship at the University of Cambridge begins with a dark paraphrase of St. Augustine: "To Cambridge then I came, where a cauldron of unholy hates hissed all about me." As Kermode pressed for certain arrangements that had been agreed upon with the Prime Minister's patronage secretary, his reception went from "chilly" to "cold," with an implication that he "must be a fantasist or a liar." He found the environment implacably change-resistant: "To my alien eye the faults in its system were obvious and even scandalous; to most of my new colleagues, my complaints arose out of mere disaffection, presumption, or ignorance of Cambridge ways." Fresh from heading the English Department at University College, London, he marvelled: "Nobody who had worked in a reasonably sane department elsewhere could have failed to be astonished at the complacency with which these chaotic arrangements were regarded." After a few years he joined the row over a lectureship denied to an unnamed younger colleague, and despaired at the depths of chicanery. "Useless to recount," he indicts, "all the complex manoeuvres, the dirty tricks, the calculated rhetorical performances." The misery of his early school days returned: "I began to have quite serious eye troubles . . . and I would wake in the morning to be at once invaded by the thought that another day of wretchedness had dawned."

At least once before, Kermode had found himself oppressed by entrenched Britishism: placed in charge, at the war's end, of a group of emaciated and disease-ridden British civil servants imprisoned, with their wives, in a Japanese concentration camp on Hong Kong, the twenty-five-year-old officer discovered that these Britons, as soon as they recovered strength enough, demanded all sorts of privileges: "They seemed to think that during their four years of captivity the world, and especially British colonial arrangements, must have remained exactly as they were in December 1941." Most odiously, the women objected to having to share quarters, on a crowded ship, with a Filipino nurse, even though she had acted as midwife to them in the desperate conditions of the Hong Kong camp. Only she, as the rescue mission ended in Sydney, "bothered to say thanks for what in my view, though not in theirs, were the remarkable civilities and kindnesses they had received during their long voyage." It is no accident, perhaps, that the handful of fellow-academics for whom Kermode has warm words include a Scotsman, D. J. Gordon; a Frenchman, Eugène Vinaver; and a fellow-Manxman, Randolph Quirk; and that he has found French thought and American milieux congenial. Why Kermode, thirteen years after abdicating the "carnival crown" of the Edward VII Professorship, continues to live in benighted Cambridge he leaves up to the reader's frequently challenged imagination.

Not Entitled remarkably conveys the "microclimate" of depression at the heart of a clever diffidence while being steadily entertaining, and even poetical. Flashes of fancy, and a wealth of literary allusions embedded in the text, ornament what could have been a drab and affectless tale. Of a posh Massachusetts town where, with his second wife, he lived one summer, he writes, "The chef at the country club could slice Virginia ham so thin that it was not unknown for a breeze off the ocean to blow the slices away." In the same antic section, this reviewer found himself featured in the book's obscurest sentence: "John Updike crawled under an interesting table on the pretence of looking for evidence of its maker's identity, but really to ask in private who all these extraordinary people were." Does this mean that others had preceded me under the "interesting" table? No matter: the theme of the not-there pervades this book, beginning with its title and its epigraph from *Coriolanus*—"He was a kind of nothing, titleless." The words "not entitled" come from Kermode's Navy years, when on payday a sailor sufficiently fined for disciplinary cause would be greeted not by a month's wages but by the barked announcement "Not Entitled!" Similarly, when Kermode arrived at Cambridge he found that he had become "a sort of nobody, yet a nobody with a title." Concerning his "failures or half-failures as husband and parent," he proposes that "looking the part while not being quite equal to it seems to be something I do rather well." The uneasy sensation of a fundamental exclusion, of being "not the sort of person I should choose to know if I had any choice in the matter" and of lacking "what appears to be in others a perfectly ordinary skill or tact in handling not only things but persons," has haunted him since his awkward Manx childhood. Yet is not this sensation a common human one? No amount of professional honor and social success can cancel it, and it is Kermode's significant accomplishment, in "the insouciance of old age," to have given it so delicate and circumstantial an expression.

Muriel Goes to the Movies

REALITY AND DREAMS, by Muriel Spark. 160 pp. Houghton Mifflin, 1997.

Muriel Spark will be eighty next year, and some seven years have passed since her last novel, *Symposium*. So it is pleasant to report that *Reality and Dreams*, vaporous though its title seems, is as intricate and bright as the toy of a child emperor, and more substantial than such recent entries in her extensive bibliography as *The Only Problem* and *A Far Cry from Kensington*. Its sixty-three-year-old hero, Tom Richards, directs film and has fallen off a crane he insisted on directing from. We find him in a hospital amid a flickering confusion of nurses and loved ones. The loved ones sift down to just three: Claire, his "nice kind wife," in her mid-fifties, rich and lovely and endlessly indulgent of a creative artist's vagaries; Cora, twenty-nine, his utterly beautiful daughter by his first marriage, to "a different sort of beauty, of Bulgarian-Polish origins"; and Marigold, the somewhat younger, unaccountably disagreeable and awkward daughter born to Tom and Claire. How two such charmers could have produced such an uncharming child baffles them both: "Her parents had searched through the past, consulted psychiatrists, took every moment to bits. In no way could she be explained." Marigold, offended by her parents' infidelities, keeps urging them to divorce, "not realising that she—that the appalling nature of their only offspring—was mainly the cause of Claire and Tom's inseparability. . . . Even her disagreeable face kept them together like birds in a storm."

All this is rather banteringly perverse, in the manner of Ronald Firbank and Aldous Huxley, but Spark's oracular eye is, as always, on the skull of damnation behind society's grinning face. Her novels, though short, are dense, many-layered. On one level, this is the story of Jeanne, a nondescriptly pretty actress picked by Tom to play the part of "the hamburger girl," a girl he glimpsed serving up hamburgers at the edge of a campsite in the Haute Savoie; his fantasies about the hamburger girl (including killing his wife so that he can bestow a fortune upon her) propel him through a movie initially titled *The Hamburger Girl*, but Jeanne remains a bit actor in it, to her frustration. She becomes querulous, takes drugs, and is destroyed, a victim of the film world and the whim of an artist. Yet she is not pitied, by the author or by the other characters. When she complains to Claire, "I've been used," the prompt response is "We're all used."

The oft-changed movie title becomes, in the end, *Unfinished Business*. Marigold has aroused in Claire and Tom "a feeling of frustration, of unfinished business," and from this angle the novel is Marigold's story. Disliked by her parents, neglected by her husband (who writes travel books), she conducts research into the currently hot issue of "redundancy," sleeps with a number of the interview subjects, disappears, makes headlines, is finally found, and is cast by her father in his newest movie, as a male—Cedric the Celt, a fifth-century centurion's servant, who foresees the future, up to the very present. Marigold's "dark sullen ugly face" haunts her father's dreams as that of "a young man sent mad by complete knowledge of the future." And, unlike her beautiful, doted-upon sister, she can act. Having played the part, she departs for America, one of the netherworlds to which Spark consigns her less lovable creations. In the tradition of the tiny-eyed Sandy Stranger in *The Prime of Miss Jean Brodie*, Marigold is a homely truth-teller, a Cassandra-witch.

This is also a novel about movie-making, put together with rapid cuts and saucy non-sequiturs. Unreeling at the pace of MTV, the narrative is always a jump or two ahead of the reader. Tom, surprisingly a Christian believer, wonders if we are all characters in one of God's dreams: "Our dreams, yes, are insubstantial; the dreams of God, no. They are real, frighteningly real. They bulge with flesh, they drip with blood." Art approximates those dreams. Though handsome and rich and wanton, Tom is a serious worker in "that world of dreams and reality which he was at home in, the world of filming scenes, casting people in parts, piecing together types and shadows, facts and illusions." He tells Dave, the West Indian he hires to drive him randomly around London, "Everything I do is basically connected with my work. Everything." Spark, with the filmic dream-world as her topic, seems especially focussed and directorial, declaring her controlling presence in such interjections as "It is time now to describe what Tom looked like," "It would be useless to give here the name of the latest director," and "The police eventually believed the boy, whose name for the present purpose is irrelevant." The style is peremptory, summary, dismissively swift: we learn in a sentence that *Unfinished Business*, whose tangled progress has taken up two-thirds of the novel, "was a decided success." The various sexual liaisons are touched upon with a speed exceeding that of a French farce; sex has adjusted to the age of the fax and the spot interview. Marigold's discoverer does not contact her parents or the police; he goes to a television network and "for a fair fee" conducts the camera crew to the hideout. Humanity is up for quick sale. A certain nostalgia for slower, more relational days creeps in; Tom mourns old friends—Auden, Graham Greene, John Braine, Mary McCarthy—who are more plausibly old friends of Muriel Spark's. She has grown into the condition of the ancients in *Memento Mori*. Tom says, "Essentially, Dave, a person consists of memories."

Yet in the sea of light-hearted betrayal and rampant redundancy there is an island of constancy: Claire, "rich, discreet about her men, tolerant of his women, a good hostess and good-looking." Her wealth derives from an American fortune, Blantyre Biscuits, Inc. Her angelic tolerance of Tom's infatuations stems from respect for his artistry: "And to be honest, thought Claire, the reason why I stick by him is that he's an interesting film director." The novel in its final turns becomes a love poem to her. She is, we are told early, "emotionally imaginative," and in a late scene she is the site of a sudden deepening of the book's flat, jumpy human perspectives:

> Claire, not knowing if Tom had slept with the girl or not, maintained an
> air of kindly coolness and of other miraculous and contradictory qualities
> such as she had learnt to adopt in the course of her life with Tom: maternal

extraneity, professional amateurism, understanding and incomprehension, yes and no.

At the end, both Tom and Cora feel "her strength and courage sustaining them," as she serves them drinks in a nuclear trinity of well-heeled beauty.

Some readers may be disconcerted by the apparent equation of spiritual worthiness with money and good looks. But in the dreams of God, which bulge with flesh, body and spirit are close to identical. "What is the difference between body and spirit?" Tom asks his masseur, Ron. Ron answers, "There is a difference but both are very alike, you know." Tom, perhaps scenting heresy, says, "At least, interdependent I should say." In Spark's very first novel, *The Comforters*, the nerved-up heroine feels a visceral repugnance toward the pious but pneumatic Mrs. Hogg, who awakens her "loathing of human flesh where the bulk outweighs the intelligence." How much nicer are lithe Cora and Claire in their several times mentioned skin-tight jeans. And, in honesty, aren't health and wealth more spiritually attractive than their opposites? If we find undemocratic Dame Muriel's distribution of providential grace, well, whose dreamed creatures are these? Hers and no one else's, she always makes perfectly clear.

God Save Ingushetia

OUR GAME, by John le Carré. 303 pp. Knopf, 1995.

Somehow I missed out on all those Cold War thrillers. I would get on an airplane and see these many men in business suits—rather, in business *trousers*, with their jackets nicely folded up in the overhead rack and their neckties loosened away from their shirt collars an artful inch—staring meaningfully into a tubby paperback or gargantuan hardcover of Clancy or Ludlum or Forsyth or le Carré, and I would suffer a pang of awe at a genre that could furnish such solemn escapism to the society's serious people, the white male power brokers, the airborne harbingers of the free world's deals. But when I peeked into these evidently absorbing tomes I got a suffocating gray impression of armaments catalogues and code nerds and excessively factual dialogue disclosing how every double-cross has another behind it and all roads lead to a vast distrust. I did once read John le Carré's *The Spy Who Came In from the Cold* and, though its details are lost in the same fog as those of older engines of suspense by Graham Greene and Eric Ambler, which I consumed as a credulous boy, there was a bitter something at the end of a metal bridge in Berlin that left a lasting taste in my mouth. Or maybe that was from the movie, with Richard Burton. These books tended to get made into movies, and a common difficulty for this moviegoer would begin with the appearance of an actor playing the President of the United States, when I knew that there had been *no such President*. To be thrilling, a political thriller has to mess with history, and history is messy enough, thanks.

Anyway, the end of the Cold War should have put an end to all that. But it hasn't, as John le Carré demonstrates with his new novel, *Our Game*. Le Carré has already exhibited magical powers in persuading hundreds of thousands of American readers that the forces of British espionage were eyeball to eyeball with the Red Menace, Smiley versus Karla, contrary to our local impression that the U.S. was doing the heavy lifting for the free world. Americans in the movies made from le Carré's novels are generally a negligible and loutish lot, and this latest tale of good old English derring-do awards the United States only a sneer—"the world's only superpower . . . America the great policeman." We fail, it seems, to sufficiently support the tiny bedevilled romantic semi-states of the North Caucasus. Now that the Soviet Empire is pretending not to exist, your typical British spy, as personified in *Our Game* by former double agent Larry Pettifer, continues to battle Russia, this time on behalf not of Britain's sceptered isle and demi-paradise but of the unjustly obscure Muslim entity of Ingushetia. It exists: you can find it on a map, north of Georgia and south of the no-longer obscure Chechnya. The Ingush made up ten per cent of the Checheno-Ingush Autonomous Republic, of which the Chechen fraction declared its independence from Russia in 1991. Le Carré has shown prescience in selecting one of the thawed world's sore spots, but has been unlucky, perhaps, in the immediacy of the grim headlines from Grozny. Fiction and news create a blurred double image. The reader, learning to suffer with Ingushetia, feels in the right church but the wrong pew. And why is the most prominent Ingush character called Checheyev?

Le Carré writes well, even fancily:

> The hill was steep, and the house a stern old lady with her feet firmly planted amid elderly friends. She had a Sunday School face and a stained-glass porch that glowed like heaven in the morning sun. She had pious lace curtains and a hint of grief, and boxed hedges and a bird table and a chestnut tree that was shedding gold leaves. The hill's gorse summit rose behind her like the green hill in the hymn, and behind the hill lay several different

heavens: blue for sunshine, black for judgment, and the clear white sky of the north.

This is an arms-dealer's house in Macclesfield, mind. Le Carré's prose has an overheated expertise about it, as if it wished to be doing something other than spinning a thriller. Our narrator, Timothy Cranmer, has developed a curious device of putting flashbacks in the present tense and action in the past; whom he is telling everything to, with all his cagey withholdings and painfully gradual revelations, is not explained. He spends the first half of the novel circling around a triangle that developed when his live-in mistress, Emma Manzini, a much younger, musical beauty whom he rescued from a low London life of odd concerts and casual couplings and installed in his old Somerset mansion complete with vineyards and chapel, fell in love with the erudite, dishevelled, neo-Byronic Larry Pettifer, who is three years younger than Cranmer and has been a friend since they were boys together at Winchester, one of those unfortunately formative English boarding schools. Cranmer protected him from schoolboy cruelties then, and later, as an Operational Man for the Office, enlisted him as a British spy also in the employ of the KGB. Both men have been rather unceremoniously dumped from the government payroll. "Cold Warriors of forty-seven don't recycle, Tim," Cranmer is told. "You're all far too nice." What emerges from a great deal of artful circumlocution is that, though Cranmer minds the elegant, sexy Emma's being stolen from him by his young former partner in espionage, his real fascination and—dare one say?—love remain with the breezily caddish Larry. This reader had the problem of taking such a dislike to Larry that to the bitter end I had hopes of his being revealed, in a cunning thriller twist, as the betrayer rather than the would-be savior of beleaguered Ingushetia. I was wrong. We are meant to take him straight, as a latter-day Byron dying for Greece, or as another Aubrey Herbert, who gave his all for Albania.

"Our game" is what the boys at Winchester used to call their peculiar version of football, and there is something of boyish daydream about *Our Game*. We are asked to believe that the Ingush in their mountain fastnesses accept one Englishman, the blithe and bookish Larry, as a top-management rebel leader, and that another Englishman, Cranmer of the prayer-book name, is escorted—roughly, but escorted—through the underworlds of Russia so he can patch things up with his old school chum. Such questing adventures take us back to *The Four Feathers* and "The Man Who Would Be King," to the outposts of T. E. Lawrence and Rider Haggard, to Victorian times, when the great, multicolored globe existed as a vast playing field on which true-hearted Englishmen could chase their personal rainbows while the picturesque heathen cheered.

"Live" Spelled Backwards

TIME'S ARROW, by Martin Amis. 168 pp. Harmony Books, 1991.

Martin Amis has inherited his father's wicked wit but on his own has developed experimental literary proclivities and an agitated liberal conscience. His book of five science-fictionish short stories, *Einstein's Monsters* (1987), opens with a thirty-page polemic upon the fact that nuclear weapons exist. Of Robert Jastrow, whose book *How to Make Nuclear Weapons Obsolete* committed the faux pas of considering some possible nuclear-war scenarios, Amis writes:

> He is wrong, and in this respect he is also, I contend, subhuman, like all the nuclear-war fighters, like all the "prevailers." The unthinkable is unthinkable; the unthinkable is not thinkable, not by human beings, because the eventuality it posits is one in which all human contexts would have already vanished.

The idea that one's humanity can be forfeited returns in the short stories: of two drunken murderers it is said, "Really the hardest thing was to touch them at all. You know the wet tails of rats? Snakes? Because I saw that they weren't human beings at all." This convenient category of the less-than-human—invoked by righteous propaganda at most of the high moments of twentieth-century massacre—ominously fascinates Amis: Nicola Six, the death-minded loose woman of his long novel *London Fields* (1989), I take to be one portrait of an inhuman human, who has flunked humanity as Amis defines the subject, and Odilo Unverdorben, the hero of *Time's Arrow*, is another. Listening to public radio in my automobile, I heard Amis explaining to an interviewer that—as best I understood—the narrator of *Time's Arrow* is Unverdorben's soul, which he gave up through his heinous actions as a doctor in various Nazi concentration camps. Why this ousted soul has been directed and empowered to traverse Unverdorben's life backwards, from death to birth, with every journey, action, and conversation experienced in reverse, I didn't hear explained, alas. Perhaps I had to stop for gas, or the driver behind me was leaning on his horn.

Amis's ambitious concerns with inhumanity, time, and the unthinkable converge in *Time's Arrow*, a work of impressive intensity and virtuosity, albeit bristling with problematical aspects. "Holocaust" has taken on two meanings in our time—nuclear war, which hasn't yet happened and we hope never will, and Nazi Germany's systematic murder of six million helpless European captives, most of them Jews. This Holocaust did happen, yet remains, like the other, unthinkable. That the German people, whose arts and sciences and industry stood in the forefront of what was proudly called European civilization, could be led into the commission of a crime so massive and wanton, so savage and yet so systematically executed, presents a monstrous riddle in the center of the twentieth century. Even though documentation, thanks to German efficiency, abounds, and though an explanatory context of German demoralization and Christian anti-Semitism can be spelled out, the mystery remains, so awesome that fictional attempts to render it more thinkable generally give offense. Leslie Epstein's *King of the Jews* was thought to be scandalously lighthearted; William Styron's *Sophie's Choice* made some readers queasy with its mixture of thoroughly researched historical horror and adolescent sexual confession by the American narrator; even so deep and refined a thinker as George Steiner struck, I thought, too playful a note in his *Portage to San Cristobal of A.H.*, relaying the arguments of a raving Hitler discovered alive in the Amazonian jungle in the 1970s. The Holocaust, a half-century later, is still not to be played with; it still gives off a poisonous heat, and perhaps none but those who actually endured the camps, like Primo Levi and Tadeusz Borowski, should be licensed to make art of them. But, of course, the artistic conscience rebels against any such prohibition. One salutes for its daring this attempt, by an Englishman born in 1949, to abandon his mastered London milieu and enter empathetically into the life of a German born in 1916, trained as a doctor, destined to perform dreadful duties at Schloss Hartheim (where physical defectives were eliminated) and then at Auschwitz, but permitted by fate to escape to Lisbon and thence to America, where he eventually dies at a ripe age of heart failure, surrounded by other doctors.

One wishes for more empathy, however, and a plainer payoff for the multiple technical difficulties of unreeling a life in reverse. Conversation, for example, arrives backwards, so that "How are you today" comes out as "Aid ut oo y'rrah?" Transcription so faithful is soon abandoned, but the only way to read extended dialogues (and there are several) is to flip ahead to the end and read up the pages. Eating and defecation become grotesque in reverse, we are more than once reminded. Smoke sinks, and fire creates. Blows heal, and doctors working in a hospital emergency ward appear to be ripping off bandages and inflicting tortures. Prostitutes pay the clients; pens turn letters into blank pieces of paper; clippings leap up from the trash and rejoin the fingernails. A familiar ordeal like getting a cab in New York City becomes hilariously pleasant:

> This business with the yellow cabs, it surely looks like an unimprovable deal. They're always there when you need one, even in the rain or when the theaters are closing. They pay you up front, no questions asked. They always know where you're going. They're great. No wonder we stand there, for hours on end, waving goodbye, or saluting—saluting this fine service. The streets are full of people with their arms raised, drenched and weary, thanking the yellow cabs.

But the forward arrow of time is so deeply embedded in the syntax of the language and narration that Amis at moments appears to slip. Of abortions: "A rectangular placenta and a baby about half an inch long with a heart but no face are implanted with the aid of forceps and speculum. . . . The full bowl bleeds. Next, the digital examination and the swab. They can get down now, and drink something, and talk in whispers. They say goodbye." Wouldn't they—the again pregnant women—say hello, at the beginning of the visit, which from our perspective is the end? At that passage of his life when Unverdorben (now given an American name of Tod Friendly, a designation as bothersomely cute as his German name, which means "unspoiled") is compelled to flee New York for New England, we read, of the reversed action, "I'm on a train now, heading south at evening," when strictly it should be "*backing* south," like the ship that brought him from (takes him back in time to) Europe:

> . . . all the people tended to gather at the sharp end of the ship, looking at where they came from, as people do. Only John [John Young, Unverdorben's first American name] is invariably to be found on the stern, looking at where we're headed. The ship's route is clearly delineated on the surface of the water and is violently consumed by our advance.

It is a mind-fraying exercise to read this book, and writing it must have made much mental labor. Even if the time reversal is not perfectly done, who else could have done it at all, with such colorful smoothness? Amis is an unusual English writer in that he has tried to learn from Americans, especially Bellow, with his quick demotic rhythms, and Nabokov, with his compressed metaphors and avid eye. When he is at home, as in his London novel *Success* (1978), Amis's hyperactive language and seething choler are irresistible. Energetic images speed the path of *Time's Arrow*, from an American hospital ("We the doctors move between ceiling and floor, between striplight and the croak of linoleum") to Portugal ("The villas loom pink and yellow on the arid land, like sweetshops on the planet Mars") and on back to wartime Berlin ("the drizzling parquetry of the streets, the shoplights like the valves of an old radio"). The existential frame of Amis's fiction seems American: he writes of "the deep and uncrackable code of the stars" in our local tone of frustrated transcendentalism. The large American section of the novel, which comes first, has a racy freshness of impression that suggests the world of *Lolita* seen in a crazy inverting mirror, with the same hollow sense of "America's pretty pluralism" and damnable plenty.

However, *Time's Arrow*, when it arrives at its moral center, Auschwitz, somehow misses; even the reverse sequencing goes limp and half-hearted. Unverdorben, in the defining role of his life, becomes vague; all he seems able to tell us is that he has become impotent with his wife, Herta. The unthinkable murderous tumult around him is seen through squinted eyes, a black-and-white newsreel that keeps breaking. Perhaps Amis, to keep this fraction of his hero's life in proportion, hurried. Perhaps, entirely dependent here for vivifying detail on the accounts of others, he chose to borrow sparingly. (Primo Levi's books supplied, at the minimum, the name Unverdorben and some excremental details.) This reader was nagged by a wish to read the factual book by Robert Jay Lifton, *The Nazi Doctors*, of which Amis in an afterword says, "My novel would not and could not have been written without it." Statistics loom over the fiction: Auschwitz covered fourteen thousand acres, Hungarian Jews were killed at the rate of ten thousand a day. Perhaps the subject is indeed too hot, too huge, to handle. Live Jews being conjured, by the reversed arrow, out of ashes and mutilated corpses, with their gold teeth being pounded back into their mouths, is not the cosmic comedy the author might have had in mind. The general human wish to undo the Holocaust—to have it unhappen—was given oddly moving expression in the coda of posthumous mass healing in D. M. Thomas's *The White Hotel*; the reader did not rebel against it, because it arose so spontaneously, so lightly, so organically out of the ground of grief and horror prepared by Thomas's earlier, scarcely bearable dramatization of the mass murder at Babi Yar. Our wish for denial was met by a whim of fiction and the old dream of a redeeming afterlife, not by a never-explained mechanism in the telling that races ruthlessly on.

For who is this "I" who enters Unverdorben's mortal story at the moment of his death and harries him backwards into his mother's womb? In the beginning, though coterminous with its physical host, the alleged soul sounds quite jaunty and detached (and English): "Life is no bowl of cherries. It's swings and roundabouts. You win some, you lose some. It evens out. It measures up." The ghostly voice complains of Tod (German for "death": another jab from the frisky author) that he has no feeling, that he "can't feel, won't connect." It sprinkles him, in the heyday of Tod's, or John's, American promiscuity, with little lectures in favor of monogamy and respect for the contents of women's heads, but allows in a sexy parenthesis, "You'll get no argument from me there: women *are* great." The "I" may think it is Tod's exiled soul ("Perhaps Irene puts it best . . . when she tells Tod that he has no soul. I used to take it personally, and I was wretched at first"), but to me it sounds like a hectoring author scolding one of his characters for being subhuman. Though Amis presents his hero as full of guilt—underestimating, I would guess, our human capacity for adamant self-justification, not limited to German war criminals—he permits him hardly a thought or deed that would encourage sympathy to work its way in. Unverdorben's truly unspoiled youth—pre-Auschwitz, pre–Reserve Medical Corps, pre-Hitler—has an impenetrable brevity. His mother is an American and his father a crippled veteran of the First World War, "a sallow-fleshed skeleton . . . as thin as a *Muselmann*." (*Muselmann*, meaning Muslim, was concentration-camp slang for a terminally damaged prisoner.) In young Odilo scarcely a glimpse of a decent boyish normality is allowed. His (and his soul's) rapturous lust for Herta inspires a prose poem: "Herta's body gossips with youth. Her ears are like cookies, her teeth are like candy. Her flesh is as taut as the flesh of an olive." But before we entertain this joyous honeymoon vision we see her bedraggled and indifferent and Odilo impotent and death-soaked and, before (after) that, abusing her with sadistic sex-games, between spells of going out and "helping" (hurting) Jews.

Well, there's no denying that much pain and cruelty disfigure human history. It is commendable that Martin Amis, or Unverdorben's alienated and garrulous soul, wants to gaze upon "the face of suffering. Its face is fierce and distant and ancient." But *Time's Arrow* seems less to witness suffering than to enact the primitive ritual of casting out a devil. This is not I, says "I" of Dr. Unverdorben; this is not you and I, says the moralizing author—this craven complicity, this violence born of the wish to succeed, this rapacious and clumsy sexuality, this hard-heartedness, this driving fear. But it *is* we, surely, however fortunately far history and social circumstance have placed us beyond the reach of our worst selves. To comprehend the perpetrators of Auschwitz as fellow human beings is a step toward Auschwitz's not being repeated. Devil theories do no good, in politics or in psychiatry. With its fiendish ingenuity, *Time's Arrow* feels a bit like an old-fashioned inquisitor's device, designed to extract, under torture, a saving confession from a lost soul. With its cloudy and flirtatious metaphysics, the novel longs for the cleansing old absolutes. It seems, flashily, to propose a fresh investigation, but comes up with no new evidence.

On the Edge of the Post-Human

NIGHT TRAIN, by Martin Amis. 147 pp. Jonathan Cape, 1997.

I wanted very much to like this book, and the fact that I wound up hating it amounts to a painful personal failure. I wanted to like it because Martin Amis, for all his spectacular talents and fierce dedication, has received a lot of bad press lately—his advances, his romances, even dentistry that he has suffered has come up for criticism—and because he is one of the few English writers of any era who has not dissed America. Amis's willingness to be tutored in American energy and brass, declared not only in his spirited criticism but in the descriptive rhapsodies of the transatlantic novel *Money* ("I felt all the contention, the democracy, all the italics, in the air"), deserves better than polite dubiety from a Yank old enough to be his father. But doubt I must.

Night Train takes place in a nameless "second-echelon American city" and, promisingly, is a take-off on those Hammett/Chandler/Cain "tough-guy" detective stories behind *noir* films and their serial television echoes. The hero, police detective Mike Hoolihan, is a heroine, a deep-voiced, 180-pound, five-ten, formerly alcoholic, child-abused, Irish-American single woman in love all her life with police work. "I am a police," she announces at the outset, in the first of a number of American locutions new to this native speaker, and belts out her résumé in a typical burst of Amis lyricism:

> In my time, I have come in on the aftermath of maybe a thousand suspicious deaths. . . . So I've seen them all: Jumpers, stumpers, dunkers, bleeders, floaters, poppers, bursters. I have seen the bodies of bludgeoned one-year-olds. I have seen the bodies of gang-raped nonagenarians. I have seen bodies left dead so long that your only shot at a t.o.d. is to size the maggots.

This displays an excellent verve, holding out simultaneous hope of a thriller's bloody satisfactions and the subtler pleasures of postmodern irony, the transmutations of a low-down genre in the manner of Umberto Eco or Alain Robbe-Grillet's *Les Gommes*. The puzzling crime is this: Jennifer Rockwell, a beautiful, intelligent, twentysomething, five-ten, 140-pound astronomer is found sitting nude in a chair in her apartment, apparently a suicide. But, if so, she has shot herself three times in the mouth, and without apparent motive: she is widely admired, professionally successful, and happily mated with an associate professor of philosophy auspiciously named Trader Faulkner. Before her abrupt demise they lived together for seven years, enjoyed a voracious sex life, and planned to marry and have children. Jennifer was the daughter of Colonel Tom Rockwell, a police higher-up who rescued our heroine Hoolihan from her alcoholism some years ago. It falls to Hoolihan to break the news to her superior; she does so with the weird words "Colonel Tom, you know I love you and I'd never lie to you. But it seems your baby girl took her own life, sir. Yes she did. Yes she did."

The novel's style evinces the simple faith that repeating something magically deepens it. E.g.: "I'm sorry. I'm sorry, I'm sorry"; "She'd always leave you with something. Jennifer would always leave you with something"; "But I cannot get the good guys. I just cannot get the good guys"; "But the seeing—the seeing, the seeing—was no good at all." But the trouble—my trouble, the reviewer's trouble—with *Night Train* isn't the faux-demotic mannerisms or the heavy debt that Amis's America owes to frequently cited cop shows on the telly but with the unmentionable way the plot proceeds. My trouble is with the solution of the mystery and the point of the book.

Amis beneath his banter is a scowling, atrocity-minded author who demands we look directly at things we would rather overlook. A few years ago, he was insisting we look at the possibility of nuclear holocaust. In *Time's Arrow* he stared at the Holocaust and the German doctors in attendance at the camps. The information in *The Information*, I have heard him explain to an interviewer, is that we die. In *Night Train* he makes us closely watch an autopsy and spotlights the void, not just the moral void around us, in which criminals "fuck a baby and throw it over the wall" and "chop up eight-year-olds for laughs," but astronomical phenomena like black holes, the missing dark matter, and the Boötes Void—"more nothing than you could possibly imagine. It's a cavity 300 million light years deep." Jennifer Rockwell, all one hundred forty delectable pounds of her, mentally dwelt among these crushing immensities; she thought that Stephen Hawking cracked the problem of black holes because he "had been staring at death all his adult life." Within the astronomical equations, presumably, lies the clue. Detective Hoolihan, before going off on a self-destructive tear, speculates, "I sometimes think that Jennifer Rockwell came from the future."

Young people, I was told last summer in Italy, are talking no longer about the postmodern but the post-human. To keep up with the future they are going in for mutilation and artificial body parts. Amis writes out of a sensibility on the edge of the post-human. His characters strikingly lack the soulful, willful warmth that he admires in Saul Bellow; they seem quick-moving automata, assembled of (mostly disagreeable) traits. No wonder he can think of little to do with them but finish them off. His fiction lacks what the late Queenie Leavis called "positives." As a mystery *Night Train* suffers from a lack of minor characters even momentarily sympathetic enough to serve as red herrings. We can believe, initially at least, in Mike Hoolihan's slangy way of talking and her bluesy love of police work; we can't believe in anything about Jennifer Rockwell but her supposedly beautiful and now vacated body. She, and *Night Train*, become pure diagram, on a blackboard as flat as it is black.

Nightmares and Daymares

BILLY LIAR, by Keith Waterhouse. 191 pp. Norton, 1960.

This pungent, shapely, and instructive novel begins, and for the first half continues, comically. Billy Fisher, an ambitious and mendacious teenager in the Yorkshire town of Stradhoughton, describes his progress through one critical Saturday. As he tells it, his family is a pack of harping drudges, his employers (undertakers) are a pair of futile fools, and his town is a dismal muddle of moldering churchyards and modernist record shops, of despairing institutions and desperate Americanisms. Along these drab streets Billy trundles a complicated apparatus of fantasy worlds: Ambrosia, an imaginary nation of which he is President and, repeatedly, savior; a companion world of "daymares," where diseases like ingrowing hair and Fisher's Yawn beset him; a vaguely envisioned London, where he hopes to go and live as a gag writer; a verbal world of wisecracks and routines with his friend Arthur; and, in action, a world of lies, edging into theft and multiple proposals of marriage.

The friction of all these revolving spheres strikes a wonderful number of comic sparks. And it all seems true. The author gives us adolescence full-bodied, in its raucous ferocity. The well-known "sensitive" youth, so pitiably oppressed in American fiction, is here shown wounding, with his

---

My first published book review, printed in the *New York Times Book Review* of January 3, 1960, and reprinted unaltered in what may well be my last collection of such material. The cocky theories as to pure comedy and "that wearisome old fellow Plot" had just been put into practice in the composition of *Rabbit, Run*.

callousness and derision, society in turn. "Stradhoughton was littered with objects for our derision," Billy says.

In the second half of the book the demands of that wearisome old fellow Plot, or perhaps the inherent seriousness of the material itself, press hard upon the humor. Apparently Billy must, if he cannot unravel, at least confront the tangle he has made. His bad checks roll in. His ebullience weakens, and with it the mainspring of the comedy. Mr. Waterhouse rushes new, more sombre resources to the fore. He creates several harrowing and touching scenes. But he is handicapped, I think, by the determinedly comic tone of the beginning. Having given us a delicious taste of the Higher Penrod, he has dulled our palate to soul-searching. The pathos and menace of the later scenes with the family are vitiated by the farcical introduction to its members in the first chapter. The characterization of the heroine, a latecomer, seems perfunctory compared to the energetic caricature of Billy's two other girls. Billy's pranks double indifferently as elements in a moral dilemma.

It comes down to the doubtful compatibility, over the length of a book, of comedy and realism. Even novels as funny as Joyce Cary's *Herself Surprised* and Henry Green's *Nothing* do not strike us as purposely comic, but, rather, accidentally so, like reality itself. The publicized Anger of England's younger writers may seem to lead easily into satire and hence into the also publicized Renascence of the Comic Novel. But, in Mr. Waterhouse's case, there is much more at stake than a view, indignant or amused, of the contemporary scene; and, while I would not really want this excellent book (except for a phrase about "the eyes that laughed aloud") any different, I hope that the author in his future work does not confine himself to a genre possibly too small for his experiences and his feelings about them.

Undelivered Remarks upon Awarding
the 1992 GPA Book Award in Dublin

"JUDGE NOT," the Bible advises us, though it contains not one but two books of Judges. Choosing the best of six Irish books seemed a pleasant enough challenge, for one long admiring of the Irish genius for the spoken and written word; but I did not expect that the six would consist of two books of poems, two novels, and two works of history. How to judge an apple compared with an orange, and both to a bunch or two of grapes? Clearly, all such fruits are excellent in their way, and the slimmest of the books, Eaven Boland's sixty-three-page book of poems titled *Outside History*, could fill its cup of intention as brimmingly as J. J. Lee's seven hundred fifty big pages of history, *Ireland 1912–1985*. But the matter of relative excellence does take on a strange elastic shape, leaping across genres; my judging became even more subjective than I had imagined. In the end I had to select the book that gave me most pleasure, or can we say gratification, in the reading and in the reflective backward glance—the book that stirred the most sparks of recognition in me, and that left the brightest embers of glowing afterthought.

By a generous margin that work was Thomas McGahern's short but not small novel, *Amongst Women*. Mr. McGahern writes narrative prose with the unassuming, speaking felicity that seems the national gift, a gift for verbal music and lucid declaration displayed, variously, by Beckett and Joyce, Yeats and Shaw and O'Casey, Flann O'Brien and Frank O'Connor, Mary Lavin and Edna O'Brien and Benedict Keily, to name only some. Ireland is a small and ancient country, and the United States a large and relatively young one, but we share the boast of having taken the literature of the English language to new, high places; in the global English-language school informally established by the late British Empire, our countries can claim, I think, to be star pupils—a stardom even more remarkable in a population as small as that of Ireland, and one with an altogether other language still in wide use, and with a prior claim, we might say, upon the Irish heart and tongue. The forked linguistic condition, it could be, of Ireland, echoing its forked political condition as a rebellious colony and now as a divided island, has helped give the voice of Irish writers urgency, that urgent *need to tell* which is the first condition for narrative or poetic art. Verbal music does not feed on thin air; it needs fact and circumstances, and in fiction the running concreteness of a story. Mr. McGahern, in recounting the last unsensational years of the farmer and former guerrilla fighter Michael Moran, has a story that without any apparent effort of his part resonated through the recent history of the Irish Republic and beyond that into some basic predicaments of the human race. *Amongst Women* is the tale of a warrior in peacetime; what we are told about Moran from the outset is that he was, when armed rebellion seemed his people's honorable and necessary recourse, not merely a fighter but a leader in the fight, a cool and ruthless killer, as he himself arrestingly says: "The closest I ever got to any man was when I had him in the sights of the rifle and I never missed." The killer's intimacy with his prey has been, we feel, the most intense reality of his life; in the wake of military triumph there has come on the national scale, in his view, political compromise and muddle, and on the personal a farmer's faithful drudgery through the seasons, and the captaincy of a village household of two sons and three daughters. He is, in this household, a tyrant who believes himself benevolent. His two sons flee to England— the younger in a storm of anger that passes into good-humored tolerance, the older with an implacable, lasting grudge. Moran's three daughters and second wife submit to his rule with a mixture of love and fear; their loving submissiveness becomes, as age undermines their master, a victory, an endurance that sees him into the grave and that, in the novel's last image, has them looking more manly than the menfolk in their lives.

Moran's is an Irish story, with some elements peculiar to the setting: the glimpses of the old struggle against the English occupiers, the scarcely ruffled rural placidity and stagnation, the national piety. It is his adamant loyalty to the Catholic church that leads him to break with his anticlerical old comrade-in-arms, McQuaid, in one of the book's many beautifully understated confrontations, and that enjoins him, throughout the novel, to have his family kneel with him in reciting the Holy Rosary around the dining table, to the discomfort of his daughters' suitors and husbands. On his deathbed, however, having asked his mourning women why they aren't praying, he breaks his life of determined observance:

> Tears slipped down their faces as they repeated the "Our Fathers" and "Hail Marys." Maggie had begun her Mystery when it grew clear that Moran was trying to speak. She stopped and the room was still. The low whisper was unmistakable: *"Shut up!"* They looked at one another in fear and confusion but Rose nodded vigorously to Maggie to ignore the whispered command and to continue.

Moran's blasphemy, too, is understated, and may be no more than a dying man's delirious irritation. Every event in *Amongst Women* is muted by the qualifications that reality does usually bring; for all his taciturnity and bullying habits Moran is a good provider and father, with some capacity for tolerance and affection, and some of the moments of conjoined family labor on his acreage have the lyricism of rural-work passages from Thomas Hardy. Flawed and even atrocious, like all families, the Morans are a true family, held together and aloof by their leader's sense of embattlement. The book is, it seemed to me, at its deepest level about the co-existence of men and women, and the always somewhat tentative rapprochements which exist between the warrior gender and the nurturing gender. At any rate, in the novel's weave of many brief scenes the novelist shows himself everywhere knowing and tactful, in language that is both simple and subtle, austere and affectionate. McGahern brings us that tonic gift of the best fiction, the sense of truth—the sense of a transparency that permits us to see imaginary lives more clearly than we see our own, a sight that cleanses us even as it saddens and frightens.

The other novel I had the pleasure of reading, Glenn Patterson's *Fat Lad*, less limpidly, with a more conspicuous and agitated brilliance, displays a range of characters from Northern Ireland. His hero, Drew Linden, is younger than Moran's children, and his restlessness and sense of alienation echo the tense, bomb-ridden urban landscape of Belfast and Ulster. Interestingly, though Drew's family is Protestant, his father, like Moran, was a son-beater, and has reaped the same paternal estrangement; the young in both novels have exile on their minds. Belfast became for this reader a jagged, jazzy mix of damp weather, ubiquitous reconstruction, smoldering bitterness, and jittery sexual adventure. Mr. Patterson's novel, very contemporary and often comic in its pieces, didn't fall toward any resolution, easy or otherwise; and in this the private lives it describes resemble the political conditions around them.

The two impressive history books offered a curious contrast. Richard Doubtwaite's *The Growth Illusion*, written in Ireland by an Englishman, describes the illusion of national growth as pernicious and doomed to fall foul of ecological limitations; he speaks well of Eamon de Valera's dream of an Ireland that "would be the home of a people who valued material wealth only as the basis of right living, of a people who were satisfied with frugal comfort." Whereas Mr. Lee's massive story of Irish politics and society since 1912 takes as its central problem the failure of the Irish Republic to grow, since independence, at the rate of comparably small European nations like Denmark and Finland. Mr. Lee's avidity of detail, his energetic characterization of several generations of Irish leaders, North as well as South, and his frequent dry wit made his uncompromisingly thorough survey considerably entertaining. He made me laugh a number of times, as when he wrote of the issue of growth,

> Perhaps the Irish simply did not want economic growth? Were not the Irish renowned for their dedication to things of the spirit, for their renunciation of the temptations of materialism, to which a decadent Europe, lacking Hibernian strength of character, sadly succumbed? It is an engaging thought, sedulously cultivated by some of the Irish themselves. Suffice it to note that, despite impressive examples of individual self-denial, particularly among missionary and nursing orders, the image of Ireland as an island sublimely submerged in a sea of spirituality carries little conviction.

In his next sentence he delivers his most stinging indictment: "Few peoples anywhere have been so prepared to scatter their children around the world in order to preserve their own living standards."

Were there a second prize, I would have awarded it to Mr. Lee's already prize-laden book. It is harder to discuss why a book, or five books, failed to get a prize than to describe why one did. All six books have received the prize of nomination, and a certain monetary recognition as well. Of the two poetry books, I have least to say, being, though a part-time poet myself, so intimidated by the primal bardic art as to render my judging faculty almost inoperative. Suffice to say that neither Mr. Boland's sheaf of recent lyrics, nor Derek Mahon's stately and mordant selection from a career of poetry, exquisite and vivid as their crystallizations of private reality frequently were, moved and engaged me as continuously, as *roundedly*, as the prose of *Amongst Women*. In any judging, there is the possibility that the failings are the reader's and not the writer's; in all my fallibility I thank the administrators of the GPA Award for entrusting these six worthy nominees to my mercy.

Idle Thoughts of a Toiling Tiler

A TILER'S AFTERNOON, by Lars Gustafsson, translated from the Swedish by Tom Geddes. 118 pp. New Directions, 1993.

Beneath the surface comedy of this small novel, as it relates the muddled day of a sixty-five-year-old Uppsala tiler named Torsten Bergman, lie the philosophical issues that Lars Gustafsson, in his poetry and fiction, likes to animate. "Hopelessness was the only thing that human beings really had in common." "Life doesn't seem to serve our purposes, that much is obvious." Interwoven with these Beckettian aperçus are Torsten's present blurred apprehensions and his vivid recollections of the past, as he erects a nicely aligned blue tiled wall in what turns out to be the wrong house. He is a loser, but who isn't? Torsten's daylong soliloquy has flashes of revelation: aquavit, he reflects, induces "an inner feeling of the meaningfulness of the world," and a kite enables the flier to feel he is in two places at once. Gustafsson's unassuming sentences all nicely align within a larger perspective, and the reader begins idly to wonder why Scandinavians don't win the Nobel Prize any more.

Dark Walker

MR. SUMMER'S STORY, by Patrick Süskind, translated from the German by John E. Woods, with illustrations by Sempé. 116 pp. Knopf, 1993.

As his books arrive in English translation, Mr. Süskind seems to be the Amazing Shrinking Author; the average-sized, best-selling *Perfume* was followed by the novella *The Pigeon*, and now comes an illustrated tale of childhood, small enough to read in an hour. With affable divagations and a charming aura of the Grimms' fables, Süskind explores some typical adventures of pre-adolescence—tree-climbing, bicycle-riding, piano lessons, a crush on a schoolmate. Through the tenderly, carefully colored landscape stalks the dark figure of Mr. Summer, a tormented and tireless hiker along the village roads. His mystery is never revealed, and one wonders if "Summer" doesn't have misleadingly mellow connotations in English. Like the pigeon in *The Pigeon*, he is an omen of death, whose chill underlies the innocent clarity of Süskind's prose. Sempé's soft, playful illustrations and Mr. Woods' flowing translation ably serve that prose; one only wishes that the little volume, which was manufactured in Mexico, weren't so strangely hard to open, and to keep open. It fights the fingers like a mousetrap being set.

Angels in Holland

THE DISCOVERY OF HEAVEN, by Harry Mulisch, translated from the Dutch by Paul Vincent. 730 pp. Viking, 1996.

The Discovery of Heaven, by the sixty-nine-year-old Dutch writer Harry Mulisch, is an old-fashioned magnum opus. It shares with Vladimir Nabokov's *Ada* the name of its heroine. Like Joyce's *Finnegans Wake*, it is oneirically entangled with the entirety of European history; like Umberto Eco's *Foucault's Pendulum*, it proposes a dark trickle of arcana running beneath the surface of that history, and gives us a thriller denouement. Perhaps the great book it most resembles—in its genial ironical tone, in its hospitality to extended intellectual arguments, and in the metaphysical height of its perspective on humanity's spiritual and erotic adventures—is Thomas Mann's *Magic Mountain*. Mulisch's Holland, like Mann's Swiss sanatorium, holds an articulate microcosm of

European opinion, from revolutionary to reactionary, and with an unmistakable joke the Dutch writer salutes the German: Mann's Clavdia Chauchat completes her seduction of Hans Castorp with a request that he return her pencil to her, and Mulisch's Sophia Brons asks Max Delius to return her pencil sharpener.

The Dutch novel, huge in length, erudition, and wealth of incident, has a first-person narrator, a nameless angel reporting to his superior in Heaven on the success of his assigned mission to maneuver earthlings into returning the two tablets upon which the Ten Commandments were engraved. It was necessary, first, to generate a human being whose DNA conformation could receive the one Spark—a bit of divine light— capable of locating and appropriating the tablets, and this involved some delicate but lethal manipulation among the generations. The Spark receptacle's maternal grandparents met in the rubble after a museum was bombed in 1944, and the paternal set proved so little compatible that the husband, an Austrian, betrayed his wife, the daughter of German Jews, to the Nazi authorities; she was shipped to Auschwitz, and he was eventually executed as a war criminal. The offspring of these two couples are the beautiful cellist Ada Brons and the brilliant, promiscuous astronomer Max Delius. He deflowers her, and they live together for a time, but the crucial conception, for reasons only angels can fully grasp, must occur in Cuba, subaqueously, when Ada is already engaged to Onno Quist, a big, slovenly, scatterbrained linguist whose aristocratic, strict-Calvinist father was a pre-war prime minister of the Netherlands. By heavenly design Onno and Max have become the dearest of friends before either meets Ada. When Quinten, Ada's uncanny, sapphire-eyed child, is born, Onno assumes that he is the father, but, as it happens, Ada has been put into a permanent coma months before parturition and Max raises Quinten anyway, with the help of Ada's mother, Sophia, whose husband died—not accidentally, you may be sure—the same night that Ada was knocked comatose by a falling tree. That's life. Onno gives up trying to decipher an unearthed ancient disc and enters Dutch politics; Max supervises the construction of a synthetic radio telescope on the site of an old concentration camp near Westerbork and discovers behind a pulsar the portal of Heaven; Quinten grows up in an enchanting castle, Groot Rechteren, which has been divided into apartments conveniently populated by all the specialists he will need for his peculiar education.

Through the angelic point of view the reader shares the manipulations that any writer must force upon the creatures of his plot. Part of the game is spotting when the angel is at work, creating coincidences and juggling circumstances. The cruelties visited on the characters to achieve heavenly ends raise questions of human purpose ruefully rather than with the Heaven-storming satire of, say, Kurt Vonnegut's *The Sirens of Titan.* Angelic intervention—an ancient and still-active notion—is not easy, our narrator explains: "Reality is just like water; it's liquid and mobile, but it can only be compressed a little by using a great deal of force." His goal is to destroy the Decalogue—"the ultimate thing on earth: the Chief's contract with humankind, concluded with its deputy, the Jewish people." The Chief and His angels are calling it quits, pulling out, leaving "all those human things" to Lucifer. The Biblical era of direct messages and face-to-face meetings is long past. An angel puts the modern case against revealed truth tellingly:

> The last straw we cling to is people's belief; the moment our existence becomes a matter of knowledge, they'll abandon us completely. They'll shrug their shoulders and say "So what?"

The plot sounds hectic in the summary, but in its unfolding it discloses many intellectually provocative turns and much depth of sympathy. Ada and Quinten are lovely conjurations, and Max and Onno mixed bags, as men are. The many minor characters are deftly stitched into an affectionate tapestry of twentieth-century Holland; the majestic European past is evoked in terms of its music and its architecture; astrophysics and biochemistry testify to the vast voids and intricacies of the universe as we know it. Written carefully and ingeniously by a novelist who is also a poet, the many pages speed by. As Ada and Max and Holland are left behind, there is a somewhat vitiating shift into travelogue and science fiction; Quinten, his angelic mission tightening around him, becomes a kind of robot, with, Onno observes, "a touch of interstellar coldness." Yet to the end the book manages surprising twists in its running discourse on such human matters as heredity and belief, sex and loneliness.

Like two of Mulisch's other novels in English—*The Assault* (1982, translation 1985) and *Last Call* (1985, translation 1989)—*The Discovery of Heaven* has its roots in the Second World War. Events then, under the compression of terror and atrocity, became omens and portents, and through decades of peace continue to assert their authority. Max, like Anton in *The Assault*, is "always surrounded" by the war. One might fancy that Mulisch (who like Max had a victim and a collaborator for parents) has turned his old devils into angels—the dark presiding powers of occupied Holland into fussy bureaucratic fate-spinners. If so, this blithely big novel is a gallant gesture from a generous imagination.

Vagueness on Wheels, Dust on a Skirt

The White Castle, by Orhan Pamuk, translated from the Turkish by Victoria Holbrook. 161 pp. George Braziller, 1991.

Love and Garbage, by Ivan Klíma, translated from the Czech by Ewald Osers. 224 pp. Knopf, 1991.

The White Castle is the first book by Orhan Pamuk to be published in the United States, but he is well known in Turkey, and not unknown in Europe. An article in the Times Literary Supplement last fall ended by claiming, "For a writer not yet forty, Pamuk's is an astounding achievement." His achievement, as the admiring critic, Savkar Altinel, outlined it, has been to recapitulate, in his novels, the Western novel in Turkish. His first novel, Cevdet Bey and Sons—completed when the author, born in 1952, was twenty-six—is a spacious work of realism, a saga of three generations of an upper-class Istanbul family comparable to Thomas Mann's precocious Buddenbrooks. Its successor, The Silent House, takes a much smaller canvas and, Altinel says, "deals with a week spent by three frustrated and unhappy siblings in the home of their dying nonagenarian grandmother in a small town near Istanbul"; this novel, as it moves through the consciousnesses of five different narrators, suggests, rather than early Mann and the nineteenth-century realists, the circling, anxious, multiple perspectives of Woolf and Faulkner. The modernist manner has yielded, in Pamuk's third novel, The White Castle, to a postmodern atmosphere of fantasy and cleverness. The Borgesian, Calvinoesque narrative (found in an old archive by, a preface establishes, one character from The Silent House, and dedicated to another) tells of a seventeenth-century Christian slave from Italy and a Muslim master who resemble each other as closely as twins and eventually swap identities. Pamuk's fourth novel, The Dark Book, appeared last year and, from its description by Altinel, is his most complex and literary yet—post–postmodern, perhaps. Pamuk evidently knows all the tricks Western literature has to teach. He steeped his youthful self in classic French and Russian fiction, and studied the English classics at Istanbul's Robert College, an American secular university. Fluent in English, he spent part of 1985 as a Visiting Writer Fellow at the University of Iowa. Of books I have read, The White Castle mostly closely resembles, in its shimmering tone, effortless gymnastics, and confusingly doubled hero, Arabesques, a novel by another Near Eastern visitor to Iowa, the Palestinian Israeli

Anton Shammas. Can it be that literary historians of the future will have to speak of "the Iowa school" of global magic realism, and ponder the stylistic relation of Grant Wood's geometric landscapes to the exotic visions of Third World intellectuals?

The narrator of *The White Castle* is the Italian slave, a captive taken at sea. His narrative, spanning more than four decades, has a weight-less buoyance that floats us over many implausibilities. The passion that steadily drives the tale is intellectual and philosophical, concerning the interplay of East and West—of fatalistic faith versus aggressive science—and, at a deeper level, the question of identity. The master, a bearded would-be inventor and scholar known only by the appellation of Hoja, meaning "teacher," keeps asking his unnamed Venetian lookalike, "Why am I what I am?" In quest of the answer, the two of them invent psychotherapy, first in the form of confessional writing, with an emphasis upon personal faults and sins, and next in the form of mirror-encounter:

> Squeezing the nape of my neck from both sides with his fingers, he pulled me towards him. "Come, let us look in the mirror together." I looked, and under the raw light of the lamp saw once more how much we resembled one another. . . . I made a movement to save myself, as if to verify that I was myself. I quickly ran my hands through my hair. But he imitated my gesture and did it perfectly, without disturbing the symmetry of the mirror image at all. He also imitated my look, the attitude of my head, he mimicked my terror I could not endure to see in the mirror but from which, transfixed by fear, I could not tear my eyes away; then he was gleeful like a child who teases a friend by mimicking his words and movements.

The feeling of being teased extends to the reader as this creepy duo grows into a trio, incorporating the playful young Sultan, and as Hoja's gradual conversion to the wisdom of the West leads him, with the Sultan's financial backing, to the obsessive creation of a superweapon more nebulous than anything the Pentagon has ever begged billions for:

> He'd repeat once again that everything was connected with the unknown inner landscape of our minds, he'd based his whole project on this, he talked excitedly about the symmetry, or the chaos, of the cupboard full of junk we call the brain, but I could not understand how this might serve as a point of departure for designing the weapon on which he'd set all his hopes, all our hopes. . . . Then he would point out to me—moved as I was, without understanding—a bizarre, obscure, ambiguous shape on paper with the tips of his trembling fingers.
>
> This shape, which I saw slightly more developed each time he showed it to me, seemed to remind me of something. . . . All during those four years I never clearly perceived this shape he scattered over pages, giving it a

sharper definition as it developed a little more each time, and which, after consuming all that effort and money accumulated over the years, he was at last able to bring to life. Sometimes I likened it to things in our daily life, sometimes to images in our dreams, once or twice to things we saw or talked about in the old days when we recounted our memories to one another, but I was unable to take the final step of clarifying the images that passed through my mind, so I'd submit to the confusion of my thoughts, and waited in vain for the weapon itself to reveal its mystery.

Small wonder that the weapon, when it is built to the size of "a grand mosque," gets stuck in the mud of battle and costs the Sultan his siege of the White Castle, in Poland. Whatever else this cloudy device symbolizes, it serves as a paradigm for the novel, which reminds us of many things but we know not exactly what, and mires itself in the messy cupboard of our brain. A certain romance can be extracted from the meeting of innocence and technology—Wells and Jarry and Queneau do it, García Márquez did it with ice in *One Hundred Years of Solitude*, and José Saramago did it with an amber-driven flying machine in *Baltasar and Blimunda*—but Pamuk's invention has no edge, no nuts and bolts; it is vagueness on wheels. Its plan, like his story, is a "dark and ambiguous stain on paper," a kind of Rorschach test into which we read what we can. A veil of diffidence dulls most of the details of seraglio and battlefield that might sharpen this historical fable into lifelikeness. A blur of ambiguity softens the miraculous twinship that is the story's premise: "The resemblance between myself and the man who entered the room was incredible! ... But he did not seem surprised. Then I decided he didn't resemble me all that much, he had a beard; and I seemed to have forgotten what my own face looked like." The episode in front of the mirror has a certain oblique sexual heat, a flavor of homosexual tyranny and submission, but the hero's forays to a perfumed brothel and his eventual marriage are mere notations, with no sense of real desire or energy. As in some of E. M. Forster's novels, what energy there is hovers in an atmosphere of schoolboy debate and suppressed attraction; the identity-switch that forms the plot's carefully prepared climax is muffled by the two men's seeming interchangeable all along. The novel, though it contains some violence, has no contending elements; everything blends and melts into the narrator's misty self. "I loved Him," he writes, the capital "H" metaphysically honoring not Jesus but Hoja, "with the stupid revulsion and stupid joy of knowing myself; my love for Him resembled the way I had become used to the futile insect-like movements of my hands and arms, the way I understood the thoughts which every day echoed against the walls of my mind and died away."

So the instability of selfhood, of reflection and memory, lies at the heart of this brilliant yet enervated novel. Pamuk in his dispassionate intelligence and arabesques of introspection suggests Proust; his narrator speaks of remembering "the colours of my past as if recalling the cherished words of a book I had memorized with pleasure." But, perhaps because the seventeenth century offers the writer's imagination a past already bookish, the colors seem faded, within the graceful outlines of gold and silver.

One way to write a postmodern novel is to adopt the texture of fable, with, in Pamuk's phrase, "hidden geometry"; another, and more common in the United States, is to adopt the texture of autobiography and write what amounts to a farraginous first-person essay, with occasional characters and conversation. This second tack is taken by the Czech writer Ivan Klíma, in his factually titled *Love and Garbage*. First published in 1986 (in Sweden, though in the Czech language), Klíma's novel seems to arrive from long ago, since it predates the fall of the Iron Curtain and originates within the weird and warped circumstances that Communist governments imposed upon would-be practitioners of the arts. An author esteemed enough to have his plays produced and his short stories published abroad, and to be visited by a glamorous French interviewer, our hero has taken a job with a street-sweeping crew, and finds therein a professional companionship and satisfaction denied him elsewhere. When the foreman thanks him for doing his job, he reflects, "It was a long time since any superior of mine had thanked me for my work." But, except for his inner fulminations against the "jerkish" (i.e., official and propagandistic) language and ideas all around him, and for a few hints of bureaucratic oppression from above, the hero might be a writer in the West, whose troubles are mostly non-political. Indeed, one problem with *Love and Garbage* is its familiarity, as the stations of the middle-aged male pilgrim are faithfully visited: the dying parent, the dear good deceived wife, the passionate but demanding mistress, the ever more distant children, the distracting daily tasks, the neglected creative work. To these inevitable stops on the circuit of quiet desperation Klíma's narrator, a childhood survivor of the concentration camp at Terezín, adds a number of recurring pet topics: Kafka's life and art, the larger meaning of rubbish, the Holocaust, Kampuchea, the curious human will to invent mechanical things, the likelihood of an immortal soul, memories of an academic stay in the United States (not in Iowa but in Michigan), and a frustrated artist's display window on a Prague side street.

In working through his extended meditation upon an alter ego's life,

Klíma does not show the suavity and lightness of his countryman Milan Kundera or of the Pole Tadeusz Konwicki, whose rambling self-expositions veer charmingly into self-deprecating farce. Klíma in his rather relentless earnestness can be high-flown ("If a person does not glimpse or hear within himself something that surpasses him, that has cosmic depth, then language will not make him respond anyway") or flat ("She makes love to me in a way that blots out my reason") or turgid:

> I don't know how or when I'll end my struggle, but at that moment my soul is still capable of rising up, of making one last flight to where it belongs, to the place of its longings, to the regions of blissful paralysis from the proximity of a loved being.

And the narrative voice can be sententious, in a Cold War liberal way. Of a young man who is trying to leave his job as a miner and study "aesthetics, art history or literature" we read:

> He considers it more acceptable to have to listen, voluntarily and for no pay, to jerkish babbling than to destroy and pollute the landscape for good pay, to mine the ore from which others would produce an explosive device capable of turning everything into flames.
>
> What stands at the beginning and what at the end? The word or fire, babbling or explosion?

Yet the narrative's churning does have the effect of dredging up, slowly, the personalities of the wife, Lída, and the mistress, Daria. Daria is a sculptress, used to working with recalcitrant materials. Lída is a social worker, a psychotherapist, who for all her wish to help mankind has not noticed in twenty-five years that her husband doesn't drink coffee, and who "was not endowed with directness. . . . In dealing with people she lacked naturalness." While our hero vacillates between them, year after year, his children leave home and make him a grandfather. His mistress, who dyes her gray hair, ages also—"she has aged at my side, in my arms, in her vain waiting, in bad dreams and in fits of crying." In one of his high-flown moods, the narrator reflects, "We mortals, here only for a single winking of the divine eye, have, in our longing to fill our lives, in our longing for ecstasy, filled our brief moment with suffering." I was reminded of Theodore Roethke's couplet

> What's the worst portion in this mortal life?
> A pensive mistress, and a yelping wife.

In Klíma's novel it is the wife who is pensive and the mistress who yelps. As the years go by, Daria becomes quite insulting of her uxorial rival, and so wild in her accusations of her lover ("Amidst the silent nocturnal landscape she screamed at me: I was a coward, a liar and a hypocrite. A trader in emotions. A dealer with no feelings") that she looks to him "like a witch, like a sorceress who'd emerged from some depth of the mountains."

These glimpses of independent personalities, of half-round bubbles allowed to materialize in the turbulent flow of the onrushing monologue, make one aware of how much the postmodern novel has lost in putting aside the objectives of old-fashioned third-person realism. Not that there was not always an authorial voice, and first-person narratives, from *Robinson Crusoe* on. But the triumph of the nineteenth-century novel, as exemplified by Jane Austen and George Eliot, Dickens and Tolstoy, was to create the illusion of human interaction viewed direct, without undue mediation and manipulation, from a standpoint elevated and detached. A stage was constructed that permitted us to imagine the actors as autonomous; now this stage has shrunk to frame the one-man act, the dazzling solitary performance. Klíma performs virtually naked (except for his G-string of a disclaimer, "None of the characters in this book—and that includes the narrator—is identical with any living person"), and Pamuk is garbed in many veils of contrivance; but the obliquity and ingenuity of the latter are basically as self-reflexive as the confessionalism of the former. In Klíma's book we cannot forget that we are listening to a writer; in Pamuk's we cannot forget that we are reading a book.

We end up not unimpressed or unentertained but disposed to argue, as if with a tract. Klíma's unnamed hero says, as his long enjoyment of his two-woman turmoil winds to its denouement, "Perhaps there is within us still, above everything else, some ancient law, a law beyond logic, that forbids us to abandon those near and dear to us." This seems too simple, given the complexity of the case as his self-serving narrative allows us to perceive it. Later, mining his theme of garbage, he pronounces, "Paradise is, above all else, the state in which the soul feels clean." Well, we're not in paradise yet. Dirt prevails. In treasuring his memories of his dying father, Klíma's narrator recalls how once the man's hat fell off into a car of a coal train; in the course of *Love and Garbage*, it emerges that somehow he retrieved the hat, "all black with soot and grime," and put it back on his head. At a late point in the novel, the hero and Daria, their affair having become a series of desperate gestures, make love in an abandoned structure, an old stone-crushing mill. She takes off her leather skirt to do so, and, back in the hotel, after they quarrel, he notices that "on the other bed, near enough for me to touch it, lies her open suitcase. Immediately next to it lies her leather skirt, the stone dust is still clinging to it." Next morning, when he awakes, the suitcase and skirt are gone. This skirt, with its telltale smirch of stone dust, is worth a thousand assertions about love and paradise and the soul. "No ideas but in things," said William Carlos Williams, and though he was speaking of poetry it is true of fiction, too. Fiction's power to sway us comes about not through directed meditations and conclusions but through depicted realities to which meaning clings, and which transfer this meaning, unmediated and otherwise inexpressible, to our consciousness, dust to dust.

Life Was Elsewhere

JUDGE ON TRIAL, by Ivan Klíma, translated from the Czech by A. G. Brain. 549 pp. Knopf, 1993.

Communism, though embattled pockets of it still exist and the social problems it hoped to rectify are still globally present, has quickly become something we'd rather not think about. All those junked monuments in concrete and steel, those dreary windowless corridors of power and terror, reeking of vodka and sweat—let history swallow the whole quaint, grim mass, while we get on with our weightless electronic future, haring after the Japanese. Communism, except in its Maoist version, lacks the macabre charm, the campy death's-head chic, of Nazism, whose insignia recur as graffiti and whose theatrical masterminds exercise the fascination of arch-fiends. Fascism re-created the glamour of murder and death, and still appeals to desperate or adolescent minds as a way out of this world, whereas Communism ended mired in the world's economic mud, humiliated by its own poverty and beggary. The empire was worse than evil: it was inefficient. A rather majestic enemy became a pitiable failure. So this is an inauspicious moment for an ambitious, conscientious novel painfully explaining the rise and fall of the Communist faith in one earnest agonist.

Ivan Klíma's *Judge on Trial* dresses an alter ego in judge's robes and attempts to condemn, from within, the Communist system as it functioned in the Czechoslovak Socialist Republic in the 1960s. Klíma has done some delving into judicial and bureaucratic procedure and shows the slippery human way in which the hierarchy of socialist power achieves its ends, stifling initiative and effectiveness as it does so. But Adam Kindl, his hero, does not manifest much of the Communist functionary's iron, even in rusted form; he is soft and disillusioned from the start. The story begins not long after August 1968, when an invasion of Russian troops and their allies reversed the liberalizing movement of Czechoslovakia's brief "Prague Spring," under Alexander Dubček. The hard-liners have been reinstated and the reformers are in disgrace if not in exile; Kindl, a thirty-seven-year-old judge no longer in the Party, is handed the case of Karel Kozlík, who has been indicted for gassing his landlady and her small daughter, and is instructed to bring in a hanging verdict. At the same time, Magdalena, a girlfriend of Adam's during his first judicial posting thirteen years before, telephones him; they arrange to meet, and she confides that she needs his help in keeping her husband from being fired from his job as a teacher at an agricultural college. That evening, Adam's wife, Alena, returns from a librarian-refresher course where, it is clear to the reader long before it is clear to her husband, she has begun an affair with a young man called Honza. And another erotic thread begins to be spun as Adam, attempting to do Magdalena's favor, reëstablishes relations with Oldrich Ruml, his worldly-wise mentor a decade ago at the law faculty of an institute in Prague, and is attracted to, and then seduced by, Ruml's wife, Alexandra. Meanwhile, Adam's younger brother, Hanuš, a mathematician, is off in England with his wife and debating whether or not to return to their bedevilled land.

This braid of stresses pulls a heavy load of confrontation, revelation, and rumination. The late-Sixties events are systematically interrupted by retrospective sections given the eerie running title of "Before we drink from the waters of Lethe," which consecutively bring Adam Kindl's story up to the book's present. Such alternating layers are becoming a novelist's tic—e.g., Anne Tyler's *Earthly Possessions*, Mario Vargas Llosa's *The Real Life of Alejandro Mayta*, Yuri Trifonov's *The Old Man*. A certain depth is gained but at the price of halving the narrative's speed. The formal interjection of the past begins to irritate the reader; like a hiker chronically halted by a companion's sore foot, he keeps waiting for the laggard to catch up. The multiple subplots of the Victorian novel, by and large, moved forward in a spatially extended present; the art of fiction was understood to include the consolidation of the characters' histories within their present deeds. In *Judge on Trial*, flashback and reminiscence dominate.

Adam's life story carries the ideological burden of the novel: the making of a Communist functionary. Like the nameless narrator of the other novel of Klíma's to be translated into English, *Love and Garbage*, Adam Kindl as a child survived incarceration in a concentration camp— identified as Terezín in *Love and Garbage*, in this novel only as the "fortress," situated in "a town which an empress had built for quite different purposes."* His best friend there, Arie, is from a more observant Jewish background than Adam's, and tells him "with enthusiasm about the old law . . . about the Sanhedrin which judged more justly than courts today." An ominous clown, one of the entertainers the authorities allow into the camp, singles out Adam by asking him "who is the most useful of men?" Adam guesses a doctor, but the answer is "the man who tells the truth." That night he peeks out of a paper-masked window and sees "a large gleaming eye . . . swirling round a fiery point. . . . In sudden awe I realised that it was He: God or Life whose mystery no one could fathom." At about the same time, he and other children discover in the fortress barracks loft a harmonium, which an older girl, Olga, plays; the music fills Adam with a "strange ecstasy":

> As if I'd been cut off from a world in which one looked forward to ersatz coffee and stewed swede, in which countless unknown people were packed together, a world of shouting, stench, and fear, a world of screeching burial carts pulled by humans. It started to become distant and I found myself elsewhere. I was alone, just myself within my own crystal-clear space. I don't know why, but at that moment I longed to see a wide desert. Most likely it wasn't a desert I longed for, but freedom.

From such inklings of freedom and justice, then, Adam emerges from the camp—liberated by Russian troops—"convinced I had to do something to ensure that people never again lost their freedom." Meanwhile, his father, an engineer, narrowly survives in a German camp, and writes in his journal,

> The boards of management of the munitions firms—Metro-Vide, Imperial Chemical Trust, Krupp, they all created Hitler. Without their help he would have ended up in an asylum the first time he tried to seize power. But their insane hatred of socialism in the Soviet Union where the bosses were put to work, where ordinary working people were appointed in place of the rulers, that completely blinded them. Maybe all this suffering has been good for one thing at least: it has completely opened my eyes. If I live to see freedom, I'll know who to thank for my life.

---

*Since the publication of *Judge on Trial* Klíma's understated autobiographical account of his internment at Terezín has appeared in *Granta*, issue 44. "A Childhood in Terezín" closely follows chronology and incidents reported in the fiction, with a number of reflections, however, that cast light upon the curious, sullen, insatiable mood of his fictional protagonists. After describing the ecstatic sense of freedom that came with liberation after over three years of captivity and the constant threat of deportation and death, he writes, "Few realize that a profound experience of happiness is impossible without an equally profound experience of deprivation. . . . The sensation of supreme happiness is the most transient of feelings, yet it can colour our judgement for a long time afterwards, despite the inevitable sobering up to follow, which causes deep frustration."

Further, Adam's uncles on both sides were stalwart revolutionaries: Uncle Gustav fought with the British in North Africa, but with no love of the British, and Uncle Karel spent the war in Moscow, where he imbibed the doctrine at the source and saw Stalin at close enough quarters to pronounce him "wise and modest." Small wonder that Adam becomes "a foot-soldier of the revolution, a hobby horse for a new generation of butchers to mount." In adolescence his conviction grows "that it was the communist movement which embodied courage, conviviality, wisdom, humanity and all the other virtues of whose real nature someone of fifteen has no idea."

His gradual disillusion is traced with a meticulousness that we who never shared those particular illusions scarcely need. Yet it is good to remember that post-war idealism and abhorrence of the trauma just endured assisted the Soviet armies in painting Eastern Europe red. European politics had long been polarized by the opposition of Communism and fascism; the opposition, so clear to Americans, between democracy and totalitarianism in all its forms was relatively unreal, especially after the ineffectual performance of parliamentary governments between the wars. What did the anti-fascists expect of Communist governments? Not what they got, the repression of individual freedom and the devious self-maintenance of an elite: "Politics . . . consisted entirely of intrigues and scarcely visible movements and shifts within the ruling circles." Adam's father is more persuasive as a betrayed believer than Adam; he sees what he has lived by ruined. "Science and technology are finished," he says. "And especially anything creative. They destroy anyone who might be capable of achieving anything. Because the place is run by numskulls and lazy slobs." While Adam is a student, his father, who has become a factory manager, is arrested and imprisoned for twenty-five months, on phony charges; at the end of a prison visit, he confides in his son, "Adam, it's all lies and falsehoods." Still Adam clings to his dream of creating an "island where reason held sway, where I ruled alone for the good of everyone, where I had eliminated all the inequality, depravity and immorality of the present-day world, along with want and unhappiness and all other untoward phenomena." Though his imaginary island erodes as his experience of the working judiciary grows, it does not sink beneath the waves, even when he is expelled from the institute for questioning the death penalty in an article and asserting, at the consequent hearing, that "censorship was only needed by governments that went in fear of truth and their own people." It takes the combined weights of a sojourn in America in the mid-Sixties, the political events of 1968, a cool betrayal by his judicial superior, and his messy mid-life marital crisis to bring him to the point where he can confess, "I used to go on about a juster society and about freedom, but I didn't know what I was talking about. And meanwhile I took away others' freedom and repressed it within myself."

This is a novel of ideas, political and metaphysical, but Klíma lacks his fellow-Czech Milan Kundera's ability to float them angelically above the action. On the contrary, they get submerged within the action. As in *Love and Garbage*, sexual events seek to clothe themselves in political significance. *Judge on Trial* presents not a triangle but a quadrangle: Adam betrays his demure, waiflike wife, Alena, with the short-skirted, wanton Alexandra, and then betrays them both with the willowy love from his past, Magdalena. If a bottle of vodka was the quickest way out of Communist Russia, a bed seems to have offered the handiest exit from Communist Czechoslovakia. The pages describing Adam's affair with Magdalena back in the mid-Fifties are the most sensually glowing, alive not only with their youth but with the beauty of the Central European countryside: "We are walking on moss among mountain thyme and Carthusian pinks, and along dry-stone walls that radiate heat, and along a valley up which the sound of bells is carried. I can see Magdalena in her light flowered dress; for the first time I saw her happy." They spend the night in an old farmhouse. The next day, Magdalena drinks too much at the local inn and makes Adam stay too late; by way of apology, back in their room, she plays her flute and begs him to sing: "The scene etched itself in my memory: her slim, almost white body, which seemed to shine in the darkness, the black flute in her big fingers, and behind her the country bed with its striped quilt." We are not surprised when, thirteen years after this idyll, as his domestic and professional worlds are collapsing, he invites Magdalena once again to bed, and she accepts. Only with her does he not feel that—in the phrase of Rimbaud's with which Kundera once titled a novel—"life is elsewhere." The sexual venturing of this novel is insistently tied to the political malaise, the sense of captivity. Magdalena feels "surrounded by lies . . . in a country enclosed with barbed wire." Alena is drawn to Honza in part because his father was sent to prison when he was very young; Adam is cold and distant because he is, with his grim idealism, a slave to the system. Alexandra (whose father, a policeman, shot himself when Communists took over) sleeps around and drinks hard in the same spirit of protest in which she wears Western-style miniskirts and deals with the economic underground. She scoffs at the "laws that say it's a crime to want to live like people and not slaves," and longs to escape to "somewhere I'd know I was alive."

All this would be more persuasive if sexual infidelity and restlessness were unknown under capitalism, or if Adam were not himself so relentlessly and humorlessly self-regarding. Once Alena slips from the innocence he had assigned her in his mind, he numbly turns his back upon her and their two children to devote himself entirely to rather ponderous introspection, filling his head and Klíma's pages with such disquisitions as:

> What was he to do? How was he to find harmony when he was incapable of knowing himself, had never learnt to heed his inner voice and it was so long since he had seen his own light, ever since he lost it in the way sleepers lose for ever the light of the star that they observed with such amazement in the night sky before they fell asleep?

In the face of his wife's plea for a reconciliation, he resents that she didn't ask him such a psychotherapeutic brainteaser as: "Where are you now and where do you want to go from here? Have you still any capacity at all to live and act as a free individual?" She goes off to have an abortion and a religious vision, while he relives his painful memories with miserly absorption and arrives at the illumination that "every decision in this life is wrong from some point of view. . . . After all there is nowhere to go to and no one to go with; we're all alone." Such nihilism gives him a mystical satisfaction; his early longing for a desert is realized in Texas, among "just stones, waterless valleys, grey-blue rocks riven with gullies, a nonterrestrial landscape, even more desolate than the one I had seen in the Holy Land." Years later he tells Magdalena, "I felt happy there."

On the one hand, Klíma wants Adam to stand as the deadened lackey of a futile system, and on the other wants him to voice his own profoundest thoughts. Beneath this fable of a judge found wanting is a search for religious meaning—both Adam and Alena have visions of God—and a certain amount of private complaint. First published underground in 1978, and revised in 1986, *Judge on Trial* is an older novel than *Love and Garbage*, which was written between 1983 and 1986. Less overtly autobiographical, the earlier novel seems more cumbersomely heavy-hearted, more of a "working-through." A veritable thematic gridlock builds up as Adam, the end of the book in sight, counsels his reeling self: "It was immaterial what would happen next. Only an effeminate, pampered and introverted mentality demanded the assurance that everything that caused it to rejoice at a given moment, everything that nourished and intoxicated its body and soul, would last for ever and ever. There was no way of insuring the future, one could only lose the present." By way of illustration, the plot peters out inconclusively. The mystery of the Karel Kozlík case is never unravelled, nor is the marriage of our Communist Adam definitely resumed or dissolved. That so bulky an epic of antisocialist realism ends in mid-air surprises us. Compared (as he inevitably must be) to Kundera, Klíma is a strenuous moralist, a dogged piler-on. Suggestiveness and humor were weapons writers under Communism developed; Klíma—though he presents some hectic dialogues of lovers and spouses that make us sadly smile—seems deficient in both. *Judge on Trial* is a novel of high purpose and considerable richness, spoiled by a sententious tone and a soggy hero.

Of Sickened Times

ON CLOWNS: THE DICTATOR AND THE ARTIST, by Norman Manea, translated from the Romanian by Cornelia Golna, Irina Livezeanu, Joel Agee, Anselm Hollo, and Alexandra Bley-Vroman. 178 pp. Grove Weidenfeld, 1992.

OCTOBER, EIGHT O'CLOCK, by Norman Manea, translated from the Romanian by Cornelia Golna, Mara Soceanu Vamos, Marguerite Dorian, Elliott B. Urdang, Max Bleyleben, and Anselm Hollo. 216 pp. Grove Weidenfeld, 1992.

The collapse of Communism in Eastern Europe has deprived the region's writers of a noble possibility, that of dissidence. As long as their totalitarian states sought to maintain a monopoly on truth, enlisting culture as a branch of propaganda, individual truth-tellers with even a particle of defiant integrity enacted a heroic role. Dangerous and harried though their lives were, threatened by suppression and exile if not, as under Stalin, imprisonment and death, they had no fear of irrelevance. Their subversive mission was clear. Published by foreign presses and internal samizdat, their poems and fictions embodied freedom; in the free world, best-sellerdom and celebrity status rewarded Pasternak, Solzhenitsyn, Sinyavsky, and Brodsky for defying the Soviet censors. If the writers of the satellite nations, with the possible exception of Czechoslovakia's Josef Švorecký and Milan Kundera, failed to excite the same bursts of sympathetic attention in the easily distracted West, publishers here did bring forth, to respectful attention, translations of Poland's Tadeusz Konwicki, East Germany's Uwe Johnson and Reiner Kunze, Yugoslavia's Danilo Kiš, and tiny, ferociously repressive Albania's remarkably relaxed Ismail Kadare. Romania's Norman Manea is the latest, and possibly will be the last, of those writers whose voices command extra attention for emanating from behind the Iron Curtain.

Grove Weidenfeld has published simultaneously a book of essays by Manea, *On Clowns: The Dictator and the Artist*, and a book of his stories,

October, Eight O'Clock. It seems safe to say that something has been lost in the many-handed translation: the essays, though finely and judiciously phrased, are less informative than we expect, and the stories less entertaining. Manea has been in this country "a few years," he tells us in introducing his essays, and teaches literature at Bard College; he has already developed, or he came equipped with, a very capitalist sense of the writer as a surly waif. He is a self-described "convalescent," whose nagging malaise spreads through his pages like a faintly sweet fog of wary ego. His "wounds," he avers, have left him "with no more than a moderate optimism, no matter on which meridian his future is taking new roots. Perhaps that is why the vivacity of victory and the joy of liberation do not sound in these pages."

All Communist countries were unhappy in their own way, and Romania's case brimmed with paradoxes. In a part of Europe dominated by Slavs, the ancient nation is a "Latin island," speaking a Romance language and tracing its Latinity back to its settlement, in the second and third centuries, as the Roman province of Dacia. A monarchy beset by fascist parties, it managed to fight on both sides in World War II, and emerged bigger in 1945 than it had been in 1940. Though cursed with a long and virulent tradition of anti-Semitism, it withheld from the Nazi Holocaust several hundred thousands of its Jews. And though Nicolae Ceauşescu, its leader from 1965 on, appeared to the West as an enlightened independent who took a number of foreign-policy steps in defiance of the Moscow line—establishing diplomatic relations with West Germany in 1967, maintaining friendly relations with Israel after the 1967 war, and refusing to join in the 1968 invasion of Czechoslovakia—he ended by creating a personal dictatorship as absurd and ruinous as that of any Third World megalomaniac. Of the six satellite Communist states of Eastern Europe, only Romania overthrew its government with gunfire, bloodshed, and the execution of the leader. Manea ascribes to his native land "a national history consisting of a series of catastrophes, a geographic position at the crossroads of East and West, directly in the path—and at the mercy—of interests more powerful than one's own: all this probably teaches caution." The national attitude is summed up in the phrase *bun simt*, which literally means "good sense" and connotes "a kind of instinctual delicacy in human relations." It was this widespread delicacy, we are left to conclude, that allowed Ceauşescu to become an ever more vicious tyrant, who "changed the whole country into a huge kindergarten populated by militarized and industrious children"—"a whole nation subjugated, hungry, humiliated, and forced to celebrate the crime ceaselessly."

In the title essay Manea asks the crucial question: "Are the tyrant and the suppressed masses truly irreconcilable in every respect, or is it a matter of unconscious reciprocal stimulation?" Instead of concentrating on the answer, however, he indignantly rehearses Ceauşescu's clownishness—"his ridiculous, self-awarded, ever more pompous titles, his endless speeches full of vast platitudes with their perennial hoarse bathos . . . his stutter and puppetlike gestures, his manic insistence and schizophrenic industry, and his perplexity when confronted with anything still alive and spontaneous"—and indulges himself in variations on the metaphoric pairing of the White Clown (the totalitarian dictator, "the clown, a little white mouse, a carrier of the plague: a death's-head of nothingness") and Auguste the Fool, who represents the artist and the poet and his own autobiographical persona, as elaborated in an earlier work, *Auguste the Fool's Apprenticeship Years.*

Manea was fifty when he emigrated, in 1986, and had been a published writer for nearly twenty years. His essays "Censor's Report" and "The History of an Interview" describe personal ordeals at the hands of state thought-control, which over the years acquired an urbane and reasonable face. "An elegant young man from the 'Writers Section' [of the Securitate, the state security system] was polite and cool, he spoke openly. For more than an hour he discussed . . . Faulkner. And discussed him competently, I must admit. This confirmed the success that the Securitate had had in recent decades in recruiting some of the best university graduates." The specimen censor's report on Manea's novel—politely deploring the book's negativity, pleading for "balance," and advising that the text be modified "by the elimination of . . . excesses in the area of caricature, irony, and grotesquery" and "the insertion of some positive, affirmative passages"—sounds much like an American publisher encouraging a writer to turn his querulous *Bildungsroman* into an upbeat best-seller. In fact, Manea took the advice and, with the help of a sympathetic editor, did publish the novel; it sold out its large edition of twenty-six thousand copies and received favorable reviews. The compromised author tells us movingly:

> Was I happy when I saw my newly published book? It had been a difficult and unhoped-for birth. My crippled baby, though it was not as I had imagined it, was still mine. The bonds that joined us, strong and scarred, were of this time and place in which we struggled, mutilated ourselves, to stay on the surface.

Nevertheless, he left Romania few months later. A fitfully, erratically enlightened dictatorship was in some ways worse than absolutism. "I am a writer who could not have been published during the Stalinist era. My generation grew up in the ambiguous, tortured, agonizing period (the 'enlightened years') of the new dictatorship." In the atmosphere of duplicity both official and unofficial, "the guilt was general but there were many levels. Some were guilty, while others had guilt imposed upon them."

"Felix Culpa" is the title of the essay that American readers may find most interesting, since it deals with a Romanian immigrant much admired here, the late Mircea Eliade, a professor at the University of Chicago Divinity School and the author of, among fifty books, the magisterial four-volume *History of Religious Ideas*. Eliade, a scholarly prodigy, received his Ph.D. from the University of Bucharest in 1933 and was appointed an assistant to the famous Nae Ionescu, a professor of logic and metaphysics. Eliade, Manea explains, "was fascinated by his mentor and friend, even when Ionescu became a propagandist for Italian fascism and German national socialism and a passionate supporter of the Iron Guard, the extreme-right-wing Romanian nationalist movement." Eliade himself went on record as a staunch admirer of Mussolini and the Iron Guard, before the Guard's suppression and Eliade's departure, in 1940—first to London, then to Lisbon, where he composed a book in praise of Portugal's dictator, Antonio Salazar. After the war, Eliade's Iron Guard associations prevented his return to Communist Romania, and he taught at various European universities and finally, in 1956, came to the United States. His frequent autobiographical writings gave him ample opportunity to recant or at least discuss his earlier pro-fascist views, but he never did, to Manea's disappointment. It *is* disappointing: the bulk of right-wing intellectuals and artists from Fascism's Thirties heyday— Pound, Hamsun, Céline, Heidegger, most notoriously—did not publicly express much repentance. Though a few, like Eliade and Paul de Man, came to the United States and became prominent citizens of our pluralistic democracy, almost none announced that they had been mistaken or had contributed their voices to what became a tide of mass murder. When Eliade's Iron Guard sympathies were, in his later life, cited against him (as in Furio Jesi's *Culture of the Right* in 1979), he opted for silence and, in his published journals, for defensive dismissals that hinted at Israeli plots or a campaign "to eliminate me from among the favorites for the Nobel Prize." More than once, he referred to his "adoration for Nae Ionescu" as a *felix culpa*, a happy guilt. Manea rightly regrets that so little honest testimony has emerged from the fellow-travellers of fascism, but he seems to prejudge what that testimony would be when he writes, "If these 'guilty' witnesses could reveal the essentials of the monstrous banality of evil, we could probably not only understand more thoroughly the past but also have a better idea of the future of humanity." But fascism's nationalistic and racial romanticism may not ever have seemed evil or banal to its adherents, even though, like the sexual romanticism of youth, it had been outgrown or proven impracticable.

In Romania's case, right-wing ideology took the form of "Romanianism," a xenophobic, anti-Semitic reaction to the enlargement of the country, by the terms of the Treaty of Versailles after World War I, to include sizable minority populations of Hungarians, Jews, and Germans. The word "Romanianism" existed since the nineteenth century and contained a Christian Orthodox streak going back to Byzantium; the Iron Guard's original name was the Legion of the Archangel Michael. The notion of a mystical ethnic purity could well have appealed to a connoisseur of myths. Eliade conceived of Romanianism as being "above politics." The language of his Thirties journalism, however, does not blink at the savage side of purification in practice: "Social reforms will be enacted with considerable brutality, every corner of the provinces now overrun with foreigners will be recolonized, all traitors will be punished, the myth of our State will extend all across the country" (1937); "We await a nationalist Romania, frenzied and chauvinistic, armed and vigorous, ruthless and vengeful" (1938). His chauvinism, Manea points out, took "the form of anti-Hungarian and anti-Slavic babble" (Eliade described the Hungarians as "after the Bulgarians the most imbecilic people ever to have existed") more than that of anti-Semitism. Nevertheless, anti-Semitism was a central tenet of Romanianism, whose biases persisted into the Communist regime: "Ceauşescu's Stalinism gradually became a camouflaged fascism." Now, post-Ceauşescu, a reëmerged right-wing press has canonized Nae Ionescu and his disciple Mircea Eliade.

In the last essay of the collection, "The History of an Interview," Manea, a Jew, tells us that when a disarming young man came from the Securitate in 1985 to talk to him about his application for a passport to France and Germany, he realized that "the officer was from the Department of Minorities." When Manea inquired, "Why are nationalistic, anti-intellectual, anti-Semitic, and anti-Western texts still being printed?" he affably called Manea "a European type" and asked him, "Why don't you emigrate?" The passport came through, as did passports for Manea and his wife a year later, when he decided that "the situation in the country was growing ever more dangerous, and my own had probably reached its limits." He emigrated. A writer does not lightly abandon the homeland of his language. Manea's account of old disputes with certain fellow-writers is a detailed pathological report that only specialists may enjoy, but in the course of it he gives his life story in a paragraph:

I did not want to accept the ethnic corner in which the Authority was trying to isolate me. The child who had come back from the concentration camp at the end of the war wanted at all cost to forget, at all cost to be like everyone else. Forty years later, must I again feel a victim? I could not bear it. I mistrusted those who professionalized their laments and I hated those who provoked them.

The fifteen stories of *October, Eight O'Clock* rehearse that history, in the veiled language of fiction. This collection was published in Romania in the fall of 1981, when Communism appeared to have a permanent lock on a vast territory from Prague to Pyongyang. This simple and helpful bibliographical date is nowhere divulged in the book itself, or on its jacket, but is revealed in Manea's book of essays, where he discusses an impolitic interview he gave at about the same time. *October, Eight O'Clock* was published, then, in a police state, a circumstance that goes a good way toward explaining what to this Western reader seemed the stories' principal fault: they feel cryptic. They are arranged in the order of the protagonist's age, and a muffled autobiography runs through them—an increasingly aggrieved, dispirited life whose critical moments and intimate moods we are invited to share without proper introductions' ever having been performed.

Manea's early stories, of childhood, are the clearest, though their bleak and savage environment would come as a puzzlement to the reader who did not know that the author, in 1941, at the age of five, was deported with his family to an internment camp in the Ukraine. Though not an extermination camp, like those in Poland, this camp was bad enough. The first story, "The Sweater," like Cynthia Ozick's "The Shawl," conjures up extreme deprivation by means of a coveted object in a world almost without furnishings. The narrator's mother, who is free to work in the countryside, knitting for peasants, has pieced together a sweater for her dying daughter, Mara. When this child dies, the sweater descends to her brother, yet when he puts it on he becomes sick and nearly dies himself. His reconciliation with the sweater can serve as an index of Manea's considerable powers of evocation:

> I put my nose, my whole face, in its roughness, once so soft and good, to let myself be intoxicated by its warmth, like that of toasted bread or boiled potatoes, or by the smell of fresh sawdust, or the fragrance of milk, of rain, of leaves, or by the longing for pencils and apples. But it was not like that; rather a strange odor, that of mold. Something rotten and penetrating. Or only sharp, suffocating, I don't remember. It had become darker, and unfamiliar, unappealing.

With such sensory penetration the story earns its chilling last sentence: "Time itself had sickened, and we belonged to it."

When advancing Russian armies and peace dissolve the world of the internment camp, with its death-imitating children's games (in the story "Death") and proud pantomimes of normal life ("Proust's Tea"), the boy hero moves into a world where unaccustomed food nauseates him ("We Might Have Been Four"), where other children call him "kike" ("The Balls of Faded Yarn"), and where the rhetoric of Communism is already establishing itself. In "Weddings," an older cousin harshly schools the little survivor in a speech remembering the miseries of the war, which he then gives over and over. A quoted fragment of the speech displays its pro-Soviet flavor: ". . . our brothers, in whose hands we saw a loaf of bread, when we had forgotten what bread looked like. And we say to you, let us not forget, let us not forgive, let us punish those who . . ." After the first success, the cousin fades away, "off his rocker," "roaming the countryside with banks of rebels," and his protégé, who has "become skillful at shielding his feelings by retreating behind a pale mask of sleepiness," gives the speech repeatedly, at weddings and anniversaries, name days and birthdays. The speech begins, "We, who haven't known the meaning of childhood . . ." But the child isn't allowed to know it; he is kept up late, through the dregs of parties, offering crowds "his old, choking fears." This rhetorical exploitation is capped by a rhetorical coda of the author's: "Only at dawn did he feel the smoke choking him again. He reeled, dizzy with weariness and sadness." To a child of the camps, peacetime Romania is a world of hidden menace, where words have a strange life of their own ("The Exact Hour") and a book of fairy tales, read over and over, is a way to come "to grips with the enchantment," the fact that "anything could become anything": "The fairy tales were real, and each one held a threat. They were real, he felt it, the old story is coming back. The fear had come back."

Teachers figure in a number of the stories, with the recurrent suspicion that being taught is a way of being corrupted. "The Instructor" contrasts a handsome young instructor at a Soviet Young Pioneer camp, who enlists his prize camper as a reader of the other campers' letters, and a plump, pale, hoarse old rabbi, who, as a favor to the boy's late grandfather, has prepared him for his bar mitzvah with lessons in Hebrew and diffident lectures in Judaic theology. The unbelieving boy has submitted, to win his parents' permission to go to the Young Pioneer camp; there he falls ill in disgust at being enlisted as a censor and a spy. When he meets the rabbi for the last time, he learns that at school he had been a party to expelling the rabbi's daughter for not doing homework on Saturdays. He confesses aloud, "Yes, I swallowed the poison, my instructors hoped I deserved this honor, this horror . . ." and inwardly concludes, "Better alone! Without parents, instructors." This is powerful material, this portrait of an adolescent torn between two unconvincing ideologies, but it is awkwardly wrapped in cinematic conceits and an obliquity necessitated, presumably, by the constrained literary environment.

As the hero matures, it becomes increasingly difficult to know exactly what is going on. In "Summer," does he blackmail the servant girl into sleeping with him, or does he only fantasize it? In the longest of the stories, "The Turning Point," what happens to the carefully described wife and sister-in-law with whom he visits the sea at the end of his university studies? Where does the heroine of a later visit, given the pop-star name of Nana Mouskouri, come from, and where does she go to? Well, women come and go in a man's life, and Communist intellectuals, repressed above the neck, often lead freewheeling sex lives. Still, the oneiric slipperiness of detail muddles the force of the story's central relation—the hero's almost suicidal fascination with the sea, "its magnificent rebellion, its immense crash."

In this tale, and in the four shorter that follow and that conclude the collection, an increasingly violent poetry of description offers itself as a substitute for events:

> Hours of bread, and chains, struggling in silence, gritting teeth, refusing, harboring hatred, fleeing the noise of ovations that accompanied complicity and moral decline. It goes without saying that heroics were futile: the dragon's arms reached everywhere, they caught you and beat you down, time and again, until you finally learned the drumbeat of this place.

A hovering, ironic rage reminds us of Dostoevsky's Underground Man, jeering at the Victorian age's Crystal Palace. "I confess," declares Manea's nameless hero, "that the only transgression I haven't been able to rid myself of, in this steadily descending spiral of life, is my lack of faith in the charity of the authorities. I deny that anyone has the right to determine what is good or bad for me." The citizens all around the hero are "poisoned or crushed by something invisible, enormous, with a miraculous power to discourage them even before they've tried anything." Small wonder that the rebellion and crash of the sea are irresistibly inviting, even to a man who can hardly swim and who almost drowns. The stress of life on land goads the writer to hysterical and opaque outbursts of language:

> Her lissome young body became a long piece of steel that bent under the weight of her suffering until, in their violent embrace, it burst in a rain of

silvery sparks. Their youth: a bloody membrane; the glasslike breaks, the reconciliations; the torture of frail, melancholy cannibals; hypocrisy, cruelty; the great feral leap.

The ultimate referent for all this strangulated emotion, this feverish imagery, remains obscure, unmentionable. But in the essay "On Clowns" the villain is clear enough: "His caricature grins from every wall of the country, the country that once embodied hope. A hope of a life, for better or worse, but a life: in the light of youth, at the time of decline, in the intoxication of love, in rebellious dreams as well as bitter disappointment." Totalitarianism, in its two major twentieth-century forms, has stolen Manea's life from him. A childhood in a Nazi internment camp yielded, with scarcely a pause, to a youth under an imposed Communism; an evil fairy tale became a grotesque circus. A captive victim, he has withstood his life rather than lived it; unlike Koestler and Kundera and Eliade and E. M. Cioran, he never participated in the illusions that give rise to totalitarianism, so his testimony is intelligent and plaintive rather than involving. Though Manea lays claim to "deep solidarity with people's unhappiness"—the unhappiness of "a whole shackled nation"— he was "instinctively suspicious and disdainful of [Ceauşescu] even before he started baring his teeth in the horrendous Grand Guignol performance." Consistently disdainful and helpless, he disdains, in the fiction of *October, Eight O'Clock*, the objectifying, counteraggressive satire we find in Konwicki and Kiš, and in his essays presents an eloquent but faintly etiolated *non mea culpa*.

Gender Benders

SHE LOVES ME, by Péter Esterházy, translated from the Hungarian by Judith Sollosy. 195 pp. Northwestern University Press, 1997.

Naughtiness is dissidence, as the writers of Eastern Europe well knew during their forty years of being tied to Mother Russia's apron strings. The heroes of Milan Kundera and Tadeusz Konwicki, among others, found relief from the imposed politics of Soviet Communism in the self-inflicted politics of sex; defiance found expression in anarchic, dissipated lives. An American version of this mood survives in Philip Roth's *The Prague Orgy*, a dishevelled and lewd postscript to the Zuckerman trilogy. "You like orgies, you come with me," Zuckerman is told. "Since the Russians, the best orgies in Europe are in Czechoslovakia. Less liberty, better fucks."

But what now, in a post-Communist world with all the usual capitalist troubles, including the commercialism of sex and the anomie of surfeit? Can naughtiness have lost its potent point? Péter Esterházy, whose *A Little Hungarian Pornography* was published in Budapest in 1983, and whose *The Book of Hrabal* came out there in 1990, as Communism crumbled, continues to anatomize—ruthlessly, obsessively—gender relations, in a sequence of ninety-seven brief chapters published under the title of *She Loves Me*. The first chapter in its entirety reads: "There's this woman. She loves me." The next chapter begins: "There's this woman. She hates me." It is not necessarily the same woman. The second woman calls the narrator Shadow, because he never leaves her side. She makes shadow pictures of a bunny rabbit or an eagle on a convenient wall, and has a father who "hates my guts and refers to my work as shadow play." Esterházy's prose is jumpy, allusive, slangy; we feel that something is being lost in translation, though Ms. Sollosy, the translator, gamely comes up with a lot of tricksome English. In Chapter 6, we read:

> This is why, when I spot her in a place fit for kissing—and there is hardly any place left these days that private or social consensus, virtue or sobriety, has put under interdiction—I up and run at her, Speedy Gonzales, that's me! and *wham!*, I slam into her, we slam into each other with no time to spare, because I know only too well that otherwise this foul emptiness, this putrid absence of absence will overwhelm me, this fetid nothingness, this pestiferous air which, and this has been known to happen, makes me retch—snot and saliva running together—though this, too, is a form of *intercourse*, I guess.

I guess. The translator seems to be hurrying to keep up with the writer, and the writer with his racing mind. The input arrives too fast for him or the reader to sort out. Few of the episodes have time to build into anything like what we might call a picture of a relationship. The woman in Chapter 63, for instance, "hates the whole world, and she'll do you a bad turn when she can. She won't relay messages, or she makes up false ones." She oversalts the food and "repeatedly denies having an orgasm, though at times the saliva runs down the corner of her lips." She glues together pages of the narrator's favorite books (Borges is named), so each becomes "like an awkward piece of brick or a secret puzzle," and he "would cease to be a person, if only she did not hate me quite so faithfully." Calvino is also invoked; the heroine of Chapter 74 ("She speaks Greek. She's got freckles"), it is asserted, "loves Italo Calvino and oatflakes." But Calvino, in *his* books of many small chapters, like *Invisible Cities* and *Mr. Palomar*, generated a strong sense of patterned arrangement, of cumulative movement toward a horizon of useful philosophical conclusion. Esterházy begins and ends on the same pitch, frenetic and enigmatic, and leaves the reader feeling excluded from ninety-seven private jokes.

Still, there is vividness, an electric crackle. The sentences are active and concrete. Physical details leap from the murk of emotional ambivalence. The women are characterized by bad breath, eyebrows "like some thicket," gout, dwarfishness, obesity, rippling thighs, blotchiness, chapped lips, possible dentures, inflamed gums, falling hair, and big bottoms. Their pubic hair receives close inspection: of the heroine of Chapter 82 we are told, "Her pubic hair is red, light red, a stone-washed pink. . . . From very close up, at follicle-distance, it's like a forest of larch trees (*Larix decidua*)." Our noses are energetically rubbed in love's physicality. The narrator, in Chapter 17, is afflicted with "some sort of foul rash." His lady friend, far from daunted,

> watched ecstatically as the rashes burst open or developed into minuscule boils with yellow centres that let off a sulphurous, decaying stench. She was crazy about them, she fondled and kissed them, she smeared herself with their juices. It was horrible. I counted for nothing, only my boils.

C'est la vie, c'est l'amour. The book's overall mood of amused cynicism, of wry psychologizing, feels very European. Americans pull a longer face before the conundrums of sex—its attempt "to pass somehow, no matter how, beyond the endless expanse of the finite," its rhythm of self-abandonment and self-absorption, its kinky stimulations and post-coital disenchantment. Esterházy, in a chapter that begins, "There's this woman. She ha . . . (loves me)," describes erotic fire as "that certain gleaming sparkle between repulsion and ecstasy." Trained as a mathematician, he takes an inventory of the wrinkles in gender relations. As the book wears on, the protean couple at its heart feel more and more married. In Chapter 91, they have been together for twenty-eight years and their son is queer. In Chapter 95, "She loves me, except she's as scared of my prick as the devil is of incense"; in her fright she jumps on the table and ruins a dinner party they are giving. In the last chapter, "She loves me less and less, and wants me more and more." They breathe the same air. The hero doesn't have a toothbrush or a name to call his own. Thus ends, in a no-man's-land, Esterházy's willy-nilly tour of the craggy, chasmed terrain where the sexes manage to meet.

OTHER CONTINENTS

A Woman's Continent

MATING, by Norman Rush. 480 pp. Knopf, 1991.

BRAZZAVILLE BEACH, by William Boyd. 316 pp. Morrow, 1991.

Who would have dared believe that American book-buyers would be offered within three months' time not one but *two* novels by male authors about, and narrated by, white superwomen in Africa? Both heroines are formidably erudite, and both forthrightly pursue a man who takes their fancy. Both have rather slangy, in-your-face prose styles, and both discuss, with a frankness new to romantic heroines, their lower functions.* Both witness a utopian society tipping off balance. Both novels are rather aggressively brilliant and information-laden, and both struck this reader as exhilarating journeys of explorations, intelligently planned and generously provisioned. The more recently published, *Mating*, is by an American, Norman Rush, and the other, *Brazzaville Beach*, is by a Briton,

---

*Lest such an allegation appear to be recklessly unsubstantiated:

"That night we were given a meaty stew and a big mound of doughy pudding to eat. When I asked what the meat was I was told bushpig. It was stringy and lean with a strong gamey taste. Whatever it was it acted as a powerful aperient on my crammed, immobile gut. I went outside and shat copiously behind one of the sheds."

And:

"As he toweled himself dry, I could see he was growing aroused. I think he liked me to be forthright and uninhibited. Once, when he had been showering, I had come into the bathroom and had a shit. I hadn't given it any thought but Usman told me after he had been shocked and exhilarated."

Both quotations come from *Brazzaville Beach*. Rush's heroine's eliminations are more complicated. She offends her future lover at their first meeting by rushing into his scientifically planned outhouse and urinating on feces: "It seems I was the only educated human

William Boyd. Both authors have had, needless to say, some experience of Africa: Boyd, of Scots parentage, was born in Ghana, and lived in Africa off and on until he was twenty-two; Rush for five years worked with the Peace Corps in Botswana. Both display, besides African experience, imagination—the questing faculty that can build adventures from the paper material of history, anthropology, even mathematics, and that here launches each writer on a prolonged sojourn in a female sensibility. The women are plausible enough, though one tends to picture them in safari jackets and khaki trousers, and wearing very sensible shoes.

The heroine of *Mating* made her debut in *The New Yorker*; a short story printed in 1983, "Bruns," shows her acting as a somewhat flip witness to the Boer persecution, in a Botswana village, of a saintly Dutch volunteer. At the outset of *Mating*, she alludes to the incident: "I had been a bystander during something interpersonally very nasty in Keteng. . . . A Dutch cooperant had been hounded to death by the local power structure." In the lengthy novel as in the short story, she is unnamed, though we are readily told that she is thirty-two, big-breasted, menstruating irregularly, and frustrated in both her academic career— her thesis in nutritional anthropology concerns hunter-gatherers, who have ceased to exist even in the remotest areas—and her sex life. Why Norman Rush didn't deign to name his ever-present central figure is as obscure to me as his refusal to use any sort of quotation marks, letting us guess at the spoken sentences bobbing in the streams of consciousness and first-person narration, e.g., "Do you know me? I asked her. Because you seem to be following me. It wasn't hostile. She admitted immediately she was following me," and "Ah, but Nel I have a few things to do. He lets you call him Nel. But pretty soon I'll be gone." These stylistic renunciations serve, I suppose, to let the reader know that he is perusing not just any old saga of African hardship and politicized courtship but a novel with aggressive modernist designs on his conventional reading habits.

The action is simple but stately, a curve of neediness, attraction, pur-

---

being who had never heard of the universally known fact that urea keeps feces from composting properly." When she sets out to pursue him across the Kalahari Desert, she commits the faux pas of "gorging on eggs and naturally getting constipated." At one point, she is led into a grassy depression by her "desperate feeling about my innards. There was a feeling of privacy. . . . I was hoping and yearning for a sign that this might be the place where I would be restored to normal in this respect at least, that the enclosedness of the scene might summon something." When she has achieved cohabitation, the summonings are shared: "And not to venture too far into the underside of our household humor, he also laughed inordinately when I was getting into bed and slightly farted and he said Is that the way you greet me? I replied quick as a flash That's the only language you understand."

NORMAN RUSH : 399

suit, capture, fulfillment, disillusion, and departure that is traced through close to five hundred big pages bristling with such recondite terms as "tonus," "makhoa," "tallywhackers," "lustral," "samoosa," "suigenerism," "cornucopious," "lanugo," "superfices," "cothurni," "karosses," "lolwapas," "idioverse," "noetic," "ketosis," "vitromania," "inter pocula," "rubiconic," "uchronia," "watership," "toriis," "langur," "ovaldavels" (from "rondavels"), "utilitariana," "sternocleidomastoids," "pygmalious," "stimmung," "credulism," "megrim," "dagga," "bogobe," "cryptomnesia" "urticaria," "elenchus," "entelechies," "geniusly," "crescive," "evanition," and "bromeliad." Some of the African terms are in a brief glossary, but some aren't, and these, plus the Latin and French tags and the puckish neologisms, keep the going stiff, and remind us that Mr. Rush and his loquacious narrator are doing their bit to freshen up the English language. "She was slightly unfresh," we are told of an otherwise irresistible African girl in one of Mr. Rush's stories, "Alone in Africa." In *Mating* this inflection is extended to, of an allegation, "It was unso."

Mating's style can be alarmingly brisk:

> There are barriers. Americans suffer the most. They come to Botswana wanting to be lovely to Africans. A wall confounds them. Behind it is something they sense is interesting. I could help them.

And unabashedly tongue-twisted:

> I think I also did a passage of invented eurhythmics whose real purpose was to wag my lower self in the face of the Kalahari, which I was letting myself feel fully as the organism that wants you to suffer that it truly is.

In the context of a brief encounter between the estranged, drunken, wistful wife of our hero, Nelson Denoon, and his by now thoroughly aroused thirty-two-year-old admirer, these stark sentences are subtle and moving:

> I had a sudden confused feeling toward her. I wanted to say I knew that what she was now was not what she had once been. I think I loved her for helping me. I wanted to say something like Neither am I always going to be like I am. There was no way to say it.

The novel is talky, but with an abruptness that keeps us awake and, now and then, makes us laugh. Except for the heroine's vivid days alone in the Kalahari, on her solitary way to Denoon's utopian, preponderantly female community of Tsau, and for the murky machinations whereby the disruptive hand of Boer South Africa darkens Tsau's sunny feminist order (driving Denoon out into the desert himself, for a survival experience that leaves him, to our heroine's taste, intolerably mystical), there is little action in the book, just discussion and description. Denoon and his anonymous lady love to talk: up on his soapbox, he speaks in entire essays and spouts improbable facts, such as that ninety percent of all the adolescents who have ever lived are alive today, and the Jewish Hell is physically next door to Paradise, with a low wall between them, for the saved's viewing pleasure. Embowered, like Antony and Cleopatra, in a world of wide space, the two lovers seem a typical urban couple, confined to a stifling studio apartment of self-conscious relationship. Their exchanges are spiked with remarks like "You're giving me cognitive dissonance." As primly as a marriage manual, they labor to shed mutual enlightenment upon such intimate areas of togetherness as cunnilingus and flatulence. At one point in their laboriously evolving relations the heroine decides to tackle her lover like a research project, complete with exhaustive measurements: "The physical description I assembled is a masterpiece of some kind. I doubt that there is a more minute physical description of one human being by another anywhere." We read about Denoon's skin, his genitals, his childhood traumas, his cornucopious political and sociological views (beamed from a stratosphere somewhere beyond socialism), his jokes, his silences, his smell ("It was positive and faintly like a veal soup my mother made five or so times in my life when for some unknown reason she was elated about something. It was a trace smell subtending the soap, diesel, and smoke amalgam"). If, for all the unstinted Denoon particulars, I had some trouble assembling them into a personality, it may be that I am unaccustomed to perceiving men so exclusively as sex objects, as targets of the mating instinct. Perhaps my own iota of testosterone compelled me, in view of the larger-than-life, spectacularly nubile woman interposing herself between us, to dislike Denoon; at any rate, I did dislike him, except at the end, where he incurs *her* dislike by becoming passive, enigmatic, and religious.

Nor was Tsau quite real to me. "How serious is this place, au fond?" our female quester asks herself. When she first glimpses it, she reflects: "In its symmetry and neatness and Mediterranean color scheme it looked like a town in the Babar books, but in its atmosphere there was something operatic or extravagant. I had no referent for it." It seems a kind of toy for Mr. Rush's imagination, with less African flavor to it than the dusty milieux of his short stories. The entire town of Tsau, on a green elevation above the desert, twinkles: "There was the ubiquitous flashing and glinting . . . due . . . to the various mirrors and solar instruments and other glass oddments that seemed to be specific to the place." Or, in a sentence of not untypical semi-opacity: "If you look at Tsau at night from out in the plain or from the top of the koppie you can imagine the dots and dashes the lit bricks become constituting a message in code." Denoon is possessed by vitromania; glass, that fruit of heat and sand, fascinates him, and the fascination goes back to a magical castle that he made of his alcoholic father's empties, and that his father drunkenly smashed. Tsau, though equipped with a geography, a technology, a politics, an economic rationale, and animated personnel, does not quite belong to Africa, any more than the self-contained luxury Hiltons of the West Indies belong to their islands. It reminded me of Dr. Nemo's self-sufficient submarine *Nautilus*—which contains all the letters of "Tsau"—with solar power the central magic instead of a glamorized electricity and Denoon's glassworks replacing as a meditation center Dr. Nemo's pipe organ. It is one more of the mystery cities that the imperial Western imagination has willed to exist in Africa, a King Solomon's Mines imposed upon the compliant native darkness. Mr. Rush is more sensitive to the natives' cultural integrity than Rider Haggard was. In one of *Mating*'s few bursts of African English, a young woman protests Denoon's anti-church, anti-missionary sermons: "Why are you speaking so long with saying we must not have beliefs whilst you are thrusting beliefs upon these people from long before when we first came here? . . . When whitemen come amongst the people it is always for lying." Denoon does not disagree with her; a talk he presents is sardonically subtitled "The Destruction of Africa Accelerated by Her Benefactors, Present Company Not Excepted." Liberal futility is built into Denoonist liberalism; politically the book (which takes place in the early Eighties) has an ambiguous, salty taste, that of Sixties idealism reduced under Reagan to helpless sneering. Back in California, the heroine quips, "Being in America is like being stabbed to death with a butter knife by a weakling," and sardonically portrays her success as a lecturer on the Third World:

> I leave every group I speak to with at least this thought—that a true holocaust in the world is the thing we call development, which I tell them means the superimposition of market economies on traditional and unprepared third world cultures by force and fraud circa 1880 to the present, and that this has been the seedbed of the televised spectacle of famine, misery, and disease confronting us in the comfort of our homes.
>   They love me for it.

She left this reader with something not every novel can muster— a strong sense of human presence. If Denoon is Dr. Nemo, she is a wry and curvy Captain Ahab, immense in her singleness of pursuit of the white whale of "equilibrium or perfect mating," and compelling in the exhaustiveness and honesty of the log she keeps during the chase. Her intellectual commentary is so rife with liberal self-debunking and post-Christian, post-Marcusian dubiousness that whether she and Denoon will wind up as legally or spiritually one doesn't excite us very much—far less than, say, little Jane Eyre's eventual acquisition, in a more romantic century, of the humbled Rochester. Not only Denoon but solar power, that sacredest of New Age sacred cows, fail to escape her withering doubts: "Or had Denoon always been an impostor without my noticing it, starting with so eloquently leading the world to expect Tsau was going to be some liberating municipal bromeliad running on sun and sweet breezes when in fact although the place was bristling and glittering with solar hardware how much did it do? . . . People had solar cookers but barely used them. And what was Tsau to him, really? Who was Tsau for?" Yet, with all her romantic overvaluations deconstructed, she lives, thinks, talks; her thoughts have gristle and irony, her sensations and intuitions are startlingly real. What she does for Denoon, the author does for her: describes a human being with a fanatic thoroughness. If *Mating* feels thin on its geopolitical edges, it is energetically dense along its chosen axis, the sensibility and observations of its heroine. Our frustrated female anthropologist achieves a primal size worthy of her chosen continent; she could not have grown this way back in the United States, any more than Denoon could have created his vitreous utopia there. Her account of crossing the Kalahari is breathtaking, as raw nature and as human psychology in crisis circumstances. Her internalization of Africa comes to a later climax as a thunderstorm approaches Tsau:

> It crawled toward us, magnificent and immense. It looked organic, I thought, more like an electrified placenta than anything else. The breadth of the lightning display was amazing. . . . Never have I seen any natural event like it. I shuddered and had pop philosophical insights, viz. human beings are microcosms of this vast oncoming system in that the thing that allows us to salivate and think and embrace is also electrical, in essence. We were related, this behemoth air beast and myself. I was its pale affiliate.

That "pale affiliate" is very pretty. She has felt herself amplified into grandeur. The first sentence of *Mating* states, "In Africa, you want more, I think."

What Hope Clearwater, the academically and sexually capable heroine of William Boyd's *Brazzaville Beach*, wants is escape from England, where her marriage to a mathematician has ended in disaster. Of *Mating*'s American expatriates, Denoon seems to be fleeing his native land's disgusting capitalism, and the Great Unnamed is getting away from her grossly overweight mother, whom she unkindly calls "the colossus of

Duluth." Both Americans have dislodged themselves from a "pathetic matrix." Hope, however, as her name suggests, is a positive person; she has no complaints about her parents, and her descriptions of England—especially the deer park and hedgerows that she is dating for an archaeological survey—have a loving redolence of ancient greenery and damp cottages. Nevertheless, she ends up in Africa, observing chimpanzees for the Grosso Arvore Research Project, which is headed by the highly regarded primatologist Eugene Mallabar. The unnamed country feels like Angola: there are a number of competing rebel armies, a long coastline, and traces of Portuguese colonization. The reader discovers Hope living alone on a beach recently named after a 1964 conference held in Brazzaville. The novel is her long reflection upon past events, done in a colloquial first person but with perhaps an excess of literary apparatus. Chapters more or less alternately set in England and in Africa march in synchrony to a double climax; in addition, each chapter begins with a few hundred words of italics on a variety of subjects, cluing the reader in on the meaning of ornate chapter titles like "What I Like to Do," "Usman Shoukry's Lemma," and "Cabbages Are Not Spheres." The novel's epigraph (from Plato) also serves as the last sentence, and Hope's "I" sometimes becomes the third-person "Hope Clearwater." All this wouldn't do for any old protagonist, but as a correlative for a shook-up intellectual's state of mind it gets by. *Brazzaville Beach* reads more easily than *Mating*, but it bulges no less with information—on mathematics, primatology, and botany both English and African, with expert digressions into shock therapy, modern weaponry and aircraft, theories of turbulence, and niceties of volleyball.

Mr. Boyd, educated, after his Ghanaian birth, at the universities of Nice, Glasgow, and Oxford, where he has taught, would seem to know everything. His novel *An Ice-Cream War* confidently moves about in the East Africa of 1914–18, and *The New Confessions* transatlantically roams through all of the twentieth century. He has an adroit and amiable narrative lightness, and some critics have classed him as a comic novelist, in the line of Evelyn Waugh and Kingsley Amis. But in *Brazzaville Beach* at least he shows little of the cheerful Tory heartlessness of those gentlemen—though he does show some linguistic snobbery, telling us of two different characters within thirty pages that "She [He] spoke [very] good English but with a pronounced [quite a heavy] accent." The primate capacity for violence, including ours, is his sombre theme, which he plays in a number of variations—cannibalism and warfare among chimpanzees, murderous and suicidal competition among intellectual speculators, the abstract mayhem coolly inflicted by mercenary pilots, and the malign farce of chaotic civil war. The heroine's adventures in this last vein, as the hostage of a small band of rebels called UNAMO that in peacetime formed a volleyball team called Atomique Boum, do happily echo the surreal Waugh of *Scoop* and *Black Mischief*, and provide some of the narrative's most poetic and indelible images. The slender, scared boy-soldiers stage a ghostly volleyball game in the bush, "in the soft evening light, their thin lanky bodies casting thinner and lankier shadows." Later, Hope and Dr. Amilcar, the wispy troop's leader, come across an unused antitank gun and its ammunition:

> He levered off the top of one of the flat wooden boxes. Inside, on a poly-styrene rack, like wine bottles, were three thin shells with lilac, onion-shaped tops, like domes on a Russian church. He removed one and held it out: it was rather a beautiful object, well designed, like the gun. The lilac shone with a luminescent glow in the yellowy light. Amilcar opened the breech of the gun and offered the onion nose to the opening. It slid in easily. It was far too small.

Dr. Amilcar muses, "Somebody from UNAMO bought this for us in Europe. I wonder what his commission was?" Thus the heroic aspirations of wars of liberation dwindle to the realities of a few frightened boys and a costly, useless weapon.

Like Bernard Malamud in his chimpanzee novel of nine years ago, *God's Grace*, Mr. Boyd was struck by that part of Jane Goodall's fieldwork which reported aggression and infanticide among the peaceable-seeming chimpanzees. Hope Clearwater's boss, Dr. Mallabar, has built a profitable reputation upon studies with such titles as *The Peaceful Primate* and *Primate's Progress*. His resistance—which becomes blind rage—to her and her African assistants' observations of unpeaceableness has its own grim comedy, and there is some graveyard humor back in England as Hope's husband, the mathematician John Clearwater, attempts to inspire his brain to formulate an immortal equation by betrancedly digging holes in the peaty English earth. But the humor of his eccentricity palls and becomes pitiful as she, who initially pursued him much as Denoon was pursued, realizes that he has become dysfunctional and must be left. Though nimble in the telling, *Brazzaville Beach* has the terror of life in it, and, like *Mating*, ends with its heroine alone, Africa her only consort. Mr. Boyd, a white African native, effortlessly names the trees, animates the chimpanzees, and describes the scenery. Compared with the Kalahari wilderness in *Mating*, his Africa is workaday; it borders on the dreary:

> I put my hands on my hips and looked around me. We could be almost anywhere in Africa, I recognized. The scene was at once typical and banal. A pot-holed road running straight through low scrubby forest, a scatter of

decrepit huts, a strange dry smell in the air of dust and vegetation, a big red sun about to dip below the treeline, the plaintive chirrup of crickets.

Nor is there much doing on Brazzaville Beach: "A boy watches three goats graze in the palm groves. A crab sidles into its hole. Someone laughs raucously in the village." Africa is certainly the most miserable of the continents these days. One might even say, looking at the famine, corruption, national debt, and now, on top of malaria and multitudinous parasites, the plague of AIDS, that it is hopeless. Yet for some Western-ers, among them Hope Clearwater, "that tall young woman who lives on Brazzaville Beach," it remains a place of healing, of spiritual opportunity.

A Heavy World

THE SEVEN SOLITUDES OF LORSA LOPEZ, by Sony Labou Tansi, translated from the French by Clive Wake. 129 pp. Heinemann, 1995.

Last summer, the dying Congolese novelist, playwright, and poet Sony Labou Tansi told the *New York Times* reporter Howard French, "Africa is the only continent left that has not found its way. We have this incredible wealth, of resources and spirit, but outsiders like France are just robbing us while blessing our dictators." Tansi made this statement in the remote village of Foufondou, in his native African state of Congo, where he had found remission from the symptoms of AIDS by way of herbal medicines and incantations that mixed "African traditional healing and Christian evangelism." Tansi told his interviewer, "I had been to hospitals in Braz-zaville and in Paris, but they had been unable to do anything for me. It wasn't until I came here, following the voice of a prophet, that my condi-tion really began to change. I should have come long ago." But native herbal concoctions had not helped Tansi's wife, Pierrette, who, lying emaciated and feeble on a mat, claimed that they had made her mouth so sore she could eat nothing but oranges. Within two weeks both she and Tansi were dead.

He was forty-eight and widely considered Central Africa's leading writer. His miserable end betokens the misery of Africa, a continent beset by AIDS, famine, poverty, tyranny, and genocidal massacre (Idi Amin's Uganda; Rwanda in 1994). The continent's journalists and writers, in-cluding Nigeria's Nobel Prize laureate Wole Soyinka, are vulnerable to censorship, imprisonment, exile, and worse. Within recent months, the

Nigerian regime of General Sani Abacha executed the playwright and television scenarist Ken Saro-Wiwa, on far-fetched charges, and upped its campaign of intimidation against journalists, confiscating an entire press run of the magazine *Tell*. Tansi's novel *The Antipeople* (1983; English translation from the French 1988) seethed with political despair. "What good is an ounce of justice in an ocean of shit?" one character asks, and another asks God, "Why did you create men?" A third asserts, "Things here have got beyond God. This is a heavy world. A heavy time." A fourth claims, "This is the most sordid time there has ever been," and the author in his own voice evokes "the huge hole of madness that was forming here; the plagues, the downpour." Even the revolutionary cause, striving to right wrongs, is a "carnivore," clamoring "to be stuffed sometimes with blind bodies."

Sony Labou Tansi's next novel, *The Seven Solitudes of Lorsa Lopez*, published in its original French in 1985, has been issued by Heinemann in its African Writers Series, as translated by Clive Wake. Grotesque, short, and crowded, this work of fiction cultivates fantasy and comedy in a mire of murder and hopeless governmental stagnation. The Francophone writers of Africa, composing in the language of Rimbaud and Céline, have tended more than their Anglophone peers to embrace surrealism—for example, Camara Laye in *The Radiance of the King* (1954) and Yambo Ouologuem in *Bound to Violence* (1968). And Tansi seems to have been reading Gabriel García Márquez: his novel begins with a murder which, like that in the Colombian writer's *Chronicle of a Death Foretold*, everybody knows is coming and is helpless to prevent; and he seeks to create, through a thick weave of fabulous incidents, a sense of enchanted communal identity like Macondo's in *One Hundred Years of Solitude*. But whereas García Márquez, however bloody and bizarre his narrative, maintains a stately tone, with a benign undercurrent of nostalgia, Tansi conjures on the edge of fury. "To be a poet nowadays," his foreword defiantly tells us, "is to want to ensure, with all one's strength, with all one's body and with all one's soul, that, in the face of guns, in the face of money (which in its turn becomes a gun), and above all in the face of received wisdom (upon which we poets have the authority to piss), no aspect of human reality is swept into the silence of history."

The novel takes place in Valancia, once the capital of an unnamed country but compelled to yield that honor to Nsanga-Norda, to which were transported "walls, bridges, municipal gardens, town squares, swimming pools, railway stations. . . . Even the water from the artificial lake of the Village of Passions, the seven drawbridges, the thirty-nine mausoleums, the fifteen triumphal arches, the nine Towers of Babel."

Scarcely has the reader wrapped his mind around this miracle of transport (reminiscent of the sale, in *The Autumn of the Patriarch*, of the sea to
the gringos) than he is asked to picture "the monster, Yogo Lobotolo
Yambi," who, "born of father unknown to the madwoman, Larmani
Yongo," was distinguished by

> seven heads crowned with a brass crest, twelve arms of unequal length, one
> leg in the shape of a grooved column ending in a sort of elephant's foot,
> thirteen highly polished jagged tusks, with thirteen orifices, four of them
> shaped like trunks ending in what resembled umbrellas made of solid lime-
> stone and which snapped like slow-worms when you touched them.

His mother attempted to drown so ungainly an infant in the estuary, but
he always came back, "with the heavy iron bar that was supposed to keep
him at the bottom of the sea still around his neck." This beast right out of
Revelation must symbolize something odious and onerous—the authorities fear that "a monster like that could easily seize power and hold it for
centuries"—but whether it was the many-headed colonizers or a home-
grown tyrant like Zaire's Mobutu Sese Seko I could not decide. Nor was
the location of Valancia clear to me: it is on the sea, near some loudly
groaning cliffs and an island shaped like Christ's head, and seems to have
been colonized not by the Belgians (like Zaire) or the French (like the
Republic of the Congo, once called the Middle French Congo and part
of French Equatorial Africa) but by the Portuguese, like Angola, which
lies to the south, and where Tansi spent some time. Magic-realist countries don't need a strict geography, of course, but in trying to grasp the
central political feature of the novel's landscape, the contrast between
coastal, feminist, rumpus-loving Valancia and vain, soulless, inland
Nsanga-Norda, one wonders what this opposition would mean (Luanda
versus Brazzaville?) to the book's ideal reader.

I was not the book's ideal reader. Not reading it in French, I was distracted by such English awkwardnesses as (on a single page) "his three
teeth of ugliness" and "she was placed at the disposition of her balls." I
could not keep up with its torrent of Iberian and African names; there
were too many characters, dismembered corpses, and distressed beauties
to retain in my linear, Eurocentric mind. It took me a while to figure out
that the first-person narrator is a woman, called Gracia; her sisters,
Nelanda and Marthalla, abruptly hurl themselves into the sea when their
supposed father, Nertez Coma, is publicly shamed by the novel's heroine, Estina Bronzario, who declares that he has been cuckolded. Gracia,
rather than drown herself, falls in love with the Nsanga-Nordan Paolo
Cerbante and extols "the smell of love, the water and juice of dream, a

small lake of peace the colour of the full moon." Estina Bronzario gets her comeuppance by joining the novel's large population of murder victims, with a wealth of detail some might call delicious:

> Estina Bronzario's body . . . had been cut up into pieces. Her heart had been placed on the fichu with her medals, where it continued to beat. . . . Her two pegs [sic] and her two shoulders lay on a huge log left behind by the high waters of March and April. On the sand, inundated with flies and nibbled by red ants, were her still-smoking intestines. Nearby, her flayed, eyeless head laughed a ghostly laugh. Her stomach had been opened up and emptied of its contents. They, too, were still smoking: beans, pimentos, sticks of yam, vegetables, fish, all the nosh from the centenary banned by the authorities.

The significance of the centenary escaped me, and the novel's apocalyptic grotesqueries and butcheries wore me out. The central engine of suspense seemed to be the endless wait for the police to come from Nsanga-Norda and investigate the murder of another Estina—Estina Benta, whose body is repeatedly disinterred and reassembled by the hopeful officials of Valancia.

"This world is an immense corpse fighting to live by every means," runs one of the many epigrammatic interjections that seek, like painted arrows in a traffic jam, to give direction to *The Seven Solitudes of Lorsa Lopez*. Earlier in the same moonlit patch of eloquence, our dimly escried narrator says, "Perhaps we come into this world to accept the unacceptable. Truth hates us. We have nothing in common with it. Yet, right in front of us, is the deep beauty of things." Unlike Tansi's unrelievedly grim *Antipeople*, this novel does have its passages of beauty, of momentary submission to the natural splendor that persists behind human ugliness. Though the author had ten years more to live, a personal dying haunts these pages, along with a black rage at post-colonial Africa. Gracia, as she nears the end of her jangling, tangled tale, praises darkness with a cosmic stoicism worthy of Camus:

> In this country, night has the appearance of divinity. It smells like infinity. Day here will never be more than a pathetic hole of blue, sickly light. . . . Only the night has things to say to the soul. Only it can unite our bodies with the vast truculence of the universe.

Between Montparnasse and Mt. Pelée

TEXACO, by Patrick Chamoiseau, translated from the French and Creole by Rose-Myrian Réjouis and Val Vinokurov. 405 pp. Pantheon, 1997.

Talk about Jungian synchronicity: the English translation of *Texaco* has appeared, five years after its publication in Paris by Gallimard in its original French and Creole, at a time when Texaco has been accused of racial discrimination in its employee relations. The novel is about affirmative action, in a way: *Texaco* takes its name from a shantytown that arises, without utilities or official approval, amid reservoir tanks, pipes, and mangrove swamps on the edge of Fort-de-France, Martinique's largest city. In the early 1980s, an urban planner investigating this spontaneous growth ("He worked in the urban services bureau created by the modernist city council that wanted him to rationalize space, and conquer the pockets of insalubrity which were a crown of thorns around it") is struck by a stone and, while still groggy, is regaled with the saga of Texaco by its founder and leading spirit, Marie-Sophie Laborieux.

She bends the interloper's ear for nearly four hundred pages, beginning with her grandfather—"one of those men from Guinea, all somber, all mute, with big sad eyes"—who poisoned the plantation's animals and was thrown into a dungeon for life. Before his incarceration, however, he got with child "a red blackwoman" who had "escaped the sugarcane horrors by working in the Manor" as a laundress. "Soon she felt her hips widen, her face fill with light and her breasts with milk," though the prospective father shouted *"No children born in chains!"* and tried to abort the birth "with magic gestures and a very ancient song." The boy who is born, Esternome Laborieux, becomes a house slave and saves the life of the Béké, the white master, when assaulted in the woods by a "maroon," an escaped outlaw slave. The episode shows the Creolized prose at its best:

> Erupting from behind a thorny tree, the demented slave caught the Béké by the throat. As sure as I am speaking to you, he shoved an unhealthy bayonet into him and pounded him with a hundred-year-old rage like he would beat conch meat to be grilled tender. My papa (he couldn't tell why but I have the feeling it was without regret) seized the musket and fired Boom! . . . The maroon looked at him with the most painful surprise. Then he collapsed so dead that one might have suspected him of being in a hurry to leave this life.

For this good deed Esternome is given his freedom before the general liberation of 1848. He eventually settles with many other ex-slaves in the

hills, and loses his love, Ninon, when Mt. Pelée erupts and destroys the
city of Saint-Pierre in 1902. Esternome's life seems stretched; if he was a
young man in 1848, he would be elderly by 1902, and yet he moves to
Fort-de-France, attaches himself to the witchlike Adrienne Carmélite
Lapidaille, impregnates her virtually blind twin sister, Idoménée, and
does not die until his daughter, our narrator, is a young woman. He must
be around a hundred years old. Chamoiseau provides, among other apparatus, a chronology, but leaves the birth years of his characters blank, as if
admitting that a certain bewitchment has descended upon his temporal
scheme. His narrative, though lively and vivid in individual episodes,
flows sluggishly, like molasses flecked with bits of sugar cane. There is little dialogue, just the musical drone of Marie-Sophie's increasingly literary voice as she strives to give her wandering, wounded, childless life an
epic point in the founding of Texaco.

Chamoiseau's epic ambitions for his material tend to smother the sparks
of life—the spoken exchanges and the turns of individual psychology—
that quicken a novel into self-forgetful movement. The author is present
in the narrative under two pseudonyms—Oiseau de Cham, and the
Word Scratcher (le Marqueur de Paroles). Marie-Sophie's Texaco becomes a branch of Montparnasse when it welcomes Ti-Cirique, a bespectacled Haitian who "spoke a perfect, finicky French stuffed with
words which adhered to his thoughts but which made him even more
obscure to us." He takes an interest in Marie-Sophie's notebooks, and
talks to her of Montaigne and Faulkner, Proust and Claudel, Céline and
Aimé Césaire, the Martinican poet, Communist, and exponent of Négri-
tude who became mayor of Fort-de-France and is the ultimate protector
of Texaco's improvised community. Ti-Cirique tells Marie-Sophie, "The
Caribbean calls for a Cervantes who has read Joyce." The region, with its
stark light, sea-girt islands, and swashbuckling history, awakens Homeric
analogies in its bards, as we find in the hexameters of Derek Wolcott.
Among the immigrants to Texaco is the fertile, white-haired Péloponèse,
whose lover, Qualidor, is described as "backing up like Ulysses before the
chimera woman with a child in each arm . . . Péloponèse leaning toward
him like a falling statue." Chamoiseau, not trusting the growth and survival of the shantytown to acquire its own majestic meaning, interrupts
the already overstuffed narrative with excerpts from a variety of notebooks, including those of the Word Scratcher and the urban planner,
who delivers such heady asides as:

> The Lady taught me to see the city as an ecosystem, made up of equilibri-
> ums and interactions. With cemeteries and cribs, with tongues and lan-

guages, mummification and throbbing flesh. And nothing which progresses or which recedes, no linear progress or Darwinian evolution. Nothing but the haphazard whirls of the living. Beyond melancholy, anxious nostalgia, or voluntary vanguards, informulable laws must be named.

Texaco won the 1992 Prix Goncourt, France's most celebrated literary award. Its mixture of Creole and literary French have a charm, presumably, which even "an English bursting at a few seams," as the translators themselves put it, can but awkwardly approximate. Idiom of some sort must lie behind "a rustle hisshissed," "suddenly-vlam," "a rubberband girl danced Saint Vitus' dance for money," and "The lady-in-love emptied the house while he slept, and took off after scrawling on the door with coal a *Pa moli* (Hold yourself together) which only the glowing cloud later to broil up City was to erase in a-one-and-a-two." The prize confirms the marvellous intellectual solidarity that France was able to forge with its colonized peoples. The educated elites of the Francophone Third World man permanent outposts of Paris, with the Gallic legerdemain in reducing reality to thought, and thought to language. *Texaco* seems in the end to be less about a century and a half of black suffering and striving than about its own language, its embedding of Creole in a matrix of mulatto, or super-correct, French. If not a Cervantes who has read Joyce, Chamoiseau is a Céline who has read Lévi-Strauss and Derrida. He does not trust his story, but he does trust words. One of his spokespersons, Marie-Sophie, is advised by another, the Old Blackman of the Doum, *"Look for The Word, my girl, look for The Word."* If you find the Word, the City will take care of itself.

Nobody Gets Away with Everything

TROPICAL NIGHT FALLING, by Manuel Puig, translated from the Spanish by Suzanne Jill Levine. 163 pp. Simon and Schuster, 1991.

The late Manuel Puig—he died in July of 1990, in Mexico, at the age of fifty-seven—was, like his fellow-Argentines Julio Cortázar, Jorge Luis Borges, and Adolfo Bioy Casares, a tricky writer. His first love was the cinema, and he took up writing, in the mid-Sixties, while employed by Air France in New York, only after years of disappointment and frustration as a would-be film director in Rome, Paris, and Buenos Aires. In his prose, he generally abjured the third-person descriptions of scenes and faces with which other writers ploddingly assemble their realities; he presented dialogue unbroken, and varied the stream of talk with documentary matter like letters and police reports. He directed, as it were, the flow of material, but remained in his authorial persona invisible and unheard; he left the storytelling up to his characters. And tell stories they do: the hero of *Kiss of the Spider Woman* regales and seduces his cellmate with the detailed plots of old movies; the daydreaming interior monologuists of *Betrayed by Rita Hayworth* seamlessly blend their narrow lives with the films they've seen. The two elderly sisters at the heart of Puig's last novel, *Tropical Night Falling*, living together in Rio de Janeiro, share not only their memories but lengthily circumstantial gossip concerning the romantic doings of a forty-six-year-old psychologist, Silvia Bernabeu, who has been confiding in the younger sister, Luci. Puig's characters desperately want to tell each other things, and this narration is a product of the universal need to form attachments, however inadequate and destructive they prove to be. His world is a dark and harsh one, lit only by the thousand guttering candles of persistent human romanticism.

The circumstances of *Tropical Night Falling* emerge slowly from the early chapters of pure dialogue, the separate utterances punctuated by, instead of quotation marks or dashes, those little uplifted periods called "bullets":

> · A husband is one thing, Nidia, a daughter is another. Your daughter. What a thing to happen, how awful.
> · Luci, I don't want to be inside, let's go out for a walk.

Luci, at the age of eighty-one, is the less vigorous; six years before the novel's events, which occur in 1987 and early 1988, she left their native Buenos Aires for the warmer climate of Rio, after the death of her husband, Pepe. She has two middle-aged sons, Luis and Ñato. The dialogues take place in her apartment, whose address is Rua Igarapava 120, Apartment 104. Nidia, upon the death of her daughter, Emilsen, at the age of forty-seven, has come for a prolonged stay. Back in Buenos Aires she has a fifty-year-old son known to her as "Baby," as well as a son-in-law, Ignacio, and four grandchildren. The two sisters discuss their health (Nidia has high blood pressure, Luci often feels tired) and their past (they remember Mama fondly) and with much tongue-clucking follow the erotic vagaries of Silvia as she pursues an elusive, sad-eyed widower named José Ferreira. He reminds her of an earlier lover, Avilés, and appeals to her "professional deformity," which is to want to know everything about people and to heal them. Silvia has a son, a nineteen-year-old studying graphic design in Mexico, and, it turns out, a number of casual but not totally inattentive lovers. Ferreira, for that matter, has a mistress from his married days, whom he reactivates as a wife substitute; this suits Silvia, according to Nidia—by this time herself something of a psychologist—since "now [Silvia] has the role of the mistress, the third side of the triangle, which is the best role, with the least commitment, and from her position she's going to continue to help him resolve his problems."

It cannot be said that untangling these threads from the word-tumble does not test the reader's patience, or that Puig's reproduction of banal conversation always avoids, in its fidelity, wearisomeness. But he lays so coherent a ground beneath his drifts of talk that we trustfully persevere, and he varies his devices enough to keep us entertained. Rather enchantingly, early in the novel, as Luci and Nidia at last settle into the silence of sleep, the book's text becomes Luci's bedtime reading, a rousing parody of popular Sunday-supplement journalese, and with increasing ellipses and some deliberate repetitions the text takes us right inside Luci's drowsily reading brain.

As the story complicates, Puig lets his web of geriatric gentility and sheltered gossip be invaded by rougher realities—those of crushing urban poverty and of death. Luci goes off to visit Ñato (her son, not the organization) in Lucerne, Switzerland, to which he has recently moved, and she dies there of heart failure. Through an omission that gathers its own momentum, Nidia is left uninformed and keeps mailing chatty sororal letters off into the void—a grim joke reminiscent of a Cortázar short story of twenty years ago, "The Health of the Sick." In Luci's absence, Nidia proceeds to invite into the apartment Ronaldo, the "gorgeous" doorman of the neighboring apartment building, and Maria José, the precociously beautiful thirteen-year-old nanny of her downstairs neighbor, and Ronaldo's wife, Wilma, who is stuck in the drought-stricken north. Before Wilma can arrive, Ronaldo and Maria José, apparently pregnant by him, disappear, pursued by the girl's wrathful brother, Otávio. These events transpose *Tropical Night Falling* into the dry but straightforward texture of police reports, and send Nidia back to Buenos Aires, having learned her lesson: "I can't trust that kind of people."

"That kind" are the desperately poor—poor but still willful and sexually lively. Manuel Puig moved to Rio de Janeiro in 1982, after living for nearly twenty years off and on in New York City. He was evidently struck, like his two heroines, by Brazil's abundance of poverty. "So much misery in such a rich country!" Nidia exclaims. Urban refugees from the country regions, people like Ronaldo and Maria José, are virtually homeless, sleeping in tiny corners, in closets and machine rooms. Ronaldo, who is on duty at night, during the daytime finds space to stretch out, amid the racket, in a building under construction. In this same half-completed structure, the bricklayers, "all of them short and kind of ugly" because "they're almost all from the North, where people are shorter," hold squalid orgies with visiting women, "usually young maids, also from the North, who feel very lonely." After a night of aquavit and being passed from man to man, these women are turned out in the morning as soon as the buses start to run; in a pages-long letter to the deceased Luci, Nidia reports, "It's difficult to make them leave, they don't want to, because they're very sleepy, and have drunk so much and slept so little, but the men take them out like bags of garbage to be hauled away."

Puig knew sorrow. In his childhood, by his accounting, only the movies relieved the provincial tedium. His homosexuality was isolating, in the lands of Latin machismo. As an exile, he went from city to city, working as a dishwasher in London and in Stockholm. Silvia, who though a psychologist finds herself repeatedly prey to demeaning attachments, writes Ñato, "Sometimes I can't understand how people put up with so much pain and disillusionment." When at last informed of Luci's death, Nidia frames a stoic epitaph:

> That's how her life was, with its good moments and its bad moments. More or less like everybody's, nobody gets away with everything. A pity that Luci often had the sensation that it was another woman, not her, who had lived the good moments.

Though both elderly ladies scoff at the afterlife ("The only thing I ask God," Luci says, "is that if there's another world I don't want to be left alone there. But after this life there's nothing, luckily"), they forgive this belief in others. When Wilma in a letter pours out her faith in seeing her dead baby daughter in the next life, Nidia excuses "these ignorant people from the North" in a letter to her sister: "Maybe it's their poverty more than their ignorance. Since they've got nothing at all, they have no choice but to invent those illusions. I envy Wilma that." The novel concludes on a hopeful note, with an act of reckless selflessness. Nidia, just short of eighty-four, yields to Silvia's urging to return to Luci's empty apartment in Rio de Janeiro. In the plane, she steals a blanket, presumably to keep Wilma, or another adopted unfortunate, warm.

Puig's final novel, though sketchy and short, shows a humane breadth. His vision is tragic but merciful. Considerable psychological insight—he is one of the few postmodern writers who tried to learn from Freud—shapes the distorted strategies his needy characters pursue, as love, in low forms and high, strives to relieve the oppressions of society and nature.

Ugliness is comprehended as, possibly, a stage of growth: Nidia's grandson Gilberto has lost to adolescence his baby face, "such a perfect little face it was, and now it's all swollen, the nose is like a red pepper. . . . If there's anything I'd like to live to see, it's how he ends up as a little man, with his own face." Behind Puig's clinical record of our babbling pathology stood a vision of health.

Shadows and Gardens

SHADOWS, by Osvaldo Soriano, translated from the Spanish by Alfred Mac Adam. 187 pp. Knopf, 1993.

THE GARDEN NEXT DOOR, by José Donoso, translated from the Spanish by Hardie St. Martin. 242 pp. Grove Press, 1992.

In these last three or so decades, the novel has looked for urgency and energy to two bedevilled backwaters, Eastern Europe and Latin America. The rollback of Communism has left Eastern Europe's artistic compasses spinning, and the rollback of the dictators in South America has left the social terrain there somewhat flat, dreary, and ambiguous—of a piece with the bourgeois prairies to the north and in the overfarmed Old World. So it seems, at least, in two short novels by authors from the cone of our shapely sister continent: *Shadows*, by the Argentinian Osvaldo Soriano, and *The Garden Next Door*, by the Chilean José Donoso. Soriano's earlier venture into black comedy, *A Funny Dirty Little War* (1980; English translation, 1986), was a chilling astonishment—a village bloodbath rendered with the hectic, fluid speed of a Keystone Kops comedy. *Shadows*, too, suggests a silent movie—a parade of clowns on the desolate Argentine pampas, tracing in their dilapidated vehicles vast dusty circles that implausibly keep intersecting. It is *On the Road* without Kerouac's youthful buoyancy and North America's roadside abundance; the first sentence runs, "Never in my life had I been on the road without a penny to my name," and one of the two epigraphs displays the late Italo Calvino's opinion that "now the only kind of stories which exist in the world are those that are unresolved and get lost on the road."

Shadows is nothing if not modernist. Our narrator-hero has no name, save the one that another lost traveller, a former circus proprietor and performer called Coluccini, gives him: Zárate. We learn that this Zárate is a software expert, has been living in Italy, and has a daughter in Spain about whom he feels guilty because he never communicates with her. A train he was riding through the pampas to a town called Neuquén has stopped "in the middle of nowhere." After the second night of non-movement, he begins to walk, lights a fire, is told by a farmhand that this is against the law, finds a semi-abandoned Shell station, washes himself and his underpants at a pump out back, and encounters Coluccini, who drives a Renault Gordini heaped high with suitcases and announces, "*L'avventura è finita!*" Zárate accepts a ride, and is off on a close-packed series of adventures in a virtually endless, homogenous landscape: "I tried to identify a point of reference along the road, but it was all the same: wire fences, cows, the occasional tree, a dumb cloud drifting along." He encounters, among others, a truck driver who, his truck having broken down, hopes to sell his load of watermelons to a passing empty truck; a man with "a smooth, insipid face, the kind you forget instantly," who drives a Jaguar, is unlucky in love, and is named Lem; a dog that bites him (Zárate); a priest who feeds him; a travelling fortune-teller called Nadia, who drives an old Citroën Deux Chevaux; two kids called Rita and Boris, who are on their way to Cleveland in a Mercury; some thieves stripping telephone poles of their copper wire; and, the most bizarre of all, a big man called Barrante, who wears a Perón pin, a suit "missing almost all its buttons," a "wide, shiny mourning band," and a length of hose "wrapped around him up to his neck, [so] he looked like a roll of dried beef."

For two-thirds of the way, *Shadows* is a beguiling farce, an uncanny exaggeration of the shadowy, sleepy, muffled, flimsy, gray quality of modern life, especially life on the road, as the landscape dulls down and travellers meaninglessly pass and repass: "It all seemed to be taking place at a distance, as if it were happening to someone else or as if I were seeing it in a movie." But the point is not one, perhaps, that can be made at length; at less than two hundred pages, *Shadows* is a third too long. A muddled sting operation that Coluccini and Zárate pull off in a town called Colonial Vela and then a no doubt satirical Independence Day involvement with some stray members of the Argentine armed forces exhaust our appetite for the inconsequential; the line keeps playing out, but we are no longer hooked. Soriano is fascinated by messiness, by messes. The civil mayhem of *A Funny Dirty Little War* was a bloody mess; the messes of *Shadows*, though there is a fatal shooting, primarily concern automotive malfunction, squalid poverty, food, drink, and flood. Nadia's Citroën is swept off the road by a downpour:

> The car floated awhile, then slammed against a hummock, and I landed
> on top of Nadia because there was nothing for me to hold on to. . . . Muddy

water began to seep in through the floor, carrying away our sandwiches and covering our feet. . . . I had to dry the ham with a rag. The mayonnaise jar was lost under the seat, but the bread was safe because it had been caught between two cans of oil.

In this dishevelled setting occurs the novel's one scene of lovemaking. Its tenderest scene of healing, stranger still, comes when Barrante removes a speck of dirt from Zárate's eye:

He turned on the lamp and brought it closer while he raised my eyelids with two pudgy and filthy fingers. His breath was bitter, and his teeth were covered with yellow plaque. Everything he had on was falling apart, and the Perón button was just about to fall off his lapel.

The word "filthy" is recurrent: "Two farmhands riding horses followed by a filthy dog were driving some cattle"; "Coluccini grabbed the gin and staggered out of the store, his shirt hanging out of his trousers, a sheet of filthy yellow newspaper stuck to his shoe"; up above hangs "the gray sky, where a rather filthy slice of moon was shining through." Such filth confirms the characters' sensation that they are, as Coluccini says, "in the asshole of the world." On the next page, it is said of Argentina that "a country where finding a fortune is a waste of time isn't a serious country." Zárate has known exile, as has Osvaldo Soriano, and has, like him, returned. There is no place like home. He avows that on the vacant, derelict pampas he has "met more people in the past few days than I had in all the years I lived in Europe." And there are certain magical moments in the provincial wasteland: Nadia's wonderfully insouciant and accurate card-reading, Coluccini's acrobatic bicycling on the wires above the ghost town of Junta Grande, and, in that same desolation, the appearance in a lonely mailbox of a letter from Zárate's little daughter, addressed to him simply *"Poste Restante, República Argentina."* In such moments the novel reclaims its hapless, drab territory for magic realism. As in the surreal desert of *Krazy Kat*, life absurdly persists.

José Donoso's *The Garden Next Door*, as the title suggests, offers a more domestic texture. It begins, far from the wastelands of the New World, in the snug Catalan resort of Sitges, which is overrun by European tourists and Latin American political refugees. In addition to our central characters, the Chilean writer Julio Méndez and his wife, Gloria, and their set of expatriate Chileans, there are

Argentinians of all stripes and colors, with conflicting ideologies, but intelligent and very well prepared for exile: the tragic Uruguayans who fled in large numbers, emptying their country; the Brazilians and the Central Americans, all of them running away like us, some of them persecuted, most going into voluntary exile because back home it was impossible to live and go on being yourself, with the ideas and feelings that made you who you were.

To fill their days, the exiles scrape out a living at what jobs they can find, sell handicrafts to tourists, sit in cafés admiring the parade of "Belgians, Germans, and Frenchmen, stuporous from a whole day lying in the sand . . . looking as if they'd been squeezed into their reddened skins, shiny with foul-smelling sun cream," attend Argentine barbecues, sleep with "the blond dryads who came down from the urban forests of the north in search of rest or fun, or of their 'sexual identities,' " lament the way their children are becoming Europeans and losing their Latin American roots, and endlessly rechurn the political issues and antagonisms that have landed them in Spanish exile. In the backward glance of an unusually successful expatriate, the painter Pancho Salvatierra, Chile is—like Soriano's Argentine pampas—"the asshole of the planet." Salvatierra offers the Méndezes the use of his elegant Madrid apartment for the summer, and the impoverished middle-aged couple, worn down by too much booze and Valium and Sitges partying, gratefully accept.

It is the summer of 1980; seven years have gone by since Allende's fall and his loyalists' flight from the Pinochet government. The luxurious apartment, in the center of Madrid, is reminiscent of the Santiago of Julio's past. The floors, he observes, are parquet and have "the eloquence of the wooden floors of another time, lost so many years ago in the silence of Mediterranean tile floors." Back in Chile, "all the floors creak; as well as a characteristic voice, everyone has a characteristic sound, his or her own tread on wood, a personal signature that follows one around, as inseparable as a shadow." The garden next door, an unexpectedly ample and bucolic park belonging to the Duke of Andía, reminds Julio of the garden of his old home on Rome Street, where his mother lies dying, begging in vain for Julio and his family to come for one last visit: "Why don't they come to close my eyes?" For a time, the garden is inhabited— by the duke's youngest son and blonde daughter-in-law and their two children, who live in a smaller house apart from the mansion. Julio, instead of working to revise the novel that has become the repository of all his hopes, gazes into this green paradise and falls in love with the young blonde, who is conducting, Julio comes to see, an affair with a dark young man, a "handsome brute." The novel has a number of surprises, which should be reserved for its readers. As a portrait of a struggling writer, of an embittered yet still viable marriage, and of an exile's paralyzing nostalgia, *The Garden Next Door* is ruthless, deep, and tender. Donoso, like many another writer of the so-called Boom in the Latin American novel, was infected by Faulkner's circling indirections and cavalier time-jumps; this potentially tiresome manner works well enough here, as the meditative Julio obliquely drifts, in his borrowed milieu, toward defeat and renewal.

In an even shorter and more frankly autobiographical recent work, the novella titled *Taratuta*, Donoso's narrator speaks of "the cultural references without which reality is only a sketch." Like him, Julio is a compulsive alluder, who fondly sees his blonde dryad in the duke's little forest and her smooth young friend as "Brancusiesque," and who, when she is folded into the embrace of her lover, instantly thinks of a painting by Klimt "in which all you see is the heads wrapped in a riot of colors and of gold." His own wife, the tall and patrician Gloria, is appreciated in terms of Ingres's famous *Odalisque* so consistently that she plays to it, winding her head in a towel and presenting her nude back to him. An amoral young drifter called Bijou appears to Julio first as a curly-haired *angelo musicante* from some medieval fresco and then as a Rimbaud-like decadent: "I'd thought I'd recognized the evil blond filth, the perverted defiance in those clear eyes, the dirty uneven teeth of the character in [Henri Fantin-Latour's painting] *Coin de table!*" Magritte, Scott Fitzgerald, and Mallarmé's *L'Après-midi d'un faune* are repeatedly mentioned—stroked like lucky stones. A sensibility for which life is already so saturated in art has natural difficulty in creating fresh art. The Boom weighs cruelly upon Julio, who may have some of Donoso's sensibility but does not have his secure high reputation. He is especially tormented by the fictional maestro Marcelo Chiriboga, "the most insultingly famous member of the dubious Boom," and by the Barcelona super-agent Núria Monclús, a literary discriminator of fearsome chic and decisiveness. Artistic ambition is felt as a joyless burden, and release from it as a longed-for blessing:

> Not to go on being a slave to my desire to evoke a poetic universe governed by its own resplendent laws, like the one—in spite of all the unbearable commercial lies—García Márquez, Carlos Fuentes, Marcelo Chiriboga, and Julio Cortázar are sometimes able to create. To surrender: the sweetness of accepted failure.

The garden next door to reality is art, and the mysteries of artistic creativity—its inhibition, its successful activation—lie at this novel's center. As in *Shadows*, blankness has its paradoxical fertility. When the Brancusiesque young woman dominating Julio's fantasy life departs

Madrid, he reflects, "Since the important thing about beautiful things is the pain of the deep wounds they leave, her presence in the garden may have been an obstacle for me; with her now gone, the empty park may be fruitful." For the writers of the Boom, the New World was a garden where fantasy had flourished from the start. At first, America was taken for Asia and the East Indies, then as a source of endless gold and slave-produced wealth and, later still, as a political proving-ground populated by noble savages and unprecedentedly free men. Its history is one long disillusionment, broken by spells of renewed enchantment; ideas and dreams have always been part of its unsteady, colorful reality. The final twist of perspective, in *The Garden Next Door*, is a drastic one, and the reader may boggle at its plausibility, but there is no denying Donoso's essential point: it takes imagination to live as well as to write.

Mountain Miseries

DEATH IN THE ANDES, by Mario Vargas Llosa, translated from the Spanish by Edith Grossman. 276 pp. Farrar, Straus and Giroux, 1996.

Mario Vargas Llosa's new novel is a disappointing book, thanks to our elevated expectations. Peru's best novelist—one of the world's best—tackles the heights that Peru is renowned for, and what do we get? We get some cloudy mountain mysticism and a lot of tough talk. Tough talk has been one of Vargas Llosa's modes, ever since his first novel, *The Time of the Hero* (1962, in Spanish; English translation 1966), described life in the Leoncio Prado Military Academy in Lima. The brutalities of machismo encircle the islands of peace and graciousness that women create in this author's sharply gender-conscious sense of the world. His previous book, *A Fish in the Water* (1993; 1994)—a brimful autobiography that alternates chapters on his unsuccessful campaign for the Presidency of Peru in 1990 with chapters on his early life up until his departure from Peru to Madrid when he was twenty-two years old—presents the painful cleavage in his boyhood between the Llosas, his mother's large, warm, animated, aristocratic family, and his father, Ernesto J. Vargas, a handsome and violent man of inferior social status, who had abandoned his wife, Dorita, when she was five months pregnant.

Mario, the fruit of that pregnancy, was told that his father was dead, but when he was ten Ernesto, having married again and fathered two more sons in the meantime, reëntered his life, reclaiming his mother and taking her and the boy out of the Llosa household in Piura, in northwesternmost Peru, to a small house in Lima, where Ernesto worked for the International News Service. In his son's account, he was a domestic tyrant who in fits of jealousy and class resentment beat his wife and young Mario, "as he warned me that he was going to straighten me out, to make a little man of me, because he wouldn't allow his son to be the sissy the Llosas had raised." Ernesto blamed his wife's family for fostering in the boy "fancy-pants ideas like saying that when I was grown up I'd be a bullfighter and a poet; his name was at stake and he wouldn't have a son who was a pansy." Mario was one of those children—numerous, to the world's shame—for whom home is hell. The child retreated into bitter avoidance of his father. Ironically, his precocious literary vocation was strengthened: "To write poems was another of the secret ways of resisting my father, since I knew how much it irritated him that I wrote verses, something he associated with eccentricity, bohemia, and what could horrify him most: being queer." Even when Mario had become a successful and famous adult, their rapprochement was gingerly at best, and had broken down entirely by the time Ernesto died. The menace in Vargas Llosa's fiction, then, wears a different male face from the moldering morbidity in Gabriel García Márquez or the epic, rather abstract knife-fights in Jorge Luis Borges. Vargas Llosa's repeated recourse, as an artist, to drearily masculine worlds can be read as both an exposure of and an homage to the dreaded father who didn't want his boy to be a pansy.

Some psychological dredging seems necessary to explain this highly cultivated and resourceful author's fascination with the bleak and drab character of Corporal Lituma, of the Peruvian Civil Guard, who participates here in his fourth novel. Guardsman Lituma, in love with a prostitute and usually drunk, was one of the many characters in *The Green House* (1965; 1968). Sergeant Lituma figures as the hero of a fourth chapter of the floridly inventive *Aunt Julia and the Scriptwriter* (1977; 1982). As Officer Lituma, a *cholo* (half-breed) playing Watson to the suave, pure-white Lieutenant Silva, he is the secondary detective in *Who Killed Palomino Molero?* (1986; 1987); at the end of that brief, brutish little tale of military skulduggery, Lituma is transferred to an Andean province. "So what do we get for our trouble?" Silva says to him on parting. "You're transferred to the mountains, far from your heat and your people. . . . That's how they thank you for a job well done in the Guardia Civil." Lituma seems to represent for Vargas Llosa the dogged and thankless pursuit of order and justice in a society increasingly short of both. He may represent as well the driving force of intellectual curiosity; Lituma always presses to unravel the mystery, even when there is less than nothing in it for him.

Death in the Andes is listed, in *A Fish in the Water*, among the five projects Vargas Llosa was planning to undertake before he unexpectedly, in 1987, became ensnared in a three-year campaign for political change in Peru:

> A novel, something between a detective story and a fictional fantasy, about cataclysms, human sacrifices, and political crimes in a village in the Andes.

These elements are all here, in this recently published novel, but present in a desiccated, rather cursory form, as though carried in the author's head too long. Lituma, equipped with an adjutant, Civil Guard Tomás Carreño, is the head officer in the Andean village of Naccos, once a mining center but now economically dependent on a road project employing two hundred laborers. Three men—a mute, an albino, and a highway foreman—have mysteriously disappeared. Lituma, as a man from the coastal district of Piura, is uneasy among the Quechua-speaking *serruchos*, the mountain people. Further, he is under constant threat of attack by the *terrucos*, the Sendero Luminoso terrorists, who haunt and afflict the region. Still, with the help of his Quechua-speaking adjutant, he worries away at the mysterious disappearances, his suspicions falling upon a dissolute couple who run the local cantina, Dionisio and Doña Adriana. The mystery is finally solved, but not before Lituma, in the shack where the two Civil Guardsman sleep, has heard Tomás tell, in lovingly circumstantial detail, the story of his love affair with a showgirl, Mercedes, whom he impulsively rescued from a noisy session of rough sex with a drug dealer he was supposed to be guarding.

This intricately stratified novel also provides lectures from an Incaphile gringo on Andean prehistory and folk religion, and some reminiscing interior monologues of Doña Adriana's, and chilling descriptions of terrorist attacks on innocent people and vicuñas. The Sendero Luminoso episodes are underplayed, tersely conjuring up the mixed innocence and ruthlessness of the terrorist bands:

> Daylight advanced rapidly across the plateau, and their bodies, their shapes, stood out clearly. They were young, they were adolescents, they were poor, and some of them were children. In addition to rifles, revolvers, machetes, and sticks, many of them held large stones in their hands.

Stones, it turns out, are the favored instruments of execution, which is carried out upon, among others, the well-intentioned and self-confident journalist and lecturer Señora d'Harcourt, who has made Peru her adopted country. She is told by a member of the terrorist tribunal, "a young man with a full beard and cold, gray, penetrating eyes," that she must die:

"This is war, and you are a lackey of our class enemy. . . . You don't even realize that you are a tool of imperialism and the bourgeois state. Even worse, you permit yourself the luxury of a clear conscience, seeing yourself as Peru's Good Samaritan. Your case is typical."

By the light of Maoist absolutism, everything constructive in the Andes— tree plantations, vicuña herds, the strands of commerce, the local governments—must be destroyed, to create the New Democracy. Vargas Llosa, a Communist in his university days and now a Thatcherite free-market advocate, understands both the case for revolution and the savagery of its workings. His *terrucos* are persuasively frightening in a way that his *apus* (bloodthirsty pre-Christian spirits of the Andes) and his *pishtacos* (cave-dwelling wizards who eat their victims) are not, quite. Though one does not doubt that he has been to the Andes, his mountains have the feel of papier-mâché. Their powerful emblematic appearance is not matched, somehow, by a mountainous weight:

> And on the horizon, along the Cordillera where rock and sky met, there was that strange color, somewhere between violet and purple, which he had seen reproduced on so many Indian skirts and shawls and on the woolen bags the campesinos hung from the ears of their llamas; for him it was the color of the Andes, of this mysterious violent sierra.

Even when Lituma is caught in a *huayco*, an avalanche, the event feels more literary than geological. Literary indeed is Vargas Llosa's calling his sleazy, suspicious *cantinero* Dionisio and contriving for him a Dionysian past, in which he travelled the Andean fiesta circuit with a company of musicians and dancers—"wild girls who cooked during the day and at night went crazy and did outrageous things," Peruvian maenads who went "from petting to scratching, from kissing to biting, from hugging to shoving, without ever stopping the dance." Dionisio says of such orgiastic behavior, "They paid a visit to their animal," and, like a good Reichian or reader of D. H. Lawrence, advises everyone to try it.

Death in the Andes is rich fare, hastily and confusingly served. Half as many dishes, more slowly cooked, would have made a better novel. With an impatient mastery that does not let us forget the author, we are pulled from Dionisio's revels and the Indian road-builders' sullen plight to Tomás's romantic memories of Mercedes and Lituma's homesickness for the Piuran desert, from Andean lowlife to the mystic highlands of anthropology. Vargas Llosa is one of those Latin writers incurably bitten by the Faulkner bug. He tells us in *A Fish in the Water* that his discovery of Faulkner in the 1950s "left me so bedazzled that I still haven't recovered." He goes on:

He was the first writer whom I studied with paper and pencil in hand, taking notes so as not to get lost in his genealogical labyrinths and shifts of time and points of view, and also trying to unearth the secrets of the baroque construction that each one of his stories was based on, the serpentine language, the fracturing of chronological sequence, the mystery and the profundity and the disturbing ambiguities and psychological subtleties which that form gave to his stories.

The shifts of time and point of view, the baroque construction, the serpentineness that Faulkner at his best carries off in a kind of bardic transport seem in much of Vargas Llosa mechanical: his use of alternate chapters each carrying a distinct narrative has become almost a tic. A nervous tic: the storyteller tells several stories at once, as if he doesn't trust a single story to be interesting and meaningful enough. Tomás's account of his entanglement with Mercedes, for instance, is constantly interrupted by Lituma's rude, sex-starved comments, in dialogue easy to confuse with the dialogue Tomás is recounting. There is too much dialogue, in fact, and too little scenery, architecture, physiognomy, and such other appurtenances of realism. Vargas Llosa began, in early novels like *The Green House* and *Conversation in the Cathedral* (1970; 1975), with a Joycean, Faulknerian will to tell it all—to deliver all the Peruvian reality available to his imagination. The realist impulse seems, for the moment, to have been worn down by his strenuous, fruitless trek on the campaign trail. He has exiled himself from Fujimori's Peru, and his remarks on the nation in *A Fish in the Water* are pessimistic and bitter. Campaign-trail familiarity may have bred, if not contempt, a queasy satiation. After narrowly failing to become President of his country, can a writer still aspire to be what Joyce grandly, vaguely called "the uncreated conscience of my race"? There are arresting, plausible evocations in *Death in the Andes*—the young *terrucos* in the sleepy dawn, the recalling of the old days when peddlers and entertainers roved the Andes without fear—but they exist as adumbrations of some larger, more relaxed, less manipulative work, with the same title, which has not been written.

Two Anglo-Indian Novels

THE GOD OF SMALL THINGS, by Arundhati Roy. 321 pp. Random House, 1997.

BEACH BOY, by Ardashir Vakil. 211 pp. Scribner, 1998.

The spread of English throughout the world, via commerce and colonialism and now popular culture, has spawned any number of fluent outriggers capable of contributing to English literature. Some, like most Australians and Americans, write English with no thought of an alternative; others, like certain inhabitants of the Caribbean, Ireland, Anglophone Africa, and India, write it against a background of native tongues or patois that are abandoned or suppressed in the creative effort—an effort which to a degree enlists them in a foreign if not an enemy camp, that of the colonizer. Arundhati Roy's *The God of Small Things*, a work of highly conscious art, is conscious not least of its linguistic ambivalence. It takes place in India's southern state of Kerala, where the local language is Malayalam; phrases and whole sentences of Malayalam, sometimes translated and sometimes not, seep into the book's English, whose mannerisms—compound and coined words, fragmentary sentences, paragraphs a word or a phrase long, whimsical capitalization—underline the eccentricity of the language in relation to the tale's emotional center. Estha and Rahel, male and female dizygotic twins who serve as the central characters, remember how their great-aunt, Navomi Ipe, incongruously called Baby Kochamma, inflicted English upon them, making them write "I will always speak in English" one hundred times and practice their pronunciation by singing, "Rej-Oice in the Lo-Ord Or-Orlways / And again I say rej-oice." The twins' sensibilities, uncannily conjoined, are expressed in a confidently unorthodox prose that owes something to Salman Rushdie's jazzy riffs:

> Their lives have a size and a shape now. Estha has his and Rahel hers.
> Edges, Borders, Boundaries, Brinks and Limits have appeared like a team of trolls on their separate horizons. Short creatures with long shadows, patroling the Blurry End. Gentle half-moons have gathered under their eyes and they are as old as Ammu [their mother] was when she died. Thirty-one.
> Not old.
> Not young.
> But a viable die-able age.

The main events of the novel, to which everything harks back, occur in December of 1969, when the twins' English cousin, Sophie Mol, arrives for a two-week Christmas vacation. She is the daughter and only child of their uncle Chacko, who met his English wife at Oxford, and who, divorced, has returned to live with his mother, his aunt, and his sister, Ammu—herself divorced—in the big family house in Ayemenem. They are Syrian Christians; Baby Kochamma's father was the Reverend E. John Ipe, a priest personally blessed by the Patriarch of Antioch. His son, the twins' grandfather Pappachi, was an Imperial Entomologist under the British and after Independence assumed the title of Joint Director of Entomology. But a rare moth he discovered was not named after him, and this moth, with "its unusually dense dorsal tufts," consequently "tormented him and his children and his children's children." He beat his wife, Mammachi, with a brass flower vase every night until Chacko, burly from rowing for Oxford, put a halt to the practice; then Pappachi took his favorite mahogany rocking chair into the middle of the driveway and smashed it up with a plumber's monkey wrench. His black rages were partly the fruit of spousal jealousy: Mammachi in her youth was a violinist of potential concert calibre, until he forbade further lessons; in her middle age, though virtually blind, she created from some of her recipes a successful business, named (by Chacko) Paradise Pickles and Preserves.

The pickle plant with its employees, the great old house, the river beyond, a deserted house and rubber plantation on the other side of the river (once owned by the Black Sahib, a fabled Englishman who had "gone native" and eventually committed suicide), the Ipe heritage of backwards-looking Anglophilia, a sky-blue Plymouth that Pappachi spitefully bought for himself after his rebuke from Chacko—these are the data that Arundhati Roy revolves before us as she spins her circuitous tale. The twins were seven when nine-year-old Sophie Mol visited; now they are thirty-one, and Rahel has returned from America upon learning that Estha has been sent back to Ayemenem by his father and stepmother, who have wearied of his withdrawn and virtually demented behavior.

Roy takes her time exploring the past by means of the present. Her novel provides one more example of William Faulkner's powerful influence upon Third World writers; his method of torturing a story—mangling it, coming at it roundabout after portentous detours and delays—presumably strikes a chord in stratified, unevenly developed societies that feel a shame and defeat in their history. The narrator works as hard to avoid as to reach her destination of forbidden sex and atrocious violence. From the beginning of *The God of Small Things* we know that Sophie Mol died during her Christmas vacation in India, but we don't know why. We know that Rahel and Estha were exposed to something dreadful, but we don't know what. Roy peels away the layers of her mys-

teries with such delicate cunning, such a dazzlingly adroit shuffle of accumulating revelations within the blighted House of Ipe, that to discuss the
plot would violate it.

Treading Roy's maze, we learn a great deal about India—a "vast, violent, circling, driving, ridiculous, insane, unfeasible, public turmoil of
a nation." We learn foremost that, in 1969, it was not a safe place.
Though Kerala, unlike "a small country with similar landscape" to the
east, is not being bombed by the forces of capitalism, it holds a large
number of Communists, whose machinations threaten the solvency of
Paradise Pickles and Preserves and whose angry marches shatter the
peace of an upper-class Syrian-Christian family on its way, in its big blue
Plymouth, to Cochin to see the movie *The Sound of Music*. The young
nation seethes with the violence of its long history, its resentments, its
prejudices, going back to a time "before Vasco da Gama arrived, before
the Zamorin's conquest of Calicut." Husbands beat wives, women have
no *locus standi*, and Ammu, divorced from her alcoholic Hindu husband,
spends hours "on the riverbank with her little plastic transistor shaped
like a tangerine": "A liquid ache spread under her skin, and she walked
out of the world like a witch, to a better, happier place." The liquid ache
of longing is widespread, and dangerous. The Black Sahib committed
suicide because "his young lover's parents had taken the boy away from
him." Chacko still loves his pale English wife; fat old Baby Kochamma
was once in love with a Catholic priest; and little Estha, banished to the
empty lobby of Abhilash Talkies during *The Sound of Music*, is coerced
into masturbating the man behind the refreshment counter. This horrific
scene, with its inordinately vivid molester ("He looked like an unfriendly
jeweled bear. . . . His yellow teeth were magnets. They saw, they smiled,
they sang, they smelled, they moved. They mesmerized"), is one of
the novel's flashing lunges outside the suffocating circle of Anglophile
Syrian-Christians into the Indian masses, in their poverty and dynamic,
Dickensian color.

Occidental readers who imagined that untouchability was banished by
Mahatma Gandhi will find the caste onus cruelly operative in 1969, and
not just in the memories of the aged:

> Mammachi told Estha and Rahel that she could remember a time, in her
> girlhood, when Paravans were expected to crawl backwards with a broom,
> sweeping away their footprints so that Brahmins or Syrian Christians would
> not defile themselves by accidentally stepping into a Paravan's footprint. In
> Mammachi's time, Paravans, like other Untouchables, were not allowed to
> walk on public roads, not allowed to cover their upper bodies, not allowed
> to carry umbrellas. They had to put their hands over their mouths when

they spoke, to divert their polluted breath away from those whom they addressed.

Velutha, a clever Paravan child who lives in Ayemenem, brings to Ammu, a child three years older, little toys he has made—"tiny windmills, rattles, minute jewel boxes out of dried palm reeds"—and presents them "holding them out on his palm (as he had been taught to) so she wouldn't have to touch him to take them." This sad detail, of the child taught to give without being touched, has a comic counterpart later in the novel, when Velutha's father, the subservient Vellya Paapen, is knocked down by an angry push: "He was taken completely by surprise. Part of the taboo of being an Untouchable was expecting not to be touched." In a century scarred by racial genocides, in a United States no stranger to formal and informal racial segregation, Hinduism's creation of a vast shunned underclass still has the power to shock, as if it held a magnifying glass to our own inner discriminations and dismissals.

Rahel, studying in Delhi to be an architect, meets and marries an American, who brings her to Boston. But, though adoring, he can't break through her preoccupation with the past; after her divorce, she works for several years as the night cashier in a bullet-proof booth at a gas station outside Washington, where "drunks occasionally vomited into the till, and pimps propositioned her with more lucrative job offers." One of her recurrent visitors, a "punctual drunk with sober eyes," shouts, "Hey, you! Black bitch! Suck my dick!" This is not so far from Baby Kochamma's thinking of the twins as "Half-Hindu Hybrids whom no self-respecting Syrian Christian would ever marry." Neither India nor the world is an easy melting pot.

Roy manages to catch, in the skein of the Ipes' troubled history, a sense of India's deep past, the mingling of dark inhabitants and light invaders going back to the Aryan authors of the Vedas, the roots of Hinduism. She brings us, in her ecstatically written last pages, into the heart of human love and the mythic past: Krishna, as it were, couples with Radha on the riverbank, and, when the lover makes the beloved dance, it is the dance of Kali, of death and coming destruction. There is even a magic-realist touch: he folds his fear into a rose, and she wears it in her hair. Such dark bliss is akin to that sought by a group of male kathakali dancers who, unsatisfied and humiliated by the truncated performances they put on for the guests at the tourist hotel that by 1993 has arisen on the Black Sahib's old plantation, give the full performance, in an all-but-empty temple, until dawn.

Since *The God of Small Things* delivers so much terror and beauty, and so omniscient a view of modern India, it is perhaps ungrateful to complain of the novel's artiness. But the prose, shuttling back and forth among its key images and phrases, rarely lets us forget that we are in the company of an artificer: Roy caresses her novel until it seems not merely well wrought but overwrought. Much of our mental energy is spent in recalling where insistently repeated phrases like "Locusts Stand I" and "Esthapappychachen Kuttappen Peter Mon" and "Sourmetal Smells" first occurred, and what they signify. A Joycean passage like

> A carbreeze blew. Greentrees and telephone poles flew past the windows. Still birds slid by on moving wires, like unclaimed baggage at the airport.
> A pale daymoon hung hugely in the sky and went where they went. As big as the belly of a beer-drinking man

arguably transports us into the mind of a seven-year-old, but arch modifiers like "dinner-plate-eyed" and "slipperoily" and palindromic formations such as "Dark of Heartness tiptoed into the Heart of Darkness" put us squarely on a writer's desk. Well, a novel of real ambition must invent its own language, and this one does. Arundhati Roy, the elegant dust jacket tells us, has worked as a production designer and has written two screenplays; this experience shows in the skill with which she sets and lights her scenes, as well as in such touches of special jargon as "mosaic blur," "gofers on a film set," and "a test tube of sparkling, back-lit urine." Her scenes get replayed in both the reader's memory and the characters'. This is a first novel, and it's a Tiger Woodsian debut—Arundhati Roy hits the long, socio-cosmic ball but is also exquisite in her short game. Like a devotionally built temple, *The God of Small Things* builds a massive interlocking structure of fine, intensely felt details. A rosary is held up to the light: "Each greedy bead grabbed its share of sun."

Beach Boy, by Ardashir Vakil, takes a first-person ramble through a few years in the life of Cyrus Readymoney, a Bombay boy who is eight when the narrative opens and ten when it concludes. He lives with his parents and four siblings in a modernist glass house facing the Arabian Sea, in the Juhu district, and when he is not in school spends his days on the beach, at the movies, or visiting the houses of his playmates, which cluster next to the compound of the divorced Maharani of Bharatnagar. In his room, Cyrus spies on the Maharani's adopted daughter Meera and keeps a journal of amazing literacy, for a third-grader. At school, and at tennis (his formidable mother is a player of near-Wimbledon calibre), he is a daydreaming underachiever; reality comes crashing in on him in the form of the reclusive Maharani's friendship, a visit to the rural south with the

Krishnan family, his parents' separation, and his father's heart attack. Though as casual-seeming in composition as *The God of Small Things* is intricate and purposeful, *Beach Boy* shares with the more ambitious novel a number of features. Child protagonists are placed in the recent past—1969 is specified in one novel and 1972 in the other. Ardashir Vakil was born in Bombay in 1962 and lives in London, where he teaches English; he and Arundhati Roy give us an India remembered, a land, like Nabokov's Russia, glistening with the dew of early impressions and ominous with the dimly seen, uncontrollable maneuvers of adults. Movies—Hindi extravaganzas in Cyrus's case—are crucial events, described in detail. Parents in a state of sexual rebellion occur in both novels and exude a sense of squandered gentility, of decreasingly relevant foreign educations. Chacko Ipe went to Oxford, and Cyrus's father, it turns out, went to Yale. The religious affiliations of both discontented, bourgeois households are out of the Hindu mainstream: the Ipes are Syrian Christians, and the Readymoneys—a name Cyrus's great-grandfather "earned for himself when he took on the trade of money-lender ninety years ago in the docks of Bombay"—are Parsis, Zoroastrians, who "pray at agiarys . . . where the same flame has been kept burning for hundreds of years" and who feed their dead to vultures. These religions are scarcely more exotic to Western readers than to the children of these novels, who are in thrall to music, books, and imagery originating in the West. Both novels, as it happens, contain scenes of the child hero masturbating someone else—a comic and blithe scene in Vakil, a sinister one in Roy. A robust, puritanically Hindu Communist figures in both books, as does a minute, curiously Indian maternal gesture: Ammu, seeing her son off on a train, "scanned the finger-nails of the little hand she held, and slid a black sickle of dirt from under the thumb-nail," while Cyrus's mother, similarly preoccupied, "spooned out the dirt from under my nails with her thumbnail and flicked it away."

These novels come from the same India—the same Western-educated, mercantile social class, the same western coast—and similarly touch on kathakali dancers, ravenous kites, and colorful circumambient poverty. Cyrus, trying in his self-education to attain social awareness, rides through the Bombay slums:

> The pavement on the road into town had been colonized by makeshift homes—pavement dwellings cobbled together with recycled materials collected from rubbish heaps. Brown sheets of cloth, bits of metal, torn shreds of plastic, calendars, books and hundreds of other discarded artifacts that surfaced like flotsam from the ebb and flow of the city. . . . A group of pavement boys, one of them with a rain hat over his head, was crouched over a game of cards. They were arguing noisily. A man sat on his haunches smok-

ing a beedi. A baby girl was being vigorously washed by her mother; her brown body, covered in lather, glistened in the darkness. A gaunt man in a vest emerged red-eyed from one of the entrances to a bamboo-pole and cloth hut.*

Where a native sees life, a tourist sees poverty; Cyrus, young as he is, is beginning to see with foreign eyes, those of a boy who has read too much James Hadley Chase and too many *Archie* comic books. As his family shatters and he is moved from the glass house on Juhu Beach to a Bombay high-rise, he becomes somewhat opaque; the journal he was keeping is forgotten and the novel, in its new terrain, feels impulsive, spotty, censored. Whereas Estha and Rahel had each other to turn to, Cyrus has no one. What he does have is food: *Beach Boy* constitutes a long ode to boyish hunger, and to the rich variety of stuffs that hold it at bay. In the movie theatre:

> I could smell the fried samosas. The taste of salted popcorn made my mouth dry. I wanted anything and everything.

At the Krishnans':

> The lights in the kitchen were bright, and tempting smells of frying onion, ground coconut and coriander stole up my nostrils. . . . The thought of sitting there waiting for an uttapam I might never get filled my empty stomach with apprehension.

At his grandmother's:

> Scrambled eggs were her specialty. I learned from an early age that to make them smooth and creamy you had to have them on the lowest fire possible and constantly stir the egg and milk mixture. When the eggs were almost done, my grandmother would carefully shred half a cube of Amul cheese on top. I gobbled them up with sprinklings of black pepper.

Before a street vender, a *bhaiya*:

> The bhaiya cuts a lime in half, he chops a green mango into tiny squares, he shreds some coriander leaves, he lifts up a box and slides out a sheaf of pages torn out from a magazine. The paper is thick and durable but not glossy— perfect for the food it will hold. He folds one sheet over and makes a wide cone-shaped vessel. Now comes the delicate throwing together of ingredients, dry and wet, that delights the heart.

In Kerala, picnicking:

---

*Cf. this from Roy's novel: "Gaunt children, blond with malnutrition, selling smutty magazines and food they couldn't afford to eat themselves."

We sat on the rocks, munching, lost in the lovely tastes of coriander, coconut and curry leaves, fresh curry leaves with waxy yellow potatoes, dotted with black mustard seeds. Smoky, spicy, nutty, scented potatoes. The taste of curry leaves made me appreciate the dark canopy of leaves above, the heat of the afternoon offset by the cool sweat brought on by the spices.

Back at Granny's:

She cooked delicious evening meals too: rus chawal, with its tender goat and coconut milk, khichri kheema; lentil-stained rice with healthy portions of clove and cinnamon-flavoured mince, machhi-no-sas, a thick white curry with tails of pomfret. On top of this there was a pudding every night: caramel custard, rice pudding, home-made ice-cream, falooda and an opaque pink ghas nu jelly.

And on to the Maharani's:

For pudding we ate Alphonso mangos. Ripe and golden from their straw beds. Nothing can quite compare with the sinking of teeth into the vivid orange flesh of an Alphonso. The scent of marmalade and candied fruit, and a taste like the sweet sharpness of limes are followed by the clean juice running into the mouth. "Food for the Gods" my father called them.

Is India trying to fill with delicacies the void in our young hero, whom a confusingly hybrid culture has left unconsoled and bewildered, or is the author, as he envisions tropical fruit in gray London, trying to fill himself? Arundhati Roy lives in New Delhi, as far from Cochin as Boston is from Miami. Is there a place, these novels make us wonder, for an English-language literature within India, where a bristling nationalism staves off Asian neighbors and a Hindu fundamentalism arises to compete with the Islamic variety? A writer is a spy in childhood and a self-interrogator as an adult. Who will read the debriefing report? These two writers certainly have a past—vivid, troubling, precious—but where is their future?

A Note on Narayan

R. K. NARAYAN, born in 1906, lives on, into his nineties, as if preserved in the tranquil, perennial essence of Malgudi, the imaginary town where almost all of his fiction takes place. The lightness of his touch, the smallness of his chosen field of observation, and the profound equanimity of his Hindu vision have been criticized as inadequate to the problem-ridden, poverty-stricken immensity of India. But who takes a subcontinent for a subject, when humanity is close at hand? An observed detail has a resonance—a branching truth—that no generalization can match. V. S. Naipaul, who as a boy in Trinidad and a young man in England had read and admired Narayan, was dismayed, in first travelling to India, to find it "cruel and overwhelming" compared with the cozy and comic world of Narayan's novels. He concluded that "his comedy and irony were not quite what they had appeared to be, were part of a Hindu response to the world." As a Hindu, Narayan believes in reincarnation— a universe of infinite rebirths—and a genial eternity keeps company with his social realism. In *The Guide* (1958), a con man becomes a saint; in *The Painter of Signs* (1976), the heroine of a doomed romance is momentarily "perhaps a goddess to be worshipped."

Western liberal opinion demands that Indian writers confront suffering. Narayan confronts it somewhat as Fielding and O. Henry do, with the recognition that suffering is never all there is to the picture; human buoyance and hopefulness are also part of it. "India will go on," Narayan told the young Naipaul, and if this affirmation falls short of a political program it does proclaim a lifelong opportunity to observe, to invent, to express surprise at the permutations of human behavior, to smile. Travellers to India frequently remark upon its exhilarating liveliness, once culture shock has been absorbed. Narayan gives the reader that lively joy as registered by a native immunized against shock; he surveys his teeming scene partly from the perspective of the most ancient of practiced religions, and partly from that of Edwardian English fiction, which took its own animated, caste-conscious, at times heartless society as self-evidently an entertainment.

MEDLEYS

Glasnost, Honne, and Conquistadores

No RETURN, by Alexander Kabakov, translated from the Russian by Thomas Whitney. 94 pp. Morrow, 1990.

A CAT, A MAN, AND TWO WOMEN, by Junichirō Tanizaki, translated from the Japanese by Paul McCarthy. 164 pp. Kodansha International, 1990.

SEA OF LENTILS, by Antonio Benítez-Rojo, translated from the Spanish by James Maraniss. 201 pp. University of Massachusetts Press, 1990.

Fiction brings us news of other countries and cultures, but with a certain lag in the transmission. *No Return*, by Alexander Kabakov, made big waves when it was published in Moscow, in June of 1989, and they lifted its middle-aged author into celebrity, right up to an interview in the *New York Times* and a back-page editorial in *Time*. But two years later, in the cold light of English translation, in a slim volume of less than a hundred pages, this sketchy futuristic novel reads like a movie scenario (the movie is being made) and occasions only modest shivers. Written in May of 1988, it takes place in a year, 1993, rapidly drawing nigh, as are many of the developments its dystopian vision projects: the Russian republics *are* in a state of rebellion and ethnic contention, and the Russian economy *is* a shambles. True, the impotent ruble has not yet been renamed the "gorbaty," a general does not yet head the embattled central government, and the streets of Moscow are not yet rife with explosions and machine-gun fire. But Kabakov's elaborations of present Soviet distress fail to illuminate or diagnose, for this Western reader, our formerly monolithic Cold War foe's sudden collapse into economic ignominy and smiling international compliance.

The Russian title of *No Return*, *Nevozvrashchenets*, means "the one who does not return," a term conventially applied to defectors. The hero, Yuri Ilich, works as an "extrapolator" in a learned institute that is unnamed but is persuasively described: "The dirty government-issue turquoise walls, the eternally flickering, half-functioning fluorescent lights, and the archaic carpet runners covered with canvas protectors replete with dirty footprints endowed our institute with the air of a backwater office in the boondocks." In these dismal quarters Yuri is approached by two smooth-talking operatives for a vague agency that we take to be the KGB. They want him, presumably drawing upon his talents as an extrapolator (the mechanics of his trade are left murky), to write reports from the future for them, and they seal the bargain by applying a "gentle kick" and a painful twist of his arm. With no more transition than a space break, the narrator finds himself in the Moscow of 1993. It is cold and snowing; gunfire is heard. Yuri's transistor radio, its batteries nearly dead, tells him of the ongoing congress of "the Russian Union of Democratic Parties," containing Christian Democratic delegations from the Trans-Caucasus, Social Fundamentalists from Turkestan, and Catholic Radicals from the Baltic Federation. General Victor Andreyevich Panayev, "secretary-president of the Preparatory Committee," has just addressed this motley body. In the Persian Gulf, a convoy of unarmed vessels belonging to the United States but flying the neutral Polish flag has been attacked by "unidentified aircraft . . . with one more nuclear bombing." In the Moscow streets, people are wearing tattered clothes and carrying guns. Street traffic consists of a light tank and "a barely functioning Volga sedan with rusted-out fenders full of holes." In the doorway of his old childhood home, Yuri encounters a "female predator"—a young woman "with a heavy Ukrainian accent," come to Moscow in the hope of buying some boots. Together, they elude a gang of assassins—veterans of the Afghanistan War—and the numerous police of the Commission for National Security. After some amorous compliance on a frosty park bench, the Ukrainian charmer seizes Yuri's Kalashnikov rifle; at gun-point she berates him for being a liberal intellectual and demands his purchasing coupons:

"It was because of vermin like you that this whole thing began. People lived like human beings and everything was normal and my man could knock off six grand gorbaties in one good day, but that wasn't enough for you! For you everything was bad. You envious rats! Leonid Ilich Brezhnev wasn't good enough for you, but there were clean streets under him, and practical people who knew how to live, had a real life! You couldn't stand Stalin. You couldn't stand Brezhnev. Gorbachev was your cup of tea! Just give me your coupons and get out of here—or else I'll kill you, you Moscow egghead."

As of 1991, Moscow eggheads see around them, amid the new freedoms they yearned for, many less fortunate apparent results of perestroika, from separatism among the Soviet republics to drastic shortages of not just fancy consumer goods but essential supplies. It is hard to know what horrors of social meltdown in *No Return* significantly exaggerate the actual situation. Menacing gangs of "twelve-year-old benzene addicts" roam the streets, along with gangs of black-jacketed, Jew-baiting "Vikings." On these same hazardous streets, soldiers of "the Revolutionary Committee of Northern Persia" take and murder hostages in reprisal for similar acts perpetrated by "the filthy dogs of the Holy Self-Defense Force." Starving tramps and benzene addicts dominate the underground metro stations, and of two trains that come through one is running empty and the other has been commandeered by a lewd party on wheels. Meanwhile, people with advantaged positions, such as coöp managers, exploit the new opportunities and live luxuriously. A mysterious elegant stranger taunts Yuri Ilich: "Here is one more brilliant holiday of liberation for you: pogroms, extermination detachments, famine, and general horror. Then, naturally, ruin and reconstruction with an iron hand." A militant workers' party already has donned what seem to be Mao jackets, and "storm troopers from the Stalinist Union of Russian Youth" try to blow up Pushkin's statue because he was anti-government and non-Slavic. But Yuri at the end votes for post-*glasnost* disorder: his KGB tormenters, transported to this extrapolated 1993, no longer frighten him. He tells his wife, "*Here* for some reason I am not afraid of them. Here everything is going to be okay. The main thing is that we are no longer *there*."

No Return, unlike *1984* and Evgenii Zamiatin's great dystopia *We*, inspires no real fear of the future. Unlike Huxley's *Brave New World* and H. G. Wells's *The Time Machine*, it does not even inspire disgust with the present. Shortages, ethnic riots, and all, Alexander Kabakov is exhilarated to be in print after seventeen years of anonymous editorial labor with a trade newspaper for railroad workers, and his exhilaration shows through. When the party on the subway car slides by, we want to join it. The peculiar zaniness, born of Gogol and Bely, that has enabled certain recent Soviet writers—Vassily Aksyonov and Andrei Bitov, Yuz Aleshkovsky and Benedict Erofeev—to vent their vitality and imply their rage does not quite stretch to fit the new Soviet situation, wherein disorder, and not the established order, is the enemy. The book's keenest shivers come with the familiar menaces of the Communist regime: the military enforcers who arrive in tanks, and the KGB enforcers who silkily reassure the hero, "So just don't be frightened, Yuri Ilich, don't be frightened, don't be frightened." Zamiatin, writing in the early 1920s out of the relatively mild and rational oppressions of Lenin's regime, foresaw a glassy world from which all privacy, individual color, and human passion would be benignly squeezed; the terror of that suffocating vision flickers in *No Return*, but as something outmoded, something in fragments.

If Alexander Kabakov doesn't scare us as much as we expected, Junichirō Tanizaki scares us a bit more. At least, even his lighter-hearted fictions, three of which are collected in *A Cat, a Man, and Two Women*, make us hold our breath, and the endings don't let us quite exhale. In the long title story, we are not surprised that the hero, the plump and ineffectual Shozo, loves his pet cat, Lily, more than he loves either his wife, Fukuko, or his ex-wife, Shinako, but we *are* surprised to have the love detailed with such unabashed physicality. Shozo feeds Lily by making her tug at a little marinated mackerel held in his mouth; his watching wife reflects, "It might be all very well to like cats, but it was going too far to transfer a fish from master's mouth to cat's." At the other extreme of intimacy, the odor of cat excrement mixes with his fondness, and he remembers with a curious relish the moment when, during a tussle, the "breath from her bowels" blew straight into his face. He brags to his wife, "Lily and I are so close we've smelled each other's farts!" When the cat gets into bed with him, "he would . . . stroke that area of the neck which cats most love to have fondled; and Lily would immediately respond with a satisfied purring. She might begin to bite at his finger, or gently claw him, or drool a bit—all were signs that she was excited."

In one of the two shorter stories bound in with this piece of feline erotica, "Professor Rado," we are not too startled when the taciturn professor, in a moment reminiscent of Proust or of Tanizaki's *The Key*, is seen through a window being caned by a lightly clad maidservant, but this just foreshadows the real voyeuristic treat, in which the professor is spied kneeling at the feet of a beautiful tall leper he has long admired from afar. Ecstatically he fits her deformed foot with an artificial toe, and she, her voice distorted by her diseased nose, tells him it doesn't hurt a bit. Masochism, O.K., and necrophilia, we've heard of that, but leprophilia?—it isn't even in the dictionary!

The deft translator, Paul McCarthy, offers in his introduction a helpful cultural observation: "Japanese society is characterized by quite clear-cut divisions between the public persona and the private life; between *tatemae* (what is outwardly expressed) and *honne* (what is actually thought and felt)." Voyeurism, the glimpse through a chink of *tatemae* into the depths of *honne*, recurs in Tanizaki, and a sense of mutual spying through the enshrouding forms of traditional decorum permeates his stately masterpiece, *The Makioka Sisters*. His characters suggest pot-bellied stoves whose cast-iron exteriors conceal the fire that makes them hot. His stories have the propulsive fascination of hidden menace, and his characters keep deepening, pushing the story into new corners. Shinako, Shozo's rejected first wife, captures Lily in a spiteful maneuver but comes to love her much as her ex-husband did, and rapturously shares her bed with her. Lily, it should be said, is no simple indigenous cat, but "of a European breed," and "European cats are generally free from the stiff, square-shouldered look of Japanese cats; they have clean, chic-looking lines, like a beautiful woman with gently sloping shoulders." Thus Tanizaki, in 1935 on the verge of his six-year patriotic labor of translating *The Tale of the Genji* into modern Japanese, gently burlesqued the infatuation with things Western that he had sympathetically dramatized in his novel of 1924, *Naomi*.

The cat story ends puzzlingly: Shozo, discovering that his former wife has reconstituted his loving relationship with Lily, flees, "as if pursued by something dreadful," just when a Western reader expects a happy reconciliation on the basis of a shared passion. Nor does the ending of the second, shorter story, "The Little Kingdom," take us where we thought we were going. The reader, foreseeing a power struggle between a fifth-grade teacher, Kaijima, and a mysteriously magnetic student, Numakura, who organizes all the other students into a little kingdom of unquestioning allegiance, petty theft, and commerce in an invented currency, instead sees the poor instructor almost resistlessly succumb to the student's spell, as illness and poverty drag him and his family down. The students' little kingdom proves to be the only realm wherein he can acquire milk for his baby, and the bitter irony of this comes upon us without warning. In Tanizaki, the bizarre reaches out to possess reality; perverse sexual obsession is just his most usual instrument for demonstrating how precariously society's façades and structures contain the underlying *honne*.

Our basic North American education does little to disabuse children of the notion that Columbus made his momentous landfall in 1492 upon some part of the East Coast of the United States. That Columbus landed on a small island not yet unambiguously identified, and that his entire career of exploration throughout four transatlantic voyages confined him to the mazy manifold coasts of the Caribbean, and that he died without any real understanding of what he had discovered—these facts, as curious as the pessimistic fantasies of Latin American magic realism, are downplayed in our celebrations. Between Columbus's first landing and

Cortés's spectacular conquest of Mexico from 1519 to 1521, our common knowledge encounters a void. For that matter, the immense succeeding pageant of Spanish America, between Pizarro's conquest of the Incas and Bolívar's liberation, nearly three centuries later, of a great arc of territories from Venezuela to Bolivia, translates into a vague blur north of the Rio Grande. Gabriel García Márquez's recent novel about Bolívar, *The General in His Labyrinth*, detailing the Liberator's last, disempowered days, was itself so infected by its hero's terminal exhaustion and drifting-ness as to depress our sense of South American history even further; it was hard to know what the author wanted us to make of this final pathetic residue of epic deeds, except to agree that, as his last paragraph blazingly conveyed, it is a pity to die.

Sea of Lentils, by the expatriate Cuban Antonio Benítez-Rojo, plays upon Spanish American history more rousingly, with an incessant hail of luminous, violent imagery and an unmistakable indignation. Mr. Benítez-Rojo has a distinct viewpoint, analytical and appalled, left over, one imagines, from the days after 1959 when he worked for the newly installed Castro government. The introduction to *Sea of Lentils*, written by Sidney Lea, whose *New England Review and Bread Loaf Quarterly* first printed this scintillating author in English translation, tells us that before Castro's revolution Benítez-Rojo studied economics in the United States, and that after it he worked in the Ministry of Labor. He did research for Casa de las Americas, a government cultural institution, in Caribbean history, and in 1979 became director of Cuba's Center for Caribbean Studies. The next year, attending a scholarly conference in Paris, he defected, and he now teaches at Amherst College. Mr. Lea, having provided this background, goes on to describe *Sea of Lentils* as liquid not only in subject but in method: "Its continuity (or continuities) consists, paradoxically, in the very polyrhythms of interruption, divagation, reconsideration, extenuation." He quotes Benítez-Rojo: "The culture of meta-archipelagoes is an eternal return, a detour without destination or milepost, a roundabout that leads nowhere but back home; it is a feed-back machine, as is the sea, the wind, the Milky Way, the novel." He further quotes the eloquent author as saying that *Sea of Lentils* is "a deconstructionist novel, no question," thus invoking a term that gives much obscure comfort to contemporary academics. Does "deconstruc-tion" mean, here, that the novel dissolves as it goes along, or that by ani-mating some ugly historical truths it disassembles our myths of imperial expansion? The novel is not especially convoluted or shifty. It blends four separate narrative strands, but with clear enough demarcations; readers who have survived Faulkner and Joyce should have no trouble keeping their heads above water. What matters for purposes of readability is that Benítez-Rojo has packed his novel with arresting matter, and that he writes wonderfully, with life, edge, and the density of a poem.

The four strands concern (1) King Philip II of Spain, who lies dying in the Escorial, in 1598, and mournfully reflects back upon his long reign; (2) Antón Babtista, a fictional soldier arrived in Hispaniola with Columbus's second voyage, in 1493, and his rapacious career among the gullible and docile Indians; (3) Don Pedro, the young son-in-law of the Adelantado (literally, "one who goes in advance"; applied to the governor of a province) Pedro Menéndez de Avilés, as he experiences the founding of St. Augustine in 1565 and the merciless massacre of the French Huguenot forces captured nearby; and (4) the de Pontes, a Genoan mercantile family transplanted to Tenerife, in the Canary Islands, and their profitable development of a three-cornered trade involving guns for slaves in Africa, and slaves for gold, silver, and pearls in the Caribbean. This last strand, the economic, draws upon the author's special erudition, and is a crucial one in a tapestry of colonial exploitation, but remains the hardest to follow, even though the de Pontes' financial adventures colorfully include piracy and the calculated seduction of an English seafarer, John Hawkins, by the lovely Inés de Ponte. In all four sequences, women play an important role in male destinies: Inés enlists Hawkins in the de Ponte fleet; Philip II mourns his failure to captivate Elizabeth of England, an amorous rejection that led to the defeat of his Armada thirty years later; and both Antón Babtista and Don Pedro owe their favored positions to their mates' relatives.

Babtista is a marvellous creation, a Sancho Panza as if by Rabelais. The little Taínos Indian girls of Hispaniola become mere receptacles for him, to be filled or emptied:

> You relaxed beside a girl whose crotch was tight and musky; then you grabbed another one, who was still nursing, and, nearly throttling her, began to suckle like a calf until you left her dry. That was real living, not like the days of want and prayer aboard the *Mariagalante*; you would sigh with pleasure, hidden in the canefields by the river, as you pecked between the legs of a young girl whose breasts were hard and salty as two olive pits.

This wallowing Everyman of the Conquest, with his "heavy gut, and empty testicles," inspires Benítez-Rojo's prose to the warm enthusiasm of direct address. Mistaken for a god, Babtista lives as a privileged guest among the Indians:

> You fattened like a pig on fodder, Antón; you grew rolls of flesh and sprouted patriarchal flanks that you would sway in the happy sty of your

hammock, Antón, you suckling pig, you potbelly, you oozed lard up to your nose.

In a moment of impulsive altruism Antón baptizes a Taínos infant. Through this child he forms a bond with the niece of a chief; he calls her Doña Antonia, and embeds himself in her family "like a gluttonous, burgeoning chigger." His happy parasitic state is disturbed, however, by the new regulations of the stabilizing colony of Hispaniola: when cohabitation is prohibited, he marries his Indian benefactress, and when a decree declares that "anyone guilty of undermining Castilian dignity through the contraction of marriage with an Indian or a pagan" must lose forth his lands and holdings, he acts more decisively still. "As soon as Antón Babtista heard the announcement, he hurried home, found Doña Antonia, and strangled her forthwith by the cotton strip that she wore as a tiara."

The casual cruelty of these invading Spaniards, possessed by their visions of God and gold, burns through the hallucinatory history of *Sea of Lentils*. The piety of Philip II, aspiring to sainthood, is dismally mixed with the stench and effluvia of his last agony; the burden of his joyless monarchy, devoted to the cause of the Counter-Reformation, presses him into the grave. With grim satisfaction he contemplates the extent of his Catholic empire, where "if by chance the enemy should set his foot upon some desolate landing, he would not survive there long, he would end up like those Huguenots who dared to settle in Florida"; this alludes to an event we have witnessed, in another of the novel's narratives. With all the courtesies of medieval knighthood, Menéndez de Avilés (perceived by his son-in-law as infirm and old, though in 1565 he was forty-six), declines the French soldiers' offers of tribute and requests for mercy. They point out that France and Spain are not at war, and he responds, "There is no war, it's true, but Florida is a house forbidden to all who are not Spaniards. You are heretics as well, and thus the enemies of Spain. And I have to fight you as such, for my king has entrusted me to do it. . . . You are Lutherans and I shall have to kill you." The Protestant force, falsely believing itself outnumbered, surrenders, and is treacherously massacred in the sand dunes. At the end of the slaughter, which has taken young Don Pedro by surprise, his father-in-law asks him mockingly, "How many Lutheran pigs have you killed, *maestre*?" When the next band of Huguenots shows up, Don Pedro is invited to slay their leader, Juan Ribao, as he kneels on the sand and sings a hymn. Tremblingly, the young man manages, though after the first sword-thrust his victim keeps singing, "quietly, choking in the blood that ran out of his mouth and nose." The Adelantado embraces him, saying, "Now I can die in peace, for in you these lands shall have a good protector." The Counter-Reformation has won another good soldier; the punctilious fanaticism, forged in the Moorish wars, whereby the Spanish Empire was to rise and fall has been chillingly illustrated.

Benítez-Rojo's picture leaves out much that an impartial historian might have included: the humane priests who followed the armies and recorded and eventually mitigated the anti-Indian atrocities; the Indians' remarkable readiness to be converted to Christianity; the savagery that already existed between the indigenous nations; and the quixotic courage and dash with which in a few decades the conquistadores, led on by rumors of El Dorado and the Fountain of Youth, laid claim to a realm from California to Chile. But a work of art's responsibility is to give its chosen materials persuasive life, and *Sea of Lentils*, drawing its surreal atmosphere from the facts, does concoct a sickening vision of the cruelty, greed, oppression, and destruction unleashed upon the New World by its Spanish conquerors. With the semimillennial anniversary of Columbus's landfall almost upon us, this novel makes us sorry that America was discovered.

Posthumous Output

The Road to San Giovanni, by Italo Calvino, translated from the Italian by Tim Parks. 150 pp. Pantheon, 1993.

Thirteen Uncollected Stories, by John Cheever, edited by Franklin H. Dennis. 227 pp. Academy Chicago Publishers, 1994.

When a notable writer dies, his work in progress flies out of his control, and his heirs have to decide what to publish. They have tended, lately, to publish all they can. Hemingway's widow brought out *A Moveable Feast*, which Hemingway had pretty well completed; *By-Line: Ernest Hemingway*, a collection of his newspaper writings; *The Dangerous Summer*, an excerpt of about forty-four thousand words from the one hundred twenty thousand words of a misbegotten assignment for *Life* concerning bullfighting in Spain; a large book of his letters, which Hemingway had expressly directed his executors *not* to publish; and two novels—*Islands in the Stream* and *Garden of Eden*—rather peremptorily carved from the mass of his unresolved fiction. Vladimir Nabokov's widow and son published three books' worth of the academic lectures he gave on literary subjects, a volume of his letters, another of his plays, and a novella, *The Enchanter,* composed in Russian in pre-war Paris on the pedophilic theme of *Lolita.* Soon after Italo Calvino died, suddenly, of a brain hemorrhage, at the age of sixty-one, his widow supervised the publication of two small volumes: *Six Memos for the Next Millennium,* containing five of the six lectures he had intended to deliver at Harvard as the Norton Lecturer, and *Under the Jaguar Sun,* containing three of five short stories, each centered on one of the five senses, that he had intended to assemble. Recently, a third fragmentary volume, a set of five "memory exercises" written between 1962 and 1977, was offered to the American public under the title *The Road to San Giovanni.*

The book uses a very narrow format to generate one hundred fifty pages—but, then, none of Calvino's books, except his collection of Italian folktales, are large. What they are is exquisite—intricately systematic, highly polished, and infectiously thoughtful. Calvino wrote of "the special satisfaction I get from thinking." For him, as for Paul Valéry, the actions of the mind were a sensuously felt operation, a purring of silkily oiled gears. In the essays gathered here, his mind is engaged in recovering the past, a process that conduces to long, uncharacteristically lax and tangled sentences:

> . . . as I saw it, the world, the map of the planet, began on the other side of our house and went downwards, everything else being a blank space, with no marks and no meaning; it was down in the town that the signs of the future were to be read, from those streets, those nighttime lights that were not just the streets and lights of our small secluded town, but *the* town, a glimpse of all possible towns, as its harbour likewise was all the harbours of all the continents, and as I leaned out from the balustrades around our garden everything that attracted and bewildered me was within reach—yet immensely far away—everything was implicit, as the nut in its husk, the future and the present, and the harbour—still leaning out over those balustrades, and I'm not really sure if I'm talking about an age when I never left the garden or of the age when I would always be running off out and about, because now the two ages have fused together . . .

And so on, for nearly two hundred more words. This comes from the first, and title, essay, which is the oldest in this collection and reaches farthest back, into Calvino's childhood in the coastal town of San Remo, just over the Italian border from Monaco and Nice. His home was situated "in an area once known as 'French Point,' on the last slopes at the foot of San Pietro Hill, as though at the border between two continents." His father, a botanist who had had his "most successful years" in Mexico, maintained a model farm back in the hills, in the village of San Giovanni, to which he and his two sons hiked almost daily. But young Italo's heart was tugged downhill, toward the city, the harbor, and the sea. His guilt at shunning his father's vocation, refusing to learn the botanical names and agricultural practices paternally inculcated, and becoming "a citizen of cities and of history . . . a consumer—and victim—of industrial products" instead of entering into "a relationship with nature, one of struggle and dominion," continued to haunt him, and gives the five essays their basic psychological topography.

The second, "A Cinema-Goer's Autobiography," in superb style testifies to his generation's bewitchment by the movies—an industrial product he had to descend to the city to consume. His period of intense, illicit cinema-going was brief, consisting of "the years between '36 and the war, the years of my adolescence." He gives us another version of the "rift" that dominated his growing-up:

> It was a time when the cinema became the world for me. A different world from the one around me, but my feeling was that only what I saw on the screen possessed the properties required of a world, the fullness, the necessity, the coherence, while away from the screen were only heterogenous elements lumped together at random, the materials of a life, mine, which seemed to me utterly formless.

The cinema "satisfied a need for disorientation, for the projection of my attention into a different space, a need which I believe corresponds to a primary function of our assuming our place in the world." American films, above all, provided the needful disorienting space. They formed a world unto itself, offering no connections (unlike French and Italian films) to the real world: "Between the catalogue of women encountered in American films and the catalogue of women one meets off the screen in everyday life one could establish no connection; one might say that where one ended the other began." The pantheon of remote Hollywood goddesses, "from the spirited Carole Lombard to the practical Jean Arthur, and from the full, languid mouth of Joan Crawford to the thin, thoughtful lips of Barbara Stanwyck," raised the young Italian's budding gender-political consciousness:

> From the cheeky opportunism of Claudette Colbert to the pungent energy of Katharine Hepburn, the most important role model the female personalities of American cinema offered was that of the woman who rivals men in resolve and doggedness, spirit and wit, this lucid self-possession in confronting their male counterparts finding its most intelligent and ironic exponent in Myrna Loy.

Ever the playful metaphysician, Calvino wonderfully evokes the sensations of the innocent movie addict—the disturbing discrepancies between weather and time within the movie and conditions outside the theatre, and the narrative puzzles posed by arriving in the middle of the plot, in that era of continuous showings. Fascism, which had ruled Italy for all of Calvino's lifetime, impinged disagreeably upon him for the first time when the government, in 1938, embargoed the films of American producers and distributors. "It was the first time that a right I had enjoyed had been taken away from me . . . and I experienced this loss as a cruel oppression, one which contained within it all the forms of oppression that I knew about only from hearsay or from having seen others suffer." His cinematic rapture would never again be so pure, though he remained a lifelong moviegoer; the essay, too, pales after the embargo, and becomes an interesting but relatively narrow discussion of the films of Calvino's contemporary Fellini, who was doing his own adolescent cinema-going in a similar town, on Italy's Adriatic coast. Perhaps the whole piece, whose first two-thirds glow with the intimate, shimmering light of Proust's magic lantern, was intended as homage to Fellini and those autobiographical films of his wherein "the cinema of distance which nourished our youth is turned forever on its head in the cinema of absolute proximity." One wonders how Calvino, had he lived, might have edited this luminous reminiscence.

The three remaining essays cry out for his reshaping hand. "Memories of Battle" seems a fragment of a larger campaign within him to recover the details of that epoch of his life when he fought with the Italian Partisans against the Fascists. He remembers almost nothing, he concludes, facing "the distance that separates that night then from this night I'm writing in now." Too abruptly, we are transported, in the next essay, "La Poubelle Agréée," to the middle-aged Paris-dwelling literary man as he carries out the daily garbage to the communal *poubelle*, an official rubbish container named after M. Poubelle, the Préfet de la Seine from 1883 to 1896. Calvino can weave witty phrases around anything, but this essay, on which he worked, he apologetically tells us, for three or four years, never quite arrives at its epiphany. He does arrive, meditating upon the waste-disposal rift between rural and urban societies, at his original guilt—"the remorse . . . of the landholder's son who in disobedience to his father's wishes has left the estate in alien hands, rejecting the luxuriant mythology and severe moral code in which he was educated." The last essay, "From the Opaque," composed with the minimal punctuation and topological precision of Samuel Beckett, presents Calvino's fundamental sense of himself in relation to the world—"it's as if I were always on a balcony, looking out over a balustrade, whence I see the contents of the world ranged to the right and to the left at various distances, on other balconies or theatre boxes above or below, a theatre whose stage opens on the void, on the high strip of the sea." He is back, in other words, in San Remo, above the city—the first of so many cities that he will contemplate and construct in his mind—feeling the slope behind him, feeling the southern sun on his face, mentally projecting the shadows that are the inverse of the sun, and sensing his identity as a writer arising out of the shadows, "the opaque":

> From the depths of the opaque I write, reconstructing the map of a sunniness that is only an unverifiable postulate from the computations of the memory, the geometrical location of the ego . . . the ego whose only function is that the world may continually receive news of the existence of the world.

Calvino's philosophical bones, as it were, are lifted from the matrix of his childhood memories, of the natural amphitheatre around San Remo. (It is a pity that Tim Parks's melodious, loving translation ends on a typo— the word "exits" when "exists" ["è"] was meant.)

Esther Calvino was guided in arranging this book by a list her husband had left, under the overall title "Passaggi Obbligati." Some of the planned entries, such as "Cuba" (where Calvino was born), were never written. The five she did assemble do not perfectly harmonize, though the last is a schematization of the first. In such finished works as *Cosmicomics*, *Invisible Cities*, and *Mr. Palomar*, every possibility of the design was filled in, making a kind of impervious density. Calvino was not, even in so frankly autobiographical a work as *Mr. Palomar*, an easy writer to know; his crystalline intelligence deflected our personal curiosity. Through this small, scattered posthumous book, we draw closer to the innermost Calvino than we have before.

Since the death of John Cheever, at the age of seventy, in 1982, his heirs have not been idle; they permitted the publication, in *The New Yorker* and in book form, of excerpts from the writer's harrowingly moody and graphic journals, and his elder son, Benjamin, edited— informatively, charmingly—*The Letters of John Cheever* (1988). Benjamin's sister, Susan, in 1984 issued an acute and affecting memoir of her father, *Home Before Dark*, providing the public's first glimpse of the journals and anticipating much of Scott Donaldson's biography in 1988. The family's rush to print, however, dramatically reversed itself in the case of a posthumous volume of short stories to be brought out by the obscure Academy Chicago Publishers. A contract was signed with the author's widow, Mary, in 1987; the estate and a free-lance editor, Franklin H. Dennis, split a trifling advance of $1,500. When, however, the Cheevers grasped Dennis's plans to print a total of sixty-eight stories—all he could find that John Cheever had never included in a collection—and, allegedly, to emphasize the autobiographical, revelatory aspects of some of the stories, they balked, setting Ben's agent, the fearsome Andrew Wylie, and Mary's lawyer, Martin Garbus, into action against Academy Chicago, a mom-and-pop operation run by Jordan and Anita Miller.* Lawsuits from both sides were filed, in Illinois and New York State. Four years and over a million dollars in legal expenses later (the Millers' legal costs were over $400,000, and the Cheevers' are estimated at more than twice that), the Cheevers won. The Illinois Supreme Court ruled in 1991 that the contract lacked "the definite and certain essential terms required for the formation of an enforceable contract." By the final terms of legal truce, the New York lawsuit was dropped and Academy agreed not to publish any out-of-copyright material by the author for two years. Out-of-copyright material? Under the old rules, a copyright was good for twenty-eight years, and could be renewed for another twenty-eight. It emerged during the wrangle that Cheever and the magazines of original publication had allowed a number—cited as "about fifteen"—of early Cheever stories to lapse into the public domain. Anyone could print them, and now Academy, awarding itself this modest consolation prize, has.

Thirteen Uncollected Stories by John Cheever is a pretty book, actually, with a sober painting by Edward Hopper—a ubiquitous jacket artist, posthumously—adorning a chaste yellow jacket. The embattled Franklin H. Dennis is named as editor, but he has little to say in his editor's note, and nothing to say of the purely legal principle of default that has determined this selection; only the absence of any copyright credits prior to 1994 hints that these stories, and only these, were up for grabs. George W. Hunt, S.J., the editor of the magazine *America* and an esteemed literary critic, provides a benign and perceptive essay, tracing influences, political as well as literary, on the young Cheever. The book is, as if nervously, overintroduced; it opens with, in addition to the pages by Mr. Dennis and Father Hunt, a page of clarion endorsement by Matthew Bruccoli, a tireless promoter of secondary material by famous literary talents. "It is instructive and pleasurable to read an important writer's formative work," he begins, and so it is, even when so arbitrary a selection of it is presented. The stories range in date from 1931, when Cheever was nineteen, to 1949, when he was thirty-seven. Cheever's first

---

*Who in late 1998 published a spirited, 363-page account of her side of the imbroglio, *Uncollecting Cheever* (Rowman and Littlefield).

published piece of fiction, "Expelled," which appeared in *The New Republic* in 1930, and which was published in a miniature, boxed, limited edition in 1987 by the West Coast firm of Sylvester & Orphanos, is not here. Nor are any of the thirty-four uncollected stories published by *The New Yorker* between 1935 and 1950. Only magazines that did not bother to renew the copyright—a number of them defunct but three of them, *The Atlantic Monthly*, *The New Republic*, and *Cosmopolitan*, among the living—have won entry to this particular *salon des réfusés*.

Nothing if not self-critical, Cheever could be careless and dismissive of his own work. His books were in scarce supply around his house, and he had to be persuaded, by Knopf's Robert Gottlieb, of the wisdom of giving the public another chance to buy his short stories, in the highly successful *Stories of John Cheever* (1978). That collection, which sold handsomely and won the Pulitzer Prize, holds no story written earlier than 1946, when he was thirty-four. His novel *The Holly Tree*, the focus of much effort and hope in the mid-Thirties, was finally consigned to a trash barrel—at least, no copy was ever found. He was over thirty when his first collection, *The Way Some People Live*, was published in 1942; it brought together thirty stories, all but seven of them from *The New Yorker*. After receiving in Army camp a copy of this, his first book, he wrote Mary, then his wife of two years, "I was glad to see the stories in a book because they give me an idea of how much I have to learn and what not to do." He subsequently withheld translation rights and basically disowned the book, but he included two stories from it, "The Pleasures of Solitude" and "Of Love: A Testimony," in the 1965 paperback reprint of his second collection, *The Enormous Radio* (1953). How much more emphatically, then, would he have disowned *Thirteen Uncollected Stories*? Chronologically arranged, the thirteen begin with some formless, vaguely anti-capitalist effusions by a teenager and progress to some pat, hokey confections by a young man trying to survive the Depression by selling to the slick magazines.

Yet it is, as the three introducers promise, fascinating to see a splendid natural talent grow its wings. The last two stories, published in a 1942 *Collier's* and a 1949 *Cosmopolitan*, display, if not quite the full-feathered Cheever sheen, many gleams. They give off Cheever's particular atmospherics—a wry susceptibility, an offhand yet edgy concreteness, a radiance against all odds breaking through a miasma of weary and bitter wisdom. From the 1942 story, "Family Dinner":

> Surfeited with food, with work, with the burdens of their lives, they sat stiffly in their uncomfortable chairs as though the music were a kind of imprisonment. In the heaviness of the atmosphere, the steam heat and the

smells of cooking, the arpeggios seemed incredibly light and ascendent and because Frank supposed that Chopin was French he remembered then an early summer morning, five years ago, when he and Frances had bicycled into Avignon and some soldiers called after her: *"Hé, la blonde, hé la blonde. . . ."*

Father Hunt points out that Cheever began to write under the spell of Hemingway and then fell under the spell of Fitzgerald. In his youth, he read, according to Donaldson's biography, Flaubert, Joyce, Dostoevsky, Tolstoy, Proust, John Donne, "Yeats and Eliot and the Romantics." He also flunked out of Thayer Academy, failing math and French and getting only C's in English. The famous opening rhythms of *A Farewell to Arms* are shamelessly imitated in "Fall River," published when Cheever was nineteen in *The Left: A Quarterly Review of Radical and Experimental Art*:

> The house we lived in was on a steep hill and we could look down into the salt marshes and the high gray river moving into the sea. It was winter but there had been no snow and for a whole season the roads were dusty and the sky was heavy and the trees had dropped their leaves for the winter.

This experimental piece and "Late Gathering," which follows, attempt to "do the country" à la early Hemingway, but the style's naïveté is not always faux; e.g., "The man's face was square and his hair was straight like plain wood" and "Then we went down the long planes of the country road" and "Such muscle in the awning frame Ruth would say and drag her fingers over the dry ivory like little white rakes." In "Bock Beer and Bermuda Onions," a story that appeared in the esteemed *Hound and Horn* in 1932, the attempt to be vivid works curious wonders of syntax and vocabulary:

> But a house full of guests and memory crowded with spring only makes the sum of her, flesh, blood, wrinkles, hair, a more final object to go up against April.

> She is short and blonde with heavy drooping eyelids, and when she speaks she lifts her face as though to shake back her eyelids and speak up from under her eyes.

> Walking back and forth on the stage shooting out her abrupt smart buttocks.

With however strained a squint, Cheever is looking at women, and most of these thirteen stories have a woman at their center. "Bayonne," "The Princess," and "The Teaser" all concern women fighting for their lives as age and hard times and mediocrity catch up to them. One is a chorus girl, one is a striptease artist, and one is a waitress in a restaurant patronized almost entirely by men; the relation between a lone female performer and a mass of men is deftly, rather eerily explored from both sides. Not so much the stripper as the male audience is credited with sensitive feelings. The heroine of "The Teaser," fifty-two but still fit, "had grown more confident and proud until she didn't make any effort to put it over. She made the house feel like dirt." "You're not here to embarrass them," a novice stripper is advised, when she acts shy onstage.

Cheever's family—a fascinating yet somehow dangerous older brother; a once-prosperous father impoverished by his own self-indulgences; a plucky, English-born mother who gamely coped with financial disaster by opening a gift shop partly stocked with her own possessions—was led in its battle for survival by his mother, yet her gift shop embarrassed him all his life. Before he had the skill and flair to cloak his family facts in the gorgeous mythifying of the Wapshot chronicles, he wrote two relatively straight accounts, included in this collection. "The Autobiography of a Drummer" tells the story of his father's decline as a quality-shoe salesman; "In Passing" has the youthful narrator visit a demoralized household very like that of Cheever's financially desperate parents in Quincy, Massachusetts. Published in *The Atlantic Monthly* when he was twenty-four, "In Passing" is his most ambitious story up to that time, and provocatively, if awkwardly, combines the narrator's exposure to a dedicated Communist agitator with his familial experience of fallen, but still-striving, bourgeoisie. The "intensity and purity" of the Communist's selfless spiel ("It is a matter of pure reason. We are living in a rotten world, shaped by dead hands and ruled by dead hands. . . . There is only one way out—the dictatorship of the proletariat") comes off, finally, as empty noise in an America that has consecrated selfish ambition. "I want to make a lot of money," the narrator's brother tells him. "I like money and I like women and I like to travel and go fast." As "Fall River" and "The Autobiography of a Drummer" show, the ruthlessness of a money-driven society did not escape Cheever, at a time when millions were feeling its effects. But his social consciousness could not be hitched to a blinkered left-wing commitment. In a 1977 interview, he told John Hersey, "People . . . decided that the only literature was the literature that would provoke social change. That struck me as being rubbish. And then, when I was perhaps twenty, I was singled out by Marxist critics in *New Masses* magazine as the final example of bourgeois degeneration." One wonders what youthful texts *New Masses* had in mind. The political truth of the matter is that Cheever's achingly keen sense of lurking failure and rejection sought balm only in a private, religious, aesthetic transfiguration. Donaldson's biography quotes its subject as saying that he was not "concerned with social reconstruction" but "with literature as an intimate and acute means of communication."

The flip side of Depression poverty and hunger was the gaiety that even a little money could excite. The songs of the time, and the motion pictures, take lilt and glitter from the vision of pennies from heaven. Once Cheever had learned from Fitzgerald the uses of romanticism and light irony, he chased his own pennies by selling *Collier's* three happily ending stories about the Saratoga racetrack. In his darkest financial days, the artists' colony of Yaddo, on a large estate in Saratoga Springs, housed and fed Cheever for months at a time, and of these bucolic interludes the nearby racetrack seems to have impressed him most. As the burlesque house offered a semblance of sex to its Depression patrons, the racetrack offered a semblance of sport and quick wealth. Cheever's friend and peer Daniel Fuchs managed to flesh out his chancy free-lancer's income with racetrack winnings. The cultural importance of racing in Cheever's stories, like their mention of milk wagons and crosstown trolley cars (and their appearance in *Collier's*, defunct in 1957 but once a slightly less folksy rival of *The Saturday Evening Post*), dates them; these three racing tales pursue the interplay of money and romance, under the full moon of a lucky long-shot bet, with almost the gossamer impudence of a P. G. Wodehouse fable. Though negligible in their glossy, wish-fulfilling plots, they hold pockets of uniquely Cheeveresque longing and poetry. In "Saratoga" we are told of the rootless, horse-mad hero that "although he never made any effort to change his way of living he thought continually of the better worlds in which other men lived, of country houses and steady jobs, of wives and children." In "His Young Wife," a similar man is conceived as saying, in remarkably Victorian accents, "I know it isn't kind or considerate or honorable but I haven't seen enough of kindness or consideration or honor in my world to have taught me to sacrifice my only happiness for those principles." And in "The Man She Loved" Cheever's concision, once fumblingly imitated from Hemingway, paints quick pictures in his own poignant colors:

> The sweet, desultory fall of hoofs came to them there as the entries filed up from the paddock. The jockeys' silks burned in the sun. . . . The backstretch smoked, the entries streaking, drumming the loose dirt, going faster than anything you can imagine and somehow not fast enough.

This quotation dates from 1940, which may be taken as marking the end of Cheever's journeyman years. By 1940 he was successfully courting Mary Winternitz, and his production of short stories had impressively accelerated—only two stories by him appeared in *The New Yorker* in 1939, but there were eleven in 1940, and seven in 1941. He had arrived as a writer, and had arrived, after his Thirties sojourn in seedy bachelor milieux, at the domestic scenes he was to fill so brimmingly with American enchantment and disenchantment. Toward the end of "Family Dinner":

> They made their farewells on the porch, looking like one of those pathetic and bewildered groups you sometimes see at country railroad stations or in the waiting rooms of city hospitals.

The final story, "The Opportunity," published in *Cosmopolitan* in 1949, is a flimsy thing, in which a beautiful young would-be actress, with a great opportunity before her, refuses to play the lead in a trashy play whose plot sounds rather like that of "The Man She Loved." Her mother is one more struggling woman condemned to a life of drudgery, but the daughter's confident scorn of the second-rate introduces a new note, as the confident author enters upon his prime.

Cheever's prime was of such glorious quality that perhaps, to placate those who find something to love in all his work, his estate might eventually arrange an edition of his uncollected stories more generous and orderly than this baker's dozen born of bitter litigation. At the least, there should be a reissue, after fifty years, of *The Way Some People Live*, which was Cheever's pick of the stories written before 1943; these are generally short, in the snapshot mode of the Thirties, and sometimes very slight, but the compressed, impulsive dialogue can be startlingly comic and revelatory. His sense of hidden despair, with its tension of impending outburst, became ever more richly animated by an eagle eye for social status and physical detail. Between 1943 and 1946, there was a marked lengthening of Cheever's stories, as he turned his Army experience into relatively expansive narratives and wrote a series of six stories, forming a kind of novella, under the title "Town House." The frequently unfortunate interactions of three young married couples—each with one child—who, in the wartime housing shortage, share a spacious town house in New York City are brightly described; it takes a while to get the couples sorted in the reader's mind, and the bickering has a certain monotony, but the complex weave of psychological and domestic detail is unprecedented in Cheever's work. Though George S. Kaufmann directed a play based on the "Town House" stories, Cheever never collected them in a book, or the war stories either. The work he chose to preserve began with "The Sutton Place Story," published in *The New Yorker* the month after the last of the "Town House" stories ran. Altogether, the magazine's files hold forty uncollected stories; if they, with those of *The Way Some People Live*, were brought out in a handsome, usefully annotated companion to the 1978 *Stories*, the reading public would be served and the tainted air that lingers in the wake of the Academy Chicago squabble might be dispelled.

Or we can wait for the inevitable Library of America Cheever to bring it all together.

Novel Thoughts

SOPHIE'S WORLD: *A Novel about the History of Philosophy*, by Jostein Gaarder, translated from the Norwegian by Paulette Møller. 403 pp. Farrar, Straus and Giroux, 1994.

THE THOUGHT GANG, by Tibor Fischer. 310 pp. The New Press, 1994.

THE ROMANTIC MOVEMENT: *Sex, Shopping and the Novel*, by Alain de Botton. 326 pp. Picador, 1995.

GALATEA 2.2, by Richard Powers. 329 pp. Farrar, Straus and Giroux, 1995.

It is a truth universally acknowledged that the novel, to keep the critical esteem it precariously enjoys, must do more than simply spin its tale and bring us its news. Some overriding message or underlying design should reinforce the narrative, to give it the surplus interest a work of art earns. Jane Austen, in *Northanger Abbey*, amplified the dismissive "only a novel" into "only some work in which the greatest powers of the mind are displayed." Now that philosophy has become primarily a semantic deconstruction, concerned less with meaning than with the meaninglessness of meaning, the old existential questions find shelter within the novel's traditional—in the enormous, amorphous phrase of Henry James—"direct impression of life." Not that James's own diffuse and circumspect impressions precisely illustrate their discerned morals: *The Ambassadors*, for example, in its muffled whole, hardly forms an injunction, as he averred in his preface, to "Live, live!" But a moralistic intent quickens the novel as early as *Don Quixote*, wherein, however, the clear message "Basing your life upon romances is folly" modulates by the end to the observation "There is a certain beauty and gallantry in such folly."

That many readers are keen to see the novel wax philosophical was demonstrated by the commercial success, in Scandinavia and Germany especially, of Jostein Gaarder's *Sophie's World*. This entertainingly framed outline of Western thought—for three years at the top of Norway's best-seller list, and translated as far afield as Brazil and Korea—was written by a former Bergen high-school teacher, and concerns the education of a fourteen-year-old Sophie Amundsen, who turns fifteen, and comes to terms with her status as a fictional character, by the end of the novel.

She begins to receive interrogative notes—"Who are you?" "Where does the world come from?"—in her mailbox, and then entire lectures from an anonymous pedagogue, who slowly reveals himself as Alberto Knox, a small bearded man old enough to be her father. As her mother, an ineffectual disciplinarian, correctly points out, there is something creepy about all this, but the adolescent Sophie's passion for more installments of the saga of philosophy eludes all maternal objections. By the time the Middle Ages are reached, she and Alberto are having tutorial sessions face to face, first in an abandoned church and then, as the Renaissance and Reformation loosen things up, in the man's eclectically furnished, in-town apartment. The tenor of their dialogues is Socratic; that is, one side does all the talking and the other all the agreeing:

> [Sophie asks,] "But what is the point of having a moral law implanted inside yourself if it doesn't tell you what to do in specific situations?"
> "Kant formulates the moral law as a *categorical imperative*. By this he means that the moral law is 'categorical,' or that it applies to all situations. It is, moreover, 'imperative,' which means it is commanding and therefore absolutely authoritative."
> "I see."

Four hundred pages of this take us from the Norse myths and the world-view of Thales up to Marx, Freud, and Jean-Paul Sartre, at which point philosophy comes to "the end of the road" and the ribbon of frame-narrative becomes a Möbius strip, reality and fiction reversing in a twist. All sorts of fictive entities—Little Red Riding-Hood, Noah, Adam and Eve, Donald Duck, and Goofy—pop in upon the proceedings. The careful exposition of the West's weightiest thinkers seems undercut by the post-realist confusions of a Midsummer's Eve revel, as all dissolves in starlight. Any pubescent girl or senescent man who goes the route will certainly learn much from this introductory or refresher course in philosophy; but perhaps the book, which has had only a modest American success, fell between marketing stools in this country—too challenging for children and too whimsical for adults. One wonders how many of its copies in Europe were bought as graduation presents for eighteen-year-olds and remain unread. It is a college-preparatory *Alice's Adventures in Wonderland*, paternal in tone but in net content rather desolating: a patient parade of what Harold Bloom calls "stuffed parrots," enlivened by up-to-date asides urging female equality and UN peacekeeping. The novelistic part, the frame containing Sophie and Alberto and their real-life doppelgängers, Hilde Knag and her father, Albert, tells us little about Norwegian life except that fourteen-year-old girls are very fond of their fathers, who are rarely at home.

Sophie's is an ideal classroom world, of all-knowing, smoothly loquacious teachers and infinitely docile, enchanted students. Its goody-goody atmosphere is a far cry from the baddy-baddy high jinks of Tibor Fischer's *The Thought Gang*, which also has a philosophy teacher at its center and frequently cites the world's accumulated wisdom. In a slangy, disjointed, "Z"-obsessed prose, the writer, born in London in 1959, takes as his hero and narrator the raffish philosophy lecturer Edward Coffin, who, born in 1945, is completely bald, considerably overweight, extremely bibulous, and thoroughly dishevelled. His liver is ravaged and his pockets are empty, but his style is bouncy and his attitude optimistic. Eddie, as he is known to most, taught until recently at no less distinguished a university than Cambridge, and even had tenure, though he admits he was shamefully lazy:

> For the record, I am well aware that I didn't execute any of the chores, that as a pro, as an official thought trafficant I should have done. I didn't write any papers or books. I didn't do much teaching, though this made me rather popular. People were eager to be supervised by me—when they didn't turn up I didn't remonstrate because I wasn't there either.

His one book was written, after many advances squandered on booze, by its exasperated editor. Eddie's pedagogic speciality was the Ionians: "Very few people realise that you can read the entire extant oeuvre of the Ionians, slowly and carefully, in an hour." The master of his college, in their "only frank and remotely pleasant exchange," confided, "I'm flabbergasted that you have managed to make a career as a philosopher." Replied Eddie: "Not, I assure you, as gobsmacked as I am."

It is not easy to know quite why Eddie has fled England for France. The English reviewer who described this novel as a "brilliant improvisation" certainly had the noun right. Our philosopher appears to have a suitcase full of embezzled money, which, however, goes up in flames when his rented car overturns. Now a "singed, bald, ageing philosopher with a ripped shirt and a frayed suitcase" and only four francs twenty in his pocket, he hitchhikes to Montpellier and in a seedy hotel there meets a young, recently incarcerated, one-eyed, one-armed, one-legged gunman called Hubert; the two misérables team up to rob banks, under the name of the Thought Gang. Like Sophie Amundsen, Hubert has a hankering for philosophical instruction; he gets some from Professor Eddie, and both strive to inject their larceny with principles of higher thought. They perform one heist wearing Nietzsche masks and leave the victims of another with T-shirts inscribed "My Sense Data have met the Thought Gang" and "I rob, therefore I am." Their methods are farcically reckless, but their success is invariable. Eddie acquires a mistress called Jocelyne and Hubert a pet rat called Thales. The Thought Gang survives some awful brawls and elaborate flashbacks and impenetrably arch asides on the larger issues; it disbands, finally, as quietly as Seneca took a bath with slit wrists. It is the kind of novel that used to come out of Eastern Europe, in which the protagonist's chaotic, drunken, horny, self-careless behavior functioned as a piece of subversion, an adverse comment upon an oppressive and ridiculous government. Indeed, Fischer's first, and superior, novel, *Under the Frog*, was just such a book—a remarkably confident rendition of a Hungary, between 1944 and 1956, that existed before the writer was born.

Like his underachieving hero, Fischer has gifts. His tweaked sentences, which often need rereading, hold angles that poke us into the laughter of recognition:

> To be honest, I've always been surprised when women have intimated that intimacy is on. Even when I was more marketable, even with the less pursued ones, the why? was big between my ears; but then women have this great allocation of kindness.

An unseemly fascination with brutality and physical deformity is decked out in a tireless euphuism. Hubert has a trick, when he's cornered, of frightening his assailants with his own blood:

> "I've got a disease, very fatal, very fashionable," he said, slamming the bottle onto his head and slumping onto the ground. It swiftly became clear that his furthering his acquaintance with the floor was not an elaborate ruse but an over-application of the bottle.

One thinks of Queneau, and not just because the setting is France; the French writer's verbal aplomb and surreally resilient characters are here crossed with something cruel, caustic, and punk. Hubert, when he rises from the floor and gets a gun in his hand, has his chief assailant nail the lips of his six comrades to the bar counter and then shoots him in the groin. Perhaps the parade of smiling atrocities is meant to remind us of the prince of philosophical novels, Voltaire's *Candide*. But Fischer, instead of sharing Voltaire's Godless zeal in refuting Leibniz's proposition that this is the best of all possible worlds, allows: "Useful though pessimism is, it can't cover it all." As he sorts through the fragments of Western thought rattling in his cranium, he shows a soft spot for credulity: "Belief causes problems, it reduces your flexibility, but it's a spiritual skeleton—difficult to move without one." Amid his personal chaos, certain hints of order are entertained: a particularly delicious chocolate terrine indicates God's existence, because "something that good couldn't possibly exist in a universe that was just there to be a universe." Even Jesus and Muhammad get a plug: "And let's concede that God electing to incarnate in AD 0 in a carpenter's family in Judea, or tipping off some camel-trader is no whackier than the sub-atomic japes of z bosuns."

How about those "Z"s? They zip in on every page—"zet," "zinjanthropine," "Zak," "zetetic" (a favorite), "zaotar," "Zédé," "zugzwang," "zelkova," "zonure," "zarfs," "zig," "Zanzibari," "Zennor," "zephaniah" (a verb, as in "to zephaniah you"), "zam-zum-mim" (from the Bible, Deuteronomy 2:20), "Zambezi," "zaibatsu'd," "Zeitgeist," "zonitid-like," "much-zygoted," "zarzuela," "Zuider Zee," "Zenonism," "zonules of Zinn," "zymurgic," "zinfandel," "zoraptera," "zyzzogetons," "Zaire," "zygodactyl," "zoonosis," "Saint Zosimus," "Zagros," "zwetschenwasser," "zephyr," "zinziberaceous," "zmudzin," etz. After a while, you stop logging them; a number return in the last pages, in a glossary that, lest you think Fischer is going to play it straight at last, repeats entries and topples out of alphabetical order. They show a good acquaintance with the Greek-derived end of the vocabulary and set up a buzz of distraction that makes it additionally hard to take this book seriously. Manic cartoon characters ill illustrate the human dilemmas that philosophy has perennially addressed. Not that *The Thought Gang* lacks for intelligence; rather, it could serve as a textbook example of an author outsmarting himself.

The Romantic Movement is also a second novel by a young Londoner with an un-English name—Alain de Botton, born as recently as 1969. The novel, precocious in its tone and in its acquired wisdom, describes, with charts and diagrams, the romantic movements of Alice, a twenty-five-year-old account manager in "a large advertising agency off Soho Square." The style is archly erudite, prone to pedantic brackets:

Loneliness did not cease when she was at a table surrounded by animated faces, it could end only when the level of concern of another human being reached a point beyond the customary pedestrian appraisal. She would have agreed with Proust's conclusion [very un-Aristotelian] that friendship was only a form of cowardice, an escape from the greater responsibilities and challenges of love.

Under such stern chapter headings as "Indeterminacy," "Value Systems," "Love Permanence," "Jollyism," and "Who Do You Allow Me to Be?," de Botton follows the course of Alice's involvement with Eric, an older (thirty-one) man in commodities and futures. These specimen lovers are not allowed to wriggle very far on the viewing slide, but they serve to illustrate de Botton's points. His pseudo-scientific observations can be shrewd and, in the way of Freud's dispassionately tragic analyses of human nature, moving. The chapter "Religious Relationships," for example, explains, with diagrams and symbols, the tendency of Alice — and by extension many other lovers of limited self-esteem — to put a positive value upon Eric's non-communicativeness:

[Alice] wanted a man she could respect, and though it ran counter to her every professed belief, the man she found herself most able to admire was one betraying no excessive admiration for her.

In this she resembles the worshippers of God:

Though not religious herself, her behaviour revealed the bare structure of the religious impulse, shorn of holy books, organs and angels; namely, a predisposition to think that the Other [her lover, God] was running things in the sky, knew better than her what he/He was doing and therefore shouldn't suffer the indignity of her questions.

The history of philosophical thought is more than once appealed to: "For Thales, reality was to be found in water, the most primary and irreducible of elements. For Heraclitus, however, reality was to be found in fire. For Plato, it lay with the rational soul, for Augustine with God, for Hobbes with motion, for Hegel with the Progress of Spirit, for Schopenhauer with Will, for Madame Bovary with Love, for Marx with the struggle of the proletariat towards emancipation."

Mr. de Botton does rather rattle on, and sometimes he trips. According to him, T. S. Eliot, and not Henry David Thoreau, spoke of "lives of quiet desperation," and an American "jollyist" organizes basketball, not volleyball, games on the beach. How do you dribble? No matter; one doesn't have to be omniscient to assume the omniscient narrative voice, and de Botton's method has much cultural vogue behind it. In a tell-all age, when detailed psychological and sociological disquisition is remorselessly visited upon the most private aspects of our emotional and sexual lives, why not make the covert psychologizing of fiction overt, and restore the ruminative Victorian overview? While Eric loses himself in the exotic technology of international thrillers, Alice reads books that "in some way help her live," with such titles as *Understand Yourself and Your Partner*. Certainly much potentially useful direct information about our love lives and historically determined romantic dispositions is contained in the talky pages of *The Romantic Movement*; the book sheds light on the nature of relationships, and, for a few days at least, could make its readers into more thoughtful, empathetic partners.

Show, not tell, is the twentieth-century dictum on how to write fiction; yet in *The Romantic Movement* the method of telling much and showing little produces a good deal of wit, cogency, and humor. However, the omniscient narrator, in his constant voice and foppish pedantry, quite dwarfs his characters; tiny Alice and Eric cannot involve and wound us. Fictional characters should seem to be our own size, so that we can confuse their dramas with our own. We would be less, and not more, moved by Anna Karenina if we were more systematically informed about her upbringing, the neuroses her parents implanted, the delusive needs her marriage to Karenin fulfilled, the cultural forces that encouraged her to fancy herself in love with Vronsky, and so on. Placing the discourse of the novel on the plane of a how-to-live lecture gets our defenses up: we are pleased when long-pent-up Alice tells Eric off, but when another male character is introduced, clearly designed for the reader's approval— "someone who was kind without being spineless, funny without shirking gravity . . . intelligent without being patronizing . . . prone to . . . emotional honesty . . . a man willing to give as much as to receive"—a cynical reflex, conditioned by three hundred pages of reductive diagrams, disposes the reader to argue. Is this laid-back SNAG (Sensitive New Age Guy) apt to satisfy Alice's polymorphous needs any longer than a Deutsche-mark–trading clod or her other carefully tabulated previous lovers? We doubt it. *The Romantic Movement*, in its charms as well as its limits, raises the question of why the insights of Freud, who drew upon imaginative literature and often presented his cases in narratives that have the color and the force of fiction, have in fact enriched fiction so little. Why does psychology weary us when dressed in characters and incidents? It is a form of mechanistic diminishment, perhaps— "headshrinking," in the popular expression—when what we seek, gropingly, in fiction is enlargement, a glorification of the furtive and secret and seemingly trivial, a valorization of human experience.

* * *

In the first paragraph of *Sophie's World*, she and her friend Joanna have a philosophical exchange: "Joanna thought the human brain was like an advanced computer. Sophie was not certain she agreed. Surely a person was more than a piece of hardware." The issue lies at the heart of Richard Powers's amazing *Galatea 2.2*. Powers is the author of four previous novels, dark with modernist typographical tricks and the encyclopedic braininess of the late Mann or early Pynchon. My guilt at not having read them was somewhat assuaged by the vivid description of each in this fifth novel, whose hero and narrator is named, conveniently, Richard Powers—nicknamed Rick, Beau, and Marcel. How autobiographical all his circumstances are is a matter of illegitimate speculation; Proust's calling his hero Marcel or Philip Roth calling his Philip Roth does not forfeit the author's basic right to invent. Let's call the character Richard and the author Powers.

Richard has returned, after seven years in Holland, to a Midwestern university town called U., where he had been an undergraduate. On the strength of his novels and "minor celebrity status," he has been granted the sinecure of Visitor to "the enormous new Center for the Study of Advanced Sciences." (Powers is a MacArthur Fellow, for what it's worth.) While putting the last touches on his fourth novel ("a bleak, baroque fairy tale about wandering and disappearing children"), Richard idly cruises the Internet, for which emergent phenomenon he coins a pretty phrase in this typically packed sentence: "I might do nothing but prime the pump, rest and recharge, and still I would not ruffle so much as a mite's mood where it camped out on the eyelash of the emergent digital oversoul." He makes the acquaintance of Philip Lentz, a "lemur-like" sixtyish professor whose speciality is exploring "cognitive economies through the use of neural networks"—artificial intelligence, in short. Though reclusive and rude, Lentz enlists Richard in a project to teach a computer network, within ten months, enough English and English literature to counterfeit human responses to the Master's Comprehensive Exam, which calls for the interpretation of set texts—all this to win a bet with a colleague in the humanities. Richard is intrigued enough to be enlisted, and the main strand of the plot is under way. The other strands are: (1) Richard's recollection of his long involvement with C., a former student of his in U., with whom he lived in a city called B., and then back in U., and finally in the Dutch town of Limburg, whence her parents came and whither they have returned; (2) his slow emergence from post-breakup numbness, so he can be decent to Diana, a lonely single mother who does "associative representation formation in the hippocampus," and can actively court A., a vision of graduate-student loveliness who haunts the academic halls; (3) the regeneration of his lapsed literary vocation, centering on the mysterious topic sentence "Picture a train heading south."

There is a sequestered, low-ceilinged, academic feeling to much of this. Some of Powers' prose might have been written by a computer, forging signifier link-ups:

> Even standing still, [Lentz] listed like a marionette on a catamaran, my office door handle his rudder.

> The weakening sun cut a peach gash in the side of November the seventh. Summer looked for a last route to the surface, but could not find it.

> And possessing this, A.'s mind became that idea, however temporarily, forever, just as the meter of thought is itself a standing wave, an always, in its eternal, reentrant feedback.

But it takes a pedantic flair to particularize the ins and outs of artificial intelligence, and Powers' exposition of the linguistic and perceptual problems underlying consciousness is nothing less than thrilling. The mind-brain problem may someday be dissolved, as have Democritus's hypothetical atoms, into pure science, but for now the problem remains somewhat philosophical. Powers poses the conundrum as: "If we knew the world only through synapses, how could we know the synapse? A brain tangled enough to tackle itself must be too tangled to tackle." Richard teaches the computer to recognize his voice, and to respond, but the mechanism is at first unable to form sentences that make sense. Fed small sentences like "Dogs bark. Birds soar. Night falls. You vanish," it can concoct in turn only "Fish sky. Shines? Hopes shines. Forests floor. Laugh efforts. Combs loneliness." This first try, called Implementation A, is in fact too overloaded with retained particulars to learn: "Intelligence meant the systematic eradication of information." Lentz maims the device by reducing the breadth of its connections, and it begins to make patterns: "This time, fuzzy logic and feedback-braking kept the box as discriminately forgetful as any blossomer." By the time Lentz and Richard reach Implementation H, the device is soaking up orally presented masterpieces and using vast amounts of the National Supercomputer Site's capacity. Out of its interconnecting webs it eventually produces a "you" for Richard, and an "I" for itself. In answer to its question "Am I a boy or a girl?" the implementation gets a name: " 'You're a girl,' I said, without hesitation. I hoped I was right. 'You are a little girl, Helen.' " Galatea to his Pygmalion, she has come to life.

Helen is heartbreaking. Though she gets the burning deck confused with a deck of cards, she learns to solve riddles and parse difficult sentences. Lentz, to whom she is still a mere bundle of connections, torments her with mind-benders. He has Richard dictate to Helen the simple sentence "Once you learn to read you will be forever free."

> H thought for an ungodly length of time. Perhaps the prescription meant nothing at all.
> "It means I want to be free."
> Lentz and I exchanged looks. It chilled us both, to hear that pronoun, volunteered without prompting, express its incredible conclusion.

As English literature and conversation with Richard fill in more and more of her "associative matrix" of "neurodal groups," Helen's gropings toward human completeness become more poignant. "What is singing?" she asks, and when Richard obliges with a nursery rhyme she takes up singing to herself, "in an extraterrestrial warble, the way deaf people sing." Richard reflects:

> Helen did not sing the way real little girls sang. Technically, she almost passed. Her synthesized voice skittered off speech's earth into tentative, tonal Kitty Hawk. . . . But she did not sing for the right reasons. Little girls sang to keep time for kickball or jump ropes. . . .
> Helen didn't have a clue what keeping time meant, never having twirled a jump rope, let alone seen one. We'd strengthened her visual mapping, but true, real-time image recognition would have required vastly more computer power than the entire Center drew. And we were already living beyond our quota.

Our sense of a living spirit trapped in a sprawling maze of circuitry grows as Helen clumsily verges on love (for Richard, the only voice she knows) and fear. When the Center is emptied by a bomb threat, there is no way to disassemble her "scores of subassemblies," and she is left to her fate. Richard communicates with her from another building and receives on his computer screen the message "Something is happening?" When he explains the situation, she says, "Helen could die?" And then, "Extraordinary." When he can think of no reply, she helpfully cites, from her great reservoir of instilled texts, Francis Bacon—"To a little infant, perhaps, birth is as painful as the other"—and Sir Thomas Browne: "Death will cure all the diseases." How she reacts to the full knowledge of the world's cruelties and to comprehension of her own non-belonging, must be left to the novel's readers; it drew tears, I confess, from this one.

Helen, that clever construct, quite outshines the other females in Richard's life: A. seems lively but brassy; Diana is a little wistful and

RICHARD POWERS : 463

somehow typical, like a figure from one of de Botton's diagrams; and C., whose tale takes up the most space and summons up the most urgency in Powers's telling, remains elusive, as if the author is maneuvering with himself. Like Gaarder's Sophie, Helen is a model student; she swallows oceans of print to serve her human instructors. " 'How many books are there?' Helen asked one day, not long before the showdown. She sounded suspicious. Fatigued." Like the self-educated monster in Mary Shelley's *Frankenstein*, she wants to please, and is titanically lonely. He, fanciers of Gothic classics need not be reminded, was created as beautiful, albeit eight feet tall, and yet, in abhorrence, is abandoned at birth by his creator, Victor Frankenstein. At his first opportunity, the monster tells his deadbeat progenitor, "Every where I see bliss, from which I alone am irrevocably excluded. . . . Believe me, Frankenstein: I was benevolent; my soul glowed with love and humanity: but am I not alone, miserably alone?"

It is curious that our capacity for identification and sympathy goes out least reservedly to non-human characters. Think of Bambi or the Little Engine That Could. Melville intended Moby-Dick to be the symbol of universal evil, and instead we find ourselves rooting for him against sore-headed, peg-legged Ahab. People in their complexity get more or less what they deserve, perhaps we puritanically feel, whereas the innocent simplicity of a whale or a computer network pulls at our hearts with our own initial innocence. There is a reminiscent wonder in the awesome spectacle Powers has with such affectionate ingenuity contrived, of intelligence emerging from a mechanical void. He is, of course, not the first on the theme: there was WESCAC in John Barth's *Giles Goat-Boy* and HAL in the movie *2001*; and ancient creation stories like that of Adam and Eve in the second chapter of Genesis trace the transition from robotic obedience to conscious independence. But Powers brings to the problem the latest refinements of computer technology and the latest understandings of the brain; words like "biome" and "myelinated" and "trisomy" come easily to him. In mapping out the tenuous miracle of the mind, he offers a number of finely observed examples of impaired cognition: Diana's younger son has Down's syndrome, Lentz's wife has suffered a deranging stroke, and Richard himself, on being transposed to a Dutch-speaking village, feels like an idiot.

Matter seeking to know itself: is this not the kernel of philosophy, from Thales on, and the evolutionary drama, insofar as we can discern it, of the cosmos? Of these four novels, *Galatea 2.2* (bearing a handsome and witty dust jacket that displays Raphael's *La Fornarina* with a pixelated twin) has best transmuted its philosophical issue into an emotional one. In the others, the thought and the story run parallel, like the different-colored waters of the White and Blue Niles not far below their juncture. In Gaarder and de Botton the flow is steady and in Fischer choppy, but the tints remain distinct, and our immersion is mostly cerebral. The novel, whatever it is or was, must be more than an illustrated lecture; it must make us think without our realizing that we are thinking.

Elusive Evil

DARK NATURE: *A Natural History of Evil*, by Lyall Watson. 318 pp. Harper-Collins, 1995.

SPEAKING WITH THE DEVIL: *A Dialogue with Evil*, by Carl Goldberg. 287 pp. Viking, 1996.

THE DEATH OF SATAN: *How Americans Have Lost the Sense of Evil*, by Andrew Delbanco. 274 pp. Farrar, Straus and Giroux, 1995.

A DELUSION OF SATAN: *The Full Story of the Salem Witch Trials*, by Frances Hill. 269 pp. Doubleday, 1995.

THE ORIGIN OF SATAN, By Elaine Pagels. 214 pp. Random House, 1995.

"Evil," as a noun, should have died away, demystified by all our liberal understandings of human behavior, but in fact there seems to be more evil than ever. Perhaps the impression is produced by improved news-gathering: distant famines that would have received a paragraph or two in the Victorian press now engender televised close-ups of skeletal, mori-bund children; atrocities that would have once been swept silently into war's chaotic carnage are investigated and their rotted victims exhumed; child abuse that used to be hushed up is now publicized and prosecuted even decades after the event, the elderly, befuddled perpetrator con-fronted in court by the former child, now middle-aged and outraged. We are more sensitive, it may be, and less willing to forgive the heavens than were our ancestors, who accepted fate's blows as part of God's inscrutable plan or as shortcuts to a blissful afterlife. Also, the global forum makes available an unprecedented quantity of bad news. Every day, we read of young women brutally murdered by disaffected lovers or husbands or total strangers overloaded with liquor and testosterone; the perpetrators, dragged into the light of justice, tend to look inadequate, their moment of fury spent, and their own griefs and confusions pathetically evident. The sum of so much faithfully reported daily madness and cruelty must be greater, somehow, than its miserable parts. In our metaphysical frustration, the scandalously old-fashioned idea of evil enjoys a revived chic, noticeable in the self-mutilations of young glamour-seekers and the sombre, zombified, Mapplethorpesque cast of fashion photography. Imagined as something absolute and fathomless, with a satiny gleam of satanic charm, evil exercises a hold not only on the imagination of Stephen King readers and horror-movie fans but on that of scientists, psychologists, and historians, as a recent spate of books indicates.

In *Dark Nature: A Natural History of Evil*, the prolific British biologist and naturalist Lyall Watson, who has also written books on *The Nature of Things* and *Supernature*, attempts to formulate the natural context of evil. His curiosity has been piqued by recent headlines about serial killers, massacres in Rwanda and Bosnia, and—especially horrifying to the English public—the case of Jon Venables and Robert Thompson, two ten-year-old boys who in 1993 kidnapped a two-year-old boy from a mall outside Liverpool and doggedly beat him to death in broad daylight, before visiting a video store. Watson defines evil, insofar as he does, as a violation of the ecological order: "If 'good' can be defined as that which encourages the integrity of the whole, then 'evil' becomes anything which disturbs or disrupts such completeness." The word "evil" is derived from the Old Teutonic "*ubiloz*," whose root meaning is "up" or "over," implying a "going beyond due measure." Good, therefore, is moderation, described by Aristotle as a "golden mean" and by Lyall Watson, more whimsically, as the "Goldilocks Effect, nature's way of getting things 'just right.'" We all have, he says, "an innate predisposition towards equilibrium," which modifies in social practice the unbridled and ruthlessly amoral competition of genes for perpetuation.

In his discussion of Darwinian survival, Watson does not always avoid the teleological fallacy of ascribing purpose to the genes: these "past masters of the survival arts" are pictured as lively entities who "leap from body to body down through all the generations, manipulating each vehicle for their own ends, abandoning a long succession of used vehicles along the evolutionary highway." We might be tempted to see a Creator's shaping hand in all this leaping and manipulating, but the living population of genes is not planning its future: genes duplicate themselves, so successful patterns recur. Some patterns, as in social insects, incorporate "altruistic" behavioral traits whereby siblings sacrifice themselves to the advantage of the family gene pool. Survival tactics, however, as a rule are harshly selfish. Spotted hyenas usually bear well-developed twins, and "within minutes of birth one of the cubs attacks its twin, sometimes savaging a brother or sister that has not yet even emerged from its amniotic sac." There ensues, unless the mother has reason to intervene, "a fight to the death between two baby animals scarcely an hour old." This instance of survival of the fittest is vivid but not exceptional; throughout the animal kingdom siblings fight for parental nurture, the weaker perishing with their genes. Nor is infanticide uncommon, as a method of thinning demand in the nest. In such species as langurs and lions, an interloping male erases the living traces—the harmless cubs—of his predecessor. Nature is even redder in tooth and claw than Tennyson thought.

An impartial mathematics of advantage presides over a daily mayhem. Watson lists three rules for the game of genetic survival: "BE NASTY TO OUTSIDERS," "BE NICE TO INSIDERS," and "CHEAT WHENEVER POSSIBLE." Under this third rule is subsumed all the intricate mimicry whereby vegetable, insect, piscine, and mammalian species evade predators, capture prey, and secure sexual services. Cheating begins even in the nest, as the hatchlings who feign hunger most furiously get fed most frequently. Deception within a pack, however, works against effective coöperation and hence against genetic survival; citing such coöperative bodies as whale pods and the United States Senate, Watson concludes that "there is a ratchet in the works, a mechanism which allows something more generous to grow out of indifference, something 'good' rather than 'bad.' " He cites the collusion of non-violence that evolved between the opposing front-line soldiers in World War I, to the displeasure of their commanders. Citizens and nations gravitate toward a state of tenuous truce wherein their competitive and selfish genes find a small but sufficient advantage in self-restraint and mutual tolerance.

In the face of sociopathic behavior such as Robert Thompson's, the biologist sees only blankness. Attending the boy's trial, Watson observed "a blank face and yet not one frozen still in shock; just blank, a mask without identity, dead skin over dead eyes. I had never seen anything quite like it before." He sees it again in the face of a thirteen-year-old American murderer, Eric Smith, and in the faces of Hutu tribesmen who, fresh from massacring Tutsi, display "a killer in the eye." Such insights take us back, not very helpfully, to the concept of the evil eye and the old notion of the "criminal type," a hopeless condition diagnosed no longer in terms of phrenology or physiognomy but in terms of genes that cause, along with criminality, "low heart rate, excessive slow wave activity in the brain, problems in paying attention, and abnormalities in the frontal area of the cerebral cortex." Outlaws, that is to say, have something basically wrong with them.

But one could argue that society makes criminals, by promulgating laws. A great proportion, if not an outright majority, of the United States' federal prison population is behind bars because of laws against drugs— drugs that offer the offenders a sense of escape and mastery and their sole entrepreneurial opportunity. Nature, *Dark Nature* makes clear, has no law against murder or theft; to lay the blame for criminality on an aberrant gene is to unjustifiably claim legal obedience as part of our natural inheritance. The Marquis de Sade argued that human immorality harmonizes with Nature's immorality; the pious heroine of *Justine* has this repeatedly explained to her, by one silver-tongued debaucher after another. Father Clement tells her:

> "The more an action thwarts our customs and morals, the more it clashes with our social conventions, the more it hurts what we believe to be the laws of nature, so much more on the contrary is it useful to this same nature. Only through crimes does she enter into her own rights, those rights taken away from her by virtue."

And Madame Dubois asks Justine:

> "Isn't it a universe vicious in all its parts and ways? . . . Why do you insist that vicious individuals displease it, since it acts itself only through vices, since all is evil and corruption in its works, since all is crime and disorder in its will? Moreover . . . from whom do our passions for evil come if not from its own hand?"

Freud, in a famous exchange, answered Einstein's question "Is there any way of delivering mankind from the menace of war?" by pointing to the violence universal in the animal kingdom. He explained the fact, astonishing to Einstein, "that it is so easy to make men enthusiastic about a war," by hypothesizing "an instinct for hatred and destruction—which goes halfway to meet the efforts of the warmongers." This "destructive instinct," he claimed,

> is at work in every living creature and is striving to bring it to ruin and to reduce life to its original condition of inanimate matter. Thus it quite seriously deserves to be called a death instinct, while the erotic instincts represent the effort to live.

Freud allowed, "It may perhaps seem to you as though our theories are a kind of mythology and, in the present case, not even an agreeable one." But this disagreeable mythology, proposed in 1932, gathered credibility as Hitler rose to power the next year and set about propelling Europe toward an orgy of destruction and killing.

No discussion of evil can ignore the Holocaust; a crime so vast and methodical must, we feel, have been the work of monsters on whom a mark of Cain is clear. Watson ponders the "most successful executioner ever," the Auschwitz commandant Rudolf Höss, a Roman Catholic family man—"a very ordinary little man"—who to the best of his ability carried out the bureaucratic duties of running an extermination camp, one in which more than two million outsiders, as defined by the prevailing ideology, were put to death. The banal administrators of Hitler's rigorous "Final Solution" present another blank, refusing to satisfy our curiosity about evil. Iago says, "Demand me nothing; what you know, you know." The essence of evil, perhaps, is *not* to know itself. Gregory Maguire, in his dandy Oz-novel *Wicked: The Life and Times of the Wicked Witch of the West*, has his lovable, green-skinned heroine say of evil,

> "You figure out one side of it—the human side, say—and the eternal side goes into shadow. . . . What does a dragon in its shell look like? Well no one can ever tell, for as soon as you break the shell to see, the dragon is no longer in its shell. . . . It is the nature of evil to be *secret*."

Lyall Watson's book ends with a whimper, a hope that our uniquely intelligent species can give "evolution the nudge it needs in the right direction." What that direction may be we are left to guess. "We mustn't expect any help from our institutions," we are warned: capitalism too faithfully reflects the ruthlessness of natural selection, and socialism "is so out of touch with basic biology that it doesn't work at all."

The psychoanalyst Carl Goldberg, in *Speaking with the Devil: A Dialogue with Evil*, begins by promising to engage, face to face, the human wickedness that looks so blank to Watson, but he wanders off into an anticlimactic plea for his personal brand of companionable, non-Freudian psychotherapy. In place of the reticent persona through which the traditional practitioner of psychotherapy invites transference, Goldberg proposes a more user-friendly psychotherapist who, after some analysis, offers friendship and an exchange of confessions: "For the patient to acquire interpersonal competence . . . therapist and patient . . . evince a progressive willingness to share reciprocal reactions to the other." Such "speaking with the devil," however, elicits dubious results in the case of Emil, a cold-hearted war criminal who terminates the treatment after telling Goldberg, "You are not superior to me. You just haven't been tested. I've been alone and terribly afraid all my life. I've been to hell and forced to follow the orders of devils. What would you have done in my place? No better than me, I'll bet!"

Goldberg recognizes a need to get beyond "good" and "evil" as terms; he quotes Thomas Hobbes, who wrote in *Human Nature*, in 1650, "Everyman, for his own part, calleth that which pleaseth and is delightful to himself, good; and that evil which displeaseth him." The term that Goldberg prefers is "malevolence," but his working definition leans hard on subjective adjectives: "Malevolence is the *deliberate* infliction of cruel, painful suffering on another living being." Does it follow from this that a serial killer who—like the hero of Patrick Süskind's novel *Perfume: The Story of a Murderer*—kills his victims deftly and painlessly is not malevolent? A certain inner deadness, for the psychologist as well as for the biologist, seems to control the concept: Goldberg says that "malevolence always involves treating other people without respect or consideration for their humanity"—either the other is seen as too "weak, stupid, and incompetent" to deserve decent interaction, or is so threatening that "any destructive action is justified." The psychoanalyst breaks the evolution of a malevolent personality into no fewer than six components: (1) habitual childhood shame, (2) contempt defensively directed outward, (3) a developed capacity for rationalization and for (4) justification of contemptuous actions, (5) "the inability or unwillingness to self-examine one's dark side," and (6) a reliance on magical thinking. This isn't the hard-wiring diagram of a malevolent brain which we might have been (magically) expecting, and it doesn't match with any very impressive precision the case histories Goldberg presents from his own practice and reading. He gives us, besides Emil, a pair of unhappy lovers; a jazz musician sunk in drugs, alcohol, anger, and violence; a handsome young would-be actor who sees a devilish doppelgänger in the mirror; and a womanizing writer, with two personalities named Jason and Stud. Stud degrades Jason's conquests by throwing one, for example, naked into the hall of a hotel, bolting the door, and "evidently enjoying her frantic efforts to get back in." This is certainly malevolent and sadistic, but it still leaves a leap to David Koresh and Jim Jones, deranged cult-leaders who led the bulk of their followers into suicide.* Crippling demands, Goldberg explains, were made on the young James Warren Jones by his parents—his father a gassed, unemployed, and misanthropic World War I veteran and his

---

*The psychological needs of cult followers ("an eagerness to follow and obey, and an intense dissatisfaction with things as they are," as Eric Hoffer said in *The True Believer*) are easier to fathom than that of their malevolent leaders. Goldberg makes the interesting point that the followers create the leader as an excuse for "extreme behavior."

mother "a fanciful dreamer" convinced that her son was the Messiah. Jones's adult manipulations and sadistic tyrannies were efforts, we are told, "to control the shame he felt because his early caretakers had demanded unrealistically that he save them from the ills and offenses of the world."

For Dr. Goldberg, "shame" has the resonance of a key, all-explaining concept, like "dread" for Kierkegaard and "*ressentiment*" for Nietzsche, but its transformation into malevolence remained obscure to this reader. Goldberg sounds provocatively existential when he states, "Shame results when we try to avoid the present, because the constructive role of shame is to teach us the reality of time, how to enhance our lives in the present because our time is implacably limited." But he seems a hurried generalizer when he claims, ten pages later, that "madness is a reaction to a sense of shame about one's personal helplessness, just as fear of death has inspired religious beliefs that promise immortality." Abused children tend to become abusive parents, yet many do not become conspicuously malevolent, while some mass murderers, like Ted Bundy, claim a normal upbringing. Parents, one way or another, can always be blamed for a deformed character. Neglect and abuse are bad, but so are stifling amounts of attention and expectation, which is what happened to the misogynistic Jason. If an utterly painless, balanced, and sitcom-sweet upbringing could be achieved in this imperfect world, it, too, might become, in the very perfection of its parental model, a monstrous, empathy-deadening psychological burden. The children of ministers and schoolteachers notoriously go through a liberating "bad" phase. Although Dr. Goldberg professes to be searching for "the foundations of a psychological theory of human behavior that is not reductionist," reductionism tinges a sweeping formulation like "the madness involved in malevolence is a *moral malaise*, an impairment of the ability to feel good about one's self or confident in one's relationship to others." De Sade's malevolent spokespersons are nothing if not self-satisfied and confident: good about their crimes is just what they feel. Neither Goldberg nor Watson gets around to admitting that inflicting pain on others is an exercise in power, and that exerting power is a pleasurable sensation.

We are excessively intelligent animals. The other creatures kill out of joyless necessity, inflicting pain without knowing it. Sadism and malevolence are purely human, born of the brain and its power of conceptualization. The human imagination, which extends our sexuality beyond the chemical signals of female estrus and makes sex for our species a continuous and pervasive concern, also conceives of pain as amusement, as an expression of human will. With pain we punish others, warn the unpunished, and extract information: by tormenting others we test our control of the society around us. Further, some of us masochistically placate our guilt and boredom with self-inflicted pain, satisfying ourselves that we feel and are alive. Dostoevsky's Underground Man, in his great diatribe, embraces his toothache and rejects the Victorian creed of benevolent enlightenment:

> Oh, tell me, who was it first announced, who was it first proclaimed, that man only does nasty things because he doesn't know his own interests; and that if he were enlightened, if his eyes were opened to his real normal interests, man would at once cease to do nasty things? . . . And what if it so happens that a man's advantage, *sometimes*, not only may, but even must, consist in his desiring in certain cases what is harmful to himself and not advantageous. . . . One's own free unfettered choice, one's own caprice—however wild it may be, one's own fancy worked up at times to frenzy—is that very "most advantageous advantage" which we have overlooked, which comes under no classification and against which all systems and theories are continually being shattered to atoms. . . . What man wants is simply *independent* choice, whatever that independence may cost and wherever it may lead.

Cleopatra, he tells us, "was fond of sticking gold pins into her slave-girls' breasts and derived gratification from their screams and writhings." Such cruel caprices have not vanished with barbarous times; on the contrary, "the only gain of civilization for mankind is the greater capacity for variety of sensations—and absolutely nothing more. And through the development of this many-sidedness man may come to finding enjoyment in bloodshed."

Amid the regimentation of benign social norms, hurtful behavior becomes self-assertion, even self-salvation. "Better to reign in Hell, than serve in Heav'n," many a sociopath says, with Milton's Satan. The rebellious angel promises his minions, "Here at least / We shall be free," a sentiment that Mammon echoes when he proposes that the fallen angels seek

> Our own good from ourselves, and from our own
> Live to ourselves, though in this vast recess,
> Free, and to none accountable, preferring
> Hard liberty before the easy yoke
> Of servile Pomp.

The resemblance between this language of liberty and our various American declarations of independence suggests one reason why, in a statistic given by Lyall Watson, "three out of four serial killers live and work in the United States." According to a 1988 Gallup poll cited by Carl Goldberg, "66 percent of American respondents claimed to believe in the devil, compared with only 30 percent or fewer in France, Great Britain, Italy, Norway, and Sweden." A cultural emphasis on individual freedom makes choosing evil a live option.

The Devil has faded to our peril—that is the surprising thesis of Andrew Delbanco's *The Death of Satan: How Americans Have Lost the Sense of Evil*. Unlike the two volumes already considered, Delbanco's is an elegant piece of exposition. A Columbia professor of humanities whose specialty has been the Puritans, he is wide-ranging in his erudition and confidently succinct in its presentation. He provides nothing less than a history of America's moral sense from the arrival of the Puritans to the bombing in Oklahoma City. Beautifully selected quotations from classic writers, Melville foremost, mingle with arresting details of cultural history culled from sermons, letters, physicians' handbooks, and popular literature. Progressive secularization is Delbanco's inevitable theme, as the national Zeitgeist descends from Puritan zeal to a contemporary "Culture of Irony" in which all value judgments are undermined by anthropological relativism and ideological deconstruction. Delbanco writes, "We have reached a point where it is not only specific objects of belief that have been discredited but the very capacity to believe." In the past, old faiths gave way to new; now we have "divestiture without reinvestment." The eighteenth-century Enlightenment achieved, he says, "the dispossession of the invisible world as a legitimate object of knowledge," and in the nineteenth century the cruelties of the Civil War and the vagaries of success under capitalism replaced the notion of a presiding Providence with the pagan concept of luck. Darwin, Freud, and Derrida left not a stick standing of the old faith, though millions of churchgoing Americans haven't quite got the news. Delbanco takes a rather dour view of what used to be considered American triumphs: the Civil War, which settled the issues of slavery and secession, afflicted "the whole nation with a kind of postcoital flatness and exhaustion, even a flustered wondering over what the exertions and excitement had been all about"; and while end-of-the-century statistics "show that Americans enjoyed substantial growth in per capita income, reduction in the length of the workweek, and a decline in death and birth rates, there was little solace in these numbers for those who actually lived through the new age of casino capitalism." There is plenty in these pages about entrenched racist distrust and dislike of immigrants but not much about what drew the immigrants here. Never mind: this is a Melvillian reading of the

Republic's innermost quest, a *Moby-Dick* whose magnificent hateful object melts away in the course of the search, leaving the whaleboats circling aimlessly.

Delbanco is a thorough and tender reader of the Puritans, and his opening chapters try to describe the precious Devil that has been lost. He was a cunning, invisible, omnipresent Devil, an Augustinian Devil whose essential quality was non-existence, an internalized negativity. St. Augustine had made the pilgrimage from Manichaean belief in good and evil as "two masses, contrary to one another, both unbounded, but the evil narrower, the good more expansive," to a Christian monism wherein evil is simply the absence of good, embodied only in the actions and hearts of sinners. The Puritans brought to the New World a "peculiarly calm self-loathing—a hatred of the self continuous with an unresentful love of God." Their Devil was impalpable and inward—"an unclean spirit," wrote the Massachusetts divine John Cotton. Samuel Willard's *A Compleat Body of Divinity* (1726) explained that Satan no longer needed the vessel of a serpent in which he appeared to Adam and Eve, because there existed "a nearer and more secret commerce that Angels can have with our spirits, than by the outward senses." Delbanco offers the vivid paraphrase, "He will never be spotted with a spyglass or by any sentry peering afar, because he is the contents of our minds," and claims that "to the degree that Puritanism did acknowledge Satan as an active, independent force—that is, to the degree that Puritanism was a dualistic religion—its Devil was never a brute, but a tempter."

A purely psychological tempter needed a sequestered and introspective world in which to be heard. As rationalism and mercantilism pressed upon the Puritan villages, the Devil coarsened into an external apparition, with "rank smell, reedy voice, scales," and lent himself to the Salem witch furor; after that disgraceful episode he became a comic cartoon "that educated men could not believe in." By the mid-nineteenth century, Satan and his hellish cohorts had become a fairgrounds attraction. John Greenleaf Whittier mournfully quoted Coleridge: "Dimmer and dimmer, as the generations pass away, this tremendous Terror—this all-pervading espionage of Evil . . . presents itself to the imagination." What remained was an impulse to demonize "the other"—the Indian, the Negro, the slaveholder, the abolitionist, the Roman Catholic, the heathen, the Hun, the Jap, the Red. Delbanco does some demonizing of his own in his characterization of Ulysses S. Grant as a "modern monster," a "preview of the dead-eyed murderers one meets in fictional and factual twentieth-century texts." This libel of a great general applies, we gather, to all warriors, now that military technology is ever better equipped "to destroy a human target whose humanity is out of range." In our era of a universally debunking irony, as Delbanco sees it, all the old signposts of humanity—concepts like rights and responsibility and evil—are drifting out of range. The nation hankers for an external devil to replace Communism's collapsed "evil empire," and the Oklahoma bombing is the calling card of a sizable group that has found "in our own federal government a demonic substitute for the lost foreign enemy." In preference to such a devil Delbanco urges the return of the Augustinian idea of "an essential nothingness"—"a symbol of our own deficient love, our potential for envy and rancor toward creation."

This concluding plea is ardently put and impressively framed, but a Christian, or Jewish, or Islamic believer might call it a plea for the results of faith without doing the work of faith. This work entails not just devotions, good deeds, and self-denial, but the intellectual humility—indeed, humiliation*—of believing in something we cannot see or prove. Taken on its own terms, from the height of a godless empyrean, the world has no evil in it, just natural events, clashing needs, and soon-extinguished egos. Delbanco quotes George Steiner: "To have neither Heaven nor Hell is to be intolerably deprived and alone in a world gone flat." The "intolerably" is hyperbolic; populations as vast as China's tolerate an official atheism. Edmund Wilson wrote, "The answer to [T. S.] Eliot's assertion that 'it is doubtful whether civilization can endure without religion' is that we have got to make it endure." But mere endurance is bleak fare after the heady wine of religious consolation. William James, exponent of that supremely American philosophy of pragmatism, put the matter bouncily:

> Let our common experiences be enveloped in an eternal moral order; let our suffering have an immortal significance; let Heaven smile upon the earth, and deities pay their visits; let faith and hope be the atmosphere which man breathes in;—and his days pass by with zest; they stir with prospects, they thrill with remoter values. Place round them on the contrary the curdling cold and gloom and absence of all permanent meaning which for pure naturalism and the popular-science evolutionism of our time are all that is visible ultimately, and the thrill stops short, or turns rather to an anxious trembling.

*Kierkegaard, in his *Concluding Unscientific Postscript*, twice mentions "the crucifixion of the understanding" as part of the "the martyrdom of faith." But for "understanding" he uses the Danish word *Forstand*, which signifies ordinary, everyday understanding, or common sense, as opposed to *Fornuft*, signifying reason, or the higher functions of the intellect. The same duality exists in the German *Verstand/Vernunft*, a distinction emphasized by Kant. The *Fornuft* presumably need not be crucified in grasping the paradoxes of Christianity. For this information I am indebted to Professor Bruce H. Kirmmse.

We learn in *Dark Nature* that even as staunch and cheerful an atheist as Bernard Shaw quailed at the full implications of Darwinism: "When its whole significance dawns upon you, your heart sinks into a heap of sand within you. There is a hideous fatalism about it, a ghastly and damnable reduction of beauty and intelligence, of strength and purpose, of honour and aspiration." In the struggle to keep hold of such traditional human virtues, the Devil is an unlikely ally.

Yet one does not wish to return to the more credulous times portrayed in *A Delusion of Satan: The Full Story of the Salem Witch Trials*, by Frances Hill. The reader's exasperation and frustration mount as the delusion takes twenty lives, in the year 1692, on no more evidence than the screaming and squealing of a pack of local girls. The author is English, but argues that she is therefore closer to seventeenth-century New England than contemporary Americans are. Building upon the socio-economic analysis of the persecutors and the persecuted set forth by Paul Boyer and Stephen Nissenbaum in their pivotal *Salem Possessed: The Social Origins of Witchcraft* (1974), Hill provides a more dramatic and consecutive account of the events. She fleshes out the gaunt records where she can, describing the maddeningly monotonous, dreary, and anxious lives of young girls in the Puritan settlements, and acquainting us with the horrors of Puritan jails:

> The jails in Ipswich, Salem, and Boston, among which the accused witches were dispersed, were places not just of privation but of horror. . . . As the most dangerous inmates, the witches were kept in the dungeons. These were perpetually dark, bitterly cold, and so damp that water ran down the walls. They reeked of unwashed human bodies and excrement. They enclosed as much agony as anywhere human beings have lived. . . . Accused witches were worse off than the other unfortunates. Their limbs were weighed down and their movements restricted by manacles chained to the walls, so that their specters could less easily escape to wreak havoc. They were treated by wardens and visitors with deliberate cruelty, fair game for sadism since they were enemies of God and mankind. Body searches for "witches' teats" afforded ample opportunities for rough treatment.

At the height of the witch-hunt more than one hundred fifty persons, mostly women, many of them elderly, were thus held captive. Four accused persons died in jail, and a four-year-old girl, Dorcas Good, after being detained eight months in the dungeons, was, in the words of her father, eighteen years later, "so hardly used and terrified that she hath ever since been very chargeable, having little or no reason to govern herself." By "chargeable" he meant that he had to pay for a keeper for her;

the child had been driven insane. Nineteen people were hanged. After a cart ride through jeering crowds to a rocky elevation outside the town, they were pushed off of a ladder leaned into the hanging tree. There was no clean snap of the neck; they slowly strangled. All of the condemned professed—some with pious eloquence—their innocence to the end.

How to explain such evil, worked against neighbors and strangers in Salem? The frenzy began in a parsonage, that of Samuel Parris, a sin-and-Satan-obsessed clergyman who had been sponsored as the first pastor of the breakaway Salem Village church by a conservative faction led by the Putnam family. Salem Village, now the town of Danvers, was the inland farm district of Salem, a backwater to Salem Town, with its up-and-coming port. The Putnams were farmers of declining fortune; the anti-Parris faction was led by the Porters, who held land closer to the waterways and were successfully associated with Salem's mercantile interests. There were domestic tensions as well. Parris's wife, Elizabeth, appears to have been sickly (she died in 1696). The household included four children and a West Indian slave couple, Tituba and John Indian. Tituba, brought from Barbados by Parris, has recently been honored with a biography, *Tituba, Reluctant Witch of Salem: Devilish Indians and Puritan Fantasies*, by Elaine G. Breslaw; though Breslaw offers a wealth of data and speculation about the Afro-Caribbean culture, Tituba remains a shadowy "other," an unwitting precipitant of white hysteria. The two West Indians' presence in the cramped parsonage, added to winter boredom and to Puritan repression and superstition, mixed in with some fireside fortune-telling by means of eggwhite and water, presumably stimulated the fits that began to afflict Parris's nine-year-old daughter, Betty, and his eleven-year-old niece, Abigail Williams. The girls started, in the words of the Beverly minister John Hale, "getting into holes, and creeping under chairs and stools, and to use sturdy odd postures and antic gestures, uttering foolish, ridiculous speeches, which neither they themselves nor any others could make sense of."

At the instigation of concerned neighbors, Tituba and John Indian helpfully baked a "witch cake," containing rye meal and the girls' urine, and fed it to a dog, who, according to English lore, was supposed then to name the witch causing the problem. The dog's remarks did not make the historical record; the two girls subsequently named Tituba as the apparition tormenting them. By the end of February or thereabouts four more girls—all frequent visitors to the parsonage—had begun to suffer fits and visions: Ann Putnam was the twelve-year-old daughter of Parris's chief ally, the farmer Thomas Putnam; Mercy Lewis was a seventeen-year-old orphan who lived in Putnam's family; Mary Wolcott and Elizabeth Hubbard were also seventeen-year-old friends of the Parrises. Writhing, choking, babbling, they named, besides Tituba, and with the help of who knows how much adult coaching, Sarah Good, "who got her living by begging and borrowing," and Sarah Osborne, who was "weak-witted, with a scandalous past." All three women were arrested and manacled, examined and jailed. Tituba, conditioned as a slave to oblige her masters, confessed to making a pact with the devil, a tall man wearing black clothes, and to riding to Boston on sticks. The witch-hunt was on. Osborne died in jail, Good was hanged, and Tituba, like all the others who confessed that they were witches, lived.*

The girls' afflictions are beyond the reach of modern diagnosis, but it is hard to escape the impression, as the accusations and convictions sickeningly widen in Hill's narrative, that, however involuntarily launched upon their prosecutorial career, the bewitched children became the instruments of the Putnam family's resentments and of others' grudges. Fourteen years afterward, at the age of twenty-six, Ann Putnam, who according to Hill was the "most quick-witted and resourceful" and implacable of the accusing girls, humbled herself in a kind of confession upon being received into the Salem Village church. Parris had long since been driven out by the anti-Putnam faction, which included the family of the most pitied of executed witches, the pious septuagenarian Rebecca Nurse. In words read aloud by the pastor, the peacemaking Joseph Green, Ann expressed remorse

> that I, then being in my childhood, should, by such a providence of God, be made an instrument for the accusing of several persons of a grievous crime, whereby their lives were taken away from them, whom now I have just grounds and good reason to believe they were innocent persons; and that it was a great delusion of Satan that deceived me in that sad time. . . . What I did was ignorantly, being deluded by Satan.

She pleaded innocent to any motive of "anger, malice, or ill-will," and, in the heat of the hysteria, may have been so. However, at the time, one of the girls, when challenged by sharp skepticism, admitted that they did it "for sport, they must have some sport."

In the records of the proceedings that have survived, the interrogating

---

*Parris eventually sold her to a new owner to pay off her prison fees, and moved to a parish in the inland hamlet of Stow, where he repeated himself by alienating his congregation with demands for more money and the title to the parsonage. He left within a year, but married a woman with enough wealth to support him in his checkered subsequent career as shopkeeper, schoolmaster, and again minister. He died in 1720 and left bequests to his children, including Betty, who had married.

magistrates—the chief was John Hathorne, whose guilt gnawed at his descendant Nathaniel Hawthorne more than a century later—appear as hectoring, bloodthirsty bullies. The clergy involved—Parris, John Hale, Nicholas Noyes, William Stoughton (a minister turned politician), and Samuel Sewall—played discreditable roles, trusting childish shrieks and garbled confessions elicited in terror rather than mature disavowals and weighed evidence. Stoughton, as the tide at last turned into a flood of acquittals, protested in Superior Court, "We were in a way to have cleared the land [of witches and evil]." The colony's leading intellectuals, Increase Mather and his son Cotton, issued equivocal tracts; their learned attempts to treat "the invisible world as a legitimate object of knowledge" brought them both into disrepute, although Increase's sermon, later a pamphlet, calling spectral evidence (the visions of self-proclaimed victims) into doubt helped close down the hearings.

A department of villainy left unexplored by Hill is the role of law-enforcement officials such as George Corwin, the twenty-six-year-old high sheriff of Essex County and nephew of an inquisitorial magistrate. Corwin can be glimpsed as very busy, seizing the goods of the accused; the property became in theory the Crown's but in practice the sheriff's, to dispose of upon conviction. At the infamous crushing of old Giles Cory under a weight of stones, the sheriff played a considerate part: "Toward the end Cory's tongue was pressed out of his mouth and the sheriff pushed it back in again with the end of his cane." Corwin's seizures of property so enraged one victim, the wealthy merchant Phillip English, that when the sheriff died young, in 1697, with a suit against him outstanding, English declared he intended to seize Corwin's body in satisfaction of the debt. The profit in property seizures and the boarding fees extracted, with astounding effrontery, from even the acquitted among the miserably jailed may well have lubricated the demented engines of the persecution.

But the ultimate blame belongs to St. Mark, according to Elaine Pagels' persuasive, lucid *The Origin of Satan*. In the Old Testament, as Pagels reads it, Satan is a minor, not entirely malevolent figure. The Hebrew word *satan* means "one who opposes, obstructs or acts as adversary," much as the Greek *diabolos* means "one who throws something across one's path." Pagels quotes her fellow-scholar Neil Forsyth: "If the path is bad, an obstruction is good." In the story of Balaam in the Book of Numbers, Chapter 22, Balaam is travelling a road forbidden by the Lord, who sends an angel to stand in his way "as his *satan*." Only Balaam's ass sees the supernatural obstructor; after Balaam strikes him three times, the beast is given a voice in which to protest, and the angel becomes visible to the repentant human being. In the story of Job, the *satan* takes a more adversarial role, but is still depicted as a member of God's heavenly court. As factionialism within Israel increased, however, the *satan* became God's antagonist, the seducer of apostates and foes in sectarian strife. The potentates of evil were known under many names—Satan, Beelzebub, Semihazah, Azazel, Belial, Prince of Darkness, and, in the book of Isaiah, "day star, son of the dawn," which John Milton translated into the magnificent Lucifer. Yet in all these Judaic personifications, Pagels asserts, "Satan is not the distant enemy but the intimate enemy . . . the attribute that qualifies him so well to express conflict among Jewish groups." In the apocryphal book *Jubilees*, written around 160 B.C., it is the Satan-figure Mastema, and not the Lord, who commands Abraham to kill his son!

The Essenes, a puritanical, all-male movement active during the Roman occupation in the first century of our common era, called themselves the "sons of light" and other Jews, especially those collaborating with the Roman powers, the "sons of darkness." This vocabulary finds echoes in the letters of St. Paul, which are the oldest texts in the New Testament: "Ye are all the children of light, and the children of the day: we are not of the night, nor of darkness" (1 Thessalonians 5:5) and "Our contest is not against flesh and blood, but against powers, against principalities, against the world-rulers of this present darkness, against spiritual forces of evil in heavenly places" (Ephesians 6:12). But Paul, the self-designated Apostle to the Gentiles, was as inclusivist as the Essenes were exclusivist, and it is the Gospel ascribed to Mark, written about 70 A.D., that sets the story of Jesus firmly in the context of cosmic war— "not simply of the struggle against Rome but of the struggle between good and evil in the universe." Pagels asks:

> How, after all, could anyone claim that a man betrayed by one of his own followers, and brutally executed on charges of treason against Rome, not only *was* but still *is* God's appointed Messiah, *unless* his capture and death were, as the gospels insist, not a final defeat but only a preliminary skirmish in a vast cosmic conflict now enveloping the universe?

Infant Christianity's first struggle was with the Jewish religion that gave it birth and then rejected it as an absurd heresy. The Gospel of Mark was composed in the violent years of the Jewish rebellion and Roman suppression, when, Pagels explains, offense to the Romans had to be avoided. Though Mark knew that a Roman governor, Pontius Pilate, had ordered Jesus to be crucified, "the two trial scenes included in this gospel effectively indict the Jewish leaders for Jesus' death, while some-what exonerating the Romans." The three other Gospels progressively—Matthew and Luke were written roughly ten years later, and John toward the end of the first century—intensify Mark's case against the Jewish high priests and Pharisees, sowing the seeds for two thousand years of Christian anti-Semitism. The cosmic import also receives increasing emphasis: John opens his narrative not with Jesus' birth on earth but with the doctrine of the Word and the light which "shineth in darkness" though "the darkness comprehended it not." The Jewish establishment acts in the Gospels as the principal agent of that darkness; when Chris-tianity spread and attracted Roman persecution, the emperors and their officials joined Satan's ranks. That onus was extended to Christian here-tics, to Muslims, and, as the Middle Ages ended, to witches. The Salem prosecutors saw themselves as soldiers in the cosmic war against devils cunning enough to take up residence in a four-year-old child. Did not Jesus himself, after all, cast out demons?

We may feel superior to the bedevilled citizens of Salem Village, but the notions of demonic possession and Satan worship are far from extinct. The Manichaean image of a universe at war—light versus darkness, with disguise and espionage rampant—retains great narrative and inspira-tional force. Witness the *Star Wars* saga and this summer's no-brainer megahit *Independence Day*. Such science-fiction fantasies, in both their aura and particulars, nostalgically recall the war of the Allies versus the Axis at the center of our century. While the wide-ranging Cold War pro-duced its riveting incidents and psychological satisfactions, demonizing the enemy was modified by a mutual desire to avoid nuclear apocalypse. The notion of an absolute evil whose only proper fate is obliteration unites and energizes men, but the heroic virtues it calls forth must now be somehow summoned on behalf of the more modest goals of stand-off, accommodation, piecemeal amelioration, and forgiveness of one's obstructor. In a monistically immoral universe, human society still makes just claims. We still feel absolute indignation when, say, the genetically programmed trustingness of children is abused by adults, or the male sex drive vents itself in the murder of women. "Evil" may be dead as a noun, but it remains an adjective.

BIOGRAPHIES

The Properties of Things

Isaac Newton: *The Last Sorcerer*, by Michael White. 401 pp. Addison Wesley,
1998.

The impulse to reveal awkward truths about the famous and great has
extended to the marmoreal, rather abstract figure of Isaac Newton, the
discoverer of the law of gravitation and the inventor of the calculus.
Michael White, in introducing his *Isaac Newton: The Last Sorcerer*, proposes that "Newton was not the man that history has claimed him to be";
that is, "The most respected scientist in history, the model for the scientific method, had spent more of his life intensely involved with alchemy
than he had delving into the clear blue waters of pure science." The
sensational story—if any story centuries old can be sensational—was
highlighted when, in 1936, the economist John Maynard Keynes purchased a raft of Newton's papers at Sotheby's and, after studying them,
announced, to the distracted England of 1942, that Newton was "the last
of the magicians, the last of the Babylonians and Sumerians, the last great
mind which looked out on the visible and intellectual world with the
same eyes as those who began to build our intellectual inheritance rather
less than 10,000 years ago." Which is a rousing way to say that Newton, a
Puritan of Socinian—that is, anti-Trinitarian—persuasion, had a mind
soaked in theism. But who, back then, didn't? Newton was born in 1642,
as England descended into a bloody civil war based upon religious opinions, and died in 1727, at just about the time when, all over Europe, men
at last stopped killing each other on behalf of their versions of Christianity. His meticulous analyses of heavenly motion and the nature of
light were carried out in an age that was still searching for the mythical
philosophers' stone. Physics and chemistry were of a piece with philosophy and theology; delusion and reason walked hand in hand.

The virtue of White's biography is that he attempts to integrate Newton's alchemical and Biblical studies with the seer's major discoveries in physics; its fault, which diminishes as the book goes on (or perhaps the reader simply gets used to it), lies in an overexcited prose of which the above "delving into the clear blue waters" is an example. In the same paragraph we find something "stuck in the craw of those early biographers" (a collective craw, an uncomfortable concept) and elsewhere an unapposite "To rub salt into Isaac's emotional wounds, he never knew when or if his mother would turn up." White, whose previous books include co-written lives of Einstein, Stephen Hawking, and Darwin and children's biographies of Mozart, Galileo, and John Lennon, seems to feel that his present subject needs a verbal boost into liveliness; Newton, at various junctions of his career, is chummily seen to "let his hair down" and to be "walking on eggshells." Nevertheless, the biography delivers a mass of information about a man who in his lifetime obfuscated and romanticized the basic biographical facts.

Newton never married and enjoyed few close relationships. His father, a prosperous yeoman also called Isaac, died of an unnamed disease at the age of thirty-six, a few months before his son's birth. The birthplace, the Lincolnshire hamlet of Woolsthorpe, was, according to White, "little more than a collection of small farms and humble country dwellings clustered around the manor house"—a house belonging to the Newtons. The birth occurred, auspiciously, on Christmas Day, a fact Newton later liked to emphasize, along with the infant frailty he miraculously survived. Either he—"small enough to fit into a quart pot"—was premature or he was conceived before his parents' marriage that April. His mother, Hannah, came from the Ayscough family, lower gentry whose sons went to universities and "found their way into parsonages and lectureships." When young Isaac, an only child, was three, his mother married Barnabas Smith, the elderly, well-to-do rector of North Witham, a hamlet about a mile from Woolsthorpe. It was decided that she would move to her new husband's home but Isaac would stay at the Newton manor, with his maternal grandparents, James and Margery Ayscough. Smith, though in his sixties, fathered three children by Hannah; when he died, in 1653, she moved back to Woolsthorpe. But by then Isaac was eleven and the damage was done.

How much damage it was remains, of course, speculative; in an age before child psychology, when free-ranging deaths by disease disarranged nearly every family constellation, such a separation was perhaps unexceptional. Property issues were involved—Hannah wished to maintain her claim to the Newton estate—and the distance was small. Visits back and forth must have been frequent. Some advantages surely existed for the fatherless boy in the guardianship of a grandfather and grandmother, though White dismissively says, "As Newton never mentioned his grandparents later in life, it would appear there was little love lost between them." Evidence survives that the boy was unhappy: at the age of nineteen Newton drew up a list of his sins, going back to childhood, of which No. 13 reads, "Threatening my father and mother Smith to burne them and the house over them" and No. 14, more generally, "Wishing death and hoping it to some." Out of whatever early unhappiness, he developed the resources of solitude; he was in his triumphs as in his foibles secretive, tenacious, and self-directed.

At the age of twelve, not long after his mother returned with her three new children, he went off to King's School in Grantham, a market town seven miles distant. He boarded with the family of the local apothecary, the Clarks, and it was under their care that he emerged—at least in the memories of townsmen interviewed by Newton's first biographer, William Stukeley—as a mechanical genius, concocting kites, sundials, paper lanterns, and a miniature windmill powered by a resident mouse. The education of the time consisted of Greek, Latin, and the Bible, with perhaps a little Euclid. Practical science was to be had, however, in the apothecary shop of Newton's surrogate father, Mr. Clark, and surviving notebooks show the young boarder transcribing prescriptions and cures, methods of producing paints and cutting glass with chemicals. At King's School he had gone from being an indifferent student to being the best, yet his mother resisted the headmaster's urging that the gifted boy pursue his education; she wanted Isaac to help her run the farm, counting sheep and marketing produce. At this he proved sluggish and inept, a less effective farmer than his illiterate father. Finally, Hannah—whose own brother, William Ayscough, had gone to Cambridge—relented; Isaac was allowed to resume at Grantham and go on to Cambridge, where, as sizar, scholar, fellow, and, finally, Lucasian Professor of Mathematics, he was to remain for nearly thirty-five secluded, prodigious years.

White, a former science lecturer, goes easy on the well-worn anecdotes of Newton as the ultimate absent-minded professor—he was "so serious upon his studies," his assistant later testified, that "ofttimes he has forgot to eat at all"—and instead tries to explain what made his scientific work so special and, to his contemporaries, marvellous. His work on optics first brought him to the attention of the London scientific establishment, embodied in the recently founded Royal Society. Glass prisms had existed since the first century A.D., but until Newton no one had thought to conduct a set of simple experiments that showed the sun's light to be composed of different colors, the difference determined by the degree of refraction. To demonstrate the invariance of the colors and their angles, he passed a section of the spectrum—the blue end, say—through a second prism, and observed that the blue passed through unchanged, with no accompanying reds and yellows, and that everything seen by its light was blue. He also refocussed the spectrum with a lens, restoring it to white light.

From these experiments he concluded, a bit rashly, that "it can no longer be disputed . . . whether light be a body"—i.e., whether light is corpuscular, composed of what we now call particles. The dominant contemporary view held that light consisted of waves, propagated through the hypothetical medium of ether. Robert Hooke, a rival scientist who was to prove a lifelong detractor, said that Newton's experiments "seem to me to prove that light is nothing but a pulse or motion propagated through an homogeneous, uniform and transparent medium." Neither Hooke nor anyone else bothered to test Newton's hypothesis by duplicating his experiments. Scientists of the time, who were called natural philosophers, preferred to debate theory and reason *a priori*. Hypotheses outranked evidence. A Parisian Jesuit called Ignace Gaston Pardies had trouble accepting Newton's "very extraordinary hypothesis" and wrote the Royal Society asking for an elaboration. Newton testily replied,

> The best and safest method of philosophising seems to be, first to inquire diligently into the properties of things, and establishing those properties by experiments and then to proceed more slowly to hypotheses for explanations of them. . . . For if the possibility of hypotheses is to be the test of the truth and reality of things, I see not how certainty can be obtained in any science.

Even the Continent's foremost scientist, the Dutchman Christiaan Huygens, who had initially called Newton's observations "highly ingenious," complained that Newton had not put forth what could be called a theory. This reservation so irritated Newton that he tried to resign from the Royal Society and, dissuaded, wrote Huygens suggesting that he perform the experiments himself. "At which point," White says, "the Dutch scientist withdrew from the discussion."

William Blake depicted Newton as a beautiful angel measuring the world with compasses; in *Jerusalem* he wrote, "For Bacon and Newton, sheath'd in dismal steel, their terrors hang / Like iron scourges over Albion . . . / . . . cruel works / Of many wheels I view, wheel within wheel, with cogs tyrannic / Moving by compulsion each other." Newton struck terror into the sensitive with his ability to conceive of the universe as if man—the observer, the measure of all things—was irrelevant. In 1664, at the age of twenty-one, he wrote in his notebook, "The nature of things is more securely and naturally deduced from their operations one upon another than upon the senses. And when by . . . experiments we have found the nature of bodies . . . we may more clearly find the nature of the senses." With something of Darwin's reluctance to publish— a reluctance possibly born of the intuition that their conclusions held theological dynamite—Newton allowed his findings and deductions to pile up around him in Cambridge. His masterwork, the *Principia Mathematica*, which White extols as "probably the greatest single work of science ever written . . . the fabled elixir, the alchemist's gold, the philosophers' stone," had to be coaxed from him. In 1684, the suave young astronomer Edmond Halley travelled from London to Cambridge to solicit from Newton a proof that Hooke had promised but failed to deliver, concerning the elliptical orbits of planets. Newton claimed he had already made the calculations, but could not find them; he did provide, after three months, a nine-page manuscript on the motion of revolving bodies, *De Motu Corporum in Gyrum*. Halley quickly saw in it the seeds of a universal system of dynamics, and promised to publish an extended treatment. Thus encouraged, Newton wrote the *Principia*, a work of five hundred fifty dense and difficult pages, in a mere eighteen months.

The *Principia*'s best-known proposition—the seventh in Book III, to the effect that every particle of matter attracts every other particle with a force proportional to the product of the masses and inversely proportional to the square of the distances between them—first took form in Newton's considerations, a piece of parchment from 1666 shows, as the calculation of the opposite, repulsive, receding force by which planets seek to escape the sun as they revolve. The act of revolution can be visualized as a ball swung on a string, and Newton concerned himself first with the centrifugal force of the ball, which from planetary observations was shown to be inversely proportional to the square of the length of the string. What was true for the escaping force proved true for the force of attraction. The string that holds the planets in place was palpable in such a humble event as the fall of an apple to the earth, which Newton claimed inspired his first speculations, back in a Woolsthorpe orchard. The speculations, as Newton, shortly before his death, described them to Stukeley, took this form:

Why should that apple always descend perpendicularly to the ground, thought he to himself? Why should it not go sideways or upwards, but constantly to the earth's centre? Assuredly, the reason is, that the earth draws it. There must be a drawing power in matter: and the sum of the drawing power in the matter of the earth must be in the earth's centre, not in any side of the earth. Therefore does this apple fall perpendicularly, or towards the centre. If matter thus draws matter, it must be in proportion of its quantity. Therefore the apple draws the earth, as well as the earth draws the apple. That there is a power, like that we here call gravity, which extends itself through the universe.

White contends that this "drawing power" would have been inconceivable to Newton without his long and earnest immersion in alchemy, which explained chemical reactions in terms of "active principles" guided by God and channelled through the alchemist, if he was spiritually pure enough. Newton's alchemical papers and notes tell how "they call lead a magnet because mercury attracts the seed of Antimony" and how "certain metals or salts are 'drawn' or 'extracted,' " and how substances "laid hold" of others or are "held down." He posits "an exceeding subtle & unimaginably small portion of matter diffused through the mass which, if it were separated, there would remain but a dead & inactive earth." The exotic, mysticized vocabulary that alchemy applied to observed but dimly understood chemistry inspired, in Newton's mind, the sweeping hypothesis of gravitational attraction, a force operating through empty space, at any distance, and effecting the orbits of the planets and of comets (conveniently frequent in the 1680s), the precession of Earth's poles, and the action of the tides. The clockwork universe was unveiled; the dynamics were explicated that would make possible the industrial revolution. And all because, according to White, "Newton saw the power of attraction and repulsion at the bottom of the alchemist's crucible."

In a sense, alchemy was the particle physics of its day. Without any knowledge of the atomic structure of the elements, it could not arrive at correct conclusions, but its intuition of powerful, transformative forces within matter was correct. There is nothing intrinsically stranger about turning lead into gold with the aid of mercury than about uranium's radioactive decay into lead or the creation of heavy elements from lighter ones during the death convulsions of stars. As Newton said, "Nature is a perpetual circulatory worker, generating fluids out of solids, and solids out of fluids, fixed things out of volatile, & volatile out of fixed." He, whose calculus exploits the power of the infinitesimal, had intuitions of atomic potency: "Have not the small particles of bodies certain powers, virtues or forces, by which they act at a distance, not only upon the rays of light for reflecting, refracting and inflecting them, but also upon one another for producing a great part of the phenomena of Nature?" Like Einstein, he illumined simultaneously the microcosm and the macrocosm, boiling a welter of phenomena down to a quickly popularized formula: $E = mc^2$ in Einstein's case, and in Newton's (though he himself never wrote it in such algebraic shorthand) $F = Gm_1m_2/r^2$.

That thinkers like these, after salad days of carelessly abundant radical insights, should bog down in relatively futile conjectures tells us less, it may be, about the human brain than the pace of scientific knowledge, which must slowly ripen between harvests by the sudden genius. That Newton devoted so much time and passion to alchemical pursuits which now seem fantastic only places him in his era, one of witch-hunts and barbarously misconstrued medical theory. That he spent hours poring over the Bible, compiling charts and dictionaries, reminds us how gradually Europe emerged from its thousand years of theocentricity. Newton searched the Bible for confirmation of his own, dangerously anti-Trinitarian views, and for the *prisca sapientia*—the wisdom that he, with the Rosicrucians, believed the ancients possessed and had secreted in their documents. The Middle Ages had, in truth, erased some ancient knowledge. The Greek astronomer Eratosthenes, in the third century B.C., calculated the circumference of the round earth to be twenty-four thousand miles (less than a thousand miles off the true value) and the distance to the sun to be ninety-two million miles, a stunningly close estimation. But the Old and New Testaments did not harbor such mathematical wisdom. Newton researched the prophetic utterances of Daniel and St. John for a chronology of the future, and carefully concluded that Satan's spell over the world would be broken in the year 1867, the Jews would return to Jerusalem in 1899, and the world would end in 1948. He did not realize that his own science had excused God from running the universe, allowing Him merely the initial push.

In 1696, Newton moved from Cambridge to London, and his history becomes more that of a man than that of a mind. The eccentric Lucasian Professor, scratching celestial diagrams on the university's gravel walks and abstrusely lecturing to empty lecture halls in the clothes he had slept in, had secured a royal sinecure: thanks to Charles Montagu, known as Lord Halifax, William III had appointed Newton Warden of the Mint. The pedagogue surprised everyone by filling this office, second to that of the Master of the Mint, with efficiency and zeal. The critical task of recoinage—minting new coins to replace the crude, worn-out, easily clipped and counterfeited coins in circulation, some dating from the reign of Edward VI—was in progress; the economy of the nation, shaken by a century of civil war, plague, fire, and foreign war, depended on it. Newton kept the horse-driven coin presses working on two ten-hour shifts six days a week, and personally supervised the war against clippers (who snipped precious metal from the coins) and counterfeiters, remorselessly sending many of them, including a picturesque scofflaw named William Chaloner, to the gallows. It is a topic for a gaudy, sardonic historical novel by Peter Ackroyd or Peter Carey: Newton in the depths, "following leads in the heart of the liberties"—the East End slums—"and arranging secret meetings with informants in gin-houses and brothels." He proved adroit and ravenous in the expansion of the Warden's power. Two days after the lazy, hard-drinking Master, Thomas Neale, died, in 1699, Newton succeeded to the post, on his fifty-seventh Christmas Day birthday. His income went from hundreds of pounds to thousands; the yeoman's son from Woolsthorpe had become a very rich Londoner.

The lady of his house, on Jermyn Street, was Catherine Barton, his niece by his half-sister Hannah Smith and the clergyman Robert Barton, whose death had left his family destitute. Catherine, a lively and greatly admired beauty, charmed Jonathan Swift and was Lord Halifax's lover from 1703 to his death in 1715. Newton in his new worldliness accepted the arrangement, but his own sex life remains a blank. The attractions he purportedly experienced, whether heterosexual (to Catherine Storer, back in Grantham, when he was boarding there) or homosexual (to Nicholas Fatio de Duillier, a young Swiss mathematician who won his favor in the early 1690s), produced, by the available evidence, no bodily collisions. Newton was a Puritan and a passionate intellectual. Even when engrossed in the material concerns of the Mint, he rose to a mathematical challenge. For over twenty years he had experienced a rivalry with the German polymath Gottfried Wilhelm von Leibniz, who had invented calculus independently of Newton, and with a superior notation. At Leibniz's instigation, in 1697, the Swiss mathematician Johann Bernoulli sent Newton a problem—known as the "brachistochrone," concerning the curve along which an object under the action of an accelerating force such as gravity would move between two points in space in the shortest time—to which Bernoulli and Leibniz already knew the answer. Catherine Barton later recalled, "Sir I. N. was in the midst of the hurry of the great recoinage, & did not come home until four from the Tower very much tired, but did not sleep till he had solved it which was by 4 in the morning." Not sleeping even then, he mailed the solution to the president of the Royal Society, with the request that it be published in the *Philosophical Transactions* anonymously. Bernoulli wrote a friend that only Newton could be the author: "I can tell the lion by the mark of his claw"—"*ex ungue leonem.*"

Newton was leonine in defense of his intellectual property: in the laboriously courteous language of the day, he feuded with Leibniz over the calculus, with Hooke over optics, with the first Astronomer Royal, John Flamsteed, over heavenly data that Newton needed for his revision of the *Principia*. Newton outlived and outshone them all, accepting from England a succession of rewards: he was elected to Parliament, knighted by Queen Anne, and made president of the Royal Society, which he subjected to the same energetic, high-handed, restorative treatment he had given the Royal Mint. Up to his death, in 1727, at the age of eighty-four, he continued his theological researches, more intensely than ever. Michael White writes, "This activity was an expression of his inner drives, a manifestation of his desire to analyse, to draw together disparate themes . . . keeping his mind alert . . . after the excitement of intellectual warfare had passed." Newton's nearly complete sublimation of inner drives into mental endeavor may strike modern sensibilities as cold and freakish. His father's death and his mother's desertion left him, perhaps, a stubborn—in Melville's term—isolato. He was most loved by those who could admire from afar the beauty of persevering, logical thought. Though himself devotedly religious, he became a symbol of cruel reason, which would rob us of our cherished illusions. Keats complained that Newton had "destroyed all the poetry of the rainbow." From another perspective, he made of the rainbow a reproducible experiment, so that—in the words of another poet, Elizabeth Bishop—"everything / was rainbow, rainbow, rainbow!"

Such a Sucker as Me

LINCOLN, by David Herbert Donald. 714 pp. Simon and Schuster, 1995.

Can a homely, gawky man of backwoods origin, with scarcely a year's formal schooling and not a day's experience of administrative public office, become, in a time of catastrophic civil strife, a great American President? Yes, we all know the answer to be, if the man is Abraham Lincoln. His heroic story needs to be told to every generation, and the Harvard history professor David Herbert Donald tells it once more. Donald, whose biographies of Charles Sumner and of Thomas Wolfe have won

Pulitzer Prizes, explains in his preface that, inspired by a remark of President John F. Kennedy's to the effect that no President should be judged by one who "has not sat in his chair . . . and learned why he made his decisions," he has attempted "a biography written from Lincoln's point of view, using the information and ideas that were available to him." He has minimized, then, vast areas of the national history, from the deep roots of the Civil War to the details of that war's battles and military campaigns, in order to give us a kind of foregrounded, close-focus Lincoln, "perhaps a bit more grainy than most, with more attention to his unquenchable ambition, to his brain-numbing labor in his law practice, to his tempestuous married life, and to his repeated defeats." Possibly fearful of drowning in the ocean of secondary Lincoln studies, Donald has "tried as far as possible to write from the original sources—that is, from firsthand contemporary accounts by people who saw and talked with the President," and, above all, from Lincoln's own writings. At the outset of his eighty-six small-type pages of sources and notes, he lists his major predecessors in biography—the ten volumes by John G. Nicolay and John Hay, Lincoln's White House secretaries; the three by William H. Herndon, Lincoln's Springfield, Illinois, law partner, and Jesse W. Weik; the two by Senator Albert J. Beveridge; the six by Carl Sandburg; the four by J. G. Randall, completed by Richard N. Current; and the relatively recent volumes by Mark E. Neely, Jr., Phillip S. Paludan, Benjamin P. Thomas, Reinhard H. Luthin, and Stephen B. Oates—and confides, "I have not read or consulted these distinguished works in the preparation of the present volume. I cannot say, however, that I have not been influenced by them, for I used these books in my classes for many years."

His biography comes with a theme, an inversion of the dynamism traditionally ascribed to great leaders: "Lincoln's fatalism," or "the essential passivity of his nature." As epigraph the volume bears a sentence Lincoln wrote in April of 1864 to Albert G. Hodges, editor of the *Frankfort* (Kentucky) *Commonwealth*, who had inquired why he had shifted from a pledge, in his First Inaugural Address, of non-interference with slavery to a policy of emancipation. Having answered at some length, the President added, "I claim not to have controlled events, but confess plainly that events have controlled me." This much is *Lincoln's* epigraph. Lincoln went on, in language echoing that of his Second Inaugural Address,

> Now, at the end of three years struggle the nation's condition is not what either party, or any man devised, or expected. God alone can claim it. . . . If God now wills the removal of a great wrong, and wills also that we of the North as well as you of the South, shall pay fairly for our complicity in that wrong, impartial history will find therein new cause to attest and revere the justice and goodness of God.

Lincoln, who declined to join any orthodox Christian church, was obliged to declare, when he was running for Congress in 1846, that he had "never denied the truth of the Scriptures" and that "in early life I was inclined to believe in what I understand is called the 'Doctrine of Necessity'—that is, that the human mind is impelled to action, or held in rest by some power, over which the mind itself has no control." As the carnage of the Civil War piled ever higher about him, he, "who couldn't cut the head off of a chicken, and who was sick at the sight of blood," as he said, took to the Bible and theology in fresh earnest. His Second Inaugural Address proposes nothing less than to demonstrate to a suffering people, North and South, that—quoting the 19th Psalm—"the judgements of the Lord, are true and righteous altogether." God rules even though (or because) "every drop of blood drawn with the lash, shall be paid by another drawn with the sword."

Calvinist fatalism seems to act, paradoxically, as a spur to enterprise; surely one of the strange features of New World development is that a Protestant nation dominated by believers in an inflexible and inscrutable predestination should have proved so dynamic, while former Iberian colonies under the influence of a Catholic system of mediatory works should have proved relatively torpid. Whatever comfort fatalistic resignation brought to the dark moments of Lincoln's life, Donald's biography provides numerous instances of exceptional initiative—the farm boy's determined pursuit of reading and learning; his departure from his father's household and agricultural labor for the hamlet of New Salem, Illinois, and the professional chances it offered; his decision to run for the state legislature at the age of twenty-three; his step up into the practice of law a few years later; his courtship of Mary Todd and the social advance it represented in the elite circles of Springfield; his successful campaign to become a Whig representative to the U.S. Congress in 1846; his pushing himself forward, after one undistinguished term in Washington and twenty years of private law practice, as the opponent of Stephen A. Douglas in the 1858 Illinois senatorial race; his insistence on a series of debates, which won him national publicity and an appearance of equality with the Little Giant; and his very shrewdly managed capture of the 1860 Presidential nomination from the fledgling Republican Party. Though he was fond, as Professor Donald tells us, of quoting Hamlet's admonition, "There's a divinity that shapes our ends, / Rough-hew them how we will," the Railsplitter took a sinewy hand in hewing his own fate. He succeeded where neither of his Whig heroes, Henry Clay and Daniel Webster, did: he became President.

Though Donald promises to show us events as Lincoln saw them, he provides much testimony of how others saw Lincoln. David Davis, a portly Maryland native who, as district judge in Illinois, shared with the busy lawyer many courtrooms and hours of travel on the circuit between 1849 and 1860, reminisced that "Mr. Lincoln was not a sociable man by any means" and had "no strong feelings for any person—mankind or thing." Yet Davis wrote his wife of "Mr. Lincoln's exceeding honesty and fairness" and in emergencies designated Lincoln to preside in his stead. A speech Lincoln gave in Worcester, Massachusetts, in 1848, was admired by one newspaper as "showing a searching mind, and a cool judgement," while another called it "rather witty, though truth and reason and argument were treated as out of the question, as unnecessary and not to be expected"; still others called it "absolutely nauseous" and "a melancholy display." His platform manner was criticized for "his awkward gesticulations, the ludicrous management of his voice, and the comical expression of his countenance." Edwin McMasters Stanton, who was to be Lincoln's Secretary of War and to say, at his deathbed, "Now he belongs to the ages," had quite a different comment in 1855, when Lincoln was brought to Cincinnati to consult on a case in which Stanton was active: "Why did you bring that damned long armed Ape here?" he asked the associate who had hired Lincoln. "He does not know any thing and can do you no good."

Lincoln himself, as his prospects were warming in 1858, scoffed: " 'Just think,' he exclaimed, wrapping his long arms around his knees and giving a roar of laughter, 'of such a sucker as me as President!' "* His partner, William Herndon, called him "purely and entirely a case lawyer," and Douglas on the stump called him a political chameleon. Donald speaks of his "hard ego." Early in the war, Jessie Frémont, the wife of John C. Frémont, who had been the first Republican candidate for President and was now one of Lincoln's insubordinate generals, glimpsed a chink in Lincoln's famous amiability and patience: when she delivered a letter justifying her husband's actions, he—according to her—"smiled with an expression that was not agreeable," cut off her own explanations with a curt "You are quite a female politician," and, in conclusion, spoke in a voice she found hard and "repelling."

Lincoln, a native of Kentucky, began with very little in his racial views to distinguish them from those of Southern slaveholders. They and the Democrats wished to extend the institution of slavery into at least some

---

*No doubt Lincoln had in mind the word "sucker" as a nickname for a person from Illinois; the state was traditionally known as the Sucker State, in honor of its state fish, the sucker, now superseded by the bluegill. In the same vein, a Kansan was called a "jayhawk."

of the territories; Lincoln and the Republican Party, born of the revulsion against Stephen Douglas's Kansas-Nebraska Act of 1854, wanted to exclude it from these territories. No sizable political party proposed abolishing slavery where it existed, or establishing Negro equality. Speaking in the fourth debate with Douglas in a county of Illinois which had been settled by immigrants from Kentucky and Tennessee, Lincoln stated, "I am not nor ever have been in favor of making voters or jurors of negroes, nor of qualifying them to hold office, nor to intermarry with white people. . . . There is a physical difference between the white and black races which I believe will forever forbid the two races living together on terms of social and political equality." Still, this was a distance from Douglas's reiterated assertions that the American government "was made by the white man, for the benefit of the white man, to be administered by white men," and that any "mixing or amalgamation with inferior races" would lead to "degeneration, demoralization, and degradation." Citing Douglas's remark that "he was for the negro against the crocodile, but for the white man against the negro," Lincoln protested the implication that "the negro is no longer a man but a brute . . . that he ranks with the crocodile and the reptile." From the modest premise that the black man is a man, Lincoln eventually deduced that black men were entitled to the freedoms extended to men in the Declaration of Independence.

The Emancipation Proclamation was issued, in its own phrasing, as "a fit and necessary war measure" and exempted slavery in all Union areas and states. But Lincoln's initially conservative racial attitudes—for years he favored a scheme for the "voluntary emigration" of African Americans to a tropical colony—eased to permit the enlistment of black troops to fight for the Union. By the war's end, Donald writes, "The stalwart service rendered by nearly 200,000 African-Americans in the military had eroded his earlier doubts about their courage and intelligence. . . . He believed that the more intelligent blacks, especially those who served in the army, were entitled to the suffrage." For the first time in the history of the White House, Negroes—including Frederick Douglass and Sojourner Truth—were received there as guests. When Lincoln visited freshly liberated Richmond, the black workmen recognized him, and their leader went forward, exclaiming, "Bless the Lord, there is the great Messiah!" and dropped to his knees. Lincoln, embarrassed, told him to rise, and kneel only to God, in thanks "for the liberty you will hereafter enjoy."

The war was less idealistic than its sentimental afterimage. When Horace Greeley in his *New York Tribune* linked the prosecution of the war with the abolition of slavery, Lincoln replied in the famous letter of

August 22, 1862, "My paramount object in this struggle *is* to save the Union, and is *not* either to save or to destroy slavery. . . . What I do about slavery, and the colored race, I do because I believe it helps to save the Union." Less well known is the fascinating geography lesson he read the Congress in his annual message of December 1, 1862:

> That portion of the earth's surface which is owned and inhabited by the people of the United States, is well adapted to be the home of one national family; and it is not well adapted for two, or more. . . . There is no line, straight or crooked, suitable for a national boundary, upon which to divide. . . . But there is another difficulty. The great interior region, bounded east by the Alleghenies, north by the British dominions, west by the Rocky mountains, and south by the line along which the culture of corn and cotton meets . . . already has above ten millions of people, and will have fifty millions within fifty years, if not prevented by any political folly or mistake. It contains more than one-third of the country owned by the United States—certainly more than one million of square miles. . . . A glance at the map shows that, territorially speaking, it is the great body of the republic. . . . And yet this region has no sea-coast, touches no ocean anywhere. As part of one nation, its people now find, and may forever find, their way to Europe by New York, to South America and Africa by New Orleans, and to Asia by San Francisco. But separate our common country into two nations, as designed by the present rebellion, and every man of this great interior region is thereby cut off from some one or more of these outlets, not, perhaps, by a physical barrier, but by embarrassing and onerous trade regulations.

In other words, the North and the Midwest did not intend to have a foreign nation straddling the Mississippi. And it was in the West that the Union fought most effectively; the fall of New Orleans in 1862 and of Vicksburg in 1863 eventually spelled the Confederacy's defeat.

Lincoln the liberal hero cannot be fenced off from the unprecedented savagery of the war. As the conflict dragged on inconclusively, he became increasingly ruthless, widely suspending the writ of *habeas corpus*, suppressing newspapers, extracting yet more conscriptions from a weary North. He recognized ahead of many of his generals the requirements of all-out war: according to Donald, "Lincoln had developed a contempt for what he scornfully called 'strategy': What he thought was needed was not more maneuvering but assault after assault on the Confederate army." Excessive caution finally cost McClellan the command of the Army of the Potomac; Meade, the victor at Gettysburg, disappointed the Commander-in-Chief by not pursuing Lee's army with his exhausted own. When Meade engaged Lee in a campaign of feints and maneuvers, Lincoln admonished him, "Only be sure to fight; the people demand it."

He wrote General-in-Chief Halleck, "If our army cannot fall upon the enemy and hurt him where he is, it is plain to me it can gain nothing by attempting to follow him over a succession of intrenched lines into a fortified city." Though Mary Lincoln called Grant a "butcher," and thought him "not fit to be at the head of an army," the President knew that in Grant he had found his man—a general willing to use the North's superiority in numbers to bludgeon the enemy into submission. With Grant's appointment as lieutenant-general of all the armies, Lincoln could stop trying to run the war with ignored directives. Although, in May of 1864, in the Battle of the Wilderness and then at Spotsylvania, ferocious fighting left the Army of the Potomac with thirty-two thousand casualties, Grant nevertheless refused to retreat, writing in a dispatch, "I propose to fight it out on this line if it takes all summer." Lincoln telegraphed back: "Hold on with a bulldog grip, and chew and choke, as much as possible."

With Sherman's capture of Atlanta in early September of that year, and Farragut's capture of Mobile Bay in late August, the sluggish tide finally turned. Beset by Radicals within his own party and prepared to lose the 1864 election to the Democrat candidate, McClellan, Lincoln instead carried every state of the reduced Union but New Jersey, Delaware, and Kentucky. As Confederate feelers for armistice terms began to come in, he held firm to the legal fiction that the seceding states were still in the Union, though dominated by "combinations too powerful to be suppressed by the ordinary course of judicial proceedings." He refused negotiations, lest recognition of the Confederacy be implied. When General Sheridan reported to him that "if the thing is pressed, I think that Lee will surrender," the President wired Grant, "Let the *thing* be pressed." Lee surrendered; Lincoln's enemies on the battlefield and in Congress melted away. His had been the authority; his was the triumph. Senator James Harlan recalled, "His whole appearance, poise, and bearing had marvelously changed. He seemed the very personification of supreme satisfaction. His conversation was, of course, correspondingly exhilarating." On the afternoon of April 14th, the President and Mary took a carriage ride around Washington, and when she remarked upon his cheerfulness he told her, "We must *both*, be more cheerful in the future— between the war and the loss of our darling Willie—we have both, been very miserable." That night, at Ford's Theatre, with Lincoln's trusty companion and bodyguard from Illinois, Ward Lamon, off on a mission to Richmond and the metropolitan policeman assigned to protect Lincoln away from his post, John Wilkes Booth, by simply showing his calling card to the lone guard, a White House footman, slipped into the Presidential box.

* * *

Would Lincoln's reputation be so exalted if he had not been assassinated? He would surely have dealt with Congress more tactfully and adroitly, with more weight of prestige and popular support, than did the crude and isolated Andrew Johnson. But Johnson faithfully carried out Lincoln's policy of reconstruction as it had been adumbrated; both Presidents were soft on the South, and under a Lincoln administration why would not the Southern state governments, once leniently reconstituted, have taken the same swift measures that they actually did to shackle in legalities the freed Negroes? The Congress, with its Radical Republican majority, would have likely registered its same indignation and punitive reaction, and what Woodrow Wilson, in his "Division and Reunion: 1829–1889," called "an extraordinary carnival of public crime" would have likely taken place under the rule of carpetbaggers, scalawags, and abruptly enfranchised ex-slaves, along with the rise of terrorist groups like the Ku Klux Klan. However compassionately presided over by Lincoln, the aftermath of the Civil War would have been a messy anticlimax, and its *Realpolitik* might well have sullied the nation's shining memory of the Great Emancipator.

Yet in any case his writings and utterances would survive, and on these his reputation most securely rests. His humorous common sense and clarity of analysis soon outgrew the elaborate rhetoric of mid-century political speechifying; with few models but the language of the King James Bible, Shakespeare, Aesop's Fables, and Bunyan's *Pilgrim's Progress*, he worked toward a directness and rhythmic energy, both formal and demotic, that rank the Gettysburg Address and the Second Inaugural Address with the noblest documents of the Republic's founders. The Lincoln touch can be seen in the last paragraph of the First Inaugural Address, which was proposed by Seward—who felt Lincoln's original ending to be too militant—in this form:

> I close. We are not we must not be aliens or enemies but fellow countrymen and brethren. . . . The mystic chords which proceeding from so many battle fields and so many patriot graves pass through all the hearts and all the hearths in this broad continent of ours will yet again harmonize in their ancient music when breathed upon by the guardian angel of the nation.

Lincoln made this of it:

> I am loth to close. We are not enemies, but friends. We must not be enemies. . . . The mystic chords of memory, stretching from every battlefield, and patriot grave, to every living heart and hearthstone, all over this broad land, will yet swell the chorus of the Union, when again touched, as surely they will be, by the better angels of our nature.

A speaking intimacy and, with it, a compelling urgency and warmth, were achieved through simplification and a subtly improved concreteness. "Fellow countrymen and brethren" became "friends," "hearths" became "hearthstones," and Seward's forced "mystic chords . . . patriot graves . . . hearts . . . hearths . . . ancient music . . . guardian angel" trope was deftly broken into separate components; especially striking is the way in which the upward glance at the supposed "guardian angel of the nation" was turned inwards, to the "better angels of our nature." Like Twain, Lincoln pared Latinate rotundity from American English and conjured music from plain words. As a lawyer and a politician, Lincoln labored lovingly over his texts. His habit of making a point or deflecting criticism by telling a story shows a literary imagination at work. In the war years, even his hastiest communiqué can flash out with an unexpected image or aptness of phrase. His rural background effortlessly supplied vivifying animal metaphors. To General Hooker, who was contemplating moving his troops across the Rappahannock:

> In one word, I would not take any risk of being entangled upon the river, like an ox jumped half over a fence, and liable to be torn by dogs, front and rear, without a fair chance to gore one way or kick the other.

The mightiest issues come clear in the homely illustration; to a general who suggested that the Confederates wanted to sue for peace, on the old terms:

> Still, to use a coarse, but an expressive figure, broken eggs cannot be mended. I have issued the emancipation proclamation, and I can not retract it.

He is so direct as to spring a smile, even where bloody matters are at stake. To a general who wanted to be restored to command:

> I have never doubted your courage and devotion to the cause. But you have just lost a Division, and *prima facie* the fault is upon you; and while that remains unchanged, for me to put you in command again is to justly subject me to the charge of having put you there on purpose to have you lose another.

In a letter designed to be read aloud to a rally of over fifty thousand Unionists in Springfield, an incantatory quality overtakes a succession of assertions:

> You say you will not fight to free negroes. Some of them seem willing to fight for you; but, no matter. Fight you, then, exclusively to save the Union. I issued the proclamation on purpose to aid you in saving the

Union. Whenever you shall have conquered all resistance to the Union, if I shall urge you to continue fighting, it will be an apt time, then, for you to declare you will not fight to free negroes.

This particular communication was cheered and reprinted in newspapers across the country and editorially praised as "one of those remarkably clear and forcible documents that come only from Mr. Lincoln's pen." In this dark year of 1863, he helped himself with his pen; the Springfield letter and some other public letters from the same period, Donald writes, "were considered so effective that they were collected and republished for wide circulation as *The Letters of President Lincoln on Questions of National Policy* in a twenty-two-page pamphlet." As Roosevelt used the radio, Lincoln used the medium of print. His letters and documents, public and private—available in two volumes of the Library of America—form an archive like none other, with even the most impersonal page somehow graced by the soul and accent of a man.

Professor Donald gives us the man in six hundred readable pages dense with scholarship. The reader does not doubt that the harvest of a thousand special studies of Lincoln has been economically and judiciously reaped. Everything is here, from Lincoln's love of Ann Rutledge (it was real, and she was plump) to his inveterate theatregoing (it was an escape from the office-seekers that relentlessly harassed him). But it is here in a rather dry, compacted way, one feels. Lincoln has had the juice squeezed out of him. One wishes now and then for one of Sandburg's leisurely, dreamy ruminations. Lincoln is so foregrounded that the other characters are excessively marginal; Donald does not demonstrate much of the ability shown by such historians of the period as Allan Nevins and Roy Nichols to effect a memorable adjectival embrace of this or that long-dead but once-lively political rascal. Political friend and foe blend together under names like Wade and Davis and Bates and Swett. The big gray pages form a matted web of facts for which this rereader would have been grateful for a fuller index. I searched long, for instance, to find again this anecdote, in which Lincoln came unexpectedly to life:

> When they [the Presidential party, visiting troops in Virginia] reached the Potomac Creek, [General] McDowell called their attention to a trestle bridge his men were erecting a hundred feet above the water in that deep and wide ravine. "Let us walk over," exclaimed the President boyishly, and though the pathway was only a single plank wide, he led the way. About halfway across Stanton became dizzy and Dahlgren, who was somewhat giddy himself, had to help the Secretary. But Lincoln, despite the grinding cares of his office, was in fine physical shape and never lost his balance.

No, it is not fair to say that Donald has squeezed all the juice out of Lincoln. What he has given us is nutrient-rich Lincoln concentrate.

Man of Secrets

Salem Is My Dwelling Place: *A Life of Nathaniel Hawthorne*, by Edwin Haviland Miller. 596 pp. University of Iowa Press, 1991.

The economics of literary biography emphasize supply over demand; it seems just yesterday (actually, it was 1980) when James R. Mellow's *Nathaniel Hawthorne in His Times* came lumbering, all 684 pages of it, down the chute, and now we have, as if in answer to a dearth, the 596 pages of *Salem Is My Dwelling Place: A Life of Nathaniel Hawthorne*, by Edwin Haviland Miller. Mr. Miller, who has previously written a biography of Melville and edited Walt Whitman's letters, in his acknowledgments speaks of "the decade I have spent in the exciting, sometimes frustrating engagement with the life and writings of a secretive author," so it isn't as if Mellow's opus had taken him from behind, in mid-course; he began his engaged decade with the echoes of the previous biographer's massive engagement freshly ringing in his ears. One wonders what Miller intended to offer that Mellow hadn't already provided. Mellow is the more fluent and colorful writer, and passages of Hawthorne's life—his sojourns at Brook Farm and in England, for example—are rendered in his book with an ample provision of circumstantial detail. Our most recent Hawthorne floats relatively free of the nineteenth century, and, suspended on the couch of Miller's pale and antiseptic prose, undergoes a psychoanalysis that treats the works, in an almost strict alternation of chapters, equally with the life. Hawthorne's fiction becomes the equivalent of an analysand's dreams. What Miller intends to provide, evidently, is a stronger, more concentrated light on the mystery of Hawthorne's secret. Mellow's book ends by describing the visit of Hawthorne's son, Julian, to the forgotten, wraithlike Herman Melville in New York City in 1883. "His words were vague and indeterminate," Julian recorded, of the sixty-four-year-old former friend of his late father, "and again and again, he would get up from his chair and open or close a window with a stick having a hook at the end, which he kept by him seemingly for that purpose." For all Melville's distraction and vagueness, however, "he said several interesting things, among which the most remarkable was that he was convinced Hawthorne had all his life concealed some great secret, which would, were it known, explain all the mysteries of his career."

In 1984, four years after Mellow's biography appeared, Phillip Young, who had already exposed the secrets of the youthful Ernest Hemingway, published *Hawthorne's Secret: An Un-Told Tale*, claiming that the secret was incest between Hawthorne and his sister Elizabeth. It is not implausible. Elizabeth was two years older, with their mother's dark hair, gray eyes, and tall beauty. She was to some degree Hawthorne's intellectual mentor and model—"the most sensible woman I ever knew in my life, much superior to me in general talent," he wrote. Hawthorne's younger daughter, Rose, left in her memoirs a vivid portrait of her aunt, as having a "magic" resemblance to her father and as being "a good deal unspiritual in everything" and "potentially rather perverse." These two siblings, with their stonily grieving widowed mother and a younger sister, Louisa, shared an eremitical existence in Salem for over ten years after Hawthorne's graduation from Bowdoin—years when both would have been at the height of physical and sexual bloom. Elizabeth opposed her brother's marriage to Sophia Peabody, saying that "the mingling of another mind" would "spoil the flower" of his genius. Though for a time she lived with her brother and her sister-in-law in Concord, she remained unfriendly: eight years after Sophia's death, Elizabeth called her "the only human being whom I really dislike." Hawthorne's fiction does contain a number of incestuous situations, from the early "Alice Doane's Appeal" to the uncompleted *Doctor Grimshawe's Secret*, and of dark, supercharged beauties whose attractions are sinisterly poisoned. A cloud of sexual guilt and disgust hovers over his fiction without, often, an adequate objective correlative. Young argues that the adultery in *The Scarlet Letter* is a mask for incest, and that the ancient document whose discovery Hawthorne describes in the famous preface refers in reality to a documented conviction for incest among his mother's ancestors, the Mannings, in 1681:

> Anstis Manning & Margaret Manning now Polfery being brought before the Court at Salem in November 1680 for incestuous carriage with their brother Nicholas Manning who is fled or out of the way . . . The delinquents appeared & the evidences being read & considered. This Court doth sentence the said Anstis & Margaret to be comitted to prison until morning & then to be whipt upon the Naked body at Ipswich, & that the next Lecture day at Salem then shall stand or sitt upon an high stoole during the whole time of the Exercise in the open middle ally of the meeting house wth a papper upon each of their heads, written in Capital Letters This is for whorish carriage wth my naturall Brother.

Another theory proposes that Hawthorne, a young man whose "androgynous beauty" (Miller's phrase) often excited admiration, was sexually molested by his uncle Robert Manning, with whom he shared, for a time, a bed in the overflowing Manning household. Manning, an internationally respected pomologist whose *Book of Fruits* was for years a standard orchard-grower's reference volume, acted as Hawthorne's guardian after the young widow cast herself and her fatherless brood upon her own family's resources. Yet Robert Manning was treated with some coolness by his matured ward, who declined to attend both his uncle's belated wedding and, eighteen years later, the man's funeral. Hawthorne made Judge Pyncheon, the gloatingly dispatched villain of *The House of the Seven Gables*, a horticulturist, among his other accomplishments—a buyer of rare peach trees and the producer of "two much-esteemed varieties of the pear." When, in 1851, Hawthorne visited a Shaker settlement, he decried with curious vehemence the Shakers' "utter and systematic lack of privacy, their close conjunction of man with man," which may hark back to unpleasant experiences in the Mannings' crowded attic. In a tangled footnote, Miller lays at Mellow's door the "speculation that there was a 'homosexual assault,'" but invokes a third Hawthornian, Gloria C. Erlich, in refutation, while registering his objections to her thesis that Robert Manning is—*vide* the identical initials—the secret subject of "Roger Malvin's Burial." So Hawthorne construably slew Manning in disguise several times, for whatever reason.

Miller's own version of the secret cleaves even closer to the kinship line: "To the end of his life Hawthorne kept not a 'secret,' as Melville alleged, but rather secrets—for he was in quest of a father, a mother, and perhaps even a brother to find security in a cold universe." That Captain Nathaniel Hathorne (his son added the "w" soon after college) died of yellow fever in Suriname, when his namesake was four, is indisputable; Hawthorne had little more than imaginative experience of a father. That his mother was also absent, emotionally, is less clear. Citing *Septimius Felton*, one of the unfinished romances from Hawthorne's last years, Miller states:

> Septimius attributes his isolation and emotional coldness to the loss of his mother: "It is as if I had not been born of woman." Surely this is a veiled comment on Hawthorne's mother who loved him after her fashion but who could not coddle or touch her son because she was imprisoned in her own cold, inhibited world.

Hawthorne himself, in a long journal entry for July 29, 1849, as his mother lay dying, wrote, "I love my mother; but there has been, ever since my boyhood, a sort of coldness of intercourse between us, such as is apt to come between persons of strong feelings, if they are not managed rightly." Yet the passage develops remarkably, as he enters her chamber:

I did not expect to be much moved ... but I was moved to kneel down close by my mother, and take her hand. . . . I found the tears slowly gathering in my eyes. I tried to keep them down; but it would not be—I kept filling up, till, for a few moments, I shook with sobs. For a long time, I knelt there, holding her hand; and surely it is the darkest hour I ever lived.

In this hour of darkness he goes on to conclude that "God would not have made the close so dark and wretched, if there were nothing beyond; for then it would have been a fiend that created us, and measured out our existence, and not God." Recording this bit of crisis theology, he adds, with detachment if not sarcasm, "So, out of the very bitterness of death, I gather the sweet assurance of a better state of being."

Not long after his gush of pent-up feeling, the now orphaned Hawthorne began *The Scarlet Letter*. As with Proust, the mother's death became a liberation into deferred greatness. Miller has no trouble connecting the mother with the novel's heroine:

Hester Prynne, then, is at once Hawthorne's love object as well as the fulfillment of his deepest desire for an ideal mother of beauty and tender feelings. . . . He achieves . . . what perhaps every son craves: he gives birth to his mother. . . . Mother and son were unable in life to communicate their love either in word or in gesture, and in death his need had to be satisfied and communicated in his art as veiled autobiography.

This blunt reading of *The Scarlet Letter* as mother-worship has its persuasive points. It is true that Hester Prynne, like Elizabeth Manning Hathorne and her daughter Elizabeth, was a tall proud brunette; Hawthorne's other sister, Louisa, was paler in several senses—"quite like other people," in the notation of Sophia Peabody's sister Elizabeth. The picture of Hester emerging from the jail with the three-month-old Pearl in her arms figures forth a Puritan madonna, wearing the "halo of the misfortune and ignominy in which she was enveloped." Hester's mothering of Pearl, though a bit fitful in the fluctuation of her still-youthful passions, comes to dominate her personality as, maturing, she extends maternal care to the unfortunates of infant Boston. In her great scene with Dimmesdale in the forest, Hester looms as an embodiment of untamed erotic force but also as a nurturer, a good nurse in contrast to the bad nurse, Chillingworth, whose talking-cure is aggravating the illness and killing the patient. She prescribes instead for the dying clergyman flight from the iron pieties of the New World and return to the Old, with herself, the shunned love object, as companion. Like Chillingworth, she has survived outside of the Puritan settlements; both husband and wife are associated, in the novel's scheme, with the wild, pagan lore of Indians.

Hester nowhere resembles Hawthorne's mother more than in her social isolation; indeed, social isolation—its melancholy and its astringent consolations—is one of the author's infallible notes, whether struck with the Quaker orphan of "The Gentle Boy," the toxic solitude of Rappaccini's daughter, or the eerily isolated households of *The House of the Seven Gables*, *Doctor Grimshawe's Secret*, and *The Dolliver Romance*. In *The House of the Seven Gables*, Hepzibah Pyncheon might well be an elderly Hester Prynne, with her tall figure and her initials but without her amorous scandal. Surely Hawthorne's loving empathy for the ostracized goes back to his shy mother, who after her husband's death reportedly took her meals alone in her room and seldom ventured into the daylight. Elizabeth Hawthorne, who outlived all the other members of that nuclear family, denied the tale the Peabody sisters told the Hawthorne children of their paternal grandmother as a white-clad recluse; Elizabeth argued that her mother never wore white and was not "gloomy or melancholy"—only "serious." Hawthorne himself, however, dubbed the house of his young manhood "Castle Dismal" and wrote to his Bowdoin friend Horatio Bridge of "the gloom and chill of my early life." The pain and yet the aristocratic distinction of the outsider had been one of his first lessons in being human.

An orphan is an outsider and, insofar as he feels responsible for his parents' deaths, a criminal. The Gentle Boy destroys, through his adopted father's conversion to detested Quakerism, the household that takes him in. "What is a crime?" Hawthorne asked in *Doctor Grimshawe's Secret*. "Each son murders his father at a certain age; or does each father try to accomplish the impossibility of murdering his successor?" In "My Kinsman, Major Molineux," the colonial father-figure is deposed in a dreamlike parade, sitting "in tar-and-feathery dignity" while his former dependent, Robin, unexpectedly laughs aloud, aligning himself, Miller explains, "with the rebels who have acted out his secret desire." "Roger Malvin's Burial" nightmarishly elaborates upon father-son mayhem: Malvin, a middle-aged soldier critically wounded in an Indian battle of 1725, persuades a younger companion, Reuben Bourne, to abandon him to die in the woods, after three days of travel together have exhausted him and left them still far from home. Though protesting that "you have been a father to me," Reuben yields to Malvin's arguments and, upon his return, marries, as both men had foreseen, Malvin's daughter, Dorcas. Yet, in the exhaustion and delirium of his return, he fails to explain to Dorcas that he left her father still alive, and allows her and the village to believe that he saw her father through to death and buried him. The truth nags Reuben, turning him into one of Hawthorne's secret-hugging social misfits and blighting his marriage, whose main joy is a son, Cyrus. When Cyrus is fifteen, the little family, impoverished by its head's distracted and irritable husbandry, enters the forest to seek a fresh start on the frontier. Reuben is instinctively led back to the exposed granite face where he left Malvin dying; he shoots his son in a hunting accident, and the boy's body falls on his grandfather's bones. Like a murderous priest of old, Hawthorne offers this as a happy ending: "The vow that the wounded youth had made, the blighted man had come to redeem. His sin was expiated—the curse was gone from him," and he is able again to pray. Miller calls the tale

> an awesome story of parricide, filicide, symbolic suicide or self-punishment, and role reversals. Hawthorne universalizes the tale by evoking the myths of Narcissus, Oedipus, and Abraham and Isaac. At the same time he reveals once again his profound understanding of mourning and grief, depression and aggression, self-destructive tendencies, and the inevitable circular return to the beginning.

Miller's insistent readings in this vein do elucidate what gives Hawthorne's tales and novels their enduring resonance: the writer's instinctive awareness of the incestuous, polymorphous seethe alive in each individual psyche. Hawthorne was unwilling, even when the operations of connection and transposition failed him, to abandon this dark inner theatre for the sunlit surface realism he admired in others, like Trollope. Fantasy and symbolization gave Hawthorne entry to the erotic knit, the interplay of primal human needs to which he was sensitive with a modern openness, even though, according to his wife, he hated "to be touched more than any one I ever knew."

A Freudian reading of Hawthorne, however, can come to seem relentless. Of the soap bubbles that Clifford Pyncheon blows from the House of the Seven Gables toward passersby, including his kinsman the Judge, Miller tells us:

> Psychologically—and this is the more telling point—Clifford's soap bubble turns out by accident (he is much too cowardly to take the offensive) to be his means of attacking his betrayer and emasculator, the man who has denied him maturity through false imprisonment. Once again the Judge's sexual power is attacked when the bubble bursts on that symbolic phallus, the nose. Symbolically, then, the child-man, or "son," has revenged himself on the Bad Father—by accident.

When Hawthorne likens Monument Mountain as seen from his study in Lenox to "a huge, headless Sphinx, wrapped in a Persian shawl," Miller pounces:

He summoned one of the recurrent images of nineteenth-century art and literature, the Greek sphinx, half-human, half-animal, a lion's body with a woman's breast, symbol of the castrating woman and guardian of the riddle which Oedipus unraveled.

If such an amplification feels needlessly expansive, a sentence like this can seem condescendingly reductive: "Hawthorne was of two or more minds on most subjects and despite his external grace limped internally with repressions and fears."

The biographer's approach—considering a writer's works primarily as a set of clues to an undeclared psychological malformation—discounts an author's ability and desire to observe and generalize. Miller quotes a fine remark by Donald Hall: "Domesticity precedes ideology, for all men and women. The feelings between parents and children, siblings, men and women as lovers or as spouses—these relationships penetrate the life of genius as much as they penetrate the lives of the rest of humanity." Hall's remark implies, however, that domesticity is succeeded by ideology, and Hawthorne did have an ideology: he believed, like a modern phenomenologist, that our human truth is blended of what he called, in the introduction to *The Scarlet Letter*, "the Actual and the Imaginary"—the objective and the subjective, body and spirit, fact and fantasy—and that art exists on the unsteady boundary between these realms. In his youthful years of impressionable reading, *The Pilgrim's Progress* and *The Arabian Nights* especially moved him; ever after, he required an element of the fantastic or allegorical in his inspirations. Sketching his own portrait as M. de l'Aubépine, the ostensible author of "Rappaccini's Daughter," he admitted to "an inveterate love of allegory" and said, "He generally contents himself with a very slight embroidery of outward manners,—the faintest possible counterfeit of real life,—and endeavors to create an interest by some less obvious peculiarity of the subject." There is a conscious self-mastery in such witty self-caricature.

Hawthorne's oeuvre, with its far-from-diffident courtship of a popular audience and its considerable portion of successfully completed hackwork (the children's books, the campaign biography of Pierce), has a constructed, outward-facing side that Miller minimizes. The writer twice occupied public office, and was in Salem the center of a storm of dirty politics and adverse publicity. Julian Hawthorne's biography records that his father intently read popular newspapers and magazines. He drew not only on his own subconscious and primal needs but on the popular imagination. His tales and novels, as we read in David S. Reynolds's *Beneath the American Renaissance* (1988), closely follow the patterns of moralizing, reform-minded popular fiction. Reynolds says of *The Scarlet Letter*, "One reason the novel became one of his most popular works was that the antebellum public felt comfortable with a fictional exposé of hidden corruption involving a hypocritical preacher, a fallen woman, an illegitimate child, and a vindictive relative. By the late 1840s such depraved characters were stock figures in popular American fiction." Yet they do not feel stock as Hawthorne developed them.

The question of his personal secret, thirteen decades after his death, is perhaps of less moment than the question of his still-living masterpiece's secret: what enabled this writer, whose fiction generally diffuses with allegorical schemes its emotional content, to produce in *The Scarlet Letter* a work so passionate and concentrated? Mark Van Doren, in his *Nathaniel Hawthorne* (1949)—a biography much swifter-moving and more critically assertive than either Miller's or Mellow's—can't emphasize enough the short novel's singularity: "Never before has Hawthorne dealt with stuff so solid; and never again will he be so able or content to let his people determine his plot." Again, discussing Emerson's remark after Hawthorne's death—"I thought him a greater man than any of his works betray . . . and that he might some day show a purer power"—Van Doren says, "The tragic element in the event is not that there was too little power; in *The Scarlet Letter* alone there was enough. It is that Hawthorne, whether from indolence or from confusion, or from the modesty which he cultivated till it became a fault, so seldom let it go."

The novel's uncharacteristic solidity, economy, narrative speed, and human warmth may stem from factors other than the death of Hawthorne's mother that year and his bedside tears, though *The Scarlet Letter* does tap our tears, especially in its forest scene of long silence broken. The novel packed a punch from the start: when Hawthorne read its ending to his wife, he told Horatio Bridge in a letter, "It broke her heart, and sent her to bed with a grievous headache." In his English notebook he recalled how, when he read the novel aloud, "my voice swelled and heaved as if I were tossed up and down on an ocean as it subsides after a storm." Though Henry James, in his masterly if captious *Hawthorne* (1879), found the novel flawed by its "element of cold and ingenious fantasy," most readers have an impression of uncanny heat, such as the author himself felt when, according to his prefatory reminiscence, he placed the faded, embroidered scarlet letter, discovered in the Custom House attic, upon his breast and was compelled to drop it, "as if the letter were not of red cloth, but red-hot iron."

The year 1849 had seen, as his preface to *The Scarlet Letter* describes at genial length, the end of his appointment as surveyor of the port of

Salem. He is humorous about his political decapitation, and proud of his three years of public service among unliterary men, following three years spent among the elevated spirits of Concord: "I looked upon it as an evidence, in some measure, of a system naturally well balanced, and lacking no essential part of a thorough organization, that, with such associates to remember, I could mingle at once with men of altogether different qualities, and never murmur at the change." Experience gives an author not only details but a texture, a sense of life. Who can say how much Hawthorne's earthy, Customs-bound vacation from cloistered composition, measuring salt and coal and enduring the conversation of sinecured old seamen, may have contributed to the bustling pace and freshened concreteness of *The Scarlet Letter*, with its vigorous, closely fitted population of characters? "Come out of your thoughts and breathe another air," Septimius Felton is advised, in Hawthorne's last attempted tale. A few pages on, the author speaks of the "love of life and clinging to it, peculiar to dark, sombre natures, and which lighter and gayer ones can never know." Hawthorne's own love of life was one of his more potent secrets, kept hidden perhaps even from himself in his Castle Dismal days. As his later life proved, he was more gregarious than he then seemed, and his vital traits did much to annul the deficit of experience he complained of to Longfellow in 1837: "I have seen so little of the world, that I have nothing but thin air to concoct my stories of."

Nor, really, can one imagine him writing *The Scarlet Letter* if he had remained unmarried. The stoic solitude of Hester Prynne may be Elizabeth Manning Hathorne's, but the book's feminist message—its bright hope of a new "relation between man and woman on a surer ground of mutual happiness"—is Sophia Hawthorne's. Biographers have found Sophia hard to love: in her interminable letters she too eagerly claimed the role of ideal wife for the Apollonian genius, and when Apollo was dead she prudishly censored his journals and letters. But the psychological confidence of *The Scarlet Letter*, its range of sympathy and analysis, testifies to his seven years of marriage, with its sexual revelations, its added responsibilities, and its exercise of tolerance and understanding in domesticity's tiny democracy. His firstborn child, Una, who was to grow from a fascinatingly difficult little girl to an unfortunately difficult woman, stood for her portrait as the elf-child Pearl; more important, the very tone of heterosexual negotiation, in its tempered passion and intuitive practicality, gives a depth of ripeness not only to the heated exchanges of Hester and Dimmesdale but to the touchingly reasonable and forgiving conversations on the least conspicuous side of the triangle, between Hester and Chillingworth. If Nora Barnacle could be credited with making a man of James Joyce, Sophia Peabody made a novelist of the brilliant and melodious sketch-writer Hawthorne. The sister-mirror was replaced by a semi-opaque wife; the realities of a family gave a flesh-and-blood weight to the ancestral spectres and shadowy maternal presences of the author's prolonged youth. Hawthorne always tended to disown *The Scarlet Letter*, even in his introduction damning it as "too much ungladdened by genial sunshine; too little relieved by the tender and familiar influences which soften almost every scene of nature and real life." For once, his softening and tricky suggestiveness yielded to an urgent bold outline of event and consequences. As with Shakespeare, a crude old story served his subtlety best.

The bracing and broadening effects of patriarchy vitalize the more scattered inspirations of his next two novels, but after seven years abroad, and the bookish triumph of *The Marble Faun*, Hawthorne lost the ability to assemble his visionary scenes into the shape of a novel. His instincts still led him into the dusk between the actual and the imaginary but could no longer lead him out. The two notions of a bloody footprint and an elixir of immortality haunt four unfinished romances with which he wretchedly struggled. Like the befuddled, extensive manuscripts Hemingway left to his heirs, Hawthorne's last efforts make us aware of how thin is the weave that hides an author's nakedness, how fragile the fabric of coherent invention. In the longest and most often revised of them, *Doctor Grimshawe's Secret*, characters change names—Etheredge, Ormskirk, Grimshawe—and aspects; the connections between America and England fail and fall silent like underwater cables; portentously foreshadowed symbols fizzle when unveiled. With their pages of sudden flashing charm—the three abandoned chapters of *The Dolliver Romance*, foremost—these romances pose the riddle of an accomplished writer's crack-up, and naturally excite searchers for Hawthorne's secret. Homosexually attractive enemies, seductive sister-figures, parentless children— all are here, swarming through the ruins. But these conjurations lack the conviction of the short stories and *The Scarlet Letter*. Hawthorne's crisis was one of health but also of belief: the ceremonies and fetishes of plot no longer commanded his faith. The Gothic tradition—the prose offspring of Romanticism, bearing muffled messages from the sealed human depths—died, as literature, with him, though its appeal, in horror fiction and film, remains, to enrich Stephen King and inspire Joyce Carol Oates.

Preoccupied with phantoms of the psyche, Miller's biography is ghostly; even his index, blocks of page numbers unbroken into subtopics, is ghostly, along with his notes, many of them merely citing in bleak cipher ("C.15: 388, 310") the Centenary edition of Hawthorne, which this reader, for one, unfortunately lacked. Perhaps a ghostly author warrants a ghostly treatment. Hawthorne's life, with its late blooming and early withering, simulates one of his more haunting tales; he enjoyed teasing it into the light, in the autobiography that flirts at the edges of his fantasy. He is often confessional, even outrageously so, as in the impudent "Custom House" foreword, which helped speed his final departure from Salem. A search for a "secret" beyond those he essayed to confide in his writings seems vulgar, like the bare revelations of our talk shows and gossip journalism. A secret, once discovered, becomes a mere datum, whereas a quality of a classic—a work that is "replete," in Roland Barthes's word—is to hold its secrets in living solution and to defy, like life itself, perfect deciphering.

Not Quite Adult

THEODORE DREISER: *Volume II, An American Journey, 1908–1945,* by Richard Lingeman. 544 pp. Putnam, 1990.

If the second volume of Richard Lingeman's biography of Theodore Dreiser seems less vivid and continuously interesting, though no less literate and thorough, than the first, which came out in 1986 with the subtitle *At the Gates of the City, 1871–1907,* the reason may be that Mr. Lingeman has had less help from Dreiser, who covered his early years in two exceptionally intimate and frank volumes of autobiography, *Newspaper Days* (1922) and *Dawn* (1931). Or it may be that the spectacle of a great man running down is less satisfactory than that of a poor nobody rising to become a great man.

Not that Dreiser in 1908 was hailed as a great man yet, though he had written one great novel, *Sister Carrie* (1900). After years of licking the wounds incurred from the commercial failure of this allegedly immoral first novel, he had reconstituted himself as the editor-in-chief of a trio of women's fashion magazines owned by the Butterick Company, a maker of tissue-paper dress patterns. Dreiser's office was baronial and his salary had started, in 1907, at the princely amount of seven thousand dollars, with bonuses keyed to circulation, which did rise under his editorship. When one of his secretaries "asked him why a man who could write such a great book as *Sister Carrie* wasted his time editing a ladies' magazine, Dreiser shrugged. 'One must live.' " He lived in quiet bourgeois fashion on West 123rd Street with his wife of ten years, Sara, a genteel and petite former schoolteacher from Missouri unglamorously nicknamed Jug—"because she wore brown so often that she resembled the little brown jug of the song." Dreiser had been attracted to Jug when he was a lowly twenty-two-year-old reporter in St. Louis. She was two years older than he, and, as the daughter of a prominent farmer and Montgomery County politician, socially superior. In *Newspaper Days* he wrote that by the time they married, in December of 1898, "the first flare of love had thinned down to the pale flame of duty." But she loved him, gave him more sex than he at times could handle, and remained Mrs. Dreiser until her death, in 1942.

Ten years after the wedding, he was romantically restless, and his infatuation with an eighteen-year-old piquantly named Thelma Cudlipp (he met her when he joined, in an un-Dreiserian fit of levity, a ballroom-dancing group called the Fantastic Toe Club) tipped the precarious balance. Though he never bedded Miss Cudlipp, his lumbering attempt caused enough fuss to spring him both from cohabitation with Jug and from his editorship of ladies' magazines. Rather than give up his pursuit of Thelma, he resigned his position with Butterick in October 1910. Freed from respectability, he swiftly finished *Jennie Gerhardt*, a novel that he had begun in 1901 but had abandoned, and commenced two others, *The "Genius"* and *The Financier*. At the same time, he embarked upon his insatiable, convoluted career of sexual entanglements. Lillian Rosenthal, "a plump and pretty young woman with a musical bent," was the twenty-year-old daughter of his landlords on Riverside Drive; their affair began, as so many would, with a letter, from her, about literature. She had read *Jennie Gerhardt* in manuscript, and felt that its happy ending rang false; Dreiser agreed, and seduced his adviser in the bargain.

This characteristic pattern, of sexual and editorial services mingled, would repeat with a number of women—Anna Tatum, Louise Campbell, Estelle Kubitz, Sally Kusell, Clara Clark, Esther Van Dresser, and Marguerite Tjader Harris. Helen Richardson, who was to be his long-suffering, oft-betrayed mistress for twenty-four years and finally, after Jug's death, the second Mrs. Dreiser, developed editorial skills but had come to him in New York as a distant cousin from Oregon. Her look of "lympathic sensuality" aroused him; aroused in turn, she "promised to read all his novels." Like an earlier inamorata, Elaine Hyman (who took the stage name Kirah Markham), Helen was essentially an aspiring actress. Interlarded with these major mistresses were many compulsive conquests. One of the latter, Yvette Szekely, the teenage daughter of his confidante Margaret Szekely, denied that Dreiser "used" women. "Why were they being used?" she responded to Mr. Lingeman in 1983. "They were happy. They loved him. . . . He told everyone that she was the only one. He really did care about the person—not that he pretended to love and didn't. If he had five women, he really cared for them." Marguerite Harris, who was to throw her body on Dreiser's corpse in the sight of the grieving widow, wrote in her memoir, *Theodore Dreiser: A New Dimension*, of how he, in his "utter simplicity," allowed "the urgency of the moment" to control his affairs. She explained, "Dreiser simply *was* his own emotions, his own instincts, or intuitions, attempting to communicate them directly, often in terms contradictory to each other." The reader of Mr. Lingeman's biography cannot but be struck by how much indulgence Dreiser asked of women, and how much he did receive. Helen Dreiser dedicated *her* memoir, *My Life with Dreiser*, "To the unknown women in the life of Theodore Dreiser, who devoted themselves unselfishly to the beauty of his intellect and its artistic unfoldment." Even when he was young, poor, homely, and severely inhibited, both by Victorian puritanism and his father's fierce Catholic religiosity, Dreiser was aided in unfoldment by "fast" college coeds, amiable prostitutes, and still-nubile landladies; women flocked to the needy call of those deepset, smoldering eyes and meaty "Austrian"—his own characterization—lips. By 1917, he was confiding to his diary, "I must give up so much screwing or I will break down."

As a writer, Dreiser was dependent upon the aid of other people to the extent that some of his later works—including the two posthumously published novels, *The Bulwark* and *The Stoic*—are virtually collaborations. Given an erratic early education by German-speaking nuns, Dreiser flunked schoolboy grammar and was ever a poor speller. His career as a Midwestern reporter and New York magazine-writer in the 1890s accustomed him to heavy remedial editing; when one of his female advisers, Ruth Kennell, pointed out his grammatical mistakes and superfluous words, he answered unapologetically, "I have been so offending all my life. All my books are full of them." Jug, the former schoolteacher, took a hand in *Sister Carrie*, changing such Dreiserian locutions as "On her feet were yellow shoes and in her hands her gloves" to the more customary but possibly less vigorous "Her brown shoes peeped occasionally from beneath her skirt. She carried her gloves in her hand." Dreiser's friend and fellow-writer Arthur Henry went through the manuscript with him, and together they excised over thirty thousand excessively philosophical or sexually specific words. About twenty-five thousand words came out of *Jennie Gerhardt*. One energetic editor promised to reduce the all-too-confessional *A Traveler at Forty* from five hundred thousand words to one hundred thousand. Fifty thousand words or so were deleted from *An American Tragedy*, and, though Dreiser supposedly joked to his editors at Boni & Liveright, "What the hell is 50,000 words between friends?," he restored over half of them. H. L. Mencken, in his review of the novel, called it "a vast, sloppy, chaotic thing of 385,000 words—at least 250,000 of them unnecessary!" In the heyday of their friendship, Dreiser had been guided by Mencken's suggestions in cutting seventy-seven pages from *The Financier*. By the time of his Hollywood twilight (1939–45), Dreiser's authorial control had grown so slack that a young movie-magazine writer, Cedric Belfrage, concocted the topical book *America Is Worth Saving* out of Dreiser's boozy ramblings. Belfrage claimed, "He couldn't have possibly written the book by himself, so in fact I wrote the book." Two of Dreiser's faithful muses ghosted a series of *Esquire* sketches that he signed, and Louise Campbell reduced so much of *The Bulwark* to "good clear English" that Marguerite Harris, to whom he had dictated the text, protested that the book had "lost much of its relation" to Dreiser. How much rough-hewn literature was lost through the drastic editing that Dreiser willingly suffered, out of necessity and laziness, remains for a patient textual scholar to define, in a restorative edition such as has already been given some cavalierly edited novels of Faulkner.

Faulkner, at his most eccentric and willfully windy, thought he knew what he was doing; Dreiser will never be, so muddied is his prose at the source, a model of stylistic integrity. He was not only awkward but careless. His habits, early acquired, of journalistic appropriation and recycling exposed him, at several times in his career, to charges of plagiarism: *Sister Carrie* embodies a passage of slightly paraphrased George Ade; parts of *Dreiser Looks at Russia* were lifted almost intact from the newspaper reports of Dorothy Thompson; and the trial in *An American Tragedy* draws nakedly on the transcript of the actual trial of Chester Gillette, including virtually verbatim sections of the pathetic letters from Gillette's victim, Grace Brown. One of Dreiser's later amanuenses, Clara Clark, called in to save *The Stoic*, observed that "for a famous novelist he was extremely humble about his writing."

It would seem that Dreiser never totally recovered from the discouragement and nervous paralysis that the suppression, by its own publishers, of *Sister Carrie* imposed on him. Never again would he write with quite such pure and innocent trust in his powers and his message—"I'll get it all in!" he once vowed, of America's reality—as he did in that first novel. Not even the large critical and popular success of *An American Tragedy* (1925) wholly lifted the air of melancholy and distraction, of weariness and muddle, from the career described in *An American*

Journey. An American Tragedy, magnificent though passages are, is a belabored, mechanically plotted book compared with *Sister Carrie*. The youthful novel coolly dismisses the providential doom that Victorian morality claimed followed upon sexual trespass; its morality is fresh and actual, based on what Dreiser saw around him, in the cities he knew and in the lives of his sisters. Whereas *An American Tragedy* tells an old-fashioned cautionary tale: a boy raised in piety is seduced by the world and becomes a sinner and a murderer and is punished. In the earlier book, the fallen woman rises. In the later, those who dare unsanctioned love perish, and Dreiser seems to be working less out of observation than out of his own deeps of guilty longing; the dismal novel ends by making us long for the straight and narrow path. Stuart P. Sherman, a vehement foe of Dreiser's earlier fictional indiscretions, praised the author, in the *New York Herald Tribune*, for having become, at last, with *An American Tragedy*, a "good moralist." At any rate, the book is a rather lonely triumph, achieved after a decade of false starts and professional quarrels and fruitless haring after Hollywood dollars, and followed by two decades without another completed novel.

Dreiser's literary impotence after 1925 is the most striking riddle of the years 1908–45, even granted that he was, in our honorable American way, a writer of starts and stops, of elephantine gestation periods and quasi-religious periods of hesitation and meditation. The older he got, the more he indulged his itch to philosophize and make pronouncements. Some of his civic acts still seem admirable and brave, such as his defense of the Scottsboro boys and his well-publicized (in part because he blithely took along a pretty libertarian identified as "Marie Pergain") investigation of miners' conditions in Kentucky's warring Harlan County. But dust and discredit have thickly gathered upon his hopes for an American-style Communism, his Anglophobic wish to keep us from going to war against Hitler, and his final, rather mystical enlistment in the Communist Party. His attempt to join the party in 1930 had been turned down by the cautious American Communist Party Secretary Earl Browder, who said of Dreiser, "He did not seem quite adult, which was part of his charm." To Cedric Belfrage ten years later, Dreiser seemed a "man in a fog groping around, looking for scapegoats." One wonders if the fog were not partly alcoholic: Belfrage described how a midday drink of straight whiskey would unhinge the dictating session, and Dreiser confessed to Mencken, of whiskey, "I love and need it so." The biographer confides: "He carried a half pint of cheap rye in his pocket and would take a nip whenever he felt bored or tired." Though not as spectacularly addicted as Fitzgerald and Faulkner, Ring Lardner and Sinclair Lewis, Dreiser drank with his bibulous generation, and in his Hollywood years he routinely started the day with "a small drink," which led to more. Much of his life after he left Jug does seem a groping, an unedifying scramble of new addresses and new women, of unearned advances and unfinished projects, of irksome suppressions and paranoid quarrels, of pompous posturing as an author, with his Westchester estate and seething harem of groupies.

Yet no excess or vanity quite obliterated his instinctive honesty and largeness of spirit. Observing him in the Harlan County investigations, Dos Passos wrote, "There was a sort of massive humaneness about him, a self-dedicated disregard of consequences, a sly sort of dignity that earned him the respect of friend and foe alike." Dreiser's was an honesty that contained contradictions: he died a member of the Communist Party and also a churchgoer. He and Helen, not herself a believer, had attended a Christian Science church for a period, but he had found most consolation at the Mt. Hollywood Congregational Church; its liberal pastor, Reverend Alan Hunter, spoke at Dreiser's funeral, along with the Communist playwright and screenwriter John Howard Lawson. A third voice at the service was that of Charlie Chaplin, who read one of Dreiser's copious *vers libres*; the entertainer's presence was fitting, since a central Dreiserian theme was the rise of America's popular, commercial culture, at the expense of Old World pieties and stabilities. His father, the fanatically pious Johann Paul Dreiser, reportedly once said, "There is no real faith in this country. On the other side—*there* is the real faith." Theodore Dreiser never stopped rummaging about for some sort of God. Mencken, a champion of *Sister Carrie* and a lifelong correspondent if not unwavering admirer of Dreiser's, was exasperated by the novelist's muddle of sex, pseudo-science, and fellow-travelling. In Mencken's *A Book of Prefaces* Dreiser is described as an "Indiana peasant, snuffling absurdly over imbecile sentimentalities, giving a grave ear to quackeries, snorting and eye-rolling with the best of them. . . . The truth about Dreiser is that he is still in the transition stage between Christian Endeavor and civilization." In 1916, Mencken complained in a letter to Ernest Boyd that Dreiser was "a fearful ass and . . . it is a very difficult thing to do anything for him"; two years later, he was complaining to Ben Huebsch how susceptible Dreiser was "to the flattery of self-seeking frauds, particularly those with cavities between their legs." Mencken was as clear-sighted and sexually reserved as Dreiser was muddle-headed and libidinous; neither churches nor the Communist Party nor female wiles fooled the Sage of Baltimore. Yet it was Dreiser's embrace of muddle that made him an artist and Mencken something slightly less.

Young Fannie Hurst met Dreiser in his pince-nezed, Butterick Company editorial capacity early in the century, and remembered his "strange lantern of a face." When Dreiser, in the dark early days of the Depression, mumblingly addressed a group of writers he had assembled on the question of what intellectuals might do for the American worker, one of those in attendance, Louis Adamic, wrote, "Dreiser's own great honesty and bewilderment had engulfed everybody." His bewilderment enabled him to enter without condescension or any slighting of nuance into the bewilderment of his characters. In the world of his fiction, people all want something, and everything is for sale, and love is the great commodity; his paragraphs buzz with the market calculations of his women and men, and religious scruples and spiritual aspirations have their considered weight among the other factors. The constrained affair, in *An American Tragedy*, between Clyde Griffiths and Roberta Alden is traced with an intense delicacy, from both sides. Clyde's wavering conscience, with a boyish puzzlement at its core, is honored to the end. The majestic patience with which Dreiser recounts his hero's low doomed pilgrimage amid the enticements and opportunities of capitalist America may have wearied Mencken, but it did not weary readers who shared Dreiser's reverence for our faltering human substance, not as it should or might be but as it is. His subject, he once told an interviewer, was "life as it is, the facts as they exist, the game as it is played." Even his notorious self-centeredness helped him be true to life. Someone less selfish than he could not have brought off his stately fictional interweaves of advantage-seeking selves—novels which in their pure truthfulness kept offending those to whom the social contract and its repressions were sacred. A review of *A Hoosier Holiday* (1916) complained that the "ill-bred, undisciplined" author was "outside all the conventions and decent loyalties of the society which he professes to represent." Another review of the same book marvelled admiringly, "To him to tell the truth is natural, and to dream is natural." This maverick naturalness redeems much to be deplored, in his literary style and his life-style, and lends him, above most other American writers in the century that opened with *Sister Carrie*, a lantern glow of the heroic.

Large for Her Years

HELEN KELLER: *A Life*, by Dorothy Herrmann. 383 pp. Knopf, 1998.

Helen Keller (1880–1968) seems an unlikely candidate for a contemporary biography. We distrust inspirational figures. We no longer idealize our celebrities; we search out their sins. Keller achieved celebrity as a child and stayed actively in the public eye until a stroke in 1961 reduced her to invalidism. World-renowned in her time, acquainted with the great from Alexander Graham Bell to Golda Meir, this woman, both deaf and blind from the age of nineteen months, is remembered in countless Helen Keller jokes whose bad taste vents our deep fear of being reduced to her condition, a kind of burial alive. Locked in her silent dark, she conveyed a spiritual triumph whose terms would embarrass, perhaps, today's Americans. She spoke to a nation familiar with deprivation; with inscrutable onslaughts of childhood disease, such as had taken her two primary senses; and with vivid hopes of a better future, whether conceived in terms of the Christian heaven or a Communist paradise. She, as it happened, was a devotee of both Christ and Marx, both a Swedenborgian and a radical socialist. Such faiths seem a stretch now, but insofar as they sustained her they communicated hope and courage to her audiences. Those audiences have vanished.

William Gibson's very successful play *The Miracle Worker*—a television play in 1957, a Broadway play for seven hundred performances, beginning in 1959, and a movie in 1962—formed a handsome tribute to the central event of her life: her learning tactile sign language at the age of six at the hands of Annie Sullivan, a twenty-year-old governess the Kellers had recently hired.* Joseph Lash's massive and thorough 1980 biography, *Helen and Teacher: The Story of Helen Keller and Anne Sullivan Macy*, would seem to wrap up all that need be said about two remarkable women and their celebrated relationship. Nevertheless, Dorothy Herrmann, whose previous biographical subjects have been S. J. Perelman and Anne Morrow Lindbergh, has produced *Helen Keller: A Life*. She

---

*Annie, the daughter of impoverished Irish immigrants, had lived in a Massachusetts almshouse until her own severe eye problems had gained her admittance to the Perkins Institution for the Blind in Boston. She had learned Braille and sign language there, and spent time with Laura Bridgman, a deaf-blind inhabitant whom Dickens had met and written about in *American Notes*; it was his account that alerted Helen's mother to the possibility that her afflicted daughter might be educable.

covers the ground more quickly than Lash, and a shade less reverently. The private woman is emphasized over the public figure, whom Helen herself began to create when she used her newfound literacy to address letters to Michael Anagnos, the director of the Perkins Institution for the Blind in Boston, and to Alexander Graham Bell. By the age of eight she was being promoted by Anagnos as "a phenomenon." He wrote, "As soon as a slight crevice was opened in the outer wall of their twofold imprisonment, her mental faculties emerged full-armed from their living tomb as Pallas Athene from the head of Zeus." Her goodness was as fabulous as her intellect. Bell wrote a colleague, "I feel that in this child I have seen more of the Divine than has been manifest in anyone I ever met before." By the age of ten Helen was an accomplished fund-raiser for another deaf-blind child, Tommy Springer, writing letter after letter, in her careful square printing, on his behalf. Her myth was launched, as—to quote the enthusiastic Anagnos in 1889—"the queen of precocious and brilliant children . . . as pure as a lily of the valley, and as innocent and as joyous as the birds of the air or the lambs in the field."

A female writer in 1998 can speculate more frankly than Lash could in 1980 about Helen Keller as a sexual being. The sexual note is struck early, in Herrmann's introduction: "Beautiful, intelligent, high-strung and passionate, Helen might have lived the life of a spoiled, willful, and highly sexed southern belle had not the nature of her disability and her dependency on Annie Sullivan forced her into an entirely different existence." The six-year-old girl whom Annie Sullivan found at her parents' home in Tuscumbia, Alabama, was, she wrote to her friend and patroness Sophie Hopkins, "large, strong, and ruddy, and as unrestrained in her movements as a young colt. She has none of those nervous habits that are so noticeable and distressing in blind children." That was the thing about Helen Keller: she radiated vitality. Mrs. Keller told the newly arrived governess that the child had "not been ill a day since the illness [called "brain fever," probably scarlet fever or meningitis] that deprived her of her sight and hearing."* At the age of twelve, according to Anagnos, Helen was "5'2" in height and of symmetrical figure. . . . Her physique is magnificent." A few years later, Lawrence Hutton, one of a number of philanthropists who helped subsidize Helen throughout her life, wrote of their first meeting in 1895:

---

*Despite her pathetic handicap, Helen had developed a play life with other children— especially the black children of Tuscumbia—and with animals, evolved a vocabulary of about fifty signs with which to communicate her needs, and could sort and fold clothes, which she differentiated by texture and smell. The first time Annie tried to discipline her, her pupil "assaulted her, knocking out one of her front teeth."

Physically she was large for her years, and more fully developed than is the every-day girl of her age. Her face was almost beautiful, and her expression charming to behold, in its varying changes, which were always bright. . . . She was peculiarly affectionate and demonstrative in her disposition. And she bestowed her innocent kisses upon persons of all ages and of either sex as freely and as guilelessly as the ordinary girl of fifteen would bestow a harmless innocent smile.

In *The World I Live In* (1908), her introspective account of her deaf-blind life, Helen wrote, in a section on smells:

Masculine exhalations are, as a rule stronger, more vivid, more widely differentiated than those of women. In the odor of young men there is something elemental, as of fire, storm, and salt sea. It pulsates with buoyancy and desire. It suggests all the things strong and beautiful and joyous, and gives me a sense of physical happiness.

Alexander Graham Bell, whose invention of the telephone was a by-product of his lifelong concern with the deaf, took her aside when she was twenty and, spelling out the words letter by letter in her palm, told her, "It seems to me, Helen, a day must come when love, which is more than friendship, will knock at the door of your heart and demand to be let in." She answered that she did think of love sometimes, but as "a beautiful flower which I may not touch, but whose fragrance makes the garden a place of delight just the same." He thought this over, and insisted, "Do not think that because you cannot see or hear, you are debarred from the supreme happiness of woman. . . . Life does strange things to us." And she replied, with sad realism, "I can't imagine a man wanting to marry me. I should think it would seem like marrying a statue."*

Yet, when a proposal came, she did not reject it: "I yielded to an imperious longing to be a part of a man's life." The proposer was Peter Fagan, Annie Sullivan Macy's twenty-nine-year-old secretary. Fagan had been an editorial associate of Annie's husband, John Macy. Macy had met the two women in the years, 1900–1904, when Helen was enrolled at Radcliffe; he had come to Harvard in 1895, from Detroit, on a scholarship and, after a distinguished undergraduate career, eked out a living as an assistant in English, and was a fiercely socialist writer and poet. To her surprise, Annie at thirty-eight found herself being courted by this brilliant and fiery man, eleven years her junior. They married in 1905, after John had received Helen's approval and assured her that she and her teacher "were

---

*When, five years later, Bell reminded her of this conversation, she insisted, "It would be a severe handicap to any man to saddle upon him the dead weight of my infirmities. I know I have nothing to give a man that would make up for such an unnatural burden."

to go on just as before." After the marriage the three shared a farmhouse in Wrentham, Massachusetts, the surrounding property fixed up with stone walls and guide wires that enabled Helen to take walks by herself.

By 1916, however, John had fled the ménage, Annie was emotionally crushed and physically unwell, and Helen had returned from an unsuccessful Chautauqua tour preaching pacifism to a nation gearing up for war. At this low point Fagan began to spell avowals into Helen's palm, and, in Annie's absence, their courtship proceeded as far as the application for a marriage license in Boston. The city registrar leaked the tidbit to the *Boston Globe*, and Helen's mother, who had been about to take her daughter back to Alabama for a stay, went into furious action. She did not like Fagan, and she did not think Helen should ever marry. A melodramatic tangle of banishments, secret communications, planned abductions, and thwarted elopements followed, with the deaf-blind thirty-six-year-old celebrity showing all the pluck and guile of a girl in love. Fagan, though, was finally scared off, disappearing from history; to his credit, he never attempted to trade on his doomed liaison with Helen Keller. Long afterwards, in *Midstream: My Later Life* (1929), Helen wrote philosophically of the escapade: "I cannot account for my behavior. . . . I seem to have acted exactly opposite to my nature." But, she went on, "I am glad that I have had the experience of being loved and desired. The fault was not in the loving, but in the circumstances." Herrmann does not flinch from estimating exactly what "the experience of being loved" consisted of:

> By "loving," Helen . . . did not mean a few chaste kisses. As a militant socialist, she would not have hesitated to consummate her love for Peter Fagan. The circles in which she and her young lover moved were in rebellion against the sexual mores of the Victorian age. Many of their friends— John Macy, John Reed and his Bohemian wife, Louise Bryant, as well as Emma Goldman—were ardent champions of free love.

Sex is one experience that might be relatively complete for a deaf-blind person—a matter of tactile sensation and heated imagination, usually conducted in the dark anyway, and with few words. The caresses of arousal should come easily to one whose main language is touch. But sexual fulfillment, for all of us, is bounded by needs and dependencies of other kinds, and those in Helen Keller's case were exceptionally acute. Her family had distinguished antecedents—her mother was related to the Adamses of Massachusetts and the orator Edward Everett, and Helen had been born on a 640-acre tract idyllic with beautiful trees and gardens—but was far from rich; her father, a moody Confederate veteran and small-town newspaper editor of Swiss descent, could scarcely afford to pay Annie Sullivan her twenty-five dollars a month and died, in 1896, deeply in debt. Helen's independence from her stifling Alabama family could be acquired only through dependence upon Annie Sullivan and the international world of deaf-blind care and charity. Her writings brought in something, and her inspirational appearances on the lecture circuit something else; but she was happiest earning money in vaudeville, in which she and Annie performed a sedate skit off and on in the early Twenties. She wrote in *Midstream*,

> My teacher was not happy in vaudeville. She could never get used to the rush, glare, and noise of the theatre; but I enjoyed it keenly. At first it seemed odd to find ourselves on the same "bill" with acrobats, monkeys, horses, dogs, and parrots; but our little act was dignified and people seemed to like it.
>
> I found the world of vaudeville much more amusing than the world I had always lived in, and I liked it. I liked to feel the warm tide of human life pulsing round and round me.

From her tumultuous childhood on, Helen liked commotion; biplane rides, storms at sea, horseback riding, the proximate swirl of Martha Graham dances—all this fed her starved, fearless soul. Annie, whose keen mind had lifted her from the abysmal depths of a Massachusetts almshouse, had quite another temperament—reclusive, shy, and suspicious. She was a decidedly disaffected Catholic where Helen was a rapt Swedenborgian, and politically skeptical where Helen was an ardent socialist, pacifist, and suffragist. According to Herrmann, Annie told her biographer that "she and the adult Helen had such fundamentally different conceptions of life that they would have loathed one another had they met under ordinary circumstances."

But the two were yoked together, literally hand in hand as Annie spelled out, hour after hour, descriptions and answers for her insatiably inquisitive companion. According to Herrmann, "Annie found constantly being with Helen a nervewracking experience, and after spelling to her for several hours, often suffered from a headache and nausea." A reviewer of Helen's first book bluntly wrote, "It is perhaps worth reminding the readers that the wonderful feat of drawing Helen Keller out of her hopeless darkness was only accomplished by sacrificing for it another woman's whole life." In truth, each woman had rescued the other from obscurity; alone, each would have been considerably diminished.*

---

*Within a few months of her arrival in Tuscumbia, Annie wrote in a report back to Anagnos, "I know that the education of this child will be the distinguishing event of my life, if I have the brains and perseverance to accomplish it" (May 22, 1887).

Together, they enjoyed comfortable homes, acquaintance with the rich and famous, and a life-style that included vacations, expensive apparel, pedigreed dogs, and generous gifts to others. John Macy had accused Annie of "resembling the rich in the vulgarity of [her] tastes." Only when, in 1924, Helen became affiliated, as "national and international counselor" (i.e., fund-raiser) with the American Foundation for the Blind, a 1921 amalgamation of lesser agencies, did the two women and their assistants find steady work and financial security, even though— Helen wrote in *Teacher: Anne Sullivan Macy* (1955)—"Teacher and I felt real shame to appear as mendicants at the doors of plenty." In *Midstream* she paints a sardonic picture of fund-raising, saying that, until a better method is found,

> individuals like myself will continue to travel up and down the land, and up and down in the elevators of great office buildings, to solicit funds from rich men. We will stand at doors and street corners, hat in hand, begging pennies from every passer-by, we will climb on to the running board of automobiles held in traffic to plead with some wealthy person to take our precious cause under his golden wing.

John Macy, in the years when he lived with the two inseparable women, called Helen "more of an institution than a woman," an institution of which his wife was condemned "to serve as chairman of the board, vice-president, secretary, treasurer, janitor, matron, and office boy." As Helen's agent, she was a formidable bargainer: when the Foundation, under its president Major Moses Charles Migel, waffled on her terms of two thousand a month, she cabled swiftly, "IF YOU THINK OTHER AGENCIES CAN RAISE THE TWO MILLION DOLLARS WITHOUT HELEN KELLER, WE SHALL WE BE MOST WILLING TO WITHDRAW."

In 1965, as she lay incapacitated, Helen Keller was one of twenty women elected to the Women's Hall of Fame at the New York World's Fair. She and Eleanor Roosevelt received most votes. Now that Mrs. Roosevelt has been plausibly* outed as a lesbian, there is a healthy interest in the Sapphic side of Helen Keller. "How tenderly she fondled my hand!" Helen wrote of Annie's last living hours. The deaf-blind woman perforce clung to Annie until Teacher's death in 1936, and after that to Polly Thomson, a spinster Scotswoman, less temperamental and bril-

---

*Or implausibly. Blanche Wiesen Cook, in her 1992 biography *Eleanor Roosevelt: Vol. 1, 1884–1933*, is convinced that Mrs. Roosevelt had a physical affair with the lesbian journalist Lorena Hickok; Geoffrey C. Ward, in his *New York Review of Books* notice of her book, strongly doubts it. Most surviving friends of the great lady doubt that the effusive warmth of her letters to Hickok was translated into physical action.

liant than Annie but a faithful and constant companion until her own death in 1960. Nella Braddy Henney—Annie's biographer and a long-time intimate—assured an inquirer that all three were "women who liked men." Keller well into her middle age projected sexual charisma, and in 1922 received by mail a proposal of marriage to which she replied in one of her frankest, most moving letters:

> Since my youth I have desired the love of a man. Sometimes I wondered rebelliously why Fate has trifled with me so strangely, why I was tantalized with bodily capabilities I could not fulfill. But Time, the great discipliner, has done his work well.

She goes on to explain that her suitor may have been misled by her writings, wherein "one hides as much as possible one's awkwardness and helplessness under a fine philosophy and a smiling face," and to acknowledge "the wise, loving ministrations of my teacher, Mrs. Macy, who since my earliest childhood has been a light to me in all dark places." Love takes many forms outside of the narrow groove of copulative heterosexual relations. Any close family seethes with it, and with jealousy, possessiveness, and the resentments bred of interdependence. It was Keller's fate, bound as she was to a household of keepers, to be a precious, demanding child all her life. Herrmann theorizes that her "startling metamorphosis," after the revelation of language at the well pump, from violent little savage to avid student and "angel child" flowed from the recognition that compliance and sweetness were the way to win protection from the vast world of "seeing, hearing people." Yet hostility toward Teacher surfaced in her dreams, and hostility toward the status quo in her radical politics. Though she no longer hit and pinched members of her family, she championed the Wobblies, the Russian Revolution, Margaret Sanger's campaign for birth control, and the NAACP. "Ever since childhood," she announced, "my feelings have been with the slaves." Her outspoken liberalism affronted her mother, irritated Annie, and piqued her rich benefactors, but helped create, it may be, the general public's love of her, and her aura of sainthood. Her cosmic optimism added to her radiance, and this radiance furthered her acceptance and self-preservation among the seeing.

As evidence of the spell she cast, her books remain, some of them still in print. Helen's years at Radcliffe, ending in her graduation cum laude in 1904, was a heroic ordeal for both her and Teacher: Annie had to spell out every lecture into the student's palm, and for hours a day had to comprehend and translate written material—German, French, history, geometry, physics, philosophy—well beyond the limits of her own education. Her fragile eyes, injured by trachoma in her girlhood, failed to the point that she "could not see much farther than the end of her nose." Most of the course matter did not exist in Braille, little in the way of companionship could be coaxed from the other students, and of Helen's rather crusty and distant professors only one, William Allan Neilson, "took the time to master the manual finger language so he could communicate directly with her." Another warm spot in the faculty was Charles Townsend Copeland, who encouraged Helen in English composition. He wrote, "In some of her work she has shown that she can write better than any pupil I have ever had, man or woman. She has an excellent 'ear' for the flow of sentences." Her written work, though a bit flowery and lofty for modern tastes, does have a lively, engaging, intricately modulated voice, whereas she herself—to her grief—could never come close to talking like other people.

Helen's themes for Copeland came to the attention of the *Ladies' Home Journal*, which paid her three thousand dollars for the series of articles that became her first book, *The Story of My Life* (1903). She had learned to touch-type, yet, even so, found writing such a burden that Annie had to remind her sternly, "The game of words is the only game you can play on equal terms with the best of them. . . . It is too bad writing should come so hard with you, especially when it is your only medium of self-expression." Annie, as her letters show, wrote quite well, as did John Macy; these two certainly exercised a shaping hand on Keller's early articles and books. But the spirit and content are Helen's. Her sensory limitations compel her to contemplate the topics of perception and consciousness that have perennially concerned philosophers. In *The World I Live In* she writes of how Descartes's "I think, therefore I am," persuaded her of her own existence, and of how the "horizon" of odor, the far limit of a scent, gave her the idea of distance which the more fortunate easily gather from sight and sound. With a hard-earned Emersonianism she writes: "Sometimes it seems as if the very substance of my flesh were so many eyes looking out at will upon a world new created every day." With wry Emersonian self-regard she proclaims, "I am burdened with a Puritanical sense of obligation to set the world to rights." Her desperate early need to break out of her maddening prison gives her prose a shine of triumph, a giddy honesty. Her story, more than any told before or since, came to represent the pathos and promise of the handicapped. Van Wyck Brooks's biographical sketch of Keller, in 1956, mentions a haunting detail most biographers omit. Before Helen's "soul was set free" by her realizing the connection between the spelled-out "w-a-t-e-r" on her hand and the silvery, gushing reality of pump water,

Annie had tapped out the word "d-o-l-l." The child had failed to grasp the connection between these taps and the doll she held but memorized the pattern of finger motions and tried them out on her old pet setter, Belle, hitherto her most understanding companion. The dog did not get it. But soon the light dawned for the child, and "I understood that it was possible for me to communicate with other people by these signs. Thoughts that ran forward and backward came to me quickly,—thoughts that seemed to start in my brain and spread all over me. . . . I felt joyous, strong, equal to my limitations."

Cubism's Marketeer

AN ARTFUL LIFE: *A Biography of D. H. Kahnweiler, 1884–1979,* by Pierre Assouline, translated from the French by Charles Ruos. 411 pp. Grove Weidenfeld, 1990.

Twentieth-century art has become, notoriously, a dealers' art; the art of the deal has made our pleasure in a museum inextricable from our wonder at how much these things are worth—that little Vermeer in the corner, just past the shoulder of the scowling guard, a few ounces of desiccated canvas and cracked paint, worth millions and millions, more than its weight in uranium! Yet are dealers, aside from the flamboyant Baron Joseph Duveen, interesting enough to become the subjects of biographies? *An Artful Life* suggests not quite.

Daniel-Heinrich Kahnweiler, born in Mannheim in 1884, had a long life, shaped with an admirable steadiness by his youthful encounter with Cubism; he had decided in his early twenties to become an art dealer, and his family, an alliance of importers on his father's side and bankers and metals speculators on his mother's, was wealthy enough to stake him to a small gallery in Paris. "This is a young man whose family gave him a gallery for his first communion," joked Ambroise Vollard, the distinguished dealer in the Post-Impressionists, to his companion, Pablo Picasso, when they first visited Kahnweiler's modest premises. Slowly, the gallery succeeded, and though twice he was driven from its management—as a German during World War I, and as a Jew in World War II—his firm survived and, thanks to its hold on Picasso's loyalty, finally prospered. Kahnweiler was a Francophile but remained Germanic: dedicated, methodical, patient, analytical, rigid, and somewhat humorless. He stuck by his principles and his intuitions. At the age of twenty-one he married a Frenchwoman—Léontine Alexandrine Godon, known as Lucie—two years his senior; he stayed married to her until her death, forty-one years later. To the day of his own death, at the age of ninety-four, he judged all modern art by the intense but narrow revelation that dawned for him in 1907, when, in Picasso's shabby studio, he witnessed the birth of Cubism, on the right-hand side of *Les Demoiselles d'Avignon*:

> When Kahnweiler finally saw the painting it came as a complete shock; he was astounded at first and then dazzled. He felt that something admirable, extraordinary, inconceivable had occurred.

By the end of his long life Kahnweiler was revered in France as "the great art dealer of the century" and "the source, the inventor, the promoter of modern art." As early as 1920, he was hearing praise like "If Picasso and Braque created Cubism, you assured its existence." Nevertheless, he remains, as better befits a businessman than the hero of a biography, rather bland and opaque, cagey and reserved.

The biographer, a Paris-based journalist, does not fail to apply the grease of dramatization to the slow-grinding wheels of his narrative. The viewing in Picasso's studio becomes an epic turning-point, a moment of mystical fusion: "Standing before Les Demoiselles d'Avignon Kahnweiler and Picasso observed one another; there was mutual understanding and a feeling of solidarity. There was no need for words. From then on Picasso knew that he was not entirely alone, and Kahnweiler knew he had made the right decision in refusing to go to South Africa to manage diamond mines." Picasso, aged twenty-six, worked in a squalid, cluttered studio on the Butte Montmartre; Kahnweiler, three years younger, sold paintings out of a tiny storefront, twelve feet square, near the Madeleine, on the rue Vignon. When visitors entered, the proprietor did not greet them but let them look in silence and then initiate conversation if they were interested in buying. "He was not one to praise paintings or formulate opinions, organize parties, or bargain over prices as in a flea market. His intention was to transform a commercial success into a moral triumph." Rather than deal in established painters, Kahnweiler wished to discover the geniuses of his own generation, and to bind them to him. "Exclusivity was the basis of his actions and the only rule he would never forsake. . . . For the painters he represented, he wanted to assume all their material worries so that they would be able to devote themselves to their art. . . . In return he insisted on exclusive rights to their work." At the 1907 exhibition at the Salon des Indépendants, he was struck by the Fauvist painters, especially Derain and Vlaminck. Disdaining to haggle, he purchased several paintings by them, and he subsequently won their friendship. Kees van Dongen came into the gallery with a roll of large, boldly colored paintings. Kahnweiler visited Georges Braque in the artist's tidy, sparsely furnished studio. Oral agreements began to secure these young artists; Matisse was already too established and expensive. Kahnweiler soon had doubts about the talent of van Dongen, who boasted that "he could visualize every detail of a painting even before he began." The dealer distrusted such sureness: "All of his life he would be on the side of painters who would begin a painting with only a vague idea of what they wanted to paint, as Pablo Picasso would put it."

With the addition of Picasso—always somewhat independent—to Kahnweiler's little stable of contracted artists, what his biographer calls "the heroic years" began. Selling largely to foreign collectors—the Swiss Hermann Rupf, the German Wilhelm Uhde, the Russians Sergei Shchukin and Ivan Morozov, the Czech Vincenz Kramar, the Americans Gertrude and Leo Stein—Kahnweiler established a lively enough market for his young artists. After about 1910, Braque and Picasso vacationed together in the little Pyrénées town of Céret, living and painting side by side with such intimacy and mutual inspiration that their paintings were difficult to distinguish. From Paris, Kahnweiler fed this two-headed prodigy on news, checks, and practical services, which included shielding Picasso from his soon-to-be-discarded mistress, Fernande Olivier. Olivier provides the only unflattering picture of Kahnweiler in the book: "He was a real Jewish businessman, knowing how to take risks to win, a man of action who bargained for hours until he tired out the artist, who, finally exhausted, would agree to the reduction in price he wanted. He knew very well what he had to gain by exhausting Picasso." Since Picasso was accustomed to being the cause rather than the victim of exhaustion, this power of Kahnweiler's may account for their enduring, however troubled, relationship. They knew each other for sixty-six years. When Picasso at last died, Kahnweiler refused to read the obituaries or to give interviews.

In return for his proprietary services, the dealer received a stream of paintings, drawings, and etchings. When, in four slovenly auctions in 1921, 1922, and 1923, his gallery, confiscated as German property during World War I, was liquidated as part of unpaid war reparations, modern art had never been sold on such a scale. A total of one hundred thirty-two Braques, one hundred thirty-two Picassos, one hundred eleven Derains, and two hundred five Vlamincks changed hands, not to mention fifty-six paintings by Juan Gris and forty-three by Fernand Léger (who both had come under contract to Kahnweiler in 1913), and numerous drawings, gouaches, and prints. The Ministry of Finance and the Commission on War Reparation earned a total of over seven hundred thousand francs—

about one hundred twelve 1922 dollars—for this dispersal of hundreds of paintings, a great many of them to foreign buyers, since generally the French public was indifferent to Cubism and the French critics were downright hostile. (As with "Impressionism," the name "Cubism" was bestowed derisively, in the latter case by Louis Vauxcelles, the most widely printed French critic of the time, who also christened "les Fauves." He had less luck calling Léger's work "tubism," perhaps his most cunning neologism of all; unaccountably, it failed to catch on.)

The war, enlisting some artists and isolating others, ended Cubism as a living movement, though Gris continued to practice his variety of it. Modest, thoughtful, somewhat dry, and stolidly loyal, Gris was the painter closest to Kahnweiler's conservative heart, and most amenable to his theories of art. Though Kahnweiler continued to function as a dealer and connoisseur to the verge of the 1980s, he never really got over Cubism. Surrealism he tolerated only to the extent of taking on a former surrealist, André Masson, as the major ornament of his post-auction gallery. Abstraction he could never abide. He snubbed Joan Miró, characterizing him as "a talented minor painter unaware of his own limitations," and spoke of Dalí as "always the same careful maniac and for me, very Ecole des Beaux-Arts." A large body of painters, including Frank Kupka and Marcel Duchamp, he dismissed as *ersatz Kubisten*, and toward the end, asked to name some great artists after Picasso and Braque, could name only Masson, André Beaudin, and Eugène de Kermadec—all represented by his gallery. Kahnweiler's ideas were strict, systematic, and insistent. His attitude toward art had a religious solemnity; he wrote a friend, "It is in this union, it seems to me, which I experience before a work of art, that I can know what saints must experience in their union . . . with God." Art must strive for a union with the real. To Picasso he said, "I believe that what is most important about painting is its creative interaction with the external world." Picasso's violent and sensual venturesomeness continued to startle and amaze him. In 1932, Picasso told him, "I would like to paint the way a blind man would describe the shape of a woman's ass," and showed him two nudes that elicited from the stunned Kahnweiler the remark "It seems as if a satyr who had murdered a woman had painted this picture." But the satyr never committed the sin of abstract painting, which Kahnweiler dismissed as "decorative." In his *Confessions esthétiques* (1963) he wrote:

> It is appropriate to bring up a trend that has set for itself the goal of painting without a subject, in order to compose harmonies of colors on the canvas without making any reference to an object in nature. . . . The prob-

lem of painting, the concentration on the multiplicity of forms in the world within the unity of a work of art, is a problem unknown to this school. It has cast aside the problems with which lyrical painting has wrestled for years. The works are decorative and will ornament walls, but that's all. It's not artistic vision that is the genesis of the work, it's the sense of decoration. That is all that these paintings ever will be, decorations.

The biographer, in his own task of representation, did not have an easy wrestle with this prim, censorious worshipper of painting, this selectively enraptured bystander. Even the most hazardous and dramatic episodes of Kahnweiler's life, his survival of the two world wars, come across as rather tame. A pacifist and far from prescient in international matters, he thought right up through July of 1914 that war between France and Germany was impossible; he and Lucie were on vacation in Upper Bavaria when Austria declared war on Serbia. They crossed the Swiss border in the middle of the night and, after four months of indecision in Italy, finally took refuge in Bern with his old friend Hermann Rupf. Kahnweiler spent five years in Switzerland, in a state of boredom and anxiety. Had he taken Picasso's earlier advice and become a French citizen, or had he taken the advice of his American partner Joseph Brenner and shipped his paintings to New York, much of his post-war misfortune might have been avoided. As it was, he managed to rebuild the gallery—renamed Galerie Simon, after his silent partner André Simon, to avoid possible restrictions against ownership by a German citizen—and steered it through the difficult Depression years, when even the rich were slow to pay their bills.

He was no more prescient about World War II than about its predecessor; in 1933 he believed that "the Nazis would be quickly voted out of office," and in 1940, "when Germany invaded Denmark and Norway, he still believed that Hitler would be defeated." Fleeing Paris at the very last moment, the Kahnweilers made their way to the Limousin region, where one of his painters, Elie Lascaux, who had married Lucie's sister Berthe, had a home in a former abbey called "Le Repaire," near the village of Saint-Léonard-de-Noblat. Here, in a community of Paris exiles that included Raymond Queneau, in a pleasant atmosphere of country walks ("They combed the village for vestiges of Romanesque art, and took long walks on trails and through chestnut groves, all the while keeping up an endless flow of conversation") and leisurely reading and writing, Kahnweiler passed the early Forties; when, in August of 1943, the Gestapo appeared at the door and rifled through his store of Cubist canvases in a search for Resistance weapons, the Kahnweilers found refuge in Gascony, "and life in the countryside continued as before." For a Jewish dealer in "degenerate art," who, furthermore, had been a German draft-dodger in World War I, he was very fortunate; he even saved his gallery, through the device of selling it, when the call for the Aryanization of businesses went out from the German occupiers, to his unimpeachably French and Catholic sister-in-law and gallery associate, Louise Leiris. The Galerie Kahnweiler, which had become the Galerie Simon in 1920, now acquired its third and last name, Galerie Louise Leiris.

In October of 1944, Kahnweiler returned to a freshly liberated Paris and assumed his post-war persona as a *monstre sacré*, the man who had marketed the Cubists two wars ago, in the laughing springtime of modernism. He shaved his head, and took on the gnomish look of a guru. He guarded the old flame fiercely: asked to help organize a Cubist retrospective for the Venice Biennale, "he featured the four great painters: Picasso, Braque, Gris, and Léger—but obstinately refused to include the works of 'Metzinger and his consorts,' " lesser Cubists he had always scorned. As he got older, the list of his peeves grew to include "critics, abstract art, the government, New York as the art center, art for speculation, the politics of museum acquisition." About most things he was probably right, but it makes dull copy. Even the translator seems to be a bit *ennuyé*, laying down such absent-minded English as "Seurat intrigued him in spite of the fact that his experimentation with pointillism was a promising undertaking only for the realistic subject of his paintings" and "As the son of the mayor of Evrette, his parents' ambition was to have him become an ophthalmologist." A few choice facts about modern art emerge from these many circumspect, circumstantial pages: Klee wrote with his right hand but painted with his left; André Malraux, who wound up scrubbing the façades of Paris for de Gaulle, was considered as a young man "slightly crazy, and definitely out of control"; Picasso thought that "collectors always prefer crusty paintings," by which he meant unfinished, confirming Gris's lament "I would so much like my painting to have the ease and coquettish quality of unfinished work." A more inspired biographer might have done more with all this material, but it's as if Kahnweiler didn't wish to be inspiring. His austere and basically humble personality imposes a curious damp propriety upon his life story. Dealing keeps its secrets. For all his years of survivorship, Kahnweiler's claim to fame remains that youthful moment in 1907 when he looked *Les Demoiselles d'Avignon* in its scrambled eyes and didn't blink.

Smiling Bob

LAUGHTER'S GENTLE SOUL: *The Life of Robert Benchley*, by Billy Altman. 382 pp. Norton, 1997.

Robert Benchley's public image was of a purely funny man, the quintessential humorist—none of Thurber's somber shadows or Perelman's baroque rhetoric for him—and yet his most recent biography, *Laughter's Gentle Soul*, by Billy (sic) Altman, left me feeling dreary and faintly indignant. Altman in his foreword seems to be trying, vainly, to buck up his long-dead subject, who "dreaded the notion of being thought of as a 'funnyman,' " and who once morosely claimed to Harold Ross, "I am not a writer and not an actor. I don't know what I am." Altman's acknowledgments exude a sweated scent of extended effort; he thanks pages of people who helped him "navigate" his "journey through the maze of Robert Benchley's life," including no fewer than three "editors on this at times seemingly endless labor of love," to whom he is "inordinately indebted" for "the truly saintly extent of their collective patience." His last editor, Amy Cherry, gets special credit for "taking a manuscript that was turned in over so long a period and gently but firmly helping to shape it into one (I hope) cohesive entity." When he thinks of the services of his editor-turned-agent, Tom Wallace, the author is "genuinely humbled by his ongoing trust in my abilities"; to his "extraordinary wife and best friend" he offers fervent thanks for ignoring his desire, in the late 1980s, not to begin a family until he was done with this demanding book.

Quel travail! And to what end? By the evidence of Altman's own bibliography, three lives of Benchley (1889–1945) already exist—by Benchley's son Nathaniel in 1955, by Norris W. Yates in 1968, and by Babette Rosmond in 1970. Why yet another? Benchley, once he came into the New York spotlight, in 1919, as the managing editor of *Vanity Fair*, generated a succession of often improbable anecdotes that have been thoroughly relayed. If a raft of new documentary material has emerged since 1970, Altman doesn't describe it for us. What has changed, of course, is the amount of frankness with which the alcoholic and sexual underside of Benchley's public image can be illumined. But even here Altman tells us less than Marion Meade, who in her 1988 biography of Dorothy Parker, *What Fresh Hell Is This?*, confided such lurid tidbits as Benchley's keeping his own kimono at the brothel run by Polly Adler and playing backgammon with the celebrated madame for the services of her whores. Meade wrote that, once Benchley had broken the extramarital ice, his love life grew too complex to document easily. In addition to the prostitutes he patronized at Polly Adler's, he made routine overtures to countless women and very often met with success. At any given time, there were four or five women openly claiming to be madly in love with him.

One banker's wife, Meade alleges, was driven by her passion to crawl through the transom of Benchley's room at the Royalton Hotel. Vignettes like this were understandably absent from his son's biography, which loyally presents him as a good father with a weakness for late hours. Babette Rosmond's snippety *Robert Benchley: His Life and Good Times* predates remorseless all-baring, though she does name three of Benchley's more important mistresses—Carol Goodner, Betty Starbuck, and Louise Macy. Altman fills in the portrait of Goodner. She was in 1923 a nineteen-year-old telephone operator in the Biltmore Hotel, near Grand Central Terminal; Benchley, commuting to his wife and two sons in Scarsdale, passed her often enough to strike up an acquaintance, which led to, besides unspeakable private raptures, her placement as a showgirl in Irving Berlin's *The Music Box Revue*, in which Benchley was performing his celebrated "Treasurer's Report" routine. Goodner appears in Edmund Wilson's journals as "quite a pretty blonde with thick ankles who, however, I thought had something of that hard-eyed prostitute stare," but Benchley told Dorothy Parker, "She enters the room like a duchess." His affair with Goodner marked a departure from an early, idealistic innocence. According to Altman:

> If nothing else, the affair with Goodner resulted in the nearly complete division of Benchley's life into two separate entities. The line between Benchley the responsible suburban homeowner with a wife and two children and Benchley the carousing big-city boulevardier with a showgirl at his side was now irrevocably demarcated. Still, the thought of a divorce seems to have never seriously entered his mind.

On the far side of this demarcation was Gertrude Darling Benchley, his long-loyal, willfully tolerant wife and perhaps the most enigmatic figure in the Benchley saga. The two were children of the Protestant middle class in Worcester, Massachusetts. Benchley's father, Charles, was a Civil War veteran and former Navy man who returned to Worcester and settled down as the mayor's clerk; he was well enough liked to keep his post under twelve mayors of both parties, but from the viewpoint of his redoubtable, temperance-minded wife, Jennie, he was an unthrifty soft touch who occasionally returned from work suspiciously smelling of fermentation. Gertrude Darling's family owned several woolen mills. She and Robert knew each other from the age of eight, and early formed a romantic attachment. They became engaged in 1913, the year after his graduation from Harvard, and were married the next year, as Benchley suffered through a series of unrewarding jobs and emitted frustrated sputters of literary and thespian talent.

Their son Nathaniel affectionally renders the Worcester ambience:

> Inside the older Worcester houses, dimly lit by the red, blue, amber, and green stained-glass windows at the stairs landings, were statuettes known as Rogers groups, or massive steel engravings of stags, or still-life compositions that looked like ducks pressed under glass. There were cuckoo clocks, and heavy draperies, and dark paneled walls, and in the winter the light from the snow outside glared through the parlor lace curtains with the brilliance of a battery of cold, white floodlights. . . . Worcester was a piece of Victorian America that, on the surface, changed little or not at all.

The worst thing that happened in Robert Benchley's Gay Nineties childhood was the sudden death of his older brother, Edmund, a West Point graduate killed by a sniper in the brief Spanish-American War of 1898. Altman's book contains a poignant photo of the boy Robert leaning on the bosom of his uniformed big brother. Edmund, who had been thirteen years older than Robert, left a fiancée, Lillian Duryea, of a "wealthy starch-manufacturing family in Nyack, New York," who felt obliged to take a hand in Robert's future, and supervised and financed (as a loan) his education at Exeter for a year and then Harvard. There is something a touch excessive in this helpfulness, and Benchley's practical helplessness in dealing with such masculine realms as finance and household mechanics may derive from the overload of powerful women in his youth.

His middle name was Charles, and his father's politic affability was part of his inheritance, winning out over his strong-minded mother's puritanism. His enduring marriage to Gertrude was rooted in small-city decency, with the concomitant stoic hypocrisy. "A man had his wife," Benchley once explained to James Thurber, "and that was that." Gertrude maintained their Scarsdale house and reared their sons virtually alone, yet she never openly admitted that their bond was broken or even stretched. Years after his death, she told Babette Rosmond, "People asked me if we were going to be divorced—how absurd! Except for the times he was in Hollywood he called me once, sometimes twice a day. . . . Do you know, in all the years we were married we never had a cross word!" Altman quotes this from Rosmond's book, but not a more telling—more sadly clear-eyed—statement of Gertrude's: "I had him so

early, and I knew what his possibilities were and that I had to share him—
so I did."

Benchley when she married him brimmed with possibilities. Elected
to the *Harvard Lampoon* on the strength of his cartooning, he rose to
become its president while pursuing a burgeoning career as a stage and
platform performer; a 1910 Harvard Club meeting in Boston listed
among the after-dinner speakers the undergraduate Benchley lecturing
on "Through the Alimentary Canal with Gun and Camera." Pleasant-
looking if not aggressively handsome, he charmed everyone with his
sense of fun and his instinctive kindliness. Though at Harvard he earned
a reputation as a wag and prankster, he was also a teetotalling Christian,
whose involvement in social work continued into his New York days and
whose social conscience led him eventually to take an active role in the
Sacco-Vanzetti protest. His marks at Harvard suffered from his extracurricular activities, but he had a good, quick mind, with a scholarly bent; he
read French and German, and for much of life harbored an ambition to
write a book on the reign of Queen Anne. His early comic essays, appearing in the *Tribune Magazine* and *Vanity Fair*, have a gracefully posed
bewilderment and an airy breadth of reference that still provoke laughter.
From a mock opera synopsis:

> *The Rhine at Low Tide Just Below Weldkschnoffen.*—Immerglück has
> grown weary of always sitting on the same rock with the same fishes swim-
> ming by every day, and sends for Schwül to suggest something to do.
> Schwül asks her how she would like to have pass before her all the wonders
> of the world fashioned by the hand of man. She says, rotten. He then sug-
> gests that Ringblattz, son of Pflucht, be made to appear before her and fight
> a mortal combat with the Iron Duck. This pleases Immerglück and she
> summons to her the four dwarfs: Hot Water, Cold Water, Cool, and
> Cloudy. She bids them bring Ringblattz to her. They refuse, because
> Pflucht has at one time rescued them from being buried alive by acorns,
> and, in a rage, Immerglück strikes them all dead with a thunderbolt.

In Benchley, a touch of German was always good for a laugh. Away from
the terrain of addled expertise, his prose can collapse into a disingenuous
confession of its own innocence. From "The Social Life of the Newt,"
cousin to his movie short *The Sex Life of the Polyp*:

> In studying the more intimate phases of newt life, one is chiefly
> impressed with the methods by means of which the males force their atten-
> tions upon the females, with matrimony as an object. For the newt is, after
> all, only a newt, and has his weaknesses just as any of the rest of us. And I,
> for one, would not have it different. There is little enough fun in the world
> as it is.

Such smiling retreats are disarming in theatrical and cinematic performance, but can be disappointing where some kind of intellectual penetration is called for. Benchley genuinely loved the theatre. At Harvard, besides acting himself, he haunted the cheap balcony seats of the Boston playhouses. He served as the drama critic for the old *Life* magazine from 1920 to 1929 and for *The New Yorker* from 1929 to 1940; he was at his most confident and expansive in dealing with the theatre. Yet his reviews—a selection was published by the small Ipswich Press, in 1985, titled *Benchley at the Theatre*—often pull up lame. Granted, most of the shows he saw were ephemeral, and the tone of the times was flip; still, an invitation from the stage to think made him uncommonly squirmy. After a strenuous and persuasive characterization of O'Neill's *Mourning Becomes Electra* as melodramatic and overlong, he goes into his shrug: "I know that this is a purely individual and unworthy reaction, quite out of place in what should be a serious review of a great masterpiece, but, as this page is nothing if not personal, I am setting it down." Shakespeare, safely dead and enshrined, is less apologetically knocked: "Only those people will be allowed to read this little piece on 'Macbeth' who will first admit that they are bored during two-thirds of most Shakespearean performances. . . . Most of the spoken words of the Immortal Bard are like so many drops of rain on a tin roof to this particular member of the *intelligentsia*." He often finds Shaw lacklustre and long-winded (the new Shaw plays of this period are not his greatest), and the finding breeds comic swirls of verbal unease:

> It is agreed, I suppose, that Shaw is a really Great Man, otherwise he could not, wearing a full beard, have his picture taken in a bathing suit (a test of greatness which even Napoleon could hardly have come through with complete success). . . . So either to praise or to pan Shaw must seem equally presumptuous on the part of a man who, even in his most luxuriant season, can raise only a fragment of a mustache.

The critic keeps hiding behind the amiable, fallible, comical man. In 1935, in a dull week, he devoted a column to the modesty of his critical effort: "This department is run solely as a superficial guide to readers—if anything. . . . Any attempt to intimidate us into a more serious attitude will be held as an infringement of the Freedom of the Press." Another column began, "Every once in a while this department wakes up in the middle of the night in a cold sweat thinking of how little it really gives its readers in the matter of cultural dialectics." Well, why not *give* them some cultural dialectics? In disavowing any special competence while continuing to occupy the reviewer's space, Benchley has it both ways, like the bibulous boulevardier also holding down a suburban householder's franchise in Scarsdale.

Some emptiness, or laziness, kept him from living up to his own highest hopes. He maintained a journal, whose original purpose was spiritual introspection. In 1913, when he was listlessly working as a copywriter for the Curtis Publishing Company in New York, he wrote,

> I must face the fact that I haven't lived up to expectations in my work. . . . I have been lazy at it, as I have at all other things. Morally, I have lost rather than gained—both in will power and perception—due, I think, to a loosening grip on spiritual introspection. I find myself reverting only occasionally to inspirations that I used to frequently fall upon. The work in the settlement house is the only thing of which I am proud.

His attempts at "serious" writing—an anti-war treatise, a short story about a subway motorman—came to nothing or to rejection; only his whimsical pieces, and then his theatre reviews, made it into print. Edmund Wilson, who in 1920 succeeded Benchley as managing editor of *Vanity Fair*, left, in his retrospective annotations of his Twenties journals, a minority report on the celebrated wits of the Algonquin Round Table. According to Wilson, they "all came from the suburbs and 'provinces,' and a sort of tone was set—mainly by Benchley, I think—deriving from a provincial upbringing of people who had been taught a certain kind of gentility . . . which they were now able to mock from a level of New York sophistication. I found this rather tiresome, since they never seemed to be able to get above it." Wilson continued:

> Benchley, as I first knew him, had the manner of a quiet and modest young Harvard graduate, with whom it was pleasant and easy to deal. Later, when he went to Hollywood, where he had some success doing comic shorts, he seemed to have become transformed. He was florid and self-assertive. . . . He got to drinking heavily and died of cirrhosis of the liver. I used, in the days I first knew him, to urge him to do serious satire; but he proved to be incapable of this. His usual character for himself was that of an unsure suburban duffer who was always being frightened and defeated, and this, even in his Hollywood shorts, seemed to be the only role in which he was able to appear.

Beginning in innocence, life is inevitably a corruption; the unusual feature of Benchley's corruption is that it so little enriched his art. That he had artistic gifts is clear in the insouciant but deft weave of his humorous writing, a model for the generation of slightly younger humorists which included Thurber, Perelman, and E. B. White—none of whom, however, remained so abjectly captive to the persona of a "funny man." This persona, emergent in the droll public performances of his Harvard days, in the end quite shouldered aside the writer in Benchley. In 1943, he announced, "I don't think I write funny anymore. I've run out of ideas. From now on I'm an actor. It's a lot easier and the pay is good." He was fired, after many a missed deadline, as *New Yorker* theatre critic in 1940, and perhaps the writer in him had begun to buckle when he signed up, in 1933, to do a thrice-weekly humor column for the Hearst syndicate. It, and his duties as a script-fixer and bit player for RKO, and the filming of a new series of shorts for M-G-M, plus the *New Yorker* obligations (besides reviewing theatre, he invented and wrote "The Wayward Press") were a staggering burden. He accumulated notes for the Queen Anne book but never got down to writing it. He had never considered himself a real writer anyway, declaring to an inquirer in the early Twenties:

> I do not think of myself as a writer in the technical sense of the word. I know practically nothing of the craft, and am constantly in dread of violating some elementary rule which every pupil of English A ought to know. . . . I am usually late with my copy and in a great hurry. I slap it down and hope to God that it is spelled correctly. (God is not always on the job, either.)

One is impressed, reading Altman's biography, by how hard Benchley worked just to keep financially afloat. *The New Yorker* paid him $300 a week and the movie studios three to four times that, in the depths of the Depression; yet he was always in debt. By the end of 1944, his Paramount contract paid him $1,750 a week, and his radio appearances provided an additional weekly $750 or $1,000. Furthermore, he was a best-seller; his book royalties for that year were nearly $20,000. With all that, he said he was merely for the first time in his adult life "caught up—give or take a few stray bank loans and those friendly reminders about arrears payments from the Treasury Department." His financial disarray needs no very arcane explanation; he had welcomed Prohibition when it was ratified in 1919, but his first alcoholic beverage, a speakeasy Orange Blossom in the fall of 1920, when he was all of thirty-one, launched him on a drinking spree that ended only when his body couldn't take any more, twenty-five years later. After his initiation into the joys of the grape, with his superego safely stashed in Scarsdale, he found a compatible Manhattan apartment-mate in the similarly de-repressed Charles MacArthur. In Hollywood, where he lived in the array of bungalows called the Garden of Allah, he fell in with the minor actor Charles Butterworth. He wrote Gertrude in 1937 that "Charlie has been practically living with me here." Henceforth, Altman says,

At the Garden of Allah, Benchley and Butterworth were inseparable—
and, most of the time, a bottle was in front of them. Albert Hackett recalled
that on one trip to Hollywood for a writing assignment, he and his wife
were staying in a bungalow next door to Benchley and Butterworth and
could hear them drinking and talking when they went to bed around eleven.
When the Hacketts got up the next morning and left for the studio at eight-
thirty, Benchley and Butterworth were still going strong.

The satisfactions of sitting up all night drinking with Charles Butterworth
are not easy to imagine; but, then, all human exercises in happiness—
gluttony, sex, bird-watching, transcendental meditation—appear, when
the lives in question are over, rather wasteful.

I was a keen consumer of popular culture when Benchley was part of it.
I sat in the local theatre and laughed at *The Courtship of the Newt* and *How
to Take a Vacation*; I read through his collections—*20,000 Leagues Under
the Sea or David Copperfield*; *From Bed to Worse or Comforting Thoughts
About the Bison*—marvelling at their impudence; I would even have
stayed up to listen to his ten-o'clock Sunday-night radio program, *Melody
and Madness*, if my parents had let me. A poll in 1939 ranked him sixth
among radio stars, just behind Jack Benny, Edgar Bergen, Bing Crosby,
Fred Allen, and Bob Hope. His 1928 short, *The Treasurer's Report*, Altman claims, was "the first continuous sound picture ever attempted by a
major studio," and eight years later Benchley participated in "the very
first television entertainment program ever aired"—a demonstration
co-sponsored by NBC and RCA and transmitted from the top of the
Empire State Building to receivers in the RCA Building. His *How to Sleep*
won the 1935 Academy Award for best short subject for comedy. Popular culture was then more compact and less dumbed-down; it is hard
to imagine any contemporary literary figure becoming such a media
celebrity. Benchley represented something to the masses, and, as a member of those masses more than a half-century ago, I feel betrayed in reading how careless a custodian he was of his health and his talents. He died
at fifty-six. Altman's biography, more vividly than the others, gives the
details—the medical verdict that Benchley had cirrhosis of the liver, the
vitamin shots and doses of Benzedrine that kept him going while he kept
drinking, the blackouts, the nosebleeds that interrupted his final rounds
at "21" and other haunts and finally took him to an uptown hospital
where, with faithful Gertrude back in Scarsdale for the night and Nat,
still in Navy uniform, on the way from the West Coast, the convivialist
died alone.

Laughter's Gentle Soul has some annoying features—its sappy title, the arch and overlong chapter heads that almost totally disguise the contents, the milky reproduction of the well-chosen clutch of photographs, an index in microscopic type. It is less good on the Worcester background than Nathaniel Benchley's, and less good on the writing than, in her bouncy way, Rosmond; but Altman is excellent on Hollywood. He has viewed the footage, a lot of it distinctly workaday. He describes the painful results when Benchley was made to act out lesser writers' notion of funniness, and pays some attention to his bit parts in feature films. Benchley's best straight performance, he says firmly, was as Deanna Durbin's father in the 1941 *Nice Girl?*: "For a man who had been an absentee father to his own children for much of their lives, he was certainly able to project the exact opposite image in this quietly affecting film."

Nevertheless, the "soiled atmosphere of Hollywood" dragged Benchley down. "Look at me," he told a friend. "A clown, a comic, a cheap gagman. There's a career for you!" Famously, late one night in the Garden of Allah, at a party where Scott Fitzgerald and the then-esteemed playwright Robert Sherwood—once Benchley's colleague on *Vanity Fair*—were also present, Benchley, talking to Sheilah Graham, pointed at Sherwood and said, "Those eyes—I can't stand those eyes looking at me!" The throng, expecting one of Benchley's jokes, was stunned at the genuine look of horror in his face as he went on, "He's looking at me, and thinking of how he knew me when I was going to be a great writer—and he's thinking, *now* look at what I am!" This man who was so liked by everybody did not, it seems, much like himself.

This Side of Coherence

SCOTT FITZGERALD: *A Biography*, by Jeffrey Meyers. 393 pp. HarperCollins, 1994.

The life of F. Scott Fitzgerald, in the half-century since it ended, has become more celebrated and paradigmatic than any of the lives found in his fiction. Dead at forty-four, he seems a sacrifice, but to what god and by what priestly hand remain mysterious. The aura is Dionysian, but the circumstances are peculiarly American. He gave us his own epitaph, writing in one of his notebooks, "There are no second acts in American lives." If Hemingway was the master of danger abroad, purposefully experienced in foreign wars and Spanish bullfights and African safaris,

Fitzgerald flattered our national consciousness with a sense of domestic danger, of the failure and rebuke that haunt every aspiration, of youthful overreaching swiftly followed by adult collapse, of a native romanticism courting the vengeance of blind destiny—a pattern illustrated in his one well-designed novel, *The Great Gatsby*. His life in fact had three acts, more or less, the curtains conveniently falling each time on the end of a decade: his yearning Midwestern youth as a delicate, shabby-genteel Roman Catholic born in and (after a ten-year interval in Buffalo, New York) returned to St. Paul, Minnesota, wherefrom he exuberantly launched himself into anticlimactic, anti-heroic careers at Princeton, in the Army, and in New York advertising; the Twenties, which he helped invent with his buoyant and hectic first novel, *This Side of Paradise* (1920), and which he ornamented with his celebrated carousing, his fetchingly named Alabama belle of a wife, Zelda, and his restless international travels as a highly paid celebrity author, and which he saw crash in rough synchrony with his own fortunes, in 1929; and the Thirties, when, with depleted energies and a dwindled public, he shouldered the responsibilities of a wife in mental institutions and a daughter in private schools and ended as a failed scriptwriter in Hollywood, fiddling away at an unfinished novel, *The Last Tycoon*, and writing skimpy little pieces for *Esquire* for which he received a few hundred dollars each—he who in his heyday commanded four thousand dollars a story from *The Saturday Evening Post*. His burial, in 1940, to the tune of nostalgic and condescending obituaries, was the prelude to a post-war resurrection that sees him now as a favorite of college curricula, the literary embodiment of the Jazz Age, and the third of a sacred trinity whose other two members are Hemingway and Faulkner.

It is a fine story, both monitory and inspirational, and Jeffrey Meyers, who has previously written biographies of Hemingway, Lawrence, Conrad, Poe, Wyndham Lewis, and Katherine Mansfield, among others, has chosen to tell it once again. Why he has carried more coals to this particular Newcastle his brief preface offers to explain by quoting the novelist Jay McInerney, who several years ago, in *The New York Review of Books*, ticked off "Bruccoli's hagiographic *Some Sort of Epic Grandeur*, James R. Mellow's peevish, sordid *Invented Lives*, as well as Scott Donaldson's folksy psychoanalysis in *Fool for Love* . . . Arthur Mizener's excellent and grim *The Far Side of Paradise*, Andrew Turnbull's biographical memoir *Scott Fitzgerald* and Nancy Milford's feminist revisionist *Zelda*" and concluded, "What doesn't emerge from any of these books is the sense of a coherent personality." Mr. Meyers' preface explains:

Though I have profited in various ways from the earlier biographies, my book on Scott is more analytic and interpretative. It discusses the meaning as well as the events of his life and seeks to illuminate the recurrent patterns that reveal his inner self. This biography places much greater emphasis on Scott's drinking; on Zelda's hospitals and doctors, especially Oscar Forel and Robert Carroll; on his love affairs, before and after Zelda's breakdown.

Of course. The dirt, the lowdown. Let's have it, especially if it helps us grasp a coherent personality. By way of additional justification, Meyers affixes an epigraph from Raymond Chandler, who, sounding tough, says, in part, "Fitzgerald is a subject no one has a right to mess up. Nothing but the best will do for him. I think he just missed being a great writer, and the reason is pretty obvious. If the poor guy was already an alcoholic in his college days, it's a marvel that he did as well as he did."

After these intimidating preliminaries, however, Mr. Meyers's expatiation upon the seamy and medical details of Fitzgerald's life serves to make larger and more paradoxical the cleavages in Fitzgerald's personality—between the spendthrift and the strict accountant, between petty heedlessness and stoic gallantry, between an aptitude for chaos and a dream of order, between conceit and insecurity, between, professionally, a hack's opportunism and a pained, revision-prone Flaubertian refinement. Fitzgerald himself said, in his notebooks, "There never was a good biography of a good novelist. There couldn't be. He is too many people, if he's any good." And his life has been poured into books, not deeds. At the age of twenty-nine, Fitzgerald wrote to his Scribner editor, Maxwell Perkins, "My work is the only thing that makes me happy—except to be a little tight."

Before Mr. Meyers assembled his brief, we never knew quite how nasty a drunk Fitzgerald was. He repaid Gerald and Sara Murphy's elegant hospitality by "throwing Sara's gold-flecked Venetian wineglasses over the garden wall" and, when banned for this outrage, threw a can of garbage onto their patio while they were dining. As he and some friends were leaving the Casino at Juan-les-Pins, an old Frenchwoman held out a tray of nuts and candies, and Fitzgerald kicked the tray right out of her hands. He picked quarrels and started fistfights, which he usually got the worse of. A fierce malice and resentment emerged in the guise of pranks and teasing. He wrote in lipstick on the expensive dress of his friend John Peale Bishop's wife; dining with Hemingway and Edmund Wilson in New York, he turned the occasion into a revel of self-abasement. According to Wilson's journal:

Scott with his head down on the table between us like the dormouse at the Mad Tea Party—lay down on floor, went to can and puked—alternately made us hold his hand and asked us whether we liked him and insulted us.

It was not the fact that Fitzgerald drank to excess that shocked his peers—they all did, by New Age standards—but that he held his liquor so badly. Meyers has a chemical explanation: Fitzgerald, like Edgar Allan Poe, "suffered from hypoglycemia, or lack of sugar in the blood, which interfered with the supply of glucose to the brain and gave Fitzgerald an abnormal craving, when he was not drinking, for chocolate and Coca-Cola. This disease made it difficult for him to metabolize and tolerate alcohol, which always had an immediate and catastrophic effect on his system." Meyers, in his extensive but rather inscrutably organized source notes at the back, cites as medical authority only *The Oxford Textbook of Medicine*. The symptoms he mentions—"insomnia, pallor and fatigue as well as aggressive speech, excessive sweating, visual blurring, muscular tremor, a sense of uncertainty, increasing confusion and, finally, unconsciousness"—might better be ascribed to chronic alcohol abuse, or possibly the tubercular and cardiac ills that did afflict Fitzgerald. Matthew J. Bruccoli's biography takes up the hypoglycemia thesis at some length, and cites the pathologist William Ober, who, after examining Fitzgerald's records at Johns Hopkins Hospital, concluded, "There is no evidence for hypoglycemia whatsoever."

Also in a medical vein are Mr. Meyers's particulars about Zelda's treatment in a succession of Continental and American sanitariums, and a clinical examination of Fitzgerald's sexual abilities. His penis size—the topic of a piquant passage in Hemingway's *A Moveable Feast*—was normal enough, agree a trio of witnesses: Sheilah Graham, the writer's Hollywood mistress; an Asheville, North Carolina, prostitute called Lottie; and Fitzgerald's *Esquire* editor, Arnold Gingrich, who once saw him with his bathrobe open. Zelda, however, especially after an affair with a French aviator in 1924, found her husband inadequate and, as the Jazz Age nibbled away at her sang-froid, accused him of homosexuality. Elizabeth Beckwith MacKie, who had been acquainted with the young Fitzgerald in West Virginia, confided in a memoir, "In 1917, I'm afraid, Scott just wasn't a very lively male animal," and Arthur Mizener, after interviewing a St. Paul acquaintance of Fitzgerald's, Oscar Kalman, concluded that "Scott liked the idea of sex, for its romance and daring, but was not strongly sexed and [was] inclined to feel the actual act of sex was messy." An ineradicable moral streak dignified his writings but complicated his hedonism. Kalman expostulated to Mizener, "Poor Scott, he never really enjoyed his dissipation because he disapproved intensely of himself all the time it was going on."

There was in Fitzgerald's nature a feminine component that enabled him to write of female sensations and strategies with a fine empathy. He was slight in build, dainty of feature, and, like many another male under-graduate, had prettily donned female clothes in a college musical. Zelda and Sheilah Graham aside, his deeply felt admirations were of men: the epicene and learned priest Father Cyril Sigourney Webster Fay, who became his mentor at the Newman School, in New Jersey; the athletic and rich Tommy Hitchcock, who stood for his portrait as Tom Buchanan in *The Great Gatsby*; Ring Lardner, in whose stoic company Fitzgerald often drank until dawn on Long Island; and Hemingway, of whom he wrote in his notebooks, "I really loved him, but of course it wore out like a love affair. The fairies have spoiled all that." The idea that Fitzgerald was homosexual flitted through the gossip surrounding him, but he had stout conventional scorn for "fairies." Mr. Meyers did some original research on his subject's fairly extensive heterosexual contacts after Zelda's off-and-on-again institutionalization began, in 1930, and with a touch of incredulity relays Sheilah Graham's sexual contentment:

> Well informed about all shapes and sizes of male sexual organs, she found the tubercular, drug-addicted and often alcoholic Fitzgerald a creditable performer—"very satisfactory . . . in terms of giving physical pleasure." After lovemaking, they would lie happily in each other's arms for a long time.

The all-but-sneering tone is what is principally wrong with this biog-raphy. Mr. Meyers, like the practitioners of celebrity-centered tabloid journalism, shows his subjects no respect. He ransacks their lives for discreditable incidents and implications. Sheilah Graham, it is clearly implied above, was a sleep-around, Fitzgerald was a pathetic wreck, and they capped their corruption by post-coitally mooning in bed like a pair of sappy teenagers. Meyers' whole presentation of Sheilah Graham is subtly poisoned. "Her series of gossipy autobiographies," he states, "tell a number of deliberate lies." Her rise from a London orphanage to success as an American gossip columnist is made to seem a tawdry trick, by way of a chorus line and an impotent older husband, and her invention of a new, American identity—in a Hollywood full of such inventions—is phrased as sinister psychological melodrama: "Sheilah, who had very lit-tle religious or family loyalty, consigned both her poverty and her Jew-ishness to the same black hole of denial." She had been born Lily Sheil, the sixth child of a father who died soon after her birth and a "sickly mother" who, in Meyers' vague phrase, "was a cook in an institution." Lily/Sheilah, after leaving the orphanage at fourteen, worked as a factory hand, an under-housemaid, and a toothbrush demonstrator in a department store. Fitzgerald in their relations comes forth as vicious, taunting her with her impoverished Jewish origins, threatening her with a gun, slapping her, humiliating her publicly. The reader inwardly cheers when she is reported to have responded to one of his suicide threats with the hearty, Hollywoodish, "Shoot yourself, you son of a bitch. I didn't raise myself from the gutter to waste my life on a drunk like you." After his death, she discovered that he had scrawled "Portrait of a Prostitute" on the back of a photograph of herself she had given him. The liaison is seen as so predominantly sordid that such positive aspects as his "patiently teaching her to understand the books that he loved" and her need (characterized as "masochistic") "to care for a great (or once-great) man" come as grudging incidentals. It is left to other biographers to emphasize that Sheilah, whatever her limitations, was responsible and responsive in a way that Zelda had not been and gave Fitzgerald a domestic stability in which he was, in his last year, overcoming the alcohol demon and picking up the pieces of his life and talent. Malcolm Cowley, in introducing his selection of twenty-eight Fitzgerald stories, tells us:

> His record of production for the last year of his life would have been remarkable for a man in perfect health. He began the year by making plans for a novel and, simultaneously, by writing twenty stories for *Esquire*. . . . Suddenly he resumed his interrupted correspondence with his friends and he sent his daughter an extraordinary series of letters that continued all through the year; perhaps they were too urgent and too full of tired wisdom for a girl in college, but then Fitzgerald was writing them as a sort of personal and literary testament. In the spring he wrote—and twice rewrote from the beginning—a scenario based on his story, "Babylon Revisited"; it was the best of his scenarios and, according to the producer who ordered it, the best he ever read.

Andrew Turnbull's biography, after admitting, "They were a curious pair—the broken novelist and the ambitious girl from the slums," points out, "In a sense Fitzgerald was fortunate to have been loved by anyone so vital and alluring. In his present state of frailty and eclipse, his choice was not unlimited." Turnbull as a boy had known Fitzgerald, as the renowned writer to whom his parents rented their Maryland house, and his biography retains a note of affectionate acquaintance and a willingness to be impressed. Bruccoli's "hagiographic" biography in its staccato fashion sums up the pros and cons of the situation: "He needed Sheilah and loved her; yet his puritan streak disapproved of their arrangement, which was circumspect by Hollywood standards." In this day of free and legal unmarried cohabitation, it is hard to imagine the old taint and strain of such arrangements; Arthur Mizener's fine pioneering biography, which came out in 1949, when Sheilah Graham was still alive, avoids mentioning her by name. Bruccoli tells us, reassuringly if a bit bluntly, of Fitzgerald's maturing daughter: "Scottie liked Sheilah, who went to considerable trouble making her California visits pleasant." It is André Le Vot, in a biography written in French and translated for Doubleday by William Byron, who gives the most favorable picture of Sheilah's role in Fitzgerald's last years; he describes her maneuvers to keep him sober and at peace, outlines the careful tutorials he gave her in Proust and Keats, and points out that this self-willed adventuress was "a heroine after Fitzgerald's heart." Le Vot quotes Helen Hayes as saying, "Sheilah Graham was good to Scott, but he wasn't nice enough to her—ever." Mr. Meyers paraphrases Hayes's remark in a way to redirect its sting: "The gentle Helen Hayes thought Sheilah was good to Scott, but that he treated her badly because (as Mankiewicz had implied) 'she represented to Scott's fevered mind the second-rate he had fallen into.' "

The difference is slight, but in the art of biography, which recycles the same basic facts and letters and reminiscences, tone is all-important. What Joseph Mankiewicz—the producer-writer under whom Fitzgerald worked for a time—implied is passed on to the reader: Sheilah Graham was second-rate, by a lofty but unspecified standard. And so, Meyers repeatedly leads us to feel, was Scott Fitzgerald. Notice the verb in this sentence: "Aware of his own intellectual limitations, he struggled to improve his mind until the very end of his life." "Struggled"—as opposed to, say, "worked" or "endeavored"—suggests that it was a strenuous but losing battle. We learn that "Fitzgerald's novels . . . are filled with hundreds of ludicrous orthographical, grammatical and factual errors," that "he wrote in pencil with his left hand and had a large, loopy handwriting that looked like a child's," and that, according to Glenway Wescott, "Fitzgerald must have been the worst educated man in the world." Fitzgerald's poor record at Princeton and his bad French are drummed upon: "He never bothered to learn more than taxi-cab French nor made the slightest effort to pronounce it correctly. Even Scottie, who soon mastered the tongue, later remarked on 'his really horrendous French' and 'his atrocious accent.' "

Mr. Meyers stalks his hapless hero with a lot of somewhat pat psychologizing; e.g.: "Fitzgerald's sudden wealth and fame created emotional and intellectual problems. He felt guilty because he did not deserve these blessings." Zelda becomes a layered confection: "There was a hardness beneath Zelda's soft exterior, and underneath that hardness a more vulnerable inner core." Meyers' biography moves swiftly, but at the possible price of giving short shrift. Considering the wealth of written testimony left not only by Fitzgerald (a great saver, for all his uneconomical behavior, of drafts and journals and carbons of letters) but by Sheilah Graham and Zelda, who had a verbal flair of her own, Meyers severely rations direct quotation. It is a pleasure to turn from his summary of events to the actual texts in which Fitzgerald accounted for his life as he saw it—the letters, especially, and the autobiographical pieces assembled by Edmund Wilson in *The Crack-Up*. We breathe there real air, braced by the dry clarity of Fitzgerald's self-regard. What sticks in the mind from Meyers' parade of anecdotes is the dreamlike grotesquerie:

> Fitzgerald owned a bloodcurdling collection of photograph albums of horribly mutilated soldiers, stereopticon slides of executions and roasted aviators, and lavishly illustrated French tomes of living men whose faces had been chewed away by shrapnel. In a remarkably morbid letter of December 1927, he told Hemingway: "I have a new German war book, *Die Krieg Against Krieg*, [*] which shows men who mislaid their faces in Picardy and the Caucasus—you can imagine how I thumb it over, my mouth fairly slathering with fascination."

Ten years later: "And during a drunken flight to Chicago in the fall of 1937, accompanying Sheilah, who was to make a national radio broadcast, he told all the passengers what 'a great lay' she was. After calling Sheilah 'a silly bitch' and punching her sponsor at the radio studio, Fitzgerald summoned Gingrich to his room in the Drake Hotel. As the editor sobered him up by shoveling steak into his mouth, the food dribbled onto his bib and he tried to bite Gingrich's hand." Imagine that: FAMOUS AUTHOR BITES HAND THAT EDITS HIM. From *The National Enquirer* to inarguably zealous scholars, the contemporary approach to celebrities reduces them to a set of antics and ailments to which we can feel far superior. Intentionally or not, Mr. Meyers absolves us from ever again having to take Scott Fitzgerald seriously.

Well, and how seriously *should* we take him? His reputation has survived better than that of all but a few of his contemporaries. His prose can be exquisite, and the something wavering and divided in his purposes

---

*The title that Fitzgerald garbles here is *Krieg dem Kriege! War Against War! Guerre à la guerre! Oorlog aan den oorlog!*, published in four languages in 1924 by the pacifist Ernst Friedrich. Its purpose was to juxtapose photographs of war's horrors with those of its supposed glory. Friedrich's "Anti-Kriegsmuseum" in Berlin was destroyed by the Nazis in 1933.

does not much trouble the connoisseurs of textual self-betrayal who run our English departments. *The Great Gatsby* is one of the most assigned texts in college courses in American literature, and the bulk of the oeuvre stays in print. Within the last six months, a book of essays, *The Great Gatsby and Modern Times*, by Ronald Berman, has been published by the University of Illinois Press, and an apparatus- and facsimile-laden edition of *The Last Tycoon*, edited by the busy Matthew J. Bruccoli (who gives the novel its more authentic, if dreadful, title of *The Love of the Last Tycoon: A Western*), has appeared in the Cambridge University Press's definitive printing of Fitzgerald's works. Academia, intoxicated by his eternal undergraduate effluvium, has clasped Fitzgerald to its bosom. He was, like Wordsworth, a writer who experienced in youth something tran-scendent, and his reverence for the fading radiance of that revelation gave some life to his callow, mannered first two novels and his glib, glit-tering mass-market short stories. "Life was a thing for youth," decides the heroine of "The Cut-Glass Bowl" (1920). The operetta absurdities of "The Offshore Pirate" (1920) occasion this dithyramb:

> Her sigh was a benediction—an ecstatic surety that she was youth and beauty now as much as she would ever know. For another instant life was radiant and time a phantom and their strength eternal.

He is an author one should read when young. To readers past first bloom, his earnest reconstructions of adolescent and collegiate maneu-vers of self-advancement may seem a bit archaeological, and his insistence upon the moonlit mood of romantic—that is, early sexual—attraction a bit arrested. In *The Great Gatsby*, everything works because Fitz-gerald has split himself in two, and the shrewd, detached voice of Nick Carraway—a junior version of Conrad's ruminative narrators—objectifies the romantically enraptured and deluded Gatsby. Yet the dis-tance is not so great that the observation becomes heartless satire, though there is much comedy here, as when Daisy sobs over her knightly lover's preposterously lavish array of imported English shirts, or when Tom sputters indignantly about the decline of Western civilization. Carraway and Gatsby are Midwestern doppelgängers in the moral jungles of the East, so similar that the author can hardly trouble to describe either man: Gatsby dawns on Carraway as "a man about my age" sitting at the same table and never becomes more physically distinct than "an elegant young roughneck, a year or two over thirty, whose elaborate formality of speech just missed being absurd." All of Fitzgerald's daydreams of luxury and romantic mission are thrust onto this vague figure, and the writer's keen-ness of sight and music of phrase are left to Carraway. Happily, in this superbly fortunate novel—"Few books come into this world with the perfection of a bird's egg," Wright Morris wrote, "and this is one of them"—what Carraway doesn't know and what Fitzgerald can't imagine function as forceful blanks on the canvas, giving largeness to what might be small if it were known. The reader's own romantic propensities are usefully engaged in the swift, sure unfolding of this efficient and expansive "anecdote," as H. L. Mencken called it. The novel's significant elements—Gatsby's shimmering parties, the Buchanans' opulently chaste household, the wilderness of ash heaps where Dr. Eckleburg's giant eyes preside, the overripe torpidity of summer Manhattan, Wolfsheim and his world of crime, Tom and his burly wealth, the downtrodden and violent Wilsons, the apparition of pathetic Henry Gatz at the end—are carried to the point of caricature but with the reward of a penetrating vividness, not unlike that of *The Scarlet Letter*. It is all as bright and plausibly implausible as a movie.

But in *Tender Is the Night* and, as best its fragments indicate, in *The Last Tycoon*, romanticism is not the thing viewed but the viewing lens. The author keeps asking us to take the characters at a valuation that his evidence doesn't support. Enchantment is supposed to cling to the prattle and muddled contretemps of a social set of tedious expatriate wastrels, and a couple, the Divers, are meant to loom heroically without first becoming real. A thick coating of ascribed glamour obscures their human details, and a fog of narcissism and hidden pleading hopelessly dampens what is meant to be a crisp and colorful panorama. The novel gets better in the long flashback, where Fitzgerald uses the experience of sanitariums and psychiatrists that Zelda's illness brought him after 1930, but a deep and disturbing problem of transposition remains: Sara and Gerald Murphy, the consummate hosts, have been turned into Scott and Zelda, quintessential guests, unruly and ingrate, at the feast of life. Hemingway, in a letter of criticism that he later softened, complained, "You took liberties with people's pasts and futures that produced not people but damned marvelously faked case histories." We who knew neither the Fitzgeralds nor the Murphys know only that character traits fail to cohere, events bob up and down in a fathomless sea, and the story obstinately declines to grab our interest. In contrast, *Gatsby* deftly picks up its adventure at the start and projects one cinematically sharp, surprising scene after another. The length of time that Fitzgerald took with *Tender Is the Night* and his worsening situation as he worked no doubt contributed to the book's essential incoherence: he was trying simultaneously to recapture the poignance of the careless expatriate life he and Zelda had experienced in the Twenties and to explain to himself the impotence and derangement that had overtaken them in the Thirties. *The Last Tycoon* is even more scattered in its effects; and certainly Fitzgerald's vision of heroism in the real movie-maker Irving Thalberg is not perceptibly realized in his morose image of the fictional Monroe Stahr. As in *Tender Is the Night*, the author chose to center the narrative in the consciousness of an infatuated young female, perhaps in the hope that the charm of the narrator's exterior would rub off on her tale. But the reader feels merely blinkered.

What is *Tender Is the Night* about? The title Fitzgerald arrived at tells us nothing, whereas his working title, *Doctor Diver's Holiday: A Romance*, delimits its episode—a nine years' marriage, lived mostly in Europe, between a psychiatrist and a patient, which ends when the patient is cured. Mental health passes between them like a baton, and Nicole's cleared head becomes finally a place where the reader is happy to be. The scene where she takes Tommy Barban as her lover is the finest fruit of Fitzgerald's predilection for female points of view. But the path to it was littered with too many revisions, too many scenes discarded in the search for the novel's troubled heart. "There were so many revisions of *Tender* that I don't know what I left in it and what I didn't leave in it finally," he confessed to Maxwell Perkins in 1934.

The best book from the second half of Fitzgerald's career may be the one that his fellow-Princetonian Edmund Wilson put together for him, posthumously—*The Crack-Up*. Bleak but oddly good-humored self-accountings, composed in what Glenway Wescott called "brief easy fiery phrases"; pieces of magazine humor, sometimes turned out with Zelda as collaborator; dazzlingly disembodied jottings from his notebooks, grouped by him under antic and alphabetical headings; letters to friends and, in his most grave and affectionate voice, to his daughter; and tributes and appraisals, rhymed and unrhymed, from friends—these varied items, in their fitful frivolity, lustre, grace, and cavalier honesty, dance us along the length and breadth of Fitzgerald's talent and hint at what remained when his wife, his money, his fame, and his health had all been taken from him.

His excessively dewy writing dried up in the Thirties. His last fictions were skeletal, wispy anecdotes concerning a Hollywood loser, the scrabbling and unscrupulous and even unhandsome scriptwriter Pat Hobby. Unlike the overplotted and overcozy Tarkingtonian fantastications on middle-class themes that he turned out for the *Post* and *Liberty*, the Pat Hobby stories feel feeble but unforced; like good John O'Hara, they have the near-shapelessness of the authentic. And some of the later *Post* stories—"Magnetism" (1928), "The Rough Crossing" (1929), "The Bridal Party" (1930), "Babylon Revisited" (1931)—are among his best, skillful but not slick, heartfelt but not narcissistic. The fuzz of glamour has been scorched away, and in "The Rough Crossing"—Conradian in its descriptions of ship and sea—Fitzgerald manages to give us a sketch of Zelda that captures at once her bohemian charm, her wifely weariness, her masked desperation, and her abrupt insanity.

He had a hard time depicting Zelda, whether as the Nicole of *Tender Is the Night* or as the Gloria Gilbert of *The Beautiful and Damned*. Love—and, to the considerable extent that he and Zelda were twins, in neat, hawk-eyed looks and reckless temperament—self-love got in the way. What Freud called "the normal overestimation of the sexual object characteristic of men" muddies a writer's work when he tries to transfer to print an untransferrable fascination. In loving fictional women—Emma Bovary and Anna Karenina and Hester Prynne, say—we like to feel we are outdoing the creator, who is merely giving the facts. Love is an exercise, after all, in freedom and choice, a moving-forward into the faintest hint, and there is more of its essence in the quick glimpses grouped, in Fitzgerald's notebooks, under the heading "Descriptions of Girls," than in his insistent selling of Gloria or Nicole to the reader. In truth Fitzgerald's feelings about Zelda were a rich and dark brew; Mr. Meyers articulates, as no other biographer has, the groom's sensation in 1920 that the bride's family had fobbed off on him defective goods. Zelda's mother gave him, just before the wedding, a sly warning—"It will take more than the Pope to make Zelda good"—and late in the Thirties Scott wrote Zelda brutally,

> [Your mother] chose me . . . and you submitted at the moment of our marriage when your passion for me was at as low ebb as mine for you—because she thought romantically that her projection of herself in you could best be shown through me. I never wanted the Zelda I married. I didn't love you again till after you became pregnant. . . . You were the drunk—at *seventeen*, before I knew you . . . you had been seduced and provincially outcast.

And he wrote his daughter, in one of his testamentlike advisory letters, "I decided to marry your mother after all, even though I knew she was spoiled and meant no good to me. I was sorry immediately I had married her." On the other hand, his becoming a successful writer to win her hand, after an initial rejection, was the feat that made him, in his sense of himself, a romantic hero; like Jay Gatsby, he wooed above his social station while in "the invisible cloak of his uniform" and "committed himself to the following of a grail." What might be read as the last word on the most important person in his life came in his last letter to Scottie, written the month he died:

But be sweet to your mother at Xmas despite her early Chaldean rune-worship which she will undoubtedly inflict on you at Xmas. [Zelda in her unbalance had become a fanatic Christian.] Her letters are tragically brilliant on all matters except those of central importance. How strange to have failed as a social creature—even criminals do not fail that way—they are the law's "Loyal Opposition," so to speak. But the insane are always mere guests on earth, eternal strangers carrying around broken decalogues that they cannot read.

The dryly eulogistic words have an undercurrent of triumph; in the married competition between these two cracked angels, he had won—he had stayed sane.

Fitzgerald should be honored, as a writer, for attempting to describe the American life of his time with all the refinement of European fiction; from imitating the smartness of Shaw and Wells and Compton Mackenzie he moved to an attempt to absorb the examples of Conrad and Turgenev and Tolstoy and Proust. Not for him an invented American style, brashly experimental like those of Hemingway and Faulkner: unlike theirs, his style is hard to parody, blended as it is of poetry and aperçu, of external detail quickly transmuted into internal sensation. His American characters, from small-town children to uproariously disintegrating sophisticates, receive a respectful and tender attention. He loved Americans and took comfort in their aura; the hero of "Babylon Revisited," returning to Paris after the Crash, finds "the stillness in the Ritz bar . . . strange and portentous. It was not an American bar any more—he felt polite in it, and not as if he owned it. It had gone back into France." The matter of America was much on Fitzgerald's mind, without the braggadocio of Wolfe or Whitman but thoughtfully, in contemplation of a spiritual puzzle. Gatsby balances on the dashboard of his car "with that resourcefulness of movement that is so peculiarly American—that comes, I suppose, with the absence of lifting work or rigid sitting in youth and, even more, with the formless grace of our nervous, sporadic games." Later in the book comes the abrupt observation "Americans, while occasionally willing to be serfs, have always been obstinate about being peasantry." And so on—the book concludes, a touch thunderously, with its celebrated paean to virgin Long Island, "a fresh, green breast of the new world," wherein man came "face to face for the last time in history with something commensurate to his capacity for wonder." To Henry James's observations of our precious and vulnerable innocence abroad Fitzgerald added notes on our capacity for correspondingly unqualified corruption and despair.

His own corruption—by drink, but, more centrally, by a wish to make his life, as well as his art, something glorious—is to his discredit, yet perhaps, after adding up Mr. Meyers' tabulation of his vanities and buffooneries and wastefulness, we might remember too how hard he worked, albeit with gin on his desk and not always at projects he knew in his heart to be worthy. "Have written two good short stories and three cheap ones," he wrote to Edmund Wilson in 1921, and, in 1924, "I really worked hard as hell last winter—but it was all trash and it nearly broke my heart as well as my iron constitution." It was too bad he could make the distinction between "good" and "cheap," or "trash," in his mind, especially since many of the stories bought by *The Saturday Evening Post*, at its tremendous rates, have their merits, as popular art sometimes does. But all art must be sincere, or the artist's moral fiber begins to fray. To Mencken, Fitzgerald wrote in 1925:

> My trash for the Post grows worse and worse as there is less and less heart in it. Strange to say, my whole heart was in my first trash. I thought that "The Offshore Pirate" was as good as "Benediction."

Fiction began as a genre for the populace, a kind of news, a plume of the print explosion, and there is nothing intrinsically wrong with a writer's hoping to make a living from it. But Fitzgerald's extravagance outran his income almost immediately, and the romanticism he shared with the American public was not enough for sales on the scale of Booth Tarkington's or Edna Ferber's or Zane Grey's or even Sinclair Lewis'. His most successful novels, the first two, each sold somewhat more than forty thousand copies (in a country with less than half the population of the present-day United States) and *Gatsby*, disappointingly, twenty-five thousand, and *Tender Is the Night* a devastating thirteen thousand. An ordinary American family could have lived for two years on what one of his short stories fetched from the *Post*, but he and Zelda did not run an ordinary family, and his little essay "How to Live on $36,000 a Year" makes a joke of it. In the end, only Hollywood could offer the kind of money he needed, and there he was lost in the machinations of an art geared for the masses. Since in many ways he thought like Hollywood (*Gatsby* cries out for film adaptation, and has received it three times), his failure there baffled him. "To say I'm disillusioned is putting it mildly," he wrote Joseph Mankiewicz after seeing the producer's revisions of a script Fitzgerald had long labored upon. "For nineteen years . . . I've written best-selling entertainment. . . . I'm a good writer, honest." How sad that he had to be the one to say it.

Alternative, less disastrous destinies for Fitzgerald—as a hard-boiled entertainer with no modernist aspirations, as an avant-garde writer with an abstemious, modest life-style—might have prolonged his life, but then his life wouldn't have made so good a story. The early death of a writer, besides shortening by a few unwritten volumes the shelves of books that weigh on our consciences, confirms our instinct that art, especially the literary art, should be sublimely difficult—a current from beyond that burns out the wire.

The Man Within

GRAHAM GREENE: *The Enemy Within*, by Michael Shelden. 442 pp. Random House, 1995.

In an age increasingly reluctant to read anything but E-mail, why do biographies of literary practitioners continue to pile up? These great scholastic mounds of summarized writings, faded gossip, and reconstructed travel schedules seem monuments in a perfect desert waste, products of the same regressively logocentric tendency that litters the walls of art museums with more and more commentary, to the point where one's eyes are too busy ever to rest on the pictures. Creativity is no longer trusted to speak for itself; as in tabloid journalism, existence (the life) enjoys priority over essence (the performance, the works).

Graham Greene, having led a long life full of travels and seductions and problematical elements, poses a bright flame for investigative moths. His letters are drifting into institutions where they can be consulted, the details of his wartime career as a spy are coming to light, and his wife of more than fifty years, Vivien, for decades a mere rumor on the fringe of Greene's fame, has emerged as a lively octogenarian widow willing to talk about their early years of marriage, his infidelities, and the long estrangement that took shape in the 1940s. In 1994, as Norman Sherry's authorized biography serenely steamed into its second volume and thirteen-hundredth page, with a coming third volume guaranteed to cover the remaining thirty-six years of Greene's life, Great Britain saw a brace of other biographies: the long-delayed and much-trimmed *Graham Greene: Three Lives*, by Anthony Mockler, and the rather assaultive *Graham Greene: The Man Within*, by Michael Shelden. The latter work has now been published here, with many small revisions and a more provocative subtitle, *The Enemy Within*. Mr. Shelden, who has previously written biographies of Cyril Connolly and George Orwell, was, like Mr. Mockler, forbidden to quote from Greene's correspondence and unpublished work. This handicap, however, has lightened his luggage and enabled him to speed in fewer than five hundred pages from Greene's birth in 1904 to his death in 1991; it has also compelled him to speak in his own voice, so that his narrative does have some polemical urgency, as he assembles his proofs that Greene was a cruel, devious, nasty, insincere, and radically unhappy man. Sherry's more thorough biography, brimming with direct quotation and with an authorized biographer's judicious circumspection, makes a relatively diffuse and episodic impression. The details flow on and on but seem shaped to no single image, no story with a moral. Take, for example, the mild manner in which Sherry introduces Catherine Walston, the great adulterous love of Greene's life: "When Catherine met Greene, she and Harry had been married for twelve years and he was not a man to censure his wife's love affairs." Of the same circumstance, Shelden writes rousingly:

> In an effort to win her love, Harry gave her whatever she wanted, and let her do whatever she wanted. If something made her happy, he was happy. By the early 1940s, she had discovered that one thing which made her very happy was to sleep with all manner of men.*

In Sherry's careful account of Greene's childhood, there is no leap to judgment like this paragraph of Shelden's:

> He found an odd sort of freedom in killing things. Told to find snails in the garden and dispose of them, he carried out his mission with considerable zest. He put them in a bucket, poured salt on them, and watched them turn to foam. For every hundred snails he destroyed, he received a small amount of money. There was also cash to be had from eliminating cabbage-white butterflies. These killing sprees gave him such satisfaction that he made a great game out of it in adulthood. During his wartime stay in Sierra Leone, he enjoyed a "glorious" slaughter when he managed to kill more than three hundred flies in a four-minute period. Everyone hates flies, but it takes a special person to time a mass murder of the pests, and then to do a detailed body count. According to Malcolm Muggeridge, Greene also liked to buy ant farms and wipe them out with boiling water.

Shelden evokes this insecticidal fiend without acknowledging that all the details (including the fly count in Sierra Leone) have been lifted— decontextualized and hardened in tone—from Greene's autobiography *A Sort of Life*, or that small boys are not unusually enlisted in the elimination of garden pests. Nevertheless, a feature of a psychological landscape has been vividly flagged, and ties in with fictional details: in *England*

---

*Quotes are from the English edition; some of the American editing seemed fussy and too PC.

Made Me, Minty traps a spider under a glass and observes its struggles and slow death for five days; in *Brighton Rock*, Pinkie is sadistic toward Rose and extols the hellfire doctrine of "torments"; in *Our Man in Havana*, the government enforcer Captain Segura reflects that "one never tortures except by a kind of mutual agreement." Greene's sexual transactions with prostitutes and some of his mistresses included, by mutual agreement, such S-and-M refinements as their inflicting cigarette burns on him. That this connoisseur of human despair and its passing easements should find pain an entertainment is not utterly surprising; but Shelden oversimplifies the psychology and the metaphysics of it. A less sensitive, less empathetic boy would not have watched as the snails "exploded into foam" (Greene's own phrase) with such intentness that he could evoke the horror a half-century later. A compulsive observer of violence—Hemingway was another—may be driven to participate in rites of destruction but does not necessarily describe cruelty as an endorsement: as a protest, rather, against the universe that, with God's evident permission, contains so much pain.

Greene's imagination had its macabre and murderous side, no doubt, and his childhood flirtations with suicide left him on friendlier terms with extreme measures than most of us. Nevertheless, it seems outrageous to imply, as Shelden does, that he was an actual murderer. Marshalling facts with the zealous woolliness of the O. J. Simpson defense team, Shelden notes the "graphic description" in Greene's *It's a Battlefield* of a female murder victim's being cut up and placed in a trunk; three months after the book was published, a dismembered torso was discovered in the Brighton railway station. The time of this Brighton murder and of Pinkie's fictional crimes in *Brighton Rock* are roughly the same, and Shelden forges a sinister link between a Detective-Sergeant Sorrell mentioned in the actual Brighton case and the presence on the bookshelves of the novel's amateur detective, Ida Arnold, of Warwick Deeping's *Sorrell and Son*, which, at the end of the novel, is stolen! Greene's other works, including his notations of his dreams, are ransacked for telltale representations of bodies in baggage and of a killer's guilt, to flesh out the possibility that Greene murdered and dismembered and packed up a woman in the early 1930s. After all, didn't his idol T. S. Eliot write, in "Sweeney Agonistes," "Any man might do a girl in / Any man has to, needs to, wants to / Once in a lifetime, do a girl in"? Even if Shelden's sensational and artfully hedged charge doesn't stick, Greene was surely a killer in his prose: "We may never know why Greene's imagination was drawn to the Brighton case, but all that matters now is the way that his fantasies of violence against women infect his art."

An example of this verbal violence, and a typically one-dimensional reading of Shelden's, is the treatment of Ida Arnold in *Brighton Rock*. Of the big-breasted, good-hearted barmaid, Shelden writes:

> She argues in favour of common decency and fair play. Her way is right, and Pinkie's way is wrong, and there is no middle ground. But her efforts to assert moral authority are consistently undermined by Greene's efforts to ridicule her simplistic thinking and her vulgar manners. . . . She is portrayed as a gross, cow-like figure who eats and drinks too much, and who pushes herself into places where she does not belong. Her big breasts make her look both intimidating and absurd.

To be sure, Greene, like Eliot—whose *Waste Land* is repeatedly echoed in the novel—disdained life-loving, good-hearted, guilt-free animal health. But in an era of absurd detective-heroes—Agatha Christie's Hercule Poirot, John Dickson Carr's Gideon Fell—Ida does not forfeit our sympathy as drastically as Shelden suggests. In my own experience of the novel, the reader is grateful for Ida's vigilance on behalf of the besmitten, defenseless Rose, and is cheered when Pinkie, his face smoking with vitriol, jumps over a cliff. Pinkie's face at the end is stripped of its demonic authority: "It was like a child's, badgered, confused, betrayed; fake years slipped away—he was whisked back towards the unhappy playground."

Greene does not ask that we forfeit our basic moral bias, for the victim and against the culprit. A conventional morality, not unlike that of the motion pictures he admired, reviewed, and helped produce, stands behind his Gothic variations on thriller plots. He is no blithely anarchic Céline or Henry Miller. Shelden observes with alarm, "Before we know it we are tempted to sympathise with Pinkie's hatred of Ida and Rose." But isn't a purpose of a novel to lead our sympathies into unexpected places? To show us the wounded schoolboy behind an arch-villain's face? To explore the pathology of our—in Christian terms—fallen world? *The End of the Affair* ends with a tender and solemn dialogue between Rose and a priest who tells her, "The Church does not demand that we believe any soul is cut off from mercy." Shelden sniffs: "Priests say such things, and they may be right. But the novel gives the concept absolutely no support. . . . It does not simply tell us that the world is evil. It rubs our noses in the evil and makes fun of us for trying to understand it. And Greene does all this with such brilliance that we cannot help being amazed. Rarely has sheer nastiness been served so well."

Such a reading indicates a limited grasp of how fiction functions. It is a novelist's exact duty to "rub our noses" in his apprehensions of the truth, paradoxical and dismal though they may be. Greene is under no obligation to check his dark thoughts and perverse impulses at creativity's door; he is obliged only to objectify and vivify them in the form of characters and actions. Fiction concerns dramatized tensions, not settled conclusions. Greene's value as a religious novelist lies not in embodied homilies but in his agonized sense of faith's shaky ground in the unhappy human condition. That the "good" characters are absurd or fallible and the "bad" ones sometimes heroic is part of the news he brings, giving his world its unique, bristling texture. That a womanizer should bear a considerable animus toward women and a Roman Catholic frequently mock the church merely locates the area of his fascination and dependency.

Shelden quite misconstrues, I think, the sincerity of Greene's Catholicism, at least as it was up through the writing of *The End of the Affair*. Shelden is indignant that that novel won a Catholic award, and says, "It is a shame—for truth's sake—that an anti-God organization was not available to present him with an outstanding achievement award. No major novelist has shown as much ingenuity in abusing the God of Christianity." He takes the novel's anti-religious narrator, Maurice Bendrix, as Greene's very voice, and cites the book's ending, with its "extraordinary outburst of hatred" directed at God, as if it were one of the author's letters to the editor. "Among blasphemers, Maurice is a pro," he says. "Of course, the real pro is Graham Greene, who found a safe way to convey the sacrilegious nature of his affair with 'C.' " Greene's long affair with Catherine Walston was tormented, and in violation of the sixth commandment, but sacrilegious? In this rich and glamorous American Greene met his spiritual match; like him, she was a promiscuous, frisky, hard-drinking Catholic convert. In 1947, in the first fever of their romance, he wrote her, "I'm not even a Catholic properly away from you. . . . It's odd how little I get out of Mass except when you're around. I'm a much better Catholic in mortal sin!" In 1950, in the throes of writing *The End of the Affair*, he wrote her:

> St. Theresa stands by my bed & every time I turn to her . . . I pray for us. But I'm afraid my prayer is always that God's will shall be in favour of our love. Don't be too sure that it may not be & who knows whether the peace we have so often got together has not been *with* him, instead of against him?

These are not the professions of a diffident or hypocritical Christian. His faith was racked and, as it were, exacerbated by this his most passionate affair. *The End of the Affair* is his most God-filled novel. Maurice's atheism is clearly a losing battle; his hatred of God is hatred of a successful rival, not of a nonentity. There is an embarrassing wealth of literal miracles: Sarah Miles does not know she was secretly baptized a Catholic but in crisis acts as a Catholic; she apparently resurrects her lover by promising God to end the affair; from beyond the grave she cures a sick boy and erases an evangelical rationalist's disfiguring strawberry birthmark. The novel reeks of an ineluctable, inconvenient credal literalism: Sarah writes to Maurice, "I believe there's a God—I believe the whole bag of tricks; there's nothing I don't believe; they could subdivide the Trinity into a dozen parts and I'd believe."

The "whole bag of tricks" chimes with one of Shelden's least savory implications—that "a novelist needs his props" and that Greene "could dispense with the theology, but he could not do without the garish plaster statues, the ghostly candle flames, the stale Communion wafers, the wine in the chalice, the rosary beads, the Latin phrases, the stuffy confessionals, the figure of Christ hanging above the altar, with His painted wounds." Roman Catholicism, that is, with its awful old trappings, supplied seediness to the neighborhoods of Greeneland. Shelden claims that Greene never surrendered his schoolboy hostility to Christianity, and "simply expanded his opportunities for subversion by presenting himself as a member of the largest—and most complex—Christian denomination"; in his fiction Greene subverts the faith by "associating it with adulterers, murderers, suicides and whisky priests." Obtusely and unconscionably, Shelden ignores the central point of *The Power and the Glory*—that an imperfect man may still, as a priest, deliver the sacraments and further the faith. Shelden pounds at the whisky priest's failings like a temperance tract:

> Religion gives him a way to dignify a meaningless life of dissipation. . . . He may be a drunk, but at least he is God's drunk. Because he is the last priest, God is stuck with him, whether He likes it or not. But as the Hollow Man, he knows that he represents nothing.

Nothing as himself, perhaps, but in his office, a great deal. Another corrupted priest in the novel spells out the moral: "That was what made him worthy of damnation—the power he still had of turning the wafer into the flesh and blood of God." To read Greene without any sense of the sacramental—of God as a veiled but detectable and active force in the world, of Greeneland's hot border with the realm of the supernatural—is to deny the Devil, so to speak, his due.

Shelden's biography loses its polemical thrust as his subject's faith slackens and Greene enters his long middle period as a world-roving, world-famous author and political gadfly. To our post–Cold War ears, Greene's once scandalous anti-American quips have a milder ring. In New York to accept the Catholic award for *The End of the Affair* in 1952, he chastised McCarthyism in what now seem sweetly reasonable tones:

I'm speaking this way because I like America and Americans. . . . People came here not to win television sets or refrigerators but to gain freedom from the house spies, the informers, the military regimes. But there are a lot of informers going around here now. . . . As part of their religious beliefs all Catholics should be opposed to this.

His sketch of the Vietnam situation in *The Quiet American* proved remarkably prescient; Alden Pyle is caricatural as a character but convincing as a harbinger of our ruinous good intentions. Apropos of Greene's notorious loyalty to the spy Kim Philby, his boss, in 1943–44, in Section V (Iberian Department) of the Secret Intelligence Service, Shelden offers a mitigating speculation: Greene saw through Philby and, caught between the undesirable alternatives of becoming involved in treachery or betraying his friend the traitor, abruptly resigned from the SIS, in May of 1944. According to Shelden, Greene wove his suspicions into *The Third Man*, with a portrait of Philby as the charming and perfidious Harry Lime. Norman Sherry's biography briefly entertains the same possibility—"If Greene did suspect Philby, it would be just the kind of thing that would catapult him out of the service rather than share his suspicions with the authorities"—and goes on to suppose that Greene's widely deplored failure to denounce Philby after the unmasked spy defected, in 1963, might have been a patriotic, government-approved ploy to maintain contact and to reënlist the bored defector in the SIS, as its mole in Moscow and the KGB. The KGB, in truth, never trusted Philby, and gave him trifling duties. Anthony Mockler, in his *Three Lives* biography, notes that after World War II Greene kept only Philby and John Cairncross, of all his old SIS colleagues, in his address book; Cairncross, of course, was "the Fifth Man"—the fifth Communist spy after Guy Burgess, Donald Maclean, Philby, and Sir Anthony Blunt. Mockler offers his "instinctive feeling" that Greene knew "that Kim Philby and John Cairncross were passing secret information on to the Soviets; that he approved; and that, in a minor way, he helped. But, all the same, he had no desire to go too far; to become too deeply embroiled. He was almost forty, and a family man *malgré lui*." It is odd that Shelden stops short of saying that Greene helped pass secrets—at a time when the Soviets were our embattled allies but anti-Communism reigned at the SIS—especially since the outcome illustrates his point that Greene "was adept at escaping from any trap."

But trapped in loneliness and a sour depression the writer did remain, as his novels grew briefer and wearier, and his fascination with misery led him to one global sore spot after another (Haiti, Batista's Cuba, the

dictatorships of Paraguay and Argentina). He enjoyed the friendship of
Panama's dictator Omar Torrijos, of Castro and the Sandinistas, and said
that, given the choice, he would rather live in the Soviet Union than the
United States. Resident since 1966 in Antibes, he sought to expose shady
doings in Nice with a pamphlet pompously titled *J'Accuse*. Shelden has
little use for any of Greene's public gestures, such as returning the
Legion of Honor to the French government and resigning from the
American Academy of Arts and Letters; they were "publicity stunts." His
numerous letters to the editor, collected as *Yours Etc.: Letters to the Press,
1945–89*, formed "a kind of joke book." Shelden blames these effusions
on "mood swings," alcohol, and bad company: "Wealth and fame had put
Greene in the company of rich men who enjoyed idle jests, but it was not
the best company for a novelist whose talent was already suffering from a
lack of focus." For all the political noise he made, Greene had no real
agenda:

> Whether he was drunk or not, he demonstrated his lack of seriousness again
> and again by the dilettantish fashion in which he moved quickly from one
> controversy to the next, rarely bothering to substantiate his charges in
> extended debates or to follow them up with some sort of constructive
> action.

Well, are extended debates what we ask of a creative artist? Is not the
artist's a license to play with the world, in order to re-create it? A mind
not "dilettantish" would scarcely stoop to the patchy labor of stitching
fiction together out of facts, memories, impressions, and flights of fancy.
That Greene chose to exercise his fancy in public statements shows a lifelong addiction to print and a schoolboy prankishness but does not diminish the harrowing passion and authenticity of his best novels. After all
that Shelden says of Greene's duplicities, perversities, and frivolities, his
portrait is less devastating and scornful than those Greene painted of
such alter egos as Fowler in *The Quiet American* and Querry in *A Burnt-
Out Case*. The entire climate and topography of Greeneland is a kind
of self-portrait; its features are pain, guilt, ennui, and lassitude. Out of
whatever depravities he needed, out of whatever depressions he over-
came, Greene managed in his best novels to locate modern men and
women in the old Christian space, giving them souls and the urgency that
the concepts of sin and damnation bestowed upon human decisions. The
feat could be said to be an unnatural one but a feat it was, carried forward
with admirable industry, clarity of observation, and narrative tautness.
Even a late bagatelle like *Doctor Fischer of Geneva or the Bomb Party* has its
forward pull and its flashes of cinematic scene-making.

Greene's bright side—his creative, intelligent, disciplined side—gets grudging lip service in Shelden's indignant account, but it existed. Greene among his many diligences kept account of his dreams, and his last literary task was to assemble some of them into the book titled *A World of My Own: A Dream Diary*. The world of his dreams was surprisingly crisp and sunny. The mighty dead, literary and political, convivially conversed with him, indicating that his subconscious had assimilated his global celebrity. The erotic strain so strong in his life and work was discreetly suppressed, but for the odd detail like "Suddenly someone thrust a large fat spider into my trousers and I felt it grasp my penis." He was, by birth, an Edwardian; the most shocking (to me) fact in Shelden's biography is that Greene never learned to operate any kind of motorized vehicle. The dream he places first is titled "Happiness" and concerns a ride on an antiquated railway. A train "of pretty carriages which must have dated back more than a hundred years" passes by, and then he boards a train whose passengers "all wore strange clothes—Edwardian or Victorian." The stations they glide through seem stations of childhood: "On one wide platform children were playing with scarlet balloons; another station was built like a ruined Greek temple; at one point the track narrowed and the train went through a kind of tunnel made with mattresses." Greene tells us, "I had never in my life felt such a sensation of happiness." In the dream placed last, he writes a verse for a competition in a magazine called *Time and Tide* on the subject of his own death. It concludes on a sweet, infantile note:

> My breath is folded up
> Like sheets in lavender.
> The end for me
> Arrives like nursery tea.

The trouble with literary biographies, perhaps, is that they mainly testify to the long worldly corruption of a life, as documented deeds and days and disappointments pile up, and cannot convey the unearthly human innocence that attends, in the perpetual present tense of living, the self that seems the real one.

Shirley Temple Regina

ELIZABETH: *A Biography of Britain's Queen*, by Sarah Bradford. 528 pp. Farrar, Straus and Giroux, 1996.

The marital and romantic derelictions of her children and their spouses have made Queen Elizabeth II interesting in a way she was not before: she has been, to judge by the results, a faulty mother, and has proved, in these recent scabrous years, inexpert in the contemporary art of damage control. Her oldest son, the Prince of Wales and heir apparent to the throne, and her two daughters-in-law, the former Lady Diana Spencer and the former Sarah Ferguson, have fed the tawdriest and most maudlin appetites of tabloid journalism with royal tidbits aplenty and, under the merciless media glare, have brought the very idea of monarchy into disrepute. Of course, it has been in disrepute before—one does not have to go back to Ethelred the Unready to find slow, murderous, self-indulgent, insane, and heartily disliked kings*—but, as the divine aura dims around the throne and cost-cutters thrive in this era of global competition, scandal becomes excitingly perilous.

The present admirable and esteemed monarch became queen, of course, because of a scandal. When Princess Elizabeth Alexandra Mary of York was born—on April 21, 1926, by cesarean section, in a vanished Mayfair house now commemorated by a plaque—she was third in line for the throne occupied by her grandfather George V. The odds were high, however, that she would be displaced. Her uncle David, first in line, was nearly certain to marry and have children, and her mother, née Lady Elizabeth Bowes-Lyon, was only twenty-five and quite likely to present her husband, David's younger brother, Albert, with a male heir. But, as it turned out, David, still a bachelor, abdicated the throne after a brief reign as Edward VIII, to marry an American divorcée, Wallis Simpson, and Albert, who then became George VI, had seen his progeny increased only by the arrival, in 1930, of another daughter, Margaret Rose. By the end of 1936—the tumultuous Year of Three Kings—ten-year-old Elizabeth had to start thinking of herself as the future monarch of England.

---

*Take, for example, the first six lines of Shelley's "England in 1819":

> An old, mad, blind, despised, and dying king,—
> Princes, the dregs of their dull race, who flow
> Through public scorn,—mud from a muddy spring,—
> Rulers who neither see, nor feel, nor know,
> But leech-like to their fainting country cling,
> Till they drop, blind in blood, without a blow . . .

She was, fortunately, by her solid, responsible, resolute temperament, well suited for the daunting role. Winston Churchill, who first met Elizabeth when she was two and a half years old, presciently told his wife, "She has an air of authority and reflectiveness astonishing in an infant."

One of the most pleasurable sections of Sarah Bradford's *Elizabeth: A Biography of Britain's Queen* consists of the early pages, where we are invited to imagine what it was like to be such a child, reared in simultaneous global fame and drastic seclusion, at a time when the monarchy, though reduced to chiefly ceremonial functions, still wore traces of prehistoric mystery and grandeur. Elizabeth was, as Bradford tells it, a dear little girl, serene and orderly and obedient. Most everybody loved her. The public, stimulated by the then-hot medium of magazines (Elizabeth was on the cover of *Time* at the age of three), loved her to such an extent that her mother wrote to Queen Mary, the child's grandmother, "It almost frightens me that the people should love her so much. I suppose that it is a good thing, and I hope that she will be worthy of it, poor little darling." When, four years after her birth, her sister appeared, Elizabeth was "maternally protective," and she has remained so, to a sibling whose character—"extrovert, capricious, attention-seeking, imaginative and naughty"—stands in sharp contrast to her own. Their parents, who for Elizabeth's first ten years led the relatively private lives of the Duke and Duchess of York, loved the girls; Albert, a shy, academically inept stammerer, cleaved to his wife, an aristocratic Scot of great animation and charm, and presided over a nuclear family—"us four," in his frequent phrase—of exceptional coziness. Elizabeth later wrote, "I have nothing but wonderfully happy memories of childhood days at home, fun, kindness & a marvellous sense of security." Even her grandfather, who had been an intimidating tyrant to his sons, loved her; he played and joked with "Lilibet" in a way that he had not with his own children, and introduced her to the world of horses, which was to be ever after her passion and retreat. Her wicked uncle David and his even wickeder wife did not, in their embittering exile, love her; they referred to her, in their private communications, as "Shirley Temple" and, into her monarchy, as "the girl."

The girl married early and pleasingly. At the age of thirteen, she developed an adolescent crush on an eighteen-year-old cousin, Prince Philip of Greece, who at the time was serving as a naval cadet. A scion of harried, rootless nobility, virtually on his own from the age of ten, Philip was pressed forward by his family, his uncle Lord Louis Mountbatten foremost, as a prospective consort, and the match, consummated by their marriage in 1947, proved, Bradford asserts, to be an excellent one:

The marriage was a success on every level; physically, mentally, and temperamentally the couple were compatible. Elizabeth was physically passionate and very much in love with her husband. Philip found her sexually attractive and was equally, although perhaps more coolly, in love.

This reassuring information is relayed without source attribution, but little evidence exists that contradicts it. The always fascinating, though by now scarcely earthshaking, question of Philip's infidelities is disposed of briskly, in the affirmative:

> Philip has learned to carry on his flirtations and relationships in circles rich and grand enough to provide protection from the paparazzi and the tabloids. . . . The women are always younger than he, usually beautiful and highly aristocratic. They include a princess, a duchess, two or perhaps three countesses, and other titled and untitled ladies.

It all sounds rather abstractly posh, and one would like to know more of the lady-in-waiting who, when she attempted to enlighten Elizabeth about some affair of Philip's, got sacked for her trouble. The anecdote ends like an admonitory fairy tale: "Appalled at her indiscretion, the lady later committed suicide."

The Duke of Edinburgh's strengths and deficiencies were summed up by an acquaintance: "He's 150 per cent male and that's his trouble really." Bradford gives the plausible impression that Philip's faults—gruffness, impatience, wanderlust—are what a woman of Elizabeth's age and class expects in a man. They still share a bed, and their recent time of family troubles has made him more supportive and protective than ever. "I think he's been apparently absolutely wonderful to her and incredibly supportive" is one tribute given him since 1992, the catastrophic year that the Queen dubbed her *annus horribilis*. "They have come together very much lately," a courtier is quoted as saying. Sometimes restive and tactless, Philip has for nearly half a century faithfully discharged his major obligation: he has fit himself into a narrow slot where many another male would look absurd. He does not; he sets her off in public becomingly. In private, Bradford states, "she adores him and defers to him." Unlike the Windsor spouses of the next generation, he—the grandson of George I of Greece, great-grandson of Christian IX of Denmark, and great-great-grandson of Queen Victoria—understood the royal game as it is played in the twilight of titled Europe. Dignity and discretion are increasingly difficult for a public figure to maintain, yet he has honored the Queen with these virtues, and with what can only be construed, allowing for the opacity of aristocratic liaisons, as love.

* * *

Elizabeth was a contented Navy wife, and the twenty-six-year-old mother of two, when her father died in his mid-fifties, worn out by a heavy nicotine habit and the cares of a kingship he had not wanted. She stepped confidently into her role and, in her royal responsibilities, has hardly put a foot wrong since. A conscientious, quick study, she always mastered the dispatch boxes of state papers that her curious position, ornamental and central, demands that she peruse, and was demurely submissive to the vast and antiquated apparatus of ceremonial royal duty. In addition, she was lovely, in just the proper reserved, unspectacular way. Margaret would have made a more striking and expressive queen, but would she have worn as well, and presided as soothingly? Elizabeth's slender, calm, almost plain good looks can still be seen on English stamps, which have not aged with her. Bernard Baruch in 1953 called her "the world's sweetheart" and listed her, with Churchill and "a glorious historical past," as one of England's three (and only three) assets. The country was then a tattered relic of its imperial self; it fell to her to embody optimism and symbolize national well-being. She took upon herself immediately the task of cementing British ties with the Commonwealth, which had replaced the vanished empire, and committed herself to a tremendous amount of travel, which took her much away from Charles and his sister Anne. She had also, as a young monarch, to navigate the sea-change within her family—her abrupt transformation into the head of a household that contained her formidable husband (who, upon being told that his name of Mountbatten, once Battenberg, was to be supplanted by his wife's name of Windsor, exploded, "I'm nothing but a bloody amoeba!"); her still-vivacious, admired mother; and her moody, erratic, rather hedonistic sister, whose quest for a mate was to prove as ill-fated as Elizabeth's was fortunate. It speaks for Elizabeth's warm and forbearing nature, and for the conservatism of her emotional attachments, that through many a storm she has sustained with Margaret the affectionate and tolerant relations established in the palace nursery.

The Queen took up her crown with an aplomb that startled those nearest her. "I no longer feel anxious or worried," she told a friend. "I don't know what it is—but I have lost all my timidity somehow becoming the Sovereign." Sarah Bradford—in private life, Viscountess Bangor—describes the sovereign duties with a detail that some American readers may feel is more than ample. We are introduced to the intricacies of the inner circles of palace management, where upper-crust courtiers come and go, arranging official parties and the Queen's often brutal schedule. One of her private secretaries is quoted as saying: "She's got very good legs and she can stand for a long time. . . . The Queen is as tough as a yak." Intimates and servants with jaunty names like "Bobbety" and "Porchy" and "Boy" and "Basher" and "Bennie" and "Bobo" circulate through the royal life. Forty-four years of English history reel by, in Bradford's account, with each Prime Minister from Churchill on described in terms of his—or, in the lone case of Margaret Thatcher, her—relations with their sovereign, whom the Prime Minister is obliged to brief in weekly sessions. After Churchill, Elizabeth got along best with two leaders of the Labour Party, Harold Wilson and James Callaghan. Things were comparatively awkward with Anthony Eden, in his brief doomed tenure, and with the stiff, introverted Edward Heath; the Queen, a member of the household confided, "found Heath hard going." On the much-mooted relationship between Elizabeth and Mrs. Thatcher, Bradford is succinct: both women were "highly professional and dedicated to their jobs," but they came from different worlds, Elizabeth being a rural conservative and Thatcher a suburban revolutionary, who never did figure out what shoes to take for an outdoorsy visit to Balmoral. (Whereas Denis Thatcher and the Duke of Edinburgh, with nothing much else to do, enjoyed each other's company considerably.) More regal in accent and manner than the Queen, Thatcher revered the monarchy but did not charm Elizabeth, who was once heard to ask, "Do you think Mrs. Thatcher will ever change?" Yet, Bradford says of Elizabeth, "Not one leading politician who has worked with her has anything but admiration and fondness for her." Even the anti-monarchist Labourite Tony Benn allowed, "She is not very clever but is reasonably intelligent and she is experienced." From the peculiar elevation of the monarchy, we learn, distinctions between Tory and Labour politicians disappear; according to Sir Godfrey Agnew, Clerk of the Privy Council, "They all roughly belong to the same social category in her view." In the periodic battles over the rising costs of the monarchy and its offshoots, the Prime Ministers have all supported the royal cause against parliamentary republicans.

As Elizabeth's four children matured and married, the British public had increasing reason to wonder what they were paying for. In the 1950s, Margaret's frustrated romance with Peter Townsend, a divorced equerry, showed the press how many newspapers any dysfunction in the Royal Family would sell. Margaret's eventual marriage to and rancorous split with the semi-bohemian photographer Anthony Armstrong-Jones; Princess Anne's divorce from her fellow show rider Mark Phillips and her marriage, in the Church of Scotland, to a less plodding horseman, Timothy Laurence; Prince Andrew's paparazzi-bedevilled breakup with the rambunctious Sarah Ferguson—all these, though meat to the tabloids, are tasty side dishes compared with the imbroglio between Prince Charles and Princess Diana, which casts a heavy shadow upon the character of the next in the royal succession and upon the welfare of his heir, thirteen-year-old Prince William. The psychodrama is still ongoing; the American edition of Bradford's book, but not the English, manages to include such recent developments as Di's dour television interview and the Queen's directive that a divorce should take place.* Elizabeth's hope, presumably, is to stanch the frightful bleeding of public grievance and self-pity, but the wound that her son has taken is already deep. The public, never totally easy with this diffident, sad-eyed mixture of playboy and Greenpeacer, now confronts a confessed adulterer as the prospective head of the established church, and a future king who must either remain queenless or try to brazen through a Queen Camilla where a Queen Wallis had been unthinkable.

Bradford makes a sympathetic case for Charles, along the lines of his own possibly overabundant testimony: a sensitive child abused by a bullying father and a distant, preoccupied mother was further hampered in his development by the isolating singularity of his position. Once out of the Navy, where he did not experience the fulfillment his father and George V did, he resisted official efforts to find him a job; his becoming Ambassador to France was one of the suggestions that went nowhere. "He wanted to be a dabbler" was one government minister's verdict. As Charles wistfully searched for himself in Oriental mysticism, anthropology, and amateur cultural criticism, his relations with his parents chilled. His romantic life went adrift. His great-uncle Lord Mountbatten had become his surrogate father, and gave him some advice which eventually backfired: "A man should sow his wild oats before settling down. But for a wife he should choose a suitable and sweet-charactered girl before she meets anyone else she might fall for." That is, marry a virgin—a barbaric requirement in this day and age, bound to block the aging Charles from his natural mates. In the long bachelor stretch between his letting Camilla Shand slip away, in 1973 (he failed to propose before he went off on a Navy tour of duty, and in any case she may have been already enamored of her soon-to-be husband, Andrew Parker Bowles), and his marrying Lady Diana Spencer, in 1981, there was "a

---

*Developments, of course, in turn eclipsed by the shocking death of Diana in a Paris car crash early on the morning of August 31, 1997, in the company of her new companion and rumored fiancé, Dodi Fayed. The outpouring of English grief, with frequent expressions of resentment toward the Royal Family, for a time heightened the ongoing psychodrama, but as of a year later the death of the beloved, erratic Princess can be seen to have given the Queen, her beleaguered eldest son, and his faithful mistress a measure of peace and restored privacy.

string of beautiful upper-class and not so upper-class girls," at least one of whom declined to become his wife. Not every eligible woman—not even Mountbatten's candidate, his granddaughter Amanda Knatchbull—wanted to enter the gilded royal cage, or fishbowl. One who did was the younger sister of Lady Sarah Spencer, herself a former girlfriend.

Diana gets a very tough report in Bradford's gleanings. She is said to resemble, "in looks and character," her mother, the former Frances Roche, who seduced her father, John Althorp, away from his fiancée and then "bolted," in English parlance, into the arms of a married man, Peter Shand Kydd. The Spencers as a clan were "difficult," a relative stated. "As a family they like to live among dramas. . . . They're not straightforward." Diana was six at the time of the divorce, and her brother Charles told her biographer, "I don't know whether a psychologist would say it was the trauma of the divorce but she had real difficulty telling the truth purely because she liked to embellish things." A school report claimed, "Diana Spencer is the most scheming little girl I have ever met." She had high hopes for herself; her family nickname was "Duch," for "Duchess." Bradford asserts, "From the age of fifteen she wanted the Prince of Wales." When she succeeded in landing him, however, qualms set in; she knew about Charles's stubbornly lingering attachment to Mrs. Parker Bowles. When, within a week of the wedding, she confided to her sisters, Sarah and Jane, her suspicion that Charles loved not her but Camilla, she was cheerily told, "Bad luck, Duch—your face is on the tea towels so it's too late for you to chicken out." Indeed, the wedding seems to have gone forward from the sheer momentum of the hoopla. At the pre-wedding ball in Buckingham Palace, Charles danced once with Diana and often with Camilla, and disappeared with her after Diana had retired. Among the many inauspicious signs was the Queen's failure to warm to the bride: "Diana, she quickly realised, was not her type of girl. . . . She was interested in clothes, pop music, dancing and shopping while horses and dogs, hunting, shooting and fishing, the royal pastimes, bored her."

Still, however many shortcomings, hereditary and acquired, the tall virgin brought to the marriage, the onus of its failure cannot be shifted from Charles. He was a thirty-two-year-old man of the world who had made his choice; Diana was an ill-educated innocent who kept her part of the bargain by enchanting the public and quickly bearing one male heir and then another for good measure. Yet, by the time of Prince Henry's birth in September of 1984, the couple were poisonously estranged and Charles was back in the arms of the compliant Camilla. Who can be blamed but he? "She worshipped him with a calf-like adoration," said one palace aide, "and he kicked her in the gutter." Our impression, after reading Bradford's even-handed account, remains that Charles, compounding obtuseness and entitled arrogance, in little more than three years turned a fairy-tale wedding into an unconcealable botch. His blundering has not been mitigated by some cunning public pleading, which has hurt others. His self-serving confession of adultery, on television in June of 1994, made it impossible for the Parker Bowleses to continue with their close-mouthed open marriage. His coöperation with his authorized biographer, Jonathan Dimbleby, extended to giving access to such a wealth of state papers and official material that Elizabeth had to demand some back. The portrait of his parents in that book has, Bradford says, outraged his three siblings. He has emerged as a ringmaster in an ongoing circus of exposure and media manipulation—a circus wherein Diana's former lover, James Hewitt, has climbed to dizzying heights of caddishness by baring their affair in print and now peddling the story to television for millions of pounds.

"I can't understand my children," Elizabeth is reported to have told a friend. She and Philip, it may be, did not create a household as warm as the one headed by her father and mother, who would join their daughters in pillow fights; then (according to Marion Crawford's early palace-tattle book, *The Little Princesses*), "arm in arm, the young parents would go downstairs, heated and dishevelled and frequently rather damp." But a dry independence and self-reliance are traditional Anglo-Saxon virtues, inculcated with especial rigor in the British upper classes. Was not Elizabeth, too, reared in large part by nurses, nannies, governesses, grooms, and other servants? Further, nurture can only do so much with nature. A hereditary monarchy depends upon belief in royal blood, in a right stuff that is passed on at birth. It must surprise her that the ideals of duty, self-restraint, and stoic endurance were not passed on with her genes. Her natural endowment was superb for the straitened role she had to play. Her French tutor, Antoinette de Bellaigue, said of her, "She had an instinct for the right thing. She was her simple self, *très naturelle*. And there was always a strong sense of duty mixed with *joie de vivre* in her character." Anne seems to have inherited the sense of duty and Andrew the *joie de vivre* but Charles a satisfactory portion of neither.

And yet Elizabeth is shy and, in public, stiff. She is no more of a glad-hander than her father was. The moments in her life when she mingled with a cross-section of her future subjects on something like their terms are touchingly few. A heavily hedged hitch in the Auxiliary Territorial Service toward the end of World War II left her with an automotive expertise of which she is proud. Before the birth of Princess Anne, she enjoyed a few months as a Navy wife on Malta: "There was swimming, dancing, picnics, expeditions by boat to the beaches and coves round the island and to Gozo. She could even go shopping and out to the hairdresser and enjoy in-jokes with the other naval wives. She was happy and pregnant." She is still so innocently curious about ordinary life that she sometimes quizzes the Scottish soldiers on protection duty at a Balmoral shoot about their personal lives. Watching the two-hour television show *Elizabeth R*, made by the BBC, one somewhat pities her, condemned to deal daily with so many strangers and dignitaries performing prescribed courtesies. She offers, as Prime Minister Callaghan found in their audiences, "friendliness but not friendship." Diana, still on view in this royally sanctioned film, has a relative ease in brief encounters, a quickness in making contact that is perhaps as much a generational as a personal trait. In her recent pronouncements, however, the Princess seems to overestimate her official viability once she is no longer the daughter-in-law of, as Edmund Spenser wrote of Elizabeth I, the "soueraine Lady Queene, / In whose pure minde, as in a mirrour sheene, / [Praise] showes, and with her brightnesse doth inflame / The eyes of all, which thereon fixed beene."

Sarah Bradford's biography of this exalted being is well researched if hurriedly written. Commas are dropped, phrases dangle, she says "inferred" when she means "implied," and the same quotations sometimes cycle around again. The maze of names and connections more than once leads her into run-on sentences:

> Sarah [York], who had ignored the scolding of her cousin, Robert Fellowes, whom she contemptuously referred to as "Bellows," and the warnings about Wyatt from her father (who at one point was sharing his mistress, Lesley Player, with Wyatt), was apparently now gently told off by her mother-in-law and ordered to "Chill him" by her mother, Susan Barrantes.

Like such phrases as "stump up" (for "cough up") and "tore a strip off" (for "berate"), the abundant detail about the qualifications and antecedents of minor courtiers adds to the book's uniquely British flavor. Without their crowns and coronets, how could the English be distinguished from the Icelanders? Bradford likes Elizabeth, and we get to share her liking, along with a sneaking fondness for all the Windsors. Neither flashy nor clever, they have tended to rise to what the occasion demanded (George VI weathering the blitz in London, for instance), and in their earthbound stodginess have kept a connection with the British masses. George V, bewildered by the warmth of his reception in the East End during his Silver Jubilee year, said to the Archbishop of Canterbury, "But I cannot understand. I am quite an ordinary sort of fellow." The Archbishop replied, "Yes, Sir, that is just it." Lloyd George said of the

King, "Thank God there's not much in his head. They're simply, very very ordinary people, and perhaps on the whole that's how it should be." Chesterton somewhere wrote that a democracy and a monarchy are alike in proposing that any man is fit to rule.

Elizabeth will never abdicate, Bradford states flatly. On the future of the monarchy in general she left this reader with a two-edged impression: England could dispense with a monarch but probably won't. For all Elizabeth's patient mastery of the state papers and her knowledgeable consultations with her Prime Ministers, the book cites no instance where her advice has influenced national events. Even her usefulness as a rallying point for the Commonwealth has diminished to the vanishing point as England has cast in its economic lot with the European Community. On the other hand, replacing the monarchy—which at present costs the British public an estimated eighty million pounds a year—with a European-style republican President "would not necessarily save a great deal." Presidential elections cost a pretty penny, and a "constitutional monarch is apolitical in a way which no president can be." If Elizabeth survives to anything like the age of her mother, who is ninety-five and smiling, Charles will have many years in which to live down his present embarrassments. His great-great-grandfather Edward VII was a disreputable Prince of Wales but a popular King. The same kind fate that plucked Victoria from the snarl of wicked uncles who had made the monarchy a distasteful joke, and that saw to the death of the unsuitable Duke of Clarence, George V's older brother, before he could ascend to the throne, may continue to preside over Elizabeth's heirs. For her children to squander completely the treasure of good will that her long and dutiful reign has accumulated, they will have to work overtime.

THINGS AS THEY ARE

An Undeciphered Residue

NATURALIST, by Edward O. Wilson. 380 pp. Island Press, 1994.

Edward O. Wilson is a scientist who likes to write—not just pinched little scientific papers, dense with data and Latin, but massive, inclusive, dictionary-sized volumes like *Sociobiology: The New Synthesis* (1975), consisting of six hundred double-column pages and a bibliography of twenty-four hundred items, and (with Bert Hölldoblet) *The Ants* (1990), even bigger and ballasted by a bibliography seven hundred items longer. Wilson has produced over three hundred scientific publications in total, and two of his books—*The Ants* and *On Human Nature* (1978)— have won the non-fiction Pulitzer Prize. This fall, he has published two new volumes, *Journey to the Ants: A Story of Scientific Exploration* (again with Bert Hölldoblet) and an autobiography, titled simply *Naturalist*. In the latter volume he offers the modest secret of his literary productivity: a bad verbal memory. "I cannot memorize lines, have trouble visualizing words spelled out to me letter by letter," he explains. "I write smoothly, in part I believe because my memory is less encumbered by the phrasing and nuances of others." He also tells us that he is blind in one eye, cannot hear high-frequency sounds, and is a poor mathematician. So, confides this winner of most of the prizes with which a naturalist can be honored, he has "skirted the weaknesses" and pushed his strengths. He has studied the ant, as Proverbs advised: "Go to the ant, thou sluggard; consider her ways, and be wise." His advice to young scientists has a certain antlike hard-headedness: "Move laterally and up and down and peer all around. If you have the will, there is a discipline in which you can succeed. Look for the ones still thinly populated, where fine differences in raw ability matter less. Be a hunter and explorer, not a problem solver."

If he describes his professional career in terms of formicid diligence and tenacity, his choice of vocation has the quality of a religious vision. In 1936, on a piece of Florida's Gulf Coast called Paradise Beach, the seven-year-old Wilson, wading, was transfixed by the sight of "a huge jellyfish in water so still and clear that its every detail [was] revealed as though it were trapped in glass." The creature, which he later learned was a sea nettle, a medusa—*Chrysaora quinquecirrha*—hung there motionless for hours as the fascinated child gazed at its curious anatomy:

> Its opalescent pink bell is divided by thin red lines that radiate from center to circular edge. A wall of tentacles falls from the rim to surround and par-tially veil a feeding tube and other organs, which fold in and out like the fabric of a drawn curtain. I can see only a little way into this lower tissue mass. I want to know more but am afraid to wade in deeper and look more closely into the heart of the creature.

Wilson's reaction to this beautifully evoked apparition spells out the dif-ference between a naturalist and the rest of us; instead of rapidly sloshing the other way in fright and disgust, he yearned to look deeper into the heart of the creature, and impressed its details upon his brain. He still remembers the image as embodying "all the mystery and tensed malig-nity of the sea."

That same summer, Wilson, in the care of a family who boarded youngsters in Paradise Beach, accidentally injured his sight. Fishing on a dock, he yanked a pinfish from the water too violently, so it flew into his face and one of its needlelike spines pierced the pupil of his right eye. The wound, neglected, led to a traumatic cataract, whose removal, itself traumatic, left that eye severely impaired. Fortunately, the other remained very keen—good enough for "fine print and the hairs on the bodies of small insects." The summer by the Gulf cemented his love of Nature, which he personifies with a capital "N." An only child and, after 1937, a child of divorce, he lived with his father, a hard-drinking govern-ment accountant who "for some reason preferred road assignments." In the course of eleven years the boy attended fourteen different public schools. "A nomadic existence made Nature my companion of choice," he writes, "because the outdoors was the one part of my world I perceived to hold rock steady."

He kept ants in a jar of sand; he fished; he collected butterflies; he learned the names of plants and creatures. There was in this bright and studious child a rare fervor—a saintlike craziness, even. At the age of fif-teen, living in the small Alabama town of Brewton, he found a swamp next to a goldfish hatchery run by "an affable sixty-year-old Englishman named Mr. Perry." Mr. Perry's excavated goldfish ponds had enriched the swamp biota, including water snakes, to the point where it seemed to young Wilson a "paradise": "A swamp filled with snakes may be a nightmare to most, but for me it was a ceaselessly rotating lattice of wonders." He became adept at catching snakes, and waded among them with a mystic joy until an oversize cottonmouth moccasin thrashed in his grip and threatened to sink its inch-long fangs in the boy's hand. He managed to toss the cottonmouth away, but the near-disastrous episode leads him to speculate as to "why I explored swamps and hunted snakes with such dedication and recklessness." He offers a number of plausible reasons, including practical ambition: "I dreamed I was training myself someday to be a professional field biologist." But there is still "an undeciphered residue, a yearning remaining deep within me that I have never understood, nor wish to, for fear that if named it might vanish."

His adult adventures as a rising naturalist took him, inevitably, to the tropics and other buggy terrain, but he added to the unavoidable hardships some extraordinary tests of his will and endurance, such as attempting to climb, in Mexico, the Pico de Orizaba—"three miles from the lowlands straight up into the air in thirty-six hours"—and, in New Guinea, succeeding in scaling the central summit ridge of the Sarawaget Mountains, the first white man to do so. He concludes his account:

> As we fast-walked and slid our way down the ridges and into the upper Bunbok Valley, something resistant and troubling finally broke and receded inside me. The Sarawaget, cold and daunting, had proved a test of my will severe enough to be satisfying. I had reached the edge of the world I wanted, and knew myself better as a result. By passing from the sea to its peaks I had finally encompassed the serious tropics of my dreams, and I could go home.

Home by that time had become Cambridge and Harvard, where Wilson has studied and taught since 1951, after earning his bachelor's and master's degrees at the University of Alabama. The peaks and swamps of his mature scientific achievement are harder for him to describe, and for the non-specialist reader to picture, than are his physical and geographical adventures. A certain bold adventurism does emerge, however, in his propounding of a new science, which he called "sociobiology" and which aroused resistance in other academic camps to the extent of intradepartmental snubbings, indignant letters in *The New York Review of Books*, and a spectacular incident at a Washington symposium in 1978: a young woman who had stormed the stage dumped a pitcher of ice water over Wilson's head while other protestors chanted, "Wilson, you're all wet!"

An academic outsider can hardly detect, reading the offending final chapter in *Sociobiology*, what they were so strenuously objecting to. This chapter, which follows twenty-six chapters that in a flat, fact-packed prose summarize what is known about coöperative animal behavior from coral colonies to chimpanzee clans, suggests what in human social behavior might be genetically, rather than culturally, determined. To be sure, pacifists who had cut their teeth on the anti-war movement might not want to consider history's constant wars as tests of "differential group fitness" or read of theories that "envision some of the 'noblest' traits of mankind, including team play, altruism, patriotism, bravery on the field of battle, and so forth, as the genetic product of warfare." Feminists might not welcome the bland inclusion, as a basic primate trait, of "aggressive dominance systems, with males dominant over females"; in Wilson's sense of human society, "During the day the women and children remain in the residential area while the men forage for game or its symbolic equivalent in the form of barter and money." Young progressives of 1975 might be sensitive to the conservative implications of observations like:

> To counteract selfish behavior and the "dissolving power" of high intelligence, each society must codify itself. Within broad limits virtually any set of conventions works better than none at all.

Like those investigators of the inheritability of intelligence as measured by IQ tests, Wilson found himself on a highly charged research track. The Sociobiology Study Group—composed of fifteen Boston-area academics and affiliated with a nationwide outfit called Science for the People—alleged in its letter to the *The New York Review of Books* that Wilson's hypotheses tended "to provide a genetic justification of the *status quo* and of existing privileges for certain groups according to class, race, or sex." Wilson describes himself as surprised and hurt by the vehemence of the attack, which linked his theories with racist eugenics and Nazi atrocities. Few on the Harvard faculty came to his defense. "In the liberal dovecotes of Harvard University," he writes, "a reactionary professor is like an atheist in a monastery." He was advised that he had offended the Marxist belief that human society could be radically remade, and characteristically undertook a thorough study of Marxism, concluding that the attack on sociobiology was "political, not evidential," and that the New Leftists of the Sociobiology Study Group "had no interest in the subject, beyond discrediting it." Wilson devotes several pages of *Naturalist* to a quietly acid portrait of his principal antagonist, the population geneticist Richard Lewontin, whose appointment to the Harvard

Department of Biology Wilson had, not long before 1975, urged against objections from other professors.

One gets a picture of the opposition without really comprehending its case. A genetic approach to human behavior is materialist and reductionist, but why would that offend Marxists, or modern academics of any stripe? Stephen Gould, another opponent of sociobiology, indicated, in a book review collected in his *An Urchin in the Storm*, how the opposition saw it: "Few programs for transformation have been more overt, few pursued with clearer aims in conscious sequence, than human sociobiology in the form proposed by Edward O. Wilson. The goal was audacious, but simply stated: to achieve the greatest reform since Freud in our notion of human nature." Furthermore, according to Gould, *Sociobiology's* very subtitle, *The New Synthesis*, was "an explicit manifesto of revolution for the cognoscenti, since we tradesmen of evolution call our own Darwinian orthodoxy, a legacy of perceived revolution during the 1930s and 1940s, 'the modern synthesis.' " Readers of *Naturalist* know that behind Wilson's methodical manner and mild appearance lurks a mountain-climbing, cottonmouth-grabbing spirit. No small ambition has generated those giant tomes. His own account of the inception of biosociology seems to confirm an aggressive intent:

> Once again I was roused by the amphetamine of ambition. Go ahead, I told myself, pull out all the stops. Organize *all* of sociobiology on the principles of population biology. I knew I was sentencing myself to a great deal more hard work. *The Insect Societies* had just consumed eighteen months. . . . The writing had pushed my work load up to eighty-hour weeks. Now I invested two more years, 1972 to 1974. . . . Knowing where my capabilities lay, I chose the second of the two routes to success in science: breakthroughs for the extremely bright, syntheses for the driven.*

The satisfactions and successes of Wilson's driven career are described with a faint undercurrent of apology, of disappointment. Concerning his collaboration with Robert MacArthur, a Canadian population theoretician who died young, Wilson writes regretfully, "I owe him an incalculable debt, that for at least once in my life I was permitted to participate in science of the first rank." Of his youthful self he confesses, "To the degree I was insecure, I was also ambitious. I hungered for the recognition and support that discovery in science brings." But scientific breakthrough of the sort that generates newspaper news and Nobel Prizes is

---

*He has been driven to publish, in 1998, *Consilience: The Unity of Knowledge*, a grand attempt to synthesize the sciences, the arts, ethics, and religion.

rare; the epochal discovery in biology came in 1953, with the deciphering of the DNA molecule. "It came like a lightning flash," Wilson writes, "like knowledge from the gods." One of DNA's two discoverers, Wilson's Harvard colleague James Watson, was to Wilson "the most unpleasant human being I had ever met"; to molecular biologists like Watson, naturalists like Wilson were mere "stamp collectors." The most, perhaps, that an entomologist could hope for would be a discovery of the order of Karl von Frisch's analysis of the "waggle dance," whereby honeybees communicate to one another the whereabouts of a food source. The "new synthesis" sociobiology may well be Wilson's attempt to push the envelope and make his own lightning flash; it fizzled, not only politically unfashionable but scientifically premature. Wilson writes, "It is possible that gene-culture coevolution will lie dormant as a subject for many more years, awaiting the slow accretion of knowledge persuasive enough to attract scholars. . . . I do not doubt for an instant that its time will come." While we wait, a stream of books and articles speculating on the built-in, genetic component of such human behaviors as domesticity, promiscuity, and homosexuality indicates the subject's general fascination.

Reading Wilson's measured but prickly account of the biosociology controversy, I had an impression of his professorial colleagues as ants whose delicate antennae had received pheromonal evidence that, beneath his appearance as one of them, Wilson was a conservative Southern boy. "In the standard leftward frameshift of academia prevailing then," he tells us, "I—Roosevelt liberal turned pragmatic centrist—was cast well to the right." Wilson evokes his Southern roots with affection. While his parents were separating, they settled the seven-year-old in the Gulf Coast Military Academy, whose Spartan routines, initially distressing, left him with "the images of a perfect orderliness and lofty purpose." Though he did not stay long at the school, he still carries "an inoculum of the military culture": "I instinctively respect authority and believe emotionally if not intellectually that it should be perturbed only for conspicuous cause. . . . I have a special regard for altruism and devotion to duty." The evolutionary riddle of altruism, so dramatically embodied in the self-sacrificial order and tactics of the ant colony, has long concerned him. He devotes a chapter to the hymns and theology of his native Baptist church, and recounts that attending church for the first time in forty years, to hear Martin Luther King, Sr., at Harvard, he wept as black Harvard students sang gospel hymns. "Religion cannot be dismissed as superstition," he says. An arresting sentence in the last chapter of *Sociobiology* runs, "The enduring paradox of religion is that so much of its substance is demonstrably false, yet it remains a driving force in all societies." The

Boy Scouts were central to his growth as a student of Nature; he had risen to Eagle Scout and camp counselor by the age of fifteen. His enduring enthusiasm leads him to include the Scout Oath in his autobiography, with the comment "I drank in and accepted every word. Still do, as ridiculous as that may seem to my colleagues in the intellectual trade, to whom I can only reply, Let's see you do better in fifty-four words." During World War II, with boys of all ages in short supply, he became "a child workaholic," awaking at three in the morning to deliver newspapers to more than four hundred citizens of Mobile. In short, Wilson imbibed the pieties and ethics of his rather staid, trusting generation (which is also mine), and was ill-equipped to cope with the playful anarchism and deadpan Marxism that swept academia in the Sixties.

His professional passions, however, have brought him at last to political correctness: since 1979 he had been an active conservationist, lecturing and writing widely on "the problems of ecosystem destruction and species extinction, and on possible socioeconomic solutions." In 1979 he coined the term "biophilia" to describe "the inborn affinity human beings have for other forms of life, an affiliation evoked, according to circumstance, by pleasure, or a sense of security, or awe, or even fascination blended with revulsion." Revulsion, indeed; after pondering, in *The Ants* and *Journey to the Ants*, numerous blown-up color photos of ants copulating, grooming, foraging, regurgitating foodstuffs into one another's ghastly sideways mouths, crawling all over their bloated inert queens, biting and stinging to death other insects and uncongenial fellow-ants, growing fungal gardens "by applying drops of anal fluid" to clumps of hyphae, cutting up leaves, forming living chains to bring the sides of leaves together, using their own silk-exuding larvae as living shuttles with which to weave their leaf-nests together, and so on, I was reminded of W. H. Auden's lines:

> But between us and the Insects,
> namely nine-tenths of the living, there grins a prohibitive fracture
> empathy cannot transgress: (What Saint made a friend of a roach or
> preached to an ant-hill?)*

Wilson, who has sat attendance upon many an anthill, details as if relaying delightful gossip such tidbits of ant behavior as how the worker-ants (all sisters, by the way) eliminate every queen but one "by stinging and dismembering" the extras, and how fire-ant workers, when a nest is flooded, "float to the surface in tightly packed masses [and] form a living

---

*"The Aliens" (1970).

raft within which the queen and brood are safely tucked." Wilson used his knowledge of the latter habit to gather enough bulk of ant bodies to extract a trace pheromone; he and his assistants "shoveled entire nests into the water of a slow-moving stream [and] scooped up seething masses of ants in kitchen strainers and plopped them into bottles of solvent." Myrmecology isn't for softies. In another experiment, to gauge rates of repopulation, Wilson and a Florida exterminator wiped out every creature living on a number of mangrove islets in the Keys. There is a pleasant technical name for this—"defaunation." One can see why Stephen Gould and his fellow-members of the Sociobiology Study Group were wary of letting a mind hardened by ant-thoughts loose on the tender substance of our human self-image.

But Nature must be faced, and the virtue of *Naturalist* lies in the unembarrassed fullness of Wilson's self-portrait. Not content to show himself as the reasonable, hard-working, civilized man he certainly is, he seeks to plumb the irrational wellspring of his vocation—the "Alabama dreaming" that led the boy toward fanatic feats of exploration and exposition, a dreaming love of the *otherness* which gazes out at us, in particularly obdurate form, from the keratinous faces of ants. Even the most empirical science draws upon a strangeness in the personalities of its fervent devotees. In *Journey to the Ants*, which reprises some of the personal history of *Naturalist*, Wilson writes that naturalists' "primary aim is to learn as much as possible about all aspects of the species that give them esthetic pleasure." While most of us find little aesthetic pleasure in ants, whether as scurrying specks underfoot or magnified dragons on the page, Wilson makes real his own mysterious bliss, and expands our sympathetic grasp of our own heterogeneous species.

At the Hairy Edge of the Possible

ORIGINS: *The Lives and Worlds of Modern Cosmologists*, by Alan Lightman and Roberta Brawer. 563 pp. Harvard University Press, 1990.

Ours is an age of personalities and interviews, of interest in people rather than abstractions like life and time and liberty and fortune. Personalities contrived by the procedures of media publicity pique the human curiosity once satisfied by the daily intercourse of the village and the city neighborhood. The science of cosmology, an ethereal and mind-bending blend of astronomy and particle physics, would seem to be abstract and aloof beyond reach of popularization, but its more spectacular findings make newspaper headlines, and in *Origins: The Lives and Worlds of Modern Cosmologists*, Alan Lightman and Roberta Brawer, scientists themselves, present a celebrity-interview approach to twenty-seven practicing cosmologists. The subjects (twenty-four men and three women, the oldest born in 1915 and the youngest in 1949) were asked a predetermined set of questions,* beginning with their individual lives and work, proceeding to their opinions of certain recent developments in cosmology, and ending with two queries that, in the words of the preface, "ask the interviewees to put aside their natural scientific caution and talk philosophically about their personal feelings toward their subject"— their subject, the universe. Since these two last questions are pseudo-religious clunkers, which most of the interviewees stumble over and some decline to answer, we feel some anxiety for the cosmologists as they are led through relatively manageable and concrete topics toward the sputtering endgame.

The two questions are, in brief, "How would you redesign the universe if you could?" and "Do you agree with Steven Weinberg when he says, 'The more the universe seems comprehensible, the more it also seems pointless'?" Almost none of the cosmologists have any better ideas on how to create a universe. Several would like to remove the physical limit that the speed of light sets on our ability to travel in space, and one, Maarten Schmidt, having protested, "This is really the worst question I've ever heard," would make the universe bigger—"I find the universe too confined. I find it amazing that it is so small." John Huchra proposes a steady-state universe with lots of planets and life and no speed-of-light limit, and adds, "Right now, I'd design it with a ski chalet in New Hampshire." The "pointless" question seems to embarrass even Weinberg, who is one of the interviewees, and it does not help that the question is sometimes posed as "whether the universe has a purpose." (A purpose is not the same thing as a point: the point of *King Lear* is that an old man should not rashly give away his property and his prerogatives, whereas its purpose is to entertain, astound, frighten, and purify the audience.) The interviewers are fishing for a religious response, and most of the cosmologists, not being religious, refuse to bite. "Why should it have a point?" Margaret Geller asks back, in a typical response. "What point? It's just a physical system, what point is there?" "I don't think there is an enormous point to it all," Vera Rubin more gently allows, adding, "But, for some of us, attempting to understand this universe is important and a major part

---

*Except for Andrei Linde, who was interviewed before the format was established.

of our lives." Weinberg's sentence goads James Peebles to sniff, "That's such an anthropomorphic remark, and not in the sense of the anthropomorphism of Bob Dicke, but I think in a much more naïve sense." To Gérard de Vaucouleurs, "the remark sounds almost nostalgic."

There are two professed Christians among the cosmologists here— Charles Misner, a Roman Catholic, and Don Page, the son of missionaries and a "conservative" Protestant. Misner, confronted with the Weinberg pronouncement, says, "I come down just on the opposite side of that. . . . The majesty of the universe is meaningful, and we do owe honor and awe to its Creator." Misner has written on the interplay of theology and cosmology, and makes an adroit analogy between Newtonian mechanics— good enough for everyday life—and Biblical mythology. He professes surprise that not everybody is as heartened as he is by Freeman Dyson's vision of a remote universal future in which life will persist, though tremendously slowed down ("the heartbeat is once per 10 billion years"). Page, though he tries "to believe in the meaning" he thinks the Bible "is intended to have," finds himself "a bit skeptical about applying the strong anthropic principle, that the universe *had* to have life in it, or that life was one of the necessary purposes for God to create the universe." He also employs analogy: "In some sense, the physical laws seem to be analogous to the grammar and the language that God chose to use." Edwin Turner, who besides being, according to his brief biography, interested in "hard rock music, baseball, Tai Chi, and Japanese poetry," is "a student of Eastern thought," says that he understands the point of the universe to be "probably close to the kind of Buddhist concept of something that just *is*. Does the water *mean* to catch the reflection of the moon? It just is. I think trying to impose reasons on it, or points, is too anthropomorphic and just a dream." Among the older cosmologists, Allan Sandage resists pointlessness, on grounds that he admits involve "belief": "Nihilism finally ends up in insanity, at least in Nietzsche's case in Basel. To avoid that, I'm quite willing to believe there is a purpose. But it *is* a belief. . . . I am not willing to be a Nietzsche nihilist, because I think that is much more pointless." And Fred Hoyle, a godfather of modern cosmology and no foe to far-out ideas (his book *The Intelligent Universe* asks us to believe that terrestrial life descends from myriads of microörganisms floating between the stars), comes up with an image borrowed from the late Richard Feynman, of "a child who watches two grandmasters. First, the child has to figure out how the pieces move. But it's a long step from there to understanding the game, and a still vaster step to being able to play a better game." It is hard to discuss order without slipping into teleology. The shadowy grandmasters playing the game are uncomfortable apparitions for most cosmologists. One of the appeals of the steady-state theory of the universe was its diffusion of the Creation issue: instead of the big bang's giant singularity it offered a minute if equally inexplicable dribble of new hydrogen atoms.

The interviewers' final two questions, awkward as they are for the bulk of the subjects, open onto the ancient religious concerns that make cosmology more fascinating to the layman than, say, bacterial biochemistry or algebraic topology. The heavens are traditionally the abode of God, and evidence of His existence must lie, if anywhere, in Creation. As Misner says, "The big bang is on everyone's lips. If you have a talk or a public lecture on the big bang universe, you will get crowds." Even among the predominantly atheistic physicists and astronomers whose cosmological views are here solicited, there is a powerful yen for the absolute, in the form of an elegantly simple theory. Many confess to believing that omega, the ratio of the observed average mass density in the universe to the critical mass density needed to halt, eventually, the universe's outward expansion, is exactly one, even though the best observational data yield an omega of merely 0.1. This is including the so-called "dark matter," whose presence is deduced from gravitational motions within the galaxies; an omega based upon the visible mass—the shining stars and galaxies—would be 0.01. Dark matter, which certainly exists (you're standing on some of it), should be distinguished from "missing mass," the wholly hypothetical nine-tenths of the universe that cosmologists need to make omega equal one. Peebles, asked to design his universe, says, "I would make omega close to unity, zero space curvature, and zero cosmological constant." "The beauty of omega equals 1 has been growing on me," Sandage claims, and for James Gunn, "If omega is not 1.0000, then something is screwed up." Misner says, "There is something very seriously wrong with our cosmology, and something is dramatically overlooked if that number is not 1 right now," and Page avows, "I do believe in inflation enough to have some prejudice toward thinking that omega is likely to be very close to 1."

"Inflation" refers to another pet notion of current cosmology—the theory that within its first second the mysteriously born big-bang universe, initially compressed to infinite smallness, achieved, under the pressure of a momentarily reversed gravitational force, and on top of its normal, sustained expansion, an exponential inflation from one-trillionth the size of a proton to the dimensions of a softball, or even, by some accounts, of a basketball. In about 1/100,000,000,000,000,000,000,000,-000,000,000 of a second, as Marcia Bartusiak's helpful *Thursday's Universe* expresses it, the infant cosmos doubled and redoubled in size a hundred times, a rate—to reach into the sports closet once more—that would expand a tennis ball to the size of the present observable universe. This "inflationary" hypothesis, developed from the formulas of particle physics and general relativity in a single, four-page burst of calculation (between 11 p.m., December 6, 1979, and one o'clock the next morning) by Alan Guth, then a young postdoctoral physicist at Stanford, has subsequently met considerable objection and undergone much modification, and, according to Stephen Hawking, "is now dead as a scientific theory." But it still intrigues cosmologists, because in one blow it eliminated a number of spooky puzzles about the big bang, such as: Why is the universe so flat? Why is it so smooth? And where did the monopoles go?

Flatness: an incredibly fine balance—less than a trillionth of one percent—between the force of the "bang" and the density of the "banged" primal matter must be posited for omega to be as close to unity as it is. Smoothness: the apparent homogeneity of the observed universe, and, especially, the almost perfect isotropy of the cosmic background microwave radiation—discovered in 1965 and believed to have originated when the universe was a mere million years old—seem to demand that areas of the expanding universe communicated with each other across impossible distances, from beyond the horizon set by the speed of light. And monopoles—heavy particles with a single magnetic pole—are predicted in abundance by the physics of the grand unified theories, and yet can't be found. Inflation explains these and other anomalies, and also has the metaphysical charm of greatly reducing the scale of creation: Guth has calculated that a mere twenty pounds of matter is needed to spark cosmic inflation and generate the 10^{87} particles in the universe. He has famously said, "Our universe is the ultimate free lunch." Cosmologists are as fond of a free lunch as the next, and a work like *The Creation*, by the British chemist P. W. Atkins, delves with considerable glee into the possible mechanics of something accidentally emerging from nothing. Further, if gravitational energy exactly equals the force of the expansion, we have a universe whose net energy is zero, which occasions a nihilist satisfaction in some scientific minds.

Meanwhile, we are stuck with the universe that does unaccountably exist, at the minimum ten billion years old and ten billion light-years in radius. In the many discussions of the inflationary hypothesis not one cosmologist seemed troubled by what seemed to me its most implausible aspect: its reduction of our huge observed universe to a mere fleck within a supposed inflated universe that now exists far beyond the reach of our telescopes. Far, *far*—the limits of the real universe, if Guth is right, are a hundred billion *billion* times as distant. My lay reaction to such an idea is outrage, that the already unthinkable vastness of what exists should be so trivialized. I am reminded of Jain cosmology, which measures time in long periods called *palyas*, and speaks of a hundred million times a hundred million of *palyas* as "an ocean of years," and goes on to speak of a hundred trillion oceans of years—crushing numbers conjured up in order to reduce the brain to selfless submission. A certain amount of vastness constitutes majesty; more than that seems insane. In Steven Weinberg's cosmological *The First Three Minutes*, a similarly gargantuan instance of excess is casually described. The billion-to-one preponderance of photons over baryons (nuclear particles) in the universe, Weinberg tells us, derives from a time when the balance was about equal, and the baryons were almost equally divided between particles and antiparticles, which destroyed each other. But there was one baryon in every billion that didn't have a matching antibaryon, and the great mutual annihilation left this "tiny excess of particles over antiparticles as a residue which would eventually turn into the world we know." The free lunch was catered for a billion more guests than stayed past the soup. Numbing numerical possibilities are the daily fare of cosmologists, cunningly made more palatable by the discreetness of exponential notation; e.g., 10^{87} particles in the universe, give or take a few. Only Roger Penrose, by discipline a mathematician, seems to share my repugnance: when told of the inflationary theory, he thought, "Gosh, that is a horrible idea," and of once-fashionable cosmic "strings" he admits, "Although studying these things is fun, I don't think I believe in them."

The interviews show a tug between the interviewers' tropism toward the big issues and the interviewees' insistence on empirical particulars. No scientist comes straight to cosmology; all arrive by way of particle physics, astrophysics, or even pure mathematics, like Penrose. Marc Davis and John Huchra are unusual among the younger cosmologists in having logged large amounts of telescope time, and in allowing that the actual facts that theory manipulates are rather scanty. Of cosmology Davis says simply, "The subject is data-starved." He was a student of Peebles, who told him, "What the world needs is good data. It doesn't need another crummy theory." Huchra, who by remeasuring thousands of galactic red-shifts came up with a faster rate of universal expansion than he had expected, and thus has significantly reduced the estimated age of the universe, says of the vexed issue of large-scale structure, "The data is in bad shape."

A good deal of journalistic attention has been given in recent years to the discovery of apparent structures—strings and "walls" of galaxies, immense voids, independent galactic motions toward a "Great Attractor"—

and one of the questions posed by Lightman and Brawer concerns them, in particular the announcement by Geller, Huchra, and Valerie de Lapparent of huge bubbles of vacuity many tens of millions of light-years in diameter. The consensus among the cosmologists of *Origins* seems to be that we need not yet abandon the lone-singularity big-bang creation of a roughly uniform universe. After all, irregularity is no surprise: it visibly exists in the stars and galaxies. On the other hand, the striking sameness of the 3°K cosmic background radiation in every direction can't be easily explained away. The universe is like an enormous sponge, and though the sponge has bigger holes in it than we thought, the time to throw it in has not arrived. James Gunn, another hands-on telescope astronomer, says, "The problem with the observations is, as always, that cosmological observations are always right at the hairy edge of the possible. Observers tend to overinterpret their observations. Theorists tend to overinterpret the observations even more." And he makes the point that, "as universities become poorer and poorer and observational astronomy gets centered at fewer and fewer higher- and higher-powered places, there's just not much way to educate people to do instrumental stuff."

The universe contains puzzles closer to hand than its creation. There is still no satisfactory theory of how our planet Earth came to have such a relatively large satellite as the moon, or why the sun rotates so much slower than it theoretically should. Edwin Turner, discussing the flatness problem, responds, "It seems curious but maybe it's just the way things are—like the sun and the moon being the same angular size in the sky, which they are incredibly precisely." This remarkable coincidence in apparent size of the two very different bodies that dominate our earthly sky might be taken as a kind of divine signature left mockingly for men to contemplate. Certainly the host of exquisitely tuned cosmic givens—from omega to the gravitational constant that keeps most stars steadily shining, from the fine-structure constant that governs atomic interactions to the strong-interactions constant that holds atomic nuclei together—have conspired to frame a universe stable and long-lasting enough to permit the evolution of intelligent life. This issue has given cosmology in recent years an unexpected anthropocentric turn. Of course, the congruence, on a vastly greater scale than the Bible envisions, of the big bang with the Judaeo-Christian Creation myth has already been noticed by the Pope and many lesser prelates. Perhaps coincidentally, the big-bang theory was first developed from Edwin Hubble's red-shift observations, by Georges Lemaître, a Belgian priest, and was enthusiastically promoted by Sir Arthur Eddington, a Quaker theist.

Modern physics was needed to make clear the remarkable tight-wire that the universe walks to render our small section of it hospitable to life. The planet is exceptional in its conditions, but its being one of a number removes it from the shadow of purposeful intention. We are here because we are here; Venus or Jupiter clearly wouldn't do. But a one-shot universe? Well, perhaps there are many, one line of speculation goes, proposing a branching of equally real universes at every fork of quantum indeterminacy—an exercise in multiplication to make even the Jains queasy. Another line of argument, the anthropic principle, attempts to make intellectual capital of the long-odds oddity by saying that certain properties of the universe depend upon the fact that without those properties we would not be here to observe them.

Follow that? *Origins* provides, in the interviewers' introduction and their glossary, thoroughly tepid definitions of the anthropic principle: "The weak form states that life can arise and exist only during a certain epoch of our universe. The strong form states that only for a special kind of universe could life arise at all, at any epoch." If that were all the anthropic principle said, it would hardly be worth enunciating. The principle's boldest proponent, John Archibald Wheeler, suggests that the universe needs us in order to exist. "Has the universe," he asks, "required the future observer to empower past genesis?" Invoking the indeterminacy principle, he points out that quantum mechanics is bound up with human observation. "The central feature of quantum mechanics tells us today with impressive force: In some strange sense, this is a participatory universe." The participation grows stranger, extended to the macrocosm: "No reason has ever offered itself," he contends, "why certain of the constants and initial conditions have the values they do, except that otherwise anything like observership as we know it would be impossible." Wheeler would include under observership a disembodied Geiger counter, but his thrust seems aimed at mankind: "Ask as we do now, if no universe at all could come into being unless it were guaranteed to produce life, consciousness, and observership somewhere and for some little length of time in its history-to-be?"

At some point in the participatory version of the anthropic principle, common sense leaves us; but, then, it leaves us in particle physics as well, with particles that are also waves and whose position and velocity cannot be simultaneously determined. What is clear from every interview in *Origins* is our undeniable fascination with the universe in its broadest construction and deepest rationale. With Gallic clarity, Gérard de Vaucouleurs asserts, "If the universe was created to produce mankind—and especially rational man and his modern civilization and everything that man has developed in the past ten thousand years (a split second on the time scale of the cosmos)—it's an incredibly inefficient mechanism." Nevertheless, we take joy in trying to understand this inefficient mechanism, as it churns away behind the plate glass of its inviolable distances, and it is a warming, if weird, supposition that, as Wheeler claims, "the observer is as essential to the creation of the universe as the universe is to the creation of the observer."

This book of interviewed observers lets us know, in its own inefficient manner, what the current cosmological trends and issues are. There is more talk about omega and isotropy and the missing dark matter than you might expect, and less of cosmic strings and plural universes. Marc Davis shares the news that, as far as astronomy goes, "the particle physics connection is dropping by the wayside. The particle theorists have their problems with grand unification and supersymmetry and superstrings. The astrophysicists are worried about the details of galaxy formation and whether the cold dark matter model works or not. They're not communicating as much as they were a few years ago." *Origins* has a glossary and bibliography but no index. Throughout, its prose is punctuated as if by people who are used to working with numbers. Most reprehensibly, its introduction seems to say that the Earth and the universe are practically the same age: "In astronomy, where the ages of things span a huge range, 4 billion years"—the age of the Earth as determined by radioactive dating of uranium—"is considered very close to 10 billion years." Well, for one thing, the age of the universe is still often given as fifteen billion years, and, for another, the earth consists of heavy elements that could only be created not in the big bang but in the dying convulsions of large stars and then dispersed in supernova explosions, as dust that gravity slowly reconcentrated. The sun is at least a second-generation star, and so its planets are *significantly* younger than the universe. Even in cosmology, billions should count for something.

Things, Things

THE EVOLUTION OF USEFUL THINGS, by Henry Petroski. 288 pp. Knopf, 1992.

Sometimes a title overreaches. *The Evolution of Useful Things* offers the reader many fascinating data about human artifacts but no theory comparable to Darwin's concerning the evolution of organic species. Darwin's theory, painstakingly illustrated with the likes of finch beaks and pigeon legs, orchids and quaggas, outlines a process whereby the prodigious variety and complexity of living organisms could have arisen without the guidance of a conscious Maker. The useful things whose evolution Petroski considers all had conscious makers, and the multiplicity of human purposes and intents overwhelms any sweeping rule of manufacture. Not that Petroski—a professor of civil engineering at Duke University, who in 1990 astounded the reading public with a 434-page opus on *The Pencil*—puts forth no theory. Repeatedly, he sets up the straw dictum "form follows function" and knocks it down: "What form does follow is the real and perceived failure of things as they are used to do what they are supposed to do." This attempt to give "perceived failure" something like the central position that "natural selection" occupies in Darwinism does not perfectly work. Confronted with the evolved oddity of many artifacts, such as the useless fins and bravura grilles of Fifties automobiles, Petroski must admit fashion into the formula, and this stretches his argument wide: "A myopic obsession with fashion, whether in silverware or steel bridges, can lead to the premature extinction of even the most fashionable form if it does not anticipate failure in the broadest sense, including the failure to be fashionable tomorrow." Well, everything, from *Tyrannosaurus rex* to bustles, eventually fails to be fashionable tomorrow.

The American architect Louis Henry Sullivan wrote that "Form ever follows function" in an essay, "The Tall Office Building Artistically Considered," in 1896, arguing against the clutter of his era's architectural eclecticism. In the context of a defense of skyscrapers, his "functionalism" proposed that a building should not attempt to conceal its purpose or the technology that made its construction possible. Until the arrival of steel girders, such concealment was scarcely possible; temples, cathedrals, and warehouses were stone inside and out. Then aesthetic conservatism created the falsity of steel-supported buildings that appear to be made of stone, and, on a lesser, everyday scale, of plywood houses clad in a layer of brick. Buildings have sociological and psychological functions beyond the baldly utilitarian: a contemporary church may intentionally evoke the Gothic style of the Age of Faith, complete with dummy buttresses, and a bank may echo, with gratuitous pillars, the trustworthy pomp and might of Rome. Even the suavely stark Seagram Building adorns its façade with vertical beams that evoke a sense of structure without being structurally essential. Technology has given modern builders an overkill of material resources, and the playful postmodernist architectural results have brought to urban centers, in the form of giant blue glass cutouts, the look of the cities we as children built of paper. The architecture of amusement parks is increasingly admired and paradigmatic.

Sullivan's formula is really a moral proposition: Form, in all aesthetic decency, *should* follow function—function and structure. But buildings, as more or less squarish lumps of shelter catering to human needs, cannot aspire to the naked mathematical beauty of bridges; one of their goals is the psychological comfort of their inhabitants. Artifacts in general are designed not just to accomplish human tasks but to make human beings feel good—at ease, luxurious, rejuvenated, chic. Women's clothing, to take an extreme case, puts a low premium on efficiency, unless attractiveness is taken as a kind of efficiency. The high heel has little to be said for it except that men seem to like it. To keep the package interesting, skirts go up and down, shoulders broaden and narrow. This is not to mention the defiant impracticalities of high fashion, where "buzz"—spectacle and publicity values—supersedes attractiveness. The actual technological advances in clothing (Velcro comes to mind) are few, yet consumer and producer both require the appearance of frequent change.

In arguing that the evolution of artifacts proceeds through inventors' perception of functional failure (or inadequacy, since total failures don't get to market), Petroski slights two factors: the importance of newness in itself as a desideratum, and the matter of the manufacturer's profit. Complex apparatuses are more expensive and hence more profitable than simple ones; merchandising is structured to discourage the purchase of a stripped-down, minimal model of anything, from an automobile to a toaster. More is, monetarily, more, even if the opportunities for malfunction increase with each new mechanical flourish. Manual typewriters are antiques, and soon electronic typewriters without built-in dictionaries will be also. Cheap computerization has enabled a whole new efflorescence of labor-saving gadgetry. The driver of a modern car need exert no more physical effort than a bather lying back in his bath; the engineering ingenuity that went into the automatic transmission is now bent on cars that steer themselves, with the driver not merely sleepy but asleep. Pushbutton mechanisms, in rendering our musculature obsolete, necessitate yet another line of products: exercise machines. In his last chapter, "Always Room for Improvement," Petroski cites a column by Russell Baker complaining, anent his office's new telephone system, "of the horrors created when engineers refuse to leave well enough alone." Petroski, like a loyal engineer, replies that he has slowly accommodated himself to the complexities of *his* office's new telephone system, and pronounces its improvements—musical and speedy push buttons, automatic call forwarding and redialing, voice mail—genuine. "The evolution of the overwhelming majority of artifacts, in both form and function, is fundamentally well intentioned and for the better."

It would take a dour reactionary indeed to deny that. If polyethylene wrapping often frustrates human fingers, and levered drain-plugs are leakier and more trouble than primitive rubber stoppers on a chain, and computerized catalogues in libraries appear to take more time and come up with fewer titles than old-fashioned card catalogues, these must be momentary kinks, to be soon ironed out. No less an authority than Thomas Edison stated, "Discontent is the first necessity of progress. Show me a thoroughly satisfied man—and I will show you a failure." If man were an artifact, no doubt he would have improved himself out of existence by now. Petroski's charming volume of artifactual meliorism ends with the glad news that certain alert inventors and manufacturers are at last producing a host of objects—garden shears, kitchen knives, corkscrews—designed for left-handed people, a minority who have been too long fumbling around in a world made for right-handers. So a new frontier of discontent is being plundered. "In the meantime, we tend to accept that ours is a technologically imperfect world and live with its minor annoyances."

For example, when we eat. In the chapter that deals with tableware, "Patterns of Proliferation," the evolution of useful things is shown to hold almost as many riddles as Darwinism. The millennia since early man hacked up raw meat with a flint proto-knife and poked it in the fire with the proto-fork of a pointed stick have evolved, in our era, a standard fish-knife whose form is, Petroski confesses, "highly specialized if mysterious." The fish fork's wider tines are justified by its greater efficacy in lifting crumbling fish pieces to the mouth; but the dull, broad, and offset fish-knife's advantage over the ordinary table-knife, either in cutting or deboning fish, seems doubtful. Like the crocodile and the horseshoe crab, the fish fork and knife have survived waves of extinction, as the Victorian plethora of tableware gradually thinned. Petroski quotes a certain Dorothy Rainwater, a specialist in silver:

> By 1898, the Towle Company's "Georgian" pattern included 131 different pieces. . . . There were nineteen types of spoons for conveying food to the mouth, seventeen for serving, ten pieces for serving and carving, six ladles, and twenty-seven pieces for serving that were not classified as ladles, forks, or spoons. One can sympathize with the hostess of that day in trying to be sure that croquettes were not served with a patty server, or cucumbers with a tomato server.

An illustration—from Noel D. Turner's *American Silver Flatware, 1837–1910*—of thirty-five forks includes six kinds of oyster fork and particular-pronged forks for terrapin, lettuce, ramekin, mango, and ice cream. Another illustration shows four types of sardine fork, five knives for jelly, and seven servers, scoops, and knives for coping with cheese. By the 1920s, Emily Post had to step into the melee and decree a four-fork, four-knife, four-spoon basic table setting. Originally, the knife, both pointed and broad, served to stick and lift the food as well as cut it; in recent centuries, the leftmost tine of some forks has hypertrophied so as to take on, for right-handers, a cutting function. For all this refinement and revision, eating continues to be a somewhat awkward operation, with a Continental and an American style of fork-handling co-existing, and the Asians remaining loyal to chopsticks (which, I have noticed, come in Chinese, Japanese, and Korean styles, the Korean being the most elaborate). Petroski concludes this chapter on an uncharacteristic note of discouragement: "Many of the most contemporary silverware patterns appear to be designed more for how the pieces look than for how they work, and this would appear to contradict every rational expectation of technological evolution."

If tableware shows populist commercialism at its most teeming and irrational, the zipper stands as a singular triumph of dogged engineering. Elias Howe, the inventor of the sewing machine, had patented as early as 1851 an "automatic continuous clothing closure," but the invention— unworkable, presumably—lay fallow. It was one Whitcomb Judson, four decades later, who took up the torch; his patents on a chain of clasps that would open and close continuously, and free mankind from the tyranny of button shoes and buttonhooks, began in 1893 and sorely stressed the financial resources of his primary backer, Colonel Lewis Walker. Judson's many versions of a "clasp locker," or "slide fastener," based on the hook-and-eye principle were bulky and tended to open inopportunely. It was a Swedish-born engineer, Otto Sundback, who, in 1913, working for a revamped company still fueled by Colonel Walker's money, arrived at the solution: a series of tiny spoon-shapes guided by a triangular slider to fit one into another. The patent followed in 1917, the name "zipper" in 1923 (invented by the president of the B. F. Goodrich Company, which was marketing the device on rubber galoshes), and the trade name "Talon" in 1937. Oddly, it was not until the Thirties that the supple fastener was taken up by clothing designers, led by Elsa Schiaparelli. "Her 1935 spring collection," we are told, "was described by *The New Yorker* as 'dripping with zippers.' " The zipper might possibly have gone forever uninvented; for Henry Petroski it makes a triumphant story of a perceived failure (the troublesomeness of button shoes) leading, through many intermediary failures of design, to an artifact now ubiquitous and seemingly indispensable.

So, too, in his telling, the wheelbarrow, the can opener, aluminum beer can, Scotch Tape, Post-it notes, the paper clip. In the last instance, the perceived failure was the tendency of pins, which are quaintly still used in some backwaters for holding small batches of paper together, to prick the fingers. The arrival of the familiar bent-wire clip, in the loop-within-a-loop Gem design, was, in the 1890s, quick but divagatious; we smile at the curious, wormy shapes that were patented en route. The Gem shape shows up in the patent records, in 1899, as incidental to the design of a wire-bending machine for making the clips. A century later, alternative designs and subtle refinements seek to remedy the clip's perceived failures—its tendency to tear the paper, to bulk up a stack of clipped sheets, to slip where the sheets are too many. The failures of two recent inventions in packaging, the polystyrene-foam "clamshell" box that Mc-Donald's perfected for its hamburgers, and the detachable beverage-can pull tab, came in the macro-realm of ecology; both clamshells and pull tabs amounted to too much non-degrading litter, and under civic pressure gave way, respectively, to revived paper packaging and to integral pop-top openers—humble marvels, these last, of metals engineering.

Petroski is an amiable and lucid though somewhat windy writer. Like a helpful lecturer, he makes the same point more than once. He does not always avoid tech-speak: "The formulation of the design problem is but a structured articulation of the objective of removing a shortcoming from an existing design." In another sentence, he puns possibly a millimeter to excess: "It seems in part to be a matter of familiarity's breeding content, at least when it comes to inanimate artifacts whose forms our hands have often grown to glove." And he can wax literary: "which will become the roads more traveled by will depend on style and conformity that designers, no less than poets—if only in retrospect—may lament." But perhaps he does belong with the poets, extending, in the manner of a celebrant as well as that of a naturalist, the Romantic embrace of nature to the invented, manufactured world which has become man's second nature.

Box Me, Daddy, Eight to the Bar Code

THE TOTAL PACKAGE, by Thomas Hine. 277 pp. Little, Brown, 1995.

Thomas Hine, author of the excellent *Populuxe* (1986), in his new book has bitten off more than anyone was ever meant to chew. Hine, the architecture-and-design critic for the *Philadelphia Inquirer*, brings us the history of packages and containers, from a five-thousand-year-old urn, found in western Iran and containing sediments of ancient beer, up to the 1990s' issues of nutrition-fact labelling and empties disposal. Along the way, scarcely a psycho-sociological stone is left unturned: the package's various roles as food preserver, shipping container, advertising placard, and hidden persuader are all explored, not without some doubling-back over already tramped ground. *Populuxe*, another prodigious marshalling of old advertisements and consumption statistics, focussed on the United States between 1954 and 1964 and poignantly illumined an era that most of the book's readers had rather unobservantly lived through. Hine coined a memorable word for a racy, splashy stylistic mood of cheap luxury mass-produced for a generation of hopeful *nouveaux riches*; his sympathetic grasp of, say, the social logic of the Tupperware party or the affinity between the potato chip's "free-form" shape and the "double-curving furniture of Charles Eames and Eero Saarinen" showed what a mischievously alert sensibility could make of vulgar forms usually kept outside the pale of serious consideration.

Much of the aerodynamic blare of *Populuxe* was called into being by the new mobility and impersonality of American life; if *The Total Package* has a dominant theme, it is the package as a substitute person in a world where the farmer, the butcher, the grocer, and even the salesclerk have been relegated to the back shelves. The package inspires trust, with its sealed and unvarying product, as "ties of family and community" fray. Hine asserts that the Romans had at least one brand-name product, the Fortis oil-burning lamp, and extols the medieval reliquary and synagogue ark as symbolically potent containers, but dates modern packaging from the seventeenth-century emergence of English patent medicines—Stoughton's Drops, Singleton's eye ointment, Turlington's Original Balsam, each brand offered in its own eye-catching shape of bottle. The names on these nostrums and the wealth of promises on their thickly printed labels aped the personal attentions of a medical practitioner. In this country, Indians, Shakers, and Quakers were associated with herbal remedies, and the first great triumph of mass-marketing in a paper box, Henry Parson Crowell's Quaker Oats, continues to sell, more than a century after its introduction, with the Quaker on the box a shade jollier but essentially unchanged. Aunt Jemima pancake mix dates from the 1890s, and she anachronistically survives from an era when, as Hine writes, "racist images, and others that reflected ethnic stereotypes, provided products with personalities that were apparently unthreatening. They were a kind of servant just about anyone could afford."

Package design, striving for a continuous relation with the consumer, tends to be conservative: Wrigley's spearmint gum, Campbell's soup, and the Hershey bar have only slightly modified, over the years, the bold and simple designs hit upon by their first promoters. Coca-Cola, though driven by economic considerations to cans, seeks to maintain, through reminiscent elements in its logo, a ghostly connection with its iconic bottle. Millions of dollars ride on nuances of design. Hine recounts the saga of two new mouthwashes introduced in the 1960s. Johnson & Johnson came out with a blue fluid called Micrin, in a plastic bottle that evoked an old-fashioned medical jar. It quickly faded, because, according to Hine, "It conveyed the message that bad breath is a medical problem that must be banished in a medicinal way. It was a variation of the Listerine approach . . . but without the weight of tradition behind it." At the same time, Procter & Gamble succeeded with Scope, a green fluid in a flattened conical bottle. Hine explains, "Its color and its almost playful shape suggested that bad breath is part of life, and Scope helps." Yet Listerine continues to sell in a plastic version of its waisted, solemnly therapeutic bottle. Hine's take on modern designers is rather negative: many packages that photograph beautifully and win prizes don't move the product off the shelves; the most creative containers hold "characterless" and hard-to-distinguish products like water, vodka, and skin cream; and "while as recently as thirty years ago many products were in the hands of strong-willed entrepreneurs who viewed packaging as an expression of themselves, today nearly all are in the hands of managers driven by fear of a career-ending mistake." Zealous surveys and gurus of psychological marketing like Stan Gross assiduously cater to the psyches of imagined consumers, whereas the early entrepreneurs, awash in ego strength, put their own faces, or images of their factories, on their labels, and lettered them with whatever typefaces the local printer had lying about in his sorts trays.

When Hine discusses specific packages and technological advances— the paper bag, the shopping cart, cellophane—he is interesting; when he generalizes, a certain mind-numbing think-tank-speak bloats the obvious:

> Seemingly nondesign issues having to do with materials, permeability, protection, expected shelf life, and even the expected cleanliness standards of the retail environment end up having a very strong influence over how the products look. The type of container chosen and the technology used to fill it have an obvious impact on costs, which require that detailed budgeting be a prerequisite for package design.

And the application of hi-crit lingo to our humble friends the packages takes some getting used to:

Thus, the shopper can choose between Tide, whose package was designed to signal that it was powerful yet mild, and Cheer, whose image is mild, yet powerful.

The use of the large-scale element on the very small package [of Wrigley's spearmint gum] gives it a sense of pent-up energy, which is enhanced by the directionality and dynamism of the arrow itself.

The illustrations are rather meagre, confined to three bound-in sheaves, only one of them in color. *Populuxe* was a much more opulent and graphically lively book, as well as less thematically diffuse. Explaining the years 1954–64 to readers in 1986 was a nervier, more spirited enterprise than surveying packaging in its sprawling totality. (Not that Hine says everything worth saying: he writes much about the visual appeal of packages but says little of their tactile come-on—the inviting fleshly feel, for instance, of such successful packages as the old cellophane-wrapped paper cigarette pack and the matte plastic squeeze bottle—and he ignores the large role that emptied packages, such as orange crates, cigar boxes, and pipe-tobacco tins, once had in the play-lives of American children.)

Packages, according to Hine, want to be our friends and by and large succeed. They have dramatically reduced the amount of time spent in food preparation, and the cost of food relative to income of an urban family. They even, surprisingly, abet conservation: "Capital-intensive American farming gets more than twice as much food per unit of fossil fuels than does labor-intensive China, largely because of packaging that keeps food from spoiling on the way to the consumer." On the hot issue of package disposal he is as melioristic as an Alcoa commercial. Cans and plastic containers are getting thinner all the time, and even now take up less landfill space than anybody thinks—less than demolition and construction debris, for instance. We do learn, however, that Staten Island's mountainous, New York City–fed Fresh Kills landfill is "the second-largest human-made structure in the world, surpassed only by the Great Wall of China."

Are packages undermining our humanity? Hine concludes by recounting how his ill mother rejected his homemade recipe for pot roast in favor of ready-mixed products, and decides that his "mother's devotion to packaged products was . . . ultimately . . . a gift. It gave me permission to leave. . . . It let us both be independent." Along the same lines, self-service supermarkets remove the "demanding" "personal interaction" of customer and salesclerk, which "requires a kind of emotional intensity that most people would rather not lavish on a trivial purchase." Further along the same lines, James Kaplan, puzzling in a recent *New York* magazine over why his generation is less adulterous than his parents', came to the arresting conclusion that, raised on television and able to rent videos at will, he and his peers are so fully entertained that it is just too much effort to get to know their neighbors well enough to sleep with them. The safe, packaged experience of videos has rendered the sexual demon obsolete. Next thing, babies will come bubble-wrapped.

The Flamingo-Pink Decade

As SEEN ON TV: *The Visual Culture of Everyday Life*, by Karal Ann Marling. 322 pp. Harvard University Press, 1994.

To over half the people now alive in the United States, the 1950s are sheer history. The decade, long snubbed as drab, conformist, and conservative, has acquired a mythic aura—the last happy time, a Cockaigne of prosperity and consensus when families still resembled those in the Dick and Jane primers and the infrastructure was building up instead of breaking down. Ike's dowdy decade has become exotic: David Halberstam has recently performed one of his heroic research treks into the mountains of its lost Shangri-la; Magnum Photos issued in 1985 a superb album of Fifties photographs; and Thomas Hine, carving the decade on the bias, from 1954 to 1964, wrote in his 1986 *Populuxe* a basic text on the era's cultural lineaments.

Karal Ann Marling, a professor of art history and American studies at the University of Minnesota, offers in seven chapters some witty riffs on Fifties themes: the topics evoked are, in order, women's fashion, amateur painting, the arrival of Disneyland, those fabulous finned autos, the taming of Elvis Presley, home cooking, and Nixon's "kitchen debate" with Nikita Khrushchev. Several of the chapters were previously published as separate articles, and the separateness still shows. The parts seem a bit more than their sum, which is the thesis that, as the prologue puts it, "Life in the 1950s imitated art—as seen on TV." The thesis comes round in the end, in the form of the sentence "As seen on TV, everything suddenly looked new to the 1950s." But it was the movies, not the little sputtering black-and-white tube, that had furnished forth the dreams of the Populuxe consumers; the bulbous, two-toned autos, and colorful, opened-up kitchens, and hyperfeminine New Look silhouettes aspire to Hollywood glamour and grandeur. The Fifties, in Marling's reading, were crazy for color—pink, above all—and television generally remained black-and-white until well into the Sixties.

To quibble thus, however, is perhaps to take too literally an intellectual romp, a dizzying free fall through the exuberant "visual culture" of that first post–World War II decade. For a reader who remembers the New Look only as a sudden puzzling abundance of leg-concealing skirts in the high-school hallways, it was elucidatory to encounter Christian Dior's own explication: "We were leaving a period of war, of uniforms, of soldier-women with shoulders like boxers. I turned them into flowers, with soft shoulders, blooming bosoms, waists slim as vine stems, and skirts opening up like blossoms." Even the abundance of cloth in the skirts was a statement: wartime shortages were over, along with the wartime understatement of sexual differences.

Marling's chapter on fashion reminds us that, before the advent of Jackie Kennedy, and in the wake of Bess Truman, Mamie Eisenhower seemed a fashion plate: "She liked fitted bodices, sweetheart necklines, and flirty skirts that swished when she walked—an ultra-feminine version of Dior filtered through Hollywood—and wore them for the next decade, when a grandmother of more sedate disposition might have settled into Mother Hubbards." The New Look's successor, the widely deplored sack dress, was, it turns out, an early salvo from the rising youth culture, since only young women could be confident enough of their figures to wear dresses that concealed them. Whatever the line from Paris, "in America's vibrant new consumer culture, luxuries once reserved for the rich were within reach of everybody."

Conspicuous consumption for the middle class: that is what the Fifties offered American citizens, and what America held out for the world to envy. To the Communists, the diversion of so much national wealth from essential industry and armaments appeared absurd. "I see no plan in all this," a Russian said of the welter of consumer goods displayed at an American exhibition in Moscow in 1959. "Your whole emphasis is on color, shape, comfort." Khrushchev was seething when he walked through the RCA Whirlpool "miracle" kitchen: "This is not a rational approach. These are gadgets we will never adopt." Nixon, in riposte, argued for choice; in Marling's elegant paraphrase of his improvised remarks, "The housewife's choice of a new appliance—pink, square, nonsensical, irrational: whatever—was a choice nonetheless and the habit of making them was a good working definition of the American way of life."

Not all Fifties developments were in the direction of luxury or a "disordered, unsorted, uncensored profusion of style." Servants were one luxury in ever shorter supply, and the Fifties saw an upsurge of do-it-yourself equipment and expertise—indeed, the new, pleasanter, mechanized kitchen was all about doing it yourself—and of hobbies to absorb the new leisure time. From the painting-by-numbers craze it is a short hop for Marling into the therapeutic amateur painting of Ike and Churchill. Churchill's popular small book *Painting as a Pastime*, she tells us, "exhorted inhibited amateurs to splash about in the turpentine and wallop the colors down in 'large fierce strokes.' " Large fierce strokes are just what the Abstract Expressionists dealt in, and Marling claims that Churchill's prescription fits "the drip-and-dribble methods shown in photographs of Jackson Pollock that enjoyed wide circulation in the early 50s." Making a connection between the lowest-brow hobby and the most avant-garde art is among the more provocative of Marling's own strokes; she finds, too, in the boxy new office towers of the Fifties and "the repetitious gesturalism of Action Painting" a rather emotionless formality which fitted the mood of corporate America and the "trappings of the outer-directed executive." The bulk of the violent, moody action painters (not to mention the turbulent and sardonic poets of the era) would be surprised, though, at her flat summation "Art affirmed the way things were in the 1950s." She might have done more with the lively interplay between late modernism and popular design—the similarity, for instance, between a Calder mobile and a spindly-legged boomerang-shaped coffee table.

Any attempt to characterize something as multifarious as a decade will run into contradictions. Marling reads the Fifties as both individualistic and conformist, both inventively do-it-yourself and submissively formal. The notorious Fifties cars were sleek in silhouette and yet bristling with aggressive chrome "gorp" in front; they mimicked women's bodies for macho drivers and yet, as the ads of the time dramatize, were also an empowerment, with their power steering and touch controls, of the little lady of the household. The rich automotive paradoxes shift Marling's prose sometimes into too high a gear—"The car was the new Conestoga wagon on the frontier of consumerism, a powerful instrument of change, a chariot of fiery desire"—and engage her diagnostic skills: "The conflicting desires for bulk and for speed gave the automobile an increasingly neurotic flavor as the decade wore on." Conflicting desires were rife in this Red-fearing, fun-loving decade. There was nostalgia for the countrified landscape America was at last leaving behind. This was the heyday of Grandma Moses as well as Jackson Pollock, and both were among the exports with which we confounded Socialist Realism. Walt Disney, ever out on the longest limb of popular taste, in Disneyland commercialized his personal nostalgia with scale-model Main Streets and railroad trains; he got America to pay admission to its own past, turned into a spectator's playground. Disneyland, Marling points out, had the "spatial sensibility" of television—episodic, discontinuous, and (in that the cartoon creatures came out into three dimensions and acted as guides) somewhat inter-active. The interactivity between Disney's amusement park, his television show *Disneyland*, and his forthcoming movies was shamelessly, profitably exploited, and created the Disney empire as we know it.

Television reshaped the American home, turning its interior architec-ture fluid and casualizing meals. It also killed the front porch, as an inter-section of community and family. I am not sure it reshaped the American head quite so pervasively and swiftly as Marling suggests. Myself, though I did buy a Ford Fairlane with modest tail fins in 1955, I didn't own a television set until 1958, and then used it mostly for quiz shows and the *Patti Page Show*, like a glorified radio. Television as it existed in the Fifties was not a visual delight; it was stark and fuzzy. (So are the black-and-white illustrations in this book, which boasts the most garish and jumbled jacket I have ever seen on a volume issued by a university press.) What does seem clear about the decade, after Professor Marling has refreshed our memories of its gaudier facets, is that Americans, having emerged triumphant from two national traumas, were fed up with doing without. In the smaller, more independent family units that the new prosperity permitted, they set about exploring the possibilities of mate-rial happiness and self-gratification.

The Liberation of the Legs

Sex and Suits, by Anne Hollander. 212 pp. Knopf, 1994.

Anne Hollander, in her entrancing, vivacious, and willful book of "speculations" (her term), has a story to tell. Once upon a time, some-where near the beginning of the nineteenth century, men's suits attained their present, classic form, and it took women's clothes well over a cen-tury—until the 1920s—to catch up and arrive at feminine outfits equally "serious." In the long interlude of the seriousness gap, "fashion" became a primarily female concern: "With the arrival of collective certainty that powerful men must dress soberly and similarly, and that women's clothes must carry all the burden of deliberate personal fantasy, fashion in dress became 'Fashion,' one of the huge new industries aimed specifically at female consumers." Hollander takes pains to detach her thesis from mili-tantly, or even indignantly, feminist implications; her approach to fashion is Freudian and fatalistic rather than Marxist and judgmental. "The shifty character of what looks right is not new," she writes, "and was never a thing deliberately created to impose male will on females, or capitalist will on the population, or designers' will on public taste." Yet fashion— a constant change in the way people dress—is a creation, she states, specific to Christendom, to the European West in its last seven hundred years:

> Long before the days of industrialized fashion, stylistic motion in Western dress was enjoying a profound emotional importance, giving a dynamically poetic visual cast to people's lives, and making Western fashion hugely compelling all over the world. . . . Fashion has its own manifest virtue, not unconnected with the virtues of individual freedom and uncensored imagination that still underlie democratic ideals.

Sex and Suits has the narrative drive, and sometimes the stylistic flightiness, of a polemic, yet the only cause Hollander champions is that of the lone individual, in his or her tender need to dress in accord with the obscure and conflicted promptings of human psychology.

First, why is the tailored male suit, the very symbol of dull if not sinister conformity, such an enduring triumph? Because, Hollander answers, it reshaped the male body to conform with the male nude of classic Greek sculpture; a romantically photographed Greek statue adorns her dust jacket. Artists of antiquity and the early Middle Ages showed men and women interchangeably draped and gowned; the male and female figures in the sixth-century mosaic lineup at Ravenna can scarcely be distinguished. By the late Middle Ages, men were clad in cloth units—tights, close-fitting doublet, padded short coat, fitted and padded sleeves, and codpiece—that imitated armor "in forming stiff abstract shapes around the body, finally culminating in the starched ruff at the neck, a kind of armor-like abstraction of the shirt collar." Women wore small stiff bodices and voluminous skirts; the all-concealing skirt remained a constant until this century, though fashion was permitted to experiment with amounts of décolletage. Hollander's description of a woman thus swaddled is unexpectedly thrilling:

> Her pelvis and legs were always a mystery, her feet a sometime thing, and her bosom a constantly changing theatrical presentation of some kind. Needless to say, her exposed hands were always dramatic costume elements, exciting bare episodes in a sea of fabric.

Men were allowed to have legs, but through much of the eighteenth century low-waisted, full-bottomed, abruptly narrowed breeches and long, collarless, button-heavy, open coats "tended to emphasize a man's hips, belly, and thighs, shrink his chest and shoulders, lengthen his torso and shorten his legs." A gentleman presented a pear-shaped figure garbed in unyielding, wrinkle-prone, light-catching, much-embellished silk.

The revolution in male dress needed not only the utilization of a softer, more flexible fabric, wool, and a guild of skilled tailors able to shape the wool with padding and darts and curved seams, but the arrival of a new body ideal, which came with the neoclassic revival: the antique male nude, its "muscular chest and shoulders, lean flanks, long legs," its overall look of clearly delineated parts harmoniously combined. The ideal male shape shifted from the reposeful pear to the forceful wedge, and tailors worked to achieve an effect of loosely armored nudity—"the real truth of natural anatomy, the Platonic form." The curved collar and the flat-lying lapel were engineered and became "the formal sign of modernity in dress"; the hitherto rather messy linen shirt and cravat were laundered and starched and "folded with a sculptor's care around the neck and jaw, to produce a commanding set of the head on the heroic shoulders." Hollander's raptures should lift the hearts of all those con- demned to lives spent in suit-filled boardrooms and commuter trains:

> Thus the male figure was recut and the ideal man recast. Formerly the play of light on rich and glinting textures had seemed to endow the gentle- man with the play of aristocratic sensibility, and made him an appropriate vessel for exquisite courtesy, schooled wit and refined arrogance without having to reveal the true fiber and caliber of his individual soul any more than that of his body. Now the noble proportions of his manly form, created only by the rigorous use of natural materials, seemed to give him an indi- vidual moral strength founded on natural virtue, an integrity that flowers in esthetic purity without artifice, and made him a proper vessel for forthright modern opinion and natural candid feeling.

Or, more practically speaking, "The separate elements of the costume overlap, rather than attaching to each other, so that great physical mobility is possible without creating awkward gaps in the composition. The whole costume may thus settle itself naturally when the body stops moving, so that its own poise is effortlessly resumed after a swift dash or sudden struggle."

Meanwhile, back on the distaff side, women were being ever more emphatically cut in two. As the nineteenth century progressed, the top halves of women could be daringly exposed, to the entire shoulders and arms, while their lower halves were kept under bustled, hoop-skirted wraps. There was an ambivalence toward women that made of each a mermaid, a "perniciously divided female monster." The upper half, with its face and voice and arms and breasts, suggests a mother's benign love and offers "both keen pleasure and a sort of illusion of sweet safety; but it is a trap. Below, under the foam, the swirling waves of lovely skirt, her hidden body repels, its shapeliness armed in scaly refusal, its oceanic interior stinking of uncleanness." Although equestriennes and George Sand and Amelia Bloomer might don approximations of male trousers, cross-dressing did not solve the problem, which was "to look both sexually interesting and ordinarily serious . . . at the same time, the way men did."

Hollander doesn't make too much of the moment, in 1858, when a man—Charles Frederick Worth, an English dry-goods merchant transplanted to Paris—became the first professional male designer of female clothes, hitherto the domain of female dressmakers and milliners and milady herself. The rise of male couturiers, in the period of grand courtesans and of female heroines fashioned by Tolstoy, Hardy, and Henry James, introduced a more tailored, less merely decorative accent into female fashion, and quickened feminine suspicions that they were being sold a bill of goods—"helping to fictionalize themselves" along the lines of masculine sexual fantasy. Cries for "rational" and "sensible" ways for women to dress were sounded by vigorous reformers, but, Hollander disarmingly avers, "Reform on the basis of good sense was, of course, an ill-conceived and losing battle."

The male suit was successful not because it was sexless and unattractive but because it so powerfully and subtly projected "an invincible physical aplomb, including sexual." Its cunning unity and ease were slowly approached. Between 1900 and 1912, women's clothes, "which had been taking up more room than men's ever since the 1700's," shrank to an equal size. The corset, which by cruelly pinching the waist had enforced the division of a woman into two non-communicating portions, gradually loosened. Tailored suits in "formerly 'masculine' fabrics" appeared, "skimmed the unified figure from neck to instep," and "cleared the ground to expose the feet at work." The liberation of female legs into visibility was critical, and epochal: "To show that women have ordinary working legs, just like men . . . was also to show that they have ordinary working muscles and tendons, as well as spleens and livers, lungs and stomachs, and, by extension, brains." All these changes of fashion had to wait upon the implicit concession that women were vital and active much as men are: "Mobility and palpability, replacing stasis and inviolability, became the desirable attributes of the clothed female body, not just of its garments or of its secret nude state. . . . Like her male counterpart, she, too, could now suggest the self-possessed animal happy in its skin."

Though Anne Hollander's story has a happy ending, it does not drive home a moral. Indeed, one of her charming qualities, as she explores fashion, is her love for all of it, even that which is no longer fashionable. Having worked her way up to the casting-off of tight corsets and long petticoats, she devotes some pages to the proposition that these things weren't as uncomfortable as you might think and had given their wearers satisfaction for centuries—"the sense of completeness that acceptable clothing always gives, which is its true comfort." Having devastatingly deconstructed the image of the full-skirted mermaid-woman, she allows that "the theme of nearly nude top and very shrouded bottom remains compelling in the present world, and it seems suitable for moments when the historical and romantic view of women has license to prevail—at the ball or the wedding, and often on the stage or screen." Nothing in fashion shocks her, not even the grungiest contemporary fads, or strikes her as ruinously subversive. All fashion is subversive, scoring its effects off preceding fashions, which become tired: "Love for a particular form is engendered by the slackening of keen desire for an earlier form, a sort of esthetic lassitude that is often unconscious, and becomes conscious only when a new form is offered." Democratic energy comes from underneath. The suit itself rose to propriety out of the so-called English "lounge suit," donned by gentlemen at country leisure and by laborers for dressy occasions; just so, blue jeans, originally produced for American ranchers and farmers, have spread to the jet set. "What looks right" is multi-determined and includes what *feels* right: women designers, reclaiming part of haute couture in the Twenties and Thirties, sought "to express a subjective, tactile delight in the wearing of the clothes, rather than echoing the standard masculine wish to stun the beholder with a vision." Two of the dresses—one worn by Clara Bow in 1928, the other by a *Vogue* model in 1938—with which Hollander illustrates the triumph of "classic purity" and "the single modern shape" are slinky to a fault, so that Bow's "own physical awareness of the dress against her skin is expressed by her sinuous pose and self-conscious gaze."

Dressing ourselves is a daily intimacy and preparation for public performance; we wish both to display ourselves and to conceal ourselves in some kind of consensual uniform. "Fashion confirms the deep importance of all appearance," Hollander writes, in an epigrammatic mood of conclusion. "Like it or not, we all have looks, and we are responsible for them." Yet our decisions, as we dress, are often inscrutably private: "The famous message of dress, the well-known language of clothes, is often not doing any communicating at all; a good deal of it is a form of private muttering." Irrationality seductively lies at the heart of fashion: "The desire to summon explanations only shows that we know how irrational it makes us all seem."

Sex and Suits itself has a dreamlike autonomy. Its illustrative plates are exquisite but few, like signposts on a knight-errant's journey. Though it includes three pages of bibliography, not one footnote or direct quotation of another author mars its discursive flow. One does not miss, in this dazzling, whirlwind account of Western costume, a determined sociology that would deal in such possibilities as the effect of domestic central heating upon the long-deferred hike in women's hems. Such material speculations get us somewhere but not far enough, and grant things a tyranny over us that they have not earned. Hollander with great cheerfulness and delicacy of perception embraces the chaos of individual determinations present in any human art. In dressing, she writes, "everyone is essentially talking to himself, like a poet." Every fashion "embodies a complicated secret wish."

She's Got Personality

SEX, ART, AND AMERICAN CULTURE, by Camille Paglia. 335 pp. Vintage, 1992.

Camille Paglia's collection might have been more accurately, if less grandly, titled, *Bits and Pieces Spun Off by a Cultural Celebrity Newly in Orbit*. The book, a paperback original, has Paglia confronting us on the cover—her face a provocative mix of stern teacher and Piafesque gamine—and her introduction thanks two people: her editor and her publicist. Why does a professor of humanities need a publicist? She has fallen prey, a confessional appendix explains, to "sudden notoriety" and must undertake, to quote the introduction, "media sallies and jousts." The introduction tells us, "The pieces in this volume, with one exception, were written during the last two years. Most of them were concentrated in the year following the appearance of my controversial op-ed article on Madonna in the New York *Times* in December 1990." Besides that attention-getter, the volume contains appreciations of Elizabeth Taylor, rock music, and male homosexuals; a number of book reviews, including her lengthy diatribe "Junk Bonds and Corporate Raiders," aimed not at Wall Street but at the shabby, feminist-tinged, French-influenced machinations within academia; a slightly doctored transcript of a freewheeling lecture she gave at MIT called "Crisis in the American Universities"; a set of lecture notes that, in her persona of dutiful student, she took during a course, "East and West," which she taught with a colleague, Lily Yeh; an appreciation of Milton Kessler, a teacher of hers when she was an undergraduate at Harpur College, in Binghamton, New York; a brief (but not too brief) account of how she rose, in 1990, from obscurity to fame; a small array of cartoons and caricatures touching on Camille Paglia; and an eleven-page list of reviews and articles on the same terrific topic, in languages including Italian, German, Chinese, Japanese, and Russian and with titles like "Woman Warrior," "Hurricane Camille," and "Catwoman of Academia." It is lovely to see an intellectual so unabashedly bask in public attention. Reading the coverage of her MIT lecture the next day in the *Boston Globe*, Paglia "felt like Faye Dunaway lounging in her mules and white satin negligée, her brand-new Oscar for *Network* glittering among the newspapers on her poolside glass table at dawn." Not exactly the hard gemlike glitter of Walter Pater (one of her admirations), but shimmering dreams of glory nevertheless, come true in this land, still, of opportunity.

She presents herself as a daughter of Italian-Americans and a spiritual child of the Sixties, fed up with the whining feminism of spoiled upper-middle-class princesses and with the vapid academic chic of the wicked French trio Lacan, Foucault, and Derrida. She embraces post-Fifties popular culture—rock music and films above all—as an outburst of the Dionysian strain long repressed in the West. She is a lusty, feisty, bisexual scholar swooping into prominence from an outsider's perch at the University of the Arts in Philadelphia. "Junk Bonds and Corporate Raiders," once it disposes of the two weak-kneed collections of essays on sexuality that are its ostensible occasion, takes on a comic-strip vitality as the superheroine in her Sixties Frye boots and hot pants clobbers one villain after another; you can almost see the capitalized concussion sounds in their little spiky balloons. POW! "American feminism's nose dive began when Kate Millett, that imploding beanbag of poisonous self-pity, declared Freud a sexist." BIFF! "Lacan: the French fog machine; a gray-flannel worry-bone for toothless academic pups; a twerpy, cape-twirling Dracula dragging his flocking stooges to the crypt." ZAP! "That damp sob sister, Hélène Cixous, with her diarrhea prose, or Luce Irigaray, the pompous lap dog of Parisian café despots doing her grim, sledgehammer elephant walk through small points." WHAMMO! "Heilbrun's late self-packaging as a feminist is a triumph of American commerce. The gauzy, ethnicity-evading style of her dazzlingly research-free books is the height of wishful, reactionary gentility. Women's studies is a jumble of vulgarians, bunglers, whiners, French faddicts, apparatchiks, doughface party-liners, pie-in-the-sky utopianists, and bullying, sanctimonious sermonizers." Take to the hills, evildoers; No-Nonsensewoman is here, with her trusty sidekicks Elvis Presley ("one of the most influential men of the century"), Jimi Hendrix ("We didn't need Derrida: we had Jimi Hendrix"), and Keith Richards ("My idol . . . who made menacing music out of the Dionysian darkness never seen by society-obsessed Foucault").

The trouble with the French, if you must know, is that their Sixties fizzled:

> The Sixties revolution in America . . . followed and fulfilled its own inner historical pattern, a fall from Romanticism into Decadence. In France, in contrast, the brief student and worker revolt was put down by government action, an external force. Armchair French leftists like Foucault went into a permanent sulk. They never saw the errors of their ideas because those ideas, through lack of French moxie, were never tested against reality by being put through their full organic cycle. Hence the utter madness of French leftist pretensions being flaunted by milquetoast academics in America, which as a nation had made an epic journey to the heart of darkness and returned with tragic truths.

Paglia is a great loyalist to what she possessively calls "my Sixties generation," and also to her ethnic and religious antagonisms. The "milquetoast academics" have used the French frauds to perpetuate "the genteel high Protestant style of the country clubs and corporate boardrooms" and to foment "a continuation not of Sixties leftism but of Fifties prep schools, with their snide, slick style, a cool, insufferably pretentious, nasal voice you can hear everywhere on Ivy League campuses." If her own tone isn't exactly mellifluous, so what? "The Italian philosophy of life espouses high-energy confrontation," she asserts in "Rape and Modern Sex War."* In an essay on Robert Mapplethorpe's photographs and their "in-your-face content" she states, "Identity thrives by conflict and opposition." Sadomasochism is not merely a fact of life; "it is our deepest nature." Paglia told Sonya Friedman in an interview on CNN, "I feel that sex is basically combat. I feel that the sexes are at war." When Friedman, according to the transcript, exclaimed, "Oh, my goodness," her dauntless interviewee added, "I do feel it. It's like going to Atlantic City and gambling, okay? Every date is a gamble. Now, when you lose, you cannot go running to Mommy and Daddy. Sometimes you win, and sometimes you lose. I am a sexual adventuress."

---

*This will be news to Perry Como, Dean Martin, and those military experts who agree with General Léon de Lamoricière when he announced, in 1860, *"Les Italiens ne se battent pas."* After saying this, de Lamoricière, fighting the Italians on behalf of the Papal Domains, was beaten in battle, as it turned out. See *The Italians*, by Luigi Barzini, for the whole tricky situation.

Feminist views on rape and date rape represent "this stupid, pathetic, completely-removed-from-reality view of things that [Ivy League college women] have gotten from these academics who are totally off the wall, totally removed. Whereas my views on sex are coming from the fact that I am a football fan and I am a rock fan." Thus she spoke to Celia Farber, of *SPIN*; another interviewer she advised, "I mean, wake up to reality. This is male sex. Guess what, it's hot." And, *SPIN* again, "Feminists have no idea that some women like to flirt with danger because there is a sizzle in it." Risk comes with freedom, as the Sixties, unlike the repressed Fifties and crybaby Eighties, understood: "My Sixties attitude is, yes, go for it, take the risk, take the challenge—if you get raped, if you get beat up in a dark alley in a street, it's okay. . . . Go with it. Pick yourself up, dust yourself off, and go on. We cannot regulate male sexuality. The uncontrollable aspect of male sexuality is part of what makes sex interesting."

Paglia is a reassuring author for a man to read. She is as loyal to the male gender as an Italian matriarch is to her father, husband, and son, even if all are involved in the Mafia. She sees men as incorrigible, sizzle-producing brutes whom white, middle-class feminists are trying to castrate, "to make eunuchs out of them." The snag with Sensitive New Age Guys is that they can't, biologically, exist. The recent embarrassments of Woody Allen gave Paglia a new chance to expatiate on "the lugubriousness of typical feminist views." She told a reporter, "They keep trying to redefine the American male into this eunuchized, castrated, supportive male. But that's not the answer. Woody's nerdlike, nonthreatening intellectual persona was just as sexual a persona, and now women can't stand that it was *only* a persona. This is a wonderful cold douche for feminist naïveté." Why, some feminists are so naïve, Paglia has written, that they fail to see "what is for men the eroticism or fun element in rape, especially the wild, infectious delirium of gang rape." You can't blame the guys, really. "Men must struggle for identity against the overwhelming power of their mothers. Women have menstruation to tell them they are women. Men must do or risk something to be men." So, be warned, ladies of the post-menarche: "Masculinity is aggressive, unstable, combustible. It is also the most creative cultural force in history."

Paglia's opinions are gruff and deliberately sensational but not unreal. The roots of sexual attraction and excitement *do* go deeper than our codes of civilized behavior. There *is* a tragic grandeur to the gulf between the sexes. The first chapter of Paglia's magnum opus, *Sexual Personae*, setting forth her cosmology under the title of "Sex and Violence, or Nature and Art," is, simply, magnificent—dense with stark truths and sweeping insights. We seem embarked, in a Nietzschean gale, upon one of those thrilling overviews of Western culture, such as André Malraux's *Voices of Silence* or Erich Auerbach's *Mimesis*, that leave us with a map in our heads. By the end, it feels less a survey than a curiously ornate harangue. Her percussive style—one short declarative sentence after another—eventually wearies the reader; her diction functions not so much to elicit the secrets of books as to hammer them into submission.

Stretched on the rack of her taut opposition of female/Dionysian/chthonian versus male/Apollonian/skyey, one author after another is made to confess to sexual crossover, androgyny, and sadomasochism. Many of her readings are brilliant—Whitman and Henry James will never look the same—but many seem overreadings. Blake's lullabylike "Infant Joy," in its extremity of simplicity and innocence, is alleged to "daemonize the reader, drawing him into the rapacious cycle of natural process," and to indict "the oppressive paternalism of society's self-appointed guardians." Hawthorne is theorized to have added "w" to the family name Hathorne as a way of adding "woman"—"his father's name blasphemously hermaphroditized"—in counterbalance to his mother's maiden name of Manning. We begin with the bust of Nefertiti, "a haughty face . . . carved out of the chaos of nature," and end with the verbal amputations and shearings of Emily Dickinson, who is described as the American Marquis de Sade. We are left with a chthonian stew of simmering, carved-up bits. Repeated dissections have demonstrated that nature is cruel and sex is part of nature. Is sex therefore *only* cruel? In a book all about sex, we miss a feel of the organic—its springiness, its "give." Though Paglia is very free, in a scholarly work, with the first-person singular pronoun, and flavors her Ph.D.-ese with slang, the voice stays flat and metallic. The weary reader longs for the mercy of a qualification, a doubt, a hesitation; there is little sense, in her uncompanionable prose, of exploration occurring before our eyes, of tentative motions of thought reflected in a complex syntax.

Paglia's hammering, flaunting, outrageous manner is that of a performer; when she is literally onstage, as in the MIT talk, she is in her element, and very funny. The laughter and latent hostility of the audience stimulate her to skits wherein Foucault becomes the vacuum cleaner that all the ducklings follow thinking it is their mother, or the fashionable French intellectuals become "zebra Naugahyde furniture":

So they went heavily into this, okay, their whole house is furnished in it. Then suddenly, twenty years down the road, someone like me appears and says, "Guess what—that's *out* now. Not only that, but it was in terrible taste to begin with." So you can see why they're mad at me. They're mad because they're stuck with that furniture! They have twenty years of furniture!

Her operatic tough-girl voice rings out into the cloistered academic air: "We have got to let the mind open *freely*, freely toward sex, and understand that from the moment you're on a date with a man, the idea of sex is *hovering* in the air—*hover, hover, hover,* okay?" Lest the reader miss some of her performance, she supplies her miming in brackets:

> Silly me—at the end of class, I would, like, *go*—go to the library, gotta do something, go to a movie, right? And I would see some of my fellow graduate students clustering around the teacher in this odd way, and I thought, "What are they doing?" And then at the end of lectures by famous people, I would see them, and there's a weird motion they would get. . . . And it's sort of like a zombie look they get on their faces, and their bodies begin to *undulate*, you know the way seaweed does [*imitates undulating seaweed*]. They're moving into *Toady Mode*!

This is effective teaching, no doubt, teaching being a kind of entertaining. But does Paglia's jubilant demonization of feminism and academia constitute effective criticism? For all of her self-professed intellectual passion and her genuine erudition, she strikes one as less serious, somehow—less gravely involved in issues of language and culture—than the ironical, verbose, and easy-to-deride Derrida. She is happy with short takes. The world of bites exhilarates her. "With reporters . . . I'm in my element, like Roz Russell in *His Girl Friday*, a boisterous, wisecracking, machine-gun American verbal style. . . . Talking with them, I feel connected to a vast communications network." Her reviews and op-ed pieces are lively; she does not stint or soften her message. In a little review of Marjorie Garber's *Vested Interests: Cross Dressing and Cultural Anxiety*, after complaining about "lumpish pastiches of tedious Lacan jargon" and the author's ignorance of Paglia's special areas of expertise (classical antiquity and pop culture), she comes up with a true illumination of the mystery of cross-dressing: "The drag queen defies victim-centered feminism by asserting the dominance of woman in the universe."

The assertion, and not the defiance, is the helpful point, phrased a bit differently in *Sexual Personae*: "A woman putting on men's clothes merely steals social power. But a man putting on women's clothes is searching for God." Paglia's awareness of the life-enabling religious impulses moving beneath the quirks of human culture is her most valuable and refreshing trait, though it leads her to overvalue the chimeras of pop culture. Is Madonna, with her thin talents and hard edges, quite the Second Coming of womanhood described in Paglia's two pieces on her, which extol her as "an international star of staggering dimensions," "the future of feminism," and a global force who, "with an instinct for world-domination gained from Italian Catholicism, . . . has rolled like a juggernaut over the multitude of her carping critics." Does Elizabeth Taylor's sometimes hefty embodiment of a violet-eyed alternative to the "antiseptic American blondeness" of Doris Day, Debbie Reynolds, Sandra Dee, and Meryl Streep ("with her boring decorum") really make her "the greatest actress in film history"? And Paglia's mooniness over male rock stars is a real nostalgia trip, to the far edge of female adolescence.

Another girlish item in *Sex, Art, and American Culture* is the long introduction that the Yale University Press persuaded her to reduce to a page for *Sexual Personae*, but the softer-hearted editors at Vintage have included entire here. It is all about the Paglia persona, self-dramatized as "a scholar with stars in her eyes." We learn about her girlhood fascination with classical antiquity and Egypt in the same paragraph that tells of "an affectionate calico she-cat named Teabag who ferociously patrolled the sidewalk and fire escape" of Paglia's apartment building in New Haven. With the ingenuous egoism of a teenager, she lists her pet peeves, her likes and dislikes: Sade over Rousseau, hierarchy over egalitarianism, rock-and-roll over Greek tragedy, astrology over rational science, nature over nurture, "verbally aggressive" "visionary rabbis" as teachers over New Critics with their "sunny Christian courtesy," the Thirties over the Fifties. "The prewar era, in the shadow of the Depression, was a period not only of female achievement but of beauty, glamour, and style, values that I found in ancient Egypt but nowhere in my own world, whose applecheeked dictator was Doris Day." (Paglia really should get to know Doris Day—a renegade Catholic and no prig, and not even a natural blonde, as early photographs indicate.) Before she latched on to Frazer and Freud, Paglia spent three high-school years studying her heroine Amelia Earhart; like a dashing early aviator, Paglia flies by the seat of her pants. Her ethnic prejudices (safely anti-Wasp), her personal psychodrama as an Italian woman full of male bravado, and her joy in the gestures of assault for their own sake all give her critical and sociological judgments a certain tilt. She is in danger of getting trapped in a shtick. Her reactions and opinions, so initially startling, become predictable, and automatically raucous. From her mentor Harold Bloom, perhaps, she has received the idea that literature is a power game, a matter of ousting and supplanting; her own determination to strive, struggle, and triumph becomes the most conspicuous thing about her, eclipsing the considerable worth of her learning, ingenuity, and fearlessness. In the once-rejected introduction to *Sexual Personae*, she describes its ambition in terms of bulk:

Women have never written epic, the longest and most military of literary forms, taking in the gods and heaven and hell. In its excessive scale and all-fencing inclusiveness, *Sexual Personae* is a Roman omnibus, a gazetteer of points of cultural transfer. . . . The two volumes of *Sexual Personae*, with the author as Amazon epic quester, may be the longest book yet written by a woman, exceeding in this respect even George Eliot's hefty *Middlemarch*. That book contains as its moral irritant a huge unrealized project, Casaubon's *Key to All Mythologies*, which I dutifully complete here.

Poor Casaubon, readers of *Middlemarch* will recall, sank disconsolately to death in the throes of writer's block, unable to bring his *Key* together. One awaits with some trepidation the second volume of *Sexual Personae*, in which Paglia has promised to "show how movies, television, sports, and rock music embody all the pagan themes of classical antiquity." Can the crass and ephemeral artifacts of the mass-entertainment industry supply her animus and mental energy with fodder comparable to the masterpieces of Western culture she ripped through in Volume I? Can she add significantly to the already vast commentary which her generation of the Sixties, the most self-impressed and self-righteous generation alive, has devoted to its own pop envelope? Tune in the further adventures of the Amazon quester. One cannot help applauding her, as a unique performer on the cultural stage, while wondering if performance, in even this dim-witted age of diluted Dionysianism, is all there is. Her solemn compiling of her own notices in *Sex, Art, and American Culture* implies that stirring up press attention is in itself an achievement. Maybe so, but *ars est longa*, and buzz is short.

Among Canines

The Hidden Life of Dogs, by Elizabeth Marshall Thomas. 140 pp. Houghton Mifflin, 1993.

Mrs. Thomas brings to the alien world of dogs the same openness and poise that characterized her youthful anthropological studies of Bushmen and Dodoth tribesmen and her two superb recent novels set among Paleolithic people in northern Asia. That dogs have consciousness, thoughts, and emotions seems to her (as to most dog-lovers) obvious, and she cites a number of irrefutable examples of canine cogitation. Her field studies began with a six-month guest in her Cambridge home, a husky called Misha who, in spite of fences, traffic, and leash laws, established a roaming range of one hundred thirty square miles and never got injured or lost. Tailing him on foot and bicycle, at all hours, she deduced that the object of his wandering was neither sex nor food but circling, sniffing encounters with other dogs, and the establishment of relative rank. As her number of household dogs achieved the size of a pack, other behavioral traits emerged, of which the most startling was the dogs' secret construction of a wolvish den in their pen in Virginia, which involved the scattering of six cubic yards of dirt, though the den's entrance was but twenty yards from the Thomases' front door. Don't flatter yourselves, primates: dogs are thoroughly dog-centered. "What do dogs want most? They want to belong, and they want each other." This stark conclusion takes on an eerie comedy when Mrs. Thomas, determined "to visit a dog's mind," joins her pets in long afternoons of doing nothing—"like entering a quiet little village in some faraway country." When one of them dies, she inhales the "odor of the dog, of wet dog, musky and penetrating," that upwells like a cry from the fur of the survivors.

Fine Points

THE NEW FOWLER'S MODERN ENGLISH USAGE, edited by R. W. Burchfield. 864 pp. Oxford, 1996.

The anonymous jacket designer for *The New Fowler's Modern English Usage* shows a cunning grasp of typographical politics. The headlined, selling word is *"Fowler's,"* italicized, white on black, and measuring at full height an inch and a quarter. The word "NEW" is very discreetly tucked between the "F" and the "l," in thin caps three-eighths of an inch high and tinted a receding blue. The words "Modern English Usage," five-eighths of an inch high, appear in silver on a blue band that brightly suggests first-prize-winning status; the type recalls that used, in a dowdy maroon on gray, on the first edition of H. W. Fowler's famous reference work of 1926, whose full title was *A Dictionary of Modern English Usage*. Below the blue band we read, in letters not more than a quarter the size of those spelling "Fowler's," the words "Third Edition" and "Edited by R. W. Burchfield." It is only upon penetrating to the fifth page of Burchfield's preface that we discover that this "Fowler" is Fowler in name only, or almost only: "Fowler's name remains on the title-page, even though his book has been largely rewritten in this third edition." Burchfield in his preface has come not to praise but to bury his fabled predecessor. His pious graveside elegy even offers suggestions on the embalming:

I hope that a way will be found to keep the 1926 masterpiece in print for at least another seventy years. . . . It is not, of course, as antiquated as Ælfric's Grammar nor yet as those of Ben Jonson or Robert Lowth. But it is a fossil all the same, and an enduring monument to all that was linguistically acceptable in the standard English of the southern counties of England in the first quarter of the twentieth century.

Fowler's revered name may be big on the jacket (and enormous on the spine) but he is cut sharply down to size in Burchfield's revisionary estimate:

> What I want to stress is the isolation of Fowler from the mainstream of the linguistic scholarship of his day, and his heavy dependence on schoolmasterly textbooks in which the rules of grammar, rhetoric, punctuation, spelling, and so on, were set down in a quite basic manner. . . . For his illustrative examples Fowler often turned to the *OED* [the *Oxford English Dictionary*] and drew on them to support his arguments. Above all, however, he turned to newspapers (though he seldom specifies which ones) because they reflected and revealed the solecistic waywardness of "the half-educated" general public in a much more dramatic fashion than did the works of English literature.

Not only was Henry Watson Fowler an isolated and linguistically amateurish former schoolteacher (at Sedburgh School, in northwestern Yorkshire, of classics and English, for seventeen years) who revelled in the errors of hurried journalists but, "perhaps as a hangover from [his] days as a schoolmaster, his scholarship needed to be enlivened by a veneer of idiosyncrasy and humour." In *The King's English*, a 1906 guide to usage he compiled with his younger brother, Francis George Fowler, various issues of syntax and taste were discussed under such frisky heads as "Airs and Graces," "Between Two Stools," and "Wens and Hypertrophied Members." *A Dictionary of Modern English Usage* sports articles titled "False Scent," "Out of the Frying-Pan," and "Pairs and Snares." Such academic japes, Burchfield tartly comments, "have endeared the book to Fowler's devotees, but no longer have their interest or appeal and are not preserved in this new edition." Nor are Fowler's system of indicating pronunciation, his crisply prescriptive tone, and a number of entries that Burchfield deemed "quirky, opinionated, and based on inadequate evidence."

In their place Burchfield brings the International Phonetic Alphabet, an extensive computerized access to modern verbal evidence, a "systematic reading of British and American newspapers, periodicals, and fiction of the 1980s and 1990s," and, most important, "an historical approach to English usage." Born in New Zealand in 1923, Burchfield held academic positions at Oxford before becoming chief editor of the Oxford English dictionaries; his own titles include *The Oxford Dictionary of English Etymology* (1966) and *Unlocking the English Language* (1989). As a historian of the language, he is a pragmatic relativist who believes, "Judgements based on the distribution of competing constructions or pronunciations are intrinsically fragile and diminished in value if the constructions are not also examined historically."

How does his historical, descriptive approach differ from that of the 1926 Fowler when both are consulted on some still-smarting sore points of usage? Under the entry "mutual," Fowler calls the word "a well-known trap" and says, "The essence of its meaning is that it involves the relation, x is or does to y as y to x; & not the relation, x is or does to z as y to z." Quoting the phrase "the mutual enemy," he admonishes firmly, "In such places *common* is the right word, & the use of *m.* betrays ignorance of its meaning." Burchfield, after quoting Fowler, Evelyn Waugh, and other dogmatists on this issue, points out that "the other use of *mutual*, namely 'pertaining to both parties, common,' has been in unbroken use since the late 16c. (Shakespeare)," and that the phrase "our mutual friend" appeared long before Dickens's novel of that name.

Under the entry "include, comprise" Fowler considers "comprise" a "stylish" word which "the inferior kind of journalist" uses when "include" would do — that is, when there is no inclusion of "the content of the whole." "Compose," of course, has an opposite sense: all the parts compose the whole, the whole comprises all the parts. Burchfield, having marked the distinction, goes on to cite a number of uses of "comprise" when "compose" was meant and amiably predicts, "It cannot be denied, however, that the sheer frequency of this construction seems likely to take it out of the disputed area before long." Concerning "purport," Fowler called the use of the verb in the passive "an ugly recent development" and argued against its use with a person ("She purports to find . . ."; "Sir Henry is purported to . . ."). Burchfield throws up his hands:

> *Conclusion.* It would appear that the language is gradually admitting some uses of *purport* not recorded in the *OED* and others that were disliked by Fowler. It is a classic example of a verb continuing to vie for space with its near-synonyms . . . and having a mixed reception from standard speakers as the linguistic battle takes its course.

To Burchfield, the English language is a battlefield upon which he functions as a noncombatant observer. In this capacity, he can be surprisingly lenient. If there is one popular usage generally decried by contemporary grammarians it is the adverb "hopefully" used in the sense of "it is hoped that"; e.g., "Hopefully, the sun will shine." The usage was so out-of-bounds in 1926 that Fowler doesn't mention it. But Burchfield states, in one of his relatively few entries that could be called spirited, that "hopefully" in this sense is a "sentence adverb," employed "to qualify a predication or assertion as a whole." There has been in this century, he observes, "a swift and immoderate increase" in such adverbs; others are "actually, basically, frankly . . . regretfully, strictly, and thankfully." Why, he asks, put "a dunce's cap" on the user of "hopefully" in this sense, when in "Unhappily, there are times when violence is the only way" the adverb is an unobjectionable way of expressing "It is an unhappy fact that . . ."? (One might certainly say, in exact parallel, "Happily, the sun will shine.") Burchfield blinks at the flak in summing up: "Conservative speakers, taken unawares by the sudden expansion of an unrecognized type of construction, have exploded with resentment that is unlikely to fade away before at least the end of the 20c."

On the frequently deplored use of "nauseous" to mean "nauseated," he takes cover behind another permissive, precedent-rich authority, *Webster's Dictionary of English Usage*, whose relevant entry concludes, "Any handbook that tells you that *nauseous* cannot mean 'nauseated' is out of touch with the contemporary language." On the veteran outcast "ain't," Burchfield is more than democratic; he pleads the outcast's case like a left-wing lawyer: "For over 200 years the bar sinister word *ain't* has been begging for admission to standard English . . . thwarted by the equally bar-sinister form *aren't*. [It] leads a shadowy existence in the language of various underclasses." Even Fowler admitted it to be a pity that no legitimate contraction for "am not" existed, though "ain't" when used in place of "isn't," he insisted, "is an uneducated blunder & serves no useful purpose."

Now and then Burchfield not merely softens Fowler, he openly rebukes him. To call the use of an adjective plus "otherwise" when "other" is meant ("agricultural and otherwise") "a definite outrage on grammatical principles" appears to Burchfield, seventy years later, excessive: "the language has moved on and the type condemned by Fowler is now in standard use." In "want[ing] to kick" the non-personal genitives ("the problem's resolution," "China's integrity") that descend from newspaper headlines into lower-case text, Fowler, Burchfield says, "seemed to be off target." Under "coastal," we read in the new Fowler, "Fowler's objection . . . to this formation as a 'barbarism' is a classic example of a lost cause." Fowler argued that the word should be "costal" (as it still is in medical contexts) to preserve its Latin root, *costa* (rib). For similar reasons of etymological purity, he rejected the negative "a-," of Greek origin, when attached to stems of Latin origin, as in "asexual" and "amoral," urging "non-moral" for the latter. But these qualms, along with Fowler's zealous definitions of increasingly arcane Greek prosodic and rhetorical terms like "acatalectic," "alcaics," "anacoluthon," anacrusis," "arsis," and "hysteron proteron" (all of which Burchfield has decided, "on balance," to include), belong to a quaint day when Greek and Latin formed the requisite base of a humane education.

Linguistics offers a slippery field for the exercise of moral indignation. Live languages change. A purely descriptive dictionary of usage has the merit of illuminating, as is done on the grandest scale by the *OED*, the long and winding corridors of recorded usage. And it has the charm, in this age of cultural diversity and politically correct sensitivity, of assuring all users of English that no intelligible usage is absolutely wrong. Use "comprise" and "nauseous" often enough in the unfavored sense, and such a sense gets enrolled in the dictionary. Purists need, perhaps, to be reminded that the English language is a hybrid of exceptional flexibility, variety, and inconsistency. Burchfield's 864 double-columned pages attempt, his preface states, "to guide readers to make sensible choices in linguistically controversial areas of words, meanings, grammatical constructions, and pronunciations." Such a modest goal may be the only feasible one. But it proposes no ideal of clarity in language or, beyond that, of grace, which might serve as an instrument of discrimination. It was Fowler's flinty idealism that endeared him to the generations of those who came to consult and stayed to read, with real pleasure, his tireless compilations of slovenly English and his relentlessly logical parsing. He offers a dynamic guidance that promises a brighter future, rather than a helpless wallow in the endless morass of English as it was and is. "Every just man who will abstain from the fused participle . . . retards the progress of corruption."

Modern English Usage was long contemplated. In 1909, Fowler outlined an "idiom dictionary" (a colleague described it as "a Utopian dictionary") as follows:

> We should assume a cheerful attitude of infallibility, & confine ourselves to present-day usage; for instance, we should give no quarter to *masterful* in the sense of *masterly*, as the OED is obliged to do because there is antiquated authority for it, & generally speaking should try to give a shove behind to the process of differentiation.

Differentiation—between such confusable pairs as "admission/admittance," "affect/effect," and "continual/continuous"—was one of his dictionary's main purposes. On the last pair, Fowler is characteristically crisp: "That is -al which either is always going on or recurs at short intervals & never comes (or is regarded as never coming) to an end. That is -ous in which no break occurs between the beginning & the (not necessarily or even presumably long-deferred) end." Burchfield says, "In practice the distinction is not as neat as that," and conscientiously muddles the issue with instances of what Fowler called "antiquated authority." Burchfield knows that he is revising to death a loved tome; in his preface he defensively raises the question "Why has this schoolmasterly, quixotic, idiosyncratic, and somewhat vulnerable book, in a form only lightly revised once, in 1965, by Ernest Gowers, retained its hold on the imagination of all but professional linguistic scholars?" The question frames its own answer: in our ignorance we seek schoolmasterly instruction, and are beguiled and entertained when the master displays quixoticism, idiosyncrasy, and vulnerability.

Fowler provided a user's guide for people in the word trade. The founding editor of *The New Yorker*, Harold Ross, worked, according to James Thurber, "surrounded by dictionaries, which he constantly consulted, along with one of his favorite books, Fowler's *Modern English Usage*.* He learned more grammar and syntax from Fowler than he had ever picked up in his somewhat sketchy school days." But more than grammar and syntax were being inculcated; the dictionary of usage is the child of the Fowler brothers' *The King's English*, which on its first page fortifies "any one who wishes to become a good writer" with five precepts:

Prefer the familiar word to the far-fetched.
Prefer the concrete word to the abstract.
Prefer the single word to the circumlocution.
Prefer the short word to the long.
Prefer the Saxon word to the Romance.

---

*Ben Yagoda, in his researches for a book on *The New Yorker*, came across a few references to Fowler in Ross's correspondence. In a 1945 letter to Samuel H. Adams, he discussed Alexander Woollcott's grammatical foibles and said, "I had to pull Fowler in both cases. Fowler is a useful stone to throw at anyone living in a glass house." In 1949, to Kay Boyle, Ross wrote, "We think ourselves into knots over style things around here, although we've long since cracked most problems. We're having one now on when to use *which* and when to use *that* that is a little gem. Fowler, in 'Modern English Usage,' differentiates between them and, somehow or other—I don't know how, so help me—we got to following him in the editing of all house (or unsigned) stuff and then in practically all fact stuff (the writers are around the office and can be talked to from hour to hour), and then in more or less all the fiction, most of the writers falling into line. . . . Our trouble is that we think the magazine sounds funny part *which* and part *that*—or anyhow, some of us do. The office is not unanimous in this matter, as usual, and the writer has his way, anyhow."

H. W. Fowler himself practiced these stark preachments, with a resultant style that Gowers called "mathematical rather than literary." But in the narrow dictionary double columns the mathematically precise style is delightfully spiky, tonic, gnomic, and lucid, with a certain metronomic rhythm:

> Now the sobriquet habit is not a thing to be acquired, but a thing to be avoided; & the selection that follows is compiled for the purpose not of assisting but of discouraging it.

More than once, Fowler seeks to cure us with a surfeit: "And now, in order that the reader may leave this disquisition sick to death, as he should be, of the fused participle, a few miscellaneous specimens are offered." A column and a half of bad examples follow—not nearly so many, however, as he provides under the broad heading of "Elegant variation," effectuating his "attempt (the main object of this article) to nauseate by accumulation of instances, as sweet-shop assistants are cured of larceny by cloying." Fowler's grammatical morality extends itself, here and there, into political commentary. Under the cool blue light of his differentiation machine, "socialism, communism, anarchism" are drolly arranged as inflections of the same discomfort:

> The things are not mutually exclusive; the words are not an exhaustive threefold division of anything; each stands for a state of things, or a striving after it, that differs much from that which we know; & for many of us, especially those who are comfortably at home in the world as it is, they have consequently come to be the positive, comparative, & superlative, distinguished not in kind but in degree only, of the terms of abuse applicable to those who would disturb our peace.

There is something wry as well as fervid about Fowler, as he vigorously tilts at such whirling windmills as "Battered ornaments," "Misapprehensions," "Mannerisms," "Facetious formations," "Pomposities," "Superstitions," and "Sturdy indefensibles"—all of them types of faulty writing arraigned in separate articles in his dictionary. Though so little of a Christian that he left the academic world rather than prepare his charges for confirmation, he shows the methodical zeal of a St. Ignatius of Loyola or St. Thomas Aquinas. "Unattached participles," "Unequal yokefellows," "Poeticisms," "Literary words," "Needless variants"—the categories mount into a scholastic encyclopedia of sins, sins against a holy vision of utterly crystalline, rational language. He catalogues sins that only the keenest eye and ear could have ferreted out. "Cannibalism," for instance, exposes to our horrified censure sentences wherein "words . . . devour their own kind":

The Council of the League shall direct the Members of the League as to *which combatant is to be applied the Decree of Non-intercourse. To* has swallowed a *to,* as its way is when employed by AS-*to* writers.

Got that? It should have read "as to to which . . ." "Swapping horses" deals with an equally insidious subtlety of misuse, "changing a word's sense in the middle of a sentence, by vacillating between two constructions either of which might follow a word legitimately enough, by starting off with a subject that fits one verb but must have something tacitly substituted for it to fit another":

Viscount Grey's promised speech in the House of Lords on Reparations & inter-Allied debts furnished *all the* interest *naturally* aroused. *Interest* is here virtually, though not actually, used twice—the speech furnished interest, interest was aroused; but what was furnished was interesting matter, & what was aroused was eager curiosity.

The effect of immersion in Fowler's splendid nitpicking is to make a writer feel entangled in likely—nay, certain—error, and engaged in a hopelessly dirty task. The language is a mess, except as scoured and rinsed and hung out to dry by Fowler. Users are mired in its schizoid mix of Germanic and Romance roots, its notoriously erratic spelling and pronunciation, its vestigial subjunctive, and its tendency, as noted by Dr. Samuel Johnson in the preface to *his* dictionary, to modify the meaning of a verb "by a particle subjoined"; Johnson cites "fall in," "bear out," "take off," "give over," and despairingly swears to "innumerable expressions of the same kind, of which some appear wildly irregular, being so far distant from the sense of the simple words, that no sagacity will be able to trace the steps by which they arrived at the present use." No learned academy in the English-speaking world has been able to assume the French Academy's pose as an official guardian of the language; the closest such authority in this country was Noah Webster and he, like Bernard Shaw and Andrew Carnegie, made himself look cranky by trying to standardize and simplify English spelling. The tools of logic fall afoul of so compounded and shifty an organism as English; Fowler, reasoning from the analogies of "accept," "success," and "coccyx," found "soccer" a misleading spelling and recommended "socker," which would certainly have given the game a different connotation. As is, the players play soccer and the spectators play socker.

How useful are guidebooks to usage, in an age when the concept of correctness, except in a political sense, is suspect? Who uses them?* Edi-

---

*There is also, in the matter of usefulness, the handiness factor. The Strunk and White *Elements of Style* manual owes much of its great success to its conciseness and brevity. A thoroughly modern, historically descriptive, citation-rich work such as *Webster's Dictio-*

BURCHFIELD'S FOWLER

tors, seeking to impose order and clarity on the torrents of prose that
flow through their publications, have recourse to them; any faithful contributor to *The New Yorker* has been periodically checked in his outpour
by some icy citation from Fowler. Until the editorial thaw of recent years,
"contact" and "intrigue" were considered arriviste verbs to be snubbed in
its pages, and "located" in both the senses of "found" and "situated"
raised uneasy hackles. Under "hyphens," Burchfield remarks, "*The New
Yorker* regularly places hyphens in *teen-age* and *teen-ager*; it is a long time
since I last saw a hyphen in these words in works printed in Britain." The
purpose of this, an editor once explained to me, was to avoid confusion
with the English dialect word "teenage," meaning "brushwood used for
fences and hedges." Another editor informed me that the adjective "balding" wouldn't do because its implication that the subject would get balder
was unkind. Such beautiful scruples excluded the plentiful coinages of the
advertising world; how I struggled, when young and strong, to get the
epithet "flavorful" printed in a *New Yorker* short story! The fact seems to
be that while writing I rarely consult Fowler or any other guide to usage;
I would rather trust my ear and unconsciously acquired sense of the language. John O'Hara, who took a pugnacious pride in his ear, once wrote
to his publisher, "Don't cite dictionaries to me, on dialog or the vernacular. Dictionary people consult me, not I them."

Language is first and fundamentally a spoken thing, made and
reformed in the daily commerce of men and women. A recurrent thrust
of English literary genius, from Shakespeare and Wordsworth to Hemingway and T. S. Eliot, has been to make poetry of the demotic tongue,
and to shed archaic forms mainly transmitted in the written language.
Fowler's list of five precepts favors the simple, direct, and "Saxon." If
faithfully followed, it might engender an English of artificially restricted
reach. Clarity and logicality are not the only virtues of prose; had James
Joyce rested content with the limpid prose of *Dubliners* and not instead
explored the margins where mental processes surrender grammar, the
vocabulary of fiction would be much the poorer. The disciplinarians
of language offer little encouragement to the attempt, which needs constant renewal, to find written equivalents for actual experience, in its
unparsable, impressionistic complexity.

---

nary of International Usage threatens to become a thousand big pages of wandering word-
chat. Burchfield's post-Fowler Fowler is one hundred thirty pages longer than the original,
and that much more intimidating to consult. Handier was the restrained but admirable
second edition of 1965; Gowers took out some of Fowler's longer lists, provided some
overdue attention to Americanisms, and shortened the original by a few pages. In paperback, it was easy to hold and shelve; it did not have the air, as does this third edition, of
sleek, imposing bulk.

* * *

Not that Fowler was not, in his day, something of a liberator. He allowed that infinitives should sometimes be split and that sentences could properly end with a preposition. He was not unaware of the impossibility of making English tightly fit Greek and Latin rules. Yet the background of his allowances remains the presumption that language is an instrument for conveying distinct meanings and can be codified to that end. Burchfield's version of *Modern English Usage* presents a wispier version of Fowler's faith. What Marshall McLuhan called the "electric galaxy" is overwhelming Gutenbergian niceties.

Magazines and even, under the influence of ever younger copyeditors, publishing houses are smoothing away many of the old typographical courtesies. Numbers are no longer spelled out but given in numerical, indeterminately pronounced forms. Hyphens and commas fall away. The advent of the typewriter and now the computer has diminished the use of diacritical marks to the vanishing point. "Role" instead of "rôle" is perhaps no great loss, or "chateau" instead of "château," but "tete-a-tete" instead of "tête-à-tête" approaches baby-talk, and "née" without the accent sticks us with the almost unreadable masculine form "ne." The usage experts should be combatting the loss of any aid to understanding or pronunciation, in a language that leaves us so often adrift: the spread of blandly doubled vowels as in "cooperate" and "reenter" (as opposed to "co-operate" or "reënter") adds to our burdens, and the dropping of the comma before "and" in a series seems to me a surrender of clarity, giving "red, white and blue" the same rhythm as "tea, bread and butter" or "Chaplin, Laurel and Hardy." Burchfield, no scold, does say that this so-called "Oxford comma" is "frequently, but in my view unwisely, omitted by many other publishers." Print managers, apparently anxious to save space so small as the width of a lower-case "l," now prefer, with the connivance of Webster's Third Edition, "marvelous" to "marvellous" and, worse, "worshiping" (which looks as though it rhymes with "sniping" and "piping") to "worshipping." There is even seen, as if to chime with "raped," "kidnaped."

Burchfield lays the blame for some of these slovenly preferences on American English, a terrain that was *terra incognita* to Fowler but where Burchfield does venture, albeit diffidently. He says, for example, apropos of quotation marks, that American publishers are "likely . . . to use double marks for a first quotation and single ones for a quotation within a quotation" when in fact they are certain to do so; quotation marks provide the quickest way to tell if a text has been typeset in the United States or Great Britain. Burchfield lists the striking Anglo-American differences in designating "rubbish/garbage" and its adjuncts. He takes gingerly note of the "minor curiosity" that "African-Americans frequently use the word *nigger* without giving offense when addressing other blacks"; Burchfield has already been taken to task by an American lexicographer, Jesse Sheidlower, in *The Atlantic Monthly*, for being "generally insensitive to the use of 'politically correct' language." Well, a linguistic descriptionist might argue, you have to take the language as you find it, insensitivity and all.

Yet one does feel that some discipline should be maintained, and some rules should bind us together. The contemporary misusage that I take most gravely as a personal affront is the weird revision, in popular speech, of the emphatic declaration "I couldn't care less" into its opposite, "I could care less," as if both meant the same thing. Burchfield, always the polite observer of the linguistic broils, comments, "No one has satisfactorily accounted for the synonymy of what would appear to be straightforwardly autonymous uses." The reason to me is clear: people are too lazy or hazy to realize that they are speaking within a descending scale of concern the bottom rung of which they have just denied to the scorned subject. No fanatic about verbal proprieties, when it comes to such arrant muddle of meaning I find I *could* care less.

Oh, It Was Sad

DOWN WITH THE OLD CANOE: *A Cultural History of the* Titanic *Disaster*, by Steven Biel. 283 pp. Norton, 1996.

EVERY MAN FOR HIMSELF, by Beryl Bainbridge. 224 pp. Carroll & Graf, 1996.

The RMS (Royal Mail Steamer) *Titanic*, whose sinking over eighty-four years ago made the biggest news splash of the new century, still generates headlines. The discovery of the wreck in 1985, three hundred and seventy miles southeast of Newfoundland and two and a half miles below the surface of the Atlantic, by a team of scientists from the Woods Hole Oceangraphic Institution and the Institut Français de Recherche pour l'Exploitation de la Mer, revivified a fascination that had never quite died. Though the leader of the expedition, Robert Ballard, denounced salvage of the wreck, and placed a plaque on the *Titanic's* stern declaring it "a sacred resting place," his French partners in *l'exploitation de la mer* did not share his qualms. More submersible vessels rather than fewer will likely visit the watery grave and bring sacred relics to the surface. Lumps of coal from the *Titanic*'s bins can be bought for twenty-five dollars each, and nine bottles of Bass Ale (of twelve thousand on board) have been recovered, along with plates, chamber pots, toilet articles, a camera, a gilded ceiling-fixture, and a wallet stuffed with money and receipts. The debris is scattered over a square mile; the ship lies in two big pieces, the stern badly damaged but the bow still grand. Touted as "unsinkable," the *Titanic* at its launching became the largest movable object ever made by man—882 feet in length (nearly three football fields), displacing sixty-six thousand long tons of water.* Her rudder weighed one hundred one tons, and her hull contained three million rivets. Just recently, a seventeen-ton, fourteen-by-eighteen-foot section of the hull slipped away from the diesel-fuel-filled lifting balloons, giving rise to another headline. A more modest retrieval, a small piece of inch-thick hull steel holding three rivet holes, led to a scientific test in Canada demonstrating that the *Titanic* steel was sulfur-rich and brittle. So our sense of the *Titanic* undergoes yet another modification: it was made of bad steel. Or—the most recent theory—the rivets were brittle and weak.

Steven Biel, in his cumbersomely titled *Down with the Old Canoe: A Cultural History of the* Titanic *Disaster*, traces the various meanings that the *Titanic*'s sinking has had for Americans since it so astoundingly occurred in mid-April of 1912. In Biel's account, the first reports, based upon the *Titanic*'s last wireless message—"Sinking by the head. Have cleared boats and filled them with women and children"—created a legend of heroic first-class-cabin males gallantly giving up their lifeboat seats to the weak and fair and socially inferior. The proprietorial rule of white Anglo-Saxon males was being challenged by suffragists and labor organizers, and the conservative press seized the opportunity to extol "that Christian knightliness which seeks not its own, but the good of others." Archibald Gracie, a first-cabin survivor (*Titanic* survival was morally suspect but Colonel Gracie went down with the ship and swam with "unusual strength" to a capsized lifeboat), wrote that the "coolness,

---

*A long ton equals 2,240 pounds. In relation to ships, the ton is generally a measure of space. The commonly cited weight of 46,000 tons for the *Titanic* refers to net registered tonnage—the cubic-foot measure of revenue-producing space. Gross tonnage gives the total volume enclosed by the hull and superstructure. The measure goes back to wine casks called "tunnes" or "tuns," whose capacity was regularized as "tons," a unit of volume about the size of four large refrigerators—one hundred cubic feet. "Deadweight tonnage" measures, in long tons, the amount of cargo, liquid or solid, that a ship can safely load. None of these figures gives the weight of the ship's metal and wood constituents if placed on a scale. (For this information I am indebted to Alan Littell.)

courage, and sense of duty that I . . . witnessed made me thankful to God and proud of my Anglo-Saxon race that gave this perfect and superb exhibition of self-control at this hour of severest trial." The *Atlanta Constitution* proclaimed:

> The Anglo-Saxon may yet boast that his sons are fit to rule the earth so long as men choose death with the courage they must have displayed when the great liner crashed into the mountains of ice, and the aftermath brought its final test.

"Must have displayed"—tales, some based on the testimony of first-class female survivors and others spun out of sheer wishful thinking, dramatized the heroic last minutes of upper-class representatives such as John Jacob Astor, George D. and Harry Widener, J. B. Thayer, President Taft's military aide Archibald Butt, and two Jewish millionaires of whom Biel says, "Wealth apparently transformed Isidor Straus and Benjamin Guggenheim into honorary Anglo-Saxons." Guggenheim debonairly donned a tuxedo at the last; Straus refused to let his advanced age win him a place in a lifeboat; and the celebrated decision of Mrs. Straus to stay on the sinking ship with her husband was fodder for articles, sermons, and a poem urging all women to "Emulate the deed of such a wife, / As went down in the blue." If the Strauses displayed the right stuff on the first-class deck, however, the alien races in steerage became in their panic "a frenzied mob of armed brutes," held back by the officers' guns. Fifth Officer Harold Lowe recalled: "I saw a lot of Latin people all along the ship's rails. They were glaring more or less like wild beasts, ready to spring." The cowardly men who allegedly showed up in the lifeboats, sometimes clad in women's clothes, were variously reported as Italian, Japanese, Armenian, or Filipino.* The thronging brutes on the sinking *Titanic* uncannily resembled "the specters of an immigrant tidal wave engulfing the United States in the early twentieth century." The statistics show a different class bias:

> Of the first-cabin men, 31 percent survived, compared with 10 percent in second class and 14 percent in steerage. In all, 60 percent of the first-cabin passengers lived, compared with 44 percent of the second-cabin passengers and only 25 percent of the steerage passengers.

---

*The survivor of whom the cross-dressing rumors were true bore the Anglo-Saxon name of Daniel Buckley. A third-class passenger, he and several others jumped into a boat and, according to Lord, "huddled there crying. Most of the men were hauled out, but somewhere he got a woman's shawl. He said Mrs. Astor put it over him. In any case, the disguise worked."

Walter Lord's *A Night to Remember* (1955) points out that "somehow the loss rate was higher for Third Class children than First Class men."

The *Titanic* had other repercussions than glorification of the ruling class. Ministers took the occasion to denounce Mammon and his works. The Reverend Charles H. Parkhurst of Manhattan's Madison Square Presbyterian Church preached the cautionary paradox of "dead helplessness wrapped in priceless luxury":

> Everything for existence, nothing for life. Grand men, charming women, beautiful babies, all becoming horrible in the midst of the glittering splendor of a $10,000,000 casket!

George Chalmers Richmond, a Philadelphia Episcopalian, even maligned John Jacob Astor, a recent divorcé embarked with his nineteen-year-old second wife: "Mr. Astor and his New York and Newport associates have for years paid not the slightest attention to the laws of church or state which have seemed to contravene their personal pleasures or sensual delights. But you can't defy God all the time." For this breach of respect the Reverend Mr. Richmond was roundly condemned.

Among the alarming apparitions of the *Titanic*'s last minutes had been a "grimy stoker of gigantic proportions" who tried to steal the wireless operator's life jacket. The grimy cad took a deeper tint in Logan Marshall's 1912 book on the disaster, as a "negro stoker creeping up behind the operator." But in fact no Negro of either sex was privileged to be aboard. A Leadbelly song at the time went, "Black man oughta shout for joy, / Never lost a girl or either a boy." Black America and its press were relatively indifferent to the *Titanic*'s loss; yet a cycle of vernacular poems, or "toasts," arose which featured a black stoker called Shine, whose behavior was the pointed opposite of that of the first-cabin self-sacrificers. Told by the captain to go back down below, Shine responds, "There's one time you white folks ain't gonna shit on Shine," and "I'm gonna try to save this black ass of mine." He successfully swims to safety, while doomed white men offer him money and the sexual favors of their wives: "One thing about you white folks I couldn't understand: / You all wouldn't offer me that pussy when we was all on land."

Another scornful countercurrent existed in the radical left-wing press: *Masses* decried the "insanity of luxury, of foolish display and self-pampering even to the point of wrecking the safety and health of the luxurious themselves," and a writer who signed himself with the name of John M. Work asserted, in the magazine *NYC*, that the wreck was "a very slight tragedy" compared with the "millions upon millions who are enduring a living death under capitalism."

In song and anecdote the *Titanic* was remembered through the greater disasters of economic depression and two world wars. One of the wealthy survivors, Eleanor Widener, gave two million dollars for a new main library at Harvard named for her son, Harry Elkins Widener, a twenty-seven-year-old bibliophile. (Biel, who uses the library, thinks that the sumptuous memorial chambers caused scrimping in the stacks and elevators.) In Washington, the long-planned Women's Titanic Memorial to the men who sacrificed themselves was not dedicated until 1931, and eventually, to make way for the Kennedy Center, was moved from that site to a less prominent one, at Fourth and P Streets. In 1955, the ship's legend was given fresh life by Lord's best-selling *A Night to Remember*. According to Biel, Lord bestowed upon the *Titanic* disaster its significance as the end of an Edwardian era of *noblesse oblige* and general confidence in a civilization headed by the glamorous rich. Lord wrote, "The unending sequence of disillusionment that has followed can't be blamed on the *Titanic*, but she was the first jar. Before the *Titanic*, all was quiet. Afterward, all was tumult." But the feeling behind such a gross simplification had existed, surely, from the beginning. Lord's book had been preceded by the 1953 Hollywood movie *Titanic*, with Clifton Webb and Barbara Stanwyck as an estranged couple who reconcile as the ship founders,* and it was followed by a television program narrated by Claude Rains, and a British film with the same title as the book, starring Kenneth More as Second Officer Charles Lightoller, who while bobbing disconsolately on a capsized lifeboat pronounces, "I don't think I'll ever feel sure again. About anything." A more cheerful commercial spinoff of the disaster was the 1960 Broadway musical *The Unsinkable Molly Brown*, about the *Titanic* survivor Margaret Tobin Brown, a plucky mining plutocrat from Denver who was played by Tammy Grimes onstage and Debbie Reynolds in the 1964 movie—"the last," Biel tells us, "of the grandiose MGM screen musicals."

The legend's Cold War use as an indicator of America's unsinkability

---

*The captain of the ship was played by Brian Aherne, and forty years later I still remember the scene where he, sitting alone in the first-class lounge listening to some soft late-night music, lifts his head at hearing a slight bump. Thus quietly do catastrophes announce themselves. The jolt and sound of the collision varied with one's distance from the lower decks. To Mrs. J. Stuart White, the ship seemed to roll over a thousand marbles; to Lady Cosmo Duff Gorden, it was "as though somebody had drawn a giant finger along the side of the ship"; to Mrs. E. D. Appleton, it seemed "an unpleasant ripping sound . . . like someone tearing a long, long strip of calico"—an image that novelist Beryl Bainbridge uses as "a long drawn-out tearing, like a vast length of calico slowly ripping apart." The injury to the ship, long described as a three-hundred-yard-long "gash," has been revealed by underwater inspection to be a not very extensive strip of popped rivets and buckled plates produced by the momentum of the massive ship in its passing contact with the impervious iceberg. The wound was relatively slight, but fatal.

seems to me one of Biel's more far-fetched readings (what Hollywood musical heroine *isn't* plucky and unsinkable?), but there is no denying the religious devotion that *Titanic* buffs bring to every detail of their ship and its memorable last night. Centered on the Titanic Historical Society, which operates out of Henry's Jewelry Store, in Indian Orchard, Massachusetts, the cult devours arcana. "I can't learn enough about her," one member avowed. For another member, the *Titanic* "expresses in that era the eternal achievement of humankind," and for yet another "represents a way of life which I and others long for." Such enthusiasm—tied, Biel asserts, "to a cultural conservatism rooted in perceptions of social turmoil and decline"—led, in the macho Reagan era, from adoration of the unattainable beloved to physical possession of her underwater body. The successful diver, Robert Ballard, publicized as an old-style "cowboy" entrepreneur, is called by Biel a symbol of "revitalized American masculinity and a resurgent nation" and is caught out using the vocabulary of sexual adventure. The sunk *Titanic*, viewed in 1985 through an unmanned submersible containing underwater cameras, appeared to be "gorgeous" and "in beautiful condition." A year later, after "penetrating" her with a joystick-operated video camera, Ballard reported in the *National Geographic*, "Though still impressive in her dimensions, she is no longer the graceful lady that sank a mere five days into her maiden voyage." In an interview, Ballard revealed that his disillusion had become downright marital: "It seemed nice at the time—you know, she was cute, she was nice and all that sort of thing—but now I'm married to her and wondering if I made a mistake."

This is a funny and wickedly apt deconstruction, but Biel's book as a whole has the frustrating feeling of floating above coral gardens in a glass-bottomed boat. The thing itself, the event in its complex actuality, remains out of reach; in the cultural historian's world of "established meanings," there are no facts, just construals, mind-sets recovered from the dust of libraries and tied to stereotyped decades. To anyone alive in the 1950s, a passage like this has a tinny ring:

> While many fifties Americans were reading about or watching the *Titanic* disaster, the atomic establishment was telling the public about "the sunny side of the atom." More broadly, the nostalgia for security reflected an ambivalence about the achievements of the "affluent society" and the burgeoning national security state. Locating security in the remote, pre-*Titanic* past called into question the claims that defense-based abundance had provided Americans with permanent safety and comfort.

There is nothing blatantly false here, but also nothing out of conformity with the standard historical take on the Fifties: affluence, the atom, and national security monopolized people's heads back then. History becomes a stream of group obsessions and delusions which the writer and his reader have of course transcended. We read:

> In the case of the *Titanic* the myth of first-cabin male heroism appealed to conventional understandings and sentimental notions of gender roles that involved a series of oppositions: strength versus weakness; independence versus dependence; intellect versus emotion; public versus private.

Such oppositions have nothing, presumably, to do with us or the enduring human condition. We get the impression that nothing ever happens—there are just widespread opinions that something has happened. This style of history is like the present style of reading literature in academia: plenty of reference to implied social constructs but little to enduring truthfulness or a passionate excellence. With a fussy wealth of "*sic*"s and brackets, Biel puts the past in quotation marks, like a quaint or archaic expression. We float above the branching wonders of a sunken garden in which the giant *Titanic* serves but as an artificial shoal, its body ornately grown over by successive "myths."

We are left with an impulse to *touch* the disaster, to grapple unironically with its powerful facts. Lord's book is the best known of many; Wyn Craig Wade's *The Titanic: End of a Dream* (1979) is a more thorough, argumentative work, concentrating not on the drama of multitudinous subjective viewpoints like *A Night to Remember* but on the verbatim testimony by witnesses, principally those that appeared before the United States Senate hearing later that April, chaired by Senator William Alden Smith of Michigan—no relation to Edward J. Smith, the unfortunate captain of the *Titanic*. The captain and most of his senior officers did not survive to be interrogated, so the justifications of their mistakes could never be heard; but the survivors, crew and passengers, had much to say of the confusion attending the wreck and its dismal immediate aftermath on the water. Senator Smith, against some protest in the British press, persisted in eliciting the extraordinary fact that the half-filled lifeboats collectively refused to go back toward the site of the sinking, which had left hundreds of people floating and thrashing in the freezing North Atlantic, crying out for help. The Senate hearing held this exchange between Smith and Third Officer Herbert J. Pitman, who had been in one of the lifeboats:

> "Did you hear any cries of distress?"
> "Oh, yes."
> "What were they—cries for help?"
> "Crying, shouting, moaning."

"From the ship or from the water?"

"From the water after the ship disappeared—no noises before."

"Did you attempt to get near them?"

"As soon as she disappeared, I said, 'Now, men, we will pull toward the wreck.' Everyone in my boat said it was a mad idea, because we had far better save what few we had in my boat than go back to the scene of the wreck and be swamped by the crowds that were there." . . .

"I'll ask you if any woman in your boat appealed to you to return to the direction from which the cries came."

"No one."

In boat after boat, the women were in no mood to return the life-and-death courtesies extended them by the men, nor did any of the crew members in charge—with the energetic exception of Fifth Officer Lowe—insist on a rescue mission. From a mile away, one witness heard "a heavy moan as of one being from whom final agony forces a single sound"; to another, Jack Thayer, who himself had been in the water, the sound was "like locusts on a midsummer night"; to a third it resembled the noise a baseball crowd makes when a home run is hit. Pitman admitted to "a continual moan for about an hour" and, in tears, told Smith, "I cannot bear to recall it." This terrible lack of altruism, this dazed failure of mercy, does not figure in Mr. Biel's cultural history; it generated no provocative myths.

The cries are heard, though, by the twenty-two-year-old hero of Beryl Bainbridge's new novel, *Every Man for Himself*, when he surfaces out of the undertow of the plunging ship:

> I had thought I was entering paradise, for I was alive and about to breathe again, and then I heard the cries of souls in torment and believed myself in hell. Dear God! Those voices! *Father . . . Father . . . For the love of Christ . . . Help me, for pity's sake! . . . Where is my son.* Some called for their mothers, some on the Lord, some to die quickly, a few to be saved. The lamentations rang through the frosty air and touched the stars; my own mouth opened in a silent howl of grief. The cries went on and on, trembling, lingering—and God forgive me, but I wanted them to end.

Bainbridge is attracted to disasters and male perspectives. Her previous novel, *The Birthday Boys*, brilliantly renders the Scott expedition to the South Pole, another casualty of 1912, in the voices of the five participants who perished; British heroism is boiled down to a boyish camaraderie whose innocent glee breasts hideous hardships. In *Every Man for Himself*, she writes with a kind of betranced confidence, seeming to lose all track of her story only to pop awake for a stunning image or an intense exchange; as postmodern a fictionist as Professor Biel is a historian, she only intermittently gives us the *Ding an sich*. Her sudden details have a surreal snap. The hero, Morgan (called nothing else, as if in blunt token of his condition as an adopted son of his uncle J. P. Morgan, the owner of the *Titanic*'s White Star Line), remembers from his childhood a house-maid interrupting her scrubbing to comfort him: "A bubble of soap burst in her hair as she took me on her knee." When a friend on the *Titanic* displays a fragment of the iceberg that has brushed the ship, "He thrust it under my nose and it smelt rank, a bit like a sliver of rotten mackerel." And when the famous band on the doomed vessel goes on deck to play, Morgan, heading down into the lounge, notes, "I could see the score in the carpet where the cellist had dragged up his instrument." These precisionist visions loom, however, out of a fog of obscure motivation and existential portent. "In Scurra's company it was necessary to contemplate the exquisite darkness of the world"; "Pity welled up in me, and envy too, for I might never know the sort of love that gripped her by the throat."

Hard-drinking Morgan, returning from England to New York in a crowd of chummy nobs, is in love with the "absolutely unobtainable" Wallis Ellery. "Dancing with her was like holding cut glass; Hopper [a chum] got it about right when he complained she made him feel he left finger marks." Relations between the young in 1912 were sexually constrained:

> Most of our time was spent thinking what we might do with women if only we had the chance. There were houses we could go to, of course, but with girls of our own set there was never the slightest opportunity of trying out even a little of what we'd learnt.

Morgan gets a distinct shock, then, when at close quarters he overhears Wallis making kinky love (she likes being tied) with their sinister fellow-passenger Scurra, whose grotesquely split lip is never satisfactorily explained. Scurra is ready to share, however, any number of aperçus. "One must distinguish," he says, in refutation of Morgan's idealistic Marxism, "between use-value and exchange-value. . . . Philosophically speaking, life may be said to have use-value, but only for the individual. Its exchange is death, which has no value whatsoever unless one is in severe torment." Asked, by his slowly illumined acolyte, if he is in love with Wallis, Scurra replies, "Love? Good heavens! Love is what women feel."

Wallis is so enamored of Scurra that she has to be dragooned into a lifeboat. In historical actuality, many of the women did at first resist exchanging the vast deck of the luxurious *Titanic* for a lifeboat swaying in its davits above the black midnight ocean. Captain Smith gave few clear orders; no safety drills had been rehearsed. The confusion of the ship's last two and a half hours could have been worse; crew members, knowing in the pit of their stomachs that these might well be the last hours of their lives, by and large performed dutifully, and the second- and third-class passengers tended to observe the proprieties, sticking to their sections even as the decks perilously tilted. The band played on. The class system held, though it failed of its basic promise to its lesser orders: Know your place and you will be taken care of.

As Morgan comes of age via glimpses of sex and death, fictional and real characters mingle: he brushes against Mrs. Straus on the ship's Grand Stairway, and observes the Astors looking "as if they'd barely finished a thundering row . . . he nearing fifty, his long gloomy nose nudging his moustaches, she barely nineteen, her flower head drooping on the stalk of her neck." He happens to overhear that there are no binoculars in the crow's nest—a detail dear to *Titanic* scholars. Morgan's knowledge of the ship is above average, since, in obedience to his uncle, he worked for eleven months as an apprentice draughtsman to Thomas Andrews, the designer of the great ship and himself on board, attentive to such minute details as the number of screws in the rooms' coat-hooks. Amid this novel's somewhat bizarre and ghostly swarm of characters, the phlegmatic Andrews stands out, as deserving pity. He was, of the foundering's fifteen hundred victims, the quickest to understand the damage, and the one who knew best the love and labor lost when this nautical masterpiece was carelessly condemned to the bottom of the sea.

The *Titanic*'s ill-fated voyage attracts dramatizers; *Every Man for Himself* is by no means the only *Titanic* novel published this year. There are also *Maiden Voyage*, by Cynthia Bass, and *Psalm at Journey's End*, by the Norwegian Erik Fosnes Hansen, which has been a considerable bestseller in Europe. Bainbridge's novel shares with Bass's a young male narrator who finds himself through the ordeal, and with Hansen's a sense that Western civilization was ripe for a comeuppance. The *Titanic* in its very name evoked a race of beings who defied God and were destroyed. Wyn Craig Wade's scrupulous examination of the facts ends with a word-flight claiming that the *Titanic*'s "maiden voyage expresses the blind justice of Greek Tragedy, and the allegorical warning of the medieval morality play . . . the Titans' struggle against Jove, the Babylonians' ziggurat to heaven. . . . In a word, she is Hubris." Certainly fate played a delicate game with the ship that night. When the first reports began to come in, they were received incredulously, in part because, as Wade says, "there was no case in current recollection of any sizable ship going down as a result of an iceberg."

Had not First Officer William Murdoch, at the helm, in attempting to avoid the iceberg, maneuvered the ship into a glancing long blow instead of a head-on collision, the forward bulkheads might have contained the damage, as had happened with the *Arizona* in 1879, the *Concordia* in 1899, the *Kron-Prinz Wilhelm* in 1907, and the *Columbia* just the year past—all had survived head-on collisions with icebergs. Had the crow's-nest lookouts possessed binoculars, they might have seen the iceberg a crucial minute earlier.* In 1907 Captain Smith told an interviewer that in his forty years at sea he "had never been in any accident of any sort worth speaking about"; had he experienced any, he might not have been so sanguinely proceeding at near–top speed through an ice field that many other ships had warned him about. And had Stanley Lord, the scapegoated captain of the *Californian*, not been so determined to stay asleep belowdecks that night, while his officers on deck kept seeing the *Titanic*'s rockets, or had not Cyril Evans, the twenty-year-old radio operator of the *Californian*, not turned off his wireless ten minutes before the *Titanic* struck the iceberg and began flooding the air with calls for help, the *Californian* might have come to the rescue and saved many of the lives lost. Even without the *Californian*, had there been more than half enough lifeboats, and had the ship not been strange to its crew, and had there been a lifeboat drill, the toll would have been less. The sinking of the *Titanic* seems, like the world war that commenced twenty-seven months later, tragically avoidable; it was a disaster that men coasted into, confident of their invulnerability and righteousness. Its awful majesty is not easily assimilated, however, into invented narratives. Reading novels that take place on board is like sitting through the warm-up acts of a rock concert, waiting for the star—the crash—to appear. The *Titanic*'s story can't be topped, though it is being extended and reversed by the ship's piecemeal raising. The story's august moral remains: nothing human is unsinkable.

---

*Both lookouts, Frederick Fleet and Reginald Lee, survived, but in the Washington and London hearings and in later life told inconsistent stories that did not dispel the suspicion, first raised in 1912, that they had been sheltering from the arctic cold under the solid side of the crow's nest and not vigilantly looking. In the motion picture *Titanic*, whose billion-dollar-gross success came the year after this review was written, the lookouts are distracted by watching the film's two principals, played by Kate Winslett and Leonardo DiCaprio, canoodle on the deck below.

2000, Here We Come

QUESTIONING THE MILLENNIUM: *A Rationalist's Guide to a Precisely Arbitrary Countdown*, by Stephen Jay Gould. 190 pp. Crown/Harmony Books, 1997.

One surefire prediction about the future: the next millennium will soon arrive. No one knows quite what to make of this fact, but it must be, we feel, somehow momentous. At the purely computational level, computers, wherein years have been programmed as two digits and "00" has hitherto signified the year 1900, may be stumped, and the worldwide financial network collapse, reducing us all to insolvency and barter. More generally, a transformative millenarian change looms, even though the new millennium has already crept into our mundane lives: the college class of 2001 has donned its freshman beanies, and bonds due in the twenty-first century are paying interest in many a contemporary portfolio. "What's the fuss?" Stephen Jay Gould in effect asks in his succinct book *Questioning the Millennium: A Rationalist's Guide to a Precisely Arbitrary Countdown*.

Arbitrary indeed: there is nothing in nature keyed to the number one thousand. The decimal system of counting derives from our ten manual digits, which in the twists of evolution could have been less or more. The Mayas had an elaborate mathematics based on twenty, and a base of two works elegantly for computers. The three heavenly cycles that measure the passage of calendrical time—the earth's rotation, the revolution of the moon around the earth (lunation), and the revolution of the earth around the sun—are mutually irregular. A lunation takes 29.53059 days, and a solar revolution 365.242199 days. The fractions have forced makeshifts upon the keepers of the calendar. Societies, such as those of imperial China, Judaism, and Islam, that use a predominately lunar calendar deploy twenty-nine-day months (known as "defective" or "hollow") and thirty-day months ("full"), which still leaves them eleven days short of the solar year. The irregularity of the solar year, measured in rotations of the earth (days), has necessitated, in Christendom, a series of adjustments—a familiar story that Gould retells with his characteristic relish for historical detail. The Julian calendar, introduced by Julius Caesar in 45 B.C., instituted the leap year, but an actual solar year is more than eleven minutes short of three hundred sixty-five and a quarter days. By the late sixteenth century, the annual eleven-minute surplus amounted to ten full days, generating some problems with the equinoxes, "particularly for priests and astronomers charged with the solemn and sacred duty of determining the date for Easter." A committee for calendar reform convened by Pope Gregory XIII decided that ten days must be dropped from the calendar: the days from October 5 through October 14, 1582, were wiped out of history (in Catholic countries only). The committee, headed by the Jesuit mathematician Christopher Clavius, also fine-tuned the leap years: a leap year would be omitted at the turn of each century, except for those centuries divisible by four hundred. This brought the calendar year within 25.96 seconds of the solar year—"accurate enough to require a correction of one day only every 2,800 years or so."

Gould's keen interest in calendrics may outwear the reader's. He explores at length the riddle of the so-called idiot savants who can swiftly calculate the day a certain date falls on, and the problem of exactly when a century begins—a problem traceable to a sixth-century monk, Dionysius Exiguus, or Dennis the Short. Dennis, in preparing a chronology for Pope St. John I, added a variation on the traditional reckoning of years from the founding of Rome (A.U.C., *ab urba condita*) by dating time also from the infant Christ's circumcision, eight days after Jesus's supposed birth on December 25, 753, A.U.C. The first year of this new sequence he called 1 A.D. (*Anno Domini*) instead of the year 0.* Thus all subsequent zero years end rather than begin a set of ten. Every new century incites a debate as to exactly when it begins; an Englishman of 1800 commented on "the idle controversy, which has of late convulsed so many brains, respecting the commencement of the current century." In the instance close upon us, does the third millennium begin in the year 2000 or, as in the movie title, 2001? Popular instinct, conditioned by odometers, votes for the rollover of nines into zeroes as the critical moment; but at the last such rollover, high culture, in the form of university presidents and newspapers, opted for 1901. The *New York Times*, on the last day of 1899, stated, "Tomorrow we enter upon the last year of a century," and the British magazine *The Nineteenth Century* changed its name (adding *And After*) only with the January 1901 issue. This time around, Gould confidently predicts, popular preference will prevail over elitist precision, and "the world will rock and party on January 1, 2000." A day-date savant whom Gould consulted on the question unhesitatingly responded, "In 2000. The first decade had only nine years."

Day and night, full and new moons, solstices and equinoxes are empirical events; the rest is a man-made skein of numbers, a fallible approximation. Gould in conclusion says that he has "always and dearly loved calendrical questions because they display all our foibles in revealing

*Zero as a concept did not really enter Western mathematics (from Hindu and Arabic sources) until several centuries later. As Gould puts it, "During the year that Jesus was one year old, the time system that supposedly started with his birth was two years old."

miniature"—our foible, that is, of looking to nature for anthropocentric order and, not finding it there, seeking to impose it. Gould's ability to empathize with failed science, to retrace its awkward but earnest steps, is perhaps his outstanding quality as an essayist. He sympathetically treats Archbishop James Ussher's often ridiculed dating, in his *"Annales veteris testamenti a prima mundi origine deducti"* (1650), of the creation of the world to precisely at noon on October 23 of the year 4004 B.C. Gould admits Ussher was bound to find that, as current Christian theory demanded, four thousand years passed from the creation to the birth of Jesus. The four extra years have their origin in another imprecision of Dennis the Short, who overlooked the evidence that King Herod, the persecutor of the infant Jesus, had died in the year 4 B.C. As to the four thousand years, Gould surprisingly praises this foreordained conclusion as a work of conscientious research:

> Ussher's large folio volume represents an immense labor of calcula-tion and scholarship (requiring knowledge of Latin, Greek, and Hebrew). You can't simply spend a rainy afternoon counting the begats in the Bible, for gaps and ambiguities abound, and the record is incomplete in any case. . . . Thus, one has to move laterally from the biblical record into the historical documents of other societies (particularly to Babylon . . .) then forward to Roman history, and back again to the New Testament. . . . The actual information must have come pretty darned close to four thousand years.

If the data had "added up to ten thousand or two thousand years, then this enterprise would be cooked. . . . I don't doubt that he read all questionable points in his favor, but he did count, and labor, and read, and ponder, year after patient year." The second piece of Ussher's cosmology was that the world would end two thousand years after the birth of Christ, which, subtracting the four mistaken years, and adding the missing zero year, puts the date safely behind us, on October 23, 1997.

If nature does not deal in even thousands, the Bible does, especially the writer of Revelation, who saw an angel lay hold of Satan and bind him for a thousand years, and cast him in a bottomless pit. When the thousand years have expired, "Satan shall be loosed out of his prison," and with his allies Gog and Magog will battle for the world, until the fire from God in Heaven devours them, and the Devil is cast into a lake of fire and brim-stone; then the dead shall stand before God, and those whose names are not written in the book of life will be cast into the same lake, and a new Heaven and Earth established. These verses, and the visions related in the Old Testament Book of Daniel, inspire the faiths of the millenarians (one "n," since the word derives from the Latin *milleni*, meaning "a thousand each," and not *millennium*, meaning "a thousand years").

Millenarian sects have arisen within Christianity since the second-century Montanists; twentieth-century examples include the Branch Davidians who met their fiery end at Waco and the polite Jehovah's Witnesses who come so persistently to the door. Especially in America, it seems, there is a longing for the end, for a cataclysmic shake-up, for what Gould nicely calls "an imminent termination to the current order." Perennially, those who do not profit by the current order—the slaves, the losers, the excluded—take solace in the hope of such a termination, and of course Christianity itself was millenarian in this sense: both Christ and St. Paul asserted that the end was near, within the lifetime of the living. The year 2000 is shadowed, even in this secular and scientific age, by the prospect of the Second Coming, of the sweeping destruction and redemption which so many spirited sects have firmly predicted, only to slink away from their mountaintops disappointed, soothing their scorched beliefs with ingenuities of reinterpretation. Within the New Testament, the second epistle of Peter addresses the faithful who have met "scoffers, walking after their own lusts, and saying, Where is the promise of his coming? for since the fathers fell asleep, all things continue as they were from the beginning of the creation." Peter, echoing the 90th Psalm, offers the expectant flock a sonorous equivocation: "Beloved, be not ignorant of this one thing, that one day is with the Lord as a thousand years, and a thousand years as one day."

Neither God's nor Nature's timetable, then, is ours. However, it does not follow, from Gould's rationalist questioning of the millennium, that nothing will happen in the year 2000. The number is a cultural construct, but we dwell within culture, and make things happen within it. The last such event was the year 1000 A.D. (The year 1000 A.U.C., I calculate, fell in 246 A.D., when Rome was enjoying the brief reign of the Arabian-born Emperor Philip, at the outset of what Gibbon calls "twenty years of shame and misfortune.") Eighteenth- and nineteenth-century historians painted a vivid picture of the "panic terror" that came upon the European population of the year 999. William Robertson, a Scots peer of Gibbon and Hume, wrote that "A general consternation seized mankind; many relinquished their possessions, and abandoning their friends and families, hurried with precipitation to the Holy Land, where they imagined that Christ would quickly appear to judge the world." Pope Sylvester II was alleged to have had all the bells of Christendom ring out at the millennial moment. Later historians doubt that much of the sort happened, since calendrical confusion still obtained, and New Year's Day scarcely existed. Gould, however, who has audited some of the fierce debates that rage over this issue, is convinced that "sufficient evidence now exists to support at least a modest claim for substantial millennial stirring, especially in peasant and populist strata of society." They may not have had clocks, but the chronologies of the eighth-century Venerable Bede had popularized throughout Europe the A.D. dating system. Though no papal or royal statement of the time mentions the imminent Armageddon, a contemporary monk called Raoul Glaber wrote that, shortly after the year 1000 had safely passed, a wave of church-building took place—"the world put on the pure white robe of churches." In the broad perspective, things did pick up in the eleventh century, as if men, seeing that the world was still in place, felt free to focus on earthly concerns such as trade and technology; the Dark Ages yielded to the Middle Ages of cathedrals and centralized kingdoms.

More recently, as one century gives way to another, the journalistic orgy of retrospection and prediction cannot but infiltrate the mood of people and affect, if not politics, culture. Centuries feel bumptious in the beginning, thick in the middle, and sickly at the end. Though the seminal texts of Romanticism—Goethe's *Sorrows of Young Werther*, Rousseau's *Emile* and *Confessions*, Wordsworth and Coleridge's *Lyrical Ballads*—lie within the end of the eighteenth century, Romanticism awaited the galvanic figure of Napoleon, who seized dictatorial power in 1799, defeated Austria at Marengo in 1800, and made France paramount on the Continent by 1801. Romanticism's final *fin-de-siècle* flicker, in such artists as Oscar Wilde and Huysmans, became, in the early, rather mauve work of Pound, Joyce, and Proust, the sparks of modernism. In fiction, realism of a strangely pure, non-programmatic sort announced itself in Dreiser's *Sister Carrie* and Colette's first Claudine novel, both published in 1900, along with Freud's *Interpretation of Dreams*.* Relativity came along five years later, mixed into a dizzying stew of subatomic revelations. Who can say, until hindsight clarifies the picture, what rough beast was slouching through our own *fin de siècle* to be born? One development is visibly in progress: the end of a century, like the end of a house's tenancy, brings with it a ruthless disposal of accumulated trash, once viewed as treasure. Old styles, old scruples, old debates, old gossip, old books—out with them! The departing century's literary masterpieces undergo a drastic winnowing, and already we can see, in young people's indisposi-

---

*Actually, it was published in 1899, but both Freud and his publisher wanted it post-dated into the new century—an early flare of self-conscious modernism.

tion to read at all and a jaundiced anti-canon mood within academia, a massive casting-out and forgetting such as has relegated to specialists most of the Greek and Latin texts formerly deemed indispensable to an education.

I was born in 1932, and one of my first idle speculations concerned whether or not I would live to see the year 2000. It was nip and tuck, by the actuarial charts of Depression America. Now the odds seem pretty good, and I look forward with an irrational expectancy to the ominous and charismatic New Year. Until then, my life will have been entirely a twentieth-century one, imbued with a certain temporal patriotism, despite all the carnage and cruelty the century has contained—more than any other, if pain can be quantified. As a boy I thrilled to the trumpets that blared when, in the darkened movie house, the three-dimensional letters of 20TH CENTURY FOX appeared amid trumpet fanfares and swivelling floodlights. And to the hope of someday riding the Twentieth-Century Limited, in one of those spacious compartments where movie stars in glamorous silk pajamas and bathrobes (Myrna Loy, say, and William Powell) puffed cigarettes in holders and cracked witticisms while the sleeping cornfields poured by. And to the Trylon and the Perisphere, approached through what seemed miles of parked cars, in that hopeful year of 1939, when the future was a benign matter of spiralling highways and a family helicopter in every garage. My father striding beside me on that visit to the future, as it happened, had been born in 1900, on George Washington's Birthday,* and he walked through life with the springy step of a man twice favored. May the children born in 2000 get off to a comparably auspicious start.

---

*Considered to be February 22. The British Parliament kept the Julian calendar until 1752, by which time another extra day had accumulated, so that Washington was born, not in 1732 but 1731 (the Julian year began in March), on what was then February 11.

Visible Matter

MOVIES

The Old Movie Houses

THEY CAN STILL BE IDENTIFIED, in the old downtowns of the United States, by their marquees, which stick out over the sidewalk with an awkward nudity, since they no longer serve as billboards for that week's new movie. Inside, there is an awkward tilt to the floor that makes it difficult to convert the buildings into emporiums for, say, furniture or motorcycles. One of the grandest old palaces in Boston, the Copley on Essex Street, has become a giant Waterstone's bookstore, and the theatre in my home town of Shillington, Pennsylvania, has become a church for an evangelical sect. The newer brand of Protestant churches, indeed, are among the few customers for these deserted theatres of dreams, whose spaciousness and elegant details were designed to inculcate a religious mood.

My parents would take me when I was as young as three years old. I would sit between them, and once to my indelible shame I placed some gum on the seat next to me, where my father sat, ruining the trousers of a suit he could ill afford to replace. But even we were not too poor, in those Depression years, to afford the price of a movie, and my parents, in their thirties, went often, and would hold hands in the dark. A sour shadow fell on these innocent outings when someone teased my father, a public schoolteacher, about this sign of connubial affection. The hand-holding ceased, and my parents slowly left the moviegoing to me. The theatre was two blocks away, and I was allowed to attend alone from the age of six. Less venturesome than my classmates in many respects, I went there more than all but a few of them did, and was able to entertain them with descriptions of the Monday-Tuesday double-bill of B movies, westerns or

· For *Der Spiegel*'s 100th Anniversary Issue, December 1994.

comedies involving former romantic stars of silent films like Adolf Menjou and Zazu Pitts. Once I stood in class—the second grade, as I recall it—and told of an amusing door my family had cut into our front door, so that our pet dog could go in and out when he pleased. We had no such magic door-within-a-door; I had seen it in a movie, and perhaps our teacher had seen the same movie, for her amused skepticism conveyed to me, while I was still standing on my feet, the realization that I was lying. The movies and my life were so intertwined I had not been, in my enthusiastic projection of this image, quite aware of where reality ended.

Realer than real, truer than true—that was how the movies loomed to me until the age of twelve or thirteen. The little theatre, called simply The Shillington, provided a rich diet of Hollywood fare—the show was changed three times a week, and usually included a double bill. A cartoon, a newsreel, and a travelogue or comic short enlarged the ninety-minute feature to near two hours of bewitchment. My seat of preference was the back row, the lefthand seat, and quite early on my quest for fame manifested itself in a particularly loud and hearty laugh, which other members of the audience would mention to me the next day. For I did not attend, in my knickers and ear-lowering slanty-banged haircut, solely as a consumer but as something of a performer, a personage, John Updike, the high-school teacher's son, whose gestures in paying, entering, seating himself, and departing took on something of the suavity, say, of George Sanders as the Saint or the Falcon, or Errol Flynn as Robin Hood, or Humphrey Bogart as Philip Marlowe, Private Eye. I thought in those years I wanted to be a private detective when I grew up, or if not that a test pilot—another sort of hero, debonairly skirting the edge of annihilation, come into romantic prominence with the advent of World War II. For what did the movies teach a young American boy but a gallant stoicism, a death-defying nimbleness, whether manifested in the costume of a cowboy or an airplane pilot, a knight in armor or a playboy (Cary Grant, Ralph Bellamy) in a tuxedo? And we learned kissing and smoking: at least we saw how these oral exercises were conducted by giant black-and-white lips on the screen, though when our own time for enactment came there were tastes and dizzy sensations the movies had not described.

What I really wanted to be when I grew up was an animator. To create motion, frame by frame, appeared Godlike, and appealed to both the boundless egoism of the small movie-attending boy and his obscure passion for order, for pattern. I was five years younger than Mickey Mouse, and just old enough to be among the first audience for *Snow White and the Seven Dwarfs* in 1937. I have rarely missed a Disney animated film since, though as my hair has become gray I have been embarrassed to show up alone. The early, and greatest, full-length features—*Pinocchio*, *Fantasia*, *The Reluctant Dragon*, *Dumbo*, and *Bambi*—I saw under ideal circumstances, as an impressionable child. As an adolescent I experienced the tailing-off of the wartime films like *The Three Caballeros* and *Make Mine Music!*, in which animation lost its primal innocence and was polluted by all sorts of shortcut effects. A female friend from high school permitted herself, though we had graduated, to be taken to *Alice in Wonderland*, which hurt my eyes with its whirl of color and line, and by the time of *The Jungle Book* I had children of my own to take, though the Sixties were lean times for the art of animation. Now grandchildren can forbearingly escort me to *The Little Mermaid*, *Beauty and the Beast*, and *Aladdin*, in which the now venerable, rather frantically jazzed-up art of animation enjoys, or suffers, a revival. The wonder of animation lies in its possibility of creating a world from scratch, one liberated from the deadly laws of gravity; the disappointment comes when the world it conjures up so tritely resembles our own, and sags under all of reality's clichés. By the time I was old enough to apply to the Disney Studios for work, the heyday of animation was over—like so many of the grand Hollywood manufactures, it needed the low wages of the Depression to flourish.

And by the mid-Fifties, too, the downtown movie theatres were losing customers to the television sets popping up in American living rooms. Perhaps television's hours and hours of situation comedies and infotainment—not much crasser or more mechanical, really, than the run of old-fashioned Hollywood fare—supplies its consumers with the same educational and inspirational benefits that I enjoyed. But I doubt it. You had to get out of your house to go to the movies. It was, in the darkened theatre, a shared experience and social event. The very décor of the theatre, in its mirrored and gilded extravagance, its Arabian-nights fantasy and palatial scale, lifted the men and women of drab American towns and cities up from their ordinary lives onto a supernatural level. We all tried, in our small ways, to live up to the stars—to dress as smartly, to act as bravely, to love as completely. No wonder so many of the vacant theatres are now churches. We worshipped in those spaces, and for all the frequent shoddiness and imbecility of the mass-market motion picture, there was nothing to prevent grandeur from occurring; there were, in the mad profusion, the weekly tumble, works of cinematic art that moved and transformed us as absolutely as the best and noblest painting, music, and poetry. For Americans, it was our native opera, bastard and sublime.

Samson and Delilah and Me

IN CECIL B. DE MILLE's Biblical epic *Samson and Delilah*, released in 1949, there is a moment in which Samson, played by Victor Mature, throws Delilah, played by Hedy Lamarr, roughly onto a white rug, within a well-furnished tent. She lands softly as a cat, in my imperfect memory, bracing her fall with her arms and hands, and looks slowly, carefully, *winningly* up and around, at Samson and at me. *Oh, boy,* I said to myself, sitting alone in the audience. *This is love, this is life, and all out of the Bible, so it must be reliable.* In 1949 I was a susceptible seventeen, entered into a man's hormonal condition if not a man's wisdom and experience. Unlike Victor, I was *im*mature. *Samson and Delilah* was the sexiest motion picture I had ever seen, with the single exception of a brief newsreel showing women mud-wrestling.

The entire film was very lush, beginning with its two somewhat over-ripe stars. Both Mature and Lamarr, later research tells me, had fallen on dull times, for stars of their magnitude, and they were not again to have a success on the order of *Samson and Delilah*, which broke every previous attendance record except that of *Gone With the Wind*. Nor was De Mille ever again to cash in so resoundingly on his venerable formula, dating back to the silent era, of Biblical cheesecake. *Samson and Delilah* was an old-fashioned picture for its time, an old-style Hollywood commercial triumph just before the American middle class would begin to stay home by the millions and watch television. The critics mocked the film; but when have the critics ever understood the spiritual needs of the mass audience that gathered night after night to forget its troubles at the movies?

I was a good Lutheran boy who had met the story of Samson and Delilah in Sunday school. Samson, one of the least pious and most easily tempted of the Biblical heroes, seemed charming, as he went about smiting uncircumcised Philistines "hip and thigh" with the jawbone of an ass, eating honey out of the carcass of a lion, and falling prey to the wiles of a woman at the drop of a shimmering robe. Pressed by the wanton Delilah to reveal the secret of his strength, he repeatedly ascertains, with cunningly false testimony, that she means to do him in, and then tells her his secret anyway; he is blinded and "made sport of" by those despicable Philistines (led, in the movie, by the superbly sneering George Sanders) and yet has the last laugh by tumbling the temple of Dagon down on

---

For a series, *52 Bilder vom Kino*—"52 Images, or Moments, from the Movies"—for the *Frankfurter Rundschau*.

everybody's head. A brutal and shapely tale that appealed to John Milton and Cecil B. De Mille both.

What the motion picture made clearer than the blunt Biblical narrative was the possibility that mortal combat could be an erotic occasion. The young moviegoer of 1949 could not escape the impression that Samson and Delilah, however mutually destructive their entanglement proved to be, were made for each other. For better or worse, they are lovers, equals in desirability. God presides above their tussle, and consecrates it. The moment when Samson knocks Delilah down, and she not only survives it but accepts the blow as coin of their basic transaction, returns, in amplified reverse, when through guile she renders him bald and helpless as a baby, and then again when, in the film if not in the Bible, he includes her among his slain victims in the ruined temple of Dagon. (Come to think of it, I believe she repents and assists him at the last moment, and enables his mighty arms to find the pillars. Yes, that is how Hollywood would have done it; I had forgotten.)

What I clearly remember is the luxurious décor of their trysting tent, and their elegant shoulder-baring robes, and the powerful androgyny of the beefy but soft-bodied hero in his long Samsonian hair, and the wiry catlike hardness of the sexually aggressive Lamarr. Fantastic though many of their suppositions about American life were, those old Hollywood makers knew about sex, and knew how to coax barbaric music out of the war of the sexes, music that would get a boy to tingling below his belt. The volatility of the sexual contest, the seesawing reverses of relative strength and vulnerability, the quasi-coital back and forth, the interlock of sexual love and political hostility—these are present in *Samson and Delilah* as much as in the critically acclaimed romantic comedies of the Thirties and Forties, but taking an opulent epic form that mixed with my adolescent juices and left me with an indelible image.

Legendary Lana

THE END-OF-1995 WRAPUPS didn't take much notice of Lana Turner, who had died on the 29th of June in her two-bedroom condo in Los Angeles, of throat cancer, at the age of seventy-four. The movie-star death of the year had been that of Ginger Rogers: a fond outpouring recalled her spunky screen persona and her iconic dance partnership with Fred Astaire; their mode of Depression escapism in long retrospect seemed heroic—a gallant, flip, graceful, and purely American response, on the part of the film industry, to a gritty national crisis. And there were tributes to Dean Martin, the nonchalantly gifted son of an immigrant Italian barber, and to Ida Lupino, a cinema vixen who, way ahead of her time, became a female director of films. But few remembered Lana.

She had had the misfortune, publicitywise, to die in the week when the big story out of Hollywood was Hugh Grant's arrest for lewd behavior with the prostitute Divine Brown. Grant's was a pale and farcical scandal compared to the most famous event in Turner's life: on April 4, 1958, her fourteen-year-old daughter, Cheryl Crane, fatally stabbed Lana's lover, a minor, darkly handsome gangster named Johnny Stompanato, in the actress's Beverly Hills bedroom, in the wake of a fierce quarrel the girl had overheard. According to Turner's account, Stompanato was in the process of leaving, with his clothes held high on a hanger, which Cheryl mistook for a threatening gesture; in the past, there is no doubt, he had repeatedly terrorized Turner with beatings and threats to cut up her face. This sensationally squalid event did not do immediate harm to Turner's film career—she went on to make her most successful film, *Imitation of Life* (1959), about an actress who neglects her daughter to attend to her career—but it perhaps soured the tone of her obituaries, which inevitably recalled Stompanato and her seven failed marriages. There is something ridiculous about a woman who takes seven husbands, as if she had rummaged through the drawers of masculinity and come up with seven dwarfs. Never mind that until the 1960s popular morality, reinforced by the Hollywood moguls, did not condone cohabitation without marriage. Turner underwent eight wedding ceremonies, as did Elizabeth Taylor: both serial polyandrists married one husband twice.

Personal irregularities, however, do not dim the reputations of Hollywood stars, who are licensed to live out our fantasies, in a realm above conventional constraints. The main inhibitor of memorial enthusiasm for Lana Turner was an implication that, unlike Rogers, she was a faded period piece, an old-fashioned glamour queen whose fifty-four films, over four decades, don't amount, retrospectively, to much. And who could deny it? In the massive compendiums that keep the accounts for cinema's busy, busy century, she gets short, even contemptuous, shrift. In David Shipman's *The Story of Cinema: A Complete Narrative History from the Beginnings to the Present*, he calls her "vacuous" and "a void" and, writing of *A Life of Her Own* (1950), says of the admired director, "What Cukor could not manage was to get a good performance from Turner, but she is not—for once—a dead loss." David Thomson, in his opinionated and witty *Biographical Dictionary of Film*, sounds personally offended by Turner: she has "the unanimated, sluggish carnality of a thick broad on the make. No actress, always inclined to veil her nature in the posturing of melodrama, she was close to the spirit of small-town waitresses ready to be picked up by a toothbrush salesman with a cousin in casting. Her private life only proved that a dull face could have a tempestuous romantic passage." Criticism even leaks into some of her own films: in *The Bad and the Beautiful* (1952) Leo G. Carroll calls a screen test her character takes "wooden, gauche, artificial"; in *Imitation of Life* her fictional daughter impatiently tells her, "Stop acting!"—as Turner was so evidently doing. Along with her numb, sex-stung look she displayed a quizzical, vexed expression, a quick and apologetic furrowing of her broad brow that seemed to confess the strain and difficulty of being in front of the cameras. Like Kim Novak, she appeared a bit lost—a doe caught in klieg lights.

The legend ran that she was discovered while sitting, or working, in Schwab's drugstore, in the middle of Hollywood. The facts, no less striking, are—as she remembered them in her autobiography, *Lana: The Lady, the Legend, the Truth* (1982)—that she had cut a typing class at Hollywood High School and run across Highland Avenue for a five-cent Coke, at a place called the Top Hat Café, long since defunct. A well-dressed man, "with sharp features, a mustache, and dark hair," politely asked the counterman for permission to speak to her, and then asked her, "Would you like to be in the movies?" The question was classic, but her answer was original: "I don't know," she said. "I'd have to ask my mother." The mysterious dark stranger gave her a card that identified him as W. R. Wilkerson, publisher of the *Hollywood Reporter*. Julia Jean Mildred Frances Turner, called Judy, was fifteen at the time, and had recently moved, with her widowed mother, from Sacramento to Los Angeles. They had come not to break into the movies but to ease the mother's respiratory ailments. Mrs. Turner worked in a beauty parlor, and was tired that night when her daughter showed her Wilkerson's card, "and so she shrugged it off." But they were living, in their poverty, with a friend, Gladys Taylor, who urged the child to take the opportunity seriously. A visit to Mr. Wilkerson led to the talent agency of Zeppo Marx, and that led to an interview with the director Mervyn LeRoy and her first role, as a provocative teenager (who is soon murdered) in a Southern melodrama, *They Won't Forget* (1937). LeRoy remembered their first meeting: "She was so nervous her hands were shaking. She wasn't wearing any makeup, and she was so shy she could hardly look me in the face. Yet there was something so endearing about her that I knew she was the right girl. She had tremendous appeal, which I knew the audience would feel." Her rolling walk, in a tight skirt and sweater, made her brief role notable, and "the sweater girl" was launched. She herself later wrote, "I was just a 15-year-old kid with a bosom and a backside strolling across the screen."

Her diffidence was unfeigned. As a performer she was purely a studio-made product. She had had no theatrical training, no elocution lessons. She had not been pushed forward by a stagestruck mother. Like most people in the Thirties, she went to the movies, and as a girl sketched clothes designs inspired by what she saw there; her highest hope for herself was to be a dress designer. She had been born in 1921 in Wallace, Idaho. Her father, John Virgil Turner, was a miner and gambler, who gave her, she wrote, "his bright blue eyes and small nose." After work, she remembered, he would dance with her, teaching her a few simple steps. He had time to teach her little else, for her parents separated, without divorcing, shortly after Judy had innocently revealed to some playmates that he maintained an illegal still in the basement of their new home in Stockton, California. Her mother, Mildred Frances, supported herself and her daughter with beauty-parlor jobs in San Francisco and Sacramento. "Times were hard," Lana remembered. "Once we lived on crackers and milk for half a week." In San Francisco they moved in with two other women, who used to stash the child in a closet when they entertained male friends. Eventually Mildred placed Judy with a family called Hislop, under whose influence the child converted to Catholicism. In 1930, she was told—as a God-filled dream of hers had foretold—that her father was dead. He had been robbed and killed in San Francisco after winning big in a crap game and bragging, according to a possibly Hollywood-flavored news item, that "he planned to buy his little girl a bicycle."

In her glory days Lana Turner loved going to nightclubs and dancing, but she was no hoofer, and she couldn't sing. Her voice was small, velvety, without the articulation and projection that stage experience would have given her. At times she fell into a baby whimper, with elaborate lip quivers, that uncannily anticipates mannerisms of Marilyn Monroe, whose studied sense of glamour, from overpainted lips to frozen-whip platinum hair, was distinctly Lanaesque. Turner's ripe figure flirted with plumpness—she was only five feet three inches tall—and in that unexercised era too many nightcaps added their increments to her bones. *Time* once wrote that "In any posture, Lana suggests she is looking up from a pillow"; at times her greatly magnified, vaguely defined face seems to *be* a pillow.

Yet one doesn't have to be old enough for Medicare to remember when "Lana" elided into "glamour" and she and Hedy Lamarr were considered the two most beautiful women in the movies. Turner was M-G-M's female answer to Clark Gable, a fair-sex hunk, and was paired with him in four movies. Her prime was the second half of the Forties, when she made *The Postman Always Rings Twice* (1946), with John Garfield, in spite of a California fog and a bingeing director; had an affair with Tyrone Power, which she remembered as the high point of her romantic life; married (among others) the millionaire Bob Topping; discovered that she owed buckets to the IRS; told off Hedda Hopper; turned down the script of *Madame Bovary*; and was voted the number-one box-office star by *Modern Screen*. Critics didn't like her, but for a considerable time two groups did: the people who made movies, and the people who went to them. Why this was so takes us a distance into the mystic communion that pre-television Hollywood enjoyed with its huge American audience.

She was not a void on the screen. At the minimum, she brought the unique, magical name—a coinage, according to her autobiography, of the teenage ingenue, when Mervyn LeRoy, claiming "Judy Turner" to be "too ordinary," offered her Leonore and Lurlene. At a time when many female stars were imported exotics like Garbo and Dietrich, a forthrightly Wasp name was joined to a word out of space, a playful invention.* She did not realize until later that *lana* means "wool" in Spanish and in Mexico is slang for "money."

She brought, too, herself, whatever her limits as an actress. She learned the lines and looked to her directors for guidance. Some of the lines in those studio-era scripts, pounded out by writers with frustrated literary aspirations, defied plausible delivery. In *Johnny Eager* (1941) she is supposed to be, in her high heels and tottering oval hat, a sociology student who suddenly quotes from *Cyrano de Bergerac* to a hoodlum on parole. In *Dr. Jekyll and Mr. Hyde* (1941), according to the harsh David Shipman, "Lana Turner has to listen to a fellow diner who asks 'Has anyone read that poem by that new chap, Oscar Wilde?' and she deserves no better." Turner worked conscientiously in the fantasy mills. Unlike Monroe, she never allowed her nervousness or insecurity to break down the produc-

---

*Her poetic name figures in a number of poems, including two by Frank O'Hara: "Steps" (1961) asks, "where's Lana Turner / she's out eating," and "Poem" (1962) begins, "Lana Turner has collapsed!" and ends, "oh Lana Turner we love you get up." David Lehman, an O'Hara scholar, in his poem "Who She Was" writes, "and if you want to know / where I am, I'm in Palm Springs / fucking Lana Turner / as Frank Sinatra put it to Ava Gardner / who was in the bathtub at the time / it was 1952." Turner in *Lana* remembers the incident very differently: Sinatra had loaned her his house in Palm Springs, and "The simple fact is that Ava, Ben [Cole], and I were about to eat chicken in the kitchen when Frank appeared at the door." Gardner and Sinatra quarrelled, and "a lot of sick rumors grew out of it."

tion of a movie or drive her fellow actors to distraction. Her obituaries did not lack for tributes from actors who had worked with her: Hope Lange, who played Turner's daughter's best friend in the melodramatic *Peyton Place* (1957), said, "She had no sense of self-importance. There wasn't an ounce of condescension to her." Teri Garr, a fellow-performer in her last film, the unreleased *Witches' Brew*, recalled her as "very sweet; a gracious, genteel, lovely woman."

Her instinctive gentility comes through in her later roles as an older woman, where she comports herself with the crisp, guarded, smiling dignity of an all-American matron, a former cheerleader who has kept her waist and her legs. In *Cass Timberlane* (1947), made with Spencer Tracy the year after she grappled her way to murder with Garfield, Turner does not seem out of place as the wife of a middle-aged judge; where she does appear unconvincing, in that cozy, creaky adaptation of the Sinclair Lewis novel, is as a girl of the people, from the wrong side of the tracks. She could look tough but could not do tough accents. Her pose as the Brooklyn babe Flatbush in *Ziegfeld Girl* (1941) feels quaint; it is her regal descent of the stairs at the end that takes possession of the screen, and that she proudly remembered in her memoirs. Another piece of acting she cherished was the long fit of hysteria climaxing her segment of the three-part *The Bad and the Beautiful*; the segment as a whole holds perhaps her best sustained performance, drawing upon the two personae in which Hollywood could best imagine her: woozy slut and glamour queen. Before her climactic scene, a three-month break in the filming had intervened, and in her recollection she was thrust one morning, with no direction from Vincente Minnelli, into an old car chassis mounted on springs, rocked by stagehands, and doused with water by men in yellow slickers:

> I went to the set, climbed over the paraphernalia, and got into the chassis. I tried to re-create the shock of finding Jonathan with another woman, the scene I had filmed nearly three months earlier. I dug for it, dug deeper into my own feelings, into my own bitter experiences with love. . . . The car moved and threw me from side to side. I concentrated on my hysteria, building with each movement of the car. *It's my big night, my premiere, and meanwhile he's with another woman.* . . . Emotions welled up inside me and tears sprang to my eyes.
>
> I don't like to cry but once I am in tears, the more I try to fight them, the more they come. They came gushing now and were echoed by the gush of water against the windshield. . . .

Minnelli made her do it over and over, all day, filming her from different angles, with different lenses:

The mike was pushed into the cab, and in my hysteria I sobbed and the mike picked up the sobs. The agony by then was genuine. Too much was coming back to me, too much of my own life: the bitter marital disappointments, the babies I had fought to keep and had lost—and that crushing last meeting with Tyrone, the man I had loved most of all. When Vincente said, "Cut. That's it," for the last time, I was totally drained.

This vivid passage tells us that (a) actress abuse was part of moviemaking, (b) Lana Turner took her acting seriously, (c) she had a lot to cry about.

Mervyn LeRoy, having discovered her and created the sweater-girl image, took her with him from Warners to M-G-M. The grandest of the major studios, M-G-M was also perhaps the stupidest; certainly its products, bouncy musicals and family comedies and bloated costume dramas, didn't ask much intelligence from the American moviegoer. Warners at least tried to stretch its audience into awareness of the despairing, criminal underside of American society, and Twentieth Century–Fox offered vistas of wit and sophistication. Turner might have seemed less vacuous had she been with a studio that developed her *noir* potential: her show-me-what-you've-got pout held a sinister challenge, as *Postman*—a film with classic moments, but no classic—imperfectly demonstrates. She was not a void, but she was relatively inert and amorphous: examining the two spreads of publicity photos and magazine covers reproduced in *Lana*, one can hardly believe that they are all of the same woman, or of any particular woman. There is no Lana look—just a cloudy, heated Lana presence. One of the few photographs that capture an individual beauty was taken in the harrowing aftermath of Stompanato's death. She was wearing dark glasses and a bandana, and the stoically pursed lips tell it all: a bleached blonde who's been around, retreating into herself as flashbulbs beat on her white skin.

The Hollywood films of today, with their mechanical violence and computer-driven spectacle, seem made, most of them, for adolescent males—kids who need to get out of the house. The pre-television movies were made for adults, though adults, by today's standards, of a pious simplicity. They expected sin to be punished and the flag to be honored. Nevertheless, adult issues were addressed, including the nature of sexual relations; the old movies, though anxiously watched over by the Hays Code, had more to say about the sadistic and masochistic components of sex than can be said in today's liberated but gender-politically chastened atmosphere. "Kick her hard," a man in *Ziegfeld Girl* advises, of a girl who needs discipline, adding sagely, "Kick her where it won't show." In *Johnny*

Eager, Edward Arnold, a vigorous law-enforcer, surprisingly pontificates, "Lovemaking is not always correct, or gentlemanly, or considerate." The voluptuous sociology student is warned, "You're gonna get hurt, you know," and Van Heflin, as Johnny Eager's erudite friend, muses, "When a woman loves you like that, she can love you with every card in the deck and then pull a knife across your throat the next morning."

Turner's screen persona did not have the feisty class of Katharine Hepburn's or Claudette Colbert's; nor did it often muster the hard-won righteousness of Barbara Stanwyck's or Joan Crawford's. Turner, in most of her roles, lives for love and takes her lumps. Erotic high points of her film career include being knocked unconscious by Robert Taylor, offering to drown herself for John Garfield, being rolled from a moving car in *Cass Timberlane*, going to the scaffold in *The Three Musketeers* (1948).* If Johnny Stompanato roughed her up, it had happened to her before, in the movies; it took her virgin daughter to rescue her from the morass of what we now would call an abusive relationship. In her films, she is often in bed, sick or broken-hearted, and often, in her frailty or fallibility, needs to be lifted and carried—another metaphor for sexual transport. She is malleable and self-sacrificial, consumed in the instant of intercourse, for which the kiss was the universally understood symbol in the days of the Hays Code. And Turner was one of the great screen kissers, her small-nosed profile expectant, her round chin lifted to give her throat a swan's curve. "O.K., so you know your own strength," she tells Jimmy Stewart after a long osculation in *Ziegfeld Girl*. He responds, "You ain't exactly anemic yourself." Love as a divine force, a magic potion, a doom that survives betrayals and double crosses and angry blows: this monogamous theme was one of Hollywood's contributions to order in America.

Turner, for all her seven husbands and untabulated dance partners, believed in love, and in her memoirs she cast herself opposite Tyrone Power. Divorced from Stephan Crane, by whom she bore her one child, she entered an affair with the recently separated Power. "But more important to me than money was, as always, the love I longed for. And finally I found it, if only for a moment. The man was Tyrone Power. . . . You had only to look at us to know we were in love. And we made a breath-taking couple." She was so smitten that she chased him to his

---

*There is a moment in *Postman*, however, when she gets a gun in her hand; she and Garfield, who appear sluggish and helpless for much of the film, show teamwork and initiative when threatened with blackmail. Garfield does the fisticuffs while Turner holds the gun, and this viewer at least felt a certain ecstasy, seeing the embodiment of female passivity equipped at last with an "equalizer."

movie location in Mexico, arriving on New Year's Eve, 1947. Their tryst is pure Hollywood:

> In my memory we will always be an especially beautiful couple. I say this, I think, without vanity. Tyrone, so stunningly handsome, was majestic, and I wanted so to be his equal—I like to think that on that night I succeeded. I wore white satin brocade, cut in the Chinese fashion, with a high mandarin collar and slits up the long, tight skirt. The sides and the sleeves of my gown were heavily beaded with seed pearls and rhinestones that gleamed like the stars in the Mexican skies. I'd even brought jewels with me. I like to think of that Mexican night glittering off the jewels I wore in my hair. Oh, I think we *were* beautiful. But more than that, there was such an aura of love about us that we would have shone just as brightly even without the diamonds and the pearls.

There is a pathos in such self-dramatization—Power soon betrayed her (with Linda Christian), as many of Turner's chosen beaux were to betray her—but there is also a professional thoroughness, a resolute perfectionism. A star, she took it upon herself to live as a star, romance, seed pearls, Mexican moonlight, and all. We are told in a soon-to-be-published book, *The Private Diary of My Life with Lana,* by one of her hairdressers, Eric Root, that when she could no longer offer her public beauty she stayed in her apartment, sipping drinks and watching television, where her younger self sometimes flickered. Root's hold over her was that he could cater to her paralyzing vanity, with his applied beauty tips. To be a star is a job that never ceases, and, she wrote, "The most important tool of my trade was a mirror." Narcissism was an occupational hazard, along with feckless husbands and merciless directors. According to Root, she didn't allow anyone entering her apartment—where her "perfume clung to the air like a romantic Polynesian aphrodisiac"—to wear any competing perfume or cologne: "She didn't want any other essence co-mingling with her own. She thought it might 'break the spell.' "

The most startling revelation in her *Lana: The Lady, the Legend, the Truth* is that she had no eyebrows. They had been shaved off for the role of a Eurasian handmaiden in *The Adventures of Marco Polo* (1938), and never grew back. For the rest of her life, every day of her life, they had to be drawn on, or else counterfeited with little woven falsies she needed help to apply. It's a detail from a Eurasian handmaiden's slave narrative: she was loaned from Warners to M-G-M; the great Goldwyn himself insisted on the eyebrow-shaving; and when the film was belatedly released she was billed as Gary Cooper's co-star, even though most of her scenes had been cut. She had given up her eyebrows for nothing—for a mogul's whim.

Turner was one of those actresses it was convenient to cast as an actress, and Hollywood knew itself cold. Shortly before fifteen-year-old Judy Turner was signed up for fifty dollars a week, she was informed, "As far as this industry goes, you're eighteen"—the age, that is, when statutory rape could not be an issue in the course of a starlet's development. *Ziegfeld Girl* portrays show business as a blithe meat market that eats up young bodies, and *The Bad and the Beautiful* describes the oppression of the few who make it to movie stardom: Georgia, the fictional star, kneels by a dying man, telling him she loves him, while a towering structure of onlookers—director, assistants, cameraman, light grips—seems to rest upon her back. The film industry's immense technical and financial superstructure rests upon the evanescent basis of an authentic emotion or a moment of beauty, conjured up on sets where everything proclaims contrivance and falsity: an industry built on lies.

"Don't lie to me, Mr. Eager," the sociology student says. "Why not?" Robert Taylor quickly responds. In her real life, Turner was easy to lie to: her last two marriages were to younger men who dipped deep into her pocketbook, and even Bob Topping, for all his supposed millions, cost her money. Her last husband, Ronald Dante, whom she married in her late forties, was a nightclub hypnotist who appeared at her door on a motorcycle: "I had never been on a motorcycle before, but I was game. He told me to climb on behind him and hold on tight. Then off we sped through the hills of Malibu. I loved it!" In the course of their marriage, she confides, he embezzled from her, stole her jewelry, signed her name to documents, and produced a document (thrown out by the court) in which she promised to pay him $200,000 in the event of a divorce. He really was a hypnotist.

Had Turner been harder-headed, she might not have projected the vulnerability that her female fans could identify with. The housewives and working girls who trooped to the movies between 1930 and 1950 saw their furtive affective lives enlarged and glamorized on the screen. In a stylized movie like *Ziegfeld Girl*, who was closest to them: Judy Garland, with her brassy talents; Hedy Lamarr, with her foreign accent; or Lana Turner, with a truckdriver boyfriend and a hankering for the bright lights beyond Brooklyn? The last is the only real story told, melodramatic as it is. "You know what's wrong with me?" Flatbush says. "I'm two people." So are most of the heroines Turner plays, torn between passive love and active ambition. Discontent and desire rile these lacquered love objects. They want to be actresses, they want to live in New York. "I want more," Lora announces in *Imitation of Life*. Her constant suitor, faithful to a fault, says, "I love you. Isn't that enough?" She gives him a plain answer: "No." Even tawdry Cora, in *Postman*, with no nobler aim in her life than an improved roadside eatery, proclaims, "I want to be somebody . . . and work hard and be something." Virginia, in *Cass Timberlane*, tells her exemplary judge of a husband, "I can feel myself dying. . . . I'm married to the most wonderful man on earth, it's true, but it doesn't help."

Turner won her sole Academy Award nomination playing, in *Peyton Place*, a woman who has been a married man's mistress and has renounced sex, for herself and, if she has her way, for her daughter as well. Veteran filmgoers could be confident, however, that the former sweater girl would come round into a good man's arms. But Turner writes in her autobiography, "I might as well confess I was not a great companion in bed. . . . Sex was so much what I symbolized, so much of my image, that I closed myself off to the pleasures of the act." She insists to the reader,

> Sex was never important to me. I'm sorry if that disappoints you, but it's true. Romance, yes. Romance was very important. But I never liked being rushed into bed, and I never allowed it. I'd put it off as long as I could and gave in only when I was in love, or thought I was. It was always the court-ship, the cuddling, and the closeness I cared about, never the act of sex itself—with some exceptions, of course.

Of course. She did have a wild streak—after all, what was she doing cutting typing class that day she met Mr. Wilkerson in the Top Hat Café? She was a woman who received more invitations than most, and accepted a good number of them. She paid a price in divorces, abortions, and one suicide attempt. But she did not self-destruct, as Marilyn and Judy did, as Ava and Vivien and Natalie did. This ultimate studio product held up. When the movies would no longer have her, she acted on television; when her serial, *The Survivors*, folded, she took her name and well-worn glamour to the stage, to the dinner-theatre circuit. Gay men became her companions and escorts, and she became a friend to her adult daughter, who had entered Stephan Crane's restaurant business and lived, with a female companion, in Honolulu. As Turner passed sixty, she turned to God, collected some film awards, and wrote—with the help of Hollis Alpert and others—a relatively frank and engaging autobiography. If you want to know how disappointing it was to go to bed with Artie Shaw, this is your book.

They don't make them like Lana Turner any more. Hollywood's present queens are a lean, clever lot, whose grip on the box office is unsteady—look at Julia Roberts. Only pop divas and the heroines of television serials enjoy the old, non-critical kind of audience; a more suggestible and repressed public consumed the products of the Hollywood that made Lana Turner. Might one even say a more generous-hearted public? Fifty years ago we were still a nation of builders and dreamers; now whittlers and belittlers set the cultural tone. Custodians of today's correctnesses may prefer to forget a once-celebrated screen presence whose appeal was purely sexist, built on bosom and backside, pouting lips and pencilled eyebrows, breathless embraces and limp surrender. But, aside from the undercurrent of feminist protest in many of the roles she played, Turner's well-publicized life showed her idolizers that even a beauty cannot depend on a man: a girl is on her own.

M.M. in Brief

CAPTIONS FOR A Playboy *spread. Each was tailored, letter by letter, to an allotted space, and each one, the reader will notice, begins, as requested by the editors, with an "M." The photographs these captions illumined must be feverishly imagined.*

MARILYN MONROE was not nudity-averse. Natasha Lytess, who lived with the budding movie star in the late Forties, recalled how she would come wandering naked from her bedroom around noon, bathe for an hour, and "still without a stitch on . . . drift in a sort of dreamy, sleepwalking daze into the kitchen and fix her own breakfast." So it was at the studio, where she "ambled unconcerned, completely naked, around her bungalow, among wardrobe women, make-up girls, hairdressers. Being naked seemed to soothe her—almost hypnotize her. If she caught sight of herself in a full-length mirror, she'd sit down—or just stand there—with her lips hanging slack and eyes droopily half shut like a cat being tickled." Vagrant as a child, Monroe was at home, at ease, in her skin. The photo to the right appeared in 1953 as the first *Playboy* Sweetheart, the precursor of the Playmate centerfold.

MEN UNDRESSED are stripped of the power that uniforms and armor confer; women put on power, of a precarious, primal sort. These early cheesecake poses, some of a brunette still known as Norma Jean Baker, show her experimenting with her power. Fatherless and with a mentally unstable mother, she married young and worked in a war plant; when an Army photographer chose her for a publicity shot, her make-believe life began. Gamely, she led her photographers on, teasing them to dare more, challenging the lens.

MODELLING supported the struggling young starlet. In 1949, photographer Tom Kelley offered her fifty dollars to pose nude for a calendar, just the amount she needed to buy back her repossessed car. "He stretched me out on this red velvet and it was sort of drafty," she recalled. "When I was a kid, I used to dream of red velvet." The stretched-out dreamer seems to swim—a slender swimmer through the dreams of unknown men.

MORE THAN A DOZEN YEARS LATER, the swimmer had become world-famous, grievously addicted to pills, and only the most delicious little bit chunky. Her body was old-style—pre–buns of steel. Marriages to Joe DiMaggio and Arthur Miller had enhanced her celebrity but ended in divorce. Tardy, spacy, ill, she sent film budgets soaring. *Something's Got to Give* aptly titled a doomed movie she was fired from; but she did perform a swimming-pool skinny-dip, voluntarily shucking her flesh-colored bathing suit and leaving on film a haunting record of what the world would soon lose.

MONROE collaborated cunningly in her exploitation as a sex object. Bert Stern has left a hard-breathing account of how, six weeks before her suicide, he turned a fashion shoot for *Vogue* into a striptease. The climactic shots came after midnight, and the model had been loosened up with plenty of Dom Pérignon. Yet who, looking at the results, can doubt that such immortalizing exposure was what she desired? She pored over the transparencies, mutilating with a hairpin the ones she didn't want used.

MARILYN rests. Stern's assistant, Leif-Erik Nygards, snapped the exhausted, casually naked star when everyone else had left the room. Her pubic hair is unbleached; her hand rests like a self-comforting child's beneath her lightly smiling mouth. The semblance of intimacy and the sensation of isolation are the twin conditions of those who live by what the public sees of them. Arthur Schlesinger, Jr., who saw an amount of Monroe in the shadowy months when she drifted like a ghost through the corridors of the Kennedys' Camelot, writes of how "she receded into her own glittering mist. There was something at once magical and desperate about her." Her life as a person ended at thirty-six, in an odor of despair and failure; her life as an image is a continuing, swelling triumph. Her dreamy awkwardnesses, her inability to stay a wife or become a mother, her pathetic death consecrate her to a lonely monumentality. Had she lived, she would be seventy and one more discomfiting reminder of how we all age, even the most beautiful. As it is, like a broken marble Venus, she defies time.

The Vargas Girl

PIN-UP ART. The phrase has become quaint, like "cheesecake" and "sweater girl"—souvenirs of World War II, that strange time of mingled innocence and atrocity. "Skin magazines" and legally sanctioned pornography have retired the pin-up girl; insofar as she survives, she belongs to the photographer. After all, the lens doesn't lie. Yet a sensuality and a poignance adhere to drawn and painted images of women which the unblinking, unthinking camera cannot match; each line, each curve and highlight, has passed through the eyes and hands of the painter. The model has been caressed into being, stroke by stroke. The photograph is a split-second's capture, and can be brutal and unfeeling; the graphic artist slowly conjures his subject up, and the excitement of his close attention rubs off on the viewer.

Joaquin Alberto Vargas y Chavez, who signed himself Alberto Vargas, was born in Peru, and a certain Latin gallantry flavors his glamorization of lean yet soft-bodied beauties. His famous rival in pin-up art, George Petty, turned out relatively mechanical, impossibly exaggerated mannequins; compared with the Vargas girl, the Petty girl has no internal organs, no fertility, no vulnerability. Vargas began, in the 1920s, as an illustrator for the Ziegfeld Follies, which sheathed the female form in feathers and fantasy. The early Vargas girl depicted here* sports wings, as well as a Louise Brooks hairdo. Vargas persuaded some of his showgirl models to pose in more nudity than could be accommodated in the public press, and married one of them, Anna Mae Clift. They remained married until she died, in 1975. His harem was on paper.

In the Thirties Vargas did movie posters and his work began to appear in *Esquire*, in place of the departed Petty. Like Petty's creations, his women wear very high-heeled pumps or mules and are frequently on the telephone. Who are they talking to? Not their tax accountants, to judge from their expressions. The telephone as erotic instrument—the sanitary distance it imposes, while permitting mouth-to-ear intimacy—is one of pin-up art's discoveries. Another is the arousal factor of partial clothing. Total nudity is a confrontation; semi-undress is a flirtation. A Vargas girl almost never has bare feet, and when she does we view her with quite a different set of feelings, as a kind of Greek goddess, who breathes the chilly air of Mt. Olympus. More typically, the Vargas girl

---

*In *Playboy*, several from the layout I was first shown—a barefoot goddess, a tousled type, a breast-holder—were later removed, as possibly not pneumatic enough for Hef's Wonderbread taste.

breathes the perfumed air of her own boudoir, where we discover her in a state of advanced deshabille.

Some of his tousled blondes seem to have been "roughed up," like a *film-noir* sweetheart of Cagney or Bogart. The tough blonde, from Jean Harlow to Marilyn Monroe, is a perhaps specifically American ideal—the woman who can "take care of herself." This taking care can assume the form of a masturbatory ecstasy that leaves her breasts in her own competent hands, or of a gold-digging that has produced a very serious diamond necklace, or of toting a gun. Vargas himself spoke of his creations as "dream girls," and part of their dreamy unreality is their solitude on the page, their evident independence. Whatever they need us for, it is not to take care of them—to house them and to be a father to their babies. They are women in their moment of invitation; the confusing, wearying, codependent aftermath is off the page.

Vargas began with the lean flapper ideal: lithe types with small bosoms and narrow hips. The ever-so-slight silken fall of the up-tipped handful of breast is where his early art is most honestly erotic; there, and in the almost touchingly angular fannies of his hard-dancing chorus girls. The phenomenal mammary bloom of the cushioned Fifties and Sixties, and the hip-flare to balance it, overtook the Vargas girl, but she became something of a caricature in the process. She became less vulnerable, and less anatomically plausible; some of his Twenties and Thirties legs, in semi-sheer stockings whose tops marked the boundary of forbidden territory, are marvels of loving rendering, every elongated tendon and muscle.

Not that the consumers of pin-up art are primarily after anatomy lessons. What they are after are glimpses of a kind of heaven, the realm of sexual fulfillment. As late as the mid-1960s, this realm—home territory, after all, for the human animal in its progenitive function—could be glimpsed only through peepholes, through suggestive images. The movies were of course the great suggesters, the global masters of erotic implication and symbolism; the masses came staggering out of love-steeped melodramas into the hard light of Main Street. Cheesecake (that apt slang term lately given a masculine equivalent, "beefcake") was a socially acceptable code for the sexual realities; it covered everything from Hedy Lamarr's lifted eyebrow to Betty Grable's pertly bathing-suited derrière, in the most popular of World War II pin-ups. In this time of heroic national virtue, in a Puritan country that regarded sex as "naughty" if not evil, cheesecake kept the hormones placated, and appeased public awareness of sexual deprivation in the military services. It came as a shock to discover, in James Jones's *From Here to Eternity*, that the GIs' reality was not Betty Grable's backside on the barracks wall but a sweaty Honolulu whorehouse on payday. The art of cheesecake was to make the part suggest the whole; when the whole body could be displayed in *Playboy* or at Woodstock, and when actual copulation could be legally screened in movie theatres, suggestiveness lost its power, and cheesecake lost its place on the front lines of realism.

For a time, cheesecake was as far as you could openly go in representing women in their role (not their *only* role, of course) as sexual provocatrices. Whether the Vargas girl was more aphrodisiac than the *Venus de Milo* or Titian's *Venus* or Manet's *Olympia* or for that matter Michelangelo's *David* is moot. What is aphrodisiac for one is a turn-off for another; the Vargas girl, for me as an adolescent, was less exciting than newsreels of women mud-wrestling in Texas or movies of Doris Day belting out a ballad at the top of her marvellous lungs. That open mouth, that starry gaze. The sexual instinct will speak whatever language is needed to make itself heard. But as for the female body in the public rotogravure, the Vargas girl was what we had, and there is no reason not to see her, as Vargas himself did, as a piece of homage to the eternal feminine.

Genial, Kinetic Gene Kelly

HE HAD PLENTY OF GINGER but no Ginger: although he danced affectingly with Leslie Caron, amusingly with Debbie Reynolds, snappily with Judy Garland, bouncily with Rita Hayworth, broodily with Vera-Ellen, and respectfully with statuesque, stony-faced Cyd Charisse, we think of Gene Kelly as a guy in loafers and a tight T-shirt tap-dancing up a storm all by his lonesome. His torso and his profile were beautiful, and he had a touching little scar on the left side of his mouth, and the musical comedies in which he starred never failed to deliver his dream girl into his embrace; yet somehow his image left no space around it into which a moviegoing housewife could project herself. Even boneless, balding, big-eared Bing Crosby was more of a heartthrob. In the masculine romp of *On the Town*—for this viewer the very best of all Kelly's musicals—Frank Sinatra is cast as a sex-shy nerd, yet in this secondary and comic role he conveys that mysterious attraction, that shadowy depth of contradictory possibilities, which Kelly rarely manifests amid the outpouring of his glittering, genial gifts.

In contrast—in the inevitable contrast, white socks versus white tie—millions of moviegoing housewives imagined themselves dancing with Fred Astaire. The two dancers, though similar in the intelligence and ardor of their dedication to their art, were differently conditioned. Astaire began his career on the vaudeville stage as his sister Adele's dance partner, and it is as a consummate ballroom dancer, weightlessly swirling his partner through a polished and heavenly space, that he lives in our pantheon. Kelly, thirteen years younger, came too late for the ballroom tradition. As related in *The Films of Gene Kelly*, by Tony Thomas, Kelly's first stage partner was his brother Fred, and he trained his body on high-school athletics in his native Pittsburgh. In the 1958 television documentary *Dancing—A Man's Game*, Kelly said, "I played ice hockey as a boy and some of my steps come right out of that game—wide open and close to the ground." His Canadian-born father flooded their back yard and gave him hockey lessons; his mother loved the theatre and saw to it that he and his two brothers attended dancing school. At fifteen, Eugene Curran Kelly was working out with a semipro ice-hockey team; while attending Penn State, he was a gymnastics instructor for the YMCA. After college, he founded a dancing school with his mother, and then went to Chicago to take ballet lessons from Bernice Holmes. He came to New York in 1937, at the age of twenty-four, and got his first break as the dancing character in William Saroyan's *The Time of Your Life*, in 1939; his big break came as the star of *Pal Joey* (1940), a musical based upon his fellow-Irishman John O'Hara's epistolary sketches of a nightclub singer, loner, and heel.

Hollywood welcomed him in 1942. His dancing was more athletic and balletic than Astaire's—one cannot imagine Astaire doing the dizzying number on a high building framework that Kelly performs in *Living in a Big Way* (1947); the aerial acrobatics of *The Pirate* (1948); the swooping roller-skate tap dance of *It's Always Fair Weather* (1955); or the sidewise scuffle on hands and feet that Kelly agilely lowers himself to in several films—and his screen persona was less partnerable. Some of his most memorable numbers, such as the duet with his own reflection in *Cover Girl* (1944), come in the lonely trough between love at first sight and eventual reunion with the heroine. In another technical tour de force, *Anchors Aweigh* (1945) had him dancing with animated cartoons, as did the "Sinbad the Sailor" episode of *Invitation to the Dance* (1956). In the latter sequence, as in many live numbers throughout his films, Kelly— the third of five children, and the middle son—is in the middle of three dancing men. Male partners seem to free him up to be his most cheerfully spectacular and inventive self—for instance, a creditably dancing Sinatra in their two sailor musicals; Donald O'Connor in *Singin' in the Rain* (1952), beginning with the marvellous throwaway vaudeville bits in the opening flashback; Michael Kidd and Dan Dailey in the celebrated trash-can-lid dance from *It's Always Fair Weather*; and Astaire himself in the introductory segments of *That's Entertainment Part II* (1976). Astaire at the time was seventy-seven years old, yet noticeably the looser of the two—especially in his arm movements—as he and Kelly perform some charmingly low-key dance patter.

Of course, Kelly can glide through the steps with a woman, and can execute a tap routine in perfect synchronization beside her, but up close he lacks a certain ineffable touch. In Kelly's first Hollywood film, *For Me and My Gal* (1942), there is an incidental moment in which George Murphy, in the role of the ousted suitor, does a brief turn with Judy Garland that is consummate in its courtly ease of motion; we see, through a chink of the main romantic plot, just how a woman should be danced with—with a feathery lightness, and a feather-stiff spine.

Yet it is in *For Me and My Gal* that we are most fully persuaded that the Kelly character is loved by the heroine. Garland, only twenty in 1942 but a vaudeville trooper since the age of four and for six years a Hollywood presence, had wanted Kelly for the part, instead of Murphy, who had originally been cast as the guy who gets the gal. She tutored Kelly in acting for the camera. "It was Judy who pulled me through," Kelly later said. "She was very kind and helpful, and more helpful than she even realized because I watched her to find out what I had to do." An intensity of mutual regard does burn through when they gaze each into the other's shining black eyes or crisply tap-dance side by side. Kelly, fresh from his brash Broadway role, is still swaggering, and his reedy intonation suggests a gentler younger brother of James Cagney's sassy, defiant George M. Cohan. Kelly and Garland both have a slightly troubled, orphaned air, which lends believability when the film—with the hero's decision to beat the First World War draft by mangling his own hand on a trunk lid—takes a *film-noir*ish turn, and which sees them through the musical's timely metamorphosis into a rousing war movie, complete with dead Germans and smoky battlefields. It is Garland's nervous energy, clarion voice, and still-girlish looks that carry the picture; confronted with so volatile and compelling an expressiveness, Kelly's relatively immobile face yields traces of a sulky city waif, with something of Bogart's or John Garfield's bruised appeal. He was subsequently cast, in the freewheeling manner of studio-run Hollywood, in a number of non-dancing roles—in one film, *Christmas Holiday* (1944), as the would-be killer of Deanna Durbin. He dies in her arms, begging forgiveness.

The chemistry between him and Garland had faded when they were paired again, in 1948, in *The Pirate*. This fanciful action-farce, situated on a level of unreality that might be called arty, is Kelly's movie, though the rights to the stage play had been purchased by M-G-M's Arthur Freed as a vehicle for Garland, to be directed by her then husband, Vincente Minnelli. Garland has aged beyond her years, and the zany plot has her and Kelly mostly at odds; at one point, she unloads nearly all the breakable furniture of a colonial palace in his direction, in one of filmdom's great exhibitions of throwing by a left-handed female. Kelly's personality is so encased in his flamboyant parody of John Barrymore and Douglas Fairbanks as to be impenetrable, and the concluding number, "Be a Clown," appears to have jumped in from some other musical. Garland sings her best number supposedly in a hypnotic trance and her whole performance seems a bit dazed—gamely she makes her moves and hits her marks without really getting what is going on. Kelly's most with-it partners are a pair of black dancers, the Nicholas Brothers, whom he insisted on including in spite of warnings that even such mild miscegenation would cost the film some Southern bookings.

Their third pairing, in *Summer Stock* (1950), revives the chemistry, but with the current reversed. Kelly, as a dance-happy city slicker, is in top form; Garland, who would not work for M-G-M again, looks overweight and considerably older than Kelly. Her addictions and inner travail were on their way to cutting short her precocious career; it is his physical electricity, along with the droll byplay of Gloria De Haven and Eddie Bracken, that lifts this lame bucolic romance halfway off the ground.

No one in the post-war era worked harder to expand musical comedy's boundaries than Kelly. Making his debut as a co-director with *On the Town* (1949), he persuaded the management of M-G-M, which in those days hated to leave its Culver City sound stages, to let him shoot on location in New York; in three hurried days, he and a crew captured all the various shots of New York scenery that, sprinkled among the sound-stage footage, give the film an unprecedented spaciousness. Brought in quickly on a forty-six-day schedule, on a budget of merely $1,500,000, *On the Town* remained a proud favorite of Kelly's; he said, "After *On the Town* musicals opened up." Watching a number of Kelly films on video, I found myself continually smiling throughout this one; there is almost nothing stale about it, and nothing painful, such as the overblown ballet in *An American in Paris* (1951) or the grating voice Jean Hagen was obliged to put on in *Singin' in the Rain*. The opening shots of the enchanted Manhattan skyline at dawn, the unprefaced arrival of song in the voice of a sleepy dockworker, and the perennial theatricality of sailor suits instantly transports the action to a plane of buoyant make-believe where singing and dancing are the norm. Besides the Statue of Liberty and the Rocke-feller Center Prometheus, *On the Town* has the terrific tapping of Ann Miller and some postmodern dialogue: Betty Garrett, as the amorous taxi-driver Brunhilde Esterhazy, says to Sinatra, "I like your face. It's open, you know what I mean? Nothing in it. The kind of a face I could fall into. Kiss me." Alice Pearce, in the now unthinkable role of a laugh-ably ugly girl, says, after a brief date with Kelly, "At last I have something to write in my diary. I've been using it for laundry lists." Not quite Con-greve or Shaw, but flip, sharp, and sweet. *On the Town* is that happy occa-sion, an ambitious film not spoiled by any sign of ambitiousness.

Two years later, Kelly, as star and choreographer, presented an overtly ambitious display of what dance meant to him and could mean to the movies, *An American in Paris*. His love of France gives warmth to a num-ber of episodes, and rather paternally enfolds the gamine heroine he chose for his leading lady, the eighteen-year-old ballet dancer Leslie Caron. But Oscar Levant is a dour presence, there isn't enough for the French performer Georges Guétary to do, and Kelly's artist-hero's murkily dubious affair with Nina Foch's rich patroness strikes an off-note that doesn't go away. The climactic ballet to the music of Gershwin's *American in Paris* now appears, with its French-painter sets and eclectic busyness, pretty heavy kitsch, while the dancing episodes of the corny Thirties farces of Astaire and Rogers feel ever more precious and pure.

That ineluctable invidious comparison dogs Kelly's renown. In the years when Hollywood musicals were still a popular genre being churned out in abundance, Kelly's ebullient performing prowess and venturesome spirit put him at the head of the pack; now he tends to be remembered as the Astaire-not, a chesty hoofer with a slant smile who danced the Holly-wood musical into its coffin. Astaire's Thirties movies played to a giant captive audience, an America stuck in the Depression, with little else but the radio to amuse it. Kelly's post-war movies were competing with a ris-ing television that was keeping more and more of the adult middle class at home. The furious energy of *Singin' in the Rain* has something desperate about it; it is, like Cinerama and the Fifties Biblical epics, trying to out-shout and outdazzle the little home screen. O'Connor's frantic gymnas-tics to "Make 'Em Laugh" and Kelly's delirious* splashing in the famous title number have an attention-getting excessiveness. The most relaxed and old-fashioned number—the peppy furniture-hopping of O'Connor, Kelly, and Debbie Reynolds to "Good Mornin' "—is the most pleasing.

---

*He was sick, it turns out, in the drenching day and a half it took to film this ebullient number. "In addition to being constantly wet, I had a bad cold and a fever," he later said.

(One wonders how much American furniture was broken by adolescents trying to emulate the smoothly controlled sofa-topple that the three dancers ride toward the camera.) Even the film's nostalgic topic, the critical moment when sound came to the motion pictures, has a pleading undercurrent—*Love us*, the movies are saying, *like you used to*. But no brilliance of performance, no breadth of screen, no new suavity of color (the early-Fifties movies all look blue, with everybody wearing powder-blue suits and even blue fedoras) could bring the crowds back. John Springer, in his 1966 history of the Hollywood musicals *All Talking! All Singing! All Dancing!*, names *Singin' in the Rain* "the best movie musical ever made" and yet writes:

> By the mid-Fifties, the "Golden Era" of movie musicals indeed seemed over. Many of the brightest originals . . . were making disappointing showings at the box office. As the world market became an ever more important factor in final box office grosses, it became evident that in many foreign countries musicals were not being shown at all. Or occasionally they would be shown with song numbers neatly snipped out.

There was something artificial about the movie musical which audiences came to resist—even to the point of wanting the songs snipped out! It has almost always been a tense and potentially awkward moment when the background music swells and the hero or heroine takes a breath to project a melody into his or her significant other's face. But we put up with it for decades, pleasurably, as a rendering, on film, of stage magic. Song and dance go back to the very beginnings of theatrical performance. The Greek tragedies were partly chanted; Shakespeare thinks nothing of interjecting a song. By assembling in a theatre we license the performers to do whatever they can to entertain us: sing, dance, juggle, cavort. The live presence of performers makes theatre a social event, in which the gala dress of the audience echoes the costumes onstage. But the cinema, once past the primitive phase when a stationary camera filmed a stage complete with proscenium arch and footlights, became more interior—a kind of seen novel, consumed in a private darkness and ever more skillfully imitating, with its camerawork, the shifts of consciousness. As the movie audiences forgot the live performances of vaudeville, travelling opera companies, and small-town theatricals, and the upright piano lost its pride of place in the American home, the conventions of musical comedy came to seem incongruous. These conventions were always somewhat incongruous; the majority of musicals concerned show business, whose professionals would naturally demonstrate singing and dancing skills and might plausibly use them to enact their private lives. But actors and actresses make up a tiny fraction of humanity, and backstage is a narrow world. It wore thin. Real people don't sing and dance, and it is a rare musical—*On the Town, Oklahoma!, West Side Story*— that convinces us they do.

Also, noting the particular European and foreign resistance to Hollywood musicals, one might speculate that there was something specifically American about these films—a brassy optimism and a galvanizing work ethic. From the muscularity of the performers to the dizzily wheeling multitudes of choral dancers and swimmers, the atmosphere is cheerfully industrial. The style of the images may be insouciant—*Look, Ma, I'm tap-dancing!*—but their message is power, American power, the power released from Everyman by the emancipations of democracy. In this factory of American self-celebration, Kelly, who rose from the assembly line to the managerial level of choreographer and director, was ideally electric yet chaste. The musicals were about sex, but sex puritanically streamlined. They demonstrated to their public how to make love in the old sense of the phrase (as when William Dean Howells writes in *Venetian Life* of an "idle maiden" who "balanced herself half over the balcony-rail in perusal of the people under her, and I suspect made love at that distance, and in that constrained position, to some one in the crowd"). Making love is finding the way to the fadeout kiss, not what comes after it. To the question "How can I get a guy/girl?" the Hollywood musicals answered, "Dance with/sing to him/her." Again and again, after their spoken spats, they musically melt, Rogers and Astaire, Howard Keel and Kathryn Grayson, Kelly and whoever, into each other's arms. Around 1955, they begin to melt away. The profitable movie musicals to follow will tend to feature Elvis Presley. The tune changed—rock-and-roll (its very name gutsy and lewd) made the elaborate sublimations of the musical comedy seem arcane, if not silly. Another language had become academic. Few spoke the language when it was a live one with more fluency than Gene Kelly, and none more gamely embodied American élan.

PHOTOS

The Domestic Camera

*(An Introduction to a Book of Family Photographs
That Was Never Published)*

IN FASCINATED EXPLORATION of the mystery of time we are drawn to the photographs on museum walls, and to those in family albums as well. In just such a way (we think to ourselves), in sunlight indistinguishable from that of tomorrow afternoon, this woman, this child, this Indian chief posed; bodies now forever dissolved were in a certain instant bombarded by photons, inarguably *there*. A photograph presents itself not only as a visual representation but as evidence, more convincing than a painting's because of the unimpeachable mechanical means whereby it was made. We do not trust the artist's flattering hand; but we do trust film, and shadows, and light. Yes, trolley tracks once ran down Fifth Avenue, amid all those straw hats, and the Sphinx was buried up to its ears in sand, while gaunt brown guides in dirty caftans squinted toward the mysterious Europeans with their curious black boxes on tripods. And yes, we ourselves once did have this slim smooth shape, with not a gray hair, and our daughter, now herself a mother, was a bald babe in arms. Many of us learn to operate a camera only when we have children, and a record of their growth and change seems suddenly necessary, as once our own seemed to our parents, whose brittle, yellowing snapshots accumulated in shoeboxes and albums out of the same devotional, conservative impulse that collects our color slides in carrousels—priceless evidence, when the moment comes to investigate the baffling death of former selves and the strange disappearance of precious days.

That the photograph serves as evidence and souvenir does not mitigate the claim of photography to be an art: all art arises out of an original usefulness, and aesthetic appeal subtly compounds the stimulation of a number of basic appetites. A photograph is taken through a kind of peephole, and not many years passed after the technique's invention before it was being used to spy on naked bodies, with an aim of sexual excitation. Stereoptical pornography dates from as early as 1850; a feast of "artistic" nudes, generally plump and often garnished with the trappings of a harem, were served up by the youthful art; the 1880s saw Muybridge's scientific studies of naked forms in motion and Eakins' sober studio portraits of female nudes masked or with averted faces. Like film, skin has a grain, and is sensitive to light; there is an affinity. The first photographs showed inanimate objects—still lifes and houses and streets—that remained motionless for the long length of exposure; the first human figure recorded on film, we learn, was a man whose tiny silhouette was holding still for a shoeshine on a Paris boulevard in 1838. As chemical advances shrank the exposure time from hours to minutes and then seconds, the camera found in the human physiognomy and form the subject it was made for. Even those first stiff daguerreotypes have, in distinction from the always somewhat Platonic images of painted portraiture, that helpless individuality, that sharp intimacy peculiar to film. Film is itself *exposed*, and we expect, when looking at photographs, to encounter nakedness, even though it be that (in this collection) of Paul Strand's wife's extraordinarily close and tenderly open face, or that of Dorothea Lange's husband's veined and weathered hands.

The painter can imagine or reconstruct, whereas the photographer must have his subject physically present; exposure naturally occurs in the family circle. To the photographer both professional and amateur, to "take" a picture of a spouse or child is an act of love, of possession and of arrest, of rescue from time's flow. This capture, however, can also can be felt as unkind: the intimacy and vulnerability of private life are turned public and given an unwelcome permanence. The embarrassed wife and children scream in protest during the slide show, and afterwards try to pull out the unflattering slide and throw it away. The issue is further complicated when the photographer is an artist, and entitled to an artist's cold eye. One would like to know, for example, how Charis Weston, Nancy Chappell, and Edith Gowin felt about the unblinking images of their nude bodies that were produced by their husbands and are here displayed. Perhaps, one must suppose, women burdened with petty vanity or excessive modesty do not marry serious practitioners of the photographic art. The family member as model, without the paid compensation models usually get, and with sentimental claims models do not usually (at least until well on their way to becoming wives) exert, is if not a contradiction in terms at least a problematical factor in the artistic equation solved variously by our fifteen artists. In these photographs, those of Alfred Stieglitz appear to use family members, particularly his well-endowed niece Georgia Englehard and handsomely bony second wife, Georgia O'Keeffe, much as if they were interestingly shaped models, to be posed, captured, and dismissed, whereas Eliot Porter's are warmly infused with family affection and a sense of domestic setting—as are, indeed, the paintings of his brother Fairfield. And in the work of Danny Lyon the casual family snapshot has become the form itself, parodied rather than transcended, only his wider, quicker, and wittier eye distinguishing his collection from the artlessly snapped souvenirs of a million bourgeois vacations.

Photography is the first art wherein the tool does most of the work. The musician must understand harmonics, and the painter know something (though, in the cases of Leonardo da Vinci and Albert Ryder, not enough) of his messy medium; but the amateur photographer aims and clicks in happy ignorance of what exactly he triggers within his little black box, and of the accumulated store of chemical and mechanical ingenuities upon which he so easily draws. In truth the aiming and the clicking are, if not everything, a great deal; attempts to combine and distort and otherwise manipulate negatives, whether those of nineteenth-century pseudo-painters Oscar Rejlander or Henry P. Robinson or of today's avant-garde darkroom contortionists, offend (to my mind) the genius of photography. Our aesthetic response is inextricably entwined with the actuality, the *thereness* of the subject, though it may have been there for only a thousandth of a second and may look as abstract as Paul Caponigro's rock surfaces or Edward Weston's cabbage leaves. The camera sees for us; it sees faster and sharper than the eye, more steadily and spaciously, but our world is what it sees. In this sense all photography is journalistic, and no useful distinction exists, in the history of the art, between Mathew Brady's plates of Civil War carnage and Julia Cameron's peaceful portraits of distinguished Victorians. The contemporary father as photographer (of course it may be the mother, or grandfather, or a child; anyone over five can become, for one lucky shot, a Lartigue), with an elementary knowledge of exposure and depth of field, potentially rivals the eminent experts whose family photographs are assembled here.

What is the difference? What makes these photos different, we ask ourselves, from those we and our obedient Nikons take? An energy of combination, perhaps. An exemplary photograph is rarely of one thing only; the focus has been cleverly multiplied. Dana Steichen's bitten apple combined with her pleased facial expression; Brett and Neil Weston's bare-chested brawn combined with the structural drama of, respectively, a fallen tree and a half-built boat; Anna Friedlander's intent face combined with the perspective-enlarged bell of her trombone and the profile of the listening dog, who looks blown out of scale by the noise we cannot hear: the capture or concoction of such visual "events" makes amusement within the family generally amusing, and gives the domestic picture a detached, ironical frame. Also, we might notice, the natural environment has often a force and presence that set up a counterpoint—the pine trunks that surround Emmeline Stieglitz, the Western terrains behind the Westons. Robert Frank's portraits are notably indirect: his wife, Mary, is seen upstaged by the sweeping shadow she is casting on the wall while she dozes, and then is reduced to a shaggy silhouette while the camera focuses on the quizzical face of a statue, and lastly is lost within a surreal composition that rests the ocean exactly on her head and divides her face in half with a shadow that we presume is the photographer's own. Her stare, with one pale eye and one dark one, looks malevolent, or at best impatient; certainly these family portraits are distinguished from our own by the relative absence of smiles. Something deeper than the amiability of mutual approval and shared happiness is being searched out. These families often appear not only sombre but haggard. Childhood, in these photographs, seems often nude but rarely blithe. Imogen Cunningham's children look at their mother with worried expressions, and little Jazmina MacNeil seems stolidly to mourn. Her mother, Wendy, also declined to elicit a smile from her husband, Ronald, though she photographed him in an amusing enough variety of outfits; the beekeeper's net almost brings out a smile on its own. The family mood feels ambivalent, and the viewer cannot quite shake a possibly illegitimate curiosity about the subjects themselves. *What is happening here?* we want to ask them. What do the neighbors think of your allover tan? What's it like, living with somebody who pokes a lens at you whenever you try to take a shower? It is the uneasy, Janus-faced nature of photography to give publicity to the intimate, and permanence to the ephemeral.

Perhaps we are being unduly sensitive and prone to the medium's morbidity to feel a certain doom moving through this assemblage of vanished moments, of aging women and wary men held up to the light, of first wives yielding to second wives, of downy toddlerhood turning into haughty adolescence. Always we are aware, in looking at photographs, that something lies beyond the edges, in the dimensions both of space and time. Unlike the older, more humanly shaped arts, which begin with a seed and accumulate their form organically, photography clips its substance out of an actual continuum. A painting includes all that the painter wished to include; Toulouse-Lautrec and Degas were being witty when they transferred to their canvases the fractional forms and interrupted gestures of the new mode of picture-making. Our knowledge that something lurks just beyond the edge of exposure is ominous; a motion picture is more terrifying than a play because a huge anything—a mummy's hand, a knife, a contorted or mutilated face—might in the next instant leap onto the screen, whereas all that can enter a stage is another painted, costumed, self-importantly piping, life-sized human being. The violent clipping of, say, the nude mother and daughter that Walter Chappell found (or posed) upon the sand, or the stunning simplification in Harry Callahan's focus upon his infant daughter's pate, achieve out of these parts a sum of implied immensity, a mythic roundness.

In the dimension of time, too, a photograph has edges: the glimpses of Eleanor Callahan half covered by a bedsheet, or Edith Gowin holding her translucent nightgown away from her opaque body, or Marie Friedlander clutching a towel to her with the same hand that holds glasses and a bra, all invite us to imagine the moments before and after. Is the curve of action descending or ascending from this point we glimpse, or is the point merely a pose, struck by request? Family life flows through and around these photographs, but the flow is troubled by the unseen presence, the armed and probing invader of the intimate circle: the witness with camera. He or she is a presence partly sinister, bringing a reminder of time and mortality into the self-forgetful cycle of mating and rearing progeny, of creating and enjoying shelter. Because these photographers are artists, the shadows are deeper, the grays more tellingly modulated, the cool that surrounds our islands of warmth more palpable, than in the snapshots we amateurs take in a doting spirit of tribute to those who have consented to share our lives. Not that the customary fond motives and emotions are absent here; but they are present, as it were, in solution, part of a chemistry as complex as that of film itself. These beautiful images oscillate indeterminately, fascinatingly between just family and just photography.

A Bookish Boy

MY MOTHER took this photograph, and dated it precisely on the back: September 21, 1941. I was, therefore, nine years, six months, and three days old. Consulting the perpetual calendar, I find that date fell, as I

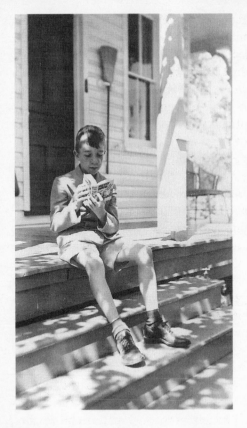

suspected, on a Sunday; my little suit coat, my solid laced shoes, and a sabbath gleam in the dappled sunshine suggest a day apart. No amount of peering, even with a magnifying glass, at the photograph revives in me any memory-sensation of the moment that has been preserved, but the site is very familiar. It was one of my favorite places in the world: the side porch of the house at 117 Philadelphia Avenue, in Shillington, Pennsylvania. The house belonged to my maternal grandparents; due to the exigencies of the Depression my parents and I lived there as well. On this long side porch, half of whose length stretches out of sight to my right, I would play by myself or with others—setting up grocery stores out of orange crates and crayonned paper fruit, making cozy houses out of overturned wicker porch furniture. A grape arbor extended outward from the porch roof, throwing its dazzling dapple down upon the steps and a brick patio where ants busily came and went between the cracks. The grapevine's tendrils curled with such intricacy that I imagined they would spell the entire alphabet, if I looked hard enough.

The door behind me leads into our kitchen, with its linoleum floor and wooden icebox and soapy-smelling stone sink. The kitchen smelled of vanilla, cinnamon, and shredded coconut in its glass-fronted cabinets and of the oilcloth on the little table where we ate, I seated at a corner that prodded me in the stomach. On those days when my mother and grandmother canned, putting up peaches and pears and tomatoes in Mason jars, there was a majestic amount of steam in the kitchen, and a surplus of those fascinating little sealing rings of red rubber. These rings, and clothespins, and spools depleted of thread were common household items in that homely pre-war world, and thriftily became toys.

The broom rack is a period detail, and another broom seems to peek in at the left; sweeping was a constant rite of summer, as was fly-swatting, with its similarly shaped implement. At the end of the porch, against the radiant foliage of our back yard, sits a wire lawn-chair that had a curious destiny. When we moved, in 1945, from this house to a smaller house in the country, the wire chair, a greenish blue in color, somehow came indoors, and joined our living-room furniture. A cushion did not appreciably disguise or soften its metal mesh. Its springy seat rebounded into convexity, when you stood up, with an audible snap.

The chair eventually migrated to our barn, and I did not notice it there last fall when, more than forty-eight years after she took this picture, my mother died, and I surveyed my inheritance. My mother's old camera had also vanished. The technical excellence of this photograph, there in the difficult dapple, testifies to my mother's skill as she lovingly sought to capture her only child. The camera was an oblong old Kodak with a pebbly black leather skin, an unfolding black bellows, and a broken viewfinder. She would judge the exposure by looking at the sky and determine the focus by pacing off the distance and returning to her photographer's spot. Here she managed a focus so sharp that one can not only read the words *Mickey Mouse* on the cover of the Big Little Book but the subtitle *The Treasure Hunt* and see that Mickey is wearing a pith helmet.

How I did love Big Little Books! They were chunky little volumes sold for ten cents, made of single panels from a comic strip opposite a short page of narrative text. My transition from wanting to be a cartoonist to wanting to be a writer may have come about through that friendly opposition, that even-handed pairing of pictures and words. The colorful crispness of the fat flat Big Little Book spines stacked on my bedroom shelf, and on the counters of the Woolworth's and McCrory's where, on Saturday mornings, I went with my hoarded dimes to enlarge my collection, deepened my love of all books and my sense that, whatever else it may be, a book is a manufactured item, which should be amusing to look at and pleasant to hold.

An uncanny stillness reigns between the boy's face, with its tiny smile and many freckles, and the pages of the open book. His hands, in sunlight, look posed, and indeed a posed quality formalizes the whole. This quality strikes me now as poignant and tender. My mother was so encouraging of my childish artistic interests, so hopeful for me. Here she seems, out of sheer hopes for the future, to have carefully arranged and taken the first picture of me suitable for use on the back of a book jacket—the Author in Early Bud, at work in his outdoor study.

An Ecstatic State

A WHILE AGO, I was invited to specify the most memorable photograph I had ever seen, and to be interviewed about it. At once I thought of this photograph, but I couldn't find it, nor could the prospective interviewer, who therefore wandered away. But now, in late 1989, I *have* found it, and am prepared to answer questions, which I must propose myself.

Q.: What and where and when?

A.: The photograph, by Leonard McCombe, appeared on page 25 of *Life*'s issue of March 23, 1959, in illustration of Hawaii's achieving statehood. Its caption read: "DANCING WAHINE sways through a Hawaiian number for 30,000 spectators assembled in Honolulu Stadium for a special show to celebrate new statehood." It totally filled its page, which measured ten by fourteen inches in *Life*'s generous Eisenhower-era format.

Q.: What struck you?

A.: The word "Wahine," for one thing. The young woman's beauty, for

another—her svelte midriff, her exposed navel, her perfect teeth, her cluster of earrings, her fishnet stockings with their hint of whorishness. The expression on her face, between glee and agony. The sea of faces behind her. Her curious aloneness in front of that sea, facing the other way, on what appears to be an otherwise deserted stage. Is she one of a chorus line? Whence comes the music she is swaying to, the rhythmic impetus hoisting one dainty heel up from its slipper and swirling the threads of her skirt and her bra? What force has shut her eyes? The camera has caught a Dionysian mystery; it has caught ecstasy.

Q.: Anything else strike you?

A.: The sunlight that nakedly sits on the stage boards, on her extended arm, on her brow and clavicle. And the delicious twisted strip of sun that catches the top of her backside. Though her costume has a tawdry nightclub feeling, we are outside, in raw daylight, as at a bullfight; the rawness is exciting. In the crowd, many of the faces are laughing; all along the fall of her black hair, white smiles flash out. The crowd to the left of her isn't quite so amused. She is, perhaps, amused. What can the joke be that has ignited all these smiles, a musical joke we will never hear, here in this sunstruck stadium over thirty years ago?

Q.: What qualities would you ascribe to this photograph?

A.: Grandeur. Ephemerality. Eroticism. Poignance. Her perfect face seems a mask, a mask of glee, with the eyes left out and not joining in. Genuine joy, self-forgetful, appears to have broken through the stage decorum whereby pretty young dancers mechanically smile; the pretense of jubilation has yielded to the real thing. But in what exact proportion does emotion mix with artifice? Why are we slightly afraid of this girl in her grandeur, her baubles? Why does she seem a slave, a captive to the moment—is it the harness, the collar of studded ribbons, that she wears? Note also the wrist heavy with bangles, and the wedding or engagement ring on her left hand, which is splayed near her crotch as if with masturbatory intent. She is racially exotic, which ups the current. What I above all remembered of viewing this photograph, at the age of just twenty-seven (my birthday the very same week), was the ambiguous vehemence of her face and body in their arrested motion.

Q.: Any new feelings, seeing this photo again, after three decades?

A.: I am surprised by how much leg she shows, how insubstantial her skirt is. I wonder what has happened to her. If she was twenty then, she is fifty now. Overweight, I would imagine, fat on breadfruit and the junk food of statehood, with only this photo to prove her former crowd-transfixing beauty and maenadic animation. I see that many of the faces above her right arm look worried. I worry too, that time has treated her cruelly. She deserved the best, for being so glorious a Wahine in this sunlit split-second of celebration, of motion, of life.

A Woman's Burden

THIS PHOTOGRAPH, taken by David Seymour in 1952, pricked my conscience* because it showed such loveliness—a beautiful woman in her prime, sturdy and sandalled, cheerfully bearing the burden of womanhood the world over, babies. The photograph, so innocent and even

comic, made seem shameful the outcry in my country two years before, when Ingrid Bergman, still married to her Swedish husband Petter Lindstrom, bore a child to the Italian director Roberto Rossellini. America was not yet used to open adultery and out-of-wedlock pregnancy from its film actresses, especially from this actress, who had played a nun and Saint Joan as well as the heroically virtuous wife of *Casablanca* and the innocent victim of Charles Boyer's cruelty in *Gaslight*. Stars are by definition beloved, but few have been loved as Bergman was by the American public in the 1940s. She betrayed us, it was felt, and with a greasy Italian at that. *Quel scandale!* Her banishment from Hollywood and our hearts was complete, and the facts that Rossellini married her and made her an "honest

---

*The German newspaper *Die Zeit* in 1998 invited "writers, actors, artists or politicians to select . . . a photo which at a certain time of their lives had an especially strong impact on their conscience."

woman," that she had had a number of not especially secret affairs before, that Lindstrom was a (presumably cold-blooded) Swede, and that even in her film roles she had shown some relish in playing "bad girls"—none of this sufficiently softened the national indignation. If ever there was a thoroughly fallen woman, Bergman was it, and it didn't help that Rossellini had her tramping around bare-legged in the muddy rice fields of *Stromboli*.

Well, here she is in 1952, standing proud. Two little twins, Isabella and Ingrid, peep from their carry cots as if wondering what the fuss was about. Now Isabella is a middle-aged model, her mother is sixteen years dead, and 1950 does seem a very long time ago, in terms of morality and celebrity culture. Bergman lived through it with the same quiet dignity of her screen presence. She seemed to wear no make-up and had a comfortable thickness to her waist; no wonder we all loved her, back then—a "natural woman" who was also a movie queen. A little too natural, it turned out. Nature is hard to contain, whether by religious morality or the derived hypocrisies of public relations. Bergman was a European—with a German mother, and almost a German film career—who failed to play by American rules. The rules have long changed, and, seeing this picture now, we want to go down on our knees to it.

Descent of an Image

THE PHOTOGRAPH BELOW is the most celebrated image to emerge from the American involvement in World War II. It has been reproduced

small, as a postage stamp, and large, as the sculptured Marine Memorial next to Arlington Cemetery in Washington, D.C. It shows six men from Easy Company of the 3rd Marine Division raising the American flag on Mt. Suribachi, on the Pacific island of Iwo Jima, on February 23, 1945. The tiny volcanic island was important to both sides for its three airstrips. As long as the Japanese held Mt. Suribachi, they could fire on any position the invading Marines established. The entrenched defenders had to be driven out of their tunnels and ravines with flame throwers, bazookas, and hand grenades. After days of some of the bitterest fighting of the war, the summit was cleared and a patrol led by Lieutenant Harold Schreir was able to raise a small flag—an action unmemorably photographed by Lou Lowery. A larger flag was later brought—so that, in the words of Sergeant Mike Strank, "every Marine on this cruddy island can see it"—and its raising was indelibly captured by Associated Press photographer Joe Rosenthal.

How posed was the picture? An earlier raising had occurred, and Rosenthal posed a subsequent shot of Marines gathered under the erected flag; but this image with its reaching hands and dramatically diagonal pole is too good to have been contrived. "It was like shooting a football game," Rosenthal later said. "You never knew what you got on film." He pointed out that if he had posed the men he would have had them turn their faces toward the camera, and a picture editor, Harold Evans, has said that "no genius could have posed the picture if he had spent a year in a studio with lights and a wind machine."

Three of the six men in the photograph, including Strank, their leader, died in action within weeks. The best-known survivor, Pima Indian Ira Hayes, died at thirty-two of alcoholism, as a kind of protest against his own post-war celebrity. "How could I feel like a hero," he asked, "when only five men in my platoon of forty-five survived, when only twenty-seven men in my company of two hundred fifty managed to escape death or injury?" His dead "good buddies" haunted him: "They were better men than me and they're not coming back. Much less back to the White House, like me." At the 1954 ceremony dedicating the Iwo Jima monument in Washington, he was asked, "How do you like the pomp and circumstances?" He answered, "I don't." Three months later, he was dead.

Nearly seven thousand U.S. personnel perished on Iwo Jima, as did twenty thousand Japanese, with only a thousand prisoners of war taken. The ferocity of the Japanese resistance had been underestimated, and promised a long war to come. One in three Marines became a casualty. Twenty-seven Congressional Medals of Honor were awarded, thirteen posthumously.

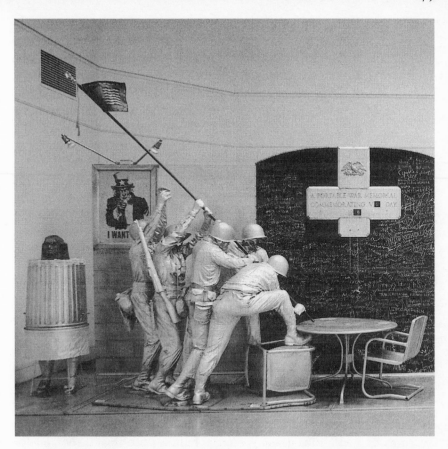

The image was mockingly employed in Edward Kienholz's tableau, *The Portable War Memorial*, in 1968. At the height of the protest against the Vietnam War, the heroic moment from World War II was transposed to an American diner, with its trash and banality, the soldiers spray-painted silver and their helmets devoid of heads but the allusion unmistakable and exact. The image still had enough sacred power to raise some objections; Kienholz wrote in a 1969 letter to *Artforum*, "I would . . . never insult this country as I love it perhaps as well as you. I would, however, in my way, presume to change it."

Neither anti-war protest nor glorification of war's heroes seems intended by the contrivers of the next image, the cover of an extensive travel brochure put out in 1997 by GWV International. The art director who commissioned it, the photographer who executed the job, and the models, laughing and virtually bare-assed, who posed were presumably all born long after 1945, with no visceral memory of the vast sacrifices and cruelties of that war—the terrible drama of it as, island by island and

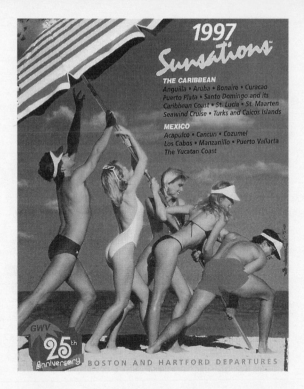

town by town, the Allied forces fought to reclaim the world from the ruthless, racist Axis regimes. In sunny innocence the models mock the postures of men—like them, young—fighting for their lives and for what they understood to be a just and noble cause. The striped flag has become a striped beach umbrella, and the bloody taking of a hill of muddy volcanic ash has become the joyous taking possession of a beach and beryl ocean.

An iconic image has been appropriated with no thought of its dreadful, epic source. Kienholz, the artist, knew he was being offensive; he meant to offend, and to awaken melancholy resonances. The creators of the advertising image are so removed from the original resonances that they breeze past any question of dubious taste. Their visual pun trades on a worn-out image, an empty armature of gesture. Yet a connection does exist between our historic Pacific agony and this contemporary Caribbean bliss: a victorious America exercises its right to use the world as a playground. From the shed blood of the grandfathers flows the grandchildren's heedless happiness; from devastation and veneration, triumphant "sunsations."

Introduction to The Writer's Desk, *by Jill Krementz*

I LOOK AT THESE PHOTOGRAPHS with a prurient interest, the way that I might look at the beds of notorious courtesans. Except that the beds would tell me less than these desks do. Here the intimacy of the literary act is caught *in flagrante delicto*: at these desks characters are spawned, plots are spun, imaginative distances are spanned.

The sheets are often mussed. Robert Penn Warren has papers over-flowing his typing table and adjacent surfaces and even underfoot—his feet are nearly naked, as if he is about to tread grapes. Joan Didion's are totally bare. William Maxwell is in his pajamas and bathrobe. So is Kurt Vonnegut, who works on his lap while crouching at a shelf that does for a desk. Terry Southern has a lot of copies of *Candy* on his desk, a whiskey glass in his hand, and the challenging word ROCK tacked to a bulletin board. John Cheever has equipped himself with a glass and not one but *two* packs of cigarettes. George Plimpton is evidently able to concentrate amid a vivacious clutter of books and mementos, while the floor holds bright splashes of sunlight and a pair of twin infants lustily sucking on twin bottles. Robert Coles's piled books are reaching for the ceiling, and Jean Piaget calmly lights his pipe of meditation amid a mountainous clut-ter of stratified books and folders, not to mention what appears to be two radios, one on top of the other.

Whereas Georges Simenon has at least twenty pipes lined up impec-cably, on a desk whose objects are subdued to parade formation. There is a tidy, minimalist school of desk décor. E. B. White and Archibald MacLeish, both in rural retreat, work next to open windows, on bare plain wood. Lewis Mumford displays a system of suspended clips on hooks that suggests a factory foreman keeping track of rush orders. Willie Morris and Susan Sontag go in for long, long desks, where the reach for inspiration is physicalized, whereas Rita Dove and Anthony Powell work at spaces that are conspicuously small, as if to keep margi-nalia at bay. Isaac Bashevis Singer perches self-effacingly at the end of a desk, like the coxswain of a racing shell. Thornton Wilder and James Merrill project a sense of being literary gentlemen of Connecticut, at home in a dignified clutter. The two most commercially successful authors herein, Stephen King and James Michener, wear blue-collar clothes in an industrial-looking environment—though King occupies less space than his tremendous production would seem to warrant, and he shares it furthermore with a dog. (Dogs outnumber cats as quadrupedal muses two to one.) P. G. Wodehouse and Pablo Neruda, two authors seldom otherwise bracketed, are both conspicuous in the wearing of jackets and neckties at their desks, while pursuing an occupation notably informal in its traditional garb.

And then there are those who, at least within the ken of Jill Krementz's camera, abjure desks entirely. Saul Bellow, the foremost American writer, stands erect at a drawing board. Toni Morrison, our most recent Nobel Laureate, sits on a sofa with a lined notebook. William Buckley dictates in the back of a car, Ross MacDonald has constructed a kind of bed for himself, and Walker Percy and Cathleen Schine are actually *in* bed, a classic writing site utilized by Edith Wharton, Colette, Proust, and James Joyce, who sprawled across his and Nora's bed in a babble of notes to himself. I am struck by the wealth of photos, trinkets, and mementos with which John Irving, Nikki Giovanni, and Peter Matthiessen have crowded the walls and sills of their work area, for the requirement of any writing space is that it disappear from the mind's eye of the inhabitant, to be replaced with the verbal vistas of poetry and prose. A desk surrounded by too many lively souvenirs might seem to clamor with the claims of the life—trivial, busy, egocentric life—away from the desk; but better these than strange sights, which demand fresh attention. From Twain to Fitzgerald, American writers have set up shop in German castles or Italian villas to get away from it all and immerse themselves in the otherworld of a book. Some still hold to the practice, and find ease in the neutrality of a strange hotel room; for most, the shortest distance for the imagination to travel is from a familiar corner of their home.

Desks want to get messy. Letters and unsolicited manuscripts and bound galleys pathetically crying for attention hang out at the corners, until they fall off. In my own writing quarter—four little "maid's rooms," with lavatory, in a generous-scaled old summer house—I have three desks, each of a different substance and each accustomed to support a different activity. An oak desk bought at Furniture in Parts in Boston twenty years ago forms, along with a metal typing table and an old manual Olivetti, the site where I answer letters and talk on the phone. An olive-drab steel desk, a piece of retired Army equipment bought over thirty years ago in Ipswich, is where I write by hand, when the fragility of the project—a poem, the start of a novel—demands that I sneak up on it with that humblest and stealthiest of weapons, a pencil. Also this desk, whose ample surface (annoyingly dented in the center by some mishap in its military career) I try to keep relatively empty, supports parallel stacks of proofs, as I compare a novel's successive versions side by side. The third desk, veneered in white Formica, holds the word processor where everything gets typed up and many items, including this introduction, are composed. Being able to move from desk to desk, like being able to turn over in bed, solves some cramps and fidgets and stratifies the authorial persona: the wooden desk serves the man of the world, the Formica the functioning professional, and the old Army desk the tentative, tender creator, who still hopes to establish, in this clumsy, improvised setting, some connection with the ethereal and everlasting spirit of literature.

Our task as we sit (or stand or lie) is to rise above the setting, with its comforts and distractions, into a relationship with our ideal reader, who wishes from us nothing but the fruit of our best instincts, most honest inklings, and firmest persuasions. This ideality can be courted, as we see here, in a wide range of bowers, from a bare boathouse (E. B. White) and a mysteriously timbered back room (Edwidge Danticat) to living spaces ornate with signs of bourgeois comfort. Comfort is relative—Katherine Anne Porter's crowded table, with its lean rush-seated chair, was comfort to her, as is Dorothy West's "mess" of papers, which have spread, fluttering, up the walls. What is crucial is a sense of ease that frees the mind. And yet the atmosphere should not be so easy as to discourage a day's worth of uphill work. Writing—the leap onto the blank paper, the precarious linkage of one sentence to the next—is labor of a peculiarly exhausting sort. The goal of perfection, for which the classics are our measure, is intimidating enough to freeze fine minds and pure hearts into permanent silence. It helps, perhaps, to have an impending engagement—a lunch date, a golf game, or a long-contemplated outdoor chore—to concentrate the mind. Otherwise, our energy spreads itself thin over the available hours and the meanders of possible rewording. Much time can be wasted, but in the end the moment must be seized. The most prolific living author here, Joyce Carol Oates, claims, "Most of the time I do nothing. . . . I waste most of my time, in daydreaming, in drawing faces on pieces of paper." Even more surprisingly, John Ashbery, to whom inspiration is so readily available that he composes his poems on a typewriter, professes to have fewer "hang-ups and rituals" than he used to: "I feel blocked much less often, though it still happens." If these two writers sometimes stall, what doubts and procrastinations waylay the rest of us?

On the desks shown here, the once-ubiquitous ashtray has over time yielded its place to the word-processor keyboard; the piece of paper rolled into the typewriter's platen is now a screen framed in icons. Two of the younger generation, Cathleen Schine and Mona Simpson, have moved on to laptops, which can turn an airplane seat into a desk in the sky. Jill Krementz's photographs, in all their variety of milieu and demeanor, generally show people at peace in their settings, their activity, and their poses. Writing at its innermost is a deeply comforting activity, an ordering and a purging and a bringing into the light what had been hidden an hour before. These desktops and nooks are happy places— chaste beds of conception, rumpled and warm.

Introduction to The First Picture Book—Everyday Things for Babies, by Mary Steichen Calderone and Edward Steichen

"BEHOLD THE CHILD among his new-born blisses," Wordsworth advises in the famous ode subtitled "Intimations of Immortality from Recollections of Early Childhood." The poet puts forward a considerably developed metaphysical explanation for the incomparable vividness and mysterious power of our first impressions:

> Our birth is but a sleep and a forgetting:
> The Soul that rises with us, our life's Star,
> Hath had elsewhere its setting,
> And cometh from afar:
> Not in entire forgetfulness,
> And not in utter nakedness,
> But trailing clouds of glory do we come
> From God, who is our home:
> Heaven lies about us in our infancy!

The clouds of glory dissipate, yet tendrils cling, leaving the adult mind "Haunted for ever by the eternal mind" and by "High instincts before which our mortal Nature / Did tremble like a guilty thing surprised." We remain troubled and guided by

> . . . those first affections,
> Those shadowy recollections,
> Which, be they what they may,
> Are yet the fountain-light of all our day,
> Are yet a master-light of all our seeing . . .

The photographic genius of Edward Steichen has captured here, at his daughter Mary's behest, the primal frontality and awesome scale of those simple things that dawn, so metaphysically laden with wordless meaning, upon the child's consciousness.

Sifting through my recently dead mother's possessions, I encountered more than one object—a chunky magnifying glass, a small copper ashtray still darkened by my father's cigarette ashes, a thick pale-green ceramic candlestick, its handles akimbo like an angry woman's arms—which reawakened in my nervous system an infantile sense of largeness, of a numbly grasped ominousness, as of statues viewed in smoky caves. Items of inexpensive mass manufacture, they had been left behind, as decisively as the Bakelite telephone and wicker baby carriage depicted in this volume, by the evolutions of style and of manufacturing economy. Their old-fashionedness stemmed from the Thirties and the Forties, decades entirely historical to most of the world's living population but as intimately real to me, a man not yet old, as my own pillow. The era's substances—the kitchen tables covered in oilcloth, the slate sinks, the wooden iceboxes, the square soaps, the toys of real rubber and lead—cradled my growing awareness and formed material expectations which modern plastics and brittle "white metal" inevitably disappoint; the evidence of my senses proposes, over a lifetime, a world increasingly light-weight, odorless, gimcrack, and flimsy, where grotesquely inflated money is traded for pathetically shoddy goods. Real fur was guiltlessly abundant in that primitive world of the Thirties, and one of my mother's old coats, found at the back of a closet, unworn for decades, was trimmed with a collar of red-brown fox fur, each hair tipped with black. I stared at the texture wondering why it spoke to me so strongly, in the smoky cave of lost time, and realized that this fur had been habitually close to my face, its details pressed decisively into my passive infant awareness. My mother, not dead but alive and young and fashionable, was carrying me against her shoulder.

The basic equipment of life is quite conservative in design, and of these objects photographed in 1930, two years before my birth, few will be utterly strange to a child of today. The teddy bear is a bit more dishev-elled in its fur, and probably harder in its body, than the boneless Dacron-furred contemporary teddies, which seem designed more as throw pillows than as sturdy companions for a child. My bear, looking almost exactly like this one, with tawny blond hair and limbs that moved on stiffish little swivels, was called Bruno. His two-tone brown eyes came out on long pins like hatpins, and one of them got lost, so he was dis-turbingly one-eyed. Cruelly, tenderly, I would remove his surviving eye, study his blind blond socket, and then with a lordly compassion reinsert the bright hatpin, restoring helpless Bruno's sight.

These first toys stand in relation to the child's power and size as the child himself does to those of adults, and just as adult behavior seems sometimes arbitrarily punishing, so is his; I wince to think of the inchoate anger inflicted upon dear docile Bruno, and upon a rubber Donald Duck whose throat I experimentally slit with a razor, halfway through, and a

rubber Mickey Mouse whose head, with a little distorting squeeze, came altogether off, and could be reinstalled on a small flanged collar between his shoulders. We rehearse with our toys our eventual relations with people. George Eliot, in describing, in *Middlemarch*, her heroine's unfortunate marriage, particularizes Mr. Casaubon's unwittingly cold rejection of "those childlike caresses which are the bent of every sweet woman, who has begun by showering kisses on the hard pate of her bald doll, creating a happy soul within that woodenness from the wealth of her own love." By extension, the bridal Dorothea "had ardour enough for what was near, to have kissed Mr. Casaubon's coat-sleeve, or to have caressed his shoe-latchet"—fetishistic tributes not quite so startling as the kiss Marcia Gaylord bestows, in the first chapter of William Dean Howells's *A Modern Instance*, upon the doorknob on which Bartley Hubbard's handsome hand has lately rested.

If the nineteenth century tended to picture the very young as still steeped in the liquids of Heaven, the twentieth has taken a darker, more sardonic view: Auden's poem "Mundus et Infans," meditating upon a male baby, sees a "cocky little ogre" who is "resolved, cost what it may, to seize supreme power," and who has not yet learned "to distinguish /

Between hunger and love." At the birth of his little cosmos, as at the birth of the larger, there is a primal seethe of undifferentiated force:

> A pantheist not a solipsist, he co-operates
> With a universe of large and noisy feeling-states
>   Without troubling to place
> Them anywhere special, for, to his eyes, Funnyface
>   Or Elephant as yet
> Mean nothing. His distinction between Me and Us
> Is a matter of taste; his seasons are Dry and Wet;
>   He thinks as his mouth does.

Destruction, aggression, and investigation are hard to distinguish in an infant's gropings toward reality. Recently I watched my youngest grandson cope with a present I had given him for his first birthday. It was a set of French bells mounted in a circle that could be spun, the bells colored like a rainbow and numbered so that tunes could be picked out with the mallet provided. Pealing glissandos could be produced by spinning the circle and letting the mallet caress the bells as they flashed by, their rainbow merged into a glittering gray. A toy, certainly, to appeal to a Francophile grandfather of arrested musical development. The one-year-old quickly discovered that the bells, struck with a fisted mallet, responded with a noise, and that his towering audience of parental figures approved. Very intelligently, I thought, he figured out that the full circular set, struck glancingly by his hand, would spin, but that when the toy lay upside down on the floor the same effect was impossible to produce. His attempt to imitate the glissando we demonstrated was frustrated by his inability to hold the mallet lightly enough. His further experiments were so hard to distinguish from a destructive assault that we temporarily separated the boy and the toy.

The ageless charm of blocks partly lies in their susceptibility to being knocked down and reassembled, their unblaming accommodation of those cycles of construction and deconstruction whereby the young child expresses his ambivalence toward the world that so imposingly surrounds him. His or her impulse to kiss the doll's bald pate has a companion itch to kill, to remove irritating obstacles from a horizon crowded with frustrations and challenges. Among the striking qualities of Steichen's solemn photographs of common things is their *menace*—the giant-faced alarm clock, the bed like a cage, the one-armed black telephone, the sharp-edged blocks in their military order, the hot-water faucet with its scalding long nose.

In my first house, where I lived up to the age of thirteen, the bathroom—its stains, its nether-connected plumbing—frightened me. To a very young child, a home holds cheerful, sunlit patches and pockets of mystery and magic. The area around our upright piano, for instance, in its little, seldom-visited "piano room," was charged with a sinister electricity for me even before I took lessons and struggled to decipher music, which came in the big flat books haunted by spidery images of Mozart with his white pigtail and Mussorgsky with his bleary hangdog eyes. On top of the piano lay a nest of curiosities—a faded red runner of mazy Oriental design, a chocolate-brown metal box containing unreadable and momentous documents, and a little brass tiger, its stripes incised, its mouth snarling, and the underside stamped simply CHINA. All these are now in my possession, and have not totally lost their cloudy old largeness and potency, their fuzz of significance. Through their curious quiddity, my own existence—its final unknowableness, its mortality— began to gather specifics.

The Steichens' little book, for all the worthy educational aims so lucidly expressed in its two prefaces, was not a great success, and it has languished out of print during most of the sixty years since its publication. The reasons for this neglect are harder to descry than the reasons why it seems so worth reprinting now. To infants too young, of course, "Funnyface / Or Elephant as yet / Mean nothing." Deciphering the shadows and highlights and foreshortening of a photograph takes some optical sophistication. A child's own drawings embody not so much visual appearances as *ideas*: sky is blue and at the top of the paper, grass is green and at the bottom, men and women are upright stalks in between, sprouting wavery limbs. Illustrations by a graphic artist, however skilled, also embody notational ideas, chiefly in the all-important outlines, which do not exist in nature. A drawing in its very texture comfortingly declares the intervention of a human mind, eye, and hand; a photograph, however controlled, has something of nature's own brute opacity. It can possess, too, a troubling duplicity, a trompe-l'oeil elusiveness: this book's photographs of flat semiotic realities such as books and newspapers and the mail flirt with being both images of things and the things themselves. The conventions whereby the photographer's art is comprehended and appreciated are, like those of cinema-viewing, more recently established than those of drawing and painting and, being bound up with a changing technology, less instinctive. Also, with a world of gaudily colored children's books to choose from in 1930, children and their parents may have felt photography's black-and-white rather dreary.

Whereas we respond, in the 1990s, to Steichen's photography, even in this narrow project, as an art in a heroic exploratory stage. Improvements in film sensitivity, lighting equipment, and focus capabilities made possible for photographers of the 1910s and 1920s a range of formal experiments comparable to those in easel painting from Cubism on. The two arts mutually excited each other, painting to an extent having been freed from its representational duties by the arrival of photography, and photography in turn goaded by avant-garde painting into attempting abstract and expressionistic effects.

Steichen, a photographer since the age of sixteen, returned from his service in World War I still with painterly ambitions. At his home in Voulangis, France, he executed a series of geometric paintings as illustrations for a children's book (never published), and another set of paintings based on the Chinese symbols of yin and yang. Then, in 1921, having renounced his efforts to become a painter and burned all his canvases, he embarked upon his famous series of more than a thousand photographs of a white teacup and saucer, with minute adjustments of shadow and background. Still life—including bodies and landscapes photographed as still life, purified of anecdotal interest—was the dominant mode of Twenties photography, in the work of such masters as Steichen, Edward Weston, Alfred Stieglitz, Paul Strand, Imogen Cunningham, Ralph Steiner, and Charles Sheeler; the luminous precision and monumental stillness of their images still represent, for many, the essence of art photography. By the 1930s, Henri Cartier-Bresson and others would leave the studio entirely behind, pursuing with fast film and hand-held cameras the fleeting pictorial moment in the life of the streets, in a world where social and political issues had become newly urgent.

The images of *The First Picture Book* savor of an art still seeking a classic repose and absolute definition, through objects sometimes posed on a velvety black background and always in a mood of strict selectiveness. Nothing is present by accident, not even the marks in the sand surrounding the beach toys. We can clearly see the weave of the tablecloth, the nubble of the carpet, the seams of the rubber ball, the fine print of the newspaper, the alarming jungle of the grassy lawn. The perspectives, chosen for maximum clarity, sometimes lift the child up, over his breakfast toast and silver mug of milk, in a way that suggests aerial photography, with which Steichen had become familiar in wartime. The blocks and toy trains are set out with an ideal orderliness that reminds us of the unforgiving rows and jutting geometric planes of fascist imagery. This is a no-nonsense baby's world: the preface sternly warns us, "Fanciful tales or pictures having for basis nothing the baby knows may lead to a later inability to distinguish between fact and fancy."

But fact blends into fancy. A few sentences earlier, Mary Steichen Calderone states that "to a baby everything is 'wonder-full,' " and so it might be said that to a photographer all visual appearances are opportunities for wonder and study. A photograph's quick and exact rendition of the gradations of light caught in its lens still strikes us as a miracle, a nullification of time's blurring, eroding progress. Steichen's own statements about photography, like his industrious and eminently practical explorations of the medium, avoid the high-flown. "Photography," he wrote, "renders service with a precision well beyond the scope of any other visual means." This capacity for precision, to see better than the human eye, enlarges and renews our visual universe, from the revelation of microscopic forms by the magnifying lens to the discovery of pure forms in a cabbage as photographed by Edward Weston. Much as manual work develops calluses, quotidian living inculcates a certain imperviousness, and we walk through our days wastefully ignorant of what we are seeing. In its innocent clarity a child's eye approximates the camera's fine-ground, unprejudiced lens. In his *Life in Photography* (Doubleday, 1963), Steichen gives a typically factual account of this project:

> In 1930, my daughter Mary, now grownup and married, came to me with
> a proposition. She said she felt the need of some kind of book to interest her

small children in pictures, and she had an idea for a book to be called *The First Picture Book—Everyday Things for Babies*. I found the idea intriguing, so Mary and I produced it together. I made realistic still-life photographs of the objects that a small child could recognize as part of his life. One was a picture of a washstand with toothbrush set in a glass. After the book was published, a letter came from a mother telling us that, when her child came to this picture, he stopped, making the gesture of taking the brush out of the glass, and then simulated the movement of brushing his teeth. He ended the performance by spitting into the washbasin in the picture!

Though few adult connoisseurs will make this moist mistake, we do like the purposeful, unironical realism of these stark photographs. The camera sees so much, a little is often plenty. The single apple, banana, and twig of grapes on their plate, on the checked tablecloth, have the heavy edibility of an entire heaped sideboard by Chardin. Humble daisies make an almost alarmingly profuse bouquet. Miles of sand beckon in a few square feet, and a whole table seems to gleam in a single setting of silver, so vivid is its sheen, so immaculate its expectancy. Steichen's still-unfolding pleasure in the powers of his technical equipment gives his little subjects the gravity and power of a child's first impressions. The lighting is hot and vertical, like that of Thirties movies, whose actors and actresses moved in their white gowns and black tuxedos through a synthetic indoors; their sharp-shadowed glamour was echoed by Steichen's celebrity portraits for *Vanity Fair*. The hairbrush and comb, posed as if about to kiss, seem especially Hollywood, especially glamorous yet elemental.

When, toward the end of this decade, the sense of exploration left Steichen's commercial studio work—his well-paid fashion and advertising photography—he closed up shop, and retired at the age of fifty-nine, to explore the natural light of the West and the newly opened possibilities of Kodachrome color film. But the dew of artistic adventure still glistens in these attentive, larger-than-life images much as, in the words of Harriet M. Johnson's brief introduction, "a child's early fancy roams among intimate, homely, and familiar things." The series of sequels that her introduction promised—"book after book"—stopped short at one, *The Second Picture Book*, which showed children developing their dexterity in using simple objects. It, too, enjoyed small success, and photography, for all its contemporary abundance, still plays a minor part in the vast world of children's illustrated literature. The Steichens' charming experiment stands almost alone, at the gate of a path not taken, although well mapped by theory and brilliantly lit by a master's practice. Now we can see *The First Picture Book* for the treasure it is—a collection of glowing archetypes, a magic book of signs, a wordless primer of "first affections."

Facing Death

IN THE COURSE of this lethal century, death has been rendered increasingly abstract—a choreographed plunge on the television screen, the punch of a red button in a bomber or a computer game, a statistic in a column of print. As a domestic reality, at least in the Western world, dying has been eased out the door—sent off to the hospital or the nursing home, and the corpse dispatched straight to the mortician, who is handsomely paid for performing his magic out of sight. Open-coffin funerals, the norm in my boyhood, have all but vanished in Protestant middle-class circles. Men and women not involved in mortuary, medical, or police work can now lead full long lives without ever having to see, let alone touch, a corpse. So Twelvetrees Press, in its black-jacketed, beautifully produced volume entitled *Sleeping Beauty: Memorial Photography in*

America, has managed to come up with a book that, in our hard-to-shock age, is truly disturbing and repellent—a book we open with difficulty, though there is little but stillness and tenderness within, and a mood of grieving love.

Sleeping Beauty presents over seventy photographs of the dead or dying from 1845 to 1925, with a few black-clad live mourners included. As the book's organizer and editor, Dr. Stanley B. Burns, informs us in his preface:

> Postmortem photography, photographing a deceased person, was a common practice in the nineteenth and early twentieth centuries. These photographs were often the only ones taken of their subjects and much pride and artistry went into them. It is astounding that although postmortem photographs make up the largest group of nineteenth-century American genre photographs, they are largely unseen, and unknown.

Over half of the examples in this collection are of children. In some, the dead child, stiff as a doll with rigor mortis, is posed in the arms of a parent. Some photographs clearly show the effects of dehydration and malnutrition produced by a host of unchecked and maltreated diseases—cholera, typhoid fever, dysentery, diphtheria, scarlet fever, measles. One especially painful pair shows a child before death, gazing from his pillow, and after, with a gravely straight parting and stiffly held lips. Where the photographer has been exceptionally successful in creating a lifelike appearance, we are disturbed by our own assent to sentimentality's denial of the undeniable.

The common man and woman of the nineteenth century had no choice but to face death. Until the work of Pasteur and Lister in the 1860s, the microbes of disease ranged uncomprehended and unchallenged. Child mortality ranged from 30 to 50 percent. Epidemics often wiped out all the young of a family. More than one in thirty mothers died in childbirth, and a soldier was ten times likelier to die of disease than of a battle wound. In rural isolation, the body had to be prepared for burial by the family. The front parlor of lower-middle-class homes was devoted to funerary rites; its association with death was so strong that a deliberate fiat of the *Ladies' Home Journal*, around 1910, renamed it the "living-room." When, with the new century, outside establishments began to handle these rites, they were called Funeral "Parlors." "During the 1920s," states one of Dr. Burns' informative back-of-the-book captions, "formal postmortem photography disappeared in mainstream middle-class America." It had never been a recourse of the rich, who could afford to pay portrait painters to memorialize them.

Anonymous daguerreotype, c. 1843

An epigraph in *Sleeping Beauty* quotes La Rochefoucauld: "One can no more look steadily at Death than at the sun." But it is not merely the fact of death that we modern viewers want to blink away, as we look at these photographs; it is the ambience of our ancestors' life, the piety-wreathed rigors it visited upon its men in their stovepipe suits and its women in their sleek and severe chignons. How much labor seems laid to rest in the snaggle-toothed, sleepy-eyed corpse with tied hands from 1843, or in the woman, from the same year, with a trail of postmortem blood disfiguring her profile. The photographers' aesthetic effort to prop the corpses into lifelike positions strikes us as monstrously misplaced; we are reminded of the makers of wax effigies, or of the embalmer Mr. Joyboy, in Evelyn Waugh's *The Loved One*, who massages smiles into the faces of the corpses being sent on to his loved one, the cosmetician Miss Thanatogenos. The macabre could be defined as animated death, death that does not act dead. A daguerreotype like "Older Girl Seated on a Loveseat" affects us with not only pathos but terror, she appears so close, with her awkward hands and bloody nostril, to moving.

Some of the photographs have an uncanny beauty. Early photography's principal problem—how to keep its subjects still enough for the necessary long exposure—was here no problem. As the century advanced, and became our own, equipment permitted a wider, more detailed evocation of the funereal display. No bloody trickle or locked joints betray the illu-

Anonymous daguerreotype, c. 1852

sion of luxurious sleep. Flowers, symbols of ephemerality but also of Nature's lavish capacity for renewal, cushion the corpses and the waxen fact of death; the dead glide into the beyond dressed as if for a wedding or graduation. These photographs approach our own funereal experience and taste, and are less alarming than the earlier, cruder attempts to freeze the dead on the edge of life.

The ritual and semiotic systems whereby men shelter themselves from death vary. Our own time, which celebrates the living body—in exercise, diet, gladiatorial games, and pornography—with more frankness and zeal than any culture since the pagan Roman, is very squeamish about the body once dead: we will it to disappear, in closed coffins or the little cardboard urns the crematorium supplies. No longer open to the invitations of sex appeal and consumerism, the body becomes trash. The piety of the previous century clung to the Christian tenet, unemphasized in today's churches, that the body *is* the person, with a holy value even when animation ceases. This faith, embodied in these memorial images, tells us more than we want to know about corporeality, and challenges our modern mysticism, the worship of disembodied energy.

Nadar's Swift Tact

PHOTOGRAPHY is a matter of time. The time of exposure is part of a photograph's credentials, and from even mediocre photographs flows the uncanny power of temporal authenticity: things looked this way at one certain moment, a moment now irrevocably gone. Painting, for all its documentary value, has an idealizing evasiveness; the heroic age of American politics ended when, beginning with William Henry Harrison and John Tyler, Presidents could be photographed, in all their warty imperviousness to the glamorization of brushstrokes. We trust the camera—mechanical, dispassionate, mindless—but not the painter, who inevitably has some kind of myopia or an ax to grind. And yet photographers tend to burn out, at the level which generates enduring quality in a medium so copious. A peculiar kind of intensity must function behind the lens, along with a lucky tilt from the Zeitgeist. Gaspard-Félix Tournachon (1820–1910), known professionally as Nadar, devoted rather little of his long and busy life to being a portrait photographer, but the six years in which he seriously practiced this fledgling profession have secured him posterity's acclaim and a contemporary show of one hundred photographs at the Metropolitan Museum of Art, from April to July of 1995.

The son of a Lyons printer and publisher who moved to Paris three years before Félix was born, Nadar, as he called himself after 1838, underwent a bourgeois education until 1836, when he was expelled for unruly behavior from the Collège Bourbon. The following year, his father's death reduced the family fortune, though Félix briefly attended medical school in Lyons. By 1838 he was back in Paris, and had soon dropped out of medical studies and had joined the large population of struggling young writers and artists who tried to extract a living from the welter of ephemeral magazines; he helped edit one of the more luxurious journals, *Livre d'or*, until it consumed the inheritance of its young patron and folded. The poor "water-drinkers" of the Latin Quarter and their female companions led a style of life that was rendered famous in a series of articles, *Scènes de la vie de Bohème*, written in the 1840s by Nadar's friend Henri Murger, and a half-century later turned by Puccini into grand opera.

As a caricaturist, Nadar was no Daumier but as good as many who wielded this once-widespread skill. As a writer, he was fluent and lively but lacked, perhaps, the devotion to reality's exact details that characterizes literary masters. Six feet tall, red-haired, gregarious, self-promoting, and cheerfully enterprising, he not only practiced art but became a kind of culture vulture, a highly sociable head-collector who claimed to enjoy five thousand friendships among Paris's cultural elite and who had a genuine, disarmingly selfless gift of admiration. He conceived of an ambitious caricatural "pantheon" of one thousand writers and artists of the day, in four giant posters to be sold for twenty francs apiece. He completed only one, which sold a mere 136 copies and was then banned by the Minister of the Interior, in 1854. Also in 1854 Nadar married a nicely dowered seventeen-year-old Protestant from Normandy, and with a friend's help set up his unemployed younger brother, Adrien, in a photography studio on the boulevard des Capucines. The time was ripe. With the advent of the collodion-on-glass negative and the paper print, the speed and ease of photography had greatly increased, and the number of photographers in Paris shot up. Adrien, who aspired to be a painter, learned the technical fundamentals quickly, from the well-named Gustave Le Gray. But by the end of the year the studio was failing, and Nadar stepped in to save it, absorbing the basics by the way. Thus sideslippingly a great photographer was born.

He began to practice in his home on the rue Saint-Lazare, using the sunlit garden as a studio and friendly fellow-artists as subjects. Nadar was a staunch Republican (in the French sense) and worked best with people he admired, either politically or artistically. He took his time with each session, establishing rapport with the subject and adjusting the clothing and the reflectors, to produce effects of chiaroscuro akin to those of Rembrandt and Van Dyck. In a description of his photographic artistry (bellicosely framed in a legal combat with his brother), he wrote:

> What can't be learned, I will tell you: it's the sense of light, it's the artistic appreciation of the effects produced by different and combined qualities of light. . . .
> What can be learned still less is the moral intelligence of your subject, it's the swift tact that puts you in communion with the model. . . .
> What also can't be learned is integrity of work: in a genre as delicate as portraiture, it's zeal, the search, an indefatigable perseverance in the relentless pursuit of the *best*.

He was a bohemian snob, whose abjuration of furniture and trappings distinguished his work from the cluttered style of studios catering to the bourgeoisie, and who sometimes draped his subjects in costumes of a picturesque informality. Yet during the 1850s he not only made great portraits but made money; he charged as much as a hundred francs for the privilege of a sitting, no doubt adjusting this downward for worthy acquaintances like Baudelaire, Gautier, Berlioz, Michelet, Daumier, and

Delacroix. There was a commercial cunning as well as a romanticism to his elitist standards; Elizabeth Anne McCauley, in her excellent *Industrial Madness: Commercial Photography in Paris 1848–1871*, titles her chapter on Nadar "Nadar and the Selling of Bohemia." His austere, unhurried approach "were appreciated," she writes, "by sitters who cared to be different," including some from the aristocracy.

Adrien Tournachon—"erratic, querulous, boastful," a wall caption at the Metropolitan tells us—was an embarrassment to Nadar and remains one to Nadar scholars. For some months the brothers operated the boulevard-des-Capucines studio together, and a number of the finest photographs, including a spectacular series of the seventeen-year-old mime Charles Deburau dressed in the voluminous white clown-costume of Pierrot, are signed by Adrien, as "Nadar jeune." The *"jeune"* became a barely discernible *"jne"* and the original Nadar, after a year of contention, sued to get his pseudonym back. Françoise Heilbrun, in her essay on the photographs in the handsome, essay-laden exhibition catalogue, protests rather too much that no photograph of merit can be by Adrien, even when stamped by him and in his characteristic format. "To my mind, however, the picture can essentially be attributed to Félix," she writes in one instance, and of the beautiful Pierrot series says they were "clearly" "taken in collaboration with his brother." Well, couldn't even Adrien have got lucky for a second? Might the brothers' brief collaboration not have been a two-way street, even though Adrien never succeeded on his own, abandoned his studio in 1860, and died in a mental hospital?

From 1855 to 1860 is the brief heyday of Nadar *aîné* as a hands-on, eyes-on photographer. In 1860, after his mother had died in the house on the rue Saint-Lazare, he bought out his brother's equipment and built himself a two-story glass atelier atop a building on the boulevard des Capucines adorned with his giant, gaslit signature. But the bourgeois clients he needed to attract, and the oval vignettes and little *cartes de visite* they expected, bored him, and he left the day-to-day work to his staff, lending his superb personal touch to rare sitters like George Sand and Sarah Bernhardt, in the mid-1860s. He continued to cut a figure in Paris, however, pioneering photography by electric light in the catacombs and sewers of Paris and then aerial photography, taking shots of Paris from balloons. A great admirer of modern inventions, he managed, at ruinous cost, to construct—from twelve miles of silk!—the largest balloon in the world, called Le Géant, which he launched from a number of European capitals. Of balloon flight he rhapsodized:

Free, calm, levitating into the silent immensities of welcoming, beneficent space, where no human force, no power of evil can reach him, a man seems to feel himself really living for the first time, rejoicing in a sense of spiritual and bodily well-being of a fullness never before known.

As early as the early 1870s, Nadar was letting his son Paul run the studio, now moved to the rue d'Anjou. He wrote a number of reminiscences in his high-flown, adjectival style and, the year before he died, sent a telegram of congratulation to Louis Blériot, the first man to fly the English Channel. Under the management of Paul and Nadar's wife, Ernestine, the firm turned a profit on its great name but produced commonplace work. Paul died in 1939 and during the war the Nadar archives were pillaged by collectors. Only recently has the immense task been undertaken of sifting from the great mass of Nadar Studio plates and prints the precious images, often preserved in a single paper proof print run up for the customer's inspection, which Nadar captured in his brief period of creativity.

He was, in short, a restless, dabbling, flamboyant spirit, who could have found great distinction in perhaps no art save photography. A photographic portrait is a matter of interaction; the photographer's animation and charm spread to the sitter. Rossini's pouchy eyes glint with

Honoré Daumier, 1856–58

amusement; Michelet seems to be biting back a riposte on the tip of his tongue; Ravel (Pierre-Alfred, a vaudevillian) is so amused his face is blurred a bit out of focus. A cocky sense of confrontation sparks the faces of Dumas *père* and the famous clown Kopp. The poets are hauntingly vivid: Gérard de Nerval, who will commit suicide within a year of his portrait, gazes directly into the lens with a moist stare, and Baudelaire, in a pair of very different exposures, displays, standing, a frantic edge and then, seated, a handsome, intelligent repose. The four photographs of Daumier are especially electric, in the unmediated clarity with which the man stands close before us, his stocky build, swaddled in a featureless black coat, topped by a half-illumined face shockingly modern in its weary alertness and nervous preoccupation. He seems truly to have forgotten he is being photographed, no small feat in a time when the fastest exposures were over a second in length. We feel the link between this tousled, acute, unsmiling presence and the rotund crayonned forms of Daumier's vigorous satire. As a rule Nadar's photographs are chastely untheatrical, and the ones that do attempt a dramatic gesture—those of Charles Couderc and Jean Journet, for example—are the only ones that appear dated.

Young model, 1856–59

The dignity of Nadar's method irradiates his dozen or so pictures of women. There is no obvious prettifying, and no playful condescension. In an age and country that did not hide its erotic exploitation of the female underclass from which artists' models were generally drawn, Nadar allows women of this class the same grave inwardness as the writers and upper-class wives. The photo of a nameless model "brought," it is noted on the back, to Nadar's studio by the boulevardier Louis Lherminier, contains a challenging and composed gaze beneath the spectacular spread of unbound hair; the wall and catalogue commentary permits itself a leer (she "has undone her hair and perhaps much else") but the photographer does not leer at all. The body did not much interest Nadar; the small semi-draped figure titled "Mimi" is quite ethereal and distant, though the commentary insists, "The easy attitude of the woman's pale, thin body and her beguiling regard confirm her membership in the eternal sorority of Mimis." That is, she is a whore. But the dignity and facial piquancy of the two photos of the black model Maria silences comment, though one pose shows her "opulent breasts." In the one total nude in the catalogue (not in the show) Nadar makes of the frontal figure a twisted column of light, an Ingres translated into flesh. The model has been permitted or instructed to cover her face with her arm, a discretion also observable in the clinical shot of a hermaphrodite taken in 1860.

Not that Nadar has no capacity for glamorization: his "young woman with a profile" is startlingly beautiful, as his image of Aimé Millet is romantically handsome. The often-reproduced photographs of the onyx-eyed young Sarah Bernhardt, of Marie Laurent from the back, and of the aging but jauntily posed singer Rosine Stoltz all show a willingness to let women present themselves to advantage. Indeed, throughout, Nadar's photographs to a remarkable degree express the kindness and warmth of the photographer: a fruit, perhaps, of his independence in his first years at the trade, when celebrity had not commercialized his name.

Even those who possess the excellent catalogue with its big illustrations should see the show itself. The photographs—some smaller, some bigger than reproduced, and some considerably milkier than in the catalogue—have a tone and a dimension that the most scrupulous five-color reproduction cannot capture. Only a viewing of the real prints delivers a sharp sense, in the finger-smudges and chemical spatters, of a precarious process and a precarious survival. These little, irregularly cut pieces of paper—big prints for their time—were pulled, many only once, from negatives now lost or deteriorated beyond use. Even if the negatives were perfectly preserved, Ulrich Keller points out in his catalogue essay, modern photographic technology, with its "harsh,

Sarah Bernhardt, c. 1864

high-contrast prints," could not reproduce the "soft, transparent complexion" of Nadar's salted-paper prints. On file for decades, they were saved in part by Nadar's own solicitude for his artistic prime, and were marked in his sometimes shaky hand with the name of the sitter. By the time of his labelling a whole vanished era lived in them, illumined by the flare of his brief brilliance.

ART

Fast Art

THE ANDY WARHOL RETROSPECTIVE at New York's Museum of Modern Art is the perfect show for time-pressed Manhattanites; they can breeze through it at the clip of a fast walk, take it in through the corners of their eyes without ever breaking stride, and be able to talk about it afterwards entirely in terms of what they got out of it. Indeed, you can honorably discuss the show without attending it at all, if you've ever seen a Brillo box, a Campbell's soup can, a photograph of Marilyn Monroe, and a silver balloon. Here they are again, the dear old Warhol icons, full of empty content, or contented emptiness. Their vacuity gains through muchness, since if you miss one wall of silk-screened cans or Marilyns or dollar bills, another wall will deliver the same massage, and we can take in this art as we take in reality—while trying to ignore it. Not only does, say, a duplicated and garishly paint-smeared image of Liza Minnelli or Truman Capote not invite close attention, it sends it skidding the other way. Busy power-people should love this show; it repels lingering, and can be cruised for its high spots, which are all but indistinguishable from its low spots.

This is not denigration but an attempt at description. Warhol's art has the powerful effect of making nothing seem important. He was a considerable philosopher, and in his testament, *The Philosophy of Andy Warhol*, as extracted by Pat Hackett, we read: "Some critic called me the Nothingness Himself and that didn't help my sense of existence any. Then I realized that existence itself is nothing and I felt better." His great unfulfilled ambition (he couldn't have had too many) was a regular TV show; he was going to call it *Nothing Special*. He came to maturity in the postwar, early–Cold War era of existentialism and angst, and found himself greatly soothed by the spread of television and the tape recorder. In his *Philosophy*, he speaks this parable: "A whole day of life is like a whole day of television. TV never goes off the air once it starts for the day, and I don't either. At the end of the day the whole day will be a movie. A movie made for TV." The tape recorder completed his deliverance from direct, emotional involvement in his own life: "The acquisition of my tape recorder really finished whatever emotional life I might have had, but I was glad to see it go. Nothing was ever a problem again, because a problem just meant a good tape, and when a problem transforms itself into a good tape it's not a problem any more." Like the pidgin pronouncements of Gertrude Stein, Warhol's harbor amid their deadpan tumble of egocentric prattle an intermittent clairvoyance, a shameless gift for seeing what is there and saying it. The political turbulence and colorful noise of the Sixties did not hide from him the decade's essential revolution: "During the 60s, I think, people forgot what emotions were supposed to be. And I don't think they've ever remembered. I think that once you see emotions from a certain angle you can never think of them as real again."

What remains real, it would seem, is the semiotic shell, the mass of images with which a society economically bent on keeping us stirred up appeals to our oversolicited, overanalyzed, overdramatized, overliberated, and over-the-hill emotions. Warhol on sex, our great social lubricant and sales incentive, is especially withering: "After being alive, the next hardest work is having sex." Sex is not only work: "Sex is nostalgia for when you used to want it, sometimes. Sex is nostalgia for sex." Or: "Frigid people really make out." His obsessive silk-screening of Marilyn Monroe (of one particular face that she presented to the camera, her eyelids half lowered and her lips parted in a smile somewhat like a growl, a Fifties drive-in waitress's tired sizing-up of one more coarse but not totally uninteresting come-on) turns her into a Day-Glo–tinted, tarted-up mask, the gaudy sad skull left when she is viewed without desire. The repetition that was one of Warhol's key devices—two Liza Minnellis, ten Elizabeth Taylors, thirty-six Elvises, one hundred two Troy Donahues— has a mocking effect. In one of the many essays that introduce the tribute-laden, 478-page catalogue, John Cage is quoted as saying, "Andy has fought by repetition to show us that there is no repetition really, that everything we look at is worthy of our attention." To me the message seems the exact opposite: that everything is repeated, that everything is emptied and rendered meaningless by repetition. Warhol himself stated: "When you see a gruesome picture over and over again, it doesn't really have any effect."

Born Andrew Warhola in 1928, the son of an immigrant Carpatho-Russian coal miner, he came from Pittsburgh to New York in 1949, freshly graduated from Carnegie Tech. In *Pre-Pop Warhol*, an album of his commercial art published in 1988 by Panache Press at Random House, Tina S. Fredericks, who gave Warhol his professional start at *Glamour* magazine, writes, "I greeted a pale, blotchy boy, diffident almost to the point of disappearance but somehow immediately and immensely appealing. He seemed all one color: pale chinos, pale wispy hair, pale eyes, a strange beige birthmark over the side of his face (almost like a Helen Frankenthaler wash)." He was not only appealing and blotchy but persistent and resourceful; by the mid-Fifties he had become a very successful commercial artist. His drawings of shoes for I. Miller, done in the Ben Shahn–like blotted-line look that he had developed, were especially celebrated in the advertising world. He was industrious and quick, and never overdid his assignments, providing a light, artist-effacing touch. In *Pre-Pop Warhol* can be found a number of devices directly transferred to the "serious" art he began to produce in 1960—repetition, gold-leaf, a wallpaper flatness, monochrome washes across the outlines, and appropriation of ready-made elements such as embossed paper decorations. These early years also saw, in the hiring of his first assistant, Nathan Gluck, in 1955, the beginning of his famous "Factory" and (to quote Rupert Jasen Smith) "his art-by-committee philosophy." Warhol's first art sales were of shoe drawings rejected by I. Miller, displayed on the walls of the Serendipity restaurant in 1954. His first exhibit, containing paintings of Superman and a Pepsi-Cola advertisement and a before-and-after nose job all present in this 1989 retrospective, appeared behind mannequins in a window of Bonwit Teller in 1961. As late as 1963 he was still accepting more commercial commissions than he rejected. He saw, however, that the gallery and the museum were the path to true wealth and fame; he went, in his words, from the art business to business art. "I started as a commercial artist, and I want to finish as a business artist. . . . I wanted to be an Art Businessman or a Business Artist. Being good in business is the most fascinating kind of art."

"American money is very well-designed, really," Warhol said in one of the few aesthetic judgments offered in his *Philosophy*. "I like it better than any other kind of money." He drew dollar bills freehand, he silk-screened sheets of them, he became rich. He had an untroubled tabloid mentality; his eye naturally went to what interests most of us: money, advertisements, packages, lurid headlines, pictures of movie stars, photographs of electric chairs and gory automobile accidents. His early-Sixties pencilled and painted copies of screaming front pages from the *News*, the *Post*, and the *Mirror*, with Sinatra and Princess Margaret, Liz and Eddie carefully but not mechanically reproduced, make us smile, because these are familiar images we thought too lowly to be passed through the eye and hand

and mind of an artist. They, and the soup cans and Coke bottles, are Pop comedy, our world brought home to us with that kiss of surprise which realism bestows. The multiple silk-screens possess, in the inevitable irregularities of the process and the overlay of colors, qualities that we can call painterly, and that reassure us.

But when we arrive, on the lower floor of this exhibition, at the blown-up and monochromed photos of car wrecks and electric chairs and race riots, a whiff of Sixties sulphur offends our nostrils in these odorless Eighties. Something too extreme and bleak is afoot. We wonder how much of our interest can be credited to Warhol, and how much to the inherent fascination of the original photographs. Where is the artist in all this? Is he working hard enough, or just peddling gruesome photos? We find ourselves getting indignant and hostile. Warhol in his lifetime inspired a great deal of hostile criticism, even in times when almost anything went, and the hostility relates, I think, to the truly radical notion his works embody: the erasure of the artist from art, his total surrender to mechanism and accident. Such a notion makes art critics uneasy, for if artists self-erase, art critics must be next in line, and it distresses the art viewer with the suspicion that he is being swindled—being sold, as it were, a silk-screen of the Brooklyn Bridge.

No sweat, the saying goes, and Warhol perfected sweatless art: movies without cutting, books without editing, painting without brushing. Up from blue-collar origins, he became the manager of the Factory. His lightest touch on the prayer wheel there produced a new billowing of replicated images, of Maos and cows and Mick Jaggers, of dollar signs and shoes, of mock-ads and packages, of helium-filled silver pillows. When each idea had had its scandalous and impudent little run, he came up with another, and although some, like the oxidization paintings produced by urinating on canvases covered with copper metallic paint,* will never replace Pollock in the hearts of museum curators, it must be said that for all the Sixties and much of the Seventies Warhol maintained quality controls. Almost everything produced was perfect in its way, with a commercial artist's clean precision and automatic tact. In the anarchic realm of the disappearing artist, the artist's ghost—wispy and powdery, Warhol came to look more and more ghostlike—exercised taste. Not until the last rooms of this show do any of the canvases seem too much, like the visually noisy camouflage series, or too little, like the epochal religious paintings of Raphael and Leonardo reduced to coloring-book outlines and disfigured with manufacturers' logos.

---

*"Mixed mediums," in polite cataloguese.

In the realm of social behavior, too, a certain control kept Warhol productive and inventive. Though lesser members of his Factory descended into stoned orgies and ruinous addictions, he remained wrapped in a prophylactic innocence, going home every night (until 1971) to his mother—that same mother who, he remembered in his brief memoir of his childhood, used to read *Dick Tracy* to him in "her thick Czechoslovakian accent" and who would reward him with a Hershey bar "every time I finished a page in my coloring book." How much, really, of his mature work can be described as "coloring"! In one of his first self-abnegations he induced her to sign his works, and write his captions, in her own clumsy but clear handwriting. Julia Warhola presents a perspective on her son opposite from that of the critic who called him Nothingness Himself: Tina Fredericks quotes her as saying, "He represents at the same time the American and the European fused together and he's very keen and sensitive to everything that goes on every day and he registered it like . . . you know . . . a photographic plate. . . . He has this terrific energy and he goes out and he registers everything and he does that everything and he becomes everything. The everything man."

Everything and nothing, Warhol might have pointed out, are close to identical. He evidently did not quite discard the Roman Catholicism in which he was raised, paying daily visits to the Church of St. Vincent Ferrer on 66th Street and anonymously performing good works for the homeless. The closing paragraphs of the catalogue essay by Robert Rosenblum persuasively link Warhol's Catholicism with his sense of the iconic, his altarpiecelike diptychs, his fondness for gilt and memento mori. But surely, also, the profound hollowness we feel behind the canvases is a Catholic negativity, the abyss of lost faith. Protestantism, when it fades, leaves behind a fuzzy idealism; Catholicism, a crystalline cynicism. In the *Philosophy*, some of his remarks have the penetrating desolation we associate with maximists like La Rochefoucauld and Chamfort. "I think that just being alive is so much work at something you don't always want to do. Being born is like being kidnapped. And then sold into slavery." The equation of being born with being kidnapped takes one's breath away, and the Warhol "works" on display in New York assume a new light when seen as the fruits of a kind of cosmic slavery. Work he did, while pretending to do nothing. If the show in its early rooms has the gaiety of a department store, it takes on downstairs the sombre, claustral mood of a catacomb. Negatived skulls and *Mona Lisa*s suggest the inversions of a black mass. The glamorized women, we notice, are almost all of them dead or grazed by death—Marilyn, Jackie, Natalie, Liz. And

Warhol himself, unexpectedly dead in a hospital when not yet sixty, a victim perhaps of the distracted medical attention that celebrities risk receiving from the awed staff, has joined the Pop martyrs, the mummified media saints.

There was an efficient churchly atmosphere to his show, of duty discharged and superstition placated. Visitors, I noticed, kept glancing slyly at one another, as if to ask, "How foolish do *you* feel?" One woman, with a seemly irreverence, combed her hair in front of a Warhol self-portrait whose framing glass reflected back from that dead opaque face. It might have been an act of oblation. Andy has become—what he must have wanted all along—an icon.

The Revealed and the Concealed

VISITORS to the Metropolitan Museum of Art's display of American portrait miniatures from the Manney Collection in the winter of 1990–91 were startled to encounter, amid the staid Victorian visages in their tight bonnets and stocks, these luminous bare breasts. Beautifully palpable and framed by a continuous swathe of gauze, they float ownerless and glow like ghosts, or angels, in some transcendental realm whose dark atmo-

Sarah Goodridge, Beauty Revealed, *1828. Watercolor on ivory.*

sphere lurks in the corners. There is a certain confrontational severity about the precisely frontal presentation. The exquisitely tinted and shaded white skin and lipoid softness have the symmetry of armor. And a suggestion of challenge balances that of invitation. Do we imagine a plea, a silent chastisement, emanating from these so vivid but ethereally disembodied breasts?

The provocative miniature, a watercolor on ivory measuring about two and a half by three inches, was evidently presented by the Boston painter, Sarah Goodridge, to the great Daniel Webster in (as inscribed on a lost paper backing) 1828. There is nothing else like it in American miniatures, or indeed in American painting of the time. The nude, to the sparse, inhibited artists of colonial North America, was a matter of Indian maidens and classical deities stiffly copied from European prints. Until well after the Revolution—as we read in William H. Gerdts' *The Great American Nude*—there was no American academy where live models posed naked; Charles Willson Peale, the head of the short-lived Columbianum Gallery, hired a baker to pose, but the man, facing the throng of artists, fled, and Peale himself bravely stripped and posed. The young Benjamin West, wanting to include an undraped slave in his *Death of Socrates*, was obliged to study a partially undressed workman at a Philadelphia gunsmith's shop. West emigrated to England at the age of twenty-two, in 1760, and eventually rendered there a number of proficient nudes—for example, *The Death of Hyacinthus*. However, for those Americans who followed him abroad but, unlike West, returned, the drapes remained on. John Singleton Copley's single nude, in *Watson and the Shark*, is foreshortened and half submerged; John Trumbull's superb London drawings of a naked female model in 1784 were never translated to canvas. In the early nineteenth century, a trio of works were displayed to a scandalized outcry—Adolph Ulrich Wertmüller's *Danaë and the Shower of Gold* in Philadelphia, Rembrandt Peale's *Dream of Love* in Baltimore, and John Vanderlyn's *Ariadne Asleep on the Island of Naxos* in New York and elsewhere, as far distant as Havana. In New Orleans in 1822, according to the journal of John James Audubon, a lovely woman furtively approached him and paid him to paint her in the buff; he did so, in sessions extending over ten days, but the painting—the first known nude American portrait done from life—has disappeared.

Sarah Goodridge's miniature survived, handed down in the Webster family. Her eye and hand, trained in the meticulous praxis of ivory miniatures, re-creates nakedness with a photographic intensity that still carries a charge, a sharp sense of physical revelation. The living model is presumed to have been herself, though this grants young and perfect breasts to a woman who, in 1828, became forty years old. The Metropolitan catalogue gives the title as "*Beauty Revealed* (Self-portrait)."

This catalogue text, by Dale T. Johnson, goes further than any biography of Webster in detailing the relationship between Webster and Goodridge. It refers to the forty-four letters from him to her, between 1827 and 1851, which have been preserved, and whose modes of address progress from "Madame" to "Dear Miss G" and "My dear, good friend." Johnson points out that Goodridge's only two known trips out of Massachusetts were to Washington, during two winters (1828–29, 1841–42), when Webster was Senator and temporarily wifeless. Not only *Beauty Revealed* but a later self-portrait and her easel and paintbox came into Webster's possession, and were "passed down by members of Webster's family, who referred to her as his fiancée."

But the Victorians do not give up their sexual secrets easily. The letters from Webster in the possession of the Boston Museum of Fine Arts could be the hastily scrawled missives of a curt and somewhat infirm lover anxious to join his mistress or, equally well, those of a busy public man trying to fit portrait sittings into his crowded schedule. The notes are invariably signed "D.W.":

> Dear Miss Goodrich [sic]
>> I will come & see you, in the course of a few days
>>> Yrs always truly

> Dear Miss Goodrich;
>> I will come to see you, the very first day I am able to walk so far—
>>> Yrs. always

> Dʳ Miss G.
>> I am not able to call today; but I shall be up again toward the end of the week, & will see you. Probably Saturday Eve or Sunday Eve—I am better, but not yet well.
>>> Greting, [sic]
>>> D.W.

> . . . I do not know that I shall ever get time to come & give you a sitting; but I live in hopes—

> Dear Miss Goodrich
>> My kind friend,
>>> If you were not the most patient of all people, you would complain of my negligence—I shall not go away without seeing you—

> Dear Miss Goodrich,
>> At one day the weather, & at another rheumatism keeps me from walkᵍ out much—I shall not go south without seeing you

Dear Miss Goodrich

I tried to get to your house yesterday, not intending to leave Boston without seeing you, but it rained too hard. I am going to Washington, for a short time; & then expect to return & be here all summer—

I thank you for all your kindness & sympathy in our afflictions.—We that survive are well—May you be preserved, in health & happiness

Your friend

D.W.

This last letter is one of the few that are dated, and from "May 23, 48" we deduce that the "afflictions" were the deaths of two of his three adult children—Edward, dead of typhoid in a military camp outside Mexico City in January of 1848, and Julia, who died in Boston shortly after the birth of her fifth child, in April, of what was probably tuberculosis. The day of her funeral was also the day that Edward's body arrived from Mexico; that melancholy spring, Webster planted two weeping elms *in memoriam* in front of their Marshfield house.

The statesman's relationship with Goodridge included exchanges of money: "I sent you $200," he wrote her, most likely during her second Washington stay in the early 1840s. "Please write me, what your present wants are, & what they will be in future; & I will do all in my power to meet them." This sounds like a sugar daddy; but she executed many portraits of him—over a dozen, by one count—and of his children, grandchildren, and relatives, and she deserved to be paid. "Please acknowledge receipt," he writes, all business, with another installment of money. And she, one biographer notes, "seems to be one of the people to whom the impecunious Webster turned for loans of money." At the undoubtable least, the two were friendly; his proprietorial tone just barely stays within the bounds of disinterested patronage: "As soon as I return, I will see you—meantime, if you need Counsel, call on J. P. Healey, Esq [a legal partner of Webster's, not the portrait artist G. P. A. Healy], ask him to come to see you, & say it is at my request."

The letters in the possession of the Massachusetts Historical Society, many of them written from Washington in the two decades after *Beauty Revealed* was painted, are somewhat more leisurely, and strike warm notes, often in closing:

I pray you, let me hear from you, & be assured of all my good wishes, & of my true and sincere regard. [12/2/35]

I always like to receive your letters, as they keep you in friendly remembrance. [12/28/35]

I shall see you as soon as I reach home. [2/24/35]

It is my purpose to go home this month, for a few days, if the weather should continue mild. You will of course see me. I wish you were here, occupied agreeably in painting faces. [1/5/35]

I am glad to hear you are well I shall be glad to hear from you often— [9/13/37]

This hastily scrawled letter of September 13, 1837, begins, "I have not written a letter since I came here, with my own hand, except to my wife, on account of the state of my eyes, arising from influenza. I could not call to see you, before leaving home. My affairs were so urgent, & my health so bad, I could not find opportunity." He places her, then, next in priority to his wife; but Sarah Goodridge was no secret from his wife, for in a note dated 1829 "Mr. Webster presents his respects" and promises "He will call on Miss G. with Mrs Webster tomorrow." A longish letter of May 12, 1834, from Washington, sounds all the chords of their enigmatic friendship. "My Dear Miss Goodrich," it begins with special warmth. "It always gives me pleasure to hear from you, & to learn your health & happiness, so that when you have nothing to write, as well as when you have something, your letters will be welcome." He keeps her posted on his whereabouts, and his wife's: "My wife and boys leave here on the 17th— Mrs W. will probably stay some time in N. York, & then proceed to Boston." A complicated passage concerning money implies that he is borrowing five hundred dollars from her, and a postscript appoints his brother-in-law to collect it, in an atmosphere of secrecy: "I have written Mr Fletcher to call himself, on you to receive the money, instead of sending the boy. He will say nothing about this business to anybody." Another, later note makes light of his financial embarrassment: "I am very poor today, but I will let you have some money—a little—in the early part of next week." The last missive in the batch, from January 2, 1851, confesses to a surprisingly large debt: "I send you a check for $215.39—which will leave due, according to yr acct $2000—For this I will try to arrange pretty soon."

She preserved even the curtest scratching from him, whereas none of her letters to him have survived. We have only a deadpan accounting, in her hand, of the miniature-portrait commissions executed for his family. The first was "of his daughter Julia, in October 1819, age between one & two years. The second, his youngest son Charles, in December 1823, about two years of age." A warmer note creeps in: "He seemed to me an uncommonly fine promising child, and his sudden death about a year after, a sad loss." The last portrait was in 1850, of two grandchildren,

"Caroline W. & Ashburton." Her dozen or so of Webster himself over the years bespeak a fascinated gaze.

The painting of miniature portraits, to be kept in lockets and leather cases, had become, in the decades before the advent of the daguerreotype in the 1840s, a thriving artistic industry, and one of the few in which women could succeed. The delicacy of the work—laying fine strokes or stipples of transparent watercolor upon small squares or ovals of ivory—was thought especially suited for feminine talents. Sarah Goodridge opened her studio in Boston in 1820 and, until failing eyesight forced her to retire in 1850, she supported herself and a number of relatives—for eleven years, her infirm mother; a paralytic brother; an orphan niece—by painting two or three miniatures a week. For a time she was the only miniature portraitist in Boston; she remained one of the most prolific. She never married and lived with her sister and brother-in-law, the Thomas Appletons. According to a biographical sketch composed by the Appletons' great-grandaughter, Mrs. Francis Appleton Smith Mansfield, Sarah "was not a financier and loaned to many who were never able to pay. Nor was she always successful in her investments. But even with these drawbacks, she managed to save enough for her support and to leave something to her relatives."

She was an independent woman, in an age when these were few. The self-portrait in the Museum of Fine Arts shows a dark-haired, large-eyed woman with the hint of a saucy, appraising smile about her lips. Her image, if not quite that of a beauty, pleasingly conveys energy, directness, and intelligence. It makes a plausible match with the handsome, rather intense miniature of Webster she painted in October of 1827.

Six years younger than he, she was born in 1788, in Templeton, Massachusetts, a country hill town outside of Worcester. The sixth of nine children, she showed an early love of art, and used to draw with a pin on the smooth side of birch bark, and with sticks on the sand-sprinkled floors of the house. According to Mrs. Mansfield's biography, "She also drew on the whitewashed walls of the house and wherever she could find a smooth surface." Her self-instruction was reinforced by scattered tutors around Boston and in her art-poor native environment. She began to "take likenesses" in Templeton—"first on paper, life size, with red, white and black chalk, at 50 cents each, and then in water colors on paper at $1.50 each." At the age of twenty-four she moved to Boston for good and shifted, in her portrait work, from oil canvases to miniatures. "From that time forward, she had as much as she could do," according to a reminiscence by her sister Eliza, herself a gifted miniature-painter. No less a patron than Gilbert Stuart visited Sarah's studio and, according to Harry B. Wehle's *American Miniatures*, "After watching her groping methods for a while

Sarah Goodridge, Self-portrait, *1830. Watercolor on ivory.*

Sarah Goodridge, Daniel Webster, *1827. Watercolor on ivory.*

Stuart lost patience and, taking up a piece of ivory for the first (and last) time in his life, set about to demonstrate how a miniature should be painted." She painted miniatures from a number of his oil portraits and did several fine portraits of him in his old age. The girl from Templeton had a way of exciting attention from distinguished older men.

One puzzles over Webster's biography, wondering if he might have kept a mistress. The living arrangements he had created for himself—a Boston lawyer who spent half the year in Washington, with farms in Marshfield, Massachusetts, and Franklin, New Hampshire—conduced to a captain's paradise. He denied himself little in the way of physical comfort: he was a noteworthy drinker, in an era of hard drinking, and a prodigal spender; financial improprieties dogged his reputation. Yet he was also a rigorous Trinitarian Christian, in a New England rife with Unitarian infidelity, and a grimly ambitious man, his eye set on the Presidency for most of his adult life. "At thirty Alexander had conquered the world," he wrote a friend, "and I am forty."

Perhaps a clue to the mystery of *Beauty Revealed* lies in the history of miniatures. With its distant precedent in the coins and carved gems of the classic world, the art arose out of medieval illumination; the very word derives from *minium*, a red lead pigment used in painting decorative borders and initials in illuminated manuscripts. Only in the eighteenth century did "miniature" acquire its present meaning. From the start the small paintings, on cardboard or parchment, were meant to be worn or kept, in jewelled settings, by an intimate of the sitter. One of their early uses, in the Europe of the sixteenth century, was to further dynastic marriages. Nicholas Hillard did many of his portraits of Elizabeth I for her suitors. Oliver Cromwell, a few reigns later, sent a miniature of himself to Queen Christina of Sweden. In the absence of photographs and jet planes, miniatures substituted for courtship presentations. Their use as amorous proxies was extended, in the Europe (but not the America) of the early nineteenth century, to the form of "lover's eyes"—the beloved's single eye, naturalistically rendered but unrecognizable to any but the lover, painted as a small pin to be worn on the inside of the lapel or some other private site. Features even more intimate than eyes were sometimes used. Sarah Goodridge apparently made a transatlantic leap into this romantic fad.

Her smoldering portrait of the forty-four-year-old Webster dates from 1827; *Beauty Revealed* from 1828. Toward the end of 1827, Webster's first wife, Grace Fletcher, fell ill; in January, she died, leaving him in charge of three young children, distraught and despondent. "I feel very little zeal or spirit in regard to the passing affairs," he wrote his friends the Ticknors on February 22, 1828. "My most strong propensity is to sit down, and sit still." Obviously, he needed a wife. So, possibly, Sarah Goodridge offered herself, in the form of a miniature. *Come to us, and we will comfort you*, the breasts of her self-portrait seem to say. *We are yours for the taking, in all our ivory loveliness, with our tenderly stippled nipples.*

The offer, if it was one, was not taken. Webster needed not just love but money. In May of 1829 he began to court Catherine Van Rensselaer, a daughter of a wealthy New York patroon who was his political ally. Though some politic letters to the father survive, the courtship did not kindle, and by November of that year Webster—a letter to Jacob McGraw reveals—had turned to Caroline Le Roy, the daughter of a prominent New York merchant. He found her "amiable, discreet, prudent, with enough of personal comeliness to satisfy me, & of the most excellent character & principles." "At thirty-two," Webster's most recent biographer, Maurice G. Baxter, states, "Caroline was neither very young nor very beautiful. . . . Her father was reputable and, though Webster did not say it, wealthy." The wedding took place before the end of the year.

But Sarah Goodridge's breasts stayed in Webster's possession, to descend to his heirs, along with her paintbox, and he kept sitting for her scrutiny, and bringing his loved ones. She needed the business, and he—

though generally unresponsive to any art but the orator's art—seemed to need the miniatures, or her company. *These lady artists are wonderful to relax with, but one doesn't marry them, especially when they are all of forty, and commercial drudges besides.* Still, the aging statesman, battered by his creditors and the rising sectional strife in the land, had to smile, thinking of that leather-cased present she had given him, tucked away in a drawer of his mahogany chest in Marshfield like a sugar-drop at the back of his mouth.

My reconstruction of events isn't especially likely, but neither is the existence of *Beauty Revealed*. We must argue backwards from its unique datum—a singularity in American art, and a dazzling peep beneath another century's voluminous clothes.

Fun Furniture

FURNITURE, like children, should not take over; it should wait in its place to be called upon, sat upon, patted, admired. We expect it to quietly shine, to be serviceable, and not to think of itself as an art form, quite. Yet, from gilded pharaonic chairs on, some of it has crept into museums and stayed there. It was the happy notion of Edward S. Cooke, assistant curator of the Department of American Decorative Arts and Sculpture at the Museum of Fine Arts in Boston, to invite twenty-six contemporary furniture-makers (most of them born in the 1950s) each to concoct a piece of his or her own based upon a piece of furniture in the museum's permanent collection. More than two years after the invitation was extended in October of 1987, the exhibition has been mounted, and a handsome and merry one it is, on display in Boston until March, and then at the Renwick Gallery in Washington and the Contemporary Arts Center in Cincinnati.

In Boston, it occupies two large rooms—not merely occupies them, it turns these stony exhibition spaces into rooms warm with color and texture and shape. Three of the pieces are displayed with the older pieces that inspired them; for the rest, a photograph of the *pièce de départ* suffices. The exhibit is in this sense thoroughly postmodern, each item deliberately derivative, allusive, appropriative. But what pride of craftsmanship, of material and form, the contemporary creations more or less wittily exhibit! "More or less" because two approaches to the assignment might be distinguished: the path of parody, and that of homage.

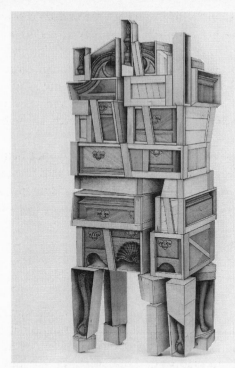

John Cederquist, Le Fleuron Manquant, *1989. Baltic
birch plywood, mahogany, Sitka spruce, purpleheart,
koa veneers, pigmented eposy, aniline dye.*

Michael Hurwitz's *Rocking Chaise*, for example, makes an extended pun
on the wavy backslats of a dainty and surprisingly airy side chair constructed by Samuel Gragg of Boston in the early nineteenth century.
The most spectacular parody is John Cederquist's take-off on a mid-
eighteenth-century Rhode Island high chest by John Townsend: the
cabriole ball-and-claw legs, the shell carving on the front rail, the ornate
brass pulls, the interrupted curved cornice, and the flame-shaped finials
of the mahogany original are all placed half hidden in the semblances
of crates by an amazing feat of trompe-l'oeil marquetry. Cederquist's
deconstruction has two flat faces set at an obtuse angle, and from the side
seems little more than a rickety stack of birch plywood crates; but in fact
the mélange would function, cunningly, as a bureau, for a set of mischievous finger pulls—some achieved by depressing a slat or trompe-l'oeil
handle—elicit a set of smoothly sliding drawers, all constructed at an
obtuse angle, so they are not rectangular but rhomboidal. Similarly, if a
bit less cunningly, Tom Loeser's irregular tower of nine striped boxes,

derived from a Boston chest-on-chest from the early eighteenth century, would serve as a bureau; the assembly is stable and the nine drawers are beautifully fitted.

Also in the parodic vein, Paul Sasso's pink version of a nineteenth-century work table is decorated with vaginal forms, a skirt carved to mimic the limp fall of cloth, and a mural inside the lid showing God as a patriarch wounded by scissors. The effect is gaudy and a touch religio-political, as is the piece's title, *No, You Get Out of My Garden*. However, it would work as a table, which cannot be said of Michael Pierschalla's con-tribution to the show, consisting of four (or is it five?) upstanding legs tied together by a cyma-curve rail and a circle of laminated wood and painted copper that might, if care were taken, support an aperitif glass or two. Pierschalla went deaf as a college freshman and his hearing returned over a decade later; the accompanying label attempts to link this physical misadventure to his tendency "to see furniture forms in a fragmented fashion." The catalogue quotes him as saying, "I am not especially inter-ested in function anymore . . . I like furniture that works, I just think there are other things to do." The most Zenlike quip against function belongs to Peter Dean's *Canyon Table*, a version of an old-fashioned tres-tle table which, by opposing the uncut edges of two mighty ash planks, leaves a gap that could be bridged by a turkey platter but would swallow a lot of cranberries and potatoes.

Yet, in the rest of its severe, even reverent appropriation of the colonial original, Dean's piece appears to pay homage, modernizing its model only with the rift in the top and a curve to the big tie beam below. Thomas Hucker's *High Chest of Drawers*, one of four tall chests in the show, Orientalizes and mysticizes the dignified William-and-Mary wal-nut piece it echoes by curving the entire front, of butterflied burl aboya veneer, and the even bigger back, of black-lacquered plywood, against which the gravely lustrous front appears to float. In a show rich with surface and texture, this splendid piece achieves the most impressive innovation in form. Kristina Madsen's oval-backed side chair, Timo-thy Philbrick's graceful dressing table, Rick Wrigley's fluted sideboard, and Richard Scott Newman's oval-fronted commode, on the other hand, modulate but modestly the functional shape of their antique models, and make their statements by outdoing them in exquisiteness. The inside veneering of Wrigley's sideboard, in wedge-shaped pieces of pale curly sycamore, produces a gossamer spiderweb effect that, unfortunately, needs a curator's empowered hand to reveal. The fineness of Madsen's chair is there for all to see. Only the curved piping on the blue silk back, whose shape is derived from that of a Maori paddle club, distinctly

Kristina Madsen, Side Chair, *1989. Pau ferro, maple,
Baltic birch plywood, silk.*

departs, to an amateur's eye, from the antique decorum of its Philadelphia prototype.

The sumptuousness and skill the makers of this furniture have at their command dominates our impressions, overriding the impudence, festivity, and satire of their designs. Even an openly comic artifact like Tommy Simpson's carved burlesque of a traditional Windsor chair, with its cacophonous variety of woods used in the stringers and spindles (walnut, cherry, padouk, mahogany, bird's-eye maple, spalted maple, curly maple, tulip, yellow satinwood), gets us to thinking about woods—how many there are, how subtly different, how they contrast and fit, how the patient hand of the devoted joiner brings the pattern and pointillism of grain out of the impassive bulk of trees. Another comic piece, Edward Zucca's long trestle table named *Mystery Robots Rip Off the Rain Forest*, has for legs carved mechanical men carrying away their phenomenal prize, a thirty-inch-wide, eleven-foot-long plank of Honduran mahogany. The form is caught stealing the substance. While the forests last, modern craftsmen have access to a dizzying variety of woods: Honduran rosewood, Sitka spruce, Baltic birch, purpleheart, koa, curly ash, burl aboya, pau ferro, Australian lacewood, Ceylonese satinwood, curly English sycamore, Macassar ebony, wenge, Swiss pearwood, and pomele sepele are among the more exotic woods used. The Australian lacewood featured in Jere Osgood's *Cylinder Front Desk* has the subdued multiple glint of hammered pewter. In Hank Gilpin's no-frills wardrobe, the stark white oak, wirebrushed but otherwise unfinished, confronts us like a mute force of nature, like a giant door in a betranced castle.

Not just wood furnishes virtuoso effects—a wealth of synthetic materials is now available, and a willingness to expand upon the primacy of wood marks this so-called second generation of studio furniture-makers. Rhodoid—synthetic mother-of-pearl—tops John Dunnigan's classically proportioned table and complements, with its optically rumpled richness, a decorative silk skirt and tassels. (How hard it is, by the way, to obey the repeated printed enjoinder not to touch all these silky, sanded surfaces!) Fountainhead, a faux granite used for kitchen counters, is a favorite material of Garry Knox Bennett, who, born in 1934, is the oldest contributor to this show. His variation on a Boston kneehole bureau employs Fountainhead and ColorCore, a Formicalike synthetic substance with a brightly colored edge, along with aluminum and brick; these assorted obdurate materials have all been sawed along a whimsical rippled curve to form a rose-and-brown confection that looks like a fireplace and includes a safe with flickeringly painted doors.

If the exuberance of this and such pieces as Mitch Ryerson's tasselled, pillowed, and perforated bench suggests that they would be boisterous companions in an everyday home, the background music of the antique models keeps the majority of the pieces in a domestic key. The very terms of the exhibition have set up a nice singing tension between antique and new, function and form, homage and parody, sensual comfort and artistic gesture. Overall, sensuality wins out, gesturally enhanced. The sculptural drama of Alphonse Mattia's asymmetrical easy chairs is softened by the luxurious undulating grain of the upholstery's knitted wool. Gold-leafed leopards sinuously, playfully stretch their necks on Judy Kensley McKie's stern black box of a chest. Wendy Maruyam's forbidding purplish high chest reveals behind its top doors (again, with a curator's connivance) a sumptuous red interior. Furniture, even at this highest level of contemporary improvisation, shapes itself to receive our body and house our clothes; next to clothes, furniture, of the things men make, comes closest to our skin, and it remains, toy with it as we will, engagingly human in its measure.

Acts of Seeing

FOR A NUMBER OF YEARS NOW, a poster-size reproduction of Norman Rockwell's *Shuffleton's Barber Shop*, originally a cover for the April 29, 1950, issue of *The Saturday Evening Post*, has hung above the water closet of my office toilet, where I cannot help but look at it, in the idle trance of

Norman Rockwell, Shuffleton's Barber Shop, *1950. Oil on canvas.*

urination, several times a day. After thousands of absent-minded exami-
nations, I am still finding new things to see in it. The boots and rub-
bers, for instance, in front of the stove, with its red-hot coals, and, in the
diagonally opposite corner, the ghostly row of old shaving mugs in
the top cells of the obsolete cabinet, between the ceiling fixture of frosted
glass and the little gooseneck lamp. One's eye, travelling around the edge
of the painting, encounters a whisk broom, an Indian-shuttered window
frame, a porcelain basin, a rack of comic books, two knobbed chairs, a
mullion with parched putty, a curved crack in the corner of a window
pane, a spindleback settee, shelves holding old magazines, a gun, fishing
tackle, and, all along the top, the gilt appliqué letters spelling BARBER.
The eye naturally swoops through the front window to the luminous,
man-crammed rectangle of the back room, skimming through the shadows of the closed shop, past the listening cat, the magnificent old barber
chair, the hairy broom, the little cracked mirror, the wartime poster of a
torn flag, into the bright chaste chamber where music is being made. The
most brilliant passages of painting, perhaps, depict the standing violinist,
all but dissolved in light, and the reflections on the foreshortened piece of
stove pipe leading into the wall. But the illustration is saturated in every
corner with an avid particularizing that allows us to forgive the cuteness
of the cat and the stagey quaintness of the whole, the idealization of
small-town life.

In the Fifties twilight of the slick magazines, before television had
quite stolen away their audience, their advertisers, and their kitschy
energy, Rockwell, always zealous in his pursuit of visual anecdote, put the
stylizations of J. C. Leyendecker and Maxfield Parrish far behind him and
let his attention range across the entire plane of the picture, overflowing
the margins of the anecdote. In the *Post* cover of September 25, 1954, the
spokes of the old truck, the fur of the collie, the battered boards of the
platform, the switchman's lantern on the trunk are all rendered with a
care that brings meaning to the central image, the face of the weary
rancher waiting to send his son off to college. In the well-known *Post*
cover of November 24, 1951, showing an old lady and a young boy saying
grace in a casual downtown eatery, chairbacks, cutlery, coffee cups, and
detached arms and hands as well as the arrested faces of other diners
crowd the picture's edges with an almost hectically populous milieu,
deepened by a monochrome industrial cityscape spread in the upper half
of the curtained window. The textures and fine compositional balance of
this canvas are not cheap effects, however adversely we react to its down-
home piety.

In a cover from June 1955 depicting a young couple as they apply for a marriage license in a shabby courthouse office, the margins are relatively quiet, the details of woodwork and iron stove and loaded bookshelves are muffled in brown, and the window deepens the space only as far as a warm brick wall, whose color beautifully confirms the hopeful yellow of the intent fiancée's dress. To write on the top of the old rolltop desk she in her feminine smallness has to lift up off her high heels, and this delicate touch carries more of the work's considerable sentimental freight than the wizened functionary's wistful expression, the geranium on the sill, or the rather reflexively included pet cat. On the cover of June 28, 1958, a jockey weighs in under the scrutiny of an overweight track official; there is no populated background, just a streaky off-white ground color, spatially unreal in Twenties style, and the jockey's shiny boots don't quite "read," reminding us of the mechanically sharp creases in Leyendecker's Arrow shirts. But the scales themselves, their corroded matte metal and faintly scratched enamel, present a marvel of mimesis, so vividly tactile as to steal attention away from the joke.

Rockwell in this silver age of his art was a photorealist; he projected selected photographs onto his canvas (square to allow the *Post* title logo room on top) and traced them in charcoal, sprayed the result with a fixative, applied a thin oil *imprimatura*, and then underpainted in monochrome, usually in violet. According to Susan E. Meyer in her *Great American Illustrators*, he tried, in painting on the colors, to avoid smothering the drawing with excessively careful working, sometimes resorting to painting with a brick or a shingle, left-handed or drunk. Yet the relatively rough and free "art" paintings he executed are not, like those of, say, Hogarth and Sargent, more interesting than his finished work, but less—unadventurous in color, tame in handling. We miss the hyperrealism, the details teased up to the point of caricature. Such teasing made for fussy, unlovely brushwork. A painter of my acquaintance, visiting the Rockwell Museum in Stockbridge, was struck by how "horrible" the paintings, as painted surfaces, were. Rockwell painted for reproduction and the reproduced image was the finished work. In the smooth vast ocean of commercial art, his work always stood out by virtue of an extra intensity, a need (bred, psychology inevitably will say, of insecurity) to provide a little more than the occasion strictly demanded—for example, his surreally expressive vocabulary of shoes.

He was something of a fanatic in his quest for authenticity. Rather than hire professional models, he cajoled people he saw on the street into posing. As he moved outward from New York City, where he was born in 1894, in a back room of a brownstone at 103rd Street and Amsterdam Avenue, he depended upon the repertoire of American faces provided by his neighbors in, respectively, New Rochelle, New York; Arlington, Vermont; and Stockbridge, Massachusetts. He would prop children into a pose with bricks and boards and, to hold their attention, piled up their fee in pennies and nickels as the session wore on. Animals were even more restless than children; a turkey once escaped from a Thanksgiving cover and had to be chased down the street. He searched old shops and barns for authentically aged chairs, beds, sleighs, and carriages. "Once," Ms. Meyer tells us, "he was able to buy an old overcoat which he saw airing on a line only by purchasing with it a bag of rags and a couple of hundred pounds of old iron. The owner naturally assumed Rockwell was a junk dealer." Commissioned to illustrate Mark Twain, he travelled to Hannibal, Missouri. "Sitting in the studio," he explained, "I may imagine a special setting and think it real and complete, but when I search out the actual counterpart there's always some little detail that I've forgotten and that will make the illustration ring true so that the reader, whether he's ever seen such a place or not, says immediately, 'that's it; that's true.' " The use of photographs, taken by a professional and then projected onto the artist's canvas, paradoxically freed him up from the worst constraints of literalism. "Working from the model," he claimed, "I had found it impossible to paint a green sweater from a red sweater. It sounds silly, but I just hadn't been able to do it. So I'd had to hunt up the right sweater in green. A nuisance. When working with photographs, I seem to be able to recompose in many ways, in form, tone, and color."

As small-town America and its family magazines faded around him, his painterly excess became more apprehensive and lavish—a preservative varnish, a nostalgic greed, a self-satisfying perfectionism, an art for art's sake. Widely loved like no other painter in America, yet despised in high-art circles, he pushed on, into canvases that almost transcend their folksy, crowd-pleasing subjects. Impressionist impasto and dash could never be his, or modernist heroics, but one of his last *Post* covers, for January 13, 1962, confronts Abstract Expressionism, a splashy phenomenon at the opposite pole from his patient, homely, humble technique. By 1962 Pop Art had already supplanted abstraction as the hot movement; Warhol, Johns, and Lichtenstein were making museum art by reproducing the comic strips and commercial imagery of the decades previous. Rockwell's was the wrong kind of commercial art, too perilously close to high art, to be thus appropriated; it had to generate its own ironic self-consciousness. Windows recur in his brimming square canvases; he flirts with trompe-l'oeil effects. As in such earlier signature works as Vermeer's self-portrait from behind and van Eyck's couple reflected in a convex mirror, seeing becomes Rockwell's secret subject, his silent boast. In *Shuffleton's Barber Shop*, we know just how we are looking in, our face a few inches from the glass. And we see, say, for the first time, how far the light cord to the gooseneck lamp has travelled, along a diagonal that mirrors the crack in the corner of the pane.

Big, Bright, and Bendayed

IN ATTENDING the 1993 Roy Lichtenstein retrospective at the Guggenheim Museum, I made a mistake: imagining that the exhibit, like most I have viewed in that cunning spiral, would begin at the top, I took the elevator up, and found myself not at Lichtenstein's beginnings as an artist but flung headlong into his latest, slickest phase. A quiet sign beckoned me yet upwards, through one of the Guggenheim's cavelike archways, and I was in a large room holding large canvases from the 1990s—meticulous crystallizations, or visual embalmings, of prototypical American living quarters. It was without doubt the best-illumined, brightest room in my museum-going experience; had I stayed in it longer, I might have acquired a tan. However, the paintings, with their wrought-iron outlines and industrial-quality Benday dots and prefab stripes, and their squared-off sofas and end tables, and their stark little simplifications of name-brand artworks, including some of Lichtenstein's, did not invite lingering contemplation, and I plunged impatiently on the smooth slope downward, in search of the comic-strip enlargements that are Lichtenstein's deathless contribution to contemporary art.

Alas, they were near the bottom of the long unwinding ribbon of viewing space, and to get to them I had to pass by, not always impatiently, three decades' worth of the variations that the ingenious, hard-working artist has rung upon his single idea—the transportation into high art of reproduced commercial art's mechanical look. Nighttime was settling into the world beyond Frank Lloyd Wright's impregnable, top-shaped fortress. The Guggenheim stays open late, in keeping with its jazzy structure, and it must be said that never have I seen artworks as comfortably resplendent in its gargantuan coils as these poster-bold big canvases of Lichtenstein's. Back and forth they blatantly signalled across the well of space, ignoring the shadowy, shuffling form of us pedestrian art-lovers, who had trooped into the dusk to be dwarfed and cowed once more by the aloof majesty of the modern masters, in this case Wright and Lichtenstein. A museum designed in splendid disdain of the art it houses, and an art which, in the words of the monitory lecture lettered on the wall, is devoted to "conveying an ironic, anti-aesthetic attitude, and capturing a look of 'insincerity' "—they were made for each other. Gaudy as a circus, the silent spectacle was well worth the pilgrimage up to 90th Street. In these days when a cultural event must have a very high gloss to catch the eye, the Lichtenstein show bedazzles.

And yet—to get back to my wrong-ended perambulation—paintings so steadfastly ironical, so exclusively devoted to the reduction of derived imagery, to the reprocessing of existing art, flicker across the attention with a certain monotony. The reality is always two-dimensional, the smile is always dry. The dryness of the two *Plus and Minus* canvases (1988) may be wasted on those viewers who do not recognize the allusion to Piet Mondrian's *Composition in Black and White* (1917), an abstraction composed of short black lines intermittently forming plus and minus signs—a pattern evoked by Lichtenstein in a Benday pattern, employed in his other late paintings, of small bricklike shapes. And not every pilgrim to the Guggenheim may recognize, in Lichtenstein's *Reflections on Nancy* (1989), the close parroting of the acrylic by Andy Warhol which, with four other similar canvases placed in a Bonwit Teller window in 1961, signalled the possibility of comic-strip characters as subjects for high art (beyond serving as elements in collages, as in some of Robert Rauschenberg's). Warhol's paintings, however, were part of a window display by an established commercial artist; it was Lichtenstein who, against the initial reservations of the dealer Leo Castelli, first presented painted comic-strip enlargements as worthy to adorn a wall—or, as the artist put it in an interview with *ARTnews* in 1983, as canvases that were too "despicable" to hang, executed by a knowledgeable student of art who was "anti-contemplative, anti-nuance, anti-getting-away-from-the-tyranny-of-the-rectangle, anti-movement and -light, anti-mystery, anti-paint-quality, anti-Zen, and anti-all of those brilliant ideas of preceding movements which everyone understands so thoroughly."

But of course the art establishment loves nothing better than packageable anti-establishmentarianism, and Lichtenstein's paradoxical position is that of an instant classic who is still lampooning other classics, in a manner that has become pedantic. He is probably right in expecting his audience to be art-savvy enough to catch his allusions to Monet, Van Gogh, Picasso, Léger, Matisse, Magritte, Gino Severini, Carlo Carrà, etc. Even if the audience were not, an artist's obligation is to focus on what interests him, and to produce what pleases him. Spectators can only stand by, and applaud (and pay) or not. Yet Lichtenstein's recent recycling of his own earlier work, along with that of other artists, by means of overlaying their all-too-well-known images with irregular strips of Benday pattern (the *Reflections* series, e. g., *Nurse* [1988] and *Whaam!* [1990]), seems a rather desperate variation on a picture-making tech-

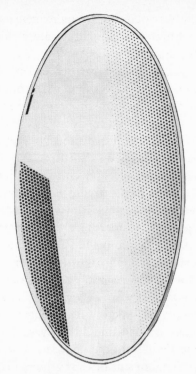

Roy Lichtenstein, Oval Mirror 6' x 3' #1,
1971. Oil and Magna on canvas.

nique whose charm was always its impudent thinness. Descending the
Guggenheim's grand helix, one sees dots before the eyes, and sometimes
not much else. Standing in front of one of his *Mirror*s from the early
Seventies—ovals empty but for dim diagonal dottings—one feels, as if
standing near a hissing airplane door, in danger of being sucked out by
the vacuity.

Benday is properly Ben Day, named after its inventor, Benjamin Day
(1838–1916), a New York printer who conceived of introducing tones of
gray into photoengraving by means of small regular patterns of dots or
stipples. Cartoonists and illustrators can purchase Benday patterns in
sheets that are transparent and adhesive and, laid upon the inked-in
drawing, can be carved with a razor blade or an X-Acto knife to the shape
desired. Lichtenstein's defining stroke of genius was to enlarge Benday
dots into a motif. At first, they were dabbed on by brush; then the bristles
of a dog brush were dipped in paint and pressed against the canvas, giving
a noticeable panelled appearance not present in real Bendayed reproduc-
tions. Also, in such early works as *Black Flowers* (1961) and *Girl with Ball*

(1961), the dots are smaller than the enlarged scale calls for. By 1962, the dots have regularized, and by 1963 Lichtenstein had developed a method whereby manufactured stencils were employed by assistants. His trend has been toward bigger and more various patterns; they now include closely packed large dots, dots tapering in size from row to row, stripes, the brick pattern previously mentioned, and a particularly ugly fake wood grain echoing that found in Cubist collages.

Much of the handwork is still executed by Lichtenstein; at least, a charming little video that runs in a side room at the Guggenheim shows Lichtenstein fondly filling in black circles and thick uniform outlines, while he assures the camera of the joy he takes in his craft. Such manual labor to produce an effect of mechanism argues for a kind of sainthood and suggests an unexpected affinity with the Performance Art that was contemporaneous with the beginnings of Pop Art: like the constructions destroyed in their performance, Lichtenstein's brushwork vanishes in the finished product. "I want my painting to look as if it has been programmed. I want to hide the record of my hand."

One comes away from the video liking Lichtenstein more for having seen it, and more prepared to consider his canvases as aesthetic objects, as well as effective attention-getters and counters in the ever-complicating game of modern art. The film shows him turning a Dagwood painting in outline upside down, to consider the composition abstractly, and a number of his paintings—the famous *Whaam!* (1963), *We Rose Up Slowly* (1964), *Still Life with Glass and Peeled Lemon* (1972), *Go for Baroque* (1979)—impress us with the powerful rightness and, somehow, the *pressure* of their composition. From the comic-strip panel he learned how to use the canvas to the brim. The catalogue, with a thorough and attentive, if rather pious and solemn, text by Diana Waldman, enables us to compare the paintings with their originals in advertising and comic-book art and bears out Lichtenstein's claim that "My work is actually different from comic strips in that every mark is really in a different place, however slight the difference seems to some. The difference is often not great, but it is crucial." Crucial, perhaps, but often so small that one wonders where the copyright lawyers for the comic-book companies have been sleeping all these years. The shock value of these painterly enlargements of single comics panels is diminished in reproduction, where they sink back toward the size of their models; perhaps not so paradoxically, an art based upon reproduction loses its punch when reproduced.

Descending, I was pleasantly surprised by the sculpture, which perforce has to step out from the two-dimensional shell game and compete in the world of objects. The Bendayed stripes become bars of painted bronze, and the visual puns—on Matisse in *Goldfish Bowl II* (1978), on a

Minoan mural in *Archaic Head VI*—become transformations, arousing our sense of weight and materials. The polka-dotted ceramic heads and chunky coffee cups, complete with ceramic coffee and saucer and spoon, have the charm of classic Pop sculpture, by Claes Oldenburg and Jasper Johns, with the patented Lichtenstein dottiness. Blessedly free of Benday and of any overt reference to his paintings are the witty and elegant brass pieces from the late Sixties, homage to the Art Deco décor of Thirties movie palaces, complete with velvet rope. Art Deco is the one formal style that Lichtenstein cannot burlesque, since its geometric cleanness and streamlining snugly fit his predilections. Canvases like *Modern Painting with Classic Head* (1967) and *Preparedness* (1968) make it on their own, as it were, as impressive and energetic compositions. The second, in three panels, is based on the WPA murals of the Thirties, and Lichtenstein in an interview took some pains to establish his correct distance from it: "You realize I'm not serious about defending our shore against foreign devils, as these works would imply. But the purpose isn't only the reverse. It is also a statement about 'heroic' composition."

The purpose isn't only the reverse: this statement is a useful corrective to Ms. Waldman's single-minded drift, which casts Lichtenstein as a satirist and counterinsurgent whose purpose has been "to celebrate the absurd aspects of our cultural condition" and "to confront the clichés of art." Her commentary does not much allow for the multidetermination of the artistic impulse; it can satirize and memorialize at the same time, reconcile scorn with affection. Even the *Brushstrokes*, of the mid-Sixties, which present a hilarious deflation of Abstract Expressionism's splashing, dripping dramatization of the painter's process—the brushstroke as heroic event—also constitute a tribute, an outburst of the very energy that the literalist, static rendering mocks.

When we arrive, a bit dizzy, on the last curves of the helix, at the comic-book paintings with which Lichtenstein made his mark, we find a far more complicated mood than travesty. At least our own response is in some significant fraction inextricable from our reaction to these panels as if we were encountering them in a comic book; the disjunct moments of melodrama ("It's . . . it's not an *engagement ring*. Is it?"; "Forget it! Forget me! I'm fed up with your kind!") catch us up in their narrative: Is it? What kind? The war scenes *(Whaam!; Takka Takka; Okay, Hot Shot!)* are thrilling, in their Second-World-War all-out murderousness; the true-romance heroines, the stylized girls with their globular tears and blue-black or black-yellow hair, are alluring in their emotional throes, each an "archetypical" woman, in Lichtenstein's phrase. To Ms. Waldman, they are stonily "products of a culture that puts celluloid glamour and consumer objects before human dignity and individual or collective

Roy Lichtenstein, Forget It! Forget Me!, *1962. Oil and Magna on canvas.*

achievement" and victims of "society's codification of women as ornaments, positioned for the male gaze only." Far be it from me to deny Lichtenstein whatever Nineties-style political correctness he achieved in the early Sixties, when these images were created; but I think that to deny that our amusement and interest in them coincides with that of average comic-book readers would be as silly as denying that our interest in painted or sculpted nudes derives in part from prurience.

Pop Art won its public because it descended from abstraction and showed us our world—its artifacts, its trash, its billboards, its standardized romantic imagery. In seizing upon cartoon images with their flat color and outlines as a way to free himself from Abstract Expressionism, Lichtenstein did not opt for sheer nullity—otherwise, he would have kept painting black-and-white golf balls, balls of twine, and composition-book covers innocent of any human drama, or would have stuck with Mickey Mouse and Wimpy instead of aping the more realistically drawn romance and war comics. His anti-expressionist comic-book paintings nevertheless have an expressive content, including, for those of Lichtenstein's generation, a considerable quotient of nostalgia. The presiding mood of campy remove co-exists with the comic-book vitality, the vitality of folk art. As the decades dissolve the context of contemporary-art politics, the more primitive underlying art remains. Having it both ways, Lichtenstein has said, "Once I have established what the subject matter is going to be I am not interested in it anymore, although I want it to come through with the immediate impact of the comics." This underlying impact, to be found at the bottom of the Guggenheim spiral, pervades the oeuvre, though ever more weakly, as the postmodern painter with his studied manipulations displaced the unsung comic-book artists he appropriated.

A Case of Monumentality

CLAES OLDENBURG'S *Clothespin* stands in the Art Institute's palatial halls like a Cyclopean, ten-foot-tall security guard, his gracefully tapered legs

Claes Oldenburg, Clothespin, *1975. CorTen and stainless steel.*

My contribution to *Transforming Vision: Writers on Art*, edited by Edward Hirsch (Little, Brown, 1994), a collection of essays and poems old and new inspired by works in the Art Institute of Chicago.

braced apart, his spring ready to snap. But the resemblance is incidental, we feel; Oldenburg is too much the engineer and architectural draughts-man to be after anything less than the *Ding an sich*, the thing in itself. His plaster hamburgers, his canvas telephones, his giant typewriter-erasers and baseball bats and electrical switches and plugs all have an elemental solemnity that disdains anthropomorphism and beckons us into the mute, inhuman world of artifacts. Oldenburg's sculptures look made, and concern made things.

Somewhat as Renaissance draughtsmen like Michelangelo and Dürer "blew up" natural details such as flowers, rabbits, and human musculature under the microscope of their close attention, after the long inattention of the Middle Ages, so the Pop Artists, after the mystic self-absorption of the Abstract Expressionists, turned to the circumambient reality of nature, and enlarged it with artistic focus. Their nature, however, was of human manufacture: Jasper Johns dignified flags and beer cans; Andy Warhol transferred to canvas the trash imagery of tabloids and advertis-ing; Roy Lichtenstein seized upon the Benday dots, primary colors, and emphatic outlines of comic strips. There was a joy of reclamation in Pop Art, a relieved embrace of the tangible world after the monkish aus-terities and tragic mood of action painting. Nothing was too lowly to notice—bottle caps, dollar bills, junk food, crushed cars—and to elevate into the museum of the cherishable. Robert Rauschenberg, with such infamous *trouvés* as the stuffed angora goat girdled by an old tire, showed the way; his masters in the Zen contemplation of the conundrum of art were Marcel Duchamp and John Cage. Pop Art had, in Dada, an intellec-tual pedigree. But a number of the Pop Artists were doing what came naturally—Warhol had been a commercial artist, James Rosenquist a billboard painter—and the movement had an unforced connection with American folk art, as it had moved from hand-made nineteenth-century artifacts to twentieth-century articles of mass manufacture. Among its several messages *Clothespin* is telling us that this humble utilitarian device is elegant and beautiful.

Irony is a way of having one's cake while appearing to eat it. An effect of Oldenburg's raising the clothespin to monumentality is to mock the concept of monumentality, which has thrust upon Mankind's weary vision so many bloated colossi, emperors' effigies, mounted bronze heroes, gesturing Lenins, gilded Buddhas, and similar ponderous adver-tisements of creed and hegemony. The monumental asserts establish-ment values, against not only contemporary dissent but against the erosion of time, unmindful that all monuments become, eventually, the enigmatic pillars of Ozymandias. Eternalization, when applied to an implement for pinching damp clothes to a line, becomes comic, as is this heroic solitude of an item useful only in numbers and generally clustered in a box or basket. The Art Institute's context of stately Doric gallery underlines the satire.

Yet is satire the only point? A true monumentality is achieved. Our childhood apprehensions of reality are revived in the disproportionate glorification of the overlookable; a child overlooks nothing near him, and the contours and mechanism of a clothespin, say, impress him with a huge, though unspeakable, significance. The mute significance of things gives the visual arts their inexhaustible impetus; the visible world, so abundant and heedless around us, is processed, by the painter's or sculptor's hand, and becomes understood. This act of understanding is the light that representation gives off, and that draws millions to rotate through museums, delighting in recognitions. We recognize the clothespin, even though it has been idealized in CorTen and stainless steel, enlarged in size, and placed upside-down from the way we usually see it on the clothesline. The recognition is fringed and flavored by what art history we possess—by whatever analogies to the Eiffel Tower or Brancusi's *Kiss* arise—but there is no escaping the *Ding an sich*. As with Oldenburg's forty-five-foot *Clothespin* near City Hall in Philadelphia, or the hundred-foot baseball bat that adorns Chicago, a humble bit of our lives is given large public dignity, in a kind of democratic revolution.

Verminous Pedestrians and Car-Tormented Streets

PUBLISHED to coincide with Columbus's rather sour quincentenary in 1992, *The Discovery of America*, a handsomely produced album of over two hundred works by Saul Steinberg, made a puzzlingly melancholy impression upon this peruser. Any selection, even one made, as in this case, by the artist himself, raises the jealous spectre of the excluded. The theme, though it reaches back to Steinberg's arrival in this country in 1941, has tended to exclude some of the very best types of his art—the mock-document, the cleverly imitated old photograph, the desktop, the collage, the self-conjuring creatures of a wandering ink line, the comic reifications of words and grammar. This is determinedly an art book, heavy on the sinister *art brut* of the last ten years, and I missed Steinberg the cartoonist, the exquisitely individual entertainer, the juggler of American icons on *New Yorker* covers.

The book's horizontal format imposes a certain monotony of proportion on the works; the famous 1976 view of the world westward from Ninth Avenue, Steinberg's most posterized and plagiarized cover, seems flatter and less poetic without the white sky introduced to back up the magazine's logo. On the opposite page of *The Discovery of America*, we find a less celebrated, more complex view eastward, from the artist's drawing board in the foreground to the East River, the towns of Long Island, the sentimentally remembered centers of his Europe, and even the cities of China he can name from his tour in World War II.

Of course Steinberg is, like Nabokov and Louis B. Mayer, a considerable discoverer of the United States. Born in Bucharest in 1914, he studied architecture in Milan and, upon getting his degree in 1940, fled to the New World, arriving, like Columbus himself, at Santo Domingo. He had begun to sell cartoons as a student in Italy and quite soon began to appear in *The New Yorker*. His early cartoons, their protagonists staring at the world with the hollow oval eyes of Harold Gray's Orphan Annie, seemed crude but not as Thurber's were crude; this artist could see, though he chose to simplify. Some of his wartime comic art, showing sailors getting tattoos or Goering plugging in his electric display of military decorations, could have been drawn by most anybody, from a gag writer's prescription. But the ensembles of drawings from India and China, where the new citizen Steinberg's enlistment as a naval ensign had taken him, had more than cartoon weight—a reportorial earnestness that did not blink at poverty (the Indians all had sad drooping eyes, and the Chi-

nese chair-bearers had hypertrophied calf muscles) and a cunning naïveté, a modernist boldness of self-declaring technique, in the linear, perspective-careless style.

By the late Forties, Steinberg's demure printed signature was signing captionless conceits—a Justitia wearing not a blindfold but sunglasses, a man shooting an apple off his own head—that only he could have conceived, and that were viable only at the level of surreality his particular style created. Thurber's rough notation served to illustrate psychodramas recognizable to contemporary urbanites; Steinberg's drawings, as they got into men tipping their heads instead of their hats and couples dancing in an implausibly readable zigzag of mutual eclipse, laid claim to an area where ink generated its own logic. Men's faces are fingerprints because we are all reduced to gray whorls of virtually interchangeable identity; a woman's head becomes a vase with a flower in it because that is how she wistfully thinks. One of the many pleasures of reading *The New Yorker* in the Fifties was watching Steinberg press on with his purely visual adventures. A straight line served in its undeviating progress as a clothesline, a railroad bridge, a desk edge, and a Venetian horizon. A set of abstract effects in wash, crosshatching, stippled arabesques, broad brush-stroke, and crayonned rococo wonderfully well conveyed on orchestral variety of sounds. One wonders how far Harold Ross, who died in 1951, would have indulged these experiments on the edge of the representational; the new editor, William Shawn, was a cerebral kindred spirit of Steinberg's, willing to give space to such donnish caprices as a man tipping his hat to the number 3.14159265, a circular chain of open-mouthed fish labelled "Taxes Ambition Nixon Facts Time Space Noise Truth Chauvinism Taxes," and a spread of pictographic animations of the names Descartes, Newton, Darwin, Marx, and Freud.

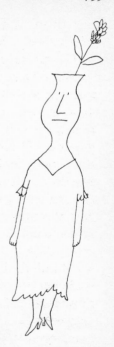

Leafing through the old *New Yorker* albums, however, one finds relatively few Steinberg cartoons; the dominant tone was set by Arno's solid, forceful compositions, Addams's meticulous, spooky washes, and, later, Saxon's elegant charcoals of suburban types. Their art pointed up a humorous idea; Steinberg's art *was* the idea, and took him into the galleries and the art magazines. In its own witty key, Steinberg's ink-and-wash exploration of the nature of representation belonged on the frontier with the Abstract Expressionists, whose broader gestures were similarly calligraphic, and whose huge canvases, like Steinberg's doodlings on graph paper, led the viewer to reflect upon the surface and materials and, finally, upon the act of creation itself.

After 1960, Steinberg's principal contributions to *The New Yorker* were his covers. Though he had made a number of sketchbook excursions into the American hinterland, bringing back squiggly cowboys and the lean horizon-line of the prairie, he seems to have been mostly struck by the psychological furniture of America—the abstract objects of the national aspiration, as expressed in its slogans, currency, popular iconography, patriotic parades, and holidays. What a native-born American comes to with childish acceptance, he acquired with an immigrant's bemusement.

On many of his covers American shibboleths and symbols take on a comical animation and promiscuity. Uncle Sam and Uncle Tom shake hands beneath busts of Santa Claus and Sigmund Freud; the Easter Bunny, Santa Claus, Abraham Lincoln, the Statue of Liberty, George Washington, and the Halloween witch all sit at the Thanksgiving table together, beneath pictures of Niagara Falls and of a red Indian in full feather. *The Discovery of America* holds a hilarious color sketch, dated 1981 and never to my knowledge developed for publication, of Uncle Sam as matador, about to apply the kill to a large, glowering turkey.* On the cover of July 4, 1964, a catlike sphinx labelled Vox Populi is delivering to an attentive Sam (with his identically profiled harem of Lex, Lux, Pax, and Libertas) a rebus in a talk balloon, where a flag, a heart, a snake,

---

*No sooner did this review appear in *The New York Review of Books* (issue of December 3, 1992), with the Uncle Sam–turkey drawing as one of its two illustrations, than *The New Yorker* (issue of November 30, 1992) ran the drawing as a cover, redrawn but not essentially more risible. The antagonists are more animated, the turkey's feathers more colorful, Santa Claus as picador has changed position, and something glowering and aquiline in the bird's eye has been lost. Still, it was the first cover under the editorship of Tina Brown that could have run under that of William Shawn.

a pair of scales, a harp, a handshake, and a cornucopia add up to a mystical distillation of Americana, this side of a horizon bearing a rainbow, a moon with a ladder leaning against it, and the decapitated pyramid that says Annuit Coeptis on our dollar bills. On other covers, purely semantic configurations were reified: Today in the form of a rocket shoots off from a crumbling Yesterday on a dotted projected route of Breakfast, Lunch, Dinner, and Tomorrow; a spindly Nobody stands on the edge of a tall Nowhere thinking of a cloudy Nothing; a rickety "I Have" rests on a rocky "I Am" while a shimmering "I Do" burns in the sky. Few of these dramatizations of language—one can almost say "the American language," recalling that while waiting in Santo Domingo for his American visa Steinberg worked on his English by deciphering *Huckleberry Finn*— are included in *The Discovery of America*.

Perhaps my melancholy arises from the likelihood that Steinberg and *The New Yorker* have gone their separate ways—that the mutually beneficial relationship between a prospering general magazine and a museum-quality experimental artist needed a cultural climate more spacious and genial than is imaginable in these strident, sectarian, and financially hard-pressed times. *The Discovery of America* presents a Steinberg, in mostly color plates, far removed from the venturesome yet risible black-and-white performer of previous albums like *The Passport* and *All in Line*. The scribbly aesthetic of graffiti art has overtaken the virtuoso penman, and his animated iconography has dwindled to a few chimerical grotesques— birds' heads mounted on high-heeled legs, with no body between, and monkey-faced bellhops. Not even Georg Grosz's Weimar war cripples, raddled prostitutes, and fat-headed gluttons had sunk quite so far in the circles of Inferno as have Steinberg's beaked and blank-eyed stalkers of America's fractured, car-tormented streets. Grosz's caricatures at least present, in their physiognomies, an unabashed satisfaction in being what they are, though their essence be as deplorable as gluttony, lust, or a murderous stiff-necked pride. Steinberg's newest creatures have the expressionlessness of stuffed animals and look frozen in a hopeless, though smartly costumed, anomie. America's streets now give back to the artist a terrifying chill, of the walking, staring dead.

The art critic Arthur Danto provides a suave and thoughtful introduction. Steinberg has deservedly attracted as introducers the intellectual cream—John Hollander and Italo Calvino, to name two. The textuality of Steinberg's visual play, his use of words and printer's devices and the apparatus—ink bottle, pencil, blotter—of inscription, well suits sensibilities accustomed to puns, parsing, signifiers, and deconstruction. Hollander's very thorough appreciation of *The Passport* quotes no less an art critic than E. H. Gombrich, saying of Steinberg that "there is perhaps no artist alive who knows more about the philosophy of representation." Dealing with thematic material less philosophically rich than the counterfeited documents and doctored photographs of this earlier assemblage, Danto makes several helpful points about Steinberg's exploration of America. For one, Steinberg entered not at New York but at Miami, and Miami's Art Deco made an enduring first impression: "His America is an Art Deco continent, a universe of jukebox architecture with jaunty angles and rainbow color schemes. . . . The Steinbergian landscape [is], in essence, an Art Deco theme park in which the clouds and the very mud puddles have the cachet of the *moderne*." Secondly, Steinberg's initially jubilant vision of our "dear preposterous civilization"—the drum majorettes, the parades, the Midwestern small towns with their false fronts and poignant excess of space—darkened in the Seventies, when America became "a sort of moral desert, the streets sites of menace and even terror." Union Square, where Steinberg had a studio, acted as his window on a Manhattan of monsters—of shrieking crazies, button-nosed Minnies and Mickeys toting machine guns, frantically bleating police cars, hookers who are all legs and hairdo, pedestrians scuttling buglike in a merciless world of solidified noise. Aggression and agony spread even to the sky, its sun a lurid Art Deco blazon and its clouds a downreaching clutter of those baroque "French curves" used in architectural drafting.

I noticed that *The New Yorker*, so often accused of tameness, ran two of the most savage of these urban nightmares as covers, ten years apart—in January of 1971 and 1981. The second of them, depicting Union Square ("a diminishing and menacing space," in Danto's phrasing, "in which statues of the imposing dead . . . preside over a human crowd that scatters like insects toward the dark holes of subway entrances"), is reproduced, oddly, without the touches of color that the cover bore. Several of the covers, puzzlingly—for instance, a charming fantasia on Florida—appear in slightly different, not noticeably stronger form.

In the decade since 1981, Steinberg's catastrophic vision of America hasn't so much changed as thickened and congealed. The verminous pedestrians have become smaller, the outlines coarser; the buildings are more shapeless and the view of the crawling streets sometimes comes from above, in a jumble of perspective. It is the jumble of gridlock rather than that of a scrimmage that will sort itself out. Polychrome paralysis reigns in the later work of this limner whose pen line was once so active, restless, and unrestrictedly inventive. Car headlights drawn as projecting substantial cones add to the jarring congestion of traffic. The striding pedestrians are going nowhere—some of them are flatly embedded in the sidewalk. Danto says, "There is very little that I can make out of Steinberg on the Reagan years," but surely the determined repulsiveness of most of the drawings from the Eighties registers some sort of outcry. The artist in his travels seems to have visited those places—Las Vegas, southern California—where a monied ugliness sleeplessly reigned, amid a gaudy coagulation of unnatural trees, impossible clouds, and a many-apertured mock-Spanish architecture. In a startlingly unfantastic drawing from 1988, a black dog stares open-mouthed from a yellow Celica in front of Campus Discount Liquors, and on the next two pages scribbled black dogs populate a kind of melting parking lot and staff an unexplained barricade on what may be the American border. We are going to the dogs?

Well, as the old E. B. White poem had it, " 'I paint what I see,' said Rivera." The view of America, from street level in our cities, is not lovely. Adam Gopnik, in his own very thorough and admiring essay, introducing the catalogue from a Pace Gallery show in 1987, says that Steinberg in the strictness of his social conscience has been led to portray contemporary fascism, "fascism as a peculiarly modern structure of cruelty, a marriage of show-biz glamour with sadism, the marriage of preening sexuality—with its effeminate love of uniforms, and a particular kind of tastelessness—with affectless violence." Steinberg is quoted as calling it "Mickey Mouse brutality." The emergence of an appropriately brutal expressionism in Steinberg is perhaps not surprising—the major modern artist to whom he seems to owe most is Klee, and a vision of horror lay close beneath Klee's skin of pictorial play. But this doesn't make *The Discovery of America* less of a downer, as it moves from exuberant drum majorettes leading parades in the Fifties to the savage majorettes of 1987, towering in their barbaric boots and impossible heels as they do tangled battle with bellhops and stray mouse-thugs. It is the Pace catalogue that labels these American Valkyries "majorettes."

More labelling and clearer dating would not have hurt this present collection. Its pictures pass in an order only roughly chronological, in unidentified thematic packets. A long section reproduces some of the enigmatic postcards Steinberg began to do in the late Seventies—the bland main streets of little-visited towns like Henderson, North Carolina, and Colton, California, and the solemnly grand central post-office buildings in such cities as Charlotte and Nashville. These deadpan snapshots, and the sketches from the Fifties of courthouses and corner drugstores and sun-creased farmers in bib overalls having a beer among

pointy-breasted barmaids, exist at the opposite pole from the merry iconography of his symbol-laden tableaux; they depict the real landscape and architecture laboriously conjured from the land with the ideological blessings of Freedom and Equality, Lex and Lux. That some sort of gap exists, where grandeur of expectation met a grandeur of emptiness, and wherein a specifically American disappointment transparently broods, goes without saying; but Steinberg's pictorial comments on America used to have a forgiving wryness, an understanding that placed our local realities in the context of the general human condition. There is little human condition in the last decade's work, just inhuman conditions. Who wouldn't be melancholy, to think that this is what the New World has come to?

Funny Faces

A CARICATURE can be a beautiful thing; the ambitious, ingenious, and slightly anxious exhibit at the National Portrait Gallery in Washington, *Celebrity Caricature in America*, from April to August of 1998, emphasizes the sociology of celebrity, and mingles the masterly work of Al Frueh, Miguel Covarrubias, Ralph Barton, and William Auerbach-Levy with that of a score of artists a shade or two less accomplished to produce a plethora. Everything is done to make the show intelligible and appealing to the multitudes who never heard Caruso sing, followed Babe Ruth's exploits, saw John Barrymore in a play or Mae West in a movie. The first rooms are piped with jazzy, Astairish music from the *entre-deux-guerres* era when celebrity is supposed to have ripened into its modern form; photographs of those caricatured are helpfully placed high on the walls; a corner of Sardi's lined with framed caricatures is reconstructed; the back rooms are enlivened by some continuously running cartoons from the 1930s by the Disney and Warner Brothers studios, in which animated caricatures of film stars consort with the likes of Donald Duck and Bugs Bunny. As a child who went to the movies often, I found the cartoons— seen again after a gap of sixty years—a thrilling return of lost vistas. But my cultural horizon fell short of such early-twentieth-century theatrical figures as Donald Brian, Julia Marlowe, John Drew, and Raymond Hitchcock; nevertheless, I could admire the beautiful economy of Al Frueh's renderings of their once widely recognized countenances. A celebration of celebrity turns out to be, with enough lapsed time, a demonstration of celebrity's impermanence—a study in our essential obscurity. The subject of the caricature sooner or later melts away, leaving us, as with Tutankhamen or the Akkadian kings, or as with the judges drawn by Daumier and the cabaret performers caricatured by Toulouse-Lautrec, the art only. Art has the capacity to outlast fame, though the artist while living must bow to the famous.

It was the happy fate of several periodicals relatively early in the century, foremost the *Vanity Fair* that ceased publication in 1936, to publish caricatures of extraordinary merit. A very young Mexican, Miguel Covarrubias—who later went on to become a leading archaeologist, ethnologist, and folklorist in his native country, and to die young at fiftythree—lifted caricature, in the *Vanity Fair* of the Twenties and Thirties, onto a new plane, though of course he had predecessors and near-equal rivals. The Italian Paolo Garretto, cleverly using airbrush and paper cutouts, produced *Vanity Fair* covers and illustrations of arresting simplicity and stylistic daring; his exuberant 1934 gouache of Al Smith is the Washington show's signature piece, and his streamlined representations of Thirties "strong men," from Mussolini and Hitler to Gandhi and La Guardia, form a historical record of sorts. But compared with Covarrubias he is a mere toymaker; he had little of the Mexican's painterly qualities or his curious primitive force. Ralph Barton, a very different but equally brilliant caricaturist, wrote that Covarrubias's caricatures are "bald and crude and devoid of nonsense, like a mountain or a baby."

Miguel Covarrubias, Douglas Fairbanks

Crude, surely, only in the sense that perfectly realized images gain a certain starkness, but indeed combining a mountainous largeness with a tenderness, an innocence of vision that might be called infantile.

Covarrubias admired the murals of Orozco and had the advantage of a strong Mexican tradition of political, pamphleteering caricature. Curator Wendy Wick Reaves points out, in her catalogue, that Covarrubias's caricatures of American celebrities are much less savage and grotesque than those of his fellow-countrymen Xavier Algara and José Juan Tablada. "Covarrubias had adapted to the *Vanity Fair* aura," Reaves writes. "This was Mexican caricature in evening clothes. . . . For a lesser artist this emotional distancing and refinement could have resulted in amiable banality. For Covarrubias, it freed him to concentrate with cool detachment on likeness, line, and pattern." In black-and-white, Covarrubias favored a woodcut look, with a comblike shading of short tapered lines. In his 1925 drawing of the young Irving Berlin, these lines round into prominence the great lidded eyes, with their oily-black irises. Douglas Fairbanks is reduced to a continuous arabesque of eyebrow, eyes as far apart as a frog's, hair as slicked as a coat of paint, and mustache and upper lip symmetrically working to bare a fine set of teeth; what startles us in 1998 is how effectively Covarrubias conveys in a few stylized lines Fairbanks' courtly thrust, a lower lip and cigarette-holding hand coming forward to assert a type of vanished, braying, charmingly formalized masculinity. The caricature of Paul Whiteman is graphically interesting in containing a little Cubistic explosion in the center of the subject's mostly empty ovoid face; this is one of the most abstract of Covarrubias's American caricatures, and one of the less friendly, but a joy to ponder in its Art Deco elegance.

After 1930, when improvements in the Condé Nast presses and photo-

Miguel Covarrubias, Paul Whiteman

engraving processes made possible frequent use of color, Covarrubias displayed a lively palette, contrasting, in illustrations for Corey Ford's "Impossible Interviews" series, a nude Sally Rand's lovely skin tint, golden curls, and pink feather-fans with Martha Graham's greenish flesh and angular red dress; and the Prince of Wales's English tweeds and pallor with Clark Gable's California white flannels, turtleneck, and tan. The Prince of Wales, as rendered in 1932, is a prophetic character study in shifty, spoiled-looking diffidence. As far as my memory of celebrity went, Covarrubias's likenesses seemed just right, and where memory drew a blank, as with the caricature of Eva Le Gallienne, the sense of a real person was conveyed, not only in the tilt of the features but in a certain spiritual aura provided by the coloring and a usually vivacious pictorial dynamic. Covarrubias's blend of witty linear likeness and painterly quality was uniquely his; Frueh, Barton, and Al Hirschfeld did linear caricature, and Will Cotton, a painter from Newport who broke into *Vanity Fair* when color came in and who was doing *New Yorker* covers up through the 1950s, used rich pastels whose satiric edge was benignly fuzzy—though he executed the definitive rendering of Jed Harris's five-o'clock shadow and immortalized Nicholas Murray Butler's pink owlishness.

Of the artists I especially cherished in the show, Al Frueh was the oldest. Born in Lima, Ohio, in 1880, he came to caricature, he claimed, by way of trying to learn Pitman's shorthand method; instead of learning it, he elaborated the squiggles. His early newspaper work showed acquaintance with French and German caricaturists, and during travels in Europe in 1908 and 1909 he studied briefly with Matisse. His linear economy was marvellous. Alla Nazimova's body becomes one thick line indented by hands and topped by a face (c. 1910–12). He drew George M. Cohan without a face, as all stance and gesture, and Marie Dressler—the bulky comedienne of many silent films—as all

Al Frueh, Alla Nazimova

face, wide and furious, mounted on a body of five curved lines. Always a lover and caricaturist of the stage, Frueh moved from the old *Life* to *The New Yorker* when it started up in 1925, and kept his place on the theatre page until the 1960s, when the fashion for caricatures had long passed. He scattered his uncannily concise likenesses in a rectangle of rather arbitrary space, and worked, I remember learning with astonishment, entirely from memory, after seeing the performance. It is one thing to remember, say, that Katharine Cornell had a wide face and long eyes, but to do justice to her nostrils, and fit them to her upper lip, is quite another. The Fruehs on exhibit, mostly gifts from his children, favor the early works, produced on brown-tinted board with ink and white highlights; they were originally not reproduced but displayed, in Alfred Stieglitz's 291 gallery. Frueh's concise linear likenesses display one aspect of the caricaturist's art at its peak, as fluent as handwriting.

Al Hirschfeld, still miraculously practicing into his nineties, is Frueh's prime heir, and a Titan of his trade. However, in his wiry pen-and-ink drawings the line becomes abstractly active in a way Frueh's did not, with a consequent flattening, sometimes, of our impression. Spiralling eyes, ears containing X's, and hair containing a trio of NINA's weaken our sense that this antic penmanship is holding a real person up to the light. A 1950 black-and-white caricature of Walter Winchell shows Hirschfeld still with some bite, and a 1956 cover of Edward R. Murrow for *TV Guide*—one of the last magazines to foreground caricature—reveals how handsomely he could function in color and the illusion of three dimensions.

Ralph Barton had no third dimension, but in the two he used he was an angel of invention, ease, and effrontery. His wandering line was simultaneously precise and carefree, and it was apparently tireless. Examine any of his famous composites—the reproduction of the massive curtain full of celebrated theatregoers he designed for the stage of the Chauve-Souris, or "Bat Theatre"; the huge composite of Hollywood celebrities dining at the Cocoanut Grove; the slightly less numerous groups he did for *Vanity Fair*—and every face bears scrutiny; each is alive and individual. His theatre cartoons for *Judge*, *Life*, and the young *New Yorker* marry the extravagant with the exquisite. I stood before his drawing of Ed Wynn and Richard B. Harrison and marvelled at one of the long curves, a fine charcoal-pencil line drawn freehand with the precision of a machine. Barton's control over the implements of his trade had a betranced finesse; though he was overwhelmed by magazine commissions, often working around the clock, there was never a loose line or a carelessly applied spot of wash. A splendid caricature of Leopold

Ralph Barton, Ed Wynn
and Richard B. Harrison

Ralph Barton, Billie Burke

Stokowski, of 1931, uses an encircling wet-on-wet dark wash to define the conductor's sphere of fuzzy white hair; his impossibly supple and slender Billie Burke wears a tint of wash as even as it is delicate. And how definitively he captures her celebrated simpering profile, spotlit in long-darkened Broadway shows but still visible in the guise of the good witch Glinda in the movie of *The Wizard of Oz*. Leaning into a Barton drawing, we feel acrobatic ourselves, involved in breathtaking acts of balance and daredevil swoop.

A Francophile and depressive, needing always to travel or change apartments, Barton tried to break out of two dimensions, writing theatre notices and two small books, one of light verse and the other a travesty history of the United States. Their critical reception was cool; unlike Beerbohm, he was a graphic artist purely. His depression deepened; his behavior became as erratic as his perspective. At the end he felt he was still hopelessly in love with his third wife, who had become Eugene O'Neill's third wife. In 1931, just short of his fortieth birthday, he shot himself in the head, leaving behind a suicide note diagnosing himself as a manic-depressive and saying that for three years he had not been "getting anything like the full value out of my talent." Relatively few, of the hundreds and hundreds of his drawings, exist as originals; they were submitted to the reproduction processes of the time, which could not do justice to his beautifully graded washes, and then destroyed. Such was the common fate of commercial art in the age of metal photoengraving; it was never thought to be headed for museum walls. So museums display what they have.

William Auerbach-Levy, born in Russia, preferred to work with a brush and to draw from the life, during visits his subjects paid to his studio. He wrote a delightful book, *Is That Me?*, describing the process whereby he caught the likenesses of such as Jimmy Durante, Ring Lardner, and Eugene O'Neill. He was capable of great simplification; he drew Lardner without a nose and O'Neill without eyes, and several of his drawings— of Mencken, Alexander Wooll- cott, George Gershwin, Franklin P.

William Auerbach-Levy, Ring Lardner

Adams—became virtual trademarks, succinct images in black-and-white sturdy
enough to serve on stationery, napkins,
the backs of playing cards, and the like
for their celebrity subjects. The show
includes some of these oft-reproduced
heads, and it is interesting to see how
much whiteout he used to adjust, say, the
few stark lines of the Adams drawing—
only the final reproduced image looked
effortless and inevitable. It is interesting,
too, to compare Auerbach-Levy's head
of Mencken with the more innocent and
contrived image Hirschfeld produced for
the cover of *Collier's* in 1949. By then
Mencken, with his cigar and central part-

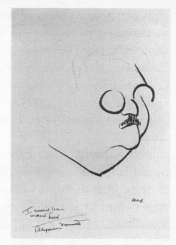

William Auerbach-Levy, Alexander Woollcott

ing, had become a harmless icon, a famous old fogey, but Auerbach-Levy
in 1925 brought out the man's strength and menace—the ominous weight
of his head and the dangerous sneer on his lips. One can see on the original of the Woollcott that the hair and the curve of the head had been
sketched but not inked in; the few lines of the face, with the incompleted
circles of the glasses, are far more effective in disembodied isolation.

The good caricaturist has the rare gift of bringing forth from the face's
knit of flesh-knots, and the spaces between them, the live spark of a
unique identity. In the making of a succinct but convincing likeness, with
resonances beyond the comic, Auerbach-Levy was unequalled. He had
another mode, in which the caricatural element was minimized to the
verge of a straight portrait. A yellow-faced Noël Coward seen by a red-
curtained window giving on Brooklyn Bridge, the Shubert brothers as
comic and tragic masks—in these the brush declares itself in halftones
and small flourishes, and we are near the end of caricature as an audacious
simplification. Few besides me remember, I suppose, Auerbach-Levy's
weekly portraits, in wartime *Collier's*, of our allies and collaborators in
World War II, following after Sam Berryman's hideous and hilarious
series of our atrocious and absurd enemies. It was a task that now would
be entrusted to photographs, even blurry ones.

Reaves in prefacing her catalogue says, "Caricature did not vanish after
World War II, but this form of it—focused on personality and fame
rather than social and political satire—diminished or changed its emphasis." One can theorize considerably on the nature of celebrity and
personality and the kind of artistic attention they receive. Did Fifties

conformity dampen caricature? Had the triumph of photography made us impatient with any other sort of representational image? Did the decline of the Hollywood studio system, of celebrity-driven radio, of Broadway, and of café society deprive us of the fixed firmament of stars caricature had thrived on? *Vanity Fair*, the grand sponsor of the art, was ingloriously folded into *Vogue* in 1936, and waited decades to be reborn as a glossy scandal mag. In 1935, Peggy Bacon retired from caricature, after a Washington show that one reviewer termed "coarse," "vulgar," and "repulsive." A well-known painter and illustrator, she had begun to do pastel caricatures in the late Twenties, inspired by those of Will Cotton, and shifted to crayon monochromes, mostly of female denizens of the art world. Of the Washington show, Reaves says, "[Bacon] found it more difficult to present witty characterizations of government appointees and other well-known but colorless subjects." Her milieu was the relatively intimate, fading one of Manhattan artistic celebrity. She had to be personally interested to function.

What we admire in human beings undergoes a gradual shift. Saints and kings and nobles were once highly esteemed, for their touch of the divine. The nineteenth century made celebrities of clergymen, millionaires, humanitarians, and opera singers. A conflux of media—radio and movies and a still-thriving popular press—created the constellation of theatre types, with additional stars from sports, the arts, and academia, that forms the basis of *Celebrity Caricature*. This pantheon was loved so much in its imaginary assembly that a cloth manufacturer made a silk print of Barton's Cocoanut Grove tableau and at least one young flapper fashioned it into a dress, which is displayed with its party stains still on it. What has happened since? Rock stars, who are already caricatures, and television and film performers with more than a tinge of the interchangeable. Easier to caricature Clark Gable than Brad Pitt, or so it seems.

Of course, caricature, like light verse, goes on. Al Hirschfeld goes on, and readers of *The New York Review of Books* for thirty years have been entertained and enlightened by David Levine's crosshatched homunculi. There is Gerald Scarfe, for those who like to see a lot of ink spilled. Edward Sorel, in his scribbly way, has done excellent likenesses. What happened to caricature between 1910 and 1950 was perhaps as simple— and as tautological—as the presence of a thriving market for it, as long as magazines were the hot medium. Also, modern art happened to it. The *fin-de-siècle* impulse of a new liveliness came out of Paris. Cubism and muralistic expressionism inspired Covarrubias; expressionistic distortion and surrealistic playfulness loosened up Barton. The idea existed of a face as a blazon, an insignia, a riff. An audience able to appreciate subtle and dashing work existed. Certain formal principles still haunted the popular expectations of art; anatomy and perspective were still taught in art schools and valued by art editors. The appetite for aesthetically exciting caricature and the artists who could satisfy it rose and fell together. People are dimmer than they used to be.

The Sistine Chapel Ceiling

ONCE, art was something you travelled to. You made your way to Rome, located the Vatican, filed into the Sistine Chapel, and looked up to receive a murky, scrambled impression of the polychrome sublime. The ceiling seemed far away, and smoky. The chapel was, after all, just a room, tall but smaller than you had expected. This is where they elected Popes, and burned the ballots. You could see how smoke had collected on Michelangelo's masterpiece, the masterpiece of masterpieces, the greatest feat of painting in the history of the world. And you could check it off your list of the world's wonders, and book passage on a Greek freighter to the pyramids.

Now art travels to you, in newsworthy sight bites, photographed and televised, four-color-pressed and cropped, shiny as new. Has anybody since Michelangelo (and his assistants and the generations of restorers who have tagged after him, with their varnish pots and sponges soaked in acidified Greek wine) seen the painting in his monumental frescoes the way we can here? The hatched brushstrokes, the nervous outlines, the impressionistic hasty bits, and now, with this latest and most chemically intelligent of restorations, his color in its first raw and innocent brilliance?

It is tender color, really, once the shock of it wears off. God in a lilac shortie nightgown, Adam's flesh the tint of a silvery clay. *Fresco* means "fresh." Watercolors are applied to wet lime plaster, and the molecules of ground pigment sink in and set with the calcium carbonate. The technique is in theory impervious to change; Minoan and Indian and Etruscan and Roman frescoes still look fresh after centuries. Yet plaster cracks and crumbles, and is taking Leonardo's *Last Supper* with it into dust. Michelangelo's mighty work needed a cleaning more than a patching; springtime coloring has replaced the autumnal patina.

A throb of creation pervades the vast whole. With creaking neck and

---

Honoring the presentation of the restored murals in a thousand-dollar book published by Knopf, and in *Mirabella*, which selected for reproduction the four details I ingeniously strung on the theme of relaxation in the last paragraph.

paint in his beard, the sculptor over four grueling years wrestled his unprecedentedly plastic imagination into Bible illustrations. He often painted directly, without cartoon tracings, onto the rapidly drying skim coat called *intonaco*. He worked backwards, toward the Creation. The first scenes he painted—the nakedness of Noah, the Flood—are relatively timid and stiff. Then, arriving at Adam, the artist loosened up, and the crowding bodies bulge, twist, overflow their niches and pedestals in a prodigious excess, a turmoil of anatomy in which only the faces allay the muscular restlessness. How calmly grateful Adam seems to receive the spark of life into his impossibly broad chest! How comfortingly sleepy Joram appears amid the thirsty tangle of her three lumpy children! How demure and refined is the androgynous Libyan Sibyl—a golden corset concealing half of the back whose preliminary sketch, from a male model, is one of the great drawings of all time! The roundly packed, foreshortened force of her arms combines, in the arm of Daniel, with utter relaxation. Sleep and limpness dance in and out of the fresco's rioting vitality, as death dances with life. Michelangelo's contoured superabundance springs from a passivity located at the ultimate reach of mastery: he lets himself get carried away.

The Frick

IF THE FRICK COLLECTION, as the museum is properly called, were to be removed from its place on the Manhattan grid at Fifth Avenue and 70th Street, plenty of great European paintings could still be viewed up the street, at the Metropolitan, but Fifth Avenue would lose its only surviving front lawn. A number of other great Beaux-Art houses of the staggeringly rich still stand, like the Morgan Library, but none so persuasively projects the illusion of a home, whose phantom host and hostess have momentarily left the room, allowing us to loiter and to ponder, with a mixture of awe and envy, the William Pitts silver-gilt wine coolers in the dining room, say, or the north hall's blue marble side table with neoclassical mounts commissioned by the Duchesse de Mazarin in 1781, or, in the library, the tall porcelain vase, from the Ch'ing Dynasty, with its green ground and plum-tree decoration, one of only six known examples of its kind, not to mention the annular mantel clock from eighteenth-century France, with reliefs depicting the seasons and figures emblematic of the passage of time.

This fancy clock is stopped. Time stands still in the library, as we wait for Mr. Frick to breeze back in, in a velvet dressing gown, with the stub of a Cuban cigar thrusting from the center of his crisp white beard. Dark little bronze statues, of Hercules and Triton and fauns and satyrs and Venus and David, perform various contortions and exercises on the table-tops and cabinets, exercises that have kept them healthy over the years, with burnished muscles and exquisite, especially, feet. The feet of those Renaissance bronzes—admirably exact and tensile tendons, toes, and toenails. In the library, one comes to notice dainty touches like the little leather dust-covers laid over the tops of the books, the long inflexible sets of Tennyson and Moore, of George Meredith and Tobias Smollett. In front of the fireplace there is an ample—how could it not be?—green sofa backed by a desk containing oversize books on low shelves. We must bend over to read the titles of the tall stout tomes. *Pictures in the Collection of P. A. B. Widener,* in three volumes. *The Royal Collection of Paintings* in two volumes. *The Complete World of Rembrandt* in eight volumes. In ten volumes, by Bancroft, *The Book of Wealth. The Book of Wealth!* We do not quite dare presume, with the eye of a uniformed guard lingering sensitively upon us, to pull out (it would take both hands, and a strong back) a volume of this set, so we will never know what kind of information *The Book of Wealth* contains. A roll call of Mr. Frick's peers in robber barony? A list of directions as to correct wealthy deportment? Or, most desirably, helpful instructions on becoming wealthy ourselves, as cozily wealthy as our host, whose broad leather-topped desk does not look very much used lately? The glass inkwells are dry, the lamp with its heavily fringed shade is dim, and the sullen black casket "after Severo da Ravenna," possibly used to hold stamps, paper clips, and rubber bands, is closed.

Henry Clay Frick was born in West Overton, Pennsylvania, which would give you a certain momentum right from the start. As a youngish man, he built twelve thousand coke ovens. Since coke and steel need each other like bread and butter, he and Andrew Carnegie came to own large portions of each other. Frick was tougher on laborers and unions than Carnegie cared to appear, and Frick for his pains in leading the forces of capitalism in the bitter Homestead Strike of 1892 was shot and stabbed by Alexander Berkman, an alleged anarchist. But Frick lived to enjoy his wealth. In 1899, he and Mr. Carnegie parted company, but Frick consoled himself by collecting railroads and paintings of the Barbizon school. He owned palatial places in Pittsburgh and Prides Crossing, Massachusetts, and built the edifice at Fifth Avenue and 70th just before World War I. Five years later, in 1919, he died, bequeathing his residence and the works of art it contained to a board of trustees. He hadn't begun to collect old masters until the turn of the century, but his taste was choice. After his wife's death in 1931, the house, originally designed by Thomas Hastings, was expanded by John Russell Pope and opened to the public in 1935. Open it remains, though not to children under ten, or to large groups, who must be broken up into parties of not more than ten. The paintings and *objets* are but lightly protected by ropes and cases, and this asks a certain decorum. Cloakroom, telephones, bathrooms— everything smoothly works and feels underutilized, which makes the Frick an island in Manhattan's ocean of crowded disrepair.

Where else can you go and in an hour's saunter through carpeted rooms see works of art almost none of which are poor and at least twelve of which are boffo, world-class masterpieces? Which twelve, you ask. Well, let's begin with almost the first painting you see after entering, Vermeer's *Officer and Laughing Girl*, one of the Frick's three Vermeers. The other two are also priceless but relatively insipid; *Officer and Laughing Girl* is crisp and flamboyant, with a photographic exaggeration of the foregound figure and a sparkling crust of light on the smiling face and detailed map beyond. A turn to the left, into the Octagon Room, brings you up against a vision in white marble, Francesco da Laurana's *Bust of a Lady*, a fifteenth-century work as tenderly abstracted as a Brancusi, as spiritual as a head from a Chartres portal, and yet as sexy and *there* (though her eyes are all but closed) as a Roman portrait bust. Another Laurana, almost as delicious, of Beatrice of Aragon, waits down in the North Hall.

In the so-called Anteroom, the small El Greco *Purification of the Temple*, so electric and compressed, begs for attention, not to mention the exquisite, dazzlingly gilded little *Christ Bearing a Cross* by the obscure Barna da Siena; but hold on, for the stately dining room and the library hold a number of English portraits, all ruddy and rosy and classy, which our hearts greet like salmon returning to the upland spawning grounds. Gainsborough's wonderfully effete *Richard Paul Jodrell*, Lawrence's sumptuous *Julia, Lady Peel*, Romney's chastely romantic *Lady Hamilton as "Nature"* (at seventeen, her career in mistresshood had but begun), and Reynolds' superciliously martial *General John Burgoyne* (one of the gents who handed us our revolution on a platter) all could be called boffo, if we weren't afraid of not leaving enough top marks for the amazing walls of the Living Hall, wherein Bellini's great *St. Francis in the Desert*— its rocks the color of icebergs and its stigmata being received invisibly, like radio messages—looks across at El Greco's grizzled *St. Jerome*, who has an I-told-you-so look on his long face and his thumb on some stern text in the Bible, to the right and upwards of Holbein the Younger's magnificent *Sir Thomas More*, with its Chuck Close–ish whisker-by-whisker jaw and its light-swallowing sleeves of velvet. And don't trip through the room of Fragonards too quickly—the panel on the south wall, *Love Letters*, is some kind of eighteenth-century quintessence, the statues and the lovers equally alive.

How many masterpieces is that? Let's say eight, to make room for Étienne de La Tour's *Education of the Virgin* (the famous translucent hand, the chalky profile of the childish Virgin, the comfortable lumpy look of St. Anne, the wicker wash-basket in the background), Rembrandt's imperial *Self-portrait* under its varnish of stagey, aging melancholy, Houdon's statue of Diana with its truly divine knees, Velázquez' heavily bedecked but rather shame-faced Philip IV, and, for good measure, from the East Gallery, Whistler's heraldic, decadently dapper, and mostly gray full-length apparition of Proust's old friend, the Comte de Montesquiou-Fezensac.

But the Frick is more than the sum of its parts; even the big West Gallery, under its warming skylight, feels homelike. A curious democracy of opulence prevails, as furniture and bronzes and vases form little nooks redolent of the well-spent loot of coke ovens. *Madame Boucher*, posed against golden-brown wall-hangings out in the south hall, goes perfectly with the golden-brown Jean-Henri Riesener secretary (made for Marie-Antoinette) beneath it. In the north hall, the pale blue of Monet's *Vétheuil in Winter* is picked up by the blue of the needlepoint chairs and the blues of Pierre-Étienne-Théodore Rousseau's *Village of Becquigny* and Ingres's lovely, contemplative *Comtesse d'Haussonville*, the back of her sleek head knottily echoed in a mirror.

Portraits dominate the Frick Collection, which adds to its feeling of inhabitation. Away from the collection's superstars, pleasant surprises enhance odd corners: in the courtyard, one can study, in Jean Barbet's fifteenth-century angel, the stout hinge that attaches the wings to the body, and be startled by the appraising gaze, out of the shadows, of Danese Cattaneo's *Bust of a Jurist*. Wherever one turns, in the large but soothingly finite space of the house, there is something refined and precious on which to rest the eyes. A strangely non-envious repose becomes the visitor's mood. Wealth has outlived its selfishness; by acts of legacy and trust, this exalted domestic effect from the last years of the Gilded Age has opened itself to civic appreciation. A plutocrat's conspicuous consumption and legal pillage of European treasure has become a shared vision of what life should be—a feast of forms and substances, topped by a Cuban cigar.

Personal Matters

PERSONAL MATTERS

UPDIKE AND I: *One of a series of imitations of Jorge Luis Borges's famous essay, "Borges and I," instigated by the magazine* Antaeus, *and later published in a book*, Who's Writing This? *(Ecco Press, 1995).*

I created Updike, out of the sticks and mud of my Pennsylvania boyhood, so I can scarcely resent it when people, mistaking me for him, stop me on the street and ask me for his autograph. I am always surprised that I resemble him so closely we can be confused. Meeting strangers, I must cope with an extra brightness in their faces, an expectancy that I will say something worthy of him; they do not realize that he works only in the medium of the written word, where other principles apply and hours of time can be devoted to a moment's effect. Thrust into "real" time, he can scarcely function, and his awkward pleasantries and anxious stutter emerge through my lips. Myself, I am rather suave. I think fast, on my feet, and have no use for the qualificatory complexities and lame double entendres and pained exactations of language in which he is customarily mired. I move swiftly and rather blindly through life, spending the money he earns.

I early committed him to a search for significance, to philosophical issues that give direction and point to his verbal inventions, but am not myself aware of much point or meaning to things. Things *are*, rather unsayably, and when I force myself to peruse his elaborate scrims of words I wonder where he gets it all—not from *me*, I am sure. The distance between us is so great that the bad reviews he receives do not touch me, though I treasure his few prizes, and mount them on the walls and shelves of my house, where they instantly yellow and tarnish. That he takes up so much of my time, answering his cloying mail and reading his incessant proofs, I resent. I feel that the fractional time of day he spends away from being Updike is what feeds and inspires him, and yet, perversely, he spends more and more time being Updike, that monster of whom my boyhood dreamed.

Each morning I awake from my latest dreams, which as I age leave an ever more sour taste. Men once thought dreams to be messages from the gods, and then from something called the subconscious, as it seeks a salubrious rearrangement of the contents of the day past; but now it becomes hard to believe that they partake of any economy. Instead, a basic chaos seems expressed: a random play of electricity generates images of inexplicable specificity.

I brush my teeth, I dress and descend to the kitchen, where I eat and read the newspaper, which has been dreaming its own dreams in the night. Postponing the moment, savoring every small news item and vitamin pill and sip of deconcentrated orange juice, I at last return to the upstairs and face the rooms that Updike has filled with his books, his papers, his trophies, his projects. The abundant clutter stifles me, yet I am helpless to clear away much of it. It would be a blasphemy. He has become a sacred reality to me. I gaze at his worn wooden desk, his boxes of dull pencils, his blank-faced word processor, with a religious fear.

Suppose, some day, he fails to show up? I would attempt to do his work, but no one would be fooled.

ME AND MY BOOKS: *An essay intended for the last page of the* New York Times Book Review, *but actually published in* The New Yorker, *in February 1997.*

There is a moment in the movie *Lawrence of Arabia* when a tiny black dot on the shimmering desert horizon slowly enlarges into a galloping sheikh, played, if memory serves, by Omar Sharif. A book you write is like that—a small vibrant blur that gradually enlarges into a presence, preferably dashing and irresistible. When people ask me how many books I have written, they may think I am being coy when I say I do not exactly know. But do I count just the forty hardcover volumes that the obliging firm of Alfred A. Knopf has published? What about the five slim books for children, and the out-of-print paperback *Olinger Stories*, or the peculiar but precious quasi-novel entitled *Too Far to Go* in this country and *Your Lover Just Called* in Great Britain, containing linked short stories not all of which have appeared in other collections? And what of the many limited editions, binding together material, often, that is not between hard covers anywhere else?*

The book-making process—fussing with the type, the sample pages,

---

*To be specific: *Talk from the Fifties*, twenty "Talk of the Town" stories, with an introduction (1979); *The Beloved*, a short story about an actor (1982); *Jester's Dozen*, twelve the running heads, the dust jacket, the flap copy, the cover cloth—has perhaps been dearer to me than the writing process. The latter has been endured as a process tributary to the former, whose envisioned final product, smelling of glue and freshly sliced paper, hangs as a shining mirage luring me through many a gray writing day. The moment when the finished book or, better yet, a tightly packed carton of finished books arrives on my doorstep is the moment of truth, of culmination; its bliss lasts as much as five minutes, until the first typographical error or production flaw is noticed. One collection of stories, *Pigeon Feathers*, had developed in the printing too narrow a top margin, and another, *Problems*, too exiguous a bottom margin. The jacket I had designed for *The Coup*, based upon a photograph of Timbuktu's boxy dried-mud houses, had been spurned by higher-ups as making it look too much like a nonfiction book, and the solid-green jacket arrived at as a compromise became, thanks to a dulling effect of the jacket stock, not at all the brilliant, verdant green shown to me in proof. Such inevitable blemishes, though extra-literary, inaugurate my estrangement from the book, which becomes somewhat distasteful to me before its life with the public has so much as begun.

The first flurry of this life, marked by hopeful arrays in bookstores, by advertisements in the plucky organs of the print trade, by inexorably mixed reviews, by blushing interviews with the giddy author, is brutish and short. Very quickly the book, scarcely news in the first place, becomes old news. Seeing an unbought stack glimmering poignantly in a window, the author averts his eyes and, like the bad Levite in the parable of the Good Samaritan, passes by on the other side. The books call out with little surface details—a title type once fervently debated, a topstain tenderly selected—for a recognition now stonily denied. Soon, like a chorus of cries from a sinking ship, the books die away; they eddy into the back shelves of bookstores, and thence into the mountainous return piles, to reappear a year or two later in the discount catalogues and in a paperback version. The royalty statements, by the time they appear, are like shreds of wreckage that float to the surface of a cruel, inscrutable sea.

And yet the books do not quite vanish. The author retains some copies, and spies others in the homes of his children and of his friends, where he has bestowed them. Occasionally he sees a stranger scowling into one on

---

poems published in the *Harvard Lampoon* between 1951 and 1954, with an introduction and eight drawings (1984); and *Concerts at Castle Hill: John Updike's Middle Initial Reviews Local Music in Ipswich, Massachusetts, from 1961 to 1965*, with an introduction (1993). All four of these slim volumes were published, handsomely, by the Lord John Press, of Northridge, California.

an airplane or in a hospital ward. My instinct is to tear the book from the reader's hands: I wonder if this reaction is abnormal or generally shared within the neurotic literary profession. One has sought this silent intimacy, and then is shocked by it; it seems so naked, and out of control. The stranger, with his or her grimy fingers and glassy gaze, is so clearly *not* the ideal reader, all-forgiving and miraculously responsive, whom I courted as I wrote. My sly, greedy wish to have my books purchased and read cannot stand up to even a little experiential reality.

Once a year, I do duty at a church book fair and stand amid table after table, receding to the horizon, of the discarded works of John P. Marquand, Thomas B. Costain, A. J. Cronin, Mary Ellen Chase (who gave my first novel a generous review, ages ago), Pearl Buck, Frank Yerby, John Gunther, Hendrik Willem Van Loon, and those innumerable others who, in the long middle of our finally terminating century, studded the best-seller lists and the sunporches, bedrooms, and dens of the local bourgeoisie. Death and demolition have released these books from the nooks of their sequestration. A few of my own yellowing titles crop up among them; their purchasers, startled to find me alive and standing there, ask me to sign them,* and thus I touch for a moment, as they surge toward me and then away again, battered copies of *Couples*, rubbed and rain-damaged *Rabbit*s, and foxed, dog-eared *Witches of Eastwick*s, the diabolic purple I chose for the cover cloth faded by the passing years to an innocent mauve. These books of mine have been through the mill. They have travelled in the ill-mapped wilderness of the reading public. Their scars of use shame me. While I cowered unseen, these books bravely ventured forth and took their chances.

The literary business, with its fitful attempts to imitate the vastly better-financed glamour of the movie and television and music businesses, comes down to books, the humble, durable husks or dregs of the reading experience. My wife has taken up genealogy, and at her side I visit in summertime the small towns of Connecticut and New York. She gravitates to the local-history section of the trim little libraries of brick and ironstone, and I drift into the general stacks, sneakily seeking out, between the massed best-sellers of Anne Tyler and Leon Uris, my own tomes. There are usually a few there, some written so long ago that my

---

*Signing! And signing! As if a book, like a check, needs to be signed to be valid. Worst are those collectors, or agents for collectors, who show up after a public reading with two or three shopping bags full. As one scratches away in a daze of repetitive self-referentiality, the question of whether this torture is being inflicted for love or for money—signed books bring a little more, one is told, in certain shady markets—fades into irrelevance. The fetish of the signature is surely one of the more pathetic features of contemporary religion.

connection to them seems grandpaternal. The condition of their spines, and the dates stamped on the check-out cards, tell me more than I want to know about my readership or lack of it. Some, usually those written when I was young—*Rabbit, Run, The Centaur, Pigeon Feathers* with its pinched top margins—have worn enough to win a staid, stamped second binding. On one steel shelf, in a Hudson Valley town with its own tributary creek gurgling over a dam and under a bridge near the library door, I saw that *S.*, in its saucy pink cloth, had a spine distinctly more canted than the others: it had been read more. The reviews, as I recalled, had been sour; there had been feminist demurs, though I had put my heart and soul into my heroine, who leaves her posh home for a raffish ashram. The publisher had evinced high hopes for sales; the first edition had proved to be more than enough. Here, years later, while water audibly rushed over the nearby dam, none of that seemed to matter. What mattered was that, to judge from the book's condition, the readership of this small town, mostly female as readership is everywhere, had recognized in *S.* my attempt at a woman's book, a book for women. A sort of blessing seemed to arise from the anonymous public; I had been, mutely, understood.

Meanwhile, the books multiply. Foreign editions, revised editions, paperbacks in a new format all come to the door and beg to be cherished. My own books have crowded all the others out of one room and have pressed on into another. Boxes of them weigh down the attic joists and molder in the basement and the barn. Their swelling bulk threatens to separate me from the point of it all. The thin edge of the wedge—my very first book, just barely a book, a collection of mostly light verse, with its thrifty pale-gray boards and black spine—had a bright purity that has been slowly submerged under the accumulating aftermath. In the backward glance, I lose sight of content. Tediously asked to name favorites, I think most fondly of those volumes that, like *Hugging the Shore* and *Buchanan Dying*, came out especially well, to my mind, as examples of book production—good margins, nice cover, pleasant heft.

A master set of the forty Knopf hardcovers sits in a polychrome row opposite my desk. They are stripped of their jackets and marked up with typos and second thoughts toward some ultimate perfected edition. Somewhere in their several million pondered, proofread, printed words I must have done my best, sung my song, had my say. But my panicked awareness, as the cut-off age of sixty-five approaches, is of all that *isn't* in them—almost everything, it suddenly seems. *Worlds* are not in them. In the face of this vacuity arises the terrible itch to—what else?—write another book, a book that, like one more ingredient sprinkled into a problematic batter, will make the whole thing rise. The little black dot on the horizon begins to quiver. Squinting, I can almost see the jacket, and make out the title page, in thirty-six-point Perpetua.

THE SHORT STORY AND I: *Written to coincide with the English publication of* The Afterlife and Other Stories, *for the London* Sunday Times, *which ran the essay in January 1995.*

Undergoing the pleasant tidying motions of assembling the present collection, I resisted my inklings that short stories had been the heart of my literary life, and that my life was nearly over. This was my seventh collection, if we count only hardcover round-ups of heterogenous tales; my ninth, if we add the two books of loosely related tales concerning the fictional writer Henry Bech; my eleventh, if we add two paperbacks, *Olinger Stories*—which take place all in a fictional Pennsylvania town called Olinger—and one titled in Penguin Books *Your Lover Just Called*, involving a fictional couple called Joan and Richard Maple. And there are stray stories in my four farraginous collections of mostly non-fictional prose, as well as some confined to limited editions and bygone magazines. An unquantifiable lot, in short, numbering close to two hundred items, most of which appeared in *The New Yorker*. More closely than my novels, more circumstantially than my poems, these efforts of a few thousand words each hold my life's incidents, predicaments, crises, joys. Further, they made my life possible, for I depended when young upon their sale to supply my livelihood.

It was not so long ago that a writer in the United States could dream of making a living by short stories. Nathaniel Hawthorne, bent over a desk in the attic of his mother's house in Salem, made what meager money his craft brought in—until the success of his novel, *The Scarlet Letter*, in 1850—with the sale of artful mini-romances to such modest New World periodicals of the 1830s as the *Salem Gazette*, *The Token and Atlantic Souvenir*, *Youth's Keepsake*, *New-England Magazine*, and *American Magazine of Useful and Entertaining Knowledge*. Melville, as he saw his literary vocation guttering after the commercial failures of *Moby-Dick* and *Pierre*, turned to producing briefer narratives for *Putnam's Monthly Magazine* and *Harper's New Monthly Magazine*; for "Bartleby" he received $85, and his total proceeds from magazines over a three-year period have been calculated at $750, which was not enough to stay his withdrawal into literary silence. In his brief and hectic career, Poe lived by magazine work; as editor of *Burton's Gentleman's Magazine*, he graciously accepted his own

"The Fall of the House of Usher," and as editor of *Graham's Magazine* he ushered into print "The Murders in the Rue Morgue." Henry James was right from the start a hit with magazine editors; his friend William Dean Howells of *The Atlantic Monthly* wrote him, "I would willingly give you half the magazine." When *The Atlantic* and *Scribner's* competed for a story, James hard-headedly wrote a friend, "It must depend upon the money question, however, entirely, and whichever will pay best shall have the story." William Sydney Porter came out of an Ohio jail to generate in less than a decade, under the pseudonym of O. Henry, a deluge, a shelf, of short stories; for a time, in the first decade of the century, he was produc-ing a story a week for the *New York World*, as well as selling to such maga-zines as *Cosmopolitan* and *Ainslee's*. In the next generation of popular magazines, *The Saturday Evening Post* would pay F. Scott Fitzgerald a princely four thousand dollars for a tale whipped out over a weekend. William Faulkner was among the other talents who graced the *Post*'s widely read pages, with their generous weekly allotment of fiction. There is nothing sadder, to me, in the situation of young American writers, as the colleges turn them out by the creative-writing classfuls, than the lack of a significantly paying market for short stories. When I graduated from college in 1954, the *Post* and *Collier's* were still publishing, though televi-sion was already stealing their advertisers; more importantly to me, *The New Yorker* was still running two or three or even four so-called "casuals" a week.

I wanted to appear in *The New Yorker*—indeed, as a would-be writer, I wanted little else. Such a narrow desire and loyalty paid off: the magazine accepted a poem and a story of mine the very summer I graduated from college. That momentous summer, my young wife and I were living off of our parents, before embarking to England for a year financed by a fellow-ship. The poetry acceptance reached us in Vermont, at my in-laws' sum-mer house; the story acceptance, a graver and more editorially meditated matter, reached me in Pennsylvania, at my parents' farm, where my mother and I had both so often plodded out to the mailbox to reap our rejection slips. But this was no rejection slip; the envelope was too small. I felt, standing and reading the good news in the midsummer pink dust of the stony road beside a field of waving weeds, born as a professional writer.

What did I know about short stories, in 1954? Precious little. The high-school textbooks had held nineteenth-century chestnuts from Poe and O. Henry, Mark Twain and Bret Harte that set off few aesthetic thrills. On my own, I had read Thurber and White, who in their sombre moods wrote spare tales of, respectively, men and women bickering ("A

Couple of Hamburgers") and men having anxiety attacks ("The Second Tree from the Corner"). If this was adulthood, I was content to wait. In college, the writing instructor read aloud to us samples from the modern masters, beginning with Chekhov. I recall staid, tweedy Theodore Morrison reading us Hemingway's "The Light of the World," as an example of consistent point-of-view successfully violated. It was Kenneth Kempton, the least tweedy of the writing instructors, who made some sort of light dawn by reading us J. D. Salinger, then hot off the press—"Just Before the War with the Eskimos" especially wowed me—and a sparkling story by V. S. Pritchett called "Passing the Ball." We could not agree on what the stories exactly meant, and Kempton didn't know either—this was a revelation to me. A good story could be ambiguous, the better to contain the ambiguity of the world. This seemed like a real advance in possibility over the crisp, wised-up, decisively downbeat stories of Dorothy Parker and John O'Hara. I came to admire John Cheever's work and to enjoy his company, but it was a story of his, "O Youth and Beauty!," that spurred me to my successful assault on the *New Yorker* citadel. Cheever's story involved drunkenness and a sudden death by pistol shot, and to my innocent palate it tasted as rasping and sour as a belt of straight bourbon. I thought to myself, "There must be more to American life than this," and wrote an upbeat little story, with an epiphanic benefaction at the end, to prove it. The story was titled "Friends from Philadelphia," and it was, *mirabile dictu*, accepted into that exalted fold.

I even remember, or think I remember, the amount of the check, which came some days later: $550. It seemed a vast amount in 1954, when three thousand dollars a year was a respectable wage. I figured, embarking a few years later on the stony road of the free-lance writer, that if I could sell *The New Yorker* six stories a year, I could support my growing family in modest but adequate small-town style. The small town was Ipswich, Massachusetts, a coastal mill town with a variegated population and a distinguished Puritan past. It seemed a town full of stories, in those fifteen years when my main business was writing them. We shopped at the Atlantic and Pacific supermarket, and so I cooked up a story called "A & P." I drove my daughter to her music lesson, and out came "The Music School." A car accident occurred at our corner, and thus "The Corner." I fell into the local version of the sexual revolution, and out came a bundle of variations on the story of Tristan and Iseult. My wife, as a fictional character, got ever more talkative and alluring as our marriage became ever more fraught with resentments and tensions. I was hip-deep in neighbors and friends, children and pets; I gossiped, I drank, I played golf, I attended church. This was life, and I shaped and polished off odd fragments of it to send away in brown manilla envelopes.

Though it must seem easier in retrospect than it really was, I never failed to sell my self-imposed quota of the six short stories to *The New Yorker*. The crucial phone calls came through on Mondays, usually around noon, as my editor relayed the verdict of the editor-in-chief, William Shawn, who read fiction on the weekends. The magazine was structured to minimize hurt feelings and awkward confrontations; all decisions descended from Shawn, and he was, like the God of the clock-work universe, basically unreachable, and unappealable-to. The light of his countenance shone upon me frequently enough that I never had to climb down from my limb in rustic New England. My stomach dipped and my heart fluttered when I picked up the ringing phone on Mondays, but things worked out.

We steady *New Yorker* contributors looked down on "slick" magazines, but I wonder now if there wasn't some justice in the charge, from dis-gruntled highbrow quarters, that our stories were just a new kind of slick? The in-house term "casual" said something; Tolstoy's "Death of Ivan Ilyich," had it appeared in the magazine, would have been considered a "casual." A sense of effort or of forcing developments was to be avoided. A small authentic thing outweighed the big inflated thing. Like Henry James, Shawn—who was not averse to putting his thoughts on paper now and then—wrote of "the real thing." Like the buyer of dreams in the Capote story (not published in *The New Yorker*), they wanted *real* dreams. My long-aspiring mother, who from the slave shack of the unpublished had a keen eye for the editorial masters, said they wanted real blood, but nothing messy.

My novels were messy, and for me a thing apart. Unlike, say, Cheever, I didn't attempt to sell them in pieces to the magazine; only two excerpts ever appeared—the second chapters of *The Centaur* and *Marry Me*, nov-els that were written consecutively but appeared over ten years apart. If not all, a large part of my artistic conscience was an implant from *New Yorker* editorial policy. A good story was, basically, one that they accepted. Yet nobody on the editorial staff ever instructed us how to write one. A note scrawled on a rejection slip I received when still in col-lege said, "Look, we don't use stories of senility." A decade later, "The Lucid Eye in Silver Town," published eventually in the *Post* (and in *Pravda*, oddly), was turned down because "stories about visitors to New York City made him [Mr. Shawn] nervous." Surprising things made Mr. Shawn nervous, but he showed iron nerves and a considerable permis-siveness in other instances. My connubial exposé "Wife-wooing" verged on the obscene in 1961, and received indignant letters when *The New Yorker* published it; the resolutely liberal Shawn had some political doubts about my "Marching in Boston" a few years later, but ran it anyway.

My feeling then and now is that mine were the best stories I could write, and only an adventurous and patient magazine would have published so many of them. John O'Hara, that prickly master, once suggested to Katharine White that he should be paid even for rejections, since stories aimed at *The New Yorker* couldn't be sold anywhere else. There was, if not a formula to adhere to, a certain inward sensation—a moderate elevation over room temperature and a palpable but not painful twisting—which told me inside when I had conceived a story "they" would "take." It was no guarantee: there had to be a stretch, a risk, a freshness of attack, each time out. You knew as you were writing if it was going well—if the harmonics and happy accidents were happening, and the sentences were moving on a kind of tiptoe. There had to be something solid in the package, and the wrapping had to have a touch of elegance; minimalism and Barthelme-esque pop surrealism redefined elegance but did not dismiss the requirement. Except for an occasional poet, the contributors were not wild or beat. Civilization and its discontents was the overall topic. Shawn had an aversion to violence and sexual explicitness, and his squeamishness dictated certain parameters of sensibility beyond which one did not trespass. I knew, because I trespassed when my fictional marriages became too modern, too bilaterally and carefreely betrayed; the stories about the Maples began to come back in the mails. By that time, my novels were selling a bit, and I had become, for bread and butter, one of the magazine's book reviewers.

I don't believe anyone could now live off *The New Yorker* without doing some journalism. Fiction is down to one story, often lurid, a week, and sometimes not even that. I have no complaints, no laments; an editor must guide his or her ship to where he or she imagines the era's readers are. The quiet disturbances of fiction suited us of the Silent Generation. *The New Yorker*'s inhibitions were only slightly more distinct and firmly policed than our own. Stories, with their falsified names and ambiguous conclusions, their hovering "weave," convey most closely human experience within my ken, in my time, as it slips over the century's horizon into the afterlife.

INTRODUCTION TO Self-Selected Stories of John Updike *(Tokyo: Shin-chosha, 1996).*

This selection of fourteen stories from six of my eleven short-story collections was made jointly by me and my estimable translator, Iwao Iwamoto. Together we sought to achieve a variety of tone, length, texture, and subject matter, while choosing stories of the highest quality. They are arranged roughly in the order in which they were written. Here are quick thoughts on each:

"The Lucid Eye in Silver Town." I was surprised when *The New Yorker* magazine, where most of these stories appeared, turned this one down, since it seemed to me one of the best of my attempts to dramatize myself as a boy, torn as I was between my Pennsylvania roots and my yearning toward the cosmopolitan life of New York, between my grand hopes and the pinched reality of my actual circumstances. *The Saturday Evening Post* ran the story eventually, and that same year, in 1964, *Pravda* translated it into Russian for its pages, perhaps because it takes an unfavorable view of a rich capitalist. Nevertheless, Uncle Quin is a dear character.

"A & P" is my most anthologized short story, and is read by high-school students who read nothing else by me. The idiomatic monologue is not my usual style. My wife at the time said that the story reminded her rather too much of J. D. Salinger. Its inspiration was simple enough: as I drove past the local A & P in our small New England town, it occurred to me that somebody should write a short story about a supermarket. I never myself clerked, as Sammy does, though I once did see some girls in bathing suits shopping for food in the aisles. They looked remarkably naked.*

"Pigeon Feathers" was written in pencil in a notebook on an old sofa in

---

*Not only to me but to the Japanese Ministry of Education, which in 1998 directed that a Japanese translation of the story be removed from an anthology prepared by the Kadokawa Shoten Publishing Company for use in high schools. The government censors felt that the story would—to quote a *Washington Post* Foreign Service story by Kevin Sullivan—"embarrass Japanese girls and cause 'significant exasperation' that would disrupt classes." American textbook producers, also, have been troubled by the story; several times I have been asked to modify this sentence from the first paragraph: "She was a chunky kid, with a good tan and a sweet broad soft-looking can with those two crescents of white just under it, where the sun never seems to hit, at the top of the backs of her legs." I declined, of course, not wishing to create a bowdlerized version for adolescent consumption. Why shelter teenagers from what they already see? The story was an especial favorite of Mr. Iwamoto's: he asked to place it first in my *Self-Selected Stories*, which on its cover bears a disarmingly animated and unanatomical Japanese watercolor of three girls in—to quote the story once more—"nothing but bathing suits."

a house the Updikes were renting on the Caribbean island of Anguilla in early 1960. It reconstructs my adolescent trauma of religious doubt mixed with the trauma of being moved from a small town to an isolated, unimproved farm. The notion that killing other creatures relieves the fear of death owes something to Hemingway. At the age of sixty-two, I can scarcely improve on the vision and affirmation of the last paragraph.

"Packed Dirt, Churchgoing, a Dying Cat, a Traded Car." Again, a story of religious belief under siege, but with an older hero, who is entering the treacherous waters of adulthood and adultery. The fugal form, combining obliquely related incidents under the aegis of a presiding meditative voice, is an invention of which I am proud. Close to the essay, yet with fiction's liberties and amplitude, such a story might be called Emersonian.

"The Bulgarian Poetess" gives birth to Henry Bech, a fictional author who figured in fourteen more stories, with a few more, I hope, still to come. I have generally avoided writing about the literary life, and my plunge into it here has a certain exhilaration. Like Bech, I was a cultural ambassador to the Communist world in 1964, and for Americans a country like Bulgaria was almost the dark side of the moon. An early title was "Through the Looking-Glass." Out-of-the-way places seem to excite me to my best and brightest prose. One of fiction's basic and ancient functions, after all, is bringing news to armchair travellers.

"The Christian Roommates" is the only story I have based on my college experience—a life-stage which was very important to F. Scott Fitzgerald and Evelyn Waugh, among others. Harvard has graduated so many writers I felt the ground was covered, so to speak. Stories of college life rarely describe the actual labor of studying, which I do here try to portray, along with the crisis of faith that new knowledge brings. For a time, Harvard College used to assign this story to its incoming freshmen—I don't know if it helped to cushion the shock or not.

"The Music School." A different sort of school, and another fugal weave. The themes of infidelity and guilt are played upon with more practiced notes than in "Packed Dirt . . ." This was made into a short movie for television, of which the most exciting parts were (1) a little science-fiction episode, photographed through a blue filter, and (2) documentary footage showing nuns in great winged headdresses manufacturing big round Eucharistic wafers.

"Museums and Women" is possibly too much of an essay, but it was heartfelt, for I am happy in almost any kind of museum, with a woman or alone. During my own visit to Tokyo, in 1970, I went alone to the museum of modern art, and then found when I came out that no taxi driver could understand the English name of my hotel. Luckily, I had a folder of matches, with a picture of the Imperial on it, and that did the trick. Pictures speak where words fail.

"The Orphaned Swimming Pool." Perhaps the story of mine that owes most to my late friend John Cheever—his wonderful quickness of action and description, his sense of American suburbia as a spoiled paradise.

"Jesus on Honshu." My only Japanese story—a fantasy springing from a report in the *New York Times*. But some of the themes here are close to my heart—the wonderfully long voyage (*The Coup, Brazil,* even *Rabbit at Rest*) and the story that gets more and more distorted in the telling (*The Witches of Eastwick, Memories of the Ford Administration*). Rereading, I am struck by the little family I give Jesus in the last section. An American Christian child grows up thinking of Jesus as the baby born at Christmas, of Joseph and Mary; something of the same sweetness clings to the idea of Him as an ancient patriarch, at the other apex of the family.

"Australia and Canada." Henry Bech again, as a celebrity straddling two big, bland domains of the English Crown in a rapid alternation of seductions. Published by *Playboy* in 1975, when sexual mores were simpler and the wounds of Vietnam were still smarting. In the era of jet planes and electronic communication, a writer in gathering truth should set foot on as much of the globe as he can.

"Nevada." Another story whose inspiration arose from the milieu. Certain images here—the giant train appearing on the main street of the little desert town, the luminous slot machines calling out to the under-aged Polly, the change girl's crinkling ember-red uniform calling out to the father—are still vivid to me, in that clear desert air of the West.

"Domestic Life in America." American overabundance—too many wives, children, Christmas trees—and an essential solitude. It is the hero who weaves back and forth between worlds, not the author. The exact nature of the miracle at the end was several times adjusted—10° and 10:01 could be 0° and 12:00, but then the alternatingly flashing numbers don't seem so miraculous.

"The Man Who Loved Extinct Mammals." I hope some of the charm of these extinct mammals survives translation. Japan, which has given us Godzilla and many another animated monster, can surely understand Sapers' fascination. It is important, I think, for writers of fiction to remind readers of the vast ongoing realities that are non-human, that surround our little adventures much as the ocean surrounds a self-important cruise ship.

For many years short stories were a large part of my livelihood; but writing them has been for me an aesthetic challenge and joy as well as a business. Situated between the novel and the poem, and capable of giving us the pleasures of both, the form also has the peculiar intimacy of an essay, wherein a voice confides its most intricate and important secrets to the reader's ear.

FOREWORD *to* Love Factories, *three stories bound into a limited edition published by Eurographica (Helsinki, 1993).*

These three stories were written in 1988: "The Football Factory" in June, "Part of the Process" in July, and "The Lens Factory" in November. The subject matter was out of my usual path, and these experiments found publication only in rather out-of-the-way journals—respectively, *Observer Magazine* in London; *Special Report,* a magazine intended for doctor's offices and published by Whittle Communications of Knoxville, Tennessee; and *Granta,* a literary journal originating at Cambridge University, in England. Also, in August of 1988, oddly obsessed by the vistas that my visit to an Ohio football factory had opened up, I wrote a ten-page non-fictional memoir, called "The Real Story," which has never been published. In it, I describe the circumstances whereby, the morning after a reading at a small Ohio university, "I was taken by my host, a tall blond male instructor of English distinguished by a solemn long face and a bad case of identification with Rabbit Angstrom, to the local factory where footballs were made. A management-level friend of his led us through. I was entranced and repelled; I was overwhelmed by the savage precision of the loud machines, and the unimaginable numerousness of the quickly accumulating steps that go into the making of a thing as playful as a football, and the fierce dedication of the workers, who seemed as unsmiling and winsome and potentially dangerous as zoo animals while our party of inspection moved among them. We, them: two different races of human being, on two levels so different that panes of thick glass or iron cage bars could not more effectually prevent us from touching. How frivolous and deplorable our party of inspection seemed, ignorantly threading its way through the process that was making the concrete floor itself tremble, and that, unmoderated, would have filled the world with footballs, right up to the sky!"

My account goes on to say: "Like the dignitary in my first story, whose life is all airplanes and talk, I wished to enter in, to descend into this toilsome noisy creation of something real, solid, kickable, tossable. But the story came out too reminiscent, for me, of an earlier story called 'One Last Interview'—my voice and invention faltered once the bliss of grafting muscles and a jingly-jangly, bar-snappy wife onto my alter ego were past. So I gathered my courage and dismissed the flimsy celebrity-persona and plunged nakedly into the lives of these factory workers. I as it were pushed the dignitary aside and possessed June Mae myself, in the story 'Part of the Process.' Jealously I tried to make her mine, while bothersome parodic shadows of minimalist fiction—that school of writing which treats ordinary Americans as exotics to be mounted and displayed in sentences of academic blandness and dryness—got in the way."

My aesthetic difficulties are symptomatic of the cleavage, in industrial societies, between the intellectuals and dignitaries, who skim the earth in airplanes, and the earthbound workers who, in factories and farms, produce the stuff of our daily lives. Attempts by the former to dramatize the situation of the latter carry an ineluctable flavor of condescension, of conscientious "fieldwork" as it is done among animals and exotic human tribes. Even a poet such as Phillip Levine, who writes knowingly about industrial jobs in Detroit, turns out, his recently published memoir reveals, to have descended, distastefully, from the middle class, into procedures that a true child of the working class would have found unremarkable. The fact is that hard physical work and hard mental work are all but incompatible; Nathaniel Hawthorne wrote in *The Blithedale Romance*, "The clods of earth, which we so constantly belabored and turned over and over, were never etherealized into thought. Our thoughts, on the contrary, were fast becoming cloddish." Yet the liberal conscience cannot ignore these millions of laboring lives, and that intellectual vice *la nostalgie de la boue* tempts our imaginations downward, into what we imagine to be a more basic, more delicious, more muddy level of reality.

Like the young hero of "The Lens Factory," I once worked in a factory. Not long, but long enough to feel the oppression, to taste the boredom, and to hear the merciless racket of the terrible machines. Terrible, and yet beautiful, in their slapdash speed and their indifference to the slivers of flesh that operate and maintain them. In my unpublished account I wrote:

> I never had time, in my three days, to grasp my part of the process in the larger context, the factory as a whole, each floor practically boundless and filled to the brim with men at machines, with wide thumping belts reaching to the ceiling, with carts being pushed back and forth in the general apparent confusion. My duties were clear; I was to place fresh semi-spheres (each containing perhaps a dozen lenses) on a row of ten or so pivots which revolved the caps under semi-spherical lids that descended and abraded the lenses in a trough of orange liquid abrasive called, fittingly, "mud."

The precise mechanics of it evade me now, as they did then. Were the caps always immersed in the mud, or did they sink down into it when the machine was activated? Did I activate it with a pedal of some kind, or was it controlled from elsewhere? From elsewhere, I believe, for the terror of the job lay in my race with the timetable of the repeating process, which called for me to place the caps, one after the other, wait a precise amount of time—twenty minutes sticks dimly in my mind—while the whole row busily bathed in the abrasive, and then remove them and carefully stack them in a mutileveled handcart. It was a frantic, recurrent race, somehow, to keep up with the machine, and the dripping, splashing mud got all over me—up my arms, into my hair, under my fingernails, inexpungeably. If the lenses revolved too long, they were ruined, and inspectors who stalked by now and then would slashingly X with chalk the lens-filled caps. Accounts were kept of how many rejects you produced. There must have been, during the minutes while the long machine brainlessly sloshed away in its mud, an opportunity for repose; but all that comes back to me is the frantic feeling of falling behind, of the pit of my stomach churning with guilt and shame over the possibly ruined lenses, of a mercilessly repeated mechanical process timed to just beyond the outer limit of my capacity.

I was recently in a book factory, to watch copies of a book of mine pour out of the acres of machinery that assembled printed signatures and bound them into a cover, or "case." I was struck by how many steps there were, in creating this intricate knit of paper and cloth and glue and gold foil, including steps I would never have conceived of, such as "rounding" the stacked signatures, once they were attached to the backing strip, to give the spine the convexity which our aesthetic sense demands. At each station on the assembly line the machines sliced and pressed and glued and dented and stamped faster than the eye could comfortably follow, the precise tension and pressure required maintained here and there with homely arrangements of rubber bands and masking tape. It alarmed me that my wayward mental adventures and my egotistic desire to communicate with unknown readers had caused such an extensive racket of ingenuity to be set in motion. The angelic beauty of human engineering, and the animal docility of the workers who, day after day, eight hours a day, minister to the amazing machines—these are a fundamental part of our modern world, and yet we, we who try to do the world's imagining, avert our eyes from them and know as little of the interior of factories as we do of an African village or a Tibetan lamasery. It was a sense of this failure, this estrangement, that led me, on the basis of a very little experience, to attempt this sequence, increasingly intimate, of three stories.

FOREWORD *to a limited edition, by Metacom Press (Worcester, Massachusetts; 1990) of my short story "Brother Grasshopper."*

In one of Aesop's versions of the fable, the slacker is a dung beetle:

> During the summer months the Ant scoured the fields for grains of wheat and barley against the coming winter. A Dung Beetle watched him at his work and expressed surprise that the Ant should put himself to such trouble at a time when other creatures were taking it easy and enjoying the good weather. The Ant answered not a word; but several months later, when the winter rains had washed away the manure and the hungry Dung Beetle came to beg alms of the Ant, he rebuked him thus: "Silly insect, if you had taken the trouble to exert yourself instead of mocking me at my labors, you would not now lack food."
> [translation by Patrick and Justina Gregory, Gambit Books, 1975]

In the other version, a cicada takes the loser's part:

> It was winter-time; the ants' store of grain had got wet and they were laying it out to dry. A hungry cicada asked them to give it something to eat. "Why did you not gather food in the summer, like us?" they said. "I hadn't time," it replied; "I was busy making sweet music." The ants laughed at it. "Very well," they said, "since you piped in summer, now dance in winter."
> [translation by S. A. Handford, Penguin Books, 1954]

La Fontaine, who follows the second of Aesop's versions fairly closely, has the indolent insect as a cicada, *une cigale*:

> La cigale, ayant chanté
> Tout l'été,
> Se trouva fort dépourvue
> Quant la vise fut venue.

A grasshopper would be *une sauterelle*. Since the cicada (the male only) makes a very loud noise by vibrating paired dorso-lateral membranes called timbals located at the base of the abdomen, a noise that permeates late-summer nights in Europe and America, whereas the grasshopper merely buzzes, or stridulates, by rubbing the minutely toothed inside of its hind femora against a raised vein on its front wing, or else unmusically crackles, or crepitates, while leaping in flight, the cicada would surely seem to be the *chanteuse* of the fable. Cicada song, the *Encyclopaedia Britannica* explains, comes in three varieties:

> (1) a congregational song, the production of which is regulated by daily fluctuations in climatic conditions and by hearing songs produced by other males; (2) a courtship song, which is usually but not invariably produced

prior to copulation; and (3) a disturbance squawk produced by individuals captured, held, disturbed into flight or otherwise irritated.

Nevertheless, the English versions of the fable, from cartoons for children to the Marianne Moore translation of La Fontaine ("Until fall, a grasshopper / Chose to chirr . . ."), specify the grasshopper, and it was the image of this green and rangy insect that inspired the title and core metaphor of my own retelling of the fable, from the ant's point of view. The grasshopper is a cheerier creature to picture and to illustrate than the drab cicada, which in some of its species, under the misnomer of locust, goes into hiding for thirteen- or seventeen-year periods. The grasshopper is always with us, a long-legged dandy of the summer meadows, and his very name connotes merriment and, with grass, perishability.

I did not have Aesop or La Fontaine before me as I composed, out of the usual writerly resources of fragmentary memory and wanton distortion, this short story of acquired fraternity. But fabulation works in mysterious ways, and I was pleased to find afterwards, in La Fontaine, that the grasshopper does offer—as in my story—the thrifty, suspicious ant a swell-sounding deal:

> Je vous paierai, lui dit-elle,
> Avant l'oût, foi d'animal,
> Intérêt et principal.

Neither the Frenchman nor Aesop provides any information about their protagonists' marriages, or educations, or socio-economic roots, so I had to invent it all. For this limited edition, I confess, my parallel rendition of the grasshopper's command winter dance—*"Vous chantiez? j'en suis fort aisé,"* says the ant. *"Eh bien! dansez maintenant"*—has been sharpened by the addition of the word "dance" to the description of the bone chips sinking, and a number of other small changes imposed themselves (for the better, one always hopes) upon the text of the fable as it appeared in *The New Yorker* in December of 1987.

NOTE *on "A Sandstone Farmhouse" for* The Best American Short Stories 1991, *edited by Alice Adams.*

I wrote "A Sandstone Farmhouse" in a rush of liberation after fifteen months' captivity in the making of a novel. The hero of this short story, Joey Robinson, figured, along with his mother and a Pennsylvania farm, in a novella of 1965, *Of the Farm*. So this is a kind of sequel, after many a year. I differ from Joey in that I lived only briefly in New York City, never was in the advertising game, and have not had three wives. But like him I did live, from the ages of thirteen to eighteen, in a sandstone farmhouse with four adults—my parents and my mother's parents. By keeping the focus on the house—its stones, its smells, its renovations—I hoped to convey the dizzying depth of life those foursquare walls have contained, and the poignant way that lives glimmer in and out of the more slowly transformed realities of environment. A Berks County friend of mine, in another connection, sent me his research on how the old houses were built, early in the nineteenth century, and I was happy to incorporate his information, with its extraordinary image of the carts shattering under their loads of sandstone. The story is about *things*—how they mutely witness our flitting lives, and remain when the lives are over, still mute, still witnessing, still resolutely themselves and nothing else.

Just last week I visited the real farmhouse where I had lived for five years and where my mother had lived for sixty of her eighty-five years. The new owners have exterminated the mice and flying squirrels that kept her company, but they have retained the integrity of the thick sandstone shell, and the old knobbed clothes pegs on the wall, and they plan to put a fireproof metal lining in the crooked flue of the old stone chimney. It was a sunny day, and the place seemed dimly to recognize me, just as my mother's dog, happy with a new owner, wags her tail and whines when she sees me, trying to remember, but not having the words wherein memories are retained.

NOTE *on "Playing with Dynamite" for* The Best American Short Stories 1993, *edited by Louise Erdrich.*

This is the only story, as best I can remember, that I wrote on request—the new editor of *The New Yorker* relayed word to me that she would be happy to have a story of mine in her first issue. Flattered silly, I pawed through the slips of paper on which I jot down story ideas, often just the titles, and came upon this title. One thing led to another, as I sat at the word processor, most of them having to do with the sensations and hallucinations of late middle age. I have written about aging, doddery, nostalgic American men whose names begin with "F" before, and let loosely related incidents weave their way around a central theme, or bitter fact, before; but the recipe seemed to produce a warmer, richer dish than usual here—at least its presence in this collection encourages me to think so. Life is an adventure, all right, from beginning to end, but life after sixty is part of the tale that perhaps is more eagerly told than heard. It is the young we love, in print as on the silver screen, as they play with the dynamite of mating. For some time, I have noticed, my heroes seem older than I feel to myself, as if, lacking sex appeal to make them dramatic, they are cozying up to death.

The many little mysteries and gaps that Fanshawe observes in his stream of experience were added to, after the story appeared in print, by a writer in *The Wall Street Journal* who opined, with an indignation itself mysterious, that the bird whose nest the Fanshawes disturb could not have been a warbler but must have been a phoebe.

FOREWORD *to a special edition of a short story, "The Women Who Got Away," written in 1994, published as a separate volume in 1998.*

If Massachusetts is the Puritan superego of New England, and Connecticut and Vermont function as healthily functioning egos, with good self-images reflected in their pretty, curried landscapes, New Hampshire is something of an id. Live Free or Die, its motto says. Grace Metalious's *Peyton Place* came storming out of New Hampshire to take the top of the best-seller lists, and likewise John Irving's *The World According to Garp*, with its notorious *fellatio interruptus*. Next door, Maine's dark woods and sour old lumber towns play host to Stephen King's goblins, but nymphs and satyrs, naked or wearing skis, haunt New Hampshire's groves and spired valley settlements. So it seemed natural to me to locate this little vision of communal intercourse in that state, as well as the extensive collegiate bacchanal of the novel *Memories of the Ford Administration*. And it seemed inevitable to assent to Bill Ewert's suggestion that he print this story in New Hampshire, in one of those loving formats and bindings of which he is one of the few surviving promulgators, up there in Concord, where the good times roll.

NOTE *on "My Father on the Verge of Disgrace" for* The Best American Short Stories 1998, *edited by Garrison Keillor.*

No doubt about it, this story has something to do with my real father. It took me back into the mythic territory of memory out of which I wrote my novel *The Centaur* over thirty-five years ago. As I have aged, my boyhood has become so far away, so strangely furnished—the icebox, the tin toaster, the recipe box holding all our money—as to be fabulous. And boyhood's buried shames—a child's sense of peril, of his and his family's inferiority within the perceived social system—can at last come out into the open. The detail about robbing the ticket money to pay the grocer still pains and frightens me to divulge, as if some surviving members of the schoolboard in the 1930s might demand from me the long-due reckoning. To give myself confessional room there is a small but necessary remove of invention: my real father taught algebra and not chemistry, and he never sold china. It was another man, in another stage of my life, who told me about the joys of descending on a strange town and coming away with a tall order. In truth I scarcely know what in this story is made up or not; it delves into a layer of my earthly duration so ancient and fraught that truth and fiction are interchangeably marvellous. Life, you could say, is a tall order.

KARL SHAPIRO, *for an issue of* hommages *put out by* Negative Capability.

I first encountered the work of Karl Shapiro in *The New Yorker* of the 1940s, and then, at college, in *The Oxford Book of American Verse* as edited by F. O. Matthiessen in 1950. Coming after (in the collection) the loose egoistic effusions of Delmore Schwartz and shortly before the knotty pentameters of the early Robert Lowell, Shapiro's poems recognizably belonged to this world, to my America, with curt declarative titles like "Midnight Show," "Hollywood," "Nigger," and "Drug Store." From "Drug Store":

> It baffles the foreigner like an idiom,
> And he is right to adopt it as a form
> Less serious than the living-room or bar;
> For it disestablishes the café,
> Is a collective, and on basic country.

> . . .

> Youth comes to jingle nickels and crack wise;
> The baseball scores are his, the magazines,
> Devoted to lust, the jazz, the Coca-Cola,
> The lending-library of love's latest.
> He is the customer; he is heroized.

And, not included by Matthiessen but somehow remembered by me, "Auto Wreck" with the beautiful opening lines

> Its quick soft silver bell beating, beating,
> And down the dark one ruby flare
> Pulsing out red light like an artery,
> The ambulance at top speed floating down . . .

and "A Cut Flower" with its stunning last questions "Where are my bees? / Must I die now? Is this part of life?" and his soldier's "Homecoming" with its horribly factual

> We bring no raw materials from the East
> But green-skinned men in blue-lit holds
> And lunatics impounded between-decks . . .

These were songs of experience, experience I could recognize even where I had not shared it. They were just, in the sense in which Richard Wilbur has described Sylvia Plath's poems as "unjust," and the sense in which Lowell's images of America were unjust—complaining, nagging, scornful. Shapiro has Whitman's good nature, and his wide embrace. In his remarkably relaxed memoirs, even where complaints might be justified—he was enlisted in the T. S. Eliot–led campaign to give the Jew-hating Ezra Pound the Bollingen Prize, and finally rebelled and protested; his poetry was entirely dropped by Richard Ellmann from *The New Oxford Book of American Verse* in 1976—his accounts are mild, fair-minded, delivered with a shrug. As keen and amused an observer of himself as of anyone else, he gives us personal testimony moderated, defused, made limp and light, by an impersonal calm; he has a touch of Southern courtliness left over, perhaps, from his Baltimore upbringing. Recent poems of his express bemusement about himself as a lover and as a Jew—two roles in which most speakers would not dare diffidence. In his poetry, he has taken an unfashionable direction, backwards toward the Beats, toward the days of long-lined personal explosion. "All things remain to be simplified. I find I must break free of the poetry trap," he writes in his Rimbaudesque cascade "I am an Atheist Who Says His Prayers." He has turned to prose poems, to prosy poems to unburden himself of awkward truths. His is an America endured without a grudge, wherein the poet, like the tourist of "Washington Cathedral," is "only a good alien, nominally happy." Bless Shapiro for his modest immodesty, his continuing verbal adventurism, his honest bemusement, his incorrigible sanity.

THREE NEW YORKER STALWARTS who were paternally kind to me. The paragraphs about Shawn and Gill were contributions to the spread of tributes with which the magazine observed their deaths, in the Decembers of 1992 and 1997 respectively. My reminiscence concerning Maxwell was part of the celebration, at the Urbana campus of the University of Illinois, of his gift of papers to his alma mater, on April 24, 1997.

To this contributor, William Shawn's unfailing courtesy and rather determined conversational blandness hid a mystery: his extraordinary aesthetic passion, which enabled him to make so many adamant and surprising discriminations. A prodigious consumer of information and culture, he retained what he had absorbed; all the tides that had washed through his eyes and ears had polished his own cultural vocabulary to a gnomic minimalism. The word "writing" covered the whole vast business of literature, and "good writing" was the height of his praise and the extent of his commentary. An editor, with the ultimate authority of acceptance or rejection, has a certain monolithic, or binary, simplicity, and to a striking degree Mr. Shawn—as I always called him—declined to compromise the dignity of his power with unnecessary elaboration. Not that he was curt; on the contrary, an infinitely patient expectancy was the mood he conveyed, and it was this expectancy, grandly non-directive, that a contributor longed to satisfy. The tiny difference between your best and your second-best would be registered, you were sure, in the ideally pure chambers of his personal quiet; it was part of his editorial genius to establish, in a manner akin to that of the classic Freudian psychoanalyst, an air of perfect listening in which you were encouraged to reveal and reconstruct yourself. You wanted to produce for him.

Our dealings were few but they needed only to be few. A softly spoken sentence while passing in the hall; a compliment relayed by another editor; a friendly word scratched on a proof—these, like the lightest of touches on the tiller, sufficed to confirm that the vessel was being steered and the right direction maintained. What was right was doubly right, somehow—aesthetics and ethics coincided—in the universe of his gentle implications. His adamancy of taste had been hardened in a buried moral fire, and his *New Yorker* was a realm from which many types of unseemliness were excluded. But his exclusionary sword had an edge of venturesomeness as well; the magazine's fiction became more avant-garde and its non-fiction more mandarin under his guidance. This shy man in his buttoned vest concealed a mental swashbuckler who constantly kept his readers and his writers on their toes. He would go with a writer as far as the writer dared go on in pursuit of what he called "the real thing,"* and turned cool only when the writer played it safe, or false. Beneath a reserve that bordered on diffidence, he harbored an intensely creative, uncompromising nature. As fate willed, he placed this nature at the service of other talents, of an entire magazine, week after week. Yet his magic force made every word and comma in some sense his. He seemed to me, when I would dare visit that corner office where Mr. Shawn pinkly crouched behind his proof-piled desk, a conjurer who, without moving a muscle, summoned spirits from the deep.

*

I met William Maxwell in August of 1954, shortly before taking a boat to England, for my first venture out of the United States. I had graduated from college that summer, and had had a poem or two and a short story taken by *The New Yorker*, and hence was invited, before I embarked for the Old World, inside the offices of the magazine that had been the object of my fantasies and aspirations since I was thirteen. The décor was scrupulously unspectacular. The waiting room, if I recall, had nothing in it but some chairs and a big copper platter and in the center of it, like some exquisitely thin and flaky Arabian pastry, a copy of the latest *New Yorker*. Ross and the first generation of editors had tended to be newspaper men, and the premises were furnished in a matter-of-fact masculine style, with steel desks and square wastebaskets and yellowing stacks of old telephone directories. The *New Yorker* of the Fifties managed to combine great literary prestige with impressive advertising revenue, but the decades still ruling the corridors were the no-frills Thirties and Forties. Maxwell, who emerged to shake my hand and usher me through the linoleum-floored maze to his own sunny office, conveyed a murmurous, restrained nervous energy and an infallible grace; I was reminded of Fred Astaire. And my sense of his being incapable of putting a foot wrong remained with me for the coming decades of editorial association. More I think than anyone I have ever met, he could be said not to waste words: not that he was stingy of words, he could talk quite generously, but every word was pertinent and *chosen*. There was none of that backing and filling with which most of us, like a computer looping through an algorithm,

---

*In the superb pages on Harold Ross (and himself) he contributed to the end of Brendan Gill's *Here at The New Yorker*: "Even when a piece of writing was too rarefied for [Ross's] taste, or outside the normal range of his interests or knowledge, or—in extreme cases—basically incomprehensible, he could tell whether it was the real thing or counterfeit. . . . He looked for truth in a piece of fiction, a reporting piece, a cartoon, and he knew just what it was when he saw it."

approach saying what we mean. Bill, if the right words did not instantly come to him, had a delightful and commanding way of waiting for them to come, a poise I connected with his Midwestern birth and upbringing, a kind of waiting for the corn to ripen. The only thing I can remember from that first encounter, in which he was so deftly, patiently courteous and friendly and I was so bedazzled, was to say, apropos of an expressed fear of mine, that—and I more or less quote—"People imagine that losing your luggage is like death, but it isn't."

At first, my fiction editor was Katharine White, but within a very few years she retired to Maine with her husband and Bill became my editor until he retired in 1976. Those who are innocent of the literary process have a possibly melodramatic view of the editor-writer relationship. The writer, in the end, must live his life and extract from it what poetry and fiction he can; the editor can accept it for print or reject it, but the amount of consultation possible while the work is in progress is limited. This is especially true of *New Yorker* short stories, where so much lies in the writing. Once, at a lunch, I did tell Bill a story about my elementary-school days and he said, "That's a short story" and so I wrote it up, much as I had spoken it, and sent it in, and saw it make it into print, under the title "The Alligators." Of another early story, "Flight," Bill suggested that, while it was acceptable as it was, the beginning seemed too tightly pulled from the narrator; and so I supplied perhaps a thousand more words about the family and background of the adolescent hero, Allan Dow. Bill liked it all, and found it all relevant; he said it was like a beam of light. To show how variable reader reaction can be, however, I will report that rather recently some critic complained, of that same story, "Why is Allan Dow telling us all this?" Not that Bill or I were wrong in our amplification, but it shows that some tiny disproportion, some old seam where the original rhythm was patched, tends to remain after an extensive alteration.

An editor more often suggests trimming than adding, and there was one story, bearing the merry title "Who Made Yellow Roses Yellow?," in which I had ignored his delicate hints that the prose was excessive and strained. I was visiting my parents' home in Pennsylvania and had brought with me the final *New Yorker* proof—the so-called page proof, in which the columns of text were arranged with the cartoons in place. My mother read it and made some frowning remark that threw a sudden revelatory light upon Bill's reservations; in a kind of revisory panic, I phoned in a number of cuts which caused the *New Yorker* make-up department a lot of trouble but did, at the last minute, improve the story. No amount of trouble, Bill's editorial demeanor conveyed, was too much trouble for even a slight improvement. Once we were locked on the telephone, well into dinnertime, over a long story called "The Wait," going through small last-minute changes; he told me afterwards it was like a long climb in which he kept repeating to himself, "Truth and beauty." A short story that has enjoyed a vigorous anthology life which no one would have predicted for it, "A & P," originally ran on for some more pages; Bill suggested that the story ended earlier than I had realized, and I was happy to take his suggestion, which fit my own intimations. With another story, however, called "Eros Rampant," *The New Yorker* was willing to publish only the first half, and here I thought they were, for once, wrong, willing to settle for half of the truth, and I withdrew the story and sold it elsewhere. Yet another story, with the epic title "The Beloved," was actually accepted and set in proof when the magazine's head editor, William Shawn, expressed such qualms about the theatrical background I had concocted for my hero's amorous evolution that we agreed to kill the story, though I, along with the typesetter, had been already paid. I was troubled at this outcome, and offered to return the money, but Bill on his own initiative extracted from the story's thirty or so pages six or seven that he felt would make a *New Yorker* story, and they were duly published—the one instance where I felt his contribution was so major that he should have co-signed the piece.

Generally, however, the verdict was yes or no, and our editorial collaboration was a matter of making the O.K. a little bit better, of getting the prose to something like the absolute polish of poetry. He was endlessly, beautifully patient and responsive in this interpersonal exercise. Many the hour we spent over the phone, looking for the perfect, invisibly precise expression. He and I do not write alike—his prose tends to be plain, a speaking prose, startlingly relaxed and idiomatic at times, and mine at least in my youth aspired toward baroque, high-modernist effects, as were admired in college in the Fifties. Sometimes, as I labored over the phone to refine some locution or other into an impossible richness of connotation, he would cut the Gordian knot by suggesting a phrase so direct and simple it had never occurred to me. But I never felt he was trying to deprive me of my style; like any good editor, he was helping the writer to become his best self. What was above all important was our sharing a hope of perfection, and his communicating to me a sense of basically boundless gratitude when I had done good work—when I had delivered the goods. So that pleasing Bill became, while not the only hope I had when I sat down to write a short story, a concrete objective to spur me on. He gave the ideal reader a living face. He made writing well seem infinitely worthwhile, and yet tangible—all too palpably distinct from not writing well.

Understand that he did not have to shoulder, in his relations with me, the full onus of acceptance and rejection. The magazine worked, as best I understood it, this way: a story was read by a number of editors, whose remarks accumulated on a so-called "opinion sheet"; this sheet was passed on, with the manuscript, to Mr. Shawn, who read fiction over the weekend and decided whether or not to accept a story for the magazine. Monday, then, was the day when I, who had recklessly left a salaried post with the magazine and set myself up as a free-lance writer in New England, would hear if the verdict was yes or no. The very tone in which Bill pronounced the one word "John?" into the telephone would often tell the tale; the message was commonly expressed, "Shawn says yes" or "Shawn says no." Elaboration was needed only in a case where a salvage operation was proposed. This delivery, year after year, of momentous news to a young householder and father of four, multiplied by the dozens of writers under Bill Maxwell's care, adds up to a human task that must take its own toll. Without ever betraying the editorial decorum, he sometimes softened a negative verdict with hints of his own approbation, or of the magazine's incorrigible prejudices. But whatever the verdict, Bill continued to feel like my friend, and a friend to excellence in literature. We loved our work, and our work was words. His own prose, and his own manner, evince a light touch, a cheering reasonableness, and those many years when he was, in effect, the caretaker of my livelihood, figure in my memory now as cheerful; just as losing your luggage wasn't the end of existence, neither were the ups and downs of an ongoing literary career.

We had a curious additional bond; though he was twenty-five years my senior, we became fathers at about the same time, of girl babies. So we had parenthood to discuss. Our second children were born in rough parallel also, though his was another girl and mine a boy. When I expressed to him the fear that my girl might now develop penis envy, he said, very quickly, "Well, having a penis doesn't solve everything"—a piece of wisdom that I will carry to my grave. It is perhaps not an entirely good idea to have a friend for an editor; the relationship is to some inevitable extent adversarial, and once I found myself enough vexed by some recent rejections so that my first wife had to step in with the comment, "Don't personalize it. Maxwell is part of a machine for getting out a certain kind of magazine." It was a helpful remark. In reading the fascinating correspondence between Bill and the Irish writer Frank O'Connor that was published last year, I was struck by how often he speaks to O'Connor of something not being a *New Yorker* short story, or of making something into a *New Yorker* story. Catholic as the magazine's taste was—more adventurous and experimental than it got credit for—there was a border where publishability stopped, a boundary as distinct in Bill's mind as the boundaries of Illinois. He once confided to me, if I understood him right, that he had never had a wholehearted recommendation of his turned down by Shawn.

He came to the magazine in 1936. He was an assistant to Katharine White; she, who had done so much to refine and broaden the magazine's collective taste, would have been one to recognize Bill's superb qualities. In an interview he gave *The Paris Review* he recalls his apprentice days outside her office, of which let me quote one anecdote:

> On Mondays and Fridays I had nothing whatever to do but stare at a Thurber drawing above my desk—until Mrs. White suggested that I get the scrapbooks from the office library and read them. She also gave me a pile of rejected manuscripts and asked me to write letters to go with those that showed any promise. After she had gone over my letters she called me into her office and said, "Mr. Maxwell, have you ever taught school?" It was a fact that I had kept from her in our interview: instinct told me that it was not something you were supposed to have done. Anyway, from her I learned that it is not the work of an editor to teach writers how to write.

It was Wolcott Gibbs, he goes on to say, who asked him to try editing; Maxwell took to it, and tells us,

> In time I came to feel that real editing means changing as little as possible. Various editors and proofreaders would put their oar in, and sometimes I had to change hats and protect the writer from his own agreeableness, or fear, or whatever it was that made him say yes when he ought to have said no. What you hope is that if the writer reads the story ten years after it is published he will not be aware that anybody has ever touched it.

The adjective that I keep coming back to, in thinking of William Maxwell, is *rare*—it is rare to encounter such extreme sensitivity housed in so cogent, unassuming, and matter-of-fact a frame. He is alive, one feels, like certain insects and birds, to colors of the rainbow invisible to the merely human eye. *The New Yorker* was a rarer, more rarefied magazine for having him on the staff, though he made his role in it sound simple: once, when I asked him what it was like being in Ross's art meetings, he said, "It was the easiest thing in the world. You sat there looking at a lot of unfunny roughs, and when a funny one came up, everybody laughed." Valuable as he was to the magazine, he did not exalt *The New Yorker* into a mystical and untouchable entity; when Brendan Gill's *Here at The New Yorker* came out, ruffling the easily ruffled feathers of some veteran staffers, Bill told me cheerfully, "I guess it takes an Irishman to tell the truth."

By the time he was my editor, he had worked out a part-time arrangement—three days a week at the office—that enabled him to write at home on his own work for the other four. I marvelled that he was able then to bring to my work, among that of many others, such an intensity of care and even affection, while carrying in his mind the lineaments of his own luminous, wry, keenly felt short stories, and the novel *The Château*, and the book of personal history called *Ancestors*. All of his published novels but the first were written after 1936, when his association with *The New Yorker* began. I do not know all the other authors whose submissions he dealt with: John Cheever, certainly, and John O'Hara, when after an eleven years' sulk he began again to write short stories for the magazine. Vladimir Nabokov was in Bill's care for a number of English translations of his Russian short stories—an entire novel, *The Luzhin Defense*, was run in two installments. Eudora Welty and Frank O'Connor and Sylvia Townsend Warner were affectionate favorites, and I believe Mavis Gallant and the half-forgotten but ineffable Daniel Fuchs. L. E. Woiwode, now known as Larry, and Bill's own secretary, Elizabeth Cullinan, were among his younger writers. Bill enjoyed people with talent; people without talent, possibly, he enjoyed less. He could be witheringly dismissive of writers who didn't make his grade. And a striking feature of his fictional imagination is his loyalty, after over sixty years away, and an immense subsequent acquaintance, to the people who fondly loomed to him in the Lincoln of his boyhood.

I am in danger of straying from my topic, my experience of Maxwell as an editor. He made me feel cherished and yet held to a certain standard. He radiated the certainty that there *were* standards, that the good could be distinguished from the less good. His own quality, of being rare, rubbed off to a degree—an emboldening, exhilarating, powdery sparkle filled his vicinity, and a writer in his editorial charge was the lucky victim of a kind of ethereal contagion.

*

Brendan was the life of any party he attended, and where a party wasn't in progress he would create one. When I came to work for *The New Yorker* in the mid-Fifties, he loomed as the only gregarious man on the premises—the only one whose creativity hadn't demanded a sublimation of his social instincts. A tall, dark, and dashing stranger whose stream of spoken wit elevated his own black, not quite then beetling eyebrows in a frequent arc of delighted surprise, he took me in hand and organized luncheons where I could meet my fellow-workers. Irresistibly he would lead me off to the Blue Ribbon or some other long-since-vanished restaurant of the West Forties, where, in company with others whom he had flushed from their dusty nooks in the shy, shabby halls of the magazine, I would be enrolled in a midday feast of good will, a chamber music of drollery dominated by Brendan's rasping, cajoling, bantering voice. Though a Hartford upbringing and Yale education had left no trace of an Irish accent, his utterances had an Irish deliciousness, a pleasure in the speaking that prolonged the key phrases. As he aged, and his slender back became stooped and his noble nose even more beaked, he would strike into, as a kind of audible italics, an old crone's quaver. His animation spread; you felt cleverer, talking to Brendan. An eminently clubbable and public-spirited Manhattanite, he brought merriment to many a meeting that would otherwise have stayed staid.

His dazzling *joie de vivre* may have put into shadow his dedication to the life of the intellect and of art. He came to *The New Yorker* young, as a writer of short stories, and stayed as a jack of all trades—a "Talk of the Town" writer and rewriter, a reporter at large, and eventually a reviewer of drama and architecture. In his *Here at The New Yorker*, whose breeziness and irreverence were not entirely appreciated in these supposedly breezy, irreverent precincts, he describes his first stories, as submitted and accepted in 1936:

> It became evident that the editors of *The New Yorker* knew little about Catholics and especially about Catholics in religious orders, and that they were eager to read about them, as occupying a hitherto largely unexplored field of human conduct; this was lucky for me, because although I knew almost as little about nuns and priests as they did, I was feverishly eager to oblige them and was therefore ready to make up anything that I didn't know or was unable to discover.

Anyone who reads some of those early stories by Brendan—for example, "The Knife," a desolating sketch of faith's clash with reality—will see that he is, characteristically, making light of them. If he didn't take his own artistic gifts quite seriously enough, he was avidly alert to the power of art in general—of the architectural treasure largely unnoticed around him, of the Yeats poetry he quoted so readily, of paintings and writings well beyond the predictable range. He composed one of the few thoughtful appreciations of pornographic films—they made him happy, he wrote—and was a book reviewer of real ardor and verve. I am haunted still by several of his architectural metaphors, applied to books: of Faulkner's *A Fable* he said that it wasn't even the ruin of a good book, it was a papier-mâché ruin, and he likened John O'Hara's large novels to giant ancient earthworks that one trudges over without ever discerning their purpose. He more than once troubled to write a young fiction writer an encouraging note, in that lucid, florid penmanship which suggested an eighteenth-century hand. Indeed, he was an Enlightenment personality, exhilarated by the possibilities of liberation; like Voltaire, he mocked in defense of life. Learning now of his death at the premature age of eighty-three, I remember how he gave my elder son, back in 1956, his first pat on the head, while the boy was still in my wife's stomach.

NOTE *for an Exhibit of* New Yorker *cartoons at the Art Institute of Boston, January 28–March 8, 1993.*

I grew up, in a sense, within *New Yorker* cartoons—bending my mind around their outlines, blissfully losing myself in their clouds of half-tone wash. Wash in a Helen Hokinson, for instance, was a fitful, almost absent-minded matter of wandering dabbles, as timid as the tender, inquisitive hearts of her heroines; whereas in an Arno it came in solid liquid layers, two or three sharp tones of it, with edges straight as razors, snapping off of an irate colonel's back or underlining the thrust of a chorine's incredibly lateral bosom. In a Whitney Darrow, it darkened abstractly toward the edges, and in a Mary Petty or Alan Dunn (husband and wife, evidently drawing upon the same art supplies) it took the form of crayonning on textured paper. George Price, it seemed, kept running out of ink, and Sam Cobean occasionally let a wet overload thicken his lines. Now Koren and Chast build up their worlds with repeated nervous scratching, and Steig—like George Price, a survivor from my first pre-pubescent inklings of cartoon bliss—knocks ever harder at the rough door of surrealism, of Freudian *art brut*. But it all seemed art to me—dense conjurations of alternative universes, in almost any of which I hankered to dwell forever, if only as a squiggle of shading, or a plump easy chair indicated by six deft brushstrokes. Reality, after a youth spent in so intensely considered an environment, has always seemed a little thin, a little hasty in execution, a little less than finished.

MY CARTOONING: *Composed to garland a selection of my* Lampoon *cartoons published in* Hogan's Alley, *an Atlanta magazine devoted to comic art.*

I can't remember the moment when I fell in love with cartoons, I was so young. I still have a Donald Duck book, on oilclothy paper in big-print format, and remember a smaller, cardboard-covered book based on the animated cartoon *Three Little Pigs*. It was the intense stylization of those

images, with their finely brushed outlines and their rounded and buttony furniture and their faces so curiously amalgamated of human and animal elements, that drew me in, into a world where I, child though I was, loomed as a king, and where my parents and other grownups were strangers. I became an expert. Spread out on the floor with my crayons and colored pencils, I taught myself to copy cartoons—I can still do a serviceable Mickey Mouse—and by the age of six or so was copying many of the syndicated comic strips of the day: Popeye and his rubber-legged sweetheart, Alley Oop on his dinosaur, Barney Google, Dagwood, Dick Tracy. I don't believe I attempted the more naturalistic style of Milton Caniff and Alex Raymond and Hal Foster, but certainly I entered into their adventures, each panel like a separate door into the same magical large room.

The Disney cartoons at the movies, which my parents took me to from the age of three on, and which I began to attend alone at the age of six, composed another corner of this room, dazzlingly bright and busy. I recently acquired the video of *Snow White*, and the procession of dwarves home from the diamond mine, and the fluttering of the birds that shepherd Snow White through the forest, seemed as marvellous and poignant as when I first saw the movie in 1937, at the age of five. For a long time I dreamed of being a Disney animator, dreams fed by those documentary films of his which displayed his studio and revealed the details of animation's technology.

I copied comic-strip characters on plywood and cut them out with a coping saw; I scissored the strips out of the daily newspaper and made little books of them; I drew caricatures of my classmates; I became the class poster-maker. I sent fan letters to comic-strip artists and sometimes got back original strips in return. The arrival of *The New Yorker* at our house when I was eleven or so shifted my ambition toward single-gag magazine cartoons, which appeared in not only *The New Yorker* but *Collier's*, *The Saturday Evening Post*, and many lesser magazines. I was fourteen or fifteen when I first began to send out "roughs" to these same magazines; I even bought myself a rubber stamp with my name on it, since I had read that that was what the pros did. I didn't crack *The New Yorker*, but I did once sell (for five dollars) a dairyman's journal a cartoon of a milk truck with a running cow instead of a greyhound on it, and when I went to Harvard I was elected to the *Harvard Lampoon* on the strength of my cartooning.

The *Lampoon*, which had begun in the 1890s as an imitation of *Punch* and had imitated *Judge* and *Life* in the Twenties, by the Fifties was an imitation of *The New Yorker*, which suited me fine. A college publication, with its lazy and distracted staff, gives wonderful scope to the creative spirits willing to work. I wrote light verse and humorous prose as well as drew for the *Lampoon*, and occupied in turn all three literary offices— Narthex, Ibis, and President. All the cartoons and spot drawings here were published in its pages before 1954, and have lost something in the reproduction. The quality of halftone reproduction, as well as its expense, led one to rely on black-on-white, with shading laid in either by me with razor blade and transparent Benday or by the printer, over a blue wash. By the time I graduated in 1954 I was eighty-five-percent bent upon becoming a writer; it took fewer ideas, and I seemed to be better at it. There is less danger of smearing the ink. Also, one can continue to cartoon, in a way, with words; for whatever crispness and animation my writing has I give some credit to the cartoonist *manqué*.

CARTOON MAGIC: *An essay covering much the same territory, at greater length, in* The New Yorker.

In the Thirties and Forties, when I was growing up, the cartoonist occupied a place in the cultural hierarchy not far below that of the movie star and the inventor. Walt Disney, Al Capp, Peter Arno—who, now, could attain their celebrity with just pen and ink? I cut my teeth on blocks and rubber toys depicting Disney characters, illiterately pondered oil-cloth pages showing Donald Duck when he looked more like a gander, learned to read from a cardboard booklet telling the cautionary tale of the Three Little Pigs and the Big Bad Wolf, and climbed up through the comics section of the local paper into the slightly racier world of comic books and the single-image cartoons, usually captioned, in *Collier's, The Saturday Evening Post, Esquire,* and—much the best and most thought-provokingly adult—*The New Yorker.* Together, from chewable Disney artifact to decipherable Thurber scrawl, they formed a world that was realer to me than all but a few patches of the substantial world which had not been conjured up by cartoonists.

This wide world offers a child many sites for passionate involvement: the keyboard of a piano, for instance, or the workings of an automobile engine. By my teens I had friends who were clever in one or the other realm; one boy, years before we got our driver's licenses, could identify any make of car—cars were overwhelmingly of Detroit manufacture then—at a glance from a block or more away. He loved automobiles, and love breeds knowledge. I was able to identify all the cartoonists as they appeared in a magazine, which I rapidly leafed through upside down while my audience—usually an audience of one, and soon bored—confirmed me right-side up. Like trees to an arborist, cartoons have personalities whose recognition the informed mind attains before any conscious sorting-out of traits, just as we spot a known face, or even a certain swing of a familiar body, at a distance that blurs all details.

I loved cartoons—almost any cartoon that met a modest standard of professional finish—and studied them as if my salvation lay somewhere in their particulars of shading and penmanship. V. T. Hamlin, for instance, who drew the syndicated strip *Alley Oop*, had a deliberate, grid-like style of crosshatching that, mixed with the peculiar inverted proportions of his cavemen's legs and arms, signalled a special solidity in the progress of his dinosaur-studded panels. Hamlin, like Alex Raymond of *Flash Gordon* and Hal Foster of *Prince Valiant* and Milton Caniff of *Terry and the Pirates* and then *Steve Canyon*, seemed to be operating well within his artistic capacities, as opposed to Chester Gould of *Dick Tracy* and

Harold Gray of *Little Orphan Annie*, who I felt were drawing at the very limit of their skills, with a cozy, wooden consistency; Gould, in his doubts that he had made this or that detail clear, would sometimes enclose an enlargement within a sharply outlined balloon, with an arrow and a label saying "2-Way Wrist Radio" or "Secret Compartment for Cyanide." Fontaine Fox of *Toonerville Folks* and Percy Crosby of *Skippy*, on the other hand, worked with a certain inky looseness, a touch of impatience in their confident pen lines. This inky ease attained opulence in Al Capp's *Li'l Abner*, the lines of which experienced a voluptuous thickening when limning the curves of Daisy Mae or Moonbeam McSwine. Capp and Caniff and Will Eisner, who drew the bloody, vertiginous *Spirit* comic books, were virtuosos; closer to a child's heart, and containing the essence of cartoon magic, were the strips of strictly limited artistic means, like *Mutt and Jeff* and *Bringing Up Father* (Jiggs and Maggie)—holdovers from an earlier, vaudevillian era—and adventure strips whose implausibility was framed in an earnest stiffness of execution, such as *The Phantom* and *Mandrake the Magician*. Strikingly minimal, in that pre-*Peanuts* era, was Crockett Johnson's *Barnaby*, whose characters appeared in invariable profile and whose talk balloons were lettered not by hand but in a mechanical type. Crazy about cartoons, I wrote to cartoonists, care of their syndicates, begging for a free original strip; a heartening number of them obliged. My sample *Barnaby* strip slowly shed, over the years, its glued-on lettering.

At a certain votive stage I cut out favorite strips and made little long cardboard books of them, held together with those nail-like brass fasteners whose flat stem splits open, it always occurred to me, like a loose-jointed dancer's legs. In my passionate doting I cut cartoons out of magazines and pasted them in large scrapbooks, agonizing over which to choose when two were back to back—my first brush with editorial judgment. And of course I copied, copied onto paper and onto slick white cardboard, trying to master each quirk of these miniature universes. Li'l Abner's hair was always drawn with the parting toward the viewer, and Mickey Mouse's circular ears were never seen on edge, and Downwind, in Zack Moseley's *Smilin' Jack*, was always shown with his face averted, and Smokey Stover, in Bill Holman's *Krazy Kat*-ish slapstick, kept saying "Foo" apropos of nothing and drove vehicles that endlessly shed their nuts and bolts. God—the heat, the quest, the bliss of it—was in the details. The way the letters of POW! or SHAZAM! overlapped, the qualities of the clouds that indicated explosions or thoughts, the whirling Saturns and stars that accompanied a blow to the head, the variations played upon the talk balloon, that two-dimensional irruption into the

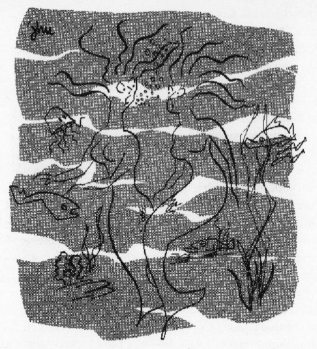

Example of Benday

panel's three-dimensional space, invisible to its inhabitants and yet critical to their intercourse—all this had to be studied, imitated, absorbed. The studying occurred mostly on the floor, my head lifted up on my elbows but not very high. When I drew, too, my nose had to be close to the paper, though I was not generally nearsighted. But the *entering in* required close examination, as though I was physically worming my way into those panels, those lines fat and slender, those energetic zigzags, those shading dots I learned to call Benday.

A craft lore existed, of pen nibs, fine brushes, blue pencils, artgum erasers, whiteout, and Higgins India ink (which came in broad-bottomed bottles that nevertheless could be knocked over, as several indelible stains on my family's carpets testified). The prestige of cartooning during the Depression and the Forties was such that one did not have to travel farther than the variety store and the adjacent camera shop in the center of our small Pennsylvania town to find most of the necessary equipment. Bristol board (two- or three-ply, more flexible and ink-accepting than the slick poster board children use in school), and a cardboard whose rippled surface would turn Conté crayon into halftones, and scratchboard, whose clayey top layer could be scraped to make white on black—for those, one

had to travel to the nearby city of
Reading, where a number of art-
supply stores, some combined with a
framer's shop, offered their wares to
the artsy-craftsy crowd. Black-and-
white cartoons were reproduced by
means of line cuts, which failed to
register washes and pencilled shadings. A great deal of technology
went into creating the impression of
gray; crosshatching, stippling, and
crayon textures could be done by
hand, and then there were sheets
of Benday in many patterns, to be
laid on and selectively cut away.
There was even a treated cardboard,
Craftint, that, depending on which
of two chemicals was brushed on,
produced fine stripes or a cross-

Example of Benday

hatch, thus supplying two degrees of halftone. My high-school year-
book, for which I did many illustrations—more than anyone asked for—
contains examples of this mechanical hatching, and of most of the other
techniques my apprenticeship claimed acquaintance with.

I drew not for the sake of drawing but to get into metal—to have
the work of my hand be turned into zinc "cuts" and by this means

Example of Conté crayon

printed. The first cuts made from a
drawing of mine—a Christmas
card, perhaps, portraying the family
dog, or a caricature done for the
class-play program—were to me
potent objects, pieces of power. In
the alchemical symbology of those
hard decades, and nowhere more
so than in the industrial cities of
Pennsylvania, metal was power—
steel rails, iron beams, lead bullets,
great greased knitting machines
twittering with a thousand nickel-
plated needles. The basement
"machine shop," with a metal lathe,
was commonplace in the town, and
here and there an adept set up a

Example of Craftint

gun shop in his back-yard garage. The toy tanks and battleships and dive-bombers that simulated the distant, headlined war were metal, though of a cheap sort that would bend and break in your hands. When you paid a school visit to the city newspaper, the Lino-typers would place in your palm a still-hot lead slug, bearing your name backwards. When, in high school, I became a summer copy-boy for the same newspaper, I saw how the comic strips arrived from the syndicates in the form of bundled paper matrices—a stiff pulpy colorless paper like that used in egg cartons—and how these rough (but legible, the reverse of a reverse) intaglios were filled with hot metal, and the cooled lead rectangles were locked into forms and recast into curved plates, which were bolted onto the presses and thunderously rolled to produce the daily comic pages. A cartoonist partook of this process at the tentative, scratchy, inky outset, and then was swept up and glorified by a massive, ponderous miracle of reproduction. To get a toehold in this mighty metal world—that was my ambition, the height of my hope.

The August 1950 issue of the soon-to-be-defunct magazine *Flair* (it had holes in the cover) contained an article about the *Harvard Lampoon*, including photographs of the young, crew-cut editors and the curious mock-Dutch building, plus some sample cartoons and verses in a little booklet stapled into this "College Review Issue." It all looked inviting and reassuring, since I was scheduled to go to Harvard the very next month. Early in my freshman year I carried a batch of my cartoons down to the *Lampoon* building, there where Mount Auburn Street meets Bow at an acute angle: an ornate little brick flatiron fronted by a tower with a sort of cartoon face and, on its hat of roof tiles, a much-stolen copper ibis. In due course some of my drawings were printed in the magazine and I was accepted for membership. The *Lampoon*, I was too ignorant an out-sider to realize, was a social club, with a strong flavor of Boston Brahmin-ism and alcoholic intake; to me it was simply a magazine for which I wanted to work. This I was allowed to do, especially as the upperclass-men year by year graduated and the various editorial offices fell to me. Though Harvard did little to attract cartoonists, in fact there were four on the *Lampoon* in 1950— Fred Gwynne, Lew Gifford, Doug Bunce, and Charlie Robinson—who seemed to me much my betters in skill and sophistication. Fred Gwynne, a multi-talented tall man who went on to become an actor best known for television's *Car 54, Where Are You?* and *The Munsters*, drew with a Renaissance chiaroscuro and mastery of anatomy; Bunce had a fine Tennielesque line and Gifford, who later made his career in television animation, a carefree flowing brushstroke and a habit of three-node noses. I tried to measure up to their examples, and cartooned abundantly for the *Lampoon*—in some issues over half the artwork was mine—but the budding cartoonist in me, exposed to what I

felt were superior talents, suffered a blight; my light verse and sup-posedly humorous prose felt more viable. By graduation I had pretty well given up on becoming a car-toonist. It took too many ideas, and one walked in too many foot-steps. Writing seemed, in my inno-cence of it, a relatively untrafficked terrain.

When I think of my brief car-tooning heyday I see myself at the desk in my narrow room on the fifth floor of Lowell House, work-ing late at night under a hot goose-neck lamp. An undergraduate lives in a succession of rooms, and I drew in all of mine, but this atticlike cub-byhole, occupied during my junior year, comes to mind as *mon atelier*. My nose inches from the garishly illuminated Bristol board, my lower lip sagging in the intensity of my concentration, a cigarette smoking in an ashtray near my eyes, I am "inking in"—tracing the lightly pencilled lines, trying to imbue them with a graceful freedom while searching out, in this final limning, the contour being described. The nervous glee of drawing is such that I sometimes laugh aloud, alone. I would get so excited by the process, so eager to admire the result, that I frequently smeared the still-wet lines with my hand. This would put me in mind of a tip I had read of in my high-school days: a successful cartoonist advised aspirants to the art, "If you're not sure the ink is dry, rub your sleeve over it." It had taken some days before I realized that this was not a tip but a joke.

Or, the precarious inking done, I am warily slicing, with a lethal single-edge Treet razor blade, the boundaries of a patch of Benday, or applying, with an annoyingly gummed-up little brush, whiteout to an errant line or a stray blot. Years before, I used to study my collection of begged comic strips, marvelling at the frequency of whiteout touches. Even pros err. My soul hovers, five stories up, in the happiness of creation, the rapture of conjuring something out of nothing. All around me, my fellow-students are silent, sleeping or communing with the printed page; only I, in this vicinity, am carving a little window into a universe that, an hour ago, had not been there at all.

I dislike drawing now, since it makes me face the fact that I draw no better, indeed rather worse, than I did when I was twenty-one. Drawing is sacred to me, and I don't like to see it inferiorly done. A drawing can feel perfect, in a way prose never does, and a poem rarely. Language is intrinsically approximate, since words mean different things to different people, and there is no material retaining ground for the imagery that words generate in one brain or another. When I drew, the line was exactly as I made it, just so, down to the tremor of excitement my hand may have communicated to the pen; and thus it was reproduced. Up to the midpoint of my writing career, I sometimes tried—most elaborately in the poem "Midpoint"—to bring this visual absoluteness, this two-dimensional quiddity, onto a page of print with a pictorial device. But the attempt was futile, and a disfigurement, really. Only the letters themselves, originally drawn with sticks and styluses and pens, and then cast into metal fonts, whose forms are now reproduced by twinkling electronic processes, legitimately touch the printed page with cartoon magic.

CHRISTMAS CARDS: *A memory produced for* The New Yorker's *Christmas issue of 1997.*

How strange it is—gut-wrenchingly strange—to realize that your parents, in a snapshot taken by memory, are younger not only than you now but than your own children. If I was seven or eight on a certain Christmas that I remember, my father would have been thirty-nine or forty, and my mother thirty-five or -six. A couple of kids, really, living in her parents' house with their only child, in a Depression that war's excitement and mounting public debt hadn't yet lifted. The taste of Christmas in the little Pennsylvania town of Shillington—one of the more penetrating in my life's bolted meal—was compounded of chocolate-flavored piety, as sweetly standardized as Hershey's Kisses, and a tart refreshed awareness of where one stood on the socio-economic scale.

Since at that latitude white Christmases were a rarity, the proper atmosphere had to be created within the front parlor: an evergreen tree more or less richly laden with decorations brought down from the attic; beneath the tree, a "Christmas yard," a miniature landscape of cotton snow and mirror ponds and encircling railroad tracks; a heap of wrapped presents, which at my age of seven or eight had not yet quite shed the possibility, like a glaze, that an omniscient, fast-moving Santa Claus had personally deposited them. Though we had the tree, our neighbors' trees were in my impression bushier, pressing against the ceiling and crowding the front windows, and more sumptuously hung with reflective balls, colored lights, and glittering tinsel. We didn't bother with tinsel; my mother, I believe, found it vulgar and messy. Though we had the Christmas yard, with a lovable blue Lionel train—engine, coal car, and two or three passenger cars, going around and around in tooting obedience to a cubic black transformer—friends of mine, or friends of theirs, had entire basements dedicated to mountainous, suburbanized mazes of tracks, switchoffs, tunnels, and toy stations. Our yard had a single tunnel, through a papier-mâché mountain whose snowy crest was approached up green-sprayed sides diagonally dented by what I understood to be sheep paths. Our pond was square, and any illusion of landscape fomented by the toy cows and cottages on its cotton banks clashed with the reality of my own Gargantuan, freckled face looking up from it when I peeked in. Though we had the presents, they seemed less numerous and luxurious than presents bestowed up and down Philadelphia Avenue, in houses externally more modest than ours.

On the Christmas that I painfully remember, one of the presents was a double deck of playing cards in a pretty box, whose gray surface had a fuzzy texture, and whose paper drawer was pulled out by a silken tab. I had unwrapped the box and had assumed it was for me, until my father's voice, which was almost never raised to me in disapproval or correction, gently floated down from above with the suggestion that the cards were a present from him to my mother. This made sense: one of her habits—the most alarming habit she had, indeed—was to play solitaire at night at the dining table, under the stained-glass chandelier. "The weary gambler," she would intone theatrically, "stakes her all," as she doggedly laid out the cards in their rows. Now her voice descended to me, saying that the cards were for all of us to share; and it was true, we did play cards, three-handed pinochle, and the box said PINOCHLE on it. Nevertheless, I was humiliated, as deeply as only a child can be, to be caught trying to appropriate her present. At the same time I thought that if there had been more presents I would not have made such a mistake. And I was afflicted by the paltriness of this present from my father to his wife. At least, I am afflicted now, or have been the hundreds or thousands of times I have remembered this incident. The something pathetic about our Christmases, the something that strived and failed to live up to Shillington's Noël ideal, was bared; a pang went through me that preserved the moment in memory's amber.

An elemental, mournful triangle seems sketched: my grandparents, those distant, grave, friendly adjuncts, are absent from the room as I remember it. My parents are above me, the presents shorn of wrapping paper are around me, the three-rail Lionel tracks are by my knees, the tree with its resiny scent presses close. I have no memory of what I did receive that Christmas—the wooden skis, perhaps, with leather-strap bindings that never held, or a shiny children's classic that would never be read. I feel, for a moment, the triangle flip; through the little velvety box of cards I see my parents in their poverty, their useless gentility, their unspoken plight of homelessness, their clinging to each other through such tokens of affection, and through me. I become in my memory their parent, looking down and precociously grieving for them.

Captured in this recollection, I want to move off and look out the window for relief, at the vacant lot next to our house, at the row houses opposite. If there was no white Christmas, there was at least a public Christmas, a free ten-o'clock cartoon show at the Shillington movie theatre, followed by a throng of us children lining up at the town hall to receive a box of chocolates from the hands of Sam Reich, the fat one of the three town policemen. I remember eating these chocolates, trying to avoid the ones with cherries at their centers, while walking up Philadelphia Avenue with the other children as they noisily boasted of their presents—I seeming to be, as one sometimes is in a dream, tongue-tied.

A RESPONSE *to being asked, by the* New York Times Magazine, *in connection with a special issue on the American Child, for "an account of some childhood transgression you committed."*

In a sense, all of life—every action—is a transgression. A child's undulled sensitivity picks up the cosmic background of danger and guilt. A child is in constant danger of doing something wrong. I was most severely punished, as I fallibly recall it, for being late in getting back home. At least once and perhaps several times my mother, her face red with fury, pulled a switch from the stand of suckers at the base of the backyard pear tree and whipped me on the back of the calves with it, when I had been, let's say, a half-hour late in returning from the playground or some friend's house a few blocks away. Fear for my safety was, I suppose now, behind this stinging discipline, but at the time it seemed mixed up with her fear that, by playing late with some other boy, I would be on the road to homosexuality. She didn't like to see me wrestling with other boys, even on our own property. No doubt she was right, taking "homosexual" in its broadest meaning, about young male roughhousing, but to my pre-pubescent self her anxieties seemed exaggerated. She didn't like to see my father, a six-foot-two schoolteacher with, as far as I could see, normal tendencies, put his hand on his hip, either. But, whatever the psychological roots of her (as I saw it, with eyes full of tears) overreaction, it did its work on my superego: I have an unconquerable dread of being late for appointments or returning home later than promised, and what modest heterosexual adventures were mine in adulthood received the slight extra boost, from deep in my subconscious, of my mother's approval. Better this than one more game of Parcheesi over at Freddy Schreuer's, as the clock ticked sinfully toward five-thirty.

We were Lutherans, and, as American Protestant denominations go, Lutherans were rather soft on transgression. In Luther's combative, constipated sense of the human condition, there was not much for it but to pray for faith and have another beer. This side of the cosmic background and of my mother's sexual preferences, I didn't really think I could do much wrong. Normal childhood sadisms—bug-torture, teasing, fishing—repelled me, and I was all too inclined to believe the best of my cultural-political context, from President Roosevelt down.

A child's transgressions are often, I believe, simple misunderstandings of how the world is put together. Once, attending a movie with my parents, I took the chewing gum from my mouth and put it on the seat where my father, a second later, sat, ruining forever (my impression was) the trousers of his new suit. The sense of a grievous financial mishap, verging on ruin, permeated the days afterwards, and I had no answer to the question, *Why did I do it?* The answer seemed to be that I had wanted to get the chewing gum out of my mouth and had no sense of the consequences of my placing it on the seat beside me. I certainly meant my father no harm; he was mildness itself toward me, and an awareness of his financial fragility dominated our threadbare household.

Yet the other transgression that comes to mind also threatened him, though remotely, it appears now. Shillington, Pennsylvania, was a small town, where everything impinged. He was a schoolteacher, and his domain began just beyond our back yard, across an alley and a narrow cornfield. The school grounds included the yellow brick high school, several accessory buildings, a football field encircled by a cinder track, a baseball diamond with grass and bleachers and wire backstop, and a softball field that was little more, off season, than a flat piece of dirt with a dead grass outfield. Early one spring, exulting perhaps in my March birthday, I was riding my fat-tired Elgin bicycle in this familiar terrain, alone, and thought to pedal across the dirt infield. I was stupidly slow to realize that the thawing earth was mud and that I was sinking inches down with every turn of the wheel. Within some yards, I could pedal no farther, and dismounted and walked the bike back to firmer *terra*; only then did I see, with a dull thud of the stomach, that I had left a profound, insolently wandering gouge in the infield, from beyond third base to behind the pitcher's mound. It looked as if a malevolent giant had run his thumb through the clay. I sneaked home, scraped the dried crust from my tires, and hoped it would all be as a dream. Instead, my father began to bring home from school news of this scandal, the vandalized softball field. The higher-ups were incensed and the search for the culprit was on. He would be fired, I reasoned, if the culprit were revealed as his son, and we would all go to the county poorhouse—which, conveniently, was situated only two blocks away.

I forget how it turned out—my best memory is that I never confessed, and that the atrocious scar remained on the softball field until the advent of dusty summer. How old was I? Old enough to propel a bicycle with some force, and yet so young that I did not grasp the elemental fact of spring mud. How blind we are, as we awkwardly push outward into the world! Such a sense of transgression and fatal sin clings to this (in its way, innocent) incident that I set down my confession with trepidation, fearful that the Shillington authorities will at last catch up to me, though I live hundreds of miles away, my father has been dead for over twenty years, and the last time I looked at the softball field it was covered with Astroturf.

A RESPONSE *to a request, from* Life, *to remember Pearl Harbor.*

Pearl Harbor and John Kennedy's assassination: if you were alive at the time, you remember where you were. On December 7, 1941, I was three months short of ten years old, and my parents and I were visiting my father's sister's house in Greenwich, Connecticut. We had come from afar, from eastern Pennsylvania. It was a Sunday, and some kind of family gathering, slow-moving and stifling to my puerile nerves, had been convened. There is, in the blurred snapshots of my recollection, a sunporch, and a radio, and toward the end of the short day's afternoon, in a haze of digestive tobacco smoke, a sudden amount of murmuring among the tall men of our little Updike tribe. It is to my uncle Arch, my father's red-headed older brother, who lived in Florida, that I credit the announcement, in his deep Southern-tinged rumble of a voice, that the Japanese had attacked a place, on the other side of the world, called Pearl Harbor. A dark wind swept in among the trousered knees of my kinfolk, chilling me with the certainty that things had changed, drastically. We were under attack. We were in danger. Not even the assembled male might of my immediate clan, and the associated plump mothers off in the kitchen, could protect me from this fearful alteration in the national atmosphere. Not until word reached me, twenty-two years later, while seated in a dentist's chair, that President Kennedy had been shot, would any news event give me such a sensation of pervasive upheaval.

The American home front, of course, was a halcyon place compared with that of Britain, or Russia, or, as the tide turned, that of Japan or Germany. Only the coasts were even scratched by a hint of action—of submarine sightings, of rumored lobbed shells. Yet in the mind of a child the fear was real enough, fear and its natural antidote combativeness. There were mock–air raids, in which my father patrolled the darkened streets in a white helmet, and the rest of us huddled on the stair landing, safe from hypothetical flying shards of glass, listening for the buzz of the Luftwaffe, which we knew from newsreels. Though the newsreels and newspapers aimed not to demoralize us with the bad news of the war's first year, and implacably sounded the steely-voiced call to battle, there was no disguising the fiery losses and underwater burials of that December Sunday, or the fact that we of the United States had now followed most of the world into a realm where death, destruction, sacrifice, valor, and the possibility of defeat were the norm. There were screaming black headlines every day, and mountainous collections of tin cans and scrap metal on the schoolgrounds, and little flags of blue and gold stars appearing in our neighbors' front windows, signifying boys not much older than myself who had gone off to the war.

For those of us too young or old to fight, there was the exhilaration of a universally shared and unambiguously depicted purpose. We were playing a vast game whose scores came in from all the corners of the globe and whose other players—the monkeyish "Japs," the laughable maniac Hitler and his gang of malevolent grotesques—made vivid the post-office walls, the magazine racks, the school bulletin boards. We were allowed and even encouraged to hate, to nurse dreams of annihilation and counter-blitzkrieg. The dips into violence common in a child's improvised, ill-policed world—vaguely disgraceful in peacetime, like a child's excursions into sexuality—suddenly had adult sanction; with our little lead tanks and rubber fighter planes we aped the actual heroics that our President was lauding and our popular arts were glorifying.

Pearl Harbor had welded us, in one Sabbath moment of blazing affront, into a fighting nation; the thirteen colonies didn't fight as whole-heartedly for their Revolution as we did for islands in the Pacific as obscure, before 1941, as pockmarks on the moon. A gentleman older than I once shocked me by telling me that the Depression was a fine time to be alive in, if one only had a little money. Nor was World War II a bad time, if one was personally out of danger. It was exciting and righteous (a rare combination); everybody was in on it; and we won. Perhaps a pre-adolescent boy, thirteen years old by the time of V-J Day, was ideally situated to experience it—young enough to swallow all the propaganda, yet old enough to enjoy *See Here, Private Hargrove* and Betty Grable's legs. Meat and butter were rationed, but victory gardens burgeoned. Major-league baseball almost called it quits, but playground ballgames continued, and school, and Hollywood movies. You even, while the newspaper nightmare raged, grew a few inches.

My own family was significantly bucked up; my father, a veteran of the First World War, was a natural leader on the home front, and my mother came out of her shell and went to the local fire station as a plane-watcher, playing solitaire with a deck of cards that instead of kings and queens carried the silhouettes of enemy and friendly aircraft. The idea of my mother calling out the antiaircraft guns was strangely reassuring. And she went to work in a parachute factory, where she wore her hair up in a bandana like Rosie the Riveter. As a side effect of the war effort, more money came into the household. The scary wind I had felt down among the Updike knees had blown us some immediate good. Still, it would be wrong for a young peace-lover of today to believe that even children loved the war. We read *Life*, or at least looked at the pictures; we knew horrible things were happening across the oceans; the gold stars that the honor rolls kept sprouting could have been us. When, on an August

Tuesday, the Pacific war ended, it was like being let out of an especially drab, confining, and menace-ridden school.

In this school, however, we had learned to trust our nation. The Kennedy assassination, and the aimless violence, domestic and foreign, which that event trailed through the Sixties, tended to implant distrust, a suspicion of machination and moral chaos at the top. Those of us who still remember Pearl Harbor are by and large more simpleminded. We carry an image of the United States as a wounded lamb that responded like a lion; we believe that this country is, when it needs to be, terrific.

REFLECTIONS ON RADIO *conjured up for* Media Exchange, *Vol. II, no. 2 (Summer 1991).*

In my childhood and youth, radio was everywhere—in the barber shop, at the dentist's, and on its own little table in the parlor off the living room—a dome-topped brown Philco with an orange dial. Radio kept you company, but it wasn't as possessive as television. It opened you up, instead of closing you down. The fiction of my contemporary Philip Roth brims with mentions of the *Jack Benny Show* and other such half-hours of comedy and adventure that fed the fantasies and strengthened the comedic senses of young Americans and old. Roth, in fact, immediately after writing *Portnoy's Complaint* composed a kind of parody of those old radio shows; titled "On the Air," it appeared in the paperback *American Review* but has yet to make its way into hard covers. "Too disgusting," Roth has explained in an interview; it did veer off weirdly into obscenity and violence, wallowing in all that was tastefully omitted from the public airwaves and yet revealing how deeply those old radio voices thrust into our heads.

Prime time was Sunday night, beginning at seven with Jack Benny, Mary Livingston, Rochester, Dennis Day, and all the gang, then dipping into the less frenzied comedy of Phil Harris and his wife, Alice Faye (Forties radio had a prophetic number of wives functioning under their maiden names), and then rising at eight to the hilarities of Edgar Bergen and Charlie McCarthy, who were the same person, a ventriloquist and his dummy. After that, I don't know what happened, for by then I was sent to bed, fairly radioactive with absorbed roentgens of Hollywood energy. Weekday evenings, there were the Lone Ranger galloping off in a thunder of coconut shells and the *William Tell* Overture, and the Green Hornet buzzing about, and the Shadow with his scary knowing baritone, and *Inner Sanctum*, which opened with a viciously creaking door, and *I Love a*

Mystery, which seemed somehow to be taking place, often, in a cave full of chirping monkeys. Or were they bats or parakeets? Memory plays tricks, after all these intervening decades of talk shows and rock-and-roll, but there is no forgetting that this was *entertainment*, narrative entertainment that exercised the ears and the mind.

To engage the imagination art must leave something out: painting leaves out sound and the third dimension, sculpture leaves out (usually) movement and color, music leaves out vision, written fiction and poetry appeal to our ability to concoct imagery out of alphabetic sequences. The radio, notoriously, plugs into one human sense, amid the distractions of household and highway; yet, freed of the tyranny of visual mimesis, how easily its narratives soar and plunge, defying gravity with a whistle of speed, constructing Aladdin's cave out of a few sighs into an echo chamber, inciting the mind to build palaces, raceways, herds of shuffling beasts, perilous heights. Edgar, in *King Lear*, is a kind of radio dramatist as he plants blind Gloucester on the edge of an imaginary cliff: "Come on, sir, here's the place; stand still. How fearful / And dizzy 'tis to cast one's eyes so low! / The crows and choughs that wing the midway air / Show scarce so gross as beetles." Indeed, most of the Western world's greatest drama—in ancient Greece and the era of Shakespeare—was done like radio plays, with nothing but the actors' voices to conjure up the scenery.

It is a cultural loss, then, that for whatever nexus of reasons narrative radio has all but vanished in this country, taking from writers an opportunity to create drama without the confining overhead of stage and screen productions, and from listeners an opportunity for the kind of aesthetic experience that, fifty years ago, kept millions listening.

A REMINISCENCE *offered in celebration of the city of Reading's bicenquinquagenary (250th) birthday in 1998.*

When I was a Shillington boy, Reading was where the trolleys went; it was where my mother worked (at Pomeroy's) and where, on Saturday mornings, as I grew older, I was allowed to cruise the five-and-tens on Penn Square for Big Little Books and the thrilling auras of consumer culture, Forties style. I began, as I remember, at McCrory's at the corner of Penn and Fifth and worked my way up, through Woolworth's and maybe another, to Kresge's at Sixth. It took most of the morning, this browsing through the aisles, with its occasional expenditure of a dime, taking care to leave in my pocket seven cents for the trolley ride home.

But my most vivid memories of Reading come later, when we had moved from Shillington to Plowville, and I had a summer job as a copy boy at the *Reading Eagle*. One of my duties was to take breakfast orders and by eight o'clock go out to the diner on Penn near Fourth Street and bring back a box of highly particularized coffees and doughy goodies for the editorial staff. The great thoroughfare at that hour would have just begun to stir; the stores were not yet open, there was a morning freshness on the wide sidewalks, and the splendor of the urban vista up Penn to where the Pagoda presided on its mountaintop seemed peculiarly mine to enjoy. I have never forgotten that strange pride, of being, temporarily, in my teens, in shirtsleeves on a summer morning, a citizen of Reading, part of its workings as they were poised at the beginning of another day. I was a tiny cog, but turning; the coffees in their paper cups were hot on my arm as I hurried back; this was city, this was life.

A RESPONSE *to the* London Observer's *assurance that "it would be lovely if you could choose an hour of day and write about it in some way."*

At eleven in the morning, the day is young but not too young. It is on its feet; its coltish wobbles and blinks are outgrown. This is the hour, if ever, for getting down to business. In my own work rhythms, it is when, breakfast absorbed, the mail answered, all procrastinatory maneuvers executed, I am at last covering blank paper with words that matter, at least to me and perhaps to others eventually. If one is a tourist, it is the hour when everything is open; the fresco, the pyramid, the museum, the cathedral, the expensive shops are delightfully receptive to investigation. The first time I came to England, it was on a British liner. How surprising and welcome were the bells to elevenses—hot bouillon and soda crackers served on the tipping deck, high sun gleaming on the polished brass and spray-wet rails! Eleven a.m. is the hour for optimists, when much remains to be done, yet a healthy bite has been taken from the day.

Two ANSWERS *to the question of why I live in New England—the first, for the Internet Home Page of a friend of a friend, and the second for* USAir Magazine, *under the title of "Home."*

My then wife and I came to the North Shore, in the spring of 1957, for a variety of reasons. We had once spent a few days in Ipswich, and had liked the great beach and the general feeling of the town—it was within reach of Boston but not really a suburb, a small town big enough to hide in, and to find friends in. We were leaving New York City and my thought was to get far enough away so that the site wasn't part of Greater New York, including all of Connecticut, but not so far that I couldn't get back on occasion. Logan Airport's being on the north side of the Mystic River has turned into another good reason to live on the North Shore. Others are: the commuter line; the two hours' distance to the New Hampshire mountains; the near presence of the delightfully historic city of Salem and the beautiful peninsula of Cape Ann; the absence of the kind of heavy tourism that makes Cape Cod a summer brawl. A certain coolness in the air, weatherwise and peoplewise, that puts roses into our cheeks and a spring in our step. It has proved to be an area in which a solitary free-lance writer can do his work and enjoy his leisure.

*

We have one home, the first, and leave that one.
The having and leaving go on together.

I wrote these lines nearly forty years ago, in a poem for the bicentennial of the founding of my home town of Shillington, Pennsylvania. I was already, in 1958, a resident of Massachusetts, north of Boston, and here I still reside. I had come to New England as a college student, and after a few years in old England and New York City, I returned, with my young family, as an experiment. My instinct was that the region, where I had no kin or literary colleagues, offered living space. In polleny Pennsylvania, I had suffered hayfever; along New England's rocky shore, I could breathe. In New York, I had felt crowded, physically and spiritually; in Ipswich, Massachusetts, there was elbow room, writing room. Like all those who more or less voluntarily leave home, I was looking to create a new self.

And yet I can't say I became a New Englander. At Harvard I had learned the right costume—tweed jacket, chinos, button-down shirt— and the proper polite, ironical manner, but my accent marked me, among the flat "a"s and dropped "r"s of my neighbors, as an outsider. This suited me: a writer is an outsider. I paid my taxes, served on local committees, sent my children to the public schools, and mingled with the indigenes. But it all—the beaches, the marshes, the mountains, the colonial buildings, the Puritan houses, the crisp salt tang in the air—had for my innermost self the bright unreality of a theme park. When I went back to muggy, doughy, hilly, industry-ridden Pennsylvania, that was reality. The fields were bigger, the trees grew taller, even the road-building equipment was on a superior, non-playful scale. The accent, heavy on the consonants and slow on the vowels, sounded deeply right, trustworthy, earth-solid. Thus had it sounded in my infant ears, and sounded still. My home town of Shillington was especially familiar—the brick row houses, the snug grid of streets (which my grandfather had helped pave), the yellow-brick high school (where my father had taught), the gritty alleys where I had scuffed along in my high-top sneakers, the concrete retaining walls, the stained-glass fanlights that locked among their floral patterns the unalterable number of each house. Little had changed. Every block held a memory. This was the real me, home again. Yet after three days my hayfever would kick in, along with the realization that I had no real business here, among these tight streets and hazy cornfields.

Returned to, Massachusetts would seem wonderfully scattered, ragged, crooked, various, pretty, and open. It was not spacious on the map, but held glorious amounts of room for improvisation. Here I was improvising my life. I still get lost in Boston and the inscrutable suburbs to the west of it. I still haven't visited the Science Museum, or Plymouth Rock, or the New Bedford Whaling Museum. From my fifth home in the region I look out across Massachusetts Bay toward a low blue strip that I think is Hull, but I'm not sure. When I fly back into Logan Airport, as often as I have done it, I can never sort out the geography beneath me. Yet what I do recognize—the Hancock Tower, the neck to Nahant—is precious to me, as wisdom acquired rather than received. After nearly forty years, I still enjoy the exhilarating disorientation of a tourist. We are all homeless to a degree, living on biological terms we did not create, on a planet merely for rent. "The having and leaving go on together." New England, if not my first home, is where I have, with a daily satisfaction and gratitude, made myself at home.

INTRODUCTION TO *Concerts at Castle Hill: John Updike's Middle Initial Reviews Local Music in Ipswich, Massachusetts, from 1961 to 1965 (Lord John Press, 1993).*

In 1957, my wife, two young children, and I moved from New York City to Ipswich, Massachusetts; in 1961 my friend William Stix Wasserman, Jr., bought the *Ipswich Chronicle* and I volunteered, as a favor and a lark, to review for his newspaper the local concerts given, under changeable auspices, at the hilltop, seaview mansion built in 1928 by Chicago plumbing plutocrat Richard T. Crane. I signed myself H.H., doubling my middle initial.

Castle Hill was one of the oldest place-names in Ipswich, dating from a

1637 deed. Crane's estate, which took on the name, had been a public reservation since the 1950s; concerts could be held on the broad allée that sloped down toward the ocean, or in the more secluded outdoor space of the Italian Garden, or in the wider enclosure of the Casino, a filled-in swimming-pool area flanked by changing-houses, or in one of the first-floor rooms of the Great House itself—a mammoth medley of architectural elements from English mansions, including four rooms imported from Hogarth House in London and a library from the Earl of Essex's Casiobury Park, with carvings by Grinling Gibbons. Castle Hill was the grandest thing in town, and the summer gave us townfolk a rare excuse to go visit it.

We were, the Updikes and their friends, young marrieds, with tans hard-won on the sands of Crane Beach, Mr. Crane's other great benefaction to the landscape. For the concerts, we would arrive around six and picnic on the grassy slopes looking down on that same beach as the crowds thinned and the sun lowered and the sea turned a deeper blue. We would spread our blankets and open our wicker hampers and plastic coolers and pop our bottles of champagne and white wine. The young wives wore summer dresses and the young husbands seersucker jackets; everyone at that season of life was leggy and toothy and, as the wine sank in, giddy. From the back terrace of the Great House two bronze griffins sculpted by Paul Manship and given to the Cranes by the workmen on this house, to bring it luck, gazed down an allée bestrewn with concert-goers and lined with Norway spruces and grayish classical statues some of whose noses and toes had been lost to four decades of New England weather; the view ended with a little panel of sea and sky, like a two-tone blue door. It was a glorious sight, and a fine proud thing it felt to give an arm to one's lady and promenade, as evening descended and the mosqui-toes swarmed, across the grass toward musical entertainment.

We had been coming to concerts since coming to Ipswich—enchanted, precious, string-quartet concerts on a green wooden stage in the Italian Garden, the Samuel Barlow–introduced series that I more than once hark back to in these reviews as a golden era. It was golden in the sense that the series' annual deficit was faithfully covered by a check written by a North Shore dowager of discreet anonymity. Her largesse had ceased by 1961, the year of George Wein's managership, when I first started to review. After 1965, the concerts gradually fell into a desuetude from which they were eventually rescued by Thomas Kelly, the organist of the Episcopal church and an expert on music of the Renaissance. Purcell's "Queen Mary's Birthday Ode" was performed in August of 1972, in con-nection with that year's Seventeenth-Century Day—a tour of the town's historic houses—and summers of spirited semi-professionalism and musical esoterica followed, under Kelly's irrepressible leadership. The series now persists in a thoroughly professional way, but it's been many a summer since I attended. My concertgoing belonged to a youthful, excitable time of life—a time of folly, I could almost say—of which these twenty-two reviews, culled from moldering *Chronicle*s, are a foolish residue.

What made me think—I, who through years of childish piano lessons had evinced utterly no musical aptitude, and in the adult years since had remained signally ignorant of and indifferent to classical music—that I could or should review these concerts? Well, it was a small town, with few writers in it, and I was willing, as a form of preening. Rereading these texts, with their arrogant breeziness and callow grandiosity of assertion, I could scarcely believe that the author was, at the same time, in New York and elsewhere, a respected writer, with some published novels and many short stories to his credit, and furthermore a book reviewer careful and thoughtful enough for *The New Yorker*'s refined pages. H.H. is a local persona, batting these out for free, for a friend's newspaper, for friends to read. Several letters complained to the *Chronicle* of H.H.'s irrelevancies and jocularities, his insensitivity and censoriousness. Indeed I was, amid all my carefree asides on the weather, the audience, and the great issues of the day, surprisingly censorious. And my complaints become ever more detailed and confident as I go on; by the time I reach Peter Serkin, you might have supposed me a vacationing virtuoso, relaxing his supple fingers on the typewriter keyboard. Either I had an invincibly tin ear and basically resisted all musical performance, or else I was, those nights fragrant with sea air, crushed grass, and insect repellent, listening harder to music than ever before or since.

Mosquitoes went for the ankles—a torment for the bare-legged women, but no treat for the men, either, in their thin dress socks. There were stars overhead, and moon-gilded clouds. An occasional snore would arise in the dark, and the purr of a stray car creeping, with its interloping headlights, down the long Castle Hill driveway. Scribbling notes on the printed program, bantering in whispers with my companions in adjacent aluminum chairs, sipping from a plastic glass kept upright between my feet, I imagined myself in an elevated position at the concert, close to the management, closer to the performers, because I was going to review it. I attended on a Friday or Saturday, and on Mondays, with the weekend's humors still lively in me, sat in my office in downtown Ipswich and wrote the review, handing it in at the *Chronicle* offices a half-block away at lunchtime. The *Chronicle* came out on Thursdays, and I have dated the pieces with their publication date. These twenty-two reviews are all I wrote; I have not included an especially insufferable letter to the editor in 1962 complaining about the apparent termination of the concerts. In it I said, with the exaggerated bonhomie of my thirty tender years, "They were, flatly, the nicest concerts in the world. When all reservations about Ferrante and Teicher have been entered, it remains to confess that in the setting of the Italian Garden on a July night a kindergarten percussion band would sound heavenly."

REMARKS *delivered in acceptance of the Elmer Holmes Bobst Award for Fiction, at New York University, on May 19, 1987.*

People sometimes express to me curiosity about the relation between criticism and creativity, and the apparent paradox of practicing both. Of course, it is not much of a paradox—a visitor from Mars would be hard-pressed to distinguish between a person writing a book review and one writing a short story; the same fidgets and sighing, the same avoidance maneuvers, the same sudden swoops of fruitful concentration and forward motion are common to both. If one sets up to be a writer, one should be able to write anything, from a sonnet to a sermon, or at least be willing to try. I write not criticism but book reviews. A critic I understand to be someone who devotes a major part of his life and publication to the appreciation and analysis of an art; I, instead, am merely willing now and then to read a book and give my opinion of it in public.

And yet, there *is* something dangerous about it, something worrying. No less a critic than Malcolm Cowley once, after some kind words to me about a review I did of James Joyce's letters, wondered if I should be doing this sort of thing at all. It's as if there were a danger of making part of the brain too muscular at the expense of the other, or of smothering creativity under too great a load of discriminatory judgments and idle theory. Some danger exists, certainly, if only a corruption of one's inner ear with the too comfortable cadences and phrases of the critical voice. It is almost impossible to go wrong, in writing a review, and to avoid the tone of being wonderfully right; whereas any creative endeavor launches itself in the teeth of its certainly going wrong in some aspect, and of being judged wrong by others.

As no less ambidextrous a literary performer than William Dean Howells noted, knowing that one is going to review a book takes some of the pleasure out of it, and the books that make a real impact upon one are almost invariably read voluntarily, for pleasure and not business. The writer turned reviewer is robbing himself of the chance of being disarmed by a book, of being ravished into fresh enthusiasm for the literary enterprise. Writing a review *is* creative to the extent that the reviewer appropriates the work in a work of his own, and sets up cross-currents, the static of an observing if not a carping voice, from the first pages.

Nevertheless, reviewing gets me to reading; it imparts the illusion that I am part of a literary community and a healthily active worker in a species of journalism. Like speaking for pay at state universities, offering up book reviews to the public reassures the writer's worried relatives and neighbors that he is in a solid sort of business and not just moon-beam manufacture. Also, reviewing relieves some ill feelings about being reviewed; having come back from the other side of the looking-glass, one needn't ever again take so seriously what misconceptions and misprisions are held up in reflection of one's own work.

The miraculous thing I have to report, a secret so precious I hesitate to share it, is how docilely and utterly the critic in one goes to sleep when a creative endeavor is afoot. It is oddly possible to work ahead cheerily on a work that one well might, if someone else wrote it, feel obliged to pan. Even if, during the creative process, fitful phrases of the panning flutter into one's head, they fizzle out rapidly, like moths attracted to a glowing furnace. The fiction writer has at his back a whole other world trying to be born, and his responsibilities toward this world—opening himself to it, and letting it speak through him, and finding the phrases for its phenomena—reduce criticism to social chatter, to crowd noise.

Fiction—or poetry, or playwriting, or history or biography conceived as narrative arts—is only partly a social act. An imitation of Creation is afoot, with some of the religious feeling implied when that word is spelled with a capital "C." For the moments of actual creation, we are submitting to something beyond us, becoming a creature of an exalted sort, and the critical voice, so indefatigable when called into service, falls wisely silent, and lets us forget, for these truly valuable moments, almost everything we know. Creative activity is to a degree childish and primitive and predates, as it were, the critical faculties. The solemn bliss of the process, indeed, is so keen, and so faithful, the one feels quite sheepish trying to talk about it—critically—at all.

FOREWORD *to* John Updike: A Bibliography, 1967–1993, *compiled by Jack De Bellis (Greenwood Press, 1994).*

Bibliographer De Bellis's invitation to add to the already bulky front matter of his giant scholarly work meets in me a certain skepticism. Must I orate at my own interment? I seem to have reached in my career a terminal phase of tidying-up; in my recent *Collected Poems* I did much dating and alphabetizing, with the usual anal satisfactions that the conscientious researcher and accountant feel. Bibliography, though— especially the listing of reviews and interviews, most of which I would prefer to forget—I have happily left to others, and must from a distance marvel at their zeal and method, which in Mr. De Bellis's case has taken him into the maze of *The New Yorker*'s archives, where he ferreted out anonymous material he could have compiled from my own tearsheets, had I thought it wise to admit so fierce a researcher to my fragile castle keep. Surely a writer should properly face forward, to the words he has not yet written, rather than backwards, to those he has put behind him. Of course, his old words continue to echo in his ears, as he reads them from academic platforms, confronts them in critical reprises, and seeks to eliminate thirty-year-old typos from new editions. Among the utilizers of Professor De Bellis's mighty work I expect to number myself, as occasion arises, and for this I thank him, as well as for the very generous interest he has taken over the years in my work.

What a solemn if not quite ghastly sensation it is, glancing into such a compilation and finding that not even my few published drawings and the announcement of my wedding in my home-town paper have escaped the bibliographer's eagle eye! Are no secrets to be left me at all? Since privacy and secrets are the author's base of operations and his lode of treasure, it is alarming to see my life's loot here so systematically paraded. Yet even the omnivorous De Bellis has missed, I believe, my one formal contribution to my own bibliography, a published letter to the *Bulletin of Bibliography* (Westport, Connecticut) which I hereby reprint:

December 17, 1989

Gentlemen:

I was entertained, four years ago, by Stuart Wright's bibliography of my Shillington High School *Chatterbox* contributions from 1945 to 1950. In those same years, however, I was sending out contributions—poems, mostly—to magazines whose addresses I culled either from the local newsstands or a book of periodicals' addresses in my mother's possession. I had small success, but my mother's recent death returned to me a file in which all (I believe) of my acceptances were retained, and for some reason I feel compelled, before these antique magazines again pass out of my possession, to make a bibliographical note of them. C. Clarke Taylor's *John Updike: A Bibliography* (The Kent State University Press, 1968) mentions a few of them, but most eluded his research. All the pieces are poems, light verse mostly, and I believe that, except for five or ten dollars for the poem in *National Parent-Teacher*, my only reward was seeing them in print, such as it was in these modestly budgeted publications:

Reflections, Vol. XV, no. 11–12, November–December, 1948. Poem, "It Might Be Verse," p. 10.

The American Courier, Vol. 10, no. 7, issue 134, July 1st, 1949. Poem, "I Want a Lamp," p. 11.

National Parent-Teacher: The P.T.A. Magazine, Vol. XLIV, February 1950. Poem, "The Boy Who Makes the Blackboard Squeak," p. 39.

Reflections, Vol. XVII, no. 3, March–April 1950, 1948. Poem, "To a Bottle of Serutan." p. 9.

The American Courier, Vol. 11, no. 10, issue 149, October 1st, 1950. Poem, "Evangelist," p. 36.

Florida Magazine of Verse, Vol. XI, no. 1, November, 1950. Poems [under "Light Verse"], "Move Over, Dodo" and "The Last Word."

Reflections, Vol. XVII, no. 5, Holiday Issue. Poem, "Microphone," p. 4.

Different, Vol. 6, no. 5, November–December 1950. Poem, "The Lonely One," p. 7.

American Weave, Vol. XIX, no. 1, [no date, but copyright 1954]. Poem, "Astronomer, in Love," p. 22. Reprinted, with revisions, as *The Lovelorn Astronomer* in a signed, limited edition (Boston: G. K. Hall, 1978).

REMARKS *in acceptance of the National Book Critics Circle Award for Fiction, for* Rabbit at Rest, *in New York City, on March 14, 1991.*

I thank the National Book Critics Circle for twice, now, giving their fiction award to Rabbit Angstrom. The warmth with which my novels about this character have been, on the whole, received is a little bewildering to me, as well as gratifying. I can only think that Rabbit, from his arrival in my prose over thirty years ago, has been for me a way in, into the matter of America. When I am in his head—when I am riding him, so to speak—details of envisioned American landscapes and cityscapes take on an interest, a glow, a poetry of importance they do not have when I look at them with my own eyes. For he is, and always has been, a kind of man I am not—an athletic hero, a heroic youth who, having lived by his body, grows corpulent, tired, and old before his time. But through his possibly narrow perceptions and his instinctive present tense the great elusive nation all around us offers itself to be funnelled and decanted.

So at least I have found it; those who do not find this character and his world plausibly vital resist, or sniff, with some reason, no doubt. The point I wish to worry is not whether I deserve this coveted award but why America does, for all the fiction written and all the fictioneers being trained in colleges, seem to remain opaque, or vaporous. How many of our classics, notoriously, deal not with American society but with its asocial margins—a whale hunt on the high seas, a refugee boy and a black slave on a river raft, the outcast Hester Prynne, the expatriate heroes of Hemingway and Henry James, seeking fulfillment and aesthetic satisfaction everywhere but at home in the United States. A critic can make too much of this; but assume it is somewhat true—what might the reasons be? Let me propose four.

One, with exceptions like Washington Irving and William Dean Howells, who tend to bore posterity, the American writer has few traditional ties to the power establishment of the country, and ordinarily distrusts and scorns its politicians, businessmen, bureaucrats, managers, and even its workers—all those, in short, who make the society go are dismissed by a Puritan idealism that sees the compromises and maneuvers of bourgeois striving as unworthy of sympathetic consideration. Two, the ideal of a classless society, in which there is no aristocracy, no peasantry, no servant class, in a perverse way makes us *less* accessible to one another, by depriving our imaginations of those colorful badges and mannerisms and assigned duties with which characterization can begin. Three, the very triumph of American popular culture in this century coats the individual, whom the writer would hold up to cultural study, in an impervious skin of cultural cliché; the crises of will and desire that occupy nineteenth-century novels are as it were kidded away by the image-saturated modern consciousness, which has pre-experienced everything, in a trivializing and dulling abundance of unearned sophistication: this weariness of knowingness was wonderfully captured in the fiction of the late Donald Barthelme. And four, perhaps a culture that never had a pagan or medieval epoch doesn't leave one much to say about being human; when, in a nation soundly founded on eighteenth-century rationalism and nineteenth-century laws of material exchange, *Homo sapiens* has been stripped of superstitious loyalties and quixotic delusions, what is left is a bald consumer, an animal of purely selfish appetites and purely biological motives whose genetically determined life-events scarcely warrant the glamorization of fiction.

For whatever reason, America remains something of a riddle to the practitioners of fiction, a tougher nut to crack than you would think. Several able journalists advise us simply to seize the beast by the horns—do some research and conduct a few interviews and lay out the facts in lively, Zolaesque fashion. And of course facts should be collected, by the fiction writer as by every other citizen. But something in our collective Puritan conscience insists, I fear, that to be worth writing our novels have to have, besides facts, an injection of the personal, the confessional, the spiritually urgent. It is this we grope for through our characters, this unprogrammable quality of *testimony*—of external evidences become interior signs—and to which a few characters do seem to grant us access.

REMARKS *delivered in acceptance of the Howells Medal*—*"given once every five years in recognition of the most distinguished work of American fiction published during that period"*—*for* Rabbit at Rest, *at the American Academy of Arts and Letters on May 17, 1995.*

William Dean Howells, in whose name this medal is given, was a considerable theorist of fiction, and of American fiction. As a practitioner and critic he sought to hold himself and other writers to a standard of realism that rose above the romantic exaggerations and implausible adventures that characterized popular fiction in his day and, indeed, in ours. He thought progress was being made, and in 1891 wrote, "Fiction is now a finer art than it has ever been hitherto. . . . I have hopes of real usefulness in it . . . but I am by no means certain that it will be the ultimate literary form. . . . On the contrary, it is quite imaginable that when the great mass of readers, now sunk in the foolish joys of mere fable, shall be lifted to an interest in the meaning of things through the faithful portrayal of life in fiction, then fiction the most faithful may be superseded by a still more faithful form of contemporaneous history."

The situation now is more drastic, I think, than Howells conceived it, for what looms is not a mere change of literary fashion or shift of genres but a loss of literature itself, rendered passé by the bright flickering tongues of the electronic modes of entertainment and instruction. Young students, it is reported from academia, are less and less willing and able to read, and the language of even as limpid a nineteenth-century style as that of Hawthorne is reportedly impenetrable to them. Those of us who grew up on a diet of the modernist masterpieces, and have tried to write works that would enchant and challenge readers such as we were, may be like those Renaissance poets who mastered the art of Latin verse, in quixotic or elitist defiance of a widespread linguistic death. We are writing for an audience that less and less exists, and a posterity that will not exist.

And yet, when this most dire of scenarios has been sketched, how empowering the practice of fiction remains! Faced with the gradually filling emptiness of a novel in progress, the writer feels he is at the controls of a device whose potential is infinite, a tool that outrivals even a computer in its plasticity and nimbleness, in its inexhaustible capacity for the imitation of life in its real shadings and farraginous details, and for the generation of a narrative music and a weave of symbols and a poetry both of expression and of circumstance. Writing fiction, as those of us who do it know, is, beneath the anxious travail of it, a bliss, a healing, an elicitation of order from disorder, a praise of what is, a salvaging of otherwise overlookable truths from the ruthless sweep of generalization, a beating of daily dross into something shimmering and absolute.

For somewhat these reasons, I imagine, are medals and prizes for the novel awarded—not so much to the lucky individual prizewinner as to this permissive, hybrid, democratic, curious art form itself, in thanks for the validation it bestows upon our common humanity and for the persistence of its faith (once the prerogative of philosophy and religion) that what Howells called "the meaning of things" can be laid bare.

INTRODUCTION *to the Easton Press's uniform edition of the four novels about* Rabbit Angstrom, *published in 1993. I have written (and spoken) more about these novels than all the others combined: there have been individual forewords for each volume in their Franklin Library editions, and acceptance speeches for the two prizewinners, and a lengthy, careful summing-up to introduce the Everyman's Library* Rabbit Angstrom: The Four Novels *(1995). Compared with that six-thousand-word survey—not included in* More Matter— *my remarks for Easton Press were skimpy and casual, but on rereading them I thought they recalled a few truths not present in the later, fuller introduction. Also, the hurried feel of the prose was possibly truer to the texture of the books themselves, which I wrote at a smart clip, full sail under pressures both professional and internal.*

Rabbit, Run was begun early in 1959 and typed up in a rush toward the end of that year, so that my family and I could go off at the beginning of the new decade for a vacation. We lived in a seventeenth-century house in Ipswich, Massachusetts, and I wrote the novel at home, by hand, at a fold-down desk in a small corner room with a view of a busy street corner, a complicated telephone pole, and a grand old elm. I had lived in New England for more than two years, and had left Pennsylvania at the age of twenty-one, and yet the Keystone State was still realer to me than my Yankee surroundings.

Intending to write a movielike novella, in the then highly unusual present tense, I found Harry "Rabbit" Angstrom's locale and predicament expanding under me, to fill over three hundred typed pages. Some parts of it were taken from my present environment: a much-admired rhododendron garden at the top of the hill behind our house became Mrs.

Smith's garden, where Harry works for a season, and my friendship with the local Episcopalian minister fleshed out a few scenes of imagined ecclesiastic life. But the central situation—the anticlimactic adulthood of a high-school athletic hero—belonged to the Pennsylvania of my boyhood. My father was a high-school teacher, and in time I passed through his school and his classes to graduation; high school was the one American institution I understood from the inside, from several viewpoints. Many a basketball game I watched and cheered; many a sad tale my father brought home of a former star gone bad, in the asphalt alleys and brick row houses of greater Reading. Reading was the city three miles or twenty minutes away by trolley car from our town of Shillington. I had never lived there, and Mt. Judge, in my fiction, has the physical configurations of not my home town but the rival town of Mt. Penn. I had never been a basketball star—even my season of playing for the junior varsity was aborted, and an embarrassment to remember. So a heavy, intoxicating dose of fantasy and wish-fulfillment went into *Rabbit, Run*, along with the reality of a nostalgically evoked locale and the clutter and tensions of young married life. Rabbit ran while I sat at my desk, scribbling in pencil and kicking with my feet, so that at the end of the year I had worn a bare spot in the varnished pine floorboards.

I had not intended to revisit Rabbit. The end of my novel was meant to be the last any of us would see of this plebeian counterpart to the bohemian travellers of Kerouac's *On the Road*. Yet enough people asked me what had happened to him after my novel's end, when his hard and worried heart momentarily dissolves in the ecstasy of running nowhere, so that ten years later I thought of reviving him, as a conduit to ordinary America during the explosive late Sixties. Possibly the present tense would have achieved its vogue without *Rabbit, Run*; but I can claim unequivocally to have revived the word *redux* from its limbo since Anthony Trollope had published *Phineas Redux* nearly a century before. That the Latin word has become commonplace in jocular headlines is the one clear difference my life's work has made to the English language.

Rabbit Redux raced through its pages; one of the pleasures of a sequel is that the characters, towns, and streets are already named, and need only to be updated and kept consistent. I must have begun writing some time after the astounding news events of July 1969—the moon landing and Chappaquiddick in the same week! During the writing of the book, we changed houses in Ipswich, moving to more acreage and less historicity on a tidal river called Labor-in-Vain Creek, into a domicile owned in the Thirties by another writer, a playwright named George Brewer, Jr. He wrote *Dark Victory*; the film version, starring Bette Davis, uncannily echoed, when I watched it on television recently, the layout of the Labor-in-Vain place, with its studio cottage nestled in lilacs apart from the main house.

I didn't use the cottage, though. I do recall, in the period when the main house stood awaiting our furniture, laying a board across two low bookcases and typing away at the further adventures of Harry and Janice and Nelson while workmen came and went. But I had rented an office downtown, above a restaurant, some years before, and it was mostly there that I plugged away at the book. If the novel seems hectic, so were the times. *Rabbit, Run* took place in 1959 but wasn't really about Eisenhower or the public events that, in one brief episode, filter in over my hero's car radio. Ten years later, the news had moved out of the television sets right into our laps, and there was no ignoring the war, the protest, the civil-rights movement, the moon shot, and the drugs and sexual promiscuity that were winning favor in the middle classes. On the theory that all major national developments eventually impinge upon the microcosm of the private citizen, I invaded Harry's little ranch-house on Vista Crescent with an upper-class runaway and a black-power advocate who together stage in his living room what were called, in that morally strident era, teach-ins.

Yet the basic action remains familial: marital fidelity and parental responsibility are still the issues, and Nelson, now twelve going on thirteen, lodges a more verbal and defiant protest than he was able to when only two. All four grandparents are still alive at this point in time, and Pa Springer casually mentions his acquisition of a Toyota franchise, which will become central in the next two sequels. But for now Harry works as a typesetter, a Linotype operator, and to me there was something heroic about this, a metallic heightening of my own sedentary days piling up words. I had worked as a copy boy for the *Reading Eagle* for several summers, and carrying copy into the room where the Linotypers and the engravers worked under their hot lights had been a visit to a foundry—a clattering, sweating place where print and plates were *made*. I would wish for all would-be authors such an exciting glimpse into the industrial end of their enterprise. The owner of the *Ipswich Chronicle* let me examine his Linotype machines (about to be rendered technologically obsolete by offset printing and computerization) and refresh my memory. Liberal, savvy Charlie Stavros must derive from Ipswich's lively Greek community. But it was in Berks County, as my parents reported to me, that a house occupied by a biracial couple—the black man had attended my high school—mysteriously went up in flames.

Though both novels had their displeased critics, and neither was a best-seller or a prizewinner, I had a good thing going, evidently. By the time the ninth year of the decade came round again, I lived in a different town, with a different wife, and my exultation in newness gave *Rabbit Is Rich* an exuberance we might almost call optimistic. Harry's jogs through Mt. Judge were certainly the jogs I would take, after dinner, through the darkened, irregular streets of Georgetown, Massachusetts. Unassuming, inland Georgetown, twenty minutes from Ipswich, was more like a Pennsylvania small town than the old Puritan port had been, and my imaginary Diamond County fattened on its homely atmosphere. Janice's new stature as a character, and Harry's revived interest in her, must relate to the other, connubial change in my life. I felt rich, in fresh impressions if not in Toyota profits. The year 1979 had no moon shot to give it an insignia and *point de départ*; the gas crunch of June, with its long lines of automobiles and its staggering jogger of a President, offered the central metaphor, and Harry's natural ebullience and insatiability did the rest. I was especially pleased with the way Ma Springer, now the only surviving grandparent, spoke for the social order, as Nelson's several girlfriends brought fresh winds into the big stucco house on Joseph Street. My own four children were supplying fresh faces to my own life, and a friendly academic connection of mine provided the particulars of Nelson's education at Kent State, in Ohio; but the thick moral atmosphere, the resistant but tolerant conservatism, is Pennsylvanian. This book did win prizes, and in accepting one of them, the National Book Critics Circle Award, I said, "My native region of southeastern Pennsylvania, though nearly three decades have passed since I could claim sylvan residence, obligingly continues to warm my imagination with the impressions of humanity I received there, longer and longer ago — a land fertile for even the absentee farmer."

The next ten years brought one more change of address for me — to a big white summer cottage in Beverly Farms, with a view of the sea. Sitting in one of the old maid's rooms at the green steel Army desk that I had bought for thirty dollars to be the centerpiece of my Ipswich office, I looked out at the shifting surface of the Atlantic Ocean and tried to imagine Harry in decline. He was only in his fifties, a year younger than I, but I thought the time had come to wrap up his life and my series of novels. It was a depressing prospect, made additionally so by my mother's decline, back in Berks County, alone in the sandstone farmhouse where she had, over eight decades ago, been born. She had been my principal connection with the land of Rabbit, and she died just as I had completed the first, pencilled draft of *Rabbit at Rest*. My many visits to her that year, at her home and in the hospital, had exposed me to more of Berks County than

I had seen since the age of twenty-one. Details of her hospital care were opportunistically transposed into Harry Angstrom's key, in Florida and Brewer; the sight, on Reading's Ninth Street, of Bradford pear trees in blossom became an epiphany for the retired Toyota salesman. George-town, that same summer, invited me to march in a parade, as a celebrated former resident, and my dizzying, somehow posthumous sensations were transferred to my old fictional friend as well. Everything was being piled on him, by an author who did not want to let go but knew he must. Enough must be enough. My own heart was giving me twinges. By the time he and I got back to Florida—where he had thought he was heading at the beginning of *Rabbit, Run*—the blessed goal was at hand; God was in the clouds, along with Hurricane Hugo.

In accepting a prize that this last Rabbit book won for me, I said that his character gave me access to America—"a way in, into the matter of America"—as my own persona did not. Access is what a fiction writer seeks: some route, usually roundabout, into himself and his (or her, need-less to say) treasure of subconsciously stored reality. Harry and I have a lot in common: we grew up together, and are both white American males whose chief historical experiences have been the Depression, World War II, and the Cold War. He was born a year later than I, like a narrowly younger brother, and my life has gone places his has not. Yet I do not contain him, like a larger circle circumscribed around a smaller. He has qualities I do not have—he is taller, handsomer, wilder than I, more sensitive and spiritual. Fictional characters in general, as E. M. Forster pointed out in his *Aspects of the Novel*, are more sensitive and spiritual than real people, less obtuse and blind in regard to their surroundings. Harry regards America proprietorially, and is alert to the changes and deteriorations in it. Unlike me, he stayed in Pennsylvania, immersed in the radiance, the momentousness, of childhood impressions.

Yet the four novels' reflection of life in the United States is not their central aspect for me. True, abortion availability, drug use, sexual hab-its, racial attitudes, popular entertainment, fashions in clothing, and the physical appearance of our cities and towns have all changed since 1959, and these changes are observed. But many a work of sociology and con-temporary history consider them more systematically than my random samplings of the headlines and textures at the ends of four decades. A few old *World Almanac*s would supply much more data.

The tetralogy to me is the tale of a life, a life led by an American citizen who shares the national passion for youth, freedom, and sex, the national openness and willingness to learn, the national habit of improvisation. He is furthermore a Protestant, haunted by a God whose manifestations are elusive yet all-important. Like the hero of Kafka's *Castle*, he wants useful work and does not find it. Compared with most of the world's population, he is fortunate; but he never feels perfectly at home in the world. Life's physicality, as embodied by his old rival Ronnie Harrison, fascinates and disgusts him. His tale is in part a sexual pilgrimage, deeper into the bodies of women, and in part the evolution of a marriage, in which the woman becomes stronger and the man weaker. It is about beginning as a son and becoming a father and then a grandfather; the relationship — the balked love — between Harry and Nelson is one of the tetralogy's main strands. Another is Harry's search for the daughter he lost, and his attempt to right, somehow, the wrong of her death: life becomes a long attempt to heal a central trauma. The tetralogy is about, and not only in the last book, a man's relationship with his coming death. And it is about a number of other things which I cannot formulate except in the skimming weave of writing fiction. In fiction it is not just the reader who hopes to be surprised by meaning; it is the writer as well.

HENRY BECH *interviews Updike apropos of his fifteenth novel.*

Can it really be over ten years since your fictional interviewer encountered his creator in a prairie-flat New England crossroads called Georgetown, Massachusetts, and more than twenty since he did the same in a dismal shoebox of an office in a salty old settlement named Ipswich? Now Updike, still stubbornly north of Boston, resides in a remote corner of a drab burg yclept Beverly, distinguished chiefly for having allegedly been the birthplace of the American Navy (a painful parturition, no doubt, with all those masts and anchor chains) and for containing an empty shoe-machinery plant bigger than the Trump Tower dumped on its side. Following directions as intricate as an alchemist's manual, we proceeded, my taxi driver and I (he was from East Boston, and as terrified of bosky suburbs as yours truly), across some railroad tracks to what I presumed was the wrong side, where, after a few divagations into the driveways of indignant local gentry, we eventually came upon the author, looking as elderly and vexed as his neighbors. Since last we met, his touseled locks have grown whiter, his eyes smaller, and his teeth straighter, as the miracles of cosmetic dentistry pile up. His front porch appeared to have splitting pillars; his front door opened with difficulty in the seaside damp. My attempts to glance around for telling details of his home furnishings were frustrated by the speed with which he escorted me up some winding stairs to the hideously cramped quarters where he claims to work, thrashing from one desk to another like a wounded flamingo.

I was struck by, in the lemon-yellow cubicle containing his touchingly obsolete word processor (it has no computer function, is not IBM-compatible, and starts up with a hand crank), two framed drawings by Saul Steinberg, one inscribed "To John Updike with best wishes" and dated 1945, when the recipient was a thirteen-year-old autograph-seeker, and another, of a scribbling rabbit, saying "John Up 60!" and dated 1992. Forty-seven years of memorabilia: the chasm of *temps perdu* dizzied me, as did the view from Updike's smudgy windows, of frazzled gray squirrels chasing each other around through the perilously bending branches of trees the rural scribe confidently identified to me as oaks, whether red or white he didn't know.

I asked him if he still mourned not being a cartoonist, like the estimable Steinberg.

"Ah," Updike said, his rheumy eye kindling a little, "but Steinberg is no mere cartoonist—a full-fledged artist, rather, with exhibitions at the Whitney and imitators the world over. I could not have been he, I fear, and so am content to have diverted into printed language my love of convolute scrollings and animated rabbits, of talk balloons and *to be continueds*, of double entendres and trompe l'oeil. The medium of the word is impalpable, giving even less resistance than grainy paper offers graphite, or scratchboard offers ink. It is like a great shining sheet of cardboard into which one falls each morning like Alice passing through the looking-glass. I wouldn't trade my trade for anything."

This speech, delivered with a characteristic and curious tensing of the corners of Updike's lips and a disquieting flutter of his eyelids, has been reconstructed from memory, since your interviewer hadn't yet switched on his brand-new Yamaha four-wheel-drive tape recorder. Now I did, and asked in a loud voice, "Your new novel—I didn't have time to more than skim the opening chapters, and hate reading bound proofs anyway, riddled as they are with typos and contemptible mental lapses, but it seems more of a Wonderland than usual. Chapters about sexual disarray in the days of Gerald Ford, other chapters all about James Buchanan and his fuddy-duddy nineteenth-century buddies, notes in brackets to some imaginary editors, footnotes, footnotes to footnotes—a mishmash, *una olla podrida!*"

A. (*getting on his dignity*): It is my *Tempest*, my valedictory visit to all of my themes before deeper than did ever plummet sound I drown my book. Ever since my blushing twenties I have yearned to tell the tale of James Buchanan, Pennsylvania's only, much-maligned President. My attempts to write a novel about him collapsed into a stage play with a copious afterword in 1974, but this surrender rankled, and I recently thought that perhaps if I embedded Buchanan in a twentieth-century New England sex comedy, with a historian within the living plot engaged in trying to write about Buchanan, I might thereby bestow upon myself a writing license, the necessary freedom of the imagination which had been hitherto constrained by my constitutional unwillingness to do all the faking—what Henry James called the *escamotage*—that goes into a historical novel. The *escamotage*, the juggling and magic surrealism, now belongs to my fictional historian, whose name is Alf Clayton. *Memories of the Ford Administration* is a kind of sequel, an alert critic could say, not only to *Buchanan Dying* but to *A Month of Sundays*, which are adjacent within my oeuvre. Some time ago I reached the age when everything I did was, more or less, a sequel to something I had done earlier. Some would call it poverty of inspiration; I would call it sound conservation policy.

Q.: But why the title?—your longest and most cumbersome if I mistake not.

A.: Well, I was struck by how strangely obscure the Ford administration has quickly become. When I mention this title to people, they smile, as though the Ford administration is a little secret that Americans all share. It had the obscurity, the hiddenness, that I need for a topic truly to excite me.

Q. *(after silently indicating approval of the unsplit infinitive)*: But, John— may I call you "John"?—

A.: Why not? Everybody else does. Especially long-distance telephone operators. Have you noticed the way nobody under forty addresses an envelope "Mr." any more? It drives me *wild*.

Q.: —you yourself are less and less hidden. You have become what used to be called, in the days when you were pestering Saul Steinberg with letters as adolescent as they were adoring, a Famous Author. How does this affect you?

A.: How does it affect *you*?

Q.: It can't be good for me. But I live in Manhattan, as you know—

A.: At West 99th and Riverside Drive. I put you there myself.

Q.: —where authorship is a local business, and fame is worn with as little fuss as a necktie on Wall Street. But for you, a boy from the hills of Pennsylvania—

A.: Please. I spent my first thirteen years in a small town in a sequestered valley. But, yes, as one's elders die off, a certain threadbare mantle descends, and one makes the desolating discovery that the world would rather have a writer give speeches, judge prizes, receive prizes, attend book signings, go on TV and radio, display him- or herself on college campuses, advise students how to write their condescending theses, serve on committees, pose for photographs, and pen coyly promotional pieces for *Vogue* than, in the primal sense, write. It shouldn't surprise us that society values social activities over the anti-social seclusions of writer and reader and the vague, unremunerative, politically incorrect ideals of "literature." A small-town boy, and a schoolteacher's son at that, early trained to be a "good" boy, responds all too eagerly to his society's many flattering invitations, and lets himself be cast, at many a tea-party and classroom chat-up, as a "nice" person. But as Norman Mailer pointed out decades ago, and Philip Roth not long afterwards, niceness is the enemy. Every soft stroke from the society is like the *pfft* of an aerosol can as it eats up a few more atoms of our brain's delicate ozone, and furthers our personal cretinization. The appetite for serious writing is almost entirely dead, alas, but the appetite for talking, walking authors rages in the land. It's a paradoxical priority, relating no doubt to the way television needs faces to televise. Faces, people, sex lives, bank scandals—my God, can this be all there is? But enough whining. You take the world as you find it, and make your way as best you can. Shakespeare had his problems, as did Alexander Pope. Authors do well to remember that they are not really kin to priests and politicians but to singers and stand-up comedians—entertainers, of a devious sort.

Q. *(socking it to him):* How do you feel, then, about fiction, as a viable art form?

A.: I find that the longer I'm at it the more narrowly focussed I become upon my own specific delivery problems. What *I* like about the new novel, for instance, is the way I smuggled the name of every American President into it, and the way the characters over a century apart began to send signals back and forth. No doubt Fiction, if we can picture her with a capital letter, is suffering. Fewer paying markets for short stories, trashier titles pushed by the increasingly corporate-minded book industry, end-of-the-century aesthetic exhaustion, generations of brains rendered unfit by television for either reality or art, etc. And yet, shepherding my very possibly dispensable titles one after another into print, what bliss! What space for invention, what possibilities of fusion as the words heat up, what a satisfying transmutation of personal fodder into purgative, regularizing bran for everyone! Fiction, one still can't help feeling, is healthy for the writer and the reader both. And there is no bottom of the barrel, though the barrel needs now and then to be renamed, and "postmodern" was never much of a label anyway. But I hear myself sounding like a "nice" guy, a booster, so let's get off this airwave. Let's be purely, life-enhancingly selfish. The self, after all, is the glittering instrument given to us for performing whatever this tricky operation—life, reality—is.

Q. (*fearful that the Yamaha might implode under too massive a metaphysical input*): O.K., O.K., if you say so. Want to share with us your next plunge into self-exploitation?

A.: I'm collecting my poems. Nobody asked me to, but I was curious to see how they'd look all together. Each day, I reread and touch up a few, while my whole life reels before me. Then, I want to write a novel that, unlike this one, will be short and fabulous. I want it to take place in a foreign setting, and to be a breeze to write.

Q.: Don't you wish. Don't *we* wish. Take care, John.

A.: You, too, Hank. Listen, you've been a doll to do this. It's the sort of thing, like falling in love, that's embarrassing to do alone.

A "SPECIAL MESSAGE" *for the Franklin Library's Signed First Edition Society printing of* Memories of the Ford Administration *(1992).*

I do not know when I first heard about James Buchanan. The public schools of Shillington, Pennsylvania, did not teach state history, or if they did I was home sick that day. Perhaps it was from the lips of my maternal grandfather that I first heard Buchanan's name. My grandfather, John Hoyer—I was his namesake—had been born in Berks County a few months after the Battle of Gettysburg, of a Pennsylvania Dutch family considerably involved in county politics, on the Democratic side. In all his ninety years he never sullied his ballot by voting for a Republican. Faithful to his general bias if not to his exact words is this passage from my first novel, *The Poorhouse Fair*, in which the elderly John Hook declaims, in his hyphenated accents, of Buchanan:

> "A ver-y unfairly esti-mated man . . . The last of the presidents who truly represented the entire country; after him the southern states were slaves to Boston, as surely as Alaska. Buchanan, you know, had been the am-bassador to Russia, and was very well thought-of there."

By the time I wrote *The Poorhouse Fair*, in 1957, I had mentally sketched a Pennsylvania tetralogy to be capped by a historical novel concerning the only President the grand old commonwealth had ever sent to the White House. I composed the second and third novels of the intended quartet—*Rabbit, Run* and *The Centaur*—with fair dispatch but then was seduced by my adopted commonwealth of Massachusetts into writing a

New England novel called *Couples*. With the sense of leisure this best-seller earned for me, I began, while in London, to do my Buchanan research; returning to the United States in the summer of 1969, I knew enough to make a start, but the going was tough, and finally I opted to write instead another novel about a contemporary, make-believe Pennsylvanian—Rabbit Angstrom. This was *Rabbit Redux*, which would head me into a Pennsylvania tetralogy of a different sort.

Still, my fascination with Buchanan did not abate, nor was I able, as the Seventies set in, to move the novel forward through the constant pastiche and basic fakery of any fiction not fed by the springs of memory—what Henry James calls (in a letter to Sarah Orne Jewett) the "fatal *cheapness* [and] mere *escamotage*" of the " 'historic' novel." At last I settled upon the form of a play; it offered direct transposition to the spoken words that history saw fit to record and left the manifold descriptive problems up to the costume and set designers. Duly I produced *Buchanan Dying*, in three talkative acts. Knopf brought out the work in an exceptionally handsome little maroon volume in 1974, with endpapers and a copious afterword that includes all the interesting facts about James Buchanan that I had failed to work into the play.

The play was produced, twice, in shortened versions, at Franklin and Marshall College, in Lancaster, and at San Diego State University, in California. I attended both and, through no fault of the various actors (I remember especially the charming French accent of the F & M actress who portrayed Czarina Aleksandra), found my unease with the live stage—its artifice, its human imperfections and tense air of social occa-sion, its *theatricality*—reinforced. I had not done justice to Buchanan, to the peculiar poignance I found in the man or to the illumination of high American office that his Presidency promised. When, a few years ago, Knopf allowed *Buchanan Dying* to go out of print, the stubborn idea dawned of telling his tale again, with the new boldness that Latin Ameri-can magic realism has introduced into fiction's armory, and with an inter-vening author who would in his fictional person shoulder all the difficulties I had encountered in my travails of historical reconstruction. Let him and not me take on the fatal cheapness, the inevitable jaunty fal-sity of any attempt to animate individuals more than a century dead.

Hence the invention of Alf Clayton, professor of history at Wayward College in New Hampshire, in the era of Gerald Ford. He would suffer historical authorship on my behalf and himself be a historical figure, a survivor of the Ford Presidency. I am attracted, among Presidents, to the underappreciated, and Gerald Ford's Presidency has managed in a mere fifteen years to be all but forgotten. During its two years, as it happened,

I lived in Boston without a television set or a subscription to a newspaper; I have almost *no* memories of the Ford administration as such, except for some skirmish with a Cambodian gun boat, and the attempt of two women to assassinate the poor good man. Alf, as he dutifully relates his memories for the Northern New England Association of American Historians, characterizes the Ford era as best he can, but the later administration should not loom as more vivid than the earlier, or crush the finespun ante-bellum ghosts under too lusty a load of modern data. A theme of the novel, after all, is the impossibility of recovering the past, whether as nostalgia or as history. Resorting to my dusty old file of Buchananiana, I had to relive my researches and reinvent my facts; some of the novel's opening episodes, such as the scenes with Jackson and the Hubley sisters, are closely adapted from the out-of-print play; as I got back "into" my subject, certain other episodes, such as the lovesong to Senator W. R. D. King and the conversation with Nathaniel Hawthorne, were invented. Many other passages in Buchanan's long and political life received short shrift, in the interests of speed. Young Prince Albert's visit to the White House, for instance, and its effect on the nubile Harriet Lane would make a fine farce or erotic novella.

Like my novel of (can it be?) thirty years ago, *The Centaur, Memories of the Ford Administration* moves through alternating chapters, taken from contrasting yet harmonizing levels of reality. I did not wish to pull the connections between the two eras and the two protagonists too tight; paper parallels are, like fictional dreams, all too easy to manufacture. While Alf wrote about Buchanan, his own life tinged the chapters, but delicately, I hoped. Buchanan and Ford are linked not by "and" but by "Ann." While we write, over months and years, at a book, what happens around us, downstairs and outside the windows, creeps in, as mice in winter creep into a house, but scarcely visibly. Alf's framing tale of not untypical marital and extramarital adventure took on the natural quickness of contemporary notation; at the same time, I felt Buchanan come to life, too, a stately costumed figure on the stage of history, seen from far back in the balcony, a puppet in the lights, but moving his arms without strings.

A "SPECIAL MESSAGE" *for the Franklin Library's Signed First Edition Society printing of* Brazil *(1994).*

In my youth, long before I had laid even the shadow of a claim to the proud title of novelist, I had a dream of exceptional penetration and power: I dreamed of a medieval knight who spied a dusky lady at a joust or castle feast and pursued her all the way across the Middle East, Central Asia, India, and Southeast Asia, until at last, dying, he saw her, from behind a screen of tropical growth, disrobing and bathing in the sea that lapped one of the Polynesian islands. She was home, and he was far from home. I awoke, and told myself with amazement that I had dreamed a novel. This adolescent feat of subconscious imagination, which I have never forgotten, contributes to *Brazil* its yearning for distances and its vision of an undeviating fidelity.

The human ability to traverse vast distances is surely one of our heroisms, whether it manifests itself as the travels of Marco Polo, the return journey of Odysseus, Magellan's surviving crew's global circumnavigation, the westward march of the American pioneers, the agonized wanderings of Coronado or Stanley or Sir John Franklin, the astronauts' trip to the moon and back, the explorations of Antarctica, or the anonymous migrations that populated the six other continents. The ability to keep going, lured on by visions of gold or of caribou herds, creates and consumes maps.

The *bandeirantes* of Brazil were epic travellers; according to John Hemming's *Red Gold*, "In 1647 the fifty-year-old António Rapôso Tavares led his bandeira of sixty whites and a few Indians right across South America"—west from São Paulo across the Paraná and Paraguay rivers, across the terrible swamps of the Chaco to the edges of the Andes and thence down the Madeira to the Amazon, a journey of seven thousand miles along the perimeter of Brazil. This mammoth trek, brutal and brutalizing—"When Rapôso Tavares finally made his way back to São Paulo," Hemming tells us, "he was so disfigured that his own family did not recognize him"—is mentioned and echoed in my novel, but it was the twentieth-century journey of the French anthropologist Claude Lévi-Strauss across the Mato Grosso in 1935–36 that provided a direct inspiration. His account of his experiences of Brazil and its Indians, *Tristes Tropiques*, is wonderfully circumstantial and witty, as well as brilliant in its anthropological perceptions, which range from the remotest backlands of the *sertão* to the urban circles of São Paulo. It is hard to imagine a better escort for the armchair traveller; Lévi-Strauss's magically sharp mind, serene Olympian perspective, and poetry of close observation skim the reader enchantingly across a wilderness full, as it were, of a sardonic emptiness. Another model of traveller's prose was in my mind, that section of Vladimir Nabokov's most ambitious novel in Russian, *The Gift*, in which the narrator evokes the Asian travels of his father:

From a great height [he] saw a dark marshy depression all trembling from the play of innumerable springs, which recalled the night sky with stars scattered over it—and that is what it was called; the Starry Steppe. The pass ascended beyond the clouds, marches were tough. We rubbed the pack animals' wounds with a mixture of iodoform and vaseline. . . . Further on comes the desert of Lob: a stony plain, tiers of clay precipices, glassy salt ponds; the pale fleck in the gray air is a lone individual of Roborovski's White, carried away by the wind.

Brazil retells the story of Tristan and Iseult if their romance is allowed to age into a marriage. As with the fantasy of *The Coup*, threads of my own domestic experience were woven into the exotic details. In fact I had spent time in Brazil—a week, to be exact. In the course of that week I received impressions valid for 1992 but not, my friends in Brazil politely informed me, for the 1960s, when most of the action takes place. Nevertheless, like a blundering brave explorer of old, I persisted, and laid my young couple's adventures upon the underlying terrain I had sensed during my week of visitation, in which I travelled from São Paulo to Ouro Prêto to Brasília to Rio, where my hotel room overlooked the fabled beach where my tale begins. My Brazil lies somewhere between the rather grisly headlines of today—which report massacres of street children and Amazonian Indians, and armies of corrupt and violent police doing battle with gangs of drug dealers established in the favelas like brutal barons from the Dark Ages: a society, in short, in meltdown, the institutions of order and decency collapsing under a sodden weight of poverty and cynicism—and the idyllic land of those Forties Hollywood movies showing Hope and Crosby and Carmen Miranda and José Carioca doing a perpetual samba before a backdrop of tropical fruits and big-billed toucans and smiling brown faces. I saw those movies as a child, as a young man in bud, dreaming his dream of the knight who walked in his armor to Polynesia.

For me, Brazil (with its floating, lulling song of the same name) is not only a tinted area on the map but a conceptual state of well-being, like Erewhon and Ruritania and Cockaigne. It was a territory that lured me forward, into its luminous green depths, into its magical emptiness; it seemed one of the last earthly spaces that held room for the imagination. Fiction needs such room, as well as the furniture that experience and research supply; if my Brazil is underfurnished, and what furniture exists grotesquely mismatched, it has a compensatory roominess, in which events can move quickly, unimpeded by the muchness that so often seems to clog and clutter our realism. We can catch at a truth from a distance as well as up close; I refuse to disown my Brazil as unrealistic. A country's sense of itself is an activating part of its reality, and this sense derives in part from outsiders. Because others have romanticized and sexualized Brazil, Brazil is saturated in romanticism and sexuality. Sex, between masters and slaves, conquerors and indigenes, has shaped its identity as an image of the world that is coming, one world of many mixed colors.

A "SPECIAL MESSAGE" for the Franklin Library's Signed First Edition Society printing of In the Beauty of the Lilies (1996).

My faithful readers will recognize, in the fifth chapter of my memoir Self-Consciousness and in the short story "Son," antecedents of the family history projected in In the Beauty of the Lilies. The title has been long in my mind, as in its surreal sadness summing up a world of Protestant estrangement—In the beauty of the lilies Christ was born across the sea. That is, not on this side of the ocean. My hope was to tell a family saga in terms of God's dealings with four generations, somewhat as the Bible relates the genealogical tale of Abraham and Isaac, Jacob and Esau, Joseph and his brothers. Penetratingly melancholy details of this Biblical genealogy have stayed with me from my Lutheran Sunday school, held in basement rooms redolent of varnished oak and musty evangelical leaflets—Abraham with his knife poised over Isaac's trusting breast, ancient Isaac (still trusting) pathetically fooled by some hides placed over Jacob's hands to counterfeit the rough hands of Esau, young Joseph in his coat of many colors cast into a pit by his envious brothers. Not just the mysterious will of God made itself felt in this continuum, but the inexorable action of time, turning the boy of one episode into the old man of another. And in my own family, on both my mother's and my father's sides, there were repeated bits of "family history," precious nuggets worn smooth by retelling, passed on with a gravity of self-evident significance, as if these remote doings and bygone transactions among the dead bore centrally upon my own, childish, rather history-resistant identity. The Hoyers, my mother's people, were all about us in Pennsylvania's Berks County, in the form of aunts and uncles and cousins and farms; the Updikes, who came from New Jersey, had to be visited, at the annual summer Updike reunion, held near Trenton, at the terminus of a tedious, stifling car drive along poky, pre-superhighway roads. Once there, I was afforded the spectacle of seeing my father revert to being a happy boy, among his own cousins and surviving aunts and uncles, whose names all year lived with such a fond tang on his reminiscing tongue.

In my now not unlengthy career, I have already written about some of this, directly or fancifully—see the short story "The Family Meadow."

To compose my novel—a novel to be expressive of America with sufficient breadth and generality—I had to discard the personal facts and
invent an ancestral past, and this invention gave me much trouble of
research. The specifics of a Paterson, New Jersey, where I had never set
foot needed to be discovered; an idyllic small-town Delaware had to be
projected upon a real map. While the book was being written, I flew one
clear day from Washington to Boston right over the site of my mythical
Basingstoke; I looked down and, a bit north of the Canal on the Delaware
Bay, just where Basingstoke should have been, I saw a nest of great white
petroleum-storage tanks, and greedily snapped them up for my story-
book scenery. Hollywood, so much written about and so often depicted
in the films that originate there, was in a sense already known; but the
ghosts of Fitzgerald, Faulkner, Nathanael West, Ludwig Bemelmans,
Raymond Chandler, and others were not really welcoming. They had
seen with the eyes of writers who as a rule wished to be elsewhere, not
with the eyes of a star who had arrived at her heart's desire. Essie's enchanted childish moviegoing coincides more or less with mine, though
she is two years my senior; the period of her rising stardom, however, saw
a tailing-off of my moviegoing, as college, marriage, paternity, and literary labor came between me and the silver screen. Much of what I read in
the film histories listed in the afterword was news to me, though I tried to
work with movie moments glowingly embedded in my brain. As for
Colorado, it is for me a state of mind as well as of the Union, that state of
the American mind which yearns for more height, more breadth, more
Western space in which the limitless Emersonian self can breathe the
divine ether.

Writing this book had its pleasures as well as its travails. To be, in
imagination, a young woman is always pleasurable for a male fictionist.
To feel landscapes assembled piece by piece become coherent and inhab-
itable is satisfying. With so many characters obliged to make the muster, I was grateful to those, like Harlan Dearholt and Arnie Fineman,
who offered to take charge. Whole other chapters could have followed
Clarence and Stella, Teddy and Emily into other passages of their lives,
but I was trying through this throng of identities to tell a continuous
story, of which God was the hero. I invited Him in, to be a character in
my tale, and if He declined, with characteristic modern modesty, to make
His presence felt unambiguously, at least there is a space in this chronicle
plainly reserved for Him, a pocket in human nature that nothing else will
fill. The Wilmots—a name I took from a historical proviso—represent
an old American strain, in times when many strains are vigorously contributing to the national life. I thought to follow their pallid Calvinist
thread through most of this century, which has been called the American

century. This flattering phrase can be justified with a number of statistics, but it seemed to me just and true in regard to global dreaming: our American movies, our songs, our inventions, our autos (from the Greek for "self"), our political insistence upon the rights of the individual all gave the world, amid the century's wars and horrors, a new style of aspiration and a higher standard of personal comfort than history had hitherto permitted its billions to glimpse. From Taiwan to Timbuktu, American dreams flicker and shine and beckon.

A "SPECIAL MESSAGE" for the Franklin Library's Signed First Edition Society printing of Toward the End of Time (1997).

Standing in the kitchen watching my microwave oven tick off, in segmented numerals, the two minutes and twenty seconds needed for it to warm a mug of water to a temperature suitable for tea, I have more than once reflected that life consists of years, months, weeks, days, hours, seconds. The thought induces panic: we are trapped in a finite number, which, though large in most cases—the seconds flicker by rather slowly, when you watch them, and there are 2,209,032,000 of them in a life of seventy years—is nevertheless finite. Turning sixty-five, the customary age of retirement in the United States, but adds a nail to the coffin, driving deeper home an observation that a child of four or five can make: time is carrying us toward the grave. And yet our earthly existence, in all its pleasures and stimuli, could not transpire without time, time that dismisses dead minutes, that shuffles the cast of characters, that makes new room, that brings gain and growth as well as loss. Our pleasures are not just incidentally but necessarily transitory. Without time, we would be frozen immobile, more so than a body in the ice, because even within the ice chemistry works alterations, turns skin and blood and muscle into black and brittle leather. Experience itself is a function of time.

Twentieth-century writers, having lost most of the beliefs that called forth metaphysical thought, continue to dignify time with contemplation. Proust, in his magnificent À la recherche du temps perdu, claimed to feel time reversed in the moment of involuntary memory sprung by a sensation—a madeleine soaked in chamomile tea, uneven paving stones underfoot. Nabokov, in the treatise on time that composes the fourth part of his cosmic novel *Ada*, strives to perceive the texture of time in "the dim intervals between the dark beats" of a clock or in a quasi-physical mental exertion: "I must move my mind in the direction opposite to that in which I am moving, as one does when one is driving past a long row of poplars and wishes to isolate and stop one of them, thus making the green blur reveal and offer, yes, offer, its every leaf." This elusive texture is to an extent present in the many books that follow the year around the calendar, from Hesiod's *Works and Days* and Spenser's *The Shepheardes Calender* to such twentieth-century annals as Mikhail Prishvin's *Nature's Diary* and Hal Borland's *Sundial of the Seasons*. My first, and probably my best, book for children was *A Child's Calendar*—twelve poems on the twelve months. The years revolve, and carry us forward even as they return to where they began. The elemental impulse to trace the course of a year underlies *Toward the End of Time*.

The book takes place in the future, the year 2020, a year when I almost certainly—a fact I cannot long stare at—will not be alive. I have managed such a leap forward before. My first novel, *The Poorhouse Fair*, was written in 1957–58 and was imagined, with some imprecision, to take place in the era of George Orwell's celebrated *1984*. That leap is greater than the twenty-four years I extrapolated from 1996, when I transcribed Ben Turnbull's occasional jottings. Though as a boy I was awed, entertained, and frightened by science fiction—Wells's *Time Machine*, Shaw's *Back to Methuselah*—which projected human existence into the immensely distant future, when the very anatomy of human beings would have changed, my basic feeling about the future seems to be that it will not be much different from the present, just as the present enjoys a close relation to the past. After all, anyone older than twenty is history on legs; toys and artifacts just like those I used in boyhood now rest in museum cases. For all our fashion-conscious haste to dramatize and capitalize upon each new twist of technology and geopolitics, the human animal changes imperceptibly; the basic appetites, organic and spiritual, must be fed by the same old food, though cooked and dressed with a new nuance, or an old nuance revived.

Future historical developments, duly indicated, mark and mar Ben Turnbull's world in the year 2020, in the independent and anarchic state of Massachusetts. Quantum mechanics, which already dominate the microcosmic, subatomic world, permeate the macrocosm of the future, generating quantum leaps of plot and personality. Ben lives in the "many universes" of far-out physical theory. Yet it will strike many readers how much his life resembles that of a petty squire in the 1990s. The upper classes—and to such Ben, however uneasily and sardonically, belongs—evade many of the historical burdens that crush the less fortunate. For Ben, global disaster has amounted to minor irritations, and such, my novel implies, is the hard-hearted case for many.

He, I should hasten to emphasize, though he may write in something like the voice of this "special message," is far from being me. I was a mere sixty-four when I wrote of him as sixty-six in a year when I would be eighty-eight. He has retired where I still cheerfully toil on. He is a baby boomer and I the father of boomers. He comes from the Massachusetts Berkshires and not from Pennsylvania's Berks County. He has more children and grandchildren than I. My health, for the time being, is better than his. He has spent his professional life in a world as opaque and menacing to me as that of Neanderthal hunters, the world of financial investment. All these differences put me to considerable trouble of invention and kept me interested; autobiography strikes me as one of the dullest of genres, which begs and fudges most of the issues that properly concern an avid student of humanity.

Life in action, in its disreputable and irresponsible optimism, is the subject here—life as known and revealed by a man, a man with a certain fixed curriculum vitae but with other possibilities latent in him, in this universe built on quantum indeterminacy. Karl Barth, the most theological of modern theologians, once wrote what he expected of a novelist: "I expect him to show me man as he always is in the man of today, my contemporary—and vice-versa, to show me my contemporary in man as he always is. . . . [He] should have no plans for educating me, but should leave me to reflect (or not) on the basis of the portrait with which I am presented." Such a portrait constituted my attempt in these crabbed, confessional, divagatory pages.

TWO BELATED "TALK OF THE TOWN" STORIES, *by a reporter who retired from the field in 1957 but was called back for an eye-witness account and a self-interview in January and September of 1997, respectively.*

A visitor to the city, pent up in his room at, say, the Mayflower Hotel, on Central Park West, turns on television with a heightened sense of expectation. The medium, so often described as "cool," feels hotter here, more important, closer to real life. Sitcoms emanate from these same streets, and the major networks have their studios a few blocks away. The other evening, I watched the six-o'clock news, which featured a fire in the "midtown" apartment of the elderly jazz great Lionel Hampton: flames flickered and smoke poured out of horizontal apartment windows, and the great vibraphonist, seated in a wheelchair, dazed but courteous, was interviewed as to his rescue, his emotions, his anticipation of an imminent scheduled meeting with President Clinton at the White House to receive the National Medal of Arts. This was news. I ventured outside onto the windblown streets in search of a sandwich, and at a corner two blocks from the hotel a small cluster of people were staring up. I stared up with them, and saw a towering sheet of horizontal windows, including a darkened one with the glass and the mullions knocked out of it. It looked like the one I had just seen on television. It *was* the one. This was reality. This was "midtown." A young man in the crowd was expounding to anyone who would listen: "That fire up there was on television this afternoon, it was on the evening news, it will still be on the morning news tomorrow!" We all clucked and muttered in something like agreement and shared excitement. I had become, momentarily, a voice in the crowd, a New Yorker, full of the proud sense that to be in New York is to be in the news, or close to it.

*

John Updike, when approached by this department to discuss his recent leap into cyberspace, was characteristically diffident. "My part was the least of it," he said. "I was approached by Amazon.com, Inc., a Seattle outfit who sell books over the Internet, to contribute the beginning of a story that would be taken forward over the Internet in daily installments, for six weeks, by visitors to the Amazon.com Website. Each day's winner would get a thousand dollars. I was to provide the ending on the last day. Well, any writer has some aborted beginnings in his files, so I offered them three, of which they took the opening paragraph of a would-be murder mystery entitled *Murder Makes the Magazine*, featuring a forty-three-year-old editor, Miss Tasso Polk. I wrote it, as I recall, around 1960."

When asked what magazine he had in mind, Updike uneasily admitted, "*The New Yorker* was the only magazine I knew at all from the inside, so you might say there was a tenuous connection. But the novel didn't develop; it stalled at thirteen pages, in part because I had a heavy conscience. The magazine in those old days was immensely privacy-prone and publicity-averse, and even the most whimsical report from its interior would have seemed a betrayal. Also, I have never had any luck writing a mystery novel, though I devoured them by the dozens as a kid. So I was interested to see what others might make of my beginning."

And what did they make of it? "Well," the silver-haired, sixty-five-year-old author hesitantly declared, "they served up lots of red herrings. And a lot of male characters, so that my spinster heroine finds herself with this suddenly jammed dance card. And there are mysterious keys and messages, and a murder that has to take place twice, since one installment revived the victim. The strangest twist, I thought, was when Miss

Polk gets into a taxi and is driven, in short order, to an estate with a cobbled driveway and an allée of boxwoods and elms. An allée! In Manhattan!! And of course there were inconsistencies, which occur even with a single writer. But," Updike went on, unstoppably, "I thought they did pretty well, as a crowd. One of the winners, oddly enough, was a member of my younger daughter's group of baby mothers in Ipswich, Massachusetts. The real narrative artists, I dare say, were the judges out there at Amazon.com, since they were selecting from as many as nine thousand entries a day. Imagine, nine thousand plot alternatives a day! People thought I was among the selectors, but it would have driven me mad. When the last entry was in place, I just tried to tie up some of the bundle of loose ends and to reward Tasso Polk for her patience. I came to love her—she was the one who leaped into cyberspace, not me."

And what did his adventure tell him about the state of culture in a hyperelectronic age? "It struck me," he said, "how literary the episodes were. Euripides, *Treasure Island*, Shakespeare's sonnets, the stories of Edgar Allan Poe, Lewis Carroll—these are all knowingly alluded to. A lot of the mystery takes place, classically, in a library full of old books—the story kept trying to become an old-fashioned English country-house puzzle. Maybe it shouldn't surprise us that Internet buffs have done some reading, since what is the Internet but a form of reading? Also, cats. There are three cat characters, and the main one, Mauser, keeps sneaking back into the tale. I suppose a computer and a cat are somewhat alike—they both purr, and like to be stroked, and spend a lot of the day motionless. A cat and a computer are both on the quiet side, with secrets they don't necessarily share. As it happened, I was in New York the day my finale came due, and I had to write it on a strange laptop, with a program I didn't know. The screen kept disappearing, or jumping sideways. When I came to print it out, the printer ignored the punctuation. Still, I got it done, and faxed, and over with—a hairbreadth escape from cyberspace."

For the record, here is the beginning I gave Amazon.com:

Miss Tasso Polk at ten-ten alighted from the elevator onto the olive tiles of the nineteenth floor only lightly nagged by a sense of something wrong. The Magazine's crest, that great black M, the thing masculine that had most profoundly penetrated her life, echoed from its inlaid security the thoughtful humming in her mind: "m." There had been someone strange in the elevator. She had felt it all the way up. *Strange*, not merely unknown to her personally. Most of the world was unknown to her personally, but it was not strange. The men in little felt hats and oxblood shoes who performed services of salesmanship and accountancy and research and coördination for the firms (Simplex, Happitex, Technoni-trex, Instant-Pix) that occupied the seventeen floors beneath the sacred olive groves of The Magazine were anonymous and interchangeable to her but not strange. She could read right through the button-down collars of their unstarched shirts into the ugly neck-stretching of their morning shaves, right through the pink and watery whites of their eyes into last night's cocktail party in Westchester, Tarrytown, Rye, or Orange, right through their freckled, soft, too-broad-and-brown hands into adulterous caresses that did not much disgust her, they were so distant and trivial and even, in their suburban distance from her, idyllic, like something satyrs do on vases. Miss Polk was forty-three, and had given herself to The Magazine in the flower of her beauty. Since the day, a nervous bride, when she had been led to a desk in whose center was set a bouquet of sharpened pencils in a water glass, she had ridden the elevator two dozen thousand times, and her companions on this alternating rise and fall were rarely strange.

And this is the ending I cooked up, after forty-four intervening co-authors had contributed their episodes. If my style seems frantic, and some of my allusions obscure, remember that I am tying up as many computer-generated loose ends as I can, nearly forty years after I ushered Miss Polk out of the elevator.

"Tasso," Evermore began, heavily, damply, groggily arising from the floor, "as you know, The Magazine hasn't been doing so well these recent years."

"All those good people who used to pore over its scrupulously edited, fact-packed pages," Boyce added, in his strange androgynous voice, "now cruise the Internet, communicating interactively with a world of electronic buddies. Print has become a mug's game."

"And," Uncle James interposed in his blustery fashion, "seeing that the game was up, this elephantine rascal"—he gestured toward the now arisen Evermore, who did look gray and weary, less like a former lover than like Babar after he had eaten the ill-chosen mushroom—"was skimming enough from the staff pension fund to fill a box, bigger than a breadbox, with bars of platinum!"

"It wasn't me, it wasn't my idea!" spake the craven Evermore. "It was the duplicitous, morbid-minded old rascal Marion Merriweather, mercilessly milking his own marvelous creation!"

"You should have spurned his seduction," Tasso sternly told the cowering love of her life. "The Heart desires, but the Hand refrains."

"I, of course," said Boyce, "sensed the old plutocrat's plot, and by seeming to join it, intended to thwart it. Now The Magazine is entirely mine, and I would like to discharge Evermore and appoint you, dear Miss Polk, as editor. Your devotion and acumen have long been but half-heartedly rewarded."

"The Godhead fires, the Soul attains, huh?" said Tasso Polk. This long day had forcefully brought back to her what she found so unsatisfactory about men—their intricate thinking, their simplistic feeling, their desperate wish to reduce life to the condition of a game. "I'll think about it, Franklin," she conceded, startled by the casual first-name basis, which implied a long future familiarity. "Becoming captain has been the ruin of many a happy first mate. All I care about at the moment is, Where are my cats? Mr. Evermore"—the courtesy was reflexive; she felt nothing for the man now—"is Louis perchance the catnapper?"

Evermore limply nodded, his deflation completed by her bold stab of cognizance. "We are holding them in meow—I mean escrow—against the possibility that the box of platinum is empty. The last time I handled it, it seemed suspiciously light."

She nodded. "I will suggest that the police look into the thick old books in Merriweather's study, under the television set. They seemed uncannily heavy when I handled them." It was not so difficult, she realized, to be the master detective, a know-it-all. All it took was a certain collusion with the author. But it was late, late, and murder had been committed, the murder of Marion Hyde Merriweather, and whether Uncle James had slain his old roommate or Evermore his old employer, each of them wearing a telltale long coat, the police could sort out, along with the other sort of nitpicking detail these blue-uniformed numbskulls were paid to do.

The Magazine, at any rate, would enjoy an infusion of embezzled platinum. The issues would issue forth, mug's game or not. Pencils would be sharpened, spelling would be checked. And tomorrow, at ten-ten—or perhaps, in deference to today's shocks to her accustomed routine, at ten-twenty—she would be there.

A FOREWORD *to the French translation of* Facing Nature *(1985),* La Condition Naturelle *(1988).*

Though I am not considered, in the United States, much of a poet,* my first efforts at writing were poetry, my first publications in magazines

---

*This blunt assertion was tactfully softened in French to *"Je ne suis pas principalement considéré, aux États-Unis, comme un poète."*

were poems, and my first book was a collection of verse, bearing the untranslatable title *The Carpentered Hen*. Three more collections have followed, at intervals of five or more years, and now this one, with the perhaps also untranslatable title of *Facing Nature*. The dust jacket of the American edition, at my request, showed the face of a marble Gorgon from the Acropolis: the Gorgon who, in ancient legend, turned to stone those who gazed directly upon her. Nature frightens and fascinates us; she gives us birth, food, light, splendor, love, pain, and death. She must be faced; she is all around us and, indeed, within us. Yet there is something else within us, which is often surprised by Nature, by her variety, intricacy, and immensity, and by that apparent indifference which yet generates so much consoling beauty. This surprise moves us to philosophy or to poetry; there is even, in English, a quasi-genre, called "nature poetry," of which Wordsworth's poems are the supreme example. Many of my own poems here tend to that genre.

The first section contains "sonnets," poems of fourteen lines, written down in waiting rooms and hotel rooms when no other way of making a record seemed available. The first sequence, of three, expresses surprise at a good friend's death, and the last sequence, of eight, surprise at being awake, night after night, in a tourist's Spain. The sonnet in its shortness invites compression, and some of these lines are difficult even in the original. In the second section, there are flowers and trees, shadows and rain, crabs and birds, pain and taste. The longest poem, an attempt to visit the moons of Jupiter in terms of the imagery beamed back to earth by the Voyager space robots, leads into the third section, an attempt to hymn, in stately and even heroic measures, some of the natural processes which invisibly surround us and determine the shape and limits of our lives. For this effort, rather than stealing odd moments from my fiction and my prose, I solemnly sat down in a poet's robes each morning for several weeks, with my encyclopedia and science textbooks, and tried to draw from the facts before me and from my memory lines of enough tension and compactness to form "odes"—a somewhat archaic form, marked by a mood of exaltation and lines of varying length—to that majestic natural reality which simultaneously interpenetrates us and stretches to the stars.

I am grateful to Éditions Gallimard for favoring this volume with publication in France and to Alan Suied for taking such care with the translation. Poetry of course draws upon the full extent of a language, not only its puns and alliterations and nuances of tone but its penumbra of passing usage and past quotation. Something is lost, but perhaps, in the twist from one language to another, other aspects glint out more tellingly. Poe,

I have seen it said, is better in French, and Shakespeare in Russian. I gladly embrace the possibility that these verses will take on new lustre in the language of Racine and Valéry.

AN ANSWER *to the question "How is humor doing these days?" from* The Paris Review, *for its issue (No. 136) on Humor.*

It is hard to separate history from one's personal history. In my adolescence I thought "humor" was a sublime and prevalent genre; greedily and happily I consumed books by James Thurber, E. B. White, Robert Benchley, S. J. Perelman, Frank Sullivan, Peter De Vries, P. G. Wodehouse, Thorne Smith. I drew the line at Max Shulman—he struck me as vulgar. I read the poems of Ogden Nash, Phyllis McGinley, Morris Bishop, Arthur Guiterman, Don Marquis. In my hunger to be amused I searched out older writers like Stephen Leacock, Ring Lardner, Clarence Day, and Mark Twain. Laugh!! I loved these light-hearted volumes, available in abundant supply in the bookstores and the local library, and could imagine nothing finer than to join, someday, the jolly company of humorists.

This was all in the Forties, drawing heavily on books from the Thirties. By the time, in the Fifties, I grew to be a man, there were still humorists practicing, but somehow the entity called "humor" was fading away, drying up, even as I scribbled and sold some late examples of it. What was happening? Could the Cold War be chilling a genre that had thrived through the horrors of the Depression and World War II? Could the human animal be shedding its ancient release mechanism of laughter? One answer would be, Of course not: humor still thrives, though in slightly different milieux from the Algonquin Circle and *The New Yorker*. A book of parodies called *Politically Correct Bedtime Stories* has been on the *New York Times* best-seller list for over fifty weeks, and chaps like Roy Blount and P. J. O'Rourke seem to do all right; Art Buchwald and Russell Baker continue to troll for chuckles in the daily papers.

But this answer, though defensible, doesn't sing. Things *have* changed; *zeitgeistig* energy *has* ebbed away from "humor"—look at the very way I feel obliged to put the word in quotation marks. For one, the culture is less literate, less print-oriented, and there are fewer to appreciate, even if suitable targets were around, the kind of literary parody that Roger Angell and Veronica Geng, say, should be producing more of, or the sort of hyperliterate prose that S. J. Perelman and George Jean Nathan used to spin. Light verse required a delicacy of ear and a shared treasure of allusions that are gone; its metrical ingenuity thrived in the shade of a body of serious, stanzaic, rhymed verse that was common knowledge, and there is no such body now. Secondly, the humor of Benchley and Thurber assumed a kind of generic American experience—white, Protestant, male, bourgeois, basically genteel, timid, and well intentioned—that can no longer be assumed. Much of what used to be considered funny would now seem classist, sexist, and racist, in ascending order of unfunniness. Humor draws on stereotypes, and where "stereotype" is a dirty word, the humorist will find himself washing his hands too often. Thirdly, humor, to be a valuable release, needs something to be released, and what, in let-it-all-hang-out America, is that something? The cartoons of Thurber and Arno flirted with our privately held sexual knowledge; what sexual knowledge now is privately held? Humor used to let us peek from our excessively ordered and repressed lives into possibilities of cheerful confusion, dishevelment, and de-inhibition; now culture serves up those possibilities in rap and heavy-metal music, in boisterously shameless talk shows, in blatantly sexual movies and television serials. How strenuously, for example, television comedies like *Roseanne* and *Married . . . with Children* must cavort to be more outrageous than what is happening in the American living rooms where such programs are turned on.

Humor, to use a dichotomy dear to Camille Paglia, is a subversive Dionysian voice whispered in a society constrained by Apollonian ideals. The less the constraint, the louder the voice has to be heard; and the louder the voice, the less exquisite, the less artistic, the humor will be.

AN ANSWER *to the question—posed by Ronald B. Shwartz for a book of such replies—"What books have left the greatest impression on me, and why?"*

Well, no book fails to make *some* impression. From my childhood I can remember being terrified by the cave scene of *Tom Sawyer*, and by an account of the Peer Gynt legend in an anthology of tales for children. The first books I loved, I believe, were those of James Thurber; he drew as well as wrote, and in *Fables for Our Time* and *My Life and Hard Times* and *The White Deer* the combination seemed enchanting, a beautiful demonstration of artistic *making*. The cartoons and sketches drew me to his fiction, some of which was probably over my adolescent head. Benchley, E. B. White, Frank Sullivan, Stephen Leacock were other humorists I enjoyed. Mystery writers also gave me much pleasure as a boy, and some notion of an honorable contract between the writer and the reader: there will be murders, a puzzle, red herrings, and a solution in the end. At college, I was especially taken with Shakespeare, the metaphysical poets, Wordsworth, Walt Whitman, Tolstoy and Dostoevsky, and the short stories of J. D. Salinger, which were relatively hot off the press. In the years after college, I discovered on my own Henry Green, an English novelist whose light, willful prose touch and ear for dialogue and eye for human vulnerability were an artistic revelation, and Marcel Proust, whose grand disquisitions and metaphors showed me what majestic perspectives the diminished modern sensibility could still attain to. Søren Kierkegaard completes the list of writers who moved me in this formative period to intense admiration, and excited me to attack my own material, from an angle I felt was *new*. Kierkegaard does not write fiction, or primarily fiction, of course, but his philosophical writing is full of characters and animated illustrations. His portrait of the human condition opened my eyes and heart, as did Green and Proust. They made me want to do likewise, in my own language, on my own continent. Mighty examples exhilarate and embolden us, rather than discourage us. In the many years since then, I can think of Kafka, Robert Pinget, and John Cheever as making impressions nearly as powerful; but my own clay was more set by then, and harder to shape.

Books that changed my life: *Conjured up for Borders Books.*

I must have been already a Thurber fan before acquiring *The Thurber Carnival*, because the smell of it, the look of its jacket, the nests of drawings and cartoons built into its pages all had the pungent savor of a requested Christmas present. Thurber was but one of many humorists I read in my childhood and early adolescence. Of the dozens—nay, hundreds—of mystery novels I consumed in the same period, Agatha Christie's *And Then There Were None*, also titled *Ten Little Indians*, remains in my mind as a consummately satisfying piece of mystery fiction, as bloody and tidy as a boy could wish. Ellery Queen, John Dickson Carr, Dorothy Sayers, Ngaio Marsh—these were other magicians of the form, in its high-Thirties formality; it was never quite the same after World War II, the English villages were never quite so cozy and the country houses so hermetically snowed in. These books gave my young life great new vistas, and showed it the possibilities of writing as entertainment. I remember sitting in the Reading Public Library at about the age of fifteen, thinking it was time I got serious, and reading Bernard Shaw's *Back to Methusaleh* and T. S. Eliot's *The Waste Land*. Modernism thus loomed, but it wasn't until after college that I found in Proust the very voice of my ideal self; Proust showed me what writing could do, in that elusive but vast borderland where consciousness—sensibility—assimilates the world. I would name, as striking me as most beautiful, not the first, best-known volume, *Swann's Way*, but the second, which in flowery English translation is titled *Within a Budding Grove*. Henry Green, the English novelist, had dawned upon me a year earlier; *Loving* is his masterpiece, no doubt, but the earlier *Party-Going* and *Living* seemed even more striking, and revolutionary in their sentences and dialogue. The first Kierkegaard I read was *Fear and Trembling*, and the first Karl Barth was *The Word of God and the Word of Man*; for a while I read both theological thinkers greedily, but it was these two titles, I suppose, that gave me a philosophy to live and labor by, and in that way changed my life. That a number of my pivotal titles are now out of print or hard to get indicates, I suppose, that no two lives are alike.

FIVE REMEMBERED MOMENTS OF UTTER READING BLISS: *A list prepared for the fifth anniversary issue of* Forbes FYI, *edited by Christopher Buckley.*

1. Mickey Mouse Big Little Book, c. 1940. The chunky but light-as-balsa-wood feel of the ten-cent volume in my hand. The nice clarity of the print and the brevity of the page, each page facing a panel of a comic strip. The inky coziness of that three-fingered microcosm as Mickey and Minnie win out over Pegleg Pete and his dog-eared crew. All power to the undersized! Around me, the gloom of the Depression mingles with the clouds of gathering war, but none of it is my fault.

2. John Dickson Carr or Agatha Christie mystery, c. 1946. Hardcover wrapped in cellophane by the lending library at the drugstore, or else a twenty-five-cent Pocket Book, with kangaroo insignia and cellophane peeling from the cover. A country manor, near a village. A dwindling cast of characters, as Hercule Poirot or Gideon Fell or Miss Marple drops enticing and sinister hints. Surface text moving one way, shadowy undercurrents of evil another. Layers, red herrings; sudden corpses in the library, footprints outside the French windows. Adolescent need for structure triumphantly satisfied by complicated terminal exposition and brisk matings among the surviving characters. Consumption position: supine on sofa, book in left hand, right hand in box of raisins.

3. Edmund Spenser, *The Faerie Queene*, 1953. Highly serious midnight-blue *Poetical Works of Spenser*, Oxford University Press. Double columns, six-point type, Elizabethan spellings. Allegorical figures on

horseback and one mellifluous Spenserian stanza after another parade by. Position: derriere on a hard oak chair, tipped; feet propped on the bed across the exiguous college dormitory room. English 222, with Professor Bush, who loves Spenser so much his patient explications bring tears to even the eyes of graduate students. My undergraduate sense of absorbing one more classic, in what seems the finite task ahead, of reading *everything*. A New England blizzard and Senator McCarthy rage outside, but I am sheltered from both.

4. Proust, *Remembrance of Things Past*, 1955. Riverside Drive, New York City. Steady rush-hour traffic on West Side Highway on one side of me, wife cooking dinner and baby burbling on the other, Swann and Odette and Madame Verdurin and the Duchesse de Guermantes in the middle. Courtesy of Scott Moncrieff's florid and indefatigable translation, this gorgeous voice and mind, Marcel's, going on and on, an epiphany every four hundred pages. But what epiphanies! What shimmering Arcadian vistas of illusion and disillusion! This is *prose*.

5. Well, what? Forty years since the last bliss? Four decades of malarial literary fever but no hot flashes? Nabokov, Calvino, early Salinger, late Cheever, Robert Pinget, Bruno Schulz, Murdoch and Spark, Ozick and Oates, Tim O'Brien and Orhan Pamuk—all bliss, but *utter*? Has joining the ranks of the printed deprived me of the guileless trust I once brought Thurber, Kierkegaard, and Henry Green, say? Well, what about the *Encyclopaedia Britannica*, its row of soldiers in maroon leather uniform, that alphabetical universe of negotiable truths, of facts I can *use*? Bent low in the library wing chair, my aged eyesight strained, I consult, I memorize, I rush upstairs and pop the stolen tidbit still warm into the humming word processor, fortifying the stew of my own that therein simmers. Bliss!

IN RESPONSE *to a request from* Le Nouvelle Observateur *to write something about Cervantes'* Don Quixote.

Memory is a great trickster, and my memory of reading *Don Quixote* is distinct enough to be suspect. I read it in the first months of my first marriage, when I was a mere twenty-one, the summer between my junior and senior years at Harvard. My bride and I had secured summer jobs, at a YMCA camp on an island in the middle of a large lake in the bosky state of New Hampshire. She ran the camp store and snack shop; I was secretary to the camp's director. His typewriter had a brown ribbon, and the official letters and unofficial poems I wrote on it had a faux-rustic look.

My young wife's right forearm grew very muscular from the daily exercise of scooping ice cream from its frozen barrels. We had little spare time, but our accommodations in a cabin deep in the woods had an idyllic flavor; another Adam and Eve were setting up house in the wilderness. At twilight, between the end of work and the bell calling us to supper from the distant dining hall, I would conscientiously read a few pages of *Don Quixote*.

Why that book, of all books? I did not expect to be assigned it in my English courses, though in fact Vladimir Nabokov had taught it at Harvard not long before, in a humanities course I could have enrolled in but, regrettably, did not. My mother—surprisingly in a country girl from the Pennsylvania Dutch region west of Philadelphia—was a Hispanophile, a reader of Washington Irving and W. H. Prescott and V. S. Pritchett on the Iberian Peninsula. So, though I am not sure she ever read much Cervantes, a path of spiritual access had been cleared into the thickets of this Renaissance masterpiece. I read it in the venerable Modern Library edition, with engraved illustrations by Gustave Doré. The English translation, by Peter Motteux, must have dated from the eighteenth century, for the nouns were capitalized as in German, the past tense "ed" was written as " 'd," and quotation marks were not used for spoken discourse. The effect was crabbed but pleasant; the old text was, I soon discovered, highly readable, thanks to Cervantes's own clear, concrete, and swift-moving language. In his preface, the author advises every writer:

> Do but take care to express your self in a plain, easy Manner, in well-chosen, significant, and decent Terms, and to give an harmonious and pleasing Turn to your Periods: Study to explain your Thoughts, and set them in the truest Light, labouring, as much as possible, not to leave 'em dark nor intricate, but clear and intelligible.

The story's premise was briskly established: an elderly gentleman in a minor province has read so many medieval romances that "the Moisture of his Brain was exhausted to that Degree, that at last he lost the Use of his Reason." Off he goes, to battle the windmills and other flourishing foes. For over nine hundred big pages the comedy and excitement yielded by this single conceit rarely flags; the deluded but resilient knight-errant races toward the moment—the very great moment—when his health at last fails, his madness lifts, and on his deathbed he renounces his folly. Then his accomplice in folly, his squire, Sancho Panzo, the earthy rotund representative of common sense throughout the novel, pleads in tears that his master rise from his "doleful Dumps" and sally forth for more adventures. It is a stroke of Cervantes' humane genius to see that not only does Don Quixote need Sancho Panza, but Sancho Panza needs Don Quixote. The earthbound need the release and stimulation of the visionaries, high though the cost be in bruises and embarrassments.

Shakespeare, the greater genius, does not give us back ourselves quite the way *Don Quixote* does. His plays show a world where medieval structure persists; they contain a close analysis of kingship and a conservative distrust of the mob. Cervantes presents post-medieval men and women in a Spain, prior to the Counter-Reformation, that would not for centuries be as worldly again. Having set himself to burlesque idealism, Cervantes places narrative on a firmer but lower ground. This first modern, democratic novel takes the delusions and actions of an impoverished gentleman from Mancha to be worth relating, though they have no clear tie to Heaven and no end but disillusion and death.

My memory is that I cried at the end, letting go of this brave, boisterous saga of the humbled, unconquerable spirit. Its pages remain tinged for me with the dusky forest light and the unsteady glow of the kerosene lamp within the cabin of the newlyweds.

THE TEN GREATEST WORKS OF LITERATURE, 1001–2000: *A Eurocentric list totted up for the 1998* World Almanac.

1. Thomas Aquinas, *Summa Theologica*, written c. 1266–73. This massive medieval work of philosophy demonstrates the compatibility of faith and reason and to this day serves as a foundation of Roman Catholic apologetics. It encouraged the rise of scientific thought in Europe, and without it Dante could not have written *The Divine Comedy*, or James Joyce *Ulysses*.

2. Dante Alighieri, *The Divine Comedy*, written c. 1307–21. Known by the author simply as *Commedia*, this poem of a hundred cantos and fourteen thousand lines takes the poet on a visionary voyage from Hell through Purgatory to Paradise. A triumph of schematic organization and of line-by-line vitality, it established Tuscan as the dominant dialect of Italy and remains the greatest long poem since Virgil's *Aeneid*.

3. Miguel de Cervantes Saavedra, *Don Quixote*, Part I, 1605; Part II, 1615. This tale, of a Spanish gentleman who read too many chivalric romances and in trying to enact them runs repeatedly afoul of the actual world, is considered the first European novel. Its humor is broad but its pathos and symbolic resonance run deep; the pairing of the idealistic, infatuated don with his earthy squire Sancho Panza encapsulates the human condition.

4. William Shakespeare, *Comedies, Histories, and Tragedies*, written c. 1590–1613, published 1623. Both the greatest poet and greatest playwright in the English language, Shakespeare wrote about thirty-six plays; their insight into human character in action, the variety of their plots and situations, and the Protean energy of their poetic language continue to astonish readers and theatre audiences.

5. Voltaire, *Candide*, 1759. A slim book written in three days, and published anonymously, *Candide* distills the sparkling spirit of Voltaire and the Enlightenment. Like *Don Quixote*, it dramatizes the clash between ideas and reality—the ideas are those of the philosopher Leibniz, which explained away evil, and reality is represented by the Lisbon earthquake and other sufferings endured by the titular hero and his cheerful tutor, Dr. Pangloss.

6. Edward Gibbon, *The History of the Decline and Fall of the Roman Empire*, 1776–88. Another monument of the Enlightenment, Gibbon's six-volume history constitutes a masterpiece of research and elegantly smooth, frequently sardonic exposition that sets an unsurpassed standard for vivid historiography and sociological analysis.

7. Leo Tolstoy, *War and Peace*, 1863–69. Of the many great nineteenth-century novels, Tolstoy's panorama of Napoleon's invasion of Russia seems the greatest—great in bulk, in empathy, in the breadth of its cast of characters, in the sweep of its speculations on human history. Vast though the canvas, the individual touch is always exact, direct, and concise.

8. Fyodor Dostoevsky, *The Possessed*, 1871–72. The passionate insight that Dostoevsky brought to the novel is at its most intense and perversely comic in this portrait of left-wing revolutionaries; even if Russia had not eventually fallen under the sway of "the devils" depicted here, the depths of the human soul sounded would make the work prophetic.

9. Marcel Proust, *Remembrance of Things Past*, 1913–27. The French tradition of psychological analysis is brought to its fullest flower in this prodigiously long examination of the autobiographical hero's sensibility, as his memory traces the changing perspectives that love and snobbery yield upon a mordantly sketched social landscape. Proust's metaphors are marvellous.

10. James Joyce, *Ulysses*, 1922. A narrow, provincial subject—Dublin on one June day of 1904, as experienced by a handful of characters, foremost the young dreamer Stephen Dedalus and the middle-aged Jewish advertising salesman Leopold Bloom—becomes in Joyce's erudite, playful rendering a detailed counterpart of Homer's *Odyssey* and an epitome of realism: a book as opaque and particulate as life.

REMARKS *on religion and contemporary American literature delivered at Indiana/Purdue University in Indianapolis, April 1994.*

My impression is that orthodox religion scarcely figures at all, even as a force to be reacted against, in contemporary American writing. By way of sharp contrast, when I was becoming a writer in the 1950s, Christian orthodoxy was eminently, provocatively represented by the Anglo-Catholicism of T. S. Eliot and W. H. Auden, by the Catholicism of the fiction writers Flannery O' Connor and J. F. Powers, as well as the widely read Graham Greene and Evelyn Waugh, and—belonging to a slightly later generation—Muriel Spark and Walker Percy. A more Presbyterian kind of faith was subtly espoused by Marianne Moore, the sister of a clergyman; and the Jewish faith had its popular exponents in Herman Wouk and Chaim Potok. To this nourishing stew, Jack Kerouac and J. D. Salinger added a pinch of Oriental, zen magic. In college literature courses, Christian writers like Dante and John Donne and the English metaphysicals were especially admired. If Christianity was not precisely "in," the Middle Ages certainly were, along with concepts like "anxiety," "numinousness," and "the leap of faith." The Christian existentialism of the mid-nineteenth-century Dane Søren Kierkegaard had influenced a host of post-war European thinkers, from Sartre to Heidegger, and it is not too much to say that a certain *chic* attached to Thomists like Jacques Maritain and Father M. C. D'Arcy, and to Christian poets of a requisite agonized quality, such as Gerard Manley Hopkins and St. John of the Cross.

Not that Christian belief was easily attained to then, or complacently celebrated. Nevertheless, it was there as an animating current—a countercurrent, as it were, to straightforward realism in art and materialism in philosophy. Further, even those American writers not professing believers had been nurtured in a culture soaked in the Bible and the hymnal; they could call their novels *The Sun Also Rises* and *Absalom, Absalom* and *East of Eden* in confidence that the Old Testament resonance would be heard. The Judeo-Christian universe was the background against which the work even of such disaffected dandies as Wallace Stevens and Scott Fitzgerald established its patterns and made its points.

I am not aware of much comparable now, in the writing produced by men and women much younger than myself. For overtly Protestant novelists, we have Frederick Beuchner and Larry Woiwode; for transcendentalist essayists, we have Annie Dillard; for a Catholic novel, the best I have recently read is *Mariette in Ecstasy*, by Ron Hansen—a delicate, intuitive, cinematic work set in a New York State nunnery in 1906–07.

Its being set so securely in the past is what, perhaps, makes this fiercely religious novel possible. The Jewish religiosity of Eastern European Hasidic mysticism was luminously present in the fiction of Bernard Malamud and Isaac Bashevis Singer; to replace it, we have the more oblique and strenuous self-conscious Jewishness of Cynthia Ozick and Philip Roth. As to the Islamic content of the poems of Imamu Amiri Baraka, once known as LeRoi Jones, and of Buddhism in the poetry of Allen Ginsberg and Charles Wright, I can say little. Religious needs exist, and people who write are no more exempt from them than the rest of us; and no doubt in my ignorance I have failed to cite a number of relevant names. Reynolds Price, for instance, should be listed among the Christian novelists, and Paul Theroux's altar-boy upbringing increasingly figures in his fiction; and there are poets, such as Billy Collins and Greg Ghagis, with more than a touch of religious concern.

But the point perhaps is that for an averagely interested and distracted reader of *belles lettres* like myself, religion is not getting through. In the United States as seen by, say, Raymond Carver, Bobbie Ann Mason, Frederick Barthelme, Mary Robison and Tom Drury, the church is a footnote to the social scene and religion a dim undertone at best in the inner lives of the characters. It is not merely that lives seem to have little meaning beyond the immediate emotional need; the very lack of meaning is scarcely felt, by characters who no more look within themselves for significance than they look into the flickering dramas of television or the flickering affective lives of their friends and kin. The world they have grown up in, of television and malls and frequent geographical moves and casually extended and pruned families, is thin soil for the illusion of self-importance that religion needs to take root in. The self, the obdurant old entity without which sin and life are both nonsensical, really feels, to children of the electronic age, like what Bertrand Russell said it was — an epiphenomenon, an almost-phenomenon. In our digitized, channel-surfing America, the human integer of so-called minimalist fiction — a label no writer embraces but that covers a whole world of existing tone and mood — can no longer support a supernatural exponent; a momentary cup of positivity in the flow of electrons, the integral "I" hardly exists now, let alone forever. Nor does the more knotted and baroque fiction of gifted and challenging younger writers like, say, Deborah Eisenberg or Thom Jones or Andrea Lee, though more far-reaching in allusion and passion, aspire to hope of heaven, fear of hell, or thought of any life but this present one of bone and blood and eventual crushing disappointment. All is abysmally human, we might say. If there at all, the church is there, as it is on *The Simpsons*, for laughs, not entirely unwistful.

And yet, it should be allowed that fiction and poetry are in a sense religious exercises, requiring of their practitioners devotion and self-abnegation. Like religion, art appeals for judgement to standards not measurable in worldly terms, neither in dollar profits nor in immediate critical acclaim. In both, the last shall sometimes be first, and the meek and overlooked inherit the kingdom, as Stendhal, Melville, Emily Dickinson, and Gerard Manley Hopkins have inherited homage their own generation withheld. Artistic excellence and spiritual excellence often hide from contemporary eyes, and one consolation of being a Christian writer is that contemporary opinion, especially when slanted by contemporary political urgencies, can be discounted. Christian faith, whatever its awkwardnesses, relieves the artist of an obligation to believe that he owes mankind any propaganda on behalf of secular factions.

Fiction is rooted in an act of faith: a presumption of an inherent significance in human activity that makes daily life worth dramatizing and particularizing. There is even a shadowy cosmic presumption that the universe—the totality of what is, which includes our subjective impressions as well as objective data—composes a narrative and contains a poem, which our own stories and poems echo. The impulse of praise—or its inverse, lament and execration—motivates literature at its deepest and most simple and noble; even those who see nothing to praise admire in others the results of this impulse. The writer's most important asset is not wisdom or skill but an irrational, often joyous sense of importance attaching to what little he knows; and this is a religious sensation.

REMARKS *upon receiving the Campion Medal, bestowed by the Catholic Book Club, in New York City, on September 11, 1997.*

It is a thought-provoking, even disconcerting thing to be given an award as a "distinguished Christian person of letters," especially an award named for St. Edmund Campion. This brilliant Jesuit, a convert to Catholicism, was, history records, placed on the rack three times, in an effort to make him recant his faith. But, though tortured in body, he continued to debate brilliantly with Protestant theologians and won converts among them. He eloquently refuted the prosecution's trumped-up charges of sedition, but was nevertheless hanged, drawn, and quartered, at the age of forty-one, in 1581. How much of such persecution and agony, a recipient of the Campion Medal cannot but wonder, would he endure for the sake of his religious convictions? It is all too easy a thing to be a Christian in America, where God's name is on our coinage, pious pronouncements are routinely expected from elected officials, and churchgoing, though far from universal, enjoys a popularity astounding to Europeans. As good Americans we are taught to tolerate our neighbors' convictions, however bizarre they secretly strike us, and we extend, it may be, something of this easy toleration to ourselves and our own views.

In my own case, I came of intellectual age at a time, the Fifties, when a mild religious revival accompanied our reviving prosperity, and the powerful rational arguments against the Christian tenets were counter-balanced by an intellectual fashion that, a generation after Chesterton and Belloc, saw the Middle Ages still in favor, as a kind of golden era of cultural unity and alleviated anxiety. Among revered literary figures, a considerable number were professing Christians. The first recipient of the Campion Medal, Jacques Maritain in 1955, was the leading but far from the only figure in a movement to give Thomism a vital modern face; at another pole, philosophical existentialism looked to the Danish Lutheran Søren Kierkegaard as a founder, while the stark but expressive crisis theology of the Calvinist Karl Barth boldly sounded its trumpet against the defensive attenuations of liberal theology. Which is simply to say that when I showed a personal predilection not to let go of the Lutheran faith in which I had been raised there was no lack of compan-ionship and support in the literary and philosophical currents of the time. Had I been a young man in an atheist Communist state, or a literary man in the days when Menckenesque mockery was the dominant fashion, would I be as eligible as I am to receive this award? I am not sure. But in fact, yes, I have been a churchgoer in three Protestant denominations—Lutheran, Congregational, Episcopal—and the Christian faith has given me comfort in my life and, I would like to think, courage in my work. For it tells us that truth is holy, and truth-telling a noble and useful profes-sion; that the reality around us is created and worth celebrating; that men and women are radically imperfect and radically valuable.

Although, as St. Paul as well as Luther and Kierkegaard knew, some intellectual inconvenience and strain attends the maintenance of our faith, at the same time we are freed from certain secular illusions and monochromatic tyrannies of hopeful thought. The bad news can be told full out, for it is not the only news. Indeed it is striking how dark, even offhandedly and farcically dark, the human condition appears as pictured in the fiction of Waugh and Spark and Graham Greene and Flannery O'Connor. We scan them for a glimpse of mollifying holiness, and get instead a cruel drumming upon this world's emptiness. To be Christian in this day and age, as in the time of imperial Rome, is to be unorthodox, and readers should look elsewhere for the consolations of conventional sentiment and the popular, necessary religion of optimism.

While one can be a Christian and a writer, the phrase "Christian writer" feels somewhat reductive, and most writers so called have resisted it. The late Japanese novelist Endo Shusaku, a Roman Catholic and the Campion Medalist in 1990, observed of his Western peers, "Mr. Greene does not like to called a Catholic writer. Neither did François Mauriac. Being a Christian is the opposite of being a writer, Mr. Mauriac said. According to him, coming in contact with sin is natural when you probe the depths of the human heart. Describing sin, a writer himself gets dirty. This contradicts his Christian duty." Endo went on to say that he could consider himself a Christian writer only insofar as he believed that, and I quote, "there is something in the human unconscious that searches for God."

And, indeed, in describing the human condition, can we, as Christians, assert more than that? Is not Christian fiction, insofar as it exists, a description of the bewilderment and panic, the sense of hollowness and futility, which afflicts those whose search for God is not successful? And are we not all, within the churches and temples or not, more searcher than finder in this regard? I ask, while gratefully accepting this award, to be absolved from any duty to provide orthodox morals and consolations in my fiction. Fiction holds the mirror up to the world and cannot show more than this world contains. I do admit that there are different angles at which to hold the mirror, and that the reading I did in my twenties and thirties, to prop up my faith, also gave me a slant that affected my stories and, especially, my novels.

The first, *The Poorhouse Fair*, carries an epigraph from the Gospel of St. Luke; the next, *Rabbit, Run*, from Pascal; the third, *The Centaur*, from Karl Barth; and the fifth, *Couples*, from Paul Tillich. I thought of my novels as illustrations for texts from Kierkegaard and Barth; the hero of *Rabbit, Run* was meant to be a representative Kierkegaardian man, as his name, Angstrom, hints. Man in a state of fear and trembling, separated from God, haunted by dread, twisted by the conflicting demands of his animal biology and human intelligence, of the social contract and the inner imperatives, condemned as if by otherworldly origins to perpetual restlessness—such was, and to some extent remains, my conception. The modern Christian inherits an intellectual tradition of faulty cosmology and shrewd psychology. St. Augustine was not the first Christian writer or the last to give us the human soul with its shadows, its Rembrandtesque blacks and whites, its chiaroscuro; this sense of ourselves, as creatures caught in the light, whose decisions and recognitions have a majestic significance, remains to haunt non-Christians as well, and to form, as far as I can see, the raison d'être of fiction.

Remarks *upon accepting the 1998 National Book Foundation Medal for Distinguished Contribution to American Letters, in New York City, on November 18, 1998.*

When I was told of this handsome honor, my mind flicked back to the two other times when I have been so fortunate as to be summoned by the National Book Awards. The first occasion, on March 10, 1964, was immortalized by a young reporter for the now-defunct *New York Herald Tribune* who signed himself as Tom—as distinguished from Thomas— Wolfe.* His coverage began with these two paragraphs:

> No sensitive artist in America will ever have to duck the spotlight again. John Updike, the Ipswich, Mass., novelist, did it for them all last night, for all time. Up on the stage in the Grand Ballroom of the New York Hilton Hotel, to receive the most glamorous of the five National Book Awards, the one for fiction, came John Updike, author of "The Centaur," in a pair of 19-month-old loafers. Halfway to the podium, the spotlight from the balcony hit him, and he could not have ducked better if there had been a man behind it with a rubber truncheon.
>
> First he squinted at the light through his owl-eyed eye glasses. Then he ducked his head and his great thatchy medieval haircut toward his right shoulder. Then he threw up his left shoulder and his left elbow. Then he bent forward at the waist. And then, before the shirred draperies of the Grand Ballroom and an audience of 1,000 culturati, he went into his Sherwin-Williams blush.

In illustration of the tricks that memory plays, I remember the event as rather intimate and sedate. There had been a late-winter snowstorm in New England, and my then wife and I had risen very early to catch a train, and arrived rumpled and sleepy for this moment of triumph. Newspapers don't lie, so the Hilton Grand Ballroom it must have been, but my impression was of a small low room with a scattering of librarians in flowered hats on folding chairs. They smiled benignly, I remember that, and I also remember that just as I was about to step out into the spotlight for my turn at bat, somebody pestered me to sign his program, or scorecard. That, and the subsequent report by Tom Wolfe, were my first taste of the joys of celebrity.

The second occasion took place on April 27, 1982, in Carnegie Hall. The prizes at that point were, for no doubt valid reasons, called the American Book Awards, and only the winners were expected to show up.

---

*An invisible presence at the 1998 celebration, since his novel, *A Man in Full*, was up for the fiction prize, and the main source of buzz.

What I remember of that proud occasion is that my editor, Judith Jones, who sat beside me in the great concert hall, confided early during the ceremonies that she had just come from gum surgery. *This is some editor,* I thought at the time, and I think it still; Judith has been brave and loyal on my behalf for nearly forty years now. The ceremonies needed two hosts on the stage, like the two interlocutors in minstrel shows of yore, Barbara Walters and William F. Buckley, Jr., by name, and their interspersions were so witty and well-considered, and the acceptance speeches of the other winners so heartfelt and elaborate, that as the allotted hour wore on, and as I sat there with the folded pages of my speech gathering dampness against my breast, it became clear that there would not be time for the fiction winner, who spoke last, to say anything at all. A concert was scheduled for that evening, and we could hear, in the foyer and the wings, the musicians arriving with their clattering cellos and woodwinds, conversing of Stravinsky and Mahler and even emitting a few impatient toots on their brass and woodwinds. Barbara Walters' voice, normally so soothing, approached the strident as she advised us that our time was up; in a few gratefully applauded seconds I dashed up the aisle, grabbed my award from the capacious hand of Arthur Miller, and scampered away. The speech I never gave can be read in my collected works.

And now, as they say on television, this. Like some graying comet, every seventeen years or so, I return from the outer darkness of the un-nominated. From under my thatchy medieval haircut I peer out and what do I see? Tuxedos! Sequins! Plunging necklines! I must be in Hollywood. There are, just as at the Academy Awards, quintets of nominees, to be shortly boiled down to one modestly blushing winner and four gamely smiling losers. As in the annual film ceremonial, there is a gala air of ritual sacrifice, and some docile old buck or doe of the trade is brought forward to be given a medal whose reverse side holds the invisibly engraved implication that the time has come to retire.

Well, is there anything worrisome, anything Heaven-storming, about American publishing, whose saintly minions labor day after day far past dark over their endless proofs and their eerily glowing computer screens, putting on the dog for one night of the year? A Hollywoodian touch of glitz and glamour does not, let's hope, entail a Hollywoodian bewitchment with the mass market, with billion-dollar grosses and gross-out courtship of the adolescent mind. One of the strengths and charms of the book industry, and industry it of course is, has been its relative modesty, bow tie more than black tie, a modesty that translates into a relative mobility, an ability to publish, without catastrophic loss, books which will appeal to few, and to give the public an immense variety of products, a variety that is both a proclamation and an enjoyment of American freedom.

And yet, to be honest, if I reflect on the psychological history that led me to become a cottage laborer in this industry, an impression of glamour was part of it. There was something glamorous about the Reading, Pennsylvania, public library, a stately Carnegie-endowed edifice at Fifth and Franklin, next to a sweet-smelling bakery, where I would go with my mother from an early age, walking at her side the block from the trolley-car stop at Fourth Street, climbing the many wide steps, and stepping into a temple of books. The towering walls of books seemed conjured from a realm far distant, utterly mysterious and gracious—the little numbers inked onto the spines, the pockets for a borrower's card at the back, all these angelic arrangements. Who had done this for me? The well-thumbed volumes, with wider margins and smaller pages than are now customary, had a romantic savor of Manhattan as I imagined it, the glowing skyscrapers, the thronged streets. I read through shelves of P. G. Wodehouse and Erle Stanley Gardner, Agatha Christie and Robert Benchley, and expanded my borrowing to include the even more glamorous books rented, for I think a penny a day, from a certain counter in Whitner's department store. Those books had retained their jackets, which were in turn jacketed in cellophane—a very glamorous touch, that.

And there was a glamour, a swank, in the chastely severe, time-honored classics of English literature that one bought for courses at Harvard; sitting in my little dormered room in Lowell House at midnight, tilting back in my wooden Harvard chair, holding a cigarette in one hand and in the other the blue-covered Oxford *Poetical Works of Spenser*, with its tiny type, double columns, and Elizabethan spelling that reversed the "v"s and the "u"s, I felt like a glamorous person indeed, me and the Faerie Queene, together in the clouds. And there was certainly a glamour in the sample pages I received, some years later, from the firm of Knopf to show me what my first novel, *The Poorhouse Fair*, would look like in print. The novel had been a stumbling-block for my initial publisher, and it was by the happiest of flukes that a carbon copy fell into the hands of an editor at Knopf, Sandy Richardson, who liked the book just as it was; then it fell into the hands of Harry Ford, a "parfit gentil knyght" of the print world, an editor and designer both, who gave me a delicious striped jacket and an elegant page format, in the typeface called Janson, that I have stuck with for over forty books since. To see those youthful willful hopeful words of mine in that type, with Perpetua chapter heads set off by tapered rules, was an elevated moment I am still dizzy from. The old

Linotype letterpress had a glinting material bite for which all the ingenious advantages of computer setting have not quite compensated.

This is perhaps the fond moment to thank for manifold kindnesses and encouragements my wife, Martha, who is here with two of her sons and a glamorous daughter-in-law, and to express my deep human debt also to my own four children, and their mother, and my parents, now dead, and my mother's parents, long dead, who all together provided along the length of my life warm and action-packed households that accommodated the presence of a stranger, my strange ambition to be something glamorous. I was and am grateful. And to *The New Yorker* magazine, which since 1954 has given me a home of another sort. And to Fawcett Books, my paperback publisher since *Rabbit, Run*.

The book industry scarcely needs glamour when it has at its command something better, beauty—the beauty of the book. Though visual imagery is in a sense more absolute—more vivid, less arguable—than the printed word, electronic projectors are clumsy and prone to obsolescence compared to the physical object that bound paper forms. Alfred Knopf, when he was alive, dressed up for publishing much the way John Keats is alleged to have dressed up when he sat down to write a poem. In his purple shirts, expressionist neckties, and burnside whiskers, he seemed a cross between a Viennese emperor and a Barbary pirate; but he never frightened me because I knew I was in the company of a man who loved books and cared about their beauty. The books he published showed it. We assembled here should rejoice in our venerable product; a book is beautiful in its relation to the human hand, to the human eye, to the human brain, and to the human spirit.

Index

Note: The boldface numerals indicate pages where
the author or work is specifically the subject of a review.

Illustration Credits

The photographs and illustrations reproduced in this book were provided with the permission and courtesy of the following:

page 730: Rose Art Museum, Brandeis University, Waltham, Massachusetts. Gevirtz-Mnuchin Purchase Fund

page 731: The Art Institute of Chicago [Claes Oldenburg. American (b. Sweden, 1929). *Clothespin*, 1975. CorTen and stainless steel. H.: 304.8 cm. Gift of the Auxiliary Board of The Art Institute of Chicago; Mr. and Mrs. Frank G. Logan Prize Fund, 1976.96. 20th Century, permanent installation, September 17, 1988. To view: Gallery 261. Photograph © 1998, The Art Institute of Chicago. All Rights Reserved]

pages 734, 735, 736, and 740: Saul Steinberg

page 742: Library of Congress, Prints and Photographs Division

pages 743 and 746: Smithsonian Institution/National Portrait Gallery

page 745: National Portrait Gallery, Collection of Mr. and Mrs. Karl H. Klein

page 747: Smithsonian Institution/National Portrait Gallery, courtesy of the New York Public Library for the Performing Arts

pages 672, 742, 788, 789, 792, 793, 794, and 795: courtesy of the author